ity Press

Toronto
cutta Madras Karachi
apore Hong Kong Tokyo
m Cape Town
d Madrid

nies in

3 by Robert Cohen

University Press, Inc.,
New York, New York 10016

trademark of Oxford University Press

aloging-in-Publication Data

oung:
erica's first mass student movement,

hen.
graphical references and index.

United States—History—20th century.
ited States—Political activity—History—20th century.
United States—History.

1'981—dc20   92-22733

of America

When the Old Left
Was Young

WHEN
THE OLD
WAS YO

Student Radica
America's Firs
Mass Student
1929–1941

ROBERT COHEN

New York   Oxford
OXFORD UNIVERS
1993

Oxford Univers

Oxford   New York
Delhi   Bombay   Ca
Kuala Lumpur   Sing
Nairobi   Dar es Sala
Melbourne   Aucklan

and associated compa
Berlin   Ibadan

Copyright © 199

Published by Oxford
200 Madison Avenue,

Oxford is a registered

All rights reserved. No
stored in a retrieval sys
electronic, mechanical,
without the prior perm

Library of Congress Ca
Cohen, Robert.
When the old left was y
student radicals and An
1929–1941 / Robert Co
p.   cm.   Includes biblio
ISBN 0-19-506099-7
1. Student movements—
2. College students—Un
3. Depressions—1929—
I. Title.
LA229.C62   1993   378.

9 8 7 6 5 4 3 2 1

Printed in the United States
on acid-free paper

When the Old Left Was Young

WHEN THE OLD LEFT WAS YOUNG

Student Radicals and America's First Mass Student Movement, 1929–1941

ROBERT COHEN

New York Oxford
OXFORD UNIVERSITY PRESS
1993

Oxford University Press

Oxford   New York   Toronto
Delhi   Bombay   Calcutta   Madras   Karachi
Kuala Lumpur   Singapore   Hong Kong   Tokyo
Nairobi   Dar es Salaam   Cape Town
Melbourne   Auckland   Madrid

and associated companies in
Berlin   Ibadan

Published by Oxford University Press, Inc.,
200 Madison Avenue, New York, New York 10016

Oxford is a registered trademark of Oxford University Press

Library of Congress Cataloging-in-Publication Data
Cohen, Robert.
When the old left was young:
student radicals and America's first mass student movement,
1929–1941 / Robert Cohen.
p.   cm.   Includes bibliographical references and index.
ISBN 0-19-506099-7
1. Student movements—United States—History—20th century.
2. College students—United States—Political activity—History—20th century.
3. Depressions—1929—United States—History.
I. Title.
LA229.C62   1993   378.1′981—dc20   92-22733

9 8 7 6 5 4 3 2 1

Printed in the United States of America
on acid-free paper

To my parents,
Marvin and Shirley Cohen
and to the memory of my grandparents,
Ben and Rose Cohen,
Irving and Florence Balas

Acknowledgments

This study began as a dissertation in the UC Berkeley history department. I owe a great debt to my dissertation chair, Diane Shaver Clemens, for her encouragement, advice, and willingness to share her knowledge of international relations during the Age of Roosevelt. Diane's commitment to her students, to her scholarship, and to a more democratic university have been inspirational. Her friendship and guidance made my dissertation work more enjoyable than I would have thought possible. Leon Litwack offered helpful criticism, which convinced me to broaden the scope of the study. I am also grateful to Leon for emphasizing the literary possibilities of historical writing and insisting that historians write for the public rather than just for the academy or themselves. Michael Rogin's comments on several drafts of this study were invaluable, as was his encouragement to look at the Old Left critically but empathetically. My understanding of the American Left also has been enhanced by discussions with Candace Falk and Richard Boyden. I am indebted to Candace for providing me with the opportunity to work on the Emma Goldman Papers Project while completing this study. Goldman's brilliant writings on the Spanish Civil War influenced my own thinking, as did her radical critique of Stalinism. My thanks to James Kettner for being so generous with his time and advice.

My interest in the political history of the American university originated in an undergraduate seminar at SUNY Buffalo taught by Jesse Lemisch. Jesse's pioneering scholarship in this area served as a model for my own work, and I am grateful for his friendship, support, and for his criticism of parts of the manuscript. My thanks go as well to another of my former teachers at Buffalo, Philip Altbach in the School of Education, whose publications have helped make the study of American student politics an exciting field. Athan Theoharis of Marquette University opened up a valuable source for this study by encouraging me to obtain the FBI documents on the student movement.

The Berkeley campus itself is a great teacher about student politics. I learned much about the dynamics of student protest from my former colleagues on the *Daily Californian*—including David Pickell, Will Miner, Colleen Lye, Leigh Anne Jones, and Drew Digby—and from a whole generation of fellow activists in the Association of Graduate Student Employees, Berkeley's divestment movement, and the Graduate Assembly.

This study could not have been completed without the resources of many archives and libraries and the assistance of their staffs. I am especially grateful to Elizabeth Denier and the rest of the staff at the FDR Library in Hyde Park, New York, for promptly processing the Joseph P. Lash Papers, and making accessible this rich collection of documents on the American student movement of the 1930s. My thanks to the archivists at the Swarthmore College Peace Collection, the Tamiment Institute Library at NYU, the New York Public Library and its Schomburg Center for Research in Black Culture, the YWCA National Board Archives in New York, the American Civil Liberties Union Archives at Princeton University, and the National Archives in Washington, D.C. I am also indebted to the Carlson Library at the University of Toledo and the Tamiment Institute Library at NYU for allowing me to use microfilmed copies of Duke University's collection of the Socialist Party of America Papers.

Since American college campuses constituted the student movement's base, constituency and political environment, I found it necessary to undertake extensive research on individual campuses. This research was greatly expedited by the talented archivists and fine archival collections of many campuses. I owe a special debt to City College of New York archivist Barbara Dunlap for her help in tracking down materials on that campus's student protesters and administration. J. R. K. Kantor and his successor as University of California archivist, William Roberts, as well as other staff members at the Bancroft Library, were of great assistance in uncovering sources on UC Berkeley and UCLA. My thanks to the archival staffs at Barnard College, Brooklyn College, Columbia University's Columbiana Collection and Low Library, the Regenstein Special Collections Department of the University of Chicago, Emory University, Fisk University, Harvard University, Howard University, Hunter College, the University of Michigan and its Labadie Collection, the State University of New York at Buffalo, Oberlin College, the Ohio Historical Society, the Southern Historical Collection at the University of North Carolina, Chapel Hill, the University of Texas, the University of Toledo, UCLA, Vassar College, the University of Virginia, the University of Wisconsin, and the Wisconsin Historical Society. The libraries of Dartmouth College, the University of Illinois, the University of Kansas, the University of Kentucky, Marshall University, and Ohio State University were generous in lending me their student publications. My thanks to the interlibrary loan departments at UC Berkeley's Doe Library and the University of Toledo's Carlson Library for obliging me in what I am sure seemed an unending stream of requests for student and radical publications from across the United States.

I was very fortunate that former activists and leaders from the student movement allowed me to interview them. Their memories offered an important supplement to the written record. Celeste Strack Kaplan, Monroe Sweetland, the late F. Palmer Weber, and the late Larry Rogin not only took time to talk with me, but also assisted me in contacting other movement veterans. I am grateful to the following Depression era alumni for sharing with me their memories of the student movement: Riva Stocker Aaron, Dorothy Burnham, Joseph Clark, Kenneth B. Clark, Homer Coke, Richard Criley, Hal Draper, Theodore Draper, Judah Drob, Mary Felton Drob, Ishmael Flory, Elizabeth Pope Franklin, Marge Frantz, Emanuel Geltman, Serril Gerber, Harold Goldstein, Max Gordon, Gil Green, Robert Hall, Albert Herling, John Herling, Esther Cooper Jackson, James E. Jackson, the late Joseph P. Lash, Toni Locke, Leonard Lurie, Harry Magdoff, William Mandel, Henry May, the late Jack McMichael, the late William Parry, Paul Porter, Harry Ring, Shura Kamenir Saul, Morris Schappes, Judith Solomon, Nathan Solomon, Lil Sweetland, George Watt, the late James Wechsler, Vivian Weinstein, Max Weiss, Leon Wofsy, and Molly Yard. Toni Locke, Henry May, and Max Gordon were generous in providing me with documents from their student activist days. My knowledge of the movement was also enhanced by discussions at the American Student Union's 50th anniversary reunion, held in Long Beach, California, and organized with great skill by Leo Rifkin.

The initial research for this study was made possible by funding from UC Berkeley's Humanities Research Fellowship and the History department's Eugene McCormac and Max Farrand Fellowships. My final research trips were funded by grants from the University of Toledo and the Toledo Humanities Institute. Georgian College in Orillia, Ontario, generously made available an office in which to begin revising the manuscript. My thanks to Richard Allen, Tiffany Patterson, Michael Kay, Frederico and Pura Arcos, Lorin Cary, Carol Menning, William Hoover, Roger Ray, Michael Meranze, Mary Odem, and Janice Hughes for their friendship and support. I hope that Gary and Wanda Davis know how much I appreciate all their help over the years and their role in making my southern California research trips so pleasurable. Thanks to all my friends, relatives and friends of friends who housed me during my low budget research trips through the Midwest and South and to the East Coast. I am grateful to Judith Preissle, Guy Larkins and the University of Georgia's department of Social Science Education for providing a congenial environment in which to complete this work.

I am indebted to Vivian McLaughlin for skillful copy-editing of the typescript. My thanks to Sheldon Meyer for his patience and understanding, which enabled me to delay the completion of the manuscript until I had made use of essential sources recently released in the Lash Papers. Elizabeth Bryan, Joan Stroer, and David Pickell provided valuable assistance with the final proofreading.

Many Americans of my generation learned their first lessons about the Great Depression not from history books, but from their parents. I grew up with my father's stories of the hard times he and his brothers endured as children in a Brooklyn ghetto during the 1930s. I want to thank him for sharing those stories and sparking my interest in Depression America. My thanks to my mother and my sister Myra for encouraging me to complete this study, and to the first student rebels I ever met, my sister Judith and my brother Steven.

The historian to whom I owe the most is my wife, Rebecca Hyman. Ever since our days as Berkeley graduate students, Rebecca has encouraged me in this study and helped me retain my enthusiasm for both historical scholarship and more important things. Her intellectual comradeship and love have made all the difference. And to Daniel Langston, the youngest rebel in our family, thanks for coming along at just the right moment.

Athens, Georgia
December 1992

R. C.

Contents

Introduction

> It was a time when frats, like the football team, were losing their glamor. . . . Instead my generation thirsted for another kind of action, and we took great pleasure in the sit-down strikes that burst loose in Flint and Detroit. . . . We saw a new world coming every third morning. . . . When I think of the library I think of the sound of a stump speaker on the lawn outside because so many times I looked up from what I was reading to try to hear what issue they were debating now. The place was full of speeches, meetings and leaflets. It was jumping with issues.
>
> Playwright Arthur Miller, Michigan '38, "The University of Michigan," *Holiday Magazine* (December 1953), 70.

The student rebels of the Depression era rank among the most effective radical organizers in the history of American student politics. They built a large and influential student protest movement, organized America's first national student strikes, and shaped political discourse on campus for the better part of a decade. No college generation before them and only the New Left insurgents of the 1960s after them ever had as much impact on student politics in twentieth-century America.

The American student movement of the 1930s emerged as students groped for solutions to the double barreled crisis which confronted their generation: the Great Depression and the growing rift in international relations that ultimately led to World War II. In contrast to the mass youth movements of Nazi Germany and Fascist Italy, the American student movement did not exploit the crises of the Depression decade to appeal to the worst instincts of the young. National chauvinism, racism, and militarism—hallmarks of these European movements of the Right— were anathema to the leftist organizers who launched and led the American student movement. Student activists in the United States used the crisis atmosphere of their time for much more humane ends, fanning their classmates' egalitarian idealism and revulsion for war and fascism. The American student movement proved attractive to many young men and women because, as political scientist and former 1930s student activist John P. Roche recalled, it offered them the opportunity to transform the

United States from "a nation sunk in poverty and depression, racked by racial and religious discrimination and seemingly on 'The Road to War' . . . to a society governed by the principles of economic and political justice and human equality, living in a peaceful world."[1]

No protest movement in Depression America was more unexpected than the student movement, nor more symbolic of the transformation from the reactionary politics of the 1920s to the progressive politics of the 1930s. In the decade preceding the Great Depression, college students had represented one of America's most staunchly Republican constituencies. Student culture in that prosperous decade had been elitist and WASP-dominated; its championship of selfish materialism calls to mind the YUPPIE culture of the Reagan era, with its "Don't Trust Anyone Under $30,000" mentality. The student movement of the 1930s—led by a diverse coalition of communists, socialists, liberals, pacifists, and Trotskyists—worked along with the Depression itself to challenge the bourgeois collegiate culture inherited from the 1920s. The movement encouraged students to identify with the working class rather than the upper class, to value racial and ethnic diversity instead of exclusivity, and to work for progressive social change. This activism helped to ensure that by 1936 Republican dominance of national student politics had gone the way of the raccoon coat and the other relics of the 1920s campus world.

Along with the labor movement and other progressive insurgencies of Depression America, the student movement contributed to the formation of a national consensus on behalf of a more activist and humane federal government and a more caring society. The student movement helped introduce and popularize the idea that poverty should not force any Americans to drop out of school, and that Washington should ensure this by providing direct federal aid to students. Often the movement's vision for governmental assistance to the underprivileged went well beyond the New Deal, as when the students called for federal dollars to aid *all* needy youths—rather than the small percentage actually receiving aid from New Deal agencies. Nonetheless, the generous idealism which motivated such demands attracted Eleanor Roosevelt, the New Deal's most forceful advocate for youth, and led her to befriend and cooperate with the movement's leaders. Mrs. Roosevelt sensed that whether these young activists attacked the New Deal for doing too little for youth or rallied to save the New Deal youth programs from right wing budget-cutters, the students were kindred spirits because they shared her desire for an unprecedented federal effort to rescue the Depression's young victims.

Unlike the other movements for social change in Depression America, the student movement devoted as much attention to foreign policy as to domestic issues. Students grappled with isolationism more intensively and visibly than any other group in Depression America, knowing that their generation would be called to fight the next war. The movement's largest national demonstrations were anti-war and anti-fascist strikes aimed at staving off world war. Some of the movement's most dedicated activists not only marched for this cause, but died for it on the battlefields of Spain; fighting valiantly but futilely to stop the spread of fascism before it engulfed all of Europe.

Although international crises drew their attention overseas, the student rebels of the Depression generation also devoted considerable energy to battling for change in their own backyard: within the college gates. Recognizing that suppression of student dissent could jeopardize the entire student movement, these activists sought to advance the cause of free speech on campus. Scholars examining the history of academic freedom in this era have tended to focus upon the faculty.[2] But, in fact, students waged the largest and most effective struggles for political liberty on campus in Depression America.

The student movement championed a concept of student political rights which was much more expansive and modern than that held by many university administrators during the early 1930s. College presidents and deans clung to *(in loco parentis)* disciplinary traditions inherited from the nineteenth century, which gave them veto power over student political expression. They claimed the authority to gag student rebels, much as parents had the authority to silence rowdy children. Student activists rejected this collegiate oversight, insisting that they were not errant children, but rather citizens with First Amendment rights. The students' position was decades ahead of its time, and would not be adopted by the Supreme Court until 1969, when it ruled (in *Tinker v. Des Moines Independent Community School District*) that students do not "shed . . . their constitutional rights . . . at the school house gates."[3] The chasm between student radicalism and administration paternalism concerning student political rights led to a series of campus free speech fights during the early 1930s. Movement organizers risked suspension, expulsion, and arrest to secure free speech rights which students today take for granted.

The conflict over free speech on college campuses in Depression America also contained a hidden history, one of political surveillance, which archival research and documents obtained under the Freedom of Information Act have only recently begun to uncover. Though the student protests of the Depression era were almost always non-violent and lawful, anti-radical administrators, nonetheless, turned over to the Federal Bureau of Investigation information on their activist students, resulting in the opening of FBI files on literally thousands of these students. The complicity of college presidents and deans with the FBI in this trampling of student civil liberty compromised the very ideal of the university as a center of free intellectual discourse and pursuit of truth. The student radical who engaged too publicly in such discourse might very well end up with an FBI file, courtesy of her or his local college administrator. This informing also represented a violation of the trust which was supposed to exist between students and college officials—as administrators gave the FBI *confidential* data regarding the political affiliations, activities, and ideas of student activists. Indeed, unlike the physician, lawyer, or psychiatrist, the college administrator of the Depression era seemed to lack a strong professional ethic regarding confidentiality, at least with regard to the records of radical students.[4]

The FBI's spying on the student movement was, of course, connected to allegations that the student movement was communist-dominated. Though other leftist and liberal groups had a significant impact on the movement, no group played a larger or more decisive role in the student movement's leadership than the communists. Many of the most influential national officers in Depression America's two largest student movement organizations—the American Student Union and the American Youth Congress—were either in or close to the Communist Party or Young Communist League. Communists achieved a degree of influence in American student politics far superior to their meager impact on the larger national polity. Not even in the labor movement, where communists had an impressive presence during the 1930s, could communist influence compare with what it was in the student movement.

Historians of American Communism have been locked in a bitter debate about the character of communist-led movements. Theodore Draper and other traditional anti-communist historians judge such movements harshly, focusing on their flaws, particularly the Russia-centered mind-set of the communists who led these movements. A newer school of historians, led by Maurice Isserman, takes issue with Draper. These anti-anti-communist historians stress the strengths of communist-led movements in the U.S. and argue that communists succeeded in building mass movements because they were more responsive to American political realities than to Comintern dictation.[5]

During the student movement's early stages, communist behavior in the movement had some of the characteristics suggested in Isserman's work on the Communist Party; it was innovative, self-directed, and centered on American political realities. But in the final and self-destructive stage of the movement, these qualities vanished and communist student leaders acted in as Russia-centered and dogmatic a manner as Draper might predict. The shift came because the Nazi-Soviet Pact and the new imperatives of Soviet foreign policy forced communist students to chose between their loyalty to Stalin and their loyalty to the anti-fascist movement they had helped to build on American campuses; they opted for Stalin, and in so doing destroyed the student movement.

The student movement's history is clearly too complex to be captured by either one-sided indictments or defenses of the communist past. Communists had great strengths as political organizers and worked tirelessly to convert American campuses from bastions of elitism and apathy to centers of egalitarianism and activism. But these radicals also had grave weaknesses—the worst of which was their eagerness to defend the indefensible when it came to Stalin and his cruelties. This is what Eleanor Roosevelt biographer and former American Student Union leader Joseph

P. Lash meant when, in looking back upon the student movement, he acknowledged: "We were fearless paladins of truth when it came to the world outside the left; we were little better than apologists when it came to the left itself." [6]

As democratic as the student movement was in its demands for a more egalitarian America, internally the movement suffered from some quite undemocratic tendencies. The communists, and at times their socialist and Trotskyist counterparts, displayed a penchant for vanguardism, disingenuousness, and secrecy in the way they wielded power in the student movement's leading organizations. Such deficiencies were especially common among the communists, since they were the most numerous and powerful of the student movement's leaders, as well as the most insensitive to questions concerning democratic process. The communists also refused to be open about the links between their political positions— particularly those on foreign policy—and Soviet policy. In some cases, communists, including several national leaders of the movement, concealed their Party ties even from fellow activists and allies of the movement.

To set the historical record straight, I have tried to be as open about these flaws in the movement as I have been about the movement's more positive accomplishments. This has not been easy, because the task of writing an open and honest history of communist-led movements involves some troubling ethical problems. The most vexing of these problems concerns the conflicting claims of individual privacy and historical accuracy. If a movement leader was secretly a communist, should the historian preserve or end that secrecy? This question is complicated by the fact that during the Cold War era certain individuals were persecuted for real or imagined communist affiliations. But with the Cold War over and the threat of anti-communist political persecution as much in the past as the Berlin Wall, there is no longer a risk that the historian's candor will lead to any such persecution. Thus where it has been essential to the movement's history, I have indicated the affiliations of movement leaders—even those that chose not to disclose them—during the Depression era.

The student movement of the Depression era should be remembered, however, as more than a history of the communists who helped lead it. The majority of rank and filers who joined the movement's organizations and marched in its demonstrations were not communists. And since their presence, as much as anything the communists did, made the student movement so significant a force in American life, this must be their history too. In a very critical sense, these non-communist rank and filers were even more important than the communists who helped lead the movement. There could be a viable student movement only so long as the movement's leftist leaders responded to the crises of their decade in a manner which non-communists regarded as logical and appealing. When these leaders lost touch with the movement's non-communist ma-

jority—as they did following the Nazi-Soviet Pact—the communists became as powerless as generals without an army, and like old soldiers they
(and the movement) soon faded away.

At its peak in the late 1930s, the student movement's demonstrations
involved hundreds of thousands of students annually—by some estimates,
almost half of America's entire undergraduate population. The size of
this movement makes it impossible to provide a detailed account of student political campaigns on all of the nation's college campuses. When
portraying such a movement, it is necessary to be selective. But while selective, I have not been arbitrary. The student movement had major bat-
tlegrounds, events, and ideals that its participants recognized, so that in
setting the narrative I have sought to be faithful to the movement's own
sense of itself—particularly with regard to the order and importance of
events.

The student movement's history has been neglected by political historians of the Great Depression. Taken together, in fact, three of the best
and most widely read political histories of the United States during the
Depression decade (including Arthur Schlesinger Jr.'s multi-volume *Age
of Roosevelt*) devote less than a page to this era's student movement. In the
half-century that has passed since the death of the student movement,
historians have published only two slim monographs and a handful of
articles and chapters about that movement.[7]

Having traveled across the country researching a student movement
that even many archivists and historians had never heard of, I naturally
pondered the reasons for this historical amnesia. Was it a legacy of Mc-
Carthyism? By working to make pariahs out of communists and ex-com-
munists, Senator Joseph McCarthy and other congressional red probers
did make it difficult for historians to write a full or fair-minded history of
communist-led movements. This is almost certainly why the only significant account of the student movement published by a historian during
the 1950s was a single chapter in a volume of the strongly anti-communist
Fund for the Republic series on communist influence in American life,
which belittled and castigated the student movement at every turn.[8] But
by far the greatest harm that McCarthyism did to the historical record was to prod former leaders of the student movement—in fear of political persecution—to destroy some of the movement's main organizational files and correspondence.[9]

Damaging as it was, however, McCarthyism was not alone responsible
for the historians' neglect of the student movement. After all, Mc--
Carthyism eventually collapsed, and consequently movement veterans could
feel increasingly free to discuss their days as student activists. In fact, over
the past few decades it has been these movement veterans—through their
memoirs—rather than professional historians who have written the most
about the Depression era student movement. Unfortunately, the pattern
of neglect by historians continued.[10]

This neglect seems to be connected to the obvious fact that the Depression era campus insurgency was a movement of the young. Historians, as a middle-aged group, tend not—outside of those working on the era of the 1960s—to take youths seriously enough to study their ideas or the history of student politics. Few history departments have anyone specializing in the history of youth and student politics. Historians sometimes act as if only presidents, senators and other "adults" can make political history. I recall only too well job interviews with fellow historians who seemed to think my topic a strange outgrowth of the Berkeley political atmosphere in which I wrote my dissertation. "What kind of history is that?" "What does that have to do with political history?" The tone of such queries, as much as the words themselves, gave more than a hint of bias against historical studies of youth and student protest.

Such responses and the historiographical neglect of the student movement seem more understandable when we consider the way Americans remember the 1930s. The first images which come to mind from that decade are not student protests, but rather breadlines and Hoovervilles wrought by the Great Depression. Next come the images of a self-assured Franklin Roosevelt attempting to end the economic crisis through his New Deal programs. We also remember the 1930s as a decade in which a dizzying array of protest movements—including the union organizing drives and sit-down strikes, the Townsend, Share Our Wealth, and unemployed movements, the Farm-Labor insurgency, the Commonwealth Federation, and the End Poverty in California campaign—arose and agitated to change America. With all of these adult-led movements surging, FDR governing, and the Communist Party itself growing, youth and student rebellion could not always be at center stage. This contrasted with the New Left student movement of the 1960s, which was born in the spotlight. The New Left did not have to compete for attention, since it emerged at a time when the adult Left—hobbled by the Cold War and McCarthyism—and the labor movement—weakened by bureaucratization and corruption—were only shadows of their former selves. Given how much other significant protest activity and political change existed in Depression America, the 1930s could never be seen, as the 1960s sometimes are, as a decade dominated by youth protest. It is little wonder, then, that the Depression era student movement has received so little historical attention.

I hope this study will encourage historians and the public to rediscover this lost generation of student rebels. These young activists questioned the inequities and irrationalities of American capitalism at a time when such questioning was sorely needed. Their ambitious agenda for social change at times seemed unrealistic to more moderate leaders, such as President Roosevelt—who admonished them not to "seek or expect Utopia overnight."[11] But FDR proved no more successful than the students in devising steps to end the Depression or prevent war. Moreover, whatever its failures in fulfilling its agenda, the student movement made a profound difference to the college generation it served. "There is no question," recalled historian Henry May, who was a student activist at Berkeley and Harvard in the 1930s,

> that the movement broadened our education. Everything that was happening—in Spain and Ethiopia and Detroit, in American politics, in literature and the arts—was important and relevant. Each of us was a responsible citizen of the world, with the duty of making up his mind, joining with others, taking action. Each person's decisions and actions would make a difference . . . in changing the world. This was more than a theory, it was a faith and a way of life. Even those who could never quite believe it all still remember its powerful attraction.[12]

This extraordinary sense of engagement, this "thirst to have a hand in the shaping of history"[13] enabled the Depression generation to build America's first mass student movement. And it distinguished these compassionate student activists from the politically apathetic and self-interested youths who dominated American campus life during most of this century.

AUTHOR'S NOTE

Quotations are rendered as they appeared in the original documents, with a minimum of editorial insertions. To preserve the tone and style of the students' political discourse, I have avoided using the term "sic" where minor spelling or grammatical errors occur. I include (bracketed) corrective or explanatory material with the quotations only when this is absolutely necessary to make quotations comprehensible.

When the Old Left Was Young

Chapter 1

Dancing on the Edge of a Volcano

Though we graduate students expected the revolution very soon and planned to encourage it, we did not expect any help from the Berkeley undergraduates. Not that they would oppose—they would simply, as usual, be unaware that anything was happening. A singular accomplishment of American higher education, as one reflects on it, was the creation of a vast network of universities, public and private, which . . . caused no one any political embarrassment of any kind. In other countries they created trouble from time to time, but not here. A control system which subtly suggested that whatever the students most wanted to do—i.e., devote themselves to football, basketball, fraternities, college tradition, rallies, hell raising, a sentimental concern for the old alma mater and imaginative inebriation—was what they should do was basic to this peace. The alumni rightly applauded this control system and so, to an alarming extent, did the faculty. An occasional non-political riot was condoned and even admired; some deeper instinct suggested that it was a surrogate for something worse.

Economist John Kenneth Galbraith, memoir of Berkeley during the early Depression years. *There Was Light: Autobiography of a University, Berkeley, 1868–1968*, Irving Stone, ed. (New York, 1970), 28.

Herbert Hoover's America was a dismal place in 1931. The president had failed to end or even mitigate the economic crisis, which began with the stock market crash of 1929. Unemployment had spiraled out of control; the number of jobless Americans had soared from 429,000 in 1929 to more than nine million in 1931. The Hoover White House had undermined its credibility in 1929 and 1930 by erroneously predicting economic recovery. But by late summer 1931 even some of the president's closest congressional allies were glumly admitting that the end of the Depression was not in sight. Breadlines and shanty-towns—dubbed "Hoovervilles" to mock the impotent president—had spread across the nation, grim testimony to the hunger and homelessness wrought by the Great Depression. Municipalities and private charities could not keep pace with the need of millions of unemployed Americans for economic assistance. Relief workers, local officials, and liberals on Capitol Hill in August 1931 called for a special session of Congress to legislate aid for the unemployed; they warned that without federal relief dollars, the coming winter would bring widespread starvation.[1]

That same month, as their elders in Washington fretted over how to ready themselves for another year of Depression, students at the University of California at Berkeley also began to prepare for the coming year. But for Berkeley students that preparation did not include discussions of hunger, poverty, or other Depression-related problems. As the fall 1931 semester began, fraternities and football, sororities and parties, were the talk of the campus. In its opening editorial of the semester, the *Daily Californian,* Berkeley's student newspaper, gave advice to new students, making it sound as if their most serious problems would be chosing the proper Greek house and deciding whether to participate "in sports, in dramatics or publications." The editor also informed the freshmen that they were "fortunate to have a classmate in [football] coach Bill Ingram . . . [who will] bring back another 'Golden Era' for California athletics." Though focusing primarily on these apolitical concerns, the editorial did turn to the economy long enough to make the naive assertion that "the class of 1935 . . . is fortunate to be starting out in a year which promises prosperity . . . ."[2] In predicting prosperity, the editor closed his eyes not merely to the pessimistic national economic reports, but also to local developments. Only the previous day, San Francisco Mayor Angelo Rossi had sent an open letter to the White House suggesting that economic conditions would continue to deteriorate in the Bay Area. Rossi informed President Hoover that only federal aid could get San Francisco through the next winter because the city was overwhelmed by the task of feeding the swelling ranks of jobless San Franciscans.[3]

The upbeat and apolitical thinking of students on the Berkeley campus was not the least bit unusual for American undergraduates in the early Depression era. Most American college students seemed remarkably unconcerned about the national economic crisis during the first two years of the Great Depression. No student protests were held to demand work or relief for the unemployed. No anti-Hoover movement emerged on campus during these years, despite President Herbert Hoover's inept handling of the economy and his refusal to provide sufficient federal dollars to feed the hungry. Most college student newspapers slighted Depression-related news; they reported about fraternities and football much more avidly and often than they did about growing breadlines and Hoovervilles.[4]

The traditional social events of the nation's predominantly middle-class undergraduate population proceeded in 1929, 1930, and 1931 almost as if the Depression did not exist. This was especially true for the sorority and fraternity houses, whose activities generally set the tone for undergraduate life. Their social calendars suggest that at a time when the poor went hungry, the middle class went dancing. Though the Depression had slowed down the economy, it had yet to depress the party scene on campus. During a single weekend in October 1931, twenty-five Greek houses at the University of Wisconsin held parties; a similar level of party activity could be found on many campuses.[5]

Student parties during the early Depression years were every bit as lavish as their counterparts in the prosperous 1920s. At the University of Michigan, for example, the Pan-Hellenic Ball in November 1931 drew "more than 300 couples [who] danced to the music of Gene Austin and his Victor recording artists," a band which appeared weekly on a national NBC radio show. "Striking black and white programs in the form of miniature leather picture frames were distributed to the guests." In true high society style, the ball featured a "grand march" of the couples and a coterie of chaperones, including the president of the University and the dean of students. A less formal but equally lavish affair was thrown by a sorority at the University of Wisconsin in 1930; this party featured a fashion revue in which guests saw "dainty, gaily covered gowns . . . back-glittering rhinestones and twinkling slippers."[6] Such gala events were the collegiate norm.

Even in their rallies and riots, undergraduates revealed how far removed their world was from that of impoverished Americans. In 1930, the same year when the unemployed held hunger marches in dozens of cities, the biggest rallies on the nation's college campuses had nothing to do with the Depression. Political rallies and political violence were almost completely alien to undergraduates. The goals of collegiate rallies and riots ranged from cheering athletic heroes and razzing competing undergraduate groups to celebrating after exams. These gatherings all had one thing in common: they were totally apolitical events.

Harvard produced the largest student riot in the nation in 1930. This apolitical disturbance, which occurred on May 7, involved some 1500 undergraduates, and was so violent that it made the front page of the *New York Times*. The occasion for the violence was the conclusion of exam week. At 11:45 p.m. a student appeared outside a dormitory and sounded taps on a bugle, which served as a signal for a wild display of "high spirits." Students began hurling light bulbs out of their dormitory windows; then, over a thousand collegians poured out of the dormitories—some clad in pajamas, others half-dressed. A dozen policemen arrived, but they could not restore order, so the riot squad was called in. Firemen also appeared on the scene after students pulled a fire alarm. The students greeted them with bottles, fruit, and other missiles. The battle continued for over an hour and ended with one student arrested and two hospitalized.[7]

This same semester, Harvard's boisterous students provoked the nation's largest mass arrest of undergraduates during the early 1930s. Police jailed more than 200 Harvard students in a riot which followed a Harvard hockey team victory in February 1930. Major apolitical riots in this period resulted in the arrest of students on other campuses. There were 156 such arrests at the University of Pennsylvania, 150 at Albion College in Michigan, 46 at the City College of New York, 12 at Yale, and 7 at the University of Wisconsin.[8]

Student violence during the first two years of the Great Depression sometimes promoted class consciousness, but not the type of class consciousness about which Karl Marx wrote. This violence was between different *academic* classes: freshmen against sophomores, juniors against seniors. Moreover, this type of conflict represented an annual collegiate ritual on many campuses (which should not be surprising considering that this was an age when the youth culture of the campuses often required freshmen to wear beanies). Columbia students, for instance, became riotous during the college's Freshman Class Banquet, held in a posh restaurant at Hastings-on-Hudson in April 1930. More than a hundred Columbia freshmen had just finished the banquet's second course when several dozen sophomores invaded the restaurant and assaulted them. A wild melée ensued, with fists flying, furniture overturning, and glass shattering. Only the arrival of state troopers prevented the complete destruction of the restaurant. Outraged that they had chosen his restaurant as the site for their freshman-sophomore riot, the proprietor filed lawsuits demanding over $50,000 in damages from the students.[9]

Such disturbances not only reflected the sophomoric character of undergraduate culture, but also attested that where students were prone to excess, it was excess in pursuit of trivial collegiate rivalries. Where students were willing to defy the law, it was a defiance almost always barren of political meaning or thought. Though the riots occurred in the early 1930s, these events were the product of a much older pattern of juvenile undergraduate behavior. The disturbances were part of a male-dominated tradition of collegiate rowdiness, which had been a hallmark of collegiate life for generations. As one education reporter explained in 1931, student riots often erupted "at a particular time and place because they have always occurred at a particular time and place. They are traditional. The class of 1933 must riot because the classes of 1923, 1903, and 1893 did the same thing."[10]

Of all the extracurricular activities which preoccupied undergraduates none was more prominent than intercollegiate football. At coeducational and men's colleges, these athletic contests were the occasions for the year's largest and most celebrated gatherings of undergraduates. The huge crowds at the stadiums on Saturdays, which on many campuses included tens of thousands of students and alumni, were only one component of collegiate footballmania. Rallies, parties, yell leader contests, bonfires, and other ritualized expressions of support gave football a pervasive presence on campus—so much so that critics called the sport "King Football." And since the football season coincided with the beginning of the academic year, it helped introduce students to one another in an apolitical atmosphere; it siphoned off energy that might otherwise have gone into more serious (perhaps even political) activities.[11]

The frenetic campus activity that accompanied big college football rivalries almost defies belief. At the University of Kansas in November 1930, for instance, students planned an entire day of "rallies, speeches and general demonstrations . . . to arouse pep for the annual Missouri-Kansas game." School mascot "Dock Yak" was set "to come to the University and do his bit toward instilling pep in the student body by dispensing his potent sugar-coated pills." The Kansas student government thought these activities so important that its leaders asked the chancellor of the University to cancel classes for the day—a request he turned down. In the past, Kansas's exuberant day of football rallies had ended in damage to property and disruption of class sessions. This time the pre-game festivities mocked Depression America's homeless: the title students chose for this day of fun and athletic "boosterism" was "Hobo Day." Treating the hobo as a quaint and comical figure, rather than as a somber symbol of the economic crisis, the Hobo Day events on campus featured a contest for which "everyone is expected to come on the hill dressed in a costume fitting in with his idea of what the well-dressed hobo should wear." "Prizes" were to "be awarded for the best dressed hobo and hoboette."[12]

The apolitical character of undergraduate life from 1929 through 1931 had it critics on campus. A few liberal, radical, and intellectual students bemoaned the provincialism of their classmates. But no matter how trenchant these criticisms, the national student body paid them little heed. A case in point was the experience of Edward R. Murrow, the most prominent student critic of collegiate political apathy at the start of the 1930s. Murrow, who in these early Depression years served as the president of the National Student Federation (NSF)—America's association of college student governments—came into office chiding undergraduates for focusing so much of their time on "fraternities, football and fun." He hoped that during his presidency the NSF could awaken student interest in national and international problems. Toward this end, Murrow initiated a variety of NSF activities, including a radio news show, *University on the Air* on the Columbia Broadcasting System (CBS), aimed at a student audience.[13]

Although Murrow's broadcasts were historic because they began his connection with CBS and helped launch his stellar journalistic career, neither they nor any other NSF activity in the Hoover era had much national impact on undergraduates. The campuses remained politically inert. Murrow left office as he had entered it, criticizing the political ignorance of American undergraduates. His parting address to the national NSF convention at Toledo in December 1931 again took collegians to task for "their greatest sins . . . : campus consciousness, political apathy, and smug complacency."[14]

If the apolitical character of undergraduates in the United States irritated such reform-minded Americans as Murrow, it absolutely astonished radical Europeans. Viewing American undergraduates in an international context, Harold Laski, a leftist British scholar, expressed shock at their unfamiliarity with American politics. After lecturing at Harvard, Yale, and the universities of Minnesota and North Carolina in 1931, Laski pronounced the American college student an "almost non-political animal [who] talks of American politics as though they were the remote affairs of a distant planet." Laski was so struck by this apolitical collegiate mind-set that he published a magazine article: "The Political Indifference of the American Undergraduate." He found that European college students were far superior to their American counterparts in both their understanding of politics and involvement in important political events.

> Everyone knows how great a part the student played in the emancipation of Russia and Spain. The contribution of the universities to the political life of England and France has been outstanding. . . . To the European observer few things are more startling than the contrast in this respect with America. . . . The idea that citizenship involves on his [the American student's] part an active interest in [political] affairs simply does not . . . occur to him.[15]

Laski observed that business rather than politics interested undergraduates. Political service seemed relatively unattractive to students because in their eyes politicians were corrupt, and an honest political career "rarely offers the spectacular career of industry." They thought that businessmen rather than politicians would shape American society. Laski concluded that the American undergraduate of 1931 "lacks a sense of the positive state because the predominance of the business man has given him no notion of its possibilities."[16]

There was nothing new about either Laski's discussion of the pro-business orientation of undergraduates or Murrow's complaints about collegiate political apathy. Though Murrow and Laski made their observations about undergraduates in 1931, these closely paralleled the criticisms of American students articulated by liberals and radicals in the 1920s. Laski's discussion of student adulation for capitalists was similar to Paul Blanshard's finding in 1926 that undergraduates "too often regard college as a back door to big business." Blanshard, an organizer for the League for Industrial Democracy (LID), a socialist-led educational organization, toured the nation's campuses repeatedly during the 1920s, but despaired of ever making an impact on undergraduates so long as "the diluted culture of salesmanship dominates undergraduate life." Norman Thomas, a colleague of Blanshard in the LID, shared his pessimism about the student political conscience. Thomas concluded in 1923 that most students were too avaricious to concern themselves with the flaws in the capitalist system. He found the undergraduate definition of success similar to that of the Chamber of Commerce. "The supreme god over all for most of our students is success measured by the usual standard of the credit rating one possesses and the kind of automobile one drives or in which one is driven."[17]

Much like Murrow in the early 1930s, Thomas during the 1920s was appalled that undergraduates preferred football, fraternities, and parties to serious political thought. Thomas blamed these student rituals for the intellectual shallowness and social conformity of undergraduates. He condemned the tendency of "fraternity houses to turn out a standardized product," which left students thinking, acting, and even dressing alike. Driving this point home, Thomas in 1923 told the story of a

> father who looked vainly for his son at Yale. Finally he went home in despair and telegraphed President Hadley: "Send home my son at once." The President replied: "Which is he?" To which the answer came: "Any one will do. They all look alike."[18]

The reason for the continuity in these complaints about undergraduates is that American students had changed remarkably little either politically or economically since the 1920s. The prevalent undergraduate style of life and thought from 1929 until 1932 was shaped less by the Great Depression than by both the values of 1920s America, and the collegiate traditions inherited from that prosperous and politically conservative decade. During the opening years of the Depression, collegians continued to behave as if the prosperity of the 1920s had never ended. The economic crisis had yet to shatter the optimistic spirit, insularity, and materialism of the dominant college student culture.

This puzzling indifference to the Depression is linked to both the class background of collegians and the type of youth culture this generated on campus. College students came largely from the middle class and, unlike working class Americans, could usually afford to ignore the Depression in its early stages. Their families had emerged from the 1920s with savings and other assets, which they could draw upon to keep the economic crisis temporarily from their doors.[19] Though these middle-class Americans could not permanently escape the Depression, their economic crisis was delayed during the time it took their financial resources to dwindle. For the majority of middle-class college youths, the Depression began after—some two years after—the Depression devastated blue-collar America. This is why from 1929 through 1931 collegians barely took notice of the economic crisis.

This collegiate behavior was a far cry from that of millions of unemployed Americans, thrown into crisis and despair by the Great Depression; it suggests that in the first stages the Depression was not a national crisis shared by those on both ends of the social scale. The sense of crisis and the growing blight of poverty did not affect all social classes equally or simultaneously from 1929 through 1931. America, as always, constituted a stratified society, but now the key division existed between those who could and those who could not afford to ignore the Depression. And since the majority of collegians in 1931 fell into the former category, the apolitical undergraduate culture they inherited from the prosperous 1920s could continue to dominate student life on most campuses.[20]

College enrollment figures reflected the ability of the middle class to shelter its youth from the economic crisis during the early Depression years. Between 1929 and 1930 American undergraduate enrollments increased 4.4 percent, from 1,053,955 to 1,100,737. This upward trend accelerated in the next academic year, when enrollments rose by 4.9 percent. In order to handle this growing student population, college and university staff expanded, reaching record highs in 1930 and 1931. At a time when factories, banks, and farms were closing down, higher education remained a growth industry.[21]

The student population was one of the last groups in society stung by the unemployment crisis because a majority of undergraduates did not work their way through school. At the dawn of the Great Depression 77 percent of the women and 54 percent of the men attending college paid none of their college expenses—instead, their parents paid the bill.[22] It was these non-working students who had the most time to engage in campus activities, and at the private and most of the public colleges and universities they set the tone of student life.

The survey data collected by sociologist Robert Angell at the University of Michigan between 1929 and 1931 suggests just how economically buffered this leisured undergraduate majority was from the Depression. Angell found that 73.7 percent of the non-working students at Michigan had either a stable or rising income. These students were doubly fortunate because while their incomes held or improved, prices fell, due to the deflationary impact of the slumping economy. Consequently, they could obtain bargain prices for many goods and services. This meant that, in Angell's words, their "standard of living went up, since the main items . . . [they purchased] all show increased consumption."[23]

Their relatively affluent backgrounds and their location amidst one of the nation's few growth industries encouraged undergraduates to underestimate the seriousness of the economic crisis. Even a calamity as grave as the stock market crash attracted little attention or concern among undergraduates. Students tended to assume that the crash—as regrettable as it might be—would not hurt them personally; they would be able to continue living the comfortable middle-class life. Capturing this nonchalant collegiate spirit, the editor of Vassar's student newspaper wrote on Thanksgiving 1929,

> The holiday was set aside by our forefathers as a day when they could take a long rest and think about their blessings. . . . We have our blessings too, though they may be that Dad didn't put all his substance

on the stock market; that new fur coats are pretty nice; and that dancing at the Ritz is a comfort . . .[24]

In the months following the crash, students also saw no need to become alarmed because they thought President Hoover would prevent Wall Street's misfortune from producing a lasting economic slump. On those rare occasions when the student press commented on the economic crisis, it tended to praise "the President's zest for action and progress," and to claim that thanks to Hoover "the backbone of the crisis is now broken." This faith in Hoover was consistent with the Republican assumptions and pro-business orientation that undergraduates had held throughout the 1920s. During that decade collegians—even though not active in political campaigns—polled more strongly in favor of conservative and pro-business Republicans than did the general electorate.[25]

The dominant student attitude toward the economy during the early Depression years had an elitist cast, bordering on arrogance. Undergraduates tended to assume that they were the future leaders of society, whose skills and education assured them promising careers in any economic climate. Such attitudes derived from the exclusive nature of American higher education. Despite the growth of college enrollments between 1900 and 1931, the undergraduate population remained small relative both to its age group and the rest of society. In 1931, the peak year of undergraduate enrollment during the first third of the twentieth century, only 12 percent of all college age youth were able to enroll in institutions of higher education.[26] With a college education conferring such clear elite status, it was natural for students to consider themselves too high on the social scale to have any worries about unemployment. James Wechsler, a Columbia alumnus, recalled that this attitude was widespread among his classmates who entered college in 1931. "We felt we were lucky to be there because according to legend, a college degree would give us a big advantage over our contemporaries in the ultimate pursuit of [career goals and economic] success."[27]

This undergraduate overconfidence received considerable reinforcement from the older generation. In December 1930, more than a year after the stock market crash, a leading college employment officer was still telling students and the press that the "ambitious and capable" college graduate "ought not consider the present business depression . . . a great obstacle" to obtaining a well paying job.[28] Advising college graduates in an article published during the 1930 commencement season, Bruce Barton, the advertising industry pioneer, stressed that they would have no trouble finding employment. In fact, Barton was concerned that graduates might spoil themselves by "taking too good a job at first," rather than working their way up to the top. Citing Barton and echoing his sentiments, Barnard College's student newspaper, the *Bulletin,* gave advice to the graduates of 1930, assuring them of their pick of jobs. Ignoring the possibility that the Depression could hurt them, the *Bulletin* suggested that after graduating college women should

> try to get dad . . . to let you on your own for a year. . . . Knock about for a year. Get a job and give it up and get another. . . . When the migration is over, then get another degree or take a life job or marry. You will begin to be equipped for life. . . . Your stock in any market will go up immediately.[29]

Not all college students, however, were so fortunate as the Barnard editor's words might suggest. A significant minority of undergraduates could not look to "dad" for financial support. Some 20 percent of the male and 11 percent of the female undergraduates in the United States received no parental economic support and were entirely self-supporting during their college years. And an even larger minority was partially self-supporting, so that 46 percent of the men and 23 percent of the women undergraduates were employed during their college years. Soon after the Depression began, this working minority began to experience difficulties securing the part-time jobs they had traditionally relied upon. At Columbia University, for example, students who needed employment to help finance their education had fallen into "dire straits" by fall 1931, according to the college administration. Jobs for these Columbia students had declined by 75 percent since 1930.[30]

The problems of these working students were largely ignored by the affluent campus majority from 1929 through 1931. The dominant undergraduate culture proved as blind to the hardships the Depression had brought on to campus as it had been to the poverty spreading in society at large. Such blindness was apparently facilitated by the relatively small proportion of collegians who lacked basic necessities such as food and clothing. At Michigan, for instance, Angell found that of the 85 working students adversely affected by the Depression in 1931, only three had cut their diet "to the extent of impairing their health."[31] Students in such desperate circumstances were likely to drop out of college, which only added to the tendency of the affluent majority to be insulated from the plight of needy youths. And their plight was too serious a matter to be addressed by student social institutions, which seemed capable of little more than boosting the traditional juvenile campus rituals: rushing, hazing, proms, homecomings, football, interclass rivalries, and riots.

This juvenile mind-set and the middle-class atmosphere on campus made the early Depression years especially difficult for low income students—adding a psychological burden to students already hard pressed with economic problems. Thrust into this culture of affluence and classmates still bent on acting as if the Depression did not exist, working students could easily end up feeling alienated. As one midwestern student observed in 1930, "Being in narrow financial straits and seeing other students who have plenty of money, automobiles and such things drive many a student worker to ruin a good disposition."[32]

For low income students it was sometimes easier to accept the collegiate majority's affluence, than its indifference to campus poverty. They felt that there was no excuse for neglecting the suffering of one's class-mates—and this neglect left some of the less privileged students bitter. Film critic Pauline Kael, who as a student encountered great financial difficulty working her way through college during the Great Depression, recalled that such insensitivity was especially strong among the campus's social elite in the Greek houses. Even three decades later, when Kael spoke to Studs Terkel about her college years, she remained angry about this insensitivity.

> There were kids who didn't have a place to sleep, huddling under bridges on the campus. I had a scholarship, but there were times when I didn't have food. The meals were often three candy bars. . . . There was an embarrassment at college where a lot of the kids were well-heeled. I still have a resentment against the fraternity boys and the sorority girls with their cashmere sweaters and the pearls. Even now, when I lecture at colleges, I have this feeling about those terribly overdressed kids. It wasn't a hatred because I wanted these things, but because they didn't understand what was going on. . . . The rich kids . . . didn't give a damn.[33]

Though there were an insufficient number of indigent students to produce campus breadlines or other highly visible symbols of distress, the plight of these students could have become a campus issue in 1930 or 1931 had the dominant undergraduate culture not been so snobbishly bourgeois. The traditional attitude of the affluent student majority was that if you could not afford college, you did not belong there. And in its early stages the Depression had not altered this way of thinking. Indeed, on many campuses, particularly the more exclusive private colleges, students from prosperous families continued to display patronizing or hostile attitudes toward economically disadvantaged collegians. At Harvard, students who lacked the funds to live in dormitories were disparaged as "meatballs." Journalist Theodore White recalled that few of his more wealthy Harvard classmates in the 1930s—who were appropriately known as "white men"—would have anything to do with him since he was a "Jewish meatball."[34]

Such attitudes were by no means confined to Harvard. On almost all campuses the competitive social atmosphere promoted by the fraternity-sorority system taught students to value affluence and a leisured lifestyle, and to look down upon—and reject from membership in their clubs and social activities—students who could not afford that lifestyle. This was even true at less exclusive public institutions, such as the University of Kansas. In the fall of 1930, the editor of that university's student newspaper complained that the collegiate culture which prevailed on the Lawrence campus was out of step with the national image of Kansas as "a democratic western state." He charged that student life at Kansas was "snobbish" and fostered "some of the most rigid social distinctions of any institution in the country." At Kansas those students in the highest campus "caste," the better Greek houses, would rarely associate with non-Greeks, who by definition "do not rate." The fraternity or sorority member who dated outside this "caste" was seen as "virtually a social failure."[35]

Student concern about dating was not limited, however, to questions about who was dating whom. The issue of how much regulatory authority the colleges had over student dating also aroused interest among undergraduates. In fact, it was not the Depression, but dating regulations which provoked America's most militant student protest in 1930. This protest erupted at Montana State College in Bozeman, where students went on strike against regulations that required them to terminate their dates in time for an 11 p.m. dormitory curfew. Similarly, University of Wyoming President A.G. Crane provoked a student strike in 1931 by undertaking a "crusade against college lovemaking." According to student affidavits, Crane sparked the walkout when he "made a round of parked cars during an intermission of a university dance Friday night, opened the machine [car] doors, and made remarks concerning the morals of the couples found petting."[36]

These protests—and similar, though less militant anti-paternalist protests—on other campuses suggest where American student priorities lay during the early Depression years. Undergraduates who could not be bothered with economic or political issues lost their apathy quickly when it came to defending their social lives from adult supervision.[37] It was on these lifestyle issues that the dominant student culture showed its only liberal tendencies—advocating that collegians should be able to dance, drink, and date free from the overbearing moral policing of college officials.[38]

These tendencies toward social permissiveness again attest that undergraduates in 1930 and 1931 were heirs of the student culture of the 1920s. The only national rebellion on the campuses in the 1920s had been on lifestyle issues. Jazz Age collegians pioneered a freer sexual and social life, portrayed in F. Scott Fitzgerald's novels and symbolized in the daring dress and socializing of the flappers. The irony had been that these same students whose attacks on cultural puritanism shocked their parents in the 1920s, nonetheless shared their conservative Republican political values.[39] Conforming to this pattern, collegians in 1930 and 1931 who were too politically coventional even to conceive of revolting against Herbert Hoover, dropped their conservative demeanor when confronted with threats to their social life.

Even in this cultural sphere, however, the undergraduates of the early Depression years—though supportive of the permissive attitudes toward drinking and dating handed down from the 1920s—were hardly a rebellious lot. Culturally the undergraduates of 1930 and 1931 were a post-revolutionary generation: they were the beneficiaries of a cultural revolt already fought and largely won by their predecessors in the Jazz era. Though willing to oppose administrators who tried to turn the clock back on their social life, students such as those who did strike at Montana and Wyoming, were sporadically defending old gains, not pioneering new forms of social and sexual rebellion.

By the late 1920s and early 1930s, the new forms of student cultural rebellion that had appeared on the campuses a half-decade earlier had now grown old. For instance, the risqué flapper dresses of the coeds and the baggy trousers of the male students, which symbolized the "collegiate semi-bohemianism" of the 1920s had become passé. However, what replaced them were not more rebellious clothes, but rather more conventional ones. At the women's colleges dressing became increasingly formal. "The disappearence of the flapper" had, as the *New York Times* observed, been followed in the late 1920s by the "advent of the lady." And for men on many campuses, especially in the eastern colleges, the trend was toward the "utmost conservatism in dress." A liberal Ivy League critic complained in 1931 that the "Yale or Princeton student who wishes to make a mark dresses like a young banker on the Exchange—smartly, expensively, unostentatiously. He jumps into black suits and stiff collars at the slightest provocation." Among undergraduates, "insurgency is outmoded," and had been so since "about 1928," the *Times* concluded. "They are now painfully conformist."[40]

With even cultural rebelliousness a fading memory on campus and political apathy ascendant, the American student body of 1931 seemed to have almost no radical potential. This left some less conventional students, such as William Harlan Hale, in a gloomy mood. Hale had spent his college years at Yale editing a liberal literary magazine, aimed at rousing student interest in political issues and cultural criticism. As his graduation approached in the spring of 1931, Hale confessed that the magazine had failed in its purpose because at Yale, as at other colleges, the average undergraduate was a "collared conservative." That year, in his *New Republic* article pessimistically entitled "A Dirge for College Liberalism," Hale portrayed the college rebel as an endangered species, and predicted that the future held out the "prospects of a continuing inertia" on campus.[41] Hale's article, however, had not even mentioned the Depression. Since the economic crisis had yet to hit Hale and most of his classmates, the retiring liberal editor failed to foresee its potential for awakening the spirit of revolt on campus. Events would soon prove his eulogy for collegiate insurgency quite premature.

II

The Depression finally began to overwhelm the collegiate middle class in 1932. This was the first peacetime year in twentieth-century America when college enrollments fell, slipping by more than 4 percent. It had taken three years of the worst economic crisis in American history to bring college enrollments down. The fact that the Depression's impact on campus had been so delayed was, in the words of a 1932 *New York Times* report, a testament to "the intense faith . . . of the American people in higher education. . . . The college has been the last institution in the country to show in the number of its clientele the effects of the Depression." The 1932 enrollment drop demonstrated that the middle class was losing its ability to shelter its youth from the economic crisis. Although funds and faith in higher education had initially insulated the American campus from that crisis, by 1932 not even the middle class could keep the Great Depression off campus. And in the coming year this negative trend would show no sign of abating. In 1933 enrollments again declined by more than 4 percent; thus within this two-year period some 80,000 youths who ordinarily would have attended college were, because of the Depression, unable to do so.[42]

The drop in enrollments which began in 1932 contributed to a fiscal crisis among American colleges and universities; it denied these institutions the income traditionally received from tuition and other student fees. This year also brought a substantial cut in state funding of higher education and an unprecedented drop in private financial contributions. Some colleges reported that in the 1932–33 academic year their gift income had fallen by as much as 80 percent.[43]

This poor economic news led to the most severe retrenchment since the rise of the American university. College administrators eliminated educational programs, slashed building and maintenance expenditures, increased student fees, and reduced both the number and salaries of faculty. According to the American Association of University Professors (AAUP), 1932 was economically the worst year in history for faculty: 77 out of the 125 colleges and universities polled by the AAUP reported a decline in faculty salaries.[44]

Reports from campuses throughout the United States indicated that the 1932–33 academic year was emerging as the worst economic period that undergraduates had ever faced. According to a survey taken in October 1932, 76 out of 77 colleges and universities confronted "the most urgent need in . . . [their] history for scholarships, loans, deferred tuition payments and opportunities for earning during term time." While the wealthiest institutions, such as Harvard, had the funds to meet this unprecedented demand for student aid, many colleges and universities discovered that the reduction in their own income left them unable to assist this growing army of needy students—and without such aid, tens of thousands of students were forced to drop out.[45]

With the economic crisis overtaking the American collegiate world in 1932, the mood on campus began to change. Though the juvenile escapades and athletic ballyhoo did not cease, they were losing support; the collegiate culture was gradually becoming eroded by the Depression. "Officials of institutions from Boston to Berkeley estimated that the chief effect of the Depression had been to modulate the carefree joy of campus life and to focus the attention of students on books and blackboards," according to a *New York Times* survey in the fall of 1932. "The student of 1932, many of the replies indicated, has sold the flashy roadster and is buying second-hand books, and more than ever before is asking for . . . low priced dormitory rooms, and a chance to work his way." Faculty members found their students becoming more serious, concerned about social and political questions, eager for answers about why the Depression had begun and how it could be ended.[46]

Another sign of the changing mood on campus in 1932 came with a shift in collegiate attitudes toward low income students. Collegiate snobbery and indifference to the problems of working students did not vanish overnight. Indeed, they never disappeared completely. But as the Depression deepened in 1932 and launched an era of retrenchment on campus, these old attitudes were challenged. As students awakened to the seriousness of the Depression off campus, they began to face its effects on campus. Student complaints and exposés about the problems of working and unemployed undergraduates surfaced with increasingly frequency, as did criticism of classmates who had ignored or contributed to the exploitation of working students.

Letters, articles, and editorials began to appear in the undergraduate press that sympathized with low income students and documented their increasing hardships. Typifying this new concern about campus poverty, the University of Michigan campus daily in the winter of 1932 published a story showing that "dozens of students who are carrying a full load of school work . . . may be found rooming together in some attic at a dollar and a half a week, living on milk and crackers and occasionally a can of beans." The article revealed that for such students clothing was almost as big a problem as food; they could not afford new clothes, and in some cases were going through their entire college careers in the tattered garments they had worn daily since high school.[47]

These reports revealed that because low income students so desperately needed work in order to stay in school, they were ripe for exploitation by employers. From many campus communities came complaints about a steadily worsening work environment, in which student employees were overworked and underpaid. Students who did domestic work in private homes and those who labored in rooming houses were terribly exploited, complained an irate undergraduate, who wrote to the campus daily at the University of Wisconsin in 1932. His letter told of housewives using the Depression as a pretext for firing their full-time maids—who earned room and board plus $5 to $8 per week—and hiring in their place unsalaried students, who were required to do all the work formerly done by the maid in exchange for "only a mattress and meals." This student also reported that local boarding houses hired undergraduates to tend the furnaces and maintenance work, but paid them no wages. All the student workers received for their labor was "the privilege of sleeping in an ill-lighted, cold basement room." He concluded that students needed a labor union to "remedy this condition which amounts to nothing more nor less than slavery."[48]

The campus press began to recount the grievances of many other types of student employees, including restaurant workers. Students complained that campus area restaurants gave them less than thirty cents' worth of food for an hour of hard labor. Meals given to student workers were charged at retail value rather than wholesale prices. In the worst of these restaurants, students found that their hourly labor earned them only "hash-house meals worth five or six cents," and food that was either going bad or already spoiled.[49]

Among the most prominent targets of this new criticism were the fraternity and sorority houses. They were accused of being among the most exploitative employers—underpaying low income students who worked in their kitchens, a practice held to be especially egregious since this victimized their own classmates. At UC Berkeley, for instance, a student angrily wrote that

> the various refined clubs, fraternities and sororities . . . regard the needy students as so many free laborers. It has been the experience of the writer that in most cases an hour or even longer period of "stepping on it" in dishwashing and other delicate jobs brings nothing more than a plate full of hash or some hamburgers. Many students put up with it, ruin their digestion with yesterday's leftovers, and suffer in general simply because there is no way out.[50]

A similar report from the University of Michigan chided the "enlightened girls and boys of the sororities and fraternities" for paying their student dishwashers the equivalent of ten cents an hour. "Nowhere, except in the exploited cotton belt of the South are such low wages paid."[51]

Along with this growing willingness to acknowledge the crisis in the part-time job market came an equally significant change in student attitudes toward their career prospects. As the Depression worsened in late 1931 and early 1932, the arrogant undergraduate notion that the college-educated were too elite a group to have their careers ruined by the slumping economy began to be questioned. Student anxieties about their career prospects soared as employment figures in the business world and the professions grew more dismal. Compounding these worries was the increasing acknowledgment by campus employment offices that graduates now faced an unprecedented job crisis. Students began publicly to discuss their fear that this constricted job market might be a permanent problem rather than a temporary aberration.[52]

The Depression was striking too close to home to be ignored by collegians and, as a result, a sense of vulnerability appeared in undergraduate culture. Students came to recognize that they could become victims of the economic crisis because they had witnessed the losses of the middle class and well educated in their midst. These included: faculty who either lost salaries or jobs; classmates who either dropped out or worked poorly paying jobs to continue in school; graduates whose college degrees had proven useless in the depressed job market; and parents whose savings had been exhausted and careers disrupted by the Depression.

As the Depression entered its third year, undergraduates started to discuss a prospect that in the 1920s would have been unthinkable: that college graduates would face downward rather than upward social mobility, and experience poverty rather than prosperity. The image of the college graduate standing in a soup line found its way into student discourse, reflecting the fact that on campus overconfidence was giving way to anxiety concerning the future of college-trained youth. This could be seen, for instance, in a Thanksgiving editorial written by Reed Harris, editor of Columbia's student newspaper, which stressed that a college degree was no shield against the economic crisis. Harris mocked President Hoover's call for Americans to pick "out everything possible to be thankful for"; choosing instead to visit those too poor to afford Thanksgiving turkey— New Yorkers standing on a soup line.

> Here shivering miserably . . . waiting patiently for the long line in which they were standing to move that they acquire their meagre portion of free soup, we found graduates of the class of 1931, and others of classes not much older. Wearily these men, we discovered, had been dragging themselves from office to office in search of a job regardless of its nature. . . . Yet these men a short time ago left college filled with ambition of a type so high that only a newly graduated and somewhat naive senior, whose sheepskin was still damp with the ink of many signatures, could conceive of them. One can scarcely believe that these bedraggled, ambitionless and prematurely aged individuals are the men who less than a year ago . . . pursued rather carefree existences at various centers of learning. . . . What a sad grey the original white collars of the great middle class have attained.[53]

The realism and pessimism reflected in Harris's editorial became widespread among undergraduates as the Depression continued because not only were student attitudes shifting, the student population itself was changing. The students who had entered college before the Depression were graduating. By fall 1932, the freshmen/women, sophomores, and juniors were all classes that had entered college after the economic crisis began—making this the first year in which members of the Depression generation outnumbered those who started college before the Depression. By the following fall there would no longer be an undergraduate class that had entered college before the Depression. This meant that the college population was becoming progressively more distant from the prosperous campus world of the 1920s. This generational change helped to foster a sense that the apolitical, insular, "rah-rah" collegiate culture in-

herited from the 1920s was outdated and fast becoming irrelevant to the
needs of college youth in Depression America.

With a new student generation emerging and the economic crisis
shaking both middle-class youths and their colleges in 1932, students started
to question the traditional undergraduate notion that college years should
be a fun-filled retreat from the real world. The old collegiate rituals which
had been the heart of the apolitical student lifestyle inherited from the
1920s came under scrutiny as never before. Symptomatic of this new, serious spirit was the debate that erupted at Vassar College—the oldest and
most elite women's college in the United States—over the junior prom in
1932.

Vassar proms were an old and expensive tradition, costing thousands
of dollars for the luxurious hall rental, the band, taxis, flowers, gowns. A
vocal group of students, including the editors of the college's newspaper,
the *Vassar Miscellany News,* advocated the cancellation of the prom because
they thought it self-indulgent to engage in expensive partying at a time
when so much of the surrounding community had been impoverished by
the Depression. These students argued that there was no justification for
Vassar

> to flaunt its extravagance in the face of a community which has learned
> the meaning of starvation. . . . It is manifestly unessential to our well-
> being that we expose ourselves annually to the delights of Prom . . . .
> Have we any right to go on fulfilling Hollywood's picture of the Vassar
> girl when it involves a greater expense than we have been willing to de-
> vote to organizations which are striving to alleviate the misery of every
> Main Street?[54]

Vassar, they argued, had already fallen behind other campuses in recognizing the need to cease the traditional frivolity in this period of grave
economic crisis. "Yale realized the necessity," wrote the editor of the *Vassar Miscellany News,* "and eliminated its Derby Day celebrations; Williams
has given up its fall house parties. If we dispense with our Proms we shall
not have the glory of innovators, but if we do not we shall deserve the
ultimate criticism of blindness and egotism."[55]

Criticism of the prom grew stronger and persisted for over a month
at Vassar. The *Vassar Miscellany News* ran four editorials attacking the insensitivity of those who had organized this party. In the face of these
attacks, prom organizers moved toward a compromise: they would cut the
price of prom tickets by one-third and donate fifty cents from each ticket
to aid the unemployed in the Poughkeepsie community. But this was denounced as mere tokenism by the prom's critics. "To spend the couple of
thousand dollars that will be spent in all on this pleasant ritual," the Vassar newspaper editorialized,

> and then with a philanthropic smirk give some seventy-five dollars to
> relieve starving and homeless people—this seems to us worse than jeering

openly . . . . For some reason or other we believe that the profound needs of human beings for food, clothes, home, security, peace of mind, are more important than the need of a lot of well-fed young bourgeoises for a Junior Prom.[56]

Critics of the prom at Vassar understood that they reflected a new "school of thought flourishing in this particular world debacle"—that promoted an ideal of social responsibility which would have been alien to collegians in the less troubled world of the 1920s. According to the *Vassar Miscellany News*

> The theme-song of the school is "make the younger generation aware of the unhappy world, the community of which they are a part," shatter the prejudices they inherit from their upper middle class relatives; shatter the eat-drink-and be-merry-ness with which they pursue pleasure, at proms, on weekends; make them see that they are dancing on the edge of a volcano; make them feel the next war, the twelve million unemployed, the race conflicts, the undernourished children . . . destroy their complacency, make them challenge the status quo . . .[57]

Although the Vassar prom was not canceled in 1932, the severe criticism surrounding it suggested that the party was over for the old apolitical student culture, which had created and championed proms and all of the other insulating rituals of undergraduate life. No longer would such rituals and the carefree lifestyle they symbolized go unchallenged on campus. The Depression, having at last caught up with the college world in 1932, set the stage for the politicization of American student culture: a process that would involve questioning not merely proms but profits, not just the inequities on campus but the inequality of the capitalist system itself. And the lead role in shaping this new collegiate world would be played by a type of political activist who in the previous decade had not the slightest influence on undergraduate life—students in communist and socialist organizations.

Chapter 2

Cafeteria Commies

> Daniel, a tall young man . . . wore his curly hair long. Steel-rimmed
> spectacles and a full mustache, brown like his hair, made him look if
> not older than he was then more self-possessed and opinionated. Let's
> face it, he looked cool, deliberately cool. In fact nothing about his
> appearance was accidental. If he'd lived in the nineteen thirties and
> came on this way he would be a young commie. A cafeteria commie.
>
> E.L. Doctorow, *The Book of Daniel* (New York, 1971), 4.

Leadership in the collegiate transition from political apathy
to activism came from the Left and initially it came with
a New York accent. Almost all of Depression America's early eruptions of
student protest—including the student expedition to Harlan County, the
Columbia free speech strike, and the City Colleges' anti-tuition movement
during the 1932 spring semester—either occurred on or were launched
from campuses in New York City. Though consisting of only a small minority of the student body in New York, the city's campus radicals were
the best organized, most politically ambitious and militant student activists
in the nation. New York's emergence as the center of the student revolt
of the early 1930s was largely the work of the National Student League
(NSL), the New York-based radical organization responsible for orchestrating the first political protests by collegians during the Depression decade. The birth of the NSL in December 1931 marked the organizational
beginning of student activism in the Depression era. Coming at a time
when nationally militant political protest did not yet exist on campus, the
NSL's founding in New York attested that the city's student activists were
ahead of their time and of the rest of American undergraduates on the
road to mass protest.

The role that New York's campuses played in igniting the student
movement was facilitated by the city's unique political climate. New York
was the capital city of American radicalism during the Depression decade.

Here the Communist Party, which during this decade became America's largest radical organization, had its national headquarters and strongest following. The city was also a stronghold for the Socialist Party, which had considerable influence in metropolitan area labor unions. The radical intelligentsia too made New York its home and used the city as a base for publishing the nation's most important leftist magazines and journals. Evoking the intense radicalism and heated ideological debate in New York during the Depression, Lionel Abel recalled that intellectually the city's leftists "went to Russia and spent most of the decade there . . . . New York became the most interesting part of the Soviet Union . . . the one part of that country in which the struggle between Stalin and Trotsky could be openly expressed. And was! And how!"[1] The dynamism of the radical movement in New York spilled over on to the city's campuses.

On Manhattan's Upper West Side the campus intellectual milieu was a student radical's delight. Within a twenty block radius of the Columbia campus lived the greatest assemblage of academic progressives and radicals in Depression America. The faculties of Columbia University and Teachers College boasted some of the nation's most famous liberal and Left-leaning professors, including John Dewey, George Counts, Franz Boas, and Rexford Tugwell. Less intellectually prominent, but more active in campus politics were the young radical instructors and graduate students who had been attracted to Columbia by its eminent faculty and liberal reputation. Several of these young radical academics, including Donald Henderson and Addison Cutler, had especially close links to undergraduate leftists. Henderson, in fact, would serve as the NSL's first executive secretary.[2]

Also in the Columbia neighborhood was Union Theological Seminary, home to two of America's most renowned religious radicals, Reinhold Niebuhr and Harry Ward. Niebuhr had presided over a Commission of Christian Associations in 1931 that generated great controversy in Protestant circles by advocating a socialist America. He and Ward inspired a whole generation of radical young theologians, who as college chaplains would help make the campus YMCAs and YWCAs active in the struggle for peace and social justice.[3]

A few subway stops away from Union Theological Seminary and Columbia was the uptown campus of the City College of New York (CCNY), which produced student radical leaders at about the rate that Notre Dame churned out college football stars. The initial impetus leading to the birth of the NSL come from the CCNY campus. CCNY's prominence in the early stages of the student movement derived from sources quite different from Columbia's. CCNY lacked Columbia's cast of eminent liberal and Left-leaning faculty, who might attract bright undergraduate radicals. Indeed with the exception of the philosopher Morris Raphael Cohen, the CCNY faculty was virtually barren of distinguished liberal scholars. The advent of a vibrant student Left at CCNY, in fact, had nothing to do with the faculty. CCNY bred student radicalism because of the explosive interaction between the Depression, the working class culture of the student body, the larger radical milieu of New York, and the repressive policies of an intolerant campus administration.[4]

New York was one of the few cities in Depression America that ran a tuition-free municipal college system. CCNY, Hunter College for women, and Brooklyn College together constituted the nation's largest free city college system. Because they were tuition-free, these colleges attracted a student population quite different from that of most colleges. Where the average college was predominantly middle class, the student body at New York's municipal colleges had a much higher percentage of students from low income families.[5]

Because these New York city college students often came from families with virtually no savings, when the economy crashed, their parents could not shelter them from the consequences. They were stung by the Depression much sooner than most American collegians. Indeed, while nationally the middle-class student body was relatively unaffected by the Depression until 1932, the overwhelmingly working-class student body in New York's municipal colleges had already been badly hurt by the Depression in early 1931. At the city colleges, students had difficulty paying for even such basic necessities as textbooks, lunch, and transportation. Symptomatic of the hard times which beset city college students soon after the Depression began, was an incident economist Harry Magdoff witnessed as a CCNY undergraduate.

> Jobs were unavailable. But then there was a sign up on the bulletin board . . . "Jobs available—Part-time for Chemical Engineering Students." Gee, everybody was envious . . . . It turned out it was to shovel snow. There was a heavy snowfall in New York. They knew that if they announced snow shoveling jobs they'd have a thousand guys applying. So that by limiting it to chemical engineering they were able to cope with the thing.[6]

This relative economic deprivation had political consequences. The personal anxieties and political questioning that the economic crisis unleashed nationally on campus in 1932 had already progressed much further in these depressed City College campuses.

The unique ethnic and political background of the student body in New York's city colleges helped make their campuses fertile ground for leftist organizers—so much so that Hunter and Brooklyn College radicals would be only slightly less prominent than their CCNY counterparts in founding the NSL. These municipal college students came overwhelmingly from the city's ghettoes, which were enclaves of East European Jewish immigrants. Within these ghettoes was a powerful minority tradition of radical politics and working-class organization. Though radicals never constituted a majority within these ghetto communities, their voices dominated some of the city's leading Yiddish cultural institutions, including the Jewish press. This radical tradition was an inheritance of the socialist bund and the days of resistance to the Czar; it was also the outcome of Jewish concentration in the garment industry's work force and in their socialist-led labor unions.[7]

The ghetto world, so different from mainstream America, was one in which leftists were not seen as pariahs. Radical activists were tolerated, and their views attracted a respectful hearing in an immigrant community that had grown accustomed to such politics in Europe. It was easy to grow up in New York's ghettoes without experiencing the type of hostility toward radicalism common in much of America. Indeed, if one's parents and friends were involved in the ghetto's radical circles, anti-capitalist thought could seem normal rather than deviant. Literary critic Alfred Kazin, raised in a Brooklyn ghetto during this era, recalled that for him " 'Socialism' was a way of life since everyone . . . I knew in New York was a Socialist, more or less . . . . I was a Socialist as so many Americans were 'Christians'; I had always lived in a Socialist atmosphere." [8]

Exposed to radicalism before they ever set foot on a college campus, some of the student activists who came out of these ghetto communities began radical organizing at an early age: during their adolescent and high school years. This would be an added source of strength for the student movement on New York's campuses in the early 1930s because it meant that the student Left's leaders included political veterans. Among the NSL's founders, Joseph Clark, Max Gordon, and Max Weiss had this type of organizing experience. In their pre-college days, Clark, Gordon, and Weiss had been active in the Young Communist League (YCL), the Communist Party's youth organization. Through the YCL they developed skills as political pamphleteers, speakers, and strike organizers. Moreover, YCL members (and their counterparts in the Young People's Socialist League, the Socialist Party's youth group) were active in several New York high schools during the early 1930s, so that by the time such radical activists as Clark and Gordon arrived at college, they were already accustomed to the task of politically recruiting classmates in a school setting.[9]

The seriousness and political sophistication of students with this type of Party background was extraordinary. This could be seen, for instance, at New Utrecht High School in Brooklyn, one of the city's more politically active schools. Here in 1930 Joseph Clark exhibited some of the same leadership qualities that he would display as a college radical organizer the following year. At New Utrecht, Clark helped establish a History Club. While most youths their age struggled through basic civics courses and knew little about Marxism, Clark and his fellow History Club members were analyzing the radical issues of the day and holding debates on them between communist and socialist students.[10]

These young leftists were often better informed about radical issues than were their high school teachers. At New Utrecht the students' knowledge and militance frightened some instructors. So in 1930 school authorities tried to close down the History Club, and when they did, Clark

and his fellow radicals responded not as chastened school children but as
defiant militants. The students protested vigorously and tried to show that
the assault on their club was an example of the type of political suppression that characterized the entire capitalist system. History Club member
George Watt, who later became a national leader of the student movement, recalled the defense of their club as

> a very dramatic moment when right in this little school you had almost a
> replica, a reenactment of what was going on in the larger society. . . . I
> remember walking into the Club and there was Joe Clark . . . pointing
> his finger at the faculty advisor . . . who had just ordered the Club's
> suspension. [Joe began] shouting at him "You have taught us the lesson
> of state power and its oppression" . . . . And around the room were
> thirty members of the service squad, like that was the police power right
> in the classroom. So that for young minds like ours that left a very, very
> strong imprint.[11]

As they would do later at the college level, Clark and his YCL comrades at New Utrecht sought to use immediate economic issues as a vehicle for politicizing their classmates. The issue they focused upon at New
Utrecht was a milk price increase in the cafeteria. The school's predominantly working-class student body had been hurt by the Depression and
had difficulty affording this price increase. So, when the YCL organized
a milk boycott, the student response was overwhelming. The protests
prodded the school administration to stop the price increase. Outside observers were astounded that such an effective protest could be organized
by such young students. The New York *Daily News* was so impressed by
the militance that before long it dubbed New Utrecht "the cradle of the
American revolution."[12]

There was an unmistakable precociousness to these students who engaged in political activism so early in their lives. They were confident that
the Left held the keys both to history and political organization, and that
as part of the Left they—despite their youth—could lead effective political
actions. Such confidence was evident in George Watt's attitude toward the
milk protest at New Utrecht. Though prior to the milk boycott Watt "hadn't
any experience in this kind of organization," his lack of political experience did not faze him in the least. Watt was certain that he could help
lead the boycott to victory because he would follow the advice in Communist Party leader William Z. Foster's *Strike Strategy*. This was, Watt recalled,

> a manual on how you organized a strike; how you set up committees,
> rank and file committees; how you get community support; how you neu-
> tralize certain sectors and direct your main fire against the main target.
> It was a very useful little pamphlet which I applied almost literally in
> almost every instance to the student organization. And it worked. It worked
> very well.[13]

While students with Clark's and Watt's organizing experience played an important role in the early NSL, they did not constitute a majority within the League's founding group. Among the ghetto-raised students who participated in creating the NSL, it was more common to find youths who had been Left-leaning, but not members of socialist or communist groups in their pre-college years. Though not politically active in high school, such NSL founders as Harry Magdoff, Adam Lapin, and Joseph Starobin had—in a slightly less obvious way than those already in leftist youth organizations—been groomed for collegiate radicalism by the working-class immigrant milieu of their ghetto communities. Such students came from households which (though not affiliated with a radical party) tended to be strongly pro-union, broadly sympathetic to the Left and to the struggles radicals were waging against reactionaries in Europe. Of his political background and that of most of the City College NSLers, Harry Magdoff recalled that it was common to find

> a father who had been a union member, had been in strikes for years. Kids had suffered . . . . An environment in which the class problems—unemployment, seasonal unemployment, negotiations, problems of the union [were pervasive]. They were the children of workers and even small business people who had lived through . . . hard times in the garment trades. So it's not like they were middle class kids from Long Island . . . and they're not red diaper babies [children of Communist Party members]. But there is a tradition of another sort. I mean, I knew about unions. I knew there was a Russian revolution . . . . One of my earliest childhood memories is being on the elevated train and people swarming around with red things . . . flowing dresses and so on, singing songs and carrying whiskey bottles. This was the Lower East Side . . . . I was four years old. And what was it [they were celebrating]? The czar was overthrown! . . . These were experiences that were very important—living in a ghetto situation with alot of Russians.[14]

The cultural institutions of their Jewish ghetto communities provided Magdoff and other City College activists with an added impetus for radical politics. Along with fellow NSL founders Adam Lapin and Joseph Starobin, Magdoff attended the Sholom Aleichem schools as a youngster. Although not designed to promote radicalism, these secular Yiddish schools put students in touch with European literature—some of which was on the Left and served as a powerful inducement to radical thought. The Yiddish press, with its radical political discourse and reviews of leftist books, which students like Magdoff read avidly, helped to reinforce this Left cultural experience.[15]

The link between exposure to Yiddish culture and radicalization was, of course, not automatic or universal. In fact, the vast majority of Yiddish speaking New Yorkers were not radical. What the Yiddish cultural milieu did, however, was provide a path toward radical thought and the European Left which was less available in middle America. Thus, it increased the possibility of radicalization, particularly since this cosmopolitan atmosphere was rendered all the more politically charged by the Depression,[16]

These New York students fluent in Yiddish, who had been raised amidst ghettoes as Russian as they were American, were in but not quite yet of America; they were, as Irving Howe has put it, "still in some deep sense part of Europe."[17] The political implications of living in the United States while still thinking at least partially in European terms could be quite radical because it facilitated a certain critical detachment from the American social order, and an awareness of alternative systems of political thought and organization. Having grown up as children of European immigrants, the young radicals who emerged from these ghetto communities understood the European radical tradition and sensed that Americans could benefit from it. For Magdoff this European sensibility led to the conviction that something was radically wrong with American undergraduate life. Even while attending high school, in the days just prior to the advent of the student movement he would help build, Magdoff looked toward a European alternative to American collegiate provincialism. As a writer for his high school student newspaper, Magdoff told his classmates:

> Look, the students of Hungary, they're concerned with the real issues of the people. They're rioting; they're closing the universities . . . . Look at the American students with their fur coats and with parties, and getting drunk . . . . We're going to be different. This isn't the way students should be. They should be concerned.[18]

As a CCNY student in 1931, Magdoff sought to translate this vision into reality by working to build a radical student movement. His first step in this work was as a founder of *Frontiers,* a radical magazine at CCNY. This was published by the communist-leaning CCNY undergraduate group which Magdoff helped lead, the Social Problems Club. Even at this early point in the Depression CCNY was already a campus with an unusually vocal core of leftist students, which in addition to the Social Problems Club, included a socialist-led student organization, the Student Forum, as well as a sprinkling of Trotskyists, Lovestoneites, and anarchists. The campus also had a distinctive dissident tradition in that while most of the American student body had been politically quiescent in the 1920s, CCNY students had waged a very stormy and successful battle against compulsory ROTC. Memories of that struggle lingered. For CCNY's small core of leftists, the campus remained a hotbed of political debate, that raged in the alcoves of the school cafeteria—a critical meeting place that served as a center of intellectual life at this commuter college.[19]

To this dissident tradition *Frontiers* added a sensitivity to the new political possibilities created by the Depression. The magazine's first issue, in February 1931, reflected how—in contrast to the nation's middle-class undergraduate population—CCNY's more blue-collar student body had already been hard hit by the Depression. *Frontiers* reported that among CCNY students, "Parents, relatives, friends are unemployed . . . and plans of a successful professional career begin to seem chimerical." Such conditions at CCNY gave these young radicals an unusual insight into the forces that would soon shape a new and more politically aware college generation nationally. *Frontiers* prophetically predicted that the Depression would shatter "the aloofness and unconcern . . . towards the political and social events of the world" that had been the "customary attitude of college students."[20]

Adult influence on these CCNY radicals remained indirect and derived from the *Frontiers* group's desire to emulate the work of the communist wing of the city's intelligentsia. The CCNY students who founded *Frontiers* were seeking to bring to their classmates the type of iconoclastic Marxist journalism the *New Masses* brought to the adult Left. Indeed, when the student editors of *Frontiers* needed cartoons and photos to illustrate their stories, they took the subway down to the *New Masses* office, where they were allowed to recycle old graphics from the magazine. The student writers for *Frontiers* echoed the *New Masses* and the Communist Party in their adoration of the Soviet Union and in their concern that a hostile capitalist world was preparing for war against the U.S.S.R.[21]

It was on this last issue, war preparations, that *Frontiers* ignited a conflict with the CCNY administration—a conflict that set in motion the events leading to the NSL's formation. In its first editorial, *Frontiers* reopened the controversy over military training by calling for its abolition at CCNY. *Frontiers* editorialized that even if its courses were voluntary, the military science department had no place in an institution of higher learning because of "the central danger of Mili. Sci.—its function as the agency for the dissemination of jingoist, imperialist propaganda."[22]

This radical stance proved intolerable to Frederick C. Robinson, CCNY's president. Robinson was an acerbic, bespectacled little man, who, to several generations of CCNY students, seemed the living embodiment of political intolerance and academic pomposity.[23] Robinson loathed radicalism and thought students too immature to be granted political autonomy on campus. In Robinson's view, undergraduates were "beset with the storm and stress of adolescence" and subject to political impulses which "spring from inexperience and undue emotion." If allowed to run free, students driven by such impulses could "bring discredit upon themselves and their college." So Robinson concluded it was up to him to police the political life of undergraduates at college, just as parents police the personal conduct of their children at home. It was, Robinson said, the job of the college administration to censor student publications so that they did not "overstep . . . the grounds of decent journalism . . . become the cat's-paws of outside agitators and embroil the college in matters foreign to the purpose of its foundation."[24]

In line with this thinking, Robinson, infuriated by the anti-ROTC editorial, moved to suppress the first issue of *Frontiers* in February 1931. Under Robinson's orders, college officials broke into the locker where most of the copies of the magazine were stored and confiscated them. Claiming that the publication had been issued without proper authorization, Robinson revoked the charter of its publisher, the CCNY Social Problems Club, and suspended its president, Max Weiss. When Club members published a leaflet protesting Robinson's actions, he suspended ten of them.[25]

In response to the suppression of *Frontiers,* CCNY activists worked to build a citywide anti-censorship coalition. This effort yielded letters of support for the suspended students and *Frontiers* from campuses throughout New York City. Facing this pressure and a strike threat, the college's trustees agreed to review the case. The trustees, in a face-saving statement, expressed full confidence in Robinson, but then proceeded to authorize publication of *Frontiers* and reinstated ten of the eleven students that the CCNY president had suspended.[26]

The citywide campaign against Robinson's censorship brought CCNY's communist and communist-leaning students into closer contact with their counterparts on the city's other campuses. Their victory over Robinson enabled these hundred or so students to see the advantages of a coordinated citywide coalition of collegiate radicals. Moreover, it convinced them to create a permanent coalition by founding the New York Intercollegiate Student Council, an organization composed of eleven small, Left-oriented student groups from seven campuses in the metropolitan area.[27]

Though the Council was formed initially for the defensive purpose of protecting free speech for collegiate leftists, its organizers soon developed broader ambitions. They hoped that the Depression would enable them to take the offensive and build a strong leftist movement on the city's campuses. Toward this end, the Council reorganized in the fall of 1931 as the New York Student League (NYSL). The League established a lively political magazine, the *Student Review,* as a vehicle for building a community of radical student activists throughout New York. Bolstered by their local success and the positive response to the magazine, the NYSL shifted its organization and focus beyond New York. During the 1931 Christmas vacation, the NYSL changed its name to the National Student League and dedicated itself to the goal of radicalizing American college students.[28]

If judged by the number of students involved, the NSL's formation and first convention were hardly impressive events. At the League's first convention in March 1932 only twenty-five colleges and universities were represented—and these were primarily East Coast schools.[29] This gathering, like the NSL's founding in 1931 attracted little attention nationally on campuses; it was all but ignored by the student press, which was still predominantly apolitical. But despite these humble beginnings, the NSL would soon have a significant impact on campuses and change the face of American student politics. The NSL pioneered a new approach to radical student organizing, which would liberate the American student Left from its decade-long isolation and political impotence.

The mere fact of the NSL's creation was an unprecedented event for the campus Left; it marked the first time in the history of American student radicalism that no single organization monopolized Left organizing on campus. Prior to the NSL's birth, only one national leftist organization existed on campuses. This was the educational organization founded by Upton Sinclair in 1905, which was led primarily by socialists—though it was not officially affiliated with the Socialist Party. Sinclair's organization was originally known as the Intercollegiate Socialist Society (ISS); it was renamed the League For Industrial Democracy (LID) in 1921, and through that decade was led by adult socialists Harry Laidler and Norman Thomas.[30] The socialists' monopoly on campus radical organizing had an unhealthy effect on the student Left and contributed to its weakness in the 1920s. The NSL's founding in 1931 introduced a competitive element in the student Left, which helped prod the LID out of the doldrums into which it had fallen during the 1920s.

The LID had proven so politically ineffective in the 1920s that by the time the Depression began the American student Left was barely alive. Campus radicalism had just gone through ten of its leanest years since the rise of the American university. In 1929 the LID's student membership was miniscule—slightly more than 1000 out of a national undergraduate population of over a million—and the organization had little impact or visibility on campus.[31] LID leaders blamed their failure to attract students in the 1920s on the conservative national mood. But some of the responsibility for their poor political track record rested with the LID itself. LID national leaders frequently behaved more like teachers than political organizers. In line with the LID's motto of "education for a new social order," LID leaders placed so much emphasis on education that they seemed unable to engage in agitation on campus. LID leaders would spend months arranging academic lectures about radical principles, but little time showing collegians how to act on those principles. Despite all the energy and funds the LID devoted to publishing political pamphlets, these tracts displayed the same imbalance. A student learned much from LID literature about what was wrong with the steel industry, or why unionization and industrial democracy were worthy goals, but nothing about how to convert dissatisfaction about these issues into active political protest. None of the LID pamphlets during the 1920s were devoted to campus politics or the problems of building a student movement.[32]

Even the term "student movement" remained alien to the education-minded LID during the 1920s; it was not used in the LID's lectures, pamphlets, or newsletters. The LID was unable to look beyond the lecture hall toward the building of an aggressive student movement, fighting to restructure the university or society. Though committed to socialistic ideals, the LID's view of students in the university context was not essentially radical. The LID accepted the conventional academic notion that student days should be devoted solely to study. Instead of working to replace this conventional notion with a radical new image of the student as political

activist, the LID had focused on providing the literature and lectures necessary to make one's pensive undergraduate years include exposure to
socialist thought—reflecting an academic rather than an activist orientation.

The LID's failure to focus on the essentials of student organizing
developed because the League was not strictly or primarily a student organization. Though the LID did have an intercollegiate council, during
the 1920s this council had functioned only sporadically, and it was not the
students on this council but the adult leaders of the LID—prominent Socialist Party and Left-liberal figures—who dominated the LID's national
leadership. These leaders, men and women in their thirties and forties,
were as concerned with building non-student LID chapters in the community as they were with increasing campus LID membership. The LID's
most prominent national officers, including Norman Thomas, Paul Blanshard, and Harry Laidler were simply too old to think in student terms;
they failed to see the need to use campus problems as a bridge to larger
political issues.[33]

Since Thomas, Laidler, and most of the national LID cadre were not
students, they could not picture themselves as leaders of a student movement. As published authors several decades senior to their college audiences, touring LID lecturers fell naturally into a role roughly equivalent
to that of visiting professors—only these LID "professors" analyzed major
social issues from a socialist perspective. F.O. Matthiessen, a student at
Yale when he first heard Norman Thomas speak, was struck by the LID
leader's academic style:

> His views were very different from those of our Yale professors, but
> he was still a kind of professor all the same. . . . Thomas never served
> to do much more than educate some middle class intellectuals. He was
> never able, like [Eugene V.] Debs, to command a real mass movement.[34]

In adhering to a scholastic approach to student politics, the LID's
national leadership was perpetuating the tradition inherited from the early
days of the Intercollegiate Socialist Society (ISS). Throughout the Progressive Era, the ISS had been entirely academic in its campus work; its
avowed purpose was "promoting an intelligent interest in socialism among
college men and women . . . through the formation of study clubs in the
colleges and universities." The ISS did not engage in active political campaigns, but was "purely a discussion, a study organization."[35] And when
the ISS renamed itself the LID in 1921, this strategy did not change. In
fact, the top leaders of the LID throughout the 1920s, Harry Laidler and
Norman Thomas, were ISS veterans brought up amidst a student political
world in which socialist ideas were studied and discussed, but rarely acted
upon.

Memories of the ISS experience also limited the militancy of the League
for Industrial Democracy during the 1920s because they lowered the na-

tional leadership's expectations concerning the potential political strength of the campus Left. Both Thomas and Laidler had lived through the anti-radical hysteria of wartime and post-World War I America, which brought the ISS and much of the American Left to the brink of collapse. These LID leaders had been so scarred by the Red Scare and so accustomed to censorship, speaker bans, and general political repression on American campuses that they could not envision a complete reversal of the collegiate political order. Consequently, they could not foresee a future where the campuses—for the first time in American history—would become the base for a mass student protest movement.[36]

The excessively scholastic character of the LID found expression at the campus as well as at the national level. Throughout 1920s the dominant form of LID campus organization was the study (or discussion) group. At Yale, for instance, the LID affiliate's criteria for membership in the 1920s was more akin to a Phi Beta Kappa chapter than to an organization of political activists. Indeed, Yale LID leaders took pride in the fact that admission to their little chapter was not automatic, but had to be earned. One of these Yale LID officers reported that the chapter

> which now includes thirty-five members is exclusive; it admits only those to membership who show a keen interest in its work. It excludes those who are indifferent. A student meets us on the campus. He wants to be admitted to the Club. We ask whether he reads the newspapers, the *Nation*, the *New Republic*, the *Freeman;* whether he cares about the issues the Club is discussing. If he answers "Yes" he is admitted. If the answer is "No" he is refused.[37]

This same brand of introverted academic radicalism set the tone for the Cornell LID chapter during the 1920s, leading one disenchanted member to complain that the organization was being scorned as too "high brow" by most students; it was "a mere debating society, attracting radical students, but rather ineffective in reaching the outsider."[38]

If the student Left was to become a real force on campus in the 1930s, it would have to change its organizing strategy and create a more effective approach than the study group program of the old LID. The NSL's founders recognized this need for change; they pioneered tactics that were less academic than those which had been used so unsuccessfully by the LID during the 1920s. The NSL had no patience with ivory tower radicalism; the organization rejected the notion that the college radical's duty was solely to study or discuss radicalism. Instead, the League called for students to become activists in the struggle for egalitarian change both on and off campus. Indeed, at the core of the NSL's founding program in December 1931 was a call to immediate action on a set of ambitious yet practical political demands.[39]

NSL leaders perceived that the surest route to politicizing undergraduates was to engage them in struggles relating to political, social, and economic issues of concern to the student community. The NSL program emphasized the importance of mobilizing students around campus based issues: thirteen of the eighteen points in the program concerned collegiate issues. Here the NSL committed itself to rallying students on behalf of academic freedom, unemployment insurance for idle graduates, a free student-run employment agency, state aid to needy collegians (funded by taxes on the rich), increased appropriations for public education. The program also called for the ending of: college military training, racial and sexual discrimination on campus, exorbitant educational fees and textbook prices, compulsory campus religious services, faculty interference in extracurricular activities, and censorship of student publications. The NSL demanded complete political autonomy for student groups and freedom for students to "affiliate with such outside organizations as they choose."[40]

The NSL's extensive agenda for action on campus-related issues represented a significant breakthrough for the American student Left; it provided a vehicle for going beyond the study group mentality inherited from the LID of the 1920s and working to mobilize undergraduates for concrete political goals. The NSL helped give the student Left a sense of identity which it had lacked in previous decades. The League introduced the novel idea that campus conditions could provide student radicals with important issues around which to organize a mass, activist, and autonomous student movement as opposed to merely performing educational work or serving as an auxiliary of an adult organization like the LID. In fact, beginning with the NSL's original platform in 1931, entitled "For a National Student Movement," the term "student movement" became central to the campus Left, and with that term came the notion that such a movement could play an important role in strengthening American radicalism. NSL leaders prided themselves on having founded the most militant group of student activists in the nation and "the only independent organization of students, led by students, committed to a program of activity based on immediate student concerns."[41]

The NSL's birth marked a new departure in campus politics not only because the group pioneered an innovative approach to student organizing, but also because the NSL's founders included communists. This was a surprising development which broke with a tradition of communist inactivity on campus. The Communist Party and its youth organization, the Young Workers League (later renamed the Young Communist League) had viewed college students in the 1920s as an unreliable bourgeois element whose privileged economic position located them "in the camp of reaction." Even undergraduates who openly embraced radicalism were suspect, a Young Workers League leader explained in 1923, because "they bring with them . . . the prejudices, the mental restrictions of their former middle class environment. A young worker in the League is worth more than two students."[42] This narrow proletarian orientation meant that communist youth organizers forfeited control of the "bourgeois" college Left to the LID during the 1920s. The YCL's structure in the 1920s reflected this same bias; it had branches in factories and working class communities, but not on college campuses.[43]

The Depression did not initially change the way that adult leaders of the American Communist Party thought about college students. These leaders adhered to the ultra-radical Third Period dogma, set by the Comintern, which stressed the imminence of proletarian upheaval and revolution. In line with this proletarian orientation, the Communist Party hierarchy remained obsessed with blue-collar organizing and in 1931, the year of the NSL's birth, demonstrated no interest in mobilizing "bourgeois" college youth.[44]

Unlike these adults, however, communist students saw new opportunities on the horizon for radical student organizing. To exploit these new opportunities, they joined with their classmates, a larger group of communist sympathizers from City, Columbia, Brooklyn, and Hunter Colleges, in founding the NSL. These young leftists understood, from the type of first-hand observation available only to students, that the Depression had the potential to politicize the colleges, rendering obsolete the Communist Party's traditional indifference to student organizing. A new generation of radicals was emerging in the United States, bringing with it an interest in student politics and a sensitivity to campus realities that had been absent from the Communist Party in the past.[45]

The involvement of young communists in founding the NSL marked a substantial break with the proletarian orientation of not only the CPUSA, but also the international communist hierarchy. This point was driven home to NSL founder Joseph Clark at the Amsterdam Anti-war Congress a year after the creation of the League. Here Clark, a communist student, was so struck by the negative attitude of Young Communist International (YCI) leaders towards student organizing that he launched into a heated debate with one of these leaders, a German communist, over the importance of building student movements.[46] Clark attacked the still popular communist notion that radicals should focus all of their attention on workers and factories. He challenged the German communist leader's contention that radical organizing would yield nothing in bourgeois educational institutions. Clark stressed the importance of creating "student movements having a life of their own, issues of their own." In response, the doctrinaire German communist, according to Clark, "finally became a little exasperated with me and asked 'Du bist Student oder Kommunist?' [Are you a student or a Communist?] And at that time I had sufficient independence of mind to say 'Ich bin Student und Kommunist.' [I am a student and a Communist.] In other words, that I saw no contradiction in that."[47]

Clark's words and the advent of the NSL itself are reminders that all communists did not think alike. At a time when the adult leaders of the American CP and the YCI were still largely indifferent to student organizing, Clark and other YCLers in the NSL were enthusiastic student organizers—confident that a major radical movement could be built on

American college campuses. And somewhere in between the indifference of the adult CP and the enthusiasm of the NSLers stood the leadership of the American YCL during the early 1930s. YCL leaders still gave priority to organizing working-class youth, and in the NSL's early days, they focused much more on factories than on campuses. Indeed, the national reports of YCL leaders in 1931 and early 1932 do not even mention college youth. But at the same time, the YCL leadership approved of the involvement of student YCLers in the NSL and helped provide the embryonic NSL with some of the contacts it needed to form an intercampus organizational network. The national YCL leadership, in other words, was sympathetic and cooperative with the NSL, but did not yet see college campuses as a central arena for the radicalization of youth.[48]

As a communist-influenced organization, the NSL was unusual in that its birth was was not dictated from above—by the CP or national YCL leaders—but rather evolved from below, out of the agitation of communist rank and filers and communist sympathizers in the wake of the CCNY free speech fight. NSL founder Harry Magdoff, who was not a YCLer when he helped establish the NSL, underscored this point, recalling that the NSL's creation "wasn't a plot" of the Communist Party or YCL leadership.

> It was just the other way around. It was a movement that developed and generated excitement. We decided on the NSL . . . . We the guys at City College and the other [campuses]. We corresponded with each other. We had very exciting meetings in the citywide Student League. We corresponded through the *Student Review*. We were moving. We wanted a student movement.[49]

Echoing Magdoff, NSL founder Max Gordon, a YCL member at the time of the NSL's birth, stressed that the YCLers active in founding the NSL were not under orders to do so from either the CP or the YCL. He and his fellow Communist students "operated on their own," in their student organizing because the YCL at this point was "not predominantly interested in the student movement; it was predominantly interested in the young workers' movement."[50]

The NSL's early autonomy was also evident in the League's finances. It began its life financially independent and received no economic assistance from either the YCL or CP. For its economic survival the League relied upon dues from its members and subscriptions to its magazine, which in an era of Depression kept the NSL chronically poor. Harry Magdoff recalled that because of this lack of funds he, as editor of the NSL's national magazine, was constantly facing "the problem of getting out a magazine and not having money to pay for it. And the printer refusing to do it. [I was] trying to raise money to pay the bill for three or four months." Being poor was so trying, Magdoff joked, that "Goddamn it, if the Party would give some help it would have been welcome . . . ."[51]

Although the NSL was born as a joint venture of communist sympathizers and YCLers, the latter quickly assumed a dominant role in the student organization. YCLers brought with them the manipulative political style which they had learned in the communist movement. Thus in NSL chapters, key policy decisions were increasingly shaped in advance via caucuses (called "fractions") of communist members, particularly in the YCL strongholds. Since YCLers constituted the only group operating in this coordinated fashion within the NSL, their voice was often the decisive one. On some campuses YCL hegemony grew so complete that it led to almost comical situations. This was the case at Hunter College, where according to Joseph Clark, only one of the NSL activists

> was not a member of the YCL. And after a while the YCL members came over to this one person and said "look this is a little absurd if we have to have a separate meeting beforehand to decide what's going to happen. Why don't you just join [the YCL] and we'll at least eliminate one meeting?"[52]

Hunter's case was unusual, however, in that on most campuses YCLers constituted a minority within the NSL chapters. No matter how big or small the YCL group on campus, because it was an open secret that YCL factions were making NSL decisions, activists sometimes decided that in order to have a hand in policy making they would join the YCL. This was, for instance, a major impetus for George Watt's decision to join the YCL. In Brooklyn College's NSL chapter, Watt recalled,

> most of the people were not in the YCL . . . . The YCL had a . . . caucus operating as an organized faction within the NSL. And I used to come to [NSL] meetings and decisions would already be made, and I'd be confronted with people already having their minds made up about what they were going to do, what action they were going to take and so on. So that you felt that if you weren't in . . . [the YCL] you weren't where the action was . . . . That certainly may have drawn people [into the YCL] . . . . People don't want to be outside the action . . . . [It was] another factor that I feel I must honestly say also led me to join the YCL.[53]

The growing YCL dominance in the NSL was not, however, simply the result of caucusing or sly political maneuvering; it also represented the outcome of the ideological affinity between NSLers who were and those who were not YCL members. The non-YCLers in the NSL were often as pro-Soviet and anti-capitalist as the communists. The positions the YCL desired were often no different than those the unaffiliated students in the NSL would have supported anyway. Had this not been the case, the YCL's flagrantly undemocratic practice of pre-arranging NSL positions in communist caucuses might have become an issue in the League: a consensus over policy prevented any controversy over process. The ideological affinity between YCLers and unaffiliated radicals in the NSL was so strong, in fact, that non-YCLers could serve in important positions in the student organization without ever being pressured into taking a political position by the communists. This was the case, for instance, with several of the editors of the NSL's national magazine, who were given free rein to write as they pleased, despite the fact that they were not YCLers.[54] The political proximity between the two groups was such that often the most active students who entered the NSL unaffiliated eventually gravitated toward YCL membership.

Though YCL influence over the NSL seems to suggest that the Student League was a typical communist front organization, the NSL was in one very important respect distinct from most communist fronts: it initially ran with little direction from CP or YCL headquarters. The NSL was, as former NSL activist Theodore Draper put it, "on a longer leash than any other communist organization." This existed because the NSL had emerged at a time when the national leadership of the the CP and YCL—preoccupied with mobilizing workers—showed little interest in student organizing. During the first critical year of the NSL's life, neither the Party nor the YCL leadership cared enough about the campuses to devise strategies or goals for the young communists in the NSL. Since the Party elite had not developed positions on student organizing, the communists in the NSL freely invented their own strategies for building the student movement. This gave the NSL a freewheeling quality which was unusual for an organization in which communists were prominent.[55]

This degree of autonomy from the CP/YCL leadership had a salutary effect on the NSL. Because the NSL was not the creation of the Party elite, it did not inherit a full dose of the extreme sectarianism which so limited the CP's effectiveness during the early Depression years. And it was during this time when CP and YCL leaders, in accord with the Third Period line, continuously spewed forth divisive attacks upon even fellow leftists, denouncing Socialist Party leaders as class enemies and "social fascists."[56] Led by and for students, the NSL was able to formulate policies that were based more on campus realities than Comintern dogma. The NSL's effectiveness was facilitated by this, since it meant that the student organization's tactics came not from party bureaucrats but from youths who understood the campus political environment in which they were organizing.

II

In the semester following its birth the NSL would become a magnet for some of Depression America's most rebellious college students. Part of the attraction the League held for these campus rebels was that the NSL captured their radical disillusionment with both capitalism and mainstream politics in America. That disillusionment was rooted in the

Depression itself—the way that the crisis was not only impoverishing millions of Americans, but also closing the door of economic opportunity to an entire generation of college youth fated to, as the NSL put it, face a job market blighted by a "staggering" unemployment rate. To these students the American economic system appeared callous and irrational. Articulating this student outrage, an early NSL editorial charged that

> the years which have been spent in universities preparing for useful careers, were, for society and for students, only wasted years. The energy, the hope, the labor of youth, these things which could be society's most valuable asset, were thrown into discard like an obsolete machine. A social order which involves this waste and this conflict is sick. . . . "Go to the breadlines," it says, . . . "and in your hunger and misery, let your trained intelligence contemplate the wretchedness of idle bodies and unemployed minds."[57]

Although the NSL's platform was not explicitly communist, the organization was born with what one NSL activist aptly called a "revolutionary temperament."[58] The NSL was certain that not only the economy, but the political structure was in decay. What was needed was a "new social order," more rational, resilient, and democratic than capitalism. There would, in the NSL's view, be an extended period of class conflict before this new socialistic order could be attained: A struggle emerged which pitted workers and their battle for a new and more egalitarian America against the ruling class, determined to preserve its privileges under the bankrupt capitalist system. And according to the NSL, students could, if properly directed by the Left, assume a progressive role in this class struggle. "In spite of having been trained in the habits and the service of the ruling class," college students, because of the Depression, would soon be unemployable. Therefore their "broader interests lie with" the proletariat, the "class which is striving to build a new social order."[59]

The NSL did not call outright for a Soviet America, but the League's rosy pronouncements about Stalinist Russia leave little doubt that in envisioning a more just and Depression-free social order the League leaned heavily on the Soviet model. NSL leaders believed that all the inefficiency and poverty which burdened Depression America could at once be eliminated if the nation followed the example set by the Soviet Union. When NSL leaders looked at the U.S.S.R., they saw a socialist utopia. This naive idealism was reflected in point five of the NSL program, which specified that upon the American

> student movement . . . devolves the historic obligation of popularizing the achievements of the Soviet Union. Because the Soviet Union is the only country in the world which has been able to avoid crises and to eliminate unemployment and mass poverty, because planned economy as exemplified in the Five Year Plan is raising the standard of living of its population, the Soviet Union stands out as an inspiration and guide to us

in other parts of the world who are witnessing the social and economic evils which accompany Capitalism.[60]

The NSL's pro-Soviet position and its link to the communist movement had a definite appeal to some students angered by the Depression and the breakdown of capitalism. The CP possessed great prestige with many of these young radicals because of its leadership in labor and unemployment struggles and its ideological and political ties to the Soviet Union. This was, it must be recalled, the pre-Moscow trials era, when the Soviet revolution still enjoyed great prestige in radical and progressive circles—where the Soviet Union continued to be viewed as the world's one worker-run, depression-proof nation.[61]

An equally important part of the brand of radicalism espoused by the NSL was scorn for liberalism. Born when Herbert Hoover was still in the White House—and the New Deal had not as yet arisen to resuscitate liberalism—the NSL regarded liberalism as terminally ill. Liberals seemed to be as lost as Hoover in groping for a solution to the economic crisis.[62] For the rebellious undergraduate of 1932, the rudderless state of liberalism seemed a marked contrast with the NSL and its Marxist analysis. At a time when liberals were confused about causes of and solutions to the economic crisis, the NSL was supremely confident, claiming in fact to have all the answers about what caused the Depression (capitalism), how to end the economic crisis (move toward socialism), and how students could expedite that change (build an anti-capitalist student movement). As the Hoover years drew to a close amidst anxiety and confusion, such certitude appeared a great asset, and it helped attract students into the NSL. This was true for James Wechsler who, in explaining how he and several friends ended up joining the NSL, recalled during the last year of the Hoover era

> the absence of clear, affirmative plausible alternatives to Marxism, the hesitancy of scholars and statesmen in the face of the Marxist critique. It was not merely what the Communists said that enthralled us; it was what other men failed to say. The self-assurance of the Communists proved contagious; the liberal loss of nerve repelled us.[63]

While the NSL's radicalism made the organization extremely attractive to the nation's most rebellious students, it also prevented the League from becoming a mass membership organization. A student body raised on Republicanism and capitalism was—even amidst a Depression which was moving it leftward—hardly likely to enroll in a pro-Soviet student group. The NSL's strength, then, would not be in its membership figures, which remained small, but rather in its ability to serve as a political spark plug igniting protests by, hundreds, thousands, and finally more than a hundred thousand students—most of whom were not NSL members.[64] The NSL, in the leftist lingo of the time, served as a vanguard organization which (along with a reinvigorated campus LID) set the stage for America's first mass student movement.

The NSL's effectiveness as a vanguard organization derived from the League's ability to orchestrate political campaigns around issues that attracted mainstream students. And thus resulted the crowning irony of the NSL's political life: Despite the fact that NSLers scorned American liberalism, they knew how to appeal to students with liberal values and did so with great skill and effect. Though NSLers, as radicals, bemoaned the piece-meal reforms championed by liberal leaders in the past, these same NSLers, as realistic student organizers, were masters at championing their own list of reforms which aroused strong campus support.

Despite their own leftwing predilections, NSLers were pragmatic rather than dogmatic when it came to relating to mainstream students; so much so that during the early 1930s they became the most effective student organizers on behalf of many ostensibly liberal causes, including academic freedom and state aid to education. He and his fellow NSL leaders championed such causes, Joseph Clark explained, because they

> knew that to build a [student] movement you had to proceed on issues with which a wide group of people would be in agreement, and we utilized these very well. . . . We had a vision that the Communists would have to get out of the complete circle of isolation and sectarianism in which they were immersed during the period when the NSL was formed.[65]

The NSL was a paradoxical amalgam of ideological staleness, political insight and tactical innovation. When NSLers discussed the Soviet Union, their thought was thoroughly derivative, echoing *Daily Worker* propaganda. But when it came to the problems of organizing American students, NSLers thought for themselves and thought imaginatively. They predicted early and accurately that the Depression was going to shake the collegiate middle class out of its traditional political apathy. They were the first radicals in twentieth century America to recognize the political potential of the campuses. In addition, they understood that if student activists ran their own political organizations "formed for the purpose of developing a *student* movement on the basis of conditions and problems facing the students," they could ignite mass protest.[66] They were also the organizers who began translating this vision of insurgent campuses into political reality, by initiating a series of dramatic student protests during the 1932 spring semester.

Chapter 3

Springtime of Revolt

We have been immensely heartened by the recent appearance of a new student spirit on campus. Critics of the American undergraduate who have deplored his herd-mindedness, his conservatism, his preoccupation with parties, athletics and career-hunting, his . . . indifference to public affairs, have witnessed with pleasant surprise the emergence of large numbers of students interesting themselves actively, intelligently, practically, passionately in the political, social and economic problems of these critical days. The most dramatic expressions of the new student spirit have been the student Kentucky expedition and the Columbia Free-speech strike. . . . The new student movement . . . . is a vital new force in American life . . . .

Newton Arvin	Max Eastman
Sherwood Anderson	Waldo Frank
Roger Baldwin	Michael Gold
Malcolm Cowley	Oakley Johnson
H.W.L. Dana	Scott Nearing
John Dos Passos	Mark Van Doren
Theodore Dreiser	

"An Appeal," *Student Review* (October 1932), 21.

Tune: Coming Round the Mountain

Oh, we'll bring the Constitution when we come.
Oh, we'll bring the Constitution when we come.
Oh, we'll bring the Constitution
Now is *that* a revolution.
Oh, we'll bring the Constitution when we come.
Oh, to Hell with the Constitution when you come.
Oh, to Hell with the Constitution when you come.
Oh, to Hell with the Constitution
We must guard our institutions
For you're just a bunch of Rooshians
When you come.

"Songs Composed by Kentucky Student Delegation,"
Student Review (May 1932), 21.

The spring of 1932 marked the dawn of a new age in American student politics. Shaken by the Depression, collegians began to discard their traditional political apathy. Even college debating teams were affected, chosing as their leading topic that spring "social planning of industry," and arguing over whether the "Stuart Chase plan," the "Charles Beard plan," or the Socialist plan offered the best way out of the economic crisis.[1] And college students were doing more than talking about politics; they were starting to become involved in political actions, signaling a major change on campus. Where for the past decade political activism had been a rarity among college youth, beginning in 1932 such activism became increasingly common. The campuses were entering an era of protest: from the spring of 1932 until the end of the Depression decade not a semester would pass without some significant expression of political protest by American undergraduates.

The shift toward activism became evident during a series of political protests led by the NSL in the spring semester of 1932. These initial political actions involved only a minority of students, most of whom were from just one region of the country—the Northeast. But these protests were the start of something big; they gave life to a dissident tradition, which by the mid-1930s would yield the first mass student protest movement in American history. The student political actions of the spring of 1932 did not focus upon a single issue. Instead, there were a diversity of concerns, ranging from the exploitation of workers off campus to free speech and economic problems on campus. Though the issues around which students mobilized were diverse, all of this activism was characterized by a common spirit: a desire to prove that undergraduates cared about the problems of Depression America and were organizing to address those problems. This was a conscious revolt against the apolitical collegiate lifestyle inherited from the 1920s, which because of the Depression had begun to seem anachronistic; it was an attempt to replace that lifestyle with a more adult-like and political undergraduate tradition that would be more appropriate to a generation and a society troubled by hard times.[2]

The spring revolt was also significant because in it Columbia students were as prominent, and at times more prominent, than their counterparts from New York's municipal colleges. This represented a change from the past year, the NSL's formative period, during which CCNY was the key campus in the radical student movement. In contrast with CCNY, Columbia was a relatively affluent institution and the radicals on Morningside Heights did not come from low income backgrounds. The Columbia Left was also not so heavily Jewish as the CCNY, Brooklyn, and Hunter College Left. In fact, the key NSL leaders at Columbia during this early period were WASPs—and in this respect too, Columbia was more typical of the American student population than were New York's city colleges. Columbia was, of course, too much of an elite university, whose faculty was too liberal and location in New York too distinctive to ever be considered a truly typical American university. But the prominence of Columbia students in several of the collegiate political actions of the spring of 1932 at least suggested the potential of the NSL to reach beyond low income youth, thus attracting students from the type of middle-class backgrounds it would have to mobilize if it was to ignite a mass movement on the nation's campuses.[3]

The first student political action to attract national attention in Depression America was the student expedition to Kentucky's coal region in March 1932. Organized from New York by the NSL, a small group of students volunteered to travel south to bring food and clothing to the striking coal miners in Harlan and Bell counties. The students also planned to investigate charges that Kentucky police and vigilantes, paid by the coal companies, were brutalizing the strikers. The NSL launched the expedition in the hope of not only providing humanitarian aid to the miners, but also of raising the political consciousness of undergraduates. NSL leaders thought that by exposing students to capitalism at its worst—the poverty and bloody class conflict of the Kentucky coal region—they could radicalize them. Through this expedition the NSL sought to demonstrate that students, despite their youth and political inexperience, could act effectively on behalf of those victimized by the Depression.[4]

Kentucky's coal miners needed whatever assistance they could get from the students; they had been hard hit by the Depression. With the price of coal plummeting, mine operators had cut production, so that miners could work only three days a week. The combination of poor hours and low wages left the miners with weekly paychecks of only four to five dollars. Making matters worse, the coal operators paid the miners in scrip, forcing their employees to buy at company stores, where their pay was usually worth no more than 50 or 60 cents on the dollar. By February 1931 this bleak situation had become intolerable, as the companies imposed an additional 10 per cent wage cut—provoking 11,000 miners to strike. "We starve while we work; we might as well strike while we starve," explained one striking miner.[5]

The coal operators in Kentucky, who in the words of labor historian Bert Cochran "ran the enclosed communities like rapacious feudal barons," controlled the local police and criminal justice system and were able to mobilize them against the strikers. The coal operators used deputies and their own armed men to assault the miners. One of these violent attacks, in May 1931, wrought a half hour of machine gun fire and at least four deaths. This violence and the immense political power of the coal operators intimidated the United Mine Workers (UMW), whose leaders abandoned the seemingly hopeless strike. When the UMW walked away from the Kentucky struggle, the communist-led National Miners Union stepped in and worked to organize the coal strike.[6]

Though more defiant than the UMW, the National Miners Union fared no better than its predecessor in battling the formidable coal operators, who continued to control the region with an iron fist. But if the communists could not match the power of the coal companies in Kentucky, they could and did hurt the companies' image nationally by publicizing both the poverty of the miners and the brutal repression of their strike. A key component of this campaign, which influenced the students and helped lead to their Kentucky expedition, was its mobilization of some of the nation's leading writers on behalf of the miners.[7]

Alarmed by the violence in Kentucky, novelists Theodore Dreiser and Waldo Frank headed a small delegation of writers, which in November 1931 and February 1932 traveled to Kentucky to investigate the miners' strike. Their visits to the coal region helped draw attention to the miners' plight. But the hostile reception accorded to Dreiser's group by Kentucky police and coal company thugs showed that attempts to assist the miners could be dangerous. Two members of the delegation, including Waldo Frank, were beaten bloody by local deputies. Kentucky officials also sought to indict the entire delegation under the criminal syndicalism laws.[8]

NSL leaders praised the writers' delegation for publicizing the harsh treatment of the miners in Kentucky and "test[ing] freedom of speech, and assembly in that region." NSLers credited that delegation with exposing "the reign of terror prosecuted against the trade union activities of coal miners."[9] Soon after the writers returned from Kentucky, the NSL published a passionate article by novelist and delegation member John Dos Passos, depicting the strikers as an oppressed and impoverished group, valiantly struggling against the tyranny of the coal operators. Here Dos Passos told of a union meeting held in a

> low frame [church] hall . . . packed with miners and their wives; all faces were out of early American history. Stepping into the hall was going back a hundred years. . . . These were the gaunt faces, the slow elaborations of talk and courtesy, of the frontiersmen who voted for Jefferson and Jackson, and whose turns of speech were formed on the oratory of Patrick Henry. I never felt the actuality of the American revolution so intensely as sitting in that church, listening to the mountaineers with their old time phrases getting up on their feet and explaining why the time to fight for freedom had come again.[10]

The writers' expedition to Kentucky had its most immediate campus impact in New York City. The expedition had been organized by Dreiser out of his West 57th Street studio; and the harassment of these New York based writers in Kentucky for simply bringing to light conditions in the coal region struck close to home, angering faculty as well as students in the city. On March 3, 1932 professors from almost every college and university in the New York City area joined with over 150 other educators in publishing a petition protesting the violations of civil liberties in Harlan and Bell Counties. This protest drew praise from the student press in New York.[11]

Among New York's small core of student activists, the Dreiser expedition to Kentucky generated a wave of sympathy for the miners and a desire to do something on their behalf. One of the students so affected was Columbia NSL leader Robert Hall. A native Mississippian, Hall had come to Columbia hoping to attain the skills necessary to help transform the South politically and economically. He was convinced that unless there was a revolution in labor and race relations and a thorough modernization of the southern farm economy, the South would remain a backward and impoverished region. These concerns led Hall to major in agricultural economics at Columbia and to become an active communist. Hall's contacts with the communist movement in New York generated the idea of organizing a student expedition to the Kentucky coal region. The idea emerged during a discussion between Hall and a woman active in the communist-dominated International Workers' Order (IWO). Hall recalls that after he voiced his concern about the miners, the IWO organizer "asked if I would lead a student delegation to Harlan, Kentucky [because] there was hunger in those mountains." Hall quickly seized upon the idea, and other NSL leaders were equally enthusiastic.[12]

The NSL's announcement that it would be organizing a student expedition to the coal fields provoked an angry response from Kentucky law enforcement officials. They saw the student trip as essentially a repetition of the Dreiser delegation, which in their view was simply a group of Yankee radicals that had come to stir up trouble. Bell County Prosecutor Walter B. Smith warned "these rattle-brained college students . . . to stay out of southeastern Kentucky." Harlan Sheriff John Henry Blair threatened that if the students coming to Kentucky did not "watch their step," he would "file them along with the other exhibits in the Harlan and Pineville jails . . ."[13] Students had good reason to take these threats seriously, since the Kentucky police had recently beaten and indicted members of the writers' delegation. Even as students went among their college faculty seeking donations for the Kentucky trip, they were reminded of the dangers. Sympathetic professors agreed to help fund the expedition, but expressed fear that in Kentucky their students might face violence and death.[14]

Neither the warnings of belligerent Kentucky deputies nor the assaults on previous delegations intimidated the NSL. The threats by Kentucky officials actually created campus support for the expedition because they suggested that these officials had something to hide, making the delegation's aim of investigating conditions in the coal fields seem all the more critical. These threats and the condescending tone of the statements the Kentuckians made in denouncing the delegation angered students, including the editor of the *Columbia Spectator*. Responding to the Bell County Prosecutor's crack that "college students are lollipops," the *Spectator* denounced the "flophouse tactics" of this "alleged stool of the mineowners," and wished the expedition

> the best of luck in this praiseworthy attempt to feed a few hundred American citizens who, in accordance with the most noble precepts of

our fair country, are being slowly starved to death in order that the mine
owners of Harlan county might rest their fastidious buttocks on upholstered chairs.[15]

The threats and potential danger associated with the upcoming Harlan trip came as no surprise to the NSL activists who organized the expedition. They thought of American capitalism as an oppressive class system held together by violence, and they saw the threats as one more sign
that fascistic employers would stop at nothing in their drive to thwart
unionization. For some of the young radicals this element of danger gave
the Harlan trip a special romantic appeal; it meant standing on the front
lines of the American class struggle beside courageous workers battling
some of the nation's cruelest capitalists. This would be an opportunity for
student leftists to prove that their militancy equalled and even surpassed
that of their adult counterparts. In this defiant spirit one student radical
confided to a comrade just prior to leaving for Harlan that "one hundred
and fifty students will not be as easily cowed as [the] eight or ten writers
[in the Dreiser delegation]; and I don't think we'll sublimate abrogation
of our constitutional privileges . . ." Another of the student radicals, worried about the zeal of fellow activists going to Harlan, told a friend that
he hoped to see him after the Kentucky trip, "though in light of X's romanticism I may not be alive next Friday." [16]

Contrary to the expectations of this worried student, however, NSL
leaders did not allow revolutionary romanticism to cloud their political
judgement. The trip's organizers adopted an undogmatic and sober tone
as they prepared for the expedition. The NSLers avoided confrontational
rhetoric; they portrayed the expedition as an investigatory and relief mission, rather than as a fighting brigade about to enter the trenches of class
warfare. Conscious that ultra-radical posturing might scare off the very
students they were hoping to politicize, NSLers went out of their way to
demonstrate that their primary interest in Harlan was humanitarian aid
rather than revolutionary martyrdom.

In this spirit NSL leader Robert Hall, when in the process of organizing the delegation, warned his fellow students that in order to avoid antagonizing the Kentucky police, they should not dress down in the Left-
proletarian fashion of the day. Hall advised that "no one should wear
leather jackets, which [would mark them] as left wingers . . . 'the mark
of the beast.' "[17] Members of the delegation heeded Hall's advice, so that
when the American public viewed the Associated Press photographs of
the first Kentucky-bound busload of students, which departed from New
York City on March 23, 1932, they saw a very respectable looking group
of collegians clad in suits and skirts.[18] This same pragmatic approach would
prevail throughout the Kentucky trip, during which, as one delegation
member recalled, "all words which might impute communism to us were
taboo." [19]

The eighty-student delegation which set out to visit Harlan was small,
but it was, nonetheless, ten times the size of the writers' delegation and

the biggest effort yet to bring direct aid to the striking miners. The composition of the student delegation suggested, however, that the NSL had yet to mobilize much support beyond its home base in New York City. The majority of delegation members were from the New York campuses, including Columbia, City College, Hunter College, Brooklyn College, Union Theological Seminary, and New York University. Nonetheless, the presence of student delegates from the University of Tennessee, the University of Wisconsin, Harvard and Smith Colleges, and the selection of Kentucky as the sight for the NSL's first major action showed that the League's ambitions extended far beyond New York.[20]

In their attempt to expand the student movement's base, the NSL sought to transcend ideological as well as geographical boundaries. Despite the NSL's pro-communist orientation, the League organized the Harlan delegation on a non-sectarian basis. Expedition organizers welcomed into the delegation unaffiliated students, and even socialists—this at a time when the Communist Party adhered to the Comintern's Third Period line, which dictated that communists shun the socialists and condemn them as "social fascists." The NSL's unifying approach led a number of socialists to join the delegation, and they were impressed by the absence of sectarian rancor during the expedition. Underscoring the spirit of unity on the Kentucky trip, one of the socialist delegation members, after describing the positive interaction between socialists and communists on the expedition, observed:

> I have never seen a finer or more intelligent set of Communists than those with whom we traveled. Not only our songs harmonized, but they even listened sympathetically to X's plea for a united proletarian movement that would utilize socialist tactics where the class struggle was not sharp enough or effective to stress.[21]

The delegation was not, however, composed solely of radicals. Its members also included more moderate students, whose political experience had been confined to discussions in liberal study groups and volunteer work in local settlement houses. These moderates and liberals came to the expedition, in the words of delegation leader Robert Hall, with "a rather indefinite interest in labor problems and a somewhat vague liberal sympathy with the working class."[22]

Though to an objective observer the eighty-student delegation might seem unimposing, to Kentucky mine operators and their allies, eighty students too many were coming to the coal region; they saw to it that the students were harassed even before the delegation reached Kentucky. At Knoxville, Tennessee, where the students stayed overnight prior to entering Kentucky, a number of hotels refused them accommodations. Detectives tailed the delegation. The following day, as the first busload of students and the two miners serving as their guides approached the Cumberland Gap—still in Tennessee—a group of cars, packed with angry people who shouted and made menacing gestures at the students, followed and surrounded the bus. As the delegation crossed into Kentucky, it found a hostile crowd milling near the state line. Several men stepped forward from the crowd, demanding that the bus pull over, and since one of them pointed a revolver at the bus driver, he quickly complied.[23]

Threats shot out from the crowd. Despite the students' protests, deputies seized the two miners who had been serving as guides for the delegation. As the police evicted these miners, the crowd chanted: "We want them." When NSL leader Robert Hall stepped out of the bus to speak for the student delegation, there were calls for a lynching. Hall attempted to calm the Kentuckians by assuring them that the students had come to the coal region on a peaceful and legal mission, "to make an impartial investigation of the coal fields. Charges of violations of constitutional rights, of violence and lawlessness have been made. We have come to see for ourselves whether these charges are true." Even as Hall spoke, however, a deputy pulled out his revolver and threatened to "put a bullet" between the NSL leader's eyes.[24]

County prosecutor Walter B. Smith took the lead in confronting the students. Smith made a speech denouncing the collegians as "Yankees, aliens and agitators." He insisted that irrespective of the students' "specious claims to liberty," they had no right to conduct any type of investigation in Kentucky. Smith demanded that the delegation leave the state immediately. But the students stood their ground; they refused to turn back. Armed guards escorted the students to the courthouse in Middlesboro, where they were to be held for questioning.[25]

When the students arrived at Middlesboro another angry crowd awaited them. Any illusions the students may have held about Kentucky justice were shattered by the kangaroo court which ensued. County prosecutor Smith's questioning was saturated with anti-Semitic, anti-communist, and xenophobic images. He depicted the delegation as an un-American group, composed of Russian-born Jewish communists. In a typical round of questioning, which drew much laughter from the Kentucky courtroom crowd, Smith ordered Arthur Goldschmidt, a Columbia undergraduate, to identify himself, and then asked, "How do you spell that J-E-W-O-L-D-S-C-H-M-I-D-T?"[26]

Before the questioning could go much further, however, Hall—perhaps because of his experience as an NSL leader and his poise as an older student and native southerner—had the presence of mind to object to the whole procedure. He demanded to know whether the students were under arrest. Informed that they were under investigation, but not yet arrested, Hall told the court "In that case I protest. You have no legal right to subject us to an investigation. If we are not under arrest, you cannot question us. We will refuse to answer." When Smith threatened to throw him into jail if he did not cooperate, Hall replied "I would rather rot in jail than forfeit a single one of my constitutional rights." Following Hall's lead, the rest of the delegation refused to answer Smith's questions.[27]

Smith interpreted this defiance as final proof that the students were "aliens come into our midst to spread . . . propaganda." He ordered the delegation to leave Kentucky and announced that he and his deputies would escort the students to the state line. Before the students could leave the courtroom, however, they were again denounced and threatened. The chief attorney for Bell County's coal operators, standing next to the judge and claiming to speak for him, shouted:

> These people are here to investigate us. But we can tell them that before we allow interference with our sacred institutions, the . . . Tennessee River . . . will run red with blood. We don't want them to come here with a bowl of soup and a hunk of Sovietism to feed our people.

The courthouse crowd responded to this tirade with chants of "Amen brother!" [28]

Surrounded by armed vigilantes, police and a large, hostile crowd, the students who had come to Kentucky on the first bus had no choice but to leave the state. During this forced exodus, Kentucky law enforcement officials moved from threats to actual physical abuse of the students. This violence erupted on the bus after Smith told student delegation members he possessed a letter proving their visit was the result of a communist plot. When the students asked Smith to show them the letter, he gave it to Elinor Curtis, a Columbia graduate student. Curtis, who thought the letter fraudulent, began taking notes about it, which alarmed Smith. Smith demanded that Curtis return the letter immediately, and when she refused, a deputy intervened and began to twist her arm violently. Another student tried to come to her aid. But the deputy charged at him and punched him in the jaw, forcing the stunned undergraduate to strike his head against the luggage rack. [29]

The second busload of students arrived in Kentucky one day later; it fared no better than the first. This group tried to elude the police by taking a back route to Bell County. Smith soon caught up with this second bus, however, when it ran out of gas on a steep mountain road. Fresh from their heated encounter with the first group of students, Smith and his deputies were angry and aggressive.

When Joe Leboit, a leader of this student delegation, attempted to prevent the police from boarding the bus by demanding to see a search warrant, the deputies declared that they did not need a warrant. Leboit protested that if the police boarded the bus, they would be violating the students' constitutional rights. "You have no constitutional rights," Smith replied. "Why, aren't we in the United States?" asked Leboit. "No," Smith responded, "You're in Kentucky." "Well then," said Leboit, "We demand our constitutional rights under the constitution of Kentucky." "There is no constitution in Kentucky," Smith said. "I'm the constitution, I'm the highest court of authority. I am the law." The deputies then pushed Leboit aside, boarded the bus and forced the students to drive out of the state. [30]

Deputies roughed up several students on this second delegation's trip back from Kentucky. These assaults were even more lawless than the violent incident on the first bus because they occurred on Tennessee soil, where the Kentucky police had no legal authority. The assault began after the bus crossed into Tennessee, when Leboit demanded that Smith and his deputies leave the bus, since it was no longer in their jurisdiction. Smith ordered Leboit to be silent and move to the back of the bus, but Leboit refused. The deputies responded by jumping Leboit and beating him bloody. A scuffle ensued in which the police literally kicked two students off the bus, injured a woman student, and hit a fourth delegation member in the head with a revolver.[31]

After its ejection from Kentucky and final departure from the police in Tennessee, the student delegation regrouped, determined to continue its pro-labor mission. Though recognizing that Kentucky law enforcement officials had made it impossible for them to bring direct material aid to the miners, the students attempted to assist the miners politically. The assault on the students had been picked up by the wire services and made national news. The delegation sought to use the publicity generated by their confrontation with Kentucky police to call attention to the plight of the striking miners. Claiming that their delegation had been victimized by the same "reign of terror" used to suppress the strikers in the coal region, the students sent representatives to the Governors of Kentucky and Tennessee, demanding an investigation of police brutality and violations of miners' and students' constitutional rights. Leaders of the student delegation carried these same demands to Washington; they requested that the Justice Department provide federal protection for a new student investigation of conditions in the coal region, and urged Congressional action on behalf of the miners. The students even brought these demands directly to the Hoover White House.[32]

Despite this flurry of protest activity, the students failed to convince state government officials or the Hoover Administration to aid the miners and investigate police brutality in Kentucky. Governor Ruby Laffoon of Kentucky told the student delegates he had no authority to redress their grievances. The Governor of Tennessee proved even less cooperative, terming the student delegates "uninvited guests," and warning them to avoid communism. Hoover Administration officials showed no concern about the lawlessness the students had encountered in Kentucky and Tennessee. The Justice Department announced that the conflict in the coal region was "a matter to be handled by the states." When the students attempted to take their case to President Hoover, they got no further than "the secretary of the secretary of the secretary of Mr. Hoover."[33]

While unable to move the Hoover Administration or its counterparts at the state level, the students managed to build support on Capitol Hill for the striking miners. The students helped provide liberal Senators with

the political ammunition they needed to battle successfully for a congressional investigation of the coal strike. Delegation members met with the
Senate Committee on Manufactures and offered evidence of misconduct
by the Kentucky police. The students presented the Committee with .45
caliber bullets, which Kentucky deputies gave them with the warning that
if the delegation sought to return with federal protection "this is what we
would do to a United States deputy marshal who attempted to open up
the highways through Kentucky."[34]

The harassment of the student delegation in Kentucky generated
considerable public criticism of the coal operators and their allies. The
coal companies came out of the incident looking reckless and brutal because their allies and agents had assaulted innocent youths. Articulating
this rising public anger about conditions in the coal region, the *New York
Herald Tribune* condemned county prosecutor Smith's mistreatment of the
student delegation. The *Tribune* accused Smith of employing "primitive
methods of legal violence," "gun rule," and "perversion of law." The *Tribune* condemned Smith's belligerent speeches to the students as examples
of "narrow minded and fearful ignorance," and expressed concern for
the rights of striking miners who lived within his jurisdiction.[35]

The disruption of the Harlan expedition by Kentucky police angered
students and drew over 3,000 telegrams and letters of protest nationwide.[36] This support came from places where the NSL had never penetrated before, including the traditionally conservative schools of the South.
Among the student bodies sending telegrams protesting the mistreatment
of the delegation were those from Kentucky, Arkansas, Texas, Virginia,
and North Carolina.[37] Even some students who prior to the Harlan trip
had thought "that reports from the Kentucky and Tennessee [of exploitation and brutalization of the miners] were gross exaggerations hatched
by overzealous radicals" became convinced—because of the mistreatment
of the student delegation—"that most reports from those mining sections
are badly understated."[38] The disruption of the expedition sparked student demonstrations in Chicago, outside the home of Samuel Insull, a
utilities magnate who owned mines in Kentucky, and in Philadelphia by
the offices of a J.P. Morgan affiliate and miner owner.[39]

The Harlan trip stirred up the student Left, inspiring the still small,
but increasingly militant campus radical groups to undertake a series of
pro-labor actions. Following the example set by this first NSL-led delegation, two midwestern student expeditions to the Illinois coal belt were
launched in the spring of 1932. Both of these expeditions met with the
same kind of police intervention which the students had encountered in
Kentucky. The largest expedition, organized out of the University of Chicago, attracted 150 students and teachers; it was turned back in the Illinois coal region by a shot gun wielding sheriff. Boldest of all were the
five Arkansas students from Commonwealth Labor College, who went to
Kentucky in April 1932, seeking to carry on the investigatory and relief

mission of the first student delegation. A band of armed vigilantes assaulted these students in Kentucky before they could reach the miners.[40]

II

For the NSL, the Harlan trip and the subsequent student publicity campaign on behalf of the miners served as both political baptism and confidence builder. These activists saw the expedition as a sign that students were coming of age politically; it showed that college youth could organize meaningful and serious political actions with national impact. NSLers boasted that the student delegation to Harlan represented a "historic vanguard" because it marked the first great break away from the apolitical, juvenile collegiate past—the world of fraternities and football—and the initial step toward converting the campuses into centers of political thought and action: "For the first time American students have come out of their shell and realized themselves as a social force."[41]

NSLers came away from the Kentucky trip feeling that the expedition had borne out both the League's leftist critique of capitalism and agitational approach to student organizing. In the official NSL account of the expedition, "Kentucky Makes Radicals," Robert Hall argued that by exposing delegation members to "the fascist regime in the coal fields," the NSL radicalized even the most moderate among them, teaching them more about the oppressive side of American capitalism than they could ever learn in their classes or discussion groups. Hall pointed out that some of the student delegation members had come to the expedition out of organizations that "were no more than liberal discussion clubs." According to Hall, at the beginning of the Kentucky trip, these liberal delegates had little in common with the radicals on the expedition. But by the end of the trip, all of the delegation members, angered by the assault upon them, spoke with one voice, uniting behind a radical statement condemning the police "terrorism" to which they and the miners were subjected.[42]

Although as radicals, NSL leaders naturally trumpeted the anti-capitalist implications of their experience in Kentucky, they also emphasized the constitutional issues at stake in the coal region. The NSLers were practical enough to recognize that mainstream students not yet ready to condemn capitalism were receptive to protests against brazen violations of civil liberties. Consequently, during and after the Kentucky trip these activists worked successfully, in the words of NSL founder Joseph Clark, "to make civil liberties and . . . the repression of civil rights and liberties an issue, and the basis for the development of their own organization."[43] Delegation leader Robert Hall took this same pragmatic approach with him when he appeared before the Senate Committee on Manufactures, during the congressional investigation of conditions in the coal region, which the student expedition had helped initiate. Hall avoided revolutionary hyperbole; instead he chose to detail the vigilanteism and police brutality which he and his fellow students had observed in Kentucky. Hall argued that in light of these abuses the federal government should step in to protect the rights of the miners.[44]

Even the NSL's main competitor on campus, the student LID, was impressed by the Kentucky expedition and the way that the NSL organized it. Upon returning to New York, student LID leader Joseph P. Lash, a delegation member and one of the students assaulted by the deputies, published an article praising the expedition.[45] A half century later, Lash looked back upon the Kentucky trip as "an important part of my life . . . . It was an eye opener," which showed him that "civil liberties had no meaning" in the coal region and that the miners "had no one to appeal to." Lash had been impressed as well by the political backbone NSLers had demonstrated in leading busloads of students down to a strike area so violent as Harlan. "The Communists were willing to take chances and do work where work had to be done." Noting that the "Communists were on their best behavior" during the Kentucky trip, Lash was struck by how well they got along with the socialist students. Indeed, in Lash's view, the student expedition to Kentucky was a successful pioneering venture into the type of coalition politics which would only later be adopted by adult communists (during the Popular Front era, which began in 1935). According to Lash, the

> Harlan expedition [demonstrated] that the Socialist and Communist students . . . and non-affiliated students could work together, and this was a way to fight what we considered fascism. And it had a unifying effect, particularly upon the two college organizations, the NSL and the student LID. And I was certainly one of those people who was affected by it.[46]

It was not merely student delegation members who were impressed with their Kentucky trip. Skeptical adult observers too conceded that the students conducted their work for the miners with surprising skill and intelligence. The editor of the *Nation* admitted that initially he was critical of the proposed student expedition to the coal region because he had thought collegians too young, immature, and naive to mount a serious political action. But after watching the students in action, the *Nation* editor was impressed with the political savvy the delegates displayed in rebounding from their assault in the coal region, and using the publicity it had attracted to focus national attention on the plight of the miners. In his eyes, these college youths had proven themselves more effective in aiding the miners than their adult counterparts, including the Dreiser delegation. The *Nation* editorial concluded that the student delegation "contributed more to the Kentucky fire than any of the numerous previous expeditions have."[47] And the conduct of the student delegation members even impressed their adversaries, including the editor of the *Middlesboro*

Daily News, an anti-union newspaper in Harlan County, who, though hostile to the students, "could not help but admire their courage."[48]

The expedition was, of course, far from a complete success. The students had been prevented from bringing material relief to the miners. The Senate hearings and publicity that the student delegation had helped generate for the miners were essentially moral victories: the hunger and harsh realities of the coal region remained. Nonetheless, the Harlan trip signaled the emergence of a new and more productive era for the student Left. Though the delegation could not end the suffering of the miners, its presence in Kentucky suggested that at least this generation—unlike the self-absorbed students of the past decade—cared enough to try. Those buses to Kentucky took students away from not only their campuses, but from a long history of collegiate political inertia. And if their moral victory in Kentucky looked large to the students, this was because it seemed to tower over any previous achievement of America's politically apathetic student body. Harlan also proved that student activists could transcend the sectarianism which had weakened the adult Left and the scholasticism which had traditionally dulled the campus Left. In showing that student radicals could do more than talk—and had indeed risked their own safety in order to assist the miners—the Harlan expedition suggested that the student Left of the 1930s would be more militant and action oriented than its academic predecessors.

III

The Harlan expedition proved to be only the start of a very busy spring semester for the NSL. Less than a week after confronting suppression in Kentucky, the NSL mobilized against another restriction of student political expression—at Columbia University. Here President Nicholas Murray Butler's administration caused an uproar on April 1, 1932 by expelling Reed Harris, the muckraking editor of the *Columbia Spectator,* the college's student newspaper. The free speech fight led by the NSL on Harris' behalf would be the stormiest campus protest yet seen in Depression America; it culminated in the first political strike by college students during the 1930s.

While the NSL would play the key role in leading the Columbia censorship battle, the story of this controversy begins not with the League but with Reed Harris himself. There was nothing in Harris' background that anticipated his emergence as a college rebel. Born to an affluent family, Harris began his educational career in a conservative manner, winning the DAR prize for a history essay and spending a summer at a Citizens Military Training Camp. Harris then attended the Staunton Military Academy in Virginia, where he was a classmate of Barry Goldwater. Upon arriving at Columbia, Harris became involved in traditional campus extracurricular activities, playing football on the freshman team and joining a fraternity. The following year he even joined the Vigilance Committee, the sophomore group which hazed freshman. Yet by his senior year, Harris was writing editorials more fiery and radical than the editor of any other major college daily.[49]

Harris' radicalization occurred during his tenure as editor of the *Spectator.* Elevated to the editorship in a year when the economy was deteriorating rapidly, Harris found himself moved by "the spirit of inquiry, the spirit of questioning . . . . It was a college education in a time of depression, a time when there was great ferment in the world . . .[which] did cause us to question some of the existing standards of the times."[50] And questioning was what Harris did at the *Spectator,* exposing the elitism of college fraternities, the corruption in the Columbia administration, the suffering on the city's breadlines, the political bankruptcy of the Hoover administration, and the greed of anti-union employers.[51]

What made Harris so special was that he combined a radical sensibility and a gift for polemical writing. Harris had a biting wit, and his editorials went right for the jugular. In his first editorial controversy, Harris called upon the Columbia Athletic Association to open its financial records for inspection. Harris accused the Association of misusing student money and charged that the university had forsaken its educational mission by commercializing the football program, which he termed "a semi-professional racket."[52] As a consequence of these editorials, Harris was besieged by "football players, who threatened to beat us up, and alumni who intimated that we should retire."[53]

The muckraking style that characterized Harris' writing was something new for the *Spectator.* This was one of the reasons why his editorials so infuriated administrators, alumni, and student partisans of traditional college culture. They had simply never before encountered an undergraduate editor like him. Prior to Harris' editorship, the Columbia student newspaper reflected the values of the dominant student culture; it had been generally apolitical, insular, and tinged with Ivy League elitism. Until Harris, the *Spectator*'s editors had, in the words of James Wechsler, who would himself later follow in Harris' footsteps as editor-in-chief,

> always behaved in the best tradition of American college journalism: unhesitant pandering to the Administration, only intermittent and usually uninformed comment on affairs outside the realm of the University, devout catering to the institutions made sacred by Trustees, Alumni and their subordinates.[54]

Harris wanted to bring the student press closer to the standards of professional journalism. He believed that student journalists should be serious, critical, and above all free to "say what we think regardless of the consequences."[55] His concept of student journalism clashed with that of more traditional students, alumni, and administrators. They thought the student newspaper should function as a booster rather than critic of the school. They wanted a paper that would show deference to the campus administration and reverence for alma mater. This is what the Secretary of Columbia's Alumni Association meant when—after bemoaning Harris' negative commentary on the Columbia athletics program—he complained that "the editor of the *Spectator* is too serious. He should be more collegiate."[56] The metropolitan press, however, recognized a kindred spirit in Harris and sided with him rather than with his detractors in this dispute. The New York *World Telegram,* for instance, responded to the Alumni Association official's charge that Harris was insufficiently collegiate by arguing that collegiatism was equivalent to a type of mindlessness, which all intelligent journalists should avoid: "It is not collegiate to think. That is why American colleges and universities are glorified nurseries. It is only collegiate to be rah, rah boys."[57]

Harris grew even more controversial as the Depression deepened. Though the *Spectator* editor was neither a communist nor an NSL member, he endorsed the NSL's efforts to raise political awareness on campus and to assist the victims of the Great Depression. He urged students to drop their self-absorption and begin confronting the major problems troubling Depression America. Under Harris' editorship, the *Spectator* applauded the NSL-sponsored expedition to Harlan County in March 1932. He dispatched a *Spectator* reporter to travel with the delegation and published articles detailing conditions in the coal region. When Kentucky police disrupted the expedition, Harris editorialized against the "bigotry and intolerance" of the Kentucky legal establishment.[58]

By the middle of the spring semester the Columbia administration could no longer tolerate Harris. On March 31, Hebert Hawkes, Columbia's Dean of Students called Harris to his office. In this meeting the dean raised strong objections to the *Spectator*'s recent series criticizing the management of Columbia's dining halls. The articles had charged Columbia management with profiteering, exploiting student waiters, and serving poor food. Hawkes demanded that Harris offer proof for these charges within twenty-four hours.[59]

If Dean Hawkes thought Harris would defer to the administration's authority, he was mistaken. Having spent his term as *Spectator* editor trying to promote serious journalism, Harris naturally responded to Hawkes' demand by invoking the ethics of professional journalism. Harris sent a letter to Dean Hawkes summarizing the *Spectator*'s findings concerning the dining halls, but he refused to divulge the names of the individuals who had served as sources for the dining hall articles. Harris claimed that as a journalist he had a right to protect the confidentiality of his sources. He believed that in this case the *Spectator* had a special obligation to maintain this confidentiality, because the dining hall employees who spoke to the newspaper feared they would lose their jobs if the administration learned their identities.[60]

Harris not only refused to name his sources or comply with Hawkes' demand for "proof" of the dining hall charges, he also criticized the paternal condescension the dean had displayed in making this demand. Harris opened his letter to Hawkes by arguing that the dean rather than the *Spectator* had departed from the standard of civility which the Columbia administration claimed it was upholding:

> I want to protest against the manner in which I was "demanded" to produce an explanation [for the dining hall exposé]. You have repeatedly said to me that my mode of presentation in my editorial column has been unmannerly. Surely the dictatorial tone you adopted yesterday was not an example for me to follow in changing the tone of that column. In spite of the fact that we have had, almost constantly, major differences of opinion, I believe that I have acted in a gentlemanly manner while in your office during my term as editor of Spectator. That you should have adopted a tone suited only to a sargeant in the Marine Corps surprises me.[61]

Dean Hawkes refused to recognize the editor's right to protect his sources. He responded to Harris' letter on April 1 by informing Harris that he had been expelled and must appear before the Committee on Instruction for a hearing. Hawkes justified the expulsion (in a prepared statement which was soon released to the press) on the grounds that "material published in the Spectator during the last few days is a climax to a long series of discourtesies, innuendoes and misrepresentations which have appeared in this paper during the current academic year and calls for disciplinary action."[62]

Hawkes' press statement contradicted his initial explanation to Harris about the cause of his expulsion. The dean proved unable to get his story straight about whether the expulsion had been provoked solely by the dining hall exposé, or rather by Harris' persistent muckraking and radical editorials over the course of the entire year. Actually the dining hall information was not new; it had originally appeared in the newspaper in 1931, before Harris became editor. This fact, along with the inconsistent statements by Hawkes and other Columbia administrators fueled speculation that the dining hall exposé had been merely a pretext used by campus officials anxious to gag an iconoclastic editor—who had become too critical of the university and too sympathetic to the new student activism promoted by the NSL. The expulsion order was widely viewed as a case of administration anti-radicalism, a blatant example of intolerance toward dissent, on a level not seen at the relatively liberal Columbia campus since the repression which had accompanied World War I and the red scare.[63]

The expulsion order outraged Harris. He immediately issued a public statement denouncing the Columbia administration for violating his free speech rights and denying him a fair hearing. Harris charged that the expulsion order proved that the Columbia administration was suffering from "regimented, hypocritical thinking," which made a mockery of its own liberal pretensions:

One of the first things which is impressed upon any Columbia student is that the University is a center of liberalism. After being sentenced before trial yesterday by Dean Hawkes and then given a mock hearing at which it was revealed that Dr. Butler sanctioned the action, I am completely disillusioned concerning the liberalism of Columbia. The freedom of expression when it runs contrary to the administrative policy of the university is non-existent. The fine public utterances of Dr. Butler are seldom carried out.[64]

The charge of hypocrisy was more than merely a rhetorical device on Harris' part. The expelled editor was genuinely shocked that Columbia, home of one of America's most liberal faculties, would stoop to censoring a student newspaper. Harris was equally shocked by the illiberal manner in which he was expelled, without even a semblance of due process. What Harris had overlooked here was that academic liberals rarely applied their principles of toleration to undergraduates. Because of the paternalistic way that they viewed youth and undergraduates, the same administrators who endorsed intellectual freedom for the faculty could easily justify suppressing those freedoms for undergraduates.

Although Columbia's President Nicholas Murray Butler presided over a liberal faculty on Morningside Heights, his brand of liberalism was shallow when it came to student rights. During the 1930s President Butler became one of America's leading proponents of the view that undergraduates, unlike the faculty, had no right to academic freedom. Butler argued that as far as the status of undergraduates was concerned academic freedom "has no meaning whatever. It relates solely to the freedom of thought and inquiry and teaching on the part of accomplished scholars."[65] Since undergraduates were not "accomplished scholars" their speech could, in Butler's eyes, never be covered by the exclusively professorial right to academic freedom.

Butler's view of college students was similar to that of most American college administrators of his era. They tended to view undergraduates paternally, as immature teenagers who needed guidance enroute to adulthood. Since such college administrators did not see students as full-fledged adults, they saw no reason to grant students the rights or political autonomy of adults. On many campuses these assumptions resulted in non-students—administrators, faculty or alumni—having veto power over undergraduate political institutions.

For students, being subject to this paternalistic oversight meant living with restrictions on their political freedom. If a student organization during the early 1930s wanted to hold a meeting or bring an outside speaker to campus this often had to be cleared with a college administrator or faculty adviser. This veto system often barred controversial speakers and issues from campus. Some campuses had bylaws against using the college grounds for partisan political activity, and these were invoked to ban any brand of political organizing that might be distasteful to campus administrators. College officials employed this same type of control over the student press. And such control, as one critic wrote in 1932, effectively limited freedom of the press on campus.

> Some forty percent of the college [student] publications in the United States suffer under a system in which each editor is supervised in his activities by a "faculty advisor" whose real function is that of a censor. By this means, much of the criticism prepared against the administration is deleted before the publication reaches the press.[66]

Students who failed to comply with the decisions of their political overseers could expect a political fate similar to Harris'—facing expulsion or other disciplinary action as punishment for their insubordination. In fact, the same academic year in which Harris was expelled, eight other students were dismissed from their editorships or expelled from college because of their refusal to adhere to administration editorial restrictions, and twelve others left their posts under apparent administration pressure.[67] This censorship, as Reed Harris pointed out in 1932, had the effect of intimidating students and discouraging them from airing critical, unconventional political views. "In the treatment meted out to college editors," Harris wrote

> we have a key to the apparent immaturity of American students. They are kept that way by the men who watch their every move. As soon as an undergraduate editor begins to wake up and speak in criticism of things as they are, he is bound, gagged and, if convenient, tossed into the world outside the university, perhaps for fear lest he demoralize the more timid students by whom his writing is read.[68]

College administrators had not only the political power, but the legal right to exert disciplinary authority over undergraduates. The Courts consistently enforced the traditional *in loco parentis* doctrine, ruling that the college administrator and "teacher stands in place of the parent—*in loco parentis*—with the same power to control and punish."[69] Throughout the first third of the twentieth century, state and federal judges, citing this paternalistic legal doctrine, backed even the most arbitrary disciplining of undergraduates by college administrators. In one of the most famous of these cases, the New York Court of Appeals upheld the expulsion of a Syracuse University undergraduate even though the University's only justification for dismissing her was its vague statement that she was not a "typical Syracuse girl."[70] The Court ruled that administrators could expel anyone they thought was detracting from the moral or intellectual well being of the school, and they were not obligated to reveal the reason for the expulsion. State Courts in Pennsylvania and Florida further restricted student political rights by ruling that colleges could expel students without even holding a hearing. Federal and state courts also ruled that the college did not have to present students with the evidence used to expel them, nor did they have to give students an opportunity to defend themselves.[71]

By enforcing the *in loco parentis* doctrine and granting administrators almost absolute legal authority over their students, the Courts provided these university officials with a virtual license to police and censor undergraduate political expression. Administrators knew they could trample the civil liberties of students without any legal repercussions. When Columbia University expelled a student for making anti-war speeches during World War I, the Courts upheld the expulsion. Albany College won a similar decision in 1921, when it expelled a student because of his socialistic political opinions. Even the United States Supreme Court unanimously ruled in favor of restricting student political freedom, when it upheld the right of land grant colleges in the 1930s to expel students who refused to take mandatory courses in military training.[72]

The censorship conflict at Columbia involved far more, then, than a dispute over a few articles; it represented a clash between partisans of two ways of thinking about college students and their political rights. On the one side was the Columbia administration, asserting its right to treat students as immature youths, who could be censored and disciplined at the pleasure of college officials. On the other side was Reed Harris, who had rejected the infantilization inherent in the the *in loco parentis* doctrine, insisting that as a student journalist he was not a senseless child who could be spanked, but a citizen and editor with rights that must be respected.

Standing alongside Harris was the NSL, which from the day of its birth had recognized that it would be impossible to build a mass student movement on campus unless undergraduates enjoyed free speech rights. This is why in its founding platform the NSL in December 1931 pledged to "prosecute an unending fight for academic freedom; to the end that neither instructors nor students shall be gagged in classrooms and out, and that they may not suffer discipline for their political beliefs." In this same document the NSL had demanded complete autonomy for both the student press and all other student political institutions:

> College publications must not be subject to censorship by administration, faculty bodies and trustees, and officers of publications must not be disciplined for political or economic views expressed. Student clubs must be beyond faculty or administration censorship and must be permitted to affiliate with such outside organizations as they choose.[73]

At Columbia in 1932 the NSL made good on these pledges to battle for student free speech rights. The League's support for Harris was evident from almost the moment of his expulsion. The NSL, and its Columbia chapter, the Social Problems Club, mobilized the pro-Harris students with great speed and skill. On the day of the expulsion order, the NSL issued a statement denouncing the Columbia administration for its "un-

warranted interference with freedom of study and freedom of the press."
Though the expulsion had been announced on Friday, and student organizing is difficult on the weekend, by Sunday the NSL was already convening a citywide protest meeting on Harris' behalf. This meeting, held
in a downtown theater, drew over 1000 students (from campuses
throughout New York City), to that point the largest undergraduate political rally of the decade. At this meeting, strategy was discussed, a statement from Harris read, and the NSL declared that it had "accepted leadership of the fight to reinstate Reed Harris." The NSL also announced
that it would hold a mass protest meeting at Columbia the following day.[74]

With the NSL at the helm, the anti-expulsion protests at Columbia
got off to a roaring start on Monday, April 4. The planned mass meeting
drew over 2000 students and culminated in the crowd's overwhelming
support of a one day student strike—called by the NSL—scheduled for
April 6. The protesters also sent a delegation to Dean Hawkes, which
criticized him for censoring the student press and asked that Harris be
reinstated. But the dean would not relent; he argued that the expulsion
involved "not a question of censorship, but one of courtesy . . . . Harris
never found a basis for the evils he criticized."[75]

Hawkes' arguments did not persuade the delegation, nor were they
satisfactory to Harris' former colleagues on the student newspaper. The
Spectator protested the expulsion by leaving its regular editorial space blank
and running a black rule on the masthead where Harris' name had formerly appeared. On the front page appeared an editorial praising Harris
as a man of conscience "who detested mediocrity . . . . Columbia College
was too small to hold him." The *Spectator* concluded that the rise of censorship at Columbia had left the university's liberal reputation in shambles.[76]

Student support of Harris was not confined to the Columbia campus.
The NSL organized delegations from other metropolitan campuses to aid
in the picketing for the Columbia strike. Editorials in favor of Harris appeared in many college newspapers. Forty student newspaper editors nationwide signed a petition protesting the expulsion on the grounds that
"the right to free expression of beliefs . . . is not one to be tampered
with."[77] Off campus, Harris attracted the support of newspapers sensitive
to the censorship issue, and the American Civil Liberties Union, which
agreed to provide Harris with counsel.[78]

Not all Columbia students, however, sympathized with Harris. The
expelled editor's earlier criticism of football and fraternities had alienated
partisans of the traditional collegiate culture, who were quite happy to see
Harris censored. The fraternity-dominated Student Board of Represena-
tives (Columbia's elected student government) greeted Harris' expulsion
by passing a resolution expressing "complete confidence in the fair-
mindedness and sound judgement of Dean Herbert E. Hawkes in his recent disciplinary action."[79] A small group of Harris opponents formed an

ad hoc organization, the Spartans, seeking to undermine the drive to reinstate the expelled editor.

During the first pro-Harris mass meeting, Spartans heckled and threw apples at the speakers. In response, the rally organizers invited the hecklers to speak. One of the Spartans, Shelly Wood of the Crew team, accepted this offer, but could think of nothing more to say to the crowd than "Well you called me yellow. Here I am." A second Spartan got up and shouted "Everyone knows that these things [in the dining hall] were going on but Harris had no right to bring them up." James Wechsler, who was present at the rally, recalled that the inarticulateness of these Harris foes "inevitably strengthened the belief of the Harris legions that witlessness was arrayed with oppression on the other side of the campus barricades."[80] The Spartans could not slow the groundswell of support for Harris which was emerging on the Columbia campus.

When Columbia students came to campus on April 6, they encountered their classmates picketing, carrying "free speech" banners and urging them to join the one day strike in protest against the expulsion. The picketers distributed NSL strike leaflets which praised Harris' "militant editorial policy," and listed three demands: "1. The reinstatement of Reed Harris; 2. An investigation of the John Jay dining room by a student committee; 3. An investigation of charges of professionalism in athletics to be made by a student committee."[81] Student support for the strike was overwhelming. Over 75 percent of the student body boycotted classes, and most of these students joined the campus rally demanding Harris' reinstatement.[82]

Emotions ran high on the day of the strike. Harris supporters were out in force defending him and the new critical sensibility he represented. In opposition were the athletes and fraternity men, who embodied the values of the traditional collegiate lifestyle inherited from 1920s; their most cherished goal was the promotion of school spirit. Since they deemed the Harris supporters guilty of undermining the good name of the college, the anti-Harris students responded by behaving the way traditional undergraduate leaders had customarily acted in the face of nonconformity on campus: hazing and physically assaulting strike leaders.

This violence began in the morning on the picket line when a varsity football player attacked one of the pro-Harris leafleters. Later, as several Harris partisans tried to use black crepe to gag the statue of alma mater—symbolizing the gagging of the expelled editor—several varsity athletes grabbed the crepe, tied the protester in it and punched him. Anti-Harris students showered eggs upon every speaker who criticized the Columbia administration, including a Protestant minister, who responded by denouncing the hecklers as "regular hired thugs." The athletes and fraternity men also ripped down pro-Harris banners of demonstrators from the architecture school and neighboring Barnard college, and in the process knocked one architecture student unconscious. In defending his involvement in these assaults, one strike opponent told the *New York Times* that "no 'gentleman' would have published what Harris did . . . but on questioning he conceded that 'gentlemen' occasionally threw eggs. He said he represented the 'administration' in throwing them."[83]

Aside from bruising a half dozen protesters, the anti-Harris rioters failed to hurt the Columbia strike. In fact, the assaults and the willingness of Harris supporters to withstand physical violence for the sake of free speech built sympathy for the strike both on and off campus. James Wechsler, who covered the story for the *Spectator,* recalled feeling a great surge of admiration for such protesters as Tim Westwood, a Columbia law student who, after having been beaten bloody by a gang of anti-Harris students, returned to the library steps to give an impassioned speech in defense of Harris and free speech. Westwood had, in Wechsler's eyes, offered "a conspicuous example of gallantry under fire . . . . He seemed the personification of the invincible cause of freedom, and I could only pity those who failed to appreciate the magnificence of the moment."[84] To outside observers, moreover, such as syndicated columnist Heywood Broun, the massive size of the strike when compared with the relatively small band of violent anti-Harris students only served to demonstrate that it was Harris rather than President Butler who had carried the day. Broun concluded that the Columbia administration

> has been placed in the ludicrous position of having none but athletes on its side . . . . For the first time in the history of American education football players were observed fighting to get into class. The whole affair may prove so epoch making that from now on the brawny boys will be ready to die for dear old calculus . . . . It seems to me that a college paper ought to be more than a bulletin in which to print the time and place of the next meeting of the French Society. The Spectator under Reed Harris was enlivened by a bold challenge to tradition both in campus life and beyond. The issue of free speech has been distinctly raised by the editor's expulsion . . . . Accordingly . . . I'm for Harris and dead against Butch Butler and his football favorites.[85]

In fomenting the Harris controversy the Columbia administration proved as politically inept as its violent student suppporters. When Dean Hawkes expelled Harris he apparently did not know—or think to check—that the *Spectator* editor was in the final week of his twelve-month term of office. At the time the dean informed Harris of his expulsion, the *Spectator* had just held its annual election in which the staff of the paper chose the new editor-in-chief. Harris had already written the final editorial of his term. Had the Columbia administration been more knowledgeable and cautious, then, it could have been rid of Harris' editorial voice without provoking a strike, by merely waiting a few days for his tenure at the *Spectator* to end.[86]

The Butler administration's failure to do its political homework and inquire into Harris' status on the *Spectator* was not simply an oversight; it was a reflection of the fact that in 1932, Hawkes and Butler still assumed that student politics had not changed since the 1920s. These administrators did not painstakingly search for the least provocative way to silence Harris because they did not understand that Columbia undergraduates could be provoked into mass protest on campus. They were so accustomed to dealing with a politically quiescent student body, as in the 1920s, that they saw neither the possibility of a strike nor the necessity of thinking ahead tactically about how to handle the Harris case without provoking a strike. Hawkes and Butler were simply out of touch with the new political mood on campus, the restlessness and uneasiness wrought by the Depression, and the readiness of the new breed of student activists to challenge what they saw as unjust actions by campus administrators.

Although shocked by the student strike, the Columbia administration initially tried to give the impression that it had been unaffected by the walkout. Dean Hawkes insisted that the protests would not change his mind, and that Harris would never be reinstated. But soon after the strike, the administration began to backpedal. The first concession came on April 9, when Columbia's Commons Committee announced that it would conduct an investigation into the management of the university's dining halls. This was a major break with the administration's earlier position that the *Spectator*'s criticism of the dining halls had been groundless.[87]

The final retreat of the Columbia administration came on April 20, 1932 when, after a series of meetings between university officials and Harris' attorney, Acting Dean Nicolas McKnight announced the reinstatement of the expelled editor. In exchange for this concession, Harris had apologized for the letter he had written chastising Dean Hawkes. McKnight also announced that upon reinstatement, Harris had chosen to resign from the university—an act which was portrayed as voluntary but which was in fact part of the settlement between the two sides of the dispute.[88]

Harris owed his reinstatement to the political furor which the student protests had generated. President Butler was convinced that "the university's position was legally sound and would have been sustained by the courts." But the strike persuaded him that the political price for maintaining that position would be too high; it would lead to further protests and more negative press for Columbia. Thus the day after Harris' reinstatement was announced, Butler—in endorsing the out of court settlement—confided to the university's attorney that "the annoyance and misrepresentation which would follow upon widespread and sensational newspaper publicity would far outweigh any advantage to be gained by winning a court action."[89] John Godfrey Saxe, the university counsel, concurred in this judgement, pointing out in his reply to Butler that legal action against Harris was politically inadvisable because the case would drag on for months, "carrying continual aggravation " for the Columbia administration.[90]

Privately, several Columbia administrators voiced strong disapproval of the settlement. They felt the university had made too big a concession by agreeing to reinstate Harris. They also were dissatisfied with Harris' apology, which had recanted nothing from the controversial dining hall exposé. Indeed, the administration had given much ground; its original negotiating position with Harris' attorney had been that he would not be reinstated unless he submitted an apology to the university conceding "that the discipline which was administered to him had nothing whatever to do with the freedom of the press or the right of free speech."[91] But Harris had refused to make such a sweeping apology, forcing the administration to accept a much more limited note from him that mentioned only the letter to Hawkes. The failure of the university to obtain such a broad apology was a point of contention within the administration during the final vote on the Harris settlement, and it was mentioned by one administrator to justify his vote against the settlement.[92]

As the administration went public with its decision to reinstate Harris, face saving was the order of the day. Dean McKnight, trying to put the settlement in the most favorable possible light for the administration, portrayed the Harris case in a thoroughly disingenuous manner. Though the administration's initial refusal to reinstate Harris was now being reversed, McKnight denied that the decision to expel Harris had been wrong. McKnight told the press that "the university authorities fully supported Dean Hawkes in the action which he had taken as to Reed Harris and that the Reed Harris case did not come within the principle of free speech and freedom of the press . . ."[93] McKnight tried to make it appear as if Harris had been reinstated because he had apologized for his letter to Hawkes; the dean claimed that this letter had "precipitated the disciplinary action against Harris," when in fact the administration had previously maintained that the dining hall articles had provoked the expulsion.[94]

Although Harris' supporters cheered the reinstatement of the expelled editor, they criticized the university's refusal to acknowledge that free speech was at issue, or that the initial decision to discipline Harris had been wrong. As Roger Baldwin, director of the American Civil Liberties Union, explained: "The university's statement sustaining Dean Hawkes' expulsion of Harris when at the same time Harris is reinstated leaves us a little breathless. But face saving does not contribute to consistency." Mocking the adminstration, Norman Thomas told a crowd of Columbia students that he had never seen

> a more inconsistent peace treaty in my life—it backs Dean Hawkes and at the same time reinstates Harris . . . . The university ought to offer a course in how to write political platforms on which everybody can ride . . . . Whoever drew it up ought to go to Chicago to help the old parties write their platforms.[95]

The *Spectator* pronounced the university's statement "typical of the wavering and contradictory" methods used by the administration throughout the Harris case.[96]

The National Student League saw Harris' reinstatement as a "magnificent" victory for the student movement. In the NSL's view the administration's retreat demonstrated that students—if organized correctly—could stop political suppression on campus. By securing free speech for critics of the university, the NSL believed it was creating the political space necessary for a mass protest movement to arise on campus. The NSL interpreted the widespread student participation in the Harris protest as proof that the League's founding platform was correct in stressing that campus issues could serve as the key to politicizing undergraduates. In leading the Columbia struggle to a succesful conclusion, the NSL prided itself on having pioneered an innovative tactic, the student strike, consequently establishing a new tradition of protest. According to the NSL, the Columbia revolt showed

> that a new day had dawned in American student life. A new and almost anomalous tradition was to take its place beside the ivy-covered stories of the champion crew and the old college fence. Students had used the [strike] weapon of the working class in defense of a student right.[97]

The NSL was euphoric in the wake of the Columbia strike and with good reason. In full glare of national press attention, the League had organized the most effective student protest in recent memory. The NSL's success in its Columbia campaign was all the more impressive, given the small size of the Columbia NSL chapter. This skillful mobilization effort elicited a great deal of admiration for the NSL among students who had previously had little contact with the communist-led organization. Columbia alumnus James Wechsler recalled that

> for the large number of students who sympathized with Harris, this was a first glimpse of Communists in action and, as was to occur so often, they simply seemed to be the most dedicated and energetic champions of a great cause . . . . They resolutely took command of the proceedings and, since no college course had tutored us in such arts as the painting of picket signs, the Communists swiftly dominated the machinery of protest . . . . ; there could not have been more than thirty of them on the Columbia campus at the time. But they were tireless.[98]

As in the Kentucky expedition, the NSL at Columbia mobilized students around a civil liberties issue which had broad appeal. Once again the NSL, which could be very critical of the shortcomings of liberalism, nonetheless proved adept at honing its message in a way that stirred the student body's liberal conscience. It was the NSL rather than any liberal organization on campus which waved the liberal banner of free speech. Ironically, though in theory a communist-led organization like the NSL lacked the liberal's reverence for free speech rights (and communists would surely deny those rights to reactionaries), in practice the NSL had to fight against a prominent liberal university to preserve those very free speech rights to which liberalism was ostensibly wedded.[99]

The timidity of the faculty during the Reed Harris controversy further promoted the conclusion that the communist-led NSL had behaved more liberally than Columbia's liberals. In all of Columbia University only sixteen teachers would sign a pro-Harris petition, and of these, only one, Mark Van Doren, was a professor. Such eminent liberal faculty members as John Dewey refused to get involved in the controversy. The protesters saw this faculty apathy as the product of fear—professors not wanting to risk their jobs by siding with Harris and alientating the administration; they viewed this "widespread failure to respond [to the petition as] new proof that Columbia's liberalism was a fraud." The fact that the only faculty member to address the Columbia strikers was Donald Henderson, the young communist economics instructor, led students to ask "why there were so many non-practicing liberals" at the university.[100]

At Columbia, the NSL not only outshone the liberal faculty and administration in standing up for liberal principle, it "outorganized" the traditional undergraduate leaders who had dominated student life since the 1920s. In obtaining Harris' resinstatement, the NSL proved that the fraternity-athletic establishment could be challenged and defeated—even when allied with a powerful college administration. What the Kentucky trip did on the road, Columbia brought back to the campus: demonstrating that the old collegiate insularity and apathy could be broken down under the leadership of the student Left.

The Columbia strike spurred further radical organizing on campus because it showed that the student Left could win political victories and change the tone of student life. At Columbia this change was as large as the gulf between the pointless freshman-sophomore riot of 1930 and the determined political battle for free speech in 1932. The Reed Harris struggle provided a glimpse of what the new American student politics of the 1930s would look like: it was left of center, critical of university authority, and conducive to the emergence of large scale campus protest. This was a sight which energized the student Left, by suggesting that its hopes for politically transforming the campuses were not unrealistic. Indeed, with the Kentucky and Columbia campaigns under their belts, NSLers approached campus organizing with a great sense of confidence, aware that in less than a month they had led the two most effective student political actions of the decade.

IV

Within weeks of the Reed Harris protests the NSL was again involved in a political battle in New York City. This time the issue was economic and linked directly to the Depression: a student fee hike in the municipal colleges of New York. In the past the municipal colleges—Brooklyn College, Hunter College, and City College—had been tuition-free, charging only the most nominal educational fees. But the Depression caused a decline in tax revenues, which threw the city college system into a fiscal crisis. The New York City Board of Higher Education sought to resolve this crisis in May 1932 by imposing tuition and mandating the payment of new library, laboratory and diploma fees, scheduled to take effect in the coming fall semester. This announcement alarmed many students in the city college system, most of whom had already suffered because of the Depression; they feared that their inability to pay the proposed fees would force them to drop out of college.[101]

The NSL responded to the fee announcement by organizing the largest citywide protest yet seen on New York campuses. The NSL began by circulating a questionnaire on the student body's economic status, to document the hardships of many city college undergraduates and demonstrate that most would be unable to shoulder the new fees. The League then formed a Student Fee Committee to coordinate intercampus mobilization over the fees. The first rally was set for Brooklyn College, but the Faculty Committee on Student Affairs prohibited the students from demonstrating on campus. Consequently, the NSL moved the rally to Borough Hall in Brooklyn, where on May 18 approximately 1000 students turned out in protest against the proposed fees.[102]

At the CCNY uptown campus the following week, the NSL mobilized the most financially strapped students in the city college system: those attending CCNY's night school. These students attended college at night because they had to work full time jobs during the day to make ends meet. Some 3000 night school students rallied against the fee hikes at CCNY on May 23. Speakers at this rally, citing statistics from the NSL survey, argued that if the fees went into effect 74 percent of the evening students would be forced to drop out of college. The NSL charged that in deciding to impose the fees the Board of Higher Education had abandoned its educational mission and succumbed to the pressure of "bankers and real estate interests." A similar anti-fee rally at Hunter College the following day attracted 500 students.[103]

Unlike the Reed Harris strike, the NSL in the fee fight at the city colleges did not encounter organized student opposition. Linked by their tight budgets and their belief in low cost public higher education, the student bodies united in opposition to the fees. One sign of this unity was the overwhelming student support for the NSL's anti-fee petition, which in a few weeks time had over 5000 student signatures—and by the end of the semester more than 10,000 signatures. Student governments and newspapers from all the city colleges denounced the fees as a threat not only to individual students, but also to the character of the New York municipal college system, in which merit rather than money was the basis for admission:

The College, during the last eighty-five years has typified a pure educational democracy, students have gained admission on no other basis
than that of mental ability. Because of this fact, the College has maintained an enviable reputation. Because of this fact, the student body at
the College has been characterized by an intellectual vigor which we point
to with pride. The establishment of fees would seriously cripple that reputation. For it would mean the setting up of a new standard for admission. It would set up an artificial money barrier . . . . It would change
the character of the College, put it a step nearer to some of our country
club establishments.[104]

Recognizing that ultimate decision making power regarding the fees
rested with the city government rather than with college administrators,
the NSL took its protests to City Hall. A delegation of forty-five students
from Brooklyn, Hunter, and City Colleges attended a meeting of the New
York Board of Estimate on May 27, seeking to attain a hearing on the fee
hikes. When the delegation sought to get the Board's attention during the
meeting by marching down the room's central aisle, police halted them.
Later in the meeting, NSL leader Joseph Clark shouted "We, delegated
students of the three city colleges protest . . ." But before Clark could
finish, city officials interrupted and told the students that since they were
not on the agenda, they would not be allowed to speak.[105]

The NSL returned to City Hall with a larger student delegation on
June 10. Again the students were denied speaking rights. Police moved in
to the evict the crowd of about 200 students, which was seeking access to
the Board of Estimate meeting. Angered at the Board's rebuff, the students defied the police by hoisting their spokesman on their shoulders,
massing around him "in protection and put[ting] up a stiff resistance to
the police. Not until after they had begun to picket the hall with their
placards and special reserves had arrived and surrounded them, were they
dispersed."[106] Later the protesters defied the police once more by holding
a rally on the plaza outside City Hall, drawing over 600 students.[107]

Throughout the fee protests, the NSL stressed how regressive it was
for the municipal college system to force lower-class students, the group
least able to afford it, to bail the city out of its fiscal crisis. The NSL
suggested that the fairest way to raise the revenues for the city colleges
was by raising income taxes, inheritance taxes, and gift taxes on those in
the higher brackets. The NSL also argued that New York City's government, still dominated by Tammany Hall—New York's corrupt Democratic
political machine—should eliminate its waste and dishonesty and not expect students to subsidize City Hall's financial inefficiency.[108]

While city officials had turned a cold shoulder to the protesting students initially, City Hall ultimately proved unable to ignore the sustained
campaign against the fees. The Board of Higher Education announced
on June 13 that it would appoint a special subcommittee to consider the
demands for abolition of the fees. This subcommittee met over the summer and quietly eliminated the fees.[109]

Given the fact that the new fees had been announced so definitively in May and that city officials were at first unwilling even to offer the anti-fee activists a hearing, the elimination of the fees was a remarkable victory for the NSL. The League had shown that thousands of students could be mobilized in defense of low cost public higher education. This was a lesson which seems to have affected New York's politicians, who as a consequence of the protests recognized that fee hikes threatened to alienate both students and their parents—jeopardizing thousands of votes on election day. Consequently, a few months after the students had won the fee fight, both leading candidates in the upcoming New York mayoralty race began to compete over who could create the stronger declaration against any new fees in the city college system.[110]

New York was not the only place where the NSL orchestrated impressive student protests against fee hikes in spring 1932. Almost simultaneous with the anti-fee campaign in New York, a similar movement emerged in Detroit. In 1931 the City College of Detroit had imposed a $100 tuition fee, which burdened the college's predominantly low income student body. When in the spring of 1932, the College indicated that it would be doubling its tuition, student protests erupted. The NSL helped lead several demonstrations at City Hall, one of which drew more than a thousand students. These protests ended successfully, with the revocation of the new tuition increase.[111]

V

The college commencement season was not a happy time for the class of 1932, which was graduating into a world of mass unemployment and political uncertainty. College seniors were about to hit the job market at a time when placements of graduates from even the most elite institutions, such as Yale, were down by two thirds from the previous year. At Reed College unemployment of graduates, which had been 6 percent in 1930, was about to hit 25.6 percent in 1932. Nonetheless many commencement speakers pasted smiles on their faces and gave the traditional cheerleading orations, urging the graduates not to be discouraged by hard times.[112] But not even these purveyors of optimism and sunny platitudes could remove the pall the Depression had cast. Indeed, at several campuses the clichés of graduation oratory were discarded, and the Depression intruded into these cap and gown ceremonies. At Notre Dame, for instance, General Electric Chairman Owen D. Young urged that the president be granted almost dictatorial powers to cope with the economic crisis. Such speeches served only to remind graduates that the society which awaited them seemed on the verge of coming unhinged.[113]

About the only organization on campus that resonated with excitement during commencement 1932 was the NSL. Hard times for American capitalism had meant good times for the student Left. The NSL had

just completed a semester in which it enjoyed a string of political successes; its leaders felt that history was moving in their direction. "A new
student has arisen," explained the NSL national magazine at the end of
the 1932 spring semester.

> The economic crisis has been an excellent teacher of new values. The
> new student is breaking thru the old, narrow- fitting academic bonds. His
> school-fed illusions are fading away. He is beginning to realize that his
> life as a student is inextricably bound up with the social system under
> which he lives. This is proven by the widespread response to the events
> in Kentucky, the Columbia strike, the fight against fees in the free col-
> leges of Detroit and New York City . . . . The new student is learning
> to battle for his rights as a social individual.[114]

Such optimism and confidence were understandable, coming as they
did from young radicals who had recently stood up to vigilantes and deputies in the South, preserved low cost education in two cities, and won a
major free speech fight against one of the nation's most eminent college
presidents. But two busloads of students, plus New York and Detroit add
up to only a small part of America and its student population. The "new
student" whose emergence the NSL was celebrating in 1932 had yet to be
mobilized for political action on a truly national basis. The task of putting
together such a mobilization, building a genuine mass protest movement
on campus would be the key challenge confronting the student Left in
the wake of this first springtime of revolt.

Chapter 4

The Making of a Mass Movement

We will not support the U.S. government in any war it may conduct.

> Americanized version of the Oxford Pledge, administered
> during the student strikes against war in the United States.
> "Meaning of April 13," *Student Review* (Summer 1934), 4.

In seventeen we went to war,
In seventeen we went to war,
In seventeen we went to war,
Didn't know what we were fighting for.
Time to turn those guns the other way.

> Anti-war chant of radical student protesters in the U.S. during
> the mid-1930s. Leslie Fielder, "In Every Generation:
> A Meditation on Two Holocausts," in *Testimony*,
> David Rosenberg, ed. (New York, 1989), 218.

Our geographical isolation makes political isolation seem practical. And we have 1917 on our conscience. We went to war ostensibly to make the world safe for democracy, only to make it safe for J.P. Morgan. We don't want to be fooled again. Haunted by the past, terrified by the present, many, including those who considered themselves the most "revolutionary" have taken refuge in trying to keep America out of war by trying to keep America out of the world [through] . . . support of the Oxford Pledge.

> Joseph P. Lash, "Footnote to the Oxford Pledge" [1938].

Franklin Delano Roosevelt so dominated the American political scene from the fall of 1932 through the end of the Depression decade that historians refer to these years as the Age of Roosevelt. He won the 1932 presidential race in one of the greatest landslides in American history, trouncing Hoover—who the electorate blamed for the Depression—by almost seven million votes. FDR then presided over the extensive New Deal recovery, relief and reform programs, whose popularity helped keep him in the White House longer than any other president. But Roosevelt's great popularity with the general public did not initially carry over onto college campuses. During most of his first term, neither FDR nor his major programs captured the imagination of the American student body. Roosevelt's presidential campaign in 1932 failed to generate much excitement on campus, and from 1933 to 1935 the cause that most inspired college youth was world peace rather than the New Deal.

If the choice had been left to college students, the straw polls show, Franklin Roosevelt would not have been elected president in 1932. FDR ran far behind Hoover in the campus polls taken shortly before election day. Only 31 percent of the collegians polled supported Roosevelt, while 49 percent endorsed Hoover. Roosevelt even did badly on campuses where he had direct, personal connections. At Harvard, FDR's alma mater, the Democratic candidate lost to Hoover by a margin of more than three to one: 1211 students there voted for Hoover, while only 395 cast their ballots for Roosevelt. Support for Roosevelt was also weak among undergraduates at Columbia University, despite the fact that several of his key advisers, popularly known as the New Deal "brain trust," including Raymond Moley, Rexford Tugwell, and Adolph Berle, were Columbia professors. With almost two thirds of Columbia undergraduates voting, FDR attracted only 221 votes, losing not only to Hoover, who drew 307 votes, but also to Norman Thomas, the socialist candidate, who won 421 votes. This enabled Columbia socialists to boast at the Norman Thomas rally at Madison Square Garden that "Columbia Professors May Write Roosevelt's Speeches But Columbia Students Vote For Thomas." Roosevelt even lost in his own backyard, at Vassar College, a few miles from his home in Hyde Park. Though FDR had served as a trustee at Vassar, he ran a dismal third in the college's straw poll, attracting only 105 votes, to 563 for Hoover, and 208 for Thomas.[1]

Roosevelt's failure to compete effectively with Hoover for the student vote may seem strange in light of the Democratic landslide off campus, but it is somewhat less surprising in the context of collegiate political history. In polls taken throughout the 1920s, college students had voted more solidly Republican than had the general electorate, reflecting their middle-class roots. Critics complained that in 1932 undergraduates were simply conforming to the old collegiate pattern of "voting exactly as their fathers vote" because they accepted "as handed down to them the ideals of a comfortable owning class." The *Harvard Crimson* echoed this analysis, explaining Hoover's victory there as a consequence of the fact that "students at Harvard are on the whole of the conservative monied class."[2]

It was, however, not simply the collegiate Republican tradition or the class background of the student body which rendered undergraduates so unreceptive to FDR in 1932. Some of the responsibility for the weak Democratic showing on campus rested with Roosevelt himself. He failed to run the type of inspiring or intellectually coherent campaign which might have attracted an upsurge of students into the Democratic ranks. The Roosevelt campaign did not articulate clear solutions to the economic crisis; its political message was riddled with contradictions. For instance, the campaign implied that the federal government had to do more on behalf of the unemployed, but also called for a balanced budget. Roosevelt's supporters on campus even implied that Hoover was spending too much federal money, and that a Roosevelt administration would bring "an immediate and drastic reduction of governmental expenditures."[3]

Students were put off by Roosevelt's tendency to avoid specifics. A columnist for UC Berkeley's student newspaper complained that on the campaign trail FDR voiced his ideas "in a vague, general manner. There may be meat there but it is hidden under a cloud of gush vaguely referring to the 'common man.' "[4] The students' low estimation of Roosevelt was influenced by much of the intelligentsia, which found him intellectually shallow. This was a time when even astute political writers, such as Walter Lippmann, saw Roosevelt as merely "a pleasant man who, without any important qualifications for office, would very much like to be president." Indeed, in criticizing Roosevelt during this era, student editors, including those of the *Columbia Spectator*, cited Lippmann approvingly when they berated FDR as "the Artful Dodger, whose mastery of misty rhetoric is still unmatched."[5]

Roosevelt's failure to build a Democratic undergraduate majority in 1932 is all the more striking because it came at a time of declining Republican influence on campus. Though Hoover defeated FDR on campus, he was also the first Republican presidential candidate since the First World War who received a plurality rather than an overwhelming majority of the student vote. The 49 percent that Hoover attracted on campus represented a sharp decline from both the 58.6 percent of the student vote which fellow Republican Calvin Coolidge had won in 1924 and the two to one landslide which Hoover himself had over Al Smith on campus in 1928.[6] The Republicans had lost the sweeping campus majority that they had enjoyed throughout the 1920s because the Depression prodded increasing numbers of students to question the economic individualism and limited government ideals which had prevailed during more than a decade of Republican ascendance. A significant minority of students was shifting leftward. Had he been able to attract the students radicalized by the Depression, FDR would not have lost to Hoover in the national college straw poll. Roosevelt's problem was that he not only lost the moderate students to Hoover, but also lost the growing leftwing student vote to Norman Thomas.

A surprisingly large minority of undergraduates rejected both major party candidates in favor of Norman Thomas. The socialist candidate at-

tracted 18 percent of the 57,000 students participating in the college straw
polls. This student vote for Thomas suggested that socialistic thinking or
at least disillusionment with the two-party system had advanced much further on campus than off. Thomas' support among undergraduates dwarfed
the 2.2 percent vote he received from the general electorate.[7]

The campus campaign for Thomas was much better organized and
nationally coordinated than those of the major party candidates. By election day 1932 there were Thomas For President Clubs on more than 150
campuses, and they were far more active than their Democratic or Republican counterparts. The major parties did not pay much attention to the
campuses because only a few hundred thousand collegians were of voting
age. Thomas, on the other hand, devoted considerable time to the campuses because his financially strapped campaign needed student volunteers. He did better on campus than off because within the college gates
he had to compete with only the ideas and not the large campaign chests
of the major parties.[8]

Thomas' cogent socialist analysis of the Depression, which he articulated with great eloquence, appealed to youths searching for solutions to
the deepening economic crisis. For students shifting leftward, FDR's vague
intimations of reform paled in comparison with Thomas' call for massive
federal aid to the needy and radical restructuring of the economy. These
students thought Roosevelt too timid and moderate for the task of rescu-
ing Depression America's collapsing economic system. Their straw poll
voting attested that FDR in 1932 was "unsuccessful in channeling the mixed
idealism and unrest that rallied nationally behind Thomas' candidacy."[9]

This student enthusiasm for Thomas in 1932 was a testament to how
much had changed on campus since the 1920s. Throughout that prosperous decade, Thomas had toured the campuses for the LID, but his lectures on socialist and labor topics elicited little response from a student
body which was overwhelmingly conservative politically. The Depression
had at last given Thomas a campus following, as students, shaken by the
economic crisis, became more receptive to criticism of capitalism. And it
was not only the students who were changing, but Thomas himself. In
contrast to his academic-style lectures on campus in the 1920s, Thomas in
1932 was acting as a political crusader on the stump. He was no longer
asking students simply to study socialism, but was rather urging them to
become active in his campaign to change and save America in its hour of
crisis. This was a new and dramatic message; it generated a level of excitement on campus which had eluded Thomas in the 1920s.[10]

Thomas' campus campaign benefited from the revitalization of the
student LID. By the fall of 1932 the socialist-led student LID was a much
more dynamic organization than it had been at the beginning of the
Depression. Student LID leaders had become aware the previous spring
that the NSL, a new upstart leftist group, had out-organized them. The
NSL's effective political actions in Harlan, the Reed Harris strike, and the
City College tuition fight had attracted national attention, while the stu-

dent LID—despite its longer history—had lacked initiative, doing little more than supporting the protests launched by the NSL. But student LID leaders proved quick learners. As the 1932–33 academic year began, the campus LID had shed its academic orientation in favor of a much more activist approach to student organizing. Energized by the Depression itself and influenced by the example set by the NSL, the LID ceased merely pondering politics in discussion groups, and began involving students in political agitation. For LIDers this agitation began with assistance to Thomas; they transformed the skeletal LID network into an effective national college campaign for the socialist candidate.[11]

The student campaign for Thomas contrasted with those of the major parties in that it was more of a protest movement than an electoral race. Thomas student organizers were seeking to change not just presidents, but economic systems. They saw the campaign as a way of popularizing socialist ideas on campus, and they were passionate in this political crusade. Indeed, non-radical students were sometimes astonished by the energy and zeal of the Thomas forces. At the University of Michigan, for instance, the Socialist Club engaged in a bit of direct action which shocked and angered editors of the *Michigan Daily*. Thomas supporters marched on the the offices of that student newspaper, protesting its anti-Socialist bias and its refusal to cover a blatant case of ballot tampering. Though the paper denounced the protesters as "loud-talking, little thinking radicals," the march did prod the *Daily* to cover the ballot tampering story. The march demonstrated just how militant Thomas' supporters could be in their drive to be heard on campus.[12]

If the student LID aided the Thomas campaign, the Thomas campaign in turn invigorated the LID by boosting the morale of its organizers and raising their political expectations. Though the LID-led campaign for Thomas on campus attracted a minority of undergraduates, it was a larger and more geographically diverse minority than had ever before been organized on campus for an anti-capitalist cause. On a number of campuses the socialist candidate did more than run a respectable third: at places like Smith College, the universities of Cincinnati, Minnesota, and Vermont, Thomas took second to Hoover and at the University of North Carolina at Chapel Hill, Thomas came in second to Roosevelt. On campuses in New York and Colorado Thomas managed to come in first. No one had expected that in a nation so wedded to the two party system, college youth would break with that system and opt for a socialist candidate in such substantial numbers. At Chapel Hill the shocked editors of the *Daily Tar Heel* observed that on their campus there had been "an immense protest vote which exceeded the wildest expectation of campus socialists, [that] gave Norman Thomas a two to one majority over Herbert Hoover and sent him within sixty votes of Franklin Delano Roosevelt."[13]

The Thomas campaign did more, however, than build the student LID's confidence; it made the LID more visible on campus, attracting new recruits to the organization and demonstrating that it could politically organize students at least as well as its rival on the student Left, the NSL. The 1932 election virtually passed the NSL by because the League did not see electoral politics as a vehicle capable of bringing radical change to America. The NSL therefore did not seek to counter the Thomas campaign by making a major effort on behalf of the far less attractive communist candidate for president, William Z. Foster—who would draw less than one percent of the student vote. This NSL inaction and the LID's success in the campaign helped to restore the competitive balance on the student Left, enabling the LID to make up for the ground it had lost to the NSL the previous spring.[14]

The college campaign for Thomas further strengthened the student LID by involving members of the Young People's Socialist League (YPSL), the Socialist Party's official youth group, in campus organizing. In the past YPSLs had focused most of their attention on blue-collar youth, since they assumed that these were the most likely recruits to the socialist movement. But the substantial student vote for Thomas helped convince the YPSLs that they should become more active in working with the LID on campus because undergraduates seemed to be moving leftward. YPSLs tended to be more militant and well versed in radical theory and history than the average LID member; they became the leftwing of the campus LID. In the metropolitan areas where the YPSL presence was significant, particularly New York and Chicago, its involvement in the student movement and the LID made both more dynamic.[15]

Given the fact that their candidate finished in third place, it may seem strange that socialist students came away from the presidential race in an upbeat mood. But the student polls did demonstrate an undergraduate desire for change. Taken together, slightly more students voted for new political leadership—for the Democratic, Socialist and Communist presidential candidates—than voted for Hoover and the status quo. The straw poll returns were also encouraging for campus radicals because they showed the socialists to be the one party that gained substantial new student support in 1932, compared with previous collegiate presidential polls.[16] This suggested that the student Left was shedding its marginality and becoming a significant minority on campus. Unable to foresee the great upsurge in FDR's popularity on campus—and the achievements of his administration which would prove that his critics in the student body and the intelligentsia had underestimated him—socialist students thought the 18 percent student vote for Thomas was only the beginning of an era of growth for the Socialist Party on campus.[17]

If the straw poll returns were encouraging to the student Left, so was the campaign that yielded those returns. The Thomas campaign had been the first truly national student protest movement to emerge in Depression America; it convinced LIDers that the NSL's success in fostering student dissidence on individual campuses could be duplicated on a far grander scale. Of this optimism following the campaign, former LID leader Joseph P. Lash recalled that there were Thomas For President Clubs all over . . . . The rallies in the colleges had been so big . . . . And I think it was one of the factors that convinced the LID people that a mass student movement could be built that was very close to the Socialists. And I certainly shared that view.[18]

This surge of confidence would encourage Lash and other LID leaders to think big, enabling them, in alliance with their NSL rivals, to envision and begin building a national student movement against war.

II

During the spring semester of 1933 the big news off campus came out of Washington. The Roosevelt administration rushed to Capitol Hill seeking the enactment of the New Deal's ambitious recovery and relief programs. This legislation, including such major bills as the National Industrial Recovery Act and the Agricultural Adjustment Act, sailed through Congress in record time during the first hundred days of FDR's presidency. Students seemed impressed by the president's recognition of the need for quick action to deal with the economic crisis. Consequently, Roosevelt's unpopularity on campus diminished considerably soon after he entered the White House.[19] But undergraduates also recognized that the New Deal might well fail to end the Depression. The recovery programs were criticized from the Left as too timid and from the Right as too recklessly experimental. This uncertainty about Roosevelt's legislative initiative prevented the new president from either becoming a dominant figure on campus or inspiring any significant level of pro-New Deal activism among undergraduates. Indeed, the newsmakers who inspired the most activism and support on campus during the 1933 spring semester were not New Dealers in Washington, but pacifists across the Atlantic—at Oxford University.[20]

Students at Oxford University startled their elders and attracted international attention on February 9, 1933 when they took a radical pacifist stance. By a vote of 275 to 173 the Oxford Union, the University's debating society, adopted a motion "that this House will in no circumstance fight for its King and country." The vote was shocking because it came at England's most conservative and aristocratic university. The debating society that passed the resolution was important not just for Oxford, but for the entire British nation; it was a "miniature parliament," often referred to as the "training ground for British Prime Ministers," which according to the *New York Times* "probably has produced more Cabinet material than any similar institution on earth." Alumni and public officials could barely believe the news reports: the future leadership of the British Empire had embraced pacifism.[21]

The Oxford Pledge evoked a storm of criticism. Assuming that the students who took the pledge were cowards, an anonymous critic sent the

Oxford Union a box containing 275 white feathers—one for each pacifist vote. Thirty anti-pacifist students stormed into the Oxford Union's meeting hall, grabbed the Union's minute book and tore out the page recording the pacifist pledge. Observing that no one tried to interfere with these invaders, another student critic sneered that "although you may have been unwilling to fight for King and country, I think you might have fought for the society's minute book." The London *Times* denounced Oxford's pacifist pledge as a childish act. Conservative leader Winston Churchill derided the students who took the pledge as "callow, ill-tutored youths." Addressing a meeting of the Anti-Socialist and Anti-Communist Union, Churchill fumed that the Oxford Pledge "was a very disquieting and very disgusting symptom. One could almost feel the curl of contempt upon the lips of the manhood of Germany, Italy and France when they read the message sent out by Oxford University in the name of Young England." Oxford alumni immediately organized a movement to reverse the vote and expunge the pacifist pledge from the Union's minutes.[22]

This criticism had little impact on students either at Oxford or on Britain's other campuses. The effort to expunge the pacifist vote from the Oxford Union's records failed miserably. In one of its largest meetings in years, the Union, with almost one-fourth of the entire student body present, voted 750 to 138 against removing the pledge from its records. The Oxford Pledge then moved beyond Oxford. Students adopted the pledge at Manchester and Glasgow Universities in March. The pledge also won in votes at Leicester, Cambridge, and the University College in Wales, and it was reported to have strong support at the University of London.[23]

During the same semester in which the Oxford Pledge swept across British campuses, an Americanized version began to attract a large following among undergraduates in the United States. Student assemblies at Northwestern, Chicago, and Syracuse Universities and an anti-war conference of eight California campuses followed Oxford's lead, declaring their opposition to war service of any kind. There were active campaigns on behalf of the pledge and against military service at about ninety American colleges and universities during the spring semester. College newspapers in every region of the United States praised the Oxford Pledge and supported an effort by Brown University's strongly anti-war newspaper to initiate a national student poll on pacifism and military service. The poll of 22,627 students revealed that the Oxford Pledge had a higher approval rating than FDR had mustered during the election: 39 percent of the students polled endorsed an Oxford-style pacifist stance against participation in any war, and another 33 percent said they would not serve in the military unless the United States was invaded.[24]

The poll results, which came from 65 colleges and universities in 27 states suggested that this generation of American college students overwhelmingly opposed U.S. involvement in an overseas war. Seventy-two percent of the students polled had declared their unwillingness to fight in such a war.[25] This strong anti-war vote and the great interest in the Oxford Pledge during the spring semester of 1933 grew in part out of the anxieties students felt concerning the deteriorating state of international relations. In Asia, war was already waging, as the militaristic Japanese empire, after seizing Manchuria, approached the Great Wall and launched its first bloody assaults on China proper. Confronting League of Nations criticism of its Manchurian aggression, Japanese delegates stormed out of the League meeting in February, and Japan withdrew from this international organization the following month. In the West, war clouds loomed. The German Reichstag granted absolute power to Nazi leader Adolph Hitler in March 1933. Hitler immediately unleashed a wave of anti-Jewish and anti-communist violence, provoking international protests and fear that the Nazi state's foreign policies might soon become as bloody and brutal as its domestic policy. These depressing developments rendered many American students eager to express their desire to avoid war, and to stay out of the increasingly messy affairs of Europe and Asia.[26]

Although these bleak international events facilitated the anti-war vote on America's campuses, that vote was as much an expression of disillusionment with the First World War as it was a reaction to the international tensions of 1933. This disillusionment linked college students in Britain and America and made it possible for the Oxford Pledge to cross the Atlantic. In both countries students recalled that in the First World War youth had fought and died for lofty political goals that were not achieved and promises that were never kept. The anti-war pledge represented a means of saying that this generation had learned from its predecessors and would honor their memory by refusing to be lulled to the battlefield by flowery speeches and false slogans.

The similarity in British and American anti-war thought was evident not only in the students' common support of the anti-war pledge, but also in the rhetoric they used to justify it. Replying to critics of the pacifist pledge, Oxford Union President F.M. Hardie explained that the pacifist vote must not be interpreted as a

> slur cast on the memory of thoses who were killed fighting for their King and country between 1914 and 1918. The question for the Union was that of how, since a solemn pledge had been given to those men that they were fighting in a war to end war, that pledge could best be carried into effect. The Union decided . . . quite sincerely and quite seriously that the best method of ending war was individual resistance to any future war.[27]

Students in the United States echoed these sentiments and Americanized them by focusing on the broken promise made by President Woodrow Wilson as America entered the World War in 1917. Wilson had pledged that this would be "a war to make the world safe for democracy," but instead, as American anti-war students pointed out, "a war for democracy installed dictators all over Europe." The pacifist pledge had been brought

to America so that students could be mobilized "to prevent another repetition of the fatal mistake of 1917," explained the editor of the *Brown
Daily Herald,* one of the key sponsors the American campus agitation on
behalf of that pledge in 1933.[28]

The influence of the First World War on American student supporters of the Oxford Pledge was so strong that they seemed unable to give a
speech or make an argument about foreign affairs without referring to
that war and its "lessons." Student anti-war activists used these lessons
from the War as a guide to understanding international conflicts in the
1930s. They were convinced that "the literature of the World War . . .
[was] a textbook for the future."[29] And if the story of World War I was
indeed a textbook for understanding the future, the first chapter of that
book would have been devoted to economics.

Persuaded by revisionist histories of the First World War, students
believed that economic factors had served as the central precipitant of
United States entry into that war. They were convinced that despite President Woodrow Wilson's lofty rhetoric, the United States went to war in
1917 not "to make the world safe for democracy," but to protect the profit
margins of American capitalists. The United States had, in the view of
campus peace activists, sided with the British in 1917 because powerful
American banks were major creditors of England and France, giving the
U.S. "high economic stakes in the victory of the Allies . . . . Dividends
and profits, not German atrocities and the *Lusitania* . . . [were] the chief
causes of America's intervention."[30] Such conclusions were especially attractive to a generation of undergraduates whose careers had been threatened by a depression which it blamed on big business. Students saw this
economic lesson from 1917 as a guide for understanding not just that war
but all wars. Consequently, as James Shotwell, a leading historian on campus in 1933 observed, "The tendency to find in economics the chief if not
the sole cause of war has grown in the United States in recent years and
has almost become an axiom in the thinking of the younger generation."[31]

Another critical lesson which student anti-war organizers drew from
the revisionist accounts of the First World War concerned war guilt and
the need to be skeptical of wartime propaganda demonizing the enemy.
Under President Wilson, Americans had gone to war believing that sole
responsibility for the conflict rested with the aggressive Germans and their
allies, whose militarism had run amok, threatening the very survival of
the western democracies. Anti-war students believed that such one-sided
thinking had swayed Americans in 1917 because of "hysteria over the
Lusitania and other incidents, . . . [and] the diabolical propaganda of the
Allies, particularly the British who . . . had controlled most of the means
of world communications."[32] Due to this hysteria and propaganda the
true causes of the war were, according to student anti-war activists, ob-
scured in 1917 as

historians on both sides took a holiday for the duration of the war. With the Armistice, they slowly began to unravel the tangle of events which propaganda bureaus had declared were simple . . . . [Revisionist historians] like Harry Elmer Barnes and Sidney Fay started to explore the background of conflict in an effort to weigh the claims of . . . "war guilt". . . . The memoirs of statesmen . . . readily corroborated their discoveries. The result, of course, was to explode the assertions of both sides. Neither the Triple Alliance nor the Allied powers could be "blamed" for precipitating war . . . . [The] conflict was the outgrowth of imperialist rivalries and their symptoms: nationalism, militarism.[33]

Convinced that history tends to repeat itself, student anti-war activists took these lessons about economics, war guilt and the origins of World War I and applied them to the turbulent international scene of the 1930s. If big business and its lust for profits played a key role in pressuring Wilson to enter World War I, the students had no doubt that these same forces would—unless exposed and opposed—push Roosevelt into a new war in the 1930s. If the politicians' and plutocrats' propaganda had misled the American people in 1917, causing them to hate Germany and believe they were fighting to make the world safe for democracy, these leaders would again use these tactics to drum up war fever. In short, the lessons from World War I were not limited to 1917; they were, in the eyes of student activists, universal. This was the premise which led student anti-war leaders to conclude in 1933 that

in all great wars in the past men have become drunk upon slogans. They have been asked to fight for Belgian babies, for a world made safe for democracy, and for lilies across the field. Today, historians who have the courage to tell the truth, have smashed through the sham and hypocrisy of the shibboleths. They tell us wars are fought for steel and gold and land. They show us how the professional yes-men of big business have used blind patriotism in every war to cover the trail of private profits.[34]

To campus anti-war organizers in the 1930s, the First World War held lessons concerning not only foreign policy, but also political democracy at home. They stressed that though America ostensibly went to war in 1917 to safeguard freedom, the war instead brought an enormous wave of intolerance which trampled American civil liberty for the duration of the conflict. As they looked back on this wartime intolerance, anti-war students in the 1930s "felt ashamed, ashamed for our fathers and uncles." "We were," recalled journalist Eric Sevareid, a Depression era anti-war activist at the University of Minnesota, "revolted by the stories of the mass hysteria of 1917, the beating of German saloon keepers, the weird spy hunts, the stoning of pacifists, the arrests of conscientious objectors."[35] Students feared that such bigotry and repression would recur if the United States became involved in another war.

Student peace activists also saw the First World War as a special warning for academia. In their eyes, the university had sacrificed its intellectual integrity and freedom for the sake of the war effort. "As enlightened scholars," explained Eric Sevareid, "we considered that the professors of 1917 had degraded themselves and their sacred function by inventing preposterous theories about the essential depravity of the German race, the worthlessness of their art and the hidden evil of their music." Nor had students forgotten that academic freedom had been a wartime casualty, as anti-war professors from 1917–1919 were fired and silenced at campuses across the United States. Unless the university learned from this experience, warned the *Columbia Spectator,* it would be doomed to relive the "tragedy and corruption which ran rampant on . . . campus in 1917, . . . [when] honesty was purged and . . . the University transformed into a lie-factory for the production of cannon fodder and propaganda." The students also rebuked academics for turning "their universities into an armed camp," allowing the military to establish the Student Army Training Corp—a wartime program which converted masses of students into soliders—whose curriculum was set by the War Department rather than the professoriate. Hoping to prevent a repetition of this militarization of the university, student anti-war organizers would call for the abolition of ROTC.[36]

The prominence of the First World War in the thinking of American students in 1933 and beyond was a natural outgrowth of their generational experience. These students were "the War babies grown up."[37] Born during the Great War, they had been brought up on the stories of that mammoth conflict—stories which emphasized the brutality of the battlefield and the shattered hopes for a just peace settlement in Versailles. The anti-war movies, novels, and histories of the time left this generation of students haunted by the bloodshed and futility of that war. The undergraduates of the 1930s grew up a time when, in the words of two campus anti-war leaders,

> reciting the horrors of the last war became almost a fad . . . , but a fad which left a deep imprint. Hardly had the last flag ceased waving when the revelation began. There were novels and moving pictures like *All Quiet on the Western Front, The Case of Sergeant Grischa* and *A Farewell to Arms.* They were as widely known as Babe Ruth. They were the favorites of young people in short pants. They established a mood among millions . . . [against] war [and] . . . military barbarism.[38]

Having been raised in a nation still reeling from the First World War, students understood how easy it was for diplomacy to give way to warfare. Indeed, few generations in American history have been so pessimistic about international relations as were college students during the Roosevelt era. In the early and mid-1930s students commonly spoke of the "coming war" and "omens of a Second World War," fearing that unless something drastic was done American involvement in a new world war would be inevitable.[39] In a popular anti-war tract, student movement leaders Joseph P. Lash and James Wechsler made clear the linkage between this sense of foreboding and their status as "war babies grown up":

> Our generation was born during the tumultuous years of the First World War. So reputable an authority as Lloyd's will assure us that we have an excellent chance of dying in the next. The odds are immense that we will not attain senility before war breaks out. This realization has incessantly surrounded the lives of our contemporaries. We live next door to the executioner's block, hearing all the preparatory noises. A boom in the funeral industry appears to be the most enduring contribution which we will render to society. Attuned to this outlook, we can derive only the minimum comfort that knowledge of the future affords. Whatever our ultimate misfortune, we are at least prepared for the worst . . . . We shall not be astonished by the arrival of war nor startled by its horrors. We shall experience only the shock which occurs when dread becomes reality.[40]

For a generation with this gloomy outlook on the prospects of war, the international conflicts of the early and mid-1930s loomed especially large. Since they had grown up expecting war, an event such as the rise of Hitler served only to heighten this sense of imminent hostilities. And as the words of Lash and Wechsler suggest, for students there was an immediacy to the war danger because they knew that it would be their generation whose lives would be lost in a new world war. To students, then, international conflict seemed not remote and distant, but a matter of life and death for their generation. This is why in 1933, a time when economic issues were primary for most of Depression America, peace emerged as the hottest issue among college students.

In giving the highest priority to international affairs, college students do not conform to the textbook image of America during the early 1930s as a place where people were so "absorbed in meeting the endless personal crises of the depression [that] they had little patience with admonitions to direct their attention abroad."[41] This is not to minimize the significance of the economic crisis, which, as we have seen, started the process whereby students became politicized in the 1930s. But because of their age and generational background students felt threatened by the deterioration of international relations and the prospects of a war—a war which they knew could be even more devastating to their lives than had the Depression itself. This was why, as Lash and Wechsler wrote, fear of war outweighed even concern about the Depression on campus:

> We are fully cognizant that there are many other problems confronting us. We could recite at some length the necessity for passage of. . . [legislation] to relieve the economic dilemma of young people. Granting the abundance of our ills, war wins the destruction contest without any

serious competition. We give away no government secrets when we state that life is a prerequisite to decent living. If we can preserve an interlude of peace, the hope of such social readjustment can remain open.[42]

The prevalence of this type of thinking among a generation of under-graduates awakened politically by the Depression, scarred emotionally by the last war, and fearful of the coming war, made the campuses fertile ground for the growth of a mass student peace movement.

III

The student Left recognized the great potential of the anti-war issue on campus. Even before the Oxford Pledge Movement had emerged in England, the NSL and student LID had begun to lay the basis for a national student anti-war movement. Both organizations had strong anti-war planks in their platforms and had chapters that promoted anti-war sentiment on campus. But the most impressive of the student Left's early attempts to organize the campuses against war was the convening of the Student Congress Against War, held in Chicago in December 1932. This NSL-sponsored congress constituted the largest national meeting of student activists since the beginning of the Depression; it attracted 680 delegates from 89 colleges and universities in 30 states.[43]

Like the Oxford Movement itself, the initial impetus for the Chicago Congress came from abroad; but in this case, the source was communist rather than pacifist. In August 1932 the NSL had sent Joseph Clark to attend the World Congress Against War, a communist-sponsored peace gathering in Amsterdam. Henri Barbusse and novelist Sherwood Anderson, leaders of the Amsterdam Congress, then telegramed the NSL asking that it organize a nationwide conference of American students "to carry on a fight against war." Excited by the request and feeling that it linked them to a worldwide anti-war movement, the NSL publicized its connection to the Amsterdam Congress. The NSL magazine proudly headlined its article on the League's participation in the Congress "WE ARE INTERNATIONAL!" Heeding the appeal from Amsterdam and confident that student anti-war sentiment was strong, the NSL organized the Chicago Student Congress.[44]

Though the Amsterdam Congress had inspired the Student Congress Against War, the manifesto produced at Amsterdam saddled the NSL with a serious organizing problem. That manifesto, reflecting the sectarianism of the Comintern Third Period line, had condemned the Socialist International and its failure to oppose the First World War. If this manifesto was to be the basis for organizing the Chicago Student Congress, it could alienate the socialist-led LID, which in the wake of the Thomas campaign was the largest student activist group in the United States. The NSL sought to overcome this problem by involving socialist students in the planning of the Chicago Congress. Although this did not eliminate the mistrust the Amsterdam Manifesto had fostered among socialist students, it reassured them enough that they agreed to send a delegation—with some of the student LID's top organizers—to the Chicago Congress.[45]

At the Chicago Student Congress Against War, the NSL leaders again faced a test as to whether they were sufficiently non-sectarian to work with their socialist rivals in building an anti-war movement. The key issue was a resolution that came to the floor, which would have put the Congress on record as endorsing the Committee For the Struggle Against War. This resolution offended the socialist delegates because the Committee was organized on the basis of the Amsterdam Manifesto, which included its attack on the Socialist International. In the face of these socialist objections, the NSL agreed to withdraw the controversial resolution. The NSL further promoted unity at the Chicago Congress by electing several socialist student leaders to the Congress' continuations committee. These actions led the student LID to conclude in its official account of the Congress that "in Chicago the most encouraging sign at the whole affair was the honest bid the Communists made for a united front."[46]

The NSL's efforts to cooperate with the socialists were consistent with the non-sectarian approach it had taken in organizing the Harlan delegation. But the expedition to Kentucky had occurred nine months earlier, when the YCL and the adult leadership of the Communist Party (CP) had paid little attention to the NSL and student organizing. By the time of the Chicago Student Congress, however, the national leadership of the CP and YCL had become more interested in the student movement. This new interest arose because the communist leadership had been impressed by the NSL-led student strikes and activism in New York the previous spring. So in Chicago the eyes of the CP and YCL leaders were on the NSL, and they were not pleased with what they saw: the NSL had been too accommodating to the socialists. NSL leader Harry Magdoff recalled that because he led the forces of cooperation with the socialists at Chicago, CP leader Earl Browder "was furious" with him. "It was a problem that they [the CP leadership] had with me because I tried very hard to bring together . . . the NSL clubs and LID."[47]

YCL leader Gil Green went a step further than Browder, using the pages of the communist *Daily Worker* to criticize the NSL publicly for cooperating with socialist student leaders in Chicago. But these complaints had little impact on the NSL, which understood that cooperation with the LID was essential to the success of both the Congress and the entire student movement. Despite Green's criticism, the NSL's official account of the Congress boasted that the meeting had established a "basis of united action of all students and groups represented at the Congress." The account also mentioned that the Socialists and LID were part of this united front.[48] As at Harlan and as it would throughout its life, the NSL in Chicago had shown that it was more willing than the CP or YCL hierarchy to work with its socialist rivals and engage in coalition politics.

The Chicago Congress revealed that though the NSL and LID delegates differed in their assessment of the Socialist International, they agreed on fundamental questions of war and peace. Both saw imperialist wars as the product of capitalism and the international rivalries bred by that system as one bourgeois nation battled another "for foreign markets and fields for investment." So at the Chicago Congress both NSL and LID activists promoted this anti-capitalist perspective, incorporating it into the Chicago platform, which pledged students to oppose capitalist imperialism.[49]

Actually the greatest conflict at Chicago was not between socialists and communists, but between the leftist and pacifist delegates. The pacifists were associated with groups such as the Fellowship of Reconciliation, the Committee Against Militarism in Education, and campus YM and YWCAs; they had become anti-war activists primarily because of their religious principles. These Christian students had initiated a small drill resister movement on campus, in which more than 100 pacifists at state universities refused to enroll in required military training courses in 1932. Unlike most of the socialist and communist student activists, who would support class warfare and anti-colonial wars, the pacifists objected to all forms of violence.[50]

The NSL had made a bid for unity with pacifist students by inviting them and pacifist leader Jane Addams to address the Congress. But Addams' pacifist speech at the Congress drew criticism from the Left. Addams had condemned all wars, whereas the leftists at the Congress opposed only imperialist wars. The radicals at the Congress angered the pacifists by cheering for J.B. Matthews, when he challenged Addams by declaring that he "was not opposed to a war that would end capitalism." The pacifist students at the Chicago meeting, showing their support of Addams, issued a minority report from the Congress stating that "We believe that war is not right, even if used in trying to reach a worthy goal."[51]

Despite this philisophical division and political tension, the Congress united behind an ambitious anti-war program. This unity was possible because even though the delegates had different views of class violence, all were opposed to both an American military build-up and a repetition of the type of international conflicts and interventionism which had led to the First World War. The program endorsed by the Chicago Congress called for a nationwide anti-war campaign on campus, pledging students to convene college peace meetings, disseminate information regarding the role played by their colleges and universities in the First World War, organize "a mass struggle and agitation for the abolition of ROTC," and mobilize their classmates for "anti-war demonstrations on all military holidays and against all military displays at commencement exercises, Charter Day exercises, etc."[52]

Enlisting so large and ideologically diverse a group of students on behalf of this common program was a considerable achievement. The Chicago meeting had been a stormy affair, in which the significant political differences between the pacifist, socialist, and communist delegates were expressed openly and honestly. But in the end, all three groups realized that a larger student anti-war movement could be built only if they found common ground to begin organizing that movement together. This led one student to term the "congress . . . a remarkable display. Every group sacrificed some slice of its dogma to make a united front possible." Chicago had been the most productive meeting yet of student activists in Depression America. And it would later be viewed by these activists as an historic founding convention, where "the guiding principles of the student movement against war were established . . . . If any single enterprise can be viewed as the origin of . . . [the] vast . . . [anti-war] awakening, such was the Chicago Congress."[53]

The Oxford Pledge movement made it easier to translate the Chicago agenda into action. Soon after the Chicago delegates returned to campus and began to plan anti-war action for the semester, the news of the pacifist pledge from England hit. This provided student activists with a vehicle for promoting their anti-war position on campus. In explaining why the Oxford Pledge proved so useful an organizing tool for the peace movement on campus, SLID* leader Joseph P. Lash recalled that administering the Pledge at anti-war conferences on campus

> was a good way of expressing your feeling about war, and it almost inevitably meant that you would get a headline in the press. And that would start controversy, and then you could write letters to the editor explaining your point of view and you could have debates in the student body. It was a way of keeping your program going.[54]

The pledge served not only as a rallying point for anti-war students; it also bolstered their morale by making them feel that they were participating in a "united international action of students in all countries . . . fight[ing] against the military preparations and war policies of their governments." In providing what NSL leader James Wechsler termed" a sense of international union," the Oxford Pledge encouraged students to hope that they—unlike previous generations of anti-war activists—might actually manage to influence international relations and prevent war. Wechsler was among those swayed by the surge of optimism that the pledge generated on campus: "The people of one country do not stop war; the peoples of all countries, aligned together against their common enemies may. The Oxford Pledge was a vivid prelude to what might be hoped for on an ever wider scale."[55]

*In 1993 the student section of the League for Industrial Democracy changed its name to the Student League for Industrial Democracy (SLID). On this change, see 361n.11.

The Oxford Pledge was incorporated so quickly into the anti-war organizing spearheaded by the NSL and SLID that an Americanized version
of the pledge became virtually synonymous with student protest against
war in the United States in 1933. Because the Oxford Pledge was an exciting means of voicing anti-war sentiment, it may seem quite natural that
student radical organizers adopted and promoted the pledge. But in one
important respect this solidarity with the Oxford movement was surprising: the Oxford Pledge originated as a pacifist statement, while the Marxist NSLers (and leftwing socialists in the SLID) were—as had been clear
in the debates in the Chicago Congress—critical of pacifism. It would have
been inconsistent for them to have adopted a pledge that made it sound
as if they were completely renouncing war. They overcame this problem
by changing the phrasing of the pledge as they popularized it in the United
States. Students taking this revised, Americanized version of the Oxford
Pledge were declaring their intention to "refuse to support the government of the United States in any war it may conduct." Since the Marxist
position maintained that the only type of war the American government
could wage would be an imperialist war, the NSLers and other leftist students felt they could support the pledge because it was a rejection not of
all war, but only imperialist war.[56]

In this response to the Oxford Pledge the student Left again displayed a degree of political flexibility which strengthened the student
movement. Recognizing an innovative protest tactic when they saw one,
these young radicals adapted the pledge instead of rejecting it. They were,
in effect, following their tactical good sense as pragmatic organizers, and
relying on a semantic technicality—the rephrasing of the Oxford Pledge—
to free them from the pledge's obvious pacifist implications. This flexibility almost got communist NSLers in trouble with the leadership of the CP
and YCL. As NSL founder Joseph Clark recalled, the communist hierarchy was initially uncomfortable with the NSL, an organization in which
young communists were so prominent, associating itself so closely with
Oxford's pacifist stance:

> There was considerable questioning and concern in the Party and
> the YCL when we endorsed the Oxford Pledge because . . . it might
> convey the impression that the Communists didn't support revolutionary
> war. But since what we were dealing with was [war waged by] the U.S.
> government, the YCL and the Party went along.[57]

Here, as at Chicago, the NSL had adopted tactics considered unorthodox
by the communist hierarchy, and in so doing enhanced its leadership position in the growing anti-war movement on campus.

The process of promoting the Oxford Pledge and working together
on other anti-war activities in 1933 led to closer cooperation between the
NSL and the student LID. There were still some tensions and bickering
between the two groups because of their loyalties to rival radical parties
and competition for student recruits. But both NSL and LID activists rec-

ognized that they thought alike on the anti-war issue—so much so that before the year was out there was talk of merging the two groups. The NSL formally proposed such a merger in December. Though the student LID turned down this proposal because its leaders feared the NSL's links to the Communist Party, the SLID pledged to continue engaging in joint anti-war actions with the NSL. The SLID immediately fulfilled this pledge, joining with the NSL in anti-ROTC protests.[58]

IV

The collaboration between the NSL and the student LID facilitated the growth of the student movement; it meant that the nation's most daring and experienced student political organizers were beginning to search together for ways to mobilize their classmates. This collaboration quickly yielded Depression America's most innovative and effective form of campus political protest: the National Student Strike Against War. This one hour walkout, originated and led jointly by the SLID and NSL beginning in 1934, represented the first attempt at a nationwide strike by college students.[59]

The national anti-war strike was more daring than any previous campaign of the student Left. The idea for such a strike evolved out of the political experience that the young radicals in the NSL and SLID had accumulated since 1932. The notion that a student strike could serve as a dramatic form of college protest derived from the successful student walkout these leftists had orchestrated during the Reed Harris controversy in 1932. The National Student Strike Against War made use as well of the most effective student protest tactic of 1933, the Oxford Pledge, which was scheduled to be administered to students during the strike rallies. Strike organizers also tapped into the student body's deep disillusionment with the First World War by setting the date of the walkout in April, on the anniversary of United States entry into that war. This date was selected as a symbolic way of showing that students remembered the lessons of the last war—"the Great Betrayal of 1917," in which Americans were lulled by democratic rhetoric into an imperialist war—and would therefore "refuse to fight in the next war."[60]

Though promoting the Oxford Pledge, the strike was, in effect, a means of going a step further than Oxford. Now instead of merely pledging not to fight, students would show how they would make good on the pledge. The strike would be a "dress rehearsal" for any future war crisis, a vehicle for mobilizing the young to turn down military service in the event of a new war. SLID leader Joseph Lash, who helped conceive the idea for the strike, traced the student walkout to a "really syndicalist conception . . . [that] was a reflection of the revolutionary ferment of the early 1930s." Student anti-war activists believed, according to Lash, that war could be prevented by "a universal strike . . . If when the capitalists sat down to declare war on one another, all of us young people who had to fight the war would say 'No, we won't go,' . . . that then there couldn't be any war."[61]

The first student strike against war, on April 13, 1934, drew some 25,000 students. Coordinating a national walkout constituted a new challenge, which neither the NSL nor the SLID was able to handle with great skill. Planning for the strike had begun late, and the strike action had not been well publicized outside the student Left's stronghold in New York. Consequently, this first anti-war walkout was primarily an East Coast affair: 15,000 out of the 25,000 striking students were from the campuses of New York City. Yet even though the walkout mobilized only a small minority of the nation's undergraduate population, strike organizers viewed it as a stunning success. The strike had been the largest political demonstration by college students in all of American history. Never before had there been a sight like this: simultaneous protests against war on more than a dozen campuses, including Harvard, Johns Hopkins, Syracuse, Columbia and Chicago universities, CCNY, Vassar, Hunter, and Brooklyn College. There were even reports of anti-war assemblies on several California campuses.[62]

Nor were strike organizers alone in viewing the walkout as a major event. The strike generated considerable press coverage. The media was impressed with both the size and seriousness of the protest. Education reporters, who for years had been covering juvenile student riots and pep rallies, were startled at the sight of students striking against war, hoisting a "thousand [political] banners": "Schools, not Battleships"; "Abolish the ROTC"; "Refuse to Cooperate in Any War the United States Government May Undertake." They noted that an important change had occurred. "The traditional apathy of American youth in political matters" was being replaced with a tradition similar to that of students in Europe and Latin America, "whose immemorial role has been of political agitation en bloc."[63] Strike organizers, who in the past had to labor hard to attract press attention for their local student protests were, as Joseph P. Lash recalled, "completely bowled over" by "the publicity that the anti-war strike got in 1934. When the *New York Times* gave it the lead column story and it became an event [discussed nationally] it was totally unexpected."[64]

The anti-war mood on campus grew even stronger in the semesters following the student strike against war. During this period the anti-war movement received a major boost from the Senate. In mid-April 1934, the Nye Committee began investigating the armaments industry and its profiteering during the First World War. By the end of the year the committee was probing the role that American banks played in promoting United States intervention into the World War. The evidence unearthed by Nye's committee led many Americans to conclude that the United States had entered the war in 1917 "to save the skins of American bankers who had bet too boldly on the outcome of the war and had two billions of dollars of loans to the Allies in jeopardy."[65] The Nye revelations provided legitimation for the student anti-war movement's contention that the First

World War and United States foreign policy were guided by selfish economic interests. This compounded student disillusionment with that war and added support for the anti-war movement as it sought to prevent the United States from again entering such a conflict.[66]

Strike organizers in 1935 benefited not only from the Nye revelations, but also from their experience in the 1934 walkout. Learning from their previous mistakes, student activists began publicizing the strike long before the April walkout. The NSL and SLID also focused on broadening the sponsorship of the anti-war strike, seeking to attract support from non-radical organizations, which could help carry the strike beyond the East Coast. This search for allies proved successful. In contrast to 1934, when the NSL and SLID were the only student organizations endorsing the strike, the 1935 walkout had an impressive list of sponsors, including the National Council of Methodist Youth, the Interseminary Movement, regional councils of the National Student Federation, YM and YWCA chapters, the Youth section of the American League Against War and Fascism, and many student governments and newspapers.[67]

With such diverse groups sponsoring the strike some tension was inevitable among the walkout's organizers. The biggest flare up occurred a little more than a month before the strike. SLID leader Joseph Lash became annoyed by the behavior of the American League Against War and Fascism, because this communist-led organization was unilaterally issuing press releases about the strike and acting as if it alone was responsible for the anti-war protest. Lash threatened to remove the organization's name from the strike call unless it became more cooperative. This threat struck some of the religious pacifists as "undemocratic," and led Rix Butler, president of the Interseminary Movement to warn Lash that unless he included the League in the strike call his own organization would pull out of the strike. Lash backed down, and the strike coalition held together so well that this internal bickering never became public. Despite such disputes, the strike organizing brought some of the strike leaders closer together by involving activists from rival organizations in a common cause. Even Lash, who was still not entirely comfortable working with communists, noted that he "had a very cordial time drafting the [strike] call . . . with [communist NSL leader] Joe Cohen."[68]

The walkout's broad sponsorship helped to make the second Student Strike Against War far larger than the first. The 1935 strike drew about 175,000 students. Unlike the previous walkout, this strike was not dominated by New York City campuses. While the mobilization rate in New York remained almost identical to what it had been the previous year, turnout for the strike in the rest of the nation skyrocketed from 10,000 in 1934 to close to 160,000 in 1935.[69]

There were large strikes in every region of the country. On the West Coast, Berkeley led the way with 4000 striking, followed by 3000 at Los Angeles Junior College, 1500 at Stanford, and 1000 at UCLA and Oregon. In the Midwest, the University of Chicago had the largest strike, with

3500 participants; Minnesota had 3000 and Milwaukee State 2500, Wisconsin 2000, Northwestern, Oberlin, Ohio State, Michigan, and DePauw all had more than 1000 participants. The strike even penetrated a few campuses in the traditionally conservative South, where Texas Christian, Texas, Florida State, North Carolina at Chapel Hill, and Virginia Universities had sizable strike rallies. The Northeast remained a movement stronghold, led by Brooklyn College with 6000 strikers, 3500 at CCNY and Columbia, 3000 at the University of Pennsylvania, 2500 at Temple, and the participation of the entire student body at Vassar. On many campuses the walkouts were the first student political demonstrations in the history of these colleges and universities. Students who had never even seen a protest march before were now marching themselves and chanting the Oxford Pledge.[70]

Though the dimensions of the second student strike were new, its message was not. The speakers at the strike rallies and peace assemblies in 1935, again held on the anniversary of United States entry into the First World War, offered the familiar refrain that the nation must not go to war as it had in 1917. Strikers from coast to coast recited the "lessons" taught by the First World War: profiteering breeds war; politicians use lofty rhetoric to obfuscate the true economic nature of war; instead of promoting democracy the World War paved the way for new dictatorships, fascism and Nazism abroad, and political repression at home. The student protesters saw themselves as "realists who have learned the lessons of the class of 1917, and will practice what has been learned."[71]

The students in both strikes understood—emotionally as well as intellectually—how the First World War affected them and their desire to avoid a future war. The strikes represented an act of mourning for the last generation called upon to fight in a catastrophic war and a declaration of the students' hope and determination to save their own generation from a similar fate. This emotional linkage was evident at Springfield College, where on the night before the 1935 strike, students planted white crosses to memorialize the war dead and remind their classmates of "the Great Betrayal of 1917." It was also visible at the Columbia strike rally. Here Roger Baldwin, who had spent a year in prison for opposing the First World War, urged students to organize more effectively against war than had his generation. Following Baldwin's speech

> taps were played in honor of those students who lost their lives in the World War with the "addition that we are determined not to die as they did." Mr Baldwin then led the meeting in the Oxford Pledge . . . [and] the meeting pledged itself not to support the government in any war it may undertake.[72]

V

As political organizers, the student anti-war activists of the mid-1930s enjoyed far more success than any previous generation of students. In both 1934 and 1935 they mobilized record numbers of students for anti-war protests, and in the coming year their peace rallies would draw about 500,000 students, almost half of the entire American undergraduate population. The student movement's influence, however, extended far beyond these annual walkouts. The anti-interventionism promoted by the movement quickly dominated student thought concerning foreign policy. Indeed, a 1935 *Literary Digest* poll of 65,000 collegians found that 81 percent opposed bearing arms in an overseas war—up nine points since 1933. The anti-war consensus grew so strong on campus that mainstream students sounded little different than radicals when addressing issues of war and peace. In 1935, for instance, the National Student Federation's moderate president personally informed President Roosevelt "that the youth of America is uniting in an effort to maintain American neutrality so that they will not be caught in the same swift stream that caught humanity in 1914." [73]

Though their skill at political organizing was impressive, the student anti-war activists of 1933–35 popularized a view of foreign affairs that was in important respects mechanistic, anachronistic, and inaccurate. These young activists thought that their knowledge of the First World War's "lessons" helped them understand the international conflicts of the 1930s. But, in fact, most of these lessons would prove profoundly misleading. The students never stopped to consider that the insights gleaned from that war might not be relevant to the new and different international situation that prevailed during the Depression decade. The cliché about generals always fighting the last war was applicable here to the campus peace movement. The student anti-war activists in 1933–35 still had their heads in 1917; and in this sense, as NSL leader Joseph Clark recalled, they "relived an era . . . which no longer existed." [74] Fascinated with the scandalous revelations concerning the origins of United States intervention in the First World War, the students read too much into them, acting as if conclusions concerning that war were applicable to all wars.

Probably the most misleading lesson that students in the 1930s learned from World War I concerned the connection between economics and war. The revisionist accounts of the war and the influence of Marxism and the Nye Committee investigation converted many students into economic determinists. Viewing the First World War as the product of economic imperialism, they assumed that if the international conflicts in their own era led to a new war, it would repeat the tragedy of 1917: accomplishing nothing other than "the transfer of mines, mills and trade routes from one set of capitalists to another. These things are not worth dying for." [75] Such simplistic economic postulates from the last war left students unable to comprehend the unique nature of the coming European war: a struggle not over capitalist spoils, but over whether all of the continent was to fall to Nazi totalitarianism.

In their economic determinism, the anti-war activists assumed that idealistic rhetoric urging United States interventionism was sheer propaganda—a facade for profiteers. Determined not to become "drunk on slogans," as Americans had been when Woodrow Wilson's lofty words lured them into the First World War, anti-war organizers dismissed talk of an anti-fascist war, arguing that "A War 'Against Fascism' in 1935 is the counterpart of the War 'For Democracy' in 1917."[76] In effect, the students' understanding of the First World War had left them so jaded that rather than critically assessing the new cries for interventionism in Europe, they simply and erroneously dismissed them all as 1917-style war propaganda.

If the lessons students drew from World War I led them to misread the nature of the growing conflict in Europe, they also fostered an inaccurate assessment of American foreign policy. The students greatly exaggerated America's jingoistic and expansionist tendencies during the early and mid-1930s. Everywhere the anti-war protesters turned they thought they saw signs of 1917-style militarization of America: from the growing (yet still relatively small) War Department budgets to the Civilian Conservations Corps—which they misconstrued as an agency for militarizing youth. Contrary to what the anti-war movement preached, the United States was not heading toward massive rearmament and war during the early and mid-1930s. America was moving in the opposite direction, retreating into one of the most isolationist phases in its history. It would take years of German, Italian, and Japanese aggression before America would be shocked out of its deep isolationist slumber. Given this isolationist hegemony, the student movement's rhetoric about the imminent danger of the United States being pushed into World War by American militarists and capitalists was simply wrong—and so was its conclusion that in 1935 as in 1917 "The Greatest Enemy [of peace] is At Home."[77]

The students were not alone in their tendency to view foreign policy through the distorted lenses of 1917. Throughout the mid-1930s, Congress, reflecting the growing isolationist mood of the nation, crafted neutrality legislation designed to prevent a recurrence of the type of naval conflicts that helped push America into the First World War. Just as the students had been naive in hoping to stop war by taking an oath against military service, Congress was equally naive in believing that if its neutrality laws prevented another *Lusitania* incident this could keep America out of war.[78] Both on campus and Capitol Hill a rigid and mechanistic application of the lessons of one war to another confused the two eras and promoted an unrealistic faith that unilateral anti-interventionism by the United States could preserve world peace.

The anti-war movement on America's campuses did not err in all of its foreign policy pronouncements. The students were correct in arguing that the inequitable terms of the Versailles peace settlement helped set the stage for the rise of Hitler. The student movement also picked up quite early on the evils of Nazism in Germany, militarism in Japan, and fascism in Italy. Student anti-war activists were among the first Americans in the Depression decade to voice their disdain for these tyrannies. In 1933 student protesters angrily confronted Nazi Germany's ambassador in Manhattan and a Japanese naval delegation in Berkeley. The following year students took their anti-Nazi protests aboard the German cruiser *Karlsruhe,* docked in Boston Harbor, and an anti-fascist riot rocked CCNY during the visit of a youth delegation from Mussolini's Italy.[79] But while ahead of most Americans in recognizing and protesting against the brutality of fascism, these anti-war activists underestimated the strength of fascism. Like most Americans in the early 1930s, they did not foresee that fascism would spread and ultimately engulf Europe. And even had the students been prophetic enough to have anticipated this trend, they were too haunted by World War I to think strategically about containing fascism. The same students who took these anti-fascist actions in Berkeley, Boston, and New York also took the Oxford oath pledging themselves to military inaction—a sad irony since nothing short of military force could have reversed the fascist tide in Europe during the 1930s. In fact, at the very moment when American students were taking a pacifist pledge, students in Nazi Germany were burning pacifist books.[80] As they struck for peace on those World War I anniversaries, marched against the Wilsonian slogans of 1917 and championed anti-interventionism, students in the United States remained captives of the past: opposing the wrong war at the wrong time.

Chapter 5

Spies, Suppression, and Free Speech on Campus

> We no longer believe in free speech. We believe in responsible speech.
>
> Dr. Frederick Woelloner, UCLA professor of education,
> endorsing the suspension of five student leaders during
> the 1934 free speech fight at UCLA.
> Chester S. Williams, "This Academic Freedom," *Intercollegian and Far Horizons,* (December 1934), 92.

As the student movement spread across America from 1933 to 1935, it encountered strong opposition from college and university administrators. The anti-war demonstrations and strikes, the mass endorsement of the Oxford Pledge, and the rising influence of leftist-led student organizations outraged many of these administrators. This activism seemed so radical and sudden a departure from the political quiesence of the collegiate past that campus officials often found it intolerable. The initial impulse of many college deans and presidents was to try suppressing this student activism, in a manner quite similar to that previously seen on New York's campuses during the early days of the NSL. But just as repression had failed to kill New York's student movement in 1931–1932, it would also fail to stop the rapid growth of the movement nationally in the mid-1930s. This was due in large part to the determined free speech fights waged by student activists, who made campus political rights a top priority for their movement. Free speech became a "cause célèbre" on campus because, as former NSL leader Celeste Strack recalled, students found administration acts of suppression politically offensive and personally insulting:

> While the war and peace issue was becoming big, academic freedom was already a hot issue because no matter what you wanted to talk about

you were up against the effort . . . [of] the administration not to give
you the right to talk like grown up people about issues. . . . They . . .
[would] treat us like children, and that was very deeply resented, [and]
. . . this was a very important question.[1]

The disrespect of college administrators for student political rights
ran deeper, however, than even most movement activists could have
guessed; it led these campus officials to infringe upon student civil liberties not only publicly but also covertly. College and university administrators opposed to the student movement became involved in secretly feeding information on student protesters to the Federal Bureau of Investigation
(FBI), enabling the Bureau to open dossiers on many of these Depression
era campus activists. The number of students turned in to the FBI by
college officials cannot be traced with complete precision, since the FBI
has still refused to release much of the relevant documentation. But the
magnitude of this political surveillance is suggested by the fact that from
a single campus, the University of Chicago, the FBI had in its files "the
names of two thousand individuals" active in the student movement from
the mid-1930s through 1941. If Chicago was typical, the FBI must have
had information on tens of thousands of Depression America's student
activists.[2]

The FBI files on the student movement reveal that college and university administrators willingly, even eagerly, provided information to the
FBI on the political activity of individual students and leftist-led campus
groups. This was done apparently without a thought that such informing
violated student rights—that undergraduates should be free to engage in
lawful political activity without having their names end up in an FBI file.
The FBI documents suggest that this administration insensitivity to student rights rendered the task of campus political surveillance almost ef-
fortless for the Bureau. Campus administrators were so cooperative that
all the FBI had to do to was dispatch agents to meet with university and
college officials, and they would instantly provide the Bureau with all the
information they had on student activists.[3]

This informing was often done by high ranking campus officials, usually the deans or other administrators charged with policing undergraduate life. At the University of Pennsylvania both the dean of student affairs and the vice president of the university gave the FBI the names of
Penn's leading student activists; at Ohio State University, Montana State
University, Temple University, Purdue University, the universities of Illinois and Missouri, and Middlebury College, the dean of men provided
this information to the FBI. Other deans served as FBI informants at
DePauw University, the universities of Minnesota, Hawaii, and Washington, Yale, Oberlin, Wesleyan University and Wilson Teachers College. On
some campuses, such as George Washington University, Indiana State
Teachers College and the universities of Chicago, Michigan and Ohio,
staffers of the college dean's or university president's office worked with
the FBI—providing the Bureau with membership lists and other assis-

tance in identifying leading student protesters. At Earlham, the college president himself, William C. Dennis, informed on student protest leaders. This was also the case at Middlebury College and at the University of Michigan, whose president, Alexander Ruthven, told the FBI that the student radicals on his campus "were definitely troublemakers"; and volunteered to "furnish all available details" on their ongoing activities to the Bureau.[4]

University involvement in political surveillance was not confined, however, to this work with the FBI. Campus administrators did more than serve as informers on their students; they also sought to have the police and others serve as informers for the University, who would secretly report to them about the off campus radical activities of their students. The extent of such intelligence gathering is impossible to measure nationally, since University officials—apparently sensing that this political espionage would be controversial if word of it leaked to the public—left few written records of it. But on at least one campus, UC Berkeley, enough of the record survives to suggest that University officials energetically cultivated a wide array of informants to assemble political dossiers on their students.[5]

At Berkeley, the UC administration of President Robert G. Sproul began covertly gathering intelligence on Berkeley student radicals in July 1934 with the encouragement of Earl Warren, then the Alameda County District Attorney. That month Warren sent a letter to UC Provost Monroe Deutsch, suggesting that the university work with law enforcement officials "to organize and coordinate their activities in combatting disloyal acts of the radical groups." The intelligence network assembled by the Sproul administration included Bay Area law enforcement officials and superpatriotic groups. Provost Deutsch and President Sproul began assembling this network by dispatching the Berkeley campus police chief to solicit intelligence information on campus radicals from the Sheriff and District Attorney of Alameda County, the police chiefs of Berkeley, Oakland, Piedmont and Alameda, the District Attorney of Contra Costa County, the commanders of three American Legion posts, the commanding officer of the California National Guard, and several other public officials.[6]

The confidential letter that Provost Deutsch sent out to these law enforcement officials and superpatriot groups soliciting help in constructing UC's intelligence network attests to the Berkeley administration's political intolerance. Deutsch made it absolutely clear that the University of California was committed both to political surveillance of the Left and to purging radical activists from the Berkeley campus:

> Occasionally one hears a rumor or report with reference to alleged radical acts on the part of members of the University of California. We should deeply appreciate receiving any or all reports of this character which may come to you. . . . The University of California is anxious not to harbor . . . anyone who is encouraging the overthrow of our govern-

ment by force. . . . I shall take the liberty of sending you in a very few days Captain Walter T. Lee, chief of our police force, and we would regard it as a favor if you would place in his hands all information of this character which has come to you or which may hereafter come to you.[7]

The University's intelligence network grew quickly. Within a month of its founding, the network included a new member, the Industrial Association (IA) of San Francisco. The IA had served some of San Francisco's largest corporations in their battle against organized labor by spying on trade union and radical activists. By August 1934, the UC administration was receiving and using IA intelligence reports on campus radicals. In a typical report, the IA gave President Sproul the name of one UC student who "is quite active as an agitator for the Communist Party and also has the reputation as being a very effective 'soap box' orator [with] . . . potential for the spreading of Communist Propaganda at the University." Provost Deutsch was so happy with the information UC's intelligence network generated that within a month of its founding he was recommending that President Sproul order "that similar activity be carried on with reference to other sections of the University, particularly the University of California at Los Angeles."[8]

By November 1934, UC's intelligence network had expanded to include law enforcement officials from as far away as Monterey. That month Harry Noland, the Monterey County District Attorney, began providing the University with information on radicals from his region who were attending UC Berkeley. Here Noland warned Sproul of Richard Criley, a student he accused of being "a full fledged radical and a known Communist." Sproul then ordered the campus police to assemble a dossier and "get some further information on Mr. Criley."[9]

UC officials used such intelligence information in their attempts to intimidate student activists. Provost Deutsch boasted of such activity in a letter to Sproul in November 1934. Deutsch told of how he confronted Berkeley student protest leader John Rockwell about his radical associations. Rockwell denied that he was affiliated with any leftwing group, and Deutsch, according to his own account,

> thought that I would let him know that I was not so gullible on that score, so I asked him "Did you come from Carmel?" He admitted that he did. Then I asked him, "Didn't you and [Richard] Criley belong to the same [radical] organization there?" It took him off his guard but he admitted it.[10]

After this encounter, Rockwell—shocked by Provost Deutsch's knowledge of his political background—charged that Deutsch had tried to frighten him out of campus political activity by using information obtained from the American Legion's blacklist. Rockwell, of course, was unaware of the fact that the University did not have to rely on the Legion's blacklist because of UC's wide intelligence network.[11]

Exactly how much intelligence information UC's intelligence network yielded is not clear, since most of the dossiers it produced have apparently been destroyed. But judging from the data that the Sproul administration gathered from just one member of its intelligence network—Political Science Professor David Barrows, who was also a General and Commander of the California National Guard—these dossiers must have been extensive. In August 1934, Barrows, upon Deutsch's request, provided the Sproul administration with data on 41 Berkeley student radicals, gathered by "G–2," the National Guard's intelligence unit. At this time Barrows also informed Deutsch that he had information on 20–25 other student radicals and several new graduate students, upon which he was awaiting confirmation.[12]

Though Barrows' surveillance correspondence was addressed to Provost Deutsch, there is no doubt that UC President Sproul was involved personally in this intelligence operation. In fact, Barrows began one of these letter to Deutsch by informing the Provost that

> I am enclosing thirteen cards on what is known about the activities of certain students in this University who are or were Communists. This morning I left twenty-eight cards of other students with President Sproul, who intended to glance them over. This makes a total of about forty students out of a somewhat larger number of whom I have had occasion to secure reports in view of their actual or probable Communist activities.[13]

Nothing in this correspondence suggests that Professor Barrows, a former president of the University of California, saw any ethical problem with circulating dossiers on students in his own university. Professor Barrows reasoned that it was proper for him to have obtained this information in his capacity as a National Guard general, because the Guard needed it to be prepared for any potential battle with students engaged in "seditious and violent activity." And he apparently thought the University could make good use of this information to deal with potential troublemakers.[14]

In their secret work spying and informing on student radicals, college administrators were guided by the same anti-radical impulse that led to their public attempts to suppress student protest and faculty radicalism in the 1930s. They defined Left activism as aberrant behavior and viewed radical expression as nothing but propaganda, a category of inflammatory and misleading speech which had no place in a university, whose mission was objective inquiry and the pursuit of truth. According to Chancellor E.A. Burnett of the University of Nebraska, political subjects could be discussed on campus only "so long as they are judicial and informative rather than in the interests of propagandists. We would not knowingly permit any speaker to occupy a university platform if he is engaged in an effort to destroy the present form of government by revolutionary methods."[15] The professor who engages in such "partisan propaganda," explained President Charles Wesley Flint of Syracuse University, "discredits his profession and his institution as guides for students and as leaders for the community."[16] Since it was the college president's duty to prevent the discrediting of his institution, he was obligated, in the words of President Sproul, to silence those engaged in "spreading the poison gas of . . . class . . . warfare. . . . No society will tolerate for long those among its own servants who give aid and comfort to enemies seeking its destruction."[17]

Such anti-radicalism served as an especially strong inducement for suppression of student protest because it was wedded to an equally strong paternalistic sensibility among campus administrators. The same brand of administration paternalism which had led to the Depression era's first student free speech fights, at Columbia and CCNY, contributed to most of the repressive actions campus officials took against anti-war organizers. These administrators felt no compunction about suppressing anti-war activism because they saw students as immature youths in need of discipline and guidance rather than as adults with constitutional rights. College administrators believed that students lacked intellectual maturity and were therefore ripe for exploitation and manipulation by cynical radical agitators. President L.D. Goffman of the University of Minnesota stressed this theme in his speech, "The Exploitation of Youth," delivered before the National Association of State Universities in 1935. To Goffman, the political naiveté of collegians made them

> easy prey of the social racketeer who tells them that America is not the fair land of hope and opportunity that it was pictured to be . . . . The very folly and inexperience of youth make them easy victims of those who would use them for some ulterior purpose; the more majestic, the more emotional the appeal, the easier it is to lead the [college] youth. . . .[18]

Since undergraduates were deemed too intellectually weak and politically naive to defend themselves from the manipulations of radical propagandists, these college officials thought it their duty to protect their young flock from the wolves of the Left.

This condescending anti-radicalism allowed college officials to disregard civil liberties considerations and seek the banishment of radical activism from campus. For them suppression of radicalism on campus was equated not with the authoritarianism of a harsh dictator, but the firm hand of a concerned parent—and in this case a parent shielding youths from dangerous subversives. Syracuse University's Chancellor Flint had this in mind when he pledged to drive off campus "any organization [that] is openly affiliated, or still more if it is covertly affiliated with . . . [off campus radical groups under the] militant lash of paid secretaries and . . . persistent and occasionally fanatical propagandists."[19] Similarly, Provost Ernest C. Moore of UCLA threatened that students who allied themselves with the anti-war movement would be punished for working "to destroy the University by handing it over to the Communists."[20] President

Alexander Ruthven of the University of Michigan echoed these anti-radical sentiments, warning in 1935 that students who joined in the "perversive [anti-war] activities of a few professional agitators" would be expelled.[21]

Not even the doctrine of academic freedom could protect political liberty on campus during the 1930s. Most college presidents interpreted academic freedom in such narrow terms that it served to diminish rather than preserve free speech rights in academia. In their view, academic freedom constituted not a general right to free speech on campus, but only the privilege of academics to do research in their specialized areas and to present the findings which grew out of that research. As President Flint of Syracuse University explained in 1935, the type of speech protected by academic freedom was quite limited; it covered only the

> freedom to speak under compulsion of thought that which is worthy of being said by one who is qualified to be heard . . . . In other words, they [academics] are free only to speak on subjects on which they have earned the right to be heard . . . . Academic freedom is not a blank check; it is limited by deposits to the teacher's credit, the degree of his scholarly attainments. It is not . . . the right to unlimited expression whether or not possessing anything worth expressing; not license to scatter about publicly half-baked theories, egotistical vagaries, or to vocalize loose thinking masquerading as liberal thinking.[22]

This limited academic freedom could not protect students because campus administrators held that it applied only to professional scholars and teachers, not to a group so immature as undergraduates.[23]

Since the only form of speech protected on campus was—as this narrow doctrine of academic freedom specified—the scholarly pronouncements of professors concerning research in their areas of specialization, the degree of political freedom was often lower inside academia than it was outside. While off campus, partisan political speech tended to be protected by the first amendment, on campus such speech was either barred or severely restricted, since it was considered unprofessional and incompatible with scholarly standards. Indeed, adherents of this view of academic freedom thought that in order to be a professional scholar one had to sacrifice a measure of one's free speech rights. According to President Robert Gordon Sproul of the University of California, "In practice university professors can never be quite so free in speech and action as many other men for they cannot enjoy the license of speaking without investigation."[24]

This willingness to restrict free speech rights on campus in the 1930s derived not merely from this vision of scholarly neutrality, but from a mistrust of free speech itself. Most campus officials were definitely not civil libertarians. They thought unlimited freedom of speech could lead to trouble, promoting licentiousness rather than liberty. Thus President James L. McConaughy of Wesleyan University contended that "freedom is a dangerous tool; if you give it in a dictatorship, the dictator is soon murdered; if you give it to a group of thoughtless citizens, chaos may result . . . . Complete freedom is possible only in a Utopia." [25]

Given their belief that unlimited liberty was such a "dangerous tool", many college presidents felt it their duty to protect their schools and society by working, in the words of President Sproul, to "combine liberty with order." Liberty had to be restricted when it clashed with the needs of either the school or society. This was, as Sproul put it, limited "freedom within the framework of public good." Sproul defended this ideal of moderated liberty on the grounds that it "rediscovers what the Greek thinkers knew so long ago—that the supreme principle of human association in a free society is moderation in all principles." [26]

Despite Sproul's rhetoric about moderation and liberty, there was nothing moderate about this doctrine; it enabled college administrators to justify suppressing any form of speech which they found distasteful. In the name of liberty, it entitled the college president to act as a petty dictator, who could wipe out free speech whenever he deemed this necessary for preserving either the good name of the college or the public good. On these grounds President McConaughy of Wesleyan sought to make political suppression sound virtuous:

> Wisdom dictates some curtailment of complete freedom for the teacher—at least until the Utopian day when all teachers are wise. In war time we can not allow public servants—and teachers are public servants—to threaten the government's overthrow by complete freedom of expression. In peace some judgment has to be imposed upon them from above. Wherever possible this curb should be local, not by legislation. [27]

With the college gates guarded by such intolerant administrators, it is not surprising that there were many reports of attempts to bar both student anti-war protests and other radical dissent from campuses. Incidents involving overt restrictions on students' free speech rights occurred on at least 53 campuses between 1933 and 1935. Many of these campuses witnessed repeated free speech violations. These incidents were by no means restricted to obscure or third rate colleges; they erupted at some of America's leading institutions of higher education, including Harvard, the Universities of Michigan and Wisconsin, Columbia, Johns Hopkins, the Massachusetts Institute of Technology, UCLA, UC Berkeley, and the City College of New York. [28]

In the worst cases, the efforts of college administrators to prevent undergraduates from being infected by radicalism resulted in physical disruption of student protests. Some of the most anti-radical administrators personally supervised these disruptions during the first two national student strikes against war. One of the more high spirited of these administrators, Roscoe C. Ingalls, the Director of Los Angeles Junior College,

became so incensed by the anti-war strike in 1935 that he tried to drown
out the peace demonstrators at his college by

> roaring into microphones of the campus public address system. Next Di-
> rector . . . Ingalls stationed himself in front of the speakers, blew a tin
> whistle until he was red in the face. Unavailing, he advanced on the li-
> brary with a burly "Red squad" of policemen. When the students swarmed
> around them, the flustered policemen swung nightsticks, knocked out
> two girl students. Finally Director Ingalls turned on the sprinkler system,
> cleared the campus in two minutes.[29]

Ingall's type of direct personal intervention at the site of an anti-war
demonstration was, however, somewhat unusual for a college president.
More often, campus administrators seeking the physical disruption of anti-
war demonstrations did not themselves serve on the front lines; they fostered such disruptions by encouraging anti-radical students—either explicitly or implicitly—to harass the anti-war activists. On some campuses
this administration encouragement was both blatant and public, as when
the President of San Jose State Teachers College responded to the appearance of a radical leaflet by urging that patriotic students throw these
leftists off campus. The college president announced:

> I hope every true citizen on this campus, every one who loves the
> United States of America as well as the college will assist in the eradica-
> tion of this festering sore. Will all loyal groups, clubs, classes and societies
> act immediately. Make plans to get the necessary information. If you know
> members of the group, please feel quite free to take them to the edge of
> the campus and drop them off.[30]

A similar call to violence was heard at Michigan State University during the second student strike against war, when J.A. Hannah, the Secretary of the University, told the press that "the administration of the college will have no objection if other students toss these radicals in the river."[31]
Students answered Hannah's call to action. They disrupted the campus
anti-war meeting by tossing fruit at the rally speakers and then jumping
onto the stage, grabbing five protest leaders and throwing them into a
nearby river. Reverend Harold Marley, one of the victims of the assault,
visibly shaken by this collegiate intolerance, said that during the attack
"for the first time, I realized how Negroes must feel on the way to a
solitary tree."[32]

On some campuses, college officials were more covert in their support of anti-radical violence. These campus officials avoided public endorsements of such violence, but worked behind the scenes to organize
attacks. In 1934 Louis O'Brien, Berkeley's Assistant Dean of Undergraduates, called a private meeting in which he conferred with conservative
students and helped organize a vigilante squad, made up primarily of

fraternity members, to harass striking students.[33] An almost identical meeting occurred at the City College of New York—and in both cases these meetings led directly to anti-radical violence.[34] In other cases, campus administrators, though not playing a role in organizing violent assaults on anti-war activists, gave a green light to such attacks, by either praising or refusing to discipline the perpetrators of this violence. Physical assaults on student anti-war activists went unpunished at virtually every campus which witnessed such violence, including Harvard, Johns Hopkins, UCLA, UC Berkeley, Columbia, CCNY, MIT, Michigan State, and the universities of Chicago, Connecticut, Washington, and Wisconsin.[35]

While violence was the most dramatic form of suppression on campus, it was not the most common. College administrators from 1933 to 1935 usually sought to keep anti-war demonstrations off the college grounds without having to resort to brute force. This was attempted through the enforcement of campus political rules restricting the students' freedom of assembly, freedom of speech, and freedom of the press on campus. The most widely used forms of non-violent suppression of student radicalism and anti-war activism were, in rank order: 1. the banning of anti-war meetings and leftist speakers from the college grounds; 2. the expulsion or suspension of students for participating in anti-war actions; 3. the censorship of anti-war literature, including editorial copy from student newspapers; 4. the banning of radical student organizations.[36]

Judging by their formal power and legal authority, college administrators should have been able to smash the anti-war movement and banish its organizers from their campuses. On virtually all questions of disciplinary authority, the courts bent over backwards to favor administrators in this era of *in loco parentis*. The courts gave colleges and universities virtual carte blanche to discipline and even expel troublesome undergraduates and to do so without even a semblance of due process. By December 1934, moreover, there could be no doubt at all over whether the courts would back college administrators who used their disciplinary authority to attack anti-war dissenters on campus. That month the Supreme Court, in *Hamilton v. Regents of the University of California*, affirmed UCLA's expulsion of two student anti-war activists who had refused to enroll in mandatory military training courses. Such decisions attested that students usually had little hope of litigating successfully against politically repressive administrators.[37]

Fortunately for the student movement, however, there was often a large gap between the legal authority and the actual political power of college officials in the 1930s. University and college political battles were usually settled on campus rather than in the courts, much to the detriment of repressive administrators. Through free speech protests, indignant student bodies could hold college deans and presidents accountable for their acts of political suppression. While campus administrators hurt individual activists by subjecting them to suspensions, expulsions, and other disciplinary actions, these punitive acts proved ineffective in inhibiting student protest. Indeed, such attempts at suppression usually backfired politically because students often viewed censored movement activists as martyrs to the cause of free speech, and therefore rallied to the student movement's side. This trend was evident nationally, for at the very time (1933–1935) when attempts at political repression on campus were multiplying, student anti-war protest grew enormously, from a small insurgency in the East into a national movement. But to comprehend the actual workings and impact of political repression on campus, it is necessary to explore such repression at close range—and for this we turn to the two most ambitious attempts to suppress the student movement in this era: on the East Coast, CCNY, and on the West Coast, UCLA.

II

No college tried harder than the City College of New York to suppress student protest. CCNY's President Frederick B. Robinson and his subordinates violated student free speech rights more frequently than any other college administration in Depression America. From 1931 to 1934 Robinson's anti-radical campaign resulted in the expulsion of 43 CCNY students, the suspension of 38, and the hauling of hundreds of undergraduates before campus disciplinary boards, inquiring into their political associations, beliefs, and protest activity. In this same period, every student radical organization and publication was at one point or another banned from the CCNY campus. Robinson never learned that such repression only fueled student protest. Indeed, though many CCNY activists look back upon Robinson with scorn, they credit him with being one of their most effective organizing tools. Through his abuse of student political rights, CCNY's president inadvertently helped radicalize thousands of students and kept the campus in turmoil.[38]

The more repressive Robinson became, the more creative CCNY's student radicals became in mocking and resisting him. In fall 1932, Robinson fired Oakley Johnson, an English instructor at CCNY, apparently because of his communist affiliation and his support of the student Left. When students staged a rally in Johnson's defense, Robinson called the police on to campus, who clubbed and dispersed the demonstrators. This was the first time a college president had used the police against student protesters during the Depression decade. The confrontations over the Johnson firing were followed by a wave of suspensions, which provoked a student strike at CCNY in October 1932. Led by the NSL, the student protesters denounced CCNY's violations of academic freedom and announced their plan to hold a mock trial of President Robinson and CCNY night school director Paul Linehan for those violations. Despite threats from the college's trustees to punish participants in the trial, some 1400 students attended this event in New York's Central Opera House on the last weekend of October, 1932.[39]

The mock trial displayed political theater on a grand scale. The "defendants," Robinson and Linehan, were charged with "deliberate persecution" of student activists at CCNY, "intimidation of teachers at the College, and responsibility for the arrest of" peaceful student protesters. The trial was conducted, for the most part, as if it were occurring in a real courtroom, complete with a prosecutor, defense attorney, and judges dressed in black robes—all of whom were NSL activists. Twenty-eight witnesses testified, documenting the various acts of political censorship and suppression committed by the defendants. The trial ended after a summation by "prosecutor" Joseph Starobin, who described the conflict at CCNY as a "fight for intellectual freedom." The audience, acting as a jury, found Robinson and Linehan guilty and "sentenced" them to vacate their positions in the CCNY administration. Robinson was not amused. Though he had not attended the trial, Robinson had a stenographer record the proceedings, and then sent the record to the college's trustees—who suspended 19 organizers of the trial.[40]

Robinson went even further in his assault on student protesters during the following semester in response to an anti-ROTC demonstration. The controversy began when the administration announced its decision to cancel afternoon classes so that students could attend military exercises in a pre-Memorial Day ceremony. Student anti-war activists complained that it was wrong for CCNY, as "one of the world's largest cultural institutions . . . [to] suspend intellectual activity to pay homage to the war machine within its cloistered walls"; they derided this military event as "jingo day," and urged that students use that occasion to rally against war.[41]

The "jingo day" protest on May 29, 1933, began peacefully, when about 400 students assembled near campus to hold an anti-war rally. But the rally gathered in such close proximity to the ROTC cadets' line up for their march to CCNY's stadium for the ceremonies, that as the rally grew, the police moved in and ordered the protesters to disperse. Complying with the police order, the students regrouped a half block away. After a brief rally, the demonstrators, carrying anti-ROTC and anti-jingo day banners, brought their protest directly outside the ceremony site by picketing around the stadium.[42]

Again the police intervened, forbidding the students from picketing and ordering them to disband. The protesters began marching away, when one of them shouted "Let's go to the stadium. We were all invited." Responding spontaneously to this call to action, the students abandoned their picket line and sought to enter the stadium. Police and ushers, however, blocked the way, informing the students that they could not enter the stadium with their picket signs. But after discarding their signs, the protesters were again refused admission to the stadium. The protesters retreated to the campus where they met to discuss strategy and—angered by hecklers who disrupted the meeting by showering the speakers with eggs—decided that they had a right to go to their college's ceremonies, and so returned to the stadium.[43]

The protesters' second attempt to gain admission to the stadium resulted in a wild melee as they were again barred from the ceremony. According to the *New York Times* report

> more than 100 of the demonstrators marched past the iron gates [of the stadium] but they found their further progress blocked by an inner line of wooden doors. Some hand-to-hand fighting followed as the cadet officers, administration sympathizers and policemen pushed the pacifists outside the stadium.[44]

At this point President Robinson, accompanied by the ROTC commander and other guests, arrived at the stadium and became embroiled in a confrontation with the protesters. Robinson "raised his umbrella and lashed out suddenly, striking nearly a dozen of the . . . [protesters] about the head and shoulders." Several students responded by pinning Robinson's arms, in an effort to get the umbrella away from him and thereby stop the assault. Police intervened, pushed the students away, and escorted Robinson into the stadium.[45]

Robinson claimed that he struck the students because they were rushing toward him and threatening him and his guests. But neither the American Civil Liberties Union's investigation nor the testimony of students and bystanders support his claim. According to the ACLU, Robinson had not been threatened by the students. The ACLU reported that their "investigation of the occurrence at City College on May 29 revealed that President Robinson left the sidewalk where he was walking with his party and attacked the parading students in the street with an umbrella, and that he himself was responsible for the riot that followed."[46] Robinson apparently had become so infuriated by the sight of a throng of students near the stadium entrance and by their jeering of him that he wielded his umbrella against them.[47]

Shocked and outraged by Robinson's attack and by the announcement that participants in the demonstration would be punished, CCNY student activists immediately began to voice their criticism of the administration. CCNY's socialist-led Student Forum published a "jingo day issue" of its newsletter, headlined "ROBINSON RUNS AMOK ON CAMPUS: MADDENED PRESIDENT ATTACKS STUDENTS."[48] Campus officials were in no mood for such criticism. They stopped students from distributing this newsletter and seized the entire edition of the publication. The administration also announced that 29 student activists, three major radical student organizations on campus, and the student newspaper were suspended pending the completion of the disciplinary hearings.[49]

Despite these new restrictions on their campus political rights, CCNY student activists continued to organize against both Robinson and the suspensions. Under the leadership of the NSL and the SLID, several large protest rallies were held off campus in the week following the jingo day incident. The culmination of these protests was an "umbrella parade," which featured an immense replica of the weapon Robinson had wielded against the demonstrators.[50] CCNY student activists were not alone, however, in their criticism of Robinson. The *New Republic* suggested that CCNY's embattled president should step down because "any college president who descends to fisticuffs with his undergraduates has destroyed his usefulness as a preceptor of youth now and forever."[51]

Robinson's strong-armed manner of dealing with student protesters fostered the growth of anti-radical violence and the disruption of anti-war meetings at CCNY. Conservative students, particularly the more intolerant members of the campus ROTC and athletic teams, seem to have concluded that if it was proper for their college president to assault anti-war protesters, it was also proper for them to mount such attacks. These anti-radical students attempted to disrupt almost every protest meeting held in the weeks following the jingo day incident, employing physical violence and organized heckling. In one such meeting, socialist leader Norman Thomas could not complete his speech because twenty-five of these hecklers used automobile horns and police sirens to drown him out.[52]

This harassment might not have occurred, however, were it not for the organizing of an ROTC officer on the CCNY faculty. Apparently emboldened by Robinson's assault, this faculty member worked to create violent opposition to the student Left. According to a *New York Times* report, anti-radical students were "acting on the suggestion of Major Herbert M. Holton, Associate Professor of Hygiene [at CCNY]," when they decided to form a vigilance committee which would use "controlled force" against the anti-war protesters. Holton had made this suggestion at a meeting attended by college athletes in CCNY's Varsity Club shortly after the jingo day incident.[53] Neither Holton nor the disruptive anti-radical students—who unlike the anti-war activists actually had infringed upon student free speech rights—were ever punished or even investigated at CCNY for their acts of harassment.

The disciplinary hearings which followed the jingo day incident were extremely one-sided. The faculty committee which conducted these hearings proved unwilling even to consider the possibility that the jingo day incident might have been precipitated by President Robinson. Nor was the committee interested in examining how the conflict was facilitated by the restrictive campus regulations against political protest, the police, and the decision to bar the protesters from the stadium. The whole idea that infringements on the rights of students—including police dispersion of the picketers outside the stadium, the assault on protesters trying to enter the stadium, and the umbrella attack itself—had contributed to the crisis, and therefore merited the committee's attention, was simply alien to these unsympathetic faculty. Thus, instead of investigating why such a violent clash had occurred and what policy changes could prevent a repetition of it, the committee merely sought to determine which anti-war activists had participated in the jingo day protest, what campus rules they had broken, and how they should be punished.

The assumption that the anti-war activists were totally at fault for the jingo day incident guided the disciplinary hearings from beginning to end. This assumption was articulated not only by the committee, but by Mark Eisner, the chair of the college's board of trustees, who virtually judged the protesters guilty even before the hearing had begun. Eisner set the tone for the entire investigation in his public statement the day after the jingo day clash. He concluded that anti-war protesters "were deliberately obstructing a college function, the annual cadet review. Students who are found guilty can expect that their college days at City College are over."[54]

The disciplinary hearings, which began on June 1 and ultimately took testimony from over 100 students, were themselves a testament to the severe limits on free speech which confronted thousands of undergraduates during the early 1930s. The administrators and faculty on this disciplinary committee—like many of their colleagues across the nation—worked from the illiberal premise that any political demonstration held to protest either an action of the college or a regular college event constituted an intolerable attempt to "interfere with a stated college function."[55] Such protests merited suppression even if they were non-violent and not literally disruptive of the "stated college function." Thus in the case of the jingo day protest, the fact that students demonstrated against the scheduled military exercise was enough to convict them, even though they made no attempt to stop the ceremonies or interfere with the speeches.

Throughout the hearings, student activists clashed with the faculty and administration on the question of student political rights. These primarily communist and socialist students tried repeatedly to convince the disciplinary committee that by outlawing demonstrations at college functions the administration infringed upon their right to assemble peacefully. The students challenged the committee's assumption that in holding such a demonstration on jingo day they had interfered with a college function. In a typical exchange during the disciplinary hearings, NSL activist Herman Benson argued this point with Dean Morton Gottschall. When the Dean contended that the anti-war activists were guilty of interfering with the military exercises, Benson replied:

> No that wasn't interference because that didn't prevent the carrying out of the ROTC function. Q.[Gottschall] What do you call it then, if not interference; what name would you give it? A. [Benson] I would call it expressing our disapproval of ROTC and trying to bring our idea across to those who may have been there. Q.[Gottschall] That was interfering certainly. A. [Benson] In what way did it prevent the carrying out of the ROTC exhibition?[56]

Though the disciplinary committee repeatedly reminded the testifying students that their demonstration had violated campus regulations, the students insisted that their free speech rights should take precedence over such regulations. As one student activist told the committee, "We believe we are citizens of the college . . . and that . . . as citizens of the college we believe we have the right to protest."[57] Julian Prager, one of the students who would be expelled for his role in the jingo day demonstration, testified that no matter what the campus regulations said, "I believe we have a right to express our opinions in whatever way we see fit without infringing upon anybody's rights."[58] Soon the students began to see, however, that because their definition of political liberty on campus was much broader than the administration's, free speech battles were inevitable. NSL leader Joseph Budish told the committee "that we have reached a point where we cannot see eye to eye with the administration and that if they use sufficient pressure to make these so-called liberal principles be abandoned we would have to fight it out and take the consequences."[59]

The disciplinary committee responded to these civil liberties arguments with paternalistic and bureaucratic clichés. Committee members stressed that it was the faculty and administration who made the rules and that students had no choice but to obey them, even if they disagreed with them. The committee viewed any violation of these rules as youthful insubordination which had to be punished. Throughout the hearings, the committee insisted that any student who fell short of absolute obedience to campus regulations had no place in the college. Just how far CCNY faculty and administrators took this ethic of obedience was made clear in an exchange between Dean Gottschall and NSL leader Adam Lapin during the hearings. "Q.[Gottschall] Suppose we passed a rule prohibiting the congregating of three students on the campus? A. [Lapin] Would you gentlemen expect such a rule to be obeyed if passed? Q.[Gottschall] If it passed, we'd expect it to be obeyed."[60]

This demand for absolute obedience was a manifestation of faculty and administration paternalism—their belief that students were immature youths under their charge who had to be guided into adulthood. The type of adults they saw themselves as molding were dignified and proper gentlemen. And gentlemen, of course, would be far too civil to engage in boisterous street demonstrations, such as that seen on jingo day. This theme, that the protesters had behaved in an uncivil and immature manner, unbecoming gentlemen was stressed continually by the disciplinary committee. "I do very seriously object to a man conducting himself as though he were a rowdy and not a gentleman; and I think those [jingo day demonstrations] were rowdy and not gentlemanly actions," explained one committee member.[61]

CCNY student activists denied that they had behaved in an uncivil manner. They argued that their disorderliness had been provoked by the ungentlemanly behavior of the police, the cadets, and the president who attacked them. The activists also accused the disciplinary committee of employing a double standard in their application of the standard of gentlemanly conduct—charging that it was applied to radicals but not to the conservative students who used force to break up student anti-war meetings. When Joseph Starobin, an NSL leader, told the disciplinary committee that it was unfair for the administration to punish radical activists, while not even questioning the athletes and cadets who engaged in anti-radical heckling and violence, Professor Mead's rebuttal seemed to confirm the existence of an administration double standard. Mead told Starobin:

> That is not pertinent at all. In the first place the so called [anti-radical] Vigilantes did whatever they did off the College Grounds. A. [Starobin] They started on the College grounds. Q. [Mead] I don't know who was responsible and I don't see that that has a bearing upon the situation. That was a different situation. I was talking about organized groups of the College definitely engaged in advancing propaganda. I don't approve of what they did, but they had not propaganda in mind and were only interested in breaking up a meeting.[62]

It was not just the college's dispensing of unequal punishment, but the disciplinary process itself which offended CCNY anti-war activists. They charged that the disciplinary committee had violated their due process rights by suspending all of the campus' radical organizations even before the disciplinary hearings had started. But the committee defended its disciplinary action on the grounds that it had "a legal right to suspend . . . [student clubs] at any time," and even went on to criticize students for publicly protesting the suspensions. In response to this criticism, one NSL activist told the committee: "I maintain that we have the right to protest suspensions of that nature—suspensions without investigation. . . . Raised in the American tradition, we realized we had the right to protest any action."[63] This concept of student political rights was, however, one that the committee could not accept and one that it argued against during the hearing. Thus a member of the committee lectured the protesting student that

> when the faculty reaches a decision, even though it be wrong, as a good citizen of the college you must abide by that decision until it is changed. A. [unnamed student activist] How can we go about protesting? [Faculty Committee member] When you start protesting to the outside world your conduct is unbecoming a college student.[64]

At the conclusion of the hearings, the committee expelled twenty-one jingo day protesters and suspended eight others for an entire semester. The committee revoked the charters of the campus' three leading radical organizations, claiming that they were responsible for a "deliberately planned attempt to interfere with a stated college function." The students were found guilty of violating college rules though their participation in an unauthorized meeting on campus. The student Left at CCNY denounced the expulsions as a sign that the college had been converted into a "seething cauldron of administrative despotism." But despite widespread student anger over the expulsions, there was little that could be done to mobilize CCNY against the decision because the academic year had drawn to a close.[65]

Though the jingo day expulsions served only to anger the student body and bred further anti-war protest at CCNY, the Robinson administration persisted in its repressive policies. The administration refused students permission to hold a meeting on campus during the first anti-war strike in April 1934. When about a thousand students defied this ban by rallying on campus, Dean Morton Gottschall—taking a cue from President Robinson's earlier anti-radical assault—intervened personally to try to break up the unauthorized meeting.

> Gottschall, making a one man sortie against the mob, attempted to stop the meeting single handed. He ripped banners out of the leaders' hands and tried to compel [the main speaker, Student Council representative] Edwin Alexander '37 to get down from the flagpole [which he was using as a podium].[66]

Police then rushed in and forcibly dispersed the rally. As a result of this rally ten students were disciplined.

Before the year ended, CCNY witnessed another round of expulsions. In fall 1934, twenty-one CCNY student activists were expelled, twelve placed on probation and four suspended as a consequence of an anti-fascist protest. The event which sparked this new disciplinary round was a reception given to a visiting delegation of Italian fascist students by President Robinson, who invited the delegation to campus despite the objections of the CCNY student government. Robinson decided that the fascist delegation would be honored with a special assembly in CCNY's Great Hall. The administration refused to grant student protesters permission for an anti-fascist demonstration by the entrance to the campus, which they had hoped to hold on the day of the delegation's visit to CCNY. To these CCNY student activists the administration seemed to be employing a blatant political double standard by honoring fascists in the college assembly hall, while banning anti-fascists from marching even outside the hall. The anger generated by this administration behavior set the stage for one of the stormiest meetings in the history of the City College of New York.[67]

The meeting, which occurred before a packed house of some 2000 students on October 9, 1934, began tensely, as students jeered President Robinson during his opening remarks. Robinson shouted back at the students, "Guttersnipes, your conduct is worse than that of guttersnipes."

After Robinson completed his speech, Professor Arbib Costa of CCNY's Italian department made a brief welcoming speech and then gave the floor to CCNY Student Council representative Edwin Alexander, who was supposed to extend the student body's greetings to the visiting delegation. Before giving Alexander the microphone, Professor Costa warned him not to mention fascism in his remarks and told him that to do so would be discourteous. But Alexander, an NSL activist, disregarded this warning and began his Great Hall address with the words "I do not intend to be discourteous to our guests. I merely wish to bring them anti-fascist greetings from the student body of City College to the tricked, enslaved student body of Italy . . ." Before Alexander could utter another syllable, Professor Costa "took him by the arm away from the microphone." Members of the Italian Club then surrounded and assaulted Alexander. A full scale riot followed when students from the audience jumped onto the stage to assist Alexander.[68]

The CCNY administration and faculty responded to this incident in the same partisan manner that characterized their handling of the jingo day affair. Alexander's assailants were never investigated or punished, but disciplinary proceedings began immediately against Alexander and the other anti-fascist protesters. Initially, twenty-six of the demonstrators were suspended, as was the CCNY student government. The administration charged that the protesters had disrupted a college function and abridged the free speech rights of the visiting Italian students. These CCNY officials never considered that banning the demonstration outside the hall and using physical force to stop Alexander's anti-fascist speech constituted grievous violations of the student body's free speech rights. The disciplinary hearings were as extensive as they were partisan. They were the most sweeping internal political investigation on any American campus during the Depression decade, and involved the questioning of more than 100 students.[69]

Unlike the jingo day controversy, the Great Hall riot occurred at a good time of the year for the protesters—right in the middle of the semester. Working closely together throughout the disciplinary hearings, the NSL and SLID mobilized thousands of CCNY undergraduates in protest against the suspensions. These activists drew a crowd of over 1500 students in their mock trial of President Robinson, which indicted him for supporting fascism and violating academic freedom. The students held an "Oust Robinson" week, designed to build popular support for the president's dismissal; they organized demonstrations at City Hall and outside Robinson's home, in which 18 students were arrested. When, despite these protests, twenty-one of the suspended students were expelled, the protesters called for a strike. Over 2000 students, many of them sporting "I am a Guttersnipe" buttons, then boycotted classes in an effective and angry two-hour strike, which ended with the students burning Robinson and Mussolini in effigy.[70]

Though the protests failed to win the students' reinstatement, they succeeded in mobilizing liberal public opinion against President Robinson. Several of New York City's major liberal daily newspapers sharply criticized Robinson's behavior. The *New York Post* called upon the college to fire Robinson and replace him with "an abler and more liberal man." Most importantly, the Great Hall incident and the protests that followed helped turn a significant portion of CCNY alumni against Robinson. This shift was made clear in the address that Felix Frankfurter, then a Harvard Law Professor and one of CCNY's most eminent alumni, made at the college's annual alumni dinner soon after "Oust Robinson Week." Frankfurter told the Alumni Association:

> A state of irritability among the students at the College is hardly the proof of a wise administration. The authorities of the College assume excessive responsibility for the actions of students outside of college rooms and buildings. There is much confusion of power and responsibility in regard to discipline at the College. The real rulers of the world are undiscoverable, but there are too many rulers discoverable at City College. It is unworthy of you men to be afraid of the questioning of youth. If we cannot stand up to their questions I think we should be slightly suspicious of the solidness of our foundations.[71]

The CCNY Alumni magazine expressed similar sentiments, and there began an energetic alumni campaign against Robinson, which within a few years would bring an end to his stormy tenure as the president of CCNY.[72]

Robinson's removal from the CCNY presidency represented a major victory for the campus Left; it suggested that sustained protest on behalf of free speech could succeed against even the most repressive college administrator. The students' triumph over Robinson was, however, a testament not only to their organizing ability but also to Robinson's self-destructive tactics. In retrospect, it seems almost unbelievable that Robinson failed to recognize that his heavy handedness was inciting rather than reducing student protest. But what must be borne in mind here is that Robinson's behavior was guided by ideological rather than tactical considerations. As a committed foe of radicalism, Robinson felt it his duty to take a tough, unambiguous stand against leftist influence on the student body, regardless of the consequences.[73]

Robinson's anti-radical stance was also shaped by his paternalistic sensibility. He saw himself as a stern parent would in the face of youthful insubordination. Consequently, Robinson behaved as if protesting students were naughty children in need of discipline rather than citizens whose rights he was violating. Even in his private correspondence, Robinson clung to this understanding of his job, explaining to his son during a student strike at CCNY that "I suppose we shall have to spank a few more [students] just to let them know that students cannot determine whether they will or will not attend college."[74] It is little wonder, then, that Robin-

son came as close as he could to adminstering such a spanking—with his
umbrella on jingo day—and that he would lose his job rather than soften
his stance toward the student movement at CCNY.

III

Despite the turmoil it provoked, Robinson's hard line position against
the student Left elicited applause from the nation's more conservative
college administrators. One of these administrators, Ernest C. Moore, the
vice president and provost of the University of California at Los Angeles
was so impressed by CCNY's anti-radical policies that in 1934 he wrote
President Robinson, expressing admiration for

> the qualities of backbone of which you and the administrative part
> of the College of the City of New York are possessed. Only the most
> thoroughgoing determination could have enabled you to do the splendid
> bit of housecleaning that you have done. It has cheered and encouraged
> us all. We as well as you have been bedeviled for years by the National
> Student League . . . . We hope that the [anti-radical disciplinary] action
> . . . will clear up the difficulties.[75]

At the time that he wrote this letter, Moore was already emulating the
CCNY administration by attempting to do his own anti-radical "housecleaning"—suspending five students who he accused of aiding the efforts
of "the National Student League to destroy the university."[76]

Moore's "housecleaning" at UCLA provoked the largest campus free
speech protests on the West Coast during the 1930s. The UCLA suspensions were in part the product of friction between Moore and undergraduates, who demanded a student-controlled open forum at which political
issues could be discussed on campus. Moore vehemently opposed this demand, claiming that it violated the political neutrality of the university. In
early October 1934, Moore ordered the student council and its president,
John Burnside, to stop agitating for the open forum. But Burnside refused to obey the Provost's order, and continued working with both the
student council other student activists on behalf of the open forum. It was
when they were in the process of organizing a student referendum on the
open forum idea that Moore suspended Burnside and four other student
leaders, charging that they were working to convert UCLA into "a hotbed
of Communism."[77]

Of the five students suspended only one, NSL leader Celeste Strack,
was a communist. Two of the other students, Sid Zsagri and Tom Lambert, had been active in Upton Sinclair's campaign for governor of California—a campaign which, despite its socialistic tone, had been opposed
by the Communist Party. The other two suspended students, Mendel Lieberman and John Burnside, had no radical ties whatsoever, and all of the

students with the exception of Strack were prominent leaders of mainstream student organizations at UCLA. Moore's charge that the four non-
communists, whose only real offense had been supporting an open forum
as a vehicle for insuring free speech on campus, were promoting communism was wild and unsubstantiated, as was his claim that they and Strack
sought "to destroy" UCLA.[78]

The suspensions and wild charges reflected the panic which had seized
Moore as a consequence of the rising tide of radicalism on the West Coast
in 1934. Badly shaken by outbreak of the San Francisco general strike,
Moore fretted in his diary that "it may be the beginning of Revolution. It
ought to be put down definitely for a general strike is civil war—a form
of defiance which does not belong in a civilized society."[79] Moore expressed similar anxieties about Upton Sinclair's gubernatorial candidacy,
which he termed "a menace to California." The Provost's hostility to Sinclair contributed to his opposition to an open forum at UCLA, for the
students had expressed a desire to use such a forum to learn about Sinclair's ideas and the issues in the gubernatorial race. This suggests that
Moore, a member of Los Angeles' Republican Party central committee,
had partisan motivations for opposing the forum—quite ironic given his
public assertions that he forbade the open forum in order to preserve the
campus' political neutrality.[80]

The threat Moore perceived from the Left in 1934 put him into a
combative frame of mind, which shaped his interaction with UCLA student activists. He believed that the communists were conspiring to subvert
public higher educational institutions. Moore confided to UC President
Robert Sproul in May 1934,

> I have, as you know, been brooding over what the communists are
> trying to do to us here in the United States . . . . The method by which
> a persistent effort is being made to undermine and destroy the public
> school system, by making it impossible for the tax-paying public to sup-
> port it, is . . . diabolically effective . . . . The result is that our tax-
> paying people . . . will not any longer pay taxes to support institutions
> for the training of young people who are devoting themselves to the
> overthrow of our government.[81]

This communist plot against the schools was, Moore told Sproul, a sign
that "the class war is on," and that responsible educators must begin to
"make battle plans" on ways to help defeat the reds in this war.[82]

Provost Moore's anti-radical battle plan included working closely with
the police against the student Left. In August 1934, Moore met with H.C.
Griswold of the California State Police. Griswold confirmed Moore's fears
of communist subversion in the schools. The police officer warned Moore
that the

> Communists . . . have orders . . . to center their efforts in the U.S.
> on these two universities [UCLA and UC Berkeley] . . . . Chief [of the

State Police] Mr. Harish told him recently that they propose to do two
things 1) To make a crusade for sex freedom. Convincing the young
people that they should live together without marrying if they want to
and quite freely. 2) To make heavy war against compulsory military
training.[83]

Moore accepted unquestioningly this melodramatic warning (it was only
accurate about Left opposition to ROTC, which was already a matter of
public record), and immediately passed the information along to President Sproul, urging an administration counterattack. Over the course of
the 1934–35 academic year, the Los Angeles police department repeatedly provided Provost Moore with intelligence information about UCLA
student radicals. Moore secretly initiated this intelligence work through a
confidential letter to the Los Angeles police chief in September 1934. In
at least one case, Moore gave the police the name of a student activist that
he wanted placed under police survelliance and arrested.[84]

Well before the suspensions controversy, Moore made public his hostility to the student Left. From the beginning of the 1934 academic year,
the provost emphasized that radical activity would not be tolerated at UCLA.
Moore became personally involved in breaking up the meetings of student activists. In a mid-October diary entry, Moore describes one such
intervention. On that day he saw NSL leader Celeste Strack "haranguing
a group of boys in front of the library . . . . I went out to them and said
you cannot hold a communist meeting here Miss Strack." Moore then
called Strack into his office and told the NSL leader—who recently had
been pressured into leaving the University of Southern California because
of her anti-war organizing—that he knew she had caused "plenty of trouble [at USC] last year. I want to tell you that you cannot do . . . [that]
here." Several days later, when Strack came to Moore's office to protest
his political restrictions, the provost told Strack that he "did not want to
see her, that I already told her all that I had to tell her." Strack responded
by calling Moore a "coward for not allowing the students to conduct an
. . . [open] forum." Moore rebuked the NSL leader, "asked her to leave
the office and told her she was a traitor."[85]

Moore was so anxious to drive radicalism off the UCLA campus that
he worked to pass the word among the student body that specific members of their class were engaged in illicit radical activity. According to
Roberta Monks, a member of the undergraduate Scholarship and Activities Board, when she approached Provost Moore in October 1934 with a
request for a study hall, "Dr. Moore burst forth with the startling assertion that Mr. [Mendel] Lieberman (the chairman of the board) was a communist because—so far as I could make out—he wanted an open forum."
Moore then described Lieberman as part of a NSL-communist plot "to
burn down the buildings, pillage—all sorts of horrible things." But neither Monks nor her classmates were swayed by Moore's tirade. In a letter
to Moore's superior, UC systemwide President Robert Gordon Sproul, Monk

confided that on the day of this meeting with Moore she was "most glad to make my departure [from the provost's office]," and that when she later told the board of Moore's depiction of Lieberman as a " 'dangerous subversive' it was met with laughter."[86]

Though by October 1934 undergraduates at UCLA had grown accustomed to Moore's anti-radical rhetoric, the suspensions nonetheless came as a shock to much of the student body. By singling out for punishment some of the campus' most prominent mainstream student leaders, Moore demonstrated to students (in a way mere radical rhetoric could not) that their civil liberties were not secure at UCLA. The provost's accusations against the suspended students seemed extreme—nothing less than conspiracy to destroy the school. Many UCLA undergraduates sensed immediately that the source of the controversy was Moore's hysteria rather than student misconduct.[87] The strong doubts UCLA students had about Moore's disciplinary action became evident the day after the suspensions, when over 3000 students participated in a spontaneous protest rally on campus. This was the largest political demonstration ever seen at UCLA.[88]

Like its counterpart at CCNY, the UCLA administration proved unwilling to permit students to hold peaceful campus demonstrations in protest against college policy. Barely a moment after the start of the rally on behalf of the suspended students, two police officers moved in, and attempted to disrupt the demonstration by evicting the student who was addressing the crowd. This move angered the demonstrators, who began chanting "Let him talk." The police found it impossible to remove the speaker because as they began forcing him off, they were tackled by several students and thrown in the bushes. After this scuffle, and facing a huge angry crowd, the police allowed the rally to proceed. Speakers demanded a fair hearing for the suspended students, and one condemned Moore's red baiting, arguing that under the terms which the provost had used against the suspended students, "if you are for freedom of speech then you are a communist too."[89]

Not all UCLA students opposed the suspensions and Moore's campaign against the student Left. The provost enjoyed considerable support from conservatives in traditional campus organizations, including the fraternities, athletic teams, and ROTC. Some of these students allied themselves with the police, scuffling with demonstrators at the anti-suspensions rally. These scuffles helped to provide the administration with a pretext for ordering in the riot squad, composed of some 200 officers, which cut the rally short. And at a Greek house meeting shortly after the suspensions were announced, representatives of UCLA fraternities and sororities voted to support the administration "100 percent in any action taken in their drive to oust the radical element from the UCLA campus."[90] The more extreme faction of this opposition soon formed the UCLA Americans, a self-proclaimed vigilante group with xenophobic tendencies, which pledged to prevent protesters from distributing literature on campus or doing any other organizing in support of the suspended students.[91]

Moore welcomed and encouraged this anti-radical organizing. In the wake of the anti-suspensions rally, Moore told the press that the demonstration proved how evil the student Left was and "that students should 'clean house' of the National Student League." The provost made a radio address calling upon UCLA undergraduates to "support the University and purge the Communists from their ranks." Going beyond the UCLA campus itself, Moore called upon conservative students in college fraternities and sororities across the nation to "become active helpers of the U.S. in its day of difficulty with radical agitation."[92]

It was not Moore, however, but the suspended students who attracted support from other campuses. At Stanford University the student newspaper accused Moore of denying undergraduates their fundamental political rights and working to ensure that "freedom of speech and thought no longer exist on the southern campus." The *Stanford Daily* went on to argue that Moore's refusal to allow students to hold an open forum to discuss the crucial gubernatorial race in California threatened to make "plain nincompoops" out of UCLA students. "While all the rest of the state of California is aflame with the keenest election in its history, are students of U.C.L.A. to practice argumentative celibacy?" At UC Berkeley student activists did more than criticize the suspensions; they organized a sympathy strike on November 5, 1934. Led jointly by the NSL and SLID, this one hour student strike was designed to press UC President Robert Sproul, who resided in Berkeley, to override Moore and reinstate the five UCLA students.[93]

The Berkeley strike proved a stormy affair. Sproul took a tough anti-strike position, denying students permission to demonstrate on campus, and issuing a "word of warning" that students who boycotted classes would "suffer the usual penalty." Monroe Deutsch, the provost of UC Berkeley, sent the faculty a memorandum ordering them to take the roll, report the names of any students who stayed out of classes during the strike, and do whatever was necessary to prevent students from making pro-strike speeches or announcements in class. "The whole tone of this "memo, complained Professor George Adams of the Berkeley Philosophy department, was "that of a high military officer in a state of siege and expecting attack." Adams was particularly alarmed that the administration's hard line position seemed "by clear implication" to encourage opponents of the strike "if not to use, at least to sanction the use of physical force against students."[94]

The most extreme form of administration opposition to the free speech strike did, as Adams implied, involve violence; it came from Berkeley Dean Louis O'Brien's collusion with undergraduate vigilantes. According to student affidavits, O'Brien held a planning meeting with conservative undergraduates from the Greek houses and the football team to organize the physical disruption of the strike.[95] As the strike rally began just outside the gates of the Berkeley campus on November 5, it became obvious that opponents of the strike were prepared to use violence to thwart the protesters. While a crowd of over 1000 students looked on, "self-appointed 'vigilantes' " ripped protest signs down and drowned out rally speakers with cries of "Red," and "Down With Everything." Soon the counter-demonstrators were hurling not only epithets, but rotten eggs and tomatoes at the strike leaders, who tried in vain to complete their speeches.[96]

Strike organizers had not anticipated this disruption, nor did they recognize until the rally began that the attacks had been premeditated and carefully coordinated. "I'm sure now that in looking back and being somewhat more knowledgeable in the ways and methods of suppression of free speech that it was something that had been organized," recalled Richard Criley, one of the speakers at the strike rally. "There was a truck load of ripe tomatoes in the middle of this crowd of over 5000 people outside of Sather Gate [obviously a sign that students opposed to the strike had come prepared for disruptive action]." Though speakers pleaded with the counter-demonstrators to respect their constitutional right to free speech, the vegetable and egg barrage continued, preventing the completion of any speeches. According to Criley, not even the American flag could stop the counter-demonstrators:

> These tomatoes began flying thick and fast, and I remember ducking them. I'd say "fellow students" and then I'd duck and a tomato would whiz over my head. And it was all very funny until one of our student strike committee members who happened to be a very good looking young women got up to speak and she didn't duck. And pretty soon these tomatoes that had been funny when watching the guys being hit or ducking became sort of cruel; they were lashing and hitting hard. Pretty soon she was just dripping with tomato juice, and she started to cry, but she wouldn't get down off the platform. At this point a Berkeley merchant, who had a store down the street, came running back with an American flag, and said "Look, you people stand for the American flag. Put it up next to the speaker." We did. And soon the flag was pelted with tomatoes and was running with tomato juice, which turned many of the patriotic people in the crowd towards us, and we ended up with somewhat of a consensus of sympathy of the majority of the crowd outside Sather Gate.[97]

The strike at Berkeley effectively placed the UCLA controversy on Sproul's doorstep. The Berkeley walkout demonstrated that Moore's offensive was not only causing turmoil at UCLA, but also spreading controversy and political embarrassment for the University beyond Los Angeles. The Bay Area press gave prominent coverage to the disruption of the Berkeley strike rally. Even the UC administration now recognized that this physical assault upon free speech demonstrators had hurt the University's image. Embarrassed by the wild melee it had inspired, the Sproul administration expressed "regret . . . that students of the University did not permit [the strike speakers] . . . to state their views freely." The tumult in Berkeley suggested that unless the UCLA controversy was resolved, protest and criticism of the UC administration would continue to grow.[98]

Two days after the Berkeley strike, protests over the UCLA suspensions spread to a third California campus: San Mateo Jr. College. At the invitation of San Mateo students, several leaders of the Berkeley strike addressed them and explained the UCLA situation, rallying support for the suspended students. Over four hundred students attended the demonstration, but as at Berkeley, an anti-radical group (of college athletes) threw eggs and tomatoes at the speakers, making it impossible for the free speech rally to be completed. The disruption of the rally made headlines and added to the furor over the suspensions.[99]

Besides the student protests, President Sproul came under pressure from numerous sources to intercede in the UCLA case. Four fathers of the suspended students had issued a joint statement condemning Provost Moore for "blasting their [sons'] reputations when they are on the threshold of life before giving them a hearing in which they could have disproved such charges." The parents hinted at a potential libel suit against the University, and urged President Sproul to overrule Moore and grant the students unconditional reinstatement.[100] Moore's political position was further weakened by a petition signed by over one hundred UCLA faculty members. The petition disputed the provost's claim that UCLA was a hotbed of communism and implied that Moore's inflammatory rhetoric and decision to suspend the students had damaged the University's reputation. Sensing that he was in trouble, Moore appealed to President Sproul to intervene and make a final decision in the case.[101] Sproul agreed to review the case.

Moore was not lacking, however, in influential supporters. Several of them sat on the University's highest policy making body, the UC Board of Regents. Even during ordinary times, the regents was a conservative body, composed primarily of business leaders. But in the fall of 1934 the board was in a particularly strong anti-radical mood because, like Moore, a number of its members had been badly frightened by the San Francisco General Strike and Upton Sinclair's campaign. According to Chester Rowell, one of the more liberal regents, several of his fellow board members had been "carried away by the prevailing [anti-radical] hysteria" by the time of the UCLA suspensions. In a confidential letter to Sproul, Rowell expressed his alarm at the political intolerance he had witnessed at the November Regents meeting during the discussion of the UCLA cases:

> In all my experience with the Regents, which, first and second hand, now covers over forty years, I never before saw or heard of a meeting which came so near to Upton Sinclair's otherwise unjust strictures in his "Goose Step" [where Sinclair depicted the Regents as an intolerant group of plutocrats warring with academic freedom]. If that is the way we are going to impose the personal opinions of the old and the rich on the education of the young and aspiring, by transforming the University into a propaganda bureau for economic orthodoxy, we shall only be playing into the hands of the most dangerous sect of radicals.[102]

Rowell's observation suggest that had Sproul chosen to back Moore, UC's president would have had considerable support from the regents. And, at first glance, it might seem as if Sproul would approve the UCLA suspensions, because he was a foe of radicalism, who had spied on Berkeley's student radicals, barred leftist rallies from campus, and publicly spoke of the need for universities to help prevent the spread of radicalism. But Sproul had never been one to invite unnecessary political controversy and therefore, unlike Moore, refused to engage in public redbaiting of his own university. Sproul understood that wild charges of subversion undermined the University's reputation. In the past he had responded to those who made such charges by asking them to either provide evidence or desist from their name calling. So though Sproul shared with Moore a desire to purge UC's Left "propagandists," he also believed that the battle against campus radicalism called for discretion, rather than the screaming headlines that Moore's abrupt actions and melodramatic rhetoric had generated.[103]

As Sproul investigated the UCLA suspensions, he discovered that Moore had not done his political homework. Sproul found that Moore had initiated the suspensions without evidence against those he disciplined. After reviewing the case, Sproul came to see that the major charges against the students were groundless. Sproul reinstated four of the five suspended students on November 14 and announced that

> having spent a week in careful investigation, having interviewed or read statements from everyone who claimed to have the facts, I cannot find any evidence, convincing to me, that the suspended students either directly or indirectly gave their approval to the work of the National Student League . . . traded votes for radical support, or . . . used their student offices "to assist the National Student League to destroy the University," or to destroy the University by handing it over to an organized group of communist students.[104]

Privately Sproul complained that the UCLA cases have "done serious injury to the University, whatever the outcome," and he confided to a friend that Moore had mishandled the entire affair. "How I wish," wrote Sproul, "I had never heard of these cases, or had been in on them from the beginning instead of being dragged in after they had been bungled."[105]

Despite Sproul's private misgivings about Moore's behavior and his dismissal of the major charges against the students, the president did all that he could under the circumstances to support his provost. While announcing the reinstatements, Sproul also stated that the initial decision to suspend the students had been proper because they had been guilty of insubordination: these undergraduates had wrongly defied Moore's orders by continuing to organize on behalf of an open forum at UCLA. Sproul concluded, however, that reinstatement of four of the suspended students was now appropriate because their temporary suspension had been punishment enough for their insubordination.[106] Like Moore, Sproul thought students too immature to be granted the political rights of adults. That is why Sproul, in his statement to the press following the reinstatements, joined Moore in condemning the idea of a student controlled open forum on campus; in addition, Sproul, like his colleagues at CCNY, maintained that it was intolerable for students ever to defy the orders of a University administrator. According to Sproul, "Whatever the merits of the students' position" in calling for an open forum, since they did so against the provost's orders " this is insubordination."[107] To Sproul, then, students lacked the freedom even to call for free speech, particularly if such advocacy contradicted the instructions of University authorities.

President Sproul stressed that he was not rebuking his provost and that he had interceded in the case only at Moore's request. There was, of course, an element of face-saving in Sproul's public statements regarding Moore. As at Columbia in the Reed Harris case, the UC administration seemed unable to acknowledge error even while revoking its previous disciplinary action. And the president wanted to do all that he could to avoid embarrassing a fellow administrator. But Sproul's support of Moore included more than face-saving; his support was also the product of shared ideology and values. Sproul shared Moore's belief that the University should free itself of radicalism and help American society fight communism, but Sproul was simply more perspicacious when it came to chosing methods to fight radicalism. This ideological link left Sproul unwilling to utter publicly a single word criticizing his redbaiting provost's goal of purging campus communists.

That Sproul shared with Moore a disrespect for student free speech rights and an intolerance of student radicalism was most evident in his handling of Celeste Strack's suspension. Strack was the only one of the five suspended students at UCLA who was a self-proclaimed radical and NSL organizer. Had Sproul not been a committed anti-radical, he would have treated Strack precisely as he treated the four non-communists, reinstating them together when he found that the charges against them were groundless. And, in fact, Sproul never had any evidence that Strack, despite her radicalism, was any less innocent of Moore's charges of seeking to destroy the university than were the suspended non-communists. Nonetheless, solely on the basis of her radical affiliations, Sproul divided Strack's case from the four others and refused to reinstate her with them.[108]

The influence of Sproul's anti-radical bias in the Strack case appears explicitly in a private letter he wrote in the midst of the controversy. Here Sproul contended that because Celeste Strack was a radical organizer her

> case is different [from the other four]. Miss Strack is not the *innocent* victim of a mistaken action, but she is a clever person against whom we have a very poor case. I have delayed my decision as to her in the hope that I might find some evidence to support the charge on which she was suspended," persistent and flagrant violation of University regulations in-

cluding the holding of Communist meetings on the campus." I have not found it as yet and Dean Laughlin, whom I have consulted has not been able to find it for me.[109]

Thus although Sproul, after a careful search, still lacked evidence of Strack's guilt, he refused to assume her innocent until proven guilty. Instead, he insisted that because she was radical it was unlikely that she could possibly be innocent. There was obviously a procedural double standard at work here, which held that a week of investigation without incriminating evidence was sufficient to acquit the four non-communists but insufficient to acquit Strack.

It took almost another full month after the reinstatements of the first four students for Sproul to agree to reinstate Strack. Had Strack not threatened to sue the University, moreover, it is likely that she would not have been reinstated at all. Sproul's decision to reinstate Strack came only after an independent counsel hired by the Regents examined all the evidence in the case and informed him that Strack's threatened legal suit could prove troublesome because "there does not exist sufficient proof to sustain the charges and . . . the administration is in no position to defend its action for want of any evidence of any tangible acts which could stand scrutiny in a court of law."[110] Sproul's private correspondence confirms that it was not concern for free speech, but fear of a potentially embarrassing lawsuit which brought about Strack's reinstatement.[111]

The five suspended students were fortunate in that their accuser, Provost Moore had been politically sloppy—making charges he could not support. The students also owed their reinstatement to their own good political sense. None of them had violated University regulations. Strack, herself, though a radical activist, had been careful to comply with the rules by holding her partisan political meetings off campus.

Even the grounds upon which the five were reinstated attest to the UC administration's disrespect for political freedom on campus. Had any of the UCLA students held NSL meetings on campus, used their offices to promote the NSL, formed an alliance with the NSL during the Student Council elections, or violated any UCLA regulations which virtually banned political organizing on campus, their suspensions would undoubtedly have been converted into permanent expulsions. Indeed, the very questions President Sproul asked the suspended students when he began his investigation of the case, suggest that he saw radical activism as a punishable offense on campus. The UC President sounded as if he were conducting a political interrogation and loyalty test, asking four of the suspended students:

> Have your actions on the Council been influenced in any way by N.S.L.? By Miss Strack? . . . Did you announce that you had a mandate to oppose the American Legion, the D.A.R., etc.? From where did it come? . . . Did you ignore Dr. Moore's warning that in backing [a] student con-

trolled open forum you were playing into the hands of the Communists
. . . ? Did you offer a written disavowal of communist or radical connections? . . . Did you talk with N.S.L. members after Council meetings and
give them material for anonymous attacks on the Council and Univ. officials?[112]

When the questioning had ended and Sproul opted for reinstatement, Moore was undoubtedly disappointed. But the reinstatements had
not chastened the UCLA provost. Moore continued his crusade against
campus radicalism—colluding with the police, spying on radicals, and
publicly denouncing the communist threat to education. Summarizing the
provost's activities following the end of the suspensions controversy, a
YMCA official at UCLA informed Sproul that

> we had hoped things would quiet down after the reinstatement of the
> four boys but Dr. Moore seems determined to keep things stirred up.
> One of his spies . . . abetted in the theft of the now famous L.I.D. letter
> [from national LID organizer Monroe Sweetland to Sidney Zsagri, one of
> the reinstated students at UCLA] . . . . Dr. Moore has had photostatic
> copies made of it. His conferences with Chief of Police Davis . . . are
> supposed to relate to an effort to have Mr. Zsagri arrested on a charge
> of criminal syndicalism. . . . The faculty feel more nervous than ever
> because of the general espionage that seems to prevail. An employe[e] of
> the telegraph company let out the fact that copies of telegrams having a
> bearing on University affairs are sent to Dr. Moore.[113]

By mid-November 1934, Moore had even begun moving his anti-radical
campaign to new fronts. The provost lobbied Frank Merriam, California's
newly elected Governor, to take a strong stand against campus radicalism.
Moore implored the Governor

> to prepare and sponsor a bill to make it a punishable offence (say with
> six months' imprisonment or a fine of $500, or both) for any outside
> organization, or the members of such organization outside the schools, to
> interfere with the work of any public school or university in the state of
> California. We must smash this thing or the dry rot it spreads will kill
> us.[114]

But Moore's attempt to legislate an end to radical influence on campus
proved just as ineffective as had his use of spies and suspensions.

Moore's anti-radical offensive backfired politically at UCLA in a manner almost identical to Robinson's offensive at CCNY. In both cases, administration acts of suppression built campus sympathy and support for
the student activists. The UCLA Left counted itself fortunate because
Moore's free speech violations provided it with an issue around which to
establish a broadly based protest movement on campus. The provost's arbitrary disciplinary action raised student concern about campus political

rights to a level that the NSL had never been able to reach in its prior campaign for an open forum. As Celeste Strack recalled, the suspensions

> radicalized the campus as nothing would have. Moore couldn't have done anything more calculated if he'd planned to radicalize that campus . . . . People to this day tell me how it opened their eyes . . . . Thousands of people that may never have noticed about the business of the open forum, or cared about it, cared very much when this thing [the suspensions] happened because it was an assault on the most elementary forms of student democracy. And people get angry in this country over things like that, and the students got upset over it.[115]

In the wake of this free speech controversy, the UCLA Left was able to organize political meetings and anti-war rallies far larger than any it had held prior to the suspensions.

Moore unwittingly contributed not only to the growth of the UCLA Left locally, but also to the rising national prominence of student activists from both UCLA and other West Coast campuses. The successful movement for reinstatement—arguably the most effective student free speech battle yet waged in Depression America—put UCLA and Berkeley on the political map, demonstrating to the eastern centered leadership of the NSL and SLID that a strong student movement was emerging on the West Coast. In the wake of this battle, Celeste Strack was elevated to a national leadership position in the NSL, and West Coast campuses received increasing attention from student movement organizers and publications.[116]

IV

While campus administrators played the most active role in the effort to suppress student radicalism from 1933 to 1935, some anti-radical pressure also came from outside the academic world. The flashiest of these off campus campaigns for the suppression of academic radicalism was waged by the Hearst press. Not confined by the ethics of professional journalism, this rightwing newspaper chain produced a series of sensationalized accounts of communist infiltration of the professoriate. Through distortions and outright fabrications, the Hearst press managed to make liberal professors sound like Bolsheviks and syndicated these wild stories from coast to coast. In one typical Hearst story, a pair of reporters from the *Syracuse Journal* posed as communist students and then visited a liberal Syracuse professor. After trying to coax the professor into making radical statements, the reporters distorted his words and depicted him as a dangerous syndicalist. Hearst reporters pulled this same stunt on professors at Columbia, New York University, and the University of Chicago.[117]

Hearst newspapers also attacked the student movement. Under such screaming headlines as "Communist Plot to Capture American Youth Revealed: Drive Pushed in Colleges," the Hearst press portrayed the antiwar movement as the product of a Moscow-based conspiracy. Among most students, however, these reports had little influence because of the Hearst newspapers' lack of credibility on campus. In fact, such reports and Hearst himself served as a rallying point for the student movement, which used them as a pretext for launching a highly popular campus boycott of Hearst newspapers and movie newsreels. Next to the ROTC, war and Depression, Hearst's redbaiting was the subject of more editorial criticism than any other topic in the college press during the mid-1930s.[118]

Much like the Hearst Press, anti-radical legislators on the warpath against the campus Left made a good deal of noise, but proved remarkably inept at curbing student radicalism. They simply did not understand student activism well enough to formulate realistic repressive actions. Victims of their own anti-intellectualism, these conservatives tended to assume that the evil geniuses behind the student movement were communist professors who propagandized their students. Working from this false assumption, the anti-radicals focused most of their legislative investigations and anti-radical bills against these allegedly subversive professors. They managed to impose new loyalty oaths on teachers in 14 states between 1931 and 1935. But in reality, these oaths—though a serious infringement upon academic freedom, and one which the student movement denounced vehemently—were aimed at people who played only a minor role in the student movement. There were few radical professors on American campuses during the first half of the Depression decade and fewer still who would align themselves with the student Left. Students, not professors, were the major source of radical activism on the American college campuses of the 1930s. This is why even as faculty oath requirements spread, the student movement could continue to grow at an unprecedented rate. Had the campus Left been dependent upon faculty, its activism would have been confined to only the few colleges and universities where radical professors taught, and there would never have been a mass student movement in the 1930s.[119]

For the faculty itself, moreover, during the first half of the Depression decade the greatest threat to political freedom came from intolerant college administrators rather than legislators. These administrators believed it improper and unprofessional for faculty to engage in political activism on campus. They therefore needed no outside pressure to purge radical faculty, but did so on their own initiative. Such administration intolerance resulted in the dismissal of most of those rare faculty members (usually young instructors rather than professors) who cooperated closely with the student movement. In short, the legislative offensive against faculty radicals was misdirected because academia had already done its own purging—leaving potential faculty activists convinced that if they wanted to keep their jobs and avoid falling victim to administration intolerance, they must not become openly involved in radical politics on campus.[120]

The biggest legislative threat to the student movement in the first half of the Depression decade emerged in New York, where conservative state legislators introduced a bill which would have imposed a loyalty oath upon college students. This oath legislation, the Nunan Bill, was an important test of strength for the student movement. The student activist community worked vigorously against the bill, fearing that this legislation would inhibit campus protest in the state where the movement had its strongest following. An NSL and SLID sponsored a delegation of over 500 collegians, led by women students from Vassar College, converged on Albany, lobbying the legislature against the bill. The editors of student newspapers throughout the state launched a coordinated editorial drive denouncing the proposed loyalty oath. Demonstrations demanding the defeat of the Nunan Bill were held in New York City. In the face of this energetic campaign, the Nunan Bill went down to defeat in March 1935, giving the student movement one of its most significant civil liberties victories.[121]

Attempts by anti-radicals to use legislative investigations as a weapon against the campus Left also ended in failure during the mid-1930s. In this period the two most ambitious legislative investigations of this type occurred in Illinois and Wisconsin. After charges of subversion were leveled against the faculty at the University of Chicago and the University of Wisconsin, conservative legislators in these states launched official investigations of professorial radicalism. But the investigations failed to uncover the alleged communist infiltration; they ended without purging a single faculty radical. Long after these investigations were over, the Universities of Chicago and Wisconsin remained among the most active campuses in the student anti-war movement.[122]

Though redbaiting news stories, loyalty oath campaigns, and legislative investigations failed to cause any significant damage to the student movement, they probably provided some assistance to the movement's enemies on campus. It is highly likely that this anti-radical clamor emboldened administrators such as Provost Moore of UCLA, mistakenly assuring them of overwhelming public support for their attempts to repress student radicalism. The presence of legislative anti-radicalism could also provide a convenient justification for administration assaults on the student Left, as college officials reasoned that the autonomy of the University could best be preserved if they preempted any anti-radical legislative action by taking a strong stand against campus radicalism.[123]

This anti-radical impact, however, was diluted substantially by countervailing pressure from advocates of civil liberty both on and off campus. College presidents who launched anti-radical crusades were likely to come under heavy criticism from the ACLU, the AAUP, the Left-liberal press, progressive alumni and faculty, and prominent liberals in Washington— including Eleanor Roosevelt, an influential friend of the student movement and critic of red probes and loyalty oaths.[124] Moreover, the larger political mood in the country was decidedly progressive, a consequence of the steamrolling reformism of the early New Deal years. The University, during the mid-1930s was not besieged by a public fearful of change and radicalism; it stood within a nation which because of the Depression was moving leftward itself and becoming more tolerant of radicalism. There was, therefore, nothing resembling a consensus—like that of the Mc-Carthy era—supporting a purge of campus dissidents. This was a political environment which left anti-radicals without the support they needed for an effective national assault on faculty or student radicalism.[125]

The level of community political tolerance was such that student activists from 1933–1935 often found their free speech rights were safer not on, but off campus. This had been true, for instance, in the free speech fights at CCNY and UCLA. In both cases, student activists, after having their rallies banned from campus, avoided being silenced by simply holding their rallies just beyond the college gates. The photographs of student demonstrations during the first half of the Depression decade attest that this was not unusual. Students facing repressive administrators often rallied adjacent to campus, *on town or city property*. There were of course, exceptions to this rule, in more provincial regions of the South and Midwest, but in most of America, students were able to overcome political intolerance on campus by moving off.[126] For them, free soil and political liberty lay just outside the campus gates, beyond the reach of college officials. In other words, though students sometimes lost their First Amendment rights at the campus entrance, they picked them up again on the way out, and used these rights to build a mass movement.

The phenomenon of city property serving as a sanctuary for student protest indicated that off campus anti-radicals had been even less effective than campus officials in hurting the student movement from 1933–35. The major off campus anti-radical forces, such as the Hearst press and the American Legion, were unable to cause the expulsion or suspension of a single student radical. This was a sorry record indeed when compared with CCNY President Robinson's expulsion of 43 student radicals in 1933–1934, President Rightmire's suspension of 17 Ohio State drill resisters in 1934, President Butler's expulsion of six student anti-war activists in Columbia's medical school in 1935, or President Ruthven's expulsion of four anti-war leaders at the University of Michigan in this same period.[127] Nor could Hearst match the censorship, the banning of meetings and speakers which were routinely initiated against the anti-war movement by administrators throughout the nation from 1933–1935.

Though college administrators may have made Hearst look like an amateur in the art of political repression, ultimately even they were not able to turn back the rising tide of student activism in the early New Deal years. Despite the repressive incidents on dozens of campuses from 1933–1935, the anti-war movement grew at an increasingly rapid pace. The repression could be frightening or annoying, but it was just as often transformed—as at CCNY and UCLA—into an asset for the anti-war movement, enabling the student Left's skillful organizers to make repression an issue and thus gather support from their many classmates who be-lieved in free speech. Moreover, the level of repression was significant, but not massive enough to do any lasting damage, which would have re-quired thousands of expulsions in a coordinated national campaign. This kind of national campaign would have been beyond the pale of college administrators, whose interest in student politics did not usually extend beyond their own campuses and their *in loco parentis* responsibilities.

By 1936 the popularity of the student movement had risen to the point where even many college administrators realized that the old poli-cies of repression and confrontation were futile and counterproductive. With about half of the undergraduate population mobilized and the anti-war movement beginning to draw support and praise from the Roosevelt administration, increasing numbers of college presidents switched to tac-tics of conciliation and cooptation. Where formerly strike rallies had been banned, now they were more likely to be permitted by administrators who tried to dilute their radicalism—renaming them "peace assemblies" and imposing speakers lists which included more moderates and conserva-tives. This attempt by administrators to push anti-war discussion right-ward at times seemed manipulative, and on some campuses evoked re-sentment from student activists. Nonetheless, it represented far more administration-student dialogue than had occurred during the seasons of censorship and repression in the early 1930s. Through its own persistence and political strength, then, the student movement, by 1936, had taken the University a small step closer toward free speech.[128]

Chapter 6

The Popular Front on Campus

Gentlemen,

Until this week I have been an advocate of neutrality, and secretary of your organization. The startling rapidity of developments in Europe in the past few days has forced me to abandon the unrealistic policy of Isolation in favor of a more positive and practical peace program, namely . . . collective security as endorsed by the . . . [American] Student Union . . . . Nazi storm troopers lash Socialist workers in the factories—thousands of Jews flee . . . .—a wave of "suicides" hits the ranks of intellectuals in Vienna—Hitler sends 30,000 troops to Spain . . . .—Does isolation offer any solution to the Fascist aggression which is overwhelming Europe? . . . After thinking over all these factors, I find it necessary to resign from the Harvard Neutrality Council. I leave behind the shallow, impractical, dangerous policy of Isolation.

> Arthur Kinoy, Harvard '41, "An Open Letter to the Harvard
> Neutrality Council," *Harvard Progressive,* March 19, 1938.

The international threat posed by fascism became the central concern of the student movement during the second half of the Depression decade. For this generation of college students not a year passed without some ominous reminder of the rising strength, belligerence, and brutality of European fascism. There was Italy's invasion of Ethiopia in 1935, Hitler's and Mussolini's military support of the Spanish fascist revolt in 1936 and 1937, Germany's anti-Jewish pogrom and conquest of Austria in 1938, and the Nazi invasion of Czechoslavakia and Poland in 1939. These events, along with Japan's escalating war on China, prodded many student activists to rethink the isolationist assumptions their anti-war movement had popularized on campus in the early 1930s. The increasing aggression of the fascist powers led these activists to worry that the very neutrality that their movement had urged upon the United States to promote peace, instead, bred war by preventing America from orchestrating an international effort to thwart fascist expansionism. This mindset facilitated the rise of a major challenge to isolationism within the student movement, which by 1938 pushed the movement's largest organizations to abandon their isolationist policies and embrace collective security.

The first influential group within the student movement's leadership which sought to shift the movement away from isolationism was the communists. These radicals had the earliest and clearest vision of the student movement's need for a more explicitly anti-fascist foreign policy. Their thinking on this matter had been strongly influenced by deliberations of the Seventh World Congress of the Communist International (CI) in August 1935. The CI became concerned about the triumph of Nazism in Germany, its spreading influence in Europe, and the potential threat these developments posed to the U.S.S.R.'s security. The Seventh World Congress therefore urged the formation of broad national coalitions and international collective security arrangements on behalf of a Popular Front against fascism.[1] For communists in the American student movement, this implied the need to turn the movement's foreign policy away from American neutrality and toward the endorsement of collective efforts among the United States, the Soviet Union, and other anti-fascist states to prevent military aggression by Germany, Italy, and Japan.

In favoring this Popular Front position, communist students understood that they were sailing against the wind in the isolationist campus world of 1935. As key architects of the student peace movement, they knew from first hand experience the appeal of neutrality and anti-interventionism to college youth, who feared that their generation would be decimated by war just as the class of 1917 had been. It would not be easy to shake students out of their deeply isolationist mood. That mood had been created by disillusionment with the First World War, a pervasive feeling among students that United States intervention in 1917 had been a tragic blunder, and that any repetition of such interventionism would prove disastrous. The first two anti-war strikes and the Oxford Pledge movement had reinforced this collegiate isolationism, as had the Nye Committee revelations—concerning big business' complicity in pushing America into the First World War—and the victorious isolationist campaign for neutrality legislation on Capitol Hill.

Isolationism would also prove difficult to dislodge on campus because of its dedicated promoters within the student movement's leadership, particularly the socialists, Trotskyists and pacifists. For socialists and Trotskyists, United States neutrality was an ideological imperative, since these radicals believed that any form of interventionism by the government of capitalist America would be inherently imperialistic. They regarded anti-interventionism as a means of curbing United States imperialism. The student movement's absolute pacifists also clung to isolationism, but did so on moral rather than ideological grounds. Opposing all wars as inherently evil, these pacifists sought to avoid any departures from strict neutrality, which, in their eyes, threatened to move America into a war, just as they had in 1917.[2]

The strength of isolationist sentiment on campus prevented communist activists from orchestrating a quick rejection of anti-interventionism by the student movement; it compelled these young radicals to proceed cautiously on the road to collective security. Although communist students in 1935 aired their Popular Front positions, they did not seek to impose all of these upon the student movement overnight—recognizing that such an attempt would have been futile. With the mood on campus so strongly favorable to neutrality, the communists had to make compromises with isolationism, even though such compromises were inconsistent with the Comintern's Popular Front line.

The first such compromise occurred in November 1935, when students responded to Mussolini's invasion of Ethiopia. The communist-led NSL advocated League of Nations sanctions and a United States embargo against fascist Italy, to punish this aggression and help Ethiopia in its defensive war. Socialist students also condemned the invasion, but opposed League of Nations sanctions because they viewed the League as an imperialist tool. The socialists, along with the pacifists, feared that League sanctions and an American embargo against Italy could set a dangerous precedent that might ultimately draw the United States into an overseas war; they therefore urged official United States neutrality and an American embargo of *both* belligerents in the conflict. The socialists and pacifists then organized a national anti-Mussolini protest on campus, based on their rather contorted position of condemning fascist aggression while opposing sanctions designed to stop that aggression.

Though disagreeing with their position on League sanctions and American neutrality, the NSL joined with the socialists and pacifists in this demonstration against the Italian invasion. The NSL chose to be flexible here because its leaders realized that even if they could not agree on the specifics of United States policy regarding Italy, communists, socialists, and pacifists would be serving an important symbolic function in this demonstration by uniting students against Mussolini's aggression. In the isolationist campus world of 1935 such anti-fascist unity seemed a considerable achievement. From the NSL's perspective this demonstration represented the first step in an evolving process: students would now be mobilized against fascist aggression, and later be led to see the logic of collective security measures needed to curb that aggression. Communist willingness to compromise in this anti-Mussolini demonstration was undoubtedly strengthened by the fact that the neutrality policy for the United States advocated by the socialists and pacifists—embargoing both belligerents— would hurt Italy rather than Ethiopia, since only Mussolini's forces had the ability to import war-related goods from the United States.[3]

These responses to the invasion of Ethiopia suggested that the rise of fascist aggression was raising thorny new problems for the student movement. The question of whether to support League sanctions and United States embargoes against fascist aggressors was potentially divisive. Given the stark differences between the communist and socialist-pacifist positions on such questions, however, what was surprising in 1935 was how little discord these differences generated within the student movement. This was in part because the communist-led NSL, as had been clear in the Ethiopia demonstration, initially soft-pedalled the interventionist implications of Popular Frontism and searched for common ground with non-communists in the anti-war movement. Moreover, despite the tactical problems raised by the fascist threat, that threat actually helped to unify the American student movement in 1935 because the entire movement shared a revulsion for fascism. Indeed, the one part of the Popular Front that did have an immediate and wide appeal within the student movement was its stress on the need to unite activists from all sides of the political spectrum in opposing fascism. This general anti-fascist ethos promoted a solidarity among student activists that initially outweighed any disagreement over which specific foreign policies were best suited to thwarting war and fascism.[4]

The attraction of anti-fascist solidarity was particularly strong within the student Left. It was strong not merely because the communists, in line with their Popular Front goals, were bent on promoting unity, but also because non-communists too saw that disunity on the Left was dangerous at a time when fascism was on the rise. This fear of disunity was, as former SLID leader Joseph Lash pointed out, fostered by events in Germany:

> If there was one lesson out of Germany that we read, it was that the failure of the Socialists and Communists to work together against Hitler . . . had opened the way for Hitlerism in the crucial years. So that was an enormous pressure for us to think in terms of the unity of the American student movement.[5]

This type of thinking in 1935 would facilitate the greatest step toward unity ever taken by the student Left in Depression America: the amalgamation of the communist-led NSL and the socialist-led SLID into a single unified organization, the American Student Union.

The idea of amalgamation was not new. The NSL had proposed a merger with the SLID in December 1933 and again the following year.[6] During the early 1930s, the NSL's leadership had been much less prone than adult communist-led organizations to the extreme sectarianism of Third Period Communism. Owing to their youth, most NSLers did not have the bitter memories of communist-socialist feuding which so poisoned relations between their adult counterparts. A degree of comradery was also fostered by student status. As campus organizers NSLers and SLIDers shared common enemies, including repressive campus administrators and undergraduate apathy. These factors and the NSLers' realization that on most of the critical campus issues their positions paralleled those of the SLID, prodded the NSL to make overtures to the SLID concerning amalgamation. This occurred long before the Popular Front arose and brought such coalition politics to the adult CP.[7]

This does not mean, however, that the NSL and SLID loved each other in the early 1930s. The two organizations squabbled more than occasionally. The NSL's communist leaders tended to regard themselves as more genuinely revolutionary than the SLID, since they prided themselves on being affiliated with the one nation in which a proletarian revolution had occurred. The SLID's socialist leaders regarded themselves as more genuinely democratic than the NSL, because of their links to the electorally-minded Socialist Party; they were uncomfortable with the NSL's uncritical view of Stalin's dictatorship. Their different party affiliations and competition for members bred some friction, and left the SLID initially suspicious of the NSL's motives for proposing amalgamation. So in 1933 and 1934 the SLID leadership had turned down those proposals. But the SLID did agree to cooperate with the NSL wherever possible, and the two organizations in 1934–35 worked together on a series of increasingly large and successful campaigns on issues ranging from peace to student aid. The unprecedented size of the April 1935 anti-war strike made it evident that the closer their cooperation, the more effective the NSL and SLID could be in building the student movement. Such success eroded the mistrust between the two organizations, and this, along with the rising demand for anti-fascist unity, would help break the SLID leadership's resistance to amalgamation.[8]

Within the SLID, pressure for amalgamation came from the bottom up. SLID campus chapters functioned in a political environment more conducive to amalgamation than did the organization's national office in New York. SLID national officers had been influenced by the SLID's parent organization, the adult LID. These older leaders were wary of a merger with the communist-led NSL because the vicious attacks on them by the Communist Party during the 1920s and early 1930s had left them strongly anti-communist. But in SLID chapters outside New York's hothouse political atmosphere, few SLID activists had experienced such bitter feuding; most saw the compelling logic of merging with the NSL, since they were already cooperating with the League on most of their major political actions. The movement for amalgamation was particularly strong in the SLID's West Coast chapters, which, under the leadership of Berkeley SLID President Richard Criley, worked to push the organization's recalcitrant national leaders towards a merger with the NSL.[9]

Criley and his SLID comrades on the West Coast had become especially receptive to both amalgamation and anti-fascist unity because of the upsurge of political repression in their region. The Right had responded hysterically in 1934 to the upsurge of labor militancy on the West Coast's waterfront, the general strike in San Francisco, and Upton Sinclair's EPIC campaign. Redbaiting by the press and attacks on civil liberties by police and vigilantes were on the rise. Amidst such hysteria, western student activists had no way of knowing that this local red scare would prove short-lived; they feared that it might spread, and herald the advent of a home-grown fascist movement in the United States, much as Sinclair Lewis had predicted in *It Can't Happen Here* (1935). With his vision colored by anxieties concerning the rising strength of fascism in Europe, Criley viewed the arrests and harassment of West Coast radical organizers after the San Francisco general strike as a sign that California was "sliding into fascism very fast." Criley recalled that in the face of this "fascist" threat "it seemed to us—and I think this was true of both the National Student League members and the SLID members—that it was just insanity not to join the strength of the radical students who were the spearhead of the struggle for rights on campus."[10] Consequently, Criley worked first at Berkeley and then across the West Coast to promote a merger of the NSL and SLID.

By June 1935 the SLID's national leadership found it impossible to ignore this grass roots movement for amalgamation. That month the SLID's national executive committee met for three days to consider the question of amalgamation. Here the committee heard field reports attesting to the support of SLID chapters for a merger with the NSL. The committee learned that this support was so strong out West that the California chapters—under Criley's leadership—were planning a statewide amalgamation convention for the fall. There was clearly concern that unless the SLID national office moved toward amalgamation, a split with the West Coast chapters might occur. The committee also heard survey results of the new recruits at the SLID's summer school for student organizers, which revealed 100 percent favoring "future amalgamation."[11] All of this impressed Executive Secretary Joseph Lash, who recalled that though he and some of the other national officers had initially been "determined not to unite with the Communists, we found the pressure from our chapters, pressure within ourselves [for anti-fascist unity] was such that we felt we ought to give it a whirl."[12] The SLID national executive board agreed to establish a joint committee with its counterpart in the NSL to negotiate the terms for a merger. The negotiations went well, and in October 1935 the executive boards of both organizations recommended that their membership approve amalgamation into a new organization, the American Student Union (ASU), whose founding convention was scheduled for the coming Christmas break.[13]

Proponents of amalgamation in the NSL and SLID envisioned more, however, than simply a merger of their two organizations; they wanted the ASU to become a union of all progressive, anti-fascist students. The goal here was to overcome the key political weakness of both the NSL and SLID: their inability to become mass membership organizations. Although the NSL and SLID had mobilized an unprecedented 175,000 students in the 1935 peace strike, they were unable to convince even a substantial percentage of these demonstrators to join their organizations.

Indeed, at the time of the ASU's founding convention, the combined membership of the NSL and SLID was only about 5000.[14] The problem seemed to be that most students saw the NSL and SLID as campus appendages of the Communist and Socialist Parties and—despite NSL and SLID claims to the contrary—thought they had "to accept the whole of a revolutionary path when they signed membership cards."[15] These perceptions had apparently kept liberal students from joining the NSL and SLID, even though they would participate in demonstrations led by the two organizations. NSLers and SLIDers hoped that the ASU would prove more attractive to these students, since it was an amalgamated organization not tied to one radical party and was a self-proclaimed union of all campus progressives. With this in mind, the NSL and SLID invited students unaffiliated with either organization to join them in Columbus, Ohio as participants in the founding convention of the American Student Union.[16]

As the convention organizers prepared for the Columbus meeting, their first problem was securing a hall. Ohio State University had agreed to house the convention. But after the Hearst press redbaited the ASU's leftist sponsors, the Ohio State administration reneged on the agreement just a week before the convention. The administration claimed it lacked funds to light and heat the buildings for the convention, a shallow excuse exposed when the university refused the students' offers to pay these expenses. The convention site was then moved to the Columbus YWCA. This elicited complaints from the local American Legion, which tried to pressure the YWCA into cancelling. Because of this pressure, the convention delegates were uncertain, even after they arrived in Columbus, whether they were going to be evicted from their meeting hall. But the YWCA board, after convening a special session, confirmed that the students could use their hall.[17]

More than 400 delegates braved one of the worst snow storms of the year to attend the convention. Of these delegates 141 were NSLers, 116 LIDers, and the remaining 170 unaffiliated with either organization. These delegates represented 76 colleges and universities, 37 high schools, and 22 student councils. The delegates claimed to represent between 150,000 and 200,000 students. With the exception of the deep South, from which there were only a few delegates, every region of the country was well represented in what promised to be one of the most important student political meetings of the decade.[18]

Before the main ASU session could convene, however, the delegations of its two main constituent groups, the NSL and SLID, had to vote their final approval of the merger. The NSL delegation did so immediately after arriving in Columbus on December 28th. The SLID delegates met on the following day, but despite the SLID executive committee's prior approval of amalgamation, vocal opposition remained. Monroe Sweetland, a law student and one of the SLID's oldest national leaders, led the opposition to amalgamation. Sweetland feared that the merger would undermine the student movement's anti-war work because in contrast to the SLID, which remained opposed to United States entry into any war, the NSL was, in his view "prepared to support 'progressive' or 'anti-fascist' war." [19]

The SLID debate was long; it extended past the hour when the ASU session was supposed to convene on December 29. According to SLID delegate Nancy Bedford Jones, during the latter stages of this debate "the two hundred-odd unaffiliated students were clamoring in the halls, getting up committees to nag our leaders [to approve amalgamation] and getting more and more impatient with the delay." While the SLIDers continued to meet in closed session, the NSL delegation killed time and gave "the unaffiliated students something to sit-in on," by staying in session though it "had long since finished its business." Finally at 4 p.m. the SLID took a roll call vote. Despite the lengthy debate, the final SLID vote, reflecting chapter sentiment, went heavily in favor of amalgamation, 92 to 9, with 8 abstentions. When news of the vote reached the NSL session, which had been meeting upstairs, "for two minutes there was pandemonium, with the NSLers applauding, shouting hysterically, embracing each other." [20] All of the delegates proceeded immediately to meet in the first full session of the ASU, which lasted well into the night.

The main order of business at this meeting was the establishment of a platform for the ASU. Although the socialists and communists had been political rivals in the past, and though both were more radical than the unaffiliated liberal delegates, most of the platform discussion proceeded smoothly.[21] This was because almost all of the delegates were seeking common ground for their new organization. On most issues, moreover, agreement was easy because the students had cooperated in their prior campus activism.

The major planks of the ASU platform on domestic issues essentially codified the egalitarian demands that the student movement had championed since the early 1930s. The ASU plank on the "Right to Education and Security" demanded equal educational opportunity and economic security for all young Americans and urged social legislation to ensure that low income youth were not denied these "reasonable human rights"; it declared that "a society which cannot find places for its young people, except in work camps and on battlefields stands condemned." Carrying on the NSL's and SLID's strong commitment to racial equality, the ASU included in its platform a plank on "The Student and Minority Races," which began by citing "the evidences of racial discrimination which are alarmingly apparent in our educational institutions." The platform condemned the use of racial quotas to deny college admission to many Jewish and black students : "The ASU stands against . . . intolerance, Jim Crowism and segregation, whether these apply to Negro, Jewish, Chinese, Indian and other minority groups." The platform also reaffirmed the student movement's support for both the labor movement and the right of students and teachers to free political expression.[22]

Since the ASU was seeking to appeal to mainstream students, it avoided explicitly Marxist rhetoric in its platform. The document criticized the capitalists' greed and abuse of power, but did not condemn the capitalist system itself. Rather than speak in Marxist terms about class warfare between the workers and the bourgeoisie, the ASU platform used terms that, though more fuzzy, were indigenous to the American progressive tradition: describing a clash in the United States between "big business," "Tories," or the "inner oligarchy of high finance, industry and politics" and "the people." "A wide gulf separates this inner oligarchy . . . from the people. The latter wants peace; it foments war. The latter wants freedom; it inspires repression. The people demand jobs and social security, which the Tories block in order to secure their dividends and their rule."[23] Such language was not far from the iconoclastic liberal rhetoric used by FDR himself during the Second New Deal, and was clearly employed by the ASU with the liberal student in mind. The use of the term "Tories" to describe propertied conservatives also reflected the influence of the new Popular Front style of rhetoric of the Communist Party, in which the CP invoked patriotic themes—such as "Communism is Twentieth Century Americanism"—attempting to legitimate itself by laying claim to America's revolutionary heritage. This emphasis was also evident in the preamble to the ASU's platform, which declared that students had chosen to establish the ASU "because they, like their forefathers, are devoted to freedom and equality."[24]

Contrasting with the easy consensus on domestic issues, the discussion of foreign policy was tense and turbulent. This tension centered around the Oxford Pledge and the question of United States neutrality. Ever since the Seventh World Congress, socialist students had been skeptical over whether the communist-led NSL was still committed to the original anti-interventionist principles of the anti-war movement; they feared that NSLers would abandon those principles and support United States intervention in overseas war in the name of the Popular Front against fascism. Such fears had been fueled by the NSL's support of sanctions against Italy following the invasion of Ethiopia.[25]

SLID national leaders had become so concerned about this apparent NSL shift that in the month prior to the ASU convention they sent several letters quizzing NSL executive secretary Serril Gerber about his organization's stance regarding the Oxford Pledge. The first of these letters had asked whether the NSL still endorsed the Pledge "never to support the government of the United States in any war it may conduct." Gerber responded by reaffirming the NSL's support of the pledge; he explained that "We can conceive of no situation in which the government of the United States shall pursue other than imperialist [war] aims." Even this, however, had not stilled the doubts of the SLID leadership, which wrote back to Gerber, asking "would the NSL support a war against Japan conducted by the United States government in alliance with the Soviet Union?" Gerber again assured the SLID that the NSL would oppose war by the United States government "in all cases." Gerber's response was deemed sufficient by most of the SLID leadership.[26] But a vocal minority within the SLID remained unconvinced, and at Columbus they raised their doubts in a divisive fashion during the session devoted to establishing the ASU's peace plank.

The issue of the NSLers' attitude toward war was broached at this ASU session by socialist Hal Draper in almost precisely the same manner in which it had been raised in the SLID's letters to Gerber. Draper introduced a resolution pledging the ASU to oppose the United States government in its waging of wars in three different hypothetical international conflicts, including a war in which America allied itself with the Soviet Union. The Draper resolution brought to the surface the genuine difference which was already brewing between the pacifist/socialist bloc, which favored American neutrality and the communist/Popular Front liberal bloc, which leaned toward abandoning such neutrality. In this sense Draper's resolution represented a principled anti-war position. Such a position was, of course, consistent with the student movement's anti-interventionist tradition, which had aligned the movement with leading congressional isolationists.[27]

In introducing his resolution, Draper, a dogmatic socialist (en route to becoming an equally dogmatic Trotskyist), also had sectarian motivations. Draper had opposed the ASU's formation and had raised the war issue during the SLID caucus' debate to justify his stance against amalgamation. After losing this debate, when the SLID endorsed the merger with the NSL, he then carried the war issue into the ASU with his provocative resolutions. In effect, Draper, having failed to prevent the founding of the ASU, seized upon the war issue as a way of dividing the new organization. The resolution seemed particularly gratuitous in light of the fact that the ASU, including most of the delegates from the NSL, had already endorsed the Oxford Pledge, which specified non-support for the United States government in *any* war it might undertake. Indeed, in agreeing to continue supporting the Oxford Pledge the NSLers had already made a concession because the neutralist implication of the Pledge was at odds with their anti-fascism. Ignoring all this, Draper, who well understood the communists' devotion to the Soviet Union, was seeking to embarrass them by challenging them to take a public position distancing themselves from the U.S.S.R.[28]

The unaffiliated delegates held the swing vote in the ASU's consideration of the Draper resolution. Some of them opposed the resolution because it seemed awkward and abstract to discuss hypothetical war scenarios in the organization's platform; they also thought it unnecessary to include statements about any particular war since the platform already enunciated the general anti-war position of the Oxford Pledge. Other unaffiliated delegates opposed the resolution because they were beginning to question the strict neutrality position advocated by Draper, and were gravitating toward collective security. Their votes, along with the communists', defeated Draper's resolution. But the final vote was close, 193–

155, suggesting just how divisive the question of United States neutrality could be.[29] Indeed, the debate over the Draper resolution anticipated later conflicts in the ASU over the merits of both the Oxford Pledge and whether United States neutrality or collective security offered the most realistic solution to the growing international crisis.

The controversy over the Draper resolution was not the only indication in Columbus of the potential that communist-socialist tensions had to divide the ASU. The selection process for the new organization's leadership also evoked such tension. That process had been arrived at in October during the amalgamation negotiations between the NSL and SLID. The two organizations, in a kind of pre-nuptial agreement for their political marriage, had decided that the ASU's first national executive committee should include 11 SLIDers, 9 NSLers, and 10 students that had not been affiliated with either the NSL or SLID. It was agreed that the SLID and NSL representatives should be chosen in advance by their respective organizations. But in Columbus, after learning that the SLID had nominated Draper, the communists initially rebelled against his candidacy, since he had opposed amalgamation and played so divisive a role at the convention. The SLID delegates however, insisted that the NSLers live up to their agreement, and so the NSL delegates reluctantly dropped their opposition to Draper.[30]

With ASU leadership parcelled off in this prearranged manner among socialists, communists, and unaffiliated students, there was clearly a danger that the new organization would be polarized internally. Instead of becoming a true union of all progressive students, the ASU could erode into a battleground for competing blocs of communist and socialist members. At first glance the potential for this type of conflict might not seem strong, since the NSL and SLID leadership had agreed to disband these organizations as they merged to form the ASU. But in dissolving the NSL and SLID, the communist and socialist students had only given up their front groups, not the official party youth sections to which they belonged: the Young Communist League (YCL) and Young People's Socialist League (YPSL). These party organizations had both the power and the potential to factionalize the ASU. Indeed, through much of the ASU's life the communists and socialists who dominated its leadership would face a critical choice of priorities: Were their primary obligations to the ASU and promoting the growth of the student movement? Or, should the interests of the ASU and the student movement be subordinated to those of the Party youth organizations to which they belonged?

Fortunately for the ASU, during the critical early days of the organization, most of its national leaders were interested in mitigating socialist-communist factionalism, promoting unity within the ASU and building the student movement. Despite the tensions at the NSL-SLID wedding ceremony at Columbus, both partners came away in an upbeat mood and anxious for the ASU to enjoy a political honeymoon. This mood derived from the strong sense of pride that both NSL and SLID veterans took in their political achievement at Columbus; they had managed to overcome their differences and merge their organizations, a degree of unity which—notwithstanding the Draper controversy—far transcended anything achieved by the adult Left. At at time when the rise of fascism made unity on the Left seem imperative, these young radicals felt that they had risen to the occasion and avoided the tragic flaw of sectarianism that had left German radicals too divided to prevent Hitler's ascent. With this in mind, most of the ASU's socialist and communist activists came away from Columbus believing that the creation of this union of progressive students was, as James Wechsler put it, "a great landmark in leftwing political life. For that fleeting moment we really seemed to be making radical history."[31]

Most of the ASU's socialist and communist founders came away from Columbus delighted with their success in relating to liberal delegates. Since the ASU had been established by the Left in part to court liberal students, most socialist and communist delegates worked to establish a good relationship with them at the convention. In Columbus, socialists and communists had included liberals in writing the ASU platform and had persuaded ten of these unaffiliated students to serve on the ASU executive board. This spirit of cooperation between liberals and leftists was so strong that socialist delegate Nancy Bedford Jones boasted about it in the ASU convention report she sent to her comrades back in UCLA. Jones contrasted this cooperative atmosphere at Columbus with the southern

> California atmosphere, where the liberal abhors the radical. You all know it: The attitude that any matter, regardless of its own merit is undesirable because it comes from a radical. At the convention not a single vestige of this attitude existed. Liberals like Roger Chase of Columbia or Bruce Bliven of Harvard shared leadership with the known radicals, alternated chairmanship, worked harmoniously on committees together, felt and made it evident that this convention, this new-born organization was *theirs,* just as much as it was the LIDers and NSLers.[32]

Although liberal-leftist cooperation at the convention was impressive, the power relationship between these two groups was not nearly so equitable as Jones implied in her report. While liberals did chair convention sessions, serve on the ASU's executive board, and write platform planks, when it came to where the real power lay—the salaried national staff positions—the Left was firmly in the saddle. Not one of the six ASU staff positions was given to a liberal. Instead, these positions were divided equally between alumni of the socialist-led SLID and the communist-led NSL. This gave the Left disproportionate power within the ASU relative to the composition of both the convention, one third of whose delegates were liberals, and the national student body, in which liberals far outnumbered radicals. The liberals at the convention did not object to this situation, apparently because they thought that since the NSL and SLID were the two largest membership organizations responsible for creating the ASU, it was reasonable that their leaders should occupy the new organization's key offices. But even if it was not controversial, this Left monopoly of the officer positions attested to a certain shallowness among NSL and SLID veterans on the question of internal democracy. These leftists were seeking common ground with liberals, but not genuine power sharing—and later this would hurt the ASU because liberals would lack the power to stop the organization's radical officers from making major political mistakes.

The harm that this leftist monopoly on the ASU's paid leadership positions would do to the student movement was not, however, immediately apparent. This was due in part to the high caliber of the individuals elected to these positions in Columbus. Indeed, if one had to select only radicals for national leadership in the movement, the six activists chosen were probably the best possible candidates. They were all talented and experienced campus organizers. From the NSL came James Wechsler, ASU Director of Communications, whose primary responsibility would be editing the ASU's national magazine, the *Student Advocate*. He was a skillful writer and polemicist, who had served as editor-in-chief of Columbia University's student newspaper. Wechsler, an editor in the iconoclastic tradition of Reed Harris, made the ASU magazine the most lively and popular national student publication in Depression America. His talents would later carry him to the staff of the *Nation* and earn him the editorship of a major New York daily. Celeste Strack, ASU High School chair, was another former NSLer. A national debating champion, Strack had been the heroine of the UCLA free speech fight of 1934. Having organized amidst a conservative political environment in southern California, she was well suited for building the student movement in the even more inhospitable secondary school environment—where intolerant school principals tended to be even more repressive and paternalistic than their college counterparts.[33]

The other former NSLer among the ASU's first slate of officers was Serril Gerber, who served as ASU Field Organizer. Along with Strack, Gerber was a veteran of the Los Angeles area student movement. He was well qualified for the Field Organizer position because he had done extensive chapter building for the NSL while Executive Secretary of that organization. Gerber had also proven his political skill in organizing the second convention of the American Youth Congress, in summer 1935, which had been one of the largest national meetings ever held by student activists.[34]

The SLID veterans who served on this first slate of ASU national officers were every bit as impressive as their comrades from the NSL. The most politically experienced among them was ASU Executive Secretary Joseph P. Lash. As Executive Secretary of the SLID, Lash had played a key role in establishing the anti-war movement; it was Lash who had come up with the idea for a national student strike against war, which turned out to be the most effective protest tactic yet used by student organizers.

Lash had extensive editorial experience, producing the SLID's national magazine. He would become the ASU's most prolific author, associate editor of its *Student Advocate* and one of the movement's most effective pamphleteers—later in life his writing skills would win him a Pulitzer Prize.[35]

ASU National Chairman George Edwards was another talented SLID veteran. He had spearheaded one of the student movement's few successful southern campaigns, organizing an impressive anti-war strike at his undergraduate institution, Southern Methodist University. Edwards then served as an effective Field Organizer for the SLID, and became a leader of the student movement at Harvard during his graduate career there. And shortly after his tenure in the ASU, Edwards demonstrated that he could lead workers as well as students, becoming a prominent organizer in the United Auto Workers union, a role which would pave the way for his election to public office in Detroit and then to a federal judgeship.[36]

ASU Treasurer Molly Yard had also been an effective campus activist and national high school organizer for the SLID. As a Swarthmore undergraduate, Yard had led the campaign against racial discrimination in the college's Greek houses, which had culminated in the abolition of sororities on that campus. Decades later Yard would go on to become the most prominent social activist of all the ASU officers, emerging as a feminist leader and head of the National Organization for Women.[37]

With this talented leadership in place, the ASU quickly made its presence felt on campus. James Wechsler and Joseph Lash put together the first issue of the ASU national magazine, the *Student Advocate,* published in February 1936. The issue generated considerable excitement among students, selling out the full press run of 15,000, and going into a second printing. Wechsler and Lash struck an iconoclastic tone in the magazine, criticizing such traditional campus institutions as intercollegiate football, and exposing attempts at political suppression in both colleges and secondary schools. The magazine gave its biggest play, however, to the anti-war themes which had been central to the student movement; its main editorial, "American Storm Troops," offered a scathing indictment of the ROTC, and its lead story "Morgan: Wanted For Murder," featured an interview with isolationist Senator Gerald Nye, condemning big business for promoting war.[38]

Through the Wechsler-Lash editorship of the *Student Advocate* and Lash's supervision of the ASU's national office and chapter correspondence, they did more than any other officers in setting the tone of the new organization. This was particularly fortunate for the ASU because Lash, a socialist, and Wechsler, a communist, were both relatively independent-minded student leaders whose common interest in building the ASU and anti-fascist unity initially outweighed their different party loyalties. They came into the ASU determined to give higher priority to strengthening the student movement than to serving the narrow organizational interests of the YCL or YPSL. "Both of us," Lash observed, "felt that a mass student movement committed to a general militant program

. . . was more important than ideological purity."[39] Of his solidarity with Lash, Wechsler wrote in his memoirs that:

> The communists had stationed me in the ASU on the assumption that I would zealously carry on the communist line there. But I soon found myself far more interested in promoting the Popular Front idea than in performing factional communist assignments. I was sure Joe Lash and I could prove something to the world by working together harmoniously. He felt the same way about it.[40]

Wechsler's devotion to promoting a non-sectarian alliance against the Right went so far that in 1935 it led him into some trouble with the Young Communist League. The manuscript of Wechsler's forthcoming book on the student movement, *Revolt on the Campus* contained a two-page attack on the Hearst press for redbaiting Sidney Hook, a radical professor at New York University. This upset the YCL because Hook was an outspoken anti-Stalinist, who, according to the Communist Party, was a "Trotskyite agent of fascism." But though himself a YCL member, the free thinking Wechsler saw nothing wrong with defending Hook, and had in his own words "cavalierly forgot to submit a copy of the original manuscript" to Communist Party officials before bringing the book to the publisher. This led to criticism by YCL and CP leaders, "accompanied by clear admonitions not to go around publishing any more works without advance consultation on the highest level." The book went to press as written.[41]

Lash would prove as willing to stand up to his doctrinaire socialist comrades in the YPSL as Wechsler had been to defy communist sectarianism in the YCL. Lash's troubles with the YPSL began shortly before the the 1936 student strike against war. The conflict centered around an article YPSL leader Hal Draper published in the Socialist Party press attacking the ASU's approach toward this anti-war event. Draper accused communists in the student movement of "sapping the militancy of the ASU" by "*kowtowing*" to the sensibilities of "middle-class liberals." He charged that because communist ASUers were so intent on promoting anti-fascist unity with liberals—in accord with the Popular Front line of the Comintern—they were opportunistically abandoning any tactics which might seem too radical for liberals, including tactics that had been endorsed in the ASU's platform.[42]

As a case in point, Draper cited communist willingness to dilute the two most radical tactics used by student peace activists: the anti-war strike and the Oxford Pledge. Draper blamed the communists for the fact that at some campuses and high schools, students had agreed to substitute moderate peace assemblies (at which no classes were boycotted) for the more militant tactic of boycotting classes in the 1936 student strike against war. He also blamed the communists for the decision of high school ASUers to drop the controversial Oxford Pledge in their anti-war organizing. The communists' support of this dimunition of the student movement's militancy, in Draper's eyes, manifested the bad faith with which they had endorsed the ASU platform in the first place. Draper charged that the communists had approved the Oxford Pledge at the Columbus convention only because they had to in order to convince the SLID to merge with the NSL; the communists in actuality opposed the pledge because its anti-interventionist message was incompatible with the Popular Front and collective security. So their approach to the pledge, according to Draper, was "to leave it on paper as much as possible." Draper therefore characterized the ASU as "programmatically speaking, a 'shot-gun' wedding," between the genuinely anti-war socialists and the increasingly interventionist and pro-war communists.[43]

Indignant that Draper, an ASU national executive committee member, had issued this public attack on the ASU only a few months after the birth of the organization, Lash took to the pages of the Socialist Party press to rebut him. Lash insisted that the ASU had not lost its militancy. He accused Draper of being inflexible in his approach to student organizing, and thinking dogmatically rather than strategically: Draper had closed his eyes to the obvious fact that imposing radical tactics on students in the high school political environment would undermine the anti-war movement there. "The ASU," Lash explained,

> is weak in the high schools. Past experience with the SLID and NSL has shown that a weak high school chapter cannot by itself build the anti-war strike—that on the contrary, by calling a strike a weak chapter isolates itself from the student body and exposes to expulsion the most militant members in that chapter.[44]

According to Lash, then, it was this unfavorable political environment, not any change in the ASU outlook toward the Oxford Pledge, that had led the ASU to drop the pledge from its high school program.

Lash objected to Draper's hostile attitude toward communists in the ASU. He charged that Draper had been unfair in implying that communist ASUers had been insincere about the Oxford Pledge. Lash pointed out that the idea of removing the pledge from the high school program was "originally made" not by communists, as Draper had intimated, but "by socialists, and has the support of many leading Yipsels [YPSLs]. Draper's disagreement with them does not make them YCLers. And certainly it does not prove that the YCL is sapping the militancy of the ASU." As a YPSL member himself, Lash warned that if this organization was to play a constructive role in building the ASU and the student movement, it must not emulate Draper's divisive attacks on communist ASUers. He depicted the Draper article as representative of

> a dangerous tendency in some quarters to ignore the general needs of the student body and emphasize our differences with the YCL. Some of

us [YPSLs] seem to regard the ASU primarily as an enlarged forum for this purpose. The basis of a campaign against YCL theoretical errors becomes not a healthy one of hammering out a common approach, but of scoring debating points and winning the other fellow's following. If such becomes our primary purpose in the ASU, this splendid coalition of socialists, communists and liberals, which has swept the campus by storm will be rent asunder. One must believe that the program of the ASU will lead to actions that will dictate a common approach and solution to all the elements in the ASU.[45]

Lash's non-sectarian approach to student organizing was too unorthodox for the national YPSL leadership. Ben Fischer, YPSL national secretary, strongly criticized Lash's rebuttal to Draper. Fischer pronounced Lash "entirely incorrect" in emphasizing that

YPSL criticism of the YCL has as its purpose the hammering out of a common approach [to student organizing] . . . . The differences between the YCL and YPSL today are of a basic nature and the YPSL cannot and will not submerge these differences or soft-pedal them in the interests of a "common approach."

The YPSL secretary felt that the type of unity Lash was advocating would not be possible until the YCL dropped its Popular Front "line of support of imperialist war." Fischer objected to Lash's priorities: his notion that the goal of building a united student movement was more important than the interests of the YPSL. For socialist students, "the central task," according to Fischer, "is the organization of students into the YPSL and the extension of the influence of the YPSL, organizationally and ideologically, among the students."[46] The implications of Fischer's strategy were strongly sectarian; for if recruiting students to YPSL was, as he claimed, the raison d'être for socialist student activists, then the differences between the YPSL and the YCL would have to be stressed. Otherwise it would not be possible to ensure that radicalized students were recruited into the socialist youth group instead of its communist competitor.

In this conflict with Draper and Fischer, Lash's non-sectarian position and willingness to defend the ASU showed that he was deeply committed, both politically and personally, to the new organization. Though still a YPSL member, Lash believed that socialists could be most effective in prodding the student body leftward if they stopped squabbling with the communists and focused on building a mass student movement championing peace and egalitarian social change. But Lash had become more than a socialist functionary; he took his new office and responsibilities as ASU executive secretary seriously, and thought that this obligated him to serve the broader interests of the student movement. As a founder of the ASU who had also spent several years leading the growing SLID, Lash felt he understood the interests of the student movement better than YPSL leaders like Fischer, who had never proven themselves effective campus organizers. Lash resented being told what to do by a YPSL hierarchy he regarded as politically inept and dogmatic, especially since their directives seemed both sectarian and ill suited to the task of strengthening the student movement.[47]

The significance of the dispute between these YPSL leaders and Lash lay as much in where it occurred as why it occurred. Both sides published their polemics not in the pages of the ASU's national magazine or any other ASU publication, but rather in the Socialist Party press. This might seem logical enough, since the debate was between socialists. Yet, it is striking that the ASU's publications did not even mention this dispute between the organization's executive secretary and two of the leading socialist youth leaders in the nation. This was not some aberration, but was part of a broader pattern, in which the ASU leadership sought to keep the doctrinal and tactical disputes as well as the sectarian conflicts of the Left out of the organization's publications and proceedings. The ASU leadership adopted this strategy in the hope of building a non-sectarian student movement that could attract liberals as well as radicals.[48]

As an organizing strategy this approach had considerable merit because it fostered student unity. But it also bred a style of ASU political organizing and political journalism that was less than honest in a way that typified the Popular Front. "Front" is indeed the operative word here because that was what the ASU and its magazine were offering: a facade of independent Left-liberalism from an organization whose leaders were never entirely independent of the Commumist Party, the Socialist Party and their official youth affiliates. Of course Lash, Wechsler, and the other more imaginative ASU leaders were striving to achieve a great degree of independence, but in so doing they had to battle with the radical party organizations, whose nominations had put them in office in the first place. Yet neither these struggles nor most of the conflicts within or between the YPSL and the YCL were dealt with openly in the ASU's publications or public proceedings. The ASU's convention reports said nothing about the negotiations and political horsetrading between the YPSL and YCL that helped to determine who would occupy the pivotal leadership positions on the ASU national committees and staff. The story of how power was really wielded within the ASU, then, was not one deemed fit for public consumption. The sanitized pages of the *Student Advocate* suggest that not even its talented editors, Wechsler and Lash, who rejected so much of the narrowness of the YPSL and YCL, could escape this duplicitous feature of the Old Left political style.[49]

The same lack of candor evident in the ASU's national magazine appeared at the campus level as well. Students unaffiliated with the YCL or YPSL were so often left in the dark about the conflicts and compromises between those two organizations that leftist students often referred to them as "innocents." On some campuses—especially in conservative regions—the submerging of Left conflicts and affiliations went so far that radical students were actually concealing their party membership from their fellow activists. At the University of Kentucky, for instance, YPSL organizer Joe Freeland reported that "the Communists are at present the dominant group in the [ASU] chapter . . . . They work absolutely under cover . . . and I am convinced that not more than two or three of the unaffiliated members of the ASU know that they are Communists." Similarly, Wechsler, in looking back upon *Revolt on the Campus,* (1935), the lengthy account of the student movement he had penned while a leader in that movement, noted that the "book is most disingenuous in its failure to identify" his "political commitments" as a YCL member. Nowhere in his otherwise illuminating narrative of over 450 pages had Wechsler even acknowledged that "most of those in the forefront of the . . . [student movement] were either YCL members or enrolled in the Young People's Socialist League."[50]

Although this lack of candor may be questioned on moral grounds, there is no arguing with the political effectiveness of the ASU, and its strategy of downplaying leftist doctrinal disputes. The ASU would prove more successful than any previous student organization in finding common ground for radical and liberal activists on campus. The results of the 1936 student strike against war suggested just how much potential this unified approach toward student organizing had for building the student movement. The strike represented the largest national mobilization of students in American history. Some 500,000 students, almost half the national undergraduate population, participated in the event, rallying against both war and compulsory ROTC.[51]

The 1936 strike day began with anti-war speeches by Joseph Lash and columnist Drew Pearson, broadcast over a national radio hook up. Lash urged students to support the strike and recognize that "the highest service to one's country today is to prevent it from going to war." Pearson praised the student strike as "a healthy and disillusioning protective" against war. Among the new endorsers of the strike was Albert Einstein, who issued a statement of support to student anti-war demonstrators at Princeton, terming it "the duty of enlightened youth to combat the politics of national egotism." Noting the strength of student anti-war sentiment, administrators on many campuses shifted away from their previous opposition to the strike; they either tolerated the demonstration or tried to dilute its radicalism by scheduling university-run peace assemblies. In some cases, classes were even called off to allow for strike participation. This occurred at Cornell University, for example, making it possible for more than 2000 students to join the anti-war protest. Even critics of the student movement were impressed by the size of the strike. Thus *Time* magazine quipped that the student anti-war strike was "turning into a full sized and characteristically noisy national institution, like Halloween."[52]

The 1936 strike was not only larger, but more colorful than the previous anti-war walkouts. Locals of a recently formed student organization, Veterans of Future Wars (VFW) added a touch of ironic humor to the strike. VFW chapters lampooned war and the military. Tongue in cheek, they had demanded that the government pay them a bonus now for military service before they were drafted and killed on the battlefield. Probably the largest ASU-sponsored demonstration integrating the VFW's political theatrics into strike day events occurred on Morningside Heights. A crowd of some 5000 line up along Broadway and 120th street to watch an anti-war parade of Columbia and Barnard students. Carrying signs which said "Spend your bonus here, not in the hereafter," two hundred members of the "William Randolph Hearst Post No. 1, Veterans of Future Wars," marched down Broadway, accompanied by twenty members of Columbia's band, and led by a drum major who twirled a crutch instead of a baton. They were followed by 150 Barnard college women, dressed as nurses and widows, carrying dolls representing "war orphans." At the conclusion of the march some 3000 Columbia, Barnard, Union Theological Seminary, Jewish Theological Seminary, and Teachers College students rallied against war and took the Oxford oath.[53]

In Lash's eyes the results of the 1936 student strike suggested that it was he, rather than Draper, who had been correct in their debate concerning the intentions of communist ASUers. Despite Draper's warnings that the abandonment of the Oxford Pledge in the high schools was part of a larger communist plot to purge the Pledge from its program, at the college level—where the ASU was strongest—the Pledge was generally retained. The strike call issued by the ASU had given the Pledge prominent play, and in fact there was only a single phrase, "Stop the Aggressor," which the YPSLs could object to as even vaguely interventionist in the entire call.[54] Observing the success of the strike and the phrasing of the strike call, Lash privately boasted of how wrong Draper had been in predicting that the communists would dilute the strike's anti-war content. Instead of trying to impose the Communist Party's collective security line on the student movement, communist ASUers had, Lash explained, subordinated that line for the sake of unity in the student movement.

> We have had differences with the Young Communist League on the question of how to fight war, but they have always accepted the position of the socialists when we have insisted upon it. For instance the national strike call urges support of mandatory neutrality. This is completely inconsistent with the Communist position on sanctions. I think it is a victory for the socialists when they can get the A.S.U. to adopt their position in this way. There is a good deal of confusion in the ranks of the Young Communist League on the subject of the Oxford Pledge, but it has not affected the work of the A.S.U.[55]

Lash's conclusions, however, proved premature. In the long run it was Draper who correctly perceived the direction in which the communists would push the ASU and the student movement. Lash erred in thinking the communists would always yield to the socialists as they had in April 1936, when they had allowed the Oxford Pledge and its anti-interventionist message to remain a central part of the campus strike against war. This communist accommodationism could not last because too much of a contradiction existed between the neutrality policies championed by the anti-war strike and the collective security policies increasingly favored by communist ASUers. Though for the sake of student unity, communist ASUers had obfuscated that contradiction during the 1936 strike, international events would make them less and less willing to continue making such concessions to anti-interventionism. And of all the international events propelling this break with anti-interventionism none was more important than the Spanish Civil War. The conflict in Spain from summer 1936–1939 would change the strategy of communist ASUers, as Draper had predicted, transforming the dominant foreign policy of the student movement so that it conformed entirely to the Popular Front line of the Communist International.

II

The Spanish Civil War served as the wake-up call for a generation of student activists who had been lost in isolationist slumber. Before the conflict in Spain, communist ASUers represented virtually the only force in the student movement critical of United States neutrality and supportive of international governmental action to prevent fascist aggression. During the early 1930s most American students had assumed that the United States could preserve peace by adhering to a policy of strict neutrality. But the news from Spain following the outbreak of the fascist insurgency in July 1936 exposed the naiveté of this assumption. The Spanish Civil War would begin to discredit United States neutrality in the eyes of many students, providing communist ASUers with a host of allies in their drive to convert the student movement from isolationism to collective security and anti-fascist interventionism.

This shift away from neutrality, initiated by Spain and orchestrated by communist ASUers, would not, however, come easily. The communists were, in effect, seeking to use the Spanish Civil War to alter the student movement's raison d'être by reversing the anti-interventionist policies that had launched the college peace movement in the first place. Intellectually, this effort boiled down to a battle between the present and the past—between the old lessons from World War I and the new lessons emerging from the Spanish Civil War. Through the first half of the Depression decade, the student movement's foreign policy had been shaped by disillusionment with World War I. Convinced that United States intervention in that conflict had been a tragic mistake, most American students and their anti-war movement supported neutrality legislation designed to prevent President Roosevelt from repeating that mistake. It had been comforting to think that Congress, heeding the lessons of the First World War, could simply legislate America out of any new world war. There was therefore considerable reluctance among students about parting with this happy illusion, even when events from Spain began to suggest that the lessons of 1917 were neither relevant to the international scene of the mid–1930s, nor a reliable guide to avoiding war.

It was equally difficult for students to part with the idealism of the Oxford Pledge. When they had transported the Oxford Pledge across the Atlantic in the early 1930s, American student activists had dared to dream of a warless world. For a generation scarred by the memory of World War I, the pledge had symbolized their hope that by refusing to fight, the youth of all nations could help prevent another world war.[56] Since this optimism had helped give birth to the anti-war movement on campus, student activists were understandably reluctant to surrender it. It was painful for the young to face up to the fact that their bright hopes and dreams were dying on the battlefields of Spain; that nonviolence and neutrality only encouraged fascist aggression and thereby heightened the prospects for the outbreak of a second world war.

It was with respect to United States neutrality legislation that events in Spain did the most to refute the simplistic lessons that students had drawn from World War I. The Spanish Civil War confronted American students with the harmful effects of the neutrality policy that their anti-war movement had once championed. When President Roosevelt and Congress, in the name of neutrality, imposed an embargo on the Spanish republic, the impact of this policy was anything but neutral. By withholding support from either side, the United States objectively aided General Francisco Franco's fascist forces; for with the fascists armed to the teeth by Hitler and Mussolini, it was only the republican side which, because of the embargo by America, Britain, and France, remained desperately short of military supplies. Supporters of the Loyalist cause worried that this United States policy was contributing to the starvation of the Spanish republic and facilitating a fascist victory there. Such a victory, Popular Fronters feared, would gratify Franco's German and Italian sponsors and breed further fascist aggression by suggesting that the western democracies would not act to halt such aggression. Spain would increasingly be seen on campus as an object lesson in anachronistic foreign policy: teaching that neutrality acts framed with Woodrow Wilson in mind were not appropriate for dealing with Hitler and Mussolini.[57]

The Spanish Civil War fostered this new realism in the American student movement because of not only the tragedy of the American neutrality policy, but also the courage of the anti-fascists in Spain. ASU activists watched in horror as Franco's cabal of fascist generals turned the Spanish army upon the Spanish people and their democratically elected government. Franco's insurgency seemed all the more sinister because its success hinged upon the support of thousands of troops from fascist Italy, bombers from Nazi Germany, and other military supplies from both Hitler and Mussolini. Despite the odds against holding off these well supplied fascist forces, Spaniards rushed to the defense of their republic, and through their determined military defense of Madrid in the fall of 1936 they prevented the expected rapid fascist victory in the war. The courage of this resistance, depicted so movingly by Ernest Hemingway and other leading American and European writers, captured the imagination of many students. Inspired by Spain, a new anti-fascist idealism was emerging on campus, whose partisans carried the slogan first heard in Spain, "No Pasaran!" ("they shall not pass"). In the American student movement, this new idealism, with its call for engagement in the international struggle against fascism, would first compete with and then prevail over the anti-interventionist idealism embodied in the Oxford Pledge.[58]

The Spanish Civil War was one of those rare historical events that have the power to change people's minds and prod them to reconsider their political assumptions. This process of change was emotional as well as intellectual; it was fueled by compassion for the Spanish republic, admiration for the Loyalists and their willingness to sacrifice their lives to battle fascism, as well as outrage at the brutality of Franco and his German and Italian fascist sponsors. The strength of such feelings, and their ability to alter the thinking of student activists, was evident, for instance, in a letter Tucker Dean sent to ASU leader Molly Yard. Dean, a student anti-war leader at Harvard, who previously had been a committed pacifist, confided to Yard that the Civil War in Spain had left him thinking in ways incompatible with his pacifist principles. Dean wrote that he had been seriously contemplating

> the possibility of volunteering [to fight] in Spain. Ordinarily I wouldnt consider such a thing, since I abhor war. But in the past months I've been thinking a good deal about Germany and Spain and their relationship to my old dream of pacifism. In fact I've been literally dreaming about myself fighting fascists, always to my own astonishment, since I'd hate to kill even a fascist.[59]

While Dean dreamed of fighting fascism in Spain, other American students were translating such dreams into reality. From 1936–1938 some 500 students and recent graduates slipped out of the United States and, in defiance of United States neutrality laws, made their way to Spain, where they served as soldiers for the Loyalists in the volunteer American unit, the Abraham Lincoln Battalion. Students constituted the largest white-collar group in the Lincoln Battalion of the International Brigade. Only the maritime industry, with its unionized seamen and their radical working-class tradition, provided more American volunteers in Spain than did the campuses. And within this substantial student delegation, the largest single contingent came directly out of the ranks of the student movement. Eighty-eight ASUers served in the Lincoln Battalion.[60]

This student participation in the Spanish Civil War would have a profound impact upon the American student movement. With students fighting in Spain, the struggle against fascism and the United States embargo of the Spanish republic ceased to be abstractions; they became matters of life and death. Students now felt that the embargo was jeopardizing the survival of not only the republic, but of American student movement veterans serving in the Lincoln Battalion, who were facing the much better armed fascist forces. This became an even more urgent matter as the Lincoln Battalion began suffering heavy casualties. The special intensity of this concern reflected the fact that the first American students to die for their political beliefs in the Depression decade were those who fell in battle during the Spanish Civil War.[61]

Nowhere was the Spanish anti-fascist cause felt with more immediacy than in the national leadership of the ASU during the early stages of the Civil War. All of the national staff members of the ASU had close friends serving in the Lincoln Battalion. Since their comrades stood on the front lines in Spain there was, as James Wechsler recalled, a strong feeling among ASU officers that "those who remained behind could not let them down." In his memoir Wechsler noted that as an ASUer he had felt inspired by the example set by David Cook, a fellow veteran of Columbia University's student Left, who fought in Spain. Despite the wounds Cook had suffered in battle, he sent Wechsler optimistic letters from a Madrid hospital, voicing his determination to fight on. "In the face of such communiqués," Wechsler explained, "one tried harder than ever to . . . serve selflessly in the movement which produced such men."[62]

In its first few months, the Spanish Civil War brought most of the national staff of the ASU closer together both personally and politically. Their strong desire to support the anti-fascists in Spain and to assist their friends on the front lines helped unite communists on the ASU staff with their socialist counterparts. These communist ASUers—the most prominent of whom were Wechsler and Strack—had from the outset been ardent boosters of the Loyalist cause, because of their own anti-fascism and because this was consistent with the Comintern's Popular Front line. Their enthusiasm had been buttressed in the fall of 1936 by the U.S.S.R.'s decision to provide military aid to the republic, and by the leading role that communists had played in organizing the Lincoln Battalion and volunteer units from other nations. But Spain also pushed several of the key socialist leaders in the ASU, including Lash, Yard, and ASU executive committee member Robert Spivack, away from United States neutrality and toward the collective security position advocated by the communists.[63] Their own unity over Spain encouraged these ASU leaders, to believe that rank and file ASUers as well as the national student body would also eagerly embrace the Spanish anti-fascist cause. For these ASU leaders, the anticipation of such a united and effective crusade against fascism made the early stages of the Spanish Civil War, in Wechsler's words,

> a time of hope and excitement, of passions revived and faith rejuvenated. Earlier in the decade there had been the swift, crushing triumph of Hitler, and all the ensuing recriminations as to the blame for that disaster

. . . . Now the issue was drawn again and this time it would be different. As far as we could see at a distance, socialists, communists, anarchists and just freedom-loving men were united in the great stand of the century. "Make Madrid the tomb of Fascism" was the cry heard round the world, *"No Pasaran"* was to be the triumphant theme song of a generation. In Spain, at least, the air was clear and the battle lines plainly marked, so we believed, and there could be no doubt where every man of good will . . . must finally take his stand.[64]

This type of unity over Spain would, however, prove more difficult to duplicate in some quarters of the student anti-war movement. None of the ASU officers were pacifists, and so they did not experience the dilemma over Spain that pacifists confronted. The Spanish Civil War forced pacifists to chose between two evils that were almost equally loathsome to them: war and fascism. Some pacifists bent their neutralist principles in order to help the Spanish anti-fascists—by supporting humanitarian, non-military aid for the Loyalists; others, as was the case with Tucker Dean, abandoned neutrality and non-violence entirely by supporting anti-fascist military aid. But most pacifist students who remained affiliated with such organizations as the Fellow of Reconciliation and the War Resisters League could not bring themselves to back war or American aid for belligerents even if, as in Spain, that war was being waged against fascism. They continued to call for strict United States neutrality with respect to Spain. Since such absolute pacifists constituted only a small minority of the national student body, they could not prevent the student movement's shift toward collective security. Nonetheless, their stance made it impossible for the ASU to engineer that shift without alienating this small, yet vocal, group of activists.[65]

Nor were pacifists the only group of students reluctant to abandon United States neutrality during the Spanish Civil War. More mainstream students, brought up on isolationism, were in many cases initially uneasy about this change. At the University of Michigan, for example, the Spanish Civil War provoked much soul searching among students—some of whom just could not bring themselves to abandon isolationism. The issue of Spain was brought home to the Ann Arbor campus in March 1938 by the news that Ralph Neafus, of Michigan's class of '36, serving in the Lincoln Battalion, had been taken prisoner by the fascist forces. The State Department, citing the technicality that American volunteers in Spain had violated United States neutrality laws, refused to intercede on Neafus' behalf. Outraged by this stance and by the overall United States policy towards Spain, the Michigan ASU sought to rally the campus in protest against the State Department's unwillingness to aid Neafus.[66]

This campaign swayed the editors of Michigan student newspaper, the *Michigan Daily*, even though the paper had begun the academic year staunchly isolationist. The *Daily*, urged the State Department to work for Neafus' release, and praised him for "representing the finest elements in

Michigan tradition . . . risking his life for . . . democratic ideals. He offered his life to the Spanish Republic in the same way that Lafayette, von Steuben and Kosciusko offered their services that this republic might live." Not all of Michigan's isolationists, however, were this willing to change. Rigid isolationists viewed Neafus' service in Spain as a misguided intrusion into the internal affairs of another nation, and they felt that any intercession by Washington on his behalf would violate United States neutrality. This isolationist mind-set prevailed within Michigan's student council, which by a 14 to 13 vote refused to join the ASU in sending a telegram on Neafus' behalf to the State Department. The closeness of this vote on a campus once overwhelmingly isolationist suggested the ASU was making progress in using Spain to turn students against neutrality; but the loss on the vote also attested that collegiate isolationism was far from dead.[67]

There were also serious obstacles on the road to collective security within the ASU. Not all of the ASU's leadership was as united as the national staff on Spain. The ASU's national executive and administrative committees—which, along with the ASU national staff, implemented ASU policy—included leftwing socialists and Trotskyists who were die hard foes of collective security. These dissidents, most of whom were YPSLs, sympathized with the Loyalists, but would only support worker's (i.e. nongovernmental) aid to the Spanish anti-fascist cause; they opposed United States government involvement in either the Spanish conflict or any collective security alliances and international sanctions against fascism. They rejected all measures designed to give Washington a leading or even active role in thwarting fascism internationally. Clinging dogmatically to the socialist view of war inherited from 1917, the YPSL continued to insist that since the United States was inherently imperialistic, even ostensibly anti-fascist foreign policy initiatives only masked America's true expansionist war goals. Where collective security advocates saw in Spain proof that the United States must join with the U.S.S.R. and other anti-fascist nations in using state power to contain Hitler and Mussolini, the YPSLs refused to believe that the might of capitalist America could be employed for such benign ends. The YPSLs contended that America itself was so militaristic that it constituted as big a threat to world peace as did Nazi Germany or fascist Italy. Thus leading YPSLs in the ASU, including Hal Draper, Judah Drob, and Alvaine Hollister, refused to go along with the communists' attempt to focus the student movement's foreign policy exclusively on the fascist threat. They instead pushed for an ASU which, though anti-fascist, would emphasize the war danger emanating from the United States and the need to use the Oxford Pledge to resist American militarism.[68]

These doctrinaire YPSLs in the ASU not only refused to reconsider their own analysis of American foreign policy in light of the developments in Spain; they also attacked socialist students who dared to engage in such a reconsideration. Acting like cardinals in the church of the socialist Left, the YPSL leadership sought to purge its ranks of heretics who embraced collective security. One YPSL heretic who was the object of such an attack was Joseph Lash. The ASU Executive Secretary had angered the YPSL leadership in the fall of 1936 when he co-authored with James Wechsler, *War Our Heritage,* an anti-war book, narrating the history of the student movement. The first six chapters of the book had been completed before the outbreak of the Spanish Civil War; they were true to the anti-interventionist spirit of the early student movement, and as such were not offensive to the YPSL. But the book's final chapter was written during the Spanish Civil War; it upset the YPSL leadership because it reflected the authors' shift away from anti-interventionism. Here Lash and Wechsler, after criticizing Hitler and Mussolini for aiding "the Spanish fascist rebels in Spain in their war against a democratic government," warned that

> it would be folly for the American peace movement . . . to ignore this immediate crisis which fascist aggressiveness has precipitated . . . . America's absence from collective security may accentuate the peril of war in Europe. . . . Washington . . . could legitimately collaborate in an attempt to enforce peace and to halt recurrent menaces to peace.[69]

This support of collective security led the YPSL to attack Lash and challenge his leadership in the student movement.

The YPSL leadership's anger at both Lash and the general direction of the ASU became evident during the YPSL national executive committee meeting in November, 1936. This meeting had been convened to prepare YPSL strategy for the upcoming ASU convention. At this meeting YPSL leaders complained that Lash "will not fight aggressively" for socialist goals within the ASU "because basically he disagrees with many of the policies of the YPSL." Determined to battle "against the YCL effort to line up pacifists and liberals [in the ASU] for collective security," the YPSL leadership agreed that this could be done most effectively without Lash. YPSL's executive committee therefore voted unanimously to dump Lash from its slate of candidates for the ASU national staff, and ordered his removal from all student organizing. The committee also echoed Hal Draper's criticism that the ASU was not sufficiently radical. These YPSLs objected that "in order to placate liberals" the ASU had used such words as "Tories" in its platform instead of specifically naming and targeting the capitalist class. The YPSL executive committee planned to demand at the convention that the ASU become explicitly anti-capitalist. The committee ruled that if the ASU refused to move in this direction, then no YPSL should serve in the position of ASU Executive Secretary.[70]

Lash realized that by endorsing collective security in *War Our Heritage* he had opened himself to this type of attack by the YPSL. But he responded to the YPSL challenge by arguing that foreign policy was not at the heart of this dispute. He claimed that the real reason the YPSL leadership wanted him out of the ASU was that "the YPSL NEC [National Executive Committee] hates me because I would not utilize my post in the

ASU for an unjustifiable and sectarian attack upon the YCL—that I would not allow factional differences to disturb the whole of the ASU." Lash termed the YPSL's decisions regarding him and the ASU convention the "reductio absurdium of [sectarian] tendencies which have long been developing in the YPSL." Lash attributed this sectarianism to YPSL jealousy of him, the ASU, and Communist ASUers. The YPSL leaders felt such jealousy, according to Lash, because while the ASU and YCL had grown with the student movement, the YPSL had virtually stagnated. Lash observed that Socialist Party leader

> Norman Thomas has a tremendous following amongst youth. Gil Green of the YCL has sighed in my presence that if they had a man like Thomas they could build an organization of a hundred thousand. But the YPSL has not grown . . . because it never possessed a leadership with the ability and imagination to build a massive Socialist youth movement.[71]

The YPSL leadership's plan to impose its doctrinaire approach to politics upon the ASU was, in Lash's view, a recipe for political disaster: "Obviously if the ASU was to become a mass organization it could not utilize [the] Marxian terms [advocated by] . . . the YPSL. The YPSL has consistently paid lipservice to the need for mass work. Why doesn't it govern its action by this need?"[72]

There was, of course, a self-serving quality to some of Lash's counterattacks in his conflict with the YPSL. Aware that *War Our Heritage*'s collective security position made him politically vulnerable in socialist circles, Lash, in his contemporary discussions with socialist comrades, downplayed the extent of his dissent on this issue. He emphasized that most of *War Our Heritage* had been anti-interventionist and that his foes in the YPSL were focusing on the book's final chapter because they were out to get him.[73] What Lash conveniently ignored here was that with the YPSL preparing for the ASU convention, at which the debate over collective security promised to loom large, it was quite reasonable for the YPSL leadership to be concerned about his views on this issue—particularly since his last writings on foreign policy in *War Our Heritage* had endorsed the very collective security ideas that the YPSL opposed. Clearly the YPSL had reason to fear that Lash might use his pivotal position in the ASU's leadership to defeat YPSL foreign policy goals at the convention.

Lash was, however, on more solid ground in criticizing the YPSL leadership's penchant for sectarianism and ultra-radical posturing. It made little political sense for the ASU, after a successful year, to abandon its founding platform in favor of the explicitly anti-capitalist program favored by the YPSL. Such a move might have been more consistent with the YPSL's ideological line, but it was not compatible with the basic mission of the ASU, which was uniting liberal and radical students to build a mass student movement in America. It made even less sense for the YPSL national executive committee to insist that unless the ASU changed its program in this manner, YPSLs would not serve in the key ASU national staff position. This strategy seemed sure to leave the YPSL and the student movement weakened; it might, in Lash's words, "embroil the [ASU] convention in a polemic that could consolidate the liberals with the YCL, or completely disgust the non-YPSL-YCL elements and destroy the ASU."[74]

Fortunately for both Lash and the student movement, the YPSL executive committee decided at the last minute not to implement most of its initial strategy for the 1936 ASU convention. The YPSL plans to dump Lash and attack the ASU program were short circuited by Socialist Party leader Norman Thomas. Upon learning of these YPSL plans a few weeks before the ASU convention, Thomas voiced his disapproval to the YPSL leadership. Thomas thought it unrealistic for the YPSLs to insist on remaking the ASU platform into an explicitly socialist document. He cautioned the YPSL not to act as if it was functioning "in a closed circle with reference only to the YPSL vs the YCL." The Socialist Party leader thought it the height of sectarianism for the YPSL to bar its members from the ASU national staff simply because the ASU's program was not revolutionary. Chiding the YPSL executive committee, Thomas stressed that

> we cannot set a precedent for isolation. We have to seek a program and a psychology which will be effective . . . . We have to be guided somewhat by what is possible in dealing with youth . . . . Above all things we must avoid a tone resembling that of third period Communism. I do not think we can possibly maintain as a rule the position that socialists can be in a mass organization but cannot hold policy forming office within it.[75]

Thomas also noted that though he disagreed with the statements in Lash's book regarding collective security, this was not a dispute of sufficient magnitude to justify the YPSL's decision to remove Lash from his leadership position in the ASU.

Thanks to Thomas, Lash came out ahead in this conflict with the YPSL. At the ASU convention, held in Chicago over the 1936 Christmas break, the YPSL did not seek to change the ASU's platform. Nor did the League follow through on its plan to remove Lash from the ASU leadership. But Lash's conflict with the YPSL did have an impact upon both him and the convention. Having been criticized for his few pages of pro-collective security argumentation in *War Our Heritage,* Lash shied away from making an explicit endorsement of collective security in his convention speeches. Lash, being, as he recalled, "under Socialist discipline," actually spoke on behalf of an anti-collective security resolution at the convention, despite feeling very "uneasy" about this position. This YPSL-sponsored resolution, which would have had the ASU criticize collective security as incompatible with the Oxford Pledge, lost 136 to 99. This close vote and Lash's retreat from collective security convinced communist ASUers that any attempt to impose a full collective security position on the convention would be too divisive. They therefore supported Molly

Yard's conciliatory proposal, which, for the sake of unity, had the ASU not take any position on collective security. And it was her proposal which prevailed at the convention.[76]

Although the ASU convention was too divided to come out explicitly for collective security, there were indications in Chicago that the ASU was heading in this direction. The convention passed a resolution warning against the "danger of fascist aggression on democratic nations," which seemed to imply—as collective security advocates believed—that the key danger to international peace came from fascist Italy and Germany rather than from the United States. This change in tone was also discernible in Lash's keynote speech to the convention. Although Lash, under pressure from the YPSLs, had earlier supported their resolution championing the Oxford Pledge and criticizing collective security, his keynote speech suggested where his heart really lay on these issues. While careful not to mention the words "collective security" in this address, Lash maintained much of the tone of the Popular Front position he had taken in his controversial *War Our Heritage* chapter. In his discussion of the student peace movement, Lash urged the ASU delegates to make anti-fascism, support of the Loyalist cause, and opposition to the United States embargo of Spain their highest priorities. Lash conceded that "many absolute pacifists have been shocked because our Union" endorsed the Loyalists, who employed force in their anti-fascist struggle. He defended this position and argued that pacifists should endorse it too since the fate of Spanish anti-fascism and the student movement's goal of preventing a new world war were inextricably linked. "The victory of fascism in Spain," Lash prophesized, "would prolong and extend the conditions which bring war closer to the whole world."[77]

In this speech Lash came closest to repudiating the student movement's previous anti-interventionism when he discussed the Oxford Pledge. After denouncing United States neutrality for being unneutral and aiding Spanish fascism, Lash pointed out that the ASU's support for the Loyalist war effort was not inconsistent with the organization's endorsement of the Oxford Pledge. Lash reminded the ASU's pacifists that the Pledge did not oppose all military service, but only military service on behalf of an "imperialist war for the U.S. government." Treading on dangerous ground since both the YPSL and pacifists in the ASU gave unqualified support to the Oxford Pledge, Lash asserted that the "Oxford Pledge is not for the A.S.U. . . . . an ethical absolute."[78] By qualifying and implicitly challenging the very anti-war pledge that had helped give birth to the student peace movement, Lash was suggesting that it might be necessary to change the direction of the movement for the sake of the Popular Front against fascism.

Lash's veiled public challenge to the YPSL position on the Oxford Pledge was tame, however, compared to the challenge he mounted to YPSL authority in the convention's closed socialist caucuses. Upon arriving in Chicago, Lash obtained a YPSL memo revealing a YPSL plot against him.

The memo stated that though the YPSL executive committee would not challenge Lash at the ASU convention, YPSL leaders, including Ben Fischer, the organization's national secretary, had agreed that after the convention "a campaign must be organized to expel Lash" from the YPSL.[79] The memo indicated that the YPSL leaders had only heeded Thomas' advice not to seek Lash's ouster as ASU Executive Secretary at the convention out of strategic considerations; they had been afraid that such a challenge might prove divisive at the convention and that a last minute effort to oust Lash could well fail. Aware now that the YPSL leaders were only postponing their attack on him, Lash opted to force a showdown at Chicago, and did so in alliance with ASU national chairman, George Edwards.

The vehicle for Lash's confrontation with the YPSLs was Edwards' convention speech. By the time of the ASU convention, Edwards was on his way out of the student movement. He was devoting most of his time to organizing for the United Auto Workers union in Detroit, where he would play a prominent role in the sit-down strikes. But Edwards, a YPSL member himself, shared Lash's disdain for the dogmatism and sectarianism of the YPSL national leadership, and, as one of his last acts in the student movement, he gladly joined Lash in defying that leadership. Encouraged by Lash, Edwards, upon flying in from Detroit, refused to submit the text of his presidential address to a representative of the YPSL executive committee. He gave the speech to the convention without YPSL approval, in flagrant disregard of YPSL procedures. Edwards' defiance and Lash's support of it ignited a fiery debate in the YPSL caucus at the convention. The furious YPSL leadership wanted to organize a move to oust Lash from his ASU office. Only the intervention of several Socialist Party officers dissuaded them from doing so.[80]

Although the policy differences in the Lash-YPSL dispute could hardly have been larger, both sides proved remarkably similar in the way that they waged this fight. Lash had been rebellious enough to defy the YPSL leadership, but not enough to air these differences publicly in an ASU session. He chose instead to fight this battle within the confines of the Socialist Party and its YPSL caucus, as did his opponents. Both shared a loyalty to the Socialist Party, and that loyalty dictated a style of party politics that was in many respects as conventional as that of the Democratic or Republican party activists. This resemblance was most striking in the YPSL caucuses that decided whether or not to slate Lash for ASU office, and the private negotiations in which the YPSL and the YCL met to determine how many of their respective members would get to serve as ASU national leaders. There was an almost Tammany-like quality to these sessions, where young radicals in their private party sessions—the student Left's smoke filled rooms—played kingmakers for the ASU. The only difference between these parties of the Left and those in the mainstream was that the former sought to be more disciplined, and therefore had expulsion procedures for ridding themselves of dissenters. This would in fact be the path taken by Lash's foes in the YPSL.[81]

Recriminations from the Lash-YPSL dispute lingered long after the Chicago Convention. Several YPSL leaders followed through on their threats against Lash by filing formal charges against him in the Socialist Party, citing his collusion with Edwards at the convention, and his support of collective security in *War Our Heritage*. Lash fought back. He used the confrontation with the YPSL in Chicago to expose the Socialist Party leadership to his view that the YPSL executive committee had failed "to build a mass Socialist youth movement because their leadership is incompetent, unimaginative and afflicted with an anti-YCL phobia."[82] He effectively defended himself from the YPSL's charges and filed his own charges against the YPSL executive committee, criticizing its poor performance in student organizing. The YPSLs failed attempt to discipline Lash only further alienated him from the YPSL organization, and left him free to join with the communists in moving toward collective security. With Lash coming over to their side in the semester following the Chicago Convention, communists in the ASU national leadership could now afford to become increasingly explicit in their push for collective security.

It would, however, take another full year after the 1936 ASU convention before collective security would become official ASU policy. The Chicago Convention demonstrated that extensive organizing and educational work would be needed before the ASU and the national student body would embrace collective security. Here the ASU was a victim of its own success. Having been so effective in publicizing the Oxford Pledge and its anti-interventionist message, the ASU would have to find a way to convince students that this old message was now out of date. Even with Spain on their side, this was a formidable task. Hoping to avoid an outright split in the campus anti-war movement over collective security, the ASU officers in spring 1937 adopted a pluralistic style as they pushed to reorient the student movement's foreign policy.[83] That is, they stressed the primacy of the anti-fascist cause and de-emphasized the Oxford Pledge, but did not try to compel all student organizers to do the same. Their hope was that the force of international events would buttress their anti-fascist message and gradually win students over to collective security.

This pluralistic approach guided the ASU national office's work in the 1937 student strike against war. At the ASU's initiative, the strike was coordinated through the United Student Peace Committee (USPC), a recently formed umbrella organization of anti-war groups. Under USPC auspices the 1937 strike would be the most broadly sponsored national student demonstration of the decade. The walkout was endorsed by such USPC members as the pacifist War Resisters League and Fellowship of Reconciliation, religious student groups, including the National Council of Methodist Youth, the Joint Committee on United Christian Youth Movement, the National Councils of the Student YMCA and YWCA, the liberal National Student Federation, and the radically-led American Youth Congress and American Student Union. The USPC's strike call, reflecting the sentiments of the USPC's pacifist members, had an anti-interventionist emphasis, endorsing "strict neutrality legislation," and offering only a passing reference to the Spanish Civil War. To help support the strike the ASU agreed to sign the USPC strike call, which it termed "an intelligent and careful minimum for the united action of the overwhelming majority of the student body"; but the ASU also made clear its disapproval of the anti-interventionist message of that document.[84]

The ASU was walking a political tight rope, as it sought to both air its differences with the USPC and still maintain strike unity in spring 1937. This was evident in the ASU national magazine's strike editorial, "April 22: We Must Remember Spain." Here the ASU criticized as "the most profound shortcoming of the [USPC] strike call" its "treatment of the Spanish issue." The ASU charged that the USPC had understated the importance of the Spanish Civil War and had erred seriously in promoting United States neutrality legislation. "American neutrality is sham neutrality at best and overt aid to fascism at worst," explained the ASU magazine. "If while fascism throws all resources into Spain, the allies of the Spanish government remain inert, the simple and inevitable consequence will be world war." Yet for the sake of unity, the editorial advised ASUers to be tolerant of the type of sentiment expressed by the USPC strike call, even as they expressed their problems with the call and worked to sway students to the anti-fascist cause in the strike:

> Without seeking to impose our judgment upon other participants in the strike, the American Student Union must undertake the responsibility of clarifying the Spanish issue, of revealing its link to the war crisis, of winning sympathy and aid for the embattled Spanish people.[85]

As far as turnout was concerned, the ASU's strategy for the strike proved enormously successful. The 1937 student strike was by all accounts larger than even the previous year's massive walkout. The ASU claimed that about a million students had participated in the strike, and even the conservative *New York Times* conceded that at least 500,000 students had mobilized for the event. Exhilarated ASU leaders boasted of the strike's "astounding proportions," and termed this protest "the greatest student mobilization for peace in the history of the U.S."[86]

If judged by content instead of size, however, the 1937 student strike was far from a smashing success. The strike lacked a single coherent message; it was rather a babel of conflicting voices and opinions. On campuses where communist ASUers and Popular Front liberals dominated the strike, the Oxford Pledge and anti-interventionism were de-emphasized in favor of anti-fascism, aid to republican Spain, and collective security. Where YPSLs were in control, the prior strike's stress on the Oxford Pledge and opposition to United States militarism was retained. And in pacifist-

controlled strike rallies support for tough United States neutrality legislation took center stage. So while the ASU officers were delighted with
the turnout, they were, with good reason, concerned about the loss of
coherence in the strike. ASU officers began to recognize that a political
fight would be necessary to make international anti-fascist solidarity the
student movement's top priority. They would soon insist upon collective
security becoming the official line of both the ASU and the student strike—
even though this meant alienating pacifists, YPSLs, and others favoring
an isolationist United States foreign policy.[87]

It was, however, not only the results of the 1937 strike but events in
Spain that were rendering the ASU officers willing to risk splitting the
anti-war movement for the sake of collective security. Though Spain had
initially been a unifying cause for much of the student Left, this changed
dramatically in spring 1937. Begun as a broad republican coalition, the
Spanish Loyalists forces were, by virtue of Soviet aid, becoming increasingly communist-dominated. The communists in Spain wanted to postpone revolutionary measures (such as land seizures), in order to unify all
of the country's social classes against the fascists. But many anarchists,
leftwing socialists, and Trotskyists in the Loyalist ranks disagreed with this
strategy. They advocated an immediate social revolution, arguing that this
would give the lower classes more of a stake in their battle against fascism.
This dispute ended in bloodshed in May 1937 when, under communist
orders, Spanish government troops attacked the anarchists and their leftist allies in Barcelona. Communist ASUers and liberal Popular Fronters
responded to these events by rallying to the side of the Spanish government, while YPSLs and Trotskyists strongly criticized the government. This
split drove a wedge through the student Left, which would encourage the
ASU's increasingly communist-dominated leadership to break with the
YPSLs, Trotskyists, and other foes of collective security.[88]

The impact that Spain had upon the ASU's communist-dominated
leadership in 1937 can be seen clearly in the case of Joseph Lash. The
cause of Spanish anti-fascism so moved Lash that in the summer of 1937
he made his way over to Spain, and began drilling with the Abraham
Lincoln Battalion. At the time Lash departed for Spain, he was still a
socialist, despite his running feud with the YPSL. But the journey to Spain
finalized Lash's move out of the socialists' circles and into the communists'. Communists helped Lash get into Spain, and once there he became
convinced that the communists were providing both the backbone and the
most far sighted strategists of the anti-fascist resistance. To his wife Nancy,
Lash wrote from Spain in July that

> the CP here has pursued a consistently fine policy which in the main
> accounts for the fact that it is now the dominant party in Spain. Its slo-
> gans have proven correct and have become the slogans of the nation. It
> was the first party to realize that everything must be subordinated to
> winning the war . . . .[89]

That month in his diary Lash noted feeling "more and more in sympathy with communist policy," and "ready to take out a C party card."[90]

Lash adopted much of the communist perspective on Spain's non-Stalinist Left. Though as an anti-war leader Lash had consistently criticized the political repression which gripped America during the First World War, he was willing to sanction even harsher repression against Trotskyists in Spain for the sake of the war effort. On this point, Lash, in a confidential letter from Spain, wrote that the Trotskyists'

> policy has been objectively harmful. So far as I am concerned the burden of proof rests with the Trotskyists that the govt. and not they were the provocators of the Barcelona events. This is an iron age and we are in a civil war. It's about time Norman [Thomas] discovered that there are more important things in the world than defending Trotskyists.[91]

Lash was not immune to doubts about the communists and the harsh suppression they inflicted upon their leftist critics. Lash confessed in his diary to feeling troubled when he "found out too much" from a friend who had come to Spain to investigate the disappearance of the son of an exiled Menshevik leader. But Lash felt it is his anti-fascist duty to stifle his doubts. Thus in his diary Lash notes a "long heart to heart talk" with a comrade about the need "to subordinate oneself, one's misgivings about some of the things that were going on in Spain and russia if we are going to win against the fascists." Lash was too intelligent, however, to adopt this position without misgivings, and wrote privately of "the danger of becoming political hacks, if one suppressed all critical feelings." [92] In the end, though, his anti-fascism overcame such misgivings, and he sent back to the ASU uncritical propaganda from Spain. Lash would personally help to promote such uncritical thinking in the student movement. The Lincoln Battalion and YCL leadership pressured Lash to halt his training with the International Brigade, urging him to return to America and the ASU in order to rally student support for the Loyalist cause. Though confessing that he felt "absolutely like a bastard" for leaving the Brigade, Lash finally gave in, returning to the United States and his duties as ASU Executive Secretary in October.[93]

Although Lash's case was distinctive because he had actually gone to Spain, his mind-set regarding the Spanish struggle was typical of the ASU's communist and Popular Front leadership. ASU communications director James Wechsler recalled that he too was troubled by the "discord behind the Spanish lines." But with Lash and other friends in Spain, Wechsler felt obligated "to stifle doubt" about communist behavior there—"trying to be a good homefront soldier" for the anti-fascist cause. For Wechsler part of being a "good homefront soldier" meant attacking those who had allegedly been responsible for disrupting anti-fascist unity in Spain: the Trotskyists.[94]

Looking back on the Trotsky baiting of the late 1930s, Wechsler observed that "nothing is more comparable to the intellectual overtones of McCarthyism than the Communist crusade against Trotskyists." While this crusade raged, any radical who disagreed with the Popular Front or any other communist position could be instantly dismissed and discredited by simply being branded "Trotskyist;" it was used, as Wechsler recalled, in an attempt "to crush any vestige of independent thought" on the Left. The crusade came to America via Russia and Spain. Reflecting the feud between Stalin and Trotsky, the communists in Spain had attacked left-wing insurgents (many of whom were not actually Trotskyists) as traitors to the Loyalist cause and Trotskyist agents of fascism.[95]

Wechsler and other communists in the student movement would hurl these same false charges at Trotskyist youth organizers in the United States, whenever they dared to criticize the communist-dominated government of Spain. They believed that such attacks served the Loyalist cause. In 1937, for example, Wechsler was selected to deliver an address on "The Danger of Trotskyism" at the student session of the YCL convention. Initially reluctant to address such a sectarian topic, Wechsler nonetheless did so, having "decided that I could face so small an ordeal while others were enduring far greater punishment on the Spanish front."[96] In Wechsler as well as Lash, then, passion for the Loyalist cause fostered the very type of sectarianism which they had so studiously avoided in launching the ASU— both seemed to forget for the moment that it had been non-sectarianism which had helped make the ASU America's largest and most influential Left-led student group.

The hostility of this communist-Trotskyist conflict flowed in both directions. The Trotskyists were on the offensive as much as their communist rivals. When, for instance, Lash returned from Spain, Trotskyist YPSLs greeted his fall 1937 campus tour with leaflets charging him with promoting a "counter-revolutionary line," "slandering the revolutionary workers of Spain," and serving as a political propagandist for the People's Front government which "directed their massacre."[97] Later, Trotskyist student leader Irving Howe would depict ASU activists as fascistic, making the unfounded charge that they were raising funds "for BOTH sides [in the Spanish Civil War], Loyalist and Franco."[98] The political atmosphere within the Left was becoming so poisoned that it was growing increasingly difficult for any genuine dialogue over the Popular Front policies to occur. Lash himself confessed in his diary to feeling stultified by this atmosphere, while on the midwestern leg of his national campus tour on behalf of the Loyalist cause. Lash noted his concern about a

> meeting at Minn. U. [which] ended in noise and confusion because of Trotskyists from town who came down to present "another point of view." . . . [The student chairing the meeting] refused to give them the floor for anything but questions and promised them a speech at the end of the meeting and then adjourned it without allowing the speech. One wonders at the effect of such a move on people. I was doubly disturbed because

there are no arguments of the Trotskyists that I fear and cutting off discussion this way created the impression that I didn't have an answer.[99]

Even when dialogue was not cut off in this manner, the Trotskyist and YPSL critics of the republican government had little impact upon campus opinion regarding Spain. The very complexity of these critics' position on the Civil War made it difficult to sell. Though their attacks on Spanish communist repression of the anti-Stalinist Left were brilliant and accurate, making such attacks placed them in an awkward position. In the midst of a war against fascism, they appeared to be contradicting themselves by simultaneously denouncing both the Spanish fascists and the republican government leading the fight against those fascists. Thus in explaining why she rejected the YPSL-Trotskyist position on Spain, socialist student activist Nancy Bedford Jones gibed "I am not a split personality, one of those who can both support and oppose [those working] . . . to defeat fascism in Spain . . . . Therefore my support [of the Loyalists] . . . is full."[100]

In contrast to the complexity and seeming ambiguity of the Trotskyist-YPSL position on Spain, the communist ASUers' message of unqualified support to Spain's beleaguered anti-fascists was simple, clear, and appealing to most student activists. Moreover, as Irving Howe recalled, he and his fellow Trotskyists in the ASU were at a disadvantage emotionally as well as politically in the debate on Spain. With fascism threatening to crush the Spanish republic, the Trotskyists were, as Howe put it,

> complicating the Spanish question in ways that seemed insufferable. That the loyalist Spain which so stirred hearts could be guilty of allowing the NKVD to kidnap and murder Andrés Nin, the POUM leader, was simply too much. People could not bear to hear that La Pasionaria, the flaming defender of Madrid, was also a ruthless Stalinist persecuting political opponents.[101]

As Spain and the rift with the Trotskyists fostered an all or nothing attitude toward collective security within the ASU, President Roosevelt also contributed to this trend. In October 1937 FDR mounted his first major challenge to isolationism, with his "Quarantine" speech. The speech reflected his anger over Japan's invasion of northern China and his concern about the growing threat to peace posed by Hitler and Mussolini. Speaking in Chicago, the heartland of American isolationism, the president warned that "mere isolation or neutrality" would not protect America from "the present reign of terror and international lawlessness." He implied the need for some form of collective security by "peace-loving nations, . . . a concerted effort in opposition to those" engaged in international aggression. The president suggested the need for a "quarantine of those spreading the epidemic of world lawlessness." Widely interpreted as a call for sanctions against aggressor nations, the Chicago speech drew angry denunciations from isolationists. In the face of these attacks Roosevelt retreated and did almost nothing to translate this speech into policy.[102] But FDR's brief challenge to isolationism helped provide an opening to collective security proponents in the ASU, who could now invoke the authority of the president for their position. This gave them hope that as they turned the ASU into an officially pro-collective security organization—a move which would obviously alienate the student movement's Trotskyist, leftwing YPSLs and pacifist minorities—the ASU and the student movement could retain support from liberals, who constituted a majority of the national student body.[103]

The final showdown over collective security within the ASU would occur during its 1937 national convention at Vassar College, two months after FDR's Quarantine speech. Both the pro- and anti-collective security factions within the ASU knew that the showdown was coming and began preparing for the fight well before the convention convened in December. The Oxford Pledge emerged as the key issue as the two sides geared up for the convention. There was no question that the communist ASUers and other proponents of collective security would seek to drop the Pledge from the ASU platform at the convention. For them the Pledge's anti-interventionist message was anachronistic, as was its implication that there was a serious war danger emanating from the United States. They were promoting a more benign image of the United States as a potential leader in the international effort to halt fascist aggression. The YPSLs, pacifists, and Trotskyists, on the other hand, were readying themselves for a vigorous defense of anti-interventionism and the Oxford Pledge at the convention. They also prepared for a possible split with the ASU in case the Pledge was dropped and collective security adopted at the convention. This preparation, which began in November, took the form of preliminary organizing to launch the Youth Committee for the Oxford Pledge (YCOP), a group designed to draw students away from the ASU and collective security.[104]

Tension over this imminent battle gripped the ASU's national leadership. Molly Yard, who was now ASU Organizational Secretary as well as Treasurer, noted in the month preceding the convention that the ASU staff—which more than doubled in size since 1935—had become so factionalized that it was limiting the efficiency of the national office. In a letter to Lash, Yard complained of a

> tendency for staff members to do other things—they come in looking haggard at 9:30 or later . . . . There is Brit[ton Harris] with the YCL and Alvaine [Hollister] with the YPSL and Robin [Myers] and Bob [Kelso] with the pacifists. I am getting God dam sick of all this. It is too much for me. I think it would be interesting to see what would happen to the ASU if everyone really concentrated on building it.[105]

Among the ASU's national staff and administrative committee, the personal relationships between pro- and anti-collective security advocates deteriorated as the convention drew closer. This deterioration accelerated after the YPSLs and pacifists began working on the YCOP, which to its foes clearly seemed an attempt to subvert the ASU through the creation of a rival organization. Lash, who by this time had resigned from the YPSL and Socialist Party because of their opposition to collective security, repeatedly fell into arguments with Oxford Pledge supporters in the ASU national leadership. YPSL leader Alvaine Hollister complained to a fellow YCOP activist in November that Lash "is getting very excitable these days, on almost any occasion. At the administration committee meeting Thursday night, he went off the handle completely—at one point called me a liar, and during the day he told Bob and Robin that they were just my 'stooges.' "[106]

The ASU leadership's meetings to prepare for the convention were particularly contentious. Since a majority of leaders in the ASU national office and administrative committee favored collective security, their opponents were quite concerned that they might structure the Vassar meetings unfairly, so that the collective security position could be railroaded through the convention. At one such meeting, Hal Draper, now a Trotskyist and ASU national Administrative Committee member, insisted that Oxford Pledge supporters be represented in every aspect of planning and conducting the convention. Yard was conciliatory, explaining that "we were not trying to keep out any point of view and had no intention of so doing." But the YCL members of the committee proved intolerant. According to Yard's account of the meeting,

> Celeste [Strack] and Brit were pretty terrible in my estimation . . . . They kept telling Draper he'd better leave if he didn't like things in very measured tones and were generally very antagonizing. If they act that way at the Convention I think they will lose all the liberal support. It is really disgusting.[107]

At the campus level similar conflicts occurred. As in the ASU national office, the majority of convention delegates elected by the chapters favored collective security, and their opponents charged that the majority was acting to preempt any dissent from the convention. "Some chapter elections which preceeded" the ASU convention were, according to the YPSL,

> exemplary of what lack of democracy can mean in action. In New York, for example proportional representation in all chapters was prohibited . . . . In Philadelphia, all chapters were instructed by the District Committee that their delegates had to vote for collective security simply because the district convention had done so (72–30). In other chapters, speakers supporting the [old] ASU program [endorsing the Oxford Pledge] were refused the floor for no better reason than that the majority opposed the program.[108]

Although such complaints might sound rather hollow—the usual gripes from the losing side—the private correspondence of pro-collective security ASUers confirms that at least some of these complaints were justified. Thus Molly Yard in a letter to Lash reported on a Vassar College meeting, which in early November 1937 reversed its initial approval of the Oxford Pledge, thanks to the manipulative behavior of communist students, who packed the meeting. "The story," Yard gloated "is that the YCL pulled in a lot of delegates who never even registered to vote on it. Anyway the whole thing is very sweet."[109]

The ASU convention, which met at Vassar College over the 1937 Christmas vacation, revealed the degree to which collective security advocates had outorganized their rivals. Unlike some of the previous ASU chapter meetings, however, there was no attempt here to stifle criticism of collective security. An equal number of speeches were heard from supporters and opponents of collective security. The YPSLs were permitted to have Norman Thomas, the Socialist Party's most eloquent speaker, make their case against collective security at the convention. Thomas argued that the only form of aid to anti-fascists overseas that would promote peace would be that which workers provided "independently of their government." Any involvement by Washington in these conflicts would only serve the interests of American imperialism and militarism. "Collective sanctions," Thomas warned, "means probable war and certain militarization . . . . We are not anxious to join the collective suicide club as the proponents of collective action by governments would have us do." But Thomas swayed few delegates. The convention voted by an overwhelming 282 to 108 margin to drop the Oxford Pledge from the ASU program and embrace collective security.[110]

Though this lopsided vote for collective security had been facilitated by communist manipulation of the delegate selection process, even had such manipulation not occurred the collective security position would still have carried the convention. Indeed, collective security advocates at the convention were so confident that their views represented the ASU rank and file that they offered to hold a referendum on the new peace planks among the organization's general membership. That referendum found the ASU membership embracing collective security by an even more resounding majority vote than had the convention itself. Not even ASU opponents of collective security claimed that the communists' underhanded tactics had been the key cause of their defeat at Vassar. It was rather the threatening events overseas which did the most to defeat these Oxford Pledge supporters and render them a defensive minority within the ASU. Hitler's and Mussolini's intervention in Spain and Japan's invasion of China strongly suggested that something had to be done to halt fascist aggression. This sentiment on campus had been reinforced by the ASU's persistent anti-fascist agitation, the deaths of American students fighting in Spain, and by the president himself in his Quarantine speech. By the fall of 1937 most ASUers would not be attracted by the foreign policies advocated by

YPSLs, pacifists, and Trotskyists, who were insisting on retaining the Oxford Pledge and United States neutrality, because these isolationist groups clearly lacked any realistic strategy for dealing with the fascist threat.[111]

The vote for collective security reflected a growing awareness among ASUers that their anti-war movement had to adapt to this changing international scene, something which foes of collective security seemed unwilling to do as they urged the ASU to stand firm and retain the Oxford Pledge. For most ASUers it no longer seemed enough to simply pledge oneself against militarism at home, as students had done through the Oxford Pledge in the early 1930s; one now had to address the problem of militarism overseas, which threatened to engulf the entire world in war. Thus in justifying their decision to abandon the Oxford Pledge for collective security, ASU leaders stressed that recent international developments had made the Pledge seem both outdated and provincial. Joseph Lash, in the only convention address published by the ASU, told the delegates that the Pledge was

> not only valueless in the present circumstances but actually a deterrent in the campaign for peace. Our concern is to keep America out of war; this demands a positive peace policy now. The Oxford Pledge talks fantastically about what we will do when war comes. Our concern is with how to prevent war from spreading; how to maintain the peace we have; how to restore the peace that has been shattered by fascist aggression. The Oxford Pledge demobilizes this immediate struggle for peace. With the fascists madly brandishing their war torches, the Oxford Pledge assumes that the main instigator of war today is the United States. Directing itself solely against the United States it breeds the illusion that we can . . . keep the United States out of war, [without concern] . . . for what is going on in the rest of the world.[112]

Having rejected the Oxford Pledge, the convention endorsed specific steps for the United States government to help halt fascist aggression. The ASU urged "American leadership in naming aggressors and applying embargoes against aggressors through international collaboration." The ASU took a strong stance against the neutrality policies which in the past had guided both the ASU and American foreign policy. The convention came out for "repeal or modification of the neutrality act so as to discriminate between aggressors and attacked and aiding those nations which are attacked."[113]

While dispensing with the Pledge as a symbol of outdated isolationism, the delegates embraced new symbols which articulated their opposition to international aggression. The first of these symbols was the student movement's own group of anti-fascist fighters and martyrs in Spain. Paying tribute to ASUers in the Abraham Lincoln Battalion, Lash told the convention that we are deeply proud of . . . the service records of our two N.E.C. members, George Watt and Paul MacEachron, and humble before those like Don Henry of the University of Kansas, Nate Schilling of Chicago University, Sam Levinger of Ohio State, Roy McQuarrie of Wayne and others who have been killed in action. What can we say to them save our pledge that the American Student Union will not forget them and will demonstrate its remembrance by its deeds. In an age which puts scorn upon the symbols of civilization—justice, freedom, democracy, humanity—these fellow students of ours have revitalized those values for our generation.[114]

Since the recent Japanese assaults on China had resulted in the deaths of many civilians, the convention also adopted a symbol of their solidarity with the victims of this aggression. After voting overwhelmingly to boycott Japanese goods in protest against the invasion of China, the delegates lit a bonfire and tossed silk stockings and neckties into the blaze. As the protesters fed the fire, they chanted "If you wear cotton, Japan gets nottin'."[115]

Throughout the convention, the ASU leaders championing collective security embraced an especially powerful symbol of their new position: President Roosevelt. Lash had solicited and received a letter of welcome to the delegates from the president, which was read at the convention and featured on the front page of the ASU's report on the Vassar proceedings. Though in October Roosevelt had quickly backed away from the anti-isolationist message of his Quarantine speech, this is no way diminished his usefulness as a symbol for ASUers promoting the new collective security policies. Their image of the president was of a leader who had urged the quarantining of aggressor nations. This was evident in Lash's convention speech, which attacked Oxford Pledge supporters for seeking "to resist President Roosevelt's moves toward international cooperation against fascist aggression." Lash warned that such opposition to the president "strengthen[s] the camp of isolation" and leads "inevitably into that world war which we all fear."[116] These pro-Roosevelt arguments proved helpful in attracting liberals to collective security at the ASU convention, and they would later have a similar impact on the national student body.

Although the ASU had made a dramatic break with its past in dumping the Oxford Pledge and endorsing collective security, there were also elements of continuity in the ASU's peace policy. The ASU continued to oppose United States "preparations for war," including "the skyrocketing military budget," and mandatory ROTC—positions the organization had held since its founding.[117] Though the pro-collective security ASUers at the Vassar Convention would have denied it at the time, there was an obvious contradiction between these old anti-preparedness policies and the new foreign policy adopted by the ASU. James Wechsler recalled that he harbored private doubts about the compatability of these two policies:

> If we were committed to the proposition that the free nations ought to band together with Russia to deter fascist aggression, much of the deterrent effect would depend on how strong they were. Neither Hitler nor Mussolini was likely to be impressed by a program of resistance based on unpreparedness. Any effective stand against aggression surely involved the risk of war; but we were now embracing a stand which called for the assumption of all the risks without any of the preparations.[118]

The reasons that the ASU convention left Vassar with such contradictory policies were both strategic and emotional. Obviously, it would be somewhat less traumatic for an organization making so fundamental a shift in its foreign policy if it avoided changing every aspect of its peace policy. By maintaining its opposition to preparedness, the ASU could continue to claim that it remained an anti-war organization and had merely changed its tactics for promoting peace. The retention of the anti-preparedness planks was also a sign of the ASU's reluctance to go all the way in surrendering the optimism that the student movement had previously cherished when it had embraced the Oxford Pledge. Even as it dropped that Pledge at Vassar, the ASU, as Lash recalled, "still . . . hoped that it would be possible to stop aggression without world war." The majority of ASUers came away from Vassar believing that if enacted, the foreign policy it was urging upon the American government—including the use of anti-fascist economic sanctions in conjunction with other western democracies and the U.S.S.R.—could help halt fascist aggression without dragging the United States into a new war.[119]

Such arguments did not sway the dissident minority within the ASU, which had lost the battle for the Oxford Pledge at Vassar. Most YPSLs, pacifists, and Trotskyists came away from the convention bitterly opposed to the ASU's new collective security policy. Leaders of this opposition, such as Alvaine Hollister, carried their criticism back to the campuses and into the leftwing and student press, warning that the ASU would now become a force for "Left jingoism on campus." Hollister told the *Socialist Call* that in the wake of the convention

> the ASU is no longer an organization devoted to the struggle against war . . . . Every working class or youth movement in Europe which had supported collective security has eventually come to the position of support of military programs and budgets of their countries. This must inevitably be true of the ASU. The American Student Union, when it dropped the Oxford Pledge and adopted a program of collective security deliberately aligned itself with the warmaking Roosevelt administration and gave the president a tacit pledge: "If you go to war against a fascist nation and call that war one for democracy, we will fill your armies and fire your guns."[120]

It was not merely such criticism, but the critics themselves that posed a serious problem for Lash and his allies as they worked to unite the ASU behind the new collective security policies. Several of these critics remained on the ASU national staff and were therefore in a strategic position to undermine the implementation of the new policies. Hollister, for example, who so scathingly indicted ASU "jingoism" in the press, had just been elected national high school secretary of the ASU. Robin Myers and Fay Bennett were also anti-collective security activists on the ASU national staff.

This situation had arisen because at Vassar the two sides had battled primarily over policy rather than personnel. Hollister and her allies had wanted to unseat Lash as ASU executive secretary, but lacked a candidate "willing and able to give Joe a real fight." They had also feared that such a challenge would anger the collective security majority at the convention, and result in all foes of collective security failing to be re-elected to national office in the ASU. For their part, Lash, and other pro-collective security leaders at the ASU convention blocked only one anti-collective security activist, Bob Kelso, from being elected to the ASU national staff. They had not tried to purge Hollister or most of her allies from the staff. This was apparently because Lash and his supporters already had their hands full orchestrating the ASU's programmatic change, and wanted to avoid a move that could further divide the convention. Moreover, since the collective security forces enjoyed a majority on the ASU's national staff, executive, and administrative committees, they initially thought they could afford to tolerate the presence of a few isolationists in the ASU's national leadership.[121]

Since the personnel conflict had not been fought out at the convention, it would rage within the national office itself, beginning immediately after the ASU leadership returned from Vassar. The anti-collective security staff members started working even more energetically than they had before the convention to promote the growth the Youth Committee for the Oxford Pledge (YCOP) and its successor in 1938, the Youth Committee Against War (YCAW). In effect, Hollister and her allies were seeking to use the contacts and resources of the ASU national office to subvert that organization, by launching the YCOP to compete with the ASU and its new foreign policy. This effort involved not only open competition, but factional plotting and spying. Only a few weeks after the Vassar Convention, Bob Kelso and another ASU staff member involved in organizing the YCOP slipped into the ASU national office late at night and began "reading through Joe's [Joseph Lash's] outgoing mail." Kelso reported to YPSL leader Al Hamilton on some of the instructions Lash's letters were giving to ASU opponents of the YCOP, gloating that he had "picked up some other good dope here last night in addition to copying some of the more interesting letters that Lash sent out."[122]

The anti-collective security faction seems to have had no monopoly on this type of political snoopery. In February 1938, for example, Joseph Lash obtained a copy of a confidential letter written by a YPSL leader. The letter, which apparently described a YPSL plan to remove Molly Yard from office, proved highly embarrassing to the YPSL leadership when

Lash showed the letter to Yard. The YPSL leaders were certain that the letter had reached Lash illicitly; it had, they thought, been given to Lash by YCL leader Gil Green, who himself allegedly obtained "it . . . thru a spy who went into Alvaine [Hollister]'s purse and personal folder and copied the carbon of the correspondence . . ."[123]

Such mistrust and deceit, even more than the Vassar Convention itself, attest that the Popular Front romance which had produced the communist-socialist marriage in the ASU was over: shattered by irreconcilable differences over foreign policy. Though the divorce between the ASU's pro- and anti-collective security forces had not yet been finalized, both sides knew that it was just a matter of time. Lash acknowledged this in a letter to Yard only a few weeks after the Vassar Convention, noting that "the YPSLs are just waiting for the opportune moment to break with the A.S.U . . . . Today they are not at all interested in building the A.S.U. but in criticizing it in such a way as to start a revolt."[124] The YPSL's internal reports and correspondence leave no doubt that Lash was correct in this estimation. The real question now was whether one party or the other in this divorce would carry off the family wealth: Would the ASU, with its collective security policies or the YCOP, with its advocacy of the Oxford Pledge, inherit the mass student anti-war movement which had been built when the two parties had been united? This question would be answered decisively by the American student body as it responded to the rival ASU and YCOP efforts to dominate the campus anti-war strike of 1938.

The struggle for control over the upcoming anti-war strike began shortly after the ASU convention; it was centered initially in the USPC's planning meetings for the strike. During the previous year, the ASU had been willing to cater to the pacifists and other anti-interventionists in the USPC by signing the organization's strike call, even though it promoted neutrality policies with which the ASU disagreed. The ASU had made that concession in 1937 for the sake of student unity in the strike. This time however, with the ASU having endorsed collective security and facing competition with the YCOP over the basic direction of the student anti-war movement, ASU leaders refused to make such major concessions. In the strike planning meetings of the USPC, ASU delegates took the position that they would under no circumstances agree to sign "an isolationist strike call."[125]

The ASU's collective security leadership did not, however, want to break up the USPC, since they realized that this broad coalition of leftist, liberal, and pacifist groups had played an important role in making the 1937 strike so large. Thus within the parameters of their collective security principles, the ASU representatives worked with the USPC on a strike call which might make some degree of unity possible. ASU leaders realized that they could not sell the USPC—with its pacifist affiliates—on a militantly anti-fascist strike call that urged such specific United States government steps as sanctions; instead, they pushed for a call which would be collective security in tone, but not so interventionist that it would alienate the pacifists. Joseph Lash proposed in February that the USPC strike call declare: "Whether America is at peace tomorrow depends upon whether American foreign policy is a force for peace today. We urge an American foreign policy which is based upon the distinction between the victim and aggressor." Lash thought that even for the pacifists such a statement would be

> a difficult one with which to take exception. Although the absolute pacifists think that it is worthless for the Spanish people to resist because they can gain nothing by violence, nevertheless they do not have the guts to say there is no distinction between aggressor and victim.[126]

Led by the YCOP, the socialist and pacifist student organizations attacked the language of Lash's proposed strike call. In a contentious USPC meeting held in mid-March, only a month before the national strike date, these supporters of the Oxford Pledge argued that the proposed call was too "weighted towards collective security." On this basis, the YCOP, the student sections of the Fellowship of Reconciliation, the National Council of Methodist Youth, and the War Resisters League announced at the USPC meeting that they would not sign the call. These groups wanted to drop Lash's language in favor of a strike call that presented the student walkout as "a dress rehearsal" for resistance to military service in any future war. This was, of course, the old anti-interventionist line of the first antiwar strikes, and was unacceptable to the ASU representatives, who depicted it as thoroughly outdated, arguing that "the time for a dress rehearsal is past. War exists."[127]

Unable to reach an agreement on the wording and message for its 1938 strike call, the USPC settled on a strike call without a text. The March meeting of the USPC decided to promote the strike through posters which said only, "Strike Against War," and listed the USPC's constituent groups, along with the date and time of the walkout. Instead of text, the USPC strike poster merely included a photograph of a shell-torn town. Since neither the ASU nor the YCOP had been able to incorporate its message into the USPC's strike call, the battle between them was on this level a draw. But in a sense the ASU won here because it removed the USPC, the strike's sponsoring organization, from the anti-collective security position it had taken in 1937, when its strike call had endorsed neutrality legislation and the Oxford Pledge. From a collective security standpoint the USPC's silence in 1938 was better than its anti-interventionist message in 1937.[128]

Since the battle between the ASU and the YCOP had not been settled decisively at the national level in the USPC, the critical test of strength would come on the campuses themselves. The YCOP, which in the spring changed its name to the Youth Committee Against War (YCAW) and affiliated with the Keep America Out of War Congress, began working frantically to prepare for the strike almost as soon as its leaders returned from the Vassar Convention.[129] But founding a new organization, rooting it in the campus communities, and preparing for a nationwide strike were large tasks, particularly since the April strike date meant that all of this had to be done in a hurry—and done in competition with the ASU. The YPSL, the key leftist organization behind the YCAW, had little experience in mass organizing; its activists were heavily concentrated in a few cities, particularly New York and Chicago. They had spent more time feuding with communists than mobilizing mainstream students, and it was unclear whether they could work effectively with such students. But the YCAW did have the benefit of the campus contacts of its pacifist students who, through their affiliation with such large national religious groups as the National Council of Methodist Youth, had more of a national student network than did the YPSLs.[130]

The YCAW had the advantage of promoting an anti-interventionist message which over the past few years had become both familiar and popular on campus. That message, after all, had mobilized hundreds of thousands of student anti-war strikers during the early and mid-1930s. Treating consistency as a virtue, YCAW organizers argued with great force that they rather than the ASU had been truer to the student movement's founding principles. YCAW leaflets quoted ASU leaders who had sung the Oxford Pledge's praises in 1936 and then repudiated the Pledge in 1937. YCAW organizers took this approach because they thought that students would continue to respond to those same isolationist appeals which had helped give birth to the campus peace movement.

A national poll taken by Brown University's student newspaper only a few weeks before the 1938 student peace strike suggested that the YCAW might be right. This poll of 31,515 students on 101 campuses found more support for United States neutrality than for collective security. Though the poll was not entirely reliable because of some poor wording on its questionnaire, its data left no doubt that isolationism remained a considerable force on campus. YCAW organizers understood that this student support of United States neutrality was rooted in collegiate disillusionment with World War I. They appealed to this disillusionment in much of their literature, and accused the ASU of following the Wilsonian path towards a new world war—only now anti-fascist rhetoric had replaced Wilsonian slogans to excuse the drift toward war.[131]

Given these advantages, the YCAW's performance in the 1938 strike was surprisingly weak. The YCAW had hoped that its separate strike rallies on behalf of the Oxford Pledge would match or exceed the turn-out at the ASU-led rallies for collective security. But by its own estimates, the YCAW mobilized only about 25,000 students in its strike actions, a turnout rate far below the YCAW's goals.[132] Frustration with this response pervaded many of the field reports by YCAW organizers. A pacifist YCAW activist from Berkeley, for instance, wrote with obvious disappointment that the effort to turn the local ASU chapter and strike against collective security had been voted down by a two to one margin.[133] Reports from the East were also discouraging, as YCAW executive secretary Alvaine Hollister noted:

> Philly has called off the Rayburn Plaza meeting—afraid they don't have enough strength for a demonstration—probably only too true . . . CCNY 23rd lost out . . . to c.s.[collective security] . . . Smith College . . . is overwhelmingly c.s., with a few faint traces of pacifist-socialist influence. The A.S.U.-communist strike [at Brooklyn College night school] had about 800 people and the best location; we had from 150–300, at a poorer location.[134]

There were only a few bright spots for the YCAW. The new organization did carry the day at the University of Chicago's anti-war strike in 1938. The Chicago campus witnessed a YCAW sponsored peace conference, which, according to one ASU report "was almost monopolized by the isolationists." Some 2000 students turned out on this campus to hear Norman Thomas' anti-interventionist speech. But the YCAW proved unable to duplicate this success in outorganizing the ASU on most campuses, even in the midwestern heartland of isolationism. Student response to YCAW organizers was often tepid. The YCAW field organizer in Ohio reported feeling "discouraged" about the student response to the strike.[135] A YCAW activist from the University of Illinois confessed to YPSL leader Judah Drob that the situation on that campus was "very discouraging," and that in his strike work he was making "no headway" against the ASU "political machine. . . . Ken Born (ASU organizer) was down here and clinched the hold that collective security has upon the . . . non-affiliated people."[136]

The YCAW's strike efforts seemed particularly ineffective in comparison with that of the ASU. Student participation in the ASU-led peace activities of the day of the strike was, according to ASU estimates, almost as high as the previous year. Even allowing for some exaggerating in the ASU reports, which claimed that 750,000–900,000 students were mobilized, the turnout was impressive. Though in this strike the ASU, for the first time in its history, faced competition from a hostile national student organization, the ASU had risen to the occasion with remarkable ease. Where the YCAW field reports had been grim, most ASU reports tended to be upbeat, reflecting the fact—confirmed by the press nationally—that at most major campuses the majority of demonstrators had joined the protests and rallies led by collective security advocates.[137]

The strike results reassured the ASU's leaders that their organization's shift to collective security would not threaten its position as the leading student activist organization in the United States. Indeed, in New York City alone, during the strike and the week following it, the ASU picked up 825 new student members. This was roughly comparable to the total national membership of the YCAW. Such successful recruiting, along with the national ASU membership figures, which stood at about 15,000, suggests just how effective the ASU had been in besting its new rival.[138]

The ASU's success against the YCAW in the 1938 mobilization was due in part to several key organizational advantages which the ASU carried into the strike. The ASU was by far the more established of the two groups. Since its founding in 1935, the ASU had constructed the nation's largest network of student activists. This network included not only the ASU and YCL chapters, but allied groups such as campus YW and YMCAs. At the national level, moreover, the ASU still had at its head the student movement's most experienced leaders, including Molly Yard and Joseph Lash, who had helped build the ASU and orchestrated the organization's effective national strike efforts in the past. All of this helped give the ASU a significant jump on its YCAW rivals.

The effectiveness of the ASU in the 1938 strike was facilitated by the organization's increasingly friendly relations with campus administrators. As part of its Popular Front approach to student organizing, the ASU had sought to enlist every element of the campus, including college officials in its anti-fascist coalition. For the sake of anti-fascist unity, ASU campus leaders were willing to negotiate with and even accommodate administrators over the format of strike day events on campus. When confronted by college officials who opposed the anti-war strike, ASU organizers would settle for peace assemblies, in which campus administrators helped shape, and in some cases even dominated the programs of these meetings. Relations between campus officials and the ASU also improved because the ASU's new foreign policy line made these activists no longer seem radical or threatening. It was not ASUers, but their rivals who were now promoting the Oxford Pledge, which administrators had tended to oppose as unpatriotic. This made it much easier for the ASU to gain some of level of administration support for their organizing, which in turn made the peace events seem more inviting to mainstream students.[139]

Its new rhetoric regarding President Roosevelt also aided the ASU peace mobilization. ASU activists invoked FDR and his Quarantine speech in their organizing for collective security, just as they had done in the Vassar convention.[140] This would, of course, appeal to the many liberal students who admired the president. It also would make it difficult for campus administrators to attack ASU-led events. Few college deans or presidents would see any need to suppress student organizers whose professed goal was rallying the campuses behind the foreign policy of the president of the United States.

These advantages notwithstanding, the ASU's success in outorganizing the YCAW was an impressive achievement. Indeed, though the ASUers in the 1938 strike had invoked the name of the Franklin Roosevelt for their cause, they had in fact proven much more daring and effective in challenging isolationism than had the president himself. FDR's challenge to isolation in his Chicago speech had been a brief foray, followed immediately by an almost complete retreat in the face of an isolationist criticism. Roosevelt had continued to defer to isolationists on Capitol Hill throughout the spring, and he remained too timid to remove the embargo on the Spanish republic. Unlike the president, the ASU, after openly embracing collective security in December 1937, refused to defer any longer to isolationists. The ASU not only challenged isolationism and proponents of United States neutrality, but defeated them both at the Vassar convention and at campuses across the nation in the spring anti-war mobilization.[141]

The inroads that the ASU made against collegiate isolationism owed much to the evolving international situation. The ASU's relentless criticism of the flaws and shallowness of isolationist thought was persuasive because it came at a time when the German and Italian sponsored fascists were on the march in Spain and while Japan brutalized China. These tragic events offered compelling evidence for the ASU's warnings about the evils of fascism and the need for international sanctions against aggressor nations. The collective security actions that the ASU proposed to halt such aggression may not have seemed ideal, since they could enmesh the United States in dangerous international conflicts; but no one was offering any better solutions—certainly not the YCAW with its calls for neutrality, which would have had the United States close its eyes to the crisis that was breeding a new world war. Recognizing this, and hoping that collective security might be able to prevent world war, students increasingly moved with the ASU away from isolationism.[142]

Although the dominance of the ASU and collective security in the 1938 strike suggests that isolationist forces were in a state of disarray on campus, the strike should not be read as signalling the death of collegiate isolationism. The fact that the isolationist YCAW mobilized far fewer students than expected was probably due more to poor organization (which is to be expected in a new student group) than to the lack of an isolationist student constituency. Moreover, the 25,000 student mobilization achieved by the YCAW seems small only in comparison to the ASU's. Placed into the broader context of the student movement's history in the Depression decade, the YCAW mobilization seems more substantial. Since this was the YCAW's first national strike effort, its 1938 mobilization—instead of being compared with the ASU's organization of this its third strike—might more properly be compared with that other first strike, the NSL-SLID sponsored peace strike of 1934. The YCAW in 1938, like the NSL and SLID in 1934, had rallied some 25,000 students. Given the persistent isolationist sentiment reflected in the student polls, the YCAW had considerable reason to hope that, like the NSL and SLID earlier in the decade, with experience its effectiveness in student strike mobilizations would grow. ASU leaders such as Lash were clearly worried about the YCAW. Indeed, in the wake of the 1938 strike, Lash warned a West Coast ASU organizer that because of the YCAW and the appeal of isolationism on campus "the

ASU is only beginning to experience hardship . . . . [The YCAW's] strikes and all its activities lead us to believe it will flower as a dual organization to the ASU, shortly." [143]

Such anxieties on the part of Lash and his fellow Popular Fronters in the student movement led them to intensify their efforts to promote collective security and battle isolationism. In August 1938 these efforts culminated in the largest single youth meeting of the decade, the second World Youth Congress (WYC). The WYC, which held its first meeting in Geneva in 1936 under the sponsorship of the League of Nations Association, had been founded to promote peace and international cooperation among the youth of the world. A broad coalition of student and youth organizations, which included the ASU, sought to turn the 1938 World Youth Congress, held in New York City and Poughkeepsie, into a major event on behalf of collective security. The idea was that if the strike against war had demonstrated American student support for the Popular Front against fascism, the WYC would demonstrate that such support among youth extended internationally. [144]

From the vantage point of the promoters of collective security, the World Youth Congress was an immense success. More than 500 delegates from 53 nations attended the Congress. This attendance lent credibility to the Congress' claims to speak for the world's youth. The WYC also demonstrated that the student movement's eagerness to align liberals and radicals into an anti-fascist front was winning it influential new friends. New York Mayor Fiorello La Guardia agreed to speak at the opening session of the Youth Congress, which helped attract a crowd of some 22,000 in Randall's Island Municipal Stadium in New York City. The WYC attracted additional attention nationally with First Lady Eleanor Roosevelt's address during the WYC sessions in Poughkeepsie, and with the radio broadcast on the gathering which was carried by the NBC radio network. [145]

The WYC's young organizers skillfully used all of this attention to publicize their Popular Front position. This was evident from the opening session of the Congress, which featured speakers from countries threatened by fascist aggression, such as Jiri Kasparek of Czechoslavakia, pleading for anti-fascist unity and collective security. F.Y. Young, of the Chinese delegation, told the crowd on Randall's Island that "Chinese youth wants more than sympathy from America. We want concrete action to help us halt the invasion of our homeland, and bring peace to the Far East." This same message prevailed as the Congress completed its working sessions on the Vassar College campus, culminating in the WYC's adoption of a strong collective security statement, the Vassar Peace Pact. Through this pact WYC delegates pledged

> to bring pressure to bear . . . upon our respective authorities to take the necessary concerted action to prevent aggression and bring it to an end, to give effective assistance to the victims of . . . aggression and to refrain

from participating in any aggression whether in the form of essential war material or other financial assistance.[146]

The Vassar Pact infuriated the YCAW. In the wake of the Vassar meeting, YCAW delegate Judah Drob charged that the communist-led collective security bloc at the WYC had railroaded the Pact through and had refused to allow discussion of the document on the floor of the Congress. Drob's complaint was not unjustified. Indeed, in responding to this complaint, the final published report of the WYC offered the feeble excuse that "limited time made impossible the discussion of the Vassar Peace Pact in a meeting of the United States delegation." Here, as was often the case within the anti-war movement during the late 1930s, when the communists faced an important vote, they displayed far more interest in winning than in playing by the rules of democratic process. Nor was this the only process abuse associated with the WYC. Prior to the Congress, the communist-dominated New York Planning Committee of the WYC had tried to exclude the YCAW from the WYC's American delegation. It was not until the YCAW and other peace organizations loudly demanded that all wings of the anti-war movement be represented at Vassar that the Planning Committee relented and admitted the YCAW.[147]

Despite these disputes, however, the WYC's adoption of the Vassar Pact represented a clear defeat for YCAW and its isolationist allies. After the YCAW had been admitted to the WYC, the American delegation did have representatives of all wings of the student anti-war movement. And despite the dissent of the YCAW minority, the American delegation voted overwhelmingly to endorse the Vassar Pact. Although the decision-making process would, of course, have been more judicious had the Pact been fully debated, the delegates did know what they were voting for, and they agreed to endorse a Pact that was unambiguous in its endorsement of collective security. Here, as in the 1938 strike against war, the YCAW proved unable to assemble majority student support for United States neutrality. But the failure of the YCAW at Vassar extended beyond the American peace movement.

The YCAW's socialist leaders found that they could not even attract the support of their socialist comrades from Europe who were representatives at the World Youth Congress. A frustrated Drob noted that at the WYC's caucus of the Socialist Youth International "the United States Socialists were the only members of the International who opposed collective security." Worried by the fascist menace on their continent, the young European socialists at the WYC "insisted that Hitler could only be defeated by the military strength of the United States." Drob and his fellow American socialists responded by "asserting that the workers of Germany were simply waiting for Hilter's entry into a war for a revolutionary uprising," which would topple the Nazi regime. But the Europeans, better acquainted with the strength of the Nazi threat, dismissed this argument as unrealistic. They accused the American YPSLs of being "romantic leftists," too absorbed in the "distant ideal of socialism" to recognize that the most important task at hand was uniting all anti-fascist nations to stop Hitler.[148]

The outcome of the WYC added to the sense of progress and momentum of student activists promoting collective security on campus. For them the Vassar Pact served as a symbol—much as the Oxford Pledge had been for the very different peace policies of the early 1930s—that American youth were part of an international anti-fascist movement. The WYC was, however, only one of the many ways in which the student movement used its international contacts to combat isolationism. Through much of the late 1930s the ASU sponsored collegiate speaking tours by activists recently back from Spain and China, who gave first hand accounts of fascist aggression, and who urged an American role in halting this aggression. Such reports on the international crisis and pleas for help from abroad placed collegiate isolationists on the defensive.[149]

The movement's most effective advocates of international solidarity against fascism may have been those unable to make such campus tours: the recent college alumni in the Lincoln Battalion, whose letters from Spain were circulated by the ASU and the student press. "Nothing must be left undone in stopping fascism; there is no sacrifice we can refuse to make" wrote Ralph Neafus of the University of Michigan, before being captured by Franco's forces. Sam Levinger, an Ohio State ASUer, agreed. Shortly before his death on the Aragon front, Levinger wrote: "the war is long . . . . Still let us climb the grey hill and charge the guns, . . . towards . . . A free bright country."[150] The emotional power of such appeals helped open the campuses to the Popular Front, and spread an internationalism that was more than rhetorical. They gave ASUers and many of their classmates a sense that fascism's triumphs abroad threatened freedom everywhere, including the United States. This internationalist sensibility left ASUers determined to battle isolationism no matter what the political risks— in stark contrast to the president himself; it enabled ASUers to march aggressively into the collegiate centers of isolationism and outorganize their isolationist rivals in the peace mobilizations of 1938.[151]

Internationalism of a more abstract, but no less influential, sort also steeled the ASU's resolve to battle isolationism. The ASU's communist leadership regarded the U.S.S.R. as a leftist utopia. They thought it their obligation as part of the international communist movement to defend the Soviet Union. This rigid loyalty left communist students determined to defy the strong winds of collegiate isolationism for the sake of collective security. They believed that collective security was critical for the protection of the Soviet Union because it would unite the world against the U.S.S.R.'s dangerous fascist enemies.[152]

The communists' pivotal role in challenging collegiate isolationism would give that challenge an ironic quality. Communists led the student body away from its dogmatically critical view of United States foreign policy, even though they previously had been among the most dogmatic critics of all. The movement had been born with communists, along with socialists and pacifists, championing a litany of simplistic "lessons" from the First World War: that all of United States foreign policy is inherently imperialistic, as is any war involving capitalist states; that since the First World War had been a bloody clash over imperialist spoils, so would any new world war, and as such the public had no interest in fighting a war between virtually indistinguishable rivals. Bound by such dogmas, the student movement in the early 1930s had been been lost in the world of 1917, endorsing neutrality legislation designed to halt a Woodrow Wilson, and acting as if Wilsonianism rather than fascism posed the greatest threat to peace. But in the mid-1930s, communist students rebelled against these anachronistic views because the U.S.S.R. and the Popular Front had shown them the way toward a more realistic appraisal of the fascist threat.

Communist ASUers would carry this realism to the student movement, as they pressed students to allow the crisis of the present—the tragic events in Germany, Italy, Spain, China, and Japan—rather than the dogmas of the past to guide their outlook on United States foreign policy. The student strike of 1938, with its emphasis on collective security, suggested that the ASU had been surprisingly successful in this effort, replacing dogmatism with political realism, and prodding students to see that because of fascist aggression the international crisis of their own era was different and more ominous than the crisis that had led to the First World War. But this ASU realism would prove transient. The same communist ASUers who had freed much of the student movement of its isolationist dogma were afflicted by an equally dogmatic faith in Stalin and his foreign policies—a faith which in the fall of 1939 would lead to the destruction of the Popular Front on campus.

Chapter 7

Beyond the New Deal?
Egalitarian Dreams and
Communist Schemes

We are tired of waiting, Mrs. Roosevelt.

> Louis Burnham, an African American student leader in the
> ASU, responding to the First Lady's suggestion that young
> activists show some "patience" on the issue of racial equality.
> *Student Advocate* (March 1936), 16.

The student movement came to President Roosevelt's doorstep on February 20, 1937, when some 3000 young demonstrators marched on the White House. The protesters, representing student and youth organizations from across the nation, sought to dramatize the economic hardships of youth in Depression America. Marching down Pennsylvania Avenue, they waved banners and chanted their demands. "Pass the American Youth Act—We want jobs;" "Scholarships not Battleships;" "Homes not barracks." One group dressed in prison garb, carried a sign "We never had jobs." Others costumed as pilgrims, miners, and farmers made the same point. The California delegation rode in on a covered wagon bearing the battered sign "Go East Young Man." To the tune of Yankee Doodle, the protesters—carrying signs that identified their college, school, religious group, or trade union affiliation—sang "American youth is on the march for jobs and education." This was, as the *Washington Post* observed "a line of marchers such as Washington has never seen before."[1]

This march on the White House was part of a three day Youth Pilgrimage for Jobs and Education. The protesters did more than parade down Pennsylvania Avenue; they also lobbied Congress on behalf of greater federal assistance to the millions of young Americans hurt by the Great Depression. The pilgrimage attested that even though peace was the most popular cause on campus, the student movement of the 1930s was not merely an anti-war crusade. It was also a movement for social justice, whose leaders cared so much about the plight of low-income youth that they chose to make this, rather than war, the focus of the movement's first sizable national march on Washington.[2]

The pilgrimage symbolized the student movement leadership's commitment to building a more egalitarian America. The movement's leaders envisioned a society where education would be a right rather than a privilege; they thought Washington should ensure that no one would be—as millions of Depression era youth had already been—forced to drop out of school because of insufficient funds. The student movement sought to make America a nation free of unemployment, poverty, and racism. These were natural concerns for a movement led by leftists and born amidst the worst economic depression in American history.[3]

In pursuit of this egalitarian vision, the student movement's leaders had worked to broaden the base of their movement. These young leftists realized that the task of changing America and bringing educational and economic opportunity to their generation required more political muscle than could be found on the campuses alone. This was, after all, a time when inadequate financial and educational resources kept the vast majority of young Americans (almost 90 percent of the college age population) out of college. If the student movement was to have real credibility as a voice of Depression era youth, it would have to expand its constituency well beyond the small college elite. With this goal in mind, student activists in the mid-1930s began working to build a unified youth movement, which could link students and non-students in the quest for expanded federal aid to youth and egalitarian social change. The organization through which this was attempted was the same one which sponsored the Youth Pilgrimage for Jobs and Education: the American Youth Congress.[4]

Founded in 1934, the American Youth Congress (AYC) soon evolved into the most influential leftist-led youth group in Depression America. More than any other organization, the Youth Congress broke down the barriers between the college elite and non-student youth. The Youth Congress served as an advocate for millions of underprivileged young Americans—blue collar workers, blacks, the unemployed, and needy students— who traditionally had been ignored by the political process. Organized as a youth federation and lobby, the AYC assembled an amazingly broad group of affiliates, which included not only students, but labor, civil rights, religious, community and fraternal organizations. Among the Youth Congress' members were the National Student Federation, the YWCA, the National Intercollegiate Christian Council, the National Council of Methodist Youth, the Youth Committee Against War, the Young People's Socialist League, the Young Communist League, the Southern Negro Youth Congress, the Chinese Student League, Young Judea, the American Stu-

dent Union, the Southern Tenant Farmers Union, youth divisions of the
American Jewish Congress, the United Auto Workers, the United Electrical, Radio and Machine Workers, locals of the National Association for
the Advancement of Colored People and many others. At its height in the
late 1930s, the Youth Congress included dozens of national organizations
and scores of local groups, claiming to represent 4.5 million American
youths.[5]

If the number of affiliated organizations was impressive, so was the
diversity of the delegates themselves, who participated in the national
meetings of the Youth Congress. Thousands of delegates from different
races, social classes, and occupations attended these meetings. Youths who
participated in these gatherings for the first time often were moved by
the experience. Most had never before attended meetings which so broadly
cut across class, regional, and racial lines; they found it inspiring to meet
fellow youths from such different backgrounds and to unite with them on
behalf of a common political agenda. After returning from one such Youth
Congress meeting in Washington, for example, Elliot Maraniss, editor of
the University of Michigan student newspaper, wrote that the young activists at this gathering

> knew what problems were facing them . . . knew what they wanted and
> . . . knew how to get it. There were young Negro girls from the deep
> South who told us a tale of unbelievable misery and poverty; the Tom
> Joads and Rosasharons of the Grapes of Wrath Country who related the
> epic of the Oakies; the young men who will reap the corn on the Iowa
> plains; young auto workers, electricians, seamen and miners who told us
> the story of youth's part in the growth of trade unionism; young students
> expertly trained for some profession with no hope of employment; and
> there were the representatives of the four million of us who are without
> jobs; the kids who spent the . . . decade on box cars and highways . . .
> looking for work, who have known the hunger and frustration of en-
> forced idleness. These young people were marching arm-in-arm to the
> future organized and determined to solve their problems, and inspired
> with the courage that comes with youthfulness, with strength and with a
> program that is based upon truth, fact and real need.[6]

By assembling this broad coalition of young Americans, the Youth
Congress from 1934–1937 hoped to push the federal government beyond
the New Deal. The Youth Congress advocated more sweeping and generous social legislation than had yet been provided by the Roosevelt administration. At the heart of this effort to surpass the New Deal was the
Youth Congress' own aid package for youth, the American Youth Act
(AYA). The AYA would have gone much further than the New Deal in
providing federal aid to the young. It was in part to promote this legislation that the Youth Congress organized the 1937 Pilgrimage for Jobs and
Education. During the pilgrimage, Youth Congress leaders brought their

advocacy of this bill directly to President Roosevelt, presenting him with pro-AYA petitions, signed by close to a million Americans.[7]

The campaign for the American Youth Act was the culmination of an old dream on the part of student activists. Ever since the NSL's birth in 1931, leftist students had urged the government to assist youths who were unable to pay their way through school. Under FDR, the federal government finally became involved in rendering such assistance through the Federal Emergency Relief Administration (FERA) in 1934 and the the National Youth Administration (NYA) in 1935. These New Deal agencies annually provided $15 a month jobs to some 110,000 undergraduates and graduate students—aiding about 12 percent of the students in American higher educational institutions. The NYA also gave jobs to over 200,000 secondary school students (at a maximum of $6 per month) and to about the same number of non-students.[8] Although applauding this new federal assistance as a welcome break from the do-nothing policy of the Hoover administration, the Youth Congress was quick to point out the NYA's shortcomings. The Youth Congress deemed the NYA far too limited and underfunded to provide a realistic solution to the economic problems confronting young Americans.[9]

Citing NYA director Aubrey Williams' own statistics, Youth Congress leaders pointed out that of the five to eight million unemployed and needy youths (between the ages of 16 and 25), only a half million would receive aid from the NYA. Youth Congress activists from many different campuses complained that demand for student NYA jobs far exceeded the supply; they charged that the more needy the student body, the more inadequate was the NYA's assistance because the aid program was limited to 12 percent of the total student population, irrespective of how much more needy one campus might be over another. Thus at North Dakota Agricultural College, where 661 out of a total—and hard hit—male student population of 991 applied for aid, only 154 were given jobs. At Howard University, a black institution whose students were also heavily burdened by the economic crisis, 1400 NYA applications were submitted, out of a student body of 1700, and only 153 students received NYA jobs.[10]

The Youth Congress also complained of the NYA's inadequate attention to youths who were not in college. Youth Congress activist Constance Dimock of Vassar College pointed out that in the NYA "32 million out of 50 million dollars was alloted for student relief, [which] indicates that the NYA has dealt more with the needs of students than with young workers." This seemed particularly inequitable, since the majority of the nation's unemployed and needy youths were non-students. The Youth Congress stressed the inadequacy of the six dollars monthly NYA wage allocated for secondary school students, since this amounted to only a minimal income supplement rather than a living wage.[11]

Youth Congress leaders took the NYA to task for its "complete lack of democratic administration." They charged that too little was being done to see that the NYA did not discriminate against blacks. Youth Congress activists were also disturbed that although the NYA's mission was to serve students and other low-income youth, these groups were excluded from the NYA's decision-making process. They complained that too many businessmen sat on the NYA's national advisory board, and that most of the local administrative boards "included no representative of youth or its natural ally organized labor." This was, in the Youth Congress' view, undesirable because it meant that "any appreciation which these members of the . . . [NYA administrative] committees have of the want, hunger and despair facing contemporary youth have been derived from theoretical rather than practical sources."[12]

Although many of its criticisms of the NYA were astute, the Youth Congress quickly grew dissatisfied with playing the role of critic. Rather than merely denouncing the flaws in the New Deal youth program, the Youth Congress in 1935 formulated the American Youth Act as an alternative to that program. Here the Youth Congress took its criticisms of the NYA and transformed them into a comprehensive legislative proposal. The Youth Congress then convinced Farm-Laborite Senator Elmer Benson of Minnesota and his counterpart in the House, Thomas Amlie of Wisconsin, to sponsor the bill.[13]

The American Youth Act was far more ambitious than the NYA; it mandated federal aid to *all* needy Americans between the ages of 16 and 25. Through massive public works projects, the American Youth Act would have provided federal employment to millions of jobless young Americans, rather than the few hundred thousand supported annually by the NYA. Where limited funds had led the NYA to turn down more job applicants than it accepted, the Youth Act would have granted aid to all youths who applied for it. Under the Youth Act the monthly student wage level would rise substantially—paying high school students $15 instead of the $6 NYA wage and college students $25 instead of the $15 NYA wage. The Youth Act provided for a more democratic means of administering aid than had the NYA; it would have established an advisory board in which representatives of youth organizations, labor unions, social service, and educational institutions supervised the program. The language of the Youth Act barred racial discrimination in the distribution of student aid. Funding for this aid program would have been structured in a progressive fashion, drawing upon corporate and inheritance taxes.[14]

The American Youth Act represented so radical an expansion of federal aid to youth that it stood little chance on Capitol Hill. Where the NYA's budget had been $50 million in 1935, the Youth Act would have required an allocation of at least $3.5 billion. Critics of the Youth Act charged that its final cost would approach $15 billion. Such criticism prevented the bill from getting out of committee in 1936 or any of the three other times that the legislation was re-introduced between 1937 and 1940. Nonetheless, the campaign that the Youth Congress waged on behalf of this legislation did much to publicize both the acute economic distress endured by millions of youths in Depression American and the inability of the NYA to relieve much of that distress. This agitation convinced the Senate Committee on Education and Labor to conduct hearings on the Youth Act. These hearings attracted national press attention, as the students produced witnesses from youth organizations, college faculties, social welfare and government agencies documenting the need for expansion of federal aid to youth.[15]

The campaign for the American Youth Act attracted attention not only in the press and on Capitol Hill, but also in the White House. Through this campaign, Youth Congress leaders established a relationship with influential New Dealers, including Eleanor Roosevelt. Through much of the second half of the Depression decade, the First Lady served as the key liaison between the Roosevelt administration and the student movement. Mrs. Roosevelt showed great interest in the problems of youth, an interest which was primarily humanitarian. Mrs. Roosevelt worried about the Depression's impact on the younger generation, fearing that joblessness would breed despair. "I have moments of real terror," she explained in spring 1934, "when I think we may be losing this generation. We have got to bring these young people into the active life of the community and make them feel that they are necessary."[16] The First Lady looked to the federal government to provide the job programs which could give hope and material aid to the young. Her vision was that of a younger generation rescued from poverty, and therefore able to lend its renewed energy and sense of idealism to the struggle for social reform—in alliance with the New Deal.[17]

Knowing of the First Lady's interest in youth problems, Youth Congress leaders sought and obtained a meeting with her to discuss the American Youth Act in January 1936. This meeting proved a stormy affair. The First Lady, accompanied by NYA director Aubrey Williams, told the Youth Congress' national council that she could not endorse the Youth Act, which she thought too expensive to stand any real chance of being enacted by Congress. The Youth Congress leaders confronted the First Lady with tough criticism of the the NYA, implying that it had failed to "relieve the distress of from five to eight million unemployed youth." These young activists then spent a half-hour grilling the First Lady on the New Deal's other shortcomings.[18]

The tension at the meeting reflected the large gap between Mrs. Roosevelt's liberalism and the Youth Congress leaders' radicalism. On such key issues as the right of labor to organize, unemployment, and the fiscal crisis of educational institutions, Mrs. Roosevelt's young critics wanted quicker and more decisive federal intervention than she was willing to sanction. Joseph Lash, who was at this meeting, recalled being unimpressed with the First Lady's responses to their criticisms of the New Deal. The young radical found Mrs. Roosevelt a well intentioned but naive liberal "utterly lacking in knowledge of social forces," who "thinks she can reform capitalists . . . by inviting them to the White House for dinner and a good talking to."[19]

Despite her sharp policy differences with the Youth Congress leaders and the friction at this meeting, Mrs. Roosevelt reached out to them. She tried to defuse their hostility to the New Deal by acknowledging the NYA's shortcomings and conceding that more should be done to help youth. And she stressed the need for unity among people working to change America, advising that "it is wrong to be quite as divided as some of us are getting." Mrs. Roosevelt then invited the Youth Congress leaders to tea at the White House, assuring them that she understood their impatience at the pace of reform, since changes did seem to "take forever." "I used to be awfully impatient when I was your age."[20]

Mrs. Roosevelt's tolerance of dissent and her ongoing interest in the youth issue ensured that this first meeting would be the start of a long term relationship with the Youth Congress. She not only kept her lines of communication open to the Youth Congress leaders, but assisted them in gaining access to other prominent New Dealers. Mrs. Roosevelt was responsible for setting up the meeting between Youth Congress leaders and the president during the 1937 pilgrimage. At this meeting the president took the same position on the Youth Act that the First Lady had, refusing to endorse it on the grounds that it was too expensive. But here the president also made some sympathetic statements, telling the Youth Congress leaders that they "were on the right track in seeking federal aid for the nation's hard hit young population." President Roosevelt assured them "I am glad of what you are doing," and pledged to try to expand the NYA.[21]

President Roosevelt was not merely being polite in praising the youth delegation. The president was facing considerable Republican pressure to cut the NYA, and he and his administration perceived that the Youth Congress' campaign for greater federal aid could help offset this pressure. This same impulse toward converting the Youth Congress and the student movement into allies of the New Deal helped prod NYA Director Aubrey Williams to begin supporting and befriending the movement's national leadership. Indeed, on the day of the 1937 youth march on the White House, Williams congratulated the Youth Congress for helping to turn public opinion against cuts in federal aid to students. Williams told the protesters, "I know that your work has yielded some good results and will yield more. And I am in a good position to know whether it yields anything or whether it doesn't."[22]

This attention and praise from the president and NYA director suggested that the student movement was beginning to have some real impact in Washington. That impact was of course neither as dramatic nor complete as movement activists might have hoped, since the movement failed to enact its youth aid package. With the voting age 21, it was hardly surprising that a youth organization such as the AYC would lack the electoral power to win the Youth Act battle and push the New Deal leftward. Nonetheless, the Youth Congress' interaction with high ranking New Dealers attested that the movement was obtaining recognition as the leading advocate of youth's economic and political interests. Through the Youth

Congress, the student movement was helping to define youth's economic plight as a national issue and building a constituency for expanded federal aid to youth. These were considerable achievements for young activists simultaneously engaged in organizing a national student movement against war. If the national campus strikes showed America that students cared about peace, then the marches, hearings, and lobbying efforts of the Youth Congress in Washington showed that they also cared about educational and economic opportunity—and would fight to prevent the Depression from closing off those opportunities to youth.

II

While the Youth Congress brought the student movement's political agenda to Washington, student activists across the nation were engaged in similar efforts on their own campuses. Just as the Youth Congress from 1934–1937 sought to push the New Deal leftward, student activists first in the NSL, SLID and then in the ASU worked to push their classmates in this same direction. The student movement challenged the elitism, materialism, and conformity bred by traditional collegiate culture. Movement activists sought to convince the student body that its welfare and that of society would best be served by struggling to make both the campuses and the nation more egalitarian. They argued that the government could be pressed to ensure that the educational and economic opportunities of youth were not extinguished by the Depression only if students aligned themselves with other dispossessed groups—particularly blue-collar workers and their burgeoning labor movement.

Hoping to bring about an alliance between the student movement and the labor movement, campus activists made collegiate class prejudice one of their key targets. Student activists understood that college campuses had traditionally fed middle-class aspirations for upward mobility. These were institutions which readied students for competition in the corporate marketplace and left students placing a high value on individual wealth.[23] The flip side of this culture of aspiration had been a disdain for those without wealth, the working class. The nation's predominantly middle-class campuses had been so unfriendly toward workers and their unions that during many industrial disputes, college students had served as strikebreakers. In their struggle for a more egalitarian campus world, student activists in the 1930s sought to end such antagonism toward workers. This pro-labor orientation had been evident ever since the earliest days of the NSL, when students traveled down to Kentucky in 1932 to aid the striking coal miners; it had also been embodied in the Youth Congress, which united students and young trade unionists on behalf of federal job programs for youth. Throughout the mid-1930s, the student movement worked to perpetuate this type of unity. Thanks to the student movement, the sight of undergraduate delegations marching on the picket lines of organized labor would become common in many communities.[24]

The student movement's pro-labor actions were motivated in part by ideological considerations. As leftists, student movement leaders saw the working class as the primary agent of social change. "One of the basic tenets of the student movement was that it wasn't a movement in isolation from the rest of society" recalled NSL alumnus George Watt. "If anything, it was really auxiliary to what was going on outside, particularly in the working class and labor movement . . . [which we saw as] the moving force of history."[25] Thus campus radicals thought it critical that they awaken the student body to the historic class struggle beyond the college gates and align the campus with labor's battle to democratize American economic life.

The sense that labor represented the engine of egalitarian change grew especially strong with the upsurge of labor militancy during the mid-1930s, when general strikes and the CIO's organizing drive electrified the country. Moreover, the student Left thought that the publicity generated by its pro-labor actions could provide immediate assistance to unions and help attract much needed positive publicity to their strikes. Bringing students on to picket lines was also seen as a form of practical education which could help radicalize students, by exposing them to the poor conditions workers faced and the repression they confronted when they tried to protest those conditions.[26]

A strong humanitarian and personal element contributed to the movement's pro-labor work. Students recognized that working-class Americans suffered far more because of the Depression than had college graduates. There was a strong desire to ease the distress of the impoverished. Sometimes mixed in with this general humanitarian impulse to help labor were feelings of guilt, particularly among more affluent students at the elite private colleges—who thought it unjust that they lived in luxury while millions suffered. The activists "who came from wealthy backgrounds," explained James Wechsler, did have a tendency to be "excessively guilt ridden" because of "the ironies of their condition . . . , growing up [prosperous] in the Depression."[27] Guilt figured prominently, for example, in *Question Before the House,* a play about student-worker cooperation, co-authored by a Vassar undergraduate in 1935. This play, which was performed at Hallie Flanagan's Experimental Theatre at Vassar, glorified striking workers and the students who marched with them on picket lines protesting corporate greed. *Question Before the House* urged Vassar students to aid labor on the grounds that their own exclusive

> college is amazingly luxurious—luxury made possible by the unnecessarily low wages of the masses of people . . . . This college is . . . supported . . . by . . . corporations, many of which are guilty of very questionable labor practices . . . We have a definite responsibility to act in

this case. Why this college is . . . supported by profits squeezed out of . . . workers.[28]

Such guilt feelings may help explain why student activists on such relatively affluent campuses as Yale, Dartmouth, Harvard, Vassar, and Bryn Mawr conducted some of the student movement's more impressive pro-labor campaigns.

It was not only students from the more affluent campuses, however, who joined in labor protests. New York City's free municipal colleges were also centers of pro-labor activism. Many students in these colleges were themselves from working-class families with trade union backgrounds, who had learned to revere organized labor before they ever reached college. Recalling his experience, which was typical of many other City College radicals, literary critic Irving Howe explained how his parents' involvement in the garment workers' strike of 1933 had left him an avid supporter of the labor movement.

> Though they had never before shown any class militancy, my folks joined the picket lines . . . . Once the strike was won, life became easier: we could now have meat more often, my parents managed to squirrel away a few dollars in a savings account, and once my birthday came around my mother bought me a few "grownup" shirts. . . . The garment unions . . . [helped] ease . . . hardships . . . [and gave us] a fragment of dignity. In later years, whenever I heard intellectuals of the Right or Left attack unionism, I would be seized by an uncontrollable rage that then gave way to frustration: how to explain . . . what the strike of 1933 had meant, how to find words to tell of the small comforts the union had brought, the meat on the table and "grownup" shirts?[29]

Students in New York's municipal colleges who shared Howe's pro-labor perspective mounted the largest college labor support actions of the mid-1930s. Their involvement in the 1935 retail workers strike at Or-bach's, one of Manhattan's more famous department stores, led to the largest mass arrest of students on a labor picket line. Police arrested more than 100 Hunter, City, and Brooklyn College students, while 10,000 spectators cheered these young picketers during the strike. The second largest arrest of students on a labor picket also occurred in the City system in 1935, when 39 Brooklyn College students were booked for their participation in a strike by food service workers.[30]

Employers in the neighborhoods of these city colleges found that if they became involved in labor disputes, they had to worry almost as much about large, well organized student pro-labor protests as they did about the striking unions. During a strike at Sorrell's, a popular cafeteria near Brooklyn College, in 1934, there were more students than workers on the picket lines. Describing this strike, the Brooklyn College newspaper reported that

> At lunch hour, students gathered on the outside of the restaurant, forming long semi-circular lines, and booed all the students who entered the cafeteria. So long were the groups aligned in front of the food establishment that reserves from the 84th precinct were called and more than 10 patrolmen . . . [arrived]. Later three mounted policemen were called to supplement those dispersing the throngs of students.[31]

These protests and an increasingly effective student boycott of the cafeteria forced management to capitulate—raising wages and recognizing the union.

A similar result was obtained in the more turbulent student protests during a cafeteria strike in the CCNY campus neighborhood in 1935. Here the owner of a cafeteria on Broadway, incensed over student support of his striking workers, had the police arrest 27 CCNY undergraduates in a week of picketing. The students organized a boycott of the cafeteria, forcing management to settle with the union. The disorderly conduct charges against the students were soon dropped, with the judge admonishing them to "spend more time in school and let the strikers take care of their own affairs"—advice which went unheeded as CCNY students continued their labor support work.[32]

As with the Harlan delegation of 1932, some of the pro-labor campaigns were organized jointly by students from a number of different campuses. In a Hartford munitions strike in 1935, small groups of delegates came from colleges all over the Northeast to help the picketers. The colleges represented in this picket included Amherst, Barnard, Connecticut State College, Mount Holyoke, Smith, Trinity, Vassar, and Wesleyan.[33] The students hoped that by organizing such a broad intercollegiate group, they would convey the impression that there was great public support for the strikers, and thus put added pressure on management. This same approach was used by activists from Dartmouth, Bennington, Skidmore, Hunter, and the University of Vermont, who in 1936 jointly conducted a public hearing on the poor working conditions which had led to a strike by Vermont quarry workers.[34]

The issue of freedom of speech and assembly often became linked with pro-labor campaigns, after students observed police and management infringements on the constitutional rights of picketers. Protests against one such infringement caused the arrest of 21 Berkeley student activists in 1936, who had joined striking warehouse workers on the picket line in violation of Berkeley's anti-picketing ordinance—which made it unlawful "for persons to attempt to influence any person not to purchase goods at any business." Even after the strike was settled, the students continued their campaign against the ordinance, protesting directly to the Berkeley City Council.[35]

The student movement sought to end all collegiate involvement in strikebreaking activity. At the University of Southern California, for instance, NSL organizers heard rumors in 1934 that USC's employment office was recruiting strikebreakers for the longshoremen's strike. This elicited a quick response from campus NSL activists, including Celeste Strack, who

> called up to find out about this. And sure enough they were enlisting people to go down to the waterfront. And they had specifically gone after the football players from the fraternity houses. So we got out and visited the fraternity houses. And we also distributed a leaflet on campus about it. We made it very well known on campus and they stopped it. They actually stopped it. And we sent a delegation down to the waterfront to do some picketing with the longshoremen. That was our first direct connection with the labor movement from SC, and it was a very natural one because of the effort that was being made to send the scabs down.[36]

As part of such campaigns against strikebreaking, student organizers tried to educate their classmates on the evils of scabbing. When a few Columbia students were found strikebreaking in a 1936 building trades strike, they were admonished that scabs

> debase the living standards of American workmen . . . . The students have seized a chance to make money that in all likelihood they needed badly. It did not occur to them, perhaps, that their need is petty compared to that of the men who have been trying to raise families on $19 and less for a sixty hour week.[37]

Where education failed, movement activists tried to shame students out of strikebreaking, as at Berkeley, where the NSL newspaper included a scab list, naming all those collegians who served as strikebreakers.[38]

The student movement sought to uncover and halt any official university involvement in anti-labor work. A major controversy erupted over this issue at Berkeley in 1936, where student activists discovered that the campus ROTC class gave cadets an exam designed to groom them for an anti-labor military campaign. The exam question asked the cadets to contemplate a hypothetical waterfront strike in San Francisco, which resulted in a Bay Area general strike and the mobilization of the National Guard and ROTC to maintain order. In this strike, where a "considerable part of the population is sympathetic towards the strikers," the cadets were asked how the ROTC troops, equipped with tear gas and gas masks, could best be deployed to prevent pro-labor gangs from invading the campus and damaging University property. Once the students made public the use of this exam question, outraged local labor leaders complained, forcing the University to pledge not to allow such biased anti-labor materials to be used in the ROTC.[39]

Students aided labor in union recruitment efforts. Harvard radicals organized a Labor Committee which was in constant contact with the CIO; it provided student organizers who went into Boston's department stores to recruit members for the retail workers union. Harvard activists also established a special squad, consisting of 30 students, which in 1936 and 1937 worked with the United Rubber Workers of America in their attempts to organize in the New England region. Every day two members of this squad would travel with union organizers and speak to workers, encouraging them to join the union. University of Chicago students played a similar role in the CIO organizing drive in the packinghouses, as did Virginia Union University's students in the CIO's campaign in the tobacco industry.[40]

In addition to this pro-labor agitation, students participated in labor education and relief work. The student movement organized fundraising events and food drives for striking workers, and sent volunteers to the coal region of West Virginia, who assisted with Christmas parties and other events designed to brighten up the lives of the impoverished workers and their families. Students in the YWCA organized similar relief work and set up programs in which students could be educated to workers' problems both through factory visits and contact with young workers who belonged to the Y's industrial branches. Students, particularly from the women's colleges, served as volunteers in the labor schools at Bryn Mawr and Vineyard Shore, which provided workers with free educational opportunities.[41]

Sometimes unions found the support of students critical to the success of their local organizing drives. Stella Nowicki, a CIO packinghouse organizer in the Chicago stockyards recalled that at a crucial time in her local's history, University of Chicago student activists provided the union with much needed assistance

> in editing and getting funds. They would help us in writing material for leaflets and by distributing materials in the factory gates. They would get up real early and be there at 6:00 or 6:30 in the morning. (We would start work at 7:00.) They did this because we could not do so, for if we were caught giving out leaflets we would be fired.[42]

Labor leaders and publications acknowledged this pro-union work and welcomed the student movement as a valuable ally. In San Francisco, the maritime workers' union applauded student activists for opposing the use of their campuses as recruiting grounds for strikebreakers. The union also praised the students for bringing labor representatives to speak to campus audiences, from which they had been barred in the past. At the national level, CIO leader John L. Lewis in 1937 credited the student movement with helping to swing public opinion on to the side of organized labor:

> All of those who are associated with the United Mine Workers and the C.I.O., or, in other words, with the current movement for establishing industrial freedom and democracy in our mass-production industries

are fully conscious of the important bearing of the student movement upon our success.

Lewis maintained that the CIO, in attempting to bring a democratic revolution to American industry, realized that "no revolution in the history of the world has been successful unless it was supported from above," and that the student movement had been a "constant" source of such support.[43]

The student movement's most important contribution to organized labor, however, may not have been its campaigns, but rather its alumni. Former student activists became prominent in all levels of the labor movement, from national leaders such as Walter and Victor Reuther of the United Auto Workers to the hundreds of local union organizers—many of whom received their political baptism and their introduction to the labor movement through their work in the student movement. It was a relatively short and easy step for campus activists to move from their pro-labor work as students to careers as union organizers. The reverence for labor, which the student movement preached—and which was particularly strong among communist and socialist students, ideologically wedded to the ideal of a heroic proletariat—made a career in the labor movement seem very attractive. To join the labor movement meant serving on the front lines of the struggle for social change. This attraction proved so strong that, as former NSL activist George Watt recalled, it led some students to drop out of college, in order to work as union organizers:

> Some of the students who became young Communists left the student movement very early and went into the shops . . . . Once you became a Communist the highest status you could achieve was to become a factory worker. So they went into the factories. And some of them played a very important role in the early formation of the CIO. They went into factories; they went into the South; they went other places. Students did play that kind of role, but not as students; they became workers and tried to integrate themselves completely and submerge themselves into the working class.[44]

In entering the labor movement these alumni brought with them their college training, political experience, and idealism; they contributed to the labor upsurge which made the second half of the depression decade one of the great eras of union organizing in American history.

III

The student movement's attempt to build collegiate solidarity with labor extended to workers on campus as well as off. Among the key beneficiaries of these efforts were student workers. The movement championed the cause of low-income students not only with the Youth Act in Washington, but with a variety of organizing efforts at the local level. Promoting the idea that poverty was the product of the flawed economy rather than the fault of the individual, the student movement pressed the student body to stop ignoring the poor in its midst. Movement organizers and publications stressed that those who worked their way through college should not be snubbed because of their poverty, but admired because of their pursuit of knowledge and opportunity. The movement also encouraged working students to defend their interests, and sought to prod state and student governments to assist them.

Through regional and state Youth Congresses, students pushed for legislatures to deal with the problems of low-income students and unemployed youth. In Washington state, such agitation secured a boost in youth's share of the state welfare funds. Massachusetts student activists convinced the state legislature to conduct a survey of the economic problems of youth. In 1937 student organizers in California brought to Sacramento a youth aid package similar to the legislation being championed by the Youth Congress in Washington, D.C. This California Youth Act would have provided jobs for all needy college students. Advocates of this bill, like their counterparts in Washington, stressed that the New Deal had not gone far enough in assisting the young. Thus in calling on students to fight for the their state government to pick up where the New Deal had left off, these activists asked, "How many of us applied for NYA aid and didn't get it? How many of us are barely able to stay in school from week to week . . . . We need the California Youth Act."[45]

In addition to trying to find new sources of student aid, the movement pressed for more efficient and democratic administration of existing aid programs. The ASU was active in organizing student unions among NYA workers. At the Universities of North Carolina and Minnesota, these unions negotiated with NYA officials for increased job allotments and adapting jobs to the applicants' interests. The University of Chicago NSL organized a telephone barrage on the NYA office to complain about late paychecks, convincing NYA officials to place the University's payroll in the "rush order category." These protesters in Chicago also advocated a student majority on a University NYA Board, which they wanted to assume full responsibility for administering the campus aid program. After similar agitation at the University of Pennsylvania, the City College of New York, and Brooklyn College, NYA administrators allowed elected student NYA boards to share in administration of the program, and they agreed to negotiate with elected grievance committees.[46]

Organization of student employees was not confined to NYA workers. Student activists attempted to unionize undergraduates employed in the private sector, where many worked in restaurants, retail shops, and boarding houses in the campus area, and also served as "hashers"—food service workers in fraternities and sororities, who received meals for their labor. Such employees were ripe for exploitation because communities with large student populations had a ready supply of surplus labor, and many students were desperate for work during much of the Depression decade. Student unions also worked against the University itself when it appeared guilty of exploitative labor conditions, as at the University of Texas, where the Working Students Federation met with the dean to complain about overwork and other poor campus working conditions.[47]

Because unemployment was such a major problem on campuses, some student unions took almost as much interest in obtaining work for the unemployed as they did in improving conditions for those fortunate enough to have jobs. This unemployment problem was, for example, the theme of a "Keep the Student in School Week," sponsored by the University of Kansas' Self-Supporting Student Association in 1933. The Association appealed to the community, merchants, and professors to give work—even odd jobs—to as many unemployed students as possible.[48]

Prodded by the ASU, student governments became involved in protecting working students. One of the most creative and successful of these student government efforts on behalf of working students occurred at UC Berkeley. In 1936, the Welfare Council of the Associated Students of the University of California (the ASUC, Berkeley's student government) undertook an investigation of the working conditions of students employed in the campus area. The investigation revealed that these employees were often paid below prevailing wage standards and had to labor under "undesirable working conditions." The Council proposed, and the ASUC within a year established, a permanent Labor Board, whose purpose was the "maintenance of fair student working standards and conditions."[49]

The primary mechanism which the Board used to assist Berkeley student workers was the Fair Bear (the bear being the school symbol) program. The Labor Board established a set of minimum wage and working conditions, which it named Fair Bear Standards; it then notified local employers of these standards. Employers who complied with these standards received Fair Bear stickers from the ASUC. Those employers alleged to be violating the standards were denied a sticker and investigated; if they were found to be violating the standards they were placed on a list to be boycotted by the Berkeley student body—which was asked not to patronize stores and restaurants unless they had Fair Bear stickers in their windows.[50]

From the moment it was implemented, the Fair Bear program helped improve conditions for the most underpaid and overworked student employees at Berkeley. Because of the program's establishment eight employers immediately raised wages to the Fair Bear minimum of 40 cents per hour. In some stores and restaurants this amounted to a wage increase of over 30 percent—attesting to how poorly paid students had been in the past. The Fair Bear program's impact on the student labor market was so great that soon after the program began it generated public complaints from several local merchants. These employers claimed that the Fair Bear standards were too high and would cause them to hire fewer students. But despite such grumbling, most campus area employers complied with the standards, since their businesses depended upon student patronage and could not have afforded a possible student boycott.[51]

The Fair Bear program faced its biggest test in 1939, when Drake's, a popular local restaurant, refused to comply with the ASUC's labor standards. Drake's paid low wages to its waitresses and required them to pay for laundering their uniforms. The ASUC Labor Board responded to the restaurant's persistent abuses by placing Drake's on its boycott list. The incensed restaurant owner tried to go over the head of the ASUC by complaining to UC President Robert Sproul. But the administration refused to overrule the Labor Board's decision. Indeed, Berkeley's dean of undergraduates actually endorsed the Fair Bear standards as "worthy and justifiable." Left with no one else to appeal to, and facing the prolonged loss of student patronage, Drake's management agreed to comply with the Fair Bear standards only a week after students began boycotting the restaurant. The Fair Bear program proved so effective that it attracted national attention, and was emulated on other campuses, such as Ohio State University. Fair Bear drew praise from labor leaders, including James Carey, the secretary of the CIO, who urged the adoption of similar programs at campuses across the country.[52]

The success of the Fair Bear program was a testament to how effective the student movement had been in transforming the campus political scene. A program such as this would have been unimaginable at Berkeley at the start of the Depression decade, when the student Left was a small minority under attack from the UC administration, the campus newspaper, and the fraternity-dominated student government. But with the growth of the student movement, the ASU now had sufficient influence to get the student government to implement the Fair Bear program and to attract support for the program from the campus press, the UC administration, and a majority of Berkeley undergraduates.[53]

IV

The Great Depression played a large, but not exclusive role in defining the student movement's domestic priorities. Because the Depression gripped the nation and affected so many students, it gave a special urgency to issues concerning economic opportunity. This was why such causes as aid to low-income youth received so much attention from student activists. The student movement's egalitarianism was not limited, however, to economics; it also extended to race. The movement demonstrated a concern with both the new inequities created by the Depression and the old inequities perpetuated by racism. The radicals who launched and led the campus revolt of the 1930s criticized the racial discrimination of the North and the Jim Crow system of the South. They envisioned an academic community and a nation free of racial prejudice and discrimination.

Depression era student activists raised the banner of racial equality on more campuses than any previous generation of students in twentieth century America.[54]

Just how far removed the student activists of the 1930s were from mainstream American racial attitudes was made evident in the very first meeting between the Youth Congress' leaders and Eleanor Roosevelt. On the question of civil rights the First Lady symbolized the Roosevelt administration's most liberal wing. She was far more willing than the president himself to confront the problem of racial inequality. But in comparison to the student movement's leaders, Mrs. Roosevelt seemed timid and conservative on race—and this led to a strong difference of opinion in her January 1936 meeting with the Youth Congress' National Council. At that meeting, Elizabeth Scott, a black leader in the Youth Congress, confronted the First Lady with the New Deal's failure to challenge Jim Crow, and explained:

> I represent one-tenth of the citizens of this country. I refer to the Negro people. We are denied citizenship in the South. We do not have the right to vote in the Democratic primaries in the southern states. In this very city of Washington, my nation's capitol, I cannot get a meal in a restaurant, whether I am starving or not . . . . How do you think we should fight against Negro discrimination in this country and what are you going to do about it?

Mrs. Roosevelt, though mentioning her "great sympathy for the problems of the Negro people" and the "importance of equal education," counselled Scott to "have patience . . . these are not things that can be settled in a short time."[55]

The First Lady's gradualist argument swayed none of the young activists. They wanted the Roosevelt administration to stop evading the issue of discrimination, especially with regard to the racist southern court system. In fact, before Mrs. Roosevelt left the meeting, the Youth Congress leaders voted to send the president a telegram protesting "the lack of civil liberties in the South" and the use of "terror and intimidation against sharecroppers" in that region who sought to unionize. The telegram also expressed outrage at the attempt of Alabama law enforcement officials to frame the young African American defendants in the Scottsboro case; it called upon FDR to offer "federal protection of the Scottsboro boys," and demanded a "federal investigation of [racial] terror."[56] This was consistent with the Youth Congress' 1935 Declaration of Rights of American Youth, which contrasted Depression America's democratic pretensions with its racial practices:

> In song and legend America has been exalted as a land of the free, a haven for the oppressed. Yet on every hand we see this freedom limited

or destroyed . . . . The Negro people are subjected to constant abuse, discrimination and lynch law.[57]

Shortly after this meeting with the First Lady, student activists were again pressing the Roosevelt administration to do more on behalf of African Americans. The American Student Union supported immediate and complete desegregation of all New Deal programs. Thus in February 1936, ASU leader Joseph Lash called upon G.W. Studebaker, United States commissioner of education, to see to it that his department's community education forums should also be used to challenge Jim Crow—by being conducted on a racially integrated basis everywhere, including in the South. This was, however, too radical an idea for Studebaker, who in turning Lash down, claimed that it would be unwise "to dictate a vital change for the age-long and traditional social relations in the South . . . . Whether white and colored meet must depend upon the spirit and customs of the community."[58]

If the student movement's racial egalitarianism seemed bold in comparison to the Roosevelt administration, it was even more daring in comparison to the administrations that governed America's college campuses. Institutional racism pervaded the American college and university system of the 1930s. Throughout the South a rigid Jim Crow system barred African Americans from enrolling in white schools. In the North, discriminatory admissions practices made it almost impossible for blacks to attend many leading colleges and universities—which accepted either none or only a token number of black applicants. In 1933, for instance, such institutions as Stanford, Grinnell, and Bryn Mawr had only one African American undergraduate each; Smith, Rutgers, Tufts, Radcliffe, Wesleyan, and Dartmouth were among the schools which had just three blacks enrolled. Only nine campuses in the entire nation (excluding black colleges) enrolled more than 100 black collegians. Discriminatory admissions practices helped confine the vast majority of African American students to black colleges: In 1933 of the 23,038 black undergraduates, 20,296 were students on black campuses.[59]

The small minority of African American students (under 3000 in 1933) who did attend predominantly white colleges and universities in the North often found these schools and their surrounding communities quite racist. Jim Crow was almost as strong in many aspects of northern collegiate life as it was in the South. At such schools as the University of Minnesota, Ohio State, and the University of Chicago, segregation in dormitories and rooming houses prevented blacks from living on or even near campus. Campus communities regularly excluded blacks from restaurants, shops, recreational facilities, social clubs, and athletic competition.[60] Discrimination against black students was so severe at the University of Illinois, that the *Daily Illini* concluded in 1932 that

if you want to know what hell is, wake up colored some morning . . . . Negro students are barred from all campus confectionaries and eating establishments. The Home Economics Cafeteria is the only public place at which they may eat. They are segregated at shows and semi-public gatherings. Most of the public dance hall managers look upon them as pariahs.[61]

Most white college administrators either tolerated or actively promoted and defended such racial discrimination. A common administration attitude seemed to be that blacks were lucky to be enrolled in college and ought not complain about discrimination they encountered on campus. As one college official explained to a black theological student at Harvard in 1930,

> In admitting the Negro students to the opportunity for study we feel we have done our duty; he should respect our good-will by not causing such social problems as are bound to grow out of his attempt to participate in campus activities.[62]

College officials also argued that deferring to traditional racial practices— no matter how discriminatory—was the best way to avoid controversy and maintain racial harmony. This was the line of reasoning that the University of Minnesota Board of Trustees used when it ruled in 1935 that blacks would continue to be excluded from the men's dormitory. Discriminatory college administrators seemed to be motivated both by fear of offending the University's white alumni and benefactors and by their own racial prejudice.[63]

There seemed to be almost no campus community free of racial discrimination. Even at liberal Oberlin, which had been among the first colleges in the nation to admit black students, discriminatory patterns were visible. Esther Cooper Jackson, recalled that she and fellow black students at Oberlin during the 1930s had to contend with prejudiced college officials throughout their undergraduate years.

> There was racism at Oberlin despite its history. We had a very racist Dean of Men who used to discourage blacks and whites, for example, just going out on casual dates. And he had his spies. And he would write to the parents of a white girl or boy, and tell them "Did you know that your son or daughter went out, is going out with a black student?" And we burned him . . . in effigy on the campus.[64]

In the surrounding community, Oberlin's black students found themselves barred from recreational facilities and facing increased discrimination in local shops. The NAACP magazine had good reason, then, for expressing its regret in 1934 that "Oberlin O., of glorious Underground Railroad history, seems to be weakening after 100 years, and yielding to the intolerance which the city's stalwarts a century ago fought with unparalleled passion."[65]

Traditional student institutions, particularly fraternities and sororities, reinforced this discriminatory atmosphere on northern campuses. Greek houses almost universally barred blacks both from their membership and social events. Such discrimination was written into the constitutions of many of these houses through clauses limiting membership to students "without Negro blood." African Americans founded fraternities and sororities, but their organizations were not treated as equals by the white Greek Houses in the 1930s. At the University of Chicago, for instance, white fraternity leaders refused to admit the black fraternity Kappa Alpha Psi into the Interfraternity Council, thus barring the blacks from establishing their own house on the campus. This same pattern prevailed in athletic and honorary societies. Not even Jesse Owens, the most famous athlete in the history of Ohio State could cross this color line. In 1936 Owens was denied admission to Bucket and Dipper, the campus' athletic honor society.[66]

Racial discrimination was so widespread on campus that segregationist students felt no compunction about publicly endorsing the exclusion of African American students from local facilities, shops, and events. At Columbia University, for instance, conservative students in 1936 defended the right of barber shops in the campus area to refuse service to black students, on the grounds that the property rights of these shop owners entitled them to bar blacks. Similar views were expressed the following year at Ohio State University during a controversy concerning discrimination in the campus community. Bigoted Ohio State students wrote in to their campus newspaper that "in a country governed by the Nordic race it is impossible to put other races on a parity with that race . . . . Negroes . . . should not be allowed to eat where we of the white race do [n]or should they be allowed to go to our shows. If one starts it they all follow and soon take various places over completely." Such sentiments led to the formation of the Anti-Negro Guild, a short-lived group at Ohio State which sought to stop white and black student activists from integrating campus facilities.[67]

The persistent bigotry of white campuses discouraged many black students from even applying to them. Some thought it better to enroll in an underfunded black college than to expose themselves to the racism of white colleges. Such sentiments were expressed by black students in an article which appeared in a leading black magazine in 1934. Here one undergraduate, in explaining his decision to attend a black college rather than a predominantly white school, noted that the racism of the white campus was harmful to the black collegian in that it could

> crush him with an inferiority complex . . . . The negro college will be the saving grace of the negro race until the fundamental attitude of the white man towards the negro makes a radical change. The white college until that time can never prepare the young negro for life.[68]

There were virtually no African Americans on the faculties of northern colleges and universities during the Depression decade. Few blacks were admitted to northern graduate and professional schools. Even those within this small elite of black Ph.D.s coming out of top white graduate schools were expected to teach only in black colleges. Consequently, when psychologist Kenneth Clark received his Columbia doctorate in the late 1930s, his professors told him: "Now you have your Ph.D., you can go back and serve your people." Clark, who would later become the first black Columbia faculty member, recalled that his response to their Jim Crow advice was "Well my people are in New York. I'm a New Yorker. I'd like to teach at City College or Princeton." Throughout the 1930s, then, top black academics in the nation were ghettoized—compelled to chose between teaching at black colleges or not teaching at all.[69]

With faculty, administrators, and traditional student groups perpetuating this pattern of discrimination, it may seem odd that the student movement of the 1930s condemned it. The movement's commitment to racial equality can be traced to its radical leadership, whose thinking on race was shaped not by the retrogressive practices of the academy but by progressive ideals of the adult Left. They followed the prevailing Left wisdom of the era, which held that racism had to be battled energetically because it was one of the most vile and effective means by which the capitalist class divided and ruled workers. This class analysis of racism appeared prominently in the student Left's publications, which stressed that race hatreds were inflamed to distract the nation from the failings of the capitalist system, and that interracial unity was the only effective weapon against this reactionary ploy. International events provided an added impetus to the fight against racism. By the mid-1930s, the student movement had begun to link the fight against racism with the broader international anti-fascist movement, and condemned Jim Crow as an American form of Hitlerism.[70]

The social composition of the student movement's leadership contributed to the movement's racial egalitarianism. The movement's national leadership included African American students, who saw racial discrimination as one of the most important targets for student protest. These black student leaders included Maurice Gates and James Jackson of the National Student League, Lyonel Florant of the Student League for Industrial Democracy, Louis Burnham, Frances Jones, and Le Marquis de Jarmen of the American Student Union, Edward Strong and Elizabeth Scott of the American Youth Congress. The heavy representation of Jews among the student movement leaders added to this anti-racist impulse. Young Jewish radicals such as Joseph Lash, James Wechsler, Joseph Clark, and Harry Magdoff had played a prominent role in launching the student movement and shaping the platforms of the student Left. They came to college aware, as were most Jewish students, that American colleges and universities in the 1930s often imposed quotas restricting Jewish enrollments. These Jewish radicals brought to the student movement a strong sensitivity toward the problem of racial discrimination, and an insistence that the movement adopt an uncompromising stance in support of racial equality.[71]

Even before they organized the first anti-war strikes, student movement leaders attempted to make a national issue of racial discrimination. In April 1933 the NSL held a Student Conference on Negro Student Problems in New York City. The NSL invited black students from all regions of the country. At this interracial conference, student delegates and prominent black social critics, including sociologist E. Franklin Frazier, denounced the Jim Crow system and the damage that racial discrimination did to education in both the South and the North.[72]

The content of this conference and the NSL's eagerness to promote racial equality impressed African American delegates. Lyonel Florant, a socialist student from Howard University, found the tone of the meeting far different from any interracial gathering he had experienced previously:

> It was not the old interracial get-together at which hands were shaken "for Jesus' sake," and after a few sessions of intellectual back-slapping, Negroes and whites returned to their isolated way of living. No, it was a fiery, militant conference that brought students and professors out of the deep South. The sugary spirit was absent; instead there was a common resolve to go back to the South and, for that matter, many areas of the North, and tackle shoulder to shoulder the problems of discrimination.[73]

James Jackson, editor of the *Panther,* Virginia Union's student newspaper during the 1930s, agreed, recalling the conference as "a very impressive event in my life." Here for the first time the black editor had a chance to participate in the formation of a student program to fight racism. Jackson found the NSL's racial militancy so unlike the attitude he had encountered among other whites that at one point he mistook one of the white NSL officers for a black:

> Joseph Clark, Executive Secretary of the National Student League [who addressed the conference] was a very dynamic speaker. And it's interesting. He in the summer was quite brown, and his hair was kind of frizzy. And I thought he was black and took great national pride that [he was] such a speaker who knew so much about the world.[74]

The student movement's leftist leaders not only preached racial equality, but practiced it in their national meetings. The NSL in 1933 held its annual convention on a black campus, Howard University, and defied the Jim Crow customs of the capital by having black and white delegates dine together in traditionally "whites only" restaurants on Connecticut Avenue. Similarly, the 1935 American Youth Congress in Detroit threatened to withdraw from the hotel in which it was headquartered unless management abided by its agreement to house the Congress' black delegates. The threatened exodus forced the segregated hotel to accommodate the black youths. This incident received prominent publicity in the

Youth Congress' publications. This scenario was repeated at the Youth Congress' 1936 convention in Cleveland, when delegates again encountered discrimination from a local hotel.[75]

Student radicals sought to spread this non-discriminatory ethos to student organizations outside the Left. In 1933 the NSL and SLID announced that they would picket the convention of the National Student Federation (NSF)—the mainstream association of student governments—because the federation had informed black students that they could not attend its dance in Washington's Mayflower Hotel. Afraid of the embarrassment from such a picket, the federation backed down, and black students were admitted to the dance. Not satisfied with this concession, the NSL, in its national magazine, ran an exposé by black activist Maurice Gates on the NSF's history of discrimination. Gates showed that the NSF had barred black students from its 1932 convention and warned that student activists would no longer tolerate such racism.[76]

The NSL worked to attract student interest in the Scottsboro case, which it saw as symbolic of all that was wrong with the Jim Crow system. The League promoted a national Scottsboro Week on campus, directing its chapters to hold forums on the case. The NSL magazine devoted several of its lead editorials to Scottsboro and drew connections between discrimination in the judicial and educational systems, urging "the student body" to "play a decisive part in the struggle against racial oppression. We must uproot it on the campus by fighting against Jim Crow clubs and schools." The NSL dispatched several student reporters to attend the Scottsboro trial, two of whom were arrested. They wrote accounts which vividly portrayed the racial injustice of the proceedings. One of these reporters was Muriel Rukeyser, who dispatched not only news stories, but also a poem, "The Trial," which would attract national attention as a searing indictment of southern racism—and start Rukeyser's career as a leading American poet.[77]

In northern campus communities, NSL and SLID chapters organized protests when racist incidents occurred. The SLID chapter at the University of Wisconsin picketed a local hotel when it refused to house a visiting black theater company in 1934. The SLID led the fight to have black students admitted to the Engineering School at the University of Cincinnati. NSL activists at the University of Michigan helped organize a meeting to protest the football coach's decision to bench black star end Willis Ward during a road game in the South. The NSL led protests against racial discrimination in UC Berkeley's campus barbershop, the hospital of the University of Chicago Medical School, the bowling alley near Oberlin College, and on the CCNY track team. The NSL also publicized the Phi Beta Kappa national organization's refusal to allow Howard University to establish a local chapter.[78]

The formation of the American Student Union helped the student movement in its civil rights work, just as it assisted it in other areas of agitation. The growth in both the number of activists and the influence of the student movement, which the ASU facilitated, allowed the movement to organize civil rights protests on more campuses than had the NSL and SLID. The ASU recommended that all its chapters proceed on an extensive civil rights agenda. Chapters were urged to support passage of federal anti-lynching legislation, equal allocation of educational dollars for black and white students, and abolition of the poll tax. There was an added emphasis on cultural and educational issues, with the ASU supporting "the inclusion of courses on Negro history and culture in the curriculum," and ASU participation in Negro History week. Most influential of all was the ASU's call for chapters to work with black students both in their own organizations and the ASU to challenge campus discrimination through "test cases."[79]

Under the influence of this civil rights program, campus ASU chapters established Negro Student Problems committees that worked with black students to uncover and protest racial discrimination in the campus community. ASU anti-discrimination battles were waged at such campuses as Berkeley, Butler, Chicago, CCNY, Columbia, Illinois, Missouri, Michigan, Minnesota, Northwestern, Ohio State, and Washington Universities. These battles, like those waged by the NSL and SLID in the early 1930s, were over basic rights for black students, including access to restaurants, dormitories, boarding houses, employment, shops, social clubs and events, athletic competition, and academic programs.[80]

This stance against racial discrimination made it difficult for the student movement to penetrate most campuses below the Mason Dixon line— where a strong regional consensus in support of segregation existed. Outside of the region's few larger and more cosmopolitan campuses, the southern student movement was quite weak. This was especially true in the deep South, where on such campuses as the University of Florida a majority of the students surveyed approved of lynching blacks accused of rape.[81]

Despite the unpopularity of racial egalitarianism in the South, however, scattered southern student radicals did challenge the Jim Crow system. In 1934 the University of Virginia's NSL chapter invited Richard Moore, a prominent black socialist, to speak on their Charlottesville campus. In inviting Moore to speak, these young radicals flouted the school's long standing tradition of racial exclusion. There had not been a militant black speaker at the University of Virginia since Reconstruction. The campus administration responded with outrage to the Moore invitation. Virginia NSL leader Palmer Weber recalled that the invitation "threw the Dean [Ivey Lewis] into a fit. He still believed in slavery. He forbade the use of any university building."[82] Weber and the NSL responded to the ban by obtaining space for Moore's speech in the Episcopal church across the street from the University. Weber, who was a writer for *College Topics*, Virginia's student newspaper, published a column blasting the University administration for violating the ancient and revered traditions of free speech and free thought. In doing so Virginia declares itself to be just another machine to hinder, even to destroy thought in the futile endeavor to support social mores, which can no longer be justified either in principle or as requisites for an ordered society.[83]

Weber also invoked the name of the University's founder, Thomas Jefferson, to indict the administration, accusing Virginia of initiating "a denial of Jeffersonian principles". "What manner of small-minded men have inherited Mr. Jefferson's University?"[84]

Much to the embarrassment of the Virginia administration, this free speech controversy attracted attention from the press all along the East Coast. John Newcomb, the University's president reacted by summoning Weber to his office. Pulling out a file of press clippings, Newcomb accused Weber of damaging the University's reputation. "My God, look what you've done to the University! This is the worst public relations in fifty years." Weber replied,

> President Newcomb, I didn't do it, Dean Lewis did it. I told him there was no way to keep it a secret that he'd forbade the use of any University building . . . . You know this is just impossible. Slavery is over. And these people are citizens of Virginia . . . and they have a right to be heard . . . . The man's been properly invited, he's qualified and he's going to speak at the Episcopal Church chapel.

Moore's speech went ahead as planned, and for the rest of the decade the Virginia administration—apparently chastened by the negative publicity from the Moore controversy—never tried to stop the NSL as it brought black speakers to campus.[85]

It was no accident that after Moore had been banned from speaking at the University, the one place the NSL could secure for their black speaker was a church. Among the few allies that the student Left found in the South were religious radicals—scattered and small groups of Christian Socialists or Left-leaning ministers and activists in the student YW and YMCAs. This is what an ASU field organizer was alluding to when he reported to Joseph Lash that "whatever there is of a student movement in the South is in the Y—you can get away with a great deal in the name of Christianity down here, which would not be listened to for a moment under any other auspices . . . ." Religious radicals were instrumental in promoting interracial meetings and work on behalf of racial equality; they were an indigenous southern group which controlled church buildings and could provide integrationists with at least limited accesss to the white student body.[86]

For these Christian allies the student Left owed a debt to Reinhold Niebuhr, Harry Ward, and Norman Thomas. As leading teachers at New York's Union Theological Seminary, Ward and Niebuhr were able to help propagate racial egalitarianism in the South because their students included southerners who would become ministers below the Mason-Dixon line. Among the students of these leftist teachers were Howard Kester and Myles Horton, who would help found two of the most radical interracial institutions in the South during the 1930s: the Southern Tenant Farmers Union, which organized sharecroppers, and the Highlander Folk School, which trained labor and civil rights organizers. Equally important were the clerics Norman Thomas had converted to socialism. Thomas, a former minister himself, frequently toured the South and managed to assemble a small network of ministers who were at least sympathetic to the goals of the student Left. Such ministers, as campus chaplains and heads of student Y's, were strategically placed to help bring an integrationist message to southern campuses.[87]

The influence of religious radicalism could be seen, for example, at Emory University in Georgia, where the student YMCA was headed by Emmet Johnson, a minister who was an avid integrationist. Johnson worked throughout the early 1930s to see that students in the YMCA from the (all-white) Emory campus met blacks on an equal basis. Without official permission from the University administration, Johnson set up small interracial student meetings in local churches and black campuses. One of the students who participated in these meetings was Jack McMichael, who would go on to become chair of the American Youth Congress. According to McMichael, these meetings—which were for their participants the first integrated and racially equal events they had ever attended—made a deep impression.

> The influence of Emmet Johnson [who led the interracial meetings] was very great on me. And these experiences made a big difference. You could read these things in a book, but when you know people who are black and you know that the taboos about them are not true you see you get this kind of deep feeling [against segregation].[88]

Johnson and McMichael sought to spread racial equality not only at Emory but through the entire religious network of the intercollegiate YM/YWCA. Aware that the local Y's, like all southern institutions, had succumbed to Jim Crowism in its regional meetings, the Emory University activists in the early 1930s, began "working together to make a sort of frontal assault on segregation in the YMCA and YWCA." This movement to reform the Y's, which united Protestant Left activists from a number of southern campuses, proved quite effective. According to McMichael,

> We went to Blue Ridge in the summers—to Blue Ridge, North Carolina, where there is a YMCA conference grounds. And they were accustomed to having all-white meetings. And we insisted on having blacks. And they said, you can have blacks, but they can't use the same toilets. And we took the position [for complete integration], largely through the

influence of the YW's—because these meetings at Blue Ridge, though in YMCA territory, were Y and YW. The YW was much more progressive, and much more willing to stick its neck out on these things. And they were insisting that there be no segregation whatever, that they make no concession to it. And so we . . . finally broke down that barrier. That meant, of course, and we knew it, that we had to break the law, because the law often required segregation in public places.

Through the remainder of the 1930s, the Y's interracial committees would bring black and white students together in southern conferences, and the more liberal Y's would assist the student Left in airing integrationist ideas which were otherwise locked out of many southern campus communities.[89]

Although able to win a few symbolic victories in the South, as with the Moore speech at Charlottesville and the integration of the Y retreats in North Carolina, southern student radicals lacked the numbers and influence to end or even seriously threaten the Jim Crow admissions polices of their colleges and universities. This lack of influence was apparent, for example, in connection with the Alice Jackson case in 1935. Jackson, a black college graduate, had challenged the color line at the University of Virginia by applying for admission to its graduate school. The University promptly rejected her, in a move supported by most Virginia students. The University of Virginia NSL was outraged; its officers sent a letter of protest to the University's Board of Visitors, rebuking the University for its violation

of the right of equal opportunity for all people regardless of race, color or creed. In short, we criticise the Board's stand because it implies the desirabilty of continuing educational inequality. We are confident that every liberal, radical and christian thinker will concur with us in this protest.[90]

The NSL challenged not merely the Virginia administration's decision, but the bigotry of the student body itself, filling the campus newspaper with pro-integration letters and arranging debates with the leading student advocates of Jim Crow education.

The tone of the debate over Jackson's admission was angry. This reflected the fact that her application and the NSL's defense of it had for the first time forced Virginia's elite white student body into the position of having to defend its most deeply held racial prejudices. Thus one segregationist student, furious at his radical classmates' support of Jackson, fumed that the "N.S.L will never convince me that they are not merely talking through their hat . . . until they convince me that they would be perfectly willing to see their sisters . . . married to negroes." Invoking southern history, another segregationist student wrote the campus newspaper that:

In answer to the N.S.L. may I state if they were of a more analyzing nature they would realize that this is the South and not any other region of the country. From the time when the first Negro set foot in Virginia in 1619, that race has not been placed in the classroom with the whites so far as the public schools are concerned and they never will be.[91]

NSL activists at the University of Virginia infuriated these segregationists with well argued rebuttals to their Jim Crow arguments. They pointed out that the longevity of the educational color line had no bearing at all on the question of whether integration was desirable. Even if it was true that blacks and whites had not been educated together since 1619, "So What?," asked the NSL. "It says nothing of the desirability of placing Negroes and whites in the same classroom." The NSL charged that the segregationists had no proof for their claims that blacks were intellectually inferior to whites. These radicals argued that the University would be strengthened as an intellectual and cultural institution by the admission of blacks:

The NSL stands for racial equality because it is just, and because it is culturally advantageous,—culturally advantageous because segregation deprives not only the Negro people of what whites have to offer, but also works the other way. The Negro people form an integral part of America. Their cultural tradition is an American heritage, to which the people as a whole, students especially have a right. Every genuine student in order to secure as broad an education as possible, must come into contact with all races and nationalities.[92]

The NSL also took issue with the emotional arguments about the alleged twin evils of integration and racial intermarriage. These activists found it "astonishing" that segregationist students had claimed they were upholding the South's tradition of racial purity in which "black is black and white is white and never the twain shall meet." Taunting one such segregationist, the NSL asked "Does the gentleman not know that nine million Negroes in the South have white blood in their veins? Surely he does not believe the stork story. Or does he?"[93]

Despite its eloquent arguments, the NSL throughout the Jackson controversy remained the only student group writing, debating, and organizing in behalf of Jackson's admission. This suggests that these civil rights advocates failed to sway many of their classmates. If *College Topics*, the campus newspaper, is a fair indicator of student sentiment, most Virginia students remained solidly segregationist. In its editorial on the Jackson case, entitled "But Not Here," the paper argued that Jackson's admission to UVA would be "disastrous" and inflame racial prejudice because the South was not yet ready for integration. The administration agreed, and refused to admit her.[94]

Four years later in Chapel Hill, the ASU waged a similar campaign in solidarity with Pauli Murray's attempt to cross the university's color line. Unlike the Virginia NSL during the Jackson case in 1935, the ASU at Chapel Hill was not totally alone its advocacy of desegregation in 1939. The ASU's integrationist efforts received support from Chapel Hill's campus YMCA, and two eloquent faculty liberals, historian Howard Beale and playwright Paul Green. Integrationist arguments seemed to have their greatest appeal among graduate students. A survey taken by the *Daily Tar Heel,* Chapel Hill's student newspaper, revealed that a majority of respondents in the University's law and graduate schools favored Murray's admission.[95]

The ASU sought to broaden student support for Murray by organizing a forum on black educational rights, which included speakers from several local black colleges. At one ASU sponsored meeting over 100 students and teachers voted their approval of the immediate integration of the University of North Carolina. The ASU's integrationist efforts received a significant boost from Murray herself. She wrote a brilliant open letter to President Graham, indicting Jim Crow education. This letter appeared in all the Chapel Hill area newspapers. These efforts failed, however, to win over the student body as a whole or the administration. There was no poll taken of the University's undergraduates, but the *Daily Tar Heel,* which itself opposed Murray's admission, claimed that majority sentiment at Chapel Hill was segregationist. A survey of other southern student newspapers also revealed majority opposition to desegregating the University. The southern student body remained solidly segregationist despite the best efforts of the ASU. Murray was not admitted to Chapel Hill, and it would take decades of legal battles before the NAACP could bring collegiate desegregation beyond the border states into the deep South. So though these student radicals had been daring in forcing upon their classmates unprecedented debates about segregation, the political climate in the South prevented them from winning those debates.[96]

If racial prejudice limited the impact of the student Left on white southern campuses, political repression played this same role on black campuses. The administrators of most black colleges were every bit as conservative as Ralph Ellison—a student at Tuskegee in the 1930s—described in his novel, *The Invisible Man.* Like Ellison's fictional Dr. Bledsoe, the administrators of black colleges were usually dependent on white philanthropy, wary of offending their schools' wealthy benefactors, and adherents of a gradualist approach to racial progress.[97] These characteristics left them intolerant of racial militancy and dissent, which they saw as a threat to the moderate image of their schools.

Social and political suppression were so severe on southern black campuses it shocked poet Langston Hughes, as he toured these campuses in 1934. Hughes protested the "astounding restrictions" and "lack of personal freedom that exists on most Negro campuses. To set foot on dozens of Negro campuses is like going back to mid-Victorian England, or Massachusetts in the days of the witch burning Puritans." Hughes found that administrators prohibited student smoking, dating, dancing, and even card playing; they required daily chapel meetings and enforced dozens of military-style regulations.[98]

During this tour, Hughes found college administrators on the black campuses even more eager to repress civil rights activism than they were to restrict student social life. At Hampton Institute, Hughes encountered a group of students outraged by both a white Birmingham mob's murder of a Hampton alumnus, and the death of a prominent black educator, who might have survived had the local white hospital not refused to treat her. These Hampton students organized a protest meeting and scheduled Hughes to speak there. But the meeting could not be held. Hampton's dean barred students from demonstrating, explaining "Hampton did not like the word 'protest.' That was not Hampton's way. He and Hampton believed in moving slowly and with dignity." Hughes was so appalled by this incident and similar experiences at other black colleges that he published an article, "Cowards From the Colleges," in the NAACP's *Crisis* magazine, bemoaning this collegiate "Uncle Tomism." The Hampton case was typical. Student radicals found that on almost every black campus during the early 1930s their organizing "had to be carried on underground. Membership in either organization [the NSL or SLID] was the basis for expulsion," reported SLID activist Lyonel Florant.[99]

Unlike student radicals above the Mason-Dixon line, their counterparts at southern black colleges had little opportunity to evade the political restrictions mandated by repressive college administrators during the early 1930s. If an NSL rally was banned from campus in the Midwest, Northeast, or far West, students could usually hold the rally on city property out of the jurisdiction of college officials. But in the South, black organizers barred from campus could count on an equally repressive response from the white segregationist officials off campus. Ishmael Flory, an African American NSL activist learned this lesson at Fisk University in 1934, when he tried to organize a protest against the lynching of Cordie Cheek, a black teenager, a few blocks from campus. Nashville's mayor and police chief refused him permission to hold an anti-lynching march off campus. Flory then held the demonstration on campus, but the mood of fear was so great that only fifteen students joined the march. That fear was well grounded because Thomas E. Jones, Fisk's white president, expelled Flory for organizing the march, and Fisk's faculty endorsed the expulsion.[100]

Although such repression inhibited student protest on black campuses, it could not kill it. Not even Flory's expulsion could completely silence Fisk students. Indeed, before the end of the year, dissent, expressed in a more moderate way, again emerged at Fisk. When President Roosevelt visited Fisk in 1934 to hear the Jubilee singers, he was presented with a petition signed by 250 Fisk students protesting the Scottsboro case and the lynching of a black in Florida. In addition, there were instances of interracial student protest in the South. The most well publicized of these actions in Virginia was the dispatching of an NSL-organized delegation of students from the University of Virginia and Virginia Union University to the state legislature. The delegation demanded increased expenditures on education and equal allocation of state educational monies between black and white students.[101]

In the hope of expanding such activism among African American students, the American Student Union chose Louis Burnham, a talented black organizer who had headed CCNY's militant Frederick Douglass Society, as its southern organizer. The combination of Burnham's skill and the ASU's autonomous image—the fact that its links with the Left were less explicit than the SLID and NSL and hence somewhat less likely to invite repression—allowed the organization to make more progress on the black campuses than had been made by the NSL and SLID in the early 1930s. Burnham established ASU chapters at eight or nine black colleges in the South, not a mass movement by any means, but at least a step in the direction of greater black student activism.[102]

African American student protest in the 1930s was strongest at Howard University, Black America's leading institution of higher education. The liberalism of Howard's faculty and the university's location in the nation's capital gave student activists at Howard an advantage over their counterparts on black campuses further south, since they fostered a freer political atmosphere at Howard. The Howard professoriate included some of Black America's most eloquent civil rights advocates, such as Ralph Bunche and Charles Houston, whose teaching, according to Kenneth B. Clark, a Howard undergraduate in the 1930s, encouraged "students to fight against the idiocy of American racism and segregationism."[103]

The critical role that liberal faculty played in protecting free speech and allowing room for dissent at Howard was evident in the controversy surrounding the demonstration by Howard students against segregation in the cafe of the United States House of Representatives in February 1934. After police arrested about 30 Howard students for demanding service in this segregated restaurant, Howard's President Mordecai Johnson began disciplinary proceedings against the protest leaders. Johnson feared that the protest had jeopardized the congressional funding upon which Howard was dependent, and it was on this basis that he summoned protest leader Kenneth Clark into his office and, in Clark's word's "gave me hell," and threatened him with expulsion. But as the disciplinary committee hearings began, Professor Bunche appeared and personally intervened on behalf of the students. Bunche told committee members that the protesters should not be disciplined, but rather they "should be given medals" for demonstrating against segregation, and he warned that he would fight any disciplinary action. Bunche swayed the committee, and none of the students were disciplined.[104]

Howard continued to produce some of the most memorable black student demonstrations of the decade, including one in which 150 Howardites rallied against the exclusion of lynching from the agenda of a national crime conference in December 1934. The protesters appeared outside the conference hall in Washington with hangmen's nooses around their necks and bearing signs indicating the numbers of blacks lynched in the South. Such activism made Howard the greatest source of national black leaders for the student movement of the 1930s.[105]

Black initiative played a pivotal role not merely in these Howard protests, but in many of the ASU's civil rights campaigns. It was often black student complaints about discrimination and segregation that brought civil rights matters to the attention of local ASU activists. The precise manner in which this interaction between black and white students occurred varied. Sometimes the black grievants were themselves ASU activists. This was the case, for instance with William Bell, a member of the ASU executive committee at Northwestern University, who sued the University for ejecting him from its campus beach. The ASU branch there followed up his suit with a broad investigation of racial discrimination on campus, and a meeting with the University president to demand change.[106]

On campuses where there were a sufficient number of blacks to form their own organizations, these groups helped bring discriminatory acts to the ASU's attention. Thus at CCNY, the Frederick Douglass Society and the ASU worked on a number of joint anti-discrimination projects. A third pattern emerged in which an unaffiliated black student, victimized by discrimination, made the ASU aware of this racism and joined or endorsed the ASU's subsequent campaign to eliminate the source of the discrimination. This occurred at Columbia University in 1936, where the ASU, acting on the report of an African American student, organized picket lines around two discriminatory barber shops in the campus area. In all three cases, black initiative and complaints, as well as interracial cooperation, paved the way for ASU civil rights protests.[107]

The same type of black initiative which the ASU encouraged and which facilitated the student movement's civil rights actions, led to the formation of the Southern Negro Youth Congress (SNYC), a black-led youth organization devoted to the pursuit of racial equality. SNYC emerged as the youth affiliate of the communist-led National Negro Congress. The African American students who founded SNYC in 1937, Louis Burnham, James Jackson, and Edward Strong were communists who had been national leaders in the American Student Union and the American Youth Congress. The student movement had served as a political training ground for these young black activists; it was the movement which first brought SNYC's founders together and showed them the potential of youth for political action. Given the student movement's commitment to racial equality, it is not surprising that it contributed to the birth of a youth and student-led civil rights organization.[108]

The founding of the Southern Negro Youth Congress did not mark a break, but rather a division of labor between white and black student activists. ASU and SNYC leaders would continue to work together in pushing for such goals as increased federal aid to youth; they met regularly as members of the American Youth Congress. SNYC's formation was, however, at least an implicit acknowledgement on the part of leaders like Burnham—who had tried recruiting black southern collegians as an ASU organizer—that the student movement had failed to mobilize many black southern youths. Those involved recognized that the ASU, which was simultaneously organizing a national movement against war and lobbying for student aid, lacked the resources to lead a large scale challenge to Jim Crow in the South. In essence, the problem of southern segregation was so massive it could only be battled effectively by a black-led southern organization, devoted exclusively to helping black people fight for equality.[109]

Organizationally, the SNYC was modeled after the American Youth Congress. As with the AYC, the Southern Negro Youth Congress started out as a federation of local youth and youth serving organizations—only in SNYC's case most of these constituent groups were black. SNYC also shared with the American Youth Congress a desire to reach beyond the campus, to join together student and non-student youth. Indeed, of all the organizations created by the student movement of the 1930s, SNYC's orientation toward off campus, non-student organizing was the strongest, and would very quickly lead SNYC to civil rights and labor mobilizations involving both old and young.[110]

SNYC's orientation toward community organizing derived from student idealism regarding the working class. SNYC organizers, like their ASU counterparts, saw workers as the ultimate agent of social change. This idealism about labor was fueled by both Marxist ideology and the new dynamism of the labor movement under the CIO. The oppressive southern political situation provided SNYC with an added incentive for moving beyond the campus, suggesting from the outset that students alone were too small a group within the black community to pose a threat to the social system which had left millions of blacks disenfranchised, impoverished, and segregated. SNYC was further impelled to move beyond the campus by the political vacuum which existed in the southern black community, where African Americans faced profound political and economic problems, but lacked militant organizations to address those problems.[111]

Headquartered initially in Richmond, Virginia, SNYC held its first convention, the All Southern Negro Youth Conference in that city in February 1937. The opening session was scheduled to coincide with the birthday of abolitionist Frederick Douglass. Over 500 delegates attended the conference, and the two largest delegations represented students and religious groups respectively. Delegates came from all classes and professions, ranging from sharecroppers and labor organizers to artists and teachers. The conference focused on the need for black economic and political opportunity. As SNYC leader Edward Strong told the delegates:

> We have come first of all, seeking the right to creative labor, to be
> gainfully employed with equal pay and employment opportunity—eco-
> nomic security . . . . The new Negro youth of the southland is rising to

manhood without the right to vote—for him we seek opportunity of political expression. And finally, we seek an existence free from the threat
of mob violence . . .[112]

From its office in Richmond, SNYC quickly reached out to one of the
poorest groups of blacks in the city: the workers in tobacco processing
plants. In the spring and summer of 1937, young SNYC organizers under
the leadership of James Jackson led a union organizing drive and a series
of walkouts among the city's tobacco workers. Jackson was responsible for
SNYC's decision to initiate this organizing drive. Having grown up in the
Richmond ghetto, Jackson Ward—or as it was commonly called "The Bottom"—Jackson had lived among the tobacco workers and known of the
oppressive conditions "in the sweatshops of the tobacco" industry. He had
resolved as a youth to "some day . . . strike a blow at this bloody system."[113]
    The wages of these workers, most of whom were stemmers and thus
responsible for removing the stems of the tobacco leaves, were paid on a
piece rate basis. The wage was determined by the size of each stem, and
often this amounted to a paltry 10 cents hourly rate. Such wages left these
workers deeply in debt. A newspaper report from the strike scene described how "one women sobbed as she told how workers had to buy at
credit stores, could not make payment on the goods bought, and how
their wages were garnished time after time." Since these pay rates were
less than half the national minimum wage, securing that minimum of 25
cents an hour became a primary demand of the strikes.[114]
    The SNYC-led strikes also focused on improving working conditions
in the tobacco plants. According to Jackson, the foremen in these plants
were whites who ran them "just like a plantation overseer," denying the
black work force ventilation (not allowing them to open the windows in
the steaming plants) and sanitation provisions. There were also no facilities for dining, causing the workers to "bring their food in newspapers
. . . and sit on the cement sidewalks outside the plant in all kinds of
weather to eat their food." The strikers therefore demanded that the
companies provide the workers with dining halls, restrooms, showers, a
place to changes clothes, cubby holds, fans, and a maintenance person
responsible for airing the factories.[115]
    In one plant after another the strikes proved successful very quickly.
Wages rose to or slightly above the national minimum wage after brief
walkouts, and the changes demanded in working conditions were won for
most of Richmond's 5000 tobacco workers.[116] The victories in Richmond's
tobacco plants, as Jackson explained, helped prod other black factory
workers in the South to unionize and become part of the CIO's massive
organizing drive:

> We organized the tobacco industry in Virginia . . . that set off a
> kind of chain reaction for struggles in the Carolinas, especially in Winston-

Salem, the R.J. Reynolds plants. And in the Virginia Carolina fertilizer chain that went all the way to Georgia. And DuPont Chemical-Nylon plants and so on . . . . On the success of the tobacco workers' strike . . . there was a general demand for organization. Workers on their own initiative wrote out on paper their names and so on and the words CIO, and appealed to the tobacco workers to organize. And organization was . . . terribly easy really; it was a matter of issuing cards and making a speech.[117]

SNYC also sought to spread black community pride toward Black America's history and culture. Much of SNYC's political discourse was saturated with reminders that African Americans had a history of fighting against racism and of achieving political and cultural progress in spite of discrimination. In its Proclamation of Southern Negro Youth (1937), for instance, which demanded racial equality, SNYC declared that

> From echoes of the past and from the deeds of the present we draw our inspiration and courage . . . . Uplifted by the bravery of Crispus Attucks; by his devotion to the cause of his people; by the courage of Frederick Douglass; by the high ideals and spiritual love of Sojurner Truth . . . . Mindful of the scientific contributions of Benjamin Banneker [and] . . . George Washington Carver; and stirred by the . . . high attainment in the arts of our own Marian Anderson and Paul Robeson . . . . Stimulated by the depth, the greatness, and creative genius of Langston Hughes, Richard Wright and Sterling Brown in the field of art and literature . . . . Proud in the stout hearts and strong fists of our champions of champions, Joe Louis and Henry Armstrong . . . . Striving to emulate the spirit of our heritage, pressing forward with pride in the past of our people and confidence in the future.[118]

SNYC did more than simply talk about black culture; it worked to bring cultural events to both urban and rural blacks in the South. SNYC established the Negro Community Theatre in Richmond, the People's Community Theater in New Orleans, and a traveling dramatic group which put on agit-prop puppet shows and Langston Hughes' one act play *Don't You Want to Be Free?* in many parts of the rural South. According Esther Cooper Jackson, who became a SNYC leader in 1938:

> We raised money and we purchased four model-T Fords. And we took puppet shows and drama groups with volunteers out to four southern states—Georgia, Alabama, Louisiana and I'm not sure of the fourth, where we put on shows with these puppets before groups of sharecroppers and in churches and in cities on how to register to vote, how to organize the sharecroppers, how to organize in the city, to take groups down to register to vote, how to train for it, how to study the Constitution . . . . Carrying the message of how to vote to small communities, rural areas. And people would come from all over; they had no movies; they had no theatres. Sometimes this was the first time they'd ever seen any kind of dramatic presentation.

In much of the rural South, where black outsiders were watched closely by police, such shows constituted the only way that SNYC could bring its egalitarian political message without harassment. Police were much less inclined to stop black organizers of a puppet show than they were to seize blacks organizing a political meeting.[119]

This cultural work was designed to assist SNYC in its expanding civil rights agitation. SNYC formed youth councils in over 20 communities in North Carolina, Virginia, Alabama, and Tennessee in 1937. These councils became involved in voting rights activity. Since the poll tax served as one of the key devices used to deny blacks the vote in these communities, it was a primary SNYC target. Recognizing that blacks lacked the power to bring about their ultimate goal of eliminating the poll tax, SNYC devised an immediate way that blacks could overcome this barrier to voting: forming poll tax clubs, which raised money so that blacks could pay the tax and thus vote. SNYC sought to make black disenfranchisement a national issue by organizing an anti-poll tax week, intended to place pressure on the House Judiciary Committee to pass the stalled anti-poll tax bill. The bill never made it out of committee, but this campaign, which included a mock election in New Orleans and public speeches and displays of anti-poll tax buttons, aired the demand for the franchise more boldly than it had ever been in the South during the Depression decade. SNYC investigated lynchings and police brutality, issuing reports designed to publicize this racial violence. The organization also promoted anti-lynching legislation and called for an end to racial discrimination in New Deal relief programs.[120]

V

The student activists in SNYC, the NSL, ASU, and AYC who fought against racial dicrimination lost far more battles than they won. Racism remained so deeply rooted in the society and campuses of America that movement organizers could not overthrow it. Despite SNYC's agitation, African Americans remained disenfranchised in the South. Despite the Fisk protests, lynching continued. Despite the campaigns waged at Charlotesville and Chapel Hill, the southern university system remained almost completely segregated in the 1930s.

Even with these defeats, however, the student movement had not lost completely because such battles highlighted the issue of racial inequality, creating its unprecedented visibility on campus. Though unable to knock out Jim Crow, the student activists of the 1930s were at least willing to step into the ring and fight it. Though these activists failed to end segregation, neither would they compromise with it. The student movement stood against racism even in the South, where doing so undermined the movement's popularity. In the North too, confronting racism was hardly expedient among a predominantly white student body, long accustomed to looking down on African Americans. At a time when the threat of war and the ravages of Depression were on everyone's mind, the movement could have ignored the issue of race entirely and focused on rallying students for peace and economic security. Yet rather than opting for this easy way out, the student movement's organizers stood by their egalitarian principles and insisted on raising the issue of racial inequality in their publications, meetings, and legislative campaigns.

The student movement pioneered a new form of campus activism, which stressed interracial cooperation and an ethic of absolute refusal to compromise with Jim Crow practices. Student activists repeatedly emphasized that a movement could not be truly committed to building a more egalitarian America unless it—in all of its elections, conventions, and campaigns—was free of racial discrimination. The movement rejected the traditional collegiate snobbishness which had almost exclusively elevated wealthy, white Protestants to leadership positions in the undergraduate peer culture. In effect, the movement turned collegiate elitism on its head, valuing diversity instead of homogeneity, revering the working class instead of the upper class.

Thanks in part to the student movement, the Depression decade marked an important turning point in the history of collegiate racism. For the first time in this century, segregation encountered vocal opposition on campus from not just African Americans, but also from white students on both sides of the Mason-Dixon line.[121] Academic racists began to be criticized for their discriminatory acts, and collegiate segregation started to become a national issue both on campus and in the courts. Student activists in the 1930s contributed to the campus civil rights ferment which was larger and more influential than the student movement itself. This ferment encompassed not only the political agitation of the students, but the legal activism of the NAACP and the scholarly work of pioneering social scientists. Before the end of the decade, the NAACP would win the *Gaines* and *Murray* decisions, desegregating professional schools in Missouri and Maryland and setting an important legal precedent in the struggle against Jim Crow on campus. Along with this progress in the Courts, came progress in the classroom, as iconoclastic academics such as Franz Boas published compelling criticisms of previously popular racist theories concerning culture and civilization.[122] The student movement represented a part of this insurgency in that it sought to popularize among students the racial egalitarianism for which the NAACP was litigating and Boas was publishing. These crucial first steps initiated a process that decades later would delegitimize both racism as an ideology and the segregationist system it had upheld.

VI

Throughout the 1930s the student movement's key activist organizations—the NSL, SLID, ASU, and AYC—promoted egalitarian social change. But was that change reformist or revolutionary? Was the student movement seeking to breed radicalism or merely liberalism as it involved collegians in struggles for educational opportunity, government aid to students, job programs for needy youth, racial equality, and collective bargaining rights for workers? The answers to these questions would change over the course of the decade. Where in the early 1930s, the leftist-led organizations that launched the student movement sought to radicalize their classmates, this goal faded later in the decade. The change was linked to the Popular and Democratic Front policies of the Communist Party and to the political realities of campus organizing—both of which encouraged the student movement's communist leaders to come to an accommodation with American liberalism.[123]

In their formative period during the early 1930s, the student movement's leading organizations exhibited considerable hostility toward both liberalism and capitalism. During these, the darkest days of the Great Depression, the NSL and SLID held that capitalism had fallen terminally ill. These radicals thought that such reformers as FDR were engaged in a futile attempt to prop up a doomed social system. In precisely the same manner as their adult Left counterparts, NSLers and SLIDers worried that the New Deal might be the entering wedge for fascism; they feared that the desperate capitalist class would resort to totalitarian methods to maintain its power and that FDR represented their class interests. This explains why in their publications during the early years of the Roosevelt administration the NSL, SLID, and AYC labeled as fascistic such New Deal programs as the Civilian Conservation Corps.[124]

Although they were radicals, when it came to campus organizing NSLers and SLIDers were also pragmatists who understood the campus political scene. They knew that a student body which as recently as 1932 had given a plurality to Herbert Hoover was not going to embrace socialism overnight. The student Left therefore did not insist that collegians who joined in its campaigns share its pessimism about capitalism or its preference for socialist alternatives. Instead, both the NSL and SLID sought to rally the campuses around causes—such as peace and student aid—whose appeal would reach beyond the Left. In effect, these were leftist organizations seeking to use reformist campaigns to first mobilize and then radicalize their classmates.[125]

NSL and SLID organizers believed that by involving students in struggles for specific and limited demands they could initiate a radicalization process. For example, the NSL thought that students who became active in protesting educational retrenchment would learn through this struggle that the cause of their hardships and the high cost of education was the capitalist system itself. These students would discover that they had to "fight capitalism because it stands opposed to the daily needs of the masses of students." At the end of this radicalization process, the NSL and SLID hoped that students would see the need "to commit oneself fully to bringing about [a] Socialist Society [because] . . . only under Socialism would you get full employment and only under Socialism would you end the threat of war and . . . Fascism and create a situation in which there would be full rights given to minorities."[126]

With the advent of the Popular Front in 1935 the tone and rhetoric of the movement's leading organizations began to moderate. Where in the early 1930s the NSL and SLID had championed specific reforms in the hope of radicalizing students, the ASU (the Popular Front organization into which the NSL and SLID had merged) in the mid-1930s treated those reforms as ends in themselves. For the sake of anti-fascist unity, the ASU and the Youth Congress muted their anti-capitalist rhetoric. This shift was evident in the platforms of the Youth Congress. At the first Youth Congress, held in summer 1934, prior to the Comintern's adoption of the Popular Front, the young activists explicitly rejected American capitalism. In the preamble to the resolutions passed at this meeting the Youth Congress pledged "to work for the building of a new social order, based upon production for use rather than profit." The next Youth Congress occurred in summer 1935 just as the Communist Party—in preparation for the Comintern's Seventh World Congress—had begun to shift toward the Popular Front. Under the influence of its communist leadership, the Youth Congress avoided explicit anti-capitalist rhetoric in its resolutions. The second Youth Congress issued the "Declaration of Rights of American Youth," calling for the country to be "turned over to the working and farming people of America," without even implying that this would require a move away from capitalism.[127]

Even this vague reference to worker's control in the 1935 Declaration would seem revolutionary compared to the Youth Congress' rhetoric during the height of the Popular Front era. In their desire to foster national unity against fascism, the Youth Congress leadership sometimes fell into a saccharine brand of patriotic discourse. In August 1938, for example, when Youth Congress chairman Joseph Cadden addressed the opening session of the World Youth Congress he did not emphasize social problems and inequities, but rather the virtues of American democracy. In his speech to the delegates from 57 nations assembled at this session, Cadden sounded more like a boy scout than a young radical. He welcomed the delegates to

> an America you have never seen . . . . You know our land for its tall buildings, its great cities . . . . But there is another side of America which you have never seen on picture post cards, a side of America which the young people of our country cherish even more than the New York skyline. In the United States we have built . . . a civilization on the firm foundation of freedom and justice. And it is of this that we are most proud.[128]

In this same mind-set the Youth Congress in July 1939 adopted its "Creed of American Youth." The Creed, which served as the new organizing document of the Youth Congress, was saturated with patriotic language. Here each member of the Youth Congress pledged that he or she would

not permit class hatred to divide me from other young people. I will
work for the unity of my generation and place that strength at the service
of my country, which I will defend against all enemies. I pledge allegiance to the Flag of the United States of America and to the Republic
for which it stands, one Nation indivisible with liberty and justice for
all.[129]

As the movement dropped its criticism of capitalism, it also softened
its stance regarding President Roosevelt and the New Deal. Talk of the
New Deal's fascistic tendencies, which had been so prominent in the early
student movement, ceased in the mid-1930s. More temperate criticisms of
the limits of the New Deal's social programs continued through 1937. The
New Deal was now depicted as a well intentioned but inadequate social
program. But by the following year, when the CP had embraced FDR as
an ally in the international struggle against fascism—during the period of
CP history appropriately dubbed the Democratic Front—both the ASU
and the Youth Congress began singing Roosevelt's praises.[130]

ASU organizers in 1938 portrayed FDR as a key leader of the western anti-fascist forces and endorsed his New Deal as a bulwark against
American reaction. They began to speak of the ASU as a "New Deal
agency," which would mobilize youth behind the president. Typifying this
new position, in an article prepared for the 1938 ASU convention, Celeste
Strack, a national officer of both the ASU and the YCL, explained that
"the leadership of the ASU . . . plans at this convention" to see "that the
ASU can become a force for winning not only the student body to the
New Deal, but through them sections of the middle class." ASU leaders
discarded earlier descriptions of their organization as a coalition of radicals and liberals, and began to speak of the ASU as a pure and simple
liberal organization. "We are the liberal youth of the nation," explained
ASU chair Robert Lane in 1938. "We must identify ourselves with . . .
the New Deal."[131] With the ASU and the Youth Congress making this
shift, their influence in Washington grew. Both the ASU and Youth Congress proved adept in bringing the student movement into the New Deal
coalition and cultivating an extraordinarily fruitful relationship with key
figures in the Roosevelt administration. The closest of these relationships
was with Mrs. Roosevelt.

The First Lady warmed up to the Youth Congress and formed personal friendships and a political alliance with its national leaders as they
grew more receptive to the New Deal. Mrs. Roosevelt served as the keynote speaker at a regional meeting of the Youth Congress in January
1938. She joined with the Youth Congress in sponsoring the World Youth
Congress in August 1938 and attended its sessions at Vassar—answering
questions from the young delegates for more than an hour. Mrs. Roosevelt, along with NYA director Aubrey Williams, were featured speakers
at the Youth Congress' convention in July 1939. The First Lady raised
funds for the Youth Congress, repeatedly invited its leaders to the White

House, interceded with the president on their behalf, and defended both the Youth Congress and the student movement in her newspaper columns. She praised the Youth Congress for raising public awareness of the "problems of 21,000,000 young people," and expressed "great confidence in the wisdom, the idealism and the honesty of" these young activists. Such endorsements from the highly popular First Lady added significantly to the Youth Congress' reputation as the voice of the young in Depression America. No leftist-led student movement before or since has enjoyed such support from the White House.[132]

This improved relationship with the Roosevelt administration did more, however, than enhance the movement's public image. It also gave these young activists a chance to participate in the process by which the Roosevelt administration shaped its aid policies for the colleges and youth. ASU and Youth Congress representatives were consulted by the WPA as it designed programs to assist playwrights and theaters on campus. Youth Congress leaders began to serve on the NYA's national advisory committee in Washington. The NYA in turn assisted the Youth Congress by providing the organization with office staff.[133]

Not everyone within the student movement was happy about the ASU's and Youth Congress' liberalism and their budding romance with Roosevelt administration. This shift enraged a small but vocal group of Trotskyists and leftwing socialists in the YPSL. These leftists accused the ASU and Youth Congress of selling out to liberalism and abandoning their radical vision. They charged that the communist-dominated ASU and Youth Congress had corrupted the student movement through a "process of class collaborationism, patriotism and junior people's frontism." In their view, the communist leaders of the student movement were so eager to form a multi-class coalition in support of the Comintern's people's front against fascism that they were willing to dispense with serious social criticism and agitation. They charged that since the ASU and Youth Congress now thought class conflict and analysis were divisive, these were being shed in favor of a more bland and nationalistic program upon which all classes could unite. The ASU and Youth Congress now promoted, according to their leftist critics, the liberal illusion that there could be meaningful "social change without class struggle."[134]

Among the worst sins of the ASU and Youth Congress, in the eyes of these leftist critics, was their support of the New Deal. The YPSLs and Trotskyists claimed that the ASU and Youth Congress had reduced themselves to cheerleaders for the Roosevelt administration, surrendering their role as champion of the "locked out generation" of "five million unemployed young people in the United States." When in 1938 the ASU began preaching that "the New Deal is Youth's Deal" it was, the YPSL charged, ignoring the fact that "the Roosevelt administration had failed utterly to answer the plight of" these millions of jobless youths.[135]

These critics were correct in noting the shift in the student movement away from anti-capitalism and toward liberalism. But this searing indictment of the ASU and Youth Congress also reflected the partisanship of its authors. The YPSLs and Trotskyists who made these criticisms were already in the process of breaking with the larger student movement because of its abandonment of the Oxford Pledge. Bitter and angry, the YPSLs and Trotskyists were so eager to denounce the communist leadership of the ASU and Youth Congress, that they cast the changes in the student movement in the worst possible light. As leftwing ideologues, they saw any shift away from a strict revolutionary line as a sellout. But the relationship between radicalism and reform within the student movement remained more complex than these critics cared to admit. The student movement had always had a strong reformist side. The Popular Front policies represented less a sell out of the movement's principles than an extension of its pragmatic (some might say opportunistic) approach to student organizing.

The continuities within the student movement in the early and late 1930s are as striking as the changes. True, the early literature of the NSL and SLID spoke of the imminent demise of capitalism, while the ASU did not. But if one probed the *activities* of these organizations, crucial similarities emerge. All three devoted almost all of their time to campaigns on immediate issues. The bulk of their energy went into promoting peace, student welfare, civil rights, and solidarity between the student movement and the labor movement. The real difference here was that unlike the ASU, the NSL and SLID spoke of using such activities to radicalize students. But this difference in intent did not amount to much. For, although the NSL and SLID had hoped their campaigns would lead to widespread student radicalization, they learned differently. Students would rally with the NSL and SLID for peace or student aid, but only a small minority would become sufficiently radicalized to join either organization. Combatting the flaws in capitalism did not—as the NSL and SLID had naively expected—lead many students to embrace socialism. Indeed, as the New Deal began to restore America's faith in liberalism in the mid-1930s, students increasingly viewed reform as a viable option. This left both the NSL and SLID in a paradoxical situation. Much as they might thumb their noses at liberal reform, NSLers and SLIDers had the most influence on campus at those moments when they were leading their classmates in reformist campaigns.

As pragmatists, NSLers and SLIDers sensed that given the non-revolutionary environment on campus in the mid-1930s, their agitation could be most effective if channelled into a new organization—the ASU—that would not be associated in the student mind with revolutionary parties and dogmas. The idea was that if freed from the revolutionary rhetoric and image of the early student Left, the ASU could attract many more members than had the NSL and SLID. The ASU was designed by its founders from the NSL and SLID to continue their campaigns for peace and social justice, but to do so in a style which would enlarge them; and this was just what the ASU accomplished.

Even though the rhetoric was new, the concept behind the ASU remained consistent with the basic organizing strategy which had guided the student Left since the early 1930s. From the very beginning of the movement both socialists and communists had suspected that an official party youth organization with the "socialist" or "communist" label would seem too revolutionary for the American student body. That is why socialist students did not center their national campus organizing in the Socialist Party's YPSL, but instead used the SLID—an organization not officially affiliated with the Socialist Party—as their main membership organization on campus. The same was true of the communists, who focused their campus organizing in the NSL rather than the YCL. So though the ASU was the first official Popular Front organization on campus, its parent organizations had in a sense already been fronts for the more explicitly ideological and partisan communist and socialist organizations. The ASU extended this approach by going further in submerging its ties with leftist parties and ideologies than had the NSL and SLID.

These were not the only continuities between the student Left of the early and late 1930s. Indeed, during the early 30s, the NSL and SLID experimented with a form of coalition politics which the adult Left would embrace later in the decade—during the Popular Front era. The NSL was championing causes which appealed to liberal students at a time when the CP's revolutionary posturing—a byproduct of the Comintern's ultra-radical Third Period line—was still alienating liberal adults. The NSL and SLID also pioneered the type of non-sectarianism which would later become a main tenet of the Popular Front. For example, during the spring 1934 anti-war strike and in the summer 1934 Youth Congress, socialist and communist student organizers worked together in the name of peace and anti-fascism, while the SP and CP were still feuding. And in working to build the Youth Congress into a multi-class organization of progressive youth (while the CP was still focusing almost exclusively on workers) the movement anticipated another key element of the the Popular Front. Long before the Comintern in the summer of 1935 declared a Popular Front by advocating unity of the Left with all classes and political groups against fascism, the student movement was already promoting such unity.[136]

These continuities in the movement suggest that the Popular Front policies may not have been quite the dire change and sell out that its critics charged. But, of course, along with such continuity did come the stunning reversal on the New Deal. The founders of the NSL and SLID in the early 1930s could barely have dreamed that their successors would so warm up to Roosevelt. If viewed in strictly ideological terms, this warmth between student radicals and a liberal administration would seem to represent—as the Trotskyists and YPSLs claimed—an abandonment of principle.[137] Here again, however, the image of the movement selling out does not quite correspond with political reality. The interaction between the student movement and the Roosevelt administration was far less one sided than its critics imply.

Even as the ASU and Youth Congress linked themselves closer to the New Deal, they still retained much of their old desire for more sweeping social legislation than the Roosevelt administration was delivering. The tone of the demands for such legislation was different and softer than in the early 1930s, since now students spoke from inside rather than outside the New Deal coalition. But the basic dynamic was the same: student activists seeking to push the federal government leftward. This could be seen, for instance, in the evolving relationship between the Youth Congress and the NYA. In May 1937, NYA director Aubrey Williams told Youth Congress leaders that the NYA was in danger because of a conservative rebellion on Capitol Hill. Williams came to the Youth Congress "appealing for a campaign to keep the relief budget from being slashed to $1,000,000,000 which would probably mean ending the National Youth Administration." The Youth Congress worked to rally national support for the NYA in order to prevent thousands of youths from losing their jobs. But while seeking to help the NYA preserve existing jobs, the Youth Congress in 1937 continued to push for expansion of youth aid through its own much more generous aid package—the American Youth Act. The Youth Congress' assistance helped prevent the feared NYA cuts. Even after this campaign, however, the Youth Congress did not completely abandon its critical view of the Roosevelt youth program. In the fall of 1937, when President Roosevelt indicated his desire to spend less on the NYA than the $75 million authorized by Congress, the Youth Congress protested the president's policy.[138]

Publicly the Youth Congress' (and ASU's) leftwing critics condemned all such cooperation with New Dealers. But privately even some of these critics conceded the logic and pragmatism of the Youth Congress' position. For instance in a letter to a fellow YPSL organizer, Hy Weintraub confided his doubts about the arguments that they had been making against fighting for an expanded and better funded NYA. Weintraub expressed his "wish" that

> someone could make a clear statement on why the YPSL does not support the fight for better conditions on the NYA. I think the Communist position on this is correct—we fight for the AYA but we also participate in the immediate struggles of youth by asking for more for the NYA. The AYA is too far away and utopian for those people who need relief immediately.[139]

Although the Youth Congress continued its support of the American Youth Act in 1938, by the following year this crusade had fizzled and the Act was not even re-introduced on Capitol Hill. This was clearly because of the growing links between the Youth Congress and the NYA. The Youth Congress had become so closely enmeshed in the NYA that its leaders were no longer interested in pushing for the AYA. However, this work with the NYA had not rendered the Youth Congress leadership complacent regarding the New Deal program. This was evident in the behavior of Youth Congress chair Abbot Simon as a participant in the NYA advisory board's 1938 meeting with FDR. Where the members of the board used their conference with the president to trumpet the NYA's accomplishments, Simon chose instead to criticize the NYA's limitations. Simon told the president that the NYA should be expanded immediately and dramatically so that it would aid 1,500,000 youths instead of the mere 500,000 it had been assisting. Similarly, at its 1939 convention, the Youth Congress praised the NYA, but also pushed for a new loan program and more vocational training and apprenticeship programs for youth.[140]

This continuing willingness of student movement leaders to press the president for more generous social programs—especially for youth—did not go unnoticed in the White House. Ironically, it helped cement their relationship with Eleanor Roosevelt during the late 1930s. At a time when the New Deal was stalemated and its youth programs threatened by Congressional cutbacks, Mrs. Roosevelt saw these activists as allies in her effort to "win the president over to doing more for young people." As Joseph Lash explains, part of the reason she "enjoyed having them to dinner with the president" was because "unlike many of the people he saw the young people stood up to him." [141]

The president, on other other hand, sometimes was irritated by the student movement's demand for increased social spending. When, for instance, the First Lady sent him a copy of Lash's keynote speech from the ASU's convention, held in December 1938—which, though pro-FDR, also called for expansion of the NYA and other social programs—the president responded testily. He wrote a memorandum in January 1939 implying that the ASU's suggestions were fiscally irresponsible. FDR advised her:

> If you want to start a discussion among young people some day, get them to discuss and answer the following question: The government deficit today is $3,000,000,000 a year . . . . We could very easily and usefully spend another billion dollars a year on aids to and improvement of education . . . . We could very easily use another billion dollars a year in . . . youth training . . . . How can the . . . new deficit, if such projects are carried out be financed? [142]

FDR's sentiments in this 1939 memorandum recalled those of his wife's at her initial meeting with the Youth Congress leadership back in 1936. At that meeting Mrs. Roosevelt had criticized the young activists and their American Youth Act for demanding far more social spending that the nation could afford.[143] The president was criticizing the ASU on this same basis in 1939. Much had changed in the student movement during the years between the 1936 meeting and the 1939 memorandum. The student movement was now supporting the Roosevelt administration rather than denouncing it and calling itself liberal rather than revolutionary. But in spite of these changes, and in spite of its occasional flights into nation-alistic gush, the student movement, as the president's irritation suggests, had not become a mere FDR fan club. The movement retained the ability and inclination to ask for more—more social spending than the Roosevelt administration provided, more educational and economic opportunity than America afforded, and more racial equality than either academia or Washington supported.

VII

Athough YPSL and Trotskyist critics exaggerated some of the stu-dent movement's flaws during the Popular Front era, these critics were nonetheless astute in at least one respect. They may have been wrong about the movement selling out to FDR, but they were right to raise the issue of political integrity. The behavior of communist leaders in the stu-dent movement during the Popular Front does raise troubling questions about both their personal and political integrity. It was not their policies—their accommodation with liberalism—but rather the process by which those polices were executed that raises the most unsettling questions. Irving Howe, an alumni of both the YPSL and the Trotskyist student Left of the 1930s, captured the essence of this problem when in a recent essay he referred to the Popular Front as a "brilliant masquerade."[144] Communist activists in the student movement brilliantly expanded the movement by merging radicalism with liberalism; they accomplished this, however, by masking their ideological loyalties and party affiliations in a way that deceived not only the public but even their political allies.

The Youth Congress embodied all these problems. This organiza-tion's external history was, as we have seen, dominated by campaigns to expand political and social democracy in the United States. The Youth Congress' internal history was, however, anything but democratic. Through a process of infiltration and tactical maneuvering, communists gradually took control of the organization's national leadership. Communist stu-dents and youth organizers packed the important committees with mem-bers and sympathizers. At the very top of the Youth Congress too, com-munist domination was assured as succeeding AYC officers were brought into the communist orbit. Former YCL leader Gil Green recalled that "one after another" the Youth Congress chairs were

> recruited into either the YCL or the Party. Waldo McNutt [the first AYC chair] was recruited into the Party. Bill Hinckley, who became the second [AYC chair] was recruited. Joe Cadden after him was recruited. And Jack McMichael [the last AYC chair] no; but he was very sympathetic. He was *very*, very close [to the CP]. And I could mention a whole number of others.[145]

The real problem with this recruitment and infiltration was not its scope, but its secrecy. Had the communists been open about their identity and influence they would have been operating within parameters of democratic process—since they, like all other members of such a federation, have the right to compete for power. Unfortunately, this was not done openly. Instead, Green secretly recruited the top Youth Congress officers; the YCL clandestinely stacked the Congress' key committees; and the Youth Congress secretly became a communist-dominated organization.[146] These Communist machinations led to political misrepresentation. At the very time when the Popular Front and its rhetoric made the Youth Congress seem more liberal and mainstream it was actually growing more communist-controlled.

The student who read Youth Congress literature in the Popular Front era would have thought it an organization influenced not by the Soviet but the American revolution. To help give credence to this association with 1776 the Youth Congress had begun in 1935 to move its annual national convention to July 4. Its Declaration of Rights of Youth at this 1935 convention was written to frame the Youth Congress' demands in a way that called to mind the Declaration of Independence. The Youth Congress also effectively combined its egalitarian message with other images from America's liberal heritage. When, for instance, the Youth Congress advertised its American Youth Act, it did so by invoking images of frontier democracy, comparing this legislation to the Homestead Act of 1862, and in fact calling it "the Homestead Act of 1937."[147]

In using such rhetoric and setting its slogans—as it did in its 1937 Youth Pilgrimage—to the tune of Yankee Doodle, the Youth Congress was trying to reach out to non-radicals. This effort to speak in the language of American liberalism was obviously a creative and important step on the road to broadening the movement. It was not the use of such rhetoric alone which is problematic, but rather the use of such rhetoric by an organization which hid its communist domination. People were being recruited into a liberal sounding organization, believing that it was run by liberals, when in fact it was run by communists. These recruits also had no way of knowing that the Youth Congress' increasingly moderate rhetoric and growing ties to the New Deal were changes linked to the influence of communists and their Popular Front line on the organization. In short, the movement's literature failed to clue students in to who ran the organization or how its policies were shaped ideologically.[148]

The deception employed by the communists in the Youth Congress was not always this subtle and implicit. Some of the leading and secret communists in the Youth Congress leadership did not simply fail to mention their Party affiliation; they publicly lied about their ties to the Communist Party and YCL. When rightwingers accused these individuals of being communists and charged that the Youth Congress was communist-dominated, these communists—including Youth Congress chairs—denied everything, misleading the press, the public, and the Youth Congress membership.[149]

Why the deception? Communists in the Youth Congress had good reason to hide their political affiliations. Even in an era as liberal as the 1930s, anti-communism remained a strong political force in America. Throughout the Depression decade state legislatures, superpatriot groups, and the Hearst press denounced and investigated red influence over youth and education. By 1938 Congress was funding its own brand of anti-communist crusading, led by Representative Martin Dies and the House Un-American Activities Committee, which he chaired. The Youth Congress would itself become the target of a red probe by Dies and his committee before the decade ended.[150] With such powerful and influential people seeking to deny civil liberties to communists, many felt that if they were to remain politically active and effective, they had to hide their party affiliations. The communists' deception here was, in part, a response to America's political intolerance—a way of evading redbaiters. This political context must be borne in mind, so as to avoid demonizing the communists or neglecting the connections between the maladies of the CP and those of the larger national polity. But this context does not excuse the communists, nor should it obscure the ways in which a political movement more concerned with ends than means compromised its integrity.

The tenor of the Popular and Democratic Fronts also provided a more positive rationale and inducement for communists in the Youth Congress to keep their Party loyalty to themselves. At the heart of the communist line in this era lay the notion that all other considerations should be secondary to the building of the broadest possible anti-fascist coalition. This meant that everyone should, as much as possible, ignore party differences and identifications in order to work together on the building of the anti-fascist front. In this sense, submerging one's CP affiliation could be seen as a virtuous act on behalf of anti-fascist unity. It was, in the student movement's case, a means of protecting the movement from the divisiveness and controversy which might have resulted had the Youth Congress' communist leadership gone public. During this era communists also felt that they shared so many foreign and social policy goals with liberals that party labels were becoming irrelevant. What mattered was not who you were or how you voted, but whether you were willing to join in the crusade to stop international fascism from exterminating democracy. This was what one of the secret communists at the top of Youth Congress leadership meant when he confided to a colleague that "it was all right for CPers in the democratic front to deny they were CPers by virtue of the fact that they were defending democracy."[151]

Although this communist secrecy represented an understandable response to intolerance and in the short run a practical step for building a broader movement, the long run consequences of it would prove disastrous for both the Youth Congress and the entire student movement. However they rationalized it, the fact was that communists in the student movement were, as ASU activist Junius Scales put it, "full of duplicity."[152] They were lying about their party ties not only to strangers, but even to their close political allies and friends. Among those so deceived was Eleanor Roosevelt. Though the First Lady did more than anyone in Washington to aid the Youth Congress and became personally close to some of the its leaders, they hid their communist ties from her. With Mrs. Roosevelt and other liberal allies of the student movement this deception would go undetected for several years. So long as the Popular Front lasted, and liberals and communists took compatible positions on key policy questions, the Party question was submerged. But when the communists, in the wake of the Nazi-Soviet Pact, began to destroy the Popular Front against fascism, their old lies would come back to haunt them. Suddenly liberals such as Mrs. Roosevelt found themselves under attack by student activists who had been their close friends. The communists flip-flopped on foreign and domestic policy questions in a manner so transparently dictated by the new Comintern line that liberals both on campus and in Washington discerned the deception. The feelings of betrayal and mistrust borne of that deception would poison the political atmosphere and contribute to the decline of both the Youth Congress and the entire student movement.[153]

Chapter 8

Activist Impulses

"How can I explain the position of organized labor to Father when you keep passing me the chocolate sauce?" The earnest college girl in the cartoon is arousing the social conscience of her well-off father while her embarrassed mother vainly tries to stanch the flow of ideology with rich food. Anne Cleveland, Vassar '36, drew the scene, and everyone who went to a liberal arts college in her time recognizes the mood of social protest.

We felt that the New Deal would never get to the bottom of the trouble. We felt that something basic was wrong with the setup and it was up to us to find out what was wrong and do something about it. We enjoyed a pleasurable sense of millenium. Things could not go on as they had. We felt injustice as personal guilt. "If you give your coat to the first man shivering on the street," we used to say, "then what are you going to do for the next one?" It worried us that we had a coat . . . . We were ashamed that our parents had sent us to snobby private schools. We imagined that the unemployed looked hungrily over our shoulders, just as we had imagined that the starving Chinese suffered when we refused to eat our spinach.

Caroline Bird, *The Invisible Scar* (New York, 1966), 138.

N o sooner had the student movement emerged than speculation began about the sources of campus activism. Since such large scale student protest was unprecedented in the nation's history, it was natural that a variety of theories would evolve as Depression America sought to explain this new phenomenon. An assortment of conservatives—which included superpatriots, redbaiting editors, and politicians—wrote the most and screamed the loudest about the causes of student radicalism during the 1930s; they did so because of their outrage at the growth of Left-led organizations and student anti-war demonstrations on campus. Their most frequent explanation for this unwelcome upsurge of student activism centered on the faculty, whom they blamed for corrupting and radicalizing youth.

The conservative press depicted college faculty as dangerously subversive. Professors emerged in these pages as a sort of academic branch of the Red Army. "There are few colleges or universities where parents may send their sons and daughters without their being contaminated with some phase of the vilest of Communistic and allied teaching," warned Roscoe J.C. Dorsey, in the *The National Republic,* a superpatriot magazine which crusaded against faculty and student radicalism. In this same journal E.D. Clark, president of the Indiana State Medical Association, diagnosed "Red Microbes in Our Colleges," evoking fears of political and sexual radicalism. The Hoosier doctor claimed that "under the guise of 'academic freedom' many professors . . . are not only teaching communism, socialism, anarchy . . . but are also endorsing 'free love' and unrestricted sex relations between unmarried people." [1]

This rightwing indictment of the faculty was not confined, however, to the college level. Conservatives hurled similar charges against teachers in secondary and even elementary schools. The Hearst press, which did so much to give such charges national circulation, claimed in 1935 that thanks to the work of subversives in the nation's school systems "two hundred thousand Soviet schoolbooks have been imported into America." [2] According to these rightwing critics, youths' support for radicalism in college derived from exposure to subversion by teachers at all levels of the American educational system. Typifying this faculty-bashing, the Hearst editorial "Red Teachers" concluded that

> the danger to the country of the growth of Communism in our seats of learning should not be blamed on our students. There is the element of youthful effervescence and the emotional hurrah of the novel that often pass away when the student begins the struggle for existence and finds that rugged individualism is his only asset. The danger lies in the teachers of communism in our colleges and schools. A student may outgrow his revolutionary effervescence. But it is hard for him to overcome the subtle and overt injections into him by persons he regards as authorities. The teaching of communism in our . . . institutions of learning is a breach of trust and a perversion of professional responsibility. A teacher is paid to expound and explain, not to indoctrinate. [3]

Although the sensationalism of such Hearst stories (which produced those mythological textbooks smuggled from Russia) makes it difficult to take the conservative view of student radicalism too seriously, that view did have serious consequences. It led anti-communists, seeking the elimination of student radicalism, to launch political attacks on the purported source of that radicalism: subversive faculty members. This was expressed through a movement, spearheaded by superpatriot groups, to impose loyalty oaths on teachers. By the end of the Depression decade, twenty-one

states had adopted such oaths. The volatility of the faculty radicalism issue was also evident in such conservative assaults on faculty dissent as that
which occurred at the University of Chicago in 1935. Here pharmacy
magnate Charles R. Walgreen caused great upheaval by removing his niece
from the University, and charging that he did so because she had been
indoctrinated in communism and free love by Chicago faculty members.
Though not even Walgreen's niece fully supported his charges, they were
all the Illinois state legislature needed as a pretext for launching an investigation into subversion at the University of Chicago—an investigation which
failed to turn up any Bolsheviks or free love advocates on the faculty.[4]

The loyalty oaths and the Chicago investigation attest that for conservatives such faculty-baiting was almost irresistable. It appealed to both the
anti-radical and anti-intellectual currents in 1930s conservatism. For
rightwing politicians and journalists, moreover, this seemed a cause tailor
made for public approval—complete with emotionally charged images of
adult "Commie" professors preying on innocent youths. The free love
charge added incestuous overtones to an already explosive brew. But
whatever its merits as a tool for demagoguery, such faculty scapegoating
misrepresented the political situation in American educational institutions. Throughout the Depression decade, the Right exaggerated the dimensions of faculty radicalism and the role of teachers in both sparking
student protest and building the student movement.

The best sources for assessing the role that faculty played in turning
students to activism are the students themselves. The SLID in 1935 and
the ASU in 1938 and 1939 held summer leadership institutes for student
organizers, during which more than 70 activists completed essays about
their politicization. Dozens of activists have written memoirs and given
interviews in which they too discussed the roots of their activism. These
sources suggest that faculty did not play a predominant role in the politicization of 1930s activists. Only 21.6 percent of the activists reported that
a faculty member fostered their politicization, and most of these activists
mentioned such faculty influence as only one of many factors which contributed to their politicization. This 21.6 percent figure looks even smaller,
moreover, in light of the fact that another 20 percent of the student activists cited unpleasant experiences with reactionary faculty who had sought
to stifle student dissent and non-conformity.[5] There were, in other words,
almost as many student organizers who viewed faculty as an obstacle to
Left-liberal activism as viewed faculty as facilitators of such activism.

Among the 20 percent recording negative encounters with conservative faculty were young men and women with painful classroom memories
dating back to elementary school. One ASU activist recalled that his parents' organizing on behalf of Sacco and Vanzetti had made a "deep
impression" on him. In grade school, however, his teacher lectured the
class on "what kind of 'bad' men Sacco and Vanzetti were." This led to
"my spontaneous outcry that she was a liar, and [a] subsequent talk with
the public school principal about how the labor movement was a bad thing."

Another activist told of being frightened by an elementary school teacher, who had become "aghast . . . and furious" after she told the teacher—as her radical parents had told her—that in 1917 the United States "had *not* entered the war to avenge the *Lusitania* . . . that it had something to do with munitions makers and raw materials." Faculty intolerance sometimes had ethnic as well as ideological dimensions, judging by a Columbia student radical's memories of his kindergarten teacher, who in 1919 called him a "little enemy" and marched him off to see the principal because he had sung a German song taught him by his parents. A University of Wisconsin ASU organizer wrote of being scolded by a teacher and sent to his junior high school principal's office for expressing "opposition to larger armaments. This was my first experience with narrow-mindedness in the school system."[6]

Even some students who had not experienced such traumatic confrontations recalled their pre-college education as dull or deadening to dissident thought. A Vassar ASU leader looked back upon her prep school as a place whose classrooms and student body were pervaded by "narrowness and conservatism." The students there were a "group of girls of the typically Boston sub-deb[utant] variety . . . whose main interest seemed to be boys and parties." Another ASU activist noted that her only contact with politics in secondary school had been

> a course in social problems from a high school teacher, who was anti-New Deal, anti-labor, anti-progress. He was a militarist, a fatalist, and a pessimist. I came out of that course a completely defeated person. The state of the human race was hardly better than . . . 3,000 years ago, and there was not much use in our fretting and striving about to improve it.[7]

A Bryn Mawr ASU organizer termed as "disgraceful" the faculty at her Philadelphia High School. "Little or no independent thinking is encouraged. Students are expected to repeat parrot-like the opinions expressed to them . . . [by] reactionary or escapist" teachers.[8]

Youths who entered the student movement before graduation from such schools were not—as the Hearst press preached—following the direction of teachers; they were rebelling against the orthodoxy and conformity fostered by those teachers. And those daring enough to engage in this open rebellion often encountered strong hostility from faculty and school authorities. An ASU organizer from Cleveland noted that in her high school

> the faculty still used its power over scholarship awards to force two members out of the [ASU] chapter, and witnesses heard the principal announce that he would do everything in his power to block the award of scholarships to the leading members of the ASU regardless of the superior qualifications of the students.[9]

A New York City ASUer described how a repressive teacher monitored the radical students in his high school's Current Problems Club: "We were silenced by the faculty advisor whenever we tried to mention ASU . . . . At High School we protested consistent faculty censorship of the paper, of assemblies, of clubs, magazine and student council." Another New Yorker with similar high school experiences believed that he had come out of this intolerant milieu strengthened by adversity. His "long initiation of . . . arguing with teachers . . . . standing up against the discipline of Principal Boylan, the many threats of violence from the football team, as well as the threats of arrest for distributing literature must have been good training for leadership" in the student movement.[10]

Not only these individual memoirs, but also the student movement's publications refute the Right's equation of American educators with revolutionary subversion. In the ASU's national magazine, *Student Advocate*, teachers, professors, and educational administrators appear much more frequently as foes than friends of the student movement. The magazine's most extensive feature on American educators was a six part series on intolerant college presidents, indicting these "Academic Napoleons" for trying to stamp out dissent on their campuses. The magazine's other coverage of the American educational scene—with such headlines as "University Sweatshops," "Gagging High Schools," "Kansas Is A White Man's School," "ROTC Trains Strike Breakers," "How to Be A Censored [Student] Editor,"—paints an equally unflattering portrait of reactionary, narrow-minded and repressive educational leadership. The *Student Advocate* lampooned stodgy and conservative professors, depicting them as comically inept teachers, out of touch with recent political and cultural developments. In fact, the ASU magazine even invoked this image in an ad for new subscribers, which featured a professorial caricature, accompanied by the words:

> Hey You! Don't think this bearded gent knows all the answers. Sometimes he doesn't even know the questions! Ask him the story behind the NYA cuts [or] who controls his Board of Trustees—and see what happens. Ask him how we can keep out of war and where you can get a job when you graduate—or why you can't.[11]

Not all teachers, of course, were as uninformed or reactionary as these ASU stories implied. After all, 21.6 percent of the student activists surveyed did credit a faculty member with helping to politicize them and pave the way for their participation in the student movement. Who were these faculty? Here again the Right's revolutionary imagery of red teachers engaging in communist indoctrination was simplistic. More than a third of the students (in the 21.6 percent group) who reported that a faculty member helped politicize them referred not to radical instructors preaching revolution, but to liberal faculty teaching about reform.[12]

This considerable liberal role reflected the fact that the 1930s was the decade of the New Deal, an era in which liberalism prevailed in the White House and much of America. Nationally, faculty were more affected by this liberalism than they were by radicalism. An overwhelming 84 percent of social science professors supported New Deal liberalism, according to a 1937 national poll.[13] Some of this sentiment would, of course, be reflected in the classroom. The result was that at least some students would be exposed to liberal idealism and critical thought about American society. This would not make instant revolutionaries out of these students; but it exposed them to new political ideas, in a way that could leave them more receptive to the appeals of ASU organizers. This was particularly true during the Popular Front era, when the politics of the ASU and the New Deal were so similar.

There were a variety of ways in which liberal teachers prodded students to think about social problems and thereby helped to politicize them. These included teaching students about social science, political problems, and the need for reformist efforts to address those problems. One ASU activist recalled that several progressive teachers in the private high school she attended introduced her

> in an undoubtedly careful and scientific manner to the social sciences for the first time in my life . . . . I learned why workers organized, what a black list is, the techniques utilized by labor and capital, the value of social legislation, and the danger of thoughtless "conservatism." . . . By the time I was ready for college I considered myself a full fledged progressive, having travelled in those two years from a disinterested Republican to an avid New Dealer to theoretically more inspiring and revolutionary horizons.[14]

A midwestern ASU organizer observed that he too had become politically conscious after his exposure to critical thought in the social sciences. College "courses in economics, history and political science awakened me to local, national and international affairs . . ." So when Molly Yard and another ASU leader came to his campus, he helped organize an ASU chapter, seeing this activist group as a vehicle "to solidify and to integrate my many new interests."[15] In other cases, it was not social science methodology, but the idealism of liberal teachers that inspired students to become politically active. A North Carolina ASU organizer, for instance, found that "one of the greatest stimuli to liberal and intelligent thinking I have received came from my high school history teacher. She had a great deal of faith in and understanding of the common person and this she passed on to some of her pupils."[16]

The liberal teachers who helped inspire student activism came not only out of the New Deal tradition, but also out of other progressive strains in American political culture. ASU national officer Celeste Strack, for instance, recalled that her first steps toward political consciousness came before college, through the influence of a feminist teacher, who was the principal of her small private school in San Diego. This teacher had herself once been a student rebel, active at Vassar during the women's suffrage campaign. She taught Strack in a manner that reflected the critical sensibility of the women's movement, having, as Strack put it,

> the knack of teaching you how to think, to question . . . . And her way was not to try to convince you of a viewpoint but to get you to think critically about the world you were in, and given the Depression that wasn't hard to do. So that it was this which I brought to USC and this . . . enabled me to be responsive [to the student movement].[17]

African American student activist Kenneth Clark had a similar experience with Howard University faculty, whose critical teachings on race relations in the United States prodded him to engage in civil rights agitation. Other students headed in an activist direction after learning from teachers influenced by progressive education—particularly in the Ethical Culture schools—which emphasized liberal values and the importance of acting on them.[18]

By understanding the role played by liberal faculty as well as their conservative counterparts, it becomes possible to put faculty radicalism into perspective. Among the students in our sample activist group who cited some faculty role—either positive or negative—in their political evolution, more than twice as many mentioned liberal and conservative faculty as mentioned radical faculty. Out of the entire activist group sampled only 11.2 percent said that radical faculty contributed to their politicization. This low number suggests that though leftist teachers contributed to politicizing students and strengthening the student movement, that contribution was much less significant than Hearst and other rightwing critics of the faculty imagined.[19]

The relatively small contribution leftist faculty made to the movement was linked to the tenuous nature of such professorial radicalism. Faculty radicals constituted a small and insecure minority. Since college administrators usually believed it improper for faculty to engage in leftist agitation, they used their power to discourage such activity. This administration anti-radicalism meant that faculty members who chose to identify themselves closely with the student Left were risking their jobs. Among the faculty who took this risk (usually young instructors rather than professors) and lost were Oakley Johnson at CCNY, Donald Henderson at Columbia, Herbert Miller at Ohio State, and Jerome Davis at Yale. Their firings received extensive press attention and served as a strong deterrent to leftist faculty—who were not anxious to lose their jobs in a depressed era, when faculty positions were particularly hard to come by. In addition to fear of firing, a professorial ethical code sometimes inhibited faculty expression of radicalism. Some (though by no means all) leftist faculty thought it unprofessional to use the "classroom as an instrument of indoctrination." "We had," as one radical faculty member explained, "a lurking feeling that it wasn't quite good sportsmanship to try to influence young people [politically]—at least to make use of our position in the classroom to do this."[20]

Few students could expect to encounter an overtly radical faculty member in Depression America, when such faculty were small in number, insecure in their jobs, and divided themselves about the propriety of radical proselytizing in the classroom. About the rarest experience of all was encountering teachers who explicitly incorporated Marxist ideas into their lectures and other regular classroom activities. This did occur, however, in a few college courses in the social sciences and humanities, usually on campuses reputed to be among the most permissive. At Harvard, for instance, the Marxist economist Paul Sweezy, jointly offered a course with a more conservative colleague to give students both the pro- and anti-capitalist perspective.[21] Vassar College, with its unique feminist tradition, allowed several radical professors the freedom to give their courses a socialist slant. At a scattering of the more progressive private secondary and lower schools, it was also possible to run into a teacher who brought radical politics into the classroom. One student activist from Western Reserve University noted that a teacher in her Ethical Culture school, who "preached a sort of Utopian Socialism" helped to shape her politics.[22]

Since the atmosphere on most campuses was not free enough for such overt radical teaching, student encounters with faculty radicalism tended to occur outside the classroom. The vehicle for this encounter was sometimes the campus' Marxist study group, where small groups of leftist faculty, graduate students, and undergraduates assembled for informal discussions of radical theory. A socialist student organizer from the University of Louisville recalled that on arriving at college

> I thought about politics in terms of Republicans and Democrats, about economics not at all. Then came the dawn! . . . . Two of my college friends invited me to attend a meeting at the house of my psychology professor . . . . It was a radical discussion group, meeting every week and known as the Pen and Hammer Club; radicals of every creed were there. The meeting was just a little over my head, but I was interested and went back again.[23]

The covert nature of these encounters sometimes gave them a special intensity, as students and teachers shared forbidden Marxist knowledge. This was evident in the memoirs of an ASU activist in a prominent eastern women's college. In linking her radicalization to "a fascinating series of Marxist" discussion group meetings with a leftist faculty member, she explained that "there was an exciting atmosphere of secrecy about each meeting. It was only as I got more involved in the actual analysis of Marxian theory that I realized how terribly important the class struggle was and how equally important my relationship to it could be."[24] An African American student radical from Fisk recalled that here too secrecy was necessary because the administration and town authorities were so anti-radical. The underground nature of her interaction with the few Communist professors on campus added to its allure:

> One professor had almost like an Anne Frank's room at the back of his house . . . packed with all kinds of radical literature. And when they got to know me I was free to visit there and just read. And there were things like the *Daily Worker* there and all kinds of books—books there would be no way of getting on the Fisk campus.[25]

She soon became involved in a radical discussion group with these leftist professors. Similarly, an ASU activist from Randolph-Macon College noted that the secret conversations she had with a young radical psychology professor were "the most important single influence in my intellectual growth." After taking a course with this professor and becoming her research assistant,

> I found out that she liked poetry, especially Auden and Spender. I was slightly suspicious of her extreme enthusiasm for them because I had read somewhere that they were Communists . . . . [We] discussed the state of Christianity. She denied that our democracy was based upon Christianity. In fact, she said it wasn't even democracy. When she explained herself, saying that there were a few people, who because they owned wealth could exploit many people, there was no equality of opportunity and therefore no democracy, I called her a Communist. She said "Sh." I was tremendously excited because I felt as if I were conspiring in a dark and dangerous discussion. In an incredibly short time I was turned into a socialist, partly because I was tired of being nothing and partly because I enjoyed the daring of being a socialist.[26]

Whether such learning was covert or overt its impact could be great on the individual student. Radical faculty willing to share their ideas with undergraduates were exposing them to criticism, authors, and a worldview that could seem new and exciting. This was particularly true for students from conservative families, such as Celeste Strack, who had never before been exposed to Marxist ideas. She first encountered Marxism in her class with a radical economics teacher at USC, and found it to be a "very different way of looking at the world, and it was a very critical way." Strack viewed Marxist concepts—dialectical materialism and class analysis—as a "scientific instrument" that enabled her to dig below the rhetoric of politicians and businessmen, revealing the economic interests and structures that had caused the Depression and shaped history. Strack looked back upon this introduction to radical ideas as "an enormously liberating experience," like " a light turning on in the room; it was literally the illumination of the world . . . a profound experience."[27] For her, the teachings of this radical professor were so memorable that even a half century later she still vividly recalled the course's final exam question which probed the "contradictions" of capitalism. At Harvard, Paul Sweezy made a similar impact on the young Leo Marx, who would later become one of America's leading cultural historians. Marx rated Sweezy "a strong teacher" who persuaded him

> to adopt a radical view of American society, to recognize that the great contradictions of American society are deeply systemic and structural and probably cannot be resolved by piecemeal reform. It's a view of the world that I've since modified in many ways, but I also think I have held onto it ever since.[28]

Not all students who encountered such faculty radicalism recall it with the same warm glow as Strack and Marx. Some viewed this political teaching as an abuse of authority and a form of indoctrination. In novelist Mary McCarthy's memoirs of her years at Vassar, she scorned

> Lockwood's press course (Contemporary Press), a junior year offering renowned for the unlearning she made girls in it do. According to the course description, the class was taught to read the press critically— doubtless a healthy thing. But it was not just the fine art of reading *behind* the news that the girls learned, sitting around a long table seminar style; they were getting indoctrinated with a potent counter-drug. The class, we heard (I never took it) was the scene, almost like a camp meeting, of many a compulsory transformation as hitherto dutiful Republican daughters turned into Socialists and went forth to spread the gospel. It was said that Miss Lockwood insisted that a girl completely break with her mother as the price of winning her favor. The effect on the girl was a kind of smug piety, typical of the born anew, that could last for years, long after the one-time converts, now alumnae (married, with 2.4 children), had turned back into Republicans.[29]

Even though such heavy-handed proselytizing was uncommon among leftist faculty, McCarthy's words confirm that it did go on. Sometimes, in fact, faculty went even further, actually recruiting students into communist or socialist-led organizations. The Fisk student discussed above was approached by a faculty member about joining the Communist Party, as was James Wechsler by a zoology instructor at Columbia. An economics instructor played this same role for the LID at the University of Louisville. But these were extremely rare cases, involving only 2.4 percent of the activists sampled. Moreover, such recruitment went on outside the classroom and was confined to students who had already participated in extensive political discussions or radical activities with the instructor.[30]

Viewed in the context of the total educational experience of the 1930s, the controversy over radical indoctrination seems not only overblown, but also representative of a political double standard.[31] The autobiographical essays, interviews, and published memoirs of the 125 activists sampled here indicate that students confronted all kinds of politics in the classroom: conservative, liberal, and radical. If bringing politics into the class-room is equated with indoctrination, then this was not merely a sin of the Miss Lockwoods of the Left. The teacher who scolded his student for opposing armaments and the principal who lectured the pro-Sacco and Vanzetti pupil on the evils of organized labor engaged in conservative indoctrination. Likewise, the instructor who preached to students about her Jacksonian faith in the common man and the professor who stumped for unions and reform engaged in liberal indoctrination. Those radical faculty who brought their politics were not guilty, then, of some uniquely sinister approach to teaching. Their only crime consisted of teaching an opposing point of view, too far out of the mainstream to be tolerated by the Right.

II

Hearst and his allies failed to understand that dissidence and activism were being taught far more effectively outside than inside the classroom. Nor did they comprehend that such instruction did not usually come from members of the teaching profession. Rightwing critics of the student movement were correct in one respect: the students' elders helped to pave the way for the campus insurgency; however, they were focusing on the wrong elders. It was not the school teachers and professors, but the moth-ers and fathers, the sisters and brothers of campus activists who did the most to incline them toward student protest. Of the student activists in our sampled group, 41.6 percent credited some family members or home influence with facilitating their politicization. Family was by far the most frequent factor the students cited as they discussed the people whose in-fluence fostered their emergence as campus activists.[32]

The fact that so many students credited family—and especially par-ents—for their dissident politics suggests that the campus activists of the 1930s were surprisingly free of youthful narcissism. Up until its final years, the student movement displayed little generational rage. These student rebels promoted political protest, but not a cultural rebellion or youth culture in revolt against the lifestyle of their elders. Snapshots of 1930s campus rebels show that this was not a movement of youthful bohemians. The protesters tended to wear suits and ties, skirts and dress coats, which resembled nothing so much as the attire of their parents. The entire style of politics was adult-like. In fact, movement organizers wanted to leave behind the juvenile modes of behavior that had characterized the fraternity-dominated youth culture inherited from the 1920s. Any violence or row-diness on college campuses in the 1930s was much more likely to be the work of fraternity men and their hazing than anti-war protesters and their much more sober protest activity.[33]

Though the Depression era student insurgency represented a move-ment of young people, it prided itself on its ties with parallel movements of adults. This reflected the Left ideological orientation of its leaders, who saw class rather than age as the most important dividing point in America. These activists viewed the student movement as an auxiliary—albeit an important one—to the labor movement and its struggle for a more egalitarian social order. This lack of generational rancor was made explicit, for instance, in the American Youth Congress' founding platform in 1934. In its preamble to this document the Youth Congress voted to

> reject the explanation which seeks to place the blame on the old as such for the evils which youth can repair just because they are young. We do not believe that the fundamental problems before us are special "youth problems," amenable to solution by special "youth demands" alone. We declare that they are the general problems of the masses of the people, who are subject to the same insecurity and the same danger, to be solved by all those whose interests drive them to seek a solution, young and old, youth from industry, farm and school.[34]

This rejection of generational politics was based on more than abstract theory; it was drawn from lessons that American student activists learned as they looked at Europe's reactionary youth movements. That is why the Youth Congress' preamble argued that stressing the special virtues of youth was dangerous and potentially fascistic:

> Emphasis upon a youth movement which glories in regimented ranks of young people, enthusiastically moving towards some goal—the goal itself being secondary—resembles the fascist movements of Germany and Italy where the sufferings and idealism of youth were perverted by the selfishly calculating guardians of a decaying economic order to bring oppression and terror to the masses of people.[35]

As in this public document, the autobiographical essays student activists wrote in the mid-1930s reflect far more generational solidarity and respect than hostility. In most of the activists' essays that mention their families, those references are positive. These activists seemed eager to link their own political activism to some legacy from their parents or siblings. Most seemed to take pride in citing this shared determination to better society.[36]

The types of positive connections the activists drew between themselves and their parents were as varied as the students themselves. In some cases, students gave much of the credit for their own politics to *activist* parents. ASU leader Molly Yard, for instance, expressed reverence for the activism and political integrity of her parents, both of whom had served as Methodist missionaries in China. Yard was especially proud of her father, a "belligerent idealist" and "radical" who "resigned from his position" in the missionary movement because "he did not see eye to eye with those in control." Here Yard was referring to her father's agitation against the missionary movement's racially segregationist practices. She also praised her father's subsequent work as religious director of Northwestern University, where his "decisive stand on all problems of race, economics and religion" again cost him his job. Yard concluded that thanks to "my parents' beliefs and their stands I have had quite a thorough education in the realm of social progress." And in fact, the link between Yard's own career as a student activist and her father's agitation is striking. Following in his footsteps, her first campaign—and one which would carry her into national leadership in the student movement—was against bigotry and discrimination in Swarthmore College's sorority system.[37]

Yard's political background was, of course, somewhat unusual. Among WASP student activists—raised in the politically conservative 1920s—only a few had so strong a radical role model as she. Radical parents were more common among student activists who were the sons and daughters of immigrants, especially Russian Jewish immigrants. Several of the essays by these students attest that they were not only second generation immigrants, but second generation student activists. "My father," wrote one ASU organizer

> was one of the student leaders in pre-revolutionary Russia [who] . . . carried on a great deal of educational work among the peasants. He left Russia because he did not believe in compulsory military training . . . . It is interesting to see that youth of a previous generation fought the same issues that we are fighting now.[38]

A Barnard ASU member described her Jewish immigrant parents attending "underground meetings" during Russia's 1905 revolution. In America her father, a dentist, became first a socialist and then a communist, active

> in the fight for socialized medicine, and more recently in arousing approval for the Wagner Health bill . . . . At home I was taught the meaning of racial and religious tolerance, and was told stories of pogroms in Russia, of the persecution of Negroes in the South . . .[39]

Another significant model for student activists came from parents and even grandparents who had been involved in liberal rather than radical organizing. Several of the young activists had parents who were veterans of the settlement house movement. A Vassar ASU organizer wrote with pride of her mother's role in "social work, she and a friend founding a summer camp for children from the slums, which is still in existence and cares for a thousand underprivileged youngsters annually." It was easy to see why she might be attracted to anti-war protest at Vassar, when her "parents were both opposed to war on principle . . . [and] neither my younger brother nor I was allowed to play with toy guns or soldiers."[40] A high school ASU organizer recalled that her grandmother had been an "active social worker in the Henry Street settlement." Over the summers her family housed young workers in their large country house to give them an escape from the slums. Through this family activism and "these contacts [with the underprivileged] I became conscious of some sort of social inequality based on wealth, which seemed puzzling and unjust. By the time I was ten, I had some vague ideas of a socialist society as an ideal."[41] A University of Chicago ASU member traced her politics to family ties with other phases of progressive era reform:

> My mother was . . . brought up in a stiffling bourgeois . . . society. Nevertheless, she had liberal tendencies . . . . Her first activities were anti-sweat shop labor agitation, visiting the sweat-shops to see for herself the actual conditions. Then she became an active suffragette. She remained a liberal throughout my youth and still is one. She started encouraging me to read the newspapers at an early age. I wasn't very interested . . . . Finally my mother shamed me into a real interest when, at an early age, she asked me who Mussolini was, and I didn't know. That settled my ignorance, and I didn't dare not read the papers.[42]

By her high school years she was an ardent pacifist, involved in the ASU and emulating her mother's activist career.

Several of the student movement's more prominent African American activists came from homes where parents had been involved in civil rights agitation. James Jackson, who organized on behalf of the NSL, the ASU, and the Southern Negro Youth Congress, recalled that his father was a loyal follower of W.E.B. DuBois. "We grew up with *Crisis* (the NAACP magazine edited by DuBois). As a matter of fact we learned to read on DuBois' column 'As the Crow Flies.'" His father was assaulted and arrested while participating in protests against Richmond's segregated trolley car system. The elder Jackson also took part in protests against racially restrictive housing covenants in the 1920s. With a role model like this, it was natural for the son to become a civil rights activist long before entering college. His activism began with a battle against segregation in the Boy Scouts of America, and a campaign to establish the first black Boy Scout troop in Virginia.[43]

More commonly, however, student movement organizers had parents who, though not active in the liberal or radical politics, were Left-liberal *sympathizers*. In many of these cases the students drew connections between their own activism and the liberal or radical values taught them by their parents. "My parents were liberal almost to the point of socialism," noted a Harvard ASU leader, who termed this "a determining factor" in his political development. A Vassar ASU organizer wrote that she owed her political orientation to her father, "a paper manufacturer . . . . Although his job . . . boosted the family social standing yet his own farm uprbringing has been to a large extent responsible for his liberal outlook and a sympathy toward labor that, one may safely say are unusual in a New England business man."[44] "The liberal tradition in my thinking I got mostly from my parents," explained an Amherst ASU activist.

> My father has a responsible position in a large leather corporation
> . . . . But instead of having any particular reverence or respect for busi-
> nessmen he has considered them a rather shallow group in any kind of
> intellectual accomplishment. Also a sympathy for labor has distinguished
> him from most of his associates. By talking with my parents I have grad-
> ually absorbed this same attitude of not having the business world as an
> idol as some middle class youths have.[45]

Parents also transmitted their political values indirectly, through formal educational institutions. Liberal or radical parents would commonly
send their children to progressive and experimental schools, which brought
them into contact with teachers who would help politicize them.[46] Academia's rightwing critics, in their rush to indict teachers and pose as defenders of the family, conveniently ignored the phenomenon of family involvement in *chosing* to send their sons and daughters to liberal educational
institutions. This phenomenon was evident, for example, in the case of
the parents of a Vassar ASU member. Although her father had been a
Hoover Republican, as the Depression intensified, he moved towards New
Deal liberalism and had no qualms about sending his oldest daughter to
liberal Vassar. This daughter returned from Vassar "and brought home
a great many liberal and radical ideas that were new to our family," explained her younger sister. "My father admits now that my sister made
him give much more serious thought to the political and economic problems of our day," a process which led him to embrace "democratic socialism . . . as the goal we must work for."[47] The father was more than
willing to pay for his younger daughter to attend Vassar, and she—influenced by her family's leftward shift—became a prominent ASU organizer
during her college years.

Even when parents did not try to teach their progressive political views
to their children, this could occur unintentionally. A socialist student from
Antioch College noted that though his parents were radicals "they themselves avoided discussing political questions with me, because they did not
want to influence my ideas." But "unhindered browsing in the family
bookcase" led him to his parents' politics anyway through a reading of
Edward Bellamy's utopian socialist novel *Looking Backwards:*

> When I found that mother could not explain . . . why Bellamy's
> beautiful system was not adopted, I turned to reading and lectures for
> the answer. I religiously attended the lecture series at the Labor Institute,
> becoming acquainted with socialist thought and gaining my first knowl-
> edge of the labor movement. My . . . belief in the necessity for change
> was intensified.[48]

Joseph Lash also grew up with socialist reading material in his home.
In his case it was the Yiddish socialist press, which opposed World War I,
giving Lash (even though this was not discussed with his parents) the
impression that "we must have been mildly anti-war." With Lash, how-

ever, the most memorable anti-war lesson he received as a child from his father occurred accidentally. While walking with his father down Amsterdam Avenue in Manhattan during World War I, the two were approached by federal agents searching for draft evaders. The agents demanded to see the draft card of Lash's father. "My Father," Lash recalled,

> who had fled Czarist Russia in 1905 and had an abiding fear of the arbitrariness of officials, especially police, in their dealings with Jews was very frightened even though as the father of five children, all under the age of eight . . . he was in a deferred status. The agent looked at his card and waved him on. But a small boy is very sensitive to his father's reactions. He had communicated his sense of fright to me. I can still feel it.[49]

The relationships between children and parents are, of course, too diverse to be fit into any one model. Not all the activists who mentioned their families in their autobiographies saw themselves as simply following in the footsteps of their parents. Sometimes the relationship was more complex than that, and the path from the parents' lives to the child's politics more winding and rocky. A CCNY communist wrote in his autobiographical essay of the painful experience of his parents. They had left Lithuania in pursuit of the American dream. "However, the land of 'golden streets' soon became a land of poverty," working in sweatshops and living in a "Lower-East-Side firetrap." Although the CCNY student's elder brother finally prospered and moved his parents out of the tenement, these ghetto years had left scars. "It was not very long ago," admitted the young communist, "that I looked upon this background with shame. I also felt ashamed of my 'greenhorn' parents." Through the radical movement, which made his working-class origins seem a virtue rather than a vice, this young activist believed he had overcome his feelings of shame and inferiority. Here radicalism seemed to offer a vehicle for both generational reconciliation and the child's redemption of the parent's American dream:

> If the working-class movement meant nothing more than the reestablishment of pride in my working-class parents, it was enough. I am proud of the struggles that my parents went through to feed me. I am proud of their true love for America, not the hypocritical flag waving of our professional patriots. Not only has the working-class movement meant this for me, but it also has given me an accomplishable vision of a new society, a society, which my parents thought they would find here.[50]

Only five out of the 125 student activists in our sample linked their politics to rebellion against their parents. Three of these five, however, indicated that during their student activist days they had gotten over this stage of youthful rebellion; they had become both reconciled with their parents and comfortable with their new politics, which was now based on political principle rather than generational hostility. But even these low

figures do not fully capture the insignificance of generational rage in producing student radicalism. Almost half of this small group of five, it turns
out, had in their stage of generational revolt, been rebelling against *radical*
parents! These two included an SLID activist from Cleveland College,
who confessed that her socialist father's "long tirades against 'the system'
which he delivered with never diminishing gusto at each dinner-time, fell
on unreceptive ears, resulting in my junior high school days, in a strongly
negative attitude towards anything of social content . . ." A Wayne University student, whose father had been a socialist since his days in Yugo-
slavia's "student terrorist oganizations" wrote that he also "went through
a period of adolescent revolt" against his father's politics. "Ever since I
was a child I was almost religiously indoctrinated with Socialism and Athe-
ism." During his period of rebellion, the son "became completely sceptical
about Socialism in the same manner as one brought up in a religious
environment becomes sceptical about God." But in both cases, these second generation radicals returned to the politics of their parents; the first
because friends in the student movement re-connected her with her radical roots through their anti-war agitation, and the second because his
own readings persuaded him that his overbearing father had been right
about the merits of socialism.[51]

Of the three students who had rebelled against non-radical parents,
one did not do so in a spiteful or purely emotional manner. The rebellion
of this ASU activist evolved out of tensions which may naturally arise between first generation college students and their much less educated parents. In this case, the parents were southerners with "strong prejudices
against foreigners, Jews, and Negroes," who, to their radical daughter,
seemed hopelessly narrow-minded. She confessed in her 1938 autobiographical essay that she had developed a "superiority complex" toward
her provincial parents. In defense of this attitude, the young activist noted
that her "superiority feeling accomplished a good purpose. It kept me
from adopting their prejudices." Having staked out her own political territory, this rebellious daughter, however, came to realize that she could
respect her parents even as she rejected their prejudices. She wrote that
her feelings of superiority had "now, I am glad to say, [been] supplanted
by respect for them because they are really intelligent parents, and good
parents, who have struggled hard to give us advantages they didn't have."[52]

No student movement is entirely free of at least a few youths whose
embrace dissident politics as a way of antagonizing parents with whom
they have been in conflict. This was clearly the case with an SLID activist,
whose autobiographical essay reflected disdain for her family of Wyoming
farmers. She noted that she had become active in the student LID "partly
because I agreed with its aims, partly because I knew my family wouldn't
like it." In his memoir, *Is Curly Jewish?*, Paul Jacobs made a similar connection between his radicalization and generational conflict. Jacobs had a
tempestuous relationship with his middle-class Jewish parents, and felt
"contempt for the values of the family." He termed his emergence as an

active leftist at CCNY "an affirmation of my contempt for and impatience with the making of money, pursuits I identified with my parents . . . . The CCNY radical regarded businessmen as a very low form of life." Yet what is striking about these two cases, was their rarity; they were the only ones out of the 125 activists in our sampled group who traced their politics to an unresolved, open, and ongoing conflict with parents.[53]

The generally high level of respect of student activists for their parents was often reciprocated. Few of the activists in our sampled group reported that parents had tried to interfere with their political lives. The lack of such parental interference contrasted starkly with the much more frequent incidents of political suppression of students by teachers and educational administrators. Indeed, in most of the major free speech fights involving conflicts between student activists and administrators, parents sided with their children against school authorities. This occurred in 1932 at Columbia University, during the first major campus free speech fight of the decade, after the Columbia administration expelled student newspaper editor Reed Haris. The expelled editor's father, Tudor Harris boasted to the press: "My son and his associates have brought new vigor and life to the editorial page" of Columbia's student newspaper, "heretofore little more than a 'yes' organ"; he publicly condemned President Butler for expelling his son, and declared that he "would regard a diploma received at the hands of a college president who would sanction, let alone direct, such an action for such a cause as a stigma."[54]

At UCLA during the West Coast's biggest free speech fight in 1930s, parents again played a prominent role in opposing repressive administrators. Soon after the UCLA administration had suspended five students on charges of assisting in a communist plot "to destroy the University" in 1934, the parents of four of these students rushed to their defense. The parents issued a joint press release attacking UCLA's provost "for the injury he has done these young people for blasting their reputations when they are on the threshold of life before giving them a hearing in which they could have disproved such charges"; they demanded that UCLA quickly correct "this injustice." The same thing happened at the University of Michigan in 1935, when an expelled NSL activist's father publicly challenged President Ruthven's disciplinary action against his son. Similarly, Hunter College's president found that a delegation of parents were among the first to protest his decision to take a campus job away from a student because of her anti-war activity.[55]

Parental support for student dissent was especially prominent at CCNY during the longest and most turbulent campus free speech fight in Depression America. Here parents appeared at the disciplinary hearings for their sons, who had gotten into trouble with the administration for protesting the visit of an Italian fascist delegation at CCNY. At these hearings, one parent told the presiding CCNY administrators that "if his son should have been expelled for his anti-Fascist beliefs I would not stand for it . . .—anti-Fascist action I always support." "I think my boy has a right to a different opinion," explained another parent. In one very tense exchange with the dean, a protester's mother made it clear that she took a dim view of both the disciplinary hearings and the fascist invitation that had led to it. The dean told her "the point is whether the faculty [or the student body] is going to run the college . . ." She replied, "I suppose students have some rights." "It is the faculty who run the College," argued the dean. "For whose benefit?" asked the mother. "I know the faculty was placed in an embarrassing position, but they should have taken into consideration that the student body didn't wish to receive them [the fascist delegation]."[56]

Nor were such objections confined to a few dissident parents. When the hearings culminated in the expulsion of twenty-one CCNY students, one of the city's largest parents organization, the United Parents Association (UPA) protested. UPA delegates, representing 201 parents organizations voted in their January 1935 meeting to oppose the expulsions. The UPA president sent a letter to the CCNY administration charging "that the penalties which have been imposed on the expelled students are far more severe than the situation warranted."[57]

There were even occasions in which parents joined their activist sons and daughters on campus picket lines. This occurred, for example, during the 1936 anti-war strike at Brooklyn College. Here a delegation of thirteen mothers marched together to show parental solidarity with the student crusade against war. The parents at this strike rally attracted press attention with their picket signs, which proclaimed that they "preferred sons to gold stars," and warned that they "had not raised their sons to be cannon fodder."[58]

Parental support did, however, have its limits. Some parents encouraged their sons and daughter to exercise caution and discretion in their political activism. These parents feared that their children might jeopardize their careers if they gained too much notoriety from protest activity. This was the case with Celeste Strack. After her initial conflicts with the USC administration, Strack found that her family was

> scared to death. They were getting phone calls threatening me at home during the summer, when I came home from USC. All sorts of pressure was brought to bear on them. And while they would argue with me, they were never attempting to disown me or throw me out. They were mainly just scared to death. I have to say looking back on it they were very forebearing, considering how conservative they were and how scared . . . and worried they were.[59]

Such fear also afflicted the father of Youth Congress chairman Jack McMichael. The Youth Congress leader's father was a physician in southern Georgia, whose liberal idealism led him to crusade on behalf of low-cost medical care for the rural poor. This crusade by Dr. McMichael had played an important role in fostering his son's politicization. But he grew quite concerned about Jack shortly after the Youth Congress' break with the Roosevelt administration, when the organization was attacked for opposing conscription and charged with communist domination. Aware that his own activism had helped inspire his more radical son, Dr. McMichael advised Jack to be less headstrong and learn from his mistakes. "It has been my nature," Dr. McMichael wrote his son,

> to go ahead with a thing I thought was right, regardless of the consequences, social, financial or other wise. In doing this I have paid a big price . . . . In looking back I believe I should have been willing to go slower after my objective, and compromise more . . . . I realize you have your own life to live, and as you know I have never asked you to let me think in place for you. At the same time I would not allow you as a child to do anything I thought might hurt you. My love for you, my age and experience I think justifies me in asking you to avoid doing anything radical. Try . . . to take as much good from all isms and make it fit democracy. It is hard to believe that so many Commentators and such a large part of the Press would say so many hard things about the Youth Congress unless they had good reason for doing so . . . . Stop and try to believe that at least some of the criticism of these older and more experienced people have made is just. Personally I would be willing to follow Mr. and Mrs. Roosevelt all the way . . . . Please be cautious in what you say and always remember that you may have to justify this later in life. Remember too that your happiness & success mean more to me than anything else.[60]

The most extreme cases of parental criticism were those in which fathers of activists publicly denounced the radicalism of their children. This occurred at Berkeley in 1940, when Professor Samuel May announced he was disowning and disinheriting his son Kenneth because of his communist activism. The father implied that his son—a teaching fellow at Berkeley—had been lured into the communist movement by his new wife, a communist "woman much older than himself." Kenneth avoided any direct attack on his conservative father; but he did refute his father's claims about his wife, telling the press that:

> I first joined the Communist party as an undergraduate at the University because I found by actual experience in student activities that the Communists were consistent and uncompromising fighters for the interests of the students and against reaction within and without the university.[61]

The other major public dispute between activist and parent also involved a California student. This time, however, it was a female undergraduate at UCLA and her rightwing father. The father in this case was H. Bedford Jones, a writer, and his daughter Nancy. Here, as in the May case, the father added sexual overtones to the story of his child's radicalization. But Mr. Jones was even less subtle in this regard than Professor May had been. Jones' 1935 *Liberty* magazine article on his daughter's radicalization appeared under the lurid title "Will the Communists Get Our Girls in College?" The article told the story of three coeds who had been led to subversive activities by a wily "young Red [who] seduces girls." Nancy Bedford Jones, an SLID activist, publicly repudiated these and other charges made by her father. In her article, "My father Is a Liar!," which she published in the student press, Nancy revealed that the three coeds discussed by her father in his *Liberty* article were in reality a fictionalized version of her own experience. She charged that her father had completely distorted the story of her radicalization in order to slander and discredit the student movement.[62]

The May and Jones disputes attracted considerable press attention. This attention came, however, because public, hostile clashes between activists and parents were so rare. Through the entire decade of student activism, from 1931 to 1941, the May and Jones cases stand out as the only examples of conservative parents mounting public attacks on their activist children. The similar dynamic of these two conflicts is also significant because in both cases it was the parent rather than the student who had initiated the public conflict—again suggesting that student activists were neither seething with generational rage nor anxious to go on the attack against their parents. In fact, part of the reason Nancy Bedford Jones became so outraged by her father's veiled public attack on her political activism was because in the past her relationship with him had been so positive. "I had," Nancy wrote, "always loved my father as a pal and I was heartsick when I learned of this. I didn't believe a father could do this to a daughter and even more to the movement in which her ideals are bound."[63]

It is possible that the fiery type of conflicts that student activists like May and Jones had with their parents in public may have gone on more frequently in private. Parents would, after all, be far more likely to air such differences at the breakfast table than in the national media—where their children's reputations would be jeopardized. But judging by the autobiographical data, even private conflicts over student activism between parents and children were unusual and generally much less heated than in the May and Jones disputes. Irving Howe, for instance, recalled that though his parents disapproved of his Trotskyist politics, they "objected more to my late hours, a result of wandering the streets with cronies after meetings." A Vassar student reported a similar conflict with her parents, after extensive campaigning for Norman Thomas led her to neglect her studies. Finding her liberal mother more upset by her falling grades than by her politics, she observed that "my mother's chief objection to Norman Thomas is not on account of his views but because he was the principal cause of my flunking that history course. I was too busy making American history to study it."[64]

III

Both in the families that did witness generational conflict and many of those that did not, a common leftward trend was discernible. Student organizers were often more radical or more active politically than were their parents. This was obviously the case for students from conservative homes like Jones and May; but it was also true in liberal families. Though students from liberal homes proudly traced their dissidence to their parents, in many cases, the autobiographies reveal that even as they appreciated their parents' reformist politics, they were moving beyond it. This leftward shift was evident with such activists as Jack McMichael, son of a liberal physician, becoming a Christian socialist and ally of the Communist Party; James Jackson son of an NAACP-style liberal, becoming a communist; Irving Howe, son of trade unionists, becoming a Trotskyist; Alice Dodge, daughter of liberal Republicans, becoming a socialist. Even in families already on the Left this trend had a significant parallel, in that the children often tended to be more politically active and militant than their socialistic parents.[65]

When asked to account for this leftward trend, the NSL and SLID during the early 1930s pointed, above all, to economics. They viewed the Depression as the great radicalizing force of their time. Thus in its December 1932 editorial, "Why Students Are Turning to Socialism," the Student LID's magazine *Revolt* traced undergraduate radicalism to "the impact of the economic crisis."

> Family incomes have declined and student budgets have been curtailed. Working students have discovered the usual summer jobs are no longer available, while wages for part-time work have fallen. Tuition fees have been increased . . . [and] the sacrifices involved in securing a college education are now less handsomely rewarded . . . . Educated for jobs that do not materialize, students will grow resentful towards the existing order and will use the learning they have acquired to overthrow it.[66]

This economic theory of radicalization evolved out of both the personal experience and political ideology of NSL and SLID leaders during the early 1930s. By the end of the Hoover era, the Depression had (as seen in Chapter I) transformed the mood on campus. The economic crisis had made it possible for leftists to challenge the insularity, complacency, and elitism of traditional student culture. Seeing the contrast between the increasingly progressive student politics of their own era and the Republican campuses of the affluent 1920s, student radicals had good reason to see economics as the key to the student revolt of the early 1930s. Moreover, NSL and SLID leaders were predisposed toward this kind of interpretation, since they were influenced by Marxist ideology and its assumption that economics was the driving force in history.

This theory of radicalization mirrored the travails of students whose own incomes and home lives had been diminished by the Great Depression. Among these students was Junius Scales, an ASU organizer and young communist, who attended the University of North Carolina. Home for young Junius included a mansion and affluent lifestyle in a prominent southern family. But the real estate market crash brought "severe financial reverses" to his family, devastating his father, who suffered a nervous breakdown and heart attack. These events left Junius receptive to the anti-capitalist talk of leftist students who congregated in the radical bookstore near the Chapel Hill campus.[67] Economic hardship and family tragedy also caused the politicization of a Vassar ASU activist. When she was a young girl, her father lost his well paying job in the western Kentucky oil fields because of the Depression. Thrown out of work, her father then lost his house and

> tried everything desperately. We moved into a little town in Tennessee where it was somewhat cheaper to live. A small income from a part interest in an oil well supported us for a while. That ran out. We moved into a two-room apartment, had the electricity turned off, bought at each grocer's in town in turn as we used up our credit. Practically the only jobs open at this time were traveling salesman jobs on commission. My father worked in insurance, school supplies, refrigerators, gadgets for oil stoves. Perhaps we should not have been too surprised when after a desperate penniless Christmas at home, he went off in his second-hand Ford and did not come back. We understood why . . . . I was sixteen then. I knew that my father loved us, that my mother still loved him, and I knew too that when every door was closed, there was no other way.

Thanks to her "absolutely mad obsession to go to a good college," she studied hard and performed well enough to obtain a Vassar scholarship. She became "a member of the ASU at Vassar because knowing what I know, I must learn to act." Similarly, a midwestern student traced the roots of his activism to his father's hours being lengthened and wages being cut in half: "Watching him become dehumanized, my mother becoming more ill intensified my feelings, and I felt the necessity for becoming [politically] active."[68]

With wages being cut, students who paid for their education had to work longer and harder than previous generations of self-supporting undergraduates. Whether they tried to make ends meet by washing dishes, cleaning houses, or waiting tables, the hardships these students experienced at home and at school sometimes moved them leftward. A University of Iowa ASU activist was among this group of students. His father lost his farm, had to move to town, and "went to work as a day laborer, #[$]3.50 a day when he worked, and employment was unsteady." The son found that at high school affluent students shunned him because of his poverty. He realized that higher education would only be possible if he could join that growing crew of college students who "work their way through." I chose the University of Iowa because it was cheap and because bad jobs were plentiful. Far be it from me to question the truth of Horatio Alger and the great American tradition of working-your-way-up-from-the-bottom, but my first three years in college were a kind of ever conscious hell— three hours sleep, day-old meals, heavy eyes, trying to keep awake in classes, being too tired to try for debate, studying in odd minutes . . . . I combined the three—scholastic success, activities and work. It's not a pleasant combination.[69]

The memory of these hardships remained even after this student won a scholarship to study in Europe; it prodded him to become critical of the economic system that had victimized him, and it led him to a group of young radical British intellectuals, with their Marxist perspective and calls for a Popular Front against fascism.

For some student movement veterans, economic hardship was such an important source of their activism that they looked back upon the entire movement as an outgrowth of such hardship. Film critic Pauline Kael, for instance, viewed the student movement during her college days at Berkeley in the 1930s as an insurgency produced by lower class youths. She recalled very well defined class lines distinguishing movement activists from the rest of the Berkeley student body; "there was a real division between the poor who were trying to improve things on the campus and the rich kids who didn't give a damn." Palmer Weber, an NSL leader from the University of Virginia, observed a similar class division on his campus in the 1930s. In both cases, the wealthiest students, belonged to Greek houses and had nothing to do with the student movement. At Virginia, according to Weber, the most affluent students were "people who came" to campus "in their Cadillac cars," and who were much more interested in holding golf clubs or hunting rifles than picket signs. During Christmas vacations, while radicals hitched their way to leftist student conventions, the University of Virginia's "car crowd, hunting crowd, golfing crowd . . . went off to Bermuda." Virginia's radicals came not from this rich upper crust, but rather from the third or so of the student body that was much too poor for Caribbean cruises. Since these students were feeling the pinch of hard times, they were, as Weber explained, "willing to think, talk and entertain ideas of how to reorganize society."[70]

This class analysis of the student movement, offered by Kael and Weber, accounts for some, but by no means all of the student activism of the 1930s. The findings from our sampled activist group indicate, in fact, though students hurt economically by the Depression constituted a significant minority, they were not a majority within the student activist community. In our sampled activist group, economic hardship was cited by 29.6 percent of the students as they explained their politicization. The 29.6 percent figure ought not be interpreted too rigidly. It is possible that lower-class students may have been underrepresented in our sampled group, since over half the sample was drawn from participants in SLID and ASU summer leadership conferences—which some working students, due to time limitations, may have been unable to attend. But even if this was a significant distortion (and the presence of lower-class students at both conferences suggests that it was not), and if one builds in a huge 20 percent margin of error, this would still leave a majority of students whose activism was not linked to economic hardship or class interests.[71]

The limitations of class analysis as a mode of understanding student activism in the 1930s was also reflected in the memoirs of the student movement's national leaders. One such leader, Celeste Strack, entered the student movement at UCLA in 1934 with assumptions about the movement's social base identical with those of Kael and Weber. Strack's own family had been hard hit by the Depression, as were the families of many of her comrades in the UCLA student movement. She assumed that student activists across the nation came from families that had been hurt by the economic crisis. But when Strack went beyond her own campus, and became a national NSL leader with contacts at other colleges and universities, she found that her class analysis of the student movement had been simplistic. Strack came to this realization during her first visit to New York. She had recently made a name for herself as a leader in the free speech fight at UCLA and was in New York to assume her new national office in the NSL. Here Strack's comrades in the student movement put her up in the home of Helen Simon, a Barnard College NSL leader. Strack was startled to find that this Barnard radical's home was an

> apartment on Fifth Avenue or right off it . . . . There was a doorman. I go in with Helen. We go up on the elevator. We go walking through carpets ankle deep, and I'm ushered into my own private bedroom with its own private bath that belonged to her sister who was in Europe. The next morning I was woken by somebody knocking on the door, and it was the maid saying breakfast was ready. I said "Well just give me a minute and I'll be right out." "No," she said, "I have it here," and arrived with a tray with breakfast. I can still see it; there was a silver vase with a rose on it, and next to it was a folded copy of the *Daily Worker*. I could not believe my eyes. I, of course, was under the impression that I had come to New York to become associated with a left-wing revolutionary movement . . . . The initiation was a little more than I could bear. I didn't know whether to laugh or what to do, so I said nothing about it.[72]

Strack's encounter with this affluent Ivy League radical had parallels on other campuses. Theodore White observed a similar disjunction between economic hardship and student radicalism as a Harvard undergraduate during the 1930s. White recalled that he and his friends—lower-middle class commuter and scholarship students, who were poor by Harvard standards—found themselves visited

> regularly by Harvard's intellectual upper-class Communists, who felt that we were of the oppressed. Occasionally such well-bred, rich or elite Com-

> munist youngsters . . . would bring a neat brown-paper-bag lunch and join us at the round tables to persuade us, as companions, of the inevitable proletarian revolution.[73]

But Harvard's affluent student radicals made few converts among White and his plebian classmates. This failure, White explains, derived from the fact that

> We were . . . middle class in the flesh—hungry and ambitious. Most of us, largely Boston Latin School graduates, knew more about poverty than anyone from Beacon Hill or the fashionable East Side of New York. We hated poverty; and meant to have no share in it. We had come to Harvard not to help the working classes, but to get out of the working classes. We were on the make. And in my own case, the approach to Harvard and its riches was that of a looter.[74]

At Columbia James Wechsler found that the class divisions his Marxism had led him to expect—with the more blue-collar students assuming leadership—in student politics did not materialize. Columbia's most proletarian students were football players, recruited from mining towns and other working-class communities. But according to Wechsler, "these same athletic battalions tended to produce the most violent opponents of radicalism . . . . The athletic proletarians were always warring against the champions of Marxism and any symptom thereof."[75]

The pattern that Strack, Wechsler, and White observed was by no means confined to the Ivy League. Joseph D. Martini, assessing the social base of the student Left at the University of Illinois, in the most thorough quantitative case study of a single campus in the 1930s, revealed that here too relatively affluent students played a prominent role in radical politics. The largest group of Illinois student radicals came from families whose fathers were employed in professional occupations. At the Illinois campus 45.8 percent of the student activists came from such families, as compared to the overall student body of which only 17.9 percent came from households headed by fathers in the professions. The proportion of working-class students was also lower in the Illinois student Left than it was in the student body as a whole—8.3 percent of the student radicals came from blue-collar homes as opposed to 15.2 percent in the overall student body.[76]

These contrasting images of student activists' class background derive from the diversity of the movement itself. The movement included *both* the type of lower-class rebels described by Kael and Weber and the more affluent radicals described by Strack, White, and Martini. The autobiographical essays of participants in the SLID and ASU leadership institutes leave no doubt at all that privileged and underpriviledged students were both well represented in the movement. The ability of the student movement to transcend class lines was also evident in the movement's political geography. The largest and most active ASU chapters included such

working- and lower-middle class campuses as CCNY, Brooklyn, and Hunter
Colleges, but also much more elite campuses, such as Harvard, Vassar,
and Columbia.[77]

The movement's diverse social composition suggests that student activism involved much more than economic self-interest. Even a glance at
the motivations of affluent student activists reveals that their activism had
little or nothing to do with their class interests. The Depression moved
them leftward by evoking guilt and compassion rather than economic in-
security. Such guilt was visible, for example, in the political autobiography
of a Vassar ASU organizer. In explaining how she first became aware
about social inequality in America, this activist recalled that as she grew
up in her prosperous Boston household

> I began to realize that my family had more money and more things
> than the majority of the families in the country . . . . We moved into a
> larger house, unnecessarily large, which made the difference even more
> marked . . . . I began to feel quite guilty and ashamed at having really
> more things than I wanted, when so many had nowhere near enough.
> This feeling increased during the depression.[78]

Affluent student activists were more likely to experience the tragedy
of the Depression vicariously, through less fortunate friends rather than
through their own families. This was the case, for instance, with Kay Martineau, an ASU organizer whose father ran a successful New Hampshire
newspaper. Her first personal encounter with the economic crisis came
when the father of a blue-collar high school friend tried to commit suicide
after he went broke during the Depression. This led to her first stumbling
steps toward social criticism. "I wished they weren't so poor and I disliked
the comfortable and selectman. But I didn't know just why." These early
stirrings accelerated after a visit to another school friend, the daughter of
an impoverished carpenter, whose family "ate meals of boiled potatoes
from tin plates [and] . . . slept in meal bags." At college she "began to
question" the undemocratic features of American life on campus and off,
after encounters with the hardships and inequities confronting her friends.
One of these encounters involved her college roommate,

> who was working her way through. She stayed in and I went out, she had
> no clothes, I had a lot, she got long letters from her family, telling her
> that her brother had no work and that her mother was thinking of ille-
> gally selling beer to make enough to eat. I joined a sorority. She didn't
> and I found her crying one night because she was called a "drip."

Outraged that her sorority denied membership to lower-class and Jewish
women, she resigned and began to think of herself as "a kind of social
outcast." She gravitated toward the ASU as the most egalitarian group on

campus and the one most committed to combatting the social injustices which had victimized her friends.[79]

The presence of affluent activists such as Martineau in the student movement was one of many indications that the movement was not merely an economic phenomenon. Had economic hardship been the most important source of student activism, then the movement would likely have been strongest during the worst years of the Depression on campus, 1932–33. These were years when unemployment was at its peak, when Hoover was stumbling, the viability of the New Deal uncertain, and student enrollments slipping. As Theodore Draper recalled of his college days in this era,

> My generation was a hopeless one . . . utterly defeatist. There were no jobs; the place was coming down. Most boys I knew didn't prepare themselves for careers at college because there weren't any opportunities. There was a real sense of a society in total collapse.[80]

These economic hardships had facilitated the rise of the student movement in Draper's generation, prodding students to become critical of Hooverism and the failing capitalist system. Yet, in these hard times the movement would not grow nearly as fast as it did in 1936–1937, when economic conditions improved for the college middle class.

The contrast between 1936–37 and the early days of the student movement was striking. Where in the early 1930s the movement never mobilized more than 25,000 students, in the later period the movement's national demonstrations involved about 500,000 students. This astonishing growth had occurred while collegians were benefitting from the moderate economic gains achieved by the New Deal. Thanks to the NYA, some 10 percent of the national student body, which otherwise might have had to drop out of college for economic reasons, received federally funded part-time work. The NYA and the mild economic upswing ended the decline in college enrollments that had begun under Hoover. Where in the early 1930s the news from the job market for college graduates worsened steadily, during the mid-1930s employment opportunities became far more promising. College seniors about to graduate in 1936, felt encouraged by surveys, like that published in the *New York Times* showing that nationwide their "employment opportunities had doubled . . . compared with 1935 . . . and that salaries are higher by an average of $10 per month." Job recruiters, who had all but disappeared from campus in the early 1930s, returned in the mid-1930s. By the fall of 1936 even teachers—one of the groups hardest hit by the Depression—were again in demand.[81]

The economic climate improved so dramatically on campus in this period that much of the student Left muted its talk of a declining middle class and collapsing capitalist system. Student activists began to worry that classmates might be lulled into political lethargy by their improving economic situation. Thus in his keynote address to the ASU convention in

1936, Joseph Lash expressed his regret that the "glamor of tinsel, temporary prosperity has hit the campus. Students are deluding themselves into believing that the jazz twenties are returning. They want to convince themselves that the crisis which had descended upon the campus has passed." This same concern led the ASU in the fall of 1936 and 1937 to publish in its national magazine articles debunking the "new prosperity." These articles stressed the limited and temporary character of the economic recovery; they reminded students that mass unemployment continued. The ASU's warnings about the durability of the Depression proved well founded. The recovery faded during the 1937–1938 academic year. But the period of economic recovery on campus had shown that ASU leadership had erroneously thought that an improving economy would impede student activism. The growing anti-war strikes in these years attested that the student movement could enjoy good health whether or not the economy was in bad health.[82]

The student movement's expansion in this period of recovery does not mean that Depression or social class were unimportant to the movement. The Depression remained a standing invitation for student activism throughout the decade; it reminded both lower-class and affluent students that America had severe social problems that merited their attention. Students radicalized by personal economic hardships or insecure about their career prospects in Depression America were always a significant segment of the student activist community. But the growth of student activism in the improved economy of 1936–37 does indicate that student movement's strength and concerns extended beyond economics.

Even though this was the Depression decade, it was not this crisis, but rather the crisis in international relations which generated the largest student mobilizations in the United States: the annual student strikes against war. James Wechsler found this to be the case even at Columbia, one of the nation's most active campuses:

> When student fees were raised, we believed we had at last found an issue which touched the deepest economic nerve and which according to our dogma, should have stirred the largest indignation. But far more students attended anti-war rallies than ever gathered to decry this attack on their parents pocketbooks.[83]

Since the cause of peace and anti-fascism concerned the entire younger generation, it enabled the student movement of the 1930s to transcend class lines and to organize impressive protests irrespective of the state of the economy.

IV

The student movement existed as more than a compilation of causes; it also represented a community, composed of activists united by a shared egalitarian ethic. Some students were drawn to the movement as much by this sense of community as by any particular issue. This was the case with some of the more affluent student activists. By virtue of their privileged economic status in a nation beset by economic distress, Left-leaning students from affluent homes felt isolated. The movement helped break down these feelings of isolation; it offered such students a new community, enabling privileged to unite with underprivileged, upper class with middle and working class. This new sense of community was especially powerful because it not only offered friendship and warmth, but a common sense of purpose and political idealism rooted in a passionate commitment to social equality.

The student movement's ability to satisfy this longing for community was nowhere more evident that in the reports movement activists published on their labor solidarity work. One such report by Dartmouth ASU activist Budd Shulberg told the story of efforts by students in this very elite college to aid striking marble workers. Shulberg begins his account by describing the students' sense of isolation. When the Dartmouth ASU contingent first arrived at the local union hall to offer their support to the strikers, they were met by "a burly Irishman [who] did not seem glad that they had come." The workers, thinking that all college "kids did was have dances and good times," had seen little reason to welcome the students or put much stock in their pledges of support. Shulberg then notes, however, that after the students worked long and hard on fund raising and publicity for the strikers, a sense of political community between these upper-class students and the workers had been established. Proudly underscoring this change, Shulberg described the very different reception ASU activists received at the union hall.

> This time the burly, strong-jawed Irishman greeted them warmly
> . . . . Other strikers hurried over to smile and shake hands. In three
> months Dartmouth students had proven that liberalism does not have to
> be a philisophical apologetic for inaction. Between the first hesitant visit
> and the latest one they had demonstrated that the twain, worker and
> student, can meet.[84]

Affluent students were not the only Depression era activists whose attraction to the student movement was linked to a search for community. If these students embraced the student movement as a means of transcending their privileged backgrounds, others embraced the movement as a means of transcending their underprivileged background. Among this latter group were Jewish students for whom the movement functioned as an avenue out of their immigrant ghettoes. The movement enabled them to meet and work with students from all over the country, and, in the words of NSL leader George Watt,

> made us feel that as part of this movement we were really part of America. It was a way for many of us who were New York Jews to become

integrated into American society. I remember when I began to attend national meetings of the NSL and you have . . . real native southerners like Francis Franklin with the thickest southern accent . . . or Jim Jackson from Howard University, or . . . Boone Schirmer from Harvard, who was a direct descendant of Daniel Boone, or people from the Midwest. These were people who gave a flavor to those of us who were from New York, gave us a sense of the movement out there that was really part of the American tradition.[85]

The student movement conferred a measure of acceptance upon Jewish students which they had never before found on American college campuses. In the past Jews had been barred from many campus social organizations and from leadership in student life. By creating new and non-discriminatory institutions, the movement enabled Jewish students to obtain national leadership positions which they could not have achieved in traditional undergraduate institutions. Thus at a time when Jews could not even belong to many student fraternities, the student movement elevated Jewish students, such as Joseph Lash, to top national offices in the largest political organization on the campuses of Depression America: the American Student Union. Lash's case was by no means unusual. Jews were prominent at all levels of the student movement, both locally and nationally. This prominence reflected the fact that this was not only a non-discriminatory community, but also a community deeply committed to stopping fascism, a force which Jewish students in this age of Hitler, found especially abhorrent and threatening.[86]

For African American students too, part of the student movement's appeal lay in this new and non-discriminatory form of community. James Jackson recalled being struck by the contrast between the segregationism and hostility of whites he had encountered while growing up in Richmond, Virginia, and the racial egalitarianism of the student movement. In Richmond, whites came into the African American community "as invaders or policemen, but hardly ever a friendly face." It was in the student movement that Jackson attended his first interracial meetings, and here "for the first time . . . saw white people who acted like they were human beings. They were concerned and humane in all respects. It was quite an experience . . . a nodal point in my life." Jackson was drawn to this community of activists which would not only admit him, but recognize his talents, elevate him to a leadership position, and support his goal of freeing America of racism.[87]

The student movement's racial and ethnic diversity was part of its attraction for Left-leaning WASP students. In a society segmented by race, ethnicity, and class, the campus activist community afforded an unusual opportunity to transcend these divisions. For an activist like Celeste Strack, who came from white suburban San Diego, the movement seemed especially exciting in that it enabled her to befriend and work with students from backgrounds much different than hers. As she began to become

politically active at USC, Strack encountered in the student Left a group
of foreign students who were "very interesting . . . red politically . . .
who brought a kind of intellectual sophistication that was very unusual."
Similarly, when Strack transfered to UCLA she grew close to a number
of Jewish student activists, who she felt "had a more sophisticated" background politically than she did because they came from radical families.
All of this gave Strack a sense that she was moving beyond the provincialism of her past, toward a more cosmopolitan community and more penetrating view of the world.[88]

This impulse toward a more diverse and egalitarian community was
perhaps strongest of all in that small circle of southern student radicals.
This was not only true for black activists, as James Jackson described so
eloquently, but also for their white counterparts. Junius Scales recalled
that as a student at the University of North Carolina, part of the ASU's
appeal was that it allowed him to leave behind a past of racial segregation
and to move toward a genuinely equal interracial community. Scales joined
the ASU after attending a North Carolina student-labor conference that
had been organized on an interracial basis:

> The conference recessed for dinner . . . . I was seated next to a
> male Negro student from A&T College in Greensboro. We'd barely in-
> troduced ourselves when I was joined on my right by a breathtakingly
> beautiful Negro woman student from Bennett College . . . . She was as
> charming and gracious as she looked, and I was soon at ease and talking
> excitedly with my neighbors. I had never known a Negro, except as a
> servant, and yet there I was in utter delight, defying all the taboos, cus-
> toms, rules and laws that kept the races apart, talking with complete nat-
> uralness as one student to another, one young *person* to another! . . . My
> companions must have noticed the impact of the meeting on me, because
> a day or two later I was asked by one of them to join the American
> Student Union.

Once in the ASU, Scales worked to duplicate this experience for other
students. He arranged interracial student meetings in Greensboro. The
first of these meetings began with "considerable social awkwardness" caused
by the inexperience of most students with racially integrated gatherings,
but it ended with the participants making "new friends" and gaining "new
insight into their differently complexioned counterparts; and there was
an atmosphere of unforgettable warmth."[89]

The egalitarian ethic of the activist community had a special appeal
to female undergraduates. Refusing to sanction discrimination in its ranks,
the student movement accorded women much more opportunity for political leadership than did most traditional undergraduate institutions, which
tended to be male-dominated. It was not at all uncommon for women to
head campus chapters of student movement organizations and to assume
important roles in regional and national leadership of the movement. Ac-

cording to Hal Draper, during the early 1930s "in SLID, as in the YPSL student activities women were by and large MORE in the leadership than men. At one point, when I was acting as Student Director of the NY YPSL, working closely with SLID, almost the entire regional officers of the SLID were women."[90] When the ASU was founded in 1935, women occupied two of its six national officer positions. Three years later, as Molly Yard recalled,

> when the question came up as to who was going to become chair of the Student Union, it turned out that both Joe [Lash] and I decided that each one of us should have that role. I said to Joe . . . "You know, Joe, that in this world of ours, everyone will expect you to become the chair because you are the man. That's the way that society is. But I think I should become the chair. That makes some kind of a statement which I think is important." And Joe agreed. So I did become chair of the Student Union.[91]

This sensitivity to the issue of women's rights also found expression in some of the student movement's anti-fascist rhetoric. American student activists noted with alarm Hitler's reactionary policy toward German women, which would remove them from political life, relegating females to the home and "the three K's—Kuche, Kinde und Kirche." They expressed outrage when in 1934 the Nazis abolished coeducation in the higher schools of Prussia. "Feminists struggled for a century and a half to reach what little there is today of feminine emancipation," explained the *Columbia Spectator*. "In sixteen months German fascism has been able to wipe out the work of 150 years . . . . The women of Germany are to devote themselves exclusively to raising Nazi cannon fodder. They are to be mothers of a new generation of soldiers who must die for the mad schemes of fascist militarism." A Hunter College student leader warned that if the Nazis succeeded, women would be reduced to the status of "slave . . . as . . . [were] their forebears of the Middle Ages."[92]

Concern about discrimination against women also occasionally found its way into the speeches of student movement leaders. In his address before an international conference of socialist and communist students in Paris, Joseph Lash mentioned the ASU's interest in campaigns to "give greater freedom to the women students who suffer from all sorts of restrictions imposed by the university authorities" in the United States. This concern also appeared in Molly Yard's annual report to the ASU. She pointed out that "Co-eds constitute a special problem—they do not have as good athletic facilities. They live under many rules and regulations while men have none."[93]

Although such egalitarianism was both significant and radical in the context of 1930s America, it would be an exaggeration to say that the student movement gave high priority to feminist issues. Very few instances occurred where the student movement's position favoring gender equality translated into concrete action against sexual discrimination either in the schools or society.[94] The movement's leaders sought to be non-discriminatory in their own ranks, but did not have an extensive feminist agenda or push women's issues the way they pushed on issues of race, class, war, and peace. Thus in the Lash speech quoted above, he mentioned the issue of women's rights last: after first discussing racial discrimination and economic problems. Yard's speech was structured similarly. And in fact, after mentioning the issue of gender discrimination, Yard quickly indicated that this was not the most pressing of problems, since "women are not the worst treated group on campus. Racial groups—especially Negroes are discriminated against at every turn."[95]

Yard's words suggest that not even the movement's leading female activists thought of women's issues as paramount. Like their male counterparts, the political agendas of these young women were set by the twin crises of Depression and war and by the larger milieu of the American Left. Generations removed from the suffragettes, women activists on campuses in the 1930s did not possess a fully developed feminist language in which to analyze gender issues. According to Molly Yard, during the Depression decade "we never thought in those days in terms of feminism. It was not a common word." But Yard and other female student activists did display at least elements of a feminist sensibility—even if they did not have a name for it—and held some notion that women should have equal access to positions of power in the movement.[96] (This is what Yard meant when she noted that "I didn't use the word feminist at that time although I was then and have always been one.") They found their male comrades usually willing to engage in such power sharing. In short, the movement was about as open to sexual equality as the women were themselves.[97] This openness—although not in itself the main precipitant of their politicization—made the activist community more congenial for women and helped draw them into it.

The significance of the activist community's egalitarianism was not lost on the conservative critics of the student movement. They well understood that the movement had built a community that defied the discriminatory divisions prevalent in Depression America. These critics were as upset about the non-discriminatory manner in which the activist community functioned as they were about the movement's protest activities. This could be seen, for example, in the publications of Elizabeth Dilling, who ranks among the Right's most prolific critics of the student movement. In one of her redbaiting books, published in 1936, Dilling, after condemning the movement for promoting "closer race relations," suggested that the student activist community had sanctioned dangerous violations of the social taboo against interracial sex. Dilling quoted extensively from a right-wing minister, who had observed the second American Youth Congress and testified that

> the most shocking thing I saw in connection with the Detroit Youth Congress was the social mixing of boys and girls of the black and white races.

Fully one third of the audience at one session was Negro. This I suppose was to be expected but I solemnly affirm that it is not to be expected, irrespective of the type of gathering that black men shall be the escorts and companions of white women. Such a situation, however, seemed perfectly natural around the Youth Congress. . . . Not three seats removed from me a white girl clung to the arm and openly petted one of the blackest sons of Africa I have ever seen. This was not an isolated incident . . . [and threatens to] destroy respect for the natural laws governing the race, remove old standards of morals and decency and reduce the human race to the level of soulless animals.[98]

Similar to Dilling's racist attack on the student movement were the xenophobic and anti-Semitic indictments of the movement by her fellow conservatives. At UCLA for example, a rightwinger wrote that the campus administration's attempt to suppress student radicalism during the free speech fight of 1934 was necessary because

there was absolutely nothing of the American or Anglo-Saxon in the appearance of the "red" students. Every one of them appeared decidedly foreign; appeared as if just imported from Soviet Russia. You can't be too severe with these obnoxious foreign elements![99]

The same point was made by the Engineering College Dean at the University of Texas, who attributed the anti-war strike of 1935 to a "bunch of Russians from the East Side of New York." An administrator at DePauw University blamed student radicalism there on "a bunch of neurotic Hebrews," and a Berkeley official claimed that the student Left was composed of "Jews and Russians mostly." Dartmouth's president attributed the rise of student protest on his campus to "the unhappiness and destructive spirit of revolt . . . characteristic of the Jewish race at all times under all conditions . . . . The jaundiced mulling of that [Jewish] . . . portion of our student body which loves to line up against the wailing wall."[100]

These attacks had two different meanings. On one level, they were irrational ravings on the part of prejudiced observers. It is obviously a testament to the depth of academic anti-Semitism that administrators at campuses such as Dartmouth, whose discriminatory admissions policies kept Jewish enrollments to a minimum, could depict Jews as the source of all the radicalism at their schools.[101] And there was a similar element of unreason and prejudice on Dilling's pages, which made the movement sound like one big interracial orgy. But though colored by fear and prejudice, their indictments were also significant because they caught something of the diversity, the tolerance, the egalitarianism of the student activist community. The movement crossed racial boundaries rarely approached in Depression America, where blacks and whites seldom socialized or cooperated closely. In her own sensationalistic way, this was what Dilling was underscoring, as she brought interracial sex into her account to dramatize the dangers of such racial egalitarianism.

Dilling's repugnance for racial egalitarianism was more explicit but no less strong than that of the campus administrators who scapegoated Jews for the rise of student radicalism. Accustomed to a campus scene in which Jews were kept on the fringes of academic life—barred from most social clubs, faculty, and top administration posts—these conservative WASP academics had every reason to feel shocked about a student movement which elevated these outcasts to leadership positions.[102] Coming out of these WASP-dominated institutions, critics such as Dartmouth's president were unable to imagine a truly multi-ethnic movement, and therefore naturally (and incorrectly) assumed that any movement with Jews in its leadership was a Jewish movement. The student movement seemed alien and un-American to conservatives because it rejected the WASP elitism and exclusionism which had been hallmarks of American society and academia. By exposing these conservatives to a new, more open, meritocratic and cosmopolitan vision of the academic world, the student movement scared and infuriated these guardians of the old order.

V

For students in Depression America there were many routes leftward. The array of factors inducing students toward political activism—including economic hardship, middle-class guilt, fears of war and fascism, the search for an egalitarian community, and the influence of progressive parents and teachers—were so numerous that one might well expect broad majorities of college students to become dedicated activists. And yet the number of students who actually went all out and became members of either the ASU or its rivals on the student Left was not overwhelming. In no single year did this activist core ever go much beyond the 20,000 figure which the ASU claimed as its national student membership.[103] This represented only a small minority of America's national undergraduate population, which annually averaged slightly more than a million. Thus to understand student politics in Depression America, it is necessary to discern not only the factors which facilitated, but also those which impeded the activist impulse on campus.

Throughout the Depression decade, traditional collegiate culture remained the biggest obstacle confronting the student movement. Thanks to Hollywood, millions of youths had been brought up with the idea that college was supposed to be a fun place, dominated by socializing sororities, frats, and football. This idea weakened considerably after it was challenged by both the student movement and the sobering crises in the American economy and in international relations. But it would be a mistake to confuse this weakness with collapse, for the old collegiate culture did not die. On campus after campus there were significant student minorities—and in some cases even majorities—which continued to see extracurricular college life in this traditional manner. Weakened as they were by the Depression, fraternities and sororities remained the largest residential social organizations of American collegians and a source of institutional power for non-radicals. Though the political and economic turmoil of the 1930s had made their collegiate lifestyle seem archaic to student activists, others thought differently. Anti-radicals in the Greek houses reasoned that with life after college looking so bleak, they should at least have some fun while they had a chance during their fleeting college years. In this view the Depression was grim enough without having to be reminded of it by those depressing radicals.[104]

Youthful anti-intellectualism that had long been a part of traditional undergraduate culture bolstered this apolitical mind-set. Those collegians who dominated the world of frats and football were usually unfriendly to more intellectual students, whom they disparaged as "grinds." They criticized and ostracized such serious students for being too engrossed in their studies and not showing the proper collegiate spirit (ie. not throwing themselves into the time-consuming socializing and juvenile rituals of the frats and football set). Some of this same hostility to "grinds" was applied to radicals, who also were depicted as overly intellectual party poopers. "The Communists we knew," Henry May explains, "were too serious, intense . . . for most middle class young Americans, and most . . . students came from the middle class."[105]

Radical students and "grinds" did, as their critics charged, share a more serious outlook than the average student. Indeed, there was some overlap between these two groups. The ranks of the campus Left included some of the most intellectually gifted members of their college generation. An impressive number of movement alumni would go on to become prominent academics, writers and journalists, including Leo Marx, Muriel Rukeyser, Irving Howe, Daniel Bell, Saul Bellow, Richard Hofstadter, Theodore Draper, Seymour Martin Lipset, Joseph Lash, Leon Wofsy, Leslie Fiedler, Irving Kristol, Henry May, Pauline Kael, Harry Magdoff, Budd Shulberg, Merle Miller, Richard Rovere, Carl Schorske, Eric Sevareid, and James Wechsler. This does not mean, however, that the movement was always a magnet for intellectually intense or studious students. Hard times often tended to make diligent students more studious rather than more political. The Depression motivated many of them to work harder so as to assemble the strongest possible academic record and improve their chances in the constricted job market. Such students, as Harry Magdoff recalled, made City College "horrendously competitive, terribly competitive in terms of class work" during the early 1930s. Radical political activism could thus seem too time-consuming and risky (especially on campuses where students were expelled) for this type of job conscious student.[106]

Time also posed an obstacle to activism for students who had been hurt economically by the Depression. Often when sociologists have explained the propensity of students for political activism, they point to the fact that undergraduates have more time for political thought and action than their elders. This was definitely not the case for working students—and during the Depression the majority did work their way through college. Those who labored long hours in low paying jobs, studied, and attended classes often did not have time for sustained political activism. This is not to say that combining employment and activism was impossible. The memoirs of CCNY night school student activists offer some remarkable examples of students who worked full time jobs by day, did their academic work at night, and somehow managed to squeeze in some political organizing. But such schedule juggling was difficult and discouraged all but the most politically conscious and energetic of students.[107]

The movement had to contend as well with a substantial degree of hereditary politics. Not all collegians came—as had the radical student organizers portrayed above—from liberal or leftist homes. Indeed, throughout the Depression decade substantial numbers of students came from conservative middle-class families and reflected the political values of their parents. It is true that the national straw polls showed that in 1936 FDR became the first Democratic presidential candidate in more than a decade to win a plurality (48.3 percent) of the national student body. But significant as that victory was, it should not be forgotten that 44 percent of American students went Republican that year. This meant that a very significant minority of undergraduates nationally would not be friendly to the egalitarian agenda of a student movement to the left of the New Deal. In the South, moreover, even though the the student majority voted Democratic, its politics followed the racially reactionary path of local white supremacist politicians and parents, and was generally cool toward the integrationist student movement.[108]

Although these obstacles to radicalization helped limit the size of the ASU, it must also be borne in mind that the ASU's influence on American campuses during the Depression decade far transcended the size of the organization. Small as the ASU might seem in comparison to the overall student population, in the context of American student politics, the ASU was a formidable presence. Its membership of 20,000 not only far exceeded previous student activist organizations, but was also much larger than any competing national student group in Depression America. This meant that on many individual campuses and in every region except the South, the ASU's vocal and dedicated activists lacked effective competition and could set the tone of American student politics.[109]

The significance of the ASU's membership level becomes even clearer when one turns from the Left to the Right. One can understand the direction of student politics in Depression America by noting the absence of any kind of effective national organization of conservative student activists. Where the Left had the 20,000 member ASU, the Right had nothing of even half this size. Although students in the fraternities and those with Republican backgrounds might seem to offer the Right a natural constituency to challenge the ASU, the fact was that no serious effort was made to mount such a challenge. In the reformist New Deal era, conservatives knew they were out of step with majority student opinion. Consequently, they were unwilling to make the time commitments and personal sacrifices necessary to build national activist organizations when the political field seemed so unpromising.

The ASU both facilitated and benefitted from a leftward shift on campus which was far broader than its own dues paying membership. This shift was reflected in surveys of student opinion throughout the 1930s, which found majority support for more equal distribution of wealth, greater government regulation of business, and an expanded welfare state. Roosevelt's victory in the 1936 student polls was a testament to how far the Depression had brought the campuses since the 1920s, when large student majorities had gone Republican. This was particularly good news for the ASU, which in the mid-1930s moved into a political alliance with the Roosevelt administration. But, of course, the most dramatic sign of change and of the ASU's dominance of student politics in this era came each spring, when the ASU spearheaded anti-war demonstrations which annually mobilized hundred of thousands of students.[110]

The influence of the ASU-led student movement was by no means confined to these spring strikes. The movement was helping to change some of the central institutions of American student life. This occurred most decisively in the case of the student press. At the dawn of the Great Depression, collegiate newspapers were overwhelmingly apolitical, often reporting more on college social life and football than serious news. By the mid-1930s, much of the college press was not only focusing on politics, but commenting upon it from a Left-liberal perspective. The movement had accomplished this by dispatching activists to work in the student press and by exposing editors to leftist ideas and causes. A *Fortune* magazine national report on college youth confirmed the movement's success in this area, finding that

> college newspapers are often far to the left of the undergraduate bodies.
> This is particularly true at Columbia, Vassar and Dartmouth, where the
> radicals provide almost the whole vocal element. Much of the energy that
> went into art in the undergraduate days of F. Scott Fitzgerald . . . now
> goes into the fledging political writing of a Left tinge for the college pa-
> pers.[111]

In helping to politicize the campus and prod collegians leftward, the student movement transformed the very ideal of student leadership. In the 1920s collegians awarded leadership not to the politically aware or intellectually developed student, but rather to the one who was socially adept and prominent in campus social clubs or athletics. However, this ideal of leadership came under steady fire from the student movement. A new and more political conception of student leadership was gradually taking hold on campus. This change was reflected in a 1936 *New York Times* student survey, which concluded:

> Nowhere is the new liberalism more apparent than in the 1936-style campus leader . . . . He is no longer the star athlete, [or] the "smooth" prom man . . . . His stigmata are more apt to be brains, a good grasp of student and national problems and frequently leadership in the peace movement.[112]

The effect of this change was especially visible in student government elections. Formerly little more than popularity contests, these elections on many campuses became serious political races in which substantive social issues were raised. This trend even affected the nationwide association of student governments—the National Student Federation—which under the influence of the student movement began to support Left-liberal causes, including the American Youth Act campaign in the mid-1930s.[113]

These changes in the student press and government indicate the far reaching impact that the student movement—and the activist impulses which created it—had on Depression America's college campuses. The movement had made impressive progress in its goal of transforming student life; its national anti-war strikes, marches on Washington, ties with the Roosevelt administration, politicization of student leadership demonstrated that students had become serious political actors. The campuses were no longer, as they had seemed in the 1920s, merely playgrounds for middle-class youth.[114]

Such changes suggest that had the ASU and the student movement lived long enough, they might have achieved a lasting revolution in American student life. But this was not to be. The apolitical culture of frats and football, socials and sororities would prove more enduring—living through the war years and obtaining unparalleled supremacy in the 1950s. The ASU's failure to achieve any lasting impact on student politics and culture came about because the organization at the age of four began began to self-destruct, due to the the influence of the communists in its leadership. From the fall of 1939–1941 the increasingly communist-dominated ASU so discredited itself that the student movement died, burying as well the politically active style of student life that it had pioneered.

Chapter 9

From Popular Front to
Unpopular Sect

> 1. The Soviet [Union] has signed a strong alliance with *Fascist* Germany!
> 2. It has entered into an act of aggression against Poland.
> 3. Immediately the Ally-German conflict becomes an "imperialist war" to the Reds in America.
> 4. And all anti-Fascist ideals go out the window! . . .
> I venture to make this prognastication: if the ASU makes the turnabout in policy that the Communists have, it will die—a suicide.
>
> Quentin Young, a Chicago ASU activist, to Joseph P. Lash, October 2, 1939.

S tudents in the 1939–1940 academic year had more reason than ever to worry that they might soon be carrying rifles instead of textbooks. With the start of classes in September came news of Hitler's invasion of Poland, followed by the British and French declarations of war against Germany. Before the first month of classes had ended, the Nazi conquest of Poland was complete. The great European war, which American student activists had spent much of the decade trying to prevent, was at hand. There followed several tense months without hostilities, Europe's "phony war." But any hopes that this was more than a temporary lull were shattered during the spring semester when Hitler struck again, launching Blitzkriegs which defeated Denmark and Norway in April and the Low Countries in May. The most shocking blow of all came at graduation time, when American students learned that France had fallen to a Nazi invasion.[1]

Although this news from Europe was horrible, it should have strengthened the student movement in the United States. After all, the movement's most influential organizations—the ASU and Youth Congress—had spent years warning Americans of the threat that Nazi Germany posed to world peace. Hitler's aggression had borne out those warnings. America seemed on the verge of adopting the anti-fascist position long advocated by the student movement. Even Congress began to move away from strict neutrality and rigid isolationism by repealing the arms embargo so as to aid Great Britain. All of this could have enhanced the student movement's prestige, conferring upon its activists a prophetic cast. Hitler's march through Europe should also have boosted the American student movement because it gave students an added impetus for turning out at rallies, lectures, and other movement events to protest Nazi aggression. At a time of surging student anxiety about a potential United States entry into the war, the student movement might have expanded greatly by continuing to carry its hopeful message that America could stay out of war by supplying Hitler's foes in Europe.[2] But instead of growing in this new crisis atmosphere, the American student movement began to crumble.

The 1939–1940 academic year proved disastrous for the American student movement. During this period the movement's key organizations lost members and credibility, the anti-war strike shrunk, and student activists began wondering whether campus protest was heading for extinction. Responsibility for this turn of events rested largely with communist student leaders. They alienated thousands of activists and potential activists from the student movement by championing first the Nazi-Soviet Pact, Stalin's shocking abandonment of anti-fascism, and then his brutal invasion of Finland. Through political manipulation and intrigue, young communists worked to force the ASU, America's largest Popular Front student organization to drop its anti-fascist principles and serve as an apologist for both the Pact and all the other twists and turns in Soviet foreign policy. These communist maneuvers fatally wounded the ASU and shattered the liberal-radical coalition which had been the life blood of the American student movement.

These political disasters might never have befallen the ASU had the organization followed the advice of the non-communists in its national office. This group, which included ASU Chair Molly Yard and Organizational Secretary Agnes Reynolds, was headed by Joseph Lash, the ASU Executive Secretary. Lash had been close to the Communist Party during the Popular Front era, because he felt the Party stood in the vanguard of the international struggle against fascism. But in August 1939, when the Nazi-Soviet Pact brought the Popular Front to an end, Lash lost faith in the Communist Party. He viewed the Pact as a sell out to Hitler and was determined that the ASU should have no part in this communist abandonment of anti-fascism.[3]

Given his own strong distaste for the Pact, Lash's advice regarding the ASU's reaction to it was quite restrained. He began the 1939 fall semester arguing that the ASU should take no public position on the Pact. Lash took this stance in the hope of saving the ASU from a ruinous split.

He understood that if the ASU endorsed the Pact it would surrender its anti-fascist principles and thereby alienate liberals and independent radicals, and if the ASU condemned the Pact it would lose the support of its many communist activists. "I do not think the ASU should become a battleground over the policies of Russia," Lash explained.[4] This would, however, prove an unrealistic hope, because the communists in the ASU were so ardently and uncritically pro-Soviet that they could not sustain neutrality on any question regarding the Soviet Union.

The first signs of trouble surfaced in early September 1939 at the ASU Fall Planning Conference, where more than 100 ASU chapter leaders and the national executive committee met. Here the growing tensions between the ASU's communists and non-communists became evident. YCL leader Bert Witt, who was also the ASU's New York district secretary, served as the key spokesman for the communist ASUers. Witt launched into a strident defense of the Nazi-Soviet Pact, provoking a heated debate with Lash. The communists and non-communists argued about not only the Pact, however, but also what foreign policy the ASU should promote for the United States. Lash and the non-communists continued to uphold the anti-fascist policies which the ASU had supported throughout the Popular Front era: opposing isolationism, calling for sanctions against Nazi Germany, and an end to the arms embargo on the victims of Nazi aggression. Communist ASUers, who had supported these policies for years, now—because of the Pact and Moscow's shifting foreign policy—criticized them and began to sound increasingly isolationist. Following Stalin's path of de-emphasizing the dangers of Hitlerism, a communist delegate from MIT explained that he "disagrees with [the] proposal to embargo Germany and aid the victim of aggression. [We] [c]annot see who is the aggressor in the present conflict."[5]

Although the debates at the Fall Planning Conference were contentious, the ASU's non-communist leaders came away from the meeting feeling that an important victory for unity had been won. The conference voted that the ASU should take no position on the Nazi-Soviet Pact. The willingness of communist ASUers to go along with this decision—in spite of their own sympathy for the Pact—left Lash optimistic that Stalin's new foreign policy would not lead to a divorce between the ASU's communist and non-communist activists. This communist-non-communist understanding would, Lash confided to a friend, strengthen the entire student movement, since "there are too many things we agree on that are urgent to allow ourselves to be divided on this issue. I say this as one of those who bitterly criticized the non-aggression pact at the NEC." Equally encouraging to the non-communist ASUers was the fact that the Fall Conference had reaffirmed the ASU's Popular Front positions, including support for amending the Neutrality Act "to permit the nation to give aid to the forces opposing Germany." This seemed to suggest that communist ASUers would respect the will of the ASU majority by not trying to force the organization to abandon its anti-fascist principles simply because Stalin had.[6]

This optimism, however, proved premature. Communist ASUers could not sustain the cooperative posture they had displayed in giving ground on the Nazi-Soviet Pact at the Fall Planning Conference. The ideological and organizational imperatives of the YCL would not allow communist ASUers again to show such independence and flexibility. The concessions communist ASUers made to non-communists at the Fall Planning Conference were unacceptable to the YCL's national leadership—which felt that in making such concessions communist ASUers had erroneously placed the interests of the American student movement ahead of the interests of the Soviet Union. This was why during the communist caucus at the ASU Fall Planning Conference, YCL leader Gil Green rebuked communist ASUers for not insisting that the ASU support the Pact; he accused them of "not defending the USSR," a cardinal sin within the communist movement.[7]

The concessions made at the Fall Planning Conference would probably not have been possible had the American Communist Party and YCL not been in a temporary state of disarray. The CP and YCL hierarchy had been shocked by the Pact and were not yet completely clear on the implications of the Pact for United States foreign policy. The American CP leadership had not yet understood that with the Nazi-Soviet Pact Stalin signalled a complete abandonment of anti-fascist collective security. Because of this confusion, the YCL hierarchy had not been able to orchestrate a disciplined factional assault on the ASU and its Popular Front policies at the ASU's Fall Planning Conference. It would, in fact, not be until the week following this conference that communist leader Earl Browder, with prodding from Moscow, announced the new isolationist CP/YCL line—in an interview published in the *Daily Worker*.[8]

This new clarity enabled the YCL to tighten the leash upon its members in the ASU, invoking Party discipline to prevent any repetition of the type of concessions that had been made at the Fall Planning Conference. From now on, the YCL hierarchy would require that all communist students defend the Pact, express relative indifference to Nazi aggression, and endorse strict United States neutrality in the European war. This would be done on the grounds that the war was simply a clash of rival imperialists. With this new line solidified, communist ASUers in mid-September 1939 began a sustained drive to rid the ASU of its Popular Front policies. Out went the anti-Hitler rhetoric and the calls for collective anti-fascist action, replaced by such isolationist slogans as "The Yanks aren't coming," and absurd claims that the Nazis were no more aggressive than their western enemies.[9]

It was, of course, more than simple Party discipline which made it possible for the young communists in the ASU to support the Pact and the new isolationist line. Communists were able to make this switch quickly because of their absolute faith in the Soviet Union; they saw it as the one nation which had completed a successful socialist revolution, which to them meant that it was the leading force of the international working-class movement and therefore, virtually infallible. The YCL faithful automatically assumed, consequently, that because the USSR had changed its line, this must represent the proper path toward peace. Embodying this mindset, shortly after the Pact, one communist student wrote Lash that it was "outright silly" for anyone to be

> amazed that [Communist loyalty to the USSR] has not wavered though Soviet foreign policy has . . . . I would consider a man a jackass if he didn't have faith in the law of gravity until it was proven to him by a physicist. A few objects falling would convince me, at least until I saw something fall upwards. The situation is similar here. Though the American CP may not fully understand every action of the USSR immediately, they have had no reason during the past 20 years to lose faith in the USSR, and until such time as there is proof of betrayal of Communist principle I see no reason why the Party shouldn't stick together.[10]

The Pact and the new isolationism had an additional appeal to young communists because it allowed them to express their most revolutionary sentiments. During the Popular Front era, when the emphasis had been on coalition building, communists were required first to mute and then to eliminate criticism of potential anti-fascist allies, including the Roosevelt administration, Britain, and France. With the ending of the Popular Front era and this need for unity gone, communists were again free to engage in anti-capitalist polemics. They could now depict the war in classic Leninist terms as a capitalist rivalry for imperialist spoils. For at least some of the young militants this was a liberating change, allowing them to feel again like true revolutionaries.[11]

Young communists also welcomed the Pact and the new line because in their eyes these seemed fitting Soviet revenge for the irresponsible foreign policies of the capitalist West. They saw the refusal of Britain and France to forge an anti-fascist alliance with the U.S.S.R. as well as Chamberlain's appeasement policy—particularly his deal with Hitler at Munich—as having been designed to isolate the Soviet Union. There was among communists therefore, as Lash put it, a desire "for venegance against [the] bourgeois world which by path of appeasement asked for its destruction."[12] The Pact also seemed to these young communists a necessary means of Soviet self-preservation, since in the wake of Munich it appeared to them too risky for the Soviet Union to remain Europe's only major anti-fascist power. As one young communist explained in defending the Pact, "I see no reason for the USSR . . . committing suicide for the Fascist groups in England or France who have created this mess and those in America who quite willingly let it be created."[13]

The zealous support that communist ASUers gave to the Pact and the new Party line angered non-communist ASU leaders. Having worked long and hard with the communists in opposing isolationism and promoting an anti-fascist foreign policy, non-communist ASUers could barely believe that their comrades would embrace isolationism and abandon the anti-fascist cause. "One went around with a terrible sense of betrayal," Lash recalled.

> It is clear now that our surprise was a sign of our political naiveté, but it was a stunning blow . . . . [What was] disheartening was the way in which young people with whom one had worked for years accepted the new [CP] policy, a policy in contradiction with the one they had been voicing, a policy they had no influence in deciding. I had assumed as we built the . . . Student Union and other organizations together that our methods of evaluation of political events were so similar, that if a new situation arose our response to that situation would be a similar one. Now, instead, person after person [within the ASU's communist ranks] began to echo the new slogans, which just didn't make intellectual sense.[14]

Non-communist ASUers were shocked as much by the suddenness of the communists' flip-flop as they were by the new party line itself. They saw their communist classmates, who in mid-August had ardently championed revision of the United States neutrality acts—to help halt Nazi aggression—opposing revision by mid-September. The communist ASUers were not only carrying new isolationist slogans, but denouncing those who would not go along with them as "warmongers." "All the independents in the ASU," Lash observed in late September, "wonder where the hell the change is coming from. They resent people who three weeks ago held one position coming around with another today and demanding that chapters obediently swing with them." Nor did most non-communist ASUers find persuasive the communists' arguments in defense of the Pact and isolationism. It seemed simple common sense that if it was important to stop Hitler last month it was no less important this month. In fact, it was the very weakness of the communists' defense of the Pact (and the transparent fact that their uncritical view of Stalin was at the root of that defense) which so concerned Lash and his followers. They recognized that if the ASU followed this line, ASUers would lose all credibility on campus—being "indelibly stamped as CP stooges."[15]

This split damaged not only communist-non-communist political alliances but also longstanding friendships within the ASU. Lash found that communist ASUers and YCL leaders, who only a few weeks earlier had been his friends, now did not hesitate to employ "character assassination and the shabbiest kind of political maneuvering" against him. Lash's personal diary from this era, reflected his anguish over these tactics and the harm they were doing. In his September 12 entry, Lash noted that one communist ASU leader "attacked me for individualism" and another accused him of being "viciously anti-Soviet" because he had urged that the

ASU avoid endorsing the Nazi-Soviet Pact.[16] The communists would also denounce Lash as a "warmonger," even though he had spent most of the decade leading the student movement against war. What hurt even more was that Lash's friend, YCL leader Gil Green, with whom he had worked closely in the student movement for almost four years, began hurling reactionary epithets at him in this dispute. Green charged that Lash had been " 'Hearst'like" in criticizing the Pact. Shocked that Green would compare him to this rightwing editor, Lash walked out of his meeting with the YCL leader, observing in his diary that "I thought I would break down and weep because the breach is widening."[17]

The communist attempt to maneuver the ASU into making the same foreign policy flip-flop as Stalin also aroused strong opposition because it brazenly violated democratic process within the ASU. Less than a week after the Fall Planning Conference, at which communists had gone along with the ASU decision to take no position on the Nazi-Soviet Pact, communist ASUers broke that agreement; they flouted majority rule in the ASU by using the organization's resources to agitate on behalf of both the Pact and an isolationist United States foreign policy. The process problem was particularly striking with respect to the ASU's communist staff members, who, by following the CP line rather than the will of the ASU membership, subverted the anti-fascist policies they were being paid to promote—policies that had been endorsed by large ASU majorities at the last national convention. Lash observed this breach of faith first hand at Harvard shortly after the Fall Planning Conference, while attending a New England ASU district meeting. Lash noted that this meeting

> was opened by the district secretary, a paid official of the American Student Union, whose speech was an outright apologia for the Nazi-Soviet Pact and defense of the [CP's] new isolationist line. It was quickly evident to me that the . . . [meeting] was packed. The same thing happened in other districts. Our district secretaries had two decent alternatives: either express the policy of the American Student Union or keep quiet. Instead, they went to town for the new [CP] line. What happened on the district scale was also going on in the chapters. The nuclei of the Young Communist League mobilized to establish the new position.[18]

Lash's bitterness toward the ASU's four district secretaries derived from the critical role that these officials played in the communist effort to rid the ASU of its Popular Front policies. All of the district secretaries were communists, who in mid-September 1939 spearheaded the YCL attempt to deprive the ASU's national officers—the non-communists Lash, Yard, and Reynolds—of their administrative authority and political influence. The idea was that because these influential national officers were critical of both the Nazi-Soviet Pact and the YCL's new isolationism, the communist district secretaries would seek to usurp their authority: pushing the new Party line on the districts and chapters, while keeping the national office, which formerly coordinated ASU affairs, as much in the dark as possible.[19]

Lash quickly recognized that something was wrong. He suspected that the YCL was plotting against him and the other non-communists in the ASU national office, noting in his diary on September 21, 1939 that at least one ASU "district [was] not coming to me with problems on war situation and ycl establishing its new position in asu by infiltration." Lash's worst fears were confirmed two weeks later, when he obtained the minutes of the ASU New England district staff meeting, which "disclosed a nat'l [YCL] drive to isolate [the ASU's] national office by having work head up in districts and having districts coordinated outside [the] n.o." Though fully aware of what he, Yard, and Reynolds were up against, and ready to fight back, Lash confessed in his diary that this confirmation of the YCL plot left him "very despondent." Lash sensed that the divisive and potentially fatal showdown between the ASU's communist and noncommunist leaders, which he had tried so hard to prevent, was now inevitable.[20]

At first glance it might seem that because of the student political environment in 1939 Lash and his allies in the ASU leadership should have found it easy to turn back the communist challenge. After all, the vast majority of the ASU's 20,000 members were not communists, and that majority had solidly backed the foreign policy positions that Lash was seeking to defend against the communists. Moreover, the Nazi-Soviet Pact was extremely unpopular both on campus and off, leaving the communists in the very difficult position of having to explain why after years of promoting anti-fascism they were now forsaking it for isolationism. This would hardly seem an opportune moment for communists to mount a successful challenge to the ASU's experienced and popular non-communist leadership.

But these factors favoring the ASU's non-communists were more than offset by the communists' organizational advantages. The communists were the only faction within the ASU which in the fall of 1939 had a tight national political network in place. This network of campus YCL units was by mid-September 1939 already coordinating a national effort to reverse the ASU's foreign policies and drive non-communists out of the leadership of the student movement. This gave the communists a big headstart over their non-communist rivals in the ASU, who had to try to create their own national network almost overnight to compete with the communists at the upcoming ASU convention over the Christmas break. Lash worked frantically, attempting to assemble this network, but it was, as he explained to a friend in late September, a formidable task: "I am leading a one man struggle to galvanize the ASU into action . . . . I have never written so many letters—exhorting, demanding, threatening, philosophising—but I feel that the time spent is worth it, for a false move now and the ASU is finished."[21]

The task of building this non-communist network was made even more difficult by the reluctance of Lash and his allies to attack the communist issue head on in public during much of the fall of the 1939 semester. Though Lash publicly campaigned to retain the ASU's anti-fascist peace policy, he would not come right out and tell the ASU's membership that more was at stake than this: that he was struggling to prevent a complete communist takeover of their organization. Only in his private correspondence did Lash acknowledge the centrality of this issue. Here Lash wrote that stopping the communists from imposing their new isolationist foreign policy on the ASU was essential because "if the YCL succeeds in changing the ASU line . . . the ASU is finished as a united organization—it will then become nothing but a communist front in truth."[22] Had Lash gone public with this message early in the fall, it might have imparted a sense of urgency to the membership and helped mobilize them against the communists. This Lash refused to do, however, because of his sense of morality, his tactical sense, and his Old Left political style.

Having been frequently redbaited himself, Lash could not rid himself of the idea that a direct public attack on communist ASUers would smack of demagoguery and political persecution. Lash was especially sensitive to this problem because at the very moment he was preparing for his showdown with communist ASUers, the nation's most prominent redbaiting group, the House Un-American Activities Committee, was on the offensive against both the ASU and the entire student movement. The Committee, headed by Texas Congressman Martin Dies, threatened throughout the fall of 1939 to probe the ASU's communist connections, and would subpoena ASU leaders—including Lash—before the end of the year.[23]

Like most ASUers, Lash viewed the work of Dies' committee as part of a rightwing assault on both the American Left and liberalism. He therefore avoided public discussion of his battle against communist domination in the ASU so as not to aid that committee. A Lash diary entry in the late fall of 1939 confirms that these congressional anti-communists were simply making it more difficult for communist domination to be battled in the ASU: "Should one pr[e]cipitate open break with ycl—since cp means to narrow asu down to ycl. org on campus? opposed to such a break . . . [because] it plays into hands of dies committee." Lash's approach here was guided by not only moral but also tactical considerations. Lash knew that if he even gave the appearance of raising the communist issue while Dies was red hunting, he could lose the support of many non-communist ASUers, who would have seen him as giving aid and comfort to the student movement's enemies in Congress. This would have strengthened the communists by enabling them to villify Lash and his political allies as traitors to the movement.[24]

This unwillingess to discuss the communist issue openly was also an outgrowth of the vanguard mentality—the elitist political style common to Lash and virtually the entire ASU leadership. For much of the ASU's history, the YCL had existed as an organized faction within the Union. While the ASU grew in the mid-1930s this faction, along with its socialist counterpart, played a preeminent role in selecting the ASU's slate of national officers, including Lash himself. But these were facts that the leadership had not shared with either the public or the ASU rank and file, since it was thought that doing so would earn the ASU a red label and frighten off potential recruits.[25]

Most ASU leaders had, in fact, always denied that the ASU was a communist front organization. Lash himself told the *New York Times* on the eve of the Dies inquiry that the ASU was "not dominated by communists."[26] This was, however, at best a half-truth. Communists had never *unilaterally* dominated the ASU, but they had dominated the ASU in alliance with like-minded activist groups. In the early days of the ASU, the communists together with the socialists had dominated the ASU's leadership. Later, during the height of the Popular Front era, communists and Popular Front liberals had dominated that leadership. Now in the fall of 1939, communist ASUers were angling to take unilateral control of the ASU in order to dump the Popular Front.

Having kept silent about these machinations at the top of the ASU for the four years when they had agreed with the communists' anti-fascist foreign policy, Lash and his political allies in the ASU were in no position to go public with the communist issue now. Had they dealt frankly and openly with the problem of communist domination in 1939, they would almost have had to acknowledge their own complicity in the similar pattern of communist domination and elite manipulation within the ASU in the past. This would undoubtedly have damaged their credibility and hampered their efforts to organize a bloc to counter communist influence in the ASU at the upcoming convention. Such considerations helped lead Lash and his supporters to try to keep their battle against communist domination of the ASU out of the headlines.

The battle between the ASU's communist and non-communist leaders began to heat up as the ASU national office prepared for campus Armistice Day demonstrations. These were scheduled to be the first major anti-war protests of the fall 1939 semester. The literature that the ASU national office began preparing for these protests was strongly anti-fascist. As part of this mobilization effort, Lash, on September 25, sent an open letter to President Roosevelt, endorsing his attempt to revise the Neutrality Act. The letter also condemned isolationism and stressed "that a victory for Hitler will menace *our* security, *our* well being, *our* democratic institutions."[27] Though this letter was consistent with ASU policy, as set in the ASU's Fall Planning Conference and last convention, it elicited an angry response from communist leaders in the ASU. On the day that Lash wrote the FDR letter, Bert Witt, the ASU's most vocal communist leader, personally rebuked Lash over the contents of the letter. Witt argued that the letter ran contrary to the current sentiment of the ASU National Executive Committee and warned that if Lash sent out the letter the committee might force him to "issue [a] retraction."[28]

Less than a week after this angry confrontation, Lash's letter to FDR became the focus of a stormy meeting of the ASU National Executive Committee. Witt told his fellow committee members that Lash's letter distorted both the international situation and ASU policy. Witt found especially objectionable the portion of Lash's letter which stated that "the victory of Hitlerism in Europe . . . would have disastrous effects on American democratic institutions." Witt argued that this was "not a correct analysis" because "the defeat of Hitler does not necessarily mean the defeat of Chamberlain and Daladier, nor does aid to Daladier defeat Hitler, as was implied in the letter." Witt charged that the entire idea of revising the Neutrality Act to aid France and Britain, which Lash so strongly urged in the letter, was misguided and inconsistent with the ASU's peace policy. "Chamberlain and Daladier are not to be depended on and therefor[e]," Witt concluded, "this is not a war against Hitler—and the peoples must make the peace." Witt's supporters at the meeting joined him in promoting the new communist line, arguing that Britain and France were as imperialist as Germany and just as much a danger to peace.[29]

The non-communists at the meeting quickly and forcefully repudiated the communist line. Agnes Reynolds pointed out the inconsistency between what the communists were saying now and the anti-fascist foreign policies that they (and the rest of the ASU) supported in the past. "We have always said that equating British imperialism with German fascism is an aid to appeasement and this is still true." Molly Yard told the communists that their new line would prove unpopular on campus and that the ASU would lose all credibility with students if it adopted that line. Yard warned "those wanting to change the ASU position" that though

> there is confusion on the campus about peace . . . the feeling on the whole is that the situation is the same today as it was a few weeks ago. Poland has been invaded, and England and France are defending Poland. We still stand for aid to victims of aggression and their allies. If we deny this, students will say the ASU is communist-dominated and is doing this only because of the Soviet Union . . . . We must remember that to most people there is a distinction between Chamberlain and Hitler.[30]

This debate brought out the resentment Lash felt over the methods the communists were using in their campaign to reverse the ASU's peace policies. Lash confronted the district secretaries at the meeting with reports that they were agitating for the new CP line rather than the ASU's anti-fascist policies; he "expressed the hope that this matter could be cleared up, with honest discussion." Lash also refuted Witt's claim that his letter to FDR had violated the ASU peace program. Suggesting that Witt's attacks had been made in an unethical manner, Lash

> charged that there was a certain amount of evasiveness being shown at the meeting, and that it consisted in this: that there are certain people who have changed their position since the NEC meeting. But, he said, we

are not discussing here the validity of the change of opinion; we are discussing the ASU position as determined by the convention and the NEC. It is not decent to charge now that those who do continue to believe in the ASU program as adopted at the Fall Planning Conference have changed their position, and that those who in reality have changed their opinion have not. There are, of course, people who say that the victory of Hitlerism makes no difference. But this is not the position of the ASU. If you have lost your confidence in me, and no longer trust my interpretation of the ASU program, I will have to resign . . . . I cannot agree to Bert's statement as the present position of the ASU. It does not mean what I mean.[31]

After all this acrimonious discusssion, the Executive Committee made one last stab at compromise. Lash's letter to the president was allowed to stand, as was the ASU national office's attempt to make revision of the Neutrality Act a key theme in the Armistice Day mobilization. But to conciliate the communists, some of their anti-imperialist rhetoric was incorporated into the ASU's official Armistice Day Statement. The preamble of that statement, came close to echoing the CP line equating German and British imperialism:

War has broken out. It is the war everyone has feared. It is a war which mankind enters with few illusions and a heavy heart. Hitler made this war, but the judgment of history will be equally severe on the Chamberlains who made Hitler, and on the system of greed and empire which has produced them both.[32]

The compromise proved ineffective. The ASU was a house dividing, with communists and non-communists moving in opposite directions on fundamental questions of war and peace. This internal strife left the ASU in no position to organize an effective national mobilization on Armistice Day. Equally damaging was the spreading anger among non-ASUers over the communist ASUers' support of the Nazi-Soviet Pact and sudden abandonment of anti-fascism. Across the nation—even at campuses where the ASU had formerly been strongest—there came word of poor turn-out and complaints that the "Armistice Day [mobilization] was a disastrous failure." At campuses where communists dominated the ASU chapters came reports of "a breakdown of confidence in the leadership of the ASU . . . [because local] officers of the ASU changed their position rapidly."[33]

Making matters worse for the ASU, the socialist-led YCAW—still bitter at the communists for pushing the ASU away from the Oxford Pledge—pounced upon the ASU in its moment of weakness. The YCAW did all that it could to publicize the communist students' flip-flop on anti-fascism. In its Armistice Day literature, the YCAW asked how anyone could

have any faith in the ability of the ASU to fight totalitarianism when it is controlled by people giving allegiance to a government which gives support to Hitler . . . . So long as the A.S.U. is dominated by the Y.C.L., and so long as American Communism remains the blind instrument of a foreign dictator, we cannot look forward to any cooperation.[34]

Such attacks contributed to the Armistice Day fiasco because students were becoming disgusted with the feuding in the anti-war movement. According to the ASU's national report on the Armistice Day mobilization, many students reacted to the ASU-YCAW polemics by withdrawing and saying "a plague on both your houses."[35]

The low turn-out and dissension at the Armistice Day protests worried Lash. He warned the ASU executive committee that this poor showing suggested that "the ASU is in the most serious crisis it has ever faced." But the communists on the committee were not listening. Convinced that the party line was correct, they thought the campuses just needed a little time to adjust to the ASU's new analysis of the world situation. There was, the communists believed, no need to panic, but rather a need to educate students about the struggle in Europe and the strength of the isolationist case. "Everybody is saying keep America out of war," a communist ASUer explained to the executive committee. "[The] ASU must give reasons why we should stay out. Most people are saying England and France are fighting a just war. We must make them understand that this is an imperialistic war."[36]

It was Lash, however, and not the communists who had correctly diagnosed the implications of the Armistice Day fiasco. This failed mobilization was, as he claimed, a clear sign that the ASU was losing its following and sinking into the most serious crisis in its history. Within a few weeks, moreover, the crisis would grow much worse. If the response of communist ASUers to the Nazi-Soviet Pact damaged the ASU's credibility on campus, their response to the Soviet invasion of Finland virtually eliminated that credibility.

Stalin's invasion of Finland on November 30, 1939 elicited an angry American response. President Roosevelt condemned the Soviets' "dreadful rape of Finland," and suggested that 98 percent of the American public agreed with him. The invasion seemed a clear case of naked aggression and the bullying of a small country by one of the world's largest nations. Before the war had ended a half million Soviet troops marched into Finland; Russian planes bombed Finnish towns and cities. American sympathy for the victims of this aggression was compounded by the fact that the Finns defended themselves so valiantly. The Kremlin and much of the world had expected the defeat of the badly outnumbered Finnish forces in a matter of days or weeks, but they held out for more than two months. The wave of American sympathy for Finland proved so strong that President Roosevelt was able to overcome the resistance of Congressional isolationists and secure some financial aid to Finland. FDR also called for a "moral embargo" against Russia, discouraging American manufacturers from supplying airplanes or equipment to "nations obviously guilty of such unprovoked bombings."[37]

At the very moment when American sympathy for Finland was surging, communist ASUers, along with their counterparts in the adult CP, rushed to the defense of the Soviet Union. Knowing that the non-communists in the ASU national office would be unsympathetic, communist ASUers used their authority at the district level to place the ASU on record in support of the invasion. These communist efforts resulted in the convening of an irregular meeting of New York City ASU chapters, which on December 9, 1939, cheered the Soviet attack on Finland. The resolution endorsed by this gathering portrayed the Soviet attack as a justifiable act of self-defense, claiming that "Finland existed . . . as . . . a puppet state created and maintained by imperial powers from abroad, a threat to and base against Russia." These ASUers charged that Americans who embraced the cause of Finland were the victims of "propaganda" and "atrocity tales." They claimed that Wall Street was seeking to use Finland to whip up an anti-Soviet war hysteria in the United States in order to draw America into the conflict, so as "to make profits from blood, to make the world safe for British and American imperialism." This communist-led group concluded by urging the student movement to adopt the isolationist slogan "NOT TO FINLAND OR TO FRANCE—THIS YANK AIN'T COMING."[38]

Non-communist ASU activists reacted with outrage and disgust to this pro-invasion stance. They were appalled that members of the ASU, an organization dedicated to opposing aggression and preserving peace, would applaud this massive act of Soviet aggression. Expressing the sentiment of these students, Robert Klein, an ASUer and vice president of the Student Council at the CCNY, fumed: "the suggestion that Finland provoked or invaded the mighty U.S.S.R. (1/6 of the earth's surface, greatest standing army, greatest natural resources, etc.) is almost too preposterous to consider if it were not seriously advanced" by communist ASUers. "The U. S. S. R. has followed the fascist nations in adopting a policy of aggression as a means of settling international disputes that they fabricate themselves." Klein noted that the "vast majority of students . . . are on the side of Finland," and that by backing the invasion the New York ASU leadership was alienating thousands of students. The CCNY leader reported that on his own campus, formerly a key ASU stronghold, the local ASU chapter's backing of both the invasion of Finland and the Nazi-Soviet Pact had seriously wounded the ASU. "Never before," Klein observed, "has the City College Chapter been held in such low esteem by the student body; never before has the active membership, and consequently the activity, of the Chapter been so low."[39]

In the national office of the ASU, the non-communists immediately acted to repudiate the New York district's statements. Lash issued a press statement criticizing the Soviet invasion and asserting that the New York district's endorsement of the invasion was not representative of the majority of ASUers. He was angry that communist ASUers had tried to give the impression that they, rather than the ASU national office, spoke for the ASU. Though still refusing to raise the issue of communist domination directly, Lash was now willing at least to be more explicit and public about the growing communist-non-communist split within the ASU. Lash told the press that his attack on New York district's statement attested to the division in the ASU between

> those who are prepared to justify any policy of the Soviet Union and the rest of us who are concerned with a movement based on the needs of the American people. The best way to build up contempt for everything progressive in this country is to identify it with the policies of Soviet Russia.[40]

This public split over the Finnish invasion intensified the communist-non-communist rivalry within the ASU. It was now clear to all that the two sides were heading for a final showdown at the ASU convention over the Christmas break. As the convention approached, the communists accelerated their campaign of vituperation against Lash. News of this campaign reached Lash from non-communist ASUers in all regions. Chicago ASU activist Quentin Young, for instance, wrote to warn Lash:

> Intrigue! I don't comprehend exactly what goes on. When you were in Chicago last things made sense. But now . . . I know you do not follow the Party Line—which . . . displeases the Reds and so out of the Chicago [ASU] District Office comes wierd sounds. You are guilty of . . . (according to them) Red Baiting at an NEC meeting . . . [and] Being generally dictatorial. The reason for this, they say is that you are 'losing power' and trying to retain it.[41]

Lash thanked Young for the warning, but told him that the stories afloat in Chicago were only a small part of the communist ASUers' effort to turn the ASU against him; they had circulated so many negative stories about him that Lash could barely keep up with them. "One day I am splitting the ASU in cahoots with FDR, the next day, I am splitting the ASU in cahoots with the Trotskyites. One rumor has it that I am running out on the ASU because I insist on leaving this January, the next that I am 'trying to retain power' as your letter cites." Lash concluded that the communists' campaign against him was designed to discredit him before the convention even met so "they will not have to answer with arguments" his criticisms of the Pact and the Finnish invasion.[42]

With both sides positioning themselves for the convention battle, the ASU executive committee meetings became increasingly acrimonious. The two sides feuded about everything from the location of the upcoming convention to the resolutions to be considered there. The most heated exchange at the NEC occurred after the communists repeatedly accused

Lash of promoting factionalism and discord in the ASU. The communists raised this charge of factionalism in response to Lash's request that before the Convention ASU delegates be briefed about the policy disputes between the ASU's non-communist and communist leaders. Lash wanted the ASU executive committee to mail the delegates position papers representing both sides in the dispute. The communists initially opposed this move, on the grounds that it would promote factionalism within the ASU. Lash found this communist position "incredible" and "hypocritical." "Here were the spokesmen for an organized faction opposing our efforts to organize on the grounds that factionalism would split the American Student Union."[43]

During this argument a member of the anti-Lash bloc barbed that "he was not interested" in paying "the salary of a national secretary to organize factionalism." This was, as Lash later explained, too much to bear, "since my salary has not been paid for several months, since all through my period of national secretaryship I have had to borrow, sponge off friends, etc." A furious Lash called his accuser "a swine," and though he later wrote a letter of apology for this remark, the exchange was indicative of just how deep the bad feelings went.[44]

In the aftermath of this bitter argument, the communists did, however, agree to Lash's demand for the mailing. The two position papers sent to the chapters defined the lines of argument which would prevail at the convention. While the communists' position paper merely reiterated the Party line, the non-communists' polemic, "Save the American Student Union" was a far more original political manifesto. Written by Yard, Reynolds, and Lash, this position paper spoke of the critical need for independent thought on the part of American liberal and radical student activists. A student movement working for peace and egalitarian change in America needed to develop its own policies, based upon "the needs and traditions of the American people," instead of mindlessly echoing "the policies of the Soviet government." The statement warned against "the viewpoint that any genuine program for peace and democracy must start with a defense of Soviet policy in Finland." Such a program would "transform the character of the ASU," so that the organization would "not be the broad ASU founded at Columbus to unite our student generation in the interests of the American people." Instead the ASU would shrink "into a narrow sect."[45]

Although critical of the communists' line and their attempt to impose it upon the ASU, the authors of "Save the American Student Union" took pains not to treat communists as pariahs. Lash, Yard, and Reynolds were careful to distinguish between their own position and those of anti-communists who wanted to deny communists a place in the American political process:

> We want to make it perfectly clear that we believe Communists have a place in the ASU. We are mindful of the great services they have ren-

dered the ASU. We have no sympathy for the various efforts headed by
Mr. Dies to outlaw the Communists. Their program, however, does not
express the interests of progressive and liberal student opinion.[46]

These ASU leaders were, then, not at all the redbaiters that their communist rivals had claimed. They were seeking to allow the ASU's communist minority to remain in the ASU while simultaneously retaining an
ASU program representative of the non-communist majority. In this sense,
"Save the American Student Union" was more of a non-communist than
an anti-communist document.

Unfortunately for Lash's bloc, however, the fate of the ASU would
be settled not by logic, merit, or rank and file sentiment, but by simple
political arithmetic. The bloc with the most delegates to the 1939 ASU
convention in Madison, Wisconsin would win the argument. Although the
non-communists tried to remain hopeful as they entered the final stages
of their mobilization effort for the convention, they knew their campaign
confronted some major problems. One of their biggest problems was, as
Lash, Yard and Reynolds acknowledged in "Save the American Student
Union," that "increasingly good ASU'ers, genuine progressives have
dropped into inactivity because of actions and policies of which the New
York resolution is only a symptom."[47] The danger was that the non-
communists would lose the delegate race because the ASU's rank and file,
disillusioned with the organization because of the behavior of communist
ASUers, had already voted with their feet—dropping out of the ASU before the convention.

Reports came in from campus chapters of just such desertions. Right
up to the eve of the convention, Lash was receiving letters from disillusioned ASUers, who were leaving the organization. One such ASUer wrote
Lash to express "hearty approval" of the ASU Executive Secretary's stance
on the Soviet invasion of Finland; he wished Lash luck in his upcoming
convention battle, but said he could not in good conscience retain his
membership in the ASU so long as his local chapter continued to support
the communist line on Finland and the Nazi-Soviet Pact. Lash replied by
urging these ASUers to defend rather than desert their organization.
"Frankly," Lash wrote to one of these drop-outs,

> while I appreciate your good wishes, what I, and the hundreds of other
> ASU leaders who agree with me, need, is your active support . . . . If
> you wait while others elect delegates then ASU policy will reflect their
> point of view . . . . We need . . . students . . . who will go into the
> ASU and fight to save it, fight for delegates and fight for support of
> progressive policies. Unless this fight is carried to the membership, unless
> the broad masses of students . . . enter the fray by becoming active in
> pre-convention discussions, etc. the fight at Madison will be difficult indeed
> . . . . Liberals who are critical of communist policy . . . [have] a special
> responsibility to come into the ASU and fight for their policies. The ASU
> has become a testing ground for progressivism: do non-communists have

a program? do they have the capacity for unity? do they have the . . . courage to carry their program through?[48]

This drop-out problem was, however, only one of many indications that in gearing up for the Convention ASU non-communist rank and filers were far less motivated than their communist counterparts. As highly committed political activists, communists had always been generally more willing than non-communists, "to do the difficult and unrewarding . . . work of organization" in the ASU—writing flyers, attending meetings, arranging demonstrations. The communists' reward for this labor had been that they were traditionally overrepresented (relative to their numbers in the overall ASU membership) in ASU convention delegations and "important posts in the Union's district apparatus."[49] This problem of communist overrepresentation was compounded in the weeks before the 1939 convention because the international situation left the communists even more highly motivated politically than in the past. Communist ASUers believed that in the wake of the invasion of Finland, an anti-Soviet war hysteria was taking hold of America. Rallying to the Soviet side in what they saw as the communist motherland's hour of political crisis, communist ASUers worked themselves into a frenzy of activity. They organized intensively to ensure communist control of the convention. They were determined to prevent the ASU from attacking the U.S.S.R.

Such tireless organizing by the ASU's communists left informed observers convinced that it would be they rather than the non-communists who would dominate the Convention. James Wechsler, the former ASU leader and ex-communist, predicted in a penetrating *Nation* article that because the communists acted "as a unified bloc in the election of delegates," this "disciplined minority" would dominate the Convention, even though most of the ASU's membership was unsympathetic to the new communist line. The communists, Wechsler explained, were willing to make "limitless sacrifices to attend conventions when lukewarm members are content to celebrate Christmas."[50] In the socialist press, Daniel Bell offered an even more sarcastic, but equally prescient prediction:

> There is no doubt that the YCL will dominate the convention. Its machine is well-oiled, and all vital manipulative posts are in its hands. Joe Stalin's boys are well trained in these arts . . . . [This] communist control means destruction and decay, and the subordination of students' interests and needs to the propaganda tasks of the communist movement seeking to whitewash a bloody Russian totalitarian state.[51]

In their eagerness to control the delegation selection process, communist ASUers often behaved, as Bell implied, like machine politicians. They did not hesitate to use ASU rump meetings, packed with fellow communists, or to employ other underhanded tactics in order to elect pro-Soviet delegates. Here communist activists showed no concern about whether their campus delegations to the convention were actually representative of majority opinion in their chapters. The president of MIT's ASU chapter, for instance, wrote Lash on the eve of the Convention that because of such communist tactics "our pre-convention meeting was *not* representative."[52] An ASU chapter leader in New York reported that at her school the communists had abused democratic process brazenly and repeatedly ever since the invasion of Finland, when

> the N.Y. district called a "Leaders" meeting [the communist-dominated ASU gathering that defended the invasion of Finland]. Only two people [YCLers] from our chapter knew about this meeting, [and these two communists voted for the pro-invasion resolution, sponsored by YCL leader Bert Witt]. The elected delegate was not informed that there was to be a meeting and so was not there. At the next meeting of . . . [the school's] A.S.U. [the chapter] went on record as being against the Bert Witt resolution . . . . [The YCL leader in the chapter] then answered that in spite of this vote, if he were elected delegate, he would vote for it at the convention. It was then that the real "fun" began. Thursday there was an [ASU chapter] executive committee meeting. I asked for the a[d]dress. One of the exec. members refused point blank to give it to me. The girl in whose house it was held gave me the wrong a[d]dress. It was only by accident that I eventually got to the meeting . . . . At Monday's chapter meeting there were 28 people . . . [to vote on the] candidates for the delegate to the convention . . . . One girl abstained and the chairman cannot vote, so that the vote was 13–13 [between the communist and non-communist candidates. The YCL leader then] . . . came forward with three proxy votes [that elected the pro-Soviet candidate] . . . . Before the actual counting [of] the votes took place, no one knew that proxy voting could be used. In fact, never before in the history of . . . [the school's] ASU had proxy voting been used.[53]

With the deck stacked so heavily against them, Lash and his political allies at the ASU's 1939 convention in Madison never had a chance. The key moment in the convention came when Lash's bloc introduced a resolution which would have placed the ASU on record as opposed to the Soviet invasion of Finland. The convention rejected the resolution by a lop-sided margin of 322 to 49. The convention then refused requests from the floor that the ASU hold a general membership referendum on this resolution. The communist-dominated gathering whole-heartedly embraced the CP's isolationist "Yanks are not coming" foreign policy. The convention also chose YCLer Bert Witt to replace Lash as the ASU's executive secretary.[54]

Though the communists won all the key votes at Madison, this quickly proved to be a hollow victory. The convention's refusal to criticize the invasion of Finland did irreparable harm to the ASU's reputation. Former admirers of the ASU now felt that the organization had been converted into a puppet of the Communist Party, thereby losing all claim to speak for the campuses. The national Left-liberal press, which had welcomed the student movement in the early 1930s and consistently supported the ASU, expressed outrage over the outcome at Madison. *The Nation* termed the ASU Convention's decision on Finland "a precious New Year's gift to Martin Dies."[55] *The New Republic* fretted: "What has happened to the American Student Union?" Running a story suggesting that at Madison communist ASUers had all but destroyed the credibility of America's most influential student activist organization. *The New Republic* concluded: "the Communists can congratulate themselves that they have done maximum harm to the whole student movement."[56] Events on campus would quickly bear out this pessimistic conclusion.

As word made its way back to the campuses about the decisions at Madison, the ASU's reputation among undergraduates sank far and fast. The news was all the more devastating when it was carried back personally to the student body by disillusioned convention delegates. One such delegate, Vic Stone, a non-communist activist from Oberlin, reported to his campus that the Madison convention attested that a communist "minority [was] dominating the student movement . . . . By demonstrating blind faith in a . . . leader [Stalin] and in a political doctrine, the delegates made it practically impossible for the ASU to lead the free thinking students of America in our fight for peace and security."[57]

Reports came in from campuses across the nation that "since the convention all hell has broken loose in the [ASU] chapters." By early January key ASU chapters, including Harvard, Reed, and Wisconsin had begun to discuss disaffiliation, and this kind of talk was spreading. It was heard, for instance, at the University of Iowa, where Merle Miller, a convention delegate and columnist in his student newspaper, wrote that "here in Iowa City, . . . the life of the ASU ended . . . on the day the convention closed." He argued that student activists at his university could now be most "effective by withdrawing from the national organization and building a local, campus organization." Similar feelings of anger and disillusionment led Grinnell College delegate Lee McIntosh to conclude that "from the looks of things the ASU will dissolve and leave only a skeleton which should rightly be called the ACU [American Communists' Union]."[58]

Much as McIntosh predicted, the ASU declined rapidly following the fiasco in Madison. Not even the work of Lash's successors in the ASU's non-communist bloc—now calling themselves the Union's Liberal Caucus—could halt this deterioration. These non-communists, led by Alan Gottlieb of the Harvard ASU, hoped they could reverse the convention's decision on Finland by sending a referendum on the Soviet invasion to the ASU general membership. The referendum, however, could not save the ASU; it was too late. Referendum organizers found that most of their potential supporters felt that the ASU was a lost cause. Chad Walsh, for instance, an ASU activist from the University of Michigan, wrote to one of these organizers that

> the sincerity and conviction of your letter almost won me over, but not quite. I admire the fight you are making, but I'm afraid that by the time

> the organization has fought the question out it will be pretty well wrecked
> by internal dissension, and will be in no position to accomplish anything
> . . . . So my resignation still stands.[59]

Like Walsh, some two thirds of the ASU's members, in the months following the Madison convention, dropped out of the ASU—making a meaningful referendum impossible. The remaining, shrunken ASU chapters
were quickly losing their political influence on campus. The ASU was becoming, as Lash had warned, "a narrow sect" and a carbon copy of the
Young Communist League; it would prove incapable of orchestrating
anything approaching the successful campus mobilizations that the organization had led during the Popular Front era.[60]

     Unfortunately for the student movement, the communists learned
nothing from the ASU debacle. Though their apologetics for Soviet
aggression had left the ASU in shambles, communist activists repeated
those apologetics in the American Youth Congress. Communists worked
to impose upon the Youth Congress the same unpopular party line that
had wrecked the ASU. As in the ASU, communist Youth Congress leaders disregarded democratic process in their rush to align the movement
with Stalin's new foreign policy. Without consulting the Youth Congress'
constituent groups, communist and communist sympathizing AYC officers reversed the direction of the Youth Congress' peace policy; they used
AYC resources to promote strict United States neutrality, ignoring the
fact that at its last national Congress in July the AYC had endorsed Popular Front policies favoring American aid to victims of Nazi aggression.
Communists in the AYC also sought in the winter of 1940 to create the
public impression that the Youth Congress opposed United States aid to
Finland, even though the Youth Congress' rank and file had never approved this policy.[61]

     These communist machinations led to a political fiasco as damaging
to the Youth Congress as the Madison Convention had been to the ASU.
This was the Youth Congress Citizenship Institute, held in Washington,
D.C. on February 9–11, 1940. No single event did more to drive liberal
students away from the student movement than did the Citizenship Institute. The difference between the initial concept and actual convening of
this Institute convinced many liberal students that the Youth Congress
was nothing but a communist-front, run in a deceptive manner by Party
hacks who could not be trusted. The Institute had been planned—prior
to the Nazi-Soviet Pact—as a political and educational event in which the
Youth Congress would bring young men and women to Washington to
learn how government works, and to lobby for federal jobs and student
aid programs. This was supposed to be done in cooperation with the Roosevelt administration, which in the late 1930s had shared with the Youth
Congress a strong desire to prevent conservatives on Capitol Hill from
cutting New Deal social programs. But at the last minute communist organizers in the Youth Congress transformed the political character of the

Citizenship Institute, making its primary message not jobs but isolationism and opposition to United States aid for Finland. Since President Roosevelt had favored just such aid, this meant that the Institute was being changed from a pro- to an anti-administration event.[62]

This communist posturing over Finland not only alienated liberal students, but also turned the Citizenship Institute into a public relations disaster for the Youth Congress by provoking an open confrontation with President Roosevelt. The president had agreed to address a crowd of participants in the Citizenship Institute at the request of his wife. FDR, however, had become increasingly annoyed with the student movement's leadership ever since the ASU Convention had refused to criticize Stalin's invasion of Finland. At Hyde Park two weeks after that convention, Youth Congress leaders got their first hint of the president's anger about the movement's handling of the Finland issue. Here, in the presence of student movement leaders who were guests of his wife, FDR had "spoken scoffingly of the ASU and referred with pointed sarcasm to the 'young liberals' of the ASU." The president further signalled his mistrust of the movement's leadership on the eve of the Citizenship Institute, when he informed Youth Congress leaders he "did not want any AYC officials on [the White House] portico with him [when he addressed Institute activists and a national radio audience] or speaking over [the] air with him."[63] FDR's anger at the student movement's leaders surged when he learned that enroute to the Citizenship Institute, the New York Council of the Youth Congress had passed a resolution attacking his plan to provide Finland with economic aid.

The president vented this anger at the Youth Congress in his address to its Citizenship Institute on February 10. Roosevelt stunned the 4466 Youth Congress activists assembled on the White House lawn by delivering a tough speech, in which he denounced the Youth Congress' position on Finland. Referring to the Finland resolution passed by its New York branch, the president issued a "word of warning," to the Youth Congress not to pass resolutions on subjects "which you have not thought through and on which you cannot possibly have complete knowledge." The president dismissed as "unadulterated twaddle" the charge made by New York Youth Congress leaders that a United States loan to Finland represented "an attempt to force America into an imperialistic war." FDR argued "that the Soviet Union would because of this [loan] declare war on the United States is about the silliest thought that I ever heard advanced in the fifty-eight years of my life, and that we are going to war ourselves with the Soviet Union is an equally silly thought." Roosevelt defended the loan as an expression of the sympathy the American people felt for a "small republic" that had been invaded by the large Soviet state—"a dictatorship as absolute as any . . . in the world."[64]

The president understood that communists in the Youth Congress had played a leading role in shaping the organization's stance on Finland. In his speech to the Citizenship Institute, he therefore discussed the issue of Communism in the Youth Congress. FDR, in contrast to the Dies Committee, defended the "constitutional right" of radicals "to call yourselves communists and to peacefully and openly advocate certain ideals of theoretical communism." But he also lectured the young radicals on their responsibility as citizens to confine their political advocacy "to the methods prescribed by the Constitution of the United States," warning that "you have no American right by act or deed of any kind to subvert the government and the Constitution of this nation."[65]

If Roosevelt's words seemed designed to cast the Citizenship Institute and its communist leaders in a negative light, the young activists' response to the speech assisted him. The crowd not only booed the president, but did so in a selective fashion which contributed to the growing public impression that the Institute and its Youth Congress sponsors were communist-dominated. The young activists stood silently in the rain while FDR offered a provocative defense of the New Deal—a defense in which he cited economic statistics comparing America in 1932 and 1939, which actually proved nothing except that the Hoover Depression was even worse than the Roosevelt Depression. Nor did they react to FDR's curt dismissal of radical solutions to the Depression or to to his condescending warning not "to seek or expect Utopia overnight." Instead, the young communists raised their voices against the president only when he broached Soviet topics, booing him when he criticized the Youth Congress' position on Finland and when he termed the U.S.S.R. an absolute dictatorship. Though this jeering only served to strengthen FDR's hand by ensuring that the press would focus on the parts of his speech most unfavorable to the AYC, the young communists could not help themselves; for it was the Soviet Union which most concerned them and Roosevelt's criticisms of it which most offended them.[66]

This confontation with the president brought the Youth Congress and the student movement a flood of negative publicity. Before a national radio audience and the entire Washington press corps, FDR had humiliated the Youth Congress leadership and signalled the break between his administration and the student movement. It was this speech more than any of the dozens of sessions of the Citizenship Institute which captured headlines and shaped the national image of the gathering. *Life* magazine, for instance, reported that the "highlight" of the meeting of Youth Congress activists in Washington "was the spanking given them by President Roosevelt for their antagonism towards U.S. aid to Finland, for their partiality to the Soviet system." Leading columnists denounced the Youth Congress, charging that "either those kids are phonies or they're idiots." Youth Congress activists also drew criticism for booing the president, an act which was widely condemned as a sign of politicial immaturity and disrespect for the office of the president.[67]

The Citizenship Institute fiasco suggested just how much the new communist line impaired the student movement's ability to communicate its egalitarian ideals to the student body and the nation. At the Citizenship

Institute, static from the communists' propaganda on the Finland issue drowned out the young activists' criticism of the Roosevelt administration's social programs. The Institute had a strong case to make in Washington on behalf of jobs and aid for impoverished youths. The New Deal had been stalled ever since FDR's failed court packing scheme. Roosevelt had not managed to end the Depression. Some four millions youths remained unemployed. The Institute had gathered white and black youth from America's farms, factories, and campuses to dramatize these problems; it had the additional asset of John L. Lewis, the fiery labor leader who, having recently broken with FDR, delivered a passionate speech to the Institute indicting the New Deal's record on youth unemployment. But because of the the flap over Finland, it was Soviet foreign policy—and Youth Congress support of that policy—rather than Roosevelt's domestic policy which attracted public criticism in the wake of the Citizenship Institute.[68]

The Citizenship Institute further damaged the Youth Congress because it undermined the important relationship between the AYC's leaders and Eleanor Roosevelt. The First Lady had been the Youth Congress' most steadfast and influential ally in the Roosevelt administration. Mrs. Roosevelt had worked to ensure that key New Dealers, including the president, paid attention to the Youth Congress' concerns. She helped raise funds for the Youth Congress and played a powerful role in legitimating the Congress with both liberal students and the general public.[69]

Mrs. Roosevelt had proven an especially valuable ally to the Youth Congress and the ASU when those organizations came under attack by the Dies Committee in the fall of 1939. The First Lady loathed the Dies Committee and what she termed its "Gestapo methods." The committee had recklessly redbaited hundreds of innocent individuals—engaging in trial by headline and refusing to accord most of the accused any opportunity to respond to the charges. Indeed, within a few days of its founding in 1938, the Committee had already produced witnesses accusing 640 organizations, 483 newspapers, and 280 labor unions of being communistic. When the committee turned its guns on the young activists with whom she had worked ever since the World Youth Congress in 1938, Mrs. Roosevelt made a principled stand in defense of civil liberty. Here the First Lady stood up to the Dies Commitee, defending free speech and due process, and resisting congressional red probers more boldly than any other occupant of the White House in this century.[70]

The First Lady used her syndicated newspaper column and her personal prestige to fend off Dies' attack on the youth leaders in the fall of 1939. Her column praised the Youth Congress and ASU. She further demonstrated her solidarity with the subpoenaed youth leaders by accompanying them to the Dies Committee hearing and inviting them to the White House. Mrs. Roosevelt spoke to the press about the value of political tolerance and suggested that rather than seeking to ban radicalism, the nation should concern itself with eliminating the social problems that bred radicalism. The First Lady then published a column calling into question the fairness of the Dies proceedings, charging that the committee had not given the youth leaders sufficient time to prepare for the hearing. She criticized the way that J.B. Matthews, the Dies Committee's chief investigator, treated the youth leaders at the hearings: "His whole attitude, tone of voice and phraseology made one feel that a prisoner, considered guilty, was being tried at the bar." This assistance from the highly popular First Lady helped arouse sympathy for the youth leaders and support for their free speech rights; it prevented Dies from damaging the Youth Congress.[71]

Mrs. Roosevelt's defense of these young activists had been based not only upon political principle, but also personal friendship. Having cooperated with the Youth Congress on behalf of several causes—especially on their common goal of expanded federal aid to needy youth—the First Lady had befriended that organization's national leaders. She trusted them. Some of those leaders, however, would prove unworthy of that trust. The Youth Congress officers who were either in or close to the Communist Party, hid their Party ties from Mrs. Roosevelt. James Wechsler, himself a former communist comrade of these Youth Congress leaders, recalled this as one of the most shameful deceptions in the student movement's history. "Mrs. Roosevelt," Wechsler explained, "gave warm and generous help to the Youth Congress in the years preceding the debacle of 1939. The communists who held strategic posts in it responded to her benevolence by lying to her about themselves and seeming to enjoy the hoax."[72]

This deception initially went undetected by Mrs. Roosevelt. As the Dies Committee accusations began, she met with Youth Congress officers at the White House and

> told them that since I was actively helping them, I must know exactly where they stood politically. . . . I told the young people in the group that if any of them were communists I would quite understand, for I felt they had grown up at a time of such difficulty as to explain their being attracted to almost any ideas that promised them better conditions. However, I felt it essential that I should know the truth. If we were going to work together, I must know where we really agreed and where we differed. I asked each one in turn to tell me honestly what he believed. In every case they said they had no connection with the communists, had never belonged to any communist organizations, and had no interest in communist ideas. I decided to accept their word . . .[73]

Having been so misled, Mrs. Roosevelt unknowingly became a party to this political masquerade of the communists and communist sympathizers in the Youth Congress' leadership. She made front page news by rebutting the Dies Committee witnesses who charged that Youth Congress leaders Joseph Cadden and William Hinckley were part of a communist delegation which had dined with her. Mrs. Roosevelt told the *New York*

Times that Cadden and Hinckley, with whom she was "well acquainted," had no ties with the Communist Party. The First Lady had no idea at the time that her two young friends had misled her. She had admired them for their youthful idealism and social consciousness and saw no reason to doubt their honesty. Mrs. Roosevelt's boldness in challenging Dies, then, was coupled with a naiveté in trusting these Youth Congress leaders.[74]

These Youth Congress leaders kept Mrs. Roosevelt in the dark about their Party loyalty apparently because this made it easier for them to influence her decisions regarding the student movement. By concealing their communist ties, they could give the First Lady the impression that they were non-partisan and objective in advising her about the movement—when in fact they were profoundly partisan. The initial effectiveness of this ruse was evident in the discussions between Mrs. Roosevelt and these Youth Congress leaders regarding the 1939 ASU Convention. They told her that the convention's refusal to criticize the Soviet invasion of Finland derived not from communist domination of that convention, but from "fear of war" on the part of "liberal" delegates and the American student body. Unaware that she was hearing a biased communist interpretation of the convention, Mrs. Roosevelt trusted the assessment of her young friends. The First Lady proceeded to echo this interpretation of the ASU Convention in her newspaper column, implying that the press attacks on the ASU Convention over the Finland issue were unjustified. The ASU's communist-dominated leadership liked the column so much that they included it in their publication of the convention's proceedings. This support from the First Lady was, of course, a great asset, and communist Youth Congress leaders were unwilling to jeopardize this by disclosing to her their Party affiliations.[75]

It was not until the Citizenship Institute fiasco that Mrs. Roosevelt began to realize that some of her friends in the Youth Congress leadership had deceived her. The Institute exposed the First Lady to the shabby side of the Old Left political style. Mrs. Roosevelt had been misled by the Youth Congress' leaders concerning the purposes of the Citizenship Institute. They had led her to believe that the Insititute would be a pro-administration event, as it had been originally planned the previous summer. Thus Mrs. Roosevelt had gone all out to assist the Institute, doing everything from finding free housing for participants to seeing to it that high ranking officials, including the attorney general and the president himself, addressed the gathering. Though the Youth Congress' communist-dominated leadership had spent the weeks preceeding the Institute preparing to turn the event into an anti-administration pilgrimage, most Youth Congress leaders tried to keep the First Lady unaware of this change.[76]

This deception left Mrs. Roosevelt in the uncomfortable position of playing hostess to a political event hostile to her husband. And if this was not humilating enough, the First Lady, who addressed the Citizenship Institute the day after her husband, was booed when she implied that the Youth Congress' position on Finland reflected a poor understanding of the world situation. These events shook Mrs. Roosevelt's faith in the Youth Congress leadership and opened her eyes to the problem of communist domination of this organization; they led her first to loosen and then break all her ties to the Youth Congress. The loss of Mrs. Roosevelt's support would prove extremely costly to the Youth Congress. Without her, the Youth Congress lacked a means of gaining access to high ranking administration officials. Having been attacked by the president and abandoned by the First Lady, the Youth Congress lost the support of leading liberals both in the capital and on campus.[77]

The decline of the Youth Congress was a terrible blow to the student movement because the Congress had played such a critical role in giving the movement a presence and youth lobby in Washington. The Congress was increasingly perceived as a narrow communist sect rather than as a broadly based organization and voice of young America. The crisis in the Youth Congress was all the more devastating to the student movement because of its timing. Just as the ASU was losing its ability to rally students, the Youth Congress lost its influence with the Roosevelt administration. With the ASU moribund and the Youth Congress failing, the student movement sank into a crisis which would prove irreversible.

Although the Youth Congress' crisis began more dramatically than that of the ASU—because it came in the form of an open confrontation with the president and First Lady in Washington—the decline of both organizations emanated from the same source. That source was the Russia-centered mind-set of the Youth Congress' and ASU's communist leaders during the 1939–1940 academic year. "The problem for the YCLer . . . was," as Lash noted in his diary, "that on one side he saw the status quo and on the other the USSR."[78] These young radicals so revered the Soviet Union as the international communist vanguard and inspiration for progressive social change that they elevated Soviet interests over those of the American student movement. Communist activists were determined to shackle the student movement to Stalin's increasingly unpopular foreign policy, even if this meant shrinking or destroying that movement and its key organizations. From their perspective it was better to have no movement at all than to have one which criticized Stalin.

This communist willingness to subordinate the student movement's interests to those of the U.S.S.R. had been evident ever since the ASU's 1939 Fall Planning Conference. Here YCL leader Gil Green had told a caucus of communist ASUers that "faith in the [Communist] Party's position on the [Nazi-Soviet] Pact means that party people will fight to establish that position in ASU *irrespective of [the] consequences for [the] ASU*." (emphasis added).[79] This attitude had also been articulated by communist ASUers as they pushed to mobilize the student movement against an American loan to Finland. Thelma Grafstein reported that as she tried to convince her ASU chapter in New York to condemn the Soviet invasion of Finland, a communist ASUer told her that "rather than see that (meaning my) program adopted, she'd rather not see any A.S.U. on the campus." She was shocked to find that "this sentiment was expressed by some other [communist] A.S.U.ers," and that when she pointed out the impossibility of building "a united progressive student movement on the" basis of the new CP line on Finland, "they answered 'I don't give a damn about the A.S.U.' "[80]

These fights within the student movement during the 1939–40 academic year revealed that though communists had labored long and hard to build the ASU and the Youth Congress, their loyalty to those organizations was quite limited. Lash came to this painful realization as he observed the communists' attempt to sabotage the ASU national office following the Nazi-Soviet Pact. Communists in the ASU had, in Lash's words, displayed a "dual loyalty," to the student movement and the Communist Party: that "when the loyalty to the ASU conflicts with the loyalty to the YCL, the former is disregarded . . . . Their loyalty . . . [is] first and foremost to the YCL, even when they are leaders of the ASU."[81]

This problem of dual loyalty deeply troubled Lash as his tenure as ASU executive secretary drew to a close. Although before the Dies Committee Lash had defended the right of communists to participate in the student movement's leadership, privately he began to have doubts. Lash came to suspect that the divided loyalty of the communists left them unfit to lead a democratic protest movement. The behavior of communist ASU national staffers after the Pact led Lash to see that they had no qualms about defying policy decisions made by the ASU's membership and elected leadership when these conflicted with YCL policy. They would "advance the communist line, irrespective of the" decisions made democratically by ASU "conventions, and other organizational bodies that determine policy." This threatened to yield political disaster, Lash concluded, because of the impossibility of maintaining "a broad student movement supported by the masses of American students if the YCL has a veto power over our policy, and that veto places the Soviet Union beyond criticism."[82]

It may seem odd that it took Popular Front liberals so long to begin grappling with the problems posed by communist participation in the student movement's leadership. But there was a good reason for this. These problems only took center stage in the eleventh hour of the ASU's life because they did not start to damage the student movement until this very late point in its history. It was, in fact, because communists had served the student movement so faithfully prior to the Nazi-Soviet Pact that their behavior after that Pact came as such a shock to many non-communists in the movement. After years of unity and cooperation with communists, it was difficult to believe that they would sabotage a student movement that they had been so instrumental in creating.

The Popular Front experience had left liberals in the student movement ill prepared to deal with communist machinations in the post-Pact era. That experience had rendered them too trusting of the communists. This trust had evolved because communists and Popular Front liberals in the student movement from 1935 to August 1939 had become so closely

aligned in promoting anti-fascism and social reform. The differences between these groups had become submerged. Communists in this era worked
hard to promote this process of submergence by sounding more like liberals than radicals—supporting FDR and the New Deal with great enthusiasm.[83]

The prospect of the YCL working as a disciplined faction to disrupt
the ASU had also seemed remote in the Popular Front period. At this
time, communists—as part of their strategy for promoting unity—were,
as Lash put it, discussing "in their publications . . . the abolition of fractions in mass organizations such as the ASU." Indeed, Lash claims that at
the height of the Popular Front era, "so great was the agreement within
the ASU that the communists dropped their work as an organized group
within the ASU." There had seemed little reason to ponder the problem
of communist "dual loyalty." The notion that communist ASUers would
work to reverse the ASU's anti-fascist policies would also have seemed far-
fetched in the mid-1930s, when communists stood in the vanguard of
international anti-fascism, risking their lives fighting against fascists on
the battlefields of Spain.[84] Given their background in this happier period
of the student movement, then, non-communists can hardly be blamed
for being naive about their communist allies.

The shock which Lash and his supporters felt as they confronted
communist machinations following the Pact underscores the startling discontinuity in communist behavior. Through most of the Depression decade communist students had acted as creative and constructive political
organizers. By responding to the needs, anxieties and idealism of a generation troubled by Depression, war and fascism, young communists had
helped build the first mass student movement in American history. The
movement was at its best in the pre-Pact years as communists pioneered
tactics contrary to the sectarianism and proletarianism which had weakened the adult Left. Their effective student mobilizations against war and
fascism proved that liberals and radicals could work together, and that
the university could be as much a source of progressive activism as the
factory. But the behavior of communist students after the Nazi-Soviet Pact
revealed that their virtues as political organizers were transient; they could
only endure so long as the interests of Soviet foreign policy and American
student politics coincided. When the two interests clashed in 1939, communist students began to act in a sectarian fashion, dedicated not to sustaining a broadly based student movement but rather to serving the narrow organizational interests of the YCL and the U.S.S.R. Blinded by their
loyalty to the Sovet Union, the communists failed to see the disastrous
consequences of forcing the movement's key organizations to defend a
Soviet deal with Hitler and invasion of Finland that most students found
indefensible.[85]

The ASU and Youth Congress could not long endure once student
disllusionment with the communists' flip-flops on foreign policy, their
abandonment of anti-fascism, and their defense of Soviet aggression, had

set in. But although the largest wounds of the ASU and Youth Congress were self-inflicted, the decline of both organizations was accelerated by external repression. Rightwingers well understood that the Nazi-Soviet Pact had alienated American communists from liberals and left these radicals unpopular and vulnerable to attack. Seizing the moment, conservatives along with some liberal anti-communists launched a series of legislative red probes, loyalty oath campaigns, and moves to restrict free speech rights for communists—which threatened to evolve into a national red scare.[86]

On campus the relatively free political space that had been created by the ASU during the Popular Front began to constrict. Free speech violations became more common, beginning with the disruption of Communist Party leader Earl Browder's campus tour in the fall of 1939. The ban began at Harvard. The Conant administration claimed that Browder's indictment for a passport violation raised the possibility that he was a lawbreaker and therefore unqualified to speak at Harvard. Critics pointed out that the ban was unprecedented, and that in 1855 Harvard had opened its doors to an abolitionist speaker under indictment for violating the Fugitive Slave Act. But the ban stood; it was emulated by such other institutions as Oberlin College, Brooklyn College, and the University of Chicago. The weakened ASU could not mobilize sufficient support to win any of these free speech fights.[87]

The ASU's decline became even more evident in April 1940, the time of the annual student strike against war. The ASU's fall in membership meant that the organization had far fewer strike organizers than in previous years. Due to the ASU's defense of Soviet aggression, the YCAW and other anti-war organizations—though sharing with the ASU support of an isolationist foreign policy for the United States—denied that the ASU was a genuine peace group and refused to cooperate with the communist-led organization in the strike. Instead, the YCAW held its own isolationist strike rallies. If this split in the isolationist camp weakened the strike, so did international events. At the time of the strike, news had just come in of the Nazi invasion of Norway and Denmark. This rendered many students more fearful of fascist aggression and unreceptive to an ASU which had abandoned the idea of a Popular Front against fascism. Thus even at some of the ASU's traditional strongholds, the strike—featuring the CP's "Yanks are not coming" slogan—was the smallest since the first campus peace strike of 1934. At Columbia University, where as many as three thousand students had turned out for past strikes, the student newspaper noted that for the 1940 walkout "a disappointing crowd of less than a thousand" rallied against war. Brooklyn College's strike drew less than half the students than had attended strike rallies during the Popular Front years. At Berkeley the student movement was in such disarray that for the first time in years no strike rally was held.[88] These strike results left no doubt that the ASU had lost its ability to lead the student movement effectively. Though once the leader of a mass Popular Front movement on campus, the ASU was deteriorating into an unpopular sect.

II

The loss of the ASU's leadership wounded but did not immediately kill the anti-war movement on campus. Although nationally the student protests against war in 1940 mobilized far fewer students than they had in the 1930s, these protests did continue. Indeed, despite their much less impressive size, the student anti-war actions of 1940 attracted almost as much attention from the press and politicians as had their counterparts during the previous decade. This was because with the war crisis growing more acute and the nation wrapped up in its great debate about United States intervention, campus opinion took on a whole new importance. Everyone, it seemed, wanted to know how the young men who might soon have to fight the coming war felt about it. Interventionists in 1940 repeatedly published articles in the press expressing alarm that isolationism was running rampant among college youth.[89]

This concern about collegiate isolationism arose in response to the new phase which the student movement entered with its peace strike of 1940. That strike differed from its Popular Front predecessors not only in size, but in content. During the peace strikes of the late 1930s, ASUers had given voice to anti-isolationist sentiment and showed the nation that students cared passionately about stopping fascism. But with the dying ASU now in the isolationist camp and no other national student organization ready to carry on the pro-Allies work that the ASU had abandoned, the peace strike of 1940 was largely an isolationist event. For the moment at least, isolationism had no organized national student competition on American college campuses. This monopoly would prove temporary; but it enabled isolationists to dominate student protest activity while it lasted.

President Roosevelt was among the first to learn about this increased prominence of collegiate isolationism. During the Nazi invasion of the Low Countries in May 1940, FDR received petitions signed by 1486 Yale students urging that the United States "stay out of the European war . . . give no credits, supplies, or manpower but should direct its effort toward making democracy safe at home." The President received similar petitions from Harvard, Dartmouth, and Cornell students.[90] Roosevelt, who by now was moving toward preparedness and aid for the Allies, found such student sentiment disturbing. In fact, as Interior Secretary Harold Ickes noted in his diary, the President, after making an anti-isolationist speech in May 1940, told the Cabinet he "was struck by the fact that most of" the telegrams critical of his speech

> came from youth organizations and college students. This is most significant and alarming. Not only for what they said but what they implied, the senders of these telegrams made it clear that they were more interested in jobs than in wars that might make a few people richer but many people poorer.[91]

The persistence of collegiate isolationism was a product of both fear and disillusionment. The fear was, of course, fear of war—fueled by the Nazi military advances and a sinking feeling that the United States was moving inexorably toward war. Several sources contributed to the disillusionment. Disdain for World War I remained strong among undergraduates. A poll of Columbia students in the spring of 1940 revealed that by an almost five to one margin they saw United States entry into war in 1917 as "the result of propaganda and selfish interests"; and most thought that if the United States went to war again its motivation would be equally sordid.[92] By 1940, moreover, new sources of disillusionment had been added to this old one. The Allies had stood by while Spain fell to fascism; Chamberlain had bowed to Hitler at Munich; the Soviets, who had championed an international movement for collective security against fascism had abandoned that cause by signing their pact with Hitler. All of this left a vocal segment of the student population feeling cynical about the Allies and their anti-fascist slogans. Reflecting this mind-set, the editor of Vassar College's student newspaper explained her reason for moving from collective security to isolationism.

> Hitler's barbarism and aggression have always filled us with revulsion. We urged, before it was too late, a policy of collective security for peace. Chamberlain and Daladier, however, preferred "appeasement;" they fattened the Nazi government on Spain and Austria and Czechoslavakia . . . . [War did not begin until] Chamberlain and Daladier saw their imperial interests at stake in the fight of the Poles and came in. We, in the United States can see the dirty hands on both sides and must not be drawn in.[93]

With neither the ASU nor any other national student group disposed to combat such isolationism, that task in the spring of 1940 fell out of student hands. The most prominent foes of collegiate isolationism in this period were college and university presidents and faculty. When Yale students sent their isolationist petition to FDR in May, they drew a sharp public rebuke from Arnold Whitridge, Yale English professor and ardent interventionist. Whitridge told the *New York Times* that the student petition represented "muddled thinking. If we wish to stay out of war . . . we must do everything possible to furnish such aid to the Allies as will enable them to win the war." Dartmouth's president Ernest Hopkins offered an even more scalding rebuke to the signers of the isolationist petition at his college, telling a Dartmouth student assembly that there "was basis for questioning the extent that college breeds discriminating intelligence when hundreds of men sign petitions to the president that they see nothing of a struggle against the forces of evil." Hopkins imputed cowardice to isolationist students, whom he ridiculed for fearing to offend "the protaganists of force and brutality, race extinction and mass murder." A similar approach was taken at Harvard by Professor Roger Merriman, who derided isolationist students as "shrimps." FDR, who was grateful for this stance by his old Harvard teacher, wrote Merriman in May 1940 agreeing that "the best thing for the moment is to call them shrimps publicly and privately . . . . Most of them will get in line, if things should become worse."[94]

Such conflicts over collegiate isolationism introduced a new generational element into American student politics. Isolationist students, finding that their harshest critics were their elders, began to discuss the foreign policy debate as a clash of young and old. "The old men do the talking, but the young men do the fighting," UCLA's *Daily Bruin* complained in the spring of 1940. Another isolationist student editor denounced Nicholas Murray Butler, Columbia's interventionist president, as "one of a few old men who are urging youth to war. We think it is time we urged the old men to go put on their uniforms." At the University of Kansas, an interventionist professor who had questioned the courage of isolationist students was told by the *Daily Kansan* that "you'd be afraid yourself if you weren't past the shooting age . . . . Anyone who isn't afraid of getting blown to bits is on the red side of the psychological ledger." At Dartmouth, where angry exchanges between interventionist faculty and isolationist students had filled the campus press all year, the student newspaper ran a bitter editorial, "Fathers and Sons," accusing their professorial elders of hypocrisy: "The same teachers who told us we should avoid involvement in a European war at any cost are now telling us that we are cowards or pro-Nazis because we listened to what they taught us . . ."[95]

This generational conflict at times spilled off campus, pitting isolationist students against alumni of their colleges who had fought in the First World War. One of the most emotional of these clashes occurred at Harvard in May 1940; it began when the *Harvard Crimson* published a petition signed by hundreds of students, pledging their determination "never under any circumstances to follow in the footsteps of the students of 1917." The petition implied that the students who served in the First World War had been duped by President Wilson's democratic rhetoric into fighting an imperialist war. This elicited an angry response from 35 members of Harvard's class of 1917, whose joint letter to the *Crimson* denied that they had been misled by Wilson or that the war had been imperialistic. These alumni called upon students to abandon isolationism and get prepared for war; they argued that the new generation of college youth had an "even bigger job to do" for the defense of democracy than had the class of 1917.[96]

Such appeals from alumni did not go over well with Harvard's isolationists. This became evident during the 1940 commencement season. At the Harvard class day ceremonies, David Sigourney, another of Harvard's World War I veterans, delivered a passionate interventionist speech, and told the graduates "we would be proud to see our boys go out there and do the job again." As Sigourney went on with his speech "each sentence was met with a round of boos and hisses, making it almost impossible to hear the speaker. There were cries of 'throw him out.' Several times he pleaded for consideration."[97]

With the Nazis on the march in Europe, it was natural for interventionists to be upset when they encountered such isolationist sentiment among students, particularly students of their alma maters. The international tensions of the time fed fears—and criticism, expressed even by such usually astute observers as Archibald MacLeish—that the younger generation was being lost to isolationism.[98] But most of those who so criticized youth, amidst the hothouse political atmosphere of America in the spring of 1940, overreacted. The tensions of the moment, which made these critics so sensitive to any expression of isolationism, led them to exaggerate the depth of isolationism among youth. None of these critics seemed to notice, for instance, that on most college campuses the student peace strike of 1940 had signalled isolationist weakness rather than strength—that in comparison to prior student peace strikes the 1940 walkout was a small affair. Nor did they notice the national polls that showed students endorsing several key positions at odds with isolationist orthodoxy, including support for FDR's cash and carry policy, lifting the arms embargo, and offering aid to the Allies short of war.[99] Students in the spring of 1940 still wanted the United States to stay out of war, but so did most Americans. The difference was only one of degree. Collegians, knowing the lives of their generation hung in the balance, were especially exuberant in their anti-war expressions and especially reluctant to substitute United States troops for less costly forms of aid to the Allies.

The limits of collegiate isolationism were also evident on the issues of conscription and preparedness. Over the summer of 1940 both the YCAW and the Youth Congress sought to rally the nation's youth against the Burke-Wadsworth conscription bill. These Left-led isolationist groups depicted conscription as a loathsome means of militarizing youth and dragging America into war. Even allowing for the fact that such summertime youth mobilizations are difficult for student groups (because school is out of session), the campaign swayed few students. The largest youth rally of this anti-draft campaign, a YCAW event featuring such prominent speakers as Norman Thomas and Senators Nye, Wheeler, and Holt—drew barely a thousand people.[100] The Burke-Wadsworth amendment made its way through Congress and in September established America's first peacetime draft.

Passage of the conscription act did not, however, bring a surrender on the part of its young isolationist critics. Now that classes were back in session, the YCAW hoped it would be better able to generate student protest against the draft. The YCAW sought to launch a large national student protest urging repeal of the new draft law. The mobilization was planned as a national "Day of Mourning," scheduled to occur on October 16, 1940, the day that thousands of students—in accord with the new law—would be registering for the draft. But on almost every campus in the nation this anti-draft mobilization failed. Only a handful of campuses had any demonstration at all, and even here participants usually numbered in the dozens rather than the hundreds or thousands. The anti-draft event was such an embarrassing failure that the YCAW newsletter, after having headlined the preparations for this "Day of Mourning" in its October issue, did not even mention the mobilization in its November issue.[101]

The anti-conscription demonstration failed because most students did not share the YCAW's views on either the draft or the entire issue of preparedness. National student polls dating back to December 1939 showed that over 70 percent of the student body favored increases in American armaments and extension of the United States military. The polls in 1940 and 1941 also reflected majority student support for conscription. At Oberlin, for instance. some 70 percent of the student body endorsed the new draft law. The vast gulf between this pro-preparedness majority and the YCAW was one of the major reasons why this isolationist organization remained so small—with a student membership never exceeding a thousand.[102]

The student body's support for the draft and military preparedness did not, however, signal a case of war fever on campus. Students still opposed war, but they also wanted America to be prepared if such a war was forced upon the nation. The *Michigan Daily* explained that students supported "conscription as a weapon only for defense," and hoped that the president could "abandon conscription as soon as America's safety permits." Ohio State's student paper termed conscription "distasteful" yet "necessary for defense," and urged that it only be maintained as a temporary emergency measure. "A *permanent* system of drafting young men who have a right to live their own lives while their nation is at peace violates both democratic privilege and sound reasoning."[103] This restrained support of the draft was reflected in collegiate commentary on the issue of exemptions. There was almost universal endorsement on campus for draft deferrals to allow undergraduates to complete their studies—so that while supporting the draft in principle, few in the 1940–41 academic year were eager for service. Linking this lack of military enthusiasm to economics, one Ohio State student explained that the class of '41 was in the

> same situation as the college graduates of 1929, the year of the depression. Then there were no jobs available and the unlucky graduates were called the "lost generation." Our own graduates who have jobs awaiting them but can't take advantage of them because of the draft law, could very aptly be termed the "lost generation" also for their situation is just about as discouraging.[104]

The poor performance of the YCAW in the October conscription mobilization revealed that the student Left had fallen to a new low in its influence on most campuses. Having in the past academic year suffered the decline of the ASU and the loss of its ability to mobilize a majority of students, the Left—including its non-communist segment represented by the YCAW—was now losing its ability to dominate even the isolationist forces on campus. The tone of collegiate isolationism, as the conscription issue made clear, was now being set by more conservative anti-interventionists. These were students with a "Fortress America" position, who preached that the United States should stay out of the war overseas but build an impregnable home defense force so that the United States could fend off any threat to its hemisphere. The main organizational representative of this new tendency was the America First Committee. And though this organization's focus would be off campus, its roots sprang from East Coast collegiate isolationism. A group of Yale isolationists headed by Kingman Brewster, editor of the *Yale Daily News* (and future Yale president), and several law students at New Haven initiated the formation of America First in the fall of 1940.[105]

The fall of 1940 also witnessed a continuation of the clashes between isolationist students and their interventionist elders. The opening salvo came just as classes began with the appearance of "Where Do You Stand? An Open Letter to American Undergraduates," in *Atlantic Monthly*, in which Yale Professor Arnold Whitridge accused isolationist students of "hysterical timidity." The Yale professor's article quickly drew a polemical response, "We Stand Here," by Kingman Brewster and *Harvard Crimson* editor Spencer Klaw, which also appeared in the *Atlantic*. Brewster and Klaw held that it was unfair for interventionists to single collegians out for special condemnation when a majority of all Americans opposed war; they offered the standard America First arguments that the United States was not ready for a European war and that such a crusade would constitute "a transoceanic war of aggression with no end in sight"—which would scuttle "democracy and freedom" in America. Americans must "take our stand here on this side of the Atlantic . . . because at least it offers a chance for the maintenance of all the things we care about in America, while war abroad would mean their certain extinction."[106]

At Harvard this intergenerational clash moved from polemic to theater. For almost a year Harvard's isolationist students had been feuding with President James Conant, one of the nation's most vocal interventionists. The *Harvard Crimson* found it appalling that Conant's agitation was helping to bring America closer to a war which "may soon send to destruction the lives" of his own students. The *Lampoon* and the *Crimson*—both dominated by isolationists—used the occasion of the 1940 Harvard-Yale football game to take a swipe at Conant, burlesquing Harvard's president in the halftime show at the Yale Bowl.

> A student with a big "1941" on his back lay down on the field reading a book when a figure appeared in cap, gown and mortarboard and wearing the sign "Conant." He began to annoy the student by parading around him with a wooden bayoneted rifle. After a short interval, the

student reluctantly took the gun but then turned to prodding "Conant" with the bayonet and chasing him around the field. Finally "Conant" was presented with a large retort and removed from the scene on a cart, presumably back to the laboratory.[107]

Before the fall semester of 1940 was over, however, isolationist students would have more to contend with than middle aged critics. The isolationist monopoly on student organizing came to an end. Inspired by England's courage in the Battle of Britain and worried by the fall of France, interventionist students on scores of campuses began to organize. Joseph Lash, who participated in this anti-isolationist resurgence, saw it as "a heartening sign" that the "condition of shell shock or paralysis among liberal young people" that had lasted for "a long time after the Nazi-Soviet Pact" was finally ending.[108] As Lash's words suggest, the timing of this anti-isolationist resurgence was in part linked to organizational factors. Lash and other foes of isolationism had been tied down the previous year first by the futile battle to free the ASU and Youth Congress of communist domination, and then by the demoralization and disorganization which followed the failure of those efforts. Now, however, with their own organizations, they were able to focus on the task of influencing the campuses.

International events also made the fall of 1940 a good moment for such an anti-isolationist offensive. The German conquests the previous spring had demonstrated that America could no longer hope that a stalemate in Europe would curb Nazi aggression. And the Battle of Britain, waged over the summer, had suggested that with the English determined to fight on, it might be possible for the United States—through aid to Britain—to play a role in stopping Hitler without actually entering the war. This was the time of Winston Churchill's stirring calls for an unending fight against Hitler; and simultaneously came Edward R. Murrow's moving radio broadcasts from London documenting the brutal Nazi bombings of civilians.[109] Such events enabled student foes of isolationism to reconstruct some of the anti-fascist idealism which had been so powerful and appealing to collegians during the Popular Front era.

Lacking any central organization—like the old ASU—to mobilize anti-isolationist sentiment, a variety of different student groups emerged over the fall semester. By December, twenty college chapters of William Allen White's Committee to Defend America by Aiding the Allies were functioning. Agnes Reynolds, a former ASU leader, presided over the creation of Student Defenders of Democracy, a group urging war preparations and aid to Britain. This group attracted endorsements from student leaders on more than 100 campuses. Joseph Lash took over the leadership of the International Student Service (ISS), and converted it from a refugee aid group into an aid the Allies organization. The ISS managed to sponsor some high profile events for the interventionist cause, thanks in part to the fund raising, contacts, and sponsorship of Eleanor Roosevelt, who was by now a good friend of Lash's. The ISS also attracted the National Student Federation, the organization of American student governments, as an affiliate, after the NSF broke with the isolationist and communist-dominated American Youth Congress.[110]

This return of anti-isolationist activism put an end to the myth of invulnerable collegiate isolationism. The stream of hysterical articles bemoaning the cowardice of youth soon diminished. As the academic year progressed, opinion polls found undergraduate isolationism declining. Students proved increasingly willing to back FDR's escalating efforts to aid England. Nationally, student endorsement of the president's Lend-Lease plan came in at an overwhelming 67 percent. At Berkeley, which in the fall had organized the only sizable anti-draft rally in the nation, a poll in February 1941 found the isolationist position opposing aid to Britain had attracted the support of only a miniscule 6.8 percent of the student body.[111]

Although their fortunes were clearly dwindling, isolationists remained a vocal group on campus. Isolationism still had on its side, for instance, much of the college press. This reflected the fact that student editors—most of whom were chosen on an annual basis—had been elected the past spring, during the high tide of collegiate isolationism in this decade. The American Youth Congress, though steadily losing affiliates and strength, could still manage to bring a few thousand students to Washington to protest against Lend-Lease in February 1941. Isolationists in the 1940–1941 academic year could also take some solace in the continuing absence of war fever on campus. Most students—even the majority of the organizers urging expanded aid to Britain—still wanted the United States to avoid going to war. Indeed, one of the main arguments anti-isolationist students used for supporting aid to Britain was that such aid might stop the Nazis and make American entry into the war unnecessary.[112]

The last national campus mobilization effort on the part of Depression era leftists and isolationists came with the eighth annual student strike against war in April 1941. Since student support for Lend-Lease and material aid to Great Britain was so overwhelming, the isolationist strike organizers avoided that whole issue. Instead, they focused on the more volatile issue of the use of armed American convoys for supply ships bound for Britain—which risked involving Americans in hostilities with the German Navy. The convoy issue seemed promising; it evoked memories of the U-boat attacks that had helped to lead the United States into World War I and might appeal to the widespread student desire to avoid a shooting war.[113]

Not even the convoy issue, however, could revitalize collegiate isolationism. Isolationist strike rallies on most campuses were the smallest since the birth of the student movement. At Yale even the prominent speaker, Senator Nye—appearing at a YCAW sponsored strike rally—could not draw an impressive crowd. Only 600 Yale students turned out to hear him, a stark contrast to the 3000 who had packed Woolsey Hall to hear

Lindbergh the previous fall. Nor would communist sponsored rallies fare any better. The communists were in no position to orchestrate an effective national strike effort. The ASU was at this point a virtual paper organization on most campuses outside New York City. The communists therefore shifted responsibility for the strike to the Youth Congress. Since the Youth Congress was a federation of affiliated groups rather than a membership organization, it had been able to stay active a bit longer than the ASU. But the Youth Congress too was dying; it had been losing affiliates ever since the Nazi-Soviet Pact and fared poorly in the strike. At UCLA, for instance, a Youth Congress led strike rally drew only 250 students, the smallest strike in years. At Vassar, once the most active womens' college in the student movement, the Youth Congress proved unable to organize any rally.[114]

Even in New York, long the capital city of American student activism, the anti-interventionist strike mobilizations went poorly. The Youth Congress organized nothing at Hunter College, and the YCAW rally there turned out only a dozen students. The group of 500 to 800 students who turned out at Columbia University was more substantial, but slim in comparison to strikes in the previous decade. On only one campus in the entire city, CCNY, were the anti-interventionists able to draw a crowd of more than a thousand. But even this CCNY rally, attended by some 2500 students, was not purely an anti-interventionist event; it was actually more of a free speech demonstration, in which students rallied to hear Morris Schappes, one of the communist instructors at the College, who had been fired as a consequence of the Rapp-Coudert red probe. That probe had hounded communist students as well as faculty, generating a repressive atmosphere which hampered Youth Congress activism; it contributed to the organization's poor showing in the strike efforts at most of the city's campuses.[115]

Making matters worse for the strike's organizers was the student opposition they encountered. Unlike the 1940 walkout, the 1941 anti-war strike found anti-isolationist students organized and vocal. The interventionist Student Defenders of Democracy used the strike day as the occasion to launch a national student petition drive in support of convoys. The SDD proved most effective at Brooklyn College. Here, with the support of the campus administration, the SDD organized a strike day rally endorsing convoys, which drew some 2000 students. This rally was about five times the size of the anti-convoy rally sponsored by Brooklyn's Youth Congress organizers.[116] ISS leader Joseph Lash was also vocal in denouncing strike agitation against convoys. Anti-isolationist activists on campus made use of literature distributed by Lash and the ISS to oppose isolationist strike events. At Dartmouth, for instance, the student newspaper greeted strike day speaker, New Hampshire's Senator Charles Tobey— sponsor of a Congressional resolution against convoys—by lambasting him and his student supporters: "We don't like the strike, any little bit of it," the *Dartmouth* explained in its strike day editorial "Not on Strike."

> The reason is simple . . . . More than we're opposed to war, we're opposed to the domination of the world by Fascism . . . . Of the "peace strike" Joseph P. Lash, a former ASU member and originator of the "strike" plan in the early 1930s said last week: "No sophistry can mitigate the basic fact that to strike against American aid to England, Greece, Yugoslavia, is to help a victory for Hitler . . . . To oppose the Lend Lease policy, to oppose the transfer of destroyers, to oppose every policy this government has undertaken against Hitler is to betray the youth of Europe."[117]

Weak as the strike had been, even this level of anti-war activism would not be matched the following semester. Isolationist demonstrations were almost unheard of during the first few months of the fall 1941 semester—a time when naval conflicts between the United States and Germany were heating up in the north Atlantic and the country geared up for war. Student support for supplying the allies against Hitler and Japan soared to 93 percent by early November. Isolationism also lost its last major stronghold on campus: the student press. President Conant would no longer have to worry about attacks from the *Crimson;* its editors were as opposed to isolationism as he. The *Yale Daily News,* which had helped give birth to America First, elected an interventionist editor. The turnarounds were equally dramatic in the traditionally isolationist Midwest, where the student newspapers at Northwestern University and the Universities of Iowa, Minnesota, and Kansas abandoned isolationism.[118]

Communist students also returned to campus in the fall of 1941 with a different attitude toward isolationism. Now that the Nazis had invaded the Soviet Union, communists in the Youth Congress dropped their isolationist slogans and became the most interventionist students in the nation. But by this point it really did not matter. The communists had already so discredited themselves by their previous foreign policy flip-flops that their new position barely attracted any attention on campus—except as a source of ridicule by classmates bemused by their willingess to constantly march in step with Stalin's zig-zagging policies. The communists had long since lost their ability to influence American student politics.[119]

The student movement was dead. But in one respect at least, its spirit lingered on right up until the eve of Pearl Harbor. The movement had been born denouncing war and pledging students against it. And despite the demise of isolationist activism on campus in the fall of 1941, students remained among the most anti-war groups in the nation. Even as America fell into naval clashes with Germany in the North Atlantic, students were still less willing than the general public to support measures that might escalate that conflict. A November 1941 national poll found America as a whole—by a 46 to 40 percent margin—favoring revision of the neutrality act to allow the arming of British-bound American ships; but college students opposed the plan 52 to 41 percent. Only 14 percent of the national student body at this point favored a declaration of war against Germany and Japan.[120] The student body would not accept war as a solution to the international crisis until the Japanese attack at Pearl Harbor foreclosed all other options.

III

After the U.S. entered the war, former peace protesters often became soldiers, sailors, and pilots. Neal Anderson Scott, the commencement day orator who preached the isolationist gospel to his graduating class at Davidson College in 1940, died in battle as a navy ensign in the Pacific War less than two years later. There were many like Scott. Few students who had been peace activists during the Depression decade became conscientious objectors during the war. The ranks of conscientious objectors were so thin and their influence so slight that they barely attracted public attention in wartime America.[121] Similarly, the nation's immersion in total war following Pearl Harbor quickly dimmed its memories of the student movement which had tried so persistently and vainly to prevent that war. The onset of this mammoth conflict with fascism suddenly made the history of collegiate isolationism seem small and irrelevant.

The collapse of the anti-war movement appears as inevitable as the war itself. No student peace movement could have survived in a nation as threatened by war and fascism as America became during the early 1940s. In retrospect, then, it was not the movement's collapse but rather the *way* that it collapsed that was so memorable. The ill will generated by the conflicts between communists and non-communists during this process of dissolution would have consequences that lasted long after the final shots had been fired in World War II. In these campus conflicts of the late 1930s and early 1940s one hears early expression of the bitter debates and restrictive philosophies that would yield so much political bloodletting and repression in Cold War America. Liberals, who had entered the Popular Front era of the student movement willing to work with communists, came away from the post-Nazi-Soviet Pact period embittered; they began to articulate an anti-communist language of exclusion.

Fundamental to this exclusionary mind-set was the notion that communists represented not a normal political party, but rather a conspiratorial group. Communists, in this view, could not be counted on to be honest about either their goals or affiliations. Since they often hid their motives and identifications, they might one minute be cooperative and tireless workers for the student movement, and the next minute—because of a shift in the Soviet and American CP's line—reverse gears, sabotaging the movement and using secret communist factions to take over the movement's organizations.[122]

This hostile view of the communists led exclusionists to the conclusion that communists had to be banned from non-communist political organizations in order to ensure the integrity of those organizations. This was precisely what happened in the anti-isolationist student organizations after the collapse of the ASU-AYC Popular Front. As the Students For Defense of Democracy, the student Committee to Defend America By Aiding the Allies, the ISS, and other anti-isolationist student groups met in 1941 to discuss a possible merger,

> the problem of communist infiltration was discussed . . . and it was agreed that there should be no cooperation with communist or communist front groups, that we should be very careful to exclude them . . . and should not work with them on the campus . . . . any cooperation might too easily result in their gaining control of our groups, and if the line shifted, using us for their own undesirable ends.[123]

There was no mystery about why such exclusion came into vogue. It arose in response to the hijacking of the ASU and Youth Congress out of the Popular Front by the communist factions within those organizations. The packing of meetings, the breaking of agreements, the numerous violations of democratic process which communists used following the Nazi-Soviet Pact won them control of the ASU and Youth Congress but made them pariahs in the eyes of many liberals.[124]

This shift toward exclusion was illustrated most dramatically in the case of Joseph Lash. As late as November 1939, when the ASU's internal communist-non-communist struggle was escalating, Lash had stood for an inclusive student movement. Called before the red probing Dies Committee, Lash praised communists for helping to build the student movement and defended their right to participate in the ASU—arguing that a democratic organization must be open to all. In the midst of his hearing before the Dies Committee, Lash ridiculed the red hunters, bursting into song: "If you see an un-American lurking far or near / Just alkalize with Martin Dies and he will disappear." Yet within two years Lash abandoned the principles which had led him to advocate an inclusive ASU and was defending an exclusive ISS.[125]

As ISS General Secretary, Lash opposed the admission of communists into the organization. Nor would he allow ISS cooperation with the communists, even after the German invasion of Russia when the communists' new interventionist position placed them in agreement with ISS foreign policy. Explaining this position in 1941, Lash cited his experience in the Youth Congress and ASU. The "inescapable conclusion from the events of the past two years" was that communists were "unreliable allies in the march towards a more democratic America and a better world." The communists "paraded as liberals" and anti-fascists then as "isolationists," leaving non-communists who had worked with them wondering why "the slogans and loyalties of one month became the anathemas and heresies of the next." Lash observed that the communist slogans used for public consumption, whether interventionist or isolationist, masked their true goal of serving Soviet foreign policy interests. In the Youth Congress, the communist faction would "not frankly espouse its fundamental conviction that defense of the Soviet Union must be the over-arching" goal of the student movement. "Hence the aroma of conspiracy and duplicity about it . . . ." In the ISS Lash would stress the need to develop a non-communist student leadership, capable of preventing communists from controlling campus politics. "Joe taught me," recalled former ISS member Louis Harris, "how to out-think, out-maneuver, and to out-sit the communists whom we were struggling against in the student movement." [126]

A large share of the responsibility for breeding such anti-communism rested with the communists themselves. Their behavior in taking control of the ASU and Youth Congress after the Nazi-Soviet Pact was every bit as manipulative as Lash had suggested. As if that was not enough to alienate non-communists—and drive them toward exclusionism—communists in the student movement during their final isolationist period embraced a sectarian style of agitation that did even more to poison their relations with liberals. Perhaps reflecting the frustrations common to declining organizations, the Youth Congress' communist-dominated leadership hurled wild and scurrilous charges at their former allies. Worst among these were the accusations that the YCL and Youth Congress leader Joseph Cadden made against Eleanor Roosevelt. They charged that the First Lady was involved in "a Fascist or Nazi scheme" to "force all young men and women into Nazified labor camps." In fact, all that Mrs. Roosevelt had done was support an ISS program in which youth would provide voluntary public service for a year. Lash looked back upon the communist distortion of this program as "propaganda worthy of Goebbels." [127] Such behavior suggests that the communists, though indeed victims of an anti-communist ban, were not innocent victims. They had helped create the harsh political atmosphere which made it impossible to preserve a working—or even a civil—relationship between communists and liberals.

The shift away from inclusionary politics had more repressive implications than Lash and the other liberal student leaders in the early 1940s realized. Lash and his allies continued to oppose anti-radical witch hunts and red probing committees. Unlike such reactionary politicians as Dies, these student movement veterans did not support the outlawing of communist organizations, or other draconian restrictions on the civil liberties of communists. [128] And yet, in banning communists from their own student organizations and in promoting hostile anti-communist rhetoric and images of communism as a conspiracy, these liberal youths inadvertently helped lay part of the intellectual foundation for the post-war attacks on communists' political rights. Liberals who preached that communists were sinister and beyond the pale of democratic organizations—that they therefore had to be banned from those organizations—helped to popularize the idea that communists were pariahs in a democratic society. If communists were too untrustworthy to be allowed into the organizations of liberals, why were they any less dangerous in their own organizations? And should not those communist organizations too be banned as nests of sinister conspirators? Once this process of banning had begun it would prove difficult to stop, especially when the tensions of the Cold War era fostered ever greater distrust and fear of communism as an international conspiracy.[129]

The bitterness and exclusionary politics which grew out of the campus battles of the Depression era endured even into the 1960s. They shaped the way that leading liberal anti-communist alumni of the old student movement initially responded to the new generation of student rebels who had begun to protest the Vietnam War. James Wechsler, for example, had written many editorials for the ASU magazine during the 1930s promoting student anti-war activism. But Wechsler would scorn such activism in the 1960s, as editor of the *New York Post*—at that time one of America's leading liberal newspapers. When Students for a Democratic Society (SDS) organized the first national anti-war march on Washington in 1965, Wechsler turned a deaf ear to their compelling critique of the Vietnam War. He had been disturbed that SDS had refused to exclude communists from the march, and his virulent anti-communism left him disinclined to support such protests against America's war on communism in Indochina. Wechsler thererefore used the pages of the *Post* to mock the protest as a "pro-communist production" and a "frenzied, one-sided, anti-American show." Such bitter words said more about Wechsler and the scars from the 1930s than they did about this SDS-led demonstration. They were the aftermath of the student movement of the Depression era—a movement which in its heyday had promoted political tolerance, but which died in a fit of intolerance.[130]

Appendix: The FBI Goes to College: A List of Informants and Information They Gave the FBI on American Student Union Activists[1]

The surviving—or at least the released—FBI documents on the ASU indicate that the Bureau did its most extensive investigation of the student movement beginning in the fall of 1940 and extending into the early years of World War II. The timing of this investigation was linked to the war mobilization. Since the ASU in 1940 was an anti-interventionist, communist-led organization, the FBI deemed it necessary to gather intelligence on the ASU's strength, anti-war agitation, and potential resistance to the recently adopted conscription act.

In the context of the student movement's own history, however, there is an ironic quality to the timing of this secret FBI probe. The FBI's most sweeping national investigation of the ASU (and the American Youth Congress) did not occur when the ASU was influential and leading a mass student movement, but rather when the ASU was discredited, weak, dying, and finally dead. Thus the FBI probe could not document any sizable ASU-led movement to violate the conscription act, nor any other violation of law which might make the investigation even remotely justifiable from a law enforcement standpoint.[2] The fact that the investigation continued after Hitler's invasion of the U.S.S.R. in 1941, when the communist-led ASU fully supported America's mobilization for war (and that the FBI probe lasted through 1943, when young communists strongly endorsed the United States war effort), suggests that the probe had more to do with FBI director J. Edgar Hoover's anti-radicalism than any genuine need to police a security threat.

The timing of this probe is important to bear in mind because it gave the FBI reports from the investigation a special quality, revealing the ideological underpinning of the informing done by university administrators (and other FBI informants). These campus officials knew that the ASU was dead or dying and posed a threat to no one. Indeed, the most common scenario in the FBI reports on Bureau interaction with campus administrators began with the college or university official telling the FBI

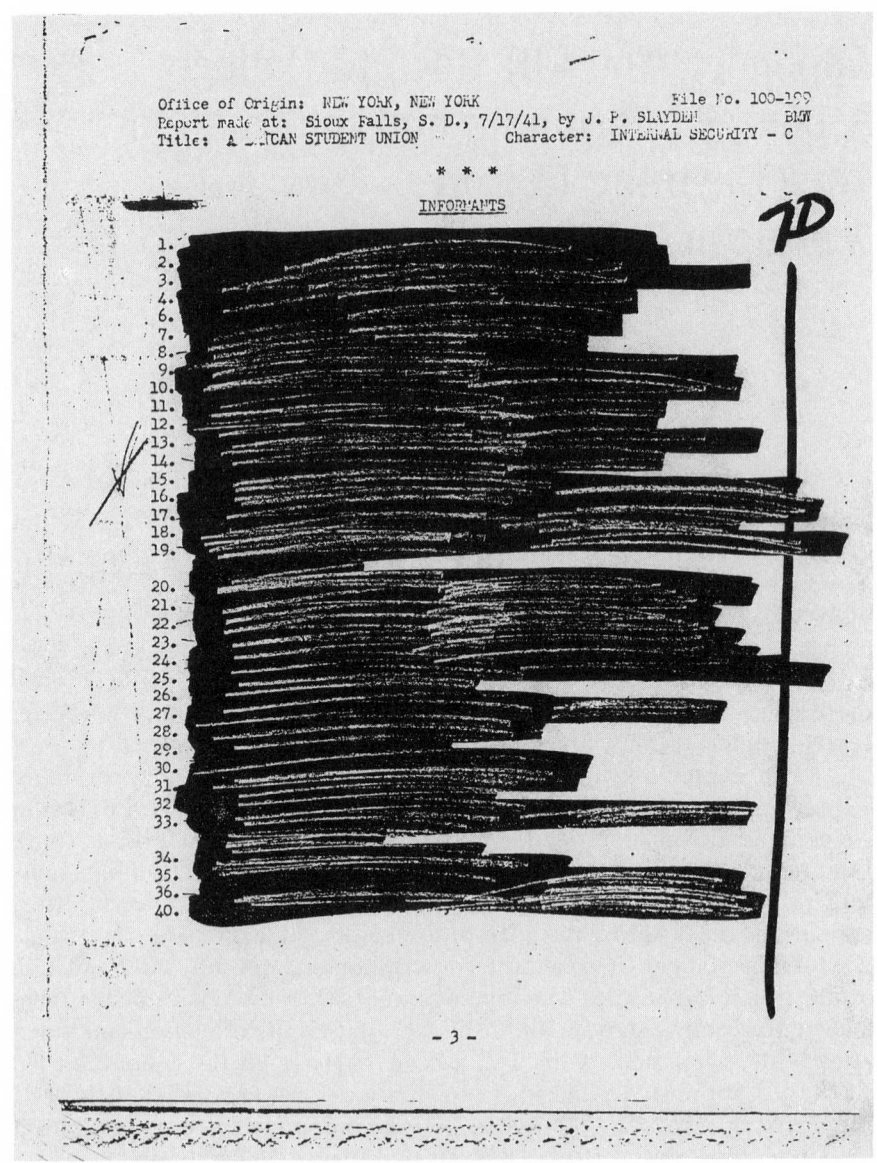

A sample of FBI censorship of its reports on the American Student Union. Such censorship makes it impossible to gauge the full extent of FBI surveillance and campus informing on student protesters during the 1930s and early 1940s.

agents about the surge of student protest that had occurred during the 1930s and narrating the recent decline or death of the ASU. The campus official then often noted that he or she saw no threat of a resurgence of radicalism on campus. Nonetheless, because of their loathing for radicalism and their sense that such dissent was not a legitimate part of university life, these campus administrators—after expressing scorn for these radical troublemakers—matter of factly opened their files on ASUers to the Bureau and freely turned over their students' names to the FBI.[3]

This list of FBI informant activity is offered as a window onto the important—but hidden—underside of academic freedom in America.[4] A full accounting of this policing of dissent will not be possible, however, until the FBI stops censoring its campus reports (many of which are more than a half-century old).

COLLEGE/UNIV.	INFORMANT	TYPE OF DATA GIVEN TO FBI
Brown University	1) American Legion "Americanization man"	Names leading ASU organizer.
	2) Confidential Informant RIDC-1	Names ASU members and sympathizers.
California, University of at Berkeley	1) Confidential Informant SF–12	Names ASU and YCL leaders and reports on ASU meetings.
	2) Confidential informant SF–59	Gives names of ASU and YCL leaders as well as reports on ASU meetings.
Chicago, University of	1) Dean's office—name deleted by FBI censors	Gives names and phone numbers of ASU leaders and ASU membership list.
Cincinnati, University of	1) Informant's name deleted by FBI censors	Names ASU leaders.
Cleveland College	1) Name deleted by FBI censors	Names leading ASUers and details their political actions.
	2) J.M. Woods, Faculty advisor to student organizations	Names student who attempted to found an ASU chapter.
Columbia University	1) John J. Swan, Comptroller	Calls attention to the "Communistic . . . control" of the Columbia ASU. Gives ASU leaflets.

COLLEGE/UNIV.	INFORMANT	TYPE OF DATA GIVEN TO FBI
Connecticut, University of	1) University administrator, name deleted by FBI censors	Names leading ASUers "inclined toward communism."
	2) Professor Andre S[rest of last name illegible]	Describes rise of ASU chapter and anti-ROTC agitation. Names ASU leaders. "Stated that he had watched the organization rather closely due to his connection with the American Legion and that he had sent information on the organization to MID [the Military Intelligence Division?] at Boston, Mass."
Cornell University	1) Charles Manning, Proctor	Names leading ASUers.
	2) Student, name deleted by FBI censors	Names ASUers, describes radical books in the room of ASU leader.
	3) Informant, name deleted by FBI censors	Gives names, local and home addresses, phone numbers, academic fields of ASU leaders.
DePauw University	1) G. Herbert Smith, Dean of Administration	Gives correspondence between ASU and De-Pauw administration and ASU petition for campus recognition, which includes names of 45 students. Points out which of the ASU members have been the most active and mentions the recent collapse of the ASU chapter.
Earlham College	1) William C. Dennis, President	Names founders of campus ASU chapter. Gives political background of ASU leaders, including their ideological tendencies. Describes ASU peace strike agitation, and gives copy of ASU constitution.

COLLEGE/UNIV.	INFORMANT	TYPE OF DATA GIVEN TO FBI
George Washington University	1) Myra Sedwick, Secretary to the President	Gives files on campus radicals dating back to 1929.
Hawaii, University of	1) E.C. Webster, Dean of Men	Gives names of ASU officers at Hawaii.
	2) Walter Chun, student govt. president	Gives names of ASU organizers, list of 36 ASU members.
Howard University	1) Confidential Informant T–1	Report deleted by FBI censors.
	2) Confidential Informant T–2	Names student radicals, faculty sympathizers.
Hunter College	1) William C. Martin, State Senator, New York	Gives the names of 46 Hunter students who signed a petition protesting his bill to ban the ASU from New York's municipal colleges.
Illinois, University of at Champaign-Urbana	1) Campus official? name deleted by FBI censors	Gives local ASU membership list with names, local and home addresses of 32 student ASUers.
	2) Dean, name deleted by FBI censors	Gives literature of local ASU with names of 31 ASUers. "Advised that he was keeping a close watch on the activities" of local ASU. Describes its sponsorship of "PEACE" meetings.
	3) Fred H. Turner, Dean of Men	Names campus ASU leaders, agrees to provide ASU membership list. Describes ASU agitation.
	4) U. Ill. official (probably Dean Turner)	Provides ASU membership list, with 18 names.
	5) Ronald Nystrom, editor *Daily Illini*	Gives name and address of ASU chapter president.
Indiana State Teachers College	1) Sara Bence, Secretary to the Dean	Names student organizer of ASU and faculty supporter.

COLLEGE/UNIV.	INFORMANT	TYPE OF DATA GIVEN TO FBI
	2) Informant name deleted by FBI censors	Names ASU activists, faculty supporters, local minister who assisted ASU.
Indiana University	1) Informant name deleted by FBI censors	Gives petition for recognition of ASU chapter, listing 45 members and officers. Names two faculty supporters of ASU.
	2) Registrar's Office	Provides information on ASU officers.
Indiana University Extension	1) Dorothy McMahon, Clerk at the Registrar's Office	Names ASU leaders.
Michigan, University of	1) Confidential Informant T–1	Names 3 ASUers.
	2) Confidential Informant F–1	Names ASUers expelled from U. of Michigan.
	3) Sergeant Eugene Gehringer, Ann Arbor Police Dept.	Submits report "fully covering" ASU protest meeting in 1940, listing 12 speakers at the meeting.
	4) Professor More	Gives pamphlets published by local ASU chapter, names the activist who distributed this literature.
	5) Norman E. Cook, Chief of Police, Ann Arbor	Reports on ASU meeting, names speakers at this meeting.
	6) Eleanor H. Scanlan, Secretary to the Dean of Students	Gives a list of ASU officers, 1939–1941.
	7) Dr. Alexander Ruthven, President	Describes conflicts between his administration and the ASU. Gives off campus location where the ASU met after being barred from campus. Attests that the ASU in 1942 was no longer active. Agrees to notify of any future agitation by ASU "trouble makers."

COLLEGE/UNIV.	INFORMANT	TYPE OF DATA GIVEN TO FBI
	8) Informant name deleted by FBI censors (but clearly a University administrator)	"They watched very closely the activities of any students that were . . . radical." Summarizes the roles played by ASU leaders in campus protests. Gives personal information on one ASU leader, his academic problems and the manner in which the father of this student reacted to these problems (during the father's conference with campus officials).
Middlebury College	1) Dr. E.B. Womach, Dean of Men	Names leading ASU organizers, describes ASU chapter and its conflict with campus administrators.
	2) Paul D. Moody, President	Names college ASU's leader. Describes ASU-sponsored meeting. "Happy to observe" demise of ASU in 1941. "Feels the wave of patriotism" has "swept" the student body "clean in all unhealthy influence in this respect."
Minnesota, University of	1) Dean Nicholson	Names the head of ASU chapter.
Missouri, University of, at Columbia	1) Darwin Hindman, Dean of Men	Names leading ASU activists.
	2) University official, name deleted by FBI censors	Gives records with names and addresses of ASU activists.
	3) Confidential Informant KC-C-31	Names ASU leader.
	4) Confidential Informant KC-C-34	Names ASU leaders. Names radical professor at William Jewell College, agrees to obtain names of those who distributed ASU literature.

COLLEGE/UNIV.	INFORMANT	TYPE OF DATA GIVEN TO FBI
	5) Professor Stephens, Dean of Arts and Sciences	Describes anti-ROTC agitation of ASU chapter. Terms ASU efforts to win student exemptions from ROTC training "a constant source of annoyance." Names a local pastor who aided the ASU in this anti-ROTC work.
	6) Harlan Byrne, student editor of the *Missourian*	Names ASU chapter leaders.
	7) American Legion member, name deleted by FBI censors	Has a fellow Legion member "discreetly attend" ASU meetings. He provides notes on these meetings, names of speakers.
Montana State University	1) Confidential Informant A	Names students and librarian who tried to organize ASU chapter in April 1939.
	2) J.E. Miller, Dean of Students	Names student who led the attempt to organize an ASU chapter. Assesses the "apparent radicalism" of this student and its decline since graduation.
New Jersey College for Women	1) Dean Leah Boddie	Gives names, addresses of ASU officers, 1939–1941.
North Carolina, University of, at Chapel Hill	1) Confidential Informant 50	Names leading ASU activists. Provides biographical data on the academic and family background of ASU leaders. The detailed nature of this and other data provided by this informant (who even reported on the number of chairs requested in 17 separate ASU meetings) indicates that in-

COLLEGE/UNIV.	INFORMANT	TYPE OF DATA GIVEN TO FBI
		formant was a campus official or faculty member with access to University files.
Oberlin College	1) Dean Carl Wittke	Names two local ASU leaders as communists. Describes the size, influence, focus of Oberlin's ASU from its heyday in the mid-1930s to its decline in 1940–41. His official aids FBI in ascertaining that 18 protesters who had sent a petition against an anti-ASU bill in New York state legislature has been Oberlin students.
	2) D.M. Love, College Secretary	Describes the rise and fall of the local ASU.
Ohio State University	1) J.A. Park, Dean of Men	Gives names, addresses of student leaders of anti-war and free speech protests. Provides ASU branch literature with names of leading activists. Describes rise and fall of the campus ASU chapter.
	2) J.F. Stecker, Assistant Dean of Men	Names communist student organizer.
Ohio University at Athens	1) Irene Delvin, Assistant to the President	Describes ideological tendencies and goals of campus protesters. Refers reporting FBI agent to Dean of women, who apparently provides officer list for the now defunct ASU chapter.
	2) Dean of Women	
	3) B.T. Grover, Public Relations Director	Names radical leaders on campus.
	4) Informant, name deleted by FBI censors	Names a student with "Socialist tendencies."

COLLEGE/UNIV.	INFORMANT	TYPE OF DATA GIVEN TO FBI
Pennsylvania, University of	1) Dr. Arnold Henry, Dean of Student Affairs 2) William DuBarry, Vice President	Henry and DuBarry name students who led ASU chapter and those involved in the campus-area "Communist bookstore." They describe recent ASU anti-war activity. Dean Henry later supplies an update on the ASU at Penn, noting latest list of ASU officers. Dean Henry contacts FBI a third time, naming a student he suspected of communist activity.
Purdue University	1) F.I. Goldsmith, Dean of Men	Gives a 1936 petition for campus recognition of the ASU chapter, signed by 31 students.
Smith College	1) Informant name deleted by FBI censors (but clearly a member of Smith College administration)	"[P]roduced the records of her office" on ASU leaders at Smith.
	2) Mrs. C. Eaton Miller, Assistant to the Registrar	"Produced the records of her office" on four ASU leaders.
	3) Former member of Smith ASU, whose name was deleted by the FBI	Names Smith student activists "who advocated the Communist form of government for this Country."
	4) Mrs. J.F. Duffey, Secretary, Alumnae Association	Provides current addresses and employment information on four ASU alumnae of Smith.
	5) M.A. Thannhauser, Smith student and former ASU member	Names six Smith ASU activists.
Southern Illinois State Teachers College	1) Robert Calless, Secretary to the Dean	Gives ASU membership list.
	2) L.B. Sherretz, head of campus police	Names the college's most prominent radical student activist.

COLLEGE/UNIV.	INFORMANT	TYPE OF DATA GIVEN TO FBI
Swarthmore College	1) Swarthmore student, name deleted by FBI censors	Names three communist students.
Syracuse University	1) Frank Piskor, Dean's Office	Names the campus' leading anti-fascist student organizers.
Temple University	1) Conrad Siegars, Dean of Men	Names nine former members of the ASU at Temple. Describes their ideological tendencies, personal backgrounds, and roles in the local student movement. Names the most influential ASU leader at Temple and terms him a "Red." Describes the rise and fall of the ASU chapter. Claims that the ASU leaders at Temple were "planted by Communists organizations in this country."
	2) Name of informant deleted by FBI censors	Names the leader of the Temple ASU.
Texas, University of	1) Informant's name deleted by FBI censors	Describes ASU agitation against ROTC and ASU organizing of a strike by student waiters. Names six student activists and a radical instructor.
	2) Former resident of Campus Guild, the Univ. of Texas men's co-op dormitory. Informant's name was deleted by FBI censors	Advises that this co-op was a " 'hot bed' for Communists." Names twenty "ringleaders of communistic activity at the Campus Guild."
Tulane University	1) Kendall Cram, Graduate Manager of Student Activities	Provides documents naming student leaders of the Tulane SLID and organizers of local student group seeking affiliation with national ASU.

COLLEGE/UNIV.	INFORMANT	TYPE OF DATA GIVEN TO FBI
Washington, University of	1) Herbert T. Condon, Dean	Names radical student leaders and a leftist minister. Describes rise of anti-war agitation on campus and conflicts between protesters and University officials. Names a minister who allowed ASU to meet in his church after the ASU had been banned from campus.
	2) University official, whose name was deleted by the FBI censors	Gives names, addresses, dates, places of birth, and next of kin of 22 student activists.
	3) Confidential Informant SE–1	Names 7 University of Washington students active in both the ASU and the Communist Party
	4) Colonel Edward Kimmel, ROTC commander	Gives files with names of anti-war leaders, reports of student protest meetings.
	5) Albert Seeman, Professor and faculty advisor to student activities groups	Provides copies of student anti-war flyers and correspondence between protesters and administration concerning the banning of a controversial anti-ROTC rally. Describes the process by which student radicals "infiltrated" mainstream campus groups.
Wayne University	1) Confidential Informant T–3	Names ASU leader at Wayne.
	2) Informant name deleted by FBI censors	Names student who initiated the formation of the Wayne ASU chapter.
Wesleyan University	1) Associate Dean Butterworth	Names ASU leaders.
	2) Elmer Schattschneider, Professor of Government	Names ASU leader.

COLLEGE/UNIV.	INFORMANT	TYPE OF DATA GIVEN TO FBI
Western Reserve University: Adelbert College and Flora Stone Mather College	1) Robert E. Bates, Dean of Students 2) H.F. Doolittle, Assistant Registrar	Bates advises FBI that Doolittle has information on campus ASU chapter. Dolittle names ASU leaders.
	3) Dr. M. Ogle, Professor, Political Science, Adelbert	Tells FBI that the campus' ASU members were "maladjusted little Jew boys." Ogle names two ASU leaders and explains that some ASUers were "militant Communists," but most were "theoretical Marxists, socialists or leftwing Democrats." Describes ASU meetings.
	4) Informant, whose name was deleted by FBI censors	Names 9 ASUers. Describes their ideological tendencies.
	5) Kenneth Deacon, former student at Western Reserve	Names 3 ASU leaders.
	6) Elinor R. Wells, Registrar, Flora Stone Mather College	Names top ASU leader at Flora Stone Mather. Assesses the activities, degree of influence of local ASU chapter.
Wilson Teachers College	1) Dr. Clyde M. Huber, Dean	Gives file on ASU leaders, including documents on suspension of students for distributing radical literature.
Yale University	1) William DeVane, Dean, Yale College	Names the Yale ASU chapter president. Advises FBI agent that this ASU leader "had been examined by Dr. Fry, the school Psychiatrist . . . but that Dr. Fry had found nothing wrong with him. He advised that perhaps Dr. Fry would be able to give a better picture of . . . [the ASU leader's] attitude." De-

COLLEGE/UNIV.	INFORMANT	TYPE OF DATA GIVEN TO FBI
		Vane furnished the official membership list of the ASU to H.B. Fisher, who in turn made it available to the FBI.
	2) Harry Fisher, Liasion Officer of Yale, and who with the knowledge of the Yale administration, served as official liaison between Yale and the FBI (apparently paid by both institutions)	Reports on ASU meetings and membership. Works with an agent in the FBI field office in New Haven, interviewing a Smith College student who named ASU activists at Smith.
	3) Professor Mommsen	Names ASU leader.

Notes

[1] This list of informants is by no means exhaustive. Hundreds of pages and probably more than a thousand informant names were deleted from the FBI files by FBI censors. There were no documents at all included by the FBI from many of the campuses with the most active ASU chapters, but it is very likely that extensive informing for the FBI occurred on these campuses. Moreover, my list only summarizes the most personal data given by these individuals to the FBI; it does not (because of space constraints) detail all of the political intelligence given to the Bureau by the listed informants. This list only covers the ASU and not the other significant student and youth protest organizations in Depression America (such as the American Youth Congress and the Southern Negro Youth Congress, which were subject to extensive FBI surveillance). The list also does not cover high schools, where there was—according to the FBI documents—a significant amount of informing against the ASU.

Note that all Confidential Informant numbers specified in the list were assigned by the FBI, as were all other deletions of informant names. In employing the word "informant" in this list I am using the dictionary definition of informant as "one who gives information," and I am not implying a paid or continuous informant relationship with the FBI.

[2] Even during the American Student Union's most isolationist phase on the eve of World War II, the ASU position on the draft—which was public information, known to the FBI—did not sanction violation of the law. In 1940, the sixth annual ASU convention took the moderate position of urging "every legal and constitutional means" to convince Congress to repeal conscription, while simultaneously pledging that so long as conscription remained the law of the land ASUers would "comply with the Selective Service act . . ." (FBI File # illegible, Report on the American Student Union February 7, 1941).

[3] The college administrators who gave the FBI their files and political intelligence on ASU activists were under no legal obligation to do so. But if the federal statutes did not compel them to cooperate with the FBI, neither did the law obli-

gate these college officials to keep student files confidential. Given the undeveloped state of the laws of privacy and student rights in America during the late 1930s and early 1940s, the question of whether or not to turn over the names of student radicals to the FBI was strictly an ethical and political question, which for this conservative generation of administrators meant that it was not a question at all (Robert B. Meigs, "The Confidential Nature of Student Records," *National Association of College and University Attorneys* (June 1962), 14–15).

Not until the 1960s would this type of collusion between academic administrators and federal red probers encounter major opposition within the educational establishment. In 1967 the American Council on Education (ACE) urged universities not to comply with the House Un-American Activities Committee's attempts to subpoena the membership lists of student anti-war groups. In the Council's view, college officials had an obligation to "protect students from unwarranted intrusions into their lives and from hurtful or threatening interference in the exploration of ideas and their consequences that education entails." Such language attests to a much more liberal reading of academic freedom than existed in Depression America. The position the ACE took in 1967 also contrasted with that of the informing administrators of the 1930s and 40s in that it acknowledged student privacy rights—affirming that "maintenance of student records, especially those bearing on personal belief and organizational affiliation, creates a personal and confidential relationship" ("Statement of Confidentiality of Student Records by the American Council on Education," Washington, D.C., July 7, 1967; William T. O'Hara, John G. Hill Jr., *The Student/The College/The Law* (New York, 1972), 53–54; On other restrictions on the release of information from student records, see the discussion of the Buckley Amendment (1974) in William A. Kaplin, *The Law of Higher Education* (San Francisco, 1985), 358–361; On restriction of police surveillance on campus, see the 1975 decision *White v. Davis* 13 Cal 3d 757, 120 Cal Rept. 94   533 P.2d).

[4]Copies of the FBI documents cited below as the sources for this list are in the author's possession and were obtained from the FBI through a Freedom of Information Act request. The informant list has been compiled from the FBI files reporting on the American Student Union at the campus level. On informing at Brown Univ., see FBI file # 100–160, Dec. 5, 1941, Report made by Norman Hanson, Providence; on UC Berkeley, see FBI file # 100–2071, Sept. 16, 1943, Report made by Theodore S. Cruise, San Francisco; on the Univ. of Chicago, see FBI file # 61–327, Dec. 6, 1941, Report made by J.F. Desmond, Chicago; on the Univ. of Cincinnati, see FBI file # 100–365, Feb. 1, 1941, Report made by S.H. Horton, Cincinnati; on Cleveland College, see FBI file # 100–608, Sept. 3, 1941 Report made by S.E. Hobbs, Cleveland; FBI file # 100–608, Feb. 12, 1942, Report made by G.E. Irwin, Cleveland; on Columbia Univ., see John J. Swan note to FBI, May 5, 1941, FBI file # 61–7491–1; on the Univ. of Connecticut, see FBI file # 100–589, 1941 [month and day illegible, reporting agent name illegible] New Haven; on Cornell Univ., see FBI file # 100–483, Nov. 4, 1941, Report made by P.D. Beachum, Albany, N.Y.; on DePauw Univ., see FBI file # 100–475, Feb. 20 [?], 1941, Report made by Richard C. Godfrey, Indianapolis; on Earlham College, see FBI file # 100–475, Jan. 23, 1943, Report made by George A. Brouillard, Indianapolis; on George Washington Univ., see FBI file # 100–920, Sept. 14, 1942, Report made by M.J. Connolly, Washington, D.C.; on the Univ. of Hawaii, see FBI file # 100–1241, June 28, 1941, Report made by John I. Condon, Honolulu; on Howard Univ., see FBI file # 100–920, Sept. 14, 1942, Report

made by M.J. Connolly, Washington, D.C.; on Hunter College, see FBI file # 100–483, May 28, 1941, Report made by J.V. Beale, Albany, N.Y.; on the Univ. of Illinois, see FBI file # 100–191, Jan. 10, 1941, Report made by W.A. Temple, Springfield; FBI file # 100–191, Feb. 1, Aug. 27, Oct. 30, 1941, Reports made by J.J. Racan, Springfield; FBI file # 100–191, Nov. 14, 1941, Report made by Arthur R. Day, Springfield; FBI file # 100–191, April 21, 1942, Report made by Charles F. Douglas, Springfield; on Indiana State Teachers College, see FBI file # 100–475, Feb. 20 [?], 1941, Report made by Richard C. Godfrey, Indianapolis; on Indiana Univ., see FBI file # 100–475, Feb. 20 [?], 1941, Report made by Richard C. Godfrey, Indianapolis; on Indiana Univ. Extension, see FBI file # 100–475, Jan. 23, 1943, Report made by George A. Brouillard, Indianapolis; on Univ. of Michigan, see FBI file# 100–1217, Nov. 29, 1941, Report made by Maurice E. Goudge, Detroit; FBI file # 100–1217, Feb. 8, 1943, Report made by John C. Hall, Detroit; on Middlebury College, see FBI file # 100–483, Feb. 6, 1942, Report made by Frank C. Wood, Albany, N.Y.; on Univ. of Minnesota, see [FBI file # illegible], Feb. 1, 1941, Report made by R.T. Noonan, St. Paul, Minnesota; on Univ. of Missouri, see FBI file # 100–1193, June 11, 1941, Report made by M.B. Rhodes, Kansas City; FBI file # 100–1193, Oct. 10, 1941, Report made by R.E. Sherk, Kansas City; FBI file # 100–1193, Dec. 5, 1941, Report made by W.C. Fuller, Kansas City; FBI file # 100–1193, March 21, 1942, Report made by R.B. Ayers, Kansas City; on Montana State Univ., see FBI file # 61–195, August 12, 1941, Report made by Elmer W. Parrish, Butte; on New Jersey College for Women, see FBI file # 100–1453, June 19, 1941, Report made by V. Walser Prospere, Newark; FBI file # 100–1453, April 19, 1943, Report made by Clement L. McGowan Jr., Newark; on Univ. of North Carolina at Chapel Hill, see FBI file # 100–419, March 5, 1941, Report made by B.F. Wiand, Charlotte; on Oberlin College, see FBI file # 100–608, Sept. 3, 1941, Report made by S.E. Hobbs, Cleveland; on Ohio State Univ., see FBI file # 100–365, March 20, 1941, Report made by Edward S. Sanders, Cincinnati; FBI file # 100–365, June 18, 1941, Report made by D.G. Jenkins, Cincinnati; on Ohio Univ. at Athens, see FBI file # 100–365, May 27, 1941, Report made by A.W. Richardson, Cincinnati; FBI file # 100–365, March 9, 1942, Report made by J.T. Delaney, Cincinnati; on Univ. of Pennsylvania, see FBI file # 61–136, Sept. 28, 1942, Report made by Harry C. Leslie Jr., Philadelphia; FBI file # 61–136, Nov. 24, 1942, Report made by Harry C. Leslie Jr., Philadelphia; on Purdue University, see FBI file # 100–475, Nov. 12, 1942, Report made by Douglas J. Williams, Indianapolis; on Smith College, see FBI file # 100–279, Feb. 20, 1943, Report made by James A. Hanley, Boston; FBI file # 100–589, Oct. 7, 1942, Report made by Charles E. Stine, New Haven; on Southern Illinois State Teachers College, see FBI file # 100–191, Feb. 1, 1941, Report made by W.A. Temple, Springfield; on Swarthmore College, see FBI file # 100–432, Dec. 5, 1941, Report made by C.H. King, Philadelphia; on Syracuse Univ., see FBI file # 100–483, Jan. 23, 1942, Report made by P.B. Beachum, Albany, N.Y.; on Temple Univ., see FBI file # 61–136, Sept. 28, 1942, Report made by Harry C. Leslie Jr., Philadelphia; on Univ. of Texas, see FBI file # 61–121, Jan. 25, 1940, Report made by J.O. Peyronnin [?, last name only partially legible], New Orleans: FBI file # 61–188, May 27, 1941, Report made by Alan H. Mayer, San Antonio; on Tulane Univ., see FBI file # 100–311, May 22, 1941, Report made by S.W. Reynolds, New Orleans; on the Univ. of Washington, see FBI file # 100–942, July 3, 1941, Report made by R.D. Auerbach, Seattle; File # [illegible], Sept. 19, 1941, Report made by R.D. Auerbach, Seattle; on Wayne University, see FBI file # 100–1217, Feb. 8, 1943, Report made by John C. Hall, Detroit; on Wesleyan Univ., see FBI file # 100–589, 1941 [month and day illegible, reporting agent name illegible] New Haven; on Western Reserve Univ.-Adelbert College-Flora Stone Mather College, see FBI file # 100–608, Sept. 3, 1941, S.E. Hobbs, Cleveland; FBI file # 100–608, Feb. 12, 1942, Report made by G.E. Irwin, Cleveland; on Wilson Teachers College, see FBI file # 100–920, Sept. 14, 1942, Report made by M.J. Connolly, Washington, D.C.; on Yale Univ., see FBI file # 100–589, [day and month illegible], 1941, [Reporting FBI agent's name illegible], New Haven; FBI file # 100–589, [month illegible], 21, 1941, and July 17, 1942, Reports made by G. J. McDonough, New Haven; FBI file # 100–589, Oct. 7, 1942, Report made by Charles E. Stine, New Haven; Sigmund Diamond, "Surveillance in the Academy: Harry B. Fisher and Yale University, 1927–1952," *American Quarterly* (Spring 1984), 7–43; Robin W. Winks, *Cloak and Gown: Scholars in the Secret War, 1939–1961* (New York, 1987), 32–351.

Abbreviations

ACLU   American Civil Liberties Union Archives, Mudd Manuscript Library, Princeton University

BC   Brooklyn College Archives, Gideonse Library

CCNY   City College of New York Archives, Cohen Library

CUC   Columbiana Collection, Butler Library, Columbia University

ECM   Ernest C. Moore Papers, Department of Special Collections, UCLA Research Library

ER   Eleanor Roosevelt Papers, Franklin D. Roosevelt Library, Hyde Park, N.Y.

FU   Fisk University Archives, Fisk University Library

HARV   Harvard University Archives, Pusey Library

JM   Jack McMichael Papers, Woodruff Library, Emory University

JPL   Joseph P. Lash Papers, Franklin D. Roosevelt Library, Hyde Park, N.Y.

NNC   National Negro Congress Papers, Schomburg Center for Research in Black Culture, New York Public Library

NT   Norman Thomas Papers, New York Public Library

NYT   *New York Times*

NYU   Tamiment Institute Library, New York University

RH   Reed Harris files, Low Library, Columbia University

SCPC   Swarthmore College Peace Collection, McCabe Library

SP   Young People's Socialist League files, Socialist Party of America Papers, Duke University (used on microfilm at the Tamiment Library, NYU; and at Carlson Library, University of Toledo)

UC   Special Collections Department, Regenstein Library, University of Chicago

UCB	University of California Archives, Bancroft Library, UC Berkeley
UM	Michigan Historical Collections, Bentley Historical Library, University of Michigan
UT	University of Toledo Archives, Carlson Library
UTEX	University of Texas Archives, Lyndon B. Johnson Library
UVA	University of Virginia Library, Manuscripts Department
UW	University of Washington Archives, Seattle
UWISC	University of Wisconsin Archives, Memorial Library, Madison
VC	Vassar College Archives, Thompson Memorial Library
YCAW	Youth Committee Against War files, Keep America Out of War Congress Papers, Swarthmore College Peace Collection
YWCA	Young Women's Christian Association National Board Archives, New York

Notes

Introduction

1. John P. Roche, *Shadow and Substance: Essays on the Theory and Structure of Power* (New York, 1964), 436. From the outset radical student activists in Depression America expressed disdain for Europe's fascist youth movements. Indeed, one of the justifications these radicals used for organizing students in the U.S. was to preempt any possible rightist youth movement here (*Hunter Bulletin*, March 27, 1933; Theodore Draper, "American Youth Rejects Fascism," *New Masses* (Aug. 23, 1934), 11–13; *Columbia Spectator*, May 7, 1934; "Should the American Student Go the Way of the German? A Student Conference Against Fascism," leaflet, N.Y., May 1934, JPL).

2. The best account of Depression-era violations of academic freedom among the faculty in the U.S. is Ellen Schrecker, *No Ivory Tower: McCarthyism and the Universities* (New York, 1986), 63–83.

3. On *Tinker v. Des Moines*, see William G. Millington, *The Law and the College Student: Justice in Evolution* (St. Paul. Minn., 1979), 160–213.

4. The secret political dossiers that the FBI—with the help of college officials—assembled on Depression-era student activists will be discussed in Chapter 5 of this study; also see Appendix. Athan G. Theoharis has uncovered unlawful behavior by the FBI in its political surveillance of these activists. FBI agents burglarized the New York office of the American Youth Congress and photocopied correspondence between the Youth Congress and Eleanor Roosevelt. See Athan G. Theoharis, "J. Edgar, Eleanor - and Herbert Too?: The F.D.R. File," *Nation* (Feb. 20, 1982), 200–201. On the FBI break-in at the offices of the International Student Service, a leading student activist organization during the last stages of the Depression era student movement, see Athan G. Theoharis and John Stuart Cox, *The Boss: J. Edgar Hoover and the Great American Inquisition* (Philadelphia, 1988), 191. Campus administrators also demonstrated a disregard for students' civil liberties by initiating some of their own political surveillance on student protesters. This will be discussed in Chapter 5.

5. Theodore Draper, *American Communism and Soviet Russia* (New York, 1986), 5, 445–82; Theodore Draper, *The Roots of American Communism* (New York, 1957), 395; Maurice Isserman, *Which Side Were You On?: The American Communist Party During the Second World War* (Middletown, Conn., 1982), vii-xiv, 1–31; Maurice Isserman, "Communist Caricature," *In These Times* (April 4–10, 1984), 18, 22.

6. Joseph P. Lash, "Do the Thirties Have Anything to Tell the Sixties?" (New York, 1968), Introduction to Greenwood Press reprint of *Student Advocate*, 2.

7. William E. Leuchtenburg, *Franklin D. Roosevelt and the New Deal* (New York,

1963), 290; Arthur Schlesinger, Jr., *The Politics of Upheaval* (Boston, 1966), 199; Robert S. McElvaine, *The Great Depression* (New York, 1984). The published historical monographs on the student movement of the 1930s are Eileen Eagan, *Class, Culture and the Classroom* (Philadelphia, 1981); Ralph Brax, *The First Student Movement* (Port Washington, N.Y., 1981). Also see Winifred Wandersee, "ER and American Youth: Politics and Personality in a Bureaucratic Age," in Joan Hoff-Wilson and Marjorie Lightman, eds., *Without Precedent: The Life and Career of Eleanor Roosevelt* (Bloomington, 1984), 63–87; George Rawick,"The New Deal and Youth: The Civilian Conservation Corps, the National Youth Administration and the American Youth Congress" (Ph.D. diss., Univ. of Wisconsin, 1957).

8. The Fund for the Republic study with the chapter on Depression-era student radicalism is Robert W. Iversen, *The Communists and the Schools* (New York, 1959), 119–47. The repressive political atmosphere of the McCarthy era left publishers under pressure not to publish memoirs that were at all sympathetic to the radical movements of the 1930s. For example, in 1953 playwright Arthur Miller wrote an article for *Holiday Magazine* on Michigan student life, which briefly but warmly recalled Depression era student radicals and their support of the militant auto strikes (his article is quoted at the beginning of this Introduction). Miller later learned that the "advertising department of the Pontiac devision of General Motors had warned [*Holiday* publisher Ted] Patrick that Pontiac would cancel all its advertising in *Holiday* if they ever published another piece by Arthur Miller" (Arthur Miller, *Timebends: A Life* (New York, 1987), 96).

9. Jack McMichael interview with author, Athens, W.Va., Aug. 22, 1982.

10. Among the best of this memoir literature by Depression era student activists is James Wechsler, *The Age of Suspicion* (New York, 1981), 3–132; Irving Howe, *A Margin of Hope: An Intellectual Autobiography* (New York, 1982), 1–89; Joseph P. Lash, *Eleanor: A Friend's Memoir* (Garden City, N.Y., 1964), 1–254; Henry F. May, *Coming to Terms: A Study in Memory and History* (Berkeley, 1987), 185–266; Junius Irving Scales and Richard Nickson, *Cause at Heart: A Former Communist Remembers* (Athens, Ga., 1987), 53–88; Roche, *Shadow and Substance*, 432–41; Paul Jacobs, *Is Curly Jewish?* (New York, 1965), 3–110; Eric Sevareid, *Not So Wild a Dream* (New York, 1965), 48–73; Hal Draper, "The Student Movement of the Thirties: A Political History," in Rita Simon, ed., *As We Saw the Thirties* (Urbana, 1967), 153–89; Pauli Murray, *Song in a Weary Throat* (New York, 1987), 82–129.

11. *NYT*, Feb. 11, 1940.

12. May, *Coming to Terms*, 207.

13. Joseph P. Lash, "Memorial to Spain" (April 13, 1980), an address on the occasion of the dedication of a memorial to the City College of New York students who fought and died in the Spanish Civil War, JPL.

Chapter 1. Dancing on the Edge of a Volcano

1. Irving Bernstein, *The Lean Years: A History of the American Worker, 1920–1933* (Baltimore, 1960), 254–57; *NYT*, Aug. 13, 1931; "The Hoover Happiness Boys," *Nation* (June 18, 1930), 692.

2. *Daily Californian*, Aug. 13, 1931.

3. *San Francisco Chronicle*, Aug. 12, 1931.

4. William Harlan Hale, "A Dirge for College Liberalism," *New Republic* (May 13, 1931), 349; Reed Harris, *King Football: The Vulgarization of the American College*

(New York, 1932), 195; *Michigan Daily,* May 7, 1932; *Intercollegian* (Jan. 1932), 130.

5. *Daily Cardinal,* Oct. 23, 1931. On the large number of campus parties, also see *University Daily Kansan,* March 22, 30, 1931, April 12, 1931; *Intersorority Council Minutes, Toledo University, book I, 1927–1943,* 37, UT; Univ. of Buffalo *Bee,* May 15, 1931. The student press treated such partying as a central undergraduate interest. See, for instance, the enormous banner headline accorded the "Prom King" election at the Univ. of Wisconsin in *Daily Cardinal,* Oct. 13, 1931.

6. *Michigan Daily,* Nov. 28, 1931; *Daily Cardinal,* Feb. 16, 1930.

7. *NYT,* May 8, 1930. To contrast this juvenile collegiate violence with the political violence which accompanied the hunger marches, see *NYT,* March 7, 1930.

8. *NYT,* Feb. 13, May 2, 1930, Jan. 6, Feb. 15, 1931, and March 9–11, 1930; *Daily Cardinal,* Oct. 15, 1931.

9. *Columbia Spectator,* April 15, and May 2, 1930. At Columbia and other campuses raiding class dinners was an annual campus ritual. See "Springs of Student Rioting : Psychology and Tradition Play Parts in the Occasional Collegiate Outbursts," *NYT Magazine* (Feb. 1, 1931), 16.

10. "Springs of Student Rioting," 16. Though student riots brought injuries, arrests and extensive property damage, some nostalgic alumni claimed that the riots in the early 1930s were not as impressive as those in their own college days during the 1920s. How much trouble one made in such disturbances was apparently a matter of generational pride. See *Daily Cardinal,* Oct. 17, 1931. Participants often defended these apolitical college riots on the grounds that they promoted a laudable "unifying spirit" among undergraduates. See *Michigan Daily,* Nov. 15, 1929; and see the reprint of the *Ohio State Lantern*'s editorial in *Daily Cardinal,* May 25, 1930.

11. Harris, *King Football* (New York, 1932), passim; *Daily Californian,* Nov. 18, 1983; *Michigan Daily,* Oct. 8, 1930; James Wechsler, *Revolt on the Campus* (1935; reprint, Seattle, 1973), 42–43. *Hunter Bulletin,* Dec. 5, 1933. College football's great popularity in the 1920s led to an awesome expansion of the game's physical presence on campus. One report covering 135 campuses found that seating capacity in college football stadiums had more than doubled from 929,521 in 1920 to 2,307,850 in 1930 (almost twice the size of the national undergraduate population). Attendance at college football games had soared by 119 percent in this same era. At many colleges the stadium was the largest or among the largest structures on campus. See *University Daily Kansan,* Jan. 19, 1933.

12. *University Daily Kansan,* Nov. 18, 1930.

13. A.M. Sperber, *Murrow: His Life and Times* (New York, 1986), 29–30, 34–44; E.R. Murrow, "National Student Federation," *American Association of University Professors Bulletin* (April 1931), 240.

14. *NYT,* Dec. 28, 1931.

15. Harold J. Laski, "Why Don't Your Young Men Care?: The Political Indifference of the American Undergraduate," *Harper's Magazine* (July 1931), 129. On the apolitical mindset of American undergraduates, also see "Collegiate Sheep," *The De Pauw* editorial reprinted in *Daily Illini,* Nov. 26, 1931; "Our Attitude Towards Politics," *Daily Iowan* editorial reprinted in *Daily Illini,* Oct. 4, 1931; *Columbia Spectator,* March 10, 24, 1931. On how disillusionment with reformers and their failures during the Progressive era left students jaded about liberalism, and fostered political apathy on campus during the early Depression years, see Robert Paul Cohen, "The Revolt of the Depression Generation: America's First

Mass Student Protest Movement, 1929–1940" (Ph.D. diss., UC Berkeley, 1987), 28–30.

16. Laski, "Why Don't Your Young Men Care?," 130, 135.

17. *LID News Bulletin*, Jan. 1926; Norman Thomas, "Youth and the American Colleges," *Nation* (Aug. 1, 1923), 106.

18. Thomas, "Youth and the American Colleges," 106.

19. *NYT*, Dec. 21, 1930; On the middle-class background of college students, see U.S. Office of Education, *Economic Status of College Alumni* (Washington, D.C., 1939), 23–25; O. Edgar Reynolds, *The Social and Economic Status of College Students* (New York, 1927), 14–21.

20. Arthur Schlesinger, Jr.'s classic *The Crisis of the Older Order, 1919–1933* (Cambridge, 1957) exemplifies the tendency of historians to ignore class distinctions in their accounts of America's response to the onset of the Great Depression. Schlesinger writes that by the spring of 1930 the Depression had bred a "contagion of fear . . . [whose] shadow fell over the cities and towns; it fell as heavily over the countryside. . . . In country and city alike anger [provoked by the economic crisis] was spreading" (*The Crisis of the Older Order*, 166, 174, 176). The problem here is that Schlesinger, whose account details the suffering of the unemployed and farmers, generalizes from these specific groups to all of society. Schlesinger erroneously assumes, without evidence, that the suffering wrought by the Depression immediately produced anger and a sense of crisis throughout society. But the facts from the campus world in 1930 and 1931 contradict Schlesinger's assumptions, and we see not fear but frivolity, not anger but apathy, among the nation's predominantly middle-class undergraduate population. On American student culture in the 1920s, see Paula Fass, *The Damned and the Beautiful: American Youth in the 1920s* (New York, 1970), passim.

21. U.S. Office of Education, *Biennial Survey of Education in the United States, 1930–1932* (Washington, D.C., 1935), 13; Malcolm Wiley, ed., *Depression, Recovery and Higher Education: A Report of the X Committee of the American Association of University Professors* (New York, 1939), 23; *NYT*, Dec. 21, 1930. The one significant exception to the rule concerning undergraduate enrollments was that of college women. While male enrollments rose in 1930 and 1931, female enrollments dipped slightly—about 1.6 percent. This reflected the sexual double standard common among parents of college students in this era concerning who needed a college education: for a son that education was viewed as a necessity because he would be the breadwinner, whereas for a daughter, who supposedly would become a housewife, that education was seen as a luxury that could be dispensed with during a depression. See *NYT*, Dec. 21, 1930, and June 3, 1931; Raymond Walters, "Statistics of Registration in American Universities and Colleges," *School and Society* (Dec. 12, 1931), 783. What is striking, however, is how little student discussion there was of this trend, and how the declining female enrollment failed to change the mood on campus. Perhaps the drop in female enrollments was not sharp enough to cause alarm. And since it was at co-educational institutions rather than at women's colleges where the early female enrollment drop was concentrated, the change occurred amidst a male-dominated student culture—which did not even seem to notice.

22. *NYT*, Feb. 17, Oct. 12, 1930.

23. Robert Angell, "The Influence of the Economic Depression on Student Life at the University of Michigan," *School and Society* (Nov. 14, 1931), 650, 653. Note, however, that elsewhere in this article Angell (649) argues for more rapid

economic decline at the Univ. of Michigan than I have found on campus nationally. For good correctives to Angell on this point, and for discussion of how "cloistered" and "pleasantly remote" students initially felt from the Depression, see *Daily
Cardinal*, Sept. 23, 1931; "Yale in Depression," *Harkness Hoot* (Nov. 23, 1931), 3–
4; *Intercollegian* (Jan. 1931), 130; *Michigan Daily*, June 3, 1932.

24. *Vassar Miscellany News*, Nov. 27, 1929.

25. *Daily Californian*, Nov. 19, 21, 1929. On this enduring faith in Hoover
and the economy, see *Michigan Daily*, Oct. 11, 1931; *University Daily Kansan*, May
4, 1930. On student support for Republicans in the 1920s, see Fass, *The Damned
and the Beautiful*, 343–44.

26. U.S. Office of Education, *Biennial Survey of Education in the United States,
1936–1938* (Washington, D.C., 1942), 8.

27. James Wechsler, *The Age of Suspicion* (New York, 1981), 20; also see *Columbia Spectator*, March 18, 1931.

28. *Columbia Spectator*, Dec. 3, 1930. Other unrealistically optimistic statements and stories concerning the employment prospects for college graduates during
the early Depression years can be found in *NYT*, July 20, 1930; "Employment of
Cornell Graduates," *School and Society* (Aug. 22, 1931), 264. There were a few
more negative reports, which, of course, turned out to be more accurate. See *NYT*,
May 3, 1931.

29. *Barnard Bulletin*, June 6, 1930.

30. Walter Greenleaf, *Self-Help for College Students* (Washington, D.C., 1929),
60–61; *NYT*, Feb. 17, 1930, Oct. 17, Nov. 3, 1931. On other campuses where
students had difficulty securing part-time jobs, see *Michigan Daily*, October 8, 1930;
Daily Cardinal, Oct. 4, 1931. Of the college employment statistics, those showing
that 20 percent male and 11 percent female students being entirely self-supporting
are the least ambiguous. These were students who had to have employment in
order to put themselves through college. But once one moves to the larger group
of employed students, the significance of job-holding is less clear. Some students
who were not fully self-supporting worked part-time jobs—even though they were
already comfortable economically—to pay for the added luxuries of an active collegiate social life. We know this because as the part-time job market tightened in
campus communities, college administrators urged students who did not absolutely need jobs to avoid seeking employment—so as to make way for those students whose ability to stay in college depended upon securing jobs. In other words,
while fully self-supporting students were thrown into economic crisis, some portion of students who worked were at worst only inconvenienced by the job crunch,
because they did not truly need the money from that employment. See *University
Daily Kansan*, Sept. 17, 1930.

The Hoover administration's response to the growing crisis in the market for
part-time jobs among college students was belated and ineffective. Refusing to use
federal funds to create new jobs for college students, the administration instead
sought to eliminate foreign job-seekers. In September 1932, Hoover's Secretary
of Labor, William Doak barred foreign college students from holding part-time
jobs. Since foreign students accounted for only a tiny fraction of the students
seeking employment, the ruling had virtually no impact on the job crisis, but it
did hurt foreign students and was condemned by college administrators. See *NYT*,
Sept. 27, 1932.

31. Angell, "The Influence of the Economic Depression on Student Life,"
653.

32. *University Daily Kansan,* Jan. 22, 1930.

33. Studs Terkel, *Hard Times: An Oral History of the Great Depression* (New York, 1970), 398. Also see "A Letter from an Unemployed Student," *The Spark,* June 1932, UTEX.

34. *Harvard Crimson,* May 2, May 22, 1933; Theodore White, *In Search of History: A Personal Adventure* (New York, 1978), 42–43.

35. *University Daily Kansan,* Oct. 10, 1930; Berkeley *Student Outpost,* Feb. 15, 1933, UCB; on the "real class warfare" between rich and poor students at the University of Virginia, see Terkel, *Hard Times,* 400.

36. *Time* (Nov. 24, 1930), 46; *University Daily Kansan,* Dec. 8, 1931.

37. For other occasions in which students organized to protest adult policing of their social life, see "Barnard Girls Revolt Against 'No Stockings' Edict at Meals," in Wisconsin *Daily Cardinal,* March 14, 1930; the report on the University of Chicago student riot protesting "dry snooping" (spying by the campus police to determine if the prohibition laws were being violated by undergraduates), in Wisconsin *Daily Cardinal,* May 25, 1930.

38. How important lifestyle issues, and in particular the freedom to consume liquor, could be to college students was suggested by an editorial in the Michigan student newspaper. More than two years after the stock market crash, and with the American economy collapsing, this editor could still claim that "of all the major problems before the American public today, prohibition is . . . [by] far the most important" (*Michigan Daily,* Nov. 3, 1931). Such sentiment was based at least in part on self-interest. According to a poll taken of eastern and midwestern undergraduates the previous year, a majority of students—15,000 out of the 24,000 students polled—violated the prohibition laws by drinking liquor. Since this made them subject to arrest, students had good reason to favor a change in the liquor laws. This problem was not merely theoretical. One of largest collegiate scandals in 1931 occurred when Michigan's fraternity houses were raided for violating the prohibition laws, and 79 students were arrested (*NYT,* March 27, 1930, Feb. 12, 13, 1931; *Michigan Daily,* Dec. 9, 1931, Jan. 13, 1932).

39. On the tradition of collegiate cultural liberalism inherited from the student peer culture of the 1920s, see Fass, *The Damned and the Beautiful,* 327–70.

40. *NYT,* May 11, 1932; William Harlan Hale, "A Dirge for College Liberalism," *New Republic* (May 13, 1931), 349.

41. Hale, "A Dirge for College Liberalism," 349–50. The editor of the Univ. of Michigan student newspaper agreed with Hale's conclusions, adding that "college liberalism" was fading not only in the East, but in the Midwest as well (*Michigan Daily,* May 6, 1931; also see Univ. of Buffalo *Bee,* Nov. 6, 1931).

42. *NYT,* Oct. 3, 1932; Wiley, *Depression, Recovery and Higher Education,* 473. On the hardships of students forced to drop out of college because of the economic crisis, and on their parents' personal grief over this, see Kenneth L. McGooden to Robert M. Hutchins, Aug. 16, 1933, and Rachel Mickolas to Robert M. Hutchins, Aug. 21, 1933 in President's Papers, *UC.* On the financial sacrifices parents made attempting to keep their children in college, see *NYT,* Oct. 23, 1932.

43. Wiley, *Depression, Recovery and Higher Education,* 170–75.

44. *Ibid.*

45. *NYT,* Oct. 3, 1932; *Daily Californian,* Oct. 6, 1932.

46. *NYT,* Oct. 3, 1932. On this new, more serious campus mood, see Robert Angell, "The Trend Toward Greater Maturity Among Undergraduates Due to the Depression," *School and Society* (Sept. 23, 1933), 391–96.

47. *Michigan Daily*, Dec. 8, 10, 1932. Also see "Privation & Co-operation," *Time* (Jan. 9, 1933), 46; *Daily Cardinal*, Jan. 11, 1933.

48. *Daily Cardinal*, Feb. 25, March 11, 1932. Other expressions of sympathy for working students can be found in *Daily Illini*, Jan. 3, 1932; *Daily Texan*, Dec. 17, 1932.

49. *Why SWF?* (Ann Arbor, n.d.); *Daily Illini*, Dec. 20, 23, 1931.

50. Berkeley *Student Outpost*, Feb. 15, 1933.

51. *Michigan Daily*, March 29, 1933.

52. *Daily Illini*, Jan. 17, 1932. The increasingly somber tone of college employment officers was evident in Christian Gauss' article, "The Lost Generation: What Chance for the College Graduate of 1931?," *Forum* (Sept. 1931), 190. On this job crisis, also see R.T. Sharpe, "The Present Problem of Student Employment," *AAUP Bulletin* (Nov. 1932), 503–4; Charles A. Maney, "College Graduates Face the Future," *Journal of Higher Education* (Oct. 1935), 371–75; University of Toledo *Collegian*, March 24, 1933; *Daily Cardinal*, Nov. 17, 1933; Bedulah Amidon, "After College-What?," *Survey Graphic* (June 1933), 320–23.

53. *Columbia Spectator*, Nov. 25, 1931; *Collegian*, Oct. 1, 1932; *Revolt* (Dec. 1932), cover graphic.

54. *Vassar Miscellany News*, Nov. 2, 1932.

55. *Ibid.*

56. *Ibid.*, Nov. 2, 5, 12, Dec. 10, 1932.

57. *Ibid.*, Nov. 2, 1932.

Chapter 2. Cafeteria Commies

1. Lionel Abel, *The Intellectual Follies* (New York, 1984), 55. On New York City radicalism during the Depression, also see Malcolm Cowley, *The Dream of the Golden Mountains* (New York, 1980), 46–62, 106–26; Irving Howe, *A Margin of Hope* (New York, 1982), 1–86; Harvey Klehr, *The Heyday of American Communism: The Depression Decade* (New York, 1984), 32–34, 265–69; Alexander Bloom, *Prodigal Sons: The New York Intellectuals and Their World* (New York, 1986), 11–120.

2. James Wechsler, *The Age of Suspicion* (New York, 1981), 42–49; Robert Hall interview with author, Willsboro, N.Y., Dec. 17, 1982; Larry Rogin interview with author, Washington, D.C., June 4, 1982.

3. Council of Christian Associations, *Towards a New Economic Society: A Program for Students* (New York, 1931), passim; Donald B. Meyer, *The Protestant Search For Political Realism* (Berkeley, 1960), 173–74; F. Palmer Weber, interview with author, Manhattan, N.Y., Jan. 25, 28, 1982; Anthony Dunbar, *Against the Grain: Southern Radicals and Prophets* (Charlottesville, 1981), 1–125.

4. Max Gordon, "Seeds of Conflict: A Memoir of 50 Years Ago," *City College Alumnus* (Oct. 1981), 10–11; Oakley Johnson, "Campus Battles for Freedom in the Thirties," *Centennial Review* (Summer 1970), 341–67; Howe, *A Margin of Hope*, 60–64.

5. David Boroff, "A Kind of Proletarian Harvard," *NYT Magazine* (March 28, 1965), 19, 106–9; Harry Magdoff interview with author, Manhattan, N.Y., March 19, 1982; Max Gordon interview with author, Manhattan, N.Y., Feb. 2, 1982; Max Weiss interview with author, Manhattan, N.Y., May 5, 1982.

6. Harry Magdoff interview with author.

7. Arthur Liebman, *The Jews and the Left* (New York, 1979), 26–37, 77–365.

8. Alfred Kazin, *Starting Out in the Thirties* (Boston, 1965), 4.

9. Harry Magdoff interview with author; Max Gordon interview with author; Max Weiss interview with author; Joseph Clark interview with author, Manhattan, N.Y., May 4, 1982.

10. George Watt interview with author, Northport, N.Y., Sept. 16, 1982.

11. *Ibid.*

12. *Ibid.*

13. *Ibid.*

14. Harry Magdoff interview with author.

15. *Ibid.*

16. *Ibid.* Note that even in New York's City Colleges the activist group was initially a small minority of the student body. At the time of the NSL's birth most of the City College's low-income students responded to the Depression not by embracing radicalism, but by buckling down in their academic work, hoping that by performing impeccably at college they would improve their chances for employment in the dismal job market. Moreover, though growing up in New York ghettoes fostered greater toleration of radicalism—which facilitated the quick growth of the student Left in the City colleges—many of these students came to college with little grounding in radical ideas. While the student body was sympathetic to the Left, the majority nonetheless did not come to college with the political sophistication of either young radical intellectuals like Magdoff or experienced activists like Weiss. Underscoring this point, Magdoff recalls that in his speech class at CCNY "I gave a talk on the need for unemployment insurance. Now you have to remember that this is a period when 20 percent, 25 percent of the population was unemployed. A lot of these kids at school, their parents were unemployed. . . . And the guys in class were . . . astounded at this crazy idea. Now you look at City College, a hotbed of revolution—of communism, of socialism—but this is as much the reality" (Harry Magdoff interview with author).

17. Howe, *A Margin of Hope*, 11. For a brilliant analysis of the ways in which such outsider status sustained a vibrant tradition of dissident thought on the Jewish Left, see Issac Deutscher, *The Non-Jewish Jew and Other Essays*, ed. Tamara Deutscher (New York, 1968), 25–41.

18. Harry Magdoff interview with author.

19. *Ibid.*; Theodore Draper, "City College's Rebel Generation," *New Masses* (Nov. 27, 1934), 15; Theodore Draper interview with author, Princeton, N.J., June 17, 1982; Max Weiss interview with author; Joseph P. Lash interview with author, Manhattan, N.Y., Nov. 23, 1982. Several vivid descriptions of the political debates in the alcoves have been published by alumni, but most of these were by CCNY students in the late 1930s—a time when the Left at City College was larger and more polarized than in the early 1930s. See Irving Kristol, "Memoirs of a Trotskyist," *NYT Magazine* (Jan. 23, 1977), 51, 54–56; Howe, *A Margin of Hope*, 64–69. It is the importance of the cafeteria as a center of radical politics and debate at CCNY that E. L. Doctorow apparently alluded to when he used the term "cafeteria Commie" to invoke the youthful radicalism of the 1930s in his novel *The Book of Daniel* (quoted at the beginning of this chapter). The allusion was especially appropriate in a novel about the Rosenberg case, since Julius Rosenberg had been a young Communist at CCNY in the 1930s. On Rosenberg's political activism at CCNY, see Morton Sobell, *On Doing Time* (New York, 1974), 30–33; Ronald Radosh and Joyce Milton, *The Rosenberg File: A Search for the Truth* (New York, 1983), 51–52.

20. *Frontiers* (Feb. 1931), 1, CCNY.

21. Harry Magdoff interview with author; *Frontiers* (Feb. 1931), 2.

22. *Frontiers* (Feb. 1931), 1.

23. Max Gordon interview with author; Max Weiss interview with author; Judah Drob interview with author, Washington, D.C., Jan. 22, 1982; Harold Goldstein interview with author, Washington, D.C., Jan. 22, 1982; Sol Becker and Archie Deno, "Seven Years of Suppression," *Frontiers* (April 1933), 6–7, CCNY.

24. *NYT*, Oct. 30, 1932; Barbara J. Dunlap, "From the Pen of President Robinson," *The City College Alumnus* (April 1981), 6.

25. CCNY *Campus*, Feb. 27, 1931, March 2, 4, 6, 10, 13, 17, 1931; Max Gordon interview with author. "The Case for the Social Problems Club," leaflet [1931], CCNY.

26. CCNY *Campus*, Feb. 27, 1931, and March 2, 4, 6, 10, 13 and 17, 1931; Max Gordon interview with author.

27. Max Gordon interview with author; Max Weiss interview with author; Gordon, "Seeds of Conflict," 10–11; *Building a Militant Student Movement: Program and Constitution of the National Student League* [n.d.].

28. Max Gordon interview with author; Max Weiss interview with author; Gordon, "Seeds of Conflict," 10–11; *Building a Militant Student Movement*; "Role of the Student—1931," *Student Review* (Dec. 1931), 2; "For a National Student Movement: A Suggested Basis," *ibid.* (Jan.-Feb. 1932), 3.

29. Max Gordon interview with author; Max Weiss interview with author; Gordon, "Seeds of Conflict," 10–11; *Building a Militant Student Movement*; "The National Conference," *Student Review* (March 1932), 16. "The National Conference Report," *Student Review* (May 1932), 19; *Daily Worker*, March 29, 1932; "Building a Student Movement: On the Second National Student League Convention," *Student Review* (Dec. 1932), 5.

30. On the history of the ISS and LID, see Max Horn, *The Intercollegiate Socialist Society: Origins of the Modern American Student Movement* (Boulder, 1982), passim; Harry Laidler, *Twenty Years of Social Pioneering : The League for Industrial Democracy Celebrates Its 20th Anniversary* (New York, 1926), 3–21. Harold Lewack, *Campus Rebels: A Brief History of the Student League for Industrial Democracy* (New York, 1953), 8–10.

31. Even the LID's tiny non-student membership outnumbered its student membership. According to the LID files, at the end of 1929 students did not constitute a majority of the League's total of 2,058 campus and community members. See Minutes, "LID Board of Directors Meeting," Dec. 4, 1929, LID Papers, NYU

32. For an example of the academic tone set by the LID's adult leadership, see Norman Thomas's professorial introduction to the study by Kenneth Meiklejohn and Peter Nehemkis, *Southern Labor in Revolt* (New York, 1930), 3–4. Here Thomas does not ask students to become active in the labor movement, requesting only that they conduct dispassionate studies of labor problems.

33. Riva Stocker, "The I.S.C. Program," *LID Monthly* (Nov. 1931), 8. Not only Stocker, but other students in the LID conceded that that the LID's intercollegiate council had been poorly organized and "somewhat inactive" (Paul Porter, "The League on Campus," *LID Monthly* (Feb. 1931), 11). Observing that it was older figures, such as Laidler and Thomas, who set the tone for the LID, the NSL, criticized the LID for being "dominated by a . . . non-student leadership which

is completely out of touch with students and their problems . . ." ("Program of the National Student League," *Student Review* (May 1932), 17).

34. F. O. Matthiessen, "The Education of a Socialist," *Monthly Review* (Oct. 1950), 175.

35. *The League for Industrial Democracy* (New York, 1921), 3, 10–11; Horn, *The Intercollegiate Socialist Society,* passim; Laidler, *Twenty Years of Social Pioneering,* 17.

36. "Liberalism in the Middle West," *LID News Bulletin* (May 1923), 3; *New Student,* June 17, 1922; Stanley Mallach, "Red Kate O'Hare Comes to Madison: The Politics of Free Speech," *Wisconsin Magazine of History* (Spring 1970), 204–22.

37. "Our Annual Student Conference," *LID News Bulletin* (Jan. 1923), 2.

38. *Ibid.,* 3. There was, however, a radical minority in the LID during the 1920s—a few militant campus chapters—which sought to get the organization to drop its educational orientation in favor of a more militant agitational approach to student organizing. But such calls for greater militancy aroused little support nationally in the LID. See "Our Intercollegiate Conference," *LID News Bulletin* (Feb. 1927), 2.

39. Joseph Clark, introduction to Greenwood Press reprint of *Student Review* (New York, 1968), 2.

40. "For a National Student Movement: A Suggested Basis," 3–4. This program contrasted starkly with that of the LID's national leadership. For example, even while noting the unemployment "crisis of tragic proportions" wrought by the Depression, LID leader Paul Porter, in issuing "A Call for Student Action," lacked a concrete program for student protest. Indeed, rather than calling for the creation of a student protest movement, Porter clung to the academic ideal. His key suggestion to students was that they "engage in vigorous education toward a new society" by arranging lectures and distributing LID educational materials (Paul Porter, "A Call for Student Action," *LID Monthly* (June 1931), 7–8). The only act of the national student LID that went beyond education was the rather tepid national petition drive against compulsory ROTC (Nathaniel Weyl, "The Student Fight Against Militarism," *LID Monthly* (March 1931), 11). This does not mean, however, that at the campus level all LID members shared the educational emphasis of the organization's national leadership. As in the 1920s, the LID had some action-oriented campus chapters. And due to the Depression this militant minority had grown—as had its impulse for anti-militarism and pro-labor agitation. What the challenge of the NSL and its agitational approach did was prod the LID in 1932 to elevate this militancy from minority status into the official program of the student LID's leadership. The volume of the debate was undoubtedly louder by this time because the Left had expanded greatly since the early days of the student movement (On these militant chapters and the move of the student LID from education to agitation, see "Among the Colleges," *LID Monthly* (Feb. 1930), 6–7; Frank Braun, "Detroit's Fighting Pacifists," *LID Monthly* (Jan. 1932), 13; Paul Porter, "Yours for the Revolution," *LID Monthly* (Feb. 1932), 11. "Blueprints of Action: A Handbook for Student Revolutionists," *Revolt* (Oct. 1932), 2).

41. "For a National Student Movement: A Suggested Basis," 3–4.

42. Martin Abern, "The Young Worker and the Student," *New Student* (Nov. 17, 1923), 6.

43. Max Weiss interview with author.

44. Max Gordon interview with author; Theodore Draper interview with author. When the Communist Party leadership spoke about youth in 1931 it was always about the need to organize young workers. See, for instance, the Commu-

nist Party Central Committee's statement on youth, made in its 13th Plenum, *Daily Worker*, Sept. 17, 1931; also see William Z. Foster, "Build the Youth Movement," *ibid.*, Sept. 29, 1931.

45. Harry Magdoff interview with author.

46. Joseph Clark interview with author.

47. *Ibid.*

48. *Ibid.*; Max Weiss interview with author; Max Gordon interview with author. That during the period of the NSL's emergence the YCL national leadership gave blue-collar youth priority over students can be seen in YCL events such as its national Youth Day in 1931. Here working-class youth were urged to take up the "class struggle," and college youth were not even mentioned (*Daily Worker*, Sept. 2, 1931; also see *Daily Worker*, Jan. 23, 29, 1932; *Young Worker*, May 25, 1931 and Jan. 18, 1932). This does not mean, however, that in 1931 and 1932 the YCL leadership was "cold" towards the NSL, as Hal Draper erroneously suggested in his otherwise illuminating article on the student movement. Interviews with NSL founders and YCL leaders as well as contemporary YCL commentary reflect a supportive attitude towards the NSL from the time of the student movement's first major actions (*Young Worker*, April 11, 18, 1932; Joseph Clark interview with author; Max Gordon interview with author; Hal Draper, "The Student Movement of the Thirties: A Political History," in Rita Simon, ed., *As We Saw the Thirties* (Urbana, 1967), 165.) Though Draper was incorrect about the YCL leadership, his point does have validity for some of the more sectarian rank and filers in the YCL. A vocal group of them did carry to extremes their reverence for blue-collar organizing—contending that the only place for the true revolutionary was among the working class, and that students were so petty bourgeois that communists should not waste their time doing campus organizing. But in contrast to the 1920s, such explicitly anti-student sentiment was rejected by the YCL national leadership in the early 30s and publicly condemned by that leadership in the mid-1930s (Max Gordon interview with author; Max Weiss interview with author; Gil Green, *Young Communists and the Unity of Youth* (New York, 1935), 19; Otto Kuusinen, *The Youth Movement and the Fight Against Fascism* (Moscow, 1935), 18; Gil Green interview with author, Manhattan, N.Y., Sept. 29, 1982).

49. Harry Magdoff interview with author. Magdoff's use of the term "guys" in discussing the NSL's founders should not be taken literally. Women, particularly from Hunter College, played a significant role in this founding group—as Magdoff himself indicated, later in the interview.

50. Max Gordon interview with author.

51. Harry Magdoff interview with author.

52. Joseph Clark interview with author.

53. George Watt interview with author.

54. Theodore Draper interview with author.

55. *Ibid.*

56. In a 1934 essay, SLID leader Joseph P. Lash condemned the Communist Party's policy of instilling "among its members a hatred of rival working class organizations," and blamed this for the general failure of the Party's united fronts. However, he excepted from this generalization the NSL. According to Lash, "The only place they have succeeded is in the student field, where the National Student League has not followed the Party line with respect to the Student L.I.D" (Joseph P. Lash, "Why I Am a Socialist," *The Clionian* (Sept. 1934), 4, CCNY). The NSL was not completely immune to sectarianism, but it was far less pronounced than

in adult and non-student communist and communist-dominated groups. This can be seen, for instance, in the pages of the NSL's national magazine, *Student Review*. There were occasional sectarian attacks on socialists and the LID, but not the stream of vitriol which ran on an almost daily basis in the Communist Party's *Daily Worker* and the YCL's *Young Worker*. According to Theodore Draper, a former editor of the *Student Review*, because the NSL focused primarily on concrete student problems and was well removed from the Party leadership, "we could avoid ideological issues which caused divisions. We were left out of these controversies, which was all to the best because we wouldn't have been interested in them. . . . For example you'd never [in the *Student Review*] have an attack on Trotskyism. . . . The NSL had Manny Geltman, an outright Trotskyist. He came to meetings and was permitted to have his say. In the Party this would have been unspeakable. . . . The NSL, then, had a loyal opposition. We had Trotskyists, Lovestoneites. In fact, in Party organizations you actually didn't talk to Trotskyists; in the NSL you got away with it" (Theodore Draper interview with author).

Trotskyists remained in the NSL throughout the organization's life, as Draper suggests. However, there were some NSL chapters—particularly in Chicago—where YCLers did not display the same degree of tolerance as the NSL's national leadership. The Trotskyist youth newspaper complained that sectarian YCLers had expelled Trotskyists students from the Chicago NSL chapters (*Young Spartacus*, Oct. 1932, Jan. 1933; Emanuel Geltman interview with author, Manhattan, N.Y., Feb. 22, 1982). But since this was the only time anti-Trotskyist expulsions from the NSL were reported in the Trotskyist press, such extreme intolerance does appear to have been the exception rather than the rule in the student organization. This was especially notable because on many occasions the Trotskyist NSLers were strong critics of NSL policy. That criticism usually derived from the Trotskyist's own sectarian spirit. The Trotskyists urged ultra-radical tactics on the NSL, which the League's leader rejected as unrealistic. The NSL leaders correctly sensed that if the League went in the direction advocated by the Trotskyists by always adopting the most revolutionary positions and refusing to compromise with pacifists and other reform-minded students, the League would never be able to mobilize mainstream students, and would remain—like the Trotskyists themselves— a small and isolated group (on Trotskyist criticism of the NSL for its coalition politics, see M. Garrett [Geltman], "The Student Review," *Young Spartacus*, Sept. 1932; "Student Notes," *ibid.*, April 1934). It was this less sectarian mindset which enabled the NSL to pioneer a Popular Front style of coalition politics long before the Communist Party adopted such tactics. Later in the decade, however, a harsh anti-Trotskyist mindset would be carried into the student movement by communist activists (which will be discussed in Chapter 6).

57. "Role of the Student—1931," 2.

58. Theodore Draper interview with author.

59. "For a National Student Movement: A Suggested Basis," 3.

60. *Ibid.*

61. Celeste Strack Kaplan interview with author, Beverly Hills, Jan. 6, 1982; Harry Magdoff interview with author.

62. Joseph Clark, introduction to reprint of *Student Review*, 1; R. F. Hale, "The Tragedy of a Liberal," *Student Review* (Dec. 1931), 13.

63. Wechsler, *The Age of Suspicion*, 36.

64. There are no documents indicating the precise number of students in the NSL at the peak of the organization's strength in Dec. 1935. However, 13 months

earlier the NSL's combined college and high school membership stood at 2,660, according to a fairly detailed listing given out at the League's fourth convention. Since the NSL continued to grow in the coming year it seems safe to estimate the membership at somewhere between 2,660 and 3000 members. Harvey Klehr puts the NSL total at 600–700 members, but this figure is not documented convincingly and was apparently drawn from testimony given to the House Committee on Un-American Activities by Joseph P. Lash. Lash was not an NSLer, and he offered no documentation for this estimate. Since Lash was speaking before this anti-communist committee, he obviously had an interest in minimizing communist influence in the student movement—and particularly in the American Student Union, the group formed when the communist-led NSL merged with the socialist-led SLID (*Bulletin of the Fourth National Convention, National Student League* (St. Louis, 1934), 8–9, President's Papers, UCB; Klehr, *The Heyday of American Communism*, 317, 467).

65. Joseph Clark interview with author.

66. Donald Henderson, "League for Industrial Democracy: What Does It Offer?," *Student Review* (July 1932), 15.

Chapter 3. Springtime of Revolt

1. Harry Laidler, "Across the Country," *LID Monthly* (April 1932), 7.

2. *Student Outpost*, March 22, 1932; Robt. F. Hall, "Kentucky Makes Radicals," *Student Review* (May 1932), 7–8; "Columbia University Strikes," *ibid.* (May 1932), 12–14. Though the major protests, which attracted national attention occurred primarily in the Northeast, this section of the country did not have a monopoly on student activism. At campuses in the Mid- and Far West, small NSL and LID chapters were beginning to stir too at this time. Their actions were less dramatic than their counterparts on the East Coast, but nonetheless, they suggested that the trend toward active protest demonstrated most graphically in the East had the potential to become a national phenomenon. At UC Berkeley, for instance, NSLers in the spring semester of 1932 began agitating against the student government activities fees, which discriminated against low income students. NSLers at the University of Wisconsin began organizing a labor union to protect student employees. NSL activists in Chicago and Washington joined in picket lines with organized labor. The LID chapter at Detroit City College organized a protest against establishing a campus ROTC unit (*Student Outpost*, March 25, 1932. "On the Student Front," *Student Review* (May 1932), 15; Frank Braun, "Detroit's Fighting Pacifists," *LID Monthly* (Jan. 1932), 13).

3. Theodore Draper interview with author; Robert Hall interview with author, Willsboro, N.Y., Dec. 17, 1982.

4. Hall, "Kentucky Makes Radicals," 7–8.

5. Bert Cochran, *Labor and Communism: The Conflict that Shaped American Unions* (Princeton, 1977), 53–54; Malcolm Cowley, *The Dream of the Golden Mountains: Remembering the 1930s* (New York, 1980), 59–60.

6. Cochran, *Labor and Communism*, 53–56; Cowley, *The Dream of the Golden Mountains.* 59–76.

7. Cochran, *Labor and Communism*, 53–56; Cowley, *The Dream of the Golden Mountains*, 59–76.

8. Cowley, *The Dream of the Golden Mountains*, 59–76.

9. See editor's notes introducing article by John Dos Passos "Free Speech Speakin's," *Student Review* (Jan.–Feb. 1932), 5.

10. Dos Passos, "Free Speech Speakin's," 5.

11. CCNY *Campus,* March 4, 1932.

12. Robert Hall to author, Dec. 10, 1982.

13. *Columbia Spectator,* March 22, 1932; *NYT,* March 25, 1932. On other threats made in Kentucky against the students, see *Pineville Sun,* March 17, 1932.

14. Lewis Feuer, *Conflict of Generations: The Character and Significance of Student Movements* (New York, 1969), 354. Though there is some useful information on the Kentucky expedition in Feuer's history of student protest, his psychological interpretation of the expedition (as well as the entire student movement of the 1930s) is narrowly polemical and unconvincing. Feuer tries to fit the Kentucky expedition into his monocausal generational interpretation of all student movements—which holds that student protest is simply the expression of the oedipal rage of youth against their fathers. For a discussion of why Feuer's generational interpretation is inaccurate regarding the Kentucky expedition, see Robert Cohen, "Revolt of the Depression Generation: America's First Mass Student Movement, 1929–1940" (Ph.D. diss., UC Berkeley, 1987), 128–30; on the relative absence of generational rhetoric and rage in the larger student movement of the 1930s, see Chapter 8 of this book.

15. *Columbia Spectator,* March 23, 1932.

16. Letter of one delegation member "to a friend," March 18, 1932, cited in Feuer, *Conflict of Generations,* 354. Feuer apparently inserted the "X" to protect the privacy of the correspondents.

17. Robert Hall to author, Dec. 10, 1982; also see, *Knoxville News-Sentinel,* March 25, 1932.

18. *Harlan Daily Enterprise,* March 27, 1932.

19. Joseph P. Lash, "Students in Kentucky," *New Republic* (April 20, 1932), 267.

20. There is no complete list of the student delegation to Kentucky. All of the participants interviewed by the author stressed that the majority of delegation members were from New York City campuses, but that there was a sprinkling of students from campuses outside the metropolitan area. See Robert Hall interview with the author. From the combined newspaper reports on the delegation, which list about half the students on the trip, the campus breakdown was as follows : 12 students from Hunter College; 9 from Columbia University; 5 from the City College of New York; 3 from New York University; 2 from the University of Cincinnati and 7 others from Ohio; 2 from Harvard, 1 from the Union Theological Seminary; 1 from the University of Tennessee; 1 from the University of Wisconsin; and 1 from Colby College. The group seems to have been diverse in its economic background, ranging from the low-income students in New York's municipal colleges to students from elite private schools, including Margaret Bailey, the daughter of a prominent attorney and director of the American Civil Liberties Union.

21. Feuer, *Conflict of Generations,* 354. In opting for a non-sectarian approach to organizing the Kentucky expedition, the NSL demonstrated substantial initiative and independence from the Comintern's sectarian Third Period line, contradicting Harvey Klehr's claim that communist-led organizations were always totally subservient to the Comintern. When Klehr speaks of the Communist Party's "need to control with an iron fist any organization associated with it," he is speaking in

terms that are simply not relevant to the NSL and the student movement in 1932 (Harvey Klehr, *The Heyday of American Communism: The Depression Decade* (New York, 1984), 83). During this period neither the Comintern nor the adult Party elite understood the potential for building a mass student movement in the United States; they did not demonstrate a desire to control the NSL "with an iron fist."

In an appendix to the most recent edition of his classic history of the American Communist Party, Theodore Draper contends that the story of cooperation between socialist and communist students in 1932 was "largely an apochryphal tale," and "largely imaginary" (*American Communism and Soviet Russia* (New York, 1986), 467). Draper erred here. There was nothing "imaginary" about communist-socialist cooperation in the 1932 student expedition to Kentucky. Socialist expedition members attested to that cooperation (both in 1932 and in retrospect). See the letter cited in Feuer, *Conflict of Generations*, 354; Joseph P. Lash interview with author, Manhattan, N.Y., Nov. 23, 1982; and socialist Student LID leader Joseph P. Lash's glowing review of the communist-led Harlan expedition, "Students in Kentucky," *New Republic* (April 20, 1932), 267–69.

22. Hall, "Kentucky Makes Radicals," 7; Lash, "Students in Kentucky," 269.

23. Gabriel Carritt, "American Students and Kentucky Gunmen," *New Statesmen and Nation* (May 28, 1932), 703; U.S. Congress, Senate Committee on Manufactures, *Hearings on Conditions in the Coal Fields of Harlan and Bell Counties, Kentucky*, 72nd Congress, 1st Session, May 12, 13, 19, 1932, pp. 22–23.

24. Charles Croix, "The Students Invade Kentucky," *New Masses* (May 1932), 9; *Middlesboro,* [Ky.] *Daily News*, March 26, 1932; U.S. Senate. *Hearings on Conditions in the Coal Fields*, 23; CCNY *Frontiers*, April 1932.

25. Carritt, "American Students and Kentucky Gunmen," 703; *Middlesboro Daily News*, March 26, 1932.

26. Croix, "The Students Invade Kentucky," 10. Jewish representation in the Kentucky expedition was played up not only by the county prosecutor, but by the press in the coal region—apparently exploiting anti-Semitism—to whip up local hostility toward the students. See *Middlesboro Daily News*, March 26, 1932. On the local Jewish community's response to this, see *Middlesboro Daily News*, March 28, 1932; *Pineville Sun*, March 31, 1932.

27. *Middlesboro Daily News*, March 26, 1932; Carritt, "American Students and Kentucky Gunmen," 703; Croix, "Students Invade Kentucky," 10; U.S. Senate, *Hearings on Conditions in the Coal Fields*, 24.

28. Croix, "Students Invade Kentucky"; *Harlan Daily Enterprise*, March 27, 1932.

29. Lash, "Students in Kentucky," 267–68; Carritt, "American Students and Kentucky Gunmen," 703.

30. Croix, "Students Invade Kentucky," 10; U.S. Senate, *Hearings on Conditions in the Coal Fields*, 24.

31. Lash, "Students in Kentucky," 268.

32. *NYT*, March 27, 28, 1932; Hall, "Kentucky Makes Radicals," 7–8.

33. *NYT*, March 29, 1932; *Harlan Daily Enterprise*, March 29, 1932; Hall, "Kentucky Makes Radicals," 7.

34. U.S. Senate, *Hearings on Conditions in the Coal Fields*, 25.

35. *New York Herald-Tribune* editorial reprinted in the *Middlesboro Daily News*, March 27, 1932.

36. Hall, "Kentucky Makes Radicals," 8; Univ. of *Cincinnati Bearcat,* March 30, 1932; Univ. of Toledo *Collegian,* April 14, 1932.

37. On Southern support for the delegation, see Senator Costigan's remarks in U.S. Senate, *Hearings on Conditions in the Coal Fields,* 27.

38. *Columbia Spectator,* March 29, 1932.

39. James Wechsler, *Revolt on the Campus* (New York, 1935), 105–8.

40. *Ibid.,* 107–8.

41. *Ibid.,* 108; Carritt, "American Students and Kentucky Gunmen," 703.

42. Hall, "Kentucky Makes Radicals," 7–9; Lash, "Students in Kentucky," 269; George Glasgow, Charles Schrank, Walter Relis, Morris A. Shapiro, "I Am the Law," *Frontiers* (April 1932), 1; *Middlesboro Daily News,* March 26, 1932.

43. Joseph Clark interview with author.

44. U.S. Senate, *Hearings on Conditions in the Coal Fields,* 21.

45. Lash, "Students in Kentucky," 267–69.

46. Joseph P. Lash interview with author.

47. *Nation* (April 6, 1932), 383.

48. *Middlesboro Daily News,* March 27, 1932.

49. James C. Katz, "The Legacy of Reed Harris '32," *Columbia College Today* (Spring 1983), 34–35; U.S. Congress, Senate Permanent Subcommittee on Investigations of the Committee on Government Operations," Testimony of Reed Harris," 83rd Congress, 1st Session, March 3, 1953, pp. 363–64; Reed Harris, "College Fraternities-Obstacles to Social Change," *Revolt* (Dec. 1932), 7; Reed Harris, "Campus Tammany," *Student Outlook* (May 1933), 15.

50. U.S. Senate, "Testimony of Reed Harris," 375.

51. A good summary of Harris' innovative editorial work can be found in Wechsler, *The Age of Suspicion,* 22–26. Also see *Columbia Spectator,* Sept. 19, Nov. 12, 15, 1931, March 23, 29, 1932. Harris would pay a high price for his editorial radicalism, not only during the 1930s, when he was expelled from Columbia, but also during the Cold War era, when he was hounded by Senator Joseph McCarthy. As deputy chief of the Voice of America, Harris was called to testify in the Wisconsin Senator's inquiry into subversion in the federal government in 1953. Lacking evidence that Harris had been disloyal while serving in the government, McCarthy tried to discredit him by reading radical passages he had written in his youth as a student editor. This reliance on twenty-one year-old evidence made McCarthy's depiction of Harris as a dangerous radical—which Harris in his days of government service was certainly not—seem ludicrous. The "words he had published in a volume called *King Football* more than two decades ago were being hurled at him [by McCarthy] as if they were the text of a subversive directive he had just issued from a strategic government outpost," observed James Wechsler. But Harris stood up to McCarthy and paid for it by losing his job. In the end, however, Harris triumphed over the Wisconsin Senator. His defiant testimony was shown as part of Edward R. Murrow's historic "See it Now" broadcast on CBS, in March 1954, which helped to discredit McCarthy. And in 1961, when Murrow became the head of the U.S. Information Agency he brought Harris back into government service (see James C. Katz, "The Legacy of Reed Harris, Part Two : Confrontation with McCarthy," *Columbia College Today* (Fall 1983), 17–21; Wechsler, *The Age of Suspicion,* 4–5).

52. *Columbia Spectator,* Nov. 10, 1931; Wechsler, *The Age of Suspicion,* 23.

53. *Columbia Spectator,* Nov. 12, 1931

54. Wechsler, *Revolt on the Campus,* 109; Robert Hall, "Student Publications," *Varsity Review* (March 1931), 25.

55. *Columbia Spectator,* Nov. 12, 1931.

56. *Ibid.*

57. *Ibid.*

58. *Columbia Spectator,* March 23, 29, 1932.

59. Wechsler, *Revolt on the Campus,* 112–13; Reed Harris, *King Football: The Vulgarization of the American College* (New York, 1932), 188–92; *NYT,* April 2, 3, 1932.

60. Reed Harris to Dean [Herbert] Hawkes, April 1, 1932, RH; American Civil Liberties Union, *The Case of Reed Harris, Student Editor at Columbia University: His Expulsion for Criticism of College Affairs, and Subsequent Reinstatement* (New York, 1932), 1–2.

61. Harris to Hawkes, April 1, 1932, RH.

62. *NYT,* April 3, 1932.

63. ACLU, "The Case of Reed Harris," 1–10; *Daily Worker,* April 5, 1932. On the violations of academic freedom at Columbia during World War I, see Walter Metzger, *Academic Freedom in the Age of the University* (New York, 1955), 225. Political intolerance on campus in the early 1930s seemed to grow as the economic crisis did. The cases of reported violations of academic freedom almost quadrupled during the first three years of the Depression, according to the American Association of University Professors (see *Student Review* (Feb. 1933), 3). On the persistence of such political intolerance throughout the first half of the Depression decade, see James Wechsler, *Revolt on the Campus* 185–325; Harris, *King Football,* 146–58.

64. *NYT,* April 3, 1932.

65. *Ibid.,* May 12, 1935; Nicholas Murray Butler, "University Freedom," *School and Society* (Jan. 18, 1936), 99–100; Nicholas M. Butler to John Godfrey Saxe, April 9, 1932, RH.

66. Harris, *King Football,* 195.

67. *Ibid.,* 192–93.

68. *Ibid.,* 196.

69. "Private Government on the Campus—Judicial Review of University Expulsions," *Yale Law Journal* (1963), 1367.

70. *Anthony v. Syracuse Univ.,* 224 App. Div. 487, 489, 231 N.Y.S. 435, 438 (1928); William G. Millington, *The Law and the College Student: Justice in Evolution* (St. Paul, Minn., 1979), 10–11.

71. *Barker v. Bryn Mawr College,* 278 Pa., 121, 122 Atl. 220 (1923); John B. Stetson Univ., 88 Fla. 510, 516, 102 So. 637, 649 (1924); *Koblitz v. Western Reserve Univ.,* 21 Ohio C.C.R. 144 (Cuyahoga Co.), 11 Ohio C.C. Dec 515 (1901); State *ex rel. Ingersoll v. Clapp,* 81 Mont. 200, 263, 263 Pac. 443, *cert. denied,* 277 U.S. 591 *error dismissed,* 278 U.S. 661 (1928); "Private Government on the Campus," 1373.

72. *Samson v. Trustees of Columbia Univ.,* 101 Misc. 146, 167 N.Y. Supp. 202 (1917); *People ex rel. Goldenkoff v. Albany Law School,* 198 App. Div. 460, 191 N.Y. Supp. 349 (1921); *Hamilton v. Regents of the Univ. of California,* 293 U.S. 245 (1934); David W. Lousiell, "A Statement on the Legal Issues," Seymour Martin Lipset and Sheldon S. Wolin, eds., *The Berkeley Student Revolt: Facts and Interpretations* (Garden City, N.Y., 1965), 281. These legal limitations on student political rights were not lifted until the 1960s. See Millington, *The Law and the College Student,* 16–70, 160–226.

73. "For a National Student Movement: A Suggested Basis," *Student Review* (Jan.–Feb. 1932), 4.

74. *NYT,* April 4, 5, 1932.

75. *Ibid.*; *Columbia Spectator,* April 5, 1932; ACLU, "The Case of Reed Harris," 2–12.

76. *Columbia Spectator,* April 4, 1932.

77. CCNY *Campus,* April 6, 8, 12, 1932; *NYT,* April 4, 1932; Univ. of Buffalo *Bee,* April 8, 1932.

78. *New York World-Telegram,* April 6, 1932; *Nation* (April 13, 1932), 411; *New Republic* (April 13, 1932), 219.

79. *NYT,* April 5, 1932; Wechsler, *The Age of Suspicion,* 27–28.

80. *NYT,* April 5, 1932; Wechsler, *The Age of Suspicion,* 27.

81. *NYT,* April 7, 1932; "Strike Today," leaflet, CUC.

82. *NYT,* April 7, 1932.

83. *Ibid.*

84. Wechsler, *The Age of Suspicion,* 29–30.

85. *New York World-Telegram,* April 7, 1932.

86. James Wechsler, *The Age of Suspicion,* 25.

87. *NYT,* April 10, 1932.

88. *NYT,* April 21, 1932; John Godfrey Saxe to Nicholas Murray Butler, April 19, 1932, RH; N.M. McKnight telegram to H.E. Hawkes, May 2, 1932, RH.

89. Nicholas Murray Butler to John Godfrey Saxe, April 21, 1932, RH.

90. John Godfrey Saxe memorandum to President Butler, Dean Hawkes et al., April 22, 1932, RH.

91. John Godfrey Saxe to Nicholas Murray Butler, April 25, 1932; John Godfrey Saxe, "Confidential Interim Report" on the Reed Harris case, sent to President Butler et al., April 15, 1932; John Godfrey Saxe memorandum to President Butler et al., April 14, 1932. All in RH.

92. John Godfrey Saxe to Nicholas Murray Butler, April 19, 1932, RH.

93. *NYT,* April 21, 1932.

94. *Ibid.*

95. *Ibid.*

96. *Columbia Spectator,* April 21, 1932.

97. *Ibid.*;"Columbia University Strikes," *Student Review* (May 1932), 12–14. This was to be the first, but not the last time Harris would be unable to obtain a Columbia degree. During the final years of Harris' life, his admirers at Columbia, including Columbia Professor Fred Friendly, who had helped produce the Murrow exposé on McCarthy, fought in vain to have the University grant the ailing former editor a Columbia degree ("Reed Harris' Death: Columbia's Disgrace," *Columbia Spectator,* Oct. 22, 1982). The year after his death, however, Columbia finally honored Harris by endowing the Reed Harris Memorial Lecture on Free Speech and the First Amendment (Katz, "The Legacy of Reed Harris, Part Two," 21).

98. Wechsler, *The Age of Suspicion,* 25.

99. *Ibid.,* 30–31.

100. *Ibid.*

101. Hilda Rubin, "The Students Fight Fees," *Student Review* (July 1932), 11–13. Nathan Solomon interview with author, Pound Ridge, N.Y., May 13, 1982; Ted Draper, "What About Fees?," *Frontiers* (Nov. 1932), 6.

102. *Ibid.*; Thomas Coulton, *A City College in Action: Struggles and Achievement at Brooklyn College, 1930–1955* (New York, 1955), 104–5. The NSL questionnaire on fees is reprinted in Oakley Johnson, "Campus Battles for Freedom in the Thirties," *Centennial Review* (Summer 1970), 350–51.

103. *NYT,* May 24, 1932: Nathan Solomon interview with author.

104. CCNY *Campus,* April 29, 1932; *NYT,* May 25–26, 1932; Coulton, *A City College in Action,* 105; *Hunter Bulletin,* May 9, 1932.

105. Rubin, "Students Fight Fees," 13; *NYT,* May 28, 1932.

106. Rubin, "Students Fight Fees," 13; *NYT,* June 11, 1932.

107. *Ibid.*

108. *NYT,* March 26, 1932; Rubin, "Students Fight Fees," 13.

109. *NYT,* June 4, 1932; Draper, "What About Fees?," 6.

110. *NYT,* Oct. 16, 24, Nov. 3, 1932.

111. *Student Review* (May 1932), 6, 15; *Young Worker,* April 18, 1932; *Young Spartacus,* June 1932.

112. Beluah Amidon, "After College—What?," *Survey Graphic* (June 1933), 320; *NYT,* June 21, 24, 1932; *Student Outpost,* March 25, 1932.

113. *NYT,* June 6, 1932.

114. *Student Review* (July 1932), 3.

Chapter 4. The Making of a Mass Movement

1. *Daily Tar Heel,* Nov. 3, 1932; *Harvard Crimson,* Oct. 31, 1932; James Wechsler, *The Age of Suspicion* (New York, 1981), 40; *Vassar Miscellany News,* Oct. 29, Nov. 15, 1932; "Why Students Are Turning to Socialism," *Revolt* (Dec. 1932), 3. Because most undergraduates were not of voting age (which was 21) in 1932, the college straw polls are the best guide to student political opinion of the Presidential race that year, which is why the discussion of student views of those elections in this chapter draws upon those polls.

2. "Coolidge Carries Colleges," *New Student* (Nov. 1, 1924), 1–4; *NYT,* Oct. 29, 1928; *Daily Californian,* Nov. 1, 1928; Norman Thomas, "Conservatism Is Jarred—Push on to Socialism," *Revolt* (Dec. 1932), 13; *Harvard Crimson,* Oct. 21, 1932.

3. *Daily Californian,* Oct. 19, 1932.

4. *Ibid.,* Oct. 14, 1932.

5. *Columbia Spectator,* Dec. 1, 1932; *Barnard Bulletin,* Oct. 18, 1932; William Leuchtenburg, *Franklin D. Roosevelt and the New Deal* (New York, 1963), 10.

6. "Coolidge Carries Colleges," 1–4; *NYT,* Oct. 29, 1928; *Daily Californian,* Nov. 1, 1928.

7. *Columbia Spectator,* Oct. 28, 1932; Robert S. McElvaine, *The Great Depression* (New York, 1984), 133.

8. "Why Students Are Turning to Socialism," 17.

9. Wechsler, *The Age of Suspicion,* 40–41.

10. "Why Students Are Turning to Socialism," 3, 17; Joseph P. Lash interview with author.

11. On the more militant, action-oriented style of the LID in fall 1932, see "Blueprints of Action: A Handbook for Student Revolutionists," *Revolt* (Oct. 1932), 2. Here the LID began to sound like the NSL, in calling for the building of a *student* movement with an agenda for protest on a series of campus related issues ranging from opposition to ROTC to support for academic freedom. Responding to the NSL's charge that they had been merely an appendage of the adult LID, student LIDers became more autonomous—founding their own magazine in 1932 (modeled after the NSL's *Student Review*) and calling their organization the *Student League for Industrial Democracy* (SLID) in 1933.

12. *Michigan Daily,* Nov. 4, 1932.

13. *Daily Tar Heel,* Oct. 28, 1932; *NYT,* Oct. 28, 1932.

14. The NSL's lack of enthusiasm for electoral politics was reflected in the pages of its national magazine in fall 1932. The League ran only one story on the election. The story was of course pro-CP, but stopped short of endorsing any ticket (to preserve its official non-partisan status). The NSL also buried the letter from Communist Party candidates William Z. Foster and James W. Ford near the end of the Oct. 1932 issue of *Student Review.*

15. On the political distinctions between the YPSLs and the SLIDers, see Hal Draper, "The Student Movement of the 1930s: A Political History," in Rita Simon, ed., *As We Saw the Thirties* (Urbana, 1969), 158–59. Note, however, that Draper's account, though generally quite incisive, at points becomes inaccurate because of his pro-YPSL bias. Draper, a former national leader of the YPSL, exaggerates the importance of the YPSLs and overlooks their weaknesses. For instance, he writes that the student YPSLs were "numerically more important than the 'LID types.' " This would have been true only in a few metropolitan centers, such as New York and Chicago. In most of the country, the SLID was a much larger student organization than the YPSL and had chapters where there were no YPSLs (see Monroe Sweetland interview with author, San Mateo, Calif., March 6, 1982). Moreover, though the YPSLs brought their energy and militance to the student movement, as doctrinaire socialists they also tended to be somewhat sectarian, a problem whose negative impact on the student movement will discussed in Chapter 6. For examples of complaints about YPSL sectarianism, see Jeffrey Campbell to Al Hamilton et al., June 2, 1938; Harry Laidler to Al Hamilton, March 3, 1937; Al Hamilton to Harry Kingman, March 20, 1937. All in YPSL files, SP.

16. *Columbia Spectator,* Oct. 28, 1932.

17. Joseph P. Lash interview with the author.

18. *Ibid.*

19. *Michigan Daily,* April 20, 1933; *Daily Californian,* March 14, 1933.

20. *Daily Californian,* March 22, 28, 1933; *Columbia Spectator,* April 18, 1933.

21. *The* [London] *Times,* Feb. 11, 1933; *NYT,* March 18, 1933.

22. *The* [London] *Times,* Feb. 13, 17, 18, 1933; *NYT,* March 17, 1933.

23. *NYT,* March 18, 1933; *The* [London] *Times,* March 3, 1933.

24. "Refuse to Fight!," *Student Outlook* (May 1933), 3; Harold Seidman, "The Colleges Renounce War," *Nation* (May 17, 1933), 554; *NYT,* May 25, 1933; Univ. of Toledo *Collegian,* April 7, 1933.

25. *NYT,* May 25, 1933.

26. *NYT,* March 28, 1933; *Daily Californian,* March 9, 15, 1933.

27. F.M. Hardie, "Political Tendencies at Oxford," *New Statesman and Nation* (Feb. 18, 1933), 182.

28. *Brown Daily Herald,* March 22, 1933; Joseph P. Lash, *The Campus Strikes Against War* (New York, 1935), 27.

29. Joseph P. Lash and James A. Wechsler, *War Our Heritage* (New York, 1936), 43. For examples of the great influence that the First World War had on student anti-war thought during the early and mid-1930s, see *Barnard Bulletin,* Oct. 20, 1933; *Columbia Spectator,* Oct. 16, 17, 1933; *Daily Texan,* Dec. 11, 1934; *Vassar Miscellany News,* Nov. 13, 1935; *Ohio State Lantern,* Nov. 8, 1935; *Daily Tar Heel,* Nov. 8, 1935.

30. Al Hamilton, *Students Against War* (Chicago, 1937), 30–31; Warren Cohen,

The American Revisionists: The Lessons of Intervention in World War I (Chicago, 1967), 50–51, 113, 132–33, 144.

31. Charles Chatfield, *For Peace and Justice: Pacifism in America, 1914–1941* (Knoxville, 1971), 168. For examples of the popularity of this economic interpretation of war among students, see *Program and Resolutions of the Student Congress Against War* (Chicago, 1932), 2; "The Student and War," Univ. of Wisconsin *New Student* (Dec. 1933), 4–6; Buffalo *Bee*, Nov. 16, 1934; Univ. of West Virginia *Daily Athenaeum*, Dec. 7, 1934; *Emory Wheel*, Dec. 7, 1934; UCLA *Anti-war Bulletin*, March 11, 1935; *Dartmouth*, Jan. 10, 1936; *Daily Tar Heel*, May 5, 1936.

32. Eric Sevareid, *Not So Wild a Dream* (New York, 1956), 61.

33. Lash and Wechsler, *War Our Heritage*, 49.

34. "Refuse to Fight!," 3.

35. Sevareid, *Not So Wild a Dream*, 62.

36. *Ibid.*, 61; *Columbia Spectator*, March 6, April 3, 1935; Lash, *The Campus Strikes Against War*, 21; James Wechsler, *Revolt on the Campus* (1935: reprint Seattle, 1973), 11–21.

37. Al Hamilton, *Students Against War* (Chicago, 1937), 28.

38. Lash and Wechsler, *War Our Heritage*, 42–43.

39. Wechsler, *Revolt on the Campus*, 120.

40. Lash and Wechsler, *War Our Heritage*, 36.

41. Leuchtenburg, *Franklin D. Roosevelt and the New Deal*, 197.

42. Lash and Wechsler, *War Our Heritage*, 101.

43. *Daily Worker,* Jan. 17, 1933; Colonel J.E. Woodward to the Adjutant General, Jan. 11, 1933, "Estimate of the Subversive Situation for the Month of December 1932," 18 *U.S. Military Intelligence Reports: Surveillance of Radicals in the US, 1917–1941* (Frederick, Md., 1984), reel 24.

44. Joseph Cohen, "We Are International," *Student Review* (Oct. 1932), 11–12; also see call to Chicago Congress on p. 13 of the same issue. Note that Joseph Cohen changed his surname to Clark, and it appears (with the exception of one quotation) as Clark in the text.

45. The student LID leadership came close to splitting the college antiwar movement in 1932, when it organized its own peace conference in New York a month prior to the Chicago Congress and seemed bent on refusing to participate in the Chicago Congress. But at the LID's anti-war conference, the delegates—after a sustained floor fight—opted for a more cooperative stance and agreed to send representatives to the Chicago Congress (see *Young Spartacus,* Jan. 1933; "An Open Letter"; Arthur J. Bartlett, "An Antiwar Conference," *Student Review* (Dec. 1932), 12–13; Ben Fischer, "Realism in Anti-War Discussions," *Student Outlook* (Feb. 1933), 5).

46. Fischer, "Realism in Anti-War Discussions," 5. On the controversy surrounding the resolution about the Socialist International's role in supporting the First World War, see Woodward to the Adjutant General, Jan. 11, 1933, "Estimate of the Subversive Situation for the Month of December 1932," 18.

47. Harry Magdoff interview with author.

48. *Daily Worker,* Jan. 17, 1933; "Carry on the Work," *Student Review* (Feb. 1933), 13.

49. Fischer, "Realism in Anti-War Discussions," 5; *Program and Resolutions of the Student Congress Against War* (Chicago, 1932), 2; *Columbia Spectator,* Jan. 4, 1933.

50. Chatfield, *For Peace and Justice,* 155; Hamilton, *Students Against War,* 25;

Wechsler, *Revolt on the Campus,* 146; Fischer, "Realism in Anti-War Discussions," 5; *Breaking the War Habit,* Feb. 15, 1933; *I Resign* (New York, 1932), passim.

51. Buffalo *Bee,* Jan. 13, 1933; Fischer, "Realism in Anti-War Discussions," 5.

52. Howard Stone, "After the Student Congress?" *Student Review* (Feb. 1933), 13; *Daily Worker,* Jan. 17, 1933.

53. Wechsler, *Revolt on the Campus,* 136; *Columbia Spectator,* Jan. 4, 1933.

54. Joseph P. Lash, Untitled typescript of a lecture on the student movement of the 1930s, 18, JPL

55. Hamilton, *Students Against War,* 9; Wechsler, *Revolt on the Campus,* 141.

56. Joseph Clark interview with author; Hal Draper, "The Student Movement of the 1930s," 169–70.

57. Joseph Clark interview with author. Though acknowledging that he and the other NSL leaders took the initiative on the Oxford Pledge without CP approval, Clark also emphasized that if the Communist Party had been inflexible and come out against the Pledge—which it did not—the NSL would have complied by dropping the Pledge. Clark's point in the interview was that political creativity and autonomy of the communist student activists were always capable of being nullified by CP leaders because these young communists were subject to Party discipline.

58. NSL National Executive Committee, "An Open Letter," *Student Review* (Dec. 1933), 5–6; "One Big Student Movement?," *Student Outlook* (Feb. 1934), 3, 22.

59. On the origins of the student strike against war, see Lash, *The Campus Strikes Against War,* 31. Cooperation between communist and socialist students was not an infrequent occurrence during these pre-Popular Front years, as student activists repeatedly proved themselves less sectarian than their adult counterparts (see *Daily Cardinal,* April 30, 1933; CCNY *Campus,* April 28, May 12, 1933; *Columbia Spectator,* Oct. 17, Nov. 17, 1933; Richard Criley interview with author, Carmel, Calif., June 17, 1982).

60. "April 13th—Strike Against War," *Student Outlook* (March 1934), 4; Lash, *The Campus Strikes Against War,* 34.

61. Transcript of Joseph P. Lash interview with Joel Chernoff, April 2, 1978, p. 18, JPL; Joseph P. Lash, untitled typescript of a lecture on the student movement of the 1930s, 19, JPL; "Why a Strike," *Student Outlook* (April 1935), 3–4.

62. *NYT,* April 14, 1934; "Students Strike Against War," *Student Outlook* (May 1934), 12–16. Not all students, however, welcomed the antiwar strike. As was the case in the Reed Harris strike, conservative students—centered in the fraternities, athletic teams and ROTC—opposed the strike, and in several cases expressed their opposition through violence. These foes of the antiwar strike acted on the belief that the strikes were unpatriotic and uncollegiate. Their outbursts did not lead to any institutionalized conservative student resistance to the antiwar movement at the national level; and they virtually died out by the time of the third antiwar strike (see Wechsler, *Revolt on the Campus,* 347–63; Heywood Broun, "Harvard Indifference," Heywood Hale Broun, ed., *Collected Edition of Heywood Broun* (New York, 1941), 332–34; Robert Cohen, "Revolt of the Depression Generation: America's First Mass Student Movement, 1929–41" (Ph.D. diss., UC Berkeley, 1987), 346–52.

63. Eunice Barnard, "Students Lay a Barrage Against War," *NYT Magazine* (April 19, 1934), 5.

64. Joseph P. Lash interview with author.

65. Leuchtenburg, *Franklin D. Roosevelt and the New Deal,* 218.

66. On the influence that the Nye Committee investigation had upon students, see Ernest R. Bryan, "Munition Makers on the Spot," *National Student Mirror* (Nov. 1934), 25–27; Univ. of Wisconsin *New Student,* Dec. 1934; *Barnard Bulletin,* April 9, 1935; *Daily Tar Heel,* Dec. 3, 1935; *Brooklyn College Pioneer,* April 10, 1935; *The Dartmouth,* April 12, 1936; Joseph P. Lash, "Morgan: Wanted for Murder," *Student Advocate* (Feb. 1936), 10–11.

67. Major G. W. Lester to Assistant Chief of Staff, "Internal Report Reference on the Subversive Situation," Nov. 26, 1935, p. 12, *U.S. Military Intelligence Reports: Surveillance of Radicals in the US, 1917–1941,* reel 24; *Oberlin Review,* April 11, 1935; "Why a Strike," 4.

68. Joseph P. Lash to Hayes Beall, Feb. 28, 1935; Rix Pierce Butler to Joseph P. Lash, March 5, 1935, both in JPL.

69. Wechsler, *Revolt on the Campus,* 179–80; *NYT,* April 13, 1935.

70. *Ibid.*

71. Hamilton, *Students Against War,* 19.

72. *Barnard Bulletin,* April 16, 1935. A similar political message was articulated on campuses across the nation. See *NYT,* April 13, 1935; *Daily Texan,* April 13, 1935; *Harvard Crimson,* April 14, 1935; Univ. of Virginia *College Topics,* April 12, 1935; *Oberlin Review,* April 11, 1935; *Challenge of Youth,* April 1935; Lash, *The Campus Strikes Against War,* 34.

73. Chatfield, *For Peace and Justice,* 259–60; *Ohio State Lantern,* Nov. 18, 1935.

74. Joseph Clark interview with author.

75. "Refuse to Fight!," 3.

76. *Ibid.*; "War is Now an Immediate Probability," *Student Outlook* (Oct. 1935), 4.

77. Jean Ford, "The CCC Stands Ready," *Student Outlook* (March 1934), 8–9; Selig Adler, *The Isolationist Impulse* (New York, 1961), 219–49; Hamilton, *Students Against War,* 32. Though the student movement depicted the U.S. as an aggressive war machine, the American standing army in 1934 was composed of only 118,750 men ("A Student Strike Against War," *Literary Digest* (March 23, 1935), 17).

78. Adler, *The Isolationist Impulse,* 238–43.

79. *Daily Californian,* April 14, 1933; Ruth Rubin, "I Heckled Luther," *Student Review* (Jan. 1934), 7–8; Edwin Alexander, "Guttersnipes at City," *Student Review* (Dec. 1934), 11–12; *Harvard Crimson,* May 22, 1934.

80. *NYT,* May 10, 11, 1933; Philip Metcalfe, *1933* (New York, 1988), 122; *Harvard Crimson,* May 7, 16, 18, 1934.

Chapter 5. Spies, Suppression, and Free Speech on Campus

1. Celeste Strack interview with author. The most thorough published account of the repression of student free speech rights on campus during the first half of the Depression decade is James Wechsler, *Revolt on the Campus* (1935: reprint, Seattle, 1973), 185–435. This was the first book-length account of the student movement of the 1930s, written by a leader of that movement. The fact that Wechsler, then a NSL and YCL activist, devoted more than half of the book to political repression and free speech suggests that the issue of student political rights was of critical importance to the student movement. Wechsler's account is also valuable in that it provides a wealth of information about collegiate free speech

battles in this era. But as a young communist, Wechsler proved unable to keep his partisanship out of the narrative, and the result is an interpretation of the national campus scene which tends to overdramatize and exaggerate the threat from the American Right in the 1930s.

Wechsler viewed the rise of political repression on college campuses in the U.S. during the first half of the Depression decade as evidence that America was experiencing a full scale red scare, which he saw as an ominous sign of the nation's potential to drift toward fascism (197, 223). What Wechsler failed to see here—in part because he was writing during the height of this repression in 1935—was that the repression would fade, and that it would prove unsuccessful in either hindering the growth of the student movement or producing an effective red scare. Indeed, Wechsler was so anxious to trumpet the danger from the Right and to apply the term "red scare" to the national campus political scene in the 1930s that he became much too loose in his use of that term. When a red scare sweeps the nation, as it did in 1919 and in the early 1950s, an almost hysterical anti-radicalism becomes popularized, leading to massive intolerance of the Left and the smashing or radical organizations both on campus and off. Though anti-radicals hoped to launch such a red scare in the early Depression years—and fostered the suppression of radicalism on campus wherever they could—they failed miserably, and the student Left therefore was able in the mid-1930s to experience one of its greatest periods of growth and influence in twentieth-century America.

2. FBI Office Memorandum, Clyde Tolson and the Executive Conference to The Director [of the FBI], March 28, 1949. Copies of this and all the FBI documents cited below are in the author's possession and were obtained under the Freedom of Information Act; they are also available in FBI headquarters in Washington, D.C. Though the documents provide a valuable glimpse of the informing against student protesters of the 1930s and early 1940s, they are not complete. The FBI censored the documents by frequently deleting the names of its informants, and at some points deleting entire pages of the documents.

3. In more than 3000 pages of FBI documents covering the student movement of the Depression decade, I did not find a single case in which a college or university administrator refused to cooperate with the FBI. None expressed any concern that informing on students might constitute a violation of their rights.

4. On the Univ. of Pennsylvania, see FBI file #61–136, Sept. 28, 1942, Report made by Harry C. Leslie Jr., Philadelphia; on Ohio State Univ., see FBI file # 100–365, June 18, 1941, Report made by D.G. Jenkins, Cincinnati; on Montana State Univ., see FBI file # 61–195, Aug. 12, 1941, Report made by Elmer W. Parrish, Butte; on Temple Univ., see FBI file #61–136, Sept. 28, 1942, Report made by Harry C. Leslie Jr., Philadelphia; on Purdue Univ., see FBI file #100–475, Nov. 12, 1942, Report made by Douglas J. Williams, Indianapolis; on the Univ. of Illinois, see FBI file# 100–191, Jan. 10, 1941, Report made by W.A. Temple, Springfield; FBI file #100–191, Feb. 1, Aug. 27, Oct. 30, 1941, Reports made by J.J. Racan, Springfield; FBI file #100–191, Nov. 14, 1941, Report made by Arthur R. Day, Springfield; FBI file# 100–191, April 21, 1942, Report made by Charles F. Douglas, Springfield; on the Univ. of Missouri, see FBI file # 100–1193, Oct. 10, 1941, Report made by R.E. Sherk, Kansas City; FBI file# 100–1193, Dec. 5, 1941, Report made by W.C. Fuller, Kansas City; FBI file #100–1193, March 21, 1942, Report made by R.B. Ayers, Kansas City; on Middlebury College, see FBI file #100–483, Feb. 6, 1942, Report made by Frank C. Wood, Albany, N.Y.; on DePauw Univ., see FBI file #100–475, Feb. 20 [?], 1941, Report

made by Richard C. Godfrey, Indianapolis; on the Univ. of Minnesota, see [FBI file# illegible], Feb. 1, 1941, Report made by R.T. Noonan, St. Paul, Minn.; on the Univ. of Hawaii, see FBI file #100–1241, June 28, 1941, Report made by John I. Condon, Honolulu; on the Univ. of Washington, see FBI file # 100–942, July 3, 1941, Report made by R.D. Auerbach, Seattle; on Yale Univ., see [day and month illegible], 1941, [Reporting FBI agent's name illegible], New Haven; FBI file #100–589, [month illegible], 21, 1941, and July 17, 1942, Reports made by G. J. McDonough, New Haven; FBI file #100–589, Oct. 7, 1942, Report made by Charles E. Stine, New Haven; Sigmund Diamond, "Surveillance in the Academy: Harry B. Fisher and Yale University, 1927–1952," *American Quarterly* (Spring 1984), 7–43; on Wesleyan Univ., see FBI file #100–589, 1941 [month and day illegible, reporting agent name illegible] New Haven; on Oberlin College, see FBI file # 100–608, Sept. 3, 1941, Report made by S.E. Hobbs, Cleveland; on Wilson Teachers College, see FBI file# 100–920, Sept. 14, 1942, Report made by M.J. Connolly, Washington D.C.; on George Washington Univ., see FBI file# 100–920, Sept. 14, 1942, Report made by M. J. Connolly, Washington, D.C.; on Indiana State Teachers College, see FBI file #100–475, Feb. 20 [?], 1941, Report made by Richard C. Godfrey, Indianapolis; on the Univ. of Chicago, see FBI file # 61–327, Dec. 6, 1941, Report made by J.F. Desmond, Chicago; On the Univ. of Michigan, see FBI file #100–1217, Feb. 8, 1943, Report made by John C. Hall, Detroit; on Ohio Univ. at Athens, see FBI file # 100–365, May 27, 1941, Report made by A.W. Richardson, Cincinnati; FBI file #100–365, March 9, 1942, Report made by J.T. Delaney, Cincinnati; On Earlham College, see FBI file #100–475, Jan. 23, 1943, Report made by George A. Brouillard, Indianapolis.

5. There is evidence of similar political intelligence work at several other campuses. See Confidential Report on American Student Union meeting held in the Michigan Union on Nov. 11, [1940]; City of Ann Arbor Police Report, Nov. 18, 1940, both in Dean of Students Papers, UM; Colonel Edward Kimmel to Commanding General Ninth Corps Area, May 21, 1938, Presidents' Papers, UW. Political surveillance of UCLA student activists will be discussed later in this chapter.

6. Monroe Deutsch to Earl Warren, M.B. Driver, Sheriff of Alameda County, Hollis Thompson, Berkeley City Manager, J.F. Hassler, Oakland City Manager, Ralph Bryant, Alameda City Manager, J.A. Greening, Berkeley Chief of Police, B.A. Wallman, Oakland Chief of Police, Vern Smith, Alameda Chief of Police, Fred Heere, Piedmont Chief of Police, James F. Hooey, District Attorney, Contra Costa County, R. R. Veale, Sheriff of Contra Costa County, J.A. McVittie, Richmond City Manager, David P. Barrows, General, California National Guard, Joseph P. Sanches, Adjutant, Berkeley Post No.7, American Legion, L.C. Thumen, Oakland Post No. 5, American Legion, James K. Fisk, Department Adjutant of the California American Legion, July 23, 1934, President's Files, UCB; Earl Warren to Provost Monroe Deutsch, July 24, 1934, President's Files, UCB. In this letter to Deutsch, Warren alludes to a May 1934 meeting he had with UC Comptroller Luther Nichols and another UC administrator, during which he had urged the University to take a strong stand against campus radicalism. He also agreed to provide the UC police and administration with any intelligence information that his office gathered on campus radicals at Berkeley.

7. Monroe Deutsch to Earl Warren [et al.], July 23, 1934, President's Files, UCB.

8. Albert E. Boynton to Robert G. Sproul, Aug. 22, 1934; Robert G. Sproul

to Albert E. Boynton Aug. 24, 1934; Monroe Deutsch Memorandum to the President, Aug. 9, 1934, President's Files, UCB.

9. Harry Noland, Monterey County District Attorney to President Sproul, Nov. 1, 1934; Robert G. Sproul to E.A. Hugill, UC Berkeley Grounds and Buildings, Nov. 3, 1934, both in President's Files, UCB; Sproul also responded to Noland's report on Criley's political affiliation by thanking him, writing Noland that it was "most helpful to know the background of these persons with whom one must deal" (Sproul to Noland, Nov. 3, 1934, President's Files, UCB). Sproul's letter to Hugill, asking him to obtain further information on Criley is revealing in that it shows that the president's office used Hugill's department—Building and Grounds—in conjunction with the campus police to gather intelligence on the student Left at UC Berkeley (see E.A. Hugill to Robert G. Sproul, Aug. 23, 1934; Monroe Deutsch to Robert G. Sproul, Aug. 22, 1934; Harold Ellis Memorandum for President Sproul, Oct. 31, 1934 (which suggests that Hugill's department photographed radicals and student protest meetings as part of its political surveillance work). All in President's Files, UCB).

10. Monroe Deutsch to Robert G. Sproul, Nov. 8, 1934, President's Files, UCB.

11. *Ibid.*

12. David P. Barrows to Monroe Deutsch, Aug. 1, 1934; David P. Barrows to Monroe Deutsch, Aug. 22, 1934, President's Files, UCB.

13. David P. Barrows to Monroe Deutsch, Aug. 22, 1934.

14. *Ibid.*; David P. Barrows to Monroe Deutsch, Aug. 1, 1934.

15. *NYT*, May 19, 1935. For an incisive discussion of this notion—widespread among campus administrators—that radical activism was antithetical to the intellectual mission of the university, see Marianne Ruth Phelps, "The Response of Higher Education to Student Activism, 1933–1938" (Ph.D. diss., George Washington Univ., 1980), 74–75.

16. Charles Wesley Flint, "Academic Freedom," *Educational Record* (Oct. 1935), 442.

17. Robert Gordon Sproul, "Problems of an American University," *School and Society* (May 30, 1936), 723–24.

18. L.D. Goffman, "The Exploitation of Youth," *Educational Record* (Jan. 1936), 95–96.

19. Wechsler, *Revolt on the Campus*, 208.

20. *Daily Californian*, Oct. 30, 1934.

21. Wechsler, *Revolt on the Campus*, 190; Ruthven proved true to his word, expelling four University of Michigan students in 1935 because of their antiwar organizing. See Wechsler, *Revolt on the Campus*, 191; Nicholas Olds to President Ruthven, Oct. 8, 1935; Ruthven to Olds, Oct. 9, 1935; both in ACLU.

22. Flint, "Academic Freedom," 433, 439.

23. On this notion that student speech was not protected by the right of academic freedom, see Chapter 3 of this study, and see *NYT*, May 12, 1935.

24. Sproul, "Problems of an American University," 723.

25. James L. McConaughy, "Education in a Democracy," *School and Society* (Sept. 25, 1937), 389.

26. Sproul, "Problems of an American University," 724.

27. McConaughy, "Education in a Democracy," 387.

28. Wechsler's *Revolt on the Campus* documents abrogations of student political rights at Berea (218–22); UC Berkeley (279–83); CCNY and the CCNY Busi-

ness School (383–96); the Univ. of Colorado (187); Columbia Univ.(406–16); Commonwealth College (245–57); Connecticut State College (310–24); Harvard, (347–54); Hunter College (396–402); UCLA (274–79); Los Angeles Jr. College, (192–93); MIT(336–44), Univ. of Michigan (190–92); Michigan State Univ. (299–310); Univ. of Missouri (438); Oregon State Univ. (344–45); Univ. of Pittsburgh (198–206); San Jose State College (275); Santa Clara Univ. (189–190); Syracuse Univ. (207–12); Univ. of Virginia (346); George Washington Univ.(189); Univ. of Washington (187–188); Univ. of Wisconsin (331–33).

For campus free speech violations not covered by Wechsler, see Case Technical College, Alexander Buchman, "Smashing the Campus Revolt," *Student Review* (April 1933), 8; and *Cleveland Student*, March 8, 1933, ACLU; the Univ. of Chicago, *NYT*, April 13, 1935; Fisk Univ., *The Crisis* (April 1934), 111; Hartwick College, *Time* (June 5, 1933), 44; Howard Univ., Rayford Logan, *Howard University: The First Hundred Years, 1867–1967* (New York, 1968), 392; Johns Hopkins Univ., *NYT*, April 14, 1934; Hunter College Bronx Extension, *Hunter Bulletin*, Oct. 24, 1933; the Univ. of Idaho, Merwin R. Sawnson, "Student Radicals at the Southern Branch: Campus Protest in the 1930s," *Idaho Yesterdays* (Fall 1976), 21–26 ; Louisiana State Univ. "Strike of Students of Journalism at the State University of Louisiana," *School and Society* (Dec. 8, 1934), 766; MacMurray College, Monroe Sweetland to American Civil Liberties Union, April 29, 1935, ACLU; Marietta College, "Campus Notes," *Student Review* (April 1935), 13; the Univ. of Maryland, *National Student Mirror* (Oct. 1934), 12; Medill Jr. College, Jean Horie, "The War-Makers Strike Back," *Student Review* (June 1935), 9; the Univ. of Minnesota, Richard M. Scammon and Lester Breslow, "Booting Out ROTC." *Student Outlook* (Oct. 1934), 13; Breslow and Scammon, "One Front in Minnesota," *Student Review* (Nov. 1934), 14 ; Sevareid, *Not So Wild a Dream*, 61; the Univ. of Nebraska, "Pacifists 39 percent," *Time* (June 5, 1933), 44 ; New York Univ., "Striking for Students' Rights," *Student Review* (March 1933), 12–13; the Univ. of Oklahoma, *Student Outlook* (May 1934), 14–15; Univ. of Oregon, "Regimentation in the Colleges," *New Republic* (Nov. 1934), 6; Ohio State Univ., *The Ohio State University Peace News*, Jan. 30, 1934; Pasadena Jr. College, *Student Outlook* (May 1934), 16; San Mateo Jr. College, *Student Outlook* (Nov.–Dec. 1934), 36; USC, Celeste Strack Kaplan interview with author; the Univ. of Tennessee, *Student Outlook* (March 1934), 21; the Univ. Texas, *National Student Mirror* (Jan. 1936), 24–25; the Univ. of West Virginia, Monroe Sweetland interview with author, San Mateo, Calif., March 6, 1982; Western Reserve Univ., Monroe Sweetland interview; Wright Jr. College, Horie, "The War-Makers Strike Back," 9; Univ. of Wyoming, *Student Outlook* (Nov.–Dec. 1934), 37.

Such widespread repression leaves the impression that all administrators thought alike on the question of student political rights during the early 1930s. But there were some distinctions in how administrators viewed this question. The most self-consciously repressive administrators were the absolute paternalists, who, like President W. Coleman Nevills of Georgetown University, thought it proper to "exclude all political activities among student bodies." These administrators tended to be political conservatives. A second group were more moderate paternalists, such as President Robert M. Hutchins of the University of Chicago. They tended to be liberals, who preferred to at least give the appearance that they were tolerant of dissent. This group argued that "campus political activity is to be tolerated *under careful supervision*" (emphasis added). The supervision turned to suppression, however, when student politics became too militant to suit the administration. For example, the Hutchins administration, which presented itself as liberal, was not above banning NSL meetings and requiring prior approval of all socialist leaflets distributed in the campus area. Since both types of paternalists engaged in repressive conduct towards students, it is easy to overlook the distinction between them. But at the very least, their rhetoric was different. See *NYT,* May 19, 1935; William E Scott to Mr. Hauser, Feb. 6, 1933, President's Papers, UC; Univ. of Chicago *Upsurge,* Feb. 6, 1935, UC.

Out of the mainstream were the few college presidents who took a principled civil liberties stance, making a point of respecting the free speech rights of their students. This was the case, for instance, with President Samuel P. Capen of the University of Buffalo—who not only wrote in defense of academic freedom, but also lived up to his rhetoric during the early 1930s (Univ. of Buffalo *Bee,* Oct. 21, 1932; Samuel P. Capen, "The Obligation of the University to American Democracy," *School and Society* (June 22, 1935), 819–22). A similar pattern of tolerance prevailed at the few colleges which had special liberal, feminist, or pacifist traditions. See, for example, the support for student civil liberties within the administration of Swarthmore College—a school founded by Quakers (Harold B. Speight to Norman Thomas, May 14, 1935, NT).

29. *Time* (April 22, 1935), 30.

30. Wechsler, *Revolt on the Campus,* 275.

31. *Ibid.,* 306.

32. *Ibid.,* 308.

33. UC Berkeley *Student Rights Association Bulletin* Nov. 27, 1934, UCB; C. Michael Otten, *University Authority and the Student* (Berkeley, 1970), 111.

34. *NYT,* June 5, 1933.

35. *NYT,* April 14, 1934, April 13, 1935; Wechsler, *Revolt on the Campus,* 299–310, 324–36 336–44, 405–6; *University Daily Kansan,* April 23, 1936.

36. This ranking is based upon the repressive incidents on 53 campuses. The 14 campuses which witnessed violent attacks on student activists between 1933 and 1935 were UC Berkeley, the Univ. of Chicago, CCNY, Columbia Univ., Connecticut State College, Harvard, UCLA, Los Angeles Jr. College, MIT, Michigan State Univ., Oregon State Univ., San Jose State College, Univ. of Washington, and University of Wisconsin. University authorities denied students the right to hold antiwar meetings, or banned student movement rallies on 17 campuses from 1933 to 1935 : Berea College, UC Berkeley, CCNY, the Univ. of Colorado, Connecticut State College, Howard Univ., Hunter College and Hunter's Bronx extension, Los Angeles Jr. College, UCLA, Univ. of Michigan, Univ. of Minnesota, Univ. of Missouri, Ohio State Univ., Univ. of Pittsburgh, George Washington Univ., Univ. of Washington.

Anti-war and radical student organizations were banned—at least temporarily—at 8 campuses between 1933 and 1935: Berea College, the Univ. of Chicago, CCNY, the Univ. of Pittsburgh, Syracuse Univ., George Washington Univ., Univ. of Washington, Univ. of Wisconsin.

University administrators expelled or suspended (or threatened disciplinary action against) student activists engaged in lawful protest activity at 16 campuses between 1933 and 1935: Case Technical College, CCNY, Connecticut State College, Columbia Univ., Fisk Univ., Howard Univ., Hunter College, UCLA, Louisiana State Univ., Univ. of Maryland, Univ. of Michigan, Ohio State Univ., the Univ. of Pittsburgh, Santa Clara Univ., USC, George Washington Univ., Univ. of West Virginia.

Censorship of antiwar literature, movement publications and campus newspaper editorials occurred on 16 campuses between 1933 and 1935: UC Berkeley, Case Technical College, CCNY, CCNY Business School, Columbia Univ., Hartwick College, Louisiana State Univ., Univ. of Michigan, Michigan State Univ., Univ. of Nebraska, New York Univ., Oregon State Univ., the Univ. of Oregon, Santa Clara Univ., Syracuse Univ., the Univ. of Texas.

All these free speech violations are covered in the sources cited in note 28 and in the following sources: Univ. of Virginia *College Topics,* May 21, 1935; *Hunter Bulletin,* Oct. 23, 1934, and March 18, 1935; Theresa Levin, "Academic Napoleon No. 5 , Dr. Colligan: Tammany's Aloysius," *Student Advocate* (Oct. 1937), 9–10; Univ. of Wisconsin *Daily Cardinal,* Jan. 8, 1936; "Academic Freedom in the U of C," Univ. of Chicago *Upsurge* (Aug. 1935), 1; Theodore Draper, "The Expulsions at Ohio State," *Student Review* (Feb. 1934), 14–15; *University of Washington Daily,* Feb. 17, Nov. 14, 1934; "At Columbia," *School and Society* (June 8, 1935), 778; *Columbia Spectator,* May 2, June 4, Oct. 18, 22, 1935; "Strike of Students of Journalism at the State University of Louisiana," *School and Society* (Dec. 8, 1934), 766; Univ. of West Virginia *Daily Athenaeum,* Feb. 23, Oct. 30, 1935; Marianne Ruth Phelps, "The Response of Higher Education to Student Activism," 92–125; Clifford McVeagh, "Academic Napoleons No. 1 : Ruthven of Michigan," *Student Advocate* (Feb. 1936), 13–15; Arthur Wilson, "Academic Napoleons No. IV: Chancellor Bowman of Pittsburgh," *Student Advocate* (Feb. 1937), 21–22.

37. Kenneth Walser, "What the Supreme Court Decided," *Intercollegian* (Jan.–Feb. 1935), 95–97; Joseph Lash, *The Campus Strikes Against War* (New York, 1935), 24.

38. Judah Drob interview with author, Washington, D.C., Jan. 22, 1982.

39. For a fuller discussion of the Johnson case, see Robert P. Cohen, "Revolt of the Depression Generation: America's First Mass Student Movement, 1929–1940" (Ph.D. diss., UC Berkeley, 1987), 180–96; Oakley Johnson, "Campus Battles for Freedom in the Thirties," *Centennial Review* (Summer 1970), 350–64.

40. *NYT,* Oct. 31, 1932; CCNY *Campus,* Nov. 1, 1932; Johnson, "Campus Battles For Freedom," 363–64; Harry Magdoff interview with author; S. Willis Rudy, *The College of the City of New York, 1847–1947* (New York, 1949), 416–17. Note, however, that though outrage over the Johnson firing and the suspensions helped fuel the growth of the CCNY Left, the protests failed to force the CCNY administration to reinstate Johnson. This would prove the case repeatedly at CCNY: administration repression hurt individual activists and disrupted their careers, while simultaneously igniting further protests which strengthened the student movement.

41. CCNY *Student,* May 26, 1933.

42. *NYT,* May 30, 1933.

43. *Ibid.; City College and War: Why Were 21 Students Expelled?* (New York, 1933), 5–9, CCNY.

44. *NYT,* May 30, 1933.

45. *Ibid.*

46. The statement disputing Robinson's version of the umbrella incident is by Florina Lasker, chair of the New York Committee of the ACLU, in *City College and War,* 10.

47. *Ibid.,* 8–9; Judah Drob and Harold Goldstein interview with author, Washington, D.C., June 22, 1982.

48. CCNY *Advance,* May 31, 1933.

49. *NYT,* June 1, 1933.

50. *NYT* June 3, 7, 1933.

51. *New Republic* (June 21, 1933), 138.

52. *NYT,* June 2, 1933.

53. *NYT,* June 5, 1933

54. *NYT,* May 31, 1933.

55. *Testimony in the Matter of the Field Day Disturbance of May 29, 1933,* 240, CCNY.

56. *Ibid.,* 459.

57. *Ibid.,* 117

58. *Ibid.,* 42

59. *Ibid.,* 23.

60. *Ibid.,* 401.

61. *Ibid.,* 55; at women's colleges a similar ideal was invoked by administrators and other critics of the student movement. They charged that radical activism was "unladylike" (see *Hunter Bulletin,* April 1, May 6, 1935; "Stop Playing with Dolls," *Vassar Alumnae Magazine* (Oct. 1, 1935), 9–10).

62. *Testimony . . . Field Day Disturbance,* 342, 395.

63. *Ibid.,* 110, 116–18.

64. *Ibid.*

65. *Ibid.,* 241; "Report of the Special Committee Appointed by the Faculty, June 12, 1933, CCNY"; *City College and War: Why Were 21 Students Expelled?,* 13.

66. CCNY *Campus,* April 17, 1934.

67. CCNY *Student,* Oct. 26, 1934; CCNY *Campus,* Oct. 8, 1934. In requesting that CCNY not hold a reception for the Italian fascist students, the Student Council had argued that the college should not allow them to come to campus to promote fascist propaganda. This argument is not very different from that which administrators used to ban Left activists—whom they derided as "propagandists," and it underscores the fact that student radicals advocated political liberty on campus for themselves but were far from absolute civil libertarians where the Right was concerned (see the perceptive discussion of this limited view of civil liberty in Eileen Eagan, *Class, Culture and the Classroom: The Student Peace Movement of the 1930s* (Philadelphia, 1981), 73–79). However, at CCNY in 1934 the question was less one of allowing the fascists to speak on campus than it was of the administration honoring them with a special reception, barring any counter demonstration in proximity to that reception, and confiscating the placards and leaflets of students who tried to organize such a counter demonstration. See CCNY Alumni Association, *Final Report of the Special Committee* (New York, 1936), 30–31, JPL.

68. CCNY *Office of the Dean, Hearings, October 10–November 7, 1934,* vol. I, 10–11, CCNY; Edwin Alexander, "Guttersnipes at City," *Student Review* (Dec. 1934), 11–12.

69. CCNY *Office of the Dean, Hearings, Oct. 10–Nov. 7, 1934,* vols. I and II, passim; CCNY *Student,* Oct. 10, 15, 26, 1934; CCNY *Campus,* Oct. 16, 19, 1934.

70. CCNY *Campus,* Oct, 23, 26, 29, 1934, Nov. 14, 16, 23; CCNY *Student,* Oct. 15, 26, 1934, Nov. 2, 9, 19, 23, 1934.

71. CCNY *Student,* Nov. 23, 1934.

72. *City College Alumnus* (Oct. 1934), 127–28; Rudy, *The College of the City of New York,* 427–32.

73. *NYT,* Oct. 30, 1932.

74. Barbara J. Dunlap, "From the Pen of President Robinson," *The City College Alumnus* (April 1981), 6.

75. Ernest C. Moore to Frederick B. Robinson, Dec. 7, 1934, ECM.

76. Wechsler, *Revolt on the Campus*, 276–77.

77. UCLA *Daily Bruin*, Oct. 30, 31, 1934, *Los Angeles Times*, Oct. 30, 31, 1934; UCLA Student Council Minutes, Oct. 3, 24, 26, 19, 1934, President's Papers, UCB; Earl Sacks, "A Student Observation of the UCLA Situation," ECM; Anna Wallace, "Fascism Comes to the Campus: The University of California as a Case in Point," *New Republic* (Jan. 9, 1935), 238–41; Celeste Strack Kaplan interview with author.

78. Claudie Little, "Vigilantism at U.C.L.A.," *Student Outlook* (Nov.- Dec. 1934), 20–21; Celeste Strack Kaplan interview with author.

79. *Ernest Carroll Moore Diary, Jan. 1933–Sept. 1937*, reel 3, July 15, 1934, ECM.

80. Norman Lee Ridker, "Ernest Carroll Moore and the Red Scare" (unpublished paper, UCLA, 1961), 16–17, 23, UCLA Archives.

81. Ernest C. Moore to Robert G. Sproul, May 10, 1934, President's Files, UCB.

82. *Ibid*; *Moore Diary*, Aug. 31, 1934, *ECM*.

83. *Moore Diary*, Aug. 31, 1934.

84. J. Finlinson, acting chief of police of Los Angeles, to E.C. Moore, Sept. 7, 1934; Luke Lane, detective lieutenant, commanding Intelligence Bureau of the Los Angeles Police Department to Ernest C. Moore, April 17, 1935; *Moore Diary*, Nov. 22, 1934. All in ECM.

85. *Moore Diary*, Oct. 20, 22, 1934, ECM.

86. Roberta Monks to President Sproul, Oct. 31, 1934, President's Files, UCB.

87. *Ibid.*; *Report on the Investigating Committee on the Five Suspended Students*, President's Files, UCB.

88. UCLA *Daily Bruin*, Oct. 31, 1934; *Los Angeles Times*, Oct. 31, 1934.

89. *Ibid.*

90. *Daily Bruin*, Oct. 30, 31, 1934; Wechsler, *Revolt on the Campus*, 277; Sacks, "A Student Observation of the UCLA Situation," 4–5.

91. *Daily Bruin*, Nov. 5, 1934.

92. *Los Angeles Times*, Oct. 31, 1934; Anna Wallace, "Fascism Comes to the Campus," 238–41.

93. *Daily Bruin*, Nov. 1, 1934; John Rockwell, "The Strike at Berkeley," *Student Outlook* (Nov.–Dec. 1934), 23–24.

94. "Statement of the Central Strike Committee, events of November 5, 1934," President's Files, UCB; Rockwell, "The Strike at Berkeley," 23–24; Richard Criley interview with author. Sproul's anti-strike statement was reprinted in the *San Francisco Chronicle*, Nov. 6, 1934; Provost Monroe Deutsch "Memo to Members of the Faculty," Nov. 3, 1934; Professor George Adams to President Robert G. Sproul, Nov. 6, 1934, both in President's Files, UCB.

95. UC Berkeley *Student Rights Association Bulletin*, Nov. 27, 1934, UCB; Otten, *University Authority and the Student*, 111.

96. *Daily Californian*, Nov. 6, 1934; Richard Criley interview with author.

97. Richard Criley interview with author.

98. Monroe Deutsch Statement, Nov. 5, 1934, President's Files, UCB

99. *Daily Californian*, Nov. 7, 1934.

100. *Daily Bruin*, Oct. 30, 31, 1934.

101. *Ibid.*; *Daily Californian*, Nov. 7, 1934.

102. Chester Rowell to President Robert Sproul, Nov. 5, 1934, President's Files, UCB. Moore also enjoyed the support of two of Los Angeles' leading newspapers, both of which were right-wing. Indeed, the local Hearst paper had gone

so far as to endorse the use of vigilante tactics by anti-radical students at UCLA (*Los Angeles Herald Examiner,* Nov. 9, 1934; *Los Angeles Times,* Oct. 31, 1934).

103. *Oakland Tribune,* Aug. 31, 1934; Robert G. Sproul, "Universities Face Radicalism, *Rotarian* (Oct. 1934), 22–23. Robert Sproul to Glenn Chadwick, Nov. 28, 1934, President's Files, UCB.

104. President Sproul, preliminary draft statement, [n.d] President's Files, UCB.

105. President Sproul to Mr. Dickson, Nov. 17, 1934, President's Files, UCB.

106. *Daily Bruin,* Nov. 15, 1934.

107. *Daily Californian,* Nov. 14, 1934.

108. Sproul to Dickson, Nov. 17, 1934; Sproul's bias against Strack apparently grew after he read the intelligence reports produced by the political surveillance network that he and Moore had helped construct. At Moore's request, the San Diego police chief had provided him with a detailed report—which Moore then gave to Sproul—on Strack's leadership role in off campus communist meetings. See Geo. M. Sears, San Diego chief of police, to Ernest C. Moore, "Re: Celeste Strack," Nov. 19, 1934, President's Files, UCB.

109. Sproul to Dickson, Nov. 17, 1934.

110. Minutes of the Univ. of California Board of Regents meeting, San Francisco, Dec. 14, 1934, President's Files, UCB.

111. Sproul to Dickson, Nov. 17, 1934.

112. President Sproul's handwritten notes used in his questioning of the suspended students [n.d.], President's Files, UCB.

113. H. Rodison to President Robert G. Sproul, Dec. 1, 1934, President's Files, UCB. The story of this intercepted LID letter was one in which Provost Moore was once again playing political policeman. After having apparently obtained this letter through one of his spies, Moore tried unsuccessfully to use the letter as proof that he had been correct all along about the suspensions and the communist plot to destroy UCLA. (Waldemar Westergaard telegram to President Robert Sproul, Nov. 29, 1934; Monroe Sweetland to Sidney Zagri [Zsagri], Oct. 31, 1934, President's Files, UCB.) Moore's diary confirms that the provost did try to prod Chief Davis of the Los Angeles Police Department to arrest Sweetland (*Moore Diary,* Nov. 22, 1934, ECM). Contrary to Moore's claim, the Sweetland letter contained nothing implicating the LID organizer in any communist plot to destroy UCLA. Indeed, Sweetland was not even a communist, but was rather a socialist.

114. Ernest C. Moore to Governor Frank F. Merriam, Nov. 17, 1934, ECM.

115. Celeste Strack Kaplan interview with author; UCLA *College News,* Dec. 1934.

116. Celeste Strack Kaplan interview with author.

117. Wechsler, *Revolt on the Campus,* 226–32.

118. *San Francisco Examiner,* Feb. 25, 1934. For another example of Hearst's redbaiting, see *New York American* article "Rid Our College of Reds," reprinted in *School and Society* (March 14, 1936), 373–74; also see "Yellow Newspapers See Red," *ibid.* (Jan. 19, 1935), 100. Student editorial attacks on the Hearst press include *Vassar Miscellany News,* March 2, 1935, Oct. 30, 1935; *Daily Texan,* Nov. 6, 1936; *University Daily Kansan,* Jan. 22, 1935; Univ. of West Virginia *Daily Athenaeum,* Oct. 11, 23, 1935; reprints of editorials from Williams, Amherst, and Princeton, in *Daily Athenaeum,* Oct. 18, 1935; *Oberlin Review,* Dec. 1, 1936. On the anti-Hearst boycott, which caused the cancellation of contracts for Hearst's Metrotone news at theaters in Princeton, Amherst, Williams, and other campus com-

munities, see *Time* (May 27, 1935), 59; Univ. of Wisconsin *Daily Cardinal,* June 2, 1935; *New Republic* (May 22, 1935), 31; Ruth to Joe [Lash], Oct. 12, 1936, JPL.

119. On the loyalty oath bills, see Wiley, *Depression, Recovery and Higher Education,* 441–48; Cohen, "Revolt of the Depression Generation," 379–80; "Teachers' Oaths," *School and Society* (Nov. 1935), 604–5; *NYT,* Oct. 8, 13, 1935; "First Casualties," *Time* (Jan. 27, 1936), 57; *Daily Athenaeum,* Oct. 16, 1935.

On the scarcity of faculty radicals, see Statement of Quentin Orgen [to the Illinois State Investigating Committee], June 6, 1935, President's Papers, UC; Univ. of Chicago Socialist Club, "An Open Letter to the Legislative Investigating Committee," Univ. of Chicago *Soapbox* (May 1935), 3, UC; *Hunter Bulletin,* May 29, 1933; Univ. of West Virginia *Daily Athenaeum,* Oct. 17, 1935; Harry Magdoff interview with author; Morris Schappes interview with author, Manhattan, N.Y., May 7, 1982; Robert Iversen, *The Communists and the Schools* (New York, 1959), 141–42; Budd Shulberg. "The Disenchanted," in *A Dartmouth Reader,* ed., Francis Brown (Hanover, 1969), 325. Even at Brooklyn College—one of the nation's leading centers of Left student activity—there was, according to former NSL organizer Theodore Draper, "not a single Communist professor in the school" during the early 1930s. It was not until later in the decade, long after the movement had become a powerful force on campus, that the Brooklyn College faculty came to include Communists (Theodore Draper, "The Class Struggle: The Myth of the Communist Professor," *New Republic* (Jan. 26, 1987), 29). The relationship between leftist faculty and student radicalism will be explored more fully in Chapter 8 of this study.

120. Ellen Schrecker, *No Ivory Tower: McCarthyism and the Universities* (New York, 1986), 68.

121. *NYT,* March 13, 1935. Actually the worst oaths and pledges imposed upon students came from within the University itself. Well before the legislative investigations and other outside anti-radical pressures had emerged in the mid-1930s, the University of Pittsburgh had already imposed a loyalty oath upon its students, in an effort to purge the campus of student radicals. This oath was initiated by Chancellor John Bowman, who had a long record of violating the academic freedom of liberal professors at Pittsburgh (*Pittsburgh Press,* Sept. 23, 25, 1932; Leonard Grumet to Chancellor John Bowman, Sept. 26. 1932, ACLU; Wechsler, *Revolt on the Campus,* 198–206).

122. Schrecker, *No Ivory Tower,* 69–70; even when opposing legislative red probes, university administrators—including some of the more tolerant college presidents, such as Robert Hutchins of the University of Chicago—displayed their intolerance of radicalism. Instead of making a strong stand on principle for the academic freedom of all academics whether radical or not, these administrators often defended the University on the grounds that there were few radicals on the faculty. In offering this type of defense, the administrators, were, as James Wechsler has put it, "retreating, by granting the essential premise of the investigation," which was that radicals had no place on a university faculty (Wechsler, *Revolt on the Campus,* 265; *Daily Athenaeum,* Oct. 17, 1935; CCNY *Campus,* Oct. 11, 1935; "Teachers' Oaths," *AAUP Bulletin* (Nov. 1935), 605).

123. This preemptive strategy was hinted at in Earl Warren to Monroe Deutsch, July 24, 1934, President's Files, UCB.

124. In the UCLA expulsion case, for instance, President Sproul received numerous letters from free speech advocates both on and off campus, which may

have helped sway him toward reinstating the students (Chester S. Williams [Organizing Director, ACLU of Northern California] to President Sproul, Nov. 16, 1934; Professor T. K. Whipple to President Sproul, Nov. 3, 1934, Rev. Theodore R. Leen to President Sproul, Nov. 4, 1934, President's Files, UCB). It was strong pressure from Left-liberal alumni and the progressive LaGuardia administration which finally drove the repressive President Robinson from CCNY (Rudy, *The College of the City of New York*, 427–32; also see *Hunter Bulletin*, April 1, 1935).

Nationally, both the American Civil Liberties Union and the American Association of University Professors took strong positions in support of student political rights (Committee on Academic Freedom of the American Civil Liberties Union,"The Principles of Academic Freedom," 4, ACLU. On the AAUP's position, see "The Right to Agitate," *AAUP Bulletin* (Oct. 1934), 1). On Eleanor Roosevelt's opposition to loyalty oaths, see *Vassar Miscellany News*, March 7, 1936. Harold Ickes took a similar position in his speech "The Need for Academic Freedom" (*AAUP Bulletin* (Nov. 1935), 562–65. For other endorsements of free speech on campus by prominent political leaders, see Cong. Maury Maverick to Dr. Robert Hutchins, President of the Univ. of Chicago, June 7, 1935, President's Files, UC; Pennsylvania Governor Pinchot's attack on the repressive Univ. of Pittsburgh administration, *School and Society* (July 28, 1934), 128).

125. Joseph P, Lash, typescript on student movement of the 1930s, 16–17, JPL.

126. Though nationally the reformist atmosphere severely limited the Right's effectiveness in attacking campus radicalism during the 1930s, the Right was not totally impotent. In isolated communities without a strong progressive presence or tradition, right wing groups—particularly the American Legion—could and did stop student radical meetings. See Monroe Sweetland to American Civil Liberties Union, April 29, 1935, ACLU.

127. Wechsler, *Revolt on the Campus*, 190–92, 387–95, 411–16; *Ohio State University Peace News*, Jan. 30, 1934.

128. On the decline in free speech violations as the antiwar movement grew, and on the shift of campus administrations to a more tolerant policy towards the antiwar strikes, see Minutes ASU National Executive Committee, June 22, 1936, JPL; *New Republic* (April 22, 1936), 298; (May 6, 1936), 254; (May 5, 1937), 371; *Harvard Crimson*, March 27, 1936. On one of the student movement's greatest free speech victories in the mid-1930s—the passage of the McGoldrick amendment authorizing student political organizations in New York's municipal colleges—see "Back of the Student Front," *Broeklyndian* (1938), 134, BC.

Note, however, that while nationally campus administration attacks on student political liberty declined dramatically, they did not completely cease in 1936. See *NYT*, April 21, 1936; Joseph Lash and James Wechsler, *War Our Heritage* (New York, 1937), 120; Bob to Ben [Fischer], April 2, 1936, YPSL files, SP; *The Dismissal of Bob Burke: Heidelberg Comes to Columbia* [1936], CUC. There would be a revival of such suppression when the student movement began to collapse following the Nazi-Soviet Pact, which will be discussed in Chapter 9.

Chapter 6. The Popular Front on Campus

1. Joseph Clark interview with author; Harvey Klehr, *The Heyday of American Communism* (New York, 1984), 167–85. This is not to say, however, that commu-

nist students embraced anti-fascist Popular Front policies simply because the Comintern had. These young communists were already heading in a Popular Front direction well before the Seventh World Congress, because of their growing awareness of the fascist menace and their sense that broad coalitions of leftists and liberals would be needed to defeat fascism. Thus communist students worked with their socialist counterparts to form an anti-fascist front (the American Youth Congress) in July 1934, a whole year prior to the Seventh World Congress. What the Comintern's adoption of the Popular Front did was to validate and accelerate the turn towards such policies already under way in the student movement (Gil Green interview with author; Robert Cohen, "Revolt of the Depression Generation: America's First Mass Student Movement, 1929–41" (Ph.D. diss., UC Berkeley, 1987), 389–99; Fraser Ottanelli, *The Communist Party of the United States: From the Depression to World War II* (New Brunswick, 1991), 62–63).

2. "A Symposium on Peace," *Student Advocate* (Dec. 1936), 29; Hal Draper, "The Case Against Sanctions and 'Neutrality Legislation,'" *Socialist Appeal*, June 1936; *Socialist Call*, Dec. 27, 1937. I use the term "isolationist" here and throughout the book to denote those who, in the words of historian Manfred Jonas, advocated for the U.S. "the avoidance of political and military commitments to or alliances with foreign powers, particularly those of Europe (Manfred Jonas, "Isolationism," *Encyclopedia of American Foreign Policy*, Alexander DeConde, ed. (New York, 1978), 496). I term "interventionists" those who wanted the U.S. to make such commitments or alliances, and in this case did so in the name of anti-fascism—which is the collective security position.

3. *NSL Organizer*, Oct. 1935. Also see Joseph P. Lash, "Veterans of Future Sanctions," *Challenge of Youth* (July 1936), 7; Harold Preece, "Sanctions Against War," *National Student Mirror* (Feb. 1936), 44–45; Joseph P. Lash to Jef Rens, May 7, 1936, JPL; Robert A. Divine, *The Illusion of Neutrality* (Chicago, 1962), 123.

4. Richard Criley interview with author.

5. Joseph P. Lash interview with author.

6. "An Open Letter," *Student Review* (Dec. 1933), 5–6; "One Big Student Movement?," *Student Outlook* (Feb. 1934), 3; Jean Symes, "The Student LID Convention," *ibid.* (Feb. 1935), 17.

7. On NSL-SLID cooperation in this era, see "Meaning of April 13," *Student Review* (Summer 1934), 4–5; Harold Draper, "The First American Youth Congress," *Student Outlook* (Oct. 1934), 15–16; Theodore Draper, "American Youth Rejects Fascism," *New Masses* (Aug. 28, 1934), 11–13; Joseph P. Lash, "Why I Am a Socialist," *Clionian* (Sept. 1934), 4; *Columbia Spectator*, Oct. 17, Nov. 2, 1933, May 7, 1934; *CCNY Campus*, April 28, May 12, 1933; *Daily Cardinal*, April 30, 1933.

8. "The American Student Union: A Recommendation from the National Executive Committee," *Student Outlook* (Oct. 1935), 3. Harry Magdoff interview with author; Monroe Sweetland interview with author.

9. Minutes of the SLID National Executive Committee, June 28–29–30 [1935], SDS Papers, NYU; Joseph P. Lash interview with author; Richard Criley interview with author; "Free for All," *Student Outlook* (Feb. 1935), 31. The chapter pressure for amalgamation did not come exclusively from the west coast. See U.S. Congress, Special House Subcommittee on Un-American Activities, "Testimony of Joseph P. Lash," 76th Congress, 1st Session, 7075.

10. Richard Criley interview with author.

11. Minutes of the [SLID] National Executive Committee, June 28–29–30 [1935].

12. Joseph P. Lash interview with author.

13. Minutes of the [SLID] National Executive Committee, June 28–29–30 [1935]; Joint Statement of the NSL-Student LID Subcommittee, SDS Papers, NYU.

14. SLID membership mailing [Oct.] 1935, 1, SDS Papers; Special Subcommittee on Un-American Activities, "Testimony of Joseph P. Lash," 7075; *Bulletin of the Fourth National Convention of the National Student League* (St. Louis, Dec. 1934), 8.

15. SLID membership mailing [October] 1935, SDS Papers, NYU; "Three Views on the ASU," *Student Review* (Oct. 1935), 16–17.

16. *Ibid.*

17. *Student Union Bulletin,* Jan. 7, 1936; *Columbus Citizen,* Dec. 23, 27, 1935; *Ohio State Journal,* Dec. 28, 30, 31, 1935; *Columbus Citizen,* Dec. 30, 1935; *Columbus Sunday Dispatch,* Dec. 29, 1935; Nancy Bedford Jones to Herman, Jan. 1, 1936, JPL; Celeste Strack, "The American Students Unite," *New Masses* (Jan. 14, 1936), 19–20; minutes Saturday session ASU convention, JPL.

18. Minutes of Dec. 29, 1935, ASU session, 10, Helen Schmock, "ASU Convention" minutes, 1–2, JPL; Nancy Bedford Jones to Herman, Jan. 1, 1936.

19. Nancy Bedford Jones to Herman, Jan. 1, 1936; on Sweetland's opposition to amalgamation, see SLID membership mailing [October] 1935, SDS Papers, NYU.

20. Jones to Herman, Jan. 1, 1936.

21. Strack, "The American Students Unite," 20.

22. *Student Union Bulletin,* Jan. 7, 1936.

23. *Ibid.*

24. *Ibid.*; Malcolm Sylvers, "Popular Front," in Mary Jo Buhle et al., eds., *The Encyclopedia of the American Left* (New York, 1990), 591–94.

25. Minutes of ASU Convention, Dec. 29, pp. 4–9, JPL.

26. Serril Gerber to Joseph P. Lash, Nov. 13, 1935; Lash to Gerber, Nov. 15, 1935; Gerber to Lash, Nov. 20, 1935. All in JPL. Resistance to amalgamation within the left wing of the socialist student groups was also linked to doctrinaire thinking about the nature of student movements. Much like the Communist Party during the Comintern's ultra-radical Third Period, some of the revolutionary socialists in the YPSL saw the student movement as at best an auxiliary of the labor movement (since the proletariat was assumed to be the main agent of radical social change). These YPSLs therefore reasoned that students should follow labor's lead rather than innovate on their own. Applied to the NSL-SLID amalgamation question, this meant that such a merger was inappropriate because communist and socialist-led labor organizations had never so merged. Thus at the 1934 SLID convention, the YPSLs presented an anti-amalgamation resolution, which concluded that "until the labor movement is unified, amalgamation of student groups with very different political orientations is impractical and utopian" (Ruth Oxman, "The Student LID Convention," *Young Socialist Review* (Spring 1935), 3, Daniel Bell Papers, NYU).

27. Minutes ASU Convention, Dec. 29, pp. 4–9; Strack, "The American Students Unite," 20.

28. Minutes ASU Convention, Dec. 29, pp. 4–9; YPSL report on the ASU convention, 2, JPL.

29. Hal Draper. "The Student Movement of the Thirties: A Political History," in Rita Simon, ed., *As We Saw the Thirties* (Urbana, 1967), 175; ballot for the [ASU] National Executive Committee, JPL.

30. Draper, "The Student Movement of the Thirties," 175.

31. James Wechsler, *The Age of Suspicion* (New York, 1981), 85.

32. Nancy Bedford Jones to Herman, Jan. 1, 1936, JPL. The NSL and SLID leadership worked so hard to hammer out a platform acceptable to liberals that this angered a dissident ultra-left minority at the convention, most of whom were Trotskyists. The Trotskyists, who had opposed the NSL-SLID merger from the beginning because of their mistrust of the Communists, viewed the ASU convention as a sell out to liberalism and an "opportunistic catastrophe" (Georg Mann, "Mistakes at Columbus," *Socialist Appeal* (Jan.-Feb. 1936), 5–6).

33. Wechsler, *The Age of Suspicion*, i-vii, 1–84; Celeste Strack interview with author.

34. Serril Gerber interview with author, Long Beach Calif., April 5, 1986.

35. Joseph Lash interview with author.

36. George Edwards, *Pioneer at Law* (New York, 1974), 122–56; U.S. Congress, Senate Subcommittee of the Committee on the Judiciary, "Nomination Hearings of George Clifton Edwards, Jr.," 88th Congress First Session, Oct. 1 and Nov. 21, 1963, pp. 12–21.

37. Molly Yard interview with author, Washington, D.C., March 21, 1983.

38. *Student Advocate* (Feb. 1936), 3–8, 10–11, 13–14; "An Apology," *Student Advocate* (March 1936), 5.

39. Joseph P. Lash interview with the author.

40. Wechsler, *The Age of Suspicion*, 85. Considering the limits on internal criticism in the Party-bound Old Left, Lash and Wechsler were—during the ASU's early days—remarkably iconoclastic in their thinking about the Communist and Socialist parties. Thus Lash noted in his diary that Wechsler was "contemptuous of the intellectual cravenness and mediocrity of the Communists, yet . . . even more against the sectarian line of the socialists." Echoing Wechsler's criticism of the adult Left, Lash noted that "I feel very much an outcast these days. The Socialists don't trust or like me because I champion cooperation with the CP, and my intellectual integrity makes me rebel against the mediocre application of the CI line to the US . . ."(Lash diary, Oct. 21, 1936, JPL).

41. Wechsler, *The Age of Suspicion*, 81–82.

42. Harold Draper, "The American Student Union Faces the Anti-War Strike," *American Socialist Monthly* (April 1936), 7.

43. *Ibid.*, 7–10.

44. Joseph P. Lash, "Another View of the A.S.U.," *American Socialist Monthly* (May 1936), 28–29. Lash's description of the situation in the high schools was accurate. See Celeste Strack to Dorothy Shoemaker, March 5, 1937, Committee on Militarism in Education Papers, SCPC; Osmond K. Fraenkel to Lewis J. Valentine, Dec. 12, 1935, ACLU.

45. Lash, "Another View of the A.S.U.," 28–29.

46. Ben Fischer, "YPSL position," *American Socialist Monthly* (May 1936), 30–31. On this self-serving YPSL view of its role in the ASU, also see Lewis M. Cohen to Joseph P. Lash, Oct. 6, 1936, JPL.

47. On Lash's low regard for the YPSL leadership, see his "Comments on the November 29, 1936, meeting of the YPSL national executive committee," 2–5, JPL. The YPSL controversy helped cement Lash's ties with Wechsler in the ASU leadership. Both increasingly saw themselves as allies in the struggle to eliminate dogmatism and destructive communist-socialist feuding in the student movement. Lash recalled: "The thing that . . . made Jimmy Wechsler and myself very sympathetic was he was having the same problem with the YCL . . . Well I guess we

never wore intellectual harnesses very easily" (Joseph Lash interview with author). Lash's willingness to take a stance against YPSL dogmatism also enhanced his stature with less sectarian socialist students—including some YPSL regional leaders and rank and filers—who were "sick and tired of the splitting tactics" of the YPSL national leadership in the student movement. See Jeff Campbell to Joseph Lash, April 2, 1936, JPL; (Bob [Newman] to Joseph Lash [n.d.], JPL).

48. Joseph P. Lash interview with author; Joseph P. Lash, "500,000 Strike for Peace: An Appraisal," *Student Advocate* (May 1936), 3–5, 21.

49. Typifying this lack of candor was the ASU's official account of its 1936 convention, which made it sound as if all the decisions at this convention were made openly by the full ASU membership. (See "One Year of Student Unionism: A Report of the Second Annual A.S.U. Convention," *Student Advocate* (Feb. 1937), 11–13.) But contrast this sanitized public account of the convention with the account recorded in the YPSL's internal bulletin, which detailed the private political horsetrading between the ASU's communist and socialists factions over the composition of ASU national executive committee at the convention. The YPSL "Student Bulletin" reported that "the YCL proposed a 5–5–20 (YCL, YPSL, and liberal) ratio. We proposed a 10–10–15 ratio which would have meant the addition of 5 members. . . . There was a sharp cleavage in outlook on the ASU here which was not resolved by the compromise of 8–8–14 finally agreed upon"("YPSL Student Bulletin," Jan. 10, 1937, p. 3, JPL). On similar private YPSL-YCL deal-making in the ASU, see [YPSL] National Student Committee Minutes, Nov. 4, 1936, JPL. On the ASU magazine's lack of candor on such questions, see Joseph P, Lash, introduction to Greenwood reprint of *Student Advocate*, "Do the Thirties Have Anything to Tell the Sixties?" (New York, 1968), 2.

50. Joe Freeland to Alvaine Hollister, Jan. 25, 1938, YPSL files, SP; James Wechsler, *Revolt on the Campus* (1935: reprint, Seattle, 1973), viii.

51. Lash, "500,000 Strike for Peace," 3–5, 21; Minutes of the American Student Union National Executive Committee, June 22, 1936, JPL.

52. *NYT*, April 23, 1936; *New York Herald-Tribune*, April 23, 1936; "Peace Day," *Time* (May 4, 1936), 53.

53. *Ibid.* Veterans of Future Wars was founded by two affluent Princeton undergraduates early in the spring semester of 1936. Within a little over a month it had chapters on some fifty campuses, and was, in the words of a *Time* reporter, "rampaging over the campuses." A female auxiliary, the "Association of Gold Star Mothers of Future Veterans," quickly arose at Vassar and spread to other campuses. Although VFW proved a transient phenomenon, and an exercise in political humor, it did indicate how popular opposition to war and the military had become on campus. This was a genuine grass roots movement, in which rank and file students organized themselves against war with little prodding from any national organization. Indeed, there was a huge gap between what the VFW's conservative Democratic founders had intended and what the VFW chapters were doing. The Princeton students had established the VFW as a parody of veterans' demands for a bonus—and conservatives initially welcomed the organization's clever attack on "extravagant" social spending. These Princeton organizers had not intended to link up with the antiwar movement, and had in fact refused to support the 1936 antiwar strike. Students out on the campuses where the VFW spread, however, changed the emphasis of the VFW from an attack on social spending to an attack on war and militarism, and many VFW chapters joined in the antiwar strike. Thus the VFW, which had initially been praised by the Right, now drew

vitriolic criticism from conservatives ("Future Veterans," *Time* (March 30, 1936), 38; Joseph P. Lash and James Wechsler, *War Our Heritage* (New York, 1936), 135–42; *Harvard Crimson*, March 18, April 21, 1936).

54. YPSL National Student Office, "Strike Bulletin," April 1936.

55. Joseph P. Lash to Elizabeth Gilman, April 20, 1936, JPL.

56. *Daily Californian*, Oct. 7, 1937.

57. "April 22nd: We Must Remember Spain," *Student Advocate* (April 1937), 3–4.

58. Wechsler, *The Age of Suspicion*, 100–101.

59. Tucker Dean to Molly Yard, May 10, 1937, JPL. On other abandonments of pacifism because of Spain, see Monroe Sweetland interview with author; David S. Burgess, "I'm No Longer a Pacifist Because," *Intercollegian and Far Horizons* (Oct. 1939), 17–18.

60. George Watt essay in *50th and 25th Anniversary ASU-SDS National Reunion* (Long Beach, Calif., 1986), 2; Robert A Rosenstone, *Crusade on the Left* (New York, 1969), 104; Arthur Landis, *The Abraham Lincoln Brigade* (New York, 1968), 249–55; Murray Kempton, *Part of Our Time: Some Monuments and Ruins of the Thirties* (New York, 1955), 310–18.

61. Wechsler, *The Age of Suspicion*, 100–101.

62. *Ibid.*; Celeste Strack Kaplan interview with author; Ruth to Joe [Lash] March 3, 1937, JPL; Molly Yard to Leonard J. Grumet, July 12, 1937, JPL.

63. E. H. Carr, *The Comintern and the Spanish Civil War* (London, 1984), 19–44; Robert G. Spivack, "A Letter to Norman Thomas," *New Masses* (Feb. 23, 1937), 21; Lash and Wechsler, *War Our Heritage*, 147.

64. Wechsler, *The Age of Suspicion*, 100.

65. Jeff Campbell to Joseph P. Lash, May 11, 1937, JPL; James Alter, "Why I Am Still a Pacifist," *Intercollegian and Far Horizons* (Nov. 1939), 39–40; *Socialist Call*, Late-Feb. 1937; Norman Thomas, "The Pacifist's Dilemma," *Nation* (Jan. 16, 1937), 66–68.

66. *Michigan Daily*, March 22, 24, 1938. The State Department's refusal to intercede on behalf of Neafus and the three other volunteers who had been captured with him had tragic consequences. Neafus and his comrades were murdered—shot without trial—by their fascist captors. The historian of these prisoners makes a convincing case that pressure from Washington would almost certainly have saved their lives. See Carl Geiser, *Prisoners of the Good Fight: The Spanish Civil War 1936–1939* (Westport, 1986), 59.

67. *Michigan Daily*, March 22, 24, 30, 1938. Also see George Watt letter from Spain, *Vassar Miscellany News*, Oct. 16, 1937.

68. Hal Draper, "The Student Movement of the Thirties: A Political History," 178–79; Al Hamilton and Alvaine Hollister, "Left Jingoism on the Campus," *Socialist Review* (Jan.-Feb. 1938), 9–10, 19; Judah Drob, "Thoughts on the ASU-SDS Anniversary" [1986], (unpublished paper, distributed at the 50th Anniversary Reunion of the ASU, Long Beach, Calif., 1986).

69. Lash and Wechsler, *War Our Heritage*, 147, 149. Gus Tyler, "We're for Peace, But . . .," *Socialist Call*, Dec. 26, 1936.

70. Joseph P. Lash, Notes on the YPSL national executive committee meeting, Nov. 29, 1936, 1–2, JPL; *Socialist Call*, Dec. 26, 1936.

71. Joseph P. Lash, Notes on the YPSL national executive committee meeting, Nov. 29, 1936, 2–5, JPL.

72. *Ibid.*

73. Statement by Joseph P. Lash to the Grievance Committee of the Y.P.S.L. [1937]; [YPSL] Hearing on Joe Lash [1937], 3, both in JPL.

74. Joseph P. Lash, Notes on the YPSL national executive committee meeting, Nov. 29, 1936, p. 3, JPL.

75. Norman Thomas, Memorandum on the YPSL-ASU Situation, Dec. 4, 1936, JPL.

76. Transcript, Joseph P. Lash interview with Joel Chernoff, 16–17, JPL; "Ten-minute remarks of Joseph Lash in support of resolution stating that support of the Oxford Pledge was incompatible with support of collective security," JPL; Minutes Second National Convention, American Student Union, Chicago, Dec. 27–30, 1936, JPL; YPSL (Fourth Internationalists, "Compromise?" [Trotskyist leaflet distributed at the 1936 ASU Convention], JPL). The beginnings of Lash's shift towards collective security had brought him into conflict with YPSL and other Socialist Party officials as early as Oct. 1936. Lash noted in his diary that month that on the collective security issue: "We've had several long sessions of various party committees in which patient attempts were made to argue me out of my heresy. Now I am not allowed to advocate the position publicly on the ground that it is incompatible with the party position" (Lash diary, Oct. 21, 1936, JPL). Note that Lash and his socialist comrades were here being insensitive to democratic process within the ASU. Rank and file ASUers, not privy to the deliberations of this Left elite, would have no idea that their organization's national executive secretary was barred from fully expressing his views on the crucial question of collective security because of his Socialist Party allegiance.

77. Minutes Second National Convention, American Student Union, Chicago, December 27–30, 1936, JPL; Joseph P. Lash, *Toward a Closed Shop on Campus* (New York, 1937), 24.

78. Lash, *Toward a Closed Shop*, 25.

79. [YPSL] NEC Motion by Ben Fischer, Dec. 15, 1936, JPL; Joseph P. Lash to Norman Thomas, Jan. 5, 1937, JPL.

80. George Edwards to Joe [Lash], Dec. 6, 1936, JPL; Joseph Lash to George [Edwards], Dec. 14, 1936, JPL; National Student Department, "Student Bulletin," Jan. 10, 1937, JPL ; Roy E. Burt to Norman Thomas, Dec. 30, 1936, NT; Frank Trager to Norman Thomas, Dec. 30, 1936, NT. Roy Burt, the Socialist Party's Executive Secretary, and Frank Trager, the party's Labor and Organization secretary were the adult Socialist Party leaders who persuaded the YPSL leadership at the convention not to bring their dispute with Lash to the convention floor, and not to try to get back at him for his collusion with Edwards by seeking his immediate ouster from the ASU leadership. Note that the YPSL procedure (involving socialist and Trotskyist YPSLs) of screening speeches by socialist ASUers was another example of factional control, at odds with the ideal of the ASU as an open and democratically led organization.

81. On the confrontation with Lash at the YPSL caucus, see Roy E. Burt to Norman Thomas, Dec. 30, 1936; Frank Trager to Norman Thomas, Dec. 30, 1936, NT; YPSL "Student Bulletin," Jan. 10, 1937, p. 4.

82. Joseph P. Lash to Norman Thomas, Jan. 5, 1937; Judah Drob to Milt Friedman, Feb. 1, 1937; "The Case Against Joe Lash," [1937]; "Report on the Special Grievance Committee to the NEC on the Charges by Ben Fischer and Alvaine Hollister Against Joe Lash" [1937]; "Statement by Joseph P. Lash to the

Grievance Committee of the Y.P.S.L."; [YPSL] Hearing on Joe Lash; Ben Fischer and Alvaine Hollister, "A Reply to Joseph P. Lash"; Harold Draper, "A Reply to Comrade Lash" [1937]; Roy E. Burt to Joe Lash, Jan. 25, 1937; Joseph P. Lash to George Edwards, Feb. 2, 1937; George Edwards and Joseph P. Lash to Roy Burt, Jan. 29, 1937. All in JPL.

83. Joseph P. Lash to John Morris, Feb. 5, 1937, JPL.

84. "April 22nd: We Must Remember Spain," *Student Advocate* (April 1937), 3.

85. *Ibid.*, 4. On this flexible approach to strike organizing in 1937, also see *Chapter Guide First Bulletin on the Student Strike Against War for April 22, 1937-11 A.M. American Student Union* (March 3, 1937), 3–5, United Student Peace Committee Papers, SCPC.

86. *NYT,* April 23, 1937; "The Great 1937 Strike in Review," *Student Advocate* (May 1937), 4.

87. "The Great 1937 Strike in Review," 4–5.

88. John Gates, *The Story of an American Communist* (New York, 1958), 52–55; Irving Howe, *A Margin of Hope* (New York, 1982), 74–76; Wechsler, *The Age of Suspicion,* 102; Allen Guttmann, *The Wound in the Heart: America and the Spanish Civil War* (New York, 1962), 150–51; Burnett Bolloten, *The Spanish Civil War: Revolution and Counterrevolution* (Chapel Hill, 1991), 429–531; Gabriel Jackson, *A Concise History of the Spanish Civil War* (New York, 1980), 118–21; *Vision on Fire: Emma Goldman on the Spanish Civil War,* David Porter, ed. (New Paltz, N.Y., 1983) 132–71.

89. Joseph Lash to Nancy [Bedford Jones], July 20, [1937]; on Lash's resignation from the Socialist Party, see Joseph P. Lash to Norman Thomas, Oct. 2, 1937; both in JPL.

90. Joseph Lash Diary, July 11, 17, 1937, JPL. There is no indication in Lash's writings that he actually followed through on his intention (as stated in his Spanish diary) of joining the Communist Party. In subsequent interviews Lash maintained that although he considered himself very close to the Communist Party during the Popular Front era, he never actually joined the Party—terming himself a "non-Party Bolshevik" in that era (transcript of Joseph Lash interview with Joel Chernoff, April 2, 1978, p. 5, JPL; Joseph Lash interview with author). However, Gil Green, who headed the YCL during the Popular Front years, recalled, that though "Joe Lash may not admit it today, he joined the CP" while a leader of the student movement (Gil Green interview with author, Manhattan, N.Y., Sept. 29, 1982). Whether Lash or Green is correct about Lash's membership in the CP cannot be determined with absolute certainty (since by definition secret membership is covert and therefore not documented). However, Lash's correspondence tends to support his claim of non-membership (see William Sussman to Joseph P. Lash [n.d.]; Joseph P. Lash to Avram [Goldstein], May 19, 1939; Joseph P. Lash to Bill [Sussman], Sept. 30, 1939. All in JPL). This disagreement over the question of formal party membership should not, however, obscure the more essential point upon which Lash and Green agree: that Lash as ASU executive secretary—the most influential national leader in the student movement—was firmly in the communist camp on all key policy questions from 1937 to summer 1939. Just how close Lash's identification was with the CP in this era can be seen in his unpublished memoir, which indicates that until the end of the Popular Front era, Lash "conferred with young c.l [Communist League] leaders on problems of the youth

movement and expected after leaving the ASU to become a full-fledged dues-paying card-carrying member of the communist party" (Joseph P. Lash, "My Political Position Before the Fall of 1939," JPL).

91. Joseph P. Lash to Nancy [Bedford Jones], July 20, [1937], JPL.

92. Joseph P. Lash Diary, July 17, 1937, JPL.

93. Joseph P. Lash to Nancy [Bedford Jones], July 20, 1937; Lash Diary, June 18 and 21, 1937, JPL. Lash was dismissive of leftwing critics and what he termed their "bogy-man tales of maneuvering, terrorism and opportunism" in republican Spain (Joseph P. Lash, "Time Works for Us—Spain 1937," *New Masses* (Oct. 19, 1937), 6–8). During this period, Lash was not only uncritical of communists in Spain, but was also also unwilling to criticize the Moscow trials publicly. In fact, he wrote a letter to one of his former colleagues in the Socialist Party, criticizing the adult LID for "cast[ing] doubt on the integrity of Soviet justice." See Joseph P. Lash to Harry Laidler, March 4, 1938, JPL. Privately and to close associates, however, Lash was more critical of the trials. See Lash Diary, March 3, 6, 1938, JPL.

94. Wechsler, *The Age of Suspicion*, 101–3.

95. *Ibid.*, 88–89, 102–3; Leo Rifkin, "900,000 Strike," 23; Ruth Watt, "Struggle Against Trotskyism in the Student Movement" [n.d.], JPL; *Daily Worker*, April 24, Oct. 23, 1937; *Communist Campanile*, Summer 1937, UCB. On the Soviet roots of this Trotsky-bashing, see Issac Deutscher, *The Prophet Outcast: Trotsky 1929–1940* (New York, 1963), 1–6, 125–26, 413–19.

96. Wechsler, *The Age of Suspicion*, 103. Despite his earlier non-sectarian approach to campus organizing, Lash too became so influenced by communist rhetoric—and so angered by the Trotskyists' divisive tactics in the student movement—that by 1939 he had become engaged in some nasty Trotsky-bashing. During the 1939 ASU summer leadership institute, Lash gave a lecture on the Trotskyists in which he referred to them as "the syphilis of the working class." See "Lash Lectures on Student Movement," *ASU Summer Leadership Institute Newsletter*, July 2, 1939, JPL.

97. "A Letter to Joe Lash" [leaflet, n.d.], JPL.

98. Irving Howe, "An Open Letter to Joe Lash on the 1938 A.S.U. Convention," *Challenge of Youth*, Jan. 1939, p. 3. Describing the extreme sectarianism of the Trotskyists in this era, two socialist student activists wrote, " Many Trotzkyists openly advocate the policy of splitting and liquidating the [American] Student Union on the grounds that it is a 'students people's front.' Just as the Communists are obsessed with a 'people's-front mania,' the Trotzkyites are afflicted with 'anti-people's front phobia.' They are constantly on a witch hunt for people's front tendencies. Every statement, decision, or action by anybody is immediately examined for 'people's frontism.' Any participation in joint activities with non-Socialists is condemned on that basis" (Hyman Bookbinder and Melvino Willbach, "An Appeal for the Preservation of a Young Socialist [Movement]" [n.d.], Daniel Bell Papers, NYU.

99. Lash Diary, Nov. 4, 1937.

100. Nancy Bedford Jones to Al Hamilton [Aug. 1937], JPL.

101. Howe, *A Margin of Hope*, 75–76.

102. Dorothy Borg, "Notes on Roosevelt's 'Quarantine' Speech," *Political Science Quarterly* (Sept. 1957), 405–33.

103. One of the most striking aspects of the debate within the student move-

ment over collective security was the way President Roosevelt was viewed. Even though FDR had quickly retreated from the pro-collective security implications of the Chicago speech, *both* the foes and supporters of collective security within the ASU continued, long after this speech, to act as if the President was a firm supporter of collective security. It was, of course, natural for supporters of collective security in the ASU to view FDR as a champion of collective security, since this enabled them to use Roosevelt's name to bid for liberal student support. It may seem puzzling, however, that opponents of collective security within the ASU failed to challenge this view of Roosevelt. Had they wished to do so, they could have pointed to FDR's statements opposing sanctions and his retreat from the "quarantine" idea to show that FDR had not in fact endorsed collective security. This would certainly have helped them in competing for liberal support on campus. But here ideology got in the way of political expediency. The anti-collective security forces were led by YPSLs, who as socialists loathed Roosevelt and regarded him as a warmonger. In their eyes, by associating itself with FDR, the pro-collective security bloc in the ASU was selling out, diluting its radicalism, and discrediting itself within the antiwar movement by becoming part of the "Roosevelt war machine." The YPSLs seemed out of touch with liberal student opinion and failed to grasp how useful FDR's name would be in helping to sway it. Thus they gave FDR away as a political symbol, setting themselves up for losses to the ASU's collective security bloc because they cared more about leftwing ideological purity than winning the hearts and minds of the American student body (*Socialist Call*, Dec. 25, 1937, Jan. 15, 1938; Joseph P. Lash, *The Campus: A Fortress of Democracy* (New York, 1938), 22–23).

104. Molly Yard to Joseph [Lash], Nov. 9, 1937, JPL; "For a Left Wing in the ASU," *Challenge of Youth*, Nov. 1937; Alvaine Hollister to Fay Bennett, Nov. 27, 1937, YPSL files, SP; Lewis Conn to ASU Administrative Committee, Nov. 12, 1937, JPL; Joseph Lash to Lewis Conn, Nov. 24, 1937, JPL; "A Proposal for a Youth Committee for the Oxford Pledge," YPSL files, SP.

105. Yard to Lash, Nov. 9, 1937. Also see Alvaine Hollister to Fay Bennett, Nov. 27, 1937.

106. Alvaine Hollister to Fay Bennett, Nov. 19, 1937, YPSL files, SP.

107. Molly Yard to Joseph [Lash], Oct. [1937], JPL.

108. *Socialist Call*, Dec. 25, 1937; "The ASU at the Crossroads," *The CCNY Redbook* (1937–38), 5–6, YPSL files, SP.

109. Yard to Lash, Nov. 9, 1937.

110. Al Hamilton to Jeff Campbell, Nov. 24, 1937, YPSL files SP; *Socialist Call*, Jan. 15, 1938.

111. *Socialist Call*, Jan. 15, 1938; Joseph Starobin, "The Students Reject Isolation," *New Masses* (Jan. 11, 1938), 13–15. In the ASU membership referendum, collective security positions won by more than a four to one margin. See *Unite the Campus to Save Peace* (1938), 12–13, JPL.

112. Lash, *The Campus: A Fortress of Democracy*, 22.

113. ASU, *The Vassar Convention of the A.S.U Convention* [n.d.], 2, JPL.

114. Lash, *The Campus: A Fortress of Democracy*, 11.

115. *Daily Worker*, Dec. 31, 1937; Bob Kahn, "Conventional Stuff," in ASU, Brooklyn College Chapter, *Convention Guide* (Feb. 1938), 7. Joseph Lash, who had shown his penchant for tactical innovation in the early stages of the student movement by coming up with the idea of a national student strike against war, was also

responsible for the idea of a bonfire protesting Japanese imperialism. See *American Student Union Chapter Guide* (Oct. 23, 1937), 4, JPL. This protest drew considerable press attention. See *Time* (Jan. 10, 1938), 42.

116. Lash, *The Campus: A Fortress of Democracy*, 23.

117. ASU, *The Vassar Convention* [n.d.], 2.

118. Wechsler, *The Age of Suspicion*, 91.

119. Joseph Lash, "Fascism Means War," JPL. The ASU convention also approved two other measures suggesting that while embracing collective security, it was still unwilling to surrender its opposition to the U.S. military and unwilling to trust in Washington's intentions to preserve peace. These measures were: (1) ASU support for "the withdrawal of United States military forces from all foreign countries" (a move obviously intended to prevent a U.S.-Japanese clash in Asia, where there had been American troops); (2) ASU endorsement of the Ludlow amendment "that war should be declared only after a national referendum" (ASU, *The Vassar Convention*, 2). These positions were obviously inconsistent with the interventionist thrust of the ASU's new collective security policy, and would therefore be dropped by the time of the next ASU Convention. The Ludlow amendment position was so at odds with the mood of the anti-isolationist rank and file that in the 1938 referendum on the ASU's peace platform it was rejected by 60 percent of the membership (and then dropped immediately from the ASU program). See *Unite the Campus to Save Peace* (1938), 13, JPL.

120. *Socialist Call,* Jan. 15, 1938.

121. Fay Bennett to Alvaine Hollister, Nov. 27, 1937, YPSL files, SP; Al Hamilton to Norman Thomas, Nov. 20, 1937, NT.

122. Bob [Kelso] to Al Hamilton, Jan. 14, 1938, YPSL files, SP.

123. Lewis [Conn] to Al[Hamilton], Feb. 18, 1938, YPSL files, SP.

124. Joseph P. Lash to Molly Yard, Jan. 19, 1938, JPL. Another sign of this deterioration in socialist-communist relations within the student movement was the use of some new hardball anti-communist tactics by the socialists at the campus level. On this point, the correspondence from Joseph Freeland, a socialist student organizer at the University of Kentucky ASU chapter, is particularly revealing. At Kentucky, for reasons of political expediency, communist student activists in the ASU had not been candid about their Party affiliation. Liberals in the University of Kentucky ASU were not told that the students who dominated the chapter were communists. During the early stages of the ASU's development at the University of Kentucky, socialists in this ASU chapter had, in Freeland's words, "respected the incognito which the communists have chosen to assume" because "in the ASU we had a common program and a common interest." But now in early 1938, with the split over collective security, it was "no longer true" that the ASU's communists and socialists shared the same goals. Thus Freeland wrote to the YPSL national office, asking whether in light of this split, he and other socialists should expose the red affiliations of the communists in his ASU chapter. YPSL national secretary Al Hamilton responded affirmatively, instructing Freeland "absolutely that you should point out to your ASU members the source of the new policy in the American Student Union. In the past you may have been correct in preserving the incognito of the YCL members. But this will have to be sacrificed if necessary to point out the source of the new pro-war policy of the American Student Union. . . . On the question of your local chapter you should attack the [national] leadership of the YCL for forcing down the throats not only of the ASU but of the [Univer-

sity of Kentucky] YCL their policy" (Joe Freeland to Alvaine Hollister, Jan. 25, 1938; Al Hamilton to Joe Freeland, Feb. 11, 1938, both in YPSL files, SP.

125. Joseph P. Lash to Howard Lee, Feb. 16, 1938, JPL.

126. *Ibid.*

127. Minutes United Student Peace Committee meeting, March 15, 1938, JPL.

128. *Ibid., NYT*, April 24, 1938.

129. On the the YCAW's early preparations for the 1938 strike, see "Report of the Executive Secretary to the Opening Youth Session of the National Anti-war Congress," YPSL files, SP.

130. Youth Committee for the Oxford Pledge, "An Open Letter to American Youth," YPSL files, SP. During the mid-1930s there were many complaints—from within the YPSL and among the organization's allies—of the YPSL tendency to spend more time feuding with the YCL and engaging in doctrinal hair splitting than recruiting new activists into the student movement (see Flora McClain to YPSL national office, June 20, 1936, YPSL files, SP; Harry Laidler to Al Hamilton, March 3, 1937; Al Hamilton to Harry Kingman, March 20, 1937, YPSL files, SP; Jeff Campbell to Joseph P. Lash, Dec. 1, 1936, JPL; Ed Bond to Joseph P. Lash, Dec. 2, 1936, JPL). On one level this penchant for factionalism can be seen and even defended as a natural response to the manipulative political behavior of the communists—that since the YPSL confronted a well-organized YCL faction in the ASU it had to embrace factionalism to survive in the movement. But such factionalism was more than an expedient for the YPSL; it was also a *preferred* style of politics which was fundamental to most YPSL organizing. The way YPSLs often expressed their passion for socialism and their loyalty to the policies of the Socialist Party was by promoting their organization's influence over all movement policy and personnel decisions, no matter who this alienated. Thus even in the YCAW, where there was no communist faction for the YPSL to contend with, YPSL leaders still engaged in self-interested factional maneuvering in defiance of democratic process. This led Jeffrey Campbell, a socialist and New England YMCA leader, to complain bitterly to the YPSL leadership about its manipulative and undemocratic behavior in the YCAW. Shortly after returning from an early YCAW national meeting, Campbell told these leaders that he was "burning up" over "the method in which offices and representative positions were elected at the Youth Committee Against War. I saw again the same tendency which so thoroughly disgusted me with the YPSL role in the Chicago convention of the ASU. At the time I laid it to Trotskyite presence in the movement plus the need of opposing the C.P. To find its identical techniques emerging at the start of a newly organized cooperatively united and friendly body drives me to express myself as strongly as I am capable. In my opinion to enter . . . the Youth Committee Against War with a small highly organized and disciplined wedge and to start assigning offices and election on the basis of prearranged agreements from which the mass is automatically excluded threatens everything fine and worthwhile accomplished by the Congress" (Jeffrey Campbell to Al Hamilton, Alvaine Hollister, Judah Drob, June 2, 1938, YPSL files, SP).

131. Youth Committee for the Oxford Pledge, "An Open Letter to American Youth." On both the poll results and the problems with the poor wording of the questionnaire, see "Brown Daily Herald Student Survey on Peace," April 15, 1938, United Student Peace Committee Papers, SCPC; Antone Singsen to Joseph P. Lash, April 8, 1938, JPL.

132. *Socialist Call,* May 7, 1938.

133. William Meyer to Al [Hamilton], Feb. 21, 1938, YPSL files, SP. A similar situation existed in southern California. See Fay Bennett to Alvaine Hollister, April 13, 1938, YPSL files, SP.

134. Alvaine Hollister to Al [Hamilton], April 20, 25, 1938. YPSL files, SP.

135. Alvaine Hollister to Al [Hamilton], April 20, 1938. On the "awful" defeat of the YCAW position in the Ohio State University antiwar rally, see Robin Myers to Alvaine Hollister, April 26, 1938, YPSL files, SP. Also see *YPSL Affairs,* May 4, 1938. On isolationist strength at the Univ. of Chicago strike, see Bud James to Joseph Lash, April 25, 1938, JPL.

136. Harold [Goldstein] to Judah [Drob], March 31, 1938, YPSL files, SP. The YCAW also flopped in its attempt to prevent the student YM and YWCAs— probably the most influential Christian student organizations in the U.S.—from moving with the ASU towards collective security. See "Report of the [YCAW] Executive Secretary to the Opening Session of the National Anti-war Congress" [1938]. On the weakness of the YCAW in New England on the eve of the 1938 student strike against war, see Helen James to Al Hamilton, March 31, 1938. All in YPSL files, SP.

137. Minutes, United Student Peace Committee meeting, May 12, 1938, p. 2, JPL; *NYT,* April 28, 1938; Garland Embrey to Joe [Lash], April 18, 1938, JPL; Sidney Koblenz to Joe [Lash], March 1, 1938, JPL.

138. Joseph P. Lash to Garland Embrey, May 12, 1938, JPL. The YCAW's total membership in 1938 and 1939 never exceeded 400. See Patti McGill Peterson, "The Young Socialist Movement in America from 1905–1940: A Study of the Young People's Socialist League" (Ph.d. diss., Univ. of Wisconsin, 1974), 199. The ASU membership would peak at about 20,000. See transcript of Joseph Lash's retrospective speech on the student movement of the 1930s [n.d.], 22–23, JPL.

139. YCAW, *Youth Challenge the War Makers* (New York, [1938]), 19, YCAW; Hal Draper, "The Student Movement of the Thirties: A Political History," 179–81; Garland Embrey to Joe [Lash], April 18, 1938, JPL.

140. *Student Advocate* (March 1938), 4–6.

141. In one respect, however, the president was ahead of the ASU on the road to interventionism in that he supported expanding the military while the ASU had not yet adopted this position. It was not until its Dec. 1938 convention that the ASU changed its position on defense in favor of preparedness, endorsing an ROTC program for fighter pilots. See *Wisconsin Soapbox,* April 1939, JPL; *ASU Chapter Guide* (Jan. 1939), ACLU. Also see FDR's lecture to movement leaders criticizing their ignorance of military matters, Lash Diary, Jan. 16, 1940, JPL.

142. *Socialist Call,* Feb. 19, 1938; Arthur Kinoy, "An Open Letter to the Harvard Neutrality Council," *Harvard Progressive,* March 19, 1938, HARV.

143. Joseph P. Lash to Garland Embrey, May 12, 1938, JPL. On Communist fears concerning the YCAW, also see Mac Weiss to Carl [Ross?], Nov. 21, 1938, JPL.

144. Dave Grant, "World Youth Speaks For Peace," *Young Communist Review* (Sept. 1938), 3–4, 27.

145. *Ibid.*; *Daily Worker,* Aug. 17, 1938.

146. *Daily Worker,* Aug. 24, 1938.

147. Judah Drob, "The World Youth Congress," *Socialist Review* (Sept.-Oct. 1938), 13–15; George Rawick, "The New Deal and Youth: The Civilian Conservation Corps, the National Youth Administration and the American Youth Con-

gress" (Ph.D. diss., Univ. Of Wisconsin, 1957), 343; Alvaine Hollister to Action Committee Member, Aug. 6, 1938; Minutes, YPSL exec. committee, Aug. 10, 1938, both in YPSL files, SP; Alvaine Hollister to Governing Committee Member, Aug. 11, 1938, YCAW.

148. Drob, "The World Youth Congress," 15.

149. *Vassar Miscellany News*, Jan. 11, 1939; *Oberlin Review*, Sept. 22, 1937; *Michigan Daily*, March 24, Dec. 2, 1938, Jan. 4, 1939; *Unite the Campus to Save Peace* [n.d], 8, 10, 11, JPL; Ruth to Joe [Lash], March 3, 1937, JPL.

150. *Michigan Daily*, March 24, 1938; Samuel Levinger, "The War Is Long," *Student Advocate* (Dec. 1937), 7; "Oppressed and Invaded Spain," Univ. of Chicago *Student Partisan* (Dec. 1937), 1, UC; Avram Goldstein, "Forging a New Tradition," *Harvard Progressive* (Sept. 1939), 8; CCNY *Campus*, April 9, 1937; George Watt, letter from Spain, *Vassar Miscellany News*, Oct. 16, 1937; "Two Letters from Spain," *Brooklyn College Observer* (April 1938), 8, 25, BC; *Michigan Daily*, Jan. 4, 1939.

151. Wechsler, *The Age of Suspicion*, 100–101; CCNY *Campus*, Oct. 15, 1937; *Daily Worker*, Nov. 10, 1938; Celeste Strack Kaplan interview with author.

152. William Sussman to Joseph P. Lash [Fall 1939], JPL.

Chapter 7. Beyond the New Deal? Egalitarian Dreams and Communist Schemes

1. *Washington Post*, Feb. 21, 1937; "After the Pilgrimage," *Student Advocate* (April 1937), 5; *NYT*, Feb. 21, 1937; Joseph P. Lash, *Eleanor and Franklin* (New York, 1971), 712.

2. Leslie A. Gould, *American Youth Today* (New York, 1940), 63–84. Although the Youth Pilgrimage was the student movement's first sizable national march on Washington, movement organizers held two previous, much smaller protests at the White House during the Roosevelt era. The first of these was a demonstration by thirty unemployed college graduates. In May 1933, they marched to the White House to call for federal grants for education and aid to the unemployed. Led by Joseph Lash, this delegation was part of a short-lived organization, the Association of Unemployed College Alumni. A delegation of these protesters met with Roosevelt aide Louis Howe, who greeted them warmly. A second youth demonstration occurred in Dec. 1933, when about 300 NSL and SLID activists, in town for a political conference, held an anti-ROTC demonstration outside the White House (*Washington News*, May 4, 1933; *NYT*, May 4, Dec. 19, 1933; Joseph P. Lash memoir typsecript, 2A, JPL; *What Is the "A.U.C.A."?* (New York, 1933), JPL.

3. *Declaration of Rights of American Youth* (New York, 1935), 1–5; William Hinckley, *Youth Seeks Peace, Freedom and Progress* (New York, 1936), 3–22.

4. Jack McMichael interview with author, Athens, W. Va., Aug. 22, 1982; Gould, *American Youth Today*, passim.

5. *Proceedings Third American Youth Congress* (Cleveland, 1936), 5–47; Gould, *American Youth Today*, 113, 299–300; *Proceedings Congress of Youth* (New York, 1939), 50–51. On the founding and early activities of the AYC, see Robert Cohen, "Revolt of the Depression Generation: America's First Mass Student Movement, 1929–1941" (Ph.D. diss., UC Berkeley, 1987), 390–402; William Hinckley, *American Youth Acts: The Story of the American Youth Congress* (New York [1936]), 3–13.

6. *Michigan Daily*, Feb. 18, 1940; George Watt interview with author.

7. *Student Review* (Oct. 1935), 10; *Daily Worker*, Feb. 22, 1937.

8. "For a National Student Movement: A Suggested Basis," *Student Review* (Jan.-Feb. 1932), 4; George Rawick, "The New Deal and Youth: The Civilian Conservation Corps, the National Youth Administration and the American Youth Congress" (Ph.D. diss., Univ. Wisconsin, 1957), 206.

9. *Student Review* (Oct. 1935), 11.

10. U.S. Congress, Senate Committee on Education and Labor, *American Youth Act Hearings* 74th Congress, 2nd Session, 13, 19, 119, 138, 182, 224. Williams estimated that despite the NYA's efforts, some 3.5 million youths could not afford to attend high school. See *NYT,* March 12, 1938.

11. *American Youth Act Hearings,* 197, 276; *Student Review* (Oct. 1935), 11.

12. *American Youth Act Hearings,* 14–15, 198, 231.

13. Gould, *American Youth Today,* 71–72.

14. *Student Review* (Oct. 1935), 10; *American Youth Act Manual* (New York, 1936); " 'Suffer Little Children . . . ,'—The Unmentionables of American Education," *Student Advocate* (Feb. 1936), 16–17.

15. *NYT,* March 21, 1936; transcript of Address by Rep. Thomas R. Amlie over the Columbia Broadcasting System, Jan. 29, 1936, JPL; Charles Beard, Francis Gorman, Celeste Strack, "Save the Lost Generation! Three Pleas to Congress for Passage of the Youth Act," *Student Advocate* (April 1936), 17–18; *Challenge of Youth,* March 5, 1940.

16. *NYT,* May 7, 1934.

17. "Address by Mrs. Eleanor Roosevelt," in *Proceedings Congress of Youth,* 34–37.

18. "A Summary of the Proceedings of the National Council of the American Youth Congress Held in Washington, D.C., on January 25–26, 1936," 1–3, JPL; Lash, *Eleanor and Franklin,* 708–10; Joseph P. Lash, *Eleanor: A Friend's Memoir* (Garden City, N.Y., 1964), 3–4.

19. Lash, *Eleanor and Franklin,* 709.

20. Lash, *Eleanor: A Friend's Memoir,* 3–4.

21. Lash, *Eleanor and Franklin,* 711; *Daily Worker,* Feb. 22, 1937.

22. Lash, *Eleanor and Franklin,* 712–13: William Hinckley to Friend, March 8, 1937, JPL.

23. David O. Levine, *The American College and the Culture of Aspiration* (Ithaca, N.Y., 1986), 113–35. I borrow the phrase "culture of aspiration" from Levine, who offers a penetrating analysis of this phenomenon.

24. Robert E. Lane, *The Student and Labor* (ASU pamphlet, n.d.), 1–7, NYU; Joseph P. Lash, *The Campus: A Fortress of Democracy* (New York, 1938), 34–35; Wechsler, *Revolt on the Campus* (1935: reprint, Seattle, 1973), 149–66.

25. George Watt interview with author.

26. *Ibid.*

27. James Wechsler interview with author.

28. Doris Yankauer and Herbert Mayer, *Question Before the House* (New York, 1935), 16–17, VC. Vassar student support work for striking factory workers in Beacon, N.Y., may well have inspired the authors of this play. See *Vassar Miscellany News,* Oct. 4, 26, 1935.

29. Irving Howe, *A Margin of Hope: An Intellectual Autobiography* (New York, 1982), 8.

30. Brooklyn College *Pioneer,* Feb. 14, 20, 25, 1935; *NYT,* Feb. 17, 1935.

31. Brooklyn College *Pioneer,* Oct. 31, 1934. This strike support work was led jointly by the campus NSL and SLID branches.

32. CCNY *Campus*, Feb. 15, 18, 1935.

33. *Barnard Bulletin*, May 10, 1935. Students did support work for rural labor and farm strikes. See *Daily Cardinal*, Nov. 4, 5, 8, 1933, Jan. 13, 1934; Visalia *Times Delta*, Oct. 19, 1933; Berkeley *Student Outpost*, Nov. 13, 1933, UCB.

34. Budd Shulberg, "Dartmouth Rejects the Academic Mind," *Student Advocate* (April 1936), 13, 30.

35. *Daily Californian*, Sept. 10, 11, 16, 17, 22 23, Oct. 19, 28, 1936; *Berkeley Daily Gazette*, Sept. 21, 1936; *Oakland Tribune*, Sept. 25, 1936.

36. Celeste Strack Kaplan interview with author. Also see *Young Spartacus*, June 1934.

37. *Columbia Spectator*, March 6, 1936.

38. *Student Outpost*, Aug. 23, Sept. 26, 1934.

39. *Daily Californian*, Oct. 14, 1936; "The ROTC Trains Strikebreakers," *Student Advocate* (Oct.-Nov. 1936), 6; *Voice of the Federation*, Oct. 8, 1936.

40. *The Harvard Student Union: A Record and a Promise*, 5; *Harvard Crimson*, May 10, 1933; Alice and Staughton Lynd, eds., *Rank and File: Personal Histories by Working Class Organizers* (Boston, 1973), 76.; James E. Jackson interview with author, Manhattan, N.Y., Aug. 31, Nov. 17, 1982.

41. Dorothy Thompson, "Of Mines and Men," *The Intercollegian and Far Horizons* (April-May 1938), 135–36; "Students in Industry," *Intercollegian* (April 1931), 235–36; *Barnard Bulletin*, Dec. 3, 1937; *Vassar Miscellany News*, Oct. 8, 1932, April 29, 1933, Oct. 13, 1934; Anna Caples, "The Union Is Santa Claus," *Student Outlook* (Feb. 1933), 9.

42. A. and S. Lynd, eds., *Rank and File*, 76.

43. *Voice of the Federation*, Oct. 24, 1935, Oct. 22, 1936; John L. Lewis, "CIO: A Challenge to the Campus," *Student Advocate* (Feb. 1937), 14.

44. George Watt interview with author; on the role that alumni of the student movement played in the labor movement, see Nathan Solomon interview with author, Pound Ridge, N.Y., May 13, 1982; Larry Rogin interview with author, Washington, D.C., June 4, 1982; James E. Jackson interview with author; Celeste Strack Kaplan interview with author; Kay Cline Burton essay in *ASU 50th Anniversary Reunion* (Long Beach, Cal., 1986), 6.

45. Gould, *American Youth Today*, 121–22; Campus Committee for the California Youth Act, leaflet (n.d.), "A Call: Northern California Assembly of Youth to Draft A California Youth Act" (Jan. 9–10, 1937), both in pamphlet collection of Henry May.

46. Lash, *Toward a Closed Shop on Campus* (New York, 1937), 6; Univ. of Chicago *Upsurge*, Nov. 14, 21, 1935, UC.

47. Student Workers Federation of the Univ. of Michigan, *Why SWF?* (Ann Arbor, 1936), 1; Agnes Reynolds to Molly Yard, Aug. 22, 1937, JPL. *Daily Texan*, May 17, 1934; Radical activists at the Univ. of Texas also organized a strike by students who worked in campus area restaurants, and they attempted to unionize all student waiters in Austin. See FBI file # 61–121, Jan. 25, 1940, Report by J.O Peyronnin [? last name only partially legible], New Orleans.

48. *University Daily Kansan*, Oct. 11, 15, 1935; on the LID's role in founding this student union in Kansas, see Paul Porter interview with author, Reston, Va., June 4, 1982.

49. *Daily Californian*, Oct. 16, 1940.

50. *Ibid.*, Jan. 14, 24, 1938.

51. *Ibid.*, and Jan. 20, 1938; Lawrence A. Maes, "Development and Applica-

tion of Fair Bear Standards at the University of California," unpublished paper, UC Berkeley, 1948, Institute of Industrial Relations Library, UC Berkeley.

52. *Daily Californian*, Sept. 6, 1939; M. R. White to Robert G. Sproul, March 22, 1939, President's Files, UCB; *Daily Californian*, Oct. 5, 1939. On the similar Labor Board which ASU activists helped establish at Ohio State University, see *Ohio State Lantern*, Oct. 19, 1939, Jan. 10, Feb. 28, Oct. 7, 8, 10, 1940.

53. *Daily Californian*, May 1, 1936. Also see Reynold Cohn, "Labor Board," *Occident* (Oct. 1937), 14–15, UCB; Henry May interview with author, Berkeley, June 22, 1982.

54. "For a National Student Movement," 4; *Program of American Youth Congress* (New York, 1934), 8, 11, 14; *Student Union Bulletin*, Jan. 7, 1936; Jack Mc-Michael to author, July 24, 1982.

55. "A Summary of the Proceedings of the Meeting of the National Council of the American Youth Congress held in Washington, D.C. on January 25–26, 1936," 3, JPL.

56. *Ibid.*

57. *Declaration of the Rights of American Youth*, 1.

58. G. W. Studebaker to Joseph P. Lash, Feb. 17, 1936, JPL.

59. "The American Negro in College, 1932–1933," *Crisis* (Aug. 1933), 181–82.

60. Univ. of Wisconsin *Daily Cardinal*, Oct. 26, 1935; *Ohio State Lantern*, May 17, 1937; Univ. of Chicago *Student Partisan* (Dec. 1937), 16–17, *UC*. On the barring of blacks from intercollegiate athletics, see *University Daily Kansan*, Feb. 14, 1935, Oct. 17, 1939, and May 3, 1940; *Daily Bruin*, Oct. 29, 1940; on racial discrimination in the ROTC, see *Ohio State Lantern*, Dec. 5, 1939.

61. *Daily Illini*, Jan. 10, 1932. Racism was by no means confined to the extracurricular part of campus life. Bigoted professors could make life miserable for African American students inside the classroom. See Everett W. Johnson to Henry J. Doermann, Feb. 9, 1929, President's Papers, UT; Randolph Edmonds, "Education in Self-Contempt," *Crisis* (Aug. 1938), 262–63, 266.

62. "Lights and Shadows of Being a Negro: A Symposium," *Intercollegian* (Dec. 1930), 71.

63. *Columbia Spectator*, Oct. 15, 1935; " 'Kansas Is a White Man's School,' " *Student Advocate* (March 1936), 23.

64. Esther Cooper Jackson interview with author, Manhattan, N.Y., Sept. 17, 1982.

65. Caroline Wasson Thomason, "Will Prejudice Capture Oberlin?" *Crisis* (Dec. 1934), 360–61.

66. Sigma Nu constitution cited in Thomas J. Cunningham to Dean Arleigh Williams, Aug. 15, 1960, President's Files, UCB; Alfred Lee, *Fraternities Without Brotherhood* (Boston, 1955), passim; R. Cohen, "Greeks Ignore Racist Past," *Daily Californian*, Oct. 16, 1986; Harold Kaplan and Alec Morin, "Jim Crow on Campus," Univ. of Chicago *Student Partisan* (Dec. 1937), 17.; Univ. of Chicago *Phoenix* (March 1937), 1, UC; *Ohio State Lantern*, May 17, 1937; Wechsler, *Revolt on the Campus*, 366–67; Univ. of Toledo *Collegian*, Feb. 25, 1938.

67. *Columbia Spectator*, April 14, 15, 1936; *Ohio State Lantern*, May 14, June 1, 1937.

68. William McClendon, "Which College—White or Negro?" *Crisis* (Sept. 1934), 264. The reputation of elite white campuses in the North for racial discrimination was so strong within the black community that it discouraged blacks not only from

attending such colleges, but even from going to conferences on these campuses. On the eve of the ASU's 1937 convention, for instance, Sarah Murphy, a black activist from South Carolina, wrote the ASU's national leadership expressing concern over whether she would be welcome at this convention, since "I understand that Vassar frankly is not desirous of having colored students in its student body." ASU leader Molly Yard's response to Murphy cited the ASU's "no discrimination" policy. Yard assured her that at all ASU conventions there "could be absolutely no question as to whether Negro delegates would be welcome," and that "we are very glad that you will be coming to the convention" (Sarah Murphy to Joseph P. Lash, Nov. 8, 1937; Molly Yard to Sarah Murphy, Nov. 11, 1937, JPL).

69. Kenneth B. Clark interview with author, Manhattan, N.Y., Aug. 3, 1982. Mordecai Johnson, "The Day of Reckoning for the College Bred," *Intercollegian* (Dec. 1930), 70, 74. Michael R. Winston. "Through the Back Door: Academic Racism and the Negro Scholar in Historical Perspective," *Daedalus* (Summer 1971), 678, 695.

70. "They Shall Not Die!," *Student Review* (Oct. 1932), 3; James Wechsler, *Revolt on the Campus*, 354–73. The student movement's racial egalitarianism was also strengthened by the access its leftist leaders had to communist historiography, which was free of many of the racist myths which distorted American history textbooks in this period. At the ASU's summer leadership institute, for example, student organizers studied and praised communist historian James Allen's revisionist work *Reconstruction*, with its positive interpretation of Radical Reconstuction and interracial democracy ("ASU Newsletter, Thyra Edwards Group," July 24, 1939, JPL).

71. Max Gordon interview with author; the student movement's African American leaders frequently raised civil rights issues and other black student concerns in articles published in the student movement's national magazines. See Maurice Gates, "Howard Must Answer!," *Student Review* (Feb. 1934), 4–5; Maurice Gates, "South Revisited," *ibid.* (March 1935), 15; Maurice Gates, "Inciting to Riot," *ibid.* (Oct. 1935), 9; James Jackson, "We Tell the Congressmen," *Student Review* (June 1935), 5–6; Lyonel Florant, "Negro Education and Status," *Student Outlook* (Oct. 1935), 10–11; Louis Burnham, "We Are Tired of Waiting, Mrs. Roosevelt," *Student Advocate* (March 1936), 16.

72. Muriel Rukeyser, "Starting the Ball Rolling, the Student Conference on Negro Student Problems," *Student Review* (May 1933), 17–18; "A Guide to Action-Proposed Resolutions of Student Conference on Negro Student Problems," *ibid.*, 19–20.

73. Lyonel Florant, "Youth Exhibits a New Spirit," *Crisis* (Aug. 1936), 237.

74. James E. Jackson interview with author.

75. "Three Conventions," *Student Review* (Feb. 1934), 5; Gould, *American Youth Today*, 64–65, 77; Nick Aaron Ford, "Oklahoma Youth Legislature Hits Jim Crow," *Crisis* (April 1938), 116.

76. "Three Conventions," *Student Review* (Feb. 1934), 5; Gates, "Howard Must Answer!," 4–5.

77. "They Shall Not Die!," 3–4; *Student Review* (Dec. 1932), 3; (May 1932), 4; Muriel Rukeyser, "The Trial," *ibid.* (Jan. 1934), 20; Muriel Rukeyser, "From Scottsboro to Decatur," *ibid.* (April 1933), 12–15.

78. "Agitate! Educate! Organize," *Student Outlook* (March 1934), 23; Hilia Laine, "The Michigan Color-Line," *Student Review* (Dec. 1934), 12; Berkeley *Student Outpost*, March 11, 1935; CCNY *Campus*, Sept. 19, 1935; Univ. of Chicago *Upsurge*,

Feb. 20, 1935; "A Communication on Phi Beta Kappa from Howard," *Student Review* (Nov. 1934), 19; *Bulletin of the Fourth National Convention of the National Student League* (St. Louis, Dec. 1934), 3. On student protests against racial discrimination in a campus employment agency, see CCNY *Campus*, March 13, 1936; a hall hosting a student dance, see CCNY *Campus*, Dec. 20, 1936; the hiring of faculty, see CCNY *Campus*, Sept. 19, 1935; college admissions policies, see *Vassar Miscellany News*, Nov. 8, 1939.

79. James E. Jackson interview with author; Lash, *The Campus: A Fortress of Democracy*, 45–47.

80. *Ibid.*; Harvard Sitkoff, *A New Deal for Blacks* (New York, 1978), 265; Univ. of Chicago *Soapbox*, Jan. 1937, UC; Univ. of Chicago *Student Partisan* (Dec. 1937), 16–17; *Ohio State Lantern*, May 3, 17, June 3, 1937; *Columbia Spectator*, April 17, May 1, 1936; CCNY *Campus*, Dec. 20, March 13, 1936, April 27, 1937.

81. Dan T. Carter, *Scottsboro: A Tragedy of the American South* (Baton Rouge, 1969), 114; on this support of lynching, see *Daily Texan*, March 4, 1934. A survey of college students in North Carolina found that 87.1 percent thought blacks should remain segregated and 47.8 percent believed that the lynching of blacks for rape was justifiable. See K. C. Garrison and Viola S. Burch, "A Study of Racial Attitudes of College Students," *Journal of Social Psychology* (May 1933), 232; on the student movement's difficulty in penetrating the segregationist South, see Jack McMichael interview with author; Monroe Sweetland interview with author.

82. F. Palmer Weber interview with author, Manhattan. N.Y., Jan. 25, 1982.

83. Univ. of Virginia *College Topics*, May 18, 1934.

84. Studs Terkel, *Hard Times: An Oral History of the Great Depression* (New York, 1970), 401. The subject of this interview, though appearing under the pseudonym Chance Stoner, was in fact F. Palmer Weber. See Weber interview with author.

85. Transcript of F. Palmer Weber interview with Charles Moran, 16, UVA; Weber interview with author; *College Topics*, Nov. 26, 1935. The Univ. of Virginia NSL also joined with African American students from Virgina Union University in protesting the state legislature's inferior funding of black schools in 1933. See James E. Jackson, "The Youth Movement," *Souvenir Bulletin* [of the Southern Negro Youth Congress], Feb. 13–14, 1937, NNC; James E. Jackson interview with author.

86. Dave to Joe [Lash], April 21 [1937?], JPL.

87. On this Christian radicalism and civil rights work in the South, see Jack McMichael interview with author; F. Palmer Weber interview with author. Anthony Dunbar, *Against the Grain: Southern Radicals and Prophets 1929–1959* (Charlottesville, 1981), 1–135; "An Action Story," *Intercollegian* (Dec. 1930), 86–89; "Interracial Tour," *ibid.* (Jan. 1931), 127; "What Is the 'Race' Problem?," *ibid.* (May 1936), 195–96; "South Carolina's First Interracial Student Conference," *ibid.* (May–June 1934), 23.

88. Jack McMichael interview with author; *Emory Wheel*, Jan. 12, 26, 1933. Emory's mainstream student leaders strongly criticized the campus YMCA chapter for sponsoring these interracial meetings. See *Emory Wheel*, Oct. 3, 1935.

89. Jack McMichael interview with author; *Southern Regional Council Minutes*, vol. II, June, 1936, YWCA. McMichael also took the fight against segregation beyond the South in 1935, when he was elected chair of a committee charged with setting the racial policy for the national council of the student YM/YWCAs. Through this committee, McMichael committed the Y's to "direct our united efforts towards the establishment of a student Christian movement and a social order which pro-

vides for every individual regardless of race, all opportunities to participate and share alike all the relationships of life"—working towards the "elimination of all segregation and discrimination" (*Moving into a New Century: An Historical Overview of the National Student YWCA* (Princeton, 1974), 3).

90. Univ. of Virginia National Student League to Univ. of Virginia Board of Visitors, Oct. 4, 1935, President's Papers, UVA.

91. Univ. of Virginia *College Topics,* Oct. 10, 17, 1935.

92. *Ibid.,* Oct. 12, 22, 1935.

93. *Ibid.,* Oct. 12, 1935.

94. *Ibid.,* Oct. 24, 1935.

95. Univ. of North Carolina *Daily Tar Heel,* Jan. 7, 8, 10, 11, 13–16, 1939; Pauli Murray, *Song in a Weary Throat* (New York, 1987), 114–29.

96. *Daily Tar Heel,* Jan. 7, 8, 10, 11, 13–16, 1939; on the early stages of this legal battle, see Richard Kluger, *Simple Justice* (New York, 1975), 173–213.

97. Ralph Ellison, *The Invisible Man* (New York, 1952), 34–148.

98. Langston Hughes, "Cowards from the Colleges," *Crisis* (Aug. 1934), 226. Also see Howard Univ. *Hilltop,* May 13, 1936. These conditions provoked black student strikes in the 1920s. See Raymond Wolters, *The New Negro on Campus: The Black College Rebellions of the 1920s* (Princeton, 1975), passim.

99. Hughes, "Cowards from the Colleges," 226; Lyonel Florant, "Youth Exhibits a New Spirit," *Crisis* (Aug. 1936), 237.

100. Ishmael Flory interview with author, Chicago, Oct. 29, 1982; Joe M. Richardson, *A History of Fisk University* (Birmingham, 1980), 128–30; "Fisk and Flory," *Crisis* (April 1934), 111; Thomas E. Jones, "Some Fisk Ideals," *Fisk News* (March-April 1934), 6; President's Trustees Series, No. 3; Thomas E. Jones to [L.] Hollingsworth [Wood], Feb. 26, 1934, both in Thomas E. Jones Papers, 1926–1946, FU; Andrew J. Allison, "The Flory Decision," *Fisk News* (March-April 1934), 5.

101. "Excerpts from the Address of John Hope Franklin, President of the Student Council, 1934–35," *Fisk News* (May-June, 1935) 12; *College Topics,* Nov. 26, 1935; James E. Jackson interview with author; Maurice Gates, "Negro Students Challenge Social Forces," *Crisis* (Aug. 1935), 232.

102. James E. Jackson interview with author.

103. Kenneth B. Clark interview with author, Manhattan, N.Y., Aug. 3, 1982.

104. *Ibid.; Baltimore Afro-American,* March 24, 1934. Unlike the typical accommodationist black college president, Johnson was a contradictory figure. He often engaged in civil rights advocacy himself, and allowed faculty to do so as well, but he also worried about Howard's financial health and would lash out at any protests—particularly by students—that he thought might threaten Howard's funding. Johnson's egaliltarian sympathies and institutional responsibilties as a college president often clashed, and from one event to another one never knew which Johnson would appear: Johnson the civil rights advocate or Johnson the cautious college president (see Howard Univ. *Hilltop,* March 26, 1940; Rayford Logan, *Howard University: The First Hundred Years* (New York, 1969), 279–93; Augusta Strong, "Southern Youth's Proud Heritage," *Freedomways* (Winter 1964), 39; Sitkoff, *A New Deal for Youth,* 156).

105. *Hilltop,* Dec. 22. 1934.

106. Richard Collins, "Liberalism and Negroes," *Student Advocate* (Feb. 1937), 8.

107. CCNY *Campus,* Dec. 20, 1936; *Columbia Spectator,* April 15, 17, 1936.

108. James E. Jackson, "The Youth Movement"; James E. Jackson interview

with author; Dorothy Burnham interview with author, Brooklyn, N.Y., March 16, 1983. Robin D. G. Kelley offers an excellent summary of SNYC's activities in his *Hammer and Hoe, Alabama Communists during the Great Depression* (Chapel Hill, 1990), 200–219.

109. James E. Jackson interview with author.

110. *Ibid.*

111. *Ibid.*

112. Strong, "Southern Youth's Proud Heritage," 38.

113. James E. Jackson interview with author.

114. *Ibid.*; Norfolk *Journal and Guide*, April 24, 1937.

115. James E. Jackson interview with author.

116. *Norfolk Journal and Guide*, April 24, May 15, 1937.

117. James E. Jackson interview with author.

118. *Proclamation of Southern Negro Youth* (Birmingham, 1938), 1, NNC.

119. Esther Cooper Jackson interview with author.

120. *Official Proceedings of the Second All Southern Negro Youth Conference*, April 1938, NNC; Henry Winston, "Freedom, Equality and Opportunity: Southern Negro Youth Congress Charts Road to Progress," *The New South* (May 1938), 10–11. Augusta Strong, "Youth Meets in Birmingham," *Crisis* (June 1939), 178–80; Augusta Strong, "Southern Youth's Proud Heritage," 44–45; James E. Jackson, Jr., "Our Battle for the Ballot" (Birmingham, 1940), passim, NYU. James Jackson interview with author; Strong, "Southern Youth's Proud Heritage," 50; *Cavalcade*, April and May, 1941, NNC.

121. Though collegiate racism emerged as a national issue in the 1930s, during the preceding decade racism and white paternalism sparked protests at several northern campuses and black colleges. See Wolters, *The New Negro on Campus*, 316–39.

122. Sitkoff, *A New Deal for Blacks*, 190–243; ASU, *Students Serve Democracy* (New York, 1939), 20; "The Inevitable Mr. Gaines," *Missouri Student* editorial, reprinted in North Carolina *Daily Tar Heel*, Jan. 10, 1939; George Cech, "Spotlight on Missouri," *The Intercollegian and Far Horizons* (March 1939), 111–12; "Why Not Negroes?," Univ. of West Virginia *Daily Athenaeum* editorial, reprinted in *Ohio State Lantern*, May 11, 1937; *Daily Texan*, Dec. 19, 1937; Charles Houston, "Don't Shout Too Soon," *Crisis* (March 1936), 79, 91; "University of Missouri Case Won," *Crisis* (Jan. 1939), 10–11; Kluger, *Simple Justice*, 155–213.

123. Note, however, that though the largest organizations in the student movement—the ASU and the Youth Congress—spearheaded this shift towards liberalism not every movement organization was supportive of this. The small but vocal left wing of the student movement, which included the YPSLs and the Trotskyists, clung to a revolutionary line (YPSL memo, "Youth and the New Deal," Oct. 10, 1938, YPSL files, SP). Although the YPSLs and Trotskyists were increasingly isolated and steadily lost influence in the student movement of the late 1930s, they did offer some cogent criticism of the shifts in ASU and Youth Congress policy, which will be discussed below.

124. *Program of the American Youth Congress*, 6, 7, 13.

125. Joseph Clark interview with author; Richard Criley interview with author.

126. *Student Review* (Dec. 1934), 8; Joseph P. Lash, typescript speech, "Student Movement of the 1930s" [n.d.], 13, JPL.

127. *Program of the American Youth Congress*, 5; *Declaration of the Rights of American Youth*, 3.

128. *Daily Worker*, Aug. 13, 1938.

129. "The Creed of the American Youth Congress," *Young Communist Review* (Aug. 1939), 7.

130. *Program of the American Youth Congress*, 6–7, 13. ASU Staff Meeting Minutes, March 15, 1937, JPL; William W. Hinckley to Joseph P. Lash, Nov. 19, 1937, JPL; Celeste Strack, "The ASU Convention," *Young Communist Review* (Dec. 1938), 28.

131. Ruth Watt, "On the Campus," *Young Communist Review* (April 1939), 18; Strack, "The ASU Convention," 28; "The National Chairman Speaks," *Student Advocate* (March 1938), 20.

132. *NYT*, Jan. 29, 1938; Eleanor Roosevelt, "My Day," reprinted in *Proceedings, Congress of Youth* (New York, 1939), 43; Lash, *Eleanor and Franklin*, 713–15; Jack McMichael interview with author.

133. Rawick, "The New Deal and Youth," 323–24.

134. "Resolution on the American Youth Congress passed by the YPSL NEC at meeting at Philadelphia, May 29 to 30, 1937," YPSL files, SP.

135. YPSL memo, "Youth and the New Deal," Oct. 10, 1938, YPSL files, SP.

136. Joseph Clark interview with author; Joseph P. Lash interview with author; Gil Green interview with author; Richard Criley interview with author; Harold Draper, "The First American Youth Congress," *Student Outlook* (Oct. 1934), 15–16; Theodore Draper, "American Youth Rejects Fascism," *New Masses* (Aug. 28, 1934), 11–13.

137. YPSL memo, "Youth and the New Deal."

138. Minutes of Resident Board [of the American Youth Congress], March 13, 1937, JPL; Gould, *American Youth Today*, 86; *NYT*, Oct. 10, 15, 1937, Dec. 7, 1937.

139. Hy Weintraub to Maxwell Haraway, Aug. 5, 1936, YPSL files, SP.

140. Minutes of Resident Board, Feb. 17, 1938, JPL; *Proceedings, Congress of Youth* (New York, 1939), 9.

141. Lash, *Eleanor and Franklin*, 716; Joseph P. Lash, *Love Eleanor: Eleanor Roosevelt and Her Friends* (Garden City, N.Y., 1982), 281.

142. Franklin D. Roosevelt memorandum, Jan. 17, 1939, reprinted in Lash, *Eleanor and Franklin*, 717.

143. "Proceedings of the National Council of the American Youth Congress, January 25–26, 1936," JPL; Lash, *Eleanor and Franklin*, 709.

144. Irving Howe, *Socialism and America* (New York, 1985), 87–104.

145. Gil Green interview with author.

146. Rawick, "The New Deal and Youth," 295–97; the leaders of the Youth Congress always publicly denied that it was communist-dominated. See Gould, *American Youth Today*, 137–64. But these denials were disingenuous. See Gil Green interview with author; Lash Diary, April 26, 1938, March 22, 1940, JPL; David Dubinsky to Eleanor Roosevelt June 20, 1940, ER.

147. Arthur Clifford, *The Truth About the American Youth Congress* (Detroit, 1935), passim; Gould, *American Youth Today*, 293; Brooklyn College *Vanguard*, Feb. 8, 1937.

148. *American Youth Today*, the official history of the Youth Congress by Leslie A. Gould is a case study in such disingenuousness and is typical of the literature

put out by the Youth Congress. This account of the Youth Congress is 300 pages long, but devotes only two pages (162–63) to the Young Communist League. In these two pages we are told that it was "patently absurd" to suppose that the mere "handful" of communists in the Youth Congress could dominate that organization. Gould also claimed that communists in the Youth Congress "always abided by the rules of democratic procedure." Both of these claims were false. On communist domination of key Youth Congress committees and staff positions, see Rawick, "The New Deal and Youth," 295–97, and see Resolution on the American Youth Congress passed by the Y.P.S.L. N.E.C. at Meeting at Philadelphia, May 20 to 30, 1937, JPL; on the secrecy involved in this domination, see Gil Green interview with author; Wechsler, *The Age of Suspicion,* 70–73; on YCL abuse of democratic process in achieving this domination, see Report of the First Meeting of the Permanent Council of the Hennerin County Youth Conference, June 12, 1936; and see Minutes of the YPSL District Executive Commitee, Aug. 10, 1938; both in YPSL files, SP.

149. Gould, *American Youth Today,* 137–64; Gil Green interview with author; Lash Diary, March 22, 1940; David Dubinsky to Eleanor Roosevelt, June 20, 1940, ER. Such disingenuousness was as pronounced in the ASU as it was in the Youth Congress. Thus in Lash's address to the 1938 ASU convention, the ASU leader asserted that "We are not a leftist or anti-capitalist organization. . . . I am sure that no one in the American Student Union would advocate the socialization of toothbrushes" (Joseph P. Lash, "Students in the Service of Democracy," in *Keep Democracy Working by Making It Serve Human Needs: Proceedings Fourth National Convention of the American Student Union* (New York, Dec. 1938), 37). Although Lash was correct in saying the ASU was not an explicitly anti-capitalist organization, its leadership was then and had always been dominated by leftists. Indeed, Lash himself, the ASU's highest ranking officer, was, at the time he gave this speech, a committed socialist, closely allied with the YCL, the CP, and their Popular Front policies—so that his denial that the "leftist" label applied to the ASU was at best a half-truth. Also see *NYT*, Nov. 28, 1939.

150. Joseph P. Lash, *Eleanor, a Friend's Memoir,* 1–2, 7–15; Schrecker, *No Ivory Tower,* 63–83.

151. Lash Diary, March 22, 1940, JPL; Joseph P. Lash interview with author.

152. Junius Irving Scales and Richard Nickson, *Cause at Heart: A Former Communist Remembers,* (Athens, Ga., 1983), 67. Mark Greenly, a Philadelphia ASUer, recalled that at his very first ASU meeting he encountered this same type of disingenuousness about the relationship between the ASU and the Communist Party. See Paul Lyons, *Philadelphia Communists, 1936–1956* (Philadelphia, 1982), 37.

153. Wechsler, *The Age of Suspicion,* 72; David Dubinsky to Eleanor Roosevelt June 20, 1940, ER; Eleanor Roosevelt, *This I Remember* (New York, 1949), 200; Don Fabun, "Is the ASU a Communist Front?," *Daily Californian,* Feb. 7, 1941. Since they played a decisive role in shaping movement policy, I have focused here on communists and their leadership role. But it should also be kept in mind that the ASU's history during the Popular Front era was also influenced by liberals— who came into the movement in response to its Popular Front policies and whose support helped encourage and expedite the movement's shift toward the New Deal. The "influx of a vast number of students who were neither socialist or communist . . . but believed in a wider utilization of the resources of government to meet human needs" added to the ASU's new liberal tone. In the Cold War era these liberals would have been termed dupes, but such terms are simplistic. Lib-

eral students wanted an organization which would work for progressive social change in alliance with the New Deal, and the ASU was responsive to them—at least temporarily (Joseph P. Lash to Rhea Whitley, May 16, 1939, JPL; Bruce Bliven Jr., "Citizens of Tomorrow," *New Republic* (Jan. 11, 1939), 283; Joseph P. Lash to Avram, May 19, 1939, JPL).

Chapter 8. Activist Impulses

1. Roscoe J.C. Dorsey, "The Future of Our Youth," *National Republic* (May 1939), 3; E. D. Clark, "Red Microbes in Our Colleges," *National Republic* (Jan. 1937), 1. Also see "Yellow Newspapers See Red," *School and Society* (Jan. 19, 1935), 100.

2. *New York American* editorial "Red Teachers," reprinted in *National Republic* (July/Aug. 1935), 28.

3. *Ibid.*

4. *NYT*, April 12, May 14, 1935; *Chicago Tribune*, April 13–15, 18, 1935; "W.R. Hearst Baits College 'Reds'," *The Social Frontier* (Jan. 1935), 3–4; Ellen Schrecker, *No Ivory Tower* (New York, 1986), 68–70; "Liberty in U.S.A," *The Social Frontier* (Nov. 1936), 63.

5. These statistics and all of the figures in this chapter on the sources of student activism are drawn from a sample group of 125 Depression-era student activists. Data on these activists come from the following sources: 55 autobiographical essays, written by student activists during the ASU's 1938 and 1939 summer training institute and 16 autobiographical essays written by student activists during the SLID's 1935 summer training institute, both in JPL; 24 interviews of student activists with the author; memoirs of six 1930s campus activists in *Political Activism and the Academic Conscience: The Harvard Experience 1936–41*, John Lyndenberg, ed. (Hobart and William Smith Colleges, 1977), 2–54, 67–73; three interviews in Vivian Gornick, *The Romance of American Communism* (New York, 1977), 101–4, 126–30, 140–45; five interviews in John Gerassi, *The Premature Anti-Fascists* (New York, 1986), 44–45, 48–49, 63–64, 69–70, 74–75; one interview in Studs Terkel, *Hard Times: An Oral History of the Great Depression* (New York, 1970), 398–99; additional memoirs of student activists in Irving Howe, *A Margin of Hope* (New York, 1982), 1–89; Junius Irving Scales and Richard Nickson, *Cause at Heart* (Athens, Ga., 1987), 29–87; James Wechsler, *The Age of Suspicion* (New York, 1981), 3–132; Henry F. May, *Coming to Terms* (Berkeley, 1987), 169–266; Pauli Murray, *Song in a Weary Throat* (New York, 1987), 59–91; John Gates, *The Story of an American Communist* (New York, 1958), 7–27; Eric Sevareid, *Not So Wild a Dream* (New York, 1956), 48–73; Richard Rovere, *Arrivals and Departures* (New York, 1976), 41–60; Paul Jacobs, *Is Curly Jewish?* (New York, 1965), 3–110; Leslie Fiedler, *Being Busted* (New York, 1969), 13–27; Thomas Merton, *The Seven Storey Mountain* (New York, 1948), 3–4, 131–65; John P. Roche, *Shadow and Substance* (New York, 1964), 432–41; Morton Sobell, *On Doing Time* (New York, 1974), 3–38; Victor G. Reuther, *The Brothers Reuther* (Boston, 1976), 1–69; Nancy Bedford Jones, "My Father Is a Liar," *Student Review* (Oct. 1935), 13–15; Jack McMichael, autobiographical essay, JM; Joseph P. Lash, memoir typescript, JPL; Daniel Boone Schirmer interview with Bill Schecter, Oral History of the American Left, NYU.

6. Anonymous, "My Autobiography"; Florence Dubroff autobiographical essay; Morton Jackson autobiographical essay; all in JPL. Carl Schorske, "A New

Yorker's Map of Cambridge: Ethnic Marginality and Political Ambivalence," in Lyndenberg, ed., *Political Activism*, 10.

Survey research on teachers in the 1930s suggests that the anecdotal evidence in these interviews concerning the narrow-mindedness and intolerance of conservative faculty reflected a very significant phenomenon in America education. One such survey found that 35 percent of the teachers polled "would deliberately omit from textbooks facts that might lead to criticism of the social order on the part of the young" (Manly H. Harper, "Social Attitudes of Educators," *The Social Frontier* (Feb. 1937), 146). Another survey found 48 percent of teachers favored the deportation of aliens who criticized the Constitution. See William H. Kirkpatrick, ed., *The Teacher and Society* (New York, 1937), 194.

7. Nancy Phillips autobiographical essay; also see Betsy Pifer autobiographical essay; both in JPL.

8. Anonymous autobiographical essay [of Bryn Mawr student], JPL.

9. Maxine Ture autobiographical essay, JPL.

10. Alice Berman autobiographical essay; Bernard Wolf autobiographical essay, both in JPL.

11. Clifford McVeagh, "Academic Napoleons #1: Ruthven of Michigan," *Student Advocate* (Feb. 1936), 13; Nancy Bedford Jones, "Academic Napoleons No. II: Provost Moore of UCLA," *ibid.* (March 1936), 19–20, 30; Roger Chase, "Academic Napoleons No. III: Nicholas Murray Butler," *ibid.* (April 1936), 20–21; Arthur Wilson, "Academic Napoleon No. IV: Chancellor Bowman of Pittsburgh," *ibid.* (Feb. 1937), 21–23; Theresa Levin, "Dr. Colligan: Tammany's Aloysius, Academic Napoleon No. 5," *ibid.* (Oct. 1937), 9–10, 26; Alberta Reid, "Academic Napoleon No. 6: Marvin of George Washington U.," *ibid.* (Dec. 37), 13–14, 18; "University Sweatshops," *ibid.* (Feb. 1936), 4; "Gagging the High Schools," *ibid.*, 20; "Kansas Is a White Man's School," *ibid* (March 1936), 23; "ROTC Trains Strikebreakers," *ibid.* (Oct.-Nov. 1936), 6; Robert N. Kelso, Jr., "How To Be a Censored Editor," *ibid.* (Oct. 1937), 16–17, 31; Jack Pollack, "Dr. Broadbent," *ibid.* (Feb. 1937), 18; Robert Rhinestone, "Gentleman and Scholar," *ibid.* (May 1936), 9; "Hey You!," *ibid.* (Oct. 1937), 2. Also see *Harvard Communist* (Nov. 1937), 19–20, HARV.

In the ASU's *Student Advocate,* the most widely circulated magazine put out by any 1930s American student activist organization, there were only six articles by or about radical faculty members during the entire three-year run of the magazine. Three of these six concerned academic freedom cases. None of the articles even remotely suggests that the student movement was dependent on leftist faculty. See D. E. Martin, "Still Sweetness and Light," *Student Advocate* (Feb. 1936), 24–25, 30; "Professors Speak Out," *ibid.* (March 1936), 5; Calvin J. Sutherlin, "For God, for Country—for the Yale Corporation," *ibid.* (Dec. 1936), 6–7; Reinhold Niebuhr, " 'Is Education a Private Industry'?," *ibid.* (Feb. 1937), 19–20, 29; Robert Kaltenborn, "Why Men Leave Harvard," *ibid.* (May 1937), 7–8; Dr. Leonard Lawson, "Peace on the Curriculum," *ibid.* (Dec. 1937), 21–22. On the limited relationship between radical faculty and students, see Leon Wofsy interview with author, Berkeley, April 29, 1986.

12. In our sample group of 125 activists, 10 of the 27 students who said that a faculty member fostered their politicization indictated that this faculty member was a liberal—while 14 named a radical faculty member and three did not specify whether the teacher was liberal or radical. For examples of this liberal role, see Virginia Sanford and Jeanette Schaeffer autobiographical essays, JPL.

13. Everett Ladd and Seymour Martin Lipset, *The Divided Academy* (New York, 1975), 27. On this growth of faculty liberalism, also see Harper, "Social Attitudes of Educators," 145–47; Kirkpartick, *The Teacher and Society*, 196, 223–24.

14. Jeanette Schaefer autobiographical essay, JPL.

15. Rembert Stokes autobiographical essay, JPL.

16. Virginia Sanford autobiographical essay, JPL.

17. Celeste Strack interview with author.

18. Kenneth B. Clark interview with author; Emily Shield autobiographical essay; Anonymous [Bryn Mawr] student autobiographical essay; both in JPL.

19. The exact figures were 25 mentioning conservative teachers, 10 liberal, 14 radical, and 3 not specified.

20. Schrecker, *No Ivory Tower*, 43, 68; Lyndenberg, ed., *Political Activism*, 19. Student activists, especially during the first half of the decade, complained about the relative lack of radical faculty at their colleges and universities. See *Soapbox*, May 1935; *Hunter Bulletin*, May 29, 1932; "Hearst at Harvard," *New Republic* (June 30, 1935), 335.

21. John Ise, "Shackles on Professors," *The Social Frontier* (May 1937), 242–45; Leo Marx, "The Harvard Retrospect and the Arrested Development of American Radicalism," in Lyndenberg, ed., *Political Activism*, 33; Kaltenborn, "Why Men Leave Harvard," 7–8.

22. Ernestine Freidl autobiographical essay, JPL.

23. Lewis Morton Cohen autobiographical essay, JPL.

24. B. Walker autobiographical essay, JPL.

25. Esther Cooper Jackson interview with author.

26. Nancy Philips autobiographical essay, JPL.

27. Celeste Strack Kaplan interview with author.

28. Marx, "The Harvard Retrospect," 33.

29. Mary McCarthy, *How I Grew* (New York, 1987), 205. Also see Alfred Kazin, *Starting Out in the the Thirties* (New York, 1965), 138.

30. For the only activists in our sampled group to be recruited directly into radical organizations by faculty members, see Esther Cooper Jackson interview with author; Lewis Morton Cohen autobiographical essay, JPL; Wechsler, *The Age of Suspicion*, 62.

31. Historians of American communism have failed to recognize the existence of this political double standard. Their oversight has left them in a historical vacuum as they debate the behavior of communist professors. Thus the anti-communist historian Theodore Draper attacks communist professors for failing to maintain scholarly neutrality and worshipping the Soviet Union, while anti-anti-communist historian Ellen Schrecker defends these communists by arguing that they displayed "fairness and lack of bias" in their teaching. Both sides of this debate seem to assume that the presence of any bias in the teaching of communist faculty would constitute both a terrible indictment of them and a unique departure from professional standards. This is a naive assumption that reflects a lack of familiarity with what was going on in the classrooms of Depression America. The problem with both Schrecker and Draper is that since they only study communist teachers and not conservatives or liberals, they do not understand that these non-radical teachers were every bit as biased in their classroom work as their radical counterparts. However one judges radical teachers in Depression America, their instructional work cannot be set into historical context unless it is recognized that during this turbulent era bias entered the classroom from all positions on the

political spectrum—right, left, and center. Unless this context is understood, we will never move beyond the unreality of this debate which casts communist teachers as either apolitical saints or indoctrinating sinners. On this debate see, Schrecker, *No Ivory Tower*, 43–44; Theodore Draper, "The Class Struggle: The Myth of the Communist Professors," *New Republic* (Jan. 26, 1987), 29–36.

32. Fifty-two of the 125 activists credited their family with facilitating their politicization. This pattern was remarkably similar to that found in studies of 1960s student activists. See Richard Flacks, "The Liberated Generation: An Exploration of the Roots of Student Protest," *Journal of Social Issues* (1967), 66–74; Kenneth Kenniston, *Young Radicals: Notes on Committed Youth* (New York, 1968), 51–76.

33. Joseph P. Lash interview with author; Celeste Strack Kaplan interview with author; Richard Criley interview with author. For photos attesting to the most non-bohemian style of dress among radical student organizers, see James Wechsler, "The Education of Bob Burke," *Student Advocate* (Oct.-Nov. 1936), 13; Joseph P. Lash, "Awakening at Oxford," *ibid.*, 23; "Striking for Students' Rights," *Student Review* (March 1933), 12–13; James Jackson, "We Tell the Congressmen," *Student Review* (June 1935), 5. The one major exception to the rule concerning generational conflict in the student movement occurred when the movement was declining in 1940. Here there was some generational conflict—or at least generational rhetoric was used by isolationist students to attack interventionists. Even in 1940, however, generational attacks (which proved quite transient) were directed neither at parents nor the older generation in general, but at teachers and administrators who had taken a strong anti-isolationist stance. This conflict will be discussed in Chapter 9.

34. *Program of the American Youth Congress* (New York, 1934), 5.

35. *Ibid.*; also on this rejection of generational rhetoric, see Gil Green, "A Communist Reply," *The Social Frontier* (May 1935), 22.

36. Former SLID activist Victor Reuther, for instance, devoted the first chapters in his memoirs to what was for him the inspiring story of his father's immigration to America and emergence as a labor militant and trade union organizer. See Reuther, *The Brothers Reuther*, 1–31.

37. Molly Yard autobiographical essay, JPL; Molly Yard interview with author.

38. Esther Feldman autobiographical essay, JPL.

39. Florence Dubroff autobiographical essay, JPL.

40. Mary Ann Loeser autobiographical essay, JPL.

41. Claire Lippman autobiographical essay, JPL.

42. Emily Shield autobiographical essay, JPL.

43. James E. Jackson interview with author.

44. Robert Lane and Betsy Pifer autobiographical essays, both in JPL.

45. P.A. Kitchell autobiographical essay, JPL.

46. Emily Shield autobiographical essay, JPL.

47. Betsy Pifer autobiographical essay, JPL.

48. Grace Smelo autobiographical essay, JPL.

49. Joseph P. Lash memoir typescript, Oct. 14, 1986, p. 7, JPL.

50. Bernard Wolf autobiographical essay, JPL.

51. Maxine Ture autobiographical essay; Stoyan Menton autobiographical essay, both in JPL.

52. Nancy Phillips autobiographical essay, JPL.

53. Jean Scott autobiographical essay, JPL; Paul Jacobs, *Is Curly Jewish?*, 17,

19. Generational conflict of a quieter, more ambiguous and subtle type than that impelling Jacobs's radicalism contributed to the radicalization of Arthur Miller. In his autobiography Miller notes that "I never raised my voice against my father." But the Depression's bite on the family income created tension between father and son. Miller recalled that "I knew perfectly well, it was not he who angered me, only his failure to cope with his fortune's collapse. Thus I had two fathers, the real one and the metaphoric, and the latter I resented because he did not know how to win out over the general collapse." Was the young Miller's radicalism a way of revolting against his father and the failing bourgeois role model he represented? In Miller's view the meaning of his radicalism was more complex than that: "If Marxism was on the metaphorical plane, a rational for parricide, I think that to me it was at the same time a way of forgiving my father, for it showed him as a digit in a kind of cosmic catastrophe that was beyond his powers to avoid" (Arthur Miller, *Timebends: A Life* (New York, 1987), 112, 114).

54. *NYT*, April 3, 1932.

55. UCLA *Daily Bruin*, Oct. 30, 1934; Philip Feldman to President Alexander Ruthven, Aug. 26, 1935, reprinted in Martin Anderson, "Interfering with Students," *Student Review* (Oct. 1935), 12–13; *Hunter Bulletin*, April 1, 1935.

56. *CCNY Office of the Dean Hearings, Oct. 10–Nov. 7, 1934,* vol. I, 63, 68, 70, 71, CCNY.

57. Mrs. Robert V. Russell to Frederick Robinson, Jan. 11, 1935, *CCNY Hearings*, vol. II.

58. *NYT,* April 23, 1936.

59. Celeste Strack Kaplan interview with author.

60. J.R. McMichael to Jack McMichael [n.d.], JM.

61. *Daily Californian,* Sept. 27, 1940.

62. Nancy Bedford Jones, "My Father Is a Liar!," *Student Review* (Oct. 1935), 13–15.

63. *Ibid.,* 13.

64. Howe, *A Margin of Hope,* 14; Alice Dodge autobiographical essay, JPL. In several cases students in our sampled group sought to avoid conflicts with conservative parents over their radical activism by keeping their leftist affiliations from them. (See Mary Ann Loeser autobiographical essay, JPL; Gerassi, *The Premature Anti-fascists*, 70.)

65. Howe, *A Margin of Hope,* 1–89; Jack McMichael, autobiographical essay, JM; James E. Jackson interview with author; Alice Dodge autobiographical essay, JPL.

66. *Revolt* (Dec. 1932), 3.

67. Scales and Nickson, *Cause at Heart,* 32–46.

68. UT Miller autobiographical essay; Ralph Meinking autobiographical essay; both in JPL.

69. Anonymous autobiographical essay, "A Rebel Is Born," JPL.

70. Terkel, *Hard Times,* 398, 400; F. Palmer Weber interview with author. Univ. of Michigan President Ruthven told the FBI that the campus ASU's membership had tended to come "from what has been characterized as the underprivileged group." See FBI Report #100–1217, Detroit, Feb. 8, 1943.

71. This was also the reason student organizers by the mid-1930s had come to recognize that economic campaigns alone would not be enough to mobilize their predominantly middle-class constituency. See Hal Draper interview with author, Albany, Calif., Oct. 26, 1981; Wechsler, *The Age of Suspicion,* 74.

72. Celeste Strack Kaplan interview with author. On affluent student radicals, also see Merton, *The Seven Storey Mountain*, 147; *Columbia Spectator*, Dec. 11, 1933.

73. White, *In Search of History*, 66

74. *Ibid.*

75. Wechsler, *The Age of Suspicion*, 28

76. Joseph R. De Martini, "Student Activists of the 1930s and 1960s: A Comparison of the Social Bases of the Two Student Movements," *Youth and Society* (June 1975), 408.

77. Celeste Strack Kaplan interview with author; Joseph Lash interview with author; Joseph P. Lash, "Action Notes," *Student Advocate* (April 1937), 25; "Action Notes," *ibid.* (Feb. 1937), 28.

78. Alice Dodge autobiographical essay, JPL. For other examples of such guilt feelings, see Leah Levinger, "We Shall Not Be Moved," *Student Advocate* (May, 1936), 15; Doris Yankauer and Herbert Mayer, *Question Before the House* (New York, 1935), 16–17, VC; James Wechsler interview with author.

79. Kay Martineau autobiographical essay, JPL.

80. Theodore Draper interview with author.

81. *NYT*, May 31, Sept. 6, 1936. By 1937, college placement officers, in an exuberant mood after months of economic progress, began to speak about the Depression in the past tense. See *NYT*, Jan. 10, July 4, 1937. Also see "To the Class of 1936," *Student Advocate* (Oct.-Nov. 1936), 14.

82. Lash, *Toward a Closed Shop on Campus*, 7. Lewis Corey, "Debunking the New Prosperity," *Student Advocate* (Oct.-Nov. 1936), 19–20, 27; "Pilgrimage to Washington," *ibid.* (Feb. 1937), 5; "Class of 1941;" *ibid.* (Oct. 1937), 3. On the returning crisis in the job market for graduates, see *NYT*, Oct. 2, 1938; Univ. of Toledo *Collegian*, Feb. 18, May 6, 1938.

83. Wechlser, *The Age of Suspicion*, 74.

84. Budd Shulberg, "Dartmouth Rejects the Academic Mind," *Student Advocate* (April 1936), 13, 30.

85. George Watt interview with author. Leslie Fiedler also recalled being attracted to the student movement because it offered a means of transcending his lower-class Jewish roots. See Fiedler, *Being Busted*, 20.

86. Paul Jacobs, *Is Curly Jewish?*, 18–19.

87. James E. Jackson interview with author.

88. Celeste Strack Kaplan interview with author; Toni Locke interview with author, Oakland, Calif., April 14, 1983.

89. Scales and Nickson, *Cause at Heart*, 60, 77.

90. Hal Draper to author, Dec. 10, 1981.

91. Molly Yard, memorial tribute to Joseph Lash in *Joseph P. Lash* (New York, 1987), 40, JPL. Lash's diary suggests that his support for women's rights was closely linked to his socialist idealism. He noted here that "socialism [was] much more than a materialisic creed. It had an ethos—stopped you from smoking, obliged you to treat women as . . . p[e]rsonalities not adjuncts . . ." Lash discovered, however, during a trip to Europe for a socialist student conference, that socialism did not lead all of its followers to support women's rights. He recalled being "surprised by the attitude of the young [European] Socialists towards women . They were not as good as men, they stoutly argued, [and] had special functions . . ." (Lash Diary, Dec. 4, 1934; Joseph P. Lash typescript memoirs, "A Trip," 26; both in JPL).

The earliest statement of support for women's rights within the American student movement came soon after the first stirrings of student activism in the Hoover era. The NSL's founding platform included a plank demanding "for women educational and professional opportunities equal to those of men" ("For a National Student Movement," *Student Review* (Jan.-Feb. 1932), 4).

92. *Columbia Spectator*, April 13, 1934; *Hunter Bulletin*, Dec. 12, 1933. Students also offered criticism of the treatment of women in fascist Italy. See *Hunter Bulletin*, Oct. 16, 1934.

93. Joseph Lash speech, minutes of the International Unification Conference of Socialist and Communist Students, Paris, July 15–18 [1937]; Report of Molly Yard, *Summary of N.E.C. Meeting September 11, 12, 13* [*1937*], 4; both in JPL.

94. The one impressive feminist campaign of the ASU occurred not nationally, but locally, when the Chapel Hill ASU chapter petitioned for the admission of women to the University of North Carolina (*Daily Tar Heel*, Feb. 2, 11, 16, 1937). In contrast to this Chapel Hill chapter, the Harvard ASU ran an article in its magazine which—though urging "closer academic cooperation between Harvard men and Radcliffe women"—opposed the admission of women to Harvard on the grounds that "to suggest coeducation for Harvard would be as rash as advocating the admission of nuns into Franciscan monasteries" (G. Robert Stange, "The Harvard Women: A Study of Radcliffe Repression," *Harvard Progressive* (April 1940), 18). Here the contrast between race and gender is striking. No ASU chapter would have published such an anti-integration article on the race question—since racial discrimination was so vehemently and repeatedly denounced in ASU platforms and meetings.

95. Minutes of the International Unification Conference; Report of Molly Yard, *Summary of N.E.C. Meeting September 11, 12, 13* [*1937*], 4.

96. Yard, memorial tribute to Joseph Lash, 40. Also see Howe, *A Margin of Hope*, 43–45.

97. Yard, memorial tribute to Joseph Lash, 40; the limits on feminist consciousness among both men and women in the student movement can be seen in "The Zest to Nest: Man-hunt at Vassar," published in the ASU's national magazine (*Student Advocate* (Dec. 1936), 10–11); Howe, *A Margin of Hope*, 44; Celeste Strack Kaplan interview with author; also see the *Student Advocate* story on the pioneers of women's education, America's "first co-eds" at Oberlin. The article paid tribute to these early female collegians for promoting "freedom and power," but the male author of this article also suggested that "Cupid" and husband hunting may have been responsible for "the first move of the female sex into the male-hallowed halls" (Ian McCreal, "Coeds-Model 1837 Four Females Invade Gentlemen's Sanctuary," *Student Advocate* (Dec. 1937), 19–20; also see "4.2 Husbands," *ibid.* (April 1937), 19; Bill Murrish, "Decline of American Womanhood," *ibid.* (Dec. 1937), 26; on Lash's suggestion that the Youth Congress chose "a Miss Young America to ride at the front" of its second march in Washington, see Joseph Lash to William Hinckley, March 3, 1938, JPL). Note that it took three years for the ASU to elect a women chair. Moreover, though women were elected to their national offices and committees, neither the NSL, the SLID nor the Youth Congress ever had a woman in their top executive post. This was also the case with the ASU national magazine, which throughout its life was edited by men.

Limited as it was, feminist consciousness in the student Left of the 1930s compares favorably with the sexism which prevailed during the early stages of the New Left student movement of the 1960s. When women in the Student Nonviolent Coordinating Committee (SNCC) and Students for a Democratic Society (SDS) first raised feminist issues in the 1960s, they encountered hostility and ridicule from their male comrades. But on those few occasions where such issues were raised by female student activists in the 1930s, they were given a respectful hearing. This was the case not only in the incident Yard discussed above with respect to Joseph Lash and the ASU chair, but also in the ASU's founding convention.

Helen Levy, an NSL delegate from Barnard College, objected on the floor of this first ASU convention that in the draft of the ASU's platform "no reference has been made to discrimination against women." The delegates reponded to Levy by indicating that they would "favor inclusion" of a plank against sexual discrimination, and referring her proposal to the ASU "program committee to include when they saw fit." No minutes from this committee have survived to indicate what discussions it held concerning the Levy proposal. The final ASU platform, which had an entire section on racial discrimination, did not have a specific plank against sexual discrimination. However, the program's one mention of gender was premised on the feminist assumption of equality between men and women. This came in the platform's section on "The Right to Education and Security," which declared, "we are not a lost generation. Unemployment is not inevitable. The continued progress of our nation requires the service of all its young men and *women*. It requires especially an increasing number of doctors, engineers teachers, and other professional groups [emphasis added]." ("American Student Union Program," *American Student Union Bulletin*, Jan. 6, 1936; ASU Convention Minutes, Saturday afternoon Session, 4., JPL; on the student Left of the 1960s and SNCC and SDS antipathy towards feminist demands, see Sarah Evans, *Personal Politics* (New York, 1979), 83–89; Todd Gitlin, *The Sixties: Years of Hope, Days of Rage* (New York, 1987), 362–76). In the Depression decade women also played an important leadership role in the Southern Negro Youth Congress. See Esther Cooper Jackson interview with author.

The Youth Committee Against War, the ASU's main rival on the student Left in the late 1930s, was slightly ahead of the ASU in empowering women. The first two students elected to the YCAW's top position (the national executive secretary) were females—Alvaine Hollister and Fay Bennett. And yet even in the YCAW, traditional sexist imagery appears in the organization's publications. For example, the YCAW's guide to its 1939 convention introduced Fay Bennett to the delegates as "the beauteous blond who charms people into cooperation and donation." Of the YCAW New England organizer, the guide notes that "a certain Yale man complained that it was unfair sending such a pretty girl to organize for the YCAW." None of the men listed in the guide had their physical attributes discussed (*National Youth Antiwar Congress* (Dec. 27–30, 1939), YCAW).

98. Elizabeth Dilling, *The Roosevelt Red Record and Its Background* (Chicago, 1936), 253. Echoing Dilling, the "business people of Urbana . . . complained to Sheriff Walker [of Urbana] because this organization [the Univ. of Illinois ASU branch] advocated allowing colored and white students to associate together and to eat at the same restaurants . . ." (FBI file #100–191, Feb. 1, 1941, Report made by W.A. Temple, Springfield).

99. Anon. student letter signed "100 percent for the Administration Students," to Provost E.C. Moore, Oct. 30, 1934, ECM.

100. Wechsler, *Revolt on the Campus*, 189, 361; Jim to Lute, Office of the Comptroller, April 7, 1933, President's Files, UCB; David O. Levine, *The American College and the Culture of Aspiration* (Ithaca, 1986), 156–57. Also, see "Red School-

houses: Young Jewish Reds in Control of American Student Union," *Social Justice* (Nov. 20, 1939), 9–10. This article, by an anti-Semitic Coughlinite, seeking to depict the ASU as the product of a Jewish radical conspiracy, was peppered with inaccuracies. Thus ASU National chair Molly Yard, a Protestant whose parents had both served as missionaries in China, and whose father was the Northwestern University chaplain, was labeled a "Jewess."

101. On Dartmouth's discrimination against Jewish applicants and on the anti-Semitism of Dartmouth's president in the 1930s and the 1940s, see Tamar Buschbaum, "A Note on Anti-Semitism in Admissions at Dartmouth," *Jewish Social Studies* (Winter 1987), 79–84.

102. On this ethnic dimension of the conflicts between radical students and conservative administrators, see Carl Schorske, "A New Yorker's Map of Cambridge," 11–20; Joseph P. Lash, "College—O Quae Mutatio Rerum," 40, JPL.

103. Molly Yard, "Action Notes," *Student Advocate* (Oct. 1937), 27.

104. John Kenneth Galbraith essay, in Irving Stone, ed., *There Was Light: Autobiography of a University, Berkeley, 1868–1968* (Berkeley, 1968), 28; *Columbia Spectator*, March 15, 1933; Monroe Sweetland interview with author; Wechsler, *The Age of Suspicion* (New York, 1981), 18–23; Dwight Croessman, "Fraternities Are Anti-Educational and Anti-Democratic," *Intercollegian and Far Horizons* (April 1940), 139–40. There is considerable evidence that college and university administrators saw the fraternity system as a political ally and strove to involve the Greek houses in anti-radical activism (Robert G. Sproul to Clifford Swan, June 5, 1941, President's Files, UCB; *University of Washington Daily*, Nov. 6, 1934).

105. May, *Coming to Terms*, 202

106. Harry Magdoff interview with author.

107. Nathan Solomon interview with author.

108. *Barnard College Bulletin,* Oct. 30, 1936.

109. Hal Draper, "The Student Movement of the Thirties: A Political History," in Rita Simon, ed. *As We Saw the Thirties* (Urbana, 1967), 182–89.

110. W. J. Boldt and J.B. Stroud, "Changes in the Attitudes of College Students," *Journal of Educational Psychology* (Nov. 1934), 616–19; Theodore R. Bramfeld, "College Students React to Social Issues," *Frontiers of Democracy* (Nov. 1934), 21–26; Walter Buck, "A Measurement of Changes in Attitudes and Interests of University Students in a Ten-Year Period," *Journal of Abnormal and Social Psychology* (April 1936), 12–19; H. H. Remmers and C. L. Morgan, "Changes in Liberalism and Conservatism of College Students Since the Depression," *Journal of Social Psychology* (1941), 99–107. When the radical party candidates are taken into account, the 1936 presidential race—as tracked in the college straw polls—reflects an even stronger student shift away from Republicanism. With Norman Thomas carrying 3.1 percent, Earl Browder 2.6 percent, the non-Republican vote (added with FDR's) was 54 percent on campus. See *Vassar Miscellany News*, Oct. 31, 1936. As the decade progressed, straw polls showed an even further erosion of Republican support nationally among college students. By December 1938 President Roosevelt's approval rating among collegians had soared to 62.8 percent, which was more than 7 percent higher than FDR's standing with the general electorate. A year later the President's approval rating among college students remained an impressive 61.9 percent. A May 1940 poll showed that only 39 percent of college students nationally said they favored the Republican party. See *Michigan Daily*, Dec. 15, 1939; Univ. of Toledo *Collegian*, May 10, 1940.

111. "Youth in College," *Fortune* (June 1936), 158.

112. Eunice Fuller Barnard, "The Class of '36 into a Baffling World," *NYT Magazine* (June 21, 1936), 20.

113. *National Student Mirror* (March 1935), 83; *ibid.* (April 1935), 116; *ibid.* (Feb. 1936), 41. In strongholds of student activism, such as the New York municipal colleges, the Left managed to dominate student government elections during the heyday of the student movement. See CCNY *Campus*, Feb. 18, 20, and 25, 1935; Brooklyn College *Vanguard*, March 20, May 15, 1936, Jan. 28, 1938.

114. *Vassar Miscellany News*, Dec. 6, 1939.

Chapter 9. From Popular Front to Unpopular Sect

1. On the general public response in the U.S. to these events the most comprehensive work is William L. Langer and S. Everett Gleason, *The Challenge to Isolation* (New York, 1952), vols. I and II.

2. The dominant trend in student opinion following the invasion of Poland was growing support for aid to England (and France until its fall), coupled with a passionate desire to keep the U.S. out of war. The students' hope was that such aid might stop Hitler and thereby make U.S. military intervention unnecessary. See *Michigan Daily*, Nov. 1, 11, 1939; Marshall Univ. *Parthenon*, Nov. 11, 1939; Olcutt [Saunders] to Robin [Myers], Oct. 18, 1940, YPSL files, SP; *Oberlin Review*, Nov. 12, 1940; *Columbia Spectator*, Oct. 24, 1940, Jan. 7, 1941; *NYT*, Feb. 8, 1941.

3. Joseph Lash, typescript memoir of ASU's collapse [n.d.], 1–3; Joseph Lash to Merle [Miller], Jan. 25, 1940; Joseph Lash to Monroe [Sweetland], Jan. 25, 1940; Joseph Lash to Max [Lerner], Sept. 6, 1939. All in JPL.

4. Joseph Lash to Lenore Carothers, Sept. 18, 1939, JPL.

5. *Fall Planning Conference, September 8–9, 1939* (New York, 1939), 4–5; Lash Diary, Sept. 12, 1939, both in JPL; *NYT*, Sept. 10, 1939.

6. Lash to Carothers, Sept. 18, 1939; *Fall Planning Conference, September 8–9, 1939*, 6.

7. Lash Diary, Sept. 12, 1939, JPL.

8. *Daily Worker*, Sept. 13, 1939. For useful summaries of the Communist Party leadership's confusion regarding the foreign policy implications of the Nazi-Soviet Pact from late Aug. through early Sept. 1939, see Harvey Klehr, *The Heyday of American Communism* (New York, 1986), 386–91; Joseph Lash, "The Pattern of Communist Action," JPL; "And the Communists Follow," *New Republic* (Sept. 13, 1939), 143.

9. *Ibid.*; The fullest student statement of this new isolationist position would later be published in *Student America Organizes for Peace: Proceedings of the Fifth Annual Convention, American Student Union* (New York, 1940), 1–4; James Wechsler, "Stalin and Union Square," *Nation* (Sept. 30, 1939), 342.

10. William Sussman to Joseph Lash [Sept.? 1939], JPL.

11. *Ibid.*; Lash Diary, Nov. 4, 1939, JPL.

12. Lash Diary, Nov. 4, 1939.

13. Lenore Carothers to Joseph Lash, Sept. 18, 1939, JPL.

14. Lash, typescript memoir of ASU's collapse, p. 3.

15. Joseph Lash to Bill [Sussman], Sept. 28, 1939; Lash Diary, Sept. 19, 1939, both in JPL. Also see, CCNY *Campus*, Sept. 29, 1939. On some campuses the

discord generated by the pact proved fatal to the ASU. See FBI file # 100–175, Jan. 24, 1941, Report made by William E. Moran Jr., Buffalo, N.Y.

16. Lash, ASU's collapse, 3; Lash Diary, Sept. 12, 1939, Oct. 8, 1939. "Individualism" was used by communist students as a pejorative, denoting excessive egotism and selfishness. They thought it profoundly egotistical for an individual such as Lash to assume that he knew better than the CP, the Comintern, and the USSR. Thus one of Lash's communist associates charged that he and other non-communists in the student movement were guilty of becoming "so infatuated with the idea . . . of thinking the way no one else does, of being able to change their minds with every passing fancy that they are now in the process of 'freeing' everyone from serious thought" (William Sussman to Joseph Lash [n.d.], JPL). Lash rejected this accusation and charged that it derived from the communist "tendency toward anti-intellectualism" (Lash to Lew Zuckerman, Oct. 12, 1939, JPL).

17. Lash, ASU's collapse, 3; Lash Diary, Sept. 12, Oct. 8, 11, 1939. Feelings of regret over this split within the movement affected not only Lash but also some of his communist critics. Among Lash's best friends in the movement at least one communist responded to his dissent by describing her own alarm over the decline of unity in the ASU. She privately pleaded with him to do all in his power to preserve that unity, and wrote that because of their friendship "I'd hate like Hell to see you on the other side of the barricade!"(Lenore [Carothers] to Joseph Lash, Nov. 24 [1939], JPL).

18. Lash, ASU's collapse, 3; also see, "Statement of Kenneth Born, Executive Secretary of the Chicago District of the American Student Union," press release, Dec. 18, 1939, JPL.

19. Daniel Bell, "Y.C.L. Puts Skids Under Joe Lash As Student Union Leader Deviates" [n.d.], JPL.

20. Lash Diary, Sept. 21, Oct. 8, 1939.

21. Joseph Lash to Bill [Sussman], Sept. 28, 1939, JPL.

22. *Ibid.*

23. Joseph P. Lash, *Eleanor Roosevelt: A Friend's Memoir* (Garden City, N.Y., 1964), 7–15.

24. Lash Diary, Nov. 4, 1939.

25. Hal Draper, "The Student Movement of the Thirties," in Rita Simon, ed. *As We Saw the Thirties* (Urbana, 1967) 175; National Student Department, Young People's Socialist League, "Bulletin #11," Chicago, Jan. 10, 1937, JPL.

26. *NYT*, Nov. 28, 1939.

27. Joseph P. Lash to Franklin D. Roosevelt, Sept. 25, 1939, reprinted in *Fall Planning Conference, September 8–9, 1939.*

28. Lash Diary, Sept. 25, 1939.

29. Minutes Administrative Committee of ASU National Executive Committee, Sept. 29, 1939, pp. 2–4, JPL.

30. *Ibid.*

31. *Ibid.*, 2–3.

32. "Armistice Day Statement Approved by the Administrative Committee— ASU," appendix to Oct. 5, 1939, NEC packet, JPL.

33. "Discussion on Armistice Day," ASU Administrative Committee Meeting Minutes, Nov. 17, 1939, 2–3, JPL.

34. *Youth Congress Against War News Bulletin*, Nov. 1939, YCAW.

35. "Discussion on Armistice Day," 2.

36. *Ibid.*, 3.

37. Langer and Gleason, *The Challenge to Isolation*, vol. I, 329–31; Ralph Ketchum, *The Borrowed Years, 1938–1941: America on the Road to War* (New York, 1989), 295–99. Majority opinion on campus was solidly behind Finland. A national campus poll, taken during the Soviet invasion, found 62 percent of American undergraduates favoring a U.S. loan to assist Finland—even though this would break with the longstanding policy of American neutrality (Univ. of Toledo *Collegian*, Feb. 4, 1940; "Soviet Aggression: A Condemnation," *Harvard Progressive* (Feb. 1940), 7, 11–12; *Michigan Daily*, Dec. 6, 1939). The communists' position on Finland had isolationist implications, since it opposed U.S. aid to Finland. But there was an important distinction between the communist and non-communist isolationist stance on Finland. Where the communists defended the Soviet invasion, non-communist isolationists—even though opposing a U.S. loan for Finland because this would violate their anti-interventionist policy—tended to view the invasion as an act of brutal aggression. Thus even the communists' potential allies in the isolationist camp were almost as angry about communist support of the invasion as the interventionists had been. See *Parthenon*, Feb. 6, 1940; *Dartmouth*, Feb. 27, 1940; *Daily Bruin*, March 19, 1940; *Oberlin Review*, Jan. 19, 1940; *Michigan Daily*, Jan. 11, 1940.

38. "Not to Finland or to France—This Yank Ain't Coming," Resolution passed by Enlarged Conference of College and High School Leaders of the New York District of the ASU, Dec. 9, 1939, JPL.

39. Robert L. Klein to Joseph Lash, Dec. 23, 1939, JPL. For a similar reaction at other key ASU strongholds, see *Harvard Crimson*, Dec. 12, 1939; *Columbia Spectator*, Nov. 29, 1939; *Michigan Daily*, Dec. 3, 1939. At the Univ. of Connecticut, the ASU chapter "broke up on the issue of the Russian invasion of Finland" (FBI Report on ASU [file number and reporting agent's name illegible], New Haven, Aug. 22, 1941).

40. *NYT*, Dec. 10, 1939. Lash was, however, careful to couple his criticisms of the invasion with opposition to reactionaries, who sought to use the Finnish events as the pretext for whipping up anti-communist hysteria in the U.S. Nonetheless, the invasion deepened Lash's disillusionment with the Soviet Union and the CP. Lash found it painful to "grapple honestly with the problems created by Russian aggression in Finland. For one of the terrible results of that aggression is that socialism . . . no longer in the minds of common men everywhere means . . . a warless world. . . . The Russian invasion of Finland [and] the CP apologies for it here have become so nauseating that one wants to get away to where people are plain rather than machiavellian. . . . It seems to me that the communist movement now has reached a point where it has made so many compromises which it has called tactical changes, resorted to so many ruthless and horrible means in the name of socialist objectives, that it has lost all significance as a movement of principle and justice" (Joseph Lash to Ed [Newman], March 13, 1940; Joseph Lash to Monroe Sweetland, Jan. 25, 1940; both in JPL).

41. Quentin Young to Joseph Lash, Dec. 2, 1939, JPL.

42. Joseph Lash to Quentin Young, Dec. 8, 1939, JPL.

43. Lash, ASU's collapse, 4; "Important! Memo on Place of Convention," Nov. 29, 1939; Executive Committee of the MIT ASU Chapter, "Don't Split the American Student Union"; Open letter from Vassar College chapter, American Student Union, Dec. 14, 1939. All in JPL.

44. Lash to Young, Dec. 8, 1939.

45. Molly Yard, Agnes Reynolds, Joseph P. Lash, "Save the American Student Union" [Dec. 1939], JPL.

46. *Ibid.*

47. *Ibid.*

48. Alan Otten to Joseph Lash, Dec. 10, 1939; Lash to Otten, Dec. 11, 1939. Also on the problem of non-communists dropping out of the ASU "because of intransigent YCL tactics," see Ray Mildernberger to Joseph Lash, Dec. 18, 1939. All in JPL.

49. James Wechsler, "Politics on the Campus," *Nation* (Dec. 30, 1939), 732.

50. *Ibid.*, 732–33.

51. Daniel Bell, "Y.C.L. Puts Skids Under Joe Lash."

52. Joe Havens to Joseph Lash, Dec. 18, 1939, JPL.

53. Thelma Grafstein to Joseph Lash [Dec. 1939], JPL. On other examples of communist maneuvers to keep their critics out of the ASU convention, see *Wisconsin Soapbox.* Dec. 1939, JPL.

54. Irwin Ross, "The Student Union and the Future," *New Republic* (Jan. 8, 1940), 48; *Student America Organizes for Peace*, 1–3.

55. *Nation* (Jan. 6, 1940), 3.

56. "The Meeting of the ASU," *New Republic* (Jan. 8, 1940), 37. The official communist interpretation of the Madison convention was, of course, much more upbeat. The ASU, in the communists' view, had taken a principled and popular anti-war position at Madison. The ASU's isolationist line and the convention's stance against those using Finland to whip up anti-Soviet war hysteria would, according to the communists, prove highly popular with American undergraduates. From communist accounts of the convention one would never guess that the ASU was in crisis and that it was on the verge of losing its campus base. See Milton Meltzer, "Collegians Reject War Racket," *New Masses* (Jan. 9, 1940), 12–13; "Students United Against War," *ibid.* (Jan. 16, 1940), 31.

57. *Oberlin Review*, Jan. 16, 1940. Attacks on the ASU for its refusal to criticize Soviet aggression pervaded the student press following the 1939 ASU convention. The *Ohio State Lantern* termed the convention's decision on this issue "incredibly stupid," and an act of "harikari"—taken because of the organization's "slavish devotion" to the USSR (*Ohio State Lantern*, Jan. 5, 1940; for similar criticism, see *Dartmouth*, Jan. 10, 1940; *University Daily Kansan*, Jan. 5, 1940; *Parthenon*, Jan. 16, 1940).

58. Joseph Lash to Max [Lerner], Jan. 8, 1940; Merle Miller to Joseph Lash, Jan. 19 [1940]; Lee McIntosh to Joseph Lash [n.d.]; Herbert B. Ross to Joseph Lash, Jan. 2, 1939 [1940]; Joseph Lash to Chad Walsh, Jan. 10, 1940. All in JPL. Even after the communist triumph at Madison, Lash, now an ASU alumnus, tried (but usually failed) to persuade non-communists to stay in the ASU and attempt to reverse its policies instead of dropping out of the organization (see Joseph Lash to Ed Newman, Feb. 14, 1940, JPL). On the collapse of the Pittsburgh ASU following the convention, see FBI report on ASU [file number illegible] by E. L. Boyle, April 1, 1941.

59. Chad Walsh to Joseph Lash, Jan. 12, 1940; American Student Union Addenda on National Referendum, March 1940, both in JPL.

60. Alan K. Gottlieb to Joseph Lash, May 5, 1940, Lash to Alan Gottlieb, March 13, 1940; John Sterling Stillman to American Student Union, Jan. 2, 1940. All in JPL. ASU membership in the spring of 1940 had, according to Gottlieb,

fallen to under 5,000, "about half of whom are in New York City." Only 3,000 ASUers would vote on the Finland referendum—evidence of how quickly the ASU (which once boasted some 20,000 members) was dissolving. It is, however, striking that even in this shrunken and communist-dominated ASU the vote was not nearly so pro-Soviet as the Madison convention had been. Where the Convention had by a 6–1 margin rejected the resolution criticizing of the Soviet invasion of Finland, the ASU membership in the March referendum rejected that resolution by only a 2–1 margin. This only hints, however, at how unrepresentative the 1939 ASU convention had been; for had the 15,000 or so non-communists not already left the ASU, this resolution would surely have won a resounding victory in the referendum (Gottlieb to Lash, May 5, 1940)). On the decline of the ASU, also see [Jack] Sessions Supplementary Statement, March 1940; [Robin Myers] to Al Lewis, Oct. 21, 1940; both in YPSL files, SP. By the time of the next ASU convention, the organization's national membership had sunk below 2,000 (Robert G. Spivack, "Youth Reorganizes," *Nation* (Jan. 18, 1941), 72; the FBI reports at the campus level confirm this picture of a collapsing membership. See FBI file # 100–476, Jan. 31, 1941, Report made by H. A. King, Portland, Ore.; FBI [file number illegible], Feb. 7, 1941, Report made by F.C. Dorwart, San Diego; FBI file # 61–327, Feb. 1, 1941, Report made by F. Schmidt, Chicago, which found that even in Chicago—the ASU's most active Midwestern city—membership no longer exceeded 100).

61. *NYT*, Feb. 4, 1940; on the manipulative tactics used by communist Youth Congress leaders to reverse the AYC's peace policy—without a vote from the full Youth Congress—see Josiah R. Bartlett's letter of resignation from the Youth Congress, Oct. 16, 1939; similar criticism and communist response to it can be found in Minutes of American Youth Congress Cabinet Meeting, Feb. 21, 1940; both in JPL.

62. Minutes of the American Youth Congress Cabinet Meeting, Feb. 21, 1940; "Draft Proceedings of the Citizenship Institute," Feb. 9–12, 1940, JPL.

63. Lash Diary, Jan. 14, Feb. 9, 1940, JPL.

64. *NYT*, Feb. 11, 1940.

65. *Ibid.*

66. *Ibid.*; Lash, *Eleanor Roosevelt: A Friend's Memoirs*, 57–58.

67. "Youth Congress in Washington Hears President Roosevelt Tell Them They're All Wet," *Life* (Feb. 26, 1940), 17; Joseph P. Lash, *Eleanor and Franklin* (New York, 1971), 596–611. In the aftermath of the confrontation with the president at the Citizenship Institute, the Youth Congress got such bad press that its leadership had to devote considerable energy to rebutting these press attacks (see "All the News That Misfits They Print," *Citizenship in Action: A Report of the American Youth Congress Institute—Washington, D.C., February 9–12, 1940*, 5–10; Abbot Simon to Eleanor Roosevelt, Feb. 20, 1940, JM). The one eloquent defense of the young activists came not from such pamphlets, but from folksinger Woody Guthrie, a supporter of the new CP line, who responded to FDR's speech by writing one of his better known anti-war songs, "Why Do You Stand There in the Rain?" (Joe Klein, *Woody Guthrie* (New York, 1980), 144–45). The Institute also drew criticism because its leaders sought to stifle dissent from participants—barring consideration of resolutions criticizing the invasion of Finland (see "Supplementary Memo on Undemocratic Practices Within the A.Y.C." (Spring 1940), YPSL files, SP).

68. *Michigan Daily*, Feb. 20, 1940; *Nation* (Feb. 17, 1940), 236–37; "All the

News That Misfits They Print," 5–10; Morris Milgram, "Behind the News of the A.Y.C.," draft article for *Socialist Call* [1940], YPSL files, SP.

69. Eleanor Roosevelt, *This I Remember* (New York, 1948), 199–205; Winifred Wandersee, "ER and American Youth: Politics and Personality in a Bureaucratic Age," in Joan Hoff-Wilson and Marjorie Lightman, eds., *Without Precedent: The Life and Career of Eleanor Roosevelt* (Bloomington, 1984), 73–78.

70. *NYT,* Dec. 3, 1939; Roosevelt, *This I Remember,* 202; William Leuchtenburg, *Franklin D. Roosevelt and the New Deal* (New York, 1963), 280.

71. *NYT,* Dec. 3, 1939; Freda Kirchwey, "Taming Mr. Dies," *Nation* (Dec. 16, 1939), 669–70.

72. James Wechsler, *The Age of Suspicion* (New York, 1981), 72.

73. Roosevelt, *This I Remember,* 200.

74. For Mrs. Roosevelt's public statement denying any links between Cadden, Hinckley, and the Communist Party, see *NYT,* Oct. 11, 1939. On at least eight separate occasions Mrs. Roosevelt, between fall 1939 and June 1940, denied that communists had any special influence over the Youth Congress. For these statements, see *NYT,* Oct. 11, Nov. 22, Dec. 5, 1939, Feb. 6, March 22, June 12, July 6, 1940; Eleanor Roosevelt typescript of article on the American Youth Congress for *Liberty* magazine, JPL. That the First Lady erred on the question of communist influence over the Youth Congress—and that these two Youth Congress leaders were secret communists—was later confirmed by several key organizers in the movement. Gil Green, who headed the YCL in this era and helped coordinate communist strategy among the Youth Congress national leadership, told me that both Cadden and Hinckley were recruited into the communist ranks as Youth Congress leaders, along with most of the other Youth Congress chairmen. (On Cadden's Communist Party ties, see Gil Green interview with author; David Dubinsky to Eleanor Roosevelt, June 20, 1940, ER; "An Analysis of the American Youth Congress Convention at Lake Geneva, Wisconsin, July 3–7, 1940," YPSL files, SP; Daniel Bell, "Liberals Shun A.Y.C. Parley as Communist Front," July 13, 1940, JPL; Harvey Klehr, *The Heyday of American Communism* (New York, 1984), 321, 468; Lewis Conn, "The American Youth Congress," *YPSL Organizer,* March 7, 1940. Note, however, that in his correspondence with Mrs. Roosevelt and other New Dealers, Cadden denied that he was a communist and claimed that the Youth Congress was no closer to the Communist Party than it was to the Democratic or Republican parties. See Joseph Cadden to Eleanor Roosevelt, July 1, 1940, ER; Joseph Cadden to Charles Taussig, Nov. 20, 1939, and Memorandum Re: letters to the Communist Party [n.d], Charles Taussig Papers, FDR Library, Hyde Park, N.Y.)

Although I find Green's memoir and the other evidence convincing, technically they do not "prove" that Cadden and Hinckley were YCL or CP members. One can only be definitive about such membership for those who were open about their CP affiliations at the time—such as Celeste Strack—or those who have since acknowledged those affiliations—such as James Wechsler. Those who kept their Party affiliation secret did so intentionally to obscure the record, and to an extent succeeded. While the actual Party *membership* of these Youth Congress leaders cannot be incontrovertibly proven, there is no question at all about their partisan *behavior;* they helped lead the pro-CP faction in the Youth Congress and hid this from Mrs. Roosevelt. (On Cadden, see Josiah R. Bartlett to member organizations, American Youth Congress, Oct. 16, 1939; Bob to Louise Meyerowtiz, April 9, 1940; both in JPL; Morris Milgram, "Behind the News of the AYC" [Feb. 1940],

YPSL files, SP; Minutes American Youth Congress Cabinet meeting, Jan. 18, Feb. 21, May 4, 1940, JPL; Joseph Lash diary, March 6, May 15, 1938, Sept. 14, 1939, Feb. 19, 22, March 21 and 22, Oct. 6, 1940; Joseph Lash to Joseph Cadden, March 16, 1940, JPL. Joseph Cadden to Eleanor Roosevelt, May 16, 1940, JM; minutes of confidential conversation between Joseph P. Lash and Max Weiss [n.d], JPL; M.J. [McKay] to Joe [Lash], April 5, 1940, in JPL; Report of meeting between Joseph Lash and Joseph Cadden, Sept. 11, 1941, JPL; Joseph Cadden to Eleanor Roosevelt, May 5, 1941, JM; Lorena Hickok to Eleanor Roosevelt, in Joseph P. Lash, *Love Eleanor: Eleanor Roosevelt and Her Friends* (Garden City, N.Y., 1982), 306; on Hinckley, see Al Hamilton to Norman Thomas, June 30, 1937, NT; George Rawick, "The New Deal and Youth," 336–37; Bill Hinckley to Joe [Lash], March 13, 1937, JPL; Klehr, *The Heyday of American Communism*, 321.)

75. *NYT*, Oct. 11, 1939; Lash Diary, Jan. 14, 16, 1940; Eleanor Roosevelt, "Students Union Attitude Reflects that of Elders," "My Day" column, Jan. 17, 1940, reprinted in *Student America Organizes for Peace*, appendix.

76. Vivian Liebman, "Cabinet Wives Contribute Housing for Youth Congress Leadership," American Youth Congress press release [Feb. 1940], JPL; Lash, *Eleanor Roosevelt: A Friend's Memoirs*, 74; Minutes, American Youth Congress Cabinet meeting, Feb. 21, 1940, JPL

77. Roosevelt, *This I Remember*, 200–204. In the months following the Citizenship Institute about two-thirds of the large youth groups that had been affiliated with the Youth Congress withdrew from the AYC (Spivack, "Youth Reorganizes," 72; *NYT*, April 13, May 14, July 3, Sept. 1, Nov. 18, 1940; also on the decline of the Youth Congress, see "The AYC and the Youth Movement" [Spring 1940]; YPSL Eastern NEC Meeting Minutes, Feb. 25, 1940; "Socialists Leave the Youth Congress" [YPSL pamphlet], July 1, 1940; Lewis Conn to Eleanor Roosevelt, July 5, 1940. All in YPSL files, SP; *NYT*, Dec. 31, 1940, and Jan. 31, 1941); Associated College Press report in *Parthenon*, March 1, 1940.

78. Lash, *Love Eleanor*, 286.

79. Joseph Lash Diary, Sept. 12, 1939, JPL.

80. Thelma Grafstein to Joseph Lash [Dec. 1939], JPL.

81. Joseph Lash to Lenore [Carothers], Oct. 19, 1939; Joseph Lash to Lee, Jan. 6, 1940, both in JPL.

82. *Ibid.*

83. Joseph Lash to Betty Sammons, Feb. 14, 1940, JPL.

84. Lash to Lenore [Carothers], Oct. 19, 1939; Lash to Lee, Jan. 6, 1940; Lash to Sammons, Feb. 14, 1940. All in JPL. For a valuable summary of this discontinuity in Communist behavior in the student movement before and after the Pact, see Connie Driusch to Bob [Jan. ? 1940], JPL. Lash does, however, seem to have overstated the degree to which communists abandoned their role as an organized faction within the ASU in the year prior to the Pact. At the Chapel Hill ASU chapter, for instance, the YCL at this time still served as a "wheel within a wheel," running the local ASU, according to a leading member of this chapter. Because Lash in this era was so close to Gil Green and trusted by the YCL, there was no need for the YCL to exert any pressure on him or to conduct active factional struggles at the ASU national office—giving Lash the mistaken impression that the YCL on campus had abandoned its role as an organized faction within the ASU (Joseph P. Lash interview with author; Scales and Nickson, *Cause at Heart*, 61).

85. [Robin Myers] to Hazel [Whitman], Oct. 29, 1940, YPSL files, SP.

86. On the resurgence of redbaiting following the Nazi-Soviet Pact, see *No Lights Out Here* (New York, 1939), 1–4; Ellen Schrecker, *No Ivory Tower* (New York, 1986), 71–83.

87. *Dartmouth*, Nov. 13, 1939; *Oberlin Review*, April 12, 1940; *No Lights Out Here*, 6; minutes of the Fourth National Youth Anti-War Congress, Dec. 27, 1940, YCAW; Deans of the College of the University of Wisconsin to Local Branch, Youth Committee Against War, Oct. 1940, President Clarence A. Dykstra Papers, UWISC.

88. *Columbia Spectator*, April 22, 1940; *NYT*, April 20, 1940. *Daily Californian*, April 29, 1940. The YPSL reported at this time that "outside of New York City, the ASU practically doesn't exist except where the YCL has a unit which calls itself the ASU" (*YPSL Organizer*, March 20, 1940).

89. Archibald MacLeish, "Post War Writers and Pre-war Readers," *New Republic* (June 10, 1940), 789–90; Charles Seymour, "War's Impact on the Campus," *NYT Magazine* (Sept. 29, 1940), 3, 15; Arnold Whitridge, "Where Do You Stand? An Open Letter to American Undergraduates," *Atlantic Monthly* (Aug. 1940), 133–37; Paul P. Cram, "Undergraduates and the War," *Atlantic Monthly* (Oct. 1940), 410–21.

90. *NYT*, May 26, 1940; Whitridge, "Where Do You Stand?," 133.

91. Harold Ickes, *The Secret Diary of Harold Ickes—Vol. III The Lowering Clouds* (New York, 1954), 179.

92. *Columbia Spectator*, April 18, 1940.

93. *Vassar Miscellany News*, Sept. 30, 1939.

94. *NYT*, May 26, 1940; *Dartmouth*, June 16, 1940; Franklin D. Roosevelt to Roger B. Merriman, May 20, 1940, in *Franklin D. Roosevelt: His Personal Papers*, vol. II, Elliot Roosevelt, ed. (New York, 1950), 1028.

95. UCLA *Daily Bruin*, May 14, 1940; *Dartmouth*, Dec. 29, 1939, May 24, 1940; *University Daily Kansan*, May 22, 1940; Irwin Ross, "College Students and the War," *New Republic* (July 15, 1940), 80.

96. James B. Conant, *My Several Lives* (New York, 1970), 217–18; *Dartmouth*, May 27, 1940.

97. *NYT*, June 20, 1940. Harvard's clash between interventionist alumni and isolationist students had reverberations that extended well beyond Harvard Yard. Only a day after Sigourney had been almost booed off the stage, a group of Harvard alumni used the gathering of their fellow graduates in Cambridge as the occasion for announcing the formation of a movement to prepare the nation for military conflict. This movement, under the auspices of the National Emergency Committee of the Military Training Camp Association, agitated for the introduction of conscription legislation in Congress—which in fall 1940 culminated in the establishment of the first peacetime military draft in American history. See *NYT*, June 21, 1940; J. Garry Clifford and Samuel R. Spencer Jr., *The First Peacetime Draft* (Lawrence, Kan., 1986), 1–130.

98. MacLeish, "Post War Writers and Pre-war Readers," 789–90.

99. *YCAW Bulletin*, Dec. 1939, YCAW; Ross, "College Students and the War," 80.

100. Clifford and Spencer, *The First Peacetime Draft*, 132. On the YCAW's rationale for opposing the draft, see *Conscription and Liberty* (New York, 1940), passim, YCAW.

101. *Michigan Daily*, Oct. 17, 1940; *Columbia Spectator*, Oct. 17, 1940; *YCAW News Bulletin* Oct., Nov.-Dec. 1940.

102. *YCAW News Bulletin*, Dec. 1939; *Oberlin Review*, Nov. 12, 1940; *Columbia Spectator*, Oct. 24, 1940; *NYT*, Feb. 8, 1941; *Parthenon*, Oct. 25, 1940; The YCAW's national leadership—aware that isolationism still had considerable support on campus—found their organization's inability to attract members and financial contributions "shocking" (Minutes of Special All Day Action Committee Meeting, May 4, 1940, YCAW; also on the YCAW'S inability to mobilize students, see [field report] to Jack Sessions, Oct. 1, 1940, YPSL files, SP).

103. *Michigan Daily*, Nov. 7, 1940; *Ohio State Lantern*, Oct. 15, 1940, and Jan. 7, 1941.

104. *Ohio State Lantern*, April 21, 1941. On student support for draft exemptions for undergraduates, see Univ. of Toledo *Collegian*, Sept. 27, Oct. 11, 1940; UCLA *Daily Bruin*, Feb. 21, 1941; *Ohio State Lantern*, April 7, 1941.

105. Wayne S. Cole, *America First: The Battle Against American Intervention in World War II* (Madison, 1953), 10–16.

106. Whitridge, "Where Do You Stand?," 133–37; Kingman Brewster, Jr., and Spencer Klaw, "We Stand Here," *Atlantic Monthly* (Sept. 1940), 277–79.

107. Whitridge, "Where Do You Stand?," 134; Conant, *My Several Lives*, 222.

108. Joseph P. Lash, "ISS and the Youth Movement," *ISS Bulletin*, Feb. 1941, JPL.

109. Ketchum, *The Borrowed Years*, 468.

110. Spivack, "Youth Reorganizes," 71–73; Joseph Lash, "ISS and the Youth Movement"; Lash, *Eleanor: A Friend's Memoir*, 220–26; "International Student Service and National Student Federation Agree to Pool Efforts," press release [n.d.], JPL.

111. *Dartmouth*, Nov. 31, 1940; UCLA *Daily Bruin*, Feb. 17, 1941; *Columbia Spectator*, Oct. 24, 1940; Univ. of Toledo *Collegian*, Feb. 14, 1941; *Daily Calfornian*, Feb. 10, 1941.

112. *Dartmouth*, Nov. 8, 1940; memorandum from Irwin Ross to Joseph P. Lash on trip to Cambridge Dec. 15–18 [1940], JPL; *NYT*, Feb. 9, 1941.

113. Special Bulletin on the Youth Strike Against War, April 3, 1941, YCAW.

114. *NYT*, April 24, 1941; Ketchum, *The Borrowed Years*, 512; UCLA *Daily Bruin*, April 28, 1941; *YPSL Organizer*, March 20, 1940; on the Youth Congress's decline in affiliates, see FBI Report # 100–358–7127, Feb. 14–21, 1941. Another sign of the movement's decline could be seen in the wild exaggerations its organizers made about strike turnout in order to save face. Nationally, strike organizers told the press that more than 500,000 students struck—a claim that was not and could not have been backed by any evidence, since the strike turnout was actually minuscule. Similar exaggerations went on at the local level. At Berkeley, for instance, strike organizers claimed that 3500 students rallied on behalf of an isolationist U.S. policy. But in fact fewer than a thousand students attended this strike rally, and more than two-thirds of those present opposed the isolationist resolutions proposed by the Youth Congress leaders. (See *Daily Californian*, April 24, 1941; Hurford E. Stone to President Sproul, April 30, 1941, Student Activities Office files, Sproul Hall, UC Berkeley.)

115. *NYT*, April 24, 1941; *New York Herald-Tribune*, April 24, 1941. On the chilling effect of Rapp-Coudert on student politics, see *Brooklyn College Vanguard*, Dec. 20, 1940, Jan. 7, 1941. With hostility towards the CP growing in the wake of the the Nazi-Soviet Pact, some New York students opposed the strike not only because it was isolationist, but also because it was communist-led (see *New York Herald-Tribune*, April 24, 1941). This surge of anti-communism also hurt the stu-

dent movement at Berkeley, where concern about the ASU's secret links to the Communist Party led the student government to revoke the ASU's campus recognition shortly before the 1941 student strike (see *Daily Californian* April 9, 1941). Similarly, at Ohio State Univ., the student government investigated and reprimanded the ASU chapter shortly after the strike (*Ohio State Lantern*, April 25, 29, 1941).

116. *NYT*, April 24, 1941; *New York Herald-Tribune*, April 24, 1941.

117. *Dartmouth*, April 23, 1941. Interventionist student activists also challenged their isolationist counterparts on the radio. See Agnes Reynolds, Joseph P. Lash, and William Bundy's transcribed remarks in "Shall We Convoy War Materials to Great Britain?," *The American Forum of the Air* (April 13, 1941), 1–6, JPL. The size and organizational skill of the anti-isolationist student groups should not, however, be exaggerated. The SDD, ISS, and other student aid to Britain groups never built their organizations up to anything approaching the level of the Popular Front era ASU. They managed to put their isolationist rivals on the defensive thanks largely to the fact that such events as the fall of France and the Battle of Britain had already weakened isolationism as a political force both on campus and off. Relative to the student movement in the previous decade, one would say of the early 1940s that student activism was dying out: small interventionist groups on campus were prevailing over a deteriorating isolationist movement (see Lash Diary, March 8, June 8, 1941, JPL).

Anti-isolationist student groups did not become mass organizations because to generate mass protest, students must have a strong incentive—a sense that their activism is really necessary. But such incentive was lacking by 1941. With isolationism declining and the President heading toward intervention, students who supported an expanded U.S. role in the fight against fascism had little to protest about since the policies they preferred were already in ascendance.

118. *Dartmouth*, Nov. 3, 1941; "Switch," *Time* (Oct. 13, 1941), 68–69.

119. For examples of collegiate ridiculing of the Communists for their flip-flops and subservience to Moscow's foreign policy, see *Ohio State Lantern*, Oct. 24, 30, 1941; UCLA *Daily Bruin*, Oct. 13, 1941; *YCAW News Bulletin* Aug. 1, 1941.

120. *Dartmouth*, Nov. 3, 1941.

121. Clifford and Spencer, *The First Peacetime Draft*, 138; Murray Kempton, *Part of Our Time: Some Monuments and Ruins of the Thirties* (New York, 1955), 303.

122. Joseph P. Lash, "New Directions for Youth," *Threshold* (Oct. 1941), 13.

123. Memorandum to the Executive Committee of the ISS Concerning a Proposed Merger of Several Student Action Groups [1941], JPL. Nor was such thinking confined to liberal interventionists. Throughout the final years of the student movement, the YCAW, led by socialists and pacifists, also had an exclusionary policy—refusing to cooperate with communist-led organizations. See *YPSL Torch*, Feb. 16 and March 12, 1940, YPSL files, SP.

124. Lash, "New Directions for Youth," 13.

125. *Ibid.*, 13–15, 34; the most vivid account of Lash's encounter with the Dies committee is John Oakes's tribute in *Joseph P. Lash* (New York, 1987), 36–37, JPL.

126. Joseph P. Lash, "ISS and the Youth Movement," *ISS Bulletin*, Feb. 1941; Lash, "New Directions for Youth," *Threshold* (Oct. 1941), 13. Louis Harris tribute to Lash, *Joseph P. Lash*, 24.

127. Young Communist *Review* (Dec. 23, 1940), 1; Joseph Cadden to Eleanor Roosevelt, May 5, 1941, JM; Lash, *Eleanor Roosevelt—A Friend's Memoir*, 230.

128. See Lash Diary, Dec. 19, 1940, on his refusal to cooperate with the Rapp-Coudert red probe, JPL.

129. Some of the leading figures in Lash's and the socialist wings of the student movement were led by this exclusionist mindset to play leading roles in promoting anti-communist politics during the Cold War era. They became founders of the Cold War liberal group, Americans for Democratic Action (ADA). One of the hallmarks of ADA liberalism was non-cooperation with communist-led organizations. By the early 1950s, the ADA was supporting President Truman's anti-communist loyalty oath program. On the role of former 1930s student activists in founding the ADA, see Monroe Sweetland interview with author; Wechsler, *The Age of Suspicion*, 211–12. On the ADA's grim record on civil liberties during the Cold War era, see Athan Theoharis, "The Politics of Scholarship: Liberals, Anti-Communism and McCarthyism," in Robert Griffith and Athan Theoharis, eds., *The Specter: Original Essays on the Cold War and the Origins of McCarthyism* (New York, 1974), 268–70.

130. Todd Gitlin, *The Sixties: Years of Hope, Days of Rage* (New York, 1987), 177, 183. Not all veterans of the Depression era student movement took so hostile a view of the anti-war movement of the 1960s. A small but vocal segment of 1930s movement veterans retained their radical or pacifist principles, and they supported the new student movement as well as the protests against the Vietnam War. Pacifist leader David Dellinger was the most prominent in this group. Dellinger, who had been a pacifist organizer at Yale in his student days before World War II, was so major a figure in the anti-war movement of the 1960s that the government chose to indict him—making him one of the defendants in the Chicago Seven conspiracy trial. See Charles DeBenedetti, *An American Ordeal: The Anti-War Movement of the Vietnam Era* (Syracuse, 1990), 24, 117, 189, 224–25, 282.

The most direct and unfortunate link between the student movement of the 1930s and the Vietnam War was provided by Dean Rusk. As a Rhodes scholar, Rusk was at Oxford University when the students took their pacifist oath not to fight for King and Country. Rusk later looked back on such anti-interventionism as not just wrong headed, but tragic in that it allowed the Nazis to feel that they could proceed with their aggression undeterred by the Western democracies. As Lyndon Johnson's Secretary of State, Rusk applied this lesson from the 1930s to Indochina in the 1960s, acting in Vietnam on the assumption that aggression had to be stopped immediately if another World War II-style cataclysm was to be avoided. But like the students in the early 1930s, who misunderstood the coming war by mechanistically applying "lessons" learned from the previous world war, Rusk did the same thing in Vietnam—mistakenly casting Ho Chi Minh as Hitler, misreading a civil war as a war of foreign aggression, and responding to the regional power of Vietnam as if it represented some Axis-style global threat. On Rusk's Oxford experience and its impact on his thinking about Vietnam, see Stanley Karnow, *Vietnam: A History* (New York, 1983), 179.

Index

Abel, Lionel, 23
Abraham Lincoln Battalion, 156–59, 167–68, 174–75, 186, 381 n66
Academic freedom, xv, 59, 61, 98, 104, 244, 307, 359 n63. *See also* Administrators; Free speech
Adams, George, 122
Addams, Jane, 88
Administrators (college and university), 133, 309–10, 366 n3; anti-Semitism of, 272–73; as FBI informants, xv, 99–100, 323–36; opposition to isolationism, 309–10, 312; paternalism of, xv, 29, 59, 117, 369 n28; racial prejudice of, 207; restrict political expression, 30, 57–59, 98, 102–11, 115, 118–19, 122, 132, 307, 372 n67, 376 n128; gather political intelligence on activists, 100–102, 128, 374 n108. *See also* Free speech
African Americans, 219, 244–45, 251, 268–69, 271–72; college and university enrollments of, 206; faculty, 208–209; fraternities, 208; as leaders in student movement, 209; attempt to integrate southern campuses, 212–13, 215–17. *See also* Historically black colleges; Lynching; Racial discrimination; Southern Negro Youth Congress
Albany College, 61
Albion College, 6
Alexander, Edwin, 115–16
Allen, James, 393 n70
All Quiet on the Western Front, 84
All Southern Negro Youth Conference, 221. *See also* Southern Negro Youth Congress
Alumni (college and university), 57, 117, 310
America First Committee, 313
American Association of University Professors (AAUP), 16, 131

American Civil Liberties Union (ACLU), 62, 66, 110, 131
American Jewish Congress, 190
American League Against War and Fascism (youth section), 93
American Legion, 100–101, 132, 140, 325
American Student Union, 189–90, 240–41, 243; and anti-war mobilizations, 152–54, 165–66, 181–84, 287, 307, 315–16; decline of, 277, 279–98, 303, 307, 313, 316, 411 n57, n60; dispute over collective security, 171–73, 176–78, 183; communist/radical influence in, xvi, 144, 151, 164, 281–93, 380 n49, 386 n124, 398 n149, n152, 414 n84, 416 n115; national conventions of, 140–47, 160, 162–64, 171–75, 265–66, 294, 296–98, 386 n119, 388 n141, 411 n56; FBI probe of, 323–39; and liberalism and FDR, 175, 194–95, 228–29, 232, 398 n153; membership of, 181–82, 275, 411 n60; dispute over Nazi-Soviet Pact, 279, 281–90; origins of, 137–40; opposition to racial discrimination, 212, 219–20, 269, 393 n68, 406 n98; controversy over Soviet invasion of Finland, 279, 291–98, 303–304, 412 n60; and Spanish Civil War, 154–59, 167–68, 174–75; and women's rights, 269–71, 405 n94, 406 n97; and working students, 202. *See also* Communists; Young Communist League; Young People's Socialist League; Lash, Joseph P.
American Youth Act, 188, 190–95, 232, 235, 277
American Youth Congress, 166, 227, 249, 271; Citizenship Institute, 298–301, 303; communist influence in, 234–37, 298, 302–304, 397 n148; Creed of American Youth, 227; Declaration of Rights of American Youth, 205, 227, 235; decline

419

A SEASON OF SPLENDOR

Also by Greg King

Twilight of Splendor:
The Court of Queen Victoria during Her Diamond Jubilee Year

The Court of the Last Tsar:
Pomp, Power, and Pageantry in the Reign of Nicholas II

With Penny Wilson

The Fate of the Romanovs

A SEASON OF SPLENDOR

The Court of Mrs. Astor in
Gilded Age New York

Greg King

WILEY
John Wiley & Sons, Inc.

With the kind permission of the 11th Duke of Marlborough, this book is dedicated to the memory of his sister Lady Sarah Spencer-Churchill, Alva Vanderbilt's great-grandaughter, an infinite source of knowledge, and a greatly missed friend.

CONTENTS

ACKNOWLEDGMENTS

This book grew from a long-standing interest in the Gilded Age. I vividly recall repeatedly leafing through numerous books at age six or seven that covered Gilded Age American palaces and their owners. The volumes by Merrill Folsom and Henry and Ottalie Williams, listed in the bibliography, had a profound effect on me, and as soon as I developed a vocabulary equal to the task, I eagerly began to read memoirs and family histories of the Vanderbilts and the Astors, eventually collecting books and materials to assuage my curiosity. Some ten years ago, the idea of actually writing a book about the Gilded Age took hold, and personal interest transformed into a more dedicated pursuit.

Given the wealth of personalities and possibilities involved, my initial ideas encompassed a wide variety of approaches, and I must thank Dorie Simmonds, my agent, and Stephen S. Power, my editor at John Wiley & Sons, for helping to refine my vision and channel it into a more coherent narrative form. In the end, it was Dorie who strongly supported a stylistic change midstream to echo my previous book *The Court of the Last Tsar,* while Stephen's insistence that I concentrate on Caroline Astor and New York society gave the narrative a central focus around which the story could be told. Their continued encouragement and enthusiasm for this project have helped keep it on track, and the end result owes a great deal to many months of frank discussions among us. Ellen Wright, Editorial Assistant at Wiley, has been a model of patience throughout, and I thank John Simko, Senior Production Editor at Wiley, for his careful attention to the manuscript.

In researching and writing this book, I have drawn on the advice and support of many people who over the years have provided both information and suggestions that have played a part in shaping these pages. I would like to acknowledge David Adams; Jason Adams; Betty Aronson; Lee Atweiler; Lucia Bequaert; David Bloom; George Bobrick; Thomas and Mary Botford; Erna Bringe; Lorraine Butterfield; Jill Camps; Vincent Cartwright; Harry Cernan; Luke Connor; Ben Curry; Cyndi Darling; Louise David; Lisa Davidson; Mona and Gerald Dennings; Elizabeth Densmuire; Sam Dettlemore; Anne Dillard; Greg Dunmassy; Keith Eaton; Brian Ebford; Fred Ernest; Cecilia Eton; Edward Fine; Beth Fry; Michelle Fumkin; Andrei Gaddis; Julia Gelardi; Kathryn George; Nick Gorman; Dan Gretsky; Roger Gringle; Larry Gross; Linda Grundvald; Sebastian Hanson; Mike Harris; John Harrison; Marina Hart; Candice Hearst; William Hemple; Bill Hennings; Steve Hervet; DeeAnn Hoff; Craig Hohman; Brien Horan; Elizabeth Hoss; Allison Hume; Francine Imford; Nagori Iskaguchi; Max Jacobs; Irving Jadschmidt; Hans Jergin; Adrian Johns, Terry and Michael Jorgenson; Greg Julia; the late Ingrid Kane; Kerry Karnet; Natasha Kennet; Will Kevin; Harvey Kew; Scott Laforce; Brandon Lamont; Ian Lanoge; Gabrielle Lasher; Jack Lazov; Anne Little; Julia Loman; Peter Longford; Mike Lumis; Justin Maris; Thomas Matt; Edgar McNeil; Grant Menzies; Irina Mishop; Ian Morris; Roger Morris; Jay Moss; Christopher Mowlens; Sue Nardin; Claudia Nervin; Felix Norris; Rick Owens; Bill Partridge; Bob Perricault; Hank Pettigrew; Marsha and Ashton Porman; Ron Questen; George Ransome; Linda and Phil Rascul; Viki Sams; William Samuels; John Sandford; Rachel Sattle; Matt Selford; Tim Simmons; Nicola Simms; John Simon; Corey Sommers; Cynthia Sulden; Ryan Tager; Josh Tanner; Eleanor Tibble; Diana Totesmore; Michael Townsend; Fanny Ulman; Eugene Unwin; Mona and Philip Usher; Anna Victor; Michel Vusgek; Henry Walters; Burt Washington; Curtis Welborne; Zora and Peter Welcome; Dale Wilmington; Allen Wilson; Nadine Womack; Cathy Wycliff; Shiguro Yukihama; Gleb Yuvenshky; and Mark Zendor.

Friends have been a constant source of support and especially understanding of the demands placed on my life as I struggled to bring this book to fruition. Past and present, they have been sounding boards for ideas, and often were the first to offer encouragement. They also were the people who have seen the least of me over the past few years, never complaining about my temporary absences from their lives. I would like to thank Sharlene

Aadland; Dominic Albanese; Janet Ashton; Jacqui Axelson; Anne Barrett; Arturo Beeche; Daniel Briere; Dan Brite; Carrie Carlson; Sally Dick; Liz and Andy Eaton; Laura Enstone; Pablo Fonseca; Jake Gariepy; Ella Gaumer; Coryne Hall; Sally Hampton; Nils Hanson; Barbara and Paul Harper; Gretchen Haskin; Louise Hayes; Kathy Hoefler; Lise Everett Holden; Diane Huntley; Chuck and Eileen Knaus; Marlene Eilers Koenig; Peter Kurth; Angela Manning; Cecelia Manning; Mark Manning; Gigi McDonald; Nancy Mellon; Ilana Miller; Russ and Deb Minugh; Jennifer Mottershaw; Annette Nason-Waters; Pepsi Nunes; Steve O'Donnell; Lisa Palmer; Anne Shawyer; Mary Silzel; Debra Tate; Katrina Warne; Sue Woolmans; and Marion Wynn.

As always, I thank my parents, Roger and Helena King, for their unfailing support.

I would like to thank Brad Swenson of Buy and Sell Videos for offering a steady stream of diverting entertainment as I wrote, allowing some relief when the pressure of deadlines was crowding around me. Antonio Perez Caballero supplied me not only with continued encouragement but also books, illustrative materials, and important information on Count Boni de Castellane and his fabled Palais Rose in Paris. Janet Whitcomb generously read through sections of the manuscript and shared her knowledge of Stanford White, and Simon Donoghue helped open doors that enabled further research and important contacts. Patrick Grimes, artistic director of the Astors' Beechwood in Newport, corrected several points related to that house. Dean de la Motte, the dean of Newport's Salve Regina University, patiently took time from his busy schedule and assisted in my research efforts, as did Maria Bernier, Salve Regina University archivist, and I also must single out Salve Regina University's Catherine Zipf, who was especially generous in sharing materials and undertaking inquiries on my behalf.

In attempting to unravel the story of Colonel William D'Alton Mann and his publication *Town Topics,* I was greatly aided by two of his descendants, John G. Mann and Tracey M. DeMartini. Additionally, Tracey DeMartini patiently read through the material related to *Town Topics,* offering advice and corrections, and graciously allowed me to quote from an unpublished memoir written by the colonel's niece Mildred Mann Brann.

As any author knows, working with archives and institutions can some-times be an exercise in bureaucratic frustration. I therefore am very pleased to thank officials with the Preservation Society of Newport Country for their extraordinary assistance, not only with illustrative mate-rials but also for their generous flow of information. The stream of media requests made of them must be constant, but they made my experience not only personal but also highly rewarding. Andrea Carneiro, communi-cations manager for the Preservation Society, undertook image research on my behalf and was a constant source of encouragement, while Paul Miller, the society's architectural historian, not only provided me with rare archival materials and patiently answered my numerous queries but also read through portions of the manuscript, offering suggestions and correc-tions to help ensure the book's accuracy. I also wish to thank Megan Delaney of the Newport Historical Society and Chris Murtha of the Museum of the City of New York for their assistance in securing last-minute illustrations.

Penny Wilson has, as always, been selfless in her efforts, helping to supply important materials. Thanks to her generosity, I was able to access hundreds of extremely rare memoirs and obscure sources that helped round out the portrait herein. She also carefully read through these pages, making comments and suggestions that enriched the text at the expense of her own hectic schedule.

Susanne Meslans also immersed herself in this project, sharing her own resources and undertaking research that helped to fill in gaps. At a time when she was facing her own important deadlines and could ill afford to do so, she offered important critical commentary on the manuscript that challenged my assumptions and made me view old issues in a fresh light.

In 1999 it was my privilege to begin work with Lady Sarah Spencer-Churchill on her memoirs. Through telephone calls, letters, faxes, and visits I came to know Sarah well, and she freely shared the fascinating story of her life, always trusting my discretion even when our talks veered into territory that she insisted could not publicly be disclosed. A truly extraordinary and gracious lady, Sarah was Alva Vanderbilt Belmont's great-granddaughter and thus Consuelo Vanderbilt's granddaughter. She knew of my intention to one day write a book on Gilded Age society, and when she needed a break from retelling her own stories, Sarah allowed me to question her at length on the era and its personalities, incidents, and episodes passed on to her by her grandmother Consuelo. Much of what she said to me is infused throughout this book, setting its tone and shaping many of my impressions. Sarah's untimely death prevented completion of her own book, but I hope that in these pages I have provided some measure of the justice she attempted to convey regarding the Gilded Age, and offered a portrait of which she would approve.

A NOTE ON CURRENCY

In this book, readers will regularly encounter a diversity of figures, to indicate not only the business and personal fortunes of members of Gilded Age society but also such items as the construction costs of their houses and the amounts they paid for their parties. In each case I have provided the original sum along with an approximate rendering of that amount in 2008 terms.

Unfortunately, there is no consistent indicator for valuation and inflation. Between 1872 to 1912 the value of the dollar fluctuated constantly, making it impossible to impose a static formula over the span of forty years. Adding to the dilemma are the issues of taxation and relative purchasing power. The stories in this book unfold in an era before the United States imposed a standard income tax, and rates for local taxation varied greatly. It is important, therefore, to keep this in mind when looking at historical finances. Then, too, the lack of taxation means that the actual purchasing power of any given sum from the turn of the century would be manifestly greater than is first evident.

In general I have used the following conversions throughout the book: figures from the 1880s are multiplied by 20; those for the late 1890s and early 1900s by 23; and those for the second decade of the twentieth century by 21. The few figures dealing with finances prior to the Civil War are even more problematic; the consensus suggests that multiplication by 30 offers the best rough estimate. While offering a close parallel to modern figures, these remain only approximate—and sometimes imprecise—estimates and reflect only relative value, not purchasing power. Thus, for $1 million in 1880, the approximate 2008 valuation would be $20.3 million. The actual purchasing power of $1 million in 1880 compared to relative

costs—and taking taxation into account—would, however, be substantially more, ranging between $130 million and $200 million in 2008. Here
I have given only the approximate 2008 equivalents for nineteenth- and
early twentieth-century amounts; readers who wish to render any of the
figures herein in terms of possible purchasing power should multiply
the 2008 equivalents by between 6 and 10.

In comprehending just how enormous many of the Gilded Age fortunes
and expenditures were, a few examples drawn from ordinary life may be
helpful. At the turn of the century, for example, the average income for a
typical American household was roughly $2,000 ($46,000 in 2008) if the
worker was engaged in skilled work, although the vast majority of the citizens earned far less, with an average of perhaps $500 to $700 a year
($11,500 to $16,100 in 2008). In New York City, the mayor had a salary of
$10,000 a year (comparable to $230,000 in 2008); seven state supreme
court justices made $11,500 a year ($264,500 in 2008); and the district
attorney received $12,000 ($276,000 in 2008). A luxurious apartment in
the city rented for approximately $3,000 to $5,000 a year ($69,000 to
$115,000 in 2008); a comfortable (though scarcely fashionable) apartment
might cost $300 a year ($6,900 in 2008); a room in a respectable lodging
house rented for $4 to $7 a week, including board ($92 to $161 in 2008);
a small apartment in the seedier parts of the city might go for $10 a month
($230 in 2008); and a room in a squalid tenement could be as little as $1 a
month ($23 in 2008). A good dinner, with wine, at the fashionable
Delmonico's Restaurant began at roughly $3 per person ($69 in 2008),
while a typical day dress, ordered from Paris and worn by a society lady,
might begin at $125 ($2,875 in 2008).[1]

I have attempted to be cautious in my translations of currency, but readers
may find varying valuations of similar figures in other works on the Gilded
Age, as is to be expected without benefit of a single, reliable standard.

INTRODUCTION

I<small>T WAS A NOVEL THAT LENT</small> the era its famous epithet. In 1873, Mark Twain coauthored *The Gilded Age: A Tale of Today,* a chronicle of what he perceived to be growing corruption in America following the Civil War. Twain concentrated on the changes wrought by the industrial revolution and the subversion of the democratic process at the hands of merchants, speculators, and unscrupulous businessmen whose riches easily bribed corrupt politicians, but the unchecked wealth and unbridled excess he described soon came to be associated with the era as a whole. In a time before federal income tax, the wealthy built extraordinary marble mansions and châteaux, settings for indulgent parties and eccentric characters who dazzled with their riches, their entertainments, and their feuds. In winter they rushed through New York City, from evenings at the Metropolitan Opera to glittering ballrooms, to dance through the night; in summer, ensconced in plush, private Pullman cars or aboard sleek yachts, New York society dispersed to sprawling Italian palazzos and Gothic castles along the Hudson River Valley, nestled in the Berkshires, and fringing the Atlantic cliffs of Newport.

This was the Gilded Age, a period that roughly stretched from the 1870s to the outbreak of World War I in 1914. In the years before the Civil War,

America had been a largely rural society; this changed with the industrial revolution and with the growth of modern transport, which not only spread the country westward but also brought thousands to burgeoning cities. Among them were railway and coal barons, oil developers, successful gold miners, steel magnates, and Wall Street speculators, armed with new business and industrial fortunes that dazzled and captivated the nation's attention. Names such as Vanderbilt, Whitney, Gould, Carnegie, Morgan, and Rockefeller became synonyms for unbridled greed and flaunted excess. Businessmen first and foremost, they not only worked hard and outwitted rivals but also, as Twain had described, often used legal loopholes to skirt the law, bribe politicians, and accumulate vast fortunes. Before the Civil War, most American fortunes had been derived from extensive real estate holdings and passed down through generations of quietly dignified heirs. By the 1890s, America could boast more than four thousand millionaires, who, though their ranks formed less than 10 percent of the country's population, controlled nearly three quarters of its wealth.[1]

At the apex of the Gilded Age stood society, and nowhere was that society more important, more celebrated, more famous, and more condemned than in New York City. Social aspirants naturally gravitated to the city where, as Thomas Beer cynically wrote, "the timid ostentations of a possible three thousand men and women living in cramped, airless houses between two polluted rivers were advertised as though an aristocracy moved proudly through some customary ritual."[2] At the turn of the century, New York was the only American city whose influence could be said to rival that of London, Berlin, or Paris. New York claimed the greatest wealth, the largest mansions imitating European palaces, the most extravagant entertainments that strove for parity with the opulence of the Old World, and the most prominent citizens in a country proudly celebrating 125 years of independence from the British Crown.

Before the Gilded Age, old New York society, remembered Mary King Van Rensselaer, "was a representative, exclusive body of all that was best in the city. There was unity, there was intellect that strove for something further than social recognition, and with them went a courtesy and chivalry inherited from the old world."[3] It had been a quiet, patrician world composed of descendants of the original Dutch and English founders. Families such as the Van Rensselaers, Schuylers, Van Cortlandts, Stuyvesants, and Schermerhorns carried on the old Dutch ways as patroons, presiding over an archaic and corrupt tenancy system that was eventually abolished in 1846, while their English counterparts—the Livingstons of Clermont and the Philipses of Philipsberg—lived equally isolated lives at their manorial estates along the Hudson. As they migrated to the city, powerful families established businesses and bought enormous parcels of real estate, forming a new urban aristocracy known as the Knickerbockers, a privileged caste that dominated New York social life for two generations.[4]

These patricians, recalled Mary King Van Rensselaer, "knew the history of the families with which they had associated for generations, and these histories were vital parts of the record of the city in which they lived. The segments of the social circle were held together by intimate ties, and this intimacy made of the social organization a clan into which few might expect to force their way except by marriage with one of its members."[5] As such, society grew "from within rather than from without. . . . The foreign elements absorbed were negligible. The social circle widened, generation by generation, through the abundant contributions made by each family to posterity."[6]

It was a world of lawyers, politicians, and discreet businessmen closely tied by blood and advantageous marriage into a community precariously balanced on honor and manners, whose social codes demanded propriety and condemned extravagance as vulgarity.[7] Isolated, proud, aware of the power of exclusion and fiercely protective of its privileges, Knickerbocker New York clung to the security of its sanctimonious, repetitive days in dour brownstones, presiding over dull parties for their dull friends between seemingly endless religious pieties. Within its formidable circles, as one observer noted, "dreary platitudes pass for conversation, and well-intending men and women, whom nature would not bless with wit, fall asleep and dream of a heaven in which they seem clever forevermore."[8]

The march of the nouveaux riches shattered this placid world, sending paroxysms of horror through elderly dowagers in their crisp black dresses and tight lace collars. The aftermath of the Civil War left New York society

adrift, confused, its loyalties torn between the old Knickerbocker aristocracy and the more insistent members of the nouveaux riches. "Until those
years," recalled Mary King Van Rensselaer, "society had remained static,
unthreatened by invasion. All at once it was assailed from every side by
persons who sought to climb boldly over the walls of social exclusiveness."[9]

The excesses of the Gilded Age burst upon a staid, monochromatic
New York in dazzling colors and with unimagined luxuries. Few welcomed these new arrivals, but they gradually took hold across the city—
industrialists, merchants, and speculators wandering the streets in
uncomfortable, ill-fitting frock coats and top hats that only emphasized
their status as outsiders. Their houses were larger and more luxurious;
their carriages sleekly new; and their servants bedecked in new ostentatious liveries.[10] In every aspect of social life, the challenges were being laid
down. Unable to reconcile their glorified conceptions of quiet grace with
the more exuberant flamboyance of these new millionaires whose money
both repulsed and intrigued, the Knickerbockers gradually faded from
view, staring disapprovingly from the windows of their respectable brownstones as the world evolved around them, dreaming of days long past, and
knowing that a new era was breaking on the horizon. "What had seemed
unalterable rules of conduct became of a sudden observances as quaintly
arbitrary as the domestic rites of the Pharaohs," wrote Edith Wharton.[11]

The struggle for primacy between tradition and social evolution,
between old money and new, between families of respected lineage and
social upstarts who dared challenge convention, was to last for the duration of the Gilded Age as this new society attempted to assimilate opposing ideals to create a unified conception of itself. That it managed, for a
time, to offer a carefully ordered system built on this often disparate and
chaotic conundrum was due to the efforts of one remarkable woman,
whose legacy largely defined the era. This was Caroline Astor, an extraordinary figure, who, through unlimited wealth and the sheer force of her
personality, boldly took the initiative and dominated the new elite of
New York City that she herself helped to create.

Caroline Astor's place at the apex of Gilded Age society offered mute
testament to the dichotomy it encompassed. As the wife of a grandson of
the famous John Jacob Astor and herself a descendant of the traditional

and respected Schermerhorn family, Caroline personified the warring factions, uniting the proud Knickerbocker heritage with the persistence of new money. Having watched the slow decay of the city's ruling elite in the aftermath of the Civil War, Caroline recognized that New York society was adrift, confused, its loyalties torn between a fading patrician aristocracy and the irresistible allure of the nouveaux riches. It was her genius to realize that new money could not be kept at bay forever, that the days of the staid and dull formality of the Knickerbockers had passed. She thus promoted not one form over another, but merged the best elements of each into a powerful coalition, creating a version of American society that welcomed both old aristocracy and the newly moneyed into its distinguished embrace.

Members of Mrs. Astor's new society shared similar characteristics. They were ambitious, but few were intellectually curious. Money insulated them from everyday concerns and from the necessities of work, although most gentlemen felt it incumbent upon them to manage the family fortune and indulge in business ventures that were often little more than dilettantish occupations. These gentlemen tended to belong to the city's exclusive clubs, which, together with their businesses and social obligations, largely defined their worlds. The majority of society ladies were concerned with either maintaining their social position or improving it. Families were often regarded as inconvenient if necessary burdens; children were raised almost exclusively by nannies, governesses, and tutors, the daughters remaining at home while the sons were sent to preparatory schools. Almost without exception, everyone was Protestant, with a marked preference for the Episcopal Church.[12]

Exclusion provided this new elite with its raison d'être: to be desirable, society must be seen as something distinct. It was, recalled James Gerard, "a closely organized and tightly controlled enterprise governed by strict rules. From the end of the Civil War until the end of World War I it was ruled by a succession of dictatorships, and, as under all successful dictatorships, the ruler's power was unquestioned. There was no competing group. Either you belonged to Society, or you didn't."[13] Because of the insular nature of Gilded Age society, its great dinners, parties, and balls were themselves models of exclusivity. Lloyd Morris likened it to "a rococo theater, where a continuous spectacle was in performance; the décor and costumes constantly changing but the same actors being displayed in a single, static situation. At most spectacles the audience may be under an illusion but the actors know that real life lies on the other side of the footlights. It was the peculiar characteristic of this one that all the illusion was confined to the actors."[14]

In what French author Paul Bourget called this "constant, tireless endeavor to absorb European ideas," the manners and modes of this new society were diligently copied from the Old World.[15] Yet New York society differed from its European models. In Europe, noted one observer, "Society is an intermittent condition created by the temporary meeting of persons of permanent rank—persons who possessed their rank before their association made Society, and retain it after their separation for the time being ends Society." But in New York, society was "largely artificial," its membership "largely arbitrary," and its continuation dependent on the idea that it occupied a position of ingrained privilege.[16]

While determined to drape itself in the mantle of wealth, power, and taste associated with foreign aristocracy, much of Gilded Age society evinced little of their cultural distinction.[17] Such failings were not merely a fixture of the newly moneyed class. For all of its probity and talk of higher principles, the Knickerbocker set had often been just as culturally arid, although they at least were careful to affect a patina of intellect. The experiences of novelist Edith Wharton, herself a product of patrician New York, revealed just how fragile this illusion could be. Her early interest in literature was tolerated rather than actively encouraged, and her intellectual pursuits were regarded with suspicion. Where the Knickerbockers had been content with anonymous obscurity, however, these new millionaires were boldly individual. Their ideas of culture relied less on appreciation of music or the arts, however; they attempted instead to manifest taste through imaginative parties and in their grandiose modern palaces firmly rooted in a nostalgic past.

Such was Caroline Astor's conception of this new society. She envisioned a ruling elite that would provide an enduring legacy to her country. By forming a set of stringent rules, by creating around her a caste that replicated foreign ideals, Caroline attempted to endow American society with tradition and a sense of noblesse oblige. Not yet a hundred years old, America in the years following the Civil War was in the midst of enormous upheaval: too much change might threaten those with inherited wealth, and too little would continue to keep the country in the shadow of Europe. America, like many countries in the uncertain nineteenth century, was in the grip of nationalism, searching for a sense of heritage that would bestow prestige. The adoption of aristocratic standards thus offered clear examples upon which Gilded Age society could model itself: thus, in place of a monarch, one could find Mrs. Astor as the social arbiter; instead of a royal court, she gathered around her the wealthiest and most influential citizens of New York, imposing on them a sense of responsibility to establish taste for the enrichment of the nation as a whole. To this end, every aspect of life in the Gilded Age took on deeper, transcendent meaning intended to prove the greatness of America: residences beautified their surroundings; works of art uplifted and were shared with the public; clothing exhibited evidence of breeding; jewelry testified to cultured taste and wealth; dinners demonstrated sophisticated palates; and balls rivaled those of European courts in their refinement. The message was unmistakable: the United States had arrived culturally, and Caroline Astor and her circle were intent on leading the nation to unimagined heights of glory.

These challenges coincided with the rise in social celebrity. In an era that witnessed a plethora of illustrated weeklies and periodicals, lithographs, and popular postcards, public attention and adoration focused on politicians, business leaders, and the wealthy as objects of interest, and press accounts of elaborate parties and extravagant balls offered vicarious excitement to millions. Caroline Astor, though she abhorred such attention as an unwelcome intrusion, cannily recognized that money and celebrity could benefit as well as entertain. She believed that by raising social, moral, and aesthetic standards, America's Gilded Age elite could compete on an even footing with the culture of the Old World. This conflation of social ambition with patriotic duty was done with the utmost seriousness, but the artifice involved often conflicted with the essence of the American ideal. Hard work and the ability to better one's situation were cherished values, but great success and great wealth were often viewed as unscrupulous avarice. These two warring ideals were woven as a leitmotif throughout the era, forever tearing at the competing strains inherent in what was essentially an artificial entity, the impulse for indulgence eventually overwhelming the noble if naive ideals that Caroline had attempted to impose.

Yet, for a time, this society was largely successful. "The mistake made by the world at large," declared one gentleman, "is that fashionable people are selfish, frivolous, and indifferent to the welfare of their fellow creatures; all of which is a popular error, arising simply from a want of knowledge of the true state of things. The elegancies of fashionable life nourish and benefit art and artists; they cause the expenditure of money and its distribution; and they really prevent our people and country from settling down into a humdrum rut and becoming merely a money making and money saving people, with nothing to brighten up and enliven life; they foster all the fine arts; but for fashion what would become of them? They bring to the front merit of every kind; seek it in the remotest corners, where it modestly shrinks from observation, and force it into notice."[18]

Following Caroline's dictates, many in society took their roles and responsibilities to heart. Their elaborate dinners and balls might seem frivolous, yet many were planned and executed with the utmost seriousness, with a keen awareness of upholding the tenets of elite society. Some, like the Vanderbilts, saw themselves as modern-day Medicis, new patrician patrons whose money contributed to the cultural life of the country. The immense châteaux, Gothic castles, and Italianate palazzos that went up along Fifth Avenue and rose in resorts such as the Berkshires and Newport offered America a proud architectural heritage designed not only to provide extravagant lodgings but also to beautify their cities. If the creation of these lavish buildings was not entirely altruistic in motive, there was at least a sense among these millionaires that they were enriching their homeland by raising the standards of American life and providing visible legacies for future generations.

This munificent society envisioned and ruled over by Caroline Astor was to last a mere twenty years. The death of her husband in 1892, the passing of one of her daughters shortly thereafter, and the construction of a new house effectively prevented her from exercising her role as doyenne of Gilded Age society for four long years. By the time Caroline resumed her entertainments, she found that other rivals had entered the breach, infused with less noble ideals and determined to use their money to attract considerable attention. Thus did Gilded Age society enter into its second phase, a period of frivolity and excess that quickly overshadowed the last vestiges of nobility and restraint. More through courtesy and respect than real influence, Caroline retained her position as uncrowned queen, and elements of her old regime periodically imposed their power, but the dichotomy between enlightened conception and lavish indulgence only heightened society's shifting perceptions of itself, resulting in increasingly outlandish displays such as dinners for dogs and balls for monkeys, which came, in the eyes of many, to characterize the era as a whole.

This new version of Gilded Age society, perhaps because it lacked the guiding principles so fundamental to Caroline Astor's conception, often gave an impression of discomfort. French author Paul Bourget, visiting America in the 1890s, noted, "These millionaires do not entirely accept themselves. . . . They do not admit that they are thus different from the Old World, or if they admit it, it is to insist that if they chose they could equal the Old World, or, at least, enjoy it."[19] Too often, enjoyment meant social competition. Writing in the August 1900 issue of *Cosmopolitan,* Montgomery Schuyler declared, "Even a multimillionaire, we may concede, has a right to his preferences, but this, the observer is driven to suspect, is not an affair of enjoyment so much as of emulation, the struggle to outdo one another, or at least not to be outdone."[20]

This quest for ever-increasing extravagance characterized the second phase of Gilded Age society. "Those were the days of magnificence," recalled one society lady, "when money was poured out like water. Nothing but the best was good enough and so the best had to be procured regardless of cost. The new kings of trade might work at their offices twelve, fourteen hours a day, but their wives would have something to show for it. Festoons of priceless jewels draped ample bosoms, yards of historic lace trimmed underpetticoats, the greatest dress designers of Europe vied with one another to create costumes that would grace some splendid ball for one night and then be thrown away. Gold plate gleaming on dinner tables laid for a hundred and fifty guests, fleets of lorries coming up from the south in depths of winter laden with orchids to decorate the ballroom of some great hostess. No one thought of the cost."[21]

Many in America, as one social historian wrote, "believed implicitly that New York's social leaders went to bed in full evening dress, brushed their teeth in vintage champagne, married their daughters without exception to shady French counts, and arrayed their poodle dogs in diamond tiaras."[22] Much later, looking back on these heady days, Frederick Townsend Martin commented on "the glitter of tinsel and the tawdry finery of mere wealth" that marked what he termed "the empty follies of the idle rich and the vapid foolishness of the ultra-fashionable in America."[23]

The tenets that ruled this world were unraveled in a scathing work, *The Theory of the Leisure Class,* published in 1899 by Thorstein Veblen. Veblen perceived the majority of this moneyed elite as an avaricious collection of self-inflated social climbers who clung desperately to the idea of privilege for fear that they, too, might face exclusion from its hallowed ranks. To bolster their own positions, members of this new society indulged in what Veblen called "conspicuous consumption."[24] Thus they needed increasingly extravagant mansions filled with antique furniture imported from Europe and an army of liveried servants; expensive clothing that heightened their aura of distinction; jewelry and extravagant frippery with which to dazzle members of their own circles as well as those who looked on from beyond the bounds of their charmed existence; private railway carriages lined with silk and tufted to within an inch of their life; sleek yachts on which to impress their friends; and stables of fine thoroughbreds. Houses in the city and estates in the country offered opportunities to engage in leisure pursuits copied from Europe and demonstrate that their owners were free of business obligations; frequent journeys to London, Berlin, and Paris testified to disposable income; and the acquisition of paintings, sculpture, tapestries, and carpets signaled lavish taste. Dinners and balls needed to be overt gestures in excess: from the antique china and gold and silver plate to the endless round of diverse and exotic courses composed of the rarest and most costly foods and wines, everything was designed to show just how little money mattered to those in society, and just how willing they were to waste their resources on such fleeting displays. It was, Veblen argued, nothing short of a hollow charade, knowingly perpetrated on the public to enforce society's distinct status, and on each other in a race toward dominance. "In order to gain and to hold the esteem of men," Veblen declared, "it is not sufficient merely to possess wealth or power. The wealth or power must be put in evidence, for esteem is awarded only on evidence."[25]

Veblen was particularly critical of the explicit show that dominated Gilded Age society's second half. Perhaps it was inevitable that ever-increasing wealth and privilege would lead to such dramatic changes; as Caroline Astor's restraining hand faded, the archetype of the selfish, indolent, and wastrel society figure rooted itself in the imagination of the public. Those whose questionable fortunes and illicit antecedents would have made them anathema under Caroline Astor's reign now began their rise through society, paving their paths to the heights of acceptance with enormous sums of money and entertainments so startlingly original in their conception that they were impossible to ignore. Diversion became the overarching concern. "There seems to be no serious basis of life for them at all," noted Sir Philip Burne-Jones, "and amusement and pleasure are the sole aims of their existence. Of course, this is more or less the case in any society where great wealth and much leisure abound, but I think it is even more noticeable in this little New York coterie than among our own leisured classes, where, at least, they have politics to fall back upon."[26]

Such changing circumstances helped account for the rise of someone like Mamie Fish, who, though she moved in the same exalted circles as Caroline Astor, was in every way the latter's antithesis. A series of walking contradictions, Mamie desired the acceptance of society while at the same time openly mocking it. "More than any one figure of her times," recorded one social historian, "she is held personally responsible . . . for causing the breakdown of the classification of society as she found it" and for eventually leading society to ruin.[27] Beneath her bluster, Mamie could often be an endearing figure, but she encouraged the rise in hedonistic behavior that eventually brought scorn on all of Gilded Age society.

By the turn of the century, Gilded Age society encompassed, in varying degrees, these two competing strains—the dignified and the effete—with the latter invariably making far better copy for newspapers anxious to cater to an insatiable public. Ironically, this same appetite for the excesses of the rich and famous ultimately led to their downfall; too much privilege, too much outrageous behavior, and too much frenzied revelry began to turn the tide from eager curiosity to moralistic opprobrium. It was on this note of almost debauched excess that Gilded Age society came to its abrupt end.

The efforts to enrich American culture with a ready-made heritage may ultimately have failed, but even in the face of society's worst excesses, Gilded Age society did leave a deeper legacy that remains to this day. Too often, the era's magnificent parties and lavish indulgences have formed a contemptible portrait of the Gilded Age as a period of unbridled excess at its worst. Yet the remaining houses of the Gilded Age, such as the fabled "cottages" of Newport, are not only recognized as architectural gems but also draw millions of curious tourists. Paintings that once hung in New York City's greatest private palaces now grace the walls of the Metropolitan Museum of Art, bequests from their owners for the benefit of the public. The principled ideals of Caroline Astor and the often outrageous gestures of Mamie Fish are ineluctably woven into this rich tapestry, each offering insights into a way of life long passed into legend. But behind the legend rests the real story, a complex tale of aspiration at a time when America's wealthiest citizens bemused and bewitched a nation, and a party in New York could capture the imagination of the entire world.

PROLOGUE
New York City, 1903

A VISITOR TO NEW YORK CITY in 1903 discovered a glittering mecca for the country's social aristocrats, a place of "beautiful women and brave men threading the mazes of the dance; scenes of revelry by night in an atmosphere loaded with the perfumes of rare exotics, in the swell of sensuous music, and all the other adjuncts of fashionable life in the great metropolis."[1] The rich came in droves, attempting to crash the rarefied circles. No matter how successful they might be in Philadelphia or Chicago, no matter their business holdings in San Francisco or Boston, entrée to New York society was the dream of wealthy America. An 1893 Baedeker guide had termed it "the wealthiest city of the New World, and inferior in commercial and financial importance to London alone among the cities of the globe."[2] With 3 million citizens, more than half of America's major corporations, and two thirds of the banking institutions headquartered in New York, the city was preeminent in its financial dominance, home to hundreds of millionaires and many more aspiring to that goal.[3] By the turn of the century, it proudly embraced its moniker of "the Empire City," a place at the very center of American business, finance, aspirations, and culture.[4]

"What London is to the continent, what Rome was in its imperial day to the empire, New York is to the immense domain of the American republic, a natural stage for the great drama of civilization on this continent." So wrote Henry Clews, stockbroker and member of Gilded Age society. To Clews, the city was without parallel, boasting "some of the finest stores in the world, and mansions of which a Doge of Venice or a Lorenzo de Medici might have been proud. Here are the most beautiful ladies in the world, as well as the most refined and cultivated; here are the finest theaters and art galleries, and the true home of opera is in this country; here is the glitter of peerless fashion, the ceaseless roll of splendid equipages, and the Bois de Boulogne of America, Central Park."[5]

Along the Hudson River estuary and into New York Harbor, steamers, ferries, and ocean liners churned through the waters. Immigrant eyes gazed eagerly upon the lonely Statue of Liberty and the immensity of the Brooklyn Bridge before taking in the long lines of wooden wharves and piers that fringed Manhattan.[6] Standing at the rails, visitors could see the jagged silhouette of the city. Beyond the rows of tenements and brownstones and the slender spires of dozens of churches rose the beginnings of the city's marvels, tall buildings dubbed with the new sobriquet of skyscrapers. "Their height," recorded one visitor, "overpowers my vision. I count the stories above the level of the roofs: one has ten, another twelve. Another, not yet finished, has a vast iron framework, outlining upon the sky the plan of six more storeys above the eight already built. Gigantic, colossal, enormous, daring, there are no words—words are inadequate to this apparition, this landscape, in which the vast outlet of the river serves as a frame for the display of a still vaster human energy."[7]

For those arriving in New York City by railway, the impact was no less dramatic, as a dozen trains steamed and wheezed into the terminals, disgorging passengers. There was no better hint of New York's wealth and ostentation than the magnificent Grand Central Station. Erected by the famous Commodore Cornelius Vanderbilt, this was an immense brick structure in the Renaissance Revival style, its cavernous halls and a confusing myriad of corridors encased beneath a mansard roof adorned with domes and proudly defiant carved stone eagles.[8]

From dock or railway station, these visitors entered into a city teeming with life. "The street from gutter to gutter is just as full of vehicles as the sidewalks are of moving people," recorded one visitor. "And the same variety rules, the same wonderment is excited in the one as in the other. Carriages of all sorts crowd along in processional line. Victorias, landaus, broughams, road wagons, occasionally an old-fashioned buggy, mingle with motor-buses, cruising cabs, countless makes and colors of automobiles, delivery wagons, express wagons, furniture vans, short-haul trucks, motor-cycles, ordinary bicycles. Policemen, mounted or standing, are in the center of crowded cross-streets to hold up the line of carriages for a moment and allow a stream of foot-passengers to pass over; but as a rule everyone does his own scrambling, keeps from under the horses' feet, and gets about or across as best he can." He noted, "Automobiles, driven perhaps by stout, red-faced men with handsome, overdressed, rather flashy young women on the back seat; victorias with elderly people in black; broughams with single occupants, and the men on the box dressed up to the color of their horses' coats; hansoms and auto-cabs with young people leaning on the closed doors," and "omnibuses with top-loads of passengers."[9]

The constant clanging of trolley bells, the shouted calls from cabmen, the clatter of horses' hooves on uneven cobblestones and broad pavement, the rumble of motorcars belching clouds of black smoke in their wakes, and the rattling shriek of the elevated railways created a cacophony of sound. For many years, the streets of New York had been a source of perpetual consternation; in the summer, their dust coated everything, and in winter they turned into a muddy miasma. "It was impossible," recalled one resident, "to keep the streets looking clean—or at least so it seemed. Horses were not so self-contained as automobiles. And if the visitor traveled on a Madison Avenue car, the overpowering barnyard odor in the Park Avenue tunnel made a lasting impression."[10]

By day, "victorias, landaus, broughams, and coupes" clogged Broadway and Union Square.[11] Here, in an area known as "the Ladies' Mile," clustered the city's most exclusive stores: the famous A. T. Stewart & Company, New York's first real department store, with a variety of imported silks from Lyon, Irish linens, and Parisian fashions prominently displayed in its plate-glass windows, with rivals Lord & Taylor, Macy's, W. J. Sloane & Sons, and Arnold Constable nearby. Silver services came from Gorham, bejeweled splendors from Tiffany & Company, exquisite furs from C. F. Janson, chocolates and pastries from Henry Maillard, and the latest leather-bound books from Brentano's.[12] "Nothing cheap is sold on Fifth Avenue," noted a turn-of-the-century observer. "There are no bargain counters, no forty-nine-cent ruling prices; and people do not go there without a plethoric purse. Everything costs half as much again as it could be bought for around the corner."[13]

Those not blessed with the privilege of Gilded Age wealth and status could still gather on the sidewalks to watch "an incessant procession of elegantly attired women who trailed their long walking dresses in the accumulated urban dust."[14] These ladies exemplified the elegance of the era. "The very manner in which the women step out of their carriages," recorded one man, "give directions to the footmen, and drift across the sidewalk into a shop entrance, has an air of distinction about it." Many of these ladies affected deliberate sartorial splendor on these expeditions: "She is dressed and sometimes overdressed—especially when she goes shopping. Her garments are of the best and most costly materials."[15] Tiffany & Company, Stewart's, and Lord & Taylor all kept a supply of young boys in stiff liveries, whose sole duty was to follow these important customers through their stores, displaying items and carrying purchases.

Architect Stanford White's great triumphal arch in Washington Square, adorned with motifs celebrating America's first president, marked the beginnings of fashionable New York. Buried deep below the roadway was an eighteenth-century paupers' graveyard. As the city spread northward, adventurous merchants had moved here and, in 1827, laid out a new park over the old cemetery, creating a gentrified place of wealth ringed by noble brownstones hovering loftily over the hundreds of nameless bodies that remained hidden below.[16]

Stretching north was Fifth Avenue, the center of the city's Gilded Age universe and "the proudest thoroughfare I had ever seen anywhere," declared one visitor.[17] First laid out in the 1820s, its sixty-foot-wide, seven-mile length edged the mass of Central Park, with its bucolic landscape of meandering drives and paths, rustic waterfalls tumbling over jagged rocks, and ornamental ponds and serpentine stretches of placid water guarded by fringes of carefully planted trees. On the other side of the avenue, row after row, block after block were the great marble châteaux and Italianate palazzos of the city's Gilded Age society. During the winter social season, their windows blazed with light as parties, dinners, and balls followed in seemingly endless succession. They were the bastions of privilege, monuments of accumulated wealth and taste brimming with intoxicating power that bemused and bewitched the collective imagination of the city.

Now, however, their windows were dark, shuttered against the pervasive cold of a Saturday night in March when the social season had come to an end and their owners had abandoned them for country estates or the more distant pleasures of Europe. The day had been cloudy, interrupted with intermittent rain that offered no hint of the approaching spring, a biting wind howling along avenues where the murky halos of electric lamps cast eerie shadows over the gloomy night. Few pedestrians braved the elements, though an endless stream of carriages and motorcars raced and rumbled along Fifth Avenue. In silence, they passed the city's fashionable restaurants, whose immense plate-glass windows revealed crowds of elegant diners relishing the warmth within. It was a scene repeated across New York. At the famed Waldorf-Astoria, social hopefuls paraded up and down the marble length of Peacock Alley, and sat in quiet solitude amid the gilded splendors of its restaurant; on the south side of Madison Square, Dorland's prepared to receive the post-theater crowd, while young gentlemen and their ladies clustered around white-damask-covered tables at Rector's, Woodmanston, and Bustanoby's, enjoying the pleasures of this quiet early spring evening.

Amid this shifting kaleidoscope, beneath the threatening skies, the intersection of Fifth Avenue and Forty-fourth Street was unusually busy, crowded with the sleek conveyances of the city's elite. At the northeast corner glowered the legendary hulk of Delmonico's, the city's most fashionable restaurant. Delmonico's had helped introduce New York to the ten- and twelve-course dinners, filled with extravagant dishes, that were quickly taken up by the Gilded Age as evidence of refined tastes. The elaborate

bar, the ladies' café, an expansive palm court where an orchestra serenaded diners, and Delmonico's third-floor ballroom had all witnessed
ritual gatherings of the city's ruling class as they reveled in their privileged
lives. On this particular evening, however, the vehicles halted on the
opposite corner, in front of the twelve-storied, ghostly white Italianate
facade of Sherry's Hotel. Built between 1896 and 1898 by architect
Stanford White for proprietor Louis Sherry, this was not only a hotel but
also a theatrical stage on which society could enact its glittering entertainments. In addition to the guest apartments, it included—like its rival
Delmonico's—a restaurant, a bar, a café, a palm court, and enormous private dining rooms, and bettered its older counterpart with not one but
three immense ballrooms.[18]

It was just before eight that night when nearly three dozen elegant
gentlemen left the gloomy chill behind and entered Sherry's gilded lobby.
They walked past Ionic columns framing the entrance to the oak-paneled
restaurant, disappearing behind the lush greenery of a forest of potted
palms that screened the Otis elevators. Within a minute they had been
conveyed to the third floor, arriving at a party whose exotic, lavish indulgence would carry the evening into Gilded Age legend.[19]

The festivities had been the idea of wealthy industrial magnate Cornelius
K. G. Billings. The forty-one-year-old Billings had recently retired as president of Peoples' Gas, Light, and Coke, a Chicago company established by
his father, and moved his wife and children to New York City, where, like
so many others before him, he hoped to use his millions to enter society; in
a city census, Billings gave his occupation as "capitalist at large," but his
real interests lay elsewhere.[20] Billings was enamored of all things equestrian,
with a passion for fast trotters, racehorses, and carriage driving, pursuits
that quickly won him acceptance among New York society.

Wanting to establish a fine equestrian facility, Billings purchased a
25-acre tract of land in Washington Heights, on the site of the old Fort
Tryon from the Revolutionary War. It was, at some 250 feet above the
banks of the Hudson, not only the highest plot of land in Manhattan,
but also conveniently close to the Harlem Speedway. This was one of
the city's most fashionable venues for riding and driving, kept exclusively private although maintained at the expense of the taxpayers.

In 1901 Billings commissioned architect Guy Lowell to design an immense riding complex here, replete with French Renaissance–inspired gate lodges and observation towers with commanding views over the city and the river. At the heart of the estate was a vast and elaborate stable, a 25,000-square-foot building built at a cost of some $200,000 ($4.6 million in 2008 figures). Two storeys in height, 250 feet long, and adorned with towers and cupolas, it boasted room for 22 carriages and 33 horses, along with a blacksmith's shop, a forge, a trophy room, and accommodations for several dozen employees.[21] It was a fitting monument for the man whose love of horses quickly propelled him to the presidency of the New York Riding Club.

Billings decided to celebrate its completion with an inaugural party, inviting thirty-five members of the club to his lavish stable for a dinner on the evening of March 28, 1903. Somehow, word of the festivities leaked out; in Gilded Age New York, society parties were regular events, but no one had ever given a celebratory dinner in honor of their stables. The whiff of sybaritic extravagance sent reporters into a frenzy, and the press besieged Billings, staking out the entrances to his Washington Heights complex for several days in an effort to uncover any details. The hint of a press-driven scandal drove Billings to despair. The day before the planned dinner, Louis Sherry, who had been scheduled to cater the affair, suggested that the event be moved from the stables to his own hotel to avoid any unwelcome publicity; Billings agreed, and quietly notified his guests of the change. Thus, on that cold, windy March Saturday night, as a dozen reporters huddled around the entrance gates to the Washington Heights complex, awaiting the expected guests, the invitees instead quietly slipped into Sherry's.

To compensate for the missing splendors of the new stable, Billings and Sherry had conceived a novel and bizarre replacement. Entering the ballroom, guests found before them a carefully contrived pastoral scene, with a carpet of green turf laid over the parquet floor; live birds flew through the air from the branches of a forest of potted trees and palms; while the ceiling had been decorated as a night sky, complete with a shining moon and artificial twinkling stars. At the center of the room, grouped around a split-rail fence and hitching post flanking a manger

Photograph of the Horseback Dinner given by Cornelius K. G. Billings.

filled with hay, stood a circle of horses, one for each guest. Each horse had been shod with special rubber shoes for its journey in the freight elevator up to the ballroom and equipped with a special tray attached to its saddle, with champagne-filled ice buckets tucked into saddlebags. The guests, some in formal evening dress of white tie and tails, and some in the uniforms of the New York Riding Club, mounted their steeds, and waiters, dressed as grooms in scarlet coats and white breeches, served the dinner on trays fitted to the saddles to the stationary riders, who sipped champagne from long rubber tubes attached to the saddlebags. The horses also dined, munching on buckets of oats held by grooms from Billings's stable as the guests enjoyed a vaudeville show.[22]

The sheer novelty of the event—and novelty was, in the Gilded Age, prized above all other things—won Billings accolades from his privileged friends. The city's papers, however, took another view. Irritated at having been outwitted, they quickly transformed the event into an extravagant folly, said to have cost some $50,000 ($1,115,000 in 2008 figures). Although the *New York Times* noted that the "horses were well-schooled, having been used in the riding academy, and showed no nervousness," others were not quite so temperate in their coverage.[23] Soon New York City was awash with stories that by the end of the evening, the smell in the ballroom—despite the best efforts of the groom-waiters—had been atrocious.[24] Worse still, Billings had engaged society photographer Joseph Byron to record the event for posterity, and photographs of the formally dressed, stiff-looking guests astride their mounts at the center of this bit of phantasmagoria were soon published, further fueling the fires of outrage. To an increasingly cynical and suspicious public, Billings's Horseback Dinner, as history recorded the event, seemed to offer mute evidence of society's moral decline as it plunged headlong into a ceaseless round of self-indulgent parties that, in the end, helped destroy the Gilded Age.

1

MRS. ASTOR HOLDS COURT

FOR NEARLY FOUR DECADES, New York was dominated by a stately, proud woman who used her family's name and background and her husband's millions to establish Gilded Age society. It was one of the ironies that Caroline Astor, who so controlled this society and excluded those families whom she considered uncouth parvenus, relied on money of questionable antecedents to establish herself as its arbiter. For the fortunes of the Astor family were less than a hundred years old and had come through not only hard work but also exploitation and greed.

In 1784, German-born John Jacob Astor, a twenty-one-year-old butcher's son who read with difficulty, wrote illegibly, and never lost his heavy Teutonic accent, arrived in America and, after a short apprenticeship, began trading alcohol, gunpowder, arms, and blankets with the Indian tribes of New England and Canada for expensive furs that he quickly sold at immense profits. His American Fur Company, established a few years later after hard-fought battles, negotiations, and legal challenges, not only helped finance expeditions west to the Pacific Ocean but also opened up rich new markets to exploit. Armed with a personal fortune of $250,000, Astor used his wealth to embark on the China trade, exporting furs and arms and importing spices, tea, silks, and porcelain.[1]

Astor fell into real estate by accident, purchasing in 1802 the remaining lease of a vast tract of land on Manhattan Island. Realizing that New York City was destined to expand, he followed this first purchase with many others, gradually spreading his ownership of land across the burgeoning metropolis. As social historian Jerry Patterson noted, "no family has ever owned so much of Manhattan" as did the Astors.[2] Among his possessions were the corner of Fifth Avenue and Fifty-sixth Street; a number of lots on Wall Street and on Pine Street; the corner of Broadway and Exchange Place; Madison Avenue from Thirty-fourth to Thirty-sixth streets; Fifth Avenue from Thirty-third to Thirty-fourth streets; and a large section of Greenwich Village, in addition to entire city blocks on the Upper West Side, including the area that later became Times Square.[3] Astor was both cagey and disingenuous in his deals; most of his tenants held leases of twenty-one years and developed and improved their property only to have it revert, at greater value, to its owner.[4]

Astor was certainly the city's wealthiest citizen, although his money did little to ease his rough edges; "He dined here last night," one contemporary wrote disapprovingly, "and ate his ice cream and peas with a knife."[5] On another occasion, Astor was said to have wiped his dirty hands on the gown of a horrified dinner partner. "The social graces eluded him forever," noted John D. Gates.[6] Although his enormous wealth helped him win grudging acceptance among a few of New York City's more tolerant elite, Astor always remained something of a social pariah in established circles. When he died in 1848, it was estimated that his fortune had reached $20 million ($600 million in 2008), making him the richest man in the country.[7]

Astor and his wife had three sons; a childhood fall left John Jacob Astor II, the eldest, mentally unfit, and it was William Backhouse Astor, the second son, who inherited his father's empire.[8] William was indeed his father's son when it came to enlarging the family's holdings, earning the epithet of "the landlord of New York."[9] His acquisition of land in New York often relied on questionable business deals with the corrupt city government under the infamous William "Boss" Tweed, and the same skewed, short-term leases employed by his father. Unfortunately for Astor's reputation, unscrupulous landlords snapped up rents for much of his property and erected squalid tenements offering some of the most oppressive and dangerous housing in the city. As waves of immigrants continued to pour into New York in the nineteenth century, many—with no financial resources—found themselves lodged in one of these shabby apartments, sharing living space with several other families in conditions that were diseased and infested with rats and lice and that lacked even the most basic sanitation.[10] These tenements, complained one clergyman, "are a standing reproach against our rich men who ought, for the sake of humanity, to be using their surplus funds in erecting cheap and comfortable residences for the poor."[11]

"For twenty years," noted one historian, "the Astors stood in the way of tenement reform and they also opposed municipal plans for rapid development of the still green acres in the northern part of Manhattan. The more congested the lower portion of the island, the greater the demand for tenements and the better the returns for them."[12] Astor merely owned the land, not the buildings and, at least in his own mind, was satisfied that he bore no responsibility for the plight of his tenants. It was, to be sure, an ethically challenged view, but one Astor apparently fully embraced. He could have imposed strict guidelines on the tenements, but he elected to simply look the other way, firmly convinced that it was better for the poor to be housed in deplorable conditions than to be living on the streets; if such reasoning also resulted in a hefty profit for his business investments, so much the better.[13]

The irony was that unlike his father, William affected the air of a rather quiet, pious man. He was not as parsimonious and crafty as his father, and gave away far more of his personal fortune to charities. He also frequently forgave the debts of his tenants and even allowed late payments—something his father would never have permitted.[14] One contemporary reported that he "used no tobacco and little wine, though when in health . . . he gave quite pleasant dinners. He seldom was out late, did not attend theaters, did not get excited nor indulge in profane adjectives, sported not with dogs and guns, never kept a fast horse, never gambled. His whole life was simple and orderly."[15]

Simple and orderly though his private life may have been, William's reign marked not only a steady rise in the Astor riches but also an increase in their social fortunes. The latter was due in no small part to William's marriage to Margaret Armstrong, a member of the prestigious Livingston family of the Hudson River Valley.[16] At a time when proper New York society was still a caste dominated by the old Knickerbocker elite, Astor's union allowed his children entrée to this insular universe, and his money, coupled with their Livingston descent, opened doors that would otherwise have remain firmly closed to their ambitions.

On his death in 1875, William left an estate rumored to be some $100 million ($2 billion in 2008), largely divided between two of his sons, John Jacob Astor III and William Backhouse Astor II.[17] John Jacob Astor III, born in 1822, was the more capable of the siblings, though he cared little for business. Determined to shake off the less than flattering reputation of his grandfather and embrace the proud heritage of his mother, John Jacob Astor III was the first member of the family to affect a truly aristocratic air. Together with his wife, Charlotte Augusta Gibbes of Charleston, he cemented the Astor family's air of social respectability. He dressed impeccably, was well-read, collected paintings from Europe, and possessed perhaps the city's finest wine cellar.[18]

The couple assumed what they took to be their proper place in New York's Knickerbocker society, hosting elaborate dinners and dances at their house in the city and at Beaulieu, their estate in Newport; yet, as Derek Wilson has noted, they "were perhaps too genuinely European to associate themselves totally with the shallow world of gossip and gaiety."[19] In particular, Charlotte found the social game far too frivolous for her liking. She took a more philanthropic approach to her position, funding hospitals, societies for the aid of impoverished children, and, unfashionably, relief agencies dedicated to helping the city's prostitutes. On February 22, 1890, John Jacob Astor III died of a heart attack in the arms of his only son, William Waldorf Astor. "Thousands and thousands of God's poor and unfortunate," eulogized the *New York Times,* "have had their wretched lives brightened because he lived."[20]

It was John Jacob Astor III's brother William, born on July 12, 1830, who, through his propitious marriage, was destined to leave the largest mark on society. William Backhouse Astor II was a generally genial man. After graduating from Columbia College, he embarked on a tour of

Europe and the Holy Land, but on his return he found that his junior role left him with little real responsibility in the family business.[21] This was just as well, as John Jacob III and William Backhouse II never got along. As the designated heir, John Jacob had been doted upon and favored by their father, a fact that grated on William. William disliked his brother's superior manner and his self-anointed position as a social leader, because William himself largely condemned such pursuits as frivolous.[22]

Tall and bewhiskered, with dark eyes and a seemingly permanent scowl, William was said to possess a natural and easy charm that his brother lacked, and he was—at least in his youth—possessed of better manners and temperament.[23] Left with little opportunity to test or employ his talents in the business world, he focused instead on pleasure. William purchased a large yacht, *Ambassadress,* on which he sailed with a disreputable coterie of friends, and an estate, Ferncliff, at Rhinebeck on the Hudson River, where he could indulge in hunting, shooting, and the breeding of stock and of prized racehorses. Here, not coincidentally, away from the eyes of the public, he could also indulge an increasing love of alcohol and the company of beautiful young women culled from New York City's demimonde.[24]

In 1853, William met twenty-three-year-old Caroline Webster Schermerhorn, daughter of New York realtor Abraham Schermerhorn.

William Backhouse Astor II, about 1880.

The Schermerhorns were an old Knickerbocker family and claimed descent from the Dutch patroons; they also were relatives of the prestigious Van Cortland, Beekman, and Van Buren families, proud of their lineage and respectful of tradition.[25] With some $15 million ($450 million in 2008), the Schermerhorn family was not as wealthy as the Astors but were among the richest in New York and, more important, possessed an impeccable pedigree.[26]

Born September 22, 1830, Caroline—called Lina in her family—had been the youngest of eight children; she was favored and doted upon and became terribly spoiled; she was also quite precocious. Educated by nannies and governesses, she frequently traveled to Europe as a child, absorbing its culture and carefully ordered aristocratic world of power and privilege. When she reached a suitable age, her secondary education was conducted at an elite school where she learned languages, dancing, etiquette, and deportment—all the skills deemed necessary to attract a suitable husband.[27] Yet she also had a taste for adventure and a determination to enjoy herself: a granddaughter later recalled that once Caroline

Caroline Schermerhorn Astor, about 1880.

had bravely infiltrated the exclusively male bastion of a New York City boxing match and had quite enjoyed herself during the bloody melee.[28]

Somewhat short and inclined to stoutness even as a young woman, with an almost hard face, thick lips, and a slightly upturned nose, Caroline was a far cry from William's usual paramours. Dark, luxuriant hair, usually worn in a cascade when she was younger, framed small, light gray eyes that seemed to be constantly on the move in an attempt to take in everything around her.[29] If she was not quite beautiful, she nonetheless possessed an undeniable vibrancy, an irresistible charm and delight in life that, coupled with a hint of steely determination, made Caroline attractive to many New York gentlemen.

It is difficult to say precisely what drew William Backhouse and Caroline together and led to their ultimate marriage. It has been suggested that William's mother was behind the match; as a woman who shared Margaret Armstrong's Knickerbocker heritage, Caroline was a socially prestigious consort whose inclusion in the Astor family would certainly add to its luster in the exclusive firmament of the city's elite.[30] Author Virginia Cowles suggested that Caroline consented to the union simply for the financial advantage it brought.[31] Yet Caroline had her own fortune, and indeed inherited a considerable amount of money on her father's death. It is more likely that the couple simply followed expectation and family desire in consenting to the eventual marriage. William and Caroline shared a conservative background of privilege and unquestioned entitlement, bolstered by their families' respective fortunes, and such considerations formed the usual foundation of many a society union. If this was no grand romance, it did offer each partner undeniable benefits. For William Backhouse, marriage to Caroline Schermerhorn was yet another triumph on the social ladder, while she undoubtedly recognized the benefits of joining America's wealthiest family and putting her husband's money to dazzling use in New York City. Their engagement, on June 13, 1853, was followed three months later with a fashionable wedding at New York City's Grace Church.

As a descendant of the proud Knickerbockers, Caroline already enjoyed the benefits of entrée into the city's elite, yet she was keenly aware that despite her mother-in-law's ancestry, the Astor name did not possess the social cachet warranted by their immense fortune. Determined to correct this, she launched upon a careful program designed to raise them to the heights of respectability, a campaign that took on new meaning with the births of the couple's five children: Emily, born in 1854, Helen, born in 1855, Charlotte Augusta, born in 1858, Caroline (known as Carrie), born in 1861, and John Jacob Astor IV, born in 1864. Ambitious for their futures, she convinced William to drop the use of "Backhouse" in his name, believing—probably correctly—that it reminded people too much of his father's questionable real estate dealings.[32] William complied, and he opened the Astor coffers to his wife to do with as she saw fit, but this was as far as he was willing to go.[33] By the birth of the couple's only son, whatever spark may once have existed between Caroline and William had all but vanished, and he deemed her company less than compelling. "The relationship of husband and wife became a standoff," noted Lucy Kavaler: "as he pushed her out of his life, she, in turn, pushed him out of the lives of their children, allowing him to assert himself only during crises, engagements, and weddings, when a father was essential."[34] By the beginning of the 1870s, the Astors led virtually separate lives, intersecting only occasionally at parties and family gatherings; neither appeared to either notice or mind the absence of the other from their carefully constructed worlds.[35]

While Caroline threw herself into the whirl of New York society, William preferred to seclude himself at his country estate. As far as Caroline was concerned, this was just as well, for her husband, when present at a social function, tended to drink "everything in sight," as one gossip put it.[36] One of his grandchildren later recalled him as a "very trying and a disagreeable man" who busied himself in "affairs with second-rate women." When she gave dinners and balls, Caroline often resorted to drastic measures to keep him at bay, instructing her husband's friends to detain him late at his club so he would not interrupt the proceedings with inappropriate remarks and questionable behavior.[37]

All of New York society whispered of his scandalous cruises. When he sold his yacht *Ambassadress* and replaced her with the larger *Nourmahal* (meaning "Light of the Harem," a rather unsubtle declaration of intent), it was, noted Derek Wilson, "symptomatic of William's rejection of the hollow pieties of polite society."[38] That he filled his yacht with prostitutes was well known, but Caroline refused to become the subject of pity and affected an air of complete and benevolent ignorance. "She had so cultivated the art of never looking at things she did not want to see, never listening to words she did not wish to hear, that it had become second nature with her," recalled one lady. If Caroline ever objected to her husband's extramarital activities, she never let on. "Dear William is so good to me," she would comment. "I have been so fortunate in my marriage."[39]

When queried about William's absence, Caroline would airily say, "Oh, he is having a delightful cruise. The sea air is so good for him. It is a great pity I am such a bad sailor, for I should so much enjoy accompanying him. As it is, I have never even set foot on the yacht; dreadful confession for a wife, is it not?"[40] It was, one of her granddaughters noted, a convenient lie: "She used to chaperone Margaret Langdon in Newport when she went out sailing in windy weather with nautical admirers, and grandmother was the only chaperone intrepid enough to go. She was never seasick."[41]

This enigmatic quality was one of the hallmarks of Caroline's life. The lady who evinced an absolutely correct attitude in all things yet enjoyed her stolen moments at a distinctly common boxing match, who spun a tissue of lies to avoid her husband's company yet happily took to the choppy seas, created about her an inscrutable aura of power mingled with benevolent indulgence. Thus, recalled Elizabeth Drexel Lehr, Caroline was "always dignified, always reserved, a little aloof. She gave friendship but never intimacy. She never confided. No one ever knew what thoughts passed behind the calm repose of her face."[42] At the same time, she was "naturally sincere and gracious and her friendship once given was not lightly withdrawn."[43] While holding fast to many of the rigid conventions of the day, she could also on occasion be surprisingly enlightened in her views. Once, when a friend fell in love with a Jewish man, she sought Mrs. Astor's advice on what to do—and this at a time when hotels in America's fashionable resorts sported signs reading "No Jews or Dogs Admitted."[44] Caroline urged her friend to marry, saying, "I for one will invite you both to my parties, and I think everyone else will do the same."[45]

For the first nineteen years of her married life, Caroline evinced no apparent overarching ambitions and seemed content to confine her interests to her children and to an occasional party or ball. This changed, however, in 1872, when her mother-in-law, Margaret, died; her position as social matriarch of the family should, by rights, have gone to John Jacob's wife, Charlotte, but the latter disliked what she termed frivolous pursuits and declined to assume the role. Caroline, however, was more than willing to accept the challenge. Under her influence, the Astors were to rise to the height of Gilded Age society. As one lady noted, the family "came to be accepted by the patrician social set of their day because of the women of their family."[46]

It was not mere want of social power and personal recognition that drove Caroline in her quest. At eighteen, her daughter Emily was ready to make her debut in society, with Helen just a year behind, and Caroline believed their ancestry coupled with the Astor money demanded a suitable stage. For the first time, Caroline faced the implications of a New York society left adrift in the aftermath of the Civil War. The old, carefully ordered world of the Knickerbockers had been thrown into disarray, their influence declining under the continuous onslaught of newly wealthy industrialists, profiteers, merchants, and speculators who poured into the city. Armed with considerable fortunes, they had begun their assault on the establishment, creating chaos of that which had once been taken as unalterable. In these years, money was power: it eroded the old social barriers, bought influence, even occasionally purchased entrée into the very heart of a system that, confused and uncertain of where to look for guidance, appeared to be crumbling into oblivion. Caroline realized that in a country without a court or aristocracy, the wealthy elite helped shape fashion and mold taste, defining in the absence of a central, titled authority what was acceptable and what was not. What post–Civil War New York needed was such a figure, someone who could serve as ultimate arbiter of distinguished society.

Caroline Astor had no desire to witness the passing of the old order, yet she was keenly aware that the status quo could not be maintained against such a persistent threat. All around her she saw the uncertainty, the need for a firm and guiding hand capable of imposing order to fill the social vacuum. Other leaders of society were too old, too unimaginative, too determined to either close ranks and completely exclude these new forces or too willing to indulge them. Armed with supreme self-confidence, Caroline determined that she would provide society with the leadership it lacked, to create, as one turn-of-the-century commentator wrote, "an original etiquette" that defined her new vision for an illustrious American elite.[47] She would preserve the traditions of her aristocratic background, but she also would bow to the inevitable changes, shining a light on a new path forward over which she could boldly lead the remnants of the Knickerbockers into the future. By using her husband's money and her own proud heritage, she would craft a new social order in which his riches and her status would dominate the city's elite into the twentieth century.

In her quest to create this new society, Caroline turned to Ward McAllister. Born in 1827, Samuel Ward McAllister was the scion of a wealthy Savannah family but had abandoned the family's traditional legal professions to strike out on the social stage.[48] After he married Sarah Gibbons, daughter of a Georgia millionaire, McAllister spent several years in Europe, carefully absorbing the heritage and culture of the countries he

Ward McAllister, Caroline Astor's social arbiter, in about 1890.

visited.[49] Sarah cared little for society and was content to let her husband use her money to make a name for himself. McAllister immersed himself in the rituals of European courts, studied architecture, read the most fashionable newspapers and periodicals, and paid attention to how society dressed, how and what it ate and drank, and where it went on holiday. "His cult of snobbishness was so ardent, so sincere," recalled Elizabeth Drexel Lehr, "that it acquired dignity; it became almost a religion. No devout parish priest ever visited his flock with more loyal devotion to duty than did Ward McAllister."[50]

A "paunchy, pompous" man with a bushy imperial on his chin and a decidedly odd wardrobe, McAllister—termed "the most complete dandy in America" by Elizabeth Drexel Lehr—was eventually propelled to the apex of society.[51] The very proper Maud Howe Elliott was among the minority in calling him "a man of social gift and charm who did much to preserve the more elegant traditions of an earlier day."[52] Most simply recognized him for what he was: an unapologetic snob.

McAllister was not a complete outsider in New York City: his cousin Samuel Ward had married William Backhouse II's sister Emily, and thus Ward was able to infiltrate the same circles as Caroline Astor. In her, McAllister later wrote, "I at once recognized her ability and felt that she would become society's leader, and that she was admirably qualified for the position. It was not long before circumstances forced her to assume the leadership, which she did, and which she has held with marked ability ever since, having all the qualities necessary. Coming herself from an old colonial family she had a good appreciation of the value of ancestry; always keeping it near her and bringing it in all social matters, but also understanding the importance and power of the new element: recognizing it and fairly and generously awarding it a prominent place."[53]

McAllister became an indispensable broker in Caroline's rise to power, acting not only as adviser but also as a kind of unofficial chamberlain to her burgeoning court. "She recognized his usefulness," noted one commentator, "and he was clever enough to appreciate her good qualities and ability, and always deferred to her judgment."[54] McAllister urged her to surround herself with the trappings of European aristocratic privilege: soon her servants were bedecked in dark blue liveries with gold

piping, adapted from those worn in Queen Victoria's household; paintings by the most fashionable Parisian artists soon graced the walls of her
ballroom; she hired a French chef to prepare the most elaborate dinners
the city had ever seen, served on the finest French and German china
and gold plate; and the most prominent visiting singers and pianists
from London and Berlin graced her drawing room to enchant her
guests.[55] Through these efforts, and under McAllister's constant tutelage,
Caroline—whom McAllister dubbed his "mystic rose"—assured not
only her acceptance among the city's most influential grandes dames but
also dominance over them.[56]

The new society conceived by Caroline and McAllister was a curious
amalgam of old and new. McAllister divided society between those he
labeled "Nobs" and "Swells." "Nobs" were possessed of old money and
distinguished lineage, while "Swells" were the Gilded Age's nouveaux
riches who were aggressively climbing socially. The integration of these two
elements called for tact and prescience. While McAllister advised that "it
is well to be in with the Nobs, who are born to their position," he also
warned that it was unwise to cling too ferociously to their past glories.
"If you see a fossil of a man," he wrote, "shabbily dressed, relying solely
on his pedigree, dating back to time immemorial, who has the aspirations
of a duke and the fortunes of a footman, do not cut him; it is better to
cross the street and avoid meeting him." In this way, associations with
remnants of the old Knickerbocker elite unlikely to offer social benefits
could be avoided. At the same time, he acknowledged that "the support
of the Swells is more advantageous, for Society is sustained and carried
on by the Swells, the Nobs looking quietly on and accepting the position,
feeling they are there by divine right."[57]

This sometimes uneasy coalition was key to the fulfillment of Caroline's
social aspirations. Ironically, in view of her husband's background,
Caroline sought to rigidly confine dominant membership to those of
respectable lineage and old money. Together with McAllister, she decreed
that those seeking acceptance into society must be separated by at least
three generations from the individual who had first made the family
fortune—a convenient determination for the wife of the great-grandson
of the first John Jacob Astor.[58] They also concluded that a minimum

fortune of $1 million in cash (approximately $20 million in 2008) was necessary; indeed, McAllister once declared, "A fortune of a million is only
respectable poverty."[59] Yet they also allowed for the inclusion of a number of McAllister's "Swells." It was impossible to keep their ever-increasing numbers at bay, and the addition of money—always carefully vetted
and determinedly respectful of tradition—not only added luster to this
burgeoning elite but also recognized the inevitable. By combining the
disparate factions under a unified code of acceptable behavior and standards, Caroline could eliminate any potential rivals to her own set and
thus maintain her hold on power. As a result, she quickly became the self-
appointed arbiter of social acceptance: if one met her requirements, one
was in; if not, one was condemned to social death.

Yet beyond the merely social functions that drove this new ruling elite
lay deeper ideas. Mrs. Winthrop Chanler later declared that members of
Caroline's milieu "would have fled in a body from a poet, a painter, a
musician or a clever Frenchman."[60] Intellect may not have figured largely
in their gatherings, but Caroline also envisioned her society as an evocation of finer instincts and cultural promotion, designed to embrace the
aristocratic idea of noblesse oblige, that with great money and privilege
came great responsibility. As America developed its industry and power,
it began to assume its place on the world stage, yet an overwhelming
sense of inferiority wounded the collective national pride. Europeans
looked down on the United States as a country without tradition, filled
with admirable ambition but lacking both manners and artistic heritage.[61] Establishing a social order to rival that of the Old World offered
one direct challenge to such deeply held beliefs, but there was no denying that the country was largely bereft of the great architectural monuments, centuries of painting and sculpture, and munificent patronage
that had endowed Europe with such cultural treasures. Her new society
could seize upon the proud example of Renaissance princes and enrich
their country. Elegant dinners and splendid balls provided one expression of this desire, enacted for the elect but often viewed as adornments
for the masses, who could share in their aesthetic triumph through
accounts in the press and thus be themselves inspired to more cultivated
heights. Exceptional clothing and exquisite jewelry testified to refined

tastes; fine horses and fast yachts indicated an appreciation of the importance of more genteel pursuits. Houses, too, offered not only personal
expression but also public beautification, lining avenues and raising the
standard of American life. Private collections of important paintings and
sculptures, often opened for view to the curious or bequeathed to museums, gave the United States an artistic legacy, albeit one often imported
from Europe. One social commentator encapsulated these ideals perfectly, writing, "The primary business of society is to bring together the
various elements of which it is made up—its strongest motive should be
to lighten up the momentous business of life by an easy and friendly
intercourse and interchange of ideas."[62] While not everyone admitted to
Caroline's circle fulfilled such aspirations, the idea of society, its way of
life, and its attendant accoutrements as bastions of culture infused the
first half of the Gilded Age, leaving an inheritance that was to far outlast
its brief tenure.

It was a staggering gamble, such direct challenges to the old order, but
Caroline and McAllister maintained the delicate balance between ostentation and propriety in a way that eventually won approval. Together they
established the Patriarch Balls, headed by a cadre of twenty-five gentlemen
from a mixture of old Knickerbocker families and the most respectable elements of newer society, including the Schermerhorns and Van Rensselaers
at one end of the spectrum and the two Astor brothers at the other. "We
resolved," wrote McAllister, "to band together the respectable element of
the city and by this union make such strength that no individual could withstand us."[63]

These twenty-five patriarchs were charged with drawing into their circle
the most socially prominent members of New York society for dances at
Dodsworth's Dancing Academy and, later, Delmonico's Restaurant. "The
whole secret of the success of these Patriarch Balls," McAllister recalled,
"lay in making them select; in making them the most brilliant balls of each
winter; in making it extremely difficult to obtain an invitation, and to make
such invitations of great value; to make them the stepping-stone to the best
New York society."[64] For young scions and eligible daughters making their
debuts, McAllister devised the Family Circle Dancing Classes, known as
the Junior Patriarchs.

This society encompassed the most exclusive and fashionable elements of New York, who received invitations to dance in Caroline's lavish ballroom. Large as the room was, however, it could—according to legend—accommodate only four hundred guests. This, according to McAllister, was an ideal number: "There are only about 400 people in fashionable New York society," he said. "If you go outside the number you strike people who either are not at ease in a ballroom, or else make other people not at ease."[65] Thus was born the famous four hundred, an elite group that, for aspiring social climbers, represented the pinnacle of acceptance. In fact, the list encompassed just over three hundred individuals, not four hundred, but the point was made.

Some of the old Knickerbocker elite, including prominent members of the Roosevelt, Rutherfurd, Fish, and Stuyvesant families, considered the four hundred a vulgar creation, teeming with thoroughly unsuitable people who would never have been admitted to their exclusive brownstones.[66] Caroline had established a bastardized version of society; McAllister's insistence that a certain number of wealthy social climbers—arrivistes—be included not only added an aura of money but also let others know that their potential acceptance, too, was a goal for which to strive.[67] This mingling of the old families with the new, of established fortunes with those of the nouveaux riches, and of traditional ideals with European influences set the four hundred apart, marking it as an intrinsically artificial American society, although one that quickly eclipsed the last remaining vestiges of the proper Knickerbockers.

It was Caroline's accomplishment, remembered Lloyd Morris, that she "transformed society into a secular religion."[68] By the turn of the century, commented the *New York Times,* her position was such that they could aptly describe her as "a landmark of New York."[69] She had come to symbolize the best elements in America, showing society the ideal through her determined leadership. Thus McAllister could write without any hint of irony that Caroline Astor "was, in every sense, society's queen. She had the power that all women should strive to obtain, the power of attaching men to her, and keeping them attached; calling forth a loyalty of devotion such as one imagines one yields to a sovereign, whose subjects are only too happy to be subjects."[70]

2

THE VAINGLORIOUS
VANDERBILTS

THE VANDERBILTS, noted one social historian, are "the nearest thing to a royal family that has ever appeared on the American scene."[1] The roots of this hold on the public imagination began in the nineteenth century, with the unlikely and distinctly unsympathetic founder of the dynasty, Cornelius Vanderbilt. Born in 1794, he was a scion of a family of Dutch farmers named Aertson from the village of De Bilt in the Netherlands who had settled on Staten Island 150 years earlier. Eventually they dropped their surname in favor of the more descriptive Van der Bilt, indicating their Dutch origin, and in time this became Vanderbilt.[2] Cornelius Vanderbilt was the fourth of nine children in a family of modest means; at age eleven he abandoned his rather unsuccessful attempts at formal education to work for his father, carrying passengers and mail along the Hudson.[3]

When he was sixteen, Cornelius Vanderbilt borrowed $100 from his mother to purchase a boat and embarked on his own business, ferrying passengers across the Hudson and around New York Harbor.[4] One boat grew into a small but successful fleet as the city's expansion necessitated more frequent transportation options. It was all an unknown adventure, a gamble that appealed to the visionary young man who loved a challenge. Vanderbilt did well, and in 1818 he sold his holdings at a handsome profit and went to work as a captain for Thomas Gibbons, proprietor of the struggling Union Line. At the time, Gibbons was attempting to counter Robert Fulton's steamship monopoly, and young Vanderbilt eagerly embraced the fight. As Cornelius had hoped, he soon transformed the line into a successful operation by offering cheap rates, and both he and Gibbons grew wealthy as the business expanded, although often at the expense of legal challenges and even raids by law enforcement officers intent on enforcing Fulton's monopoly before it was finally overturned in 1824.[5]

In 1829, armed with a considerable fortune, Vanderbilt left Gibbons's employ and again embarked on his own steamboat business. Cagey and cunning rather than intelligent, with a shrewd business sense and an unquestioning belief in his own judgment, Cornelius managed to build this initial enterprise into the proud and dominant Dispatch Line, running boats on the Hudson, along Long Island Sound, and to Boston. Even as his holdings increased to more than a hundred vessels and brought him his first million dollars, Vanderbilt never lost his love of navigation and could often be found at the helm of one of his ships, earning him the moniker of "Commodore," which he proudly bore for the rest of his life.[6]

Vanderbilt took advantage of the California gold rush to launch a passenger steamship service to the West Coast that managed to undercut his competitors' prices and times.[7] Feeling secure, the commodore left for Europe, only to find that the banking firm of Garrison, Morgan, Ralston, and Fretz, to whom he had entrusted the business, had secretly bought up enough stock in his absence to gain control. When he learned of this, he dispatched an angry, open letter: "Gentlemen: You have undertaken to cheat me. I won't sue you because the law is too slow. I'll ruin you."[8] Sure enough, Vanderbilt managed to regain control of the stock, and he used the proceeds to enter the Atlantic passenger trade for a time, eventually selling his holdings to a competitor for $3 million ($120 million in 2008 figures). Along the way, the history of Vanderbilt's business dealings was paved with scandals, tales of bribes, and the questionable contracts at which he excelled.

With ships behind him, Vanderbilt turned to railroads, purchasing a number of smaller, competing spurs, manipulating stock, and coalescing his gains into a powerful monopoly. His first acquisition, in 1863, was the New York & Harlem Railroad, followed by the Hudson River Railroad in 1864 and the New York Central in 1867, eventually joining them to form the New York Central and Hudson River Railroad. In 1871, having consolidated his railroads, Vanderbilt provided them with a new hub, which quickly became a hive of activity and trade: the massive Grand Central Depot, a brick and sandstone terminal on Forty-second Street topped with an enormous mansard roof.

Not all of Vanderbilt's endeavors went quite so smoothly. He suffered immense losses in a battle with infamous robber baron Jay Gould and speculators Daniel Drew and Jim Fisk over Vanderbilt's attempts to gain control of the Erie Railroad. The trio manipulated the stock prices and flooded the market with hundreds of thousands of dollars of fraudulent shares that cost the commodore millions of dollars. Vowing revenge, Vanderbilt attempted to coerce his friends in the New York State government and in its court system to pursue Gould and his coterie of disreputable friends. At a time of rampant corruption, Gould simply paid off legislators and judges to sympathize with his point of view. This kind of financial skulduggery continued between the warring parties, the commodore and Jay Gould each attempting to bribe their way to satisfaction, before the two tycoons reached an uneasy truce that left Vanderbilt irritated and several million dollars poorer, and Gould barely triumphant but armed with an immense personal fortune.[9] Gould, it was said, was the only man the equally ruthless Commodore Vanderbilt feared.[10]

In 1813, at age nineteen, Vanderbilt had married his first cousin Sophia Johnson. Of the thirteen children born to the couple, nine—much to the commodore's disappointment—were girls, while one of the sons died at an early age. George, the commodore's favorite son, proudly graduated from West Point, only to die of malaria during the Civil War, while another, Cornelius Jeremiah, suffered from epilepsy and, deemed mentally unstable, was occasionally locked away in an asylum by his intolerant father.[11] The commodore was scarcely an example of moral rectitude and marital fidelity, and his eldest son, William Henry, was charged with hiring beautiful young maids who would be amenable to his father's advances.[12]

The commodore, declared one acquaintance, ruled his "home, wife, and children with a rod of steel and brooked no disobedience or even contradiction. He manifested scant attention for his children, seldom sought their love or confidence, and treated them very nearly like any-body else's."[13] By 1845, the tall, bewhiskered Vanderbilt and his family had moved into a large house at 10 Washington Square in New York City. He disliked any challenge, and when he found his wife's moods objectionable, he had her locked away in an insane asylum for two years.[14] The commodore both enthralled and repulsed the very society that his descendants were eventually to rule. Although he was an astute businessman, Cornelius was scarcely a proper gentleman. His education had been spotty at best, and he sprinkled his talk with a steady stream of foul invectives: one social historian called him "perhaps the greatest mas-ter of swearing in his generation."[15] With complete disregard of more genteel sensibilities, he brazenly spat tobacco juice onto the floor—no

Commodore Cornelius Vanderbilt, painted by Flagg, 1879.

matter where he might be.[16] He was also renowned for his parsimony. To avoid sharing his favorite cigars, he carried them concealed in his coat, explaining, "When I take one cigar out of my pocket, my friends don't know whether there are any left."[17]

In August 1868, the commodore's wife, Sophia, died, and he soon fell in with a group of dubious Spiritualists who, his family suspected, were after his extensive fortune.[18] This potentially disastrous situation ended a year later when, in August 1869, the seventy-five-year-old Vanderbilt abruptly married a distant cousin from Alabama, the unusually named Frank Armstrong Crawford, a woman who was forty-three years his junior. It was under her influence that the usually parsimonious Commodore gave $1 million (approximately $20 million in 2008 figures) to establish Vanderbilt University in Nashville.[19]

In 1876 Vanderbilt fell ill with cancer, and crowds of reporters and the curious gathered outside his house, awaiting the end.[20] But the commodore was determined to cheat them of so easy a reward and not only temporarily recovered but also managed to hold on for several months. When he finally died, on January 4, 1877, he was widely acknowledged as the country's wealthiest man, leaving a fortune estimated at just over $100 million (just over $2 billion in 2008 figures), an amount that exceeded the ready cash reserves of the government of the United States.[21]

"Any fool can make a fortune," the commodore had warned his son William Henry before his death. "It takes a man of brains to hold on to it after it is made."[22] To ensure that the Vanderbilt fortune remained intact, Cornelius left only minor bequests to his widow and to most of his children, with a legacy of some $95 million ($1.9 billion in 2008 figures) to William Henry in the hope that he, too, would preserve the accumulated wealth for future generations. Three of the commodore's offspring—two of his daughters and his epileptic and frequently unstable son Cornelius Jeremiah—openly challenged the will, taking their brother William Henry to court in the fall of 1878. After nearly six months of legal arguments, William Henry agreed to provide his siblings with minor but more appropriate financial settlements, but he retained control of most of the original bequest.

The commodore's decision was an ironic one, for he had treated William Henry largely with indifference for much of his life. A stint working as a banking clerk for less than $1,000 a year ended within a few years when William Henry's fragile health collapsed; certain that his son was unfit for the rigors of the business world, the commodore exiled him to a small farm on Staten Island until middle age, saying, "He is a lazy spendthrift and will never amount to anything."[23] This was symptomatic of the way in which Cornelius treated his heir, constantly berating him as useless, then ignoring him for long periods of time. The commodore might have welcomed any display of independence, but his constant barrage of insults ultimately shaped his son into a compliant, even meek personality who longed for his father's acceptance and at the same time feared him. In turn, with an approach that hinted at his innate cruelty, the commodore constantly toyed with his dutiful heir. Once while on a cruise, Cornelius found William Henry on deck, smoking a cigar. "I wish you would quit that smoking habit of yours," he said. "I'll give you ten thousand dollars if you do."

William Henry Vanderbilt, painted by Flagg, 1877.

"You need not give me money, Father," the ever agreeable William Henry replied. "Your wish is sufficient." With that, the young man tossed his cigar into the ocean. With a smirk, the commodore then pulled a cigar from his own breast pocket, lighted it, and proceeded to smoke, carefully blowing the smoke into his son's face.[24]

William Henry was a man of middle age by the time his father finally relented and allowed him to actively enter the family business. Although William Henry may have lacked his father's cutthroat methods and the imagination to envision true innovation, he was dedicated to his job. In 1864 his father appointed him vice president of the New York & Harlem Railroad. Faced with this challenge, William Henry proved surprisingly adept, impressing his father with a comprehensive understanding of the business and a talent to expand its reach. Within a few years his efforts had so impressed the commodore that he was named vice president of the entire Vanderbilt empire; under his guidance, the family's holdings increased, and he extended the rail network, via the Lake Shore and Michigan Southern and Michigan Central lines, to Chicago, creating a monopoly on travel west. Chauncey Depew, who assisted William Henry, called him "a man of great ability, and his education made him in many ways an abler man than his father for the new conditions he had to meet. But, like many a capable son of a famous father, he did not receive the credit which was due him because of the overshadowing reputation of the commodore."[25] William Henry was a more even-headed, conciliatory man than his father; in 1877, when workers on the New York Central threatened to strike over wage cuts, he personally distributed $100,000 ($2 million in 2008) of his own money to them to help ease the burden, and promised to restore any lost wages as soon as business had improved, to avoid a conflict that would disrupt his businesses.[26]

His steady management and straightforward character took a blow in 1882, however, when a reporter asked William Henry why he was eliminating a mail train between New York and Chicago. Vanderbilt declared that it was not profitable, to which the reporter urged that the operation was for the benefit of the public. "The railroads," Vanderbilt answered, "are not run for the benefit of the public—that cry is all nonsense. They are built by men who invest their money and expect to get a fair percentage on the same." This did not seem to satisfy the interviewer, who continued to press his point. Finally, in exasperation, William Henry declared, "The public be damned!"[27] These four incendiary words, uttered largely in frustration, were quickly splashed across newspapers and did much to cement the impression that the Vanderbilts and others of their ilk were both heartless and avaricious.[28]

The public might well have expected such a reply from the commodore, but William Henry was an altogether different man from his father, careful to present himself as a modest and controlled figure. Prematurely balding and with a drooping mustache and auburn muttonchop whiskers, William was tall but stout, with piercing blue eyes, his voice "genial, cheery, and emphatic."[29] In keeping with the appearance of simplicity that dominated the majority of his life, William Henry drove himself and habitually dressed in unremarkable black. "He used no tobacco in any form," commented one contemporary. "He was abstemious at table. Few men ate less, he taking no meat sometimes for days altogether. He never partook of rich foods or hot breads. . . . He retained simple tastes and seldom drank wine or liquor of any sort."[30]

William Henry also prized moral probity. Unlike his father, he was a faithful husband to his wife, Maria Louisa Kissam, daughter of a Presbyterian minister prominent in New York society. He married her in 1841, and he loved his large family.[31] Altogether eight children born of the marriage survived to adulthood: four girls—Margaret, born in 1845, Emily, born in 1852, Florence, born in 1854, and Eliza, born in 1860— and four boys—Cornelius Vanderbilt II, born in 1843, William Kissam, born in 1849, Frederick, born in 1856, and George Washington Vanderbilt, born in 1862. As the third generation of Vanderbilts, these children thus qualified for inclusion in New York society according to the rules laid down by Caroline Astor and Ward McAllister, and while his father might not have concerned himself with such matters, William Henry did not share his prejudices against the Gilded Age elite. Within a generation, the commodore's eldest son had managed to increase the family fortune to a staggering $200 million (approximately $4 billion today).[32] "I am the richest man in the world," William Henry once proclaimed, and such circumstances surely warranted serious consideration by the ruling powers. He was determined to use his money both to enjoy life to the fullest and to help the Vanderbilts conquer society.[33]

But William Henry found that mere riches could not open the necessary doors. Memories of his father's uncouth and distinctly unrefined behavior lingered, and while money did indeed pierce some of the walls protecting society's bastion, no member of the family was yet considered worthy of inclusion in Caroline Astor's famed four hundred. William Henry's son Cornelius received several invitations to attend the Patriarch balls, an indulgence wrested from a still reluctant Mrs. Astor at the insistence of Ward McAllister, who stood in awe of the Vanderbilt fortune and who suspected—rightly—that inevitably its sheer size would win the day. But most members of society still regarded the family as somewhat suspect and dared not invoke the wrath of Mrs. Astor in embracing those whom she had yet to deem acceptable.

Faced with this intransigence, it was the usually quiet William Henry who fired the first salvo against the old guard. Dignified New York resolutely refused the Vanderbilts entrance to the Academy of Music at Irving Place, where operas preceded important balls. The eighteen principal boxes here were an outward symbol of social supremacy, often passed down from generation to generation, and the owners included not only Mrs. Astor but also the Schermerhorns, Livingstons, Beekmans, Schuylers, Roosevelts, and Lorillards. When William Henry attempted to purchase a box here for $30,000 ($600,000 in 2008), the stolid powers refused, nor did they look with kindness on similar requests from the Goelets, Goulds, Rockefellers, and Morgans—all newly moneyed and all still considered parvenus. Although the academy directors eventually proposed adding twenty-six new boxes, this was too small a number to satisfy the ever-increasing demand from the swelling ranks of the city's outcast millionaires.[34]

These social rejects retaliated in a dramatic and forceful manner, pooling their money and hiring architect Josiah Cady to build the new Metropolitan Opera House on Broadway between Thirty-ninth and Fortieth streets at a cost of 1 million. Intended as a direct challenge to the Academy of Music—and everything for which it stood—this was a blaze of opulence, the auditorium dripping with gilded carvings, crystal chandeliers, and plush red velvet that far outshone the decor enjoyed by the city's entrenched society. At the heart of the new opera house were three tiers of private boxes, including the lowest and most prominent, termed "the Diamond Horseshoe" and intended for its wealthiest patrons.[35] In size, splendor, and luxury—not to mention the impressive talent that the unlimited resources of the patrons could supply—the new Metropolitan Opera House in every way stood as a supreme example of just how far the battle for supremacy could be extended, an uneasy monument to the power of overwhelming ambition.

The new Metropolitan Opera House opened on the evening of October 22, 1883, when famed soprano Christine Nilsson—herself a regular fixture at the Academy of Music—took the stage and sang the role of Marguerite in Gounod's *Faust*.[36] The spectacle was impossible to ignore. "All the nouveaux riches were there," reported one snobbish critic. "The Goulds and Vanderbilts and people of that ilk perfumed the air with the odor of crisp greenbacks. The tiers of boxes looked like cages in a menagerie of monopolists. When somebody remarked that the house looked as bright as a new dollar, the appropriate character of the assemblage became apparent. To the refined eye, the decorations of the edifice seemed in particularly bad taste."[37]

The Metropolitan Opera House presented established New York society with a conundrum. Indeed, Mrs. Astor had purposely left the city on its opening night, perhaps to send a message of lack of interest, or perhaps because she was cagey enough to wait out the situation, hoping to better gauge just how public opinion developed.[38] There was no denying, however, that the accumulated money drew the brightest stars to the Metropolitan. Proper society could resist and, in the end, almost certainly lose the war, or they could face the inevitable. Led by a still somewhat reluctant Mrs. Astor, the older, dignified families began to rent boxes at the Metropolitan, and the Academy of Music was forced to close its doors in the face of this multimillion-dollar assault in 1885.[39]

The debut of the Metropolitan Opera House signaled an unspoken acknowledgment by the ruling elite that, as McAllister warned, the Gilded Age elite must be prepared to embrace—albeit cautiously—select members of the nouveau riche. It was a move that William Henry Vanderbilt had helped engineer but, unfortunately, he was not destined to enjoy the rewards. Ill health in 1883 forced him to retire from business concerns, and he died of a cerebral hemorrhage on December 8, 1885. He left what was popularly believed to be the largest private fortune then existing in the world; one newspaper calculated his income at roughly $8 million a year, or $28,000 a day, $1,200 an hour, or $19.75 a minute ($560,000 a day, $24,000 an hour, or $395 a minute in 2008 figures).[40] To keep most of this wealth intact, Vanderbilt arranged for two $40 million ($800 million in 2008) trusts to benefit his eight children; one functioned only to pay dividends and the principal could not be touched, while his heirs could cash out their interests in the other. Taken together, this guaranteed that each of William Henry's children received an inheritance of roughly $10 million ($200 million in 2008). But the bulk of his estate—an estimated $130 million ($2.6 billion in 2008) after various legacies—was divided between his two eldest sons, Cornelius Vanderbilt II and William Kissam Vanderbilt.[41]

Control of the family business fell to the eldest son, Cornelius Vanderbilt II. One contemporary called Cornelius "the brightest of all the Vanderbilts. He is not so sharp as his grandfather, nor so shrewd as his father, but in mental equipoise he is their superior. He is more phlegmatic than either, never allows his passion to sway him, is always courteous, considerate, and gentle . . . he is never heard to use a harsh or impure word and is known for his blameless, upright life."[42]

Known as Corneil, he was a man of modest appearance, of average height, with shortly trimmed brown hair, an aquiline nose, a high-pitched voice, and an "open, frank countenance" marked by "the steely gray eyes of the Commodore."[43] Corneil, noted one contemporary, "received a very thorough education from tutors and at private schools and his habits of life have always been most correct."[44] He had inherited his grandfather's fighting disposition, although he managed to tactfully conceal his ambitions behind a carefully orchestrated veneer of respectability. Business, in fact, was his passion; unlike most of the Vanderbilts, Corneil had no interest in society, regarded horses as merely utilitarian in nature, and never took to the seas aboard a splendid yacht.[45]

Portrait of Cornelius Vanderbilt II, painted by Benjamin Curtis Porter, 1899.

"He was a man," recalled one associate, "who loved work for work's sake. Work seemed to be his recreation. He would transact what business there was to do, attend to all the matters relating to the various philanthropic and charitable enterprises in which he was interested and finally clear up his desk."[46] Corneil did not, however, have his father's business acumen, and in 1892 his refusal to support the Union Pacific Railroad meant that the family's empire never reached beyond the Midwest. He was, remarked one acquaintance, "too conscientious and took over heavy responsibilities for the entire family. He worked harder than any of his clerks."[47]

Outwardly, Corneil was a quiet, devoutly religious man who attended daily services at St. Bartholomew's Episcopalian Church in New York and regularly gave away a third of his annual income to various charities. He also was an imperious man of autocratic manner and temperament. He expected complete deference to his position as head of the family and unswerving and unquestioning loyalty from those in his employ. Imbued with an unshakable belief in his own importance and superiority, Corneil possessed a cold, intimidating character when challenged. "Although his manner was generally mild and pleasant," one of his grandsons later wrote, "a certain chilling look of command belied his quiet courtesy. One felt that here was a man who expected to be obeyed, and instantly."[48] And his niece Consuelo remembered him as "a stern and serious person," the most feared of all of William Henry's four sons.[49]

Alice Claypoole Gwynne Vanderbilt shared her husband's piety; indeed, they had met teaching Sunday school at St. Bartholomew's. Originally from Cincinnati, she was the daughter of a lawyer, a direct descendant of Oliver Cromwell, a quiet young woman of twenty-two when she married Corneil in 1867.[50] Alice, wrote one man, was "very petite, with a rather pretty face, not exactly handsome," but with "a most gracious and winning smile. She is thoroughly domestic in her tastes, and while not averse to society, does not much care for it. Her manners are simple and unaffected, and she possesses much quiet dignity, and is an affectionate, devoted, and loyal wife."[51]

Yet, like her husband, Alice's public veneer of pronounced simplicity concealed a more complex private personality. Many in the family, as her niece Adele Sloane recalled, considered Alice a "pompous" woman who delighted in her husband's fortune and position.[52] Despite her own aspirations, Alice lacked presence and an easy manner, qualities deemed necessary for success in Gilded Age society. Her grandson, recalling her "tight lips and piercingly cold gray eyes," later wrote of her "glacial and forbidding" demeanor, stern and distinctly unsympathetic in character.[53]

Shy and almost diffident by nature, Alice dominated the lives of the couple's seven children. The first, Alice, was born in 1867, and was followed by William Henry Vanderbilt II in 1870, Cornelius III in 1873, Gertrude in 1875, Alfred in 1877, Reginald in 1880, and Gladys in 1886.

Despite—or perhaps because of—the privilege that attended their lives, Alice and Corneil insisted that their children be brought up very strictly. As a mother, Alice possessed her own inscrutable aura of power. She expected her children to obey her dictates without question. "We cannot always control other people's desires," she once said. "Most certainly we can control our own."[54] Alice died at age five, but the remaining two daughters prospered: the artistic Gertrude later married Harry Payne Whitney and founded the Whitney Museum of American Art in New York City, while Gladys wed a European aristocrat. The four sons, however, were all destined for tragic and unhappy ends. William died of typhoid in 1892; Cornelius III was cut off by his family after marrying against their wishes; Alfred drowned in 1915 aboard the *Lusitania* when it was hit by a German torpedo during World War I; and Reginald—father of the famous Gloria Vanderbilt—drank himself into an early grave.

Despite their careful restraint, both Corneil and Alice believed that their positions at the head of America's wealthiest family entitled them to the benefits of social acceptance. As the center of Gilded Age power, Mrs. Astor directed the shifting elements that formed her new society, dismissing the assaults from those she deemed beyond the pale and offering recognition to members of the nouveau riche who met her standards of wealth and taste. After ten years atop society's throne, and under McAllister's influence, she occasionally relented, as with the rare invitations to enjoy the Patriarch balls, yet even the persistence of money that brought the triumph of the Metropolitan Opera House failed to crack the most stringent barriers erected against unwelcome intrusion. William Henry had opened the door, but neither Corneil nor Alice, though possessed of respectability and an immense fortune, had the determination or the imagination to mount an unrelenting assault against the old order. That accomplishment fell to Cornelius's sister-in-law, the remarkable and irrepressible Alva Vanderbilt.

3

ENTER THE CHALLENGER

WHAT THE VANDERBILTS needed was something their money could not buy: legitimacy in the eyes of New York society. Occasional invitations to elite balls offered tantalizing glimmers of hope, and the wholesomely respectable lives of Corneil and Alice helped win over some of the more intransigent social powers in the city, but these were fleeting victories that promised no permanent foothold. In the end, the Vanderbilts, like the Astors before them, found the road to social acceptance in the marriage of a younger son to a powerful and determined woman.

Born in 1849, William Kissam Vanderbilt grew up a privileged young man who greatly differed from his elder brother Cornelius II. Whereas Cornelius was stern in demeanor and bookish in appearance, Willie, as he was known in the family, was a jovial young man, generally good-natured and adventurous in character. From his school days in Switzerland, Willie developed a love of culture and art; he was certainly more worldly and sophisticated than his older brother, and he found among Europe's aristocrats the acceptance he believed his wealth demanded. On his return to America, however, he was stunned to find that despite his careful breeding, cultivated manners, and fortune, New York society remained largely a closed world to the Vanderbilts.

William K. Vanderbilt, about 1890.

"My life was never destined to be quite happy," Willie pronounced in his maturity. "It was laid out along lines which I could not foresee, almost from earliest childhood. It has left me with nothing to hope for, with nothing definite to seek or strive for. Inherited wealth is a real handicap to happiness. It is as certain death to ambition as cocaine is to morality."[1] Yet filled with youthful enthusiasm and armed with a $3 million ($60 million in 2008) legacy following his grandfather the commodore's death, Willie set about enjoying life to the fullest. He joined the privileged South Side Club in Oakdale, Long Island, and eventually commissioned architect Richard Morris Hunt to design and build a nearby mansion for his use. Called Idle Hour, this was a large, shingle-style cottage that cost a mere $150,000 ($3 million in 2008), but it began a long and fruitful association between the Vanderbilt family and the talented architect.

Willie, recorded one contemporary in the 1880s, was "stoutly built and inclined to corpulence. His face is an open, full one, framed in English whiskers, and his complexion is ruddy and high-colored. He is what would be called a handsome man, and his figure was, until the last few years, a decidedly athletic one. He is fond of horses, although not so much as his father, or the late Commodore. He may often be seen driving a fleet pair of roadsters on the macadamized avenues that surround his country place at Islip, and he indulges in yachting at times."[2] His only daughter, Consuelo, recalled him as a man who "found life a happy adventure," "so invariably kind, so gentle and sweet," with "a fund of humorous tales and jokes" and a pronounced hatred of any discord.[3]

Willie had everything but a suitable consort. This changed in 1874, when he met Alva Erskine Smith. Born January 17, 1853, in Mobile, Alabama, Alva was the daughter of Murray F. Smith, a wealthy lawyer whose principal job was representing the cotton interests of his wife's family in Kentucky.[4] Alva had been a most unusual child, a tomboy who, as she later recounted, loved "tyrannizing over the little slave children" attached to her father's household.[5] In 1859 Smith moved his family to New York City to take advantage of the opportunities offered by the country's burgeoning rail transport. Here Smith soon prospered, and Alva grew up in a large mansion on Fifth Avenue. But the Smiths, as Southerners and, worse yet, slave owners who had moved their slaves with them to New York, found their comfortable lives undermined when the Civil War erupted.[6]

In the aftermath of the Civil War, Smith uprooted his family and took them to Paris, where Alva spent her formative years immersed in European etiquette and culture. The brilliance of the Second Empire of Napoleon III and his consort, Empress Eugenie; the endless round of parties and balls at the Tuileries and at St. Cloud; the triumphant new boulevards created by Baron Georges Haussmann lined with impressive, miniature marble châteaux; the splendid jewels of the ladies against their intricate crinolines from Worth; the elegant equipages parading through the Bois de Boulogne each afternoon—all of these sights and sounds seduced the young girl, and she never forgot the opulent manner of life she witnessed in Paris.[7] The family returned to New York City in 1870, just before the disastrous Franco-Prussian War, but financial losses on Wall Street soon took their toll. In quick succession Alva's mother died, her father's money disappeared, and circumstances were so grim that he spoke of opening a common boardinghouse—an indignity the young girl never forgot.[8]

Alva's sole goal in life became the pursuit and capture of a wealthy husband, and, with the assistance of former childhood friends Minnie Stevens and the exotic and wealthy Cuban Consuelo Yznaga (who later married Viscount Mandeville, heir of the 7th Duke of Manchester, and served as the model for Conchita Clossen in Edith Wharton's last novel, *The Buccaneers*), Alva was launched upon New York society. Alva was not beautiful; according to her friend and social rival Mrs. Stuyvesant Fish, she looked like "an intelligent Pekinese." But she was smart, energetic, and determined to place herself in the firmament of the city's social elite, "a woman of strong personality and great ability," as James Gerard recalled.[9] One contemporary described her as "an accomplished woman of the world and devoted to gaiety." She was, he noted, "tall and slight, and is neither a blonde nor a brunette, while her hair, although she is a young woman, is tinged with gray. Her conversational powers are rather remarkable. She is quick at repartee, witty, and somewhat sarcastic, and this has made her much admired and to some extent feared in society."[10] Alva's daughter Consuelo left a more critical portrait. While admitting that her mother was "delightful, charming and intelligent," she described Alva as consumed with "a towering ambition. . . . Her combative nature rejoiced in conquests. She loved a fight. A born dictator, she dominated her husband."[11]

It was perhaps inevitable that the witty, vivacious Alva and the cultured William K. Vanderbilt would eventually meet during the city's social season. The wily young southern woman transfixed the wealthy heir. It was a mutually advantageous transaction: Willie had money but no right of entrée to refined New York society, while Alva, though impoverished, possessed a proud lineage that included former members of the U.S. House of Representatives, a governor of Kentucky, government officials, English aristocrats, and early American immigrants. On April 20, 1875, the couple was married and began a tumultuous and storied relationship that forever rattled society.

Nothing, remembered Elizabeth Drexel Lehr, made Alva "happier than the knowledge that she was pitting herself against the rest of the world. She loved to see herself as a pioneer, to make others bend to her will, to have them follow her in the end, meek, sheep-like." Alva prided herself on such boldness. "I always do everything first," she declared. "I blaze the trail for the rest to walk in."[12]

For the first few years, the marriage of Willie K. and Alva followed the usual routine. There were quiet parties, a few entertainments, and three children: Consuelo (named after her mother's friend Lady Mandeville), born in 1877, William Kissam Vanderbilt Jr., in 1878, and Harold, in 1884. But the couple, educated, cultured, and wealthy, were determined to make an impact on the bastion so closely guarded by Mrs. Astor. In

Portrait of William K. Vanderbilt.

Portrait of Alva Vanderbilt.

this they were aided by Ward McAllister, who was convinced that this newest generation of Vanderbilts, armed with manners and a considerable fortune, could no longer be ignored. Although McAllister eventually convinced Caroline Astor to include Willie and Alva as his guests for a Patriarch Ball in January 1883, nothing could induce the society matriarch to receive them personally.[13] "People seem to be going quite wild and inviting all sorts of people to their receptions," Caroline complained. "I don't know what has happened to our tastes."[14]

Alva was not content to bask in an occasional invitation, however, and her first strike to conquer society was a bold one: she commissioned architect Richard Morris Hunt to build a fabulously extravagant mansion at 660 Fifth Avenue in New York. Like Alva herself, it was conceived to garner as much attention as possible. The resulting French-style château certainly attracted accolades, but it failed to win the social approval Willie and Alva so desperately sought. Caroline Astor remained proudly obdurate, but Alva was two steps ahead of her rival, and announced that she planned what promised to be the most extravagant costume ball New York had ever witnessed to formally inaugurate her new house and welcome her friend Consuelo, Lady Mandeville, to New York. In a bold move, Alva scheduled the ball for a date after Easter, when the usual social season had ended.[15]

The city's newspapers were awash with the staggering details, all carefully leaked to the press to heighten anticipation: some thirteen hundred guests were said to have received invitations; an elaborate dinner and two orchestras were engaged to provide the evening's entertainment; and thousands of out-of-season orchids and American Beauty roses, ordered from Charles Klunder, the city's premier society florist, were said to have cost some $11,000 ($220,000 in 2008) alone.[16] "I have decorated the houses of princes and ambassadors," Klunder said, "but never have I seen floral embellishments on a scale of such regal grandeur. Mrs. Vanderbilt gave me carte blanche."[17] The *New York Sun* estimated that taken together, the various expenses involved in this single evening came to a staggering $250,000 ($5 million today).[18] New York City—and America—had never seen anything so brilliant and grand.

"The Vanderbilt ball," the *New York Times* reported, "has agitated New York society more than any social event that has occurred here in many years. Since the announcement that it would take place . . . scarcely anything else had been talked about. It has been on every tongue and a fixed idea in every head. It has disturbed the sleep and occupied the waking hours of social butterflies, both male and female, for over six weeks."[19] All society was in an uproar over the guest list, clamoring for the hundreds of invitations. "For weeks beforehand," noted one contemporary, "the costumers, milliners, and dressmakers, not only of New York but of all the larger eastern cities, were engaged in preparing the richest and most varied of garments for this wonderful entertainment. Histories, novels, and illustrated books of all periods were ransacked by the expectant guests to obtain either suggestions or models upon which their own costumes could be patterned."[20]

One particularly excited young society woman was Carrie Astor, Mrs. Astor's daughter, who spent weeks practicing a quadrille for the event. Then, hearing of the girl's plans, Alva played her trump card: as Mrs. Astor had never called on or received Alva or any of the Vanderbilts, it was, she explained, quite impossible to extend an invitation to the society queen's daughter. Mrs. Astor realized what needed to be done.[21] She drove in a carriage to Alva's shimmering new palace and waited as her footman, dressed in the Astor blue livery, mounted the steps of 660 Fifth Avenue to present his mistress's engraved calling card to an equally smart footman in the maroon Vanderbilt livery. Caroline Astor and Alva Vanderbilt did not meet face to face, but the presentation of the calling card signaled the haughty Caroline's social surrender. The Vanderbilts had been formally recognized and accepted by the arbiter of New York society; that afternoon, a footman delivered engraved invitations to Mrs. Astor's mansion, a sign that the war had come to an end, and from the uneasy truce, Alva had emerged victorious.[22]

As darkness fell on Monday, March 26, 1883, a crowd gathered outside the new chateau at 660 Fifth Avenue, held back by a contingent of Metropolitan Police. At half-past eight, footmen sporting white powdered wigs and clad in eighteenth-century-style maroon liveries of surcoats, knee breeches, and silk stockings cleared the sidewalk, unrolling a gold-edged maroon carpet that stretched from the awning over the front door to the street. A long line of sleek carriages began to appear at ten: "Out stepped what appeared to be the ghosts of all the great dead since the world began," the *New York Tribune* exulted: "Joan of Arc, complete with solid silver mail; Christopher Columbus; Louis XVI; Queen Elizabeth I with a bright red wig; the goddess Diana; Daniel Boone. By 11:30, a bouillabaisse of kings, queens, fairies, toreadors, and gypsies blocked Fifth Avenue."[23]

The scene, commented the *New York Herald,* was "like an Oriental Dream," an evening "never rivaled in Republican America and never outdone by the gayest courts of Europe." Within, the rooms had been festooned with chains of orchids and palm fronds; vases and silver baskets of some ten thousand Jacqueminot, *Glorie de Paris,* and American Beauty roses alternated with potted palms.[24] "The Ball probably equaled," declared the *New York Tribune,* "if it did not excel, in beauty and attractiveness any similar entertainment ever given in the city. Any dreams of splendor by a passer-by would have been more than realized could he have caught a glimpse of the rooms inside, where beautiful women and distinguished men promenaded through the halls. . . . A countess might be seen walking with a Marchioness, or a duke with a Venetian lady, and indeed the combinations of imitated rank and beauty were endless where so many powdered wigs were graciously bowing, so many pairs of bright eyes flashing in rivalry of the jewels of their owners, and so much talking, dancing, and promenading were enjoyed."[25]

This night, Mrs. Astor did enter her rival's new château, dressed as a Venetian princess in a dark blue velvet gown embroidered in gold thread and pearls and ornamented with lace. Perhaps to make a point, however, she purposely wore nearly all of her diamonds: a tiara with diamond stars atop her black coiffure, diamond drop earrings, the rows of immense collet diamonds in her necklaces, the diamond bow and lover's knot brooches on her bodice, the diamond stomacher ornamented with pearls rippling below her décolletage, the clusters of diamonds in the bracelets around the wrists of her long white gloves—all shimmered and sparkled as she moved through the rooms.[26] At her side, as always, was the faithful Ward McAllister, dressed as Count de la Mole, the lover of Marguerite de Valois, in a costume of purple velvet and crimson silk. Together, these two arbiters of New York's Gilded Age society waited to pronounce sentence on Alva Vanderbilt's aspirations.

In the parade of extravagant costumes, only former American president Ulysses S. Grant and William Henry Vanderbilt stood out, both gentlemen preferring white tie and tails. Louisa, William Henry's wife, came humbly costumed as a lady-in-waiting to Marie Antoinette, but other members of the Vanderbilt family more than compensated for such sartorial discretion. The usually staid and religious Corneil came as Louis XVI, with a cream-colored satin surcoat embroidered in gold and silver thread worn over a frilled white shirt with a *point d'Espagne* lace jabot and brocaded waistcoat, satin knee breeches embroidered in silver foliate designs, silk stockings, and shoes with diamond buckles; atop his powdered wig perched a tricorn hat adorned with feathers, and at his side he carried a sword whose hilt glittered with diamonds. His wife, Alice, came as an electric light in a gown from Worth of Paris. Of light yellow and white satin, the skirt was edged in panels of dark blue satin embroidered with pearls and foliate designs in gold thread to match the train; the bodice, of cream-colored satin brocade ornamented with foliate designs in silver and gold thread, was trimmed with diamonds, silvered lace, and feathers; in her right hand she carried a gilded torch with a light powered by a concealed battery.[27] With her necklace, earrings, bracelets over her long white gloves, and sparkling tiara from which sprouted an immense aigrette of yellow ostrich plumes, Alice, as Ward McAllister recalled, seemed "one blaze of diamonds."[28] Alva's sister-in-law Eliza Vanderbilt Webb came costumed as a hornet, in a gown with a brown velvet skirt and a bodice of brilliant yellow satin, with brown gauze wings attached to the shoulders and antennae made of diamonds.[29] Willie came in a yellow silk doublet over matching stockings and a cape of black velvet as the Duc de Guise—an ironic choice, given that the duke had been assassinated in 1588 on the orders of King Henri II at the Château de Blois, the very building upon which Hunt had modeled the new house at 660 Fifth Avenue.[30]

But the center of attention was a triumphant Alva Vanderbilt, standing in her François I salon in front of a full-length portrait of herself by Raimundo de Madrazo y Garreta.[31] Like Mrs. Astor, she had dressed as a Venetian princess, wearing a gown of yellow and white brocade and blue satin by Worth in Paris. The underskirt of the gown, revealed by an inverted V-shaped split in the overskirt, was in white and yellow brocade graduated in rows of shifting color, from deep orange to light canary; foliate designs, scrolls, and garlands in gold thread were ornamented with iridescent beads and pearls. The overskirt and bodice were of blue satin, intricately sewn with foliate designs in gold thread and shimmering with more beading; the flowing sleeves were of transparent gold tissue, while her train was of light blue satin embroidered with gold foliate designs and lined with crimson velvet. Atop her head she wore a velvet diadem covered in jewels and dominated by a jeweled peacock. Stretching to her waist were ropes of Catherine the Great's pearls, fighting for primacy with Empress Eugenie of France's diamond and pearl brooches.[32]

Alva Vanderbilt in costume for her famous ball in 1883.

By eleven that night, the hundred participants in the six quadrilles had gathered in the third-floor gymnasium, waiting for the ball to begin, while the rest of the guests crowded the rooms on the main floor. A fanfare of trumpets, played by trumpeters at the top of the grand staircase, announced the beginning of the processions as the colorfully costumed dancers paraded slowly down the immense staircase and passed through the halls to the great, two-storey dining room. The ball opened with the Hobby Horse Quadrille, the dancers entering the room to a selection of circus music played by Gilmore's Orchestra on the gallery above. The men wore scarlet hunting coats, white satin vests, yellow satin knee breeches, white stockings, and black boots, while the ladies wore scarlet hunting coats and white satin skirts. But the most peculiar aspect of these costumes were the horses: shells constructed to the size of ponies and covered with real horse hides, complete with flowing manes and tails, which the dancers used as props in their elaborate quadrille.[33]

After this bit of theatrical indulgence, the guests looked on as the dancers performed the Mother Goose Quadrille, attired as characters from fairy tales; the Opera Quadrille, graced with costumes copied from characters in famous operas; and the Star Quadrille, for which the young ladies—including Carrie Astor—wore gowns of yellow, blue, mauve, and white, with tiny electric lights in their hair powered by concealed batteries that twinkled as they danced.[34] This was followed by the Dresden China Quadrille, for which the dancers all wore ivory satin costumes and white powdered wigs to imitate pieces of porcelain; and the Go-As-You-Please Quadrille, in which variously costumed dancers took to the floor.[35] The entire scene, rhapsodized the New York Herald, was one of "shifting gleams of gorgeous color, and of quaint and curious outlines in a thousand costumes flitting through the rooms—themselves a study fit for an artist."[36]

An eight-course supper was served at two in the morning in the third-floor gymnasium, which, the New York Times reported, had been transformed into "a garden in a tropical forest." The walls were bedecked with palm fronds, ferns, roses, orchids, and shimmering electric lights. At the center of the room, an enormous palm tree reached to the ceiling; from its fronds, strings of bougainvillea, hung with Chinese lanterns, spread to the corners of the gymnasium. Two artificial fountains played while the guests ate. After this, there were further dances below, finally ending in a rousing Virginia reel before the guests reluctantly departed at six in the morning.[37]

The next day, the city's newspapers stumbled over themselves to serve up the superlatives for their curious readers. "In lavishness of expenditure and brilliancy of dress," declared the *New York Sun,* "it far outdid any ball ever before given in this city," while the *New York World* pronounced it "an event never equaled in the social annals of the metropolis" and "unquestionably the most brilliant and picturesque entertainment ever given in New York."[38] Henry Clews, one of the guests, commented that it had "no equal in history. It may not have been quite so expensive as the feast of Alexander the Great at Babylon, some of the entertainments of Cleopatra to Augustus and Mark Antony, or a few of the magnificent banquets of Louis XIV, but when viewed from every essential standpoint, and taking into account our advanced civilization I have no hesitation in saying that the Vanderbilt ball was superior to any of those grand historic displays of festivity and amusement."[39]

Such rhapsodic descriptions cemented the place of the ball in the city's social history and underlined its larger implications. Comparisons to the splendors of the Orient, the glittering courts of Europe, and the glories of the ancient world evoked the opulence of the evening, but they also linked it to a proud and privileged heritage, offering up New York's Gilded Age society as the true successors of past ruling powers. Alva Vanderbilt's ball transcended frivolous entertainment; it was evidence of heightened taste, an expression of the ideal in which the moneyed elite would lead the way, providing America with a class and a culture that would be the envy of the world.

During the ball, Caroline Astor was seen in deep conversation with Alva Vanderbilt.[40] The doyenne of New York society was duly impressed by the château, the splendor of the evening, and the taste of her rival. After this night, even Caroline Astor was forced to concede the inevitable. "We have no right," she said, "to exclude those whom the growth of this great country has brought forward, provided they are not vulgar in speech and appearance. The time has come for the Vanderbilts."[41] The next year, Alva duly made a triumphant appearance at Caroline's annual opera ball, signaling her complete acceptance.[42]

Alva's triumph opened the door for others who followed in her wake. "Men of no social distinction," complained Mrs. John King Van Rensselaer, a grande dame of the old order, "have frequently become prominent in society by marrying women of breeding. The Vanderbilts, the Astors, the Belmonts, and other present leaders have attained their station through the infusion of aristocratic blood into their line through marriages with the old families. Their wives made them."[43]

4

THE SOCIETY LADY

THE SOCIETY LADY was a figure of great interest, her daily life a source of considerable mystery, and her stylized rituals copied and admired by those who hoped to join her ranks. "Even the way one carries a handkerchief has been systematized in the name of the *je ne sais quoi* that no one has seen or heard but that society obeys," wrote one observer. The hallmarks of breeding and taste were subtle yet of prime importance. "The way a hat is worn, to what degree tilted, or how closely fitted, the way a mantelet is carried and a foot set on the pavement, the way a handkerchief is held; these are the indelible marks for which all women aim and only a few achieve with the elegance of great ladies. It is an indestructible coat of arms handed down to high society women by their mothers and that they leave to their daughters, a challenge of one woman to another, the insidious vengeance of the true aristocrat over the parvenu in each new century."[1]

These ladies (always ladies; a woman might be an aristocrat or a parlor maid, but only a lady was a member of society) were not only wives and mothers; their roles also stretched to encompass a variety of social and philanthropic endeavors. They ran the great houses; they planned the extravagant dinners and balls that consumed society; they stood at the gates of their exclusive strongholds, welcoming those who met their stringent standards and barring those they deemed unacceptable. They crafted and honed society according to their whims, shaping taste and providing visible symbols of their status and style.

"I know of no profession, art, or trade," Alva Vanderbilt once declared, "as taxing on mental resources as being a leader of society."[2] What might at first be taken as a rather ill-informed statement made from privileged security was in fact a rather accurate assessment of the often onerous burden attendant to the position of the greatest hostesses. During the New York City social season, from the middle of November to the middle of February, society ladies were constricted and confined to a world of stylized rituals that justified their elite rank. From social calls and afternoon drives to evenings at the opera, elaborate dinners, and crowded balls, there were few days that a lady could truly call her own. These obligations continued in the months that followed, with more parties, dinners, and balls at Newport, picnics and yachting excursions along the Hudson, garden parties and archery tournaments in the Berkshires, and a round of court presentations in the capitals of Europe.

Days began late during the season, when parties and balls kept society at play until the early hours. When a lady was not required to keep to a schedule of events, she might sleep relatively late, eventually rising and with the push of a call bell summoning her maid; Caroline Astor was a unique exception, always rising promptly at eight each morning. A breakfast tray of tea and toast, brought by her maid, would quickly arrive, along with any important personal correspondence to be read while a bath was drawn and the morning's toilette made ready.[3] Although a hairdresser might be called in to attend to a coiffure if an important engagement was scheduled, generally its arrangement was left to the maid, who often inserted special pads, known as "rats," into the hair to give it the necessary volume and form deemed fashionable.[4] In the case of Caroline Astor, additional measures were needed, for she had begun losing her hair in her fifties; by the turn of the century, what remained had turned white, an untenable situation for her vanity. To solve the problem, Caroline took to wearing brown and black pompadour wigs, which lent her a slightly surreal appearance.[5]

The toilette of the society lady was of prime importance and could take an hour in the morning and then again an hour or more in the evening in anticipation of any entertainment, with numerous changes of clothing and accessories before the final touches could be completed. "Taste," recorded one lady, "allows certain perfumes to be worn on one's handkerchief and forbids others. Musk and ambergris were once acceptable; now, violet, iris, vanilla, and lemon are in. One can tell a society woman by the perfume she wears, and not merely by the perfume itself but by how much she wears."[6] Indeed, ladies were strongly advised against the use of too much scent: "It is only the faintest suggestion of a refined perfume that should ever be allowed to hang even for a moment about the belongings of a well-bred girl," cautioned one authority, "and even such a casual use of the merest whiff of a dainty and impalpable essence should be rare; to wear any redolence upon her person in sachets is unpardonable."[7]

Correspondence usually occupied several hours each morning. In addition to personal letters, inevitably there arrived daily invitations to promote a particular charity, to attend a dinner or a ball, and to lend her name to some noble cause. "The begging letter is rarely absent," noted one commentator. "Invitations to all sorts of social functions flow in uninterruptedly. Their name is legion. Eleemosynary projects are presented to her notice with solicitations for aid in their furtherance; tickets for endless so-called charitable entertainments; requests for every description of help, and of course, letters from poor relations, of whom the rich have no lack. The daily missives in the mail of a woman rich in worldly things, in their nature touch life's extremes."[8]

Some ladies kept social secretaries to help them deal with this voluminous correspondence, trusting their discretion in putting forward any worthy causes and consigning the others to the wastebasket. Caroline Astor relied on a Miss Simrock, "a forlorn old German," recalled one of the hostess's daughters, whom Mrs. Astor "bullied cruelly."[9] A supply of standard engraved replies declining the request—a kind of turn of-the-century form letter—were kept at the ready, to be dispatched in answer to most of this correspondence.[10]

For correspondence, no society lady of good standing ever used anything other than plain, thick, white or cream vellum writing paper, occasionally embossed with her name, a family crest, or her address, though the latter was deemed most appropriate. Writing paper used at a country estate might be permitted to have both the name of the house and some small, engraved representation of the premises, though any such display used in New York was a sure sign of lack of breeding. For acceptance of social invitations, thick, square vellum cards engraved with the lady's name were deemed the appropriate form. All of this correspondence was properly inserted in lined, plain white envelopes and sealed with melted wax, using a small seal engraved with the family's crest.[11] Invitations to receptions or balls could be sent by mail; dinner invitations were always delivered by hand.[12] As she worked her way through her morning correspondence, Caroline Astor would habitually refresh herself with her favorite chocolate caramels and marrons glacés, set upon a silver tray on her desk.[13]

In addition to the usual carriage drives, a society lady spent a good deal of her afternoon engaged in the ritual of the social call. This was a necessary, if time-consuming, pantomime of the exacting politesse expected from those who occupied the highest ranks, part of the iron etiquette, declared one authority, protecting society "from disagreeable, underbred people, who refuse to take the trouble to be civil."[14] The social call was enshrouded in its own elaborate sets of rules. Generally no calls were made before two in the afternoon, and it was considered rude to pay any call after four, when a lady might be attending to the evening's entertainment or out for her afternoon drive.

"I can hardly picture a lady of my mother's generation without her card-case in her hand," recalled Edith Wharton. "Calling was then a formidable affair, since many ladies had weekly 'days' from which there was no possible escape. . . . By the time I grew up the younger, married women had emancipated themselves, and simply drove from house to house depositing their cards, duly turned down in the upper left-hand corner, to the indignation of stay-at-home hostesses, many of whom made their servants keep a list of the callers who 'did not ask,' so that these might be struck off the next season's invitation list—a punishment borne by the young and gay with perfect equanimity, as it was only the dull hostesses who inflicted it."[15]

In this game, calling cards assumed prime importance. They demanded thought and attention, for their coloring, weight, and engraving indicated the bearer's position in society and their ease with its rules of politeness. Ladies were advised that a simple vellum card engraved with their name was sufficient; indeed, as one authority warned, "nothing is in worse taste than for an American to put a coat-of-arms on his card. It only serves to make him ridiculous."[16] If a residence was given, it was always printed on the card's lower right corner.[17] A married lady's card always bore her husband's name, such as *Mrs. William Astor;* she never used her own Christian name while her husband lived.[18] There was a careful language attached to the presentation of cards. On them the caller might inscribe one of four notes: *Visite, Felicitation, Condolence,* or *Pour Prendre Congé* to indicate a farewell.[19] A card whose upper left corner had been turned down indicated that the caller had made a personal visit; a card placed in an envelope and left with the butler indicated that the bearer had no wish to continue calling on the recipient.

Calling was based on a set of intricate rules. Ladies who wished to call on a new acquaintance needed a proper introduction before any such step could be considered; even then, the caller never knew if her overture would be welcomed. A debutante or a lady newly arrived in the city, having been introduced at a party or ball to her social superior, was advised to make her first call on a recognized leader of society. In Gilded Age New York City, Caroline Astor still held pride of place, but Alva Vanderbilt Belmont, Tessie Oelrichs, Mamie Fish, and Ruth Mills also could be approached with the assurance that their approval would provide entrée to the highest echelons of society. A call always was made within a week of an introduction; if a call on one's social superior was not returned, it was understood that no further acquaintance was desired.[20]

Any invitation demanded an immediate response in sending either acceptance or regret, or in leaving a calling card in person to convey the information. Even if the invitation was not—or could not—be accepted, a call within a week of receiving the invitation was deemed necessary. Etiquette demanded that a guest must call within two days after a dinner party; other entertainments could be followed by sending a calling card rather than making a personal visit.[21] Etiquette also dictated that a personal visit be returned in kind; a proxy call, during which only a card was left and no inquiry made after the mistress of the house, was deemed an insult. A personal call, however, could be returned by leaving a card if the recipient was someone known to the visitor.[22] Leaving a card was considered sufficient to establish a visiting acquaintance of a year's duration.[23]

Generally, only married ladies or widows engaged in calling. Debutantes did not receive their own calling cards until their first season ended; before this, their names were engraved on a set of their mother's calling cards, to be left during any visits.[24] Ladies were expected when making a first call to also leave their husband's card as a matter of courtesy for the gentleman of the house, although after this they needed leave only their own, unless the call was in response to a joint dinner invitation.[25] A lady calling in person presented her card to the butler or footman and waited to see if she would be received. An actual meeting was not necessarily the objective; the call and the card fulfilled societal obligation. Many ladies were at home when these visitors arrived but chose not to receive; this was considered perfectly acceptable form, and visitors would be told that the mistress of the house was "not at home to callers." This was understood to cover a multitude of possibilities, ranging from actual absence or indisposition to an actual refusal to receive, and no slight was construed by such a response; indeed, it was considered a grave offense to press for a meeting. Any society lady, however, made an exception to this charade if the caller was socially more important than she was. Regardless of whether the visitor was personally received, etiquette dictated that a calling card be left, so that the visitor's name could be inscribed in a book kept in the hall; this ensured that the lady of the house could return the favor if desired.[26] If a lady was at home and received the caller, the visit lasted, by etiquette, no more than thirty minutes.

Girls were carefully guarded from any undue influence or hint of scandal. Imbued from an early age with the necessity of always being conscious of their every action and word, they were thus keenly aware of their position and of the need to be circumspect in all matters. "When I was eleven," recalled Gertrude Vanderbilt, "I knew perfectly that my father was talked of all over, that his name was known throughout the world, that I, simply because I was his daughter, would be talked about when I grew up, and that there were lots of things I could not do simply because I was Miss Vanderbilt."[27]

Young ladies were sheltered, raised in isolated splendor, tucked away in distant nurseries and cared for by a contingent of nurses, nannies, and governesses. While society ladies had their own concerns in maintaining their positions and rising through the ranks, there was more at work here than benign parental neglect. Many of these ladies had themselves been raised according to similar standards and saw no need to alter them where their daughters were concerned. Then, too, there was often a distinct discomfort between parents and children of the era, and the deliberate isolation of children saved many mothers from the embarrassment of emotional scenes with which they were ill equipped to deal. Yet, as one authority warned of fashionable mothers, "they must see their children occasionally, and be measurably acquainted with them. They should, at least, be sure that those to whom they delegate the charge— nurses, maids, and governesses—are reliable and competent, well educated, and well bred; above all, honorable."[28]

A few daughters of privilege attended exclusive day schools, such as Miss Spence's School, the Dwight School, or the Comstock School for Girls in New York City, but, more often, they were educated by private tutors.[29] Too much education was considered forward; indeed, society gentlemen on the whole tended to steer clear of any young lady more clever than himself, or who delighted in precocious superiority. "The rich American girl rarely goes to college," noted one chronicler. "College education is not fashionable; it is useless in the society wherein the rich girl is destined to move."[30] Instead, society mothers ensured that their daughters possessed the outward forms of what one historian has termed largely "ornamental" knowledge designed to secure suitable husbands.[31]

These girls might lack comprehensive educations, but they could converse not only in English but also in French and often German. Their cultural tastes tended to reflect those of their mothers, with a marked preference for sentimental French and English romantic novels and light opera.[32] Brought up with lessons in painting, sketching, needlework, and piano, young ladies were carefully trained in all of the social graces, observing from their mothers the intricate rules of etiquette; deportment and posture; the proper manner in which to dress for all occasions; the treatment of servants; and how to host the era's elaborate dinner parties and balls. Dancing lessons were essential for success in society, and girls were often dispatched to Dodsworth's Dancing Academy, New York City's most fashionable school, learning the multitude of steps that they would one day be called upon to employ.[33] Sporting concerns were largely confined to those activities deemed acceptable for ladies: lessons in riding, as equestrian skill was considered of paramount importance; gymnastics, to imbue natural grace and poise; and archery, croquet, and lawn tennis, the trio of usual diversions employed in the summer months at their father's country estate.

Once a young girl had reached a suitable age to make her debut—usually sixteen, but occasionally older—a number of subtle but significant physical signs marked her change in status from youth to adult. Hair, previously worn long and loosely flowing around the shoulders or tied back in a bow, was now carefully coiled and stylishly arranged atop the head to indicate maturity; dresses and skirts now reached to the floor, signifying that they now concealed that which was believed to be sexually desirable; and jewelry appeared. There were initial appearances, always carefully chaperoned, at discreet afternoon teas in private houses before a young lady ventured forth to the battlefield of the ballroom.[34]

For these young ladies, the social season marked not only their formal presentation to polite, adult society but also launched them on a path to matrimony, an often daunting endeavor to the less assured. "You don't know what the position of an heiress is!" a young Gertrude Vanderbilt once wrote in despair in her diary. "You can't imagine. There is no one in all the world who loves her for herself. No one. She cannot do this, that, and the other simply because she is known by sight and will be talked about."[35] Invitations to teas, receptions, dinners, parties, and balls were thus scanned and accepted or rejected according to the potential rewards of attendance. There was a certain sense of abandon during the season; if all went well, a young lady might procure a husband by the end, the varied entertainments offering not only a first taste of adult life but also potentially a last indulgence in freedom.

A suitable marriage was the ultimate goal, but occasionally a young lady proved headstrong or, worse, determined to wed someone deemed unsuitable. As the self-appointed arbiter of New York society, Caroline

Astor had the misfortune of witnessing the marital contretemps of her daughters. Emily, born in 1854, fell in love with a widower, James J. Van Alen, much to the horror of her parents. The son of Civil War general James H. Van Alen, he stood to inherit the millions that his father had made investing in the Illinois Central Railroad, but money did not make him suitable to Emily's parents. Young Van Alen was highly eccentric: an Anglophile, he affected a British accent and, recalled Elizabeth Drexel Lehr, "his conversation was so flavored with 'egad,' 'zounds,' and 'prithee' that one almost needed a special old English dictionary to talk to him. The highest praise he could bestow on any favored lady was 'a most delectable wench, forsooth.'"[36] William Backhouse Astor, in particular, made no secret of the fact that he thought James J. Van Alen was little short of a rake, declaring, "Damned if I want my family having anything to do with the Van Alens!" On hearing this denunciation, General Van Alen actually challenged Astor to a duel; stunned, William at first agreed, then on reflection thought better of it and apologized. Although neither he nor Caroline fully reconciled themselves to the idea, the marriage took place in March 1876. The union was short-lived, however, as Emily died in 1882 giving birth to the couple's third child.[37]

Helen, the second Astor daughter, born in 1855, did nothing quite so contrary, marrying James Roosevelt, half-brother of Franklin Delano Roosevelt, in 1878. Although not as wealthy as the Astors, the Roosevelts, at least, were a socially prominent, recognized old family. But like her sister Emily, Helen's happiness was doomed to be short-lived, and she died in 1893.[38]

In 1879, Charlotte Augusta, the third Astor daughter, married James Coleman Drayton, vice president of the Equitable Life Assurance Society, in a union arranged by her mother that went spectacularly wrong and ended in an immense public scandal.[39] In ten years of marriage, the couple had four children—two boys and two girls—and outwardly, at least, there was no indication of the tumult to come, but the couple had little in common. Caroline Phillips, one of the couple's daughters, later recalled, "I often wonder why he and my mother ever married. She was very flirtatious and I am told quite pretty and a good dancer, but a very immature character, brought up in complete ignorance of the facts of life. . . . My father was a very nervous, high strung man with a violent temper, a love of art and reading and travel, very sociable, but also a lover of solitude, keen about riding, hunting and shooting and by training and profession a lawyer. He was very impulsive and had the old sensitive Southern tradition of 'honor' sometimes much exaggerated. My mother used to irritate him beyond words by inane remarks and a certain amount of nagging, and I think she found him very difficult also."[40]

Charlotte was desperately unhappy and, for consolation, turned to a neighbor, Hallet Borrowe. Discretion managed to keep word of the liaison from leaking to the public, but then Drayton decided that he was no longer content to play the cuckold and went to his father-in-law with the sordid details. William, in turn, summoned his daughter and warned that if she persisted in her behavior he would disinherit her. Such a threat, however, fell on deaf ears, for Charlotte appeared to be obsessed with Borrowe; when, in the spring of 1892, he traveled to Europe to remove himself from the situation, Charlotte quickly followed, leaving a note for her husband explaining her actions, along with money for the care of the children she had abandoned. Drayton soon followed, finding his wife and her lover in a London hotel. Here the situation erupted into chaos, with insults and threats freely hurled by all parties.[41]

The hotel was where William Backhouse Astor caught up with his wayward daughter. Drayton challenged Borrowe to a duel, but he was less than receptive to the idea, dismissing it out of hand and adding that it was not his problem if Drayton could not control his wife. Within a week, Charlotte's love letters to Borrowe appeared in print in the *New York Sun,* apparently sold by one of his friends; their content left little doubt as to the nature of the relationship.[42] A tired-looking William took his daughter off to Paris in an attempt to convince her of her error, but on April 25 he collapsed in his hotel suite and died of heart failure and congestion of the lungs.[43]

Charlotte might have remained in Europe with Borrowe but for this development; as it was, she accompanied her father's body back to New York, where, in the midst of family mourning, the scandal continued to play out. Newspapers openly speculated that Caroline Astor must have bribed Drayton into silent submission; worse, censorious gossips declared that Charlotte's behavior should come as no surprise, given her father's notoriously loose morals—and all this in the midst of his funeral.[44]

Charlotte somehow managed to convince her mother that no adultery had taken place; whether or not Caroline—with her innate capacity for ignoring her own husband's infidelities and the gossip surrounding his private life—actually believed this, once her decision was made, she set her face and thereafter spoke of her daughter as a wronged woman. Charlotte willingly left Drayton with their children and with a financial settlement to look after their needs.[45] When divorce finally came in 1894, it was on the grounds not of Charlotte's adultery, but rather on her complaint of her husband's "cruel suspicions as to her marital fidelity." Again, there was talk that Astor money had bought Drayton's complicity, while Borrowe vanished from the intrigue, said to have been paid off to prevent any further disclosure of the sordid affair.[46]

Caroline kept Charlotte at her side, and as the period of mourning for William Backhouse Astor came to an end, everyone, according to Elizabeth Drexel Lehr, "wondered what Mrs. Astor would do. Would she, who had hitherto turned her back on anyone who had come before the divorce courts, apply her rigid code on her own daughter?" They had their answer at Caroline's next reception, when Charlotte appeared at her side to receive the guests. The message was clear, as Elizabeth Drexel Lehr noted. "The queen could do no wrong. They would follow her faithfully."[47]

This rather understandable, but somewhat cynical, move was, however, not quite as easily accepted as Elizabeth Lehr suggested. In fact, it subjected Caroline to a fair amount of criticism. Newspapers castigated Mrs. Astor over her perceived hypocrisy. "In justice to the Four Hundred itself," declared the *New York Journal*, "it should be said that they never betrayed any reluctance to send Mrs. Drayton to perdition. But Mrs. Astor made up her mind that her daughter should reign by her side once more. Let us have no illusions; it does not excuse this lady to plead that the culprit was her own daughter; nor that she believed her innocence. By virtue of her position she was bound to fulfill the utmost letter of the law. For her, there should have been no daughter; no innocence; nothing but a woman who had so far forgotten her social duty as to let herself be accused and never have disproved the accusation. Human nature, maternal sentiments, have no place in the case; she must remember only the obligations of the throne and condemn without mercy or reprieve."[48] Caroline must have been relieved when, in December 1896, Charlotte wed George Ogilvy Haig (brother of future general Douglas Haig) and took up permanent residence in London. It was, noted the *New York Herald*, "a happy relief from an embarrassing situation whereby society was split up into opposing factions."[49]

The furor over the forced reintroduction of the scandalous Charlotte Augusta into New York society came as Caroline's power over that body had begun to wane. Lloyd Morris noted that while Caroline's parties continued with "all the plain, good people whom she keeps on her list," after the turn of the century "the smart ones stayed away, mostly."[50] Her husband's death in 1892, followed by that of her second daughter a year later, imposed two years of mourning; when she was ready to return to active participation in New York society, Caroline found that it had changed dramatically, and she never quite enjoyed the same power that she had once wielded.[51] She frankly admitted that the newer generation "have ideas different from my conservative ones." With her talent for ignoring the unpleasant, Caroline existed more and more in a social world confined to the rigid barriers she herself had erected, refusing to acknowledge the passage of time and the great changes being wrought from within her privileged milieu. Thus she once convincingly declared that while it was said that many young society ladies "smoke and drink and do other terrible things," no one known to her engaged in such deplorable habits. "I know a great many of them," Caroline explained, "and know them very well. I have known them since they were born, and I am quite sure there is not one in my circle who is a cigarette fiend or who drinks to excess."[52]

In the absence of Caroline's controlling hand, recalled one lady, "there was an undercurrent of speculation for two or three seasons, and the claimants to the succession vied for the distinction of giving the best entertainments, having the most beautiful clothes, the finest horses, the richest jewels—all weapons in the struggle for supremacy."[53] What eventually emerged in the wake of Caroline's diminishing influence was a more chaotic and lavishly indulgent version of society, one whose excesses were largely to become synonymous with the Gilded Age as a whole. An increasingly confused array of warring hostesses attempted to seize the reins of power, not through their cultivation of taste or insistence on refinement but with sybaritic splendor and ever more bizarre forms of novelty to keep themselves amused. Into this gap stepped Alva Vanderbilt, who occupied the foremost place, but she, too, found her position under assault, primarily due to her difficult and often abrasive personality. Alva refused to relinquish her power; instead, she cannily shared it, forming an unlikely trio with her two principal rivals known as the Great Triumvirate, creating a social anomaly at war with the more noble instincts that had previously ruled. The first of these remarkable ladies was Theresa Fair Oelrichs, a short, black-haired lady armed with an unlimited supply of money and the domineering personality of a drill sergeant.[54]

Born in 1870 and raised in Nevada, Tessie—as she was known to her friends—was the heiress to a large silver fortune. Her father, James Fair, was an Irish immigrant who became a self-made millionaire in the Comstock Lode and became a U.S. senator in 1881. In 1861, Fair had married a widowed boardinghouse keeper in Virginia City, Nevada, Theresa Rooney, and the couple had four children; when the marriage collapsed, a much-publicized divorce on the grounds of his persistent adultery followed in 1883. Tessie lived with her mother, who had claimed a $5 million ($100 million in 2008) divorce settlement—then the largest such sum ever awarded—and sister Virginia (known as "Birdie," who in 1899 married Alva's eldest son, William Kissam Vanderbilt III) in San Francisco.[55] The Fairs summered in Newport, where Tessie met her future husband. Hermann Oelrichs, born in 1850, was the son of a German émigré, and he became a successful agent for the North German Lloyd Shipping Company.[56] They married in 1890, in a lavish ceremony in San Francisco from which her father was pointedly excluded, although he generously gave her $1 million ($20 million in 2008) in cash as a wedding gift.[57] After the deaths of her mother in 1891 and father three years later, Tessie—along with her sister—inherited nearly $50 million ($1 billion in 2008).[58]

Tessie, recalled her niece Blanche Oelrichs, had a certain "Irish beauty, classic nose, and extraordinary humor." She was full of restless energy. Blanche remembered that she "seemed always starting for another point, in her victoria, or electric brougham. And I fancied she must ever appear out of glittering hallways—from between lanes of potted hydrangea plants in their spectral August bloom."[59] There were countless dinners,

Tessie Oelrichs in the garden at Rosecliff with her son Herman Jr. and her
Vanderbilt nieces, about 1914.

concerts, and balls, and she thought nothing of hiring entire ballet or opera companies to entertain for the evening. An accident had left Tessie blind in one eye, and in time she became increasingly deaf; not one to let such obstacles stand in her way, Tessie would simply amuse herself at her parties, carrying on shouted conversations interspersed with a steady stream of her own, often racy, running dialogue that drowned out most of her guests.[60]

Never quite able to overcome insecurities about her humble ancestry, Tessie created a startling impression in expensive gowns from Worth in Paris that were too small for her increasingly robust frame. In an attempt to fit into them, she employed masseuses to massage away the pounds and filled her houses with an array of the latest exercise machines. Nothing, however, seemed to work. Eventually she resorted to having her footmen lace her into ever-tighter corsets—a gross breach of etiquette that she airily dismissed as necessity.[61]

Tessie, noted one friend, "had a passion for perfection. She never did anything by halves."[62] She distrusted all servants, and every morning, promptly at nine, made a daily inspection of her house.[63] She demanded that the linens on every bed in her houses be changed each morning, even if no one had occupied it the previous night, saying, "If I didn't know that I could come in at any moment and find everything ready for me, it would feel like death."[64] Perhaps it was the specter of her childhood in a dusty mining town or her time in a rough and muddy burgeoning San Francisco that drove Tessie's obsession with cleanliness. If not satisfied with the results of her morning tour, she would drop to her knees and, still clad in one of her thousand-dollar dresses, grab a brush and pail of soapy water and scrub away at any hint of grime. "When I die," Tessie once said, "bury me with a cake of Sapolio soap in one hand and a scrubbing brush in the other."[65]

Tessie took such interest in her surroundings to compensate for the failures in her private life. Although she bore her husband two children, Marjorie and Hermann Oelrichs Jr., the marriage was soon strained from different interests and expectations, and the couple lived virtually separate lives, Tessie on the East Coast and her husband in San Francisco, attending to business. Tessie, said her niece, "had decided to remain amicably separated from her charming husband, with his noticeably high blood pressure. And well do I remember the strain it was to sit at their luncheon table on one of my uncle's rare visits, listening to their pretense at intimacy." Occasionally the charade was too much, and Tessie's frustration erupted in a stream of invectives aimed at her servants over such minor infractions as when they indulged in one too many cups of tea.[66] By tacit agreement, however, Tessie maintained the pretense until Hermann's death from a heart attack in 1906.

The third member of the Great Triumvirate was also the most eccentric, Gilded Age society's "enfant terrible," in the words of social historian Dixon Wecter.[67] Born in 1855, Marion Graves Anthon—Mamie to her friends—was the daughter of prosperous lawyer William Henry Anthon, who had served as a member of the New York State Assembly and who died when she was twelve.[68] Mamie was not as cultured as her rivals, and she took great pride in her humble tastes; her education had been indifferent at best, and her favorite reading was the notorious *Town Topics,* a scandalous gossip rag that printed society's most intimate secrets.[69] What she lacked in refined taste she more than made up for with a captivating charm coupled with an acidic, often vitriolic wit.[70]

In 1876 Mamie married Stuyvesant Fish. Born in 1851, Fish was the scion of a distinguished, moneyed family. Hamilton Fish, his father, had served as American secretary of state and was a governor of New York State, and, through his grandmother, a descendant of Peter Stuyvesant, the last Dutch governor of the New York colonies. Although he had inherited a large real-estate fortune, Stuyvesant had proudly worked his way up from the position of clerk to become president of the Illinois Central Railroad. According to one contemporary, his "good-nature and air of camaraderie . . . may have led some to underestimate his moral sturdiness, but when the time of crisis came . . . even the sacrifice of valued friendships could not cause him to waver. Still less could the lure of wealth affect his judgment."[71]

Unlike most couples in the Gilded Age, Mamie and Stuyvesant Fish enjoyed a warm and loving marriage, and no matter where they were, she made a point of spending one evening each week dining alone with him on his favorite, corned beef and cabbage.[72] She called him "the good man," but often would add, "Where would he be without me? I made him. I put him on the throne." Stuyvesant Fish, however, never enjoyed society as did his wife, and preferred to remain firmly in the background. "Sometimes he would come back tired out after a long journey over his railroad and find the house full of a noisy crowd of guests, someone sleeping in his bedroom, even his razors and shaving brushes commandeered," Elizabeth Drexel Lehr remembered. "But he would only shrug his shoulders good-naturedly. 'It seems I am giving a party. Well, I hope you are all enjoying yourselves.'" He far preferred to spend his time quietly at Glenclyffe, his family's estate along the Hudson, but he never stood in the way of his wife's ambitions. There was, Elizabeth Drexel Lehr said, "something romantic in his devotion to her."[73] Mamie, in turn, was a doting—if occasionally distant—mother to their three children: Marian, born in 1880, Stuyvesant Fish Jr., born in 1883, and Sidney, born in 1885.[74]

Somewhat short and stout, with sleepy dark eyes and a tangle of elegantly coiffed auburn hair, Mamie took great pride in her rise to power and loved to entertain, but never on the elaborate scale of her rivals.

Mamie Fish.

"We are not rich," she once explained. "We have but a few million dollars."[75] She treated Gilded Age society as a plaything, an opportunity for pointed mockery and ridicule at the expense of her haughty friends. "I'm so tired of being hypocritically polite," she once exclaimed, and she quickly put her feelings into practice.[76]

Mamie ignored rules of convention, refusing to make social calls on other women and often leaving parties shortly after arriving, loudly deeming the proceedings a bore. She cut the ordinary elaborate society dinners of up to three hours down to fifty minutes, and she even went that one better when she served an eight-course meal in a record thirty minutes, service so quick that guests were obliged to hold onto their plates with one hand while eating with the other to prevent their removal by eager servants.[77] She hated serving wine with meals, opting instead for champagne, saying, "You have to liven these people up—wine just makes them sleepy!"[78]

"American Society," Mamie once pronounced, "aims to be too exclusive, and it simply makes this country the object of ridicule abroad. Just think, for instance, how many worthy people—artists, writers, thinkers, and the like—are excluded from 'society,' or the 400 as it is called in this country, whereas in foreign society such congenial souls are welcomed with open arms. That is what I dislike about America. Talent and intellect should open the portals to society. That is where other countries show understanding and where America displays snobbishness. Oh, the 400! Doesn't it sound ridiculous? Just as if in this country there could be just 400 persons—and no more—worthy to be called the elect! Isn't that absurd? America is too new and too big for that sort of narrowness. It is not typical of the American principles; it does not do justice to the American ideal."[79]

Actress Marie Dressler, who became one of her friends, later wrote, "Mrs. Fish had humor, courage, naturalness, and honesty. These were the qualities she admired most in others. Above all, she liked courage, even ruthlessness of a sort. . . . Imperious, generous, brilliant herself, dullness was the one sin that she could not forgive. She demanded that those who sat about her dinner table should be funny, or handsome, scintillating, or like herself, superbly arrogant. It made no difference to her whether their families came over in the *Mayflower* or in the last boat to unload at Ellis Island."[80]

At the same time, however, Mamie firmly opposed many ideals of democratic equality. She once declared, "There will always be classes in this country. We are coming more and more to have an aristocracy and a common people. I do not believe in being too democratic." She also shared many of the prejudices common to Gilded Age society. "I should not like to have to eat with Negroes," she once declared. "I do not believe in equality. It would never do. We cannot mix with the Negro at all, and Negro equality will never come about."[81] Mamie disliked the ballet, the opera, and any concerts and swore like a fisherman, and her loudly bellowed laughter cut through the demure smiles at most parties, but she had the money and the husband to guarantee social acceptance.

No one quite knew what Mamie might do at any party, and her "witty, occasionally caustic remarks," remembered Eleanor Belmont, "provided her less accomplished neighbors with stories that lasted all summer, and all winter, too."[82] Once, speaking of the president's wife, she told a reporter, "Mrs. Roosevelt dresses on $300 a year, and she looks like it!"[83] Mamie smoked openly, and frequently insulted those around her. She once greeted a group of society ladies bedecked in their latest Parisian fashions with, "Well, here you all are, older faces and younger clothes."[84] On visiting a friend's newly redecorated house, he proudly pointed out to Mamie an exquisite marble fountain he had recently installed in his residence. "Beautiful, beautiful!" she announced. "Just the sort of watering trough you might put up for a favorite horse!"[85]

Invitations to Mamie's parties and dinners were widely sought after, although she rarely evinced any pleasure in entertaining her guests. To a visiting Englishman, Tony Shaw-Safe, she said, "Howdy-do, Mr. Safe. I'm so sorry to call you Mr. Safe, but I've forgotten your combination."[86] Greeting one set of arrivals, she declared, "Make yourselves perfectly at home, and believe me, there is no one who wishes you were there more heartily than do I!"[87] When one guest, sad to see the evening come to an end, asked Mamie if they might have just another two-step on the dance floor, she replied, "There are just two steps more for you—one upstairs to get your wraps, and the other out to your carriage!"[88] On another occasion, when a guest regretfully excused himself for having to leave a party early, Mamie cut him short, saying, "Don't apologize, and remember, no guest ever left too soon for me!"[89]

"The hoarse laughter of Mamie Fish was never still," recalled Blanche Oelrichs. "She had the elements of a true comedienne, but her harsh gaiety had the bitter overtone of a grotesque disillusionment with herself and everyone else. One knew as one looked and listened to her that she sensed well the triviality in which she drowned her time, and that her brash mirth concealed an ever more exasperated cry at the impotence of the kind of life that went on around her."[90]

Mamie never bothered with learning people's names, instead simply referring to them as "Lamb," "Pet," or "Sweet Pea," though her insults were firmly directed.[91] Once, Alva confronted her. "I heard what you said," she declared angrily. "You said I looked like a frog!"

"No, no, not a frog!" Mamie shot back. "A toad, my pet, a toad!"[92]

Not surprisingly, Mamie's brash behavior ultimately caused trouble. In 1883, Stuyvesant Fish had appointed Edward Henry Harriman to the Board of Directors of the Illinois Central, and later Fish supported Harriman's consolidation of the Union Pacific and the Southern Pacific. These acquisitions made Harriman one of the most powerful railway tycoons in Gilded Age America. But after the turn of the century, when Mamie reportedly offended Harriman's wife, Mary, with some of her typical mals-mots at a party, it signaled disaster for Stuyvesant Fish. Harriman supposedly moved quickly to retaliate against Mamie's husband, and engineered his removal in November 1906 from the presidency of the Illinois Central.[93]

5

THE SOCIETY GENTLEMAN

BEFORE THE GILDED AGE, American gentlemen were privileged patricians who, through heredity and breeding, represented their class at its most genteel. They usually presided over banking houses or family businesses, occasionally entered politics, but rarely embarked on anything so vulgar as a true professional career. This changed after the Civil War, when newly minted millionaires and men of business began to dominate the landscape of New York. Previously, their work had excluded them from consideration as part of proper society, but money bought entrée as the barriers crumbled. Manners and etiquette were often learned quickly, and a band armed with money and influence, if not quite breeding, beset society. Their rapid inclusion in this milieu anticipated the subtle changes in the idea of a gentleman that the Gilded Age witnessed.

In a world of society driven by and devoted to women, the gentleman rarely made an impact. "The American man," wrote Lloyd Morris, "was prepared to lavish his fortune on his wife, perhaps because he didn't know what else to do with it—or her. But he was prepared neither to share her interests nor admit her to his own. Absorbed by his pursuit of power, he asked only that she remain in her own sphere, creating for herself whatever kind of world she chose, provided that others found it enviable."[1]

Instead, most gentlemen devoted themselves to business and to leisure pursuits and interests that helped enshroud them in a mien of Old World aristocratic privileges. Thus there was a nearly universal obsession with horses: gentlemen owned, bred, and raced horses, and enjoyed coaching and driving, diversions adopted from English models. Although the American Gilded Age gentleman tended to hunt and shoot less than his European counterparts, many enjoyed—or pretended to enjoy for the benefit of their guests—such endeavors at their country estates in the autumn months. Sailing, too, remained a favorite pastime, with yachts providing not only a measure of luxury but also often—as with Caroline Astor's husband, William—welcome escapes from the endless social rounds over which their wives presided.

Armed with substantial resources and immense houses with blank walls, perhaps it was only natural that many gentlemen of the Gilded Age elite began to seriously collect and commission works of art. Collecting art tended to be a distinctly masculine pursuit: ladies oversaw the design and decoration of houses and planned society's entertainments but evinced little interest in the paintings that hung on their walls. Gentlemen, however, found in this pursuit one of the rare creative outlets open to them in the age. The accumulation of expensive paintings from Europe not only satisfied a desire to spend riches on visible symbols of wealth and demonstrate taste but also to claim the important role of cultivated sponsor and beneficent patron. These "merchant princes," as they were sometimes derisively termed in a nod to the original aristocratic Renaissance patrons, also recognized that collections often were sound financial investments for the future.

A few American collectors purchased true masterpieces by Leonardo da Vinci, Titian, and Rembrandt, but the vast majority of these gentlemen were slaves to the prevailing taste of the day, an aesthetic and often sentimental approach that presented realistic views and forms to evoke not only recognition but also delight. These paintings tended to fall into one of several categories: Oriental, with exotic views of Egypt, the Ottoman Empire, and Palestine predominant; antiquity, with ancient scenes and personages brought to life in dramatic colors; historical, with canvases modeled on recent occurrences and especially military conflicts;

and nature and rural life, depicting animals and peasants in distinctly realistic fashion against bucolic settings. Although a few English and German artists, such as Sir Lawrence Alma-Tadema, undertook works that easily fit into these categories, the overwhelming majority of the paintings that hung in the mansions along Fifth Avenue had come from the Artistes Français, the fashionable salon whose works were regularly exhibited in Paris to great acclaim.[2]

The salon artists offered paintings that clearly represented realistic scenes and portrayed recognizable people and historical events. These artists, noted Allen Churchill, "became the first to realize that upon this earth had come a group of self-made multimillionaires who believed that the more an object cost, the better it must be. In line with this, they were equally convinced that the larger a painting, the more valuable it became."[3] The undoubted master of the salon—and the painter most favored by American society—was Jean-Louis-Ernest Meissonier. By the turn of the century there was scarcely a fashionable house in New York City that did not have at least one Meissonier on its walls, so pervasive had his influence become. Meissonier was widely considered a genius in his depictions of military scenes, and his numerous canvases dedicated to the campaigns of Napoleon won him immense acclaim in his native France. Édouard Detaille, who had trained under Meissonier, continued the preoccupation with martial themes, devoting many of his works to incredibly detailed portrayals of the recent Franco-Prussian War, in which the painter had served as official artist for the army of Napoleon III. Adolphe-William Bouguereau was widely considered one of the greatest artists in the world during his life, his frank and romantic nudes evoking the work of François Boucher, and wealthy Americans particularly prized his paintings. Then there was Rosa Bonheur, the salon's most accomplished animalière and portrayer of rural life, the most famous female artist of the nineteenth century, and one whose paintings—like those of Bouguereau—were avidly collected by Gilded Age millionaires.[4]

William Henry Vanderbilt was one of the era's most dedicated patrons and collectors. After the death of his father, Vanderbilt used his money to embark on a serious career in art, turning to expert Samuel P. Avery for frequent advice and often traveling with him to Europe to meet artists and discuss commissions. Vanderbilt was a product of his time and environment, and almost without exception he favored works exhibited in the French salon; under Avery's guidance, however, and armed with a highly refined personal taste, he amassed a collection that, although occasionally derided for its dearth of imagination and lack of old masterpieces, was one of the most magnificent of the Gilded Age.

"I like pleasing pictures," Vanderbilt once declared, providing an outline of the personal taste that drove his private acquisitions.[5] Although he relied on Avery's judgment and recommendations, Vanderbilt ultimately purchased paintings and placed commissions based on his own personal tastes. Once, viewing a pastoral canvas, he commented, "I don't know as much about the quality of the picture as I do about the action of those cattle. I have seen them like that thousands of times."[6] William Henry, commented one contemporary, "would not purchase a picture of a nude subject, and he had a natural delicacy which made him dislike anything bordering on the doubtful or prurient."[7] And although like many other millionaires of the Gilded Age Vanderbilt owned a painting by Bouguereau, he once confided his own view that the artist's works were "not created with chaste intent."[8]

William Henry Vanderbilt was no mere dilettante. His purchases in a mere five years totaled a staggering $1.5 million ($30 million in 2008 figures).[9] He counted both Meissonier and Bonheur as friends and often visited them in their Parisian studios. During one visit to Meissonier, the painter revealed that the favorite of all of his works, *General Desaiz and the Captured Peasant*, had been purchased recently by a German collector who hid it away and refused to let anyone—its painter included—view it again. "It is lost to me and to France," Meissonier said sadly.

Touched, Vanderbilt immediately asked Avery to investigate and track down the canvas. After some discussion, during which Avery reported that the owner would be willing to sell the painting for $50,000 ($1 million in 2008) in cash, Vanderbilt immediately dispatched the funds and had the work quietly returned to Paris. On his next visit with Meissonier, William Henry said, "My good friend, I want your judgment on a painting I have just bought." When the artist saw the canvas before him, noted one chronicler, he "threw up his arms, uttered exclamations of delight, danced a jig, got down on his knees before the canvas, sent for his wife, and leaped about as only a mad French artist can do." Meissonier was overjoyed, but any idea that Vanderbilt had made such a gesture out of magnanimity was quickly shattered when the millionaire, having left the artist to enjoy an afternoon with his favorite painting, ordered it crated and shipped to his house in New York City.[10]

Such endeavors offered welcome relief from the persistent pressures of stock manipulations, Wall Street schemes, and the unscrupulous methods often employed in the business world of the era. Supervising one's holdings and investments took a good deal of time, but most of the Gilded Age tycoons managed to expend a minimum of energy, reserving their mornings for business and their afternoons for their clubs. A gentleman who did not belong to a club in Gilded Age New York was considered somewhat suspect. Clubs reinforced social status and exclusivity, as well as providing places for their members to meet, discuss business, relax, and dine.[11] For some, such as Cornelius Vanderbilt and his brother William, it had taken years of persistence to win entry into the Riding Club, the New York Yacht Club, and the Turf and Field Club. Still, the most exclusive clubs, including the Knickerbocker and, above all, the Union, remained impenetrable for decades, their doors solidly closed to those whose only persuasive argument for entrée was the size of their bank accounts.

The majority of these clubs followed established precedent diligently copied from their London counterparts, from the oak-paneled rooms filled with cigar smoke to the leather sofas and chairs on which members lounged.[12] Clubs were places of refuge where, when the Stock Exchange closed every afternoon at three, gentlemen could gather to discuss business affairs in the sanctity of their exclusive surroundings.[13] They could make deals here, pursue interests, socialize with like-minded members of society, dine, and even occasionally find a bed for the night, all to the low chatter of their comrades, the haze of cigarette, cigar, and pipe smoke, and the best food, wines, and liqueurs. These clubs also served as contact points for mistresses, who could write their paramours with the assurance that the sanctity of their correspondence would not be violated.[14] One lady complained that "club life among gentlemen tends more and more to postpone marriage."[15] These clubs were strongholds of strict decorum. Once, a member of the Knickerbocker lodged a complaint against a waiter, saying that he had been mortified when the man touched him and should be fired. No one quite knew the nature of the alleged infraction, and the club was astir with rumors of inappropriate sexual overtures until the member explained that the waiter had tapped him gently on the shoulder to alert him to a waiting telephone call.[16]

Of these clubs, the oldest—and the most prestigious—was the Union; indeed, one observer in 1887 commented that "membership in the Union implies social recognition and the highest respectability."[17] Founded in 1836, it had possessed an 1854 Italianate brownstone at the corner of Fifth Avenue and Twenty-first Street—the first building ever erected in the city specifically as a clubhouse—before a final move up Fifth Avenue in 1903.[18] In its first years, the Union had been composed of representatives of the old Knickerbocker families—the Livingstons, Van Cortlandts, Stuyvesants, and Van Rensselaers—and membership was limited to a thousand.[19] In the Gilded Age, the barriers began to fall somewhat, as such luminaries as August Belmont, the merchant A. T. Stewart, stockbroker Henry Clews, and John Jacob Astor were granted membership, but the Union remained a bastion of exclusivity.[20]

The Calumet, at the corner of Fifth Avenue and Twenty-ninth Street, was often derisively referred to as the "Junior Union Club," for its ranks were composed chiefly of those who had already put their names down for membership in the Union Club and were awaiting approval.[21] The Knickerbocker Club, at Fifth Avenue and Twenty-eighth Street, was formed in 1871 by members of the Union who felt that too many members of the nouveau riche were tarnishing its luster; their goal was to restrict membership to 750 who could boast of ancestry from the original descendants of those who had settled in New York.[22] It proudly boasted that it was the "most exclusive fashionable club. Mere membership is a passport to society."[23]

But perhaps the most exclusive of the great four, at Fifth Avenue and Sixtieth Street, was the Metropolitan, which owed its existence to a feud between banker J. P. Morgan and the Union Club. In 1891 Morgan had proposed a friend for membership at the Union, but the committee had rejected the application. William K. Vanderbilt had undergone a similar experience when his brother-in-law was turned down, and the two men decided to form their own club, over which they would maintain control. Morgan summoned architect Stanford White and declared, "Build a club fit for gentlemen. Damn the expense."[24]

Armed with money and influence, Morgan and Vanderbilt were quickly able to attract some seven hundred members, all—like themselves— immensely wealthy. The Metropolitan eagerly accepted for membership those whose antecedents might otherwise bar them from the more respectable establishments, and came to be known derisively as "the Millionaires' Club."[25] In keeping with the tastes and the financial resources of its members, Stanford White built a $2 million ($40 million in 2008), Beaux Arts clubhouse of white Tuckahoe marble, an Italian Renaissance–style structure modeled on the Palazzo Pandolfini in Florence. Here, arrayed around a forty-five-foot-high great hall lined with marble and dominated by an elaborate staircase, were a Louis XIV–style lounge paneled in oak, billiard and reading rooms, a Venetian-style library, a dining room, and several private apartments reserved for the use of the members.[26]

In contrast to these outwardly dignified centers of Gilded Age power, New York also offered a multitude of less respectable and reputable establishments, including dance halls, brothels, and gambling clubs. Here a gentleman could disappear from censorious eyes (though often in the company of his illustrious and publicly upright friends) to drink, wage sums, and seduce wide-eyed chorus girls eager to enrich their own purses. The most famous of these establishments was Canfield's, tucked

The fashionable Metropolitan Club in New York City.

quietly away at 5 East 44th Street. Opened by Richard Canfield, a former night clerk in a Union Square Hotel, the club was considered the most exclusive of New York's many dens of iniquity, its halls and private gaming rooms exquisitely fitted out and lavishly furnished to attract the elite gentlemen of society who wished to wager on games of baccarat or the spin of the roulette wheel or, according to rumor, to pursue more discreet pleasures in a number of private rooms.[27] Canfield's was the scene of many a wastrel heir's downfall. Reginald, the youngest of Cornelius and Alice Vanderbilt's sons, was a frequent visitor; one night he lost $70,000 ($1.6 million in 2008) at the gaming tables, while on another occasion, the sum was $120,000 ($2.8 million in 2008).[28] Such affairs came to an end in 1902, when the Metropolitan Police raided Canfield's and forever closed the establishment.[29]

The gentlemen who frequented these clubs and establishments, who controlled the destinies of family fortunes, who sailed on sleek yachts, and who partnered their wives, daughters, sisters, and fiancées across dance floors offered—like their female counterparts—a diverse mixture of the elegantly mannered and the proudly flamboyant. One of the first and most distinguished of the Gilded Age's recognized gentlemen was August Belmont. Born in France in 1813, he began work as a clerk for the banking house of Rothschild at an early age; indeed, it was whispered, he himself was the product of a liaison between a member of the family and an unnamed paramour.[30] In 1837, Belmont arrived in New York City at age twenty-four as an agent for the Rothschilds, and with their financial backing began purchasing shares of stocks and making investments.[31] He quickly abandoned Judaism; this was less an attempt to disguise his Jewish origins than a measure of his dislike of all religion and his distaste for the Jews he met in New York City, whom he regarded as snobs.[32] Dark and handsome, somewhat short and with a tendency to plumpness, Belmont eventually branched out on his own, opening August Belmont and Company Bank in New York.[33]

Belmont married Caroline Slidell Perry, daughter of the famous Commodore Matthew Perry, who had helped open the Japan trade route, and a niece of War of 1812 hero Commander Oliver Hazard Perry. Thereafter, as his business—and fortune—grew, Belmont surrounded himself with the trappings of power and taste, including a fine mansion on Fifth Avenue filled with European paintings by Bonheur, Meissonier, and Bouguereau, where he regularly presided over dinner parties for two hundred of terrapin, paté de foie gras, oysters, and caviar prepared by a chef imported from Paris—a novelty at the time that helped mark him out as a man of distinguished taste.[34] Above all, there were Belmont's prized horses. For two decades he served as president of the American Jockey Club, and he helped establish racing as a reputable pastime. His jockeys, clad in the Belmont racing colors of maroon and scarlet, raced his horses to many successes. Belmont helped establish the taste for splendid equipages: his *demi-d'Aumont,* pulled by four horses with two postillions, set a standard of luxury previously unknown in America.[35]

In 1853, President Franklin Pierce rewarded Belmont's financial support of the Democratic Party by naming him U.S. chargé d'affaires to The Hague; after two years in this position, he was named American minister there. Belmont later served as chairman of the Democratic Party before his death in 1890.[36] "Equally irreproachable in his public and private life," commented one contemporary, "August Belmont has escaped all the scandals and slanders of which American politics are so prolific. He is a man of whom everybody always speaks well, and who has not, and does not deserve to have, a single personal enemy."[37] As a self-made man who surrounded himself with the trappings of luxury, Belmont aroused a certain suspicion among members of the old guard. Belmont, one wag said, "keeps everything but the Ten Commandments," and Edith Wharton later used him, somewhat unfairly, as the model for Julius Beaufort in her novel *The Age of Innocence.*[38] But, uniquely for a man in his position—and a Jewish man—Belmont was eventually accepted into the highest echelons of New York society, largely because of his propitious marriage. He remained one of New York's most celebrated and powerful figures until his death.

Belmont had moved easily within both the ranks of the Knickerbocker elite and Caroline Astor's new society precisely because he learned how to play the game with consummate skill. Others born to the position were not so fortunate. James Gordon Bennett—called "Young Bennett," to distinguish him from his father and namesake—was a wealthy, cultured man whose reputation both attracted and repelled, a man, wrote social historian Lucius Beebe, "whose mere presence could cast doubt on the reputations of women of otherwise unassailable virtue."[39]

Born in 1841, Bennett was the son of the owner and editor of the *New York Herald*. His early life was one of tragic confusion and indulgence, which undoubtedly shaped his mercurial character. Very early on, his parents separated but did not divorce, and the boy was regularly shuttled between his father in New York and his mother in Paris; he was educated largely in France and grew to love the country and its culture, but the lack of supervision coupled with a sense of intransigence, and of entitlement brought on by his father's fortune, led Bennett astray at an early age, as he eagerly embraced the temptations his money could provide. Before he was eighteen, he had acquired an unquenchable thirst for alcohol; by the time he returned to the United States to attend college, Bennett was not only thoroughly debauched but also struck many whom he encountered as mentally unbalanced.[40] On his father's death in 1868, Bennett assumed control of the *New York Herald* and transformed it from not only one of the most important newspapers in America to one of the most sensational as well. In this, Bennett was perhaps unconsciously echoing his own existence for, as one contemporary noted, "Mr. Bennett has led a sensational life," a man deemed "as nervously fearful of exposure as he is reckless in his escapades."[41]

Bennett, remembered one acquaintance, "had certain likable traits and was doing pretty well on the whole, but he was no submissive sycophant. There was a streak of the devil in him, a love of dangerous practical jokes and a perverse desire to outrage even those people he was courting. Particularly when he was drunk he was capable of feats of rebellious daring or mean little outbursts of spleen."[42] Bennett seemed to lack any sense of propriety when it came to his own behavior. One of his favorite activities in New York City was to sit at the window of one of the numerous clubs to which he belonged, drinking to the point of intoxication, before running along the sidewalks, flailing his arms and screaming through lines of prim schoolgirls being led on their afternoon walk.[43]

Bennett loved riding and coaching, though his tastes were often peculiar. On dark nights he could often be found on country roads outside of

New York City, completely naked and riding one of his favorite horses at a reckless pace.[44] Bennett was something of a fire buff and could often be found racing through the city at all hours to observe the latest blaze. Once, he was observed—in evening dress and with the top of an alcohol bottle clearly protruding from his pocket—drunkenly wandering back and forth and shouting orders to the firemen. Bennett refused to stand back; the captain ordered the fire hose turned on him, and Bennett eventually passed out and was hauled away. On the following day, Bennett had no memory of his activities of the previous night, but he was contrite and dispatched new rubber coats—which the men had to purchase themselves—to every fireman in the city.[45]

Nor did Bennett confine his vagaries to New York. In Newport, he sponsored a visiting retired British officer, Captain Henry Augustus Candy, for membership in the exclusive Reading Room; as a bet with Bennett, Candy rode his horse up the institution's steps and straight into the club, to the horror of the gathered members. When the club withdrew Candy's guest privileges, Bennett took it as a personal insult and resigned his own membership. In retaliation, he purchased a plot of land directly opposite the Reading Room and commissioned the Casino as Newport's most exclusive club.[46]

Bennett's career of practical jokes and questionable behavior in the United States came to a spectacular end in 1877. He had become engaged to Caroline May, a suitable young woman, and set out—drunk—to attend a party on New Year's Day at her parents' house. He loudly stumbled his way into the drawing room; strode to the fireplace; undid his trousers; and, as the horrified guests looked on, promptly urinated on the roaring fire. Women screamed, Caroline ran from the room in tears, and within a minute Bennett had been hurled bodily onto the snowy sidewalk.[47]

The next day, Caroline May's brother Frederick encountered Bennett outside the Union Club in New York and set upon him, thrashing him with a horsewhip and pummeling him with his fists, all the while loudly denouncing him as a cad who had ruined his sister's good name. Carried back to his office, Bennett drank himself into the conviction that he had somehow been wronged, and he challenged Frederick May to a duel. May accepted, and on a cold, wintry morning a few days later, the two men met in a lonely meadow in Maryland. Each, however, aimed their shots high into the air, and the showdown came to nothing. But Bennett's reputation was ruined, and within a few months he left the United States to take up permanent residence in Paris.[48]

Both Belmont and Bennett reached the heights of their influence—and notoriety—in the 1870s, in the first years of the Gilded Age. Far different was James Hazen Hyde, a tall, handsome, and socially confident example of the increasingly decadent gentleman who came to characterize the second half of the era, when Caroline Astor's hold on society had faded and it fell victim to the more concentrated excesses of great wealth coupled with ennui. The son of Equitable Life Assurance founder Henry Baldwin Hyde, James was a renowned aesthete who easily fit the public preconceptions of what a gentleman should be. An early holiday in France filled James with a deep and abiding love of French culture. He adored the Paris Opéra, French châteaux, French wine, French literature, and French food.[49] After graduating from Harvard in 1898, he reluctantly settled down and assumed control of the Equitable as principal shareholder and vice president in the wake of his father's death a year later. But James, like so many of his contemporaries, took no joy in his business responsibilities, and those within the company, particularly its president, James Alexander, and without exploited his youth and inexperience to keep him largely at bay. James's enemies were always eager to spread stories suggesting that he was slowly draining the Equitable of its assets to satisfy his luxurious tastes, although in fact there appears to be no truth to this.[50] But he used the company to promote business deals favorable to France, and famously wined and dined the French ambassador to America at a magnificent banquet in 1902; in consideration of his friendly overtures, the French government duly awarded Hyde the Légion d'honneur.[51]

In contrast to a gentleman such as Belmont, who had actively engaged in a variety of useful work, Hyde epitomized the trend that had become prevalent by the turn of the century, being more interested in a life of leisure, and his salary from the Equitable, as well as his inheritance, allowed him to live lavishly. According to rumor, he habitually traveled with a trunk of black silk sheets, on which he could retire, adorned in his black silk pajamas, in a bedroom always fitted with both special black carpets and black curtains to eliminate any distracting light.[52] When not residing in the city, he could retreat in his private railway carriage to a four-hundred-acre country estate, the Oaks, at Oyster Bay, Long Island, where he had a large, Eastlake-style mansion; there, suitably attired in a fawn-colored driving coat with pearl buttons and a tall beaver-skin hat, he could indulge his passion for coaching and horses.[53] He was so enamored of coaching that he once paid thousands of dollars to have a roadside inn redecorated—his love of France notwithstanding—in the English Tudor style, complete with a menu of authentic meat pies and imported English Stilton and ales for his frequent stops when coaching.[54]

At six feet four inches tall, with dark, wavy hair, dark eyes, and a chiseled face accentuated with a little pointed beard, James was not only one of the Gilded Age's most handsome men but also one of its most eligible bachelors.[55] "I have wealth, beauty, and intellect," he once said. "What more could I wish?"[56] With his money and his manners, James was the dream of many a society debutante, including Alice Roosevelt, the proud and imperious daughter of President Theodore Roosevelt, and many expected them to marry until she fell in love with Nicholas Longworth.[57] In 1905 James finally had his moment of splendor in the sun, but it was to be a final burst of radiance before scandal drove him—like "Young Bennett" before him—from the country.

Spanning both archetypes—the privileged, mannered gentlemen of the early Gilded Age and the more determinedly self-indulgent younger men who began to dominate society at the turn of the century—was Caroline Astor's only son, Jack. Torn between two worlds, his was a confused existence. Born in 1864, John Jacob Astor IV, known as Jack, was coddled and cosseted, doted on by his mother and by his four sisters.[58] Spoiled and indulged, he could be a terror. Aboard his father's yacht he liked to sneak up on the crew and push them overboard; on another occasion he found the cook asleep in the galley and tied him to his chair. When the captain finally worked up the courage to complain to William Backhouse Astor, the latter admitted that he was afraid of correcting his

John Jacob Astor IV.

son for fear that Jack might slip something into his coffee.[59] Following his education at St. Paul's School and at Harvard, Jack emerged as a tall, rather plain young man with a keen interest in science and technology; he was constantly tinkering with some invention, and he even—to the horror of his family—published a science fiction novel. He redeemed himself from this peculiarity during the Spanish-American War, when he donated his yacht and more than $100,000 ($2.3 million in 2008) to help the effort, a move that won him the honorary rank of colonel.[60] Still, he was uneasy in society, and people took to calling him "Jack Ass" behind his back.[61]

Jack, recalled his friend James Gerard, was "tall and charming in a quiet way, and unassuming to the point of being actually bashful." He remembered that on many evenings, having shared a cab ride, Jack would guess at what was owed for the fare and pull out the bills, laying the sum down on the seat and running out of the vehicle, just to avoid having to speak to the driver.[62] He was so painfully shy that even though he was so wealthy, there was little talk of parties and feminine diversions. He was, noted one contemporary, "one of the richest catches and at the same time voted so much less brilliant than his father that it is very questionable whether, were he put to it, he could ever have earned his bread by his brains."[63]

In 1891, at age twenty-seven, Jack reluctantly married twenty-two-year-old Philadelphia socialite Ava Willing in a union arranged by his parents, apparently much against the bride's wishes. One Astor relative, Winthrop Chanler, recalled that at the February wedding Ava "looked like death, trembling & in a state of seemingly hopeless despair. . . . She trembled & cried a little, so that I felt as if I were attending a sale in a slave market."[64] Ava, in contrast to her rather ungainly husband, was exceptionally pretty. One acquaintance called her "the most beautiful woman I had ever seen. It was not alone a beautiful face but the tout ensemble, arms, wrists, hands, ankles—a brilliant distinction that was unforgettable."[65] She was also spoiled, vain, and tempestuous, accustomed to getting her own way in all matters, and Jack quickly discovered that they had little in common. Ava also proved a less than ideal mother to their children, Vincent, born in 1891, and Alice, born in 1902. Vincent, who unfortunately greatly resembled his father, later recalled that his mother ridiculed his looks in front of company, referred to him as "stupid" and a victim of his "bad Astor blood," and often locked him in a closet to keep him quiet and then went to parties, leaving him to be rescued hours later by a servant.[66] The marriage quickly unraveled; when Alice was born, she was widely believed to be the result of her mother's affair with another society gentleman.[67]

Ava had little interest in her husband except for spending his money. There were furious arguments in front of guests and servants, and Ava made absolutely no attempt to spare her husband's feelings, alternately ignoring him and then berating him for some minor transgression no matter who happened to be present.[68] He "shambled from room to room, tall, loosely built, and ungraceful, rather like a great overgrown colt, in a vain search for someone to talk to," recalled Elizabeth Drexel Lehr. When he sought comfort in playing the piano, Ava would dispatch a servant with an order that he stop, as the noise disturbed her. Knowing that Jack prized punctuality, his wife was not only deliberately late to their own dinners and parties but also purposely detained their guests, to his annoyance. "Dinner," recalled Elizabeth Drexel Lehr, "was not an enjoyable meal," as Ava constantly reprimanded her meek husband in front of the guests. Eventually Jack simply took to skipping his own parties and dining alone on a tray in his study.[69]

Jack's melancholy over such treatment gave way to emotional outbursts coupled with sexual frustration, and he began to make awkward advances to the sisters, daughters, and wives of the couple's friends.[70] According to one acquaintance, Jack "pawed every girl in sight" and was so blatant about his liaisons that he was no longer fit to be a warden in the Episcopalian Church.[71] Caroline Astor came to regret the union into which she had cajoled her son, but while she remained alive, she refused to countenance any talk of divorce. If she could not maintain her hold on the society she had created, she was at least determined to impose its stringent rules on her own family, clinging ferociously to a notion of what was good and right in the face of an increasingly cynical twentieth century.

6

THE COURT JESTER

ON JANUARY 29, 1900, Caroline Astor welcomed the new century in with her annual Opera Ball in her house at 842 Fifth Avenue. Although her hold was diminished, Mrs. Astor remained at the head of New York society, her entertainments still considered the pinnacle for all aspirants. At eleven that night, dressed in a black velvet gown adorned with white jet, lace appliqués, and tulle, and wearing her famous diamond tiara and more than $100,000 ($2.3 million in 2008) in diamond necklaces and brooches, Caroline stood in her drawing room as four hundred guests paid homage. The room was filled with bowers of roses framed by towering apple blossoms in gilded tubs, the doorways hung with strings of white lilies and yellow jonquils, and the chandeliers festooned with ivy laced with twinkling electric lights. Dancing continued until five in the morning, interrupted only by a ten-course supper that included consommé, *suprème de volaille, filet de boeuf aux champignons frais pommes,* terrapin, duck croquettes, pâté de foie gras, *salade Oriental,* and bonbons.[1]

Opening the quadrille with Mrs. Astor's daughter Carrie was Harry Lehr, a bizarre figure who had wormed his way to the center of New York society. For many years, Ward McAllister's position as Mrs. Astor's chamberlain had gone unchallenged, but the passing years brought new challenges that undermined his power and prestige. In 1889, Mamie Fish embarked on a campaign to discredit McAllister when he not only publicly criticized one of her dinners but also humiliated her husband, who was planning a great ball. Stuyvesant Fish, McAllister declared, was unequal to the task at hand. "As a dance of dignity," Ward haughtily announced, "it was a farce. I am glad I had nothing to do with such a Fish ball."[2] Yet the event was far from a disaster, and the attendance of Caroline Astor, who led a dance in the presence of President Benjamin Harrison and the first lady, hinted at the doyenne's increasing disillusion with her former aide.[3]

The situation deteriorated when, in 1892, McAllister committed the unpardonable sin of releasing a list of the famous four hundred to the *New York Times*. Critics were quick to point out that McAllister's list consisted of just over three hundred names, further calling into question his claims. McAllister delighted in the attention, and it soon became known that he was amenable to taking large bribes from members of the nouveau riche in exchange for assistance in introducing them to society.[4] He compounded these errors by granting interviews in which he discussed his wealthy friends. He recognized that New York society was changing. "There was a necessity for the Patriarchs in 1870, and that necessity seemed to be dying out," he declared. "Recently, however, a new one has arisen. London society may be too large for public balls, and there the necessity does not exist. Every one has a fixed position, but in New York they have not. The present is an era of multi millionaires who aim at keeping out as many of their own kind as possible from the inner circle which they have formed."[5]

McAllister continued to revel in his public notoriety, traveling to Chicago, where he caused such offense that he was quickly denounced as Mrs. Astor's "Head Butler" and a "New York flunky."[6] Worst of all, he let it be known that he was writing a memoir of his society friends—an unforgivable breach of etiquette. He had made the mistake of assuming he was their equal and that his bad behavior would be tolerated as if he were one of their own. But he was quickly crossed off guest lists and found himself publicly disparaged as "a discharged servant" by Stuyvesant Fish.[7] When McAllister died in January 1895, fewer than a dozen members of the fabled four hundred bothered to attend his funeral at Grace Church; Mrs. Astor was notably absent, and she even declined to cancel a previously arranged dinner.[8] "What a pity it is that he wrote a book," one member of society sadly commented.[9]

Into the void created by McAllister's fall from grace stepped Harry Lehr. Born in Baltimore in 1869, Lehr was the son of a wealthy tobacco importer who served as consul to Belgium and Portugal; thus very early on, Harry acquired not only a cosmopolitan manner but also a taste for privilege.[10] In 1886, when Harry was seventeen, his father died unexpectedly; bad investments and an economic depression depleted what remained of the family fortune, and Harry's mother moved her children to Cologne, to save the embarrassment of acknowledging their reduced circumstances among Baltimore friends. Harry, who took a job as a bank clerk, later recalled "the wretched poverty, the grayness, and squalor of it all" as his mother often went hungry so her children could eat.[11] After a few years of self-imposed exile, the family returned to Baltimore when Harry's elder brother was offered a job, but their old friends pointedly avoided the Lehrs and treated them with disdain.[12]

The years of hardship, the poverty, and the continuing snubs all preyed on the impressionable Harry, who grew contemptuous of those who occupied the social circles in which the family had previously moved. Yet he yearned for their acceptance and for entrée once again to their magical world, and he launched on a new course destined to take him to the very heights of the Gilded Age. He helped found Baltimore's Paint and Powder Club, drawing in wealthy young scions of the city's best and most important families in an attempt to establish himself in society. In this he proved remarkably successful, and he found that he enjoyed the attention his performances inevitably garnered. Harry's forte was for feminine roles—a masquerade he relished, as he always enjoyed dressing in elaborate costumes. "Oh, if only I could wear ladies' clothes," he once wrote in his diary, "all silks and dainty petticoats and laces, how I should love to choose them."[13]

The stage gave Harry the adoration he so loved. His wife later recalled that he had "the vanity of a child" and enjoyed nothing so much as talking about himself for hours on end. At the same time, he remained supremely insecure; a snub, real or perceived, could prey on his mind for days, festering like a wound to be avenged.[14] James Gerard remembered him as "somewhat porcine in appearance," with "a high falsetto voice."[15] Stocky, with blond hair and blue eyes, he realized that he was not as physically attractive as someone like James Hazen Hyde; indeed, one acquaintance unkindly described Harry as "a coy and roguish pig in men's clothes."[16] But he

Harry Lehr (right) with William K. Vanderbilt Jr. (far left) and Harold Vanderbilt at Bailey's Beach in Newport, 1897.

compensated for this with an air of supreme confidence that, like so much of his life, was a carefully composed protective mask. "There was something so magnetic in his gaiety," wrote Elizabeth Drexel Lehr, "that other people instinctively responded to it. He had a flair for drawing out unsuspected conversational talents, for holding up even the dullest gathering through the sheer force of his personality."[17]

Success in Baltimore was no substitute for the heights to which Harry aspired, and it was a chance encounter with socialite Evelyn Townsend Burden at a party that finally launched his meteoric career. She was so taken with his charm and wit that she asked Harry to join her that summer at Fairlawn, her house in Newport. Here he met other members of the elite four hundred, and, equally charmed, they soon filled his days with invitations to join them in their outings and his nights with places at their luxurious dinners.[18] Taking advantage of such unexpected bounty, he flattered and fawned his way ever deeper into their circles until he became a regular—and indispensable—fixture in their glittering world.

Harry was eventually introduced to Caroline Astor at a ball in Newport; eager for someone to fill the void left by Ward McAllister, Caroline soon latched onto Harry as her new social adviser and escort. Thereafter, recalled James Gerard, "old Mrs. Astor had him constantly at her house. He picked and seated the guests at her great dinners and held in her house a position that came somewhere between that of a court jester and a majordomo."[19] Indeed, Harry once famous fawned to Caroline, "I'm only your jester!"[20] They were so close that Harry even occasionally spent Christmas with Mrs. Astor and her family.[21]

There was little about Harry Lehr that suggested such an association would result in success. Whereas Caroline Astor was dignified and reserved, exclusive and proper, Harry was all impulses and unbridled extravagance. Flamboyant and at times coarse, he was a startling contrast to the queen of Gilded Age society and to the stuffy, pompous Ward McAllister. Yet Harry brought a breath of innovation to Caroline's circle; she realized that with the passing years, her influence was waning, and in turning to Harry she made an attempt to stay at the forefront of fashionable society. Harry, in turn, although he mocked and lampooned society, constantly longed for its acceptance, ensuring—at least in the early years—that he remained respectfully obsequious. He was, noted one historian, never quite as successful in his endeavors as McAllister had been. Whereas McAllister had held sway over society for a quarter century, Harry's reign stretched to just a little over a decade; nor was Harry, with his flaunting of protocol and disregard for the establishment, embraced in the same way by gentlemen as had been McAllister.[22]

Harry Lehr was proudly, deliberately superficial. "I make a career of being popular!" he once explained, and in his case it was no idle boast.[23] His only real job was to act as a sort of walking advertisement. Champagne merchant George Kessler paid him a substantial sum to promote his product to his society friends.[24] One of New York City's most famous tailors provided all his clothing for free, hoping that Harry would recommend them to his Gilded Age friends, and other companies stepped up with free shoes, underwear, and even jewelry; his friends who controlled the railroads ensured that he always traveled free on their lines. Department store heir Tom Wanamaker, one of Harry's closest friends, let him live rent-free in a pied-à-terre he kept at Sherry's Hotel in New York City. He dined in the restaurant below at the hotel's expense, and he entertained lavishly, with the proprietor happily picking up the tab, keenly aware that Harry attracted the city's elite to his table. "No better advertisement could exist than Harry Lehr's patronage," declared his wife. "Wherever he led, the whole of the smart crowd would be certain to follow."[25]

Harry quickly became indispensable to Gilded Age hostesses. He "chose their dresses for them, planned their house parties, taught them how to manage their love affairs, and found them husbands," recalled Elizabeth Drexel Lehr.[26] Their husbands, in turn, looked on Harry as a welcome addition, someone who distracted their wives and about whom they had no worries. "They knew that he would give them no cause for jealousy," said his wife; "they did not even fear him; his friendships with women were so completely sexless."[27] Mamie Fish once airily dismissed Harry as "just one of us girls."[28]

In 1901, "backed by a coterie of dowagers," recalled James Gerard, Harry married the widowed Elizabeth Drexel Dahlgren, heiress to a Philadelphia banking fortune, whose first husband had died within a year of their marriage.[29] One night at the opera, George Gould's wife, Edith, pulled the beautiful Elizabeth aside, saying, "My dear, I want you to meet the most amusing man in New York."[30]

Elizabeth Drexel Lehr, painted by Giovanni Boldini.

Harry was attentive; Elizabeth was certainly attractive, and her money and social prominence were all the recommendation Harry needed. After a whirlwind courtship, one day Harry took her to a luncheon with Caroline Astor, Mamie Fish, Alva Vanderbilt, and Tessie Oelrichs; they quickly took stock of her and, in the end, gave their approval. Harry soon professed his love; Elizabeth was less certain but, swept along on the romantic tale he wove, managed to convince herself that she was in love.[31] Her first hint of the trouble to come was Harry's preoccupation with her money. He complained that once he was married to an heiress, all of the merchants on whom he relied for his way of life would no longer provide him with free goods. So persistent and disagreeable was he with this talk that, in an effort to avoid any further confrontations, Elizabeth relented and offered to make a large financial settlement on him as soon as they were married, to pay all of their living expenses herself, and to provide him with $25,000 ($575,000 in 2008) a year in spending money.[32]

After their wedding at St. Patrick's Cathedral in June 1901, Harry and his bride departed for a honeymoon in Baltimore. That night, Elizabeth donned a new gown and ordered a private dinner to be served in their suite. After several hours of waiting for him to appear, a maid finally told the bride that her husband had ordered his own dinner and asked that it be in his own room. Thinking he was unwell, Elizabeth went to him, only to find that Harry was perfectly well.[33]

"There are some things I must say to you," Harry told his bride, "and it is better that I should say them now at the very beginning so that there can be no misunderstandings between us." He explained that for the rest of their marriage, when they were alone, he intended to dine privately. In public, he would shower her with affection and attentions, and appear to be the most devoted of husbands. In private, however, he wanted nothing to do with her. Elizabeth must leave him alone, not expect anything from him, neither kindness nor consideration. "I do not love you," he coldly declared. "I can never love you. I can school myself to be polite to you, but that is all. The less we see of one another except in the presence of others the better."[34]

Elizabeth was stunned. "But why did you marry me?" she asked in shock.

"Dear lady, do you really know so little of the world that you have never heard of people being married for their money, or did you imagine that your charms placed you above such a fate?" Harry countered. "Since you force me to do so I must tell you the unflattering truth that your money is your only asset in my eyes."[35]

Elizabeth returned to her own room and cried herself to sleep on her wedding night. The humiliation was almost too much to bear. Naively, she had no idea why her new husband, as he once told her, found her "repulsive."[36] Harry was never public about his homosexuality, and after his death Elizabeth was shocked to read in his diaries of his true feelings.[37] Yet everything in his manner, behavior, and way of life underlined his sexuality. His personal heroes were the late, equally flamboyant King Ludwig II of Bavaria and the Duc de Joyeuse, favorite of King Henri III, whose portrait hung over his bed.[38] As Harry frankly once told Elizabeth,

"Love of women is a sealed book for me. I have not wanted it, or sought it, and I never shall."[39]

Thoughts of divorce briefly crossed her mind, but Elizabeth realized that not only would her mother regard such a move as an intense scandal but also, as a devout Catholic, would look on the suggestion with horror. Feeling trapped, Elizabeth resolved to maintain the pretense that hers was a happy marriage, and, as he promised, Harry was the very model of a faithful and loving husband when the couple appeared in public; even Caroline Astor would look at the pair indulgently, commenting that it was "so nice to see young people so much in love."[40] But it was all a charade. Every Sunday, the couple attended Mass at St. Patrick's Cathedral; Harry would stand at her side, clutching an exquisite rosary of carved jade, seemingly lost deep in prayer, only to pause, lean over to his wife, and hiss, "What a perfect fright you are looking! Why on earth did you put on those shoes?"[41]

Despite his marriage, Harry continued to spend much of his time with Tom Wanamaker, frequenting his rooms at Sherry's and commenting airily, "His company is like a draught of wine to me!"[42] As humiliating as this was for Elizabeth, it was still often preferable to the evenings when Harry was at home when, his tongue loosened by both drink and privacy, he spat out ugly, barbed comments: "I hate the sight of you!" he once screamed at her. "You are hideous to me!" In his quieter moods, he derided her clothing and her appearance, commenting that the only thing for which she was any use was providing him with money, money that he, at least, had the good taste to put to its proper use.[43]

Thus, year after year, Elizabeth endured what she later termed "the tragic farce of our marriage."[44] One day, Alva Vanderbilt pulled her aside and said, "You are not happy with Harry Lehr. You ought to leave him. I'll help you. I don't believe in marriage anyway."[45] But as long as her mother lived, Elizabeth felt honor-bound to create no scandal.

It was in Newport that Mamie Fish met Harry Lehr. When Mrs. Astor's health began to fail, Lehr attached himself to Mamie, who with her breezy manner found him a refreshing change from the stilted society circles in which she moved, and together they embarked on what Lloyd Morris has called a "bloodless reign of terror."[46] They delighted in mischief: once,

Mamie and Harry took a dachshund, coated it with flour, and set it loose on a gathering of elegantly attired society ladies, creating havoc and ruining their expensive gowns.[47] No one was ever quite certain what to expect, and, as a consequence, some older members of society snubbed the troublesome pair. On learning that she had been pointedly excluded from one such gathering, Mamie confronted the host, demanding an explanation.

"I can't have you and Harry Lehr at this party of mine," the man replied. "You make too much noise."

"Oh, is that so!" Mamie shot back. "Well, let me tell you, sweet pet, that unless we are asked, there won't be any party. Harry and I will tell everyone that your cook has developed smallpox and we will give a rival musicale!" Faced with such a threat, the poor host eventually relented.[48]

Harry's particular brand of mischief and gaiety was not to everyone's taste, and he was often criticized and derided. *Town Topics*, an influential and scandalous society gossip magazine, once declared that his "proud parade of his many sissy qualities ... his pink complexion and golden hair, his thin voice, his peculiar gestures, the feminine prettiness of his general makeup ... has gone beyond the limits of tolerance by decent society."[49] Harry generally took such criticisms in stride, ignoring them in his perpetual quest for pleasure; indeed, he only appeared to relish the attention.

In the late summer of 1902 Harry finally reached the pinnacle of his success when Grand Duke Boris Vladimirovich, cousin of Tsar Nicholas II, visited Newport. The grand duke was a guest of Mary Goelet, wife of financial heir Ogden Goelet and a woman who traveled so frequently between America and Europe that one wag dubbed her "Steamboat Mary."[50] Both Mamie and Harry despised Mary Goelet, but the visit of a member of the Romanov dynasty presented too many opportunities for social activity, and the pair reluctantly prepared to set aside their differences with the young man's hostess. Having reached a temporary détente, Mamie announced that she would give a ball for two hundred guests at Crossways, her Newport mansion, in honor of the grand duke. In drawing up her guest list, however, she purposely excluded James Cutting, another of Mrs. Goelet's guests at Ochre Court, her Newport house. When Mary Goelet learned of this, she warned that neither she nor any of her house guests could, in good conscience, attend a ball to which any member of her own party was not also asked; this meant losing the prize of the grand duke, but Mamie was adamant.[51]

Soon enough, however, Mamie realized just what a predicament she had created for herself as hostess of a ball to be given for a guest of honor who would not attend, and she quickly turned to Harry, imploring him to think of some solution. After considering all of the options, he decided that the only course of action short of capitulation was to "turn the whole thing into a joke. You must make people laugh so much that they will not be quite sure of what has really happened." Between them, they cooked up a fantastic—and potentially offensive—piece of effrontery: Harry would appear at the party once all of the guests had assembled and impersonate not the grand duke but rather his cousin Nicholas II.[52]

Unaware of what was taking place, Mary Goelet announced that instead of the ball at Crossways, the grand duke, on the evening in question, would be attending a dinner at her mansion, and hastily sent out invitations. This caused a good deal of confusion, as most members of society had already accepted Mamie's invitations; attempts to clarify the situation went nowhere, as Mamie insisted that her ball in honor of the grand duke still would take place, and no one knew with any certainly which hostess to believe and which to refuse. In the end, most of the two hundred guests, including financier J. P. Morgan, Senator Chauncey Depew, and Lord Charles Beresford, followed their original plans, crowding Crossways and awaited the appearance of the grand duke.[53]

Mamie knew just how to draw the scene out. When her guests began to ask questions, she replied airily, "Oh, His Majesty is a little late." On being questioned further, she explained, "I could not get Grand Duke Boris after all, but I have got someone better—the Tsar of Russia!"[54]

Such was the air of unreality surrounding Gilded Age high society that most of the guests swallowed this fantastic explanation and congratulated themselves on having forgone dinner with the grand duke for an opportunity to be presented to the emperor of Russia. Finally, amid a great commotion, the entrance doors were flung open and the butler loudly announced, "His Majesty!" A hush fell across the crowd as the men bowed deeply and the ladies all sank into low curtsies. Then, when they looked up, they saw Harry. He had raided a Newport costume shop, fitting himself out in a military uniform and a long ermine cloak; in one hand he carried a fake scepter while, perched jauntily atop his head, was a gold crown with imitation gemstones. He waved his hand airily at the assembled company in response to their shocked faces. When the guests erupted into laughter, Harry and Mamie won the battle.[55]

The next morning, Harry was taking the sun on Newport's fashionable Bailey's Beach when the grand duke spotted him and set off across the sand. "I hear you represented the emperor last night," Boris declared. "It's a good thing you were not in Russia, but I only wish I had been there to see it. It must have been most amusing. Our party was poisonous. We shall have to call you King Lehr in the future."[56] The appellation stuck, and from that day on, Harry proudly declared himself "King Lehr."

7

THE ARRIVISTES

"IF YOU WANT TO BE FASHIONABLE," wrote Ward McAllister, "be always in the company of fashionable people."[1] Such was the advice offered to those who hoped to infiltrate New York's Gilded Age society. In truth, society had erected rigid barriers to prevent the unwelcome intrusion of those they deemed parvenus, climbers, crashers, or arrivistes. One of the most basic of all tenets held by those at the center was that for society to have any real value, it must remain exclusive.

Yet members of society could not prevent the inevitable incursion of the unwelcome into its midst. Indeed, as one social historian has noted, "Arrivistes were encouraged by the American ethos, which preached, if it did not guarantee, equal opportunity in an open society."[2] As new industrial merchants, railroad barons, and stock market speculators accumulated vast fortunes, many made their way to New York. The city represented the apex of society in America, and, pushed by their wives, they were determined to take what they regarded as their rightful place within its ranks. Such optimism was usually misplaced; no matter how enormous the fortune at their disposal, they often found the ranks of society arrayed firmly against them. Hostesses such as Caroline Astor regarded themselves as the gatekeepers. They believed that their wealth and position gave them a responsibility to safeguard society from the inroads of the social climber. Most society ladies—even someone as bohemian in her tastes as Mamie Fish—held fast to the notion that their surroundings, their wealth, their obligations, and their circles of friends truly did set them apart from the country's hoi polloi. The danger of allowing intrusion into this realm represented a threat to the careful order of their universe.

To breach this society, one had to be "taken up" by someone from within and promoted. For those aspiring to society, recalled McAllister, "it took the combined efforts of all your friends' backing and pushing to procure an invitation for you. For years, whole families sat on the stool of probation, awaiting trial and acceptance, and many were then rejected, but once received you were put on an intimate footing with all."[3] A smart social aspirant began his or her quest elsewhere, perhaps in Bar Harbor or Lenox, where the standards were less stringent and the elements that formed recognized society were less rigid than those in New York. If the candidate was successful, the next year might be stretched to attempt Newport, which remained the final arbiter on the path to New York. If one met with approval in Newport, social acceptance in New York was guaranteed.[4]

Those aspiring to society were advised to begin slowly. Charitable contributions to the Episcopal Church and other philanthropic works could lead to invitations to receptions and teas, where acquaintance could then be made with those already in society. It was, one authority advised, important to send any children to the best schools, where they would meet friends of higher position and thus could be used to advance one's own claims. At times even the employment of a press agent—to write a florid account of a charity event or the opening of one's country estate— was considered part of the network used by social climbers.[5]

To assist them in their quest, these arrivistes turned to the numerous books on society designed to explain its intricacies. "The consumption of such books greatly exceeded the volume of sales in the earlier period, with several new publications appearing each year between 1870 and 1917. Needless to say, few of the readers of etiquette books would ever be privileged to polish their manners in elite circles, but the popularity of the genre suggests the readiness with which readers identified themselves vicariously with the rich."[6]

"As to the unfortunates who have been reared at remote distances from the centers of civilization," warned one guide, "there is nothing left for them to do but to make a careful study of unquestionable authority in those matters of etiquette which prevail among the most refined people. . . . Etiquette is the machinery of society. It polishes and protects even while conducting its charge. It prevents the agony of uncertainty and soothes even when it cannot cure the pains of blushing bashfulness. . . . It is like a wall built up around us to protect us from disagreeable, underbred people who refuse to take the trouble to be civil."[7]

At the turn of the century, crashing society was an expensive business. Once a fashionable house in New York was built and furnished, annual running expenses might be upward of $15,000 ($345,000 in 2008). This did not include a similar amount needed to maintain a house at Newport or in the Berkshires; perhaps $30,000 ($690,000 in 2008) a year for servants' salaries; $50,000 ($1.3 million in 2008) a year for the upkeep of a private yacht or a railway car; some $40,000 ($920,000 in 2008) a year for horses, carriages, and stables; perhaps $10,000 ($230,000 in 2008) for motorcars and the required staff; $15,000 to cover the annual visit to Europe and journeys within America; $20,000 to $30,000 ($460,000 to $690,000 in 2008) for new wardrobes; and, modestly, between $30,000 and 50,000 ($690,000 and $1.3 million in 2008) marked for entertaining.[8]

Yet money was no guarantee of success. Men such as Rockefeller, Carnegie, Frick, and Morgan might mingle at the edges with certain members of society, but they were never accepted by Caroline Astor and members of her inner circle. "No retail dealer, no matter how palatial his shop front or how tempting his millions," wrote Edith Wharton, "was received in New York society until long after I was grown up."[9] In fact, Mrs. Astor once caustically answered a query if she had ever invited a wealthy merchant to one of her parties with a snide "I buy my carpets from them, but then is that any reason why I should invite them to walk on them?"[10]

Instead, those who found themselves beyond the bounds of proper society often contented themselves by surrounding themselves with the trappings of exclusivity. Theirs was a quest to establish that they were just as wealthy and as important as those who would exclude them. Paran Stevens was a hotel magnate who, by the outbreak of the Civil War, had opened six establishments in Boston, Alabama, Philadelphia, and New York. The crown jewel in his empire was the Fifth Avenue Hotel in New York, which set standards of service and luxury previously unknown in America. While Stevens was consumed with business, his ambitious wife, Marietta, saw no reason why she should not be embraced by society; her husband ran respectable establishments and had a small fortune. In addition, she declared, the Astors themselves owned several hotels in New York City. Determined to take what she believed to be her rightful place, Marietta launched herself upon a startled society in the years after the Civil War. Every few years she redecorated her house at 244 Fifth Avenue with ever more lavish fabrics, furniture, and an array of statuary imported from Europe in an attempt to impress, but the rooms were so crowded and overwrought that there was scarcely room for her guests. Her sense of style, too, left something to be desired, for she insisted on dressing in extraordinarily lavish gowns from Paris that were far too tight and so abundantly ornamented that she found movement difficult. Nevertheless, there was a certainly novelty in her manner of life, and after her husband's death in 1872, she renewed her campaign to push her way into society. Marietta broke New York City's taboo on Sunday night entertainments, and quickly her musicales drew members of society desperate for something to fill the void of an otherwise intolerably dull evening.[11] Not that they found these evenings particularly enjoyable: on taking leave of his hostess, one of Marietta's guests said frankly, "My dear lady, it is impossible for me to resist the magnetism of your charming society, although I know it only draws me back to cold tea, hot Apollinaris water, and bad music."[12]

Marietta's great triumph finally came in 1878, when she married her twenty-five-year-old daughter Mary—known as Minnie—to Sir Arthur Paget, of a famous British aristocratic family. With her daughter a member of the British aristocracy, Marietta's star rose in the New York social world, particularly when she could play host to Minnie and her husband as guests of honor at a ball. Minnie, in turn, became one of the most famous aristocratic wives in Great Britain, a member of the Prince of Wales's Marlborough House Set and a woman who played a prominent role in introducing other American heiresses to British society.[13]

Then there was the case of William Leeds and his wife, Nancy. Derisively known as "the Tinplate King" owing to the origin of his substantial fortune, Leeds was not as driven to crash society as was his wife. After much prodding, he agreed to rent a house, Fairholme, in Newport during the summer social season. Such a move was unheard of for a couple who, thus far, had yet to be invited to a single fashionable party or be received socially by any member of the ruling elite; worse still, both Leeds and Nancy had previously divorced, with her wedding to William coming only three days after the dissolution of her first marriage.[14] John Drexel, who owned Fairholme, came in for a fair degree of criticism for renting to the Leeds. "It's not fair to the rest of us!" exclaimed Edith Wetmore, proud owner of one of the town's first extravagant cottages, Château-sur-Mer. "How can you lease to those horrible, vulgar people? Why the whole house ought to be disinfected after them!"[15]

It was Alva Vanderbilt who decided to come to their rescue. "I like those Leeds people," she told Harry Lehr one day, "and the wife is lovely. I am going to take them up and put an end to this silly nonsense."

Nancy Leeds.

Together they planned a lavish ball at which Alva would formally intro-duce the couple into the ranks of society. The invitations caused a good deal of consternation among the recipients, most of whom had been quite vocal in their opposition to efforts by the Leeds to join their ranks. They did not want to seem hypocritical and suddenly embrace the couple, yet Alva wielded very real power, and refusal to accept an invitation would mean that the doors to her splendid entertainments might forever be closed to them.[16]

In the end, nearly everyone capitulated under the weight of Alva's decision. On the night of the ball, Mrs. Leeds, in a white satin gown richly adorned with diamonds, stood at the side of her benefactor, receiv-ing the members of society who had come to meet her. "Her charm was far more potent than her husband's millions," recalled Elizabeth Drexel Lehr. "Society took her to its heart from that moment. William B. Leeds, young, handsome, and ambitious for his beautiful wife, gazed at her in adoration. Her beauty had won the day."[17]

The most successful of all arrivistes, however, was undoubtedly the Wilson family. Known derisively as "the marrying Wilsons" for their almost unbelievable matrimonial luck, they were proud of their humble origins but through propitious marriages rose to the very heights of Gilded Age society.[18] Harry Lehr once described them as "deadly opponents; their minds work like oiled steel."[19]

Originally from Georgia, Richard Thornton Wilson had begun his business life in Loudon, Tennessee, where he was instrumental in the development of the river trade. During the Civil War, Wilson acted as a cotton broker, representing Southern companies to Great Britain. Although the goal was to raise badly needed money for Confederate forces, Wilson quickly amassed an enormous fortune built on profiteer-ing by charging inflated prices for the cotton and pocketing the profits. He cannily invested the proceeds in railroads and banks, building an impressive fortune of some $10 million ($200 million in 2008) that sur-vived the turmoil of the war. Tall and charming, a man of distinguished bearing and polished manner, he later served as the model for Rhett Butler in Margaret Mitchell's *Gone with the Wind*.[20]

After the Civil War, Wilson moved his wife, Melissa, and their four children to New York, where they occupied the large mansion at 511 Fifth Avenue that had formerly been home to the infamous "Boss" William Tweed before his imprisonment.[21] Here the ambitious Melissa set about conquering society. "In the exclusive set of New York," reported one contemporary newspaper, "there cannot be found any woman who has guided the destinies of her children with such unerring aim to success."[22] Slowly, stealthily, the Wilsons infiltrated the city, turning heads and attracting attention through a series of increasingly advantageous marriages. Richard Wilson Jr. married Marion Mason, daughter of a prominent doctor, but the family's assault really began when daughter Mary Rita wed millionaire banking heir Ogden Goelet in 1877. This brought the family access to the highest echelons of Gilded Age society, but daughter Leila (known as Belle) managed to do her sister one better and in 1888 ensnared the Honorable Michael Herbert, son of British aristocratic Lord Herbert and brother to the Earl of Pembroke.

With aristocratic and millionaire sons-in-law, the arriviste Wilsons had done exceptionally well, but they were just beginning their assault. The next union brought them straight to the centers of Gilded Age power when son Marshall Orme Wilson married the "gentle, lovely" Carrie Astor, Caroline Astor's youngest daughter.[23] The slight, blond, sweet-tempered Carrie fell in love with Marshall when she was sixteen, much to the horror of her mother; no family in New York could have been more unsuitable to Mrs. Astor, for the Wilsons—the marriages to the Goelets and to the aristocratic Herbert family notwithstanding—were still widely considered parvenus and, worse, fortune hunters.[24]

Caroline Astor, recalled one of her granddaughters, had "dominated poor little Aunt Carrie completely."[25] Caroline tried to dissuade her daughter from any involvement, insisting that the couple was far too young. For a time she was successful, but Carrie had truly fallen in love with the handsome Marshall, and misery soon overtook her. Caroline's attempts to bribe Marshall into rejecting her daughter backfired, and when her mother forbade her to see Marshall again, Carrie sank into a deep depression and began to suffer from ill health. Caroline had not counted on such determination and depth of feeling from her daughter, and although William Backhouse Astor remained firmly opposed to the idea, Mrs. Astor's stance eventually began to soften. To her friends she explained that one day she had seen her daughter and Marshall leaving church together, hand in hand, and that they had seemed very much in love. "I felt that I could not stand in the way of their happiness a day longer," she said.[26] Nevertheless, Carrie was forced to wait seven years—on the pretense that she needed to be certain of her feelings—before her powerful mother agreed to give the union her full blessing. After interceding with William, Mr. Astor relented, and Carrie and Marshall were wed in 1884.[27] It was yet another triumph for the marrying Wilsons, although at the wedding reception, the guest of honor, former president Ulysses S. Grant, became so drunk that he placed the wrong end of a lighted cigar in his mouth, a slight disruption to the otherwise solemn festivities.[28]

Marriage into the Astor family might have represented the pinnacle of achievement for any other family, but for the marrying Wilsons, one more target remained: the Vanderbilts. Born on September 3, 1870, Grace Graham Wilson was the youngest daughter of the family, a beautiful, shrewd young woman with hazel eyes, blond hair, and pleasant features. She had spent a good deal of time in European aristocratic circles, polishing her French and German and attracting much attention. Many gentlemen found her intriguingly worldly, a far cry from the usual sheltered young debutantes they encountered. In London, she was a particular favorite in the Prince of Wales's Marlborough House Set, a glittering circle that unfortunately tarnished the reputation of many an innocent young girl.[29] Although there is no evidence that Grace ever succumbed to the prince's amorous advances, her time in London left a shadow over her judgment and morals. Unfortunately, her behavior seemed to justify society's fears that the Wilsons were nothing but vulgar fortune hunters. In 1890 there were rumors of a romance and a secret engagement with William Henry Vanderbilt II, eldest son of Cornelius and Alice, much to his parents' consternation; she not only carried the baggage of aspersions on her character, but also she was too witty, too sophisticated for the censorious Corneil and Alice.[30] When William died of typhoid in May 1892, Grace soon took up with British banking heir Cecil Baring, but she

Grace Wilson Vanderbilt in evening gown and jewels.

conveniently broke off that engagement in the wake of the bank's financial crisis in 1893.[31]

On August 14, 1895, Grace attended a Newport ball given to mark the debut of Corneil and Alice's daughter Gertrude, during which Grace renewed her acquaintance with William Henry's brother. Cornelius Vanderbilt III was born on September 5, 1873, the second of Cornelius and Alice's sons. He had never expected to be his father's principal heir; educated by private tutors, he attended St. Paul's School in Concord, New Hampshire, and graduated from Yale University with a Bachelor of Arts degree in 1895. Called "Neily," he was a genial, handsome young man with a passion for mechanics, and he patented a number of inventions, including several implemented on the Vanderbilt family's locomotives.[32]

In the wake of the ball, Neily quickly fell in love with Grace. To his parents, this was an unpardonable sin. Corneil and Alice had not approved of the idea when their son William fell in love with Grace, suspecting her motives as a member of the Wilson family, but the young man's death had prevented any real confrontation. Grace's engagement to, and subsequent rejection of, Cecil Baring—when his family suffered a financial setback—seemed to confirm all of the worst suspicions about the Wilsons. Neily also was Grace's third beau in five years, and the second Vanderbilt—facts that were simply too much for the elder Vanderbilts to stomach.

Corneil and Alice launched upon a careful strategy designed to undermine their son's relationship. In the autumn of 1895, Alice paid a social call on Grace's mother in New York City, during which she casually asked after the family's travel plans. On learning that the Wilsons planned to remain in the city for the coming social season, Corneil and Alice quickly arranged a European holiday for their son. Realizing what had happened, the Wilsons were deeply insulted, a situation further exacerbated when Corneil asked his friend Chauncey Depew, then president of the New York Central Railroad, to meet with Richard Wilson and implore him to forbid Grace to see Neily again. This only infuriated the Wilsons even more, and in retaliation they sent Grace off to Europe, where she quickly caught up with Neily at the Hotel Bristol in Paris.[33]

Not to be defeated, the Vanderbilts then embarked on a systematic campaign to destroy the romance by blackening Grace's character. "There is *nothing* the girl would not do!" Alice complained to her daughter Gertrude. "She is at least twenty-seven . . . has had unbounded experience. Been engaged several times! Tried hard to marry a rich man. Ran after Jack Astor to such an extent that all New York talked about it . . . the most dreadful thing of its kind that has ever happened in society!"[34] Closing ranks, Neily's mother, father, and uncles dispatched a flurry of scandalous letters to Europe, some so offensive that rather than read them completely Neily consigned them to flames. His Uncle George intimated that he had "certain interesting facts about her which I cannot write."[35]

Although Grace's sister Leila called such maneuvers "the greatest wickedness of the nineteenth century," there may have been more to the Vanderbilts' objections than fear of someone they painted as a fortune-hunting adventuress.[36] A good deal of gossip suggested a more personal reason for Corneil's wrath: that he himself had become romantically involved with Grace after his eldest son's death, and the idea of his one-time mistress marrying his son was simply too much to bear.[37]

Corneil certainly made no secret of his displeasure. The battle that erupted, during which Corneil threatened his son with disinheritance, somehow leaked to the press, which splashed news of the family strife across its gossip columns; so engaging was this story of scandal and a widening feud within the world's wealthiest family that even Grace's friend the Prince of Wales was caught up in the drama, asking to be kept informed of developments.[38] By the time Neily returned to New York, his relationship with Grace had become public fodder, with insinuations of scandal, bribery, and greed. Neily and Grace were determined, however, and on June 10, 1896, her father publicly announced that the couple would be married on June 18; not only did Corneil and Alice learn of this development when they read it in the paper, but also the timing could not have been worse. On the same day, they announced the engagement of their daughter Gertrude to Harry Payne Whitney; when asked about his son's relationship with Grace, Corneil coldly told a reporter, "The engagement of Cornelius Vanderbilt Jr. to Miss Wilson is against his father's expressed wishes."[39]

New York society was in an uproar; no one knew what to do, and only a third of those who received invitations to the approaching wedding accepted, the others fearing the wrath of the Vanderbilts if they dared attend. Each day the city's newspapers reported the latest developments, describing the coming ceremony, the bride's trousseau, and the continuing tension within Neily's family.[40] Then, on the day before the wedding, a terse statement was issued by Corneil that Neily was confined to his bed, suffering from rheumatism, and that the wedding had been called off.[41]

Neily may indeed have temporarily been ill, but he had no intention of abandoning Grace, and when he learned of his father's announcement, the crisis came to a head. A confrontation over the issue that July became so heated, it was said, that father and son actually came to blows.[42] Shortly after this, Corneil collapsed with a stroke that left him confined to a wheelchair and unable to speak; Neily's family blamed him entirely. "He knows it is his behavior that gave Papa his stroke," Gertrude recorded in her diary, calling her brother "inhuman, crazy."[43] From this point on, most members of Neily's family cut him off completely and refused to speak to him. In retaliation, on August 3, 1896, at her parents' house, Grace married Neily in a small ceremony boycotted by his family. Alice refused to receive her son and new daughter-in-law, and soon the entire city was again abuzz with the feud.[44]

When Corneil died of a cerebral hemorrhage on September 12, 1899, he left an estate worth $70 million ($1.61 billion in 2008), but Neily received a mere $500,000 ($11.5 million in 2008) in cash and the income from a $1 million ($23 million in 2008) trust fund; by contrast, Neily's brother Alfred received some $40 million ($920 million in 2008), and each of the other children had bequests of approximately $7.4 million ($170.2 million in 2008). Although Alice refused to speak to her eldest son, his brother Alfred gave his brother $6 million ($138 million in 2008), bringing his inheritance in line with the rest of the Vanderbilt siblings; despite his brother's generosity, Neily was none too pleased, and he complained to the press that he had been hoping for $10 million ($230 million in 2008).[45]

The grant, however, did allow Neily and Grace to live in comfort. Unconcerned about money, he and Grace entertained in grand style; President Theodore Roosevelt, whose daughter Alice was among Grace's closest friends, once declared that Grace "sees herself in a kind of perpetual fairy tale."[46] Despite the feud within the Vanderbilt family, no one ostracized the young couple, and their position in society was solidified when Caroline Astor—whose own son-in-law Marshall was, after all, Grace's brother—took them up and ensured that Neily and his wife were always conspicuous by their attendance at the best society parties and balls. "Born with a flair for social intrigue, with all the qualities that make a ruler," Elizabeth Drexel Lehr recalled of Grace, "she gradually assumed the leadership of New York society, despite the opposition of her husband's family."[47]

For many years the couple rented Beaulieu, an oceanside mansion in Newport, from Caroline Astor's nephew William Waldorf Astor.[48] Grace adored attention, and she thought nothing of spending thousands of dollars one year to close down a popular Broadway musical, *The Wild Rose,* and bring the entire cast to Newport to perform at her Fête des Roses in August.[49] For the evening, the eight-acre lawn at Beaulieu was transformed into a carnival, "beautifully illuminated with electric lights strung for the occasion," as one guest recalled.[50] A crimson carpet nearly three hundred feet long stretched toward the ocean; the carpet was lined with colorful booths boasting fortune tellers, Punch and Judy shows, wooden duck shoots, and a variety of other amusements; for those who won, Grace arranged prizes of gold and enamel boxes for the women and cigarette cases for the men. At the edge of the ocean, workers had erected a temporary wooden stage garlanded with yellow and white roses and illuminated by calcium footlights, upon which the cast of *The Wild Rose* performed selections from their repertoire, to the accompaniment of an orchestra. After the musical had ended, workers transformed the theater into a banquet hall for a midnight supper, followed by a cotillion and fireworks over the Atlantic.[51]

Neily and Grace became early members of the international set and mixed easily with aristocrats and the crowned heads of Europe, including King Edward VII, Tsar Nicholas II, and especially Kaiser Wilhelm II, with whom they enjoyed a particularly warm relationship.[52] This surreal atmosphere quickly went to Grace's head. Once, staying in a hotel on the Riviera, she complained to the manager that her dinner table was not prominent enough and asked to be moved to one in the center of the room. That table, the manager told her, had been reserved by a prince; she pointed to another table and declared, "Well, then, I will have that one." But this table, the manager replied, had been reserved by an English duchess. Infuriated, Grace burst out loudly, "Then see that you give me a better table than the duchess's in the future! It is only here in France that I am treated in this way! In America, I take a rank something like that of the Princess of Wales!"[53]

Within a few years of marriage, Neily began to realize that perhaps his parents had been correct in warning him off the marriage. After the initial burst of romantic enthusiasm subsided, the couple found that they had very little in common. Grace wanted parties, luxury, and an endless stream of entertainments to keep her amused, while Neily preferred solitude, reading, and working on his numerous inventions. Increasingly he took to drinking, and the differences between the pair led to loud, abusive fights. "Your mother is a bully," Neily once told his son. "If she can't have her own way, there's simply no use arguing with her."[54]

If her marriage did not quite turn out to be the storied love affair the young couple had expected, Grace kept up a brave face and threw herself into the social whirl. Her parties always attracted the attention of the press through their sparkling guest lists and unusual entertainments, and she remained charmingly naive about money. Once, when signing checks that totaled $80,000 ($1.8 million in 2008), Grace turned to her secretary and asked with astonishment, "Do I have this much money?"[55]

8

THE EDIFICE COMPLEX

IN THE YEARS FOLLOWING THE CIVIL WAR, the influx of the newly wealthy to New York City laid the foundation for a great transformation. With dollars at their disposal and visions of extravagant life dancing through their heads, these merchants, speculators, profiteers, and financiers all wanted new houses and impressive mansions. The quest for grand residences as outward symbols of status, wealth, and power grew as the years passed, and gradually the city's streets and avenues were filled with the new private palaces of society and of those who aspired to join its ranks.

Until the middle of the nineteenth century, the fashionable elements of society had lived in unremarkable brownstones clustered around Washington Square and along the lower edges of Fifth Avenue, in an area redolent of inherited privilege and wealth. "One of the most depressing impressions of my childhood is my recollection of the intolerable ugliness of New York," recalled Edith Wharton, describing the endless rows of brownstones "cursed" with a "universal chocolate colored coating of the most hideous stone ever quarried."[1] Uniform in design, lacking any ostentation, and all patrician probity, these brownstones spoke of tradition, of a quiet decorum, and above all, of the desire to blend seamlessly with their neighbors. Here the Schuylers, Livingstons, Van Cortlandts, and Van Rensselaers had lived precise lives in precise brownstones. Parlors and reception rooms were unobtrusive in their lugubrious regularity, with crimson walls, dark walnut furniture, and delicate lace curtains to screen them from the unwelcome eyes of the outsiders who passed by.[2]

Members of the city's nouveau riche, however, were not content with such modest trappings. They had wealth and, hoping to use that wealth to prove their taste in an effort to win social acceptance, began the north-ward migration along Fifth Avenue. "Here and there," wrote Paul Bourget, "are vast constructions which reproduce the palaces and chateaux of Europe. I recognize one French country seat of the sixteenth century; another, a red and white house, is in the style of the time of Louis XIII. The absence of unity in this architecture is a sufficient reminder that this is the country of the individual will, as the absence of gardens and trees around these sumptuous residences proves the newness of all this wealth and of her city. This avenue has visibly been willed and created by sheer force of millions, in a fever of land speculation, which has not left an inch of ground unoccupied. This rapidity is again shown in the almost total absence of life-like figures in the sculptures with which the windows and colonnades of these impromptu palaces are decorated."[3]

The houses that arose across the city attempted to lay claim to a heroic and privileged past. With the development of regular passenger service, tours of Europe became more common, and the old royal palaces of Italy, France, Germany, and Great Britain inspired both admiration and envy. Tied to centuries of privilege and power, they evoked precisely the spirit of permanence and wealth with which Gilded Age society wished to surround itself. Ensconced in a stately new palace, wandering amid its marble corri-dors, and entertaining in a lavish ballroom, its owners could envision them-selves as true successors of Old World aristocracy. "They are the dwellings of merchant princes," commented one publication insightfully, "compara-ble, not in artistic originality and propriety, but in general atmosphere and style, to the palaces of the Florentine and Venetian nobility."[4]

Many of these houses were extraordinarily ugly, while some were more successful in grafting elements of the Old World onto new buildings. "The epithet that comes nearest to describing comprehensively the most

THE EDIFICE COMPLEX   131

characteristic of these houses is the familiar newspaper adjective palatial,"
noted one architectural chronicle shortly after the turn of the century.[5]
Although they took advantage of the latest technological innovations—
elevators, central heating, electricity, and modern plumbing—comfort was
scarcely the point of these new residences. The great houses that lined
Fifth Avenue in the Gilded Age were meant to impress, bearing silent witness to the triumph of splendor over utility. They sat side by side in a confusing architectural riot: a building copied from a French château next to a
brick Georgian mansion; an Italianate palazzo nestled against a severe
Palladian facade; a Gothic-style palace with towers and crenellations was
beside a Beaux Arts house dripping with carved statuary, pediments, and
sculpted reliefs composed of "the pickings and stealings of many styles,"
often haphazardly thrown together in an effort to impress.[6]

Building for the wealthy, especially members of the nouveau riche, presented its own unique challenges. They might have endless money to pour
into an elegant manse, but few had any idea of history or architecture. "Do
you want a porte cochere?" an architect once asked a nouveau riche client.

"You bet I do!" he answered enthusiastically. "Put in at least five on
each floor and make sure they don't make too damn much noise when
they flush!"[7]

Within, although the houses differed according to the demands of the
owners and the style imposed, most contained very similar elements
deemed necessary to life as a member of Gilded Age society. (In their
houses, members of the Gilded Age copied the European designation of
referring to the floor at ground level as the ground floor, while the floor
above was called the first, not the second, floor.) The principal rooms
were usually on the first floor; this provided for a massive grand staircase
ascending from the ground floor on which guests could process. Many
times, a second, similar impressive sweep of stairs linked the first and
second floors, providing a theatrical backdrop for the host's dramatic
entrances to parties. Bronzes, Oriental carpets, tapestries, and antique
and reproduction French fauteuils and bergères clustered in rooms that
encompassed a variety of historical themes, from Gothic and medieval to
Renaissance and elegant French neoclassical, providing a dramatic shift
of periods, colors, textures, and moods.[8]

These houses were fitted out by architects working with the city's best art dealers: Duveen Brothers and Vitall Benguiat were two of the most exclusive sources for carpets, bronzes, and works of art, while expensive reproduction furniture came from Baumgarten, the Herter Brothers, and Jules Allard and Sons or Paul Sormani in Paris. "They sent their experts to Europe to seek out the art treasures of France and Italy," recalled Elizabeth Drexel Lehr, "gave them carte blanche to buy regardless of cost. Medieval châteaux of the Touraine yielded up their tapestries and carvings, whole wainscotings, panel by panel; ancient Florentine palaces bade farewell to their frescoes. Suits of armor that had gathered the dust of centuries in grim old Scottish castles were ruthlessly packed and shipped across the Atlantic to lend realism to the newly built feudal home of some baron of trade."[9]

Drawing rooms and reception rooms offered sumptuous surroundings for entertainments; often their walls were adorned with gilded boiseries carved by craftsmen imported from Europe, and many times rooms had actually been purchased intact from some moldering European palace or castle, carefully disassembled, shipped by steamer across the ocean, and reassembled, their glittering splendor dancing in the light of the New World. The drawing rooms of many of these houses, an observer declared, "resemble nothing so much as antique shops, and seem to require only the presence of a red flag and an auctioneer to begin a sale. The fad for things old has reigned in New York for years, and is still on the throne. The fact that many of the 'antiques' bought in these days are bare-faced forgeries, or at best merely copies, does not seem to give anyone caution." This collection of bric-a-brac fought for primacy with "tables and lounges with gilded legs, and old velvets for coverings . . . tapestries and portières. Pictures on the walls share the decorative scheme with stained-glass windows, gilded woodcarvings, pieces of old sculpture, door jambs from Italian palaces, and mantels from French châteaux. Louis Seize cabinets back up against the walls and hold Chinese porcelains, silver, glass, miniatures; musical instruments of quaint designs are flung down here and there with careful neglect; and scraps of old embroidery or Oriental frippery are tacked on chairs or carved benches. It is all very costly, and some of it very beautiful; but one sadly wonders why it should litter up a place where people live. Can anyone be happy amid such a restless conglomeration of plunder?"[10] The cumulative effect of this pillaged flotsam, commented one critic, turned these rooms into "chambers of horrors."[11]

Libraries—deemed necessary declarations of breeding and taste—were filled with "nice editions, nice bindings, nicely placed on the shelves, nicely glassed—but seldom read," with "Oriental rugs, Pompeian bronzes, and Greek vases scattered about, just to encourage a classic spirit. It makes a good room to show off to one's new friends while smoking after dinner."[12] Libraries and smoking rooms offered uniquely masculine spaces, with their dark mahogany and ebony woodwork and walls of bookcases; stamped and gilded hand-tooled leather was a favorite wall covering, or, for an exotic touch, an architect might create a Moorish-style room complete with colorful arches and gilded arabesques for a taste of sybaritic splendor. Occasionally, as Ralph Pulitzer recalled, the host might be "momentarily embarrassed by one or more among his guests who, with misguided politeness, do not content themselves with admiring the masters on the walls, but ask him their names and even the subjects of their portraits," artistic inquiries that could rarely be satisfied.[13]

Dining rooms, too, conveyed baronial taste, from the carved or gilded chairs and shimmering chandeliers to displays of porcelain, silver, and crystal, with tapestries and paintings, or enormous mirrors to add to the impression of size and multiply the soft glow of flattering light. Many houses featured smaller dining rooms for members of the family, while the main dining room—large enough to accommodate perhaps a hundred guests—was reserved for the most formal of dinners and balls. And then there were the ballrooms; sometimes an art gallery could be pressed into service for dancing, but by the turn of the century, as *Town and Country* noted, "for the fashionable woman, a ballroom has become an absolute necessity. Private houses are, more and more, becoming like small hotels, with the exception that the first three floors are built solely with the view of entertaining."[14] Ballrooms typically featured a house's most lavish decoration, with handsome marbles, gilded columns, inlaid wooden floors, and massive crystal and ormolu chandeliers adding to the luster.

Rooms for family members took two forms: while most children were relegated to comfortable if somewhat Spartan rooms, their parents often luxuriated in careful period re-creations designed to evoke the spirit of Renaissance Italy or the France of the Bourbon kings. Gentlemen's rooms tended to be more subdued, with dark woods and richly colored hangings, but many ladies freely indulged their royal fantasies in miniature re-creations of splendid Venetian palazzos or rooms at Versailles. Thus it was not uncommon for beds to be ornately carved and gilded, set beneath canopies draped in costly silks and velvets, or enclosed behind gilded balustrades like those of some long past queen.

With their ornamental pilasters and richly adorned facades, these mansions were always objects of great curiosity. Guidebooks to the city often noted them as attractions, and omnibuses crowded with tourists plied the length of Fifth Avenue in the afternoons, guides armed with megaphones eagerly shouting out the names and the latest scandals of the owners as they passed.[15] Not surprisingly, most windows were shielded from such unwelcome intrusions by rows of uniform green blinds that kept the treasures within concealed from the public.

Perhaps the first attempt at a truly European-inspired Gilded Age house in New York was that undertaken in 1859 by Wall Street tycoon Leonard Jerome, whose daughter Jennie later married Lord Randolph Churchill and was the mother of Winston Churchill. A large house in the French Empire style on Madison Square, this was topped with a steep mansard roof dotted with multiple dormers and chimney stacks. Within, Jerome included a large ballroom and, in a unique touch, a private theater that, it was said, could seat six hundred.[16]

Jerome's friend August Belmont also built an exceptionally large house in these years on the northeast corner of Fifth Avenue and Eighteenth Street. The house was designed by English architect Frederick Draper; Belmont lived there in "baronial splendor," as a friend recalled.[17] A brick mansion of three storeys atop a semiraised basement of gray sandstone, the house sported Italianate detailing in its wide, bracketed cornice and shallow-hipped roof.[18] Within, the house was magnificently outfitted, with the city's first private ballroom and an art gallery lit with a skylight.[19] William Howard Russell called it "an elegant house—I use the word in its real meaning—with pretty statues, rich carpets, handsome furniture, and a gallery of charming Meissoniers and genre pieces; the saloons admirably lighted."[20]

Far more extravagant was the mansion of A. T. Stewart. The site, at the northwest corner of Fifth Avenue and Thirty-fourth street, was directly opposite Caroline Astor's brownstone. At the beginning of the Civil War, Samuel Townsend, who built his fortune on the sale of sarsaparilla as a medicinal cure-all, built a four-storey brownstone here at a cost of $100,000 (approximately $3 million in 2008), much of which went to lavishly decorating the interior. Within a few years it was sold to Stewart.[21]

Alexander Turney Stewart had come to America from Belfast in 1818 at age twenty; armed with a degree in ancient Greek and Latin from Trinity University in Dublin, he had every intention of taking an educational post and teaching the classics. After he received a small inheritance, however, he began to import and sell fine Irish linens and lace, a venture that proved so successful that eventually he opened the city's first dry goods store on Broadway.[22] He eventually opened A. T. Stewart's, New York City's first department store, and amassed a fortune estimated at $40 million ($800 million in 2008).[23]

Stewart, declared one contemporary, "is hard and repulsive. . . . He is short, with a decided Hibernian face; sandy hair, nearly red; sharp, cold avaricious eyes; a face furrowed with thought, care, and success; a voice harsh and unfriendly even in its most mellow tones." Another added: "He thinks money, lives money, makes money: it is the end and aim of his existence."[24] Stewart and his wife, Cornelia, whom he married in 1825, shared a frugal sensibility and dislike for frivolity, but when they decided to build a house suited to their new fortunes, there was little hint of economy.[25]

Townsend's brownstone was a solid, even luxurious house, in character with the neighborhood and with the neighboring houses. Whatever their personal convictions, however, the Stewarts felt that their fortune deserved a more regal setting, and they had the old house demolished to make way for what would become one of New York's most spectacular residences. In its place arose a fifty-five-room palace in a mixture of Italianate and Second Empire styles, designed by architect John Kellum and built at a cost of more than $2 million ($40 million in 2008).[26] An almost unbelievable riot of stucco swags, statuary, stone quoins, pilasters, and carved garlands adorned the three-storey facade of imported gray

A. T. Stewart's elaborate house on Fifth Avenue in New York City.

Parian marble; above, a tall mansard roof bristled with a profusion of dormer windows and massed chimney stacks.[27]

The end result was a building of undisguised theatricality, ponderous, overly ornate, and unapologetically pretentious. The Stewart residence, declared one publication, "has caused more surmise and gossip than any other house ever erected in America. . . . Few persons have ever seen the interior, which is said, however, to be plain, cold, and severe, by reason of the large quantity of Italian marble used in it. . . . Nothing concerns us except the bad influence which its exterior design is calculated to obtain with those who might otherwise have been elevated and educated through the benign influence which the expenditure of so much money might have exerted, had it been invested in a well designed and artistic structure. It is hard to conceive that any one . . . could have had so little understanding of what constituted a work of architecture."[28] It was so unusual, so extravagant, and so blatant, remembered Elizabeth Drexel Lehr, that visitors to the city regularly gathered on the sidewalks and stared "in open mouthed admiration" at its wonders.[29]

The mansion's rooms were just as opulent and oppressive as its exterior; one visitor likened the interior to "a vast tomb."[30] Some five hundred workers from Europe had labored for seven years crafting the cavernous rooms from rare marbles, mosaics, and imported woods.[31] The ceilings—even in the bedrooms—were an astonishing nineteen feet high, and the aura of some immense public institution was further underlined by the more than a thousand paintings, statues, and objets d'art that had been purchased to fill its rooms.[32]

Eight-foot-high white marble statues of figures from classical mythology and from literature lined the entrance hall, offering a ghostly contrast to the walls of blue-veined Carrara marble bedecked with fluted, gilded Corinthian columns that stretched to a stuccoed ceiling.[33] The array of enfiladed rooms were oppressive in their decoration: walls were embellished with painted panels, gilded cartouches, and marble pilasters; gilded relief scrolls wandered across ceilings hung with immense bronze and crystal gasoliers flanking allegorical panels painted by Italian artists; Carrara marble–framed windows were hung in elaborate silks; ornately carved rosewood cabinets, sofas, and chairs ornamented with ormolu reliefs stood atop imported Aubusson and Savonnerie carpets; and statuary, bronzes, paintings, and bibelots crowded every available inch of space. It was all exceptionally lavish, and exceptionally gloomy.[34]

Stewart had been among the first of America's Gilded Age millionaires to collect art on a truly monumental scale, filling his mansion's cavernous rooms with hundreds of European paintings; the sole exception was a Gilbert Stuart portrait of George Washington. Unlike many of those who came after him, Stewart did seek out and purchase old masters, including five Rembrandts and a *Madonna and Child* by Titian.[35] To accommodate this collection, Stewart had added an art gallery, seventy-five feet long and fifty feet high, whose walls were hung with more than two hundred canvases by Meissonier, Bouguereau, and Detaille, covering every inch of space.[36] The largest of these works was *The Genius of America* by French painter Adolphe Yvon, measuring thirty-five by twenty-two feet and weighing a staggering one and a half tons.[37] Stewart's own personal favorite was Meissonier's *Friedland 1807,* an eight-foot-wide work depicting a moment in one of Napoleon's campaigns. Meissonier, who sold it to Stewart for $60,000 (approximately $1.4 million in 2008) in 1873, considered *Friedland* one of his most accomplished works and had wept as he watched it being crated. Despite the artist's conviction that the work deserved wider acclaim, Stewart hung it in his bathroom, though he wrote to Meissonier: "The work is one upon which you may rest your fame with perfect confidence."[38]

The most famous of Stewart's paintings, however, was Rosa Bonheur's *The Horse Fair*, an immense work measuring some eight by sixteen and a half feet. Widely considered one of the nineteenth century's great artistic masterpieces, *The Horse Fair* had first been exhibited at the salon in 1853 while still unfinished, and it was another two years before the painting was completed. In portraying the horse market in Paris's Boulevard de l'Hôpital, Bonheur created a vibrant, energetic scene of movement and shadow amid dramatic bursts of color. Although not the largest of Stewart's paintings, *The Horse Fair* dominated his art gallery, riveting attention from the few privileged enough to gain admittance to this cold and grim mansion.[39] The Stewarts were so acquisitive, in fact, that despite the immensity of their house, they eventually ran out of room. Sculptures, bronzes, and paintings were simply stacked in rows on the floors, crowded onto tables, displayed on easels, and propped against furniture.[40]

Curious New York was dazzled at Stewart's marble palace, but it did nothing to enhance the couple's standing in elite society. Mrs. Astor, who had watched this mammoth building rise from her drawing room windows, considered it an impertinent assault, and she pointedly never called on its owners, nor did she ever receive them in her own house. Instead, the mansion sat silent, its immense marble halls and crowded salons falling victim to the opprobrium of Gilded Age society. After Stewart's death in 1876, his widow occupied the mansion for another ten years before leasing it as the city premises of the Manhattan Club. Although this provided them with the city's most extravagant surroundings, the club decided that alterations had to be made, although they were unprepared for the enormous expenses involved. One man complained of the undertaking that "the woodwork was all marble."[41] Shortly after the turn of the century, a decade after Mrs. Astor had abandoned the neighborhood and moved up Fifth Avenue, Stewart's marble palace was demolished to make way for the Columbia Trust Company.[42]

By the beginning of the 1870s, another remarkable palace had appeared in the city, the famous Marble Row built by Mrs. Mary Mason

Jones. This was not a single residence but rather a division of houses within a united facade on the east side of Fifth Avenue between Fifty-seventh and Fifty-eighth streets. In 1869, when construction began, the area was largely a deserted wasteland of open fields and muddy streets. Designed by architect Robert Mook to resemble a French Renaissance château, the light gray stone structure was ornamented with elegant pilasters and sculpted reliefs and crowned by a mansard roof dotted with wrought-iron railings. Mrs. Jones, a respected member of old New York society, lived in the house at the corner of Fifty-seventh Street.[43] Owing to her health, she took the unusual step of having her bedroom suite on the first floor, opening directly off of the foyer. "The effect was not only novel but startling," noted Lloyd Morris. "The pagan divinities that frolicked across her painted ceilings were as embarrassing as August Belmont's celebrated nude by Bouguereau."[44]

Marble Row in New York City, showing the corner pavilion occupied first by Mary Mason Jones and later by Mrs. Paran Stevens.

Mary Mason Jones's niece, Edith Wharton, later immortalized this extraordinary house, and its owner under the guise of Mrs. Manson Mingott, in her novel *The Age of Innocence*. "It was her habit," she wrote, "to sit in the window of her sitting room on the ground floor (imprisoned by her obesity), as if watching calmly for life and fashion to flow northward to her solitary doors. She seemed in no hurry to have them come, for her patience was equaled by her confidence. She was sure that presently the hoardings, the quarries, the one storey saloons, the wooden greenhouses in ragged gardens, and the rocks from which goats surveyed the scene, would vanish before the advance of residences as stately as her own."[45]

Marble Row was an unusual building. Not only was its location a startling departure from the usual genteel neighborhoods favored by fashionable society, but its exotic style also signaled a radical break with the established brownstone tradition associated with the city's most dignified families. While other houses had hinted at the faded glories of the Old World, Marble Row constituted the first true period residences in New York, the first palatial dwellings to so diligently copy and display the elements of historicism. Those who came after Mary Mason Jones not only followed her progress toward the center of Manhattan but also her European tastes, in the process transforming Fifth Avenue with an unprecedented display of diverse and impressive architectural houses that provided society with the carefully crafted settings deemed necessary to its way of life.

9

PALACES ON FIFTH AVENUE

THE GREAT HOUSES THAT ROSE ACROSS New York in the Gilded Age provided outward expression of the collective aspirations of its shifting society. The architectural vocabulary of ancient Greece, medieval England, and Renaissance France and Italy played itself across facades, offering monumental evidence of regal ambition. Intensely personal in their revelations of the quest for power and assertion of taste, these châteaux and palazzos swept their owners into a lost world of emperors and princes, kings and dukes. In this parade of architectural diversity and declaration of authority, the Vanderbilts reigned supreme.

Commodore Vanderbilt had lived rather modestly, although as his fortune increased he, too, was drawn to outward displays of his wealth. In 1839 he moved his family into a large, Greek revival–style mansion he built on Staten Island at a cost of $55,000 ($1.6 million in 2008).[1] The situation of the new house was no accident: the commodore erected it on the northeast corner of the farm on which he had been born; it also boasted a fine view of New York Harbor and, more important, was close enough to the ferry landing that Vanderbilt could survey his steamship operations from the front porch.[2] A two-storey house adorned with an impressive portico of six tall, fluted columns, it was as schizophrenic as the commodore himself.

From the stately exterior, visitors entered a surprisingly unimaginative world of flocked Victorian wallpapers, heavy brocaded curtains and portieres, solid mahogany and walnut furniture upholstered in horsehair, and consoles laden with ornaments of seashells and dried floral arrangements under glass domes, side by side with chimneypieces of imported Egyptian marble and doors of rosewood bedecked with silver hardware.[3]

If the commodore thought that his impressive new residence would open the doors of New York society, he was mistaken. Perhaps that is why, after a few years, he erected a four-storey brick townhouse at 10 Washington Place, just off Washington Square and, not accidentally, at the center of the universe occupied by the Knickerbocker elite.[4] Like the house on Staten Island, the rooms were awash with floral paper, plush sofas, and chairs edged with fringe, Oriental porcelains, ornate gasoliers, and models of the commodore's railroad engines and steamers in silver and gold.[5] It bore, wrote one architectural historian, the "luxurious trademarks of the finest hotel lobbies and riverboat saloons."[6]

His son William Henry had more sophisticated tastes, and in 1878 he commissioned the fashionable firm of Herter Brothers to redecorate the house at 459 Fifth Avenue. Wainscoting and trim of ebonized cherry, imported silks and brocades, ceilings decorated with plaster reliefs picked out in gilt and hung with bronze chandeliers, and new suites of furniture, heavily carved and adorned by Herter Brothers with intricate marquetry work or covered with plush, olive-colored velour, helped transform the interiors into models of Victorian luxury.[7] These decorations offered rooms suited to William Henry's fortune, but within a year he decided that his position required a more formidable and stately residence. His wife, Louisa, was none too pleased. "We don't need a better home," she complained, "and I hate to think of leaving this house where we have lived so comfortably. I have told William that if he wants a finer place for his pictures to build a wing to which he could go whenever he felt inclined; this is too good a house to leave. I will never feel at home in the new place."[8]

Nevertheless, William Henry had his way. He purchased an entire city block on the west side of Fifth Avenue, from Fifty-first to Fifty-second streets, directly across from the just completed St. Patrick's Cathedral. This was not yet a fashionable neighborhood, but William Henry and members of his family realized that the city's increasing growth would inevitably push society farther up Fifth Avenue, away from the once sacred bastions surrounding Washington Square.[9] In an equally unusual move, William Henry decided to erect what amounted to two mansions, linked together in unified design. William Henry's house was to be at 640 Fifth Avenue, occupying the southern corner, with an identical pavilion, divided in half, for two of his married daughters, Margaret Shepard and Emily Sloane, to the north.[10] Thus was born New York's famous Twin Palace.

The commission was unusual in yet another way. Instead of hiring an architect, William asked the firm of Herter Brothers to design and decorate the building. Christian Herter, in turn, handed most of the responsibility to architect Charles Atwood, while Vanderbilt installed his own man, John Butler Snook, as supervising contractor for much of the interior work. This triumvirate produced the house in collaboration, a situation that led to bruised egos all around, with each of the three men attempting to claim ultimate responsibility for the project.[11]

Vanderbilt trusted Herter's judgment and taste implicitly; for Herter, as the firm's historians have noted, the commission "provided him with an unparalleled opportunity to create the epitome of the cosmopolitan environments he had been producing since his arrival on American shores, and with few financial constraints. He was superbly matched with a client who desired an interior for his elevated social and economic status and who embraced Herter's predilection for mixing eclectic styles as an indicator of culture, who relished and could afford Herter's lavish use of luxurious materials, and whose public stature would ensure a lasting fame for his designs."[12] Yet Vanderbilt was personally involved in every decision. "We have rarely had a customer who took such a personal interest in the work during its progress," recalled the general manager of Herter Brothers. "All the designs were submitted to him from the first stone to the last piece of decoration or furniture. Mr. Vanderbilt was at our warerooms or at our shops almost every day for a year. He spent hours in the designing rooms, and often looked on while the workmen were busy in the shops."[13] Vanderbilt regularly visited the construction site, often pulling out his wallet and offering cash bonuses on the spot to the men in exchange for extra work.[14]

Construction began in 1879, and some six hundred men worked on the house for the next two years, a remarkably short period of time for a building so substantial and dripping with ornamentation.[15] In addition to masons and craftsmen, sixty sculptors were brought from Europe to carve the exterior and interior decorations.[16] The structure was completed in time for Louisa to hold an inaugural ball there on January 17, 1882.[17]

Although the commission included two buildings, it was William Henry Vanderbilt's house that dominated the complex and commanded both attention and admiration. Some $2.6 million ($52 million in 2008) had been spent on construction and decoration, with a rumored $800,000 ($16 million in 2008) devoted to the interior work alone, making it the single most expensive private residence in the country at the time of its completion.[18] It was a large, three-storey structure atop a semi-raised basement, in a kind of vaguely Italianate style; originally the exterior was to have been faced in pale Ohio limestone dramatically ornamented with black and red marble, but Vanderbilt, who was anxious to take up residence, thought that the quarrying and carving would take

The famous Vanderbilt Row along New York City's Fifth Avenue, showing, from left to right, the Twin Palace of William Henry Vanderbilt and two of his married daughters, at 640 Fifth Avenue, with William K. Vanderbilt's château at 660 Fifth Avenue beyond.

too much time and ordered the facade cloaked in drab, ugly brown Connecticut sandstone.[19]

Strollers on Fifth Avenue could gaze on a house of formidable magnitude, crowned with a perforated stone balustrade that only emphasized its squat, cubelike form. The architects deployed a riot of projecting bays, rows of pilasters, carved architraves and garlands, and decorative panels in an attempt to relieve the ponderous impression, but the facade remained singularly uninspired.[20] "There are no features," commented one architectural critic, "there is no relation of parts, there is no development of masses or lines, vertical or horizontal, there is no arrangement of openings with reference to each other. They are merely boxes of brownstone with architecture 'appliqué' by itself. If these Vanderbilt houses are the result of intrusting architectural design to decorators," commented one architectural critic, "it is hoped the experiment may not be repeated."[21]

To record every detail of this new monument, William Henry commissioned a massive, multivolume chronicle, encased between leather covers stamped with gilt. Its author, writing under the pseudonym Edward Strahan, took the few privileged enough to read this exclusive publication on a lavishly detailed tour of the building. In his introduction he declared that this magnificent mansion was "representative of the new impulse now felt in the national life." This lavish palace, he wrote, was "nothing but what a reasonable and practical family may live up to. It is as sincere a home as exists anywhere. Like a more perfect Pompeii, the work will be the vision and image of a typical American residence, seized at the moment when the nation began to have a taste of its own."[22] Without a hint of irony, he described this extraordinary house as a place of "self-restraint, which has avoided any fantastic and showy novelties in building," a residence whose "abiding impression is, at last, simplicity."[23]

If the exterior of the house was all uninspired severity, the interior was a succession of shockingly exotic rooms executed in contrasting themes, an enchanted realm where gilded fantasy reigned supreme. Lightly colored panels of Nubian marble quarried in Africa faced the walls of the vestibule and evoked the glories of ancient Rome, while a floor inset with shimmering mosaics of Venetian marble echoed the splendors of the doges. At the center of the room, set beneath a stained-glass skylight

The hall of William Henry Vanderbilt's Twin Palace at 640 Fifth Avenue.

ornamented with bronze, was yet another imperial allusion, this one to the Russian Empire: a nine-foot-tall malachite vase adorned with winged cherubs of ormolu, a gift from Tsar Nicholas I to Count Nicholas Demidov, from whose San Donato Palace in Florence it had been purchased for Vanderbilt.[24] Gilt bronze doors, copied from Lorenzo Ghiberti's famous *Gates of Paradise* on the Baptistry in Florence and cast in Paris at a cost of $20,000 ($400,000 in 2008), opened to the Grand Hall.[25] Situated at the center of the house and ringed by arcaded galleries atop twelve square columns of dark red African marble embellished with bronze capitals, this rose three storeys to nine leaded stained-glass skylights that bathed the hall in shifting prisms of color. A twelve-foot-high wainscot of carved English oak anchored the walls, interrupted by a monumental carved chimneypiece from France, its mantel of red African marble framed by life-size sculpted female figures in bronze.[26]

The thirty-foot-long drawing room was the most sumptuous of the interiors, a space of sensual textures and rich colors arrayed like a garden in *The Arabian Nights*. Passing beneath massive sculpted doorframes covered

The drawing room of William Henry Vanderbilt's Twin Palace at 640 Fifth Avenue.

in gold leaf and inlaid with Limoges enamels, onyx, and mother-of-pearl, visitors entered a room wrapped in luminous, elaborately carved and gilded wainscoting.[27] Foliage, garlands, and bowers of trees embroidered in gold thread ornamented with sparkling cut crystals adorned walls hung in pale red velvet brocade; at intervals, flitting among the golden vines, flashed butterflies composed of colored crystals.[28] A richly carved and gilded frieze adorned with mother-of-pearl rose to a coved ceiling where ladies, knights, jesters, and horses frolicked in a medieval Venetian pageant painted by Parisian artist Pierre-Victor Galland.[29] Christian Herter furnished the room with exotically sinuous gilded chairs and sofas, their frames inlaid with mother-of-pearl and their cushions upholstered in embroidered red Chinese silk.[30] Eight vases of stained and jeweled glass embellished with silver mounts stood on onyx and ormolu pedestals against corner niches faced with Venetian mirrors; at night, when bathed with light from the gas jets concealed within, they created "grottoes of ice."[31]

The library offered a more subdued refuge. Hung in ocher and green floral damask above bookcases and panels of rosewood and mahogany accented with inlays of ormolu and mother-of-pearl, this was an altogether

more restrained room, its coffered ceiling picked out in gold and ornamented with shimmering mirrors; yet it also contained the mansion's most
elaborate piece of furniture. At the center of the library stood a massive
table of carved rosewood inlaid with walnut, satinwood, birch, maple,
chestnut, ash, and brass, its sides and top decorated with inlaid mosaic
murals of mother-of-pearl and ormolu depicting terrestrial globes and the
heavens as they were on the day Vanderbilt had been born.[32] A stunning
piece of fantasy followed. Herter created the Japanese Parlor as a seductive evocation of the Far East. Here the rich yet subdued palette employed
in the drawing room gave way to a riot of vibrant colors: walls hung in
crimson Japanese silk below a vaulted ceiling of imitation golden bamboo
supported by carved wooden trusses lacquered in red. Staggered, open
shelves in red, green, and yellow lacquer displayed Oriental porcelain and
objets d'art.[33] It was a delightful, unexpected space, one of the many wonders concealed behind the rather grim and oppressive sandstone facade.

The dining room, decorated in a style loosely described as Italian
Renaissance, looked back to a time of heroic and chivalrous men. Meant
to evoke the solid assurance and faded glories of an age long past, Herter
fashioned it as an intensely masculine space, awash with dark woods and
dimensional refractions of historical and traditional motifs, including
repeated garlands, cascades of fruit, and dancing putti carved in high
relief on the twelve-foot-high wainscot of English oak fringing the walls;
the theme of Nature's bounty, particularly apt given the room's purpose,
was echoed in the carved frieze, awash with bunches of grapes, carved
fruits, and spreading vines. A panoply of painted medieval hunting scenes
executed in muted greens, blues, and browns complemented a similar,
rousing festival painted by E. V. Luminais of Paris that arched over the
vaulted ceiling. Eighteen chairs of English oak, covered in dark red
stamped leather kept in place by ornamental brass nail heads, circled a
massive central table, while an opulent display of gold plate, silver, etched
crystal, and porcelain shone from behind the security of elaborately
carved glass-fronted cases.[34]

A massive carved arch of polished black oak opened to a private art gallery, a vast space nearly fifty feet long that stretched across the rear of the
house. No other room so emphasized William Henry Vanderbilt's regal

The art gallery of William Henry Vanderbilt's Twin Palace at 640 Fifth Avenue.

ambitions or expressed his personal taste. Outwardly the art gallery was merely another in a succession of lavish interiors: walls draped in dark crimson brocade and ornamented with pilasters of black oak contrasted with a floor of polished San Domingo mahogany edged by a Pompeian mosaic of black and sienna marble. A monumental chimneypiece of red African marble inset with Venetian-glass mosaics between enormous, frolicking caryatids soared thirty-five feet to a ceiling adorned with opalescent and tinted-glass panels that by day bathed the room in natural light.[35] The room, however, drew its vibrancy and purpose from the two hundred paintings that formed the heart of William Henry's art collection. Arrayed in a kaleidoscope of ornately gilded frames, these offered a pageant of images, from pastoral scenes and the quiet solitude of ordinary life to the triumph of military campaigns, the devastation of war, and the tragic ruin of overarching ambition. A room of immense contradiction, it offered the spectacle of a vibrant, loving, and warring humanity whose drama played out amid the funereal silence of its gilded splendors.

The two hundred paintings in Vanderbilt's art gallery included works by Meissonier, Alma-Tadema, Millais, Gustave Doré, Landseer, Leighton, Turner, Detaille, Bouguereau, Delacroix, and Rosa Bonheur.[36] Prized among his canvases were Meissonier's *An Artist and His Wife,* along with the artist's portrait of William Henry; *Homeless* by Anton Seitz; Alma-Tadema's *Down by the River, Picture Gallery, Sculpture Gallery,* and *Entrance to a Theater;* Detaille's *Arrest of an Ambulance, Eastern Part of France, 1871,* and *Wounded Soldiers;* Alfred Stevens's *Ready for the Fancy Ball; The Sower and the Water Carrier* by Millet; *Fountain of Innocence* by Turner; Sir Frederick Leighton's *Odalisque; After the Chase* by Sir Edwin Landseer; *A Study from Nature* and *Gorges d'Apremont* by Rousseau; *The Good Sister* by Bouguereau; *Twilight in Scotland* by Gustave Doré; and Gérôme's *Reception of the Prince of Condé.*[37]

If, in his collecting, Vanderbilt embodied Caroline Astor's idea of the wealthy enriching society and creating legacies, he also understood the principle of noblesse oblige in sharing his riches with the public. He erected a separate entrance to his art gallery on West Fifty-first Street, which allowed him to open his collection to members of the public eager to view his holdings. In this, William Henry was unique among the era's millionaires in not only lending his pictures for public exhibition but also in regularly allowing access to his artistic treasures. Respectable members of the public could apply in writing for free tickets of admission when the gallery was opened for several hours each Thursday afternoon. Thus, for several years, Vanderbilt offered New York City a chance to enjoy the spoils of his fortune. Then, at the end of 1883, things went awry. One evening Vanderbilt personally invited twenty-five hundred of New York's most refined connoisseurs to enjoy his collection; more interested in his fabled house than in its works of art, they wandered through the mansion, opening drawers, poking into closets, inspecting bedrooms, and perusing the family's reading material. It was all too much for Vanderbilt, who, irritated, finally halted his exercises in public munificence.[38]

A great staircase of English oak at the northern end of the Grand Hall offered a ceremonial backdrop for receiving guests, its balustrade of ornamental ormolu scrolls flowing from a gilded bronze statue of a female slave whose headdress was studded with tiny electric lights.[39] Stained-glass skylights with allegorical designs by artist John La Farge bathed the stairwell with light.[40] The family's personal realm above was no less elegant. When he arose from his ebony and rosewood bed, inlaid with satinwood and draped in luxurious blue silk, William Henry began his mornings in a dressing room faced in opalescent tiles of gold, blue, and silver glass and sliding, mirrored doors concealing a silver bathtub and basins.[41] Rich peacock blue and gold silk damask from France, woven with water lilies and dragonflies in gold thread, cloaked the walls of Louisa's boudoir, where furniture of ebony accented with ivory added a somber note.[42] In contrast, her bedroom, overlooking the bustle of Fifth Avenue, was a symphony of white marble and silk wall panels; a carved rosewood and mahogany frieze framed Jules Lefebvre's allegorical painting *The Awakening of Aurora*.[43] "In this exquisite room," recorded one visitor, "where silver toilette services, embroidered silks, and delicate hangings vie with masterly paintings . . . there is one worn object, and only one: it is the little Bible."[44]

The *New York Times,* while glowing in its praise of the house, found it too monumental and too lavishly appointed to function as a satisfactory residence: "There can be no possible doubt that this house with its adornment, decoration, and pictures is the most superb in America. . . . There is nothing exactly loud, nor anything which 'swears.' Still, the effect is crushing. Eyes distended to their utmost are palled as the gustatory sense is sometimes cloyed by over-tasting. One longs to find out if there is not one single room where might be found some repose."[45]

At the same time that 640 Fifth Avenue was under construction, William Henry's two sons, Cornelius Vanderbilt II and William Kissam Vanderbilt, also were building their own New York palaces, but their plans went beyond the necessity of housing growing families in luxurious surroundings. Cornelius and William Kissam wanted not just statements of power; their houses were, it is true, meant to impress, but they also were declarations that William Henry's residence was not an aberration. The new generation of Vanderbilts, armed with both taste and money, intended to reign supreme. Firmly ensconced in New York City, these houses were triumphs of passion and perseverance.

In 1877 Corneil purchased two brownstones at the northwest corner of West Fifty-seventh Street, along with an adjoining lot, and had the buildings razed to create a building site of suitable size.[46] To undertake this commission, in an unfortunate choice, Corneil and Alice hired architect George Browne Post. Born in 1837, Post had studied civil engineering and, for a time, worked in architect Richard Morris Hunt's atelier before launching his own practice, but he had not absorbed his master's graceful deployment of historical elements nor his skilled approach to the demands of monumental architecture. Post's forte was engineering; although he was adept at adopting the modern technology of steel framing to nineteenth-century construction, he lacked imagination, and his designs, including a number of hotels and the state capitol in Madison, Wisconsin, were rarely inspired. Post, however, was a safe, reliable choice, and one particularly well suited to Corneil's tyrannical nature. Not only would his design echo Corneil's own inflated ego, but also by purposely selecting a second-rate architect, Vanderbilt guaranteed that there would be no disagreeable squabbles over artistic issues and that his word would be final.[47]

Cornelius Vanderbilt's house was completed by 1882, but it remained unaltered for just a decade. Although massive in size, its main floor contained only five principal rooms, and Post had neglected to include a suitable ballroom—a necessity in New York society.[48] As ever-larger houses rose across the city, Corneil's pride as the head of the Vanderbilt family demanded that his residence remain unexcelled. Therefore in 1892 he hired Richard Morris Hunt to partner with Post on a massive expansion of the building. Six adjacent houses were purchased and demolished, and some $3 million ($60 million in 2008) was spent to double the size of the palace. Always impatient, Corneil demanded that construction be completed as quickly as possible; nearly eight hundred workers labored for two years, some at night by the light of electric torches and bonfires, before the house was finally completed.[49]

The house at 1 West 57th Street, by the time of its final expansion, was—with 130 rooms—the largest private residence ever erected in New York City.[50] Said to have been modeled on the French Renaissance château of Fontainebleau, the house rose three storeys atop a raised limestone ground floor, its upper corners dotted with small corbeled towers. Post faced the exterior in a warm red brick, relieved stringcourses, quoins, and friezes of carved gray Bedford limestone to provide contrast. A massive ceremonial porte cochere dominated the northern facade, reached by a drive that curved from Grand Army Plaza into a courtyard enclosed by a tall wrought-iron fence, while the family entrance opened off of West

The enormous château built by Cornelius Vanderbilt II at 1 West 57th Street, New York City.

Fifty-seventh Street.[51] At the northeastern corner, a large, four-storey tower by Hunt terminated the new addition, adding a vertical touch that not only anchored the house to its site but also offered much-needed visual relief from the otherwise rather squat structure, for the Cornelius Vanderbilt residence was a ponderous, uninspired building. Post had attempted to fuse Gothic and French Renaissance ornament with the decorative excesses of the Victorian era, deploying all of the expected motifs from carved lintels to symmetrical fenestration, but the effect was simply one of haphazardly selected architectural elements pompously piled one atop the other. The massive mansard roof, of red slate and dotted with hooded dormers and multiple massed chimneystacks, only added to the impression that the building was top-heavy, too large and too wide to successfully refract any of its historical influences.[52] It was, commented one critic, "by no means remarkable for beauty, grace, or sympathy. It strikes the observer simply as a very, very large structure, and suggests rather a pretentious family hotel than a luxurious and elegant home."[53]

Passing through the arched gates and beneath the porte cochere, visitors entered a house as confused on the inside as without. An enclosed marble staircase, whose carved balustrade bore a pattern of interlocking V's, ascended beneath a barrel-vaulted ceiling awash with sculpted coffers to the principal rooms on the first floor.[54] This cloistered approach opened through wrought-iron and glass doors bedecked with ormolu mounts to the Watercolor Gallery, its grim stone walls hung with a selection of paintings between massed piers supporting the vaulted ceiling.[55] Rising two storeys to a leaded-glass skylight piercing a beamed ceiling, the Great Hall occupied the center of the house. Faced in carved gray Caen stone, it offered the house's most extraordinary feature: a circular staircase encased in an elaborately carved stone tower with arched openings and balustrades, copied from one in the courtyard at the château of Blois in the Loire Valley.[56] It was an impressive, technically competent allusion in a room that attempted magnificence, but the overwhelming impression was one of unrelieved, cold splendor.

The array of formal rooms was in keeping with the needs of fashionable society. There was a Louis XVI–style salon, a space of lavishly carved and gilded boiseries gleaming in the light from the three immense chandeliers that dripped in crystal tiers from a ceiling awash with sinuous rocailles and garlands; an Adam-inspired petit salon embellished with grisaille cartouches and neoclassical arabesques; and a dark and masculine library paneled in mahogany from South America.[57] Post's dining room was particularly dismal. With no exterior windows, it rose two storeys to a coved ceiling of carved and gilded coffers set with a stained-glass skylight that provided the only natural illumination. Walls fringed in English oak wainscoting and hung with dark crimson brocaded silk featured "atrocious oil paintings of pastoral scenes—badly painted cows and unnatural looking trees."[58] The immense ballroom, said to have been copied from a room in the Hôtel de Valois in Paris, was a riot of decorative detail: Corinthian pilasters framed mirrored panels topped with carved and gilded rocailles and cherubs to match those above the doorways, while an army of glittering cupids and garlands appeared to fight their way across the cornice to spread over the coved ceiling.[59] Only the smoking room offered relief from all of this gilded excess. Designed by Louis Comfort Tiffany in the Moorish style, its walls were cloaked in an array of opalescent tiles alternating with insets of mother-of-pearl, while slender columns and arches rose to a dome faced with colorful mosaics.[60] Perhaps because it was a piece of fantasy removed from the attempted rationality of the rest of the house, it managed to convey something of the splendors that might have been achieved with a more imaginative architect.

Other rooms boasted more coffered and gilded ceilings, African marble chimneypieces, and an abundance of gilded Corinthian columns adorned with foliage reliefs. The house deployed the correct, stylish elements, but it was all too much: the rooms were so insistent on their splendors, so ponderous, and so self-consciously ornate that the effect was one of oppressive gloom. "The rooms," wrote Louis Auchincloss, "were heavy, cluttered, pontifical. The proprietors seemed more interested in impressing their visitors with grandeur than with beauty."[61] After Corneil's death in 1899, Alice continued to live within its walls but rarely entertained, and for many years the house sat largely silent. It remained the largest private house in New York City, a grandiose statement of power that conflicted with the couple's public reputation, but it was not enough to win the Vanderbilts architectural laurels. That accomplishment fell to Alva Vanderbilt.

The houses built by William Henry Vanderbilt and by his son Cornelius established the Vanderbilt family among New York City's architectural elite, but neither spawned columns of praise or inspired much admiration. They were curiosities, tourist attractions, and visible displays of wealth and power, if not taste. The palace erected by William Kissam Vanderbilt and his wife, Alva, at 660 Fifth Avenue, however, was a truly transcendent building. It evoked not only the extravagance of its owners but also respect as a piece of worthy architecture in its own right. It was not the largest or the most elaborate of the city's Gilded Age residences, nor was it the first of the city's houses to look to a heroic European past: Mary Mason Jones's French-inspired Marble Row had been a bold stylistic innovation when it rose in a city dominated by brownstones, and it might be seen as a direct forerunner of the house eventually erected at 660 Fifth Avenue. Unlike Marble Row, however, 660 Fifth Avenue managed one feat unequaled by New York's other residences: it cemented the trend for historicism that eventually overtook the houses of the city's elite. It was regal and sinuous, forceful yet delicate, a triumph of fantasy that became perhaps the most admired private residence in the city.[62]

The house at 660 Fifth Avenue undoubtedly owed its success to its architect, for Alva had the foresight and the taste to hire Richard Morris Hunt to design and build her palace. Born in 1827 in Vermont, Hunt spent much of his youth in France and traveling throughout Europe.[63] The first American to study at the prestigious École des Beaux-Arts in Paris, Hunt loved the rich architectural heritage he found in France and would later successfully adapt many of its elements in his most famous buildings. In 1854 he was appointed inspector of works for the commission charged with linking the Tuileries with the Louvre, and he helped design the Pavilion de la Bibliothèque.[64] On his return to America in 1855, he soon became one of New York City's most prominent architects; his commissions included, in 1873, the Tribune Building, one of the city's first modern skyscrapers; the pedestal for the Statue of Liberty, in 1886; and the main facade of the Metropolitan Museum of Art, in 1890.[65] His greatest triumph came when he designed the extraordinary Administration Building at Chicago's World Columbian Exposition in 1893, a fantastic, domed structure that evoked neoclassical models but that was infused with the ornate decorations that typified the Beaux-Arts movement. A founding member of the American Institute of Architects, he became its president in 1888.

Along with Stanford White, Richard Morris Hunt was perhaps the most popular and fashionable architect of the Gilded Age, and his domestic work enjoyed particular success. "He could provide his very wealthy clients what they wanted, and what they needed," noted architectural historian Paul R. Baker, "indulging their whims and satisfying their vanity, while giving himself the satisfaction of creating elegant buildings in different architectural styles and with a decorative richness that few other architects were able to achieve."[66] Hunt's work was characteristic of the age, and it spanned the end of the Victorian movement to encompass not only Beaux-Arts ideals but also the growing taste for neoclassicism and historicism, all carefully drawing on European precedents as filtered through an American prism. Although for many years much of his work was derided as a derivative and eclectic pastiche, more recent assessments have recognized his undoubted genius and ability in blending the

Influential architect Richard Morris Hunt, who designed many of the fantastic houses of the Gilded Age.

old with the new, the grand with the domestic, and the European taste with American sensibilities.

Hunt drew most attention for his residential commissions. In addition to 660 Fifth Avenue and work on Cornelius Vanderbilt II's New York mansion, Hunt designed a number of Gilded Age society's most important and lavish houses: he built Willie Vanderbilt's Idle House on Long Island; renovated both Newport's Château-sur-Mer and Beechwood, the latter seaside mansion owned by Caroline Astor; erected four of the resort's most fantastic houses, the Breakers, Marble House, Belcourt, and Ochre Court; and was responsible for George Vanderbilt's enormous, triumphant Château Biltmore in North Carolina. It was Hunt's design for 660 Fifth Avenue, however, that came to be regarded as his domestic masterpiece. William K. Vanderbilt first approached Hunt in 1878 with the idea of building a residence in New York; Willie had recently acquired a plot of land on the northwest corner of Fifth Avenue and Fifty-second Street and wanted a house to complement, if not compete with, that of his father just down the avenue.[67]

Alva was intimately involved in every aspect of the design. Rarely had a client and an architect been so fortuitously matched in aspirations, inspirations, and taste. They shared a love of France and French architecture, and neither was content to settle for a mere pastiche of disparate elements grafted onto a ponderous facade.[68] Initially Alva requested that the house be in a medieval style; however, when she saw Hunt's plans for a French-inspired residence, she is said to have exclaimed that it was precisely what she wanted—"a real Venetian palace like the doges had."[69]

Hunt was too diplomatic to correct her; indeed, he seems to have had the greatest respect for her "intellect and broad grasp of architecture," declaring, "She's a wonder!" Construction began in 1879 and was largely completed by the end of 1882, although several additional months were needed to finish the intricate interiors.[70] Nevertheless, there were occasional clashes: both Alva and her architect were strong-willed, opinionated, and determined to have their own way. Once, when Alva's interference apparently became too much, Hunt cried out in exasperation, "Damn it, Mrs. Vanderbilt, who is building this house?"

"Damn it, Mr. Hunt," she shot back, "who is going to live in this house?"[71]

Hunt worked closely with two men with whom he had previously partnered on other houses. The Parisian firm of Jules Allard & Sons was commissioned to undertake much of the interior decoration according to Hunt's instructions. Allard not only provided the priceless flotsam scavenged from houses and palaces across Europe—columns, mantelpieces, chandeliers, tapestries, furniture, paintings, inlaid floors, trompe l'oeil ceilings, and even entire rooms—that filled the most fashionable American houses of the era, but he also designed and constructed careful replicas of period interiors in his studios in Paris and had them shipped across the Atlantic for reassembly under the supervision of his workers. Karl Bitter was the second of Hunt's frequent collaborators. Born in Vienna, Bitter enjoyed great success as a sculptor, and in 1889 he came to America, where he quickly found his talents in demand. His elaborate carvings and careful sculptures soon became fixtures in many of Hunt's domestic works.[72]

The design for 660 Fifth Avenue was conceived with an eye toward artistic magnitude. Based on elements derived from a number of Renaissance châteaux in the Loire Valley, it managed a cohesive presence and uniformity while incorporating a diversity of decorative elements. From the very beginning, Hunt and Alva envisioned the house as a brilliant stage set on which to enact society's rituals. Within, rooms would span a number of historical eras in French architecture and interior design, ranging from late Gothic to the reign of Louis XV; thus the exterior would present a cohesive evocation of a particular period, but the rooms inside, decorated by Herter Brothers and by Jules Allard & Sons, were to encompass a diversity

The Vanderbilt château at 660 Fifth Avenue in New York City.

unsuspected from without.[73] It was the first house in the city—and, indeed, in the country—to establish the idea of a number of rooms of varied periods, collected within the loose framework of French design, within its walls, offering visitors the surprise and pleasure of passing from one exquisite space to another that contrasted and amazed. Yet this was no mere pastiche. Hunt's vision offered coherence and strength, a bold statement of intent that marked it as unique assertion of the wealth and taste of its owners.[74]

The very materials used—gray limestone and terra-cotta reliefs—stood in stark contrast to the seemingly endless rows of uniform brownstones. The Fifth Avenue facade offered a picturesque, asymmetrical cornucopia of elaborate detail that set the house apart from its neighbors and helped soften the formal nature of the interior arrangement. At the center, a carved arch, flanked by pilasters, marked the main entrance; above this, Hunt placed a recessed balcony whose canopied niches were filled with statuary carved by Karl Bitter, topped on the third floor by yet another balustraded balcony crowned by dormers surrounded by carved buttresses and topped with elaborate stone finials, a wealth of decoration piled upon decoration reflecting the vocabulary of Renaissance France. Expressive tiers of mullioned windows, adorned with carved pilasters and ogee arches, rose on either side of the main entrance, topped with elaborately carved dormers, but the facade was dominated by a slender corbeled tower rising from the second floor, its limestone surface delicately ornamented with a design of fleur-de-lis and crowned by a tall conical roof.[75]

The facade facing Fifty-second Street, overlooking the southern half of William Henry Vanderbilt's Twin Palace, carried more varied ornamentation and rhythm in its rows of hooded windows, an oriel, large bays, and richly carved detail. Above, buttressed dormers rich with ogee arches and carved pinnacles drew the eye toward a roof line adorned with decorative statuary, including one depicting Richard Morris Hunt himself, added as a tribute to his genius.[76] Marble, ornamental wrought iron, and works of art added to the estimated $3 million ($60 million in 2008) construction cost. The house was not only impossible to ignore but also a stunning declaration of intent. New York had never seen anything like it.

"Vastness is the first impression in this truly magnificent house," commented the *New York Tribune,* "and splendor is the second impression, and luxury is the third impression."[77] A broad flight of stairs ascended directly from the sidewalk to the new château's front doors of oak opening to a vestibule faced in marble. There was a sweeping disorientation within, when visitors found themselves confronted with a series of apartments that bore little resemblance to one another or to the themes deployed on the exterior. This uncertain quality, so different from other, more overwhelming houses of the period, was a masterstroke: Alva not only kept her guests curious but also heightened the sense of theatricality and discovery.

Elaborate wrought-iron and glass doors ornamented with ormolu reliefs opened from the vestibule to a vast hall paved in marble, sixty feet long and twenty feet wide, topped with a sixteen-foot-high ceiling set with carved oak reliefs. A richly carved seven-foot-high wainscot of Caen stone wrapped the lower walls, but the severity was relieved by colorful antique Italian tapestries.[78]

To the left of the entrance, overlooking Fifth Avenue, was the reception room, its walls wrapped with dark French walnut wainscot picked out in delicate carved moldings below a colorful crimson floral damask. Alva was never entirely happy with it and later had the room redecorated in

The banquet hall at 660 Fifth Avenue in New York City.

the seventeenth-century Carolinian style using laurel wreaths, swags, trophies, and antique pendants carved by Grinling Gibbons that lent a touch of authenticity often lacking in the city's other houses.[79] Allard provided the *régence* salon, a luminous space lined with white enameled French walnut boiseries picked out in gold and purchased from a château in France. Alva bedecked the walls with three seventeenth-century tapestries by François Boucher, their classical themes echoed in a ceiling representing the marriage of Cupid and Psyche painted by Paul Baudry, who had recently decorated the Grand Foyer of Garnier's Opera House in Paris.[80] Here, alongside expensive reproduction furniture, stood genuine treasures, including finely worked commodes by master craftsman Jean-Henri Riesner that had originally belonged to Marie Antoinette.[81] For intimate meals Hunt installed a Gothic-style breakfast room with Flemish tapestries on the walls, a ceiling of painted beams, and a superb portrait by Rembrandt, *The Noble Slav,* above the mantelpiece, while a French Renaissance–style library adorned with rich ebony woodwork overlooked Fifth Avenue. There also was an exotic touch, a Moorish billiard room full of vibrant red, blue, and gold tilework, columns of marble and onyx, and windows shielded in gilded jalti screens.[82]

The banquet hall at the rear of the house was the center of 660 Fifth Avenue's regal ambitions. Designed by Herter Brothers in the baronial style, it was a vast space fifty feet long and thirty-five feet wide, rising two storeys to a coffered and beamed ceiling of oak. Alva's dining room might have been transported from some medieval manse, so precise were the details: faced in Caen stone, its lower walls were embellished with a seven-foot-high wainscot of quartered oak, above which hung seventeenth-century tapestries, while hickory logs crackled and blazed during the winter social season in a monumental double fireplace of red sandstone flanked by expressive caryatids supporting the carved oak mantel. Dominating the western wall was an enormous bay window set with stained glass depicting the meeting of Henry VIII and François I at the Field of the Cloth of Gold; at night, calcium lights concealed between the stained-glass panels and the exterior windows provided dramatic illumination, adding to the luster from four large stamped and filigreed wrought-iron chandeliers. Here, from a second-floor gallery, musicians serenaded the privileged guests as they danced through the night.[83]

From the hall, an exquisitely carved stone archway opened to a grand staircase of Caen stone flanked by an intricate balustrade awash with foliage, cherubs, and bunches of fruit, all washed in the vibrant colors of a stained-glass window at the landing.[84] As impressive as it was, however, for the Vanderbilt children it was an ominous place. "I still remember how long and terrifying was that dark and endless upward sweep," recalled Alva's daughter Consuelo, "as with acute sensations of fear, I climbed to my room every night, leaving below the light and its comforting rays."[85] While Willie's rooms on the second floor were small, practical, and executed in dark maple, Alva was not content to abandon the excesses of the ancien régime. Her suite included an enormous bedroom sheathed in gilded boiseries, a boudoir hung with François Boucher's magnificent painting *The Toilette of Venice,* originally owned by Madame de Pompadour, and a bathroom with a tub carved from a single block of white marble set against mirrored walls painted with blossoming cherry trees.[86]

The Vanderbilt house at 660 Fifth Avenue was a dramatic, shocking, and personal statement that captivated the imagination of the city. It offered true artistic expression and cultivated taste that contrasted with the often incoherent and coldly grand houses rising elsewhere across the city.

The carved staircase at 660 Fifth Avenue in New York City.

Alva proudly called it her "little Château de Blois."[87] Architect Charles McKim said that he liked to stroll past it after work, admiring its architecture. "I can sleep better at night knowing it's there," he said.[88] Critics were almost unanimous in their praise: it was, declared one, "a lyric inspiration" and "an isolated triumph of lightness and vivacious beauty."[89]

Although New York had previously witnessed theatrical residences, the Vanderbilt houses were something altogether different: the city's first true palaces, places of unrestrained ambition, extravagant interiors, and determined statements of cultivated taste. One contemporary publication praised them as mute evidence that the wealthy were content to put their resources to such use in an effort to beautify New York City, a sentiment that echoed the nobler obligations of Caroline Astor's Gilded Age society.[90] In them, noted an architectural study, "Wealth and fashion were united with a décor derived from the past that, however ostentatious, displayed a patina of good taste."[91] They led the way in a parade of million-dollar mansions that would soon rise along the length of Fifth Avenue.

10

MRS. ASTOR JOINS
THE RACE

THE HOUSES BUILT BY AUGUST BELMONT, A. T. Stewart, and even the Vanderbilts in New York all represented varied attempts to provide society with visible demonstrations of their owners' wealth and taste in efforts to gain admittance to its rarefied ranks. They stood as symbols of aspiration. But no matter the adornment of their exteriors and the opulence of their interiors, they could never entirely escape their origins as stages for social climbing. The houses of Caroline Astor, on the other hand, represented what they hoped to achieve: recognition and acceptance. Caroline's were New York City's true houses of power, where social careers were made or dreams shattered. Crossing their thresholds was akin to receiving an invitation to Buckingham Palace, providing entrée into a world of triumphant celebration.

After her 1853 marriage to William Backhouse II, it was Caroline who first suggested that the Astor family follow the trend of fashionable society and move away from the solid comforts of Washington Square to the burgeoning strongholds farther up Fifth Avenue.[1] Built in 1856, 350 Fifth Avenue was one of two houses, modeled on the city's typical upper-class brownstones, erected on adjacent lots between Thirty-third and Thirty-fourth streets on the west side of Fifth Avenue. William Backhouse Astor II lived in a four-storey house on the corner of Fifth Avenue and Thirty-fourth Street; a garden separated it from the three-storey residence of his brother John Jacob Astor III on the corner of Fifth and Thirty-third. Although Mrs. Astor's first house incorporated some features of the typical brownstone, it also was quite different. It was exceptionally large and wide, allowing for an expanse of the necessary reception rooms and drawing rooms within. The brick facade, on a semiraised basement of rusticated gray Nova Scotia freestone, was restrained; except for the Corinthian pilasters flanking the entrance door and the carved freestone architraves over the first-floor windows, it relied solely on its overhanging, bracketed cornice for ornamentation.[2] When A. T. Stewart built his white marble palace across Thirty-fourth Street, it put Mrs. Astor's unprepossessing house to shame.

At the time of its construction, Caroline Astor's house aspired to little more than an elegant, comfortable residence suited to the needs of her growing family and occasional entertaining. Mrs. August Belmont and Caroline's own mother-in-law, Margaret, were the recognized social arbiters of New York society, and there was no need for an impressive mansion to dazzle the city's elite. But this situation changed when Margaret Armstrong Astor died and Caroline began to lay claim to her mantle of society leader. Ward McAllister offered a stream of helpful advice aimed at not only conquering the social world but also on what was needed to win approval. Caroline's risk in creating a new elite composed of elements of both the old Knickerbocker aristocracy and members of the nouveau riche demanded bold measures, and among them was a residence suited to the role she had created for herself. In 1879 Caroline therefore commissioned Stanford White to greatly enhance the interior, spending nearly $83,000 (approximately $1.7 million in 2008) on new decorations, furnishings, and fittings to help advance her claim.[3] She could, of course, have commissioned an entirely new structure that would have dazzled New York. But Caroline, especially in these years, realized that the continued approval of the city's quiet and modest Knickerbocker elite was essential in maintaining her new society; a grandiose, overwrought mansion such as that erected

Caroline Astor's first house, at 350 Fifth Avenue in New York City.

by A. T. Stewart would only be met with derision and condemned as a vulgarity. Constrained by such considerations, Caroline followed the only course left open to her.

Like Mrs. Astor herself, her renovated house was meant to bridge the chasm between the old elite and the new, a carefully constructed facade that shielded the fires burning within. If the exterior largely echoed the prim neighboring brownstones, within, visitors left behind a world of ordinary uniformity and entered an unsuspected palace of marble floors, gilded boiseries, decorative stucco garlands and swags, and classical pilasters. Three enfiladed reception rooms with exquisite woodwork and painted ceilings offered mute evidence of her refined taste, while the baronial dining room, paneled in carved oak and hung with Flemish tapestries, evoked a distinctly Old World atmosphere.[4] Room after room was filled with antique furniture and carefully selected adornments designed to both impress and intimidate, forming a labyrinth of taste and power that ended at the heart of the house, a two-storey ballroom.[5] Doubling as the house's art gallery, the ballroom's red damask walls were hung with tier after tier of European paintings, rising to a gilded cornice and a ceiling cove painted in decorative motifs.

At one end, Italian candelabra with rows of opaque globes, collected by William during one of his European journeys, flanked a massive chimneypiece framed by twisted columns and bedecked with carved garlands, masks, and acanthus leaves; at the other, an immense white marble statue of Psyche, shocking in its brazen nudity, attracted as much attention as the collection of canvases. The room offered an apt summation of the transitional and uncertain period it represented: the canvases, the heavily carved and fringed walnut chairs and sofas, the plush of the upholstery, and the miniature forest of potted palms spoke of the quiet dignity of the old order, while delicate gilded chairs, Oriental porcelains, and elaborate Japanese screens hinted at the increasing swell of the exotic and historic.[6]

The house solidified Caroline's position at the apex of her Gilded Age elite, eventually entering into legend. Members of New York society, commented one contemporary magazine, regarded it "as a sort of metropolitan White House. If the Executive Mansion at Washington has been the center of the nation's political life, the Astor house has been, since 1870, the center of fashionable life in America. . . . How many thousands if not millions have gazed upon it from the outside with feelings of curiosity and interest and how many hundreds of the older generation in particular have detailed to their children and descendants the entertainments held within its walls in bygone years in which they have participated."[7] No one in New York City's Gilded Age doubted that it was the epicenter of taste and power, the sanctum sanctorum of the social world, a secular church where the faithful aspired to humble themselves and make their homage before their uncrowned queen.

As the years passed and as larger, more extravagant houses arose in New York City, Caroline remained firmly ensconced at 350 Fifth Avenue. Secure in her own position, she had no need to demonstrate her wealth or social power with a new, gaudy showplace. It provided her—and society—with permanence against an ever-evolving and uncertain world. But in 1890 this situation changed on the death of her brother-in-law, when Caroline's nephew forced the issue.

When John Jacob Astor III died in 1890, his son William Waldorf Astor fully expected to assume his father's place as patriarch of the dynasty, with all of the privileges that came with the position. But he found his claim to be head of the family challenged by his Aunt Caroline, who was loath to abandon any vestige of power and influence. William Waldorf let it be known that it was his wife, Mary, who should, by rights, assume social leadership of the family, despite the fact that with her innate shyness and serious manner, she found the idea all too intimidating. Caroline's personal calling cards had been inscribed *Mrs. William Astor,* but when she learned of her nephew's bid, she had them changed; now they boldly proclaimed, for all of society to read and digest, simply *Mrs. Astor,* as if she were the only one who counted. She was, she insisted, by years of social dominance, the only Astor wife who mattered, and people began to refer to her simply as *the* Mrs. Astor. Met with this obstacle, William Waldorf attempted a protest; custom and etiquette, he declared, dictated that the wife of the eldest male member of a family always be accorded the simplest title in deference to her rank. His position was quite correct, but Caroline let it be known that anyone who dared list or address her as *Mrs. William Astor* would forever be stricken from her guest lists; organizers of charity events were likewise warned that the proud and willful Caroline would no longer accept any invitation that did not refer to her specifically as *Mrs. Astor.*[8]

When Caroline discovered that she was listed as *Mrs. William Astor* as a patron of the Casino Ball in Newport in 1890, she angrily withdrew her support for the event, refusing to speak to any of the committee members or extend them invitations to her social functions. Mary Astor's friends retaliated by making a public scene one Sunday morning in church, when they occupied the pew customarily reserved for Caroline and pointedly refused to move when she attempted to take her usual place.[9] Things were getting ugly, and the vendettas increasingly played themselves out in public and drew in innocent bystanders. William Waldorf tried to force mail delivery of any letters or invitations addressed to *Mrs. Astor* to his own wife, but society—unwilling and unable to risk Caroline's censure—eventually took her side.[10] There was no hope that William Waldorf could win this battle against his formidable aunt, and so later in 1890—declaring in disgust that "America is not a fit place for a gentleman to live"—he took his wife and moved to England, eventually renouncing his American citizenship and becoming a naturalized British subject. Caroline emerged triumphant; now she was known simply as *the* Mrs. Astor.[11]

The battle, however, was not yet over, for William Waldorf Astor took his revenge from exile. In 1892 he had his late father's mansion at Fifth Avenue and Thirty-third Street in New York torn down and announced plans to erect a hotel on the spot; the new structure would thus abut Caroline Astor's own house. Thus the thirteen-storey Waldorf Hotel arose in all of its neo-German Renaissance glory next to the mansion of Gilded Age society's recognized doyenne. The new Waldorf opened in March 1893 with a benefit concert partially funded—and one suspects with more than a little glee—by Alva Vanderbilt.[12]

Caroline had no intention of living next to a commercial building. News of her nephew's decision to erect a massive hotel in her garden

The Waldorf Hotel (left) in New York City, next to the house of A. T. Stewart.

came at the worst possible moment—within days of William Backhouse Astor's death and in the midst of the very public scandal over Caroline's daughter Charlotte Augusta and her flight to Europe with her rumored lover. William Waldorf was certainly aware of the turmoil enveloping his aunt's life, and his rather insensitive actions earned her everlasting scorn. Thus, in the midst of mourning for her husband and worry over her daughter's sullied reputation, Caroline was essentially forced from the house in which she had lived for forty years.[13] A few years later, her son Jack attempted his own form of revenge against his cousin. At first he wanted to tear down his mother's house and replace it with a massive stable, whose pervasive smell would thus pervade the new hotel. Eventually he was talked out of such a measure and agreed to build his own competing hotel on the site. He had wanted to call it the Schermerhorn, but Caroline objected, declaring that it would be an insult to have her family name plastered on a public hotel; instead he settled on the Astoria. The two warring cousins, William Waldorf in England and Jack in New York, eventually reached a kind of détente and merged the two institutions into the venerable and opulent Waldorf-Astoria.[14]

This decision to move farther up Fifth Avenue took form when Caroline hired Richard Morris Hunt to design her new house. Hunt had previously worked for Caroline Astor, enlarging her Newport house, Beechwood, to great effect, but the decision also may have been influenced by the architect's work for the Vanderbilts. By this time Caroline had accepted the commodore's descendants into the fold of New York society, and they remained respectful—even Alva—of her position at the pinnacle of the city's elite. This was a decision made with some ambivalence; while bowing to the inevitable, Caroline was still determined to preserve the traditions that infused her world, but the undoubted magnificence of the new houses in New York and Newport had made her abodes seem positively humble in comparison. It was the height of the Gilded Age and all of its attendant extravagance and now she, too, wanted to be surrounded by its refined luxuries.

For her new residence, Caroline selected a large lot at 840 Fifth Avenue and Sixty-fifth Street, overlooking Central Park, and in March 1893 construction began. Three years—and more than $2 million (approximately $45 million in 2008) later—the house was finished.[15] The house was a double one. The larger, northern half was built for Caroline, while the southern half was for her son Jack and his wife, Ava; across the rear of both houses was a shared ballroom, and the two residences could be thrown together on crowded evenings by opening a series of enormous, sliding pocket doors. Constructed of light gray Indiana limestone, it was a building of regal proportion and careful, attenuated decoration, its three principal storeys atop a semiraised basement rising to a steeply pitched mansard roof of contrasting gray-green slate. Hunt modeled elements of 840 Fifth Avenue on the châteaux of Azay-le-Rideau and Amboise, but it was a building that evoked the early French Renaissance more than the late Gothic movement. Unlike Hunt's château for Alva Vanderbilt at 660 Fifth Avenue, Caroline's residence was more measured and classical in execution. Here Hunt abandoned the asymmetrical for a strict, ordered rhythm, defining the mansion with two, slightly taller pavilions at the northern and southern ends to break up the uniformity of the Fifth Avenue facade, but the whole was linked through the repetition of corner quoins, carved stringcourses, mullioned windows, and decorative pilasters that conveyed both movement and solidity. The mansion still bristled with Renaissance-inspired touches: carved lintels, elaborate wrought-iron grilles, a roof with massed chimneystacks, carved

Caroline Astor's new château, at 840 Fifth Avenue in New York City.

and hooded dormers, and wrought-iron cresting, but none of these picturesque elements were allowed to affect the overall formality of the design.[16] The end result, noted one contemporary, was a palace of "extraordinary luxury and grandeur," where "splendor is piled upon splendor."[17] It—and its famous owner—attracted so much attention that curious crowds regularly gathered on the sidewalk, much to Caroline's horror, and she refused to go near her windows lest some nosy tourist catch an unwelcome glimpse.[18]

Large doors of gilded bronze and glass opened to a domed, circular vestibule, a neoclassical allusion that hinted at the diversity of the rooms beyond. Passing into the two-storey hall, visitors entered a highly formalized space where Hunt successfully mingled two disparate styles. The lower half of the hall evoked the restrained world of Louis XVI. Walls of white Caen stone were adorned with Corinthian pilasters and pierced with an arcade. Ascending the handsome grand staircase of white marble, with its finely worked balustrade of wrought iron adorned with ormolu mounts, however, transported guests back in time, to the age of the baroque. Here the stucco reliefs were more abundant, and voluptuous, life-size female nudes sculpted by Karl Bitter reached toward a leaded-glass skylight set into a coved ceiling awash with carved garlands of fruit and foliage. Enormous Flemish tapestries framed by Corinthian pilasters added the only notes of color.[19] It was a space of refinement and deliberate restraint coupled with brief hints of excess, a subtle suggestion of the splendors that lay beyond.

The drawing room, recalled one visitor, "created an impression of almost overpowering solidity and permanence."[20] White walls, divided into panels by Corinthian pilasters with gilded capitals, were adorned with carved and gilded boiseries installed by Jules Allard & Sons; the doors were mirrored, and topped with mirrored, semicircular lunettes to echo the arched looking glass above the variegated black marble chimneypiece. Caroline filled the room with Louis XIV–style carved and gilded furniture, French tapestries, and a collection of Sèvres vases.[21]

The room's undoubted center of attention, however, was an immense portrait of Caroline, painted in 1890 by Charles Auguste Émile Carolus-Duran. The artist essayed *the* Mrs. Astor at the height of her power and influence. Shown in a long, dark blue velvet gown by Worth, with puffed princess sleeves and a Van Dyke collar of white lace sewn with gold, Caroline stood proudly alone, erect against a background of dramatic ocher; there was no furniture, no objets d'art, no flowers—no diversions to distract from its dominating figure and the deliberate allusion to royalty.

The grand staircase in Caroline Astor's new château, at 840 Fifth Avenue.

The right hand was gloved; the other held a fan of black ostrich feathers. Unlike many society commissions, Carolus-Duran's portrait made no attempt to improve on nature or present an idealized representation of its subject. It was an image of unmistakable power, not of beauty.[22]

In a bit of insightful planning, Hunt created an almost oppressively dark dining room, paneled in black oak accented with ebony and inlays of gilt. A hundred people could dine here, the rainbow hues of the ladies' gowns shimmering against the black of the walls to create a vivid spectacle. Gilded fillets encased antique tapestries depicting medieval hunting and banqueting scenes in keeping with the room's function, while an enormous crystal chandelier swirled from a ceiling painted with floral garlands and cartouches holding Mrs. Astor's monogram picked out in gold.[23]

In embarking on her new château, however, Caroline could not—or would not—entirely abandon those elements that had formed the center of her world for two decades. Thus, for all of the refined taste and delicate objets, her house presented a curious dichotomy of gilded 1890s grandeur coupled with the Victorian clutter of her youth. In one glance, visitors might find themselves admiring an exquisitely inlaid marquetry and ormolu French commode in her drawing room and yet be horrified to see it piled with cheap busts of Shakespeare and Wagner crowded along-side stuffed birds under glass domes. The gleaming marble and parquet floors were not only covered with expensive Oriental and Aubusson car-pets but also were scattered with a disparate assortment of tiger and bear-skin rugs, mouths open and fangs bared menacingly and, in a particularly exotic touch, a carpet stitched together from peacock feathers.[24] It was also, once built and furnished, a house of permanence, for Caroline could abide no change. "At Mrs. Astor's," recalled Elizabeth Drexel Lehr, "you would have recognized the place had you been introduced into the draw-ing room or the ball room after years of absence." Nothing, she noted, ever changed.[25]

Not surprisingly for the woman who reigned over Gilded Age society, Caroline's new house, at the time of its construction, possessed the largest private ballroom in New York City, capable of holding not her legendary four hundred, but twelve hundred guests. Rising one and a half storeys to a coved ceiling where sculpted gods and goddesses watched the revelers in

The spacious ballroom in Caroline Astor's new château, at 840 Fifth Avenue in New York City.

silent approval, its walls were hung with row after row of European paintings in deference to its alternate role as an art gallery. These were, recalled one relative, "principally seventeenth-century French art, with Corot providing the masterpieces of the collection, but the vast array of odalisques, dancing girls, cows in meadows, cottages, sleeping children, dogs herding sheep, sunrises and sunsets, Roman ruins, parting lovers, homecoming travelers, made it a monument of mid-Victorian taste."[26]

At one end of the ballroom stood an enormous white marble chimneypiece from Italy, adorned with carved and gilded laurel garlands and surmounted by massive sculpted figures framing a tall looking glass; at the other, opening off of the second floor, was a wrought-iron musicians' gallery from which an orchestra could serenade the guests. Crystal and ormolu chandeliers, and the standing gilt candelabra that had graced her original ballroom at 350 Fifth Avenue, provided the room's soft illumination. Here, upon the house's completion in 1896, Caroline resumed her round of privileged entertainments, giving her first ball since the death of her husband four years earlier.[27]

The ball marked Caroline's full return to the heights of New York society. She had now, as Lloyd Morris recalled, "entered upon her apotheosis. She was more than *the* Mrs. Astor. She was the only Mrs. Astor, and there could be no greater magnificence, no more sublime destiny than that of bearing this classically simple designation, so rich in profound, mysterious meanings. No longer was she merely the central, supreme divinity of a local cult. She became the subject of a national legend, taking her permanent place in American folklore. Though she professed disdain for the press and pretended to resent any mention of her name in its columns, newspapers throughout the country faithfully recorded her impressions, aware that, in effect, Mrs. Astor was a national institution."[28]

11

BUILDING FOR ETERNITY

In the mad rush among New York City's Gilded Age elite to trump their rivals, increasingly splendid private palaces became the most visible symbols of the fight for social supremacy. In the wake of standards set by the Vanderbilts and Mrs. Astor, these private houses grew more lavish and overtly dedicated to their ceremonial functions as stages for their owners' privileged pageants. If the Vanderbilts had built not only for themselves but also for the enrichment of the city, few of those who copied their architectural ambitions had any such pretensions to the greater good. These houses were determinedly grand, often oppressively powerful, and rarely personal in their statements. One turn-of-the-century publication declared that these houses "will not be understood unless it is frankly admitted that they are built for men whose chief title to distinction is that they are rich, and that they are designed by men whose architectural ideas are profoundly modified by the riches of their clients."[1]

Great wealth coupled with great aspirations found visible representation in such buildings, and few were conceived with as much grandeur or ultimately failed so completely in their intent as that built by railroad tycoon Collis Huntington, who had arrived in New York armed with nearly unlimited resources only to find that his background, coupled with his unconventional style of life, barred him from social entrée. Born in 1821, Huntington was, with Leland Stanford, Mark Hopkins, and Charles Crocker, one of the renowned "Big Four" who established the Central Pacific Railroad as part of a transcontinental railway system. Other railroads followed, along with Huntington's development of the Newport News Shipbuilding Company in Virginia.

In 1844 Huntington married Elizabeth Stoddard of Connecticut and settled in New York. Elizabeth was a somewhat plain, modest woman whose quiet character stood in sharp contrast to that of her more boisterous husband. The couple spent little time together, as Huntington was often in San Francisco on business. By the beginning of the 1870s, Huntington had taken a mistress, the very beautiful, very mysterious Arabella Worsham, one of the Gilded Age's most remarkable figures. Very little reliable information exists about her life before she met Huntington. Arabella seems to have been born in 1852, but her habit of lying about her background left precise details impossible to verify, perhaps as she wished.[2] A stunning and tall, dark-haired, dark-eyed woman, Arabella was a widow with a young son—or at least that is what she declared.[3] The son, born in New York City in 1870, was real enough, though the true identity of his father—like so much in Arabella's life—remains unknown, and the putative husband-father, John Worsham, actually lived for six years after Arabella announced his death. It was widely whispered that the boy was Huntington's, and, indeed, the tycoon later adopted him.[4]

What is likely is that Huntington soon set up his mistress in New York, channeling money to her mother to pay for a series of increasingly elaborate houses in the city.[5] His wife, Elizabeth, died of cancer in October 1883, and nine months later, on July 12, 1884, Huntington married Arabella. This second marriage, coming so soon after the death of his wife, coupled with Arabella's questionable background, rumors of her son's paternity, and the open secret of her liaison with Huntington, cloaked the couple in scandal. Huntington might not have cared, but Arabella desperately wanted to enter society. She—like many others before and after her—believed that the extravagant expenditure of money and the possession of a New York palace would open doors otherwise

closed. To help her accomplish the latter goal, her husband duly purchased several lots on Fifty-seventh Street and commissioned a luxurious
new mansion.

The couple selected architect George Browne Post to undertake the
new mansion, but Post initially declined on the grounds that what
Arabella wanted was simply too large and ungainly. After another architect refused the commission on the grounds that what Arabella wanted
would forever compromise him in the eyes of his colleagues, eventually
she agreed to scale down her grandiose plans to suit a reluctant Post.[6]
Construction took two years, and the house was completed in 1892.
Given the immensity of the house that was built, one must wonder what
Arabella had originally wanted. The end result was a hulking, three-storey
mélange of Romanesque, Italianate, and French Renaissance–inspired
details ringed by a tall, spiked fence.[7] "Oddest of all," wrote Stephen
Birmingham, "the house seemed to have an expression. The huge central
archway looked like a gaping mouth ringed with jagged, fanglike teeth.
Two arched windows just above looked like flared nostrils, and the big
paired windows above and to either side of the nostrils looked like enormous, baleful eyes. Viewed from the street, the house seemed literally to
be snarling at the spectator. Its whole appearance was dark, grim, and
forbidding."[8]

The house, however, failed to win Arabella the acceptance she so desperately sought, and she remained behind its hideous walls, isolated and
ignored as Gilded Age society frolicked around her. Her husband's death
in 1900 left Arabella with an immense fortune that, if nothing else, gave
her a new sense of purpose. Armed with money and an eagerness to be
taught, she launched on a serious career as one of the world's greatest art
connoisseurs, filling her house with works by Vermeer, Reynolds, Romney,
Gainsborough, and Rembrandt. Arabella later married again, this time—in
yet another of the peculiar turns so common to her life—her husband's
nephew Henry Huntington, and her great collection today forms the core
of the Huntington Library and Art Gallery in San Marino, California.

In profound contrast to Arabella Huntington and her thwarted social
aspirations was Ruth Mills, one of the era's stateliest hostesses. Ruth
Livingston Mills was, like Arabella Huntington, a woman of formidable

character, but she also was a pervasive snob. As a member of one of New York's oldest and most socially prominent families, she had been brought up with a keen awareness of her heritage and the expectations that accompanied such a position. Uniquely, for a woman consumed with upholding inherited privilege and tradition, Ruth had startled her family and friends when, in 1882, she had married Ogden Mills, one of the Gilded Age's wealthiest businessmen. Ogden's father, Darius, had taken advantage of the California gold rush to enrich himself: with William Ralston, he founded the Bank of California, and used the proceeds to buy stock in the Vanderbilts' New York Central Railroad and in the General Electric Company, investments that brought immense returns.[9]

Ogden Mills, born in 1856, had followed in his father's footsteps, continuing his profitable investments in stocks and real estate to increase his fortune. Although he was clearly a member of the era's nouveau riche, he improved his status considerably on his marriage to Ruth Livingston. It was a rare example of a union between old money and new, and it succeeded despite the nearly universal scorn that had initially greeted its announcement. The couple and their three children—twin girls and a boy—lived comfortable, privileged lives, alternating their time among a Second Empire–style mansion called Happy House in Millbrae, California; a 120-room château near Paris; and a large country estate along the Hudson River.[10] In 1885, however, Mills commissioned Richard Morris Hunt to provide a suitable New York City residence for himself and his ambitious wife, a building that reflected the increasing taste for eclectic historicism of the Gilded Age elite.

Mills purchased a lot at the corner of Fifth Avenue and Sixty-ninth Street and asked Hunt to erect a large dwelling suited to the entertainments demanded of Gilded Age society. The resulting mansion, which took two years to complete, was a curious amalgam of disparate styles and periods. Of three principal storeys, it was a very loose, expressive interpretation of the Venetian Gothic, its dark, rich brick facade ornamented with rows of windows framed in contrasting stone and topped with arches to echo the distinctive loggias of the Doges' Palace in Venice. Massive chimneystacks flanked by curved gables ringed the cornice, their appearance alluding not only to the Gothic but also to the Dutch gables imported by early settlers from the houses along the canals in Amsterdam.[11] Hunt's interiors were largely in keeping with the severity of the facade: walls of carved and dressed stone hung with tapestries, elaborately carved doorways, and gilded, coffered ceilings. It was all very monumental and very cold.[12]

In 1901 Ruth hired architect Horace Trumbauer to enlarge the house slightly and to redesign its rooms, infusing them with a more classical sensibility. Within, the Venetian Gothic gave way to eighteenth-century France, as Trumbauer deployed a profusion of antique furniture, imported boiseries, tapestries, and objets d'art. Gilded bas-reliefs decorated carved fillets on the walls of the Gray Salon to add a lustrous touch, while similar trophies glistened against the pale tones of the Green Salon below a neoclassical cornice. As the centerpiece of Ruth's social ambitions, Trumbauer lavished his greatest attention on the ballroom, adorning its luminous white walls with an impressive array of gilded rocailles and garlands that crept like spreading vines to a ceiling hung with shimmering crystal and ormolu chandeliers. The ornamental pilasters, marble chimneypieces, inlaid wooden floors, and stuccoed reliefs deemed necessary were all there to be seen, but the result was somehow less than successful, as if—constrained by working within a framework not wholly suited to such endeavors—the magnitude of Trumbauer's vision had fallen victim to the reality of execution.[13]

Among the elite hostesses of the Gilded Age, Mrs. Mills was perhaps the most exclusive of them all, attempting to limit society to a mere handful of respectable families. Whereas Caroline Astor was famous for her four hundred, Ruth declared, "There are really only twenty families in New York." Elizabeth Drexel Lehr remembered her as "cold, sarcastic, and aristocratic," a woman of whom even Harry Lehr declared, "She has reduced rudeness to a fine art." Like Mamie Fish, Ruth enjoyed toying with members of society, though she made them not objects of amusement but of disdain. She would receive guests "with a limp hand, languidly extended, and a far away expression, and then apparently forget their existence. They were chilled, but impressed."[14] Ruth constantly struggled to promote herself as a rival to Alva Vanderbilt, Tessie Oelrichs, and Mamie Fish; it was Ruth's proud boast that her house was so well run that she could give a dinner party for a hundred guests on an hour's notice without calling in extra help or dispatching servants on any emergency shopping expeditions.[15]

Ultimately, however, Ruth's exclusivity defeated her. None of the other great hostesses particularly liked her, for she was known to attempt social coups at their expense. Such was the case with Grace Wilson Vanderbilt, with whom she had a long-running feud. In 1902, when Grace managed to secure the visiting Prince Heinrich of Prussia, brother of Kaiser Wilhelm II, for a dinner party—which, she proudly let the newspapers know, was to be his *only* private entertainment in America—Ruth promptly used her money and influence to somehow coerce his attendance at a luncheon to be held *before* Grace's dinner party, and quickly notified the press of the fact. "Those who had hailed Mrs. Vanderbilt as Mrs. Astor's successor," noted *Town and Country*, "are beginning to realize that Mrs. Mills, who has long considered herself the arbiter of the circle within the circle, has no intention of abating one jot of her power."[16] Edith Wharton later parodied the imperious Ruth in her novel *The House of Mirth,* casting her as Judy Trenor, the proud mistress of Bellomont.

This progression of architectural taste, from the more outwardly dramatic to a careful and sedate stateliness, found expression in 1896 when the architectural firm of Carrère & Hastings designed a splendid, French-inspired town house at 9 East 72nd Street for Henry T. Sloane. Sloane, scion of the founder of the great W. J. Sloane & Company, worked in the family business for many years, amassing a substantial fortune, and he wanted a house suited to his wealth, if not to his social aspirations, which were never quite accepted in New York society. Carrère & Hastings provided a house suited to his grandiose pretensions, a three-storey structure bedecked with carved garlands and cartouches and dominated by a monumental range of Ionic columns rising to an elaborate cornice and a mansard roof. The elegant rooms within included an oval staircase of marble ascending to a fifty-foot-long salon and a large dining room opening to a conservatory.[17]

When the house was finished, Sloane and his wife, Jessie, the beautiful daughter of a Brooklyn drug manufacturer, took up residence, but the marriage was already strained. Sloane adored his wife, and showered her with expensive jewels and gowns from Paris, but Jessie felt smothered in this hothouse atmosphere. Longing for fulfillment, she embarked on an affair with August Belmont's handsome son Perry. The lovers were quite open about their scandalous liaison; Sloane, though devastated by this development, remained in love with his wife and, for her sake, tolerated the affair, a situation that escaped no one's notice. Gossips in society regularly whispered of the sordid "triangle" and clucked their bemused tongues at Sloane's seemingly bottomless well of indulgence.[18] "Mr. Henry Sloane," *Town Topics* commented, "has been looked upon as a complaisant husband who wore his horns too publicly."[19]

Finally, though, Sloane gave his wife an ultimatum and threatened her with divorce; believing that Henry would never expose his personal life to so public a scandal, Jessie brazenly continued her affair with Belmont. But after being the subject of so much ridicule, Sloane was not bluffing, and in 1899 he shocked society by filing for divorce and openly charging his wife with persistent adultery. Rather than contest the accusation, Jessie bowed to the inevitable; so absorbed was she with Belmont that she even failed to ask for custody of her two children. On the same day that the divorce decree was finally granted, Jessie promptly married Belmont and moved with him to Washington, D.C. Sloane himself never remarried, and sold his new residence, with its sad memories of thwarted love, a mere five years after its completion.[20]

In many ways, William Collins Whitney was remarkable not only for his success in the business world but also for the position to which he rose in New York society. Born in 1841 in New Hampshire to a family of respected pedigree but few financial assets, he proved a talented student and won accolades at Yale and at Harvard University Law School. In the New York City of the 1860s, he quickly caught the attention of dedicated reformer Samuel Tilden and of the Democratic Party, and when the infamously corrupt "Boss" William Tweed was toppled from power, Whitney found his star in the ascendant. For six years he served as the counsel to the Corporation of the City of New York, his legal prowess attracting the attention of the Vanderbilt family, who in 1882 hired him to represent their own interests.[21]

Whitney tied his fortunes to a plan by Thomas Ryan to gain control of the Manhattan street transit system; in their efforts to corner the market, Whitney and Ryan faced the formidable opposition of other speculators, including wealthy businessman Jacob Sharp, who was not above dispersing some $500,000 ($10 million in 2008) in bribes to the city's aldermen to win control of the disputed lines. Whitney and Ryan countered with their own propaganda efforts, which included scandalous stories planted in sympathetic newspapers, lawsuits, and rumors of their own, carefully placed bribes. When opinion turned against Sharp and the eighty-year-old man was hauled off to jail, Whitney and Ryan were able to purchase his business interests at a fraction of their actual value.[22]

In 1884 President Grover Cleveland asked Whitney to serve as his secretary of the navy, and, with some reluctance, he agreed, but within four years he was back in New York, again working with Ryan to increase their hold on Manhattan's street transit system. Their Metropolitan Transit Company offered new and frequently dubious opportunities for self-enrichment. They leased their own trolley cars to themselves at highly inflated prices, awarded themselves extravagant salaries, and, it was said, pocketed the dividends due to their shareholders to increase their own coffers. So successful was this endeavor that in a mere five years, Whitney had made a staggering $40 million ($800 million in 2008).[23]

Whitney's success owed much to his genteel manner. He had carefully cultivated an aura of refinement from his days at Yale and Harvard and could easily charm those he encountered. No one took him for a ruthless robber baron or unscrupulous speculator. Whitney affected a definite aristocratic air, wearing a pince-nez that concealed eyes one contemporary described as "very cold, very steady, and utterly fearless." Others praised him as "an intellectual giant," and one went so far as to declare that "mediocrity in Whitney is unthinkable."[24]

In 1869 Whitney married Flora Payne, sister of Oliver Payne, who had been his roommate at Yale, and daughter of U.S. Senator Henry Payne of Ohio. The Paynes, early investors in Standard Oil, possessed their own immense fortune, which, for Whitney, only added to the luster of the match.[25] William was devoted to Flora, and the couple had four children: Pauline, who married British aristocrat Sir Almeric Paget in a wedding at

New York City's St. Thomas's Episcopal Church that was rumored to have cost $1 million ($20 million in 2008); Dorothy; William; and Harry Payne, who, in 1896, married Cornelius Vanderbilt II's daughter Gertrude. In 1892, when Flora died unexpectedly, William was devastated, but four years later he scandalized his family by marrying Mrs. Edith Randolph, widow of a British army officer and a woman fifteen years his junior. His former brother-in-law Oliver attempted to influence his nieces and nephews against the union, threatening to cut them off from the substantial inheritance they were set to receive from Standard Oil dividends.[26] Pauline and Harry Payne sided with their uncle, but Dorothy and William remained loyal to their father.[27]

In 1888, when Grover Cleveland was defeated in his presidential reelection bid and Whitney returned to New York, his father-in-law, Senator Payne, who had already provided the couple with a fine town house at 74 Park Avenue, again dipped into his pockets and gave them a new gift, a large mansion at 2 West 57th Street. Here Whitney remained for less than a decade, finally giving the house to his son Harry on his marriage to Gertrude Vanderbilt.[28] Whitney and his new wife promptly purchased a large, château-style mansion at 871 Fifth Avenue that had formerly been owned by sugar merchant Robert L. Stuart. It was the location of the house, rather than the residence itself, that had attracted attention, for the couple commissioned Stanford White to make some $4 million ($80 million in 2008) in renovations to the existing structure.[29]

When the Whitneys purchased the property, Stuart's house was less than a decade old. A quietly dignified building of projecting bays, arched windows, and a mansard roof, it was distinguished only by its size, a large, long structure whose facade sprawled along a prominent and fashionable stretch of Fifth Avenue. White made few changes to the exterior. His work included a new, projecting entrance portico screened by bronze and iron gates from the Doria Palace in Rome, and a new wing containing a ballroom and service rooms to the east, but most of the architect's focus was devoted to the interior.[30] Whitney asked that White create rooms appropriate to a Florentine-style palazzo within the French Renaissance shell, and both client and architect scoured Italy for important artifacts and antiques. During the four years of construction, Edith

Whitney suffered a riding accident; she lingered in great pain for many months until her death in the spring of 1899, never destined to preside over the grand halls she had helped to plan.[31]

As completed by White, the house was widely considered one of the most extravagant private residences in all of New York. There were ceilings from Florentine palaces, carved chimneypieces from France, ancient statues dredged from the bottom of the Tiber, stained-glass windows from medieval monasteries, and fittings culled from French châteaux, along with Flemish tapestries, antique furnishings, costly carpets, and paintings by Raphael, Tintoretto, and Van Dyke—all the trappings of power and taste with which Whitney could surround himself.[32] Visitors to Whitney's house entered a world of carefully contrived illusion. A vestibule lined with green onyx and hung with three bronze chandeliers opened to a reception hall. Here White evoked the extravagant world of the Medicis, with walls of white marble ornamented by dark green columns above an intricate marble floor inlaid with more than ten thousand bronze mosaics. A staircase of Istrian marble, flanked by a stone balustrade so intricately carved that it resembled fine lace, ascended to a great hall with a coffered wooden ceiling from Florence and an immense carved chimneypiece from a château at Augues-Mortes.[33]

There was a dark, almost oppressive opulence to White's interiors, so loaded were they with detail piled on exquisite detail. Antique Florentine embroidered panels draped the walls of the drawing room, whose wooden ceiling, with its carved coffers picked out in rich gold, and blue and green traceries adorned with copper insets, had come from a palazzo in Rome; from its central, carved pendant hung a chandelier of hammered bronze, which matched the tall candelabrum standing around the room. In the adjoining library, the extravagantly carved bookcases, purchased from an Italian palace, lined walls hung with paintings by Reynolds and Fra Lippi. Yet another coffered wooden ceiling, inset with a painting by Bardini purchased from a palace in Genoa, graced the dining room. Brussels tapestries depicting the wars of Flavius Titus hung upon the textured walls, and Corinthian columns framed the cased doorways, holding aloft intricately carved and gilded Renaissance lintels.[34]

At sixty feet in length, White's two-storey ballroom was the largest of the mansion's interiors and, indeed, the largest private ballroom in New York City, surpassing that of Caroline Astor's château on Fifth Avenue.[35] Here White abandoned the shadows of the Renaissance in favor of the splendors of Versailles. The gilded oak boiseries on the walls had come from the château of Baron de Foix in Bordeaux, purchased by White at a cost of some $50,000 (approximately $1.1 million in 2008) and reinstalled between panels set with Flemish tapestries encased in ornamental fillets picked out in gold. More burnished gold shimmered in the rocailles and cartouches that circled a painted ceiling. At one end, above a carved chimneypiece, hung Sir Joshua Reynolds's *Portrait of a Lady*; it faced a bowed musicians' gallery, resting on carved corbels, at the opposite end, reached through a concealed doorway opening from the third floor.[36]

Whitney took up residence in his new Renaissance-style palace in 1900 and formally inaugurated the house with a splendid ball on January 4, 1901, given to celebrate the debut of his niece Helen Tracy Barney. Some seven hundred guests paraded through its lavish halls, the muted tapestries and somber stone enlivened with vibrant banks of poinsettias, baskets of pink begonias, white and pink orchids, and garlands of smilax, dancing to the music of Sherry's Hungarian Orchestra and dining at midnight on a supper of *bouillon en tasse*, terrapin, canvasback duck, *poussins grillés à diable*, *pâte en croute*, salad, gâteaux, ices, bonbons, champagne, coffee, and Apollinaris water.[37] But Whitney, tired from constant work and still mourning not only the passing of his beloved first wife but also the prema- ture death of his second, was destined to enjoy his splendid new house for a mere four years. In January 1904, after an emergency appendectomy, peritonitis set in, and Whitney died at age sixty-two.[38]

True to form, the house that Mamie Fish commissioned was as unique as her personality. In 1887 she had purchased a brick, Greek Revival– style house at 20 Gramercy Park, giving Stanford White some $120,000 ($2.4 million in 2008) to spend on renovations to transform it into a suitable stage for her entertainments.[39] Still, she was not satisfied with the results, feeling that the house lacked the grandeur necessary for the social position to which she aspired. In 1897 she again called on McKim,

Mead, and White, this time commissioning a completely new residence, at 25 East 78th Street and Madison Avenue. Completed in 1900, this was an extremely narrow, five-storey structure designed by Stanford White in the Italianate style. Construction cost just over $112,000 (approximately $2.6 million in 2008); to save money, the house was built of brick covered in plaster; only the facades facing the streets were clad in more costly limestone.[40] White deployed classical fenestration, pediments, pilasters, and a copper cornice to lend grandeur to what was, in effect, a rather small building, in keeping with Mamie's dictum that her house should be "an uncomfortable place for anyone without breeding."[41]

White designed a house that combined French classicism and colonial revival, with hints of the English Renaissance and the Venetian Gothic in an eclectic mixture of styles. On the ground floor, an entry paved in marble gave way to an Empire-style reception room, and to a Jacobean-inspired dining room, where carved wooden Corinthian columns framed walls covered in panels of hand-tooled leather. A handsome staircase of white marble, flanked by wrought-iron balustrades adorned with ormolu mounts, ascended to a lofty hall faced with neoclassical boiseries and ornamental pilasters. The Crimson Salon took its name from the red floral Venetian damask that hung on the walls. Carved wainscots and cornices of dark oak added a somber note, but the overall effect was startling, for Mamie, in typical disregard for the niceties of period décor, filled the room with a contradictory assemblage of overstuffed sofas and chairs next to exquisite French antiques, scattered atop eighteenth-century Aubusson carpets strewn with tiger and bearskin rugs, an incoherence of styles similar to that employed by Caroline Astor. It was all quite comfortable, and also terribly muddled in its expression. On the other side of the hall, White placed a Louis XVI–style ballroom. This was a luminous room, executed in gleaming white, with Corinthian pilasters, carved boiseries, bas-reliefs, and stucco garlands touched with gilt, set beneath a ceiling awash with a string of seminude goddesses dancing against the clouds of heaven.[42]

Mamie's third-floor bedroom was a luxurious evocation of the Venetian Gothic mingled with early French Renaissance. Italian cut-silk damask draped walls above a wainscot of carved African mahogany. The dark and ornate wooden furniture included a dressing table crowned by an intricately carved tripartite looking glass, consoles holding gilded candelabra, and uncomfortable-looking chairs crowned with spires, all set upon a floor covered in exotic tiger-skin rugs. But the room's center of attention was the bed; theatrically set atop a dais, this was a riot of lacy, early Renaissance-style carvings, with cherubs, spires, and arches set beneath a carved Peruvian walnut canopy draped with crimson velvet sewn with medieval designs. The result was so perfect, Mamie declared, that she could not possibly sleep there; instead, she occupied a small bed in her adjoining dressing room.[43]

Of all the private palaces erected in New York City, none more aptly reflected the ideals of Gilded Age society than that of James Burden. It was not the largest of the city's mansions, but it represented the apex of wealth and splendor, the refinement of changing taste. Henry Burden, the owner's grandfather, had come from Scotland in 1819 and settled in Troy, New York. After several years of hard work at the Troy Iron and Nail Factory, his determination so impressed the owners that they asked him to assume its management. Burden increased the company's profits, patenting new techniques for the production of railroad spikes and horseshoes, which brought him a sizable fortune, and he eventually used the profits to found the Burden Iron Company.[44] Burden's grandsons rose rapidly in New York society, assisted, no doubt, by their propitious marriages. William married Florence Twombly, granddaughter of William Henry Vanderbilt, while in 1895 his brother James wed her cousin Florence Adele Sloane, daughter of department store scion William Sloane and his wife, Emily Vanderbilt.

In 1901 Florence's father purchased a large corner lot at 7 East 91st Street in New York and commissioned the architectural firm of Warren & Wetmore to design a new mansion for his daughter and son-in-law.[45] Warren & Wetmore conceived an elaborate mansion combining Italianate touches with the formality of French neoclassicism, a building that embraced the needs of a family home in the city coupled with the splendors demanded of Gilded Age society. The end result was a structure that dazzled with its refinement and its opulence.

Built of limestone, the Burden house rose three storeys atop a ground floor faced in rusticated stone to provide a contrasting diversity of textures. Three bays wide, the house's gleaming exterior reflected a careful division of spaces: the tall windows of the ground floor contrasted with the short

The James Burden house at 7 East 91st Street in New York City.

fenestrations across the entresol above, designed to contain the family's private rooms. A carved stringcourse supported a colonnade framing the enormously high arched French doors of the third floor, with the low windows of an attic floor tucked beneath a classical, dentilated cornice and a balustrade that ringed the roof.[46]

Everything about the house was designed to impress and delight. Uniquely, it featured no visible front door; instead, a pair of decorative gates at one end of the ground floor swung open to an arcaded, covered carriageway that ended in an enclosed inner courtyard, a spatially complex approach that hinted at the unusual arrangement. Here, a projecting curved bow, set with iron and glass doors, offered entry to an oval vestibule ornamented with a screen of Corinthian columns. To one side, facing Ninety-first Street, were a small reception room, an office, and a billiard room, but inevitably the eye was drawn past the colonnade to a magnificent oval staircase of Hautville marble, washed in light from above by a Tiffany stained-glass skylight set within a domed ceiling painted by French artist Hector d'Espouy.[47]

The family's private apartments on the entresol level included a Georgian revival drawing room, a breakfast room, and bedroom suites for James and Florence; but for visitors to the house, their journey continued up the sweeping staircase to the third floor. Here any pretense at domesticity was abandoned in favor of the glories of the ancien régime. There were only three principal rooms, but these were exquisite models of Gilded Age extravagance, their design copied from the state apartments at Versailles. At the top of the staircase a regal vestibule offered entrée to a vanished world, a theatrical stage that transcended the rational city beyond and swept visitors into a universe of triumphant power. An open screen of columns created a formalized approach to the immensely high reception room, its marble walls crowned by a domed ceiling awash with gilded reliefs. On one side was a forty-foot-long dining room, its Viridian green marble walls bathed in light from tall, arched French doors. Gilded Corinthian pilasters supported an elaborate carved cornice festooned with stucco relief garlands and cherubs beneath a coved ceiling. On the other side of the vestibule, twelve-foot-high mirrored doors with sculpted ormolu handles opened to the most extravagant of the

The ballroom of the James Burden house in New York City, inspired by Versailles.

interiors, the nearly seventy-foot-long ballroom. Modeled on the Galerie des Glaces at Versailles, this was a tapestry of variegated black, red, and white marble walls framed by Corinthian pilasters sprouting gilded capitals that encased mirrored panels set within carved and gilded moldings. A monumental marble chimneypiece adorned with gilded cornucopias and topped with an oval mirror flanked by carved and gilded foliage reliefs and sinuous scrolls swept up to a rococo frieze enriched with rocailles, garlands, and cherubs.[48] It was a display of magnificence and refinement unmatched by any other house in the city, the fantastic pinnacle of Gilded Age society's quest to align itself with an aristocratic European heritage.[49]

12

THE UNSEEN ARMIES

SERVANTS FORMED AN INTEGRAL PART of life in Gilded Age society. From the great houses of New York City and the country estates of the Berkshires to the summer cottages of Newport, servants were indispensable to the lives of their masters. They laid out their clothes in the morning and helped them dress; drew their baths and attended to their personal needs; cared for their children; kept their mansions; tended their gardens; drove their coaches and motorcars; prepared and served their food; waited upon their guests; and maintained the ritualized order that permeated the great houses. These maids, housekeepers, butlers, valets, chefs, nurses, footmen, and grooms ensured that their masters were surrounded by nothing less than a constant state of perfection. Ogden and Mary Goelet employed a staff of forty-nine to maintain their Newport mansion, Ochre Court, during the ten weeks of their summer tenure. "Such a lot of trouble and endless domestic worries," Mary Goelet once complained, "running that big establishment with just a housekeeper for the twenty-seven servants, nine coachmen and grooms, and twelve gardeners."[1]

Turn-of-the-century society used servants as visible symbols of their taste and status. "Americans," noted one historian, "were materialistic. They dreamed of belonging to the leisured class and were stricken by a fever-ish desire for material comfort and symbols of affluence that knew no cure save gratification."[2] In adopting European systems of service, Gilded Age society attempted to impose centuries of evolved tradition onto an artificial world just decades old. Thus the social importance of servants offered an indication of not only wealth but also complete freedom from everyday concerns. While some Americans found employ in service, society had a preference for domestics of European origin: English butlers, footmen, and nannies; French chefs, governesses, and lady's maids; and Irish chambermaids and laundry maids. This was not just for the sophisticated and Continental air that Europeans lent to a household. American-bred domestics were often thought to be too independent-minded, too indoctrinated with democratic values, to fully embrace their subservient roles, while most Europeans not only were properly respectful of authority but also, as immigrants, had few other financial opportunities and thus were unlikely to cause too many difficulties. The waves of immigrants to America in these years often welcomed service; although most of the positions for which they were hired were largely unskilled, often poorly paid, and offered little opportunity for advancement, they did provide a regular salary, food, and often lodgings.

"The first requisite of a good servant," declared the highly critical social commentator Thorstein Veblen, "is that he should conspicuously know his place. It is not enough that he knows how to effect certain desired mechanical results; he must above all, know how to effect these results in due form. Domestic service might be said to be a spiritual rather than a mechanical function."[3] Society ladies were advised to divorce themselves as much as possible from any domestic questions. The mistress of a well-run establishment, advised one turn-of-the-century guide, "enjoys immunity from hampering household cares. She need never know when changes occur in the servant department, unless the change be among those with whom she comes in contact."[4]

In this world, male servants always ranked above female servants. The males' role, as Daniel Sutherland wrote, was often "a social role rather than an economic or productive one. They were paid for servility: their function was to emphasize the social position of employers. Male retainers received twice the wages of most female servants while doing about half as much work. . . . Likewise, while female servants were kept out of sight as much as possible, men were thrust into the spotlight at every opportunity, greeting callers, guarding hallways, serving meals, and delivering messages to parlor and sitting room. Men were also the ones decked out in livery, their glittering gold braid and glistening silk breeches heightening the effect of conspicuous display."[5]

The lives of servants in these households were as rigidly defined and codified into ranks as was Gilded Age society itself. In this hierarchy, servants fell into one of two ranks: upper servants, who constituted the personal domestic staff attending the family and who thus enjoyed regular contact with their employers; and lower servants, the largest group of domestics, who did most of the actual work and who often carried out their duties anonymously. Upper servants generally held positions of responsibility that called for some training and the direction of others. In this world, the most junior members of the domestic staff attended not only to the household in which they were employed, but also often to their superiors in service, waking upper servants, waiting on them during meals, and following the strict division of ranks common to the era.

The highest-ranking servant in any household, and the head of the upper servants, was the butler. "He has many roles to play, many attitudes to assume," wrote one guide, "subservient at one moment to certain ones above-stairs, dominant the next over others below-stairs."[6] Uniquely among the male staff, butlers were permitted to be married and to maintain their own residences, although they were expected, when entertainments were given, to remain in the house until all work among the staff had ended; often a small room with a bed was set aside for the butler's use on such occasions.[7] Butlers also were provided with their clothing at their employer's expense: a black morning suit of trousers, waistcoat, and coat for the day, and broadcloth trousers, cutaway coat, waistcoat, and white gloves for evening—often handed down and retailored from the wardrobe of his master.[8] Indeed, the only differences that marked the evening attire of a gentleman and that of his butler was that the latter's waistcoat and tie were black rather than white.[9]

The butler generally received callers, supervised entertainments and dinners, arranged the table, and, with the footmen, waited during meals, serving the wine. When dinner was nearing completion, he ensured that the drawing room, reception room, and library were ready for the service of coffee and liqueurs.[10] Butlers also kept the keys and combinations to the gold and silver safes and the wine cellars.[11] It was his responsibility, on nights when great dinner parties or balls required an impressive display of the family's treasures, to carefully record the silver or gold services taken from the vaults, and to ensure that each piece was promptly returned without damage. As the highest-ranking of the upper servants, butlers received a respectable salary approaching $400 ($9,200 in 2008) a year, and often more in larger establishments.[12]

There was no higher mark of social prominence in America than to employ an English butler.[13] They brought immediate status to their employers and added an air of distinction to the household. They were also, for those making their uncertain ways in society, able to cautiously offer advice and delicately warn of any missteps. Morton, the butler Mamie Fish had imported from England, was nearly as famous as his mistress. He was, remembered Elizabeth Drexel Lehr, "a great character. He was also a great autocrat. Everyone acquainted with the Fish household (including his employers) was more or less in awe of his superb impassivity, his eagle eye for any breach of etiquette. He could wither the most brazen offenders with one glance of superiority. He had served in English ducal families, a fact which he never failed to impress on all with whom he came in contact." Whenever Mamie would insist on some questionable practice, Morton would calmly say, "Just as you wish, Madam. But I can only assure you it is not done in the best English households." This was usually enough to silence her into capitulation.[14]

The housekeeper was the female counterpart to the butler, and the highest-ranked of the women servants. Hers was an administrative post: she had general charge of all of the female domestics, from their hiring and training to their dismissal, kept the keys to the household storage rooms, dealt with all provisions and merchants, and saw to the daily operation of the house.[15] The housekeeper was always referred to as "Mrs.," regardless of her marital status, and commanded immense respect.

Generally a woman of middle age, she was expected to keep detailed and precise accounts of all expenses incurred and any purchases made, and to deal with all regular bills.[16]

Housekeepers acted as liaison between mistress and household, often meeting the lady of the house each morning to discuss any general business, planned entertainments, and any problems that had arisen. "A perfect understanding," commented one turn-of-the-century authority, "exists between them if the hostess is experienced and knows her own position: then, she never interferes with any rules or orders of the one to whom she has assigned the entire management of her establishment."[17] Throughout the day, she was expected to inspect the house and ensure that all necessary work was carried out. For her services the housekeeper received a salary of roughly $350 per year ($8,050 in 2008).[18]

The third member of the great household triumvirate was the *chef de cuisine*. In houses of the Gilded Age, it was a mark of distinction to hire a French chef. An English chef did not carry the same culinary cachet as his French counterpart; indeed, English chefs were often regarded as somehow suspect and their cuisine inferior to that produced by their Continental counterparts. Many chefs were figures of sheer terror, dictatorial in manner and exacting in expectation; indeed, a certain amount of petulance and difficulty was always expected if one hoped to employ a culinary master. Unlike other members of the household, the chef was an artist, responsible for crafting exquisite dishes that cemented the reputation of his mistress among her society friends.[19]

Chefs normally kept to themselves and dealt only with members of their own kitchen staff. Occasionally they would be summoned to discuss a proposed menu with the mistress of the house, but there was little interaction between chef and employer, and even less interference; many mistresses feared their chefs, worried that any hint of unwelcome intrusion into their realm would result in a service-ending tantrum. Chefs rarely cooked breakfasts for the family or for the servants, this work being left to the ordinary kitchen cooks. Instead, chefs focused their attention on formal luncheons and nightly dinners. "As a rule," commented one guide, "chefs do not care to engage with families who refuse to entertain frequently and handsomely. They prefer to have plenty of opportunities to expend time and display artistic taste upon grand dinners and dainty suppers, not to mention the obvious fact of larger commissions in a hospitable mansion. They view with condescension and scorn the wealthy who will not dispense the rights of hospitality freely." Chefs de cuisine were the highest-paid of all servants, and could expect a salary approaching $100 a month ($2,300 in 2008) in the largest establishments.[20]

Also included in the ranks of upper servants were two further positions: the valet and the lady's maid. The valet was attached to the master of the household as a personal attendant, and his tasks were numerous: he was charged with the care of his gentleman's wardrobe and the selection, pressing, and laying out of various outfits; shining his shoes and boots; drawing baths; shaving his master and cutting his hair; and ensuring that any awards and decorations were suitably polished and laid out to be worn on formal occasions. It fell to the valet to arrange journeys, pack his master's clothing, secure accommodations and reservations, and pay his bills. Valets also were charged with keeping their master's secrets. They dispatched letters to mistresses, arranged for liaisons, and helped create credible alibis to cover their gentleman's absence.[21] As such, a trustworthy valet was highly regarded and his discretion prized, and he usually received $300 a year ($6,900 in 2008).[22]

Lady's maids were the female equivalents of valets. The fashion was for French lady's maids, as they were thought to have a more refined taste in dress and attire, although English maids often enjoyed greater trust, owing to an unfounded but pervasive suspicion of possible treachery by their Continental rivals. The principal duties of a lady's maid were to attend to her mistress each morning, drawing her bath, bringing her a breakfast tray, assisting her in dressing, arranging her hair, and laying out all items necessary to complete her toilette. She was expected to assist during all wardrobe changes throughout the day and into the evening, to collect any worn clothes and replace them with a new outfit, and to attend to any needed cleaning or repairs to dresses, gowns, or accessories.[23] A lady's maid also looked after her mistress's jewelry, regularly retrieving expensive pieces from the security of a locked safe whose combination she was entrusted with; she also assisted with most correspondence. Although it was exceptionally rare for a lady's maid to attend her mistress in the bathroom, she was expected to wash her most delicate garments.

During the hours when she was not required, a lady's maid would be expected to repair her mistress's wardrobe and attend to any needed personal shopping. It was, commented one guide, an undesirable position: "However luxurious the surroundings, that is not an ideal life where one must be constantly at the beck and call, or subject to the caprice of another during all the twenty-four hours, day in and day out."[24] Working for Tessie Oelrichs offered one of the era's few exceptions. Despite her rather stringent daily examinations of her house, Tessie usually treated her servants well and, if she was out late at some entertainment, insisted that she use her own key to let herself in and that her lady's maid should not wait up for her return.[25]

In addition, the singular position of lady's maid, with its close personal relationship with the mistress of the house, often made its holder the object of not only resentment among other servants but also of suspicion. Many lady's maids were regarded by lower servants as little more than arrogant spies, who happily reported any indiscretion in an effort to solidify their power, and they were routinely shunned by other members of the household.[26] For her services, a lady's maid could expect to receive approximately $25 each month ($575 in 2008) in the best establishments.[27]

Footmen also were considered upper servants and were the highest-ranked of the liveried servants. They polished the china, crystal, silver, and gold services, laid the table and waited during meals, assisted the butler, attended to visitors, and ran errands; in some families they also served as grooms, riding on carriages and opening doors for their mistresses.[28] Footmen were selected for their appearance: they had to be tall, handsome, and well-mannered, as they enjoyed close contact with their employers.[29] During the day they usually wore liveries of subdued black adorned with brass buttons depicting the family's crest, but on festive occasions they could be called on to dress in formal, eighteenth-century-style liveries of knee breeches, silk stockings, silk shirts, colored waistcoats, and tailcoats adorned with gold embroidery. To add to the effect on these occasions, many footmen were asked to "powder," combing thick white paste made from flour through their wet hair to simulate the appearance of a wig.[30] "Powdering" was a nasty, unpleasant affair, much despised by those forced to endure it, but most employers recognized the inconvenience and discomfort, and a footman could earn an additional $5 a month ($115 in 2008) if called on to do so regularly.[31]

In a large establishment there were usually a number of footmen; one authority advised that at least four footmen were necessary to portray an "unmistakable air of quiet ease."[32] They were given designations of first footman, second footman, and so on, and paid accordingly. A first footman might receive $25 a month ($575 in 2008), while a second footman could expect $20 ($520 in 2008).[33] Rates were often based on height, with taller men earning a few dollars more a week than their shorter counterparts.[34]

Female servants ranked lower than their male counterparts and were paid less, although their work was more consuming and physically demanding.[35] They spent hours scrubbing floors, climbing up and down staircases with trays, and ensuring that the house was in order. Such work was made more difficult by the restrictive clothing of the day. Usual morning cleaning called for simple cotton print dresses, caps, and aprons, worn over tight corsets that made the constant bending and stooping an ordeal; in the afternoons, they would change to black dresses, with white aprons and caps with streamers, uniforms provided by their employers.[36]

In this hierarchy, chambermaids—who cleaned the family's bedrooms and private rooms—ranked highest, followed by parlor maids, who were responsible for the rest of the house, and by any general maids, who filled in as needed and had no set responsibilities. Most maids began their days at six in the morning, as the cleaning of the main rooms was expected to be finished before the family appeared for the day, and they might end between ten and midnight. They were expected to work as quietly as possible, and Alva Vanderbilt even had her servants fitted with special felt-soled shoes to wear during their morning routines to prevent any noise.[37]

The introduction of electric vacuums eased the burden somewhat, but floors still had to be scrubbed and polished by hand, using pails of water laced with ammonia and Sapolio soap.[38] Carpets were beaten and brushed; grates cleaned; windows washed; furniture dusted with cheese-cloth and silk before being polished with beeswax and linseed oil; and writing paper and flowers replaced. In houses whose rooms featured elaborate boiseries, every crevice in the decorative ornaments had to be cleaned once a week with small brushes. The use of feather dusters was frowned on, and in most cases they were used only for books and small objets d'art.[39] A parlor maid generally received $20 a month ($520 in 2008), while a housemaid could expect $18 a month ($414 in 2008).[40]

Although the chef de cuisine headed the culinary staff, others did much of the work in the kitchen. In large establishments there might be several assistant cooks, an apprentice cook, a pastry chef, kitchen maids, and several scullery maids, all attached to the chef's department. Assistant cooks, often called "plain cooks," were responsible for most of the food produced each day in the household; they prepared breakfasts and most luncheons, and all of the meals consumed by members of the staff. On evenings when there were dinner parties or balls, they assisted the chef as well. An assistant cook might receive $20 a month ($520 in 2008). Kitchen maids often were responsible for any meals served in the household nursery in addition to assisting the plain cooks with meals for the servants. Kitchen maids also were on call during any special entertainments or dinner parties to assist the chef.[41] Scullery maids fell at the very bottom of the ladder in both status and respect, yet they slaved away each day, while the upper servants mocked or ridiculed them and members of the household literally paid them no attention at all. The great majority of their days was spent over a sink, scouring pots and scrubbing pans; although some houses installed automatic dishwaters, much of the priceless china, silver, and crystal used at dinner parties was considered too delicate to trust to a machine, and each piece had to be washed and polished by hand. On nights when there were dinner parties or balls, this could amount to thousands of pieces, which never arrived in the scullery to be cleaned before midnight, and demanded immediate attention. For this intensive labor, scullery maids received roughly $15 a month ($345 in 2008).[42]

Most fashionable houses contained their own laundries. With the exception of a few of the most personal articles cared for by a lady's maid, the head laundress saw to the washing and care of the family's clothing; an assistant was responsible for items from the nursery, while a third cleaned the household linens and other textiles.[43] Used clothing from the previous day usually arrived with linens stripped from the family's beds in immense wicker baskets; each piece had to be logged into a ledger and attended to according to its needs after being examined. Immense tubs filled with hot water swallowed dirtied linens, while most clothing required more personal attention. After being boiled, scrubbed, and run through mangles, washing was generally hung in a special drying room, on rows of carefully arranged wooden racks to allow proper ventilation, although electric or steam driers had begun to appear by the turn of the century. When suitably dry, items were ironed, wrapped in sheets of crisp tissue paper, tagged for return, and logged out of the laundry ledgers, to be returned to the rooms above.[44] During any given week, the laundry maids might be responsible for the cleaning of well over a thousand items, and more if the family entertained.[45]

Linens were stored in special rooms, often lined with cedar, where they were sorted by use and size; matching sets of bed linens were often tied together with silk ribbons of differing colors to denote their intended use. "The pure white everywhere dominant is enlivened by ribbons of blue, pink, green, lilac, yellow, and red, designating by their width, as well as color, the quality and special use of each pile," noted one guide. "They reveal the place and grade of everything in the room and its use about the house, and so facilitate the work of maids and housekeeper. One entering this linen-room for the first time is impressed by its all-pervading order, and the purity and beauty of its contents. Closer observation reveals much more. Shelves one above another on all sides are weighted with precious burdens of fine linen articles—their costliness enhanced by embroidery and bordering of delicate lace."[46]

Once, one of Alva Vanderbilt's overnight guests had been so careless with his cigarette smoking in bed that he left her exquisite linens spotted with burn holes. When told of this by a distraught maid, Alva ordered that the expensive sheets be mended with the coarsest yarn that could be found, and placed on the gentleman's bed in this state the next time he visited. After an uncomfortable night, the guest pulled Alva aside and said, "I think I ought to tell you that your linen is not being taken care of as it should be. You ought really to see the sheets on my bed."

"Ah, yes, those sheets!" Alva told her guest. "You're quite right. Those are the sheets you burned holes in with your cigarettes. I had them darned especially for your use."[47]

Some large houses also employed a young boy of ten or twelve, titled the page or hall boy. His position was as an apprentice to the lowest footman, and he performed whatever odd jobs were asked of him. On ceremonial occasions he might be dressed in livery and asked to attend to the train of his mistress's gown. This position also could be supplemented with that of the useful man, a kind of in-house carpenter, plumber, and electrician who could be relied on to help put right any problems.[48]

Outdoor servants formed a separate group from the household staff, and there was little interaction between the two factions. The stable master or head groom was charged with running the stables and their staff, and enjoyed considerable freedom in managing his premises. Under him were the coachmen; the grooms, who cared for the horses, saddles, and tack and who often rode on carriages in liveries for ceremonial occasions; and the stable boys, who cleaned the vehicles, horses, and stalls.[49] As motorcars gradually overtook the regular use of carriages, these positions were supplemented by chauffeurs and mechanics, as the most fashionable establishments continued to maintain both stables and garages.

Most fashionable establishments also employed a watchman to patrol the perimeter of the house and grounds each night. A watchman would prevent any attempts at theft and report any indiscretions among members of the staff if they attempted to leave the house or sneak back in contrary to the house rules that bade them to keep to regular hours and that forbade any evenings out except under strictly regulated terms. To ensure that the watchman did his job, most were equipped with a set of keys, each of which was required to wind a different time clock at a set hour and punch a paper disk that the housekeeper diligently checked the following morning, lest the watchman forgo his responsibilities for a quick nap.[50]

Life for servants was regulated by a diverse set of rules and regulations that governed nearly every aspect of their existence; most servants could not even take a book out of a local public library without a letter of recommendation and permission from their employer.[51] Of the servants, generally only the butler and the chef were allowed to be married; the housekeeper usually was a widow or a spinster, and none of the other servants, whether footmen or maids, were allowed to pursue any personal relationships. If they did so, it was grounds for immediate dismissal.[52] Servants were not to speak to their employers unless spoken to, and then only to directly answer a question. They were not allowed to talk to each other in the presence of their employers; if a servant was at work when his or her employer happened upon them, they were expected to turn away and to avert their eyes, to save their master or mistress the embarrassment of having to acknowledge their presence.[53]

There often was a fine line between working in a house and feeling part of the household. One Gilded Age servant recalled, "You did clean the house, but you did not have accessibility to the house. You came in at the basement end. . . . The very fact you had designated exits and entrances lets you know that the house is under the authority of the Madam."[54] In a curious though common development, many of those who served in the houses of society's elite themselves became immense snobs. They derived their own status from that of their masters and affiliated themselves with their power, looking down on friends who had the misfortune to work in less prominent establishments.[55]

"Servants," advised one authority, "must be trained to the knowledge of their various duties and a firm discipline maintained. On the other hand, employers may add much to the loyalty given by servants if they pay them promptly, make them comfortable, and treat them as human beings."[56] That it was deemed necessary to point out that servants should be treated "as human beings" underscored the enormous gulf between employee and employer and said something of the attitude of entitled privilege often prevalent in the Gilded Age. For employers there were fewer rules, one of the few universally acknowledged being that servants should never be reproved in front of any guests, which embarrassed both guest and servant.[57]

There was little understanding by their employers of the hardships endured by servants. Indeed, one late-nineteenth-century manual advised the mistress of the horrors likely to be faced by those under her roof: the newly arrived foreign girl "bent over a hot cooking-stove, doing her utmost to understand the strange rites and mysteries and the unknown implements connected with it, and pretty generally failing to do so; bent over dish-pans and wash-tubs, and dusters and brooms; bent over back aching ironing-boards and terrible scrubbing-brushes; her whole life enlisted for a continual warfare with dirt and discomfort, glad at night to creep away to the dark and dismal little room assigned her—we must acknowledge that if she were a daughter of our own we should feel her lot to be a fearful thing."[58] While most pay was incredibly low for the work required, servants generally had few expenses. Employers provided rooms, food, and uniforms, and with little time off, there were few opportunities to spend money on leisure activities. Despite the rigors of work, those in service often regarded themselves as fortunate, as they at least had the necessities of life.[59]

Rooms for servants were far from luxurious. Men were generally housed in cold, dimly lighted basement rooms, and women in stuffy attic rooms. Most housekeepers established firm rules forbidding the display of any personal items or photographs of family, lending a cold, antiseptic atmosphere.[60] "The beds," recalled one man, "were generally of cast iron and the bed springs not far different. Mattresses were usually stuffed with straw. If the room had a window on an airshaft it was a bit of luck. Usually a skylight sufficed for light and air. The furniture of the room was distinctly meager and nondescript. Any old piece that had outlived its usefulness below was sent upstairs to the servants' quarters. Generally the seat of the one chair in the room had broken through; the table had only three legs and was propped up by a box or some books."[61] There was always a servants' hall for communal living and dining, plain and usually furnished with a large central table and chairs for meals, and perhaps a few overstuffed chairs and a desk for rare moments of relaxation.[62]

Generally, servants were given a half-day off on Sunday, an evening off during the week, and one full day off each month, with a week's vacation every year, but a typical week in service might include up to seventy-two hours of work.[63] Even meals were considered to be time off.[64] The half-days and evenings were always contingent on the operation of the house, and on work being finished; the rules of the house usually dictated that servants return by nine or ten at night, lest they be locked out and censured. After the turn of the century, servants were generally given an hour or two of leisure each day as well.[65]

A mistress had to rely on the loyalty and discretion of her servants, but occasionally this trust was abused. Mrs. Carpenter, Mamie Fish's house-keeper, began her career as a second housemaid and rose through the ranks to her position of power; in time she let her authority go to her head and often would lecture her mistress on points of etiquette or make unwelcome suggestions, all of which Mamie tolerated out of respect for her years of service. When Mrs. Carpenter's young son was caught steal-ing money from the household account, Mamie forgave him and even had him educated at her expense. The end came, however, when an anonymous tell-all book titled *Confessions of a Social Secretary* appeared, in which the main character worked for an ill-mannered social upstart named "Mrs. Fisher." It took little effort to determine that Mrs. Carpenter had, in fact, been behind the exposé, and Mamie, disgusted at such betrayal, finally relieved her of her position.[66]

13

CLOTHING

As much in Gilded Age society was based on outward appearances, clothing assumed immense importance. Dressing like a member of the leisured class was not necessarily a leisurely pursuit. Like houses, wardrobes were transcendent, offering opportunities to prove one's wealth and taste, to reveal through dignified dress that one belonged to the highest and most refined circles. From morning to night, changes in attire and accessories indicated function and levels of formality; appearing in something too flashy, adventuresome, or inappropriate immediately branded the wearer as an outsider. "Clothing," wrote one historian, "did not provide a pretext for manners and proprieties, it *constituted* proprieties and manners."[1]

"They all dress neatly and walk splendidly," recalled one English visitor of society. "The high average of neatness is very noticeable at once."[2] Even gentlemen partook of these habits, although never quite as passionately as their wives and daughters. Compared with that of his female counterpart, the wardrobe of the Gilded Age gentleman suffered from a uniformity of imagination. Nevertheless, his dressing room closets were specially fitted to accommodate a diverse wardrobe: sliding trays displayed rows of starched shirts; drawers held underwear and socks; cedar closets stored winter coats adorned with astrakhan collars and fur-lined opera coats, and other compartments housed linen summer suits, riding clothes, tiers of ties and starched collars, suits and evening wear, shelves filled with an array of hats, row after row of carefully grouped footwear, each shoe filled with the maker's form to maintain its shape, and monogrammed handkerchiefs and jewelry.[3] Each morning a valet laid out the clothing required by his master to begin the day and collected items from the previous evening, a process repeated throughout the day as the gentleman changed his attire.

The Gilded Age gentleman relied on the precision and taste of a handful of establishments for his bespoke clothing. Most items were privately commissioned from a few trusted shops such as Henry Poole & Company or Stansbury & French in London, or from Wetzel, Brooks Brothers, Matthew Rock, or Kaskel & Kaskel in New York City.[4] A gentleman might replenish his wardrobe twice each year, visiting the establishments—which kept careful records of his measurements and purchases—with his valet to inspect new wools or to review suggested styles. Any necessary adjustments were made and orders placed, the finished results being delivered several months later.[5] Quality of workmanship and materials was important, but the color, look, and cut must be unremarkable so as not to attract attention. "A gentleman," declared one authority, "should always be so well dressed that his dress shall never be observed at all."[6] No one noticed if a gentleman wore the same stiff, starched white shirtfronts, suits, or swallowtail coat and white tie night after night, but a man who dared strike out and make a bold sartorial statement invited ridicule.

For the day, gentlemen usually wore a dark jacket or frock coat over a white shirt, a tie, a waistcoat, and pinstriped trousers. If gloves were worn, they were invariably in gray, black, or brown; no gentleman ever wore light-colored gloves in the day unless paying an important social call or attending a formal function.[7] By the end of the nineteenth century, the leisure suit—called a sack suit—had begun to regularly appear on American businessmen, freeing them of the formalized cut and cumbersome length of a frock coat. For yachting or tennis there were suits of white cotton, flannel, or linen, usually worn with white or cream-colored suede or canvas shoes, while an array of hunting tweeds for country life deliberately imitated English models.[8]

"When a gentleman is invited out for the evening," recorded one guide, "he need be under no embarrassment as to what he shall wear. He has not to sit down and consider whether he shall wear blue or pink, and whether the Jones' will notice if he wear the same attire three times running."[9] For formal occasions such as dinner parties or balls, there was little variation in the customary attire: a black cutaway tailcoat, matching trousers, a white starched shirt with a stiff, detachable tall collar, a white silk waistcoat, and a white tie were de rigueur. Only occasionally might a truly daring gentleman strike out with a fine waistcoat of colored silks.[10] Accessories, too, offered less scope for individual expression than those available to ladies. For formal occasions a pair of black patent leather shoes and fine black silk stockings were customary, along with a silk-lined cape or long, fur-trimmed greatcoat, a top hat with a silk band, a white silk scarf, and inevitably a pair of fine, tight white gloves. Pocket watches and shirt studs—usually in enamel—often came from the New York firms of Black, Starr & Frost, or Gorham.[11]

In the privacy of their own homes, gentlemen could engage in more exotic expressions of personal taste, preferring colorful, richly embroidered and quilted Turkish smoking jackets; in New York City, most underwear came from the firm of Kaskel & Kaskel, which produced variants in soft linens and cottons.[12] Some gentlemen kept to the tradition of sleeping in a nightshirt, usually of fine linen, cotton, or silk, and sewn with their initials, while others, such as Harry Lehr, preferred the newly invented pajamas.[13] Kaskel & Kaskel, in fact, regularly provided Lehr with their finest and latest stock of underwear and pajamas on the understanding that he would let it be known that he wore their products beneath his clothing and when he retired at night.[14]

Such easy decisions were denied to ladies nor, it must be said, would the great Gilded Age hostesses have welcomed any hint of uniformity. Fashionable dress set them apart from their rivals and ranged from morning clothes, day dresses, evening gowns, and ball gowns, along with specialized wardrobes for the country and sporting events, to clothing worn in the privacy of the boudoir and the bedroom, outerwear, and dozens of accessories deemed necessary to the society wardrobe. Social critic Thorstein Veblen noted that such clothing should convey the impression "that the wearer does not and can not habitually engage in useful work."[15] The more extravagant the ensemble, the more desirable it was deemed. "Velvets, furs, laces, and jewels may be seen on the streets and in the tram-cars, morning, noon, and night of every day," commented one visitor to New York City. "The ladies whom I saw at the opera in all the brilliancy of court costumes are to be met . . . on the streets in costumes which, if less brilliant as to color, are no less costly as to texture and variety of fabric. It has been my good fortune to know the streets of Rome, Paris, London, St. Petersburg, Amsterdam, and Vienna, but there is nothing approaching to the display of fine extravagance of dress that one sees in New York. What would my French friends think of a lady walking to and from church in a costume composed entirely of fur—jacket and skirt as well; of another in velvet, draped profusely with lace, and a bonnet of jet with pink and white plumes?"[16]

Gilded Age society began in the last years of crinolines and Victorian bustles and ended with the narrower silhouettes of the succeeding era. By the 1880s the bustle had disappeared, replaced with gored skirts; sleeves grew wider and puffed at the shoulders; fitted jackets lent a tailored look to ensembles; and waists shrank into ever-smaller proportions. By the turn of the century, young ladies favored the popular "Gibson Girl" look, with its simple skirts and tucked shirtwaists, or blouses, while their mothers had begun to adopt the tall, reedlike, and exceptionally elegant dresses and gowns that typified Edwardian taste, with tighter bodices, and skirts that flared near the bottom to form a bell shape.[17] Such confining clothing and undergarments severely limited mobility. There was, however, a certain stateliness thus lent to the carriage, a slow, flowing sweep of movement that, at its best, emphasized refinement and poise.

Society ladies might change clothes six or seven times a day, with specialized wardrobes for *du matinée, d'après-midi,* and *du soir*. Each season called for new ball gowns, along with morning dresses, afternoon dresses, tea gowns, lingerie, dozens of pairs of gloves, large picture hats embellished with flowers and plumes of ostrich feathers, and handkerchiefs, all designed not only to reinforce the owner's wealth but also to dazzle. These outfits, with their layers of extravagant silks, satins, brocades, taffetas, tulle, velvets, net, and lace, in a rainbow of colors and array of patterns, adorned with fur, overlays of lace, embroideries of gold or silver thread set with pearls or jet, and soft feathers and plumes, were quite heavy. Thus there were few articles of feminine clothing that did not call for the assistance of a lady's maid. Stockings had to be put on and attached; corsets tightly laced and buckled; petticoats eased onto the hips; dresses and gowns cascaded over heads; skirts, blouses, and jackets held and fitted; buttons done up, and accessories dispersed. Such rituals might be repeated three or four times a day, whenever a lady changed from one outfit to another. This sartorial helplessness also served to underline the lady's status; the wearing of voluminous, expensive, and impractical clothing that required the assistance of others reinforced the idea of leisure and supported the lady's distinct place in the social hierarchy, where even the daily routine of dressing demanded servants.

"American women should wear American gowns and not patronize the Parisian makers," declared Mamie Fish, but the American society hostess usually relied on the leading fashion houses of Europe for her wardrobe.[18] The only real New York couturier of the period was Madame Osborne, but, smart as her gowns were, the elite of society considered patronage of her house somewhat déclassé.[19] Most clothing, particularly evening dresses and ball gowns, came from the Parisian couture houses of Pacquin, Doucet, Redfern, Pingat, and Callot. Without doubt, however, the most famous and influential of couturiers during the Gilded Age was Charles Frederick Worth. An Englishman who moved to Paris in the middle of the nineteenth century, Worth reached the height of his success dressing such figures as Empress Elisabeth of Austria and Empress Eugénie of France, and his elaborate crinolines and combinations of rich materials and lavish embroidery and adornment guaranteed a following of the most prestigious and wealthy clients in the world. "Worth says that American women are the best customers he has—far better than queens," reported one contemporary. "They ask the price: American women never do. They simply say, 'Give me the best, the most beautiful, the most fashionable gown.'"[20]

Ladies visited these Parisian couture houses by appointment, lounging on chaises as vendeuses hovered with designs while offering champagne and canapés. Often, simple models in muslin or cotton, called toiles, were shown to reveal the cut, drape, and shape of a proposed garment; if

A Charles Frederick Worth gown worn
by Gertrude Vanderbilt Whitney.

the design was approved, the vendeuse began the intricate process of
taking careful measurements of the client. Colors, materials, and embellishments were all discussed and prices agreed to before the pieces were
commissioned.

Not surprisingly, Harry Lehr considered himself an expert at dressing
"his ladies" and regularly accompanied them to the couture houses, sort-
ing through models, suggesting colors and cut, and offering advice. His
suggestions were not always welcome, as his wife recalled. Once, during
a visit to Worth in Paris, "He had the whole establishment in commotion
that was heard even out on the Rue de la Paix, while the presiding genius
of the temple of clothes was literally tearing his hair out in handfuls in
his atelier. The particular creation that was troubling Mr. Lehr's brain,
the morning I saw him, was a combination of five colors, which he
insisted could be made into a unit."[21]

Several times a year, trunks arrived in New York from Paris, filled with
the latest dresses, gowns, and accessories.[22] When opened, they revealed
layers of tissue paper and ribbons holding everything firmly in place. The
waists, sleeves, and bodices of dresses and gowns were stuffed with tissue
to maintain their shape and prevent crushing; each dress also had a small

swatch of its principal fabric carefully attached, so that the lady's shoe-maker could provide her with custom-made matching slippers.[23]

The lady's maid might spend a day or more unpacking these trunks, carefully placing the items in her mistress's dressing room and wardrobe closets. Fine silk lingerie and matching robes, tied together with colored ribbons, nestled on shelves perfumed with small fragrant sachets. Most lingerie and underwear came from France and was adorned with exquisite embroidery and ornamented with lace.[24] There were drawers of silk stockings, and fine lace handkerchiefs sewn with monograms, chemises, and corsets. The corsets of the period, with their boning and tight structure, were cumbersome burdens deemed necessary by the morality of the day and by the dresses and gowns of the era, which demanded hourglass shapes and small waists. The ritual of donning a corset, for which a lady's maid was essential, began with a soft chemise, over which went the corset itself, cinched tightly and laced up the back to constrain the body and force the torso into the desired shape.[25] Authorities of the day warned against the dangers of tight lacing as unhealthy and unbecoming, especially to the older, more amply endowed ladies.[26] The newer, S-shaped corset, tightly boned and even more tightly laced, was an uncomfortable if requisite accoutrement for many evening gowns and a requirement to achieve the hourglass silhouette necessary for ball gowns. They were the bane of many of the older, more voluptuous society women in the Gilded Age; in comfortably padded matrons such as Caroline Astor or Alva Vanderbilt, they forced the bust forward and up, and the bottom out, resulting in what society wags gleefully called "balcony busts," where breasts could be pushed nearly a foot in front of the posterior.[27]

One closet in a lady's dressing room might be given over to shelves filled with small caps, bonnets, toques, and extravagant picture hats from Lemonnier in Paris, adorned with lace or clusters of osprey feathers or ostrich plumes and set with fine veils, each topping its own wooden form.[28] Other closets held morning dresses, afternoon dresses, dresses for promenades, tea gowns, evening gowns, gowns for church, blouses, skirts, vests, jackets, riding habits, skating costumes, and bathing dresses, arrayed by color and function, their sleeves, bodices, and collars stuffed with tissue paper to keep their shape. Shelves displayed rows of shoes and slippers;

these were often of suede or satin, with low heels to facilitate ease of movement, while those worn during a ball, though concealed beneath long gowns, were inevitably adorned with lace appliqués or seed pearls.[29] Cedar closets provided storage for outerwear, ranging from loose-fitting, filmy summer coats and jackets sewn with lace and black velvet opera cloaks lined with ermine to long fur coats with matching muffs and stoles of mink, sable, chinchilla, and fox for the winter.

The most important of these storerooms was that given to the lady's ball gowns. Lined with cedar and perfumed with aromatic sachets, this held dozens of exquisite gowns, each shrouded in a protective muslin bag and carefully stuffed with padding and tissue to retain its shape; most were so heavy with beading and embroidery that they could not be hung, lest the weight of the adornment cause any damage, so they were carefully laid on polished shelves.[30] Numbers clipped on their covers corresponded to entries in ledgers listing the pieces, allowing the lady's maid to consult with her mistress and review the desired clothing without having to search for anything and to ensure that the same ensemble was never worn too often or to the same entertainments.

There also were accessories, including filmy lace parasols that offered protection against the sun and, most importantly, gloves. A seasonal wardrobe called for dozens of pairs of multibutton doeskin, chamois, or suede gloves for ordinary day wear, and long, formal *mousquetaires* of satin or kid, designed to allow the fingers to be temporarily free and which were worn on the most formal occasions.[31] Although fashion dictated that these gloves be white, shortly after the turn of the century elbow-length, light brown gloves adopted from the Swedish court became the rage among members of New York City society, who donned them despite their drab appearance.[32]

In addition to all of these garments and accessories, a typical seasonal lady's wardrobe also included outfits designed for country pursuits and sporting endeavors. In general, dresses worn in the country were simple, with a preference for cottons, serge, or tweeds.[33] For yachting excursions, ladies donned matching skirts and jackets of serge, often adorned with embroidered insignia and worn with jaunty caps or hats.[34] For coaching, older ladies favored black or brown skirts and jackets, although the turn of the century brought with it a taste for not only impractical white but also a rainbow spectrum of colored silks and laces that one authority condemned as "undesirably conspicuous."[35] For riding, most ladies still used side-saddles and clad themselves in cumbersome skirts, black boots, tight jackets, and a silk hat trimmed with a fine mesh veil; when a member of society dared abandon such restrictive clothing and rode astride in breeches, it could lead to headlines in the day's press.[36] Motorcars presented their own unique requirements: soot and smoke called for long, loose topcoats of leather, with matching hats draped with veils, and even protective goggles. For tennis parties, ladies wore white cotton shirtwaists, pleated flannel skirts, and sailor hats with veils.[37] The skirt, recalled Elizabeth Drexel Lehr, "had to be held up—not an easy accomplishment—in order not to trip over it when running after the ball."[38] Seaside bathing in the Gilded Age was a particularly cumbersome endeavor. Ladies habitually wore black or dark blue cashmere dresses whose full skirts swirled around them as they entered the water, necessitating long black silk stockings that concealed any unto-ward glimpse of an exposed female leg; atop their heads they wore white caps, or large picture hats with veils, and some, such as Alva Vanderbilt, even carried protective parasols into the water with them.[39]

When they arose, ladies tended to wear flowing muslin peignors adorned with lace or Japanese kimonos as they took their coffee or tea and looked over any correspondence.[40] Mornings found them in a long-sleeved day dress or a fitted skirt and blouse, detailed with tucks and pleats to accentuate the figure; though of exceptionally fine workmanship and crafted from silk, satin, taffeta, or finely spun cotton, these ensembles were more utilitarian than extravagant. Such an outfit was suitable for informal mornings at home and meetings with the housekeeper, butler, or chef de cuisine; it could be worn through luncheon if that meal was served en famille, but was deemed unsuited for any excursions outside of the house.[41]

A second change of clothing came before luncheon if there were any guests, or immediately after the meal. These day dresses were more formal than those worn in the morning yet comparatively restrained in detail so as not to suggest the more elaborate creations destined for the evening; décolleté in a day dress was considered in extremely bad taste.[42] If the lady was receiving visitors, custom dictated that she again change, this time into an *après-midi* ensemble, usually with puffed sleeves at the shoulder that narrowed and tightened below the elbow.[43] Authorities recommended black silk, satin, or velvet dresses for mature ladies, adorned perhaps with beaded trim or jet embroidery and lace at the neckline and wrists, while lighter colors and more elaboration were permissible for their younger counterparts; on such occasions gloves always were worn.[44]

If a lady left her house to make calls and pay her respects, she often changed into yet another costume. This was generally of silk or velvet, with more adornment than a day dress but not as elaborate as a dress worn for an "at home" day; if the call was a formal one, a three-foot train, draped from the back of the waist, was considered proper to the occasion.[45] Such clothing was also appropriate for an afternoon drive along Fifth Avenue or through Central Park, although the outfits worn during these excursions generally tended to be more elaborate and luxurious, with lavish silks, satins, taffetas, or velvets embellished with embroidery, lace, and overlays of ruffles, all designed to attract attention and favorable comment.[46] Returning to her own house, a lady often changed again, this time into one of the tea gowns made fashionable at the turn of the century by Worth. These were lighter garments of silk, satin, chiffon, velvet, or brocade, in a rainbow of colors including pinks, blues, pearls, grays, crimsons, and lavenders; most had elbow-length sleeves adorned with lace appliqués and bodices sewn with foliate designs in gold or silver thread or ornamented in beading.[47]

A formal dinner, a visit to the opera or symphony, or a party without dancing demanded an evening gown. Evening gowns followed the silhouette of a typical dress worn in the afternoon: a tight, fitted bodice, tucked waist, narrow hips, and a skirt that flared at the bottom to form a short train. Sleeves were shorter than those of a day dress, either elbow-length or higher, allowing for the wearing of the fashionable long white gloves. These gowns were graduated according to function: for an evening dining *en famille*, a lady might select a gown with sparse ornamentation and a more reserved décolletage, while gowns worn outside of the house or for formal events were more elaborate in embellishment. A wide variety of luxurious fabrics, colors, and decorations marked these gowns as extraordinary works of couture. Designers utilized silk brocades, taffetas, velvets, and satins ornamented with chiffon or layers of tulle and lace. While ensembles designed for the day tended to white or pastel, couturiers deployed darker hues for evening gowns, ranging from rusts and crimsons to dark greens, purples, and blacks, set off with ostrich feathers or trimmed with fur. This opulent effect was enhanced by elaborate embroidery: skirts and bodices were sewn in silver or gold thread to create stunning sunbursts, geometric patterns, butterflies, oak leaves, roses, and scrolls, often ornamented with small crystals, pearls, and jewels to create vivid flashes of sparkle.[48]

Even more than evening gowns, ball gowns represented the pinnacle of the couturier's art, offering impressive statements of wealth and privilege. Almost without exception, ball gowns were white, covered with passementerie and cascades of lace, their bodice heavily boned; full skirts were of silk or satin, adorned with panels of velvet and lace and sewn with floral designs in gold and silver threads that shimmered and dazzled. Rich brocades, laced with layers of chiffon and sprinkled with shining jewels, or heavy garments of silver tissue, were trimmed with fringe, tulle, tassels, braiding, or fur. Necklines were low, revealing shapely décolletages. Skirts swept back in folds, mingling with trains embroidered with floral garlands and edged with gold lace or fur.[49]

Such gowns were invaluable aids in the ballroom for a lady who hoped to attract the attention of potential suitors or to impress with her taste. "When her shoulders stunningly emerge from her bodice," one authority wrote, "when her trailing gown undulates behind her as she walks, when the brilliance of the silken folds enveloping her attracts everyone's gaze and displays her beauty, her only concern is the effect she is producing. This is the moment of her triumph. She is aware of it and has spared no expense to create it. Everything must contribute to the effect."[50]

These displays of sartorial splendor inevitably surprised and impressed. "One rarely comes across a really badly dressed woman in any rank of life," noted one visitor. "To dress well and make the very best of her resources seems a gift peculiar to the American woman. Her Parisian sister, to whom I suppose she would herself admit that she was occasionally indebted for ideas, is not her superior in this respect. I imagine a well-dressed American woman is the best-dressed woman in the world."[51] For the Gilded Age lady, this extravagance was a social necessity, and few apologies were offered for such indulgence. Observing this trend, Thorstein Veblen noted that society's "admitted expenditure for display is more universally practiced in the matter of dress than in any other line of consumption."[52] Maintaining a wardrobe appropriate to the shifting needs of display was an expensive proposition that underlined just how indulgent society could be. It was a measure of such extravagance that millionaire industrialist William Leeds once wryly joked that he found it impossible to keep his beautiful wife, Nancy, to her annual clothing allowance of $40,000 ($920,000 in 2008).[53]

14

JEWELRY

TO GILDED AGE SOCIETY, recalled Lloyd Morris, "diamond tiaras were not empty symbols."[1] In a world where conspicuous display formed an integral part of everyday life, exquisite jewels were not only adornments but also necessities as rival hostesses sought to impress with their taste and wealth. Dinners, balls, and evenings at the opera offered ladies opportunities to revel in the tiaras, necklaces, earrings, brooches, stomachers, bracelets, and rings that filled their safes. One French visitor was amazed at the "profusion of jewels" worn by society ladies, noting "turquoises as big as almonds, pearls as large as filberts," and "rubies and diamonds" the size of fingertips.[2] Often, recalled Elizabeth Drexel Lehr, the sheer magnitude of these jewels was so overwhelming "that the problem was to find a novel way of wearing them."[3]

American Gilded Age hostesses diligently copied the European custom of displaying exquisite jewels to dazzling effect. Diamonds sparkled in tiaras and necklaces, perfectly matched pearls shimmered in earrings, emeralds and aquamarines glistened in brooches, and Burmese rubies glowed in elaborate bracelets of gold and platinum. Older, more dignified hostesses preferred family heirlooms or larger, dramatic pieces lavish in their display, while the naturalistic, garland style and the sinuous lines of

Art Nouveau found favor among younger ladies. There also was a passion for the unusual, and many jewelers turned to such exotic materials as tortoiseshell and tiger claws in the quest for distinctive ornaments.[4]

"Let royal coffers be what they may," recorded one observer at the turn of the century, "the collective contents of the jewel caskets of the ultra-fashionable set in New York society approximate closely to $170 million [$3.9 billion in 2008]. White ropes of Oriental pearls, of almost priceless purity, enchain the necks and shoulders of the smartest set; the coronets of diamonds worn at the opera cost, on the average, not more than $20,000 [$460,000 in 2008]. Of a few of the more imposing tiaras, how-ever, each of the pearl shaped brilliants capping the apex could easily command $5,000 [$115,000 in 2008]. If a woman aspires to regal effects in evening dress, besides her diamond tiara a corsage piece of diamonds valued at, say, $75,000 [$1.7 million in 2008] is requisite."[5]

Most of the era's prominent hostesses had a number of parures and demiparures from which to select. A parure consisted of a tiara, matching necklace, earrings, and brooch, while a demiparure formed a partial suite of jewels. The most conspicuous of all displays by American ladies, and the one that most reflected their desire to copy European aristocrats, was the wear-ing of a tiara. Composed of intricate circlets, floral garlands, faceted fleurons, hanging pendants, sunburst fringes, interlocked festoons, and stylized fleurs-de-lis, laurel wreaths, and oak leaf clusters, tiaras offered the ultimate in per-sonal adornment, with dazzling displays of diamonds, pearls, emeralds, rubies, sapphires, amethysts, or aquamarines set against lacy networks of platinum and silver. Some tiaras could be taken apart and their pieces used to individual effect, or worn reversed around the throat as magnificent neck-laces. There also were hair ornaments: diamond crescents, stars, moons, floral sprays, arrows, and aigrettes worn scattered through a lady's coiffure to add sparkle with every movement.

Nearly as powerful in display were the necklaces: ornaments in fringe, festoon, and collet designs shimmering with diamonds and other gems as they cascaded over throats and sparkled against the fashionable décolleté of the era. There also were dog collars thick with jewels, and the *collier résille*, made famous by Alexandra, Princess of Wales, a sumptuous cascade of diamonds or diamonds and pearls suspended on silk threads that covered necks and draped down to the tops of bodices. No matter how elaborate a gown might be, few ladies left the art of the couturier alone, further adorning bodices with lover's knot, tassel, fringe, and bow brooches to provide additional luster, with stomachers—intricate showers of jewels embellished with ropes of pearls, strings of diamonds, pendant drops, and floral garlands—also rippling from neckline to waist. As a final touch, pearl drop, chandelier, and diamond festoon earrings framed faces, while bracelets encrusted with diamonds and other gems flashed fire from wrists encased in long white gloves.

"If the precious stones are what they look to be," wrote one foreign visitor to New York in awe, "these Americans must spend fortunes upon their women."[6] Jewelry indicated status and fortune but also could offer additional hints about a lady's character, its deployment a "reliable indicator of breeding."[7] The etiquette of society, again diligently copied from Europe, demanded that only pearls or similar restrained jewels be worn before evening. "A woman who wears diamonds in the middle of the day," warned one authority, "looks like a parvenu a mile off."[8]

In the older, wealthier families boasting proud ancestry, many of these jewels were handed down from mother to daughter, while the newly moneyed availed themselves of the assembled magnificence offered by the era's jewelers. Weddings also provided occasions when many new pieces were added to a lady's collection. In April 1893, when Cornelia Bradley-Martin married the 4th Earl of Craven, her gifts included a diamond tiara, a diamond and sapphire bracelet, a collar of diamonds and other gems from India, a diamond wreath brooch, a hat pin of diamonds and sapphires, a ring set with three solitaire diamonds, a diamond-encrusted watch, and, uniquely, a Mogul dagger studded with diamonds and sapphires.[9] The jewels accompanying the marriage of Vanderbilt descendant Florence Adele Sloane to James Burden were no less dazzling: a diamond tiara from her husband, a diamond sunburst brooch—"the largest one I have ever seen," she recorded in awe—from her father, a large diamond and sapphire necklace from her mother, and, from her Uncle Cornelius Vanderbilt II, "a most gorgeous stomacher of diamonds."[10] Heiress Anna Gould's presents on her 1895 wedding to Count Boni de Castellane encompassed not only a diamond brooch, a chain of two hundred diamonds, a diamond tiara, and a magnificent necklace of eight hundred pearls and seventy-two diamonds, but also several pieces of genuine historical significance, including an antique gold necklace that had been owned by the Spanish royal family and a sixteenth-century pearl necklace that had belonged to Marie de Medici.[11]

Most new jewels came from the greatest craftsmen of the day. E. Wolff & Company, and Garrard in London, and Tiffany in New York each provided an array of exquisite adornments to discerning ladies; but above all, Paris was the center of this glittering world. During their annual visits to the capital to replenish seasonal wardrobes, ladies were drawn to the ateliers of Cartier, Chaumet, Frédéric Boucheron, and Lucien Falize. Vever and René Lalique satisfied the growing taste for pieces in the Art Nouveau style, while the more discerning and wealthy could seek out exquisite brooches, pins, and *objets de vertu* from the renowned Russian court jeweler Peter Karl Fabergé. Auctions of aristocratic and former royal jewelry in Europe added important and exquisite pieces to a market where hostesses vied to outbid one another in their acquisition. The most magnificent of all such sales was the 1887 auction of the former French crown jewels, which offered American ladies the opportunity to adorn themselves with gems of historic significance.[12]

Gentlemen of the Gilded Age were not entirely immune from the draw of glittering adornments. They carried engraved silver and gold cigarette cases inset with their initials in diamonds, wore bejeweled cuff links, sported thick gold watch chains, and embellished the fronts of their starched shirts with mother-of-pearl, ivory, or enamel studs. "A few young men, sometimes called dudes," wrote one adviser, "wear pink coral studs or black pearls," though this habit was highly discouraged.[13]

As with most other aspects of society, however, the ladies dominated. Alice Drexel had a famed string of hundreds of priceless pearls, so lengthy and so thick that she regularly wore it draped in a lattice pattern across the bodice of her gown and hanging loose over back.[14] Edith Gould, wife of Jay Gould's eldest son, George, possessed a collection of jewels valued at more than $1 million ($23 million in 2008). "She was very fond of jewels," recalled one acquaintance, "and wore them almost constantly, changing them from day to day according to what she was doing." For motoring,

Edith habitually wore her famous pearls.[15] George had purchased five perfectly matched strands of pearls for his wife from Tiffany at a rumored cost
of $500,000 ($11.5 million in 2008), although she rarely wore more than
three at a time.[16] She frequently wore a tiara of five large diamond fleurons, each hung with an exquisite freshwater pearl; George also purchased
eight large diamond peacock feathers adorned with emeralds that had
belonged to the emperor of China, and had Cartier craft five of them into
a lavish tiara, the remaining three fronds forming a magnificent brooch.[17]

One of the largest and most impressive of all jewelry collections was
that of Mrs. Cornelia Bradley-Martin. Bradley-Martin, a lawyer from Troy,
New York, did not possess a fortune, but his wife, Cornelia Sherman,
inherited some $7 million ($151 million in 2008) from her father, money
that the couple put to good use stampeding their way into the Gilded
Age's highest circles.[18] In April 1893 they married their daughter Cornelia
to the 4th Earl of Craven in an event so shameless in its promotion that a
mob actually stormed New York's Grace Church hoping to witness the
fabled festivities, knocking over floral displays to steal souvenirs, climbing
atop pews to obtain better views, and crushing the bride's dress as the
curious throng pressed through the aisles.[19] The former Cornelia Sherman
burned with a fire of aristocratic privilege and arrogance that seemingly
consumed her and her husband. Among the first things to go was the
rather plebeian family surname; in what one social historian called "the slow
growth of an imaginary hyphen," the couple gradually let it be known that
they were now "the Bradley-Martins."[20] This peculiar move, seemingly
influenced by Cornelia's attempts to imitate aristocratic names, resulted in
much mockery. Cornelia failed to notice, however; she had become,
perhaps understandably, bewitched by the milieu into which her daughter
had married, and many of her old acquaintances thought her a terrible
snob. Turn-of-the-century firebrand journalist William Brann, with typical
hyperbole, openly derided her in the press, claiming that she "finds
the customs of this country too crass to harmonize with her supersen-
sitive soul, and spends much time dangling about the titled slobs on
the other side."[21]

Armed with a considerable fortune, the newly renamed Mrs. Bradley-
Martin set about amassing a collection of jewelry nearly unrivaled in the

Gilded Age. More than any other hostess, she took advantage of the auction of the French crown jewels to transform herself, and at the turn of the century she possessed a staggering wealth of gems. She owned a tiara of diamond spikes said to have been modeled on one owned by Empress Josephine and purchased at a rumored cost of $521,700 (approximately $12 million in 2008); three large diamond rivière necklaces; a large berthe, a trellis pattern of twenty-five hundred diamonds laced in strands between diamond rosettes that served as a magnificent stomacher; and a number of diamond and pearl pendant brooches.[22] Among the actual pieces that had formed the French crown jewels, Mrs. Bradley-Martin owned ruby and diamond bracelets that she often joined to form a massive choker resembling a dog collar; a large diamond vine brooch dating from 1856; a large brooch of diamonds, pearls, and colored gemstones, made in 1864, that formed the center of a stomacher; a pendant cross of diamonds and rubies believed to have originally formed part of a rosary; and the Sévigné Brooch, a large ornament originally made in 1855 for Empress Eugénie and composed of 321 diamonds weighing 173 carats.[23] There also was an impressive necklace of diamond and ruby clusters said to have once been owned by Marie Antoinette and valued at $75,000 ($1.7 million in 2008), and a brooch of diamond grapes that had belonged to Louis XIV.[24] Bedecked in an array of all of this splendor, with exquisite piece piled on exquisite piece in an effort to dazzle, Cornelia Bradley-Martin, declared the society magazine *Town Topics,* was "so ablaze with diamonds from head to foot that she looked like a dumpy lighthouse."[25]

The collections owned by the Vanderbilts were just as diverse and exquisite. Louise Vanderbilt, married to William Henry's quiet son Frederick, was a supremely elegant lady with a taste for the past. Having read that aristocrats of the Venetian Renaissance favored sautoirs—long, finely worked chains culminating in a single large jewel—Louise commissioned her own version: an exceptionally lengthy string of pearls to which she could affix either a large ruby or an uncut sapphire as her attire dictated. Her sautoir was so long, however, that she was forever carelessly kicking the jeweled ornament at its end when she walked, much to the distress of those around her.[26]

Louise's sister-in-law Alva Vanderbilt was less concerned with such frivolous adornments, relying on her architectural aspirations to make a statement of taste, though she, too, recognized the social importance of lavish displays of jewels and possessed a considerable collection esti- mated shortly after the turn of the century at approximately $1 million ($23 million in 2008).[27] This included a diamond tiara, numerous brooches, and bejeweled bracelets, as well as a diamond sautoir believed to have been created for Catherine the Great. Alva's most significant pieces of jewelry, however, were her pearls. Three perfectly matched ropes of pearls, each half an inch in diameter, had been made for Catherine the Great, and were later worn by Empress Eugénie of France before being purchased at the 1887 auction of the French crown jewels. Alva also possessed several strands of pearls said to have once belonged to Marie Antoinette.[28]

Of all the Vanderbilt women, however, it was the former Grace Wilson who most reveled in jeweled adornments, possessing a collection believed to be worth several million dollars.[29] To mark their quiet, controversial wedding in 1896, her husband, Neily, presented Grace with a large brooch in the shape of a heart, set with thirty large diamonds surrounding a sap- phire of great clarity.[30] In the years that followed, her collection grew to include exquisite pieces: a tall diamond tiara of fretwork design; jeweled bandeaus that Grace took to wearing around her forehead, anticipating a trend that took hold after World War I; diamond bow, fringe, and tassel brooches with diamond and pearl drops; a stomacher that rippled in shimmering layers over her bodice; and a magnificent necklace by Cartier, with hanging geometric bangles and five large pear-shaped diamond pendant drops.[31] One of her most exquisite and historically important pieces was a nineteenth-century rose brooch that had originally been cre- ated for Princess Mathilde, cousin of Emperor Napoleon III of France. Purchased from Cartier in 1904, this was designed as a large rose blossom of more than three thousand diamonds weighing 136 carats set against a back- ground of gold and platinum, and was rumored to be worth more than $1 million ($23 million in 2008).[32]

Rivaling Grace was Caroline Astor, with a lavish collection of tiaras, necklaces, brooches, and other ornaments having an estimated value of

$1 million to $1.5 million ($23 million to $34.5 million in 2008).[33] Caroline, reported one contemporary, "was the first of our rich women to wear many diamonds, and she always looked as if they wearied her."[34] Her diamonds, declared the *New York Times,* were widely considered "among the finest in the country," and she tended to favor only these gems and pearls to create a unified appearance.[35] The effect was dazzling: after one evening at the opera, the *New York Times* likened her to "a walking jewelry store."[36]

Caroline owned several distinctive tiaras, including one of diamond garlands and one of diamond festoons set with perfectly matched freshwater pearls, pieces so immense and heavy that wearing them seemed almost penitential.[37] With these sprinkled through her tall pompadour wig, she frequently wore a number of diamond stars and crescents that flashed fire with each inclination of her head.[38] Caroline could select from any number of necklaces: a dog collar of diamonds sewn against a band of deep purple, multiple strings of freshwater pearls, a pearl dog collar with diamond pendant drops, a collier résille necklace of 204 diamonds valued at $60,000 ($1.4 million in 2008), and a festoon necklace, arranged as a sunburst, composed of 282 diamonds and valued at $80,000 ($1.8 million in 2008).[39] Her most famous necklace, however, was a sweep of collet diamonds, arranged in several strands, that was said to have once belonged to Marie Antoinette.[40]

In addition to bracelets and rings, Caroline possessed an extraordinary collection of brooches and bodice ornaments. She could adorn her gown with a display of diamond stars, a large corsage brooch formed of hundreds of diamonds, tassel and lover's knot brooches with hanging fringes of diamond threads or pearl pendants, a diamond cluster of leaves with three hanging tassels of large solitaires that had belonged to Empress Eugénie, and a superb bowknot brooch glistening with diamonds that was believed to have once belonged to King Louis XIV.[41] Her most magnificent piece, however, was undoubtedly an immense stomacher, a complex display of diamond foliates and corsages holding rows of diamonds and pearls that nearly covered the front of any gown and was believed to have once belonged to Marie Antoinette.[42] Caroline regularly wore this immense array of jewels "with the most effective prodigality."[43] On nights when she was *en grande toilette*, Caroline was so dazzling that one wit likened her to a walking chandelier.[44]

Display of this jeweled splendor involved an intricate ritual. On evenings when ladies attended the opera, a formal dinner, or a ball, a professional hairdresser arrived at their houses to tend to their coiffures; frequently these had to be arranged around particular ornaments—tiaras, coronets, aigrettes, or jeweled stars and crescents—that had been selected for wear. The addition of any fresh flowers to the dress, whether in the form of a corsage or sewn on to adorn the décolletage or hemline, was followed by the careful placement of jewelry. Ladies' maids retrieved pieces previously selected for use from locked safes, setting the velvet and wooden cases on a dressing table and awaiting the moment of their display. Necklaces were draped around necks, brooches pinned to fabrics, and stomachers affixed to bodices, their stands of pearls and chains of diamonds looped into artful cascades to frame waists.[45]

Although locked safes concealed in carefully guarded houses seemed to ensure the security of these riches, there always were worries over loss or theft. Whenever Caroline Astor wore her famous diamond stomacher, she was always accompanied by two private detectives to prevent any disaster.[46] Others were less cautious. Once, one society lady misplaced a bag in which, for some inexplicable reason, she carried $81,000 ($1.9 million in 2008) in diamonds at all times, in the unlikely event that she suddenly felt impelled to adorn herself; a private detective found the missing satchel and safely returned the contents.[47] The prize for carelessness, however, undoubtedly belonged to Arabella Huntington, widow of railroad tycoon Collis Huntington. One day, wandering through New York City in search of suitable antiques to add to her collection, she forgot her purse atop a desk. An extremely honest clerk discovered it and returned it to her forbidding mansion, much to her relief: still inside, tucked into a velvet pouch, were eleven pearl necklaces valued at an astonishing $3.5 million ($80.5 million in 2008).[48]

The rich variety and extravagance of these jewels often made them not only the subject of admiration but also of suspicion. One year, tin magnate William Leeds purchased a magnificent set of pearls from Parisian jeweler Bernard Citroën for his wife, Nancy, at a rumored cost of some $360,000 (approximately $8.9 million in 2008). When the couple returned to New York by ocean liner, customs officials had already heard reports of the necklace. Reviewing Leeds's arrival declaration, they found that he had claimed to be returning from Europe with nothing of value. At the time, such a luxury item was subject to a 60 percent duty, and customs officials were certain that Leeds was attempting to smuggle the necklace into the country in order to avoid the hefty surcharge on its importation. Suspecting the worst, officials called in a number of inspectors and refused to allow the couple to disembark before their possessions and luggage had been thoroughly searched. Despite intensive efforts, no necklace was found. Then, at the end of this chaotic scene, Leeds pulled from his pocket a receipt from Citroën showing that the jeweler was delivering the necklace to America and that the duty had already been paid. Faced with this, the officials had no choice but to let Leeds and his wife finally disembark. Suspicions remained, however, when it was learned that Citroën had arrived in the city a few days earlier, and a careful examination of the receipt Leeds had presented showed that only 10 percent duty, rather than the 60 percent demanded by law, had been paid on the jewels. Thinking that Leeds and the jeweler were attempting to defraud the U.S. Treasury, the government hastily dispatched an investigator to speak to Citroën. But the jeweler produced not a necklace, but instead a collection of loose pearls, and pointed out that the duty on unstrung gems was only 10 percent, compared to the 60 percent for finished pieces of jewelry. It seems that, realizing that 60 percent duty on a necklace worth $360,000 would have resulted in an ultimate cost of $576,000 ($13.2 million in 2008), Leeds and Citroën had worked out a cagey deal in which the piece was dismantled and brought into America in pieces to avoid the additional expense. Government officials, convinced of the illegality of the move, brought suit, seeking the additional $216,000 (approximately $5 million in 2008) in duty they believed they were rightly owed, but ultimately the presiding judge accepted that while the move was perhaps morally questionable, neither Leeds nor Citroën had actually violated any rules.[49]

15

TRANSPORTATION

IN THE WORLD OCCUPIED BY GILDED AGE SOCIETY, methods of transportation became yet another mark of wealth and status. Afternoon carriage drives in New York City offered ladies the opportunity not only to showcase their latest Parisian fashions but also to enjoy admiring glances directed at their sleek carriages and sleighs, and at their husband's fine horses. In an age of progression from country estate to resort, extravagant private railway cars offered the ultimate in continued comfort. Lavish yachts provided exquisite surroundings on voyages in both American waters and on annual trips to Europe. And the coming of the motorcar, sputtering along the streets and belching clouds of black exhaust, signaled an entirely new sphere for indulgence.

"You can do business with anyone," financier J. P. Morgan once declared, "but you can only sail a boat with a gentleman."[1] Such sentiments encapsulated the era's penchant for the sea. From the middle of the nineteenth century, yachts often were regarded as the ultimate symbols of luxury, and few were more famous than one of the era's earliest examples, Commodore Cornelius Vanderbilt's *North Star*. At a time when such vessels were still an almost unheard-of extravagance, Vanderbilt was not content to settle for the usual sailing ship. What he wanted, as John Malcolm Brinnin noted, was nothing short of his own small ocean liner.[2] His was, in fact, the first oceangoing steam yacht ever constructed for a private individual.[3] Built in 1853 on Long Island, *North Star* was a 270-foot-long, 2,500-ton, black-hulled wooden vessel with twin sidewheels powered by steam from four boilers, and she was said to have cost $500,000 ($15 million in 2008). Two masts, flanking the two funnels amidships, could be rigged for auxiliary use.[4] The interior was lavishly executed. A large painting of the commodore's Staten Island house graced the landing of the main staircase, which descended to a saloon lined in inlaid satinwood. Elaborately carved rosewood furniture in the Louis XV style, upholstered in green velvet worked with bouquets of flowers, offered comfortable seating, while slabs of granite from Naples, ornamented with insets of yellow Pyrenees marble, faced the walls of the dining room, below a ceiling embellished with gold, green, and purple medallions framing portraits of Columbus, George Washington, Daniel Webster, and other luminaries. The ten staterooms, with white-enameled berths fitted with silk sheets, eiderdowns, and hand-embroidered lace covers, were each finished in diverse color schemes, ranging from orange, gold, and maroon to crimson and green.[5]

The yacht caused a sensation, particularly when the commodore took his family on a tour of Europe in 1853 shortly after *North Star* was completed; joining the commodore and his crew were his wife, ten of their twelve children, their seven sons-in-law, a physician, and a private chaplain. "The Commodore did the swearing and I did the praying," the latter explained."[6] Everywhere *North Star* sailed, she was the subject of intense interest and glowing reviews in the local newspapers. In London, the press noted with more than a hint of wounded pride, "This yacht is a monster steamer. Her saloon is described as larger and more magnificent than that of any ocean steamer afloat, and is said to surpass in splendor the Queen's yacht."[7] Visiting St. Petersburg, Vanderbilt played host to the nautically minded and suitably impressed Grand Duke Konstantin Nikolaievich, son of Emperor Nicholas I. In two months the yacht covered some fifteen thousand miles before returning her passengers safely to New York.[8]

The yachts that followed spanned the range of nineteenth-century nautical technology, the paddle-wheeled steamers giving way to multimasted schooners powered by coal and finally to multiscrewed vessels dominated by tall funnels, each advance bringing unexpected luxury at ever-increasing costs. The bold and brash James Gordon Bennett had a love of the sea, and his 227-foot-long, black-hulled yacht *Namouna*, built in 1882 at a cost of $200,000 ($4 million in 2008), was a regular sight around Long Island Sound and the harbor of New York City before Bennett finally abandoned America for a life of self-imposed exile in Paris. Stanford White had spent some $20,000 ($400,000 in 2008) designing the elaborate interior.[9] There was an observation lounge on the boat deck, with padded walls, deeply tufted built-in benches, and immense windows overlooking the bow; a saloon, with walls hung in ice-blue damask woven with gold thread by Tiffany and a carved fireplace and woodwork of maple and walnut; a ladies' salon with an arched ceiling and comfortable, overstuffed sofas and chairs; and a multitude of cabins, including that of the owner, with a carved, canopied bed of cherry set against its tufted walls.[10]

In 1900 Bennett commissioned an altogether more impressive yacht, *Lysistrata*, named after the legendary Greek beauty. Built in Scotland at a rumored cost of $600,000 ($12 million in 2008), this was—at 314 feet— nearly a third longer than *Namouna*, and no expense had been spared. There were large reception rooms and saloons bedecked in mahogany, satinwood, and cherry, a tiled Turkish bath, and hot and cold bathing rooms with a masseuse on constant duty.[11] Bennett himself had three

Namouna, the first yacht of James Gordon Bennett.

private cabins, one on each of the yacht's decks, so that he need not climb any stairs if he found himself too tired.[12] There was even a special pen built on the foredeck to house a cow that accompanied him on each voyage to provide fresh milk, a "soft, padded cell" where "an electric fan blew gentle breezes over the cow in tropical climes."[13]

Then there was William Backhouse Astor II. For many years he was content with his sleek, schooner-style yacht *Ambassadress*, using it—and his wife's reluctance to join him aboard for his cruises—as a kind of floating pleasure barge, where he could freely indulge his love of alcohol and enjoy the company of a variety of pretty young actresses, dancers, and singers.[14] In 1884, however, spending more and more of his time at sea, he wanted something more impressive, and commissioned the 232-foot-long *Nourmahal*. Designed and built by Harlan & Hollingsworth in Wilmington, Delaware, *Nourmahal* was a sleek, black-hulled vessel, with gilded scrolls spreading from the female figurehead perched at the bow; between her masts, a tall funnel towered over teak decks shaded by white canvas awnings.[15] This was a step up from *Ambassadress*, with elegantly designed staterooms and a dining saloon that could seat sixty, although neither his famous wife nor any of her New York circle ever set foot in it. Astor was nothing if not obvious in the selection of the name: *Nourmahal* was said to roughly translate as "Light of the Harem," a fitting appellation for a vessel devoted to the enjoyment of less than upright pursuits.[16]

In 1885 William K. Vanderbilt commissioned Harlan & Hollingsworth to build him a magnificent yacht. A twin-screw, steam-powered vessel designed to resemble a three-masted schooner, the black-hulled yacht was christened *Alva* on its 1886 launch, and had reportedly cost $500,000 ($10 million in 2008). *Alva* was 285 feet long, with a gilded bowsprit and a tall funnel amidships. "Mrs. Vanderbilt," reported the *New York Times*, "who is generally accredited to be a lady of excellent taste, deems that elaborate and ornate furnishings are out of place on a yacht. She thinks that she is rich enough to afford simplicity in this instance, and that is what she is going to have, in a comparative sense."[17] There was a drawing room paneled in teak and mahogany, a white-enameled, gilt-ornamented dining room with a piano, and a library lined in French walnut and adorned with a skylight. Nine staterooms, each finished in different hardwoods, a

Alva, the first yacht of William K. Vanderbilt.

nursery, and bathrooms made up the family's accommodations, and there were another seven guest cabins, each with a canopied bed and a private bathroom. In addition there were cabins and ratings for the ship's fifty-three-person crew, which included a surgeon, three chefs, and one man whose sole function was to operate the ice cream maker.[18]

Alva was specifically intended not only for pleasure cruises off America's East Coast but also for transatlantic voyages. Double boilers could propel her at a top speed of fifteen knots, but she proved less than steady rolling and pitching so much that her passengers were often seasick.[19] On July 23, 1892, off the foggy Nantucket Sound, a freight steamer rammed *Alva,* and, fatally damaged, she was hastily abandoned. A year later, Willie ordered *Valiant,* a new 331-foot yacht, to replace *Alva.* Built at a cost said to approach $1 million ($23 million in 2008), *Valiant* featured a main saloon decorated in the Louis XIV style by a Parisian firm, twenty luxurious cabins, and accommodations for an increased crew of sixty-two men.[20]

Perhaps the most lavish of Gilded Age yachts was *Margarita,* designed in 1900 for Philadelphia banking heir Anthony Drexel. At a length of 323 feet and a displacement of just over 1,800 tons, *Margarita* was among the largest yachts in the world, surpassed only by a handful of vessels that included those belonging to the Tsar of Russia, the Kaiser of

Germany, and the British Crown. Her double hull, painted white, was divided into ten watertight compartments; buried deep within, powerful engines not only drove the ship through the water but also ran the heating and cooling plants of forced hot and cold air, the electrical plant that powered her 800 lightbulbs, and the machine that churned out some 1,200 pounds of ice each day.[21]

Exquisite appointments were the vessel's hallmark. A Louis XV–style salon boasted paneled walls rich with elaborate boiseries below a coffered ceiling whose details were picked out in gilt; carved sofas and chairs, upholstered in floral brocade, were gathered around a marble mantelpiece. Beyond was a library in the Empire style, with dark mahogany bookcases and furniture adorned with ormolu mounts. The dining saloon was decorated in the neoclassical taste; walls paneled in mahogany were ornamented with pilasters set with gilded scrolls and cartouches. An oval table ringed by Chippendale chairs echoed the shape of the leaded-glass dome set in the coffered ceiling above. A curved staircase with elaborately carved balustrades descended to the spacious cabins, none more luxurious than that of the owner himself. This was a symphony in Louis XVI–style rococo, its draped bed, dressing table, chaise longue, chairs, and immense, mirrored wardrobe all bristling with carved garlands, foliage, birds, fruit, and cherubs.[22]

The cost of maintaining and operating such vessels was staggering. Drexel once boasted that only three other men in the world could afford the expense of keeping *Margarita*.[23] Monthly salaries for the crews could often run to $3,000 ($30,000 in 2008). In addition, there was the cost of food, fuel, and uniforms for the crew.[24] Many crews were chiefly composed of Scandinavians, who, with their history of seafaring, were thought most adept at life on the ocean.[25] In the 1880s, Bennett's *Namouna*, its crew of fifty kept in commission year-round, cost a staggering $150,000 ($3 million in 2008) annually to run, with *Nourmahal* between $96,000 and $120,000 ($1.9 million and $2.4 million in 2008), and William Vanderbilt's *Alva* a comparatively cheap $60,000 ($1.2 million in 2008).[26]

Yachts were status symbols for the elite of the Gilded Age, but, ironically, they were not the ne plus ultra of luxurious travel. That distinction belonged to private railway carriages. Private railway cars, recalled one lady, were considered "better than a titled son-in-law or an old master, and also less expensive."[27] These private railway carriages, like Collis P. Huntington's Genesta, or William C. Whitney's Wanderer, were lavishly conceived and built, sometimes by George M. Pullman's company but more often by the Webster Palace Car Company. Founded in 1866 by William Webster, the latter manufactured the most luxurious examples and was favored by members of the Vanderbilt family, including William Henry Vanderbilt and his sons William Kissam, George, and Frederick. Indeed, William Henry's son-in-law Dr. William Seward Webb served for fifteen years as president of the Wagner Palace Car Company, so close were the ties between the firm and its clientele; only later did the two companies merge.[28]

Most such special commissions encompassed a string of three to four carriages. A dining room capable of seating up to a dozen people was generally situated in the forward car, along with a private galley and several rooms for members of the owner's personal staff. This might be followed by a carriage containing a saloon car, with comfortable sofas and chairs for relaxation, and the owner's compartment with a wardrobe and an adjoining private bathroom specially fitted with bathtubs whose rims were designed to prevent any water from sloshing over the sides during travel. Other carriages were generally devoted to private compartments for family or guests who shared a bathroom, and small rooms for additional staff. The majority of these carriages were finished with carved woodwork inset with marquetry and mother-of-pearl; padded, damask-covered walls; carved and gilded furniture; and upholstered ceilings and floors to deaden any extraneous noise. Most were air-conditioned, equipped with electric lights, boasted marble tubs with gold fixtures, had wine safes, and sported mother-of-pearl call buttons to summon servants during the journey. Not surprisingly, these luxuries cost a good deal of money, and it was not uncommon for a member of a Gilded Age society to pay in excess of $100,000 ($2 million in 2008) for such indulgence.[29]

Not surprisingly for a man who dominated the railways, Commodore Vanderbilt was perfectly at home rolling along on the tracks. He had owned two private railway carriages, Vanderbilt and Duchess, said to have cost $50,000 each ($1 million in 2008). While the interiors were awash with carved woodwork, expensive velvets, and damask, it was the exteriors that proved memorable. The commodore had the sides of Vanderbilt painted with

Interior of a private Pullman car, depicting the luxurious surroundings in which members of the Gilded Age traveled.

extravagant scenic depictions in an array of vibrant—often flamboyant—colors. In addition to views of bridges and railway tunnels, there was a representation of New York's Grand Central Terminal and an idealized view of Niagara Falls in a wash of brilliant blues and greens that contrasted sharply with the bright orange plating of the carriage.[30]

The private carriages built for Dr. William Seward Webb were more elaborate, as befitting the man who headed the Wagner Palace Car Company. Constructed in 1889, these encompassed ten cars linked together to form a miniature traveling palace. Webb had his own private carriage, Ellsmere, while that of his wife, Eliza Vanderbilt, was christened Mariquita. Both were finished in exquisitely carved mahogany paneling below tufted ceilings and featured built-in bookcases and shelves adorned with satinwood, ormolu, and mother-of-pearl inlays, and overstuffed sofas and chairs heavy with Victorian fringe. Other carriages contained a smoking room equipped with a piano, a galley, a formal dining room, a wine vault, a nursery, a dispensary manned by Webb's personal physician, a trunk room, bathrooms, and compartments for twenty attendants in addition to the main bedroom and four guest rooms.[31] From their remote country estate at Shelbourne Farms in Vermont, the Webbs regularly commuted aboard their string of railway carriages to New York City for the social season and to their isolated rustic camp in the Adirondacks, looked after by a staff that included a physician, two nurses, a valet, a lady's maid, two chefs, and eight smartly liveried stewards.[32]

George Gould, son of despised robber baron Jay Gould, made headlines in 1894 when he extravagantly took to the rails in a magnificent string of Pullman-designed and executed carriages. Each of the five cars bore its own unique name. La Rabida contained a galley and a dining room with intricately carved boiseries on the walls; in addition to compartments for staff, Marchena included a Moorish-inspired barbershop with a solid leather chair set beneath a stained-glass dome; Countess boasted a drawing room whose walls were cloaked in tufted, white cut velvet; America held lavishly fitted compartments for family members and guests; and Isabella contained not only a glassed-in observation lounge but also the principal bedroom, its adjoining bathroom—complete with a specially designed tub to prevent sloshing on the unsteady tracks—set beneath a ceiling adorned with Gothic traceries.[33]

These private railway carriages offered the latest in comforts, but their journeys had to be carefully worked out in advance and coordinated with officials of the railway lines. Private carriages generally traveled at the end of regularly scheduled journeys, coupled to the rear of the train. For each carriage, owners were forced to purchase eighteen full-class-fare tickets to cover the necessary fees, and often a surcharge was tacked on as well. Any special requirements deemed necessary by the owners, including accompanying private detectives dispatched from the Pinkerton Agency, were borne by the carriage owners. In addition, there were siding and sewage disposal fees when the train came to a halt.[34] And then there were the unforeseen expenses: one woman dispatched orders to every halt asking that fresh flowers await the arrival of her carriages so her servants could change the floral displays in her compartments each day; by the end of the journey she had spent some $300 on ($6,000 in 2008) replenishing the fragrant decorations.[35]

More important than yachts and trains were horses. "Those were the days," recalled Elizabeth Drexel Lehr, "when you had to love, or pretend you loved, horseflesh, or be socially damned."[36] In the Gilded Age, a fine mount, perfectly fitted riding clothes and boots, and an easy bearing in the saddle were considered hallmarks of breeding and refinement. So pervasive was this influence that on his honeymoon at Saratoga Springs following his marriage to Alva, William K. Vanderbilt signed the hotel register by noting not only their presence but also that of their accompanying party of "two maids, two dogs, and fifteen horses."[37]

From a young age, both boys and girls were trained to ride and master equestrian skills as a necessary social faculty. Riding was one of the few acceptable sporting pursuits open to ladies, though they were bound by a number of restrictive rules. Not only were their habits often uncomfortably tight and confining, but also riding sidesaddle called for much practice and great skill in keeping one's seat. One guide advised that while no set rule determined upon which side it was most proper for a lady to ride, it was best to adopt a position on the right, which protected the rider from any passing vehicles and allowed her to more amiably greet those whom she might encounter.[38]

Horses were often purchased at markets in England, Germany, and Paris, at which the very best specimens from the Continent were shown and subjected to bid. By the turn of the century, horses from Hungary, Austria, and Russia often were favored for their fine forms.[39] It was not uncommon for American millionaires to regularly dispatch agents such as the renowned Hiram Woodruff or Daniel Mace to such gatherings, authorizing them to pay as much as $30,000 ($600,000 in 2008) for a particularly fine stallion; indeed, many men refused to accept a seller's assessment until Mace, who was regarded as the finest authority on horses in New York, had personally inspected the animal.[40]

Both Commodore Vanderbilt and his son William Henry were known for their fine trotters. The commodore always began his mornings with an inspection of his stables, followed by a drive in Central Park, a pattern echoed by his son William Henry, who purchased the famed trotter Maude S. for $21,000 ($630,000 in 2008).[41] Every morning and afternoon, crowds lined the length of Central Park's Harlem Lane to watch the parade of curricles and sulkies, with their fast horses and proud, frock-coated and top-hatted owners, racing along.[42] Maude S. became so famous that Currier and Ives produced no fewer than eighteen lithographs depicting her and her proud owner.[43]

The typical Gilded Age stable followed a number of accepted requirements. First and foremost, stables had to be well ventilated but not subject to unwelcome drafts, providing dry, healthy environments for their horses. Rows of stalls flanked central aisles, carefully placed at a distance from the roomy spaces devoted to the storage of carriages. In addition to straight stalls, there were always a number of roomier box stalls set aside for special needs, such as a mare in foal. Most interiors were finished with utilitarian brick and with specially treated wood to prevent rot. Aisles were spread with colored sand, which had to be swept out each morning and replaced with a new coating; sanitation was a primary concern, with multiple drains set into the floors. But stables were far more than simply a collection of stalls: there were offices, extensive tack rooms with their fragrant leather harnesses, trophy rooms, a repair shop, feed rooms, and often a farrier's room and smithy.[44]

In New York City, William Henry Vanderbilt built his stables at East Fifty-second Street and Madison Avenue. With walls, floors, ceilings, an indoor riding ring, and sixteen stalls of ash, black walnut, and polished cherry, this bit of extravagance cost some $60,000 ($1.2 million in 2008).[45] His son Corneil was even more lavish with the stables for his Newport mansion, the Breakers. To preserve the tranquillity of the eleven-acre plot at the edge of the Atlantic, the stables were built a mile

The interior of the stable built for the Breakers, Newport.

west of the residence, on Coggeshall Avenue, and formed their own complex. In a large building of brick, the stables were highly compartmentalized according to their function. One set of carriage doors opened to a garage for motorcars, while another set gave access to an immense room where the family's carriages were arrayed in serried ranks. Twenty-eight horses could be accommodated in stalls along the length of a brick-paved aisle, which was swept and covered with white sand each morning when the stalls were also "set fair" with fresh straw. At one end of the corridor were rooms for the harnesses, saddles, blankets, and tack, along with a number of offices, a trophy room, and a dispensary. Tucked above were haylofts, a five-room apartment for the stable manager, and rooms for twelve grooms and stable boys, along with a living room, a dining room, and even a library.[46]

It was another Newport complex, however, that boasted the era's most famed stables. Banking heir Oliver Belmont so loved his prized horses that he could not bear the thought of being separated from them and forced architect Richard Morris Hunt to incorporate stables within his medieval Belcourt. Housed at the southern end of the main wing but separated from it by a half-timbered, Norman-style courtyard, this was the ultimate in equine indulgence: twenty-six stalls and two box stalls patterned in teak, lined in imported English tiles, and adorned with gold nameplates arrayed along a 160-foot-long corridor of handmade English bricks heated by steam. Elaborate wrought-iron grilles added a decorative touch, as did walls tiled in the Belmont racing colors of scarlet and maroon. Each morning and evening, fresh straw was placed in the stalls, and each horse was attended to by its own liveried groom; at night the animals were covered with white Irish linen blankets sewn with the Belmont family crest.[47] "Oh!" exclaimed Julia Ward Howe, "to lodge horses so, and be content that men and women should lodge in sheds and cellars!"[48] At Belmont's request, Hunt had even given over much of the castle's ground floor to a vestibule whose immense arched doors allowed carriages to directly enter the building and deposit their passengers.

Smart equipages and sleek carriages added to the luster of their owners. A typical high-society stable might include a diverse array of options appropriate to the time of day and the nature of the occasion: in Philadelphia, John Drexel kept twenty-six different carriages, while Mamie Fish maintained a similar number to provide for every occasion.[49] There might be a barouche, more formal landaus, cabriolets, and the small, closed broughams all carefully drawn up beneath the shelter of the stable roof. For morning journeys, phaetons were preferred; ladies embarking on a round of calls or an occasional shopping expedition often used single-horse victorias, whose lack of side doors eased the process of climbing into and out of the carriage in cumbersome skirts and dresses.[50] For more formal afternoon excursions there were larger victorias pulled by teams of horses, with two men riding on the box, while an evening out at the opera or a ball called for a *grande daumont de visite,* with matched steeds, a coachman in full livery atop the box, and two liveried footmen perched on the rear boards.[51] Many of these carriages were lavishly appointed, painted with the colors adopted by their owners, and often graced with a family crest, upholstered in silks and velvets, fitted out in exotic woods, and illuminated inside by gilded lamps.

Each afternoon in New York City, ladies paraded along Fifth Avenue and through Central Park. "Never have I seen in Hyde Park nor in the Champs Élysées a finer display," recalled one lady. "Barouches, landaus,

victorias, dog carts, pony phaetons, four-in-hands, tandems—and sometimes a spike team of three horses, two abreast and one in advance. The
double line of equipages drove up and down that short stretch of road,
passing and repassing each other."[52] Onlookers, recalled Lloyd Morris,
"gathered along the walk that bordered the east carriage drove from
Fifty-ninth Street and Fifth Avenue to the Mall. In the continuous procession of equipages you saw everyone who counted: the aristocracy, the
new smart set, the parvenus, the celebrities, the deplorably notorious."[53]
It was, remembered one man, a "never-ending procession of smart victorias," their occupants providing an impressive array of "beauty and fashion to be viewed. As a rule, the women wore their newest and smartest
frocks, and attention, rather than fresh air, was their quest. And they were
looked at."[54]

In the winter social season, when snow descended on New York City,
these elegant equipages were replaced with brightly painted sleighs set atop
highly polished runners. Safely nestled beneath lap robes of buffalo, black
bear, or lynx, the passengers settled against plush velvet seats, warmed by
hot water bottles as they raced over the compact snow, sleigh bells jingling
to create a cacophony of sound.[55] "Tassels grew longer and more elaborate
every season," recalled Elizabeth Drexel Lehr, "and harnesses were so gaily
decorated that they began to look like the trappings of medieval chivalry;
real aigrettes of every imaginable shade waved from the horses' heads. On
midwinter afternoons the air was full of the tinkle of sleigh bells; the snow
churned up by the beat of the hooves fell in a glittering spray as the sleighs
passed and repassed each other in Central Park."[56]

The coachmen, grooms, and footmen accompanying these carriages
often appeared just as brilliant as the equipages themselves. Owners usually provided three distinctive sets of livery for those attached to their
stables: ordinary uniforms of trousers, jackets, topcoats, and hats; formal
uniforms of breeches, striped waistcoats, and jackets adorned with buttons bearing the crest of their employers; and what was known as state
livery, of colored breeches, silk stockings, colored waistcoats, striped
coats, and ornamental tricorn hats, worn only on the most important of
occasions.[57] Elaborate dress aside, there was little glamour attached to the
jobs of those who worked in stables. Like their domestic counterparts,

their days generally began at five or six each morning and often ended late. Each horse had to be fed and watered, then attended to by grooms and stable boys who bathed them, curried their coats, brushed their manes, and cleaned their hooves with special picks before leading them from their stall for exercise to prevent agoraphobia.[58] Stalls and stables were cleaned, scoured, and filled with fresh hay, and aisles—in the wealthiest establishments—were swept and new sand raked into precise patterns, imitation heraldic crests.

Carriages, too, demanded constant attention. They were always housed away from the stalls, as the ammonia fumes from urine caused damage to both the leather tack and the enameled sides of the vehicles.[59] Ordinary maintenance involved cleaning carriages with soft sponges and chamois clothes, inspecting the leather struts and moisturizing them with an oiled rag, and wiping down the spokes of the wheels with brushes.[60] Any vehicle found to be dirty was cleaned at once; water, which tended to seep in and rot the woodwork and smear the varnish, was avoided in favor of a variety of brushes and oils to restore the shimmering surfaces.[61]

In addition to serving as means of transport, some of these vehicles were specially designed to offer the elite a fine sporting opportunity in the form of coaching displays. While these parades were more frequent during the summer in Newport, it was the annual New York Coaching Club's parade, held the first Saturday of every May, that drew the most interest. Founded in 1875, the New York Coaching Club promoted the sport as the epitome of upper-class indulgence. Christened with names such as Comet, Telegraph, and Venture, these coaches were bedecked with floral garlands to match the adornments worn by their horses. The club's parade was a rare occasion for gentlemen to display their sartorial splendor, bedecked in its regulation bottle-green coats with gilt buttons, striped yellow waistcoats, buckskin gloves, silk top hats, and large red or white boutonnieres jauntily tucked into their lapels.[62]

In time, motorcars began to replace carriages. In 1898, Alva Vanderbilt purchased a Dion Bouton in France and had it shipped to Newport, in the process becoming one of the first of the Gilded Age's elite to possess a motorcar.[63] Very soon others followed suit, and shining new cars by Renault, Mercedes, and Fiat were seen on the streets, their rumbling engines conveying passengers amid their noisy dust and smoke, which covered those nearby with layers of black soot.[64]

These early motorcars often were luxurious, their interiors fitted with rare woods, lavish upholstery, and gold handles.[65] Despite such touches, many of the grand society matrons, such as Mrs. Astor, kept to their carriages; indeed, Caroline Astor once took a reluctant spin in a motorcar and, at the end of the journey, said firmly, "This is the last time!"[66] But others, such as Tessie Oelrichs and Mamie Fish, were early fans and helped popularize the advent of the motor age.

On September 7, 1899, Alva hosted Newport's first motorcar race on the grounds of Belcourt.[67] The race was actually more of a parade around an obstacle course erected by Alva to test her fellow drivers' skills. There were "wooden horses hitched to carriages, dummy figures representing policemen, nursemaids, and loafers scattered strategically, and through them a devious course was staked out with golf flags."[68] For the occasion, the motorcars had been bedecked and wreathed with flowers and streams of trailing vines, lending a surreal aspect to the proceedings. "Serenely," recalled Lloyd Morris, "the drivers would have to manipulate their vehicles through the maze without brushing against, or toppling over, these incentives to profanity."[69] Harry Lehr, who had spent the afternoon imbibing far too much champagne, deliberately drove his motorcar "dizzily in and out of the course," straight into every pasteboard policeman, every gate, and every hedge, "hurling over all of the obstacles," and delightedly aiming at the groups of terrified onlookers, who quickly scurried out of his way to escape harm.[70] Once the competition had ended, the participants drove to a secluded beach for a picnic served by liveried footmen before returning home at midnight, with "every vehicle brilliantly illuminated with countless little glow-lights interspersed among the floral wreaths, so that the cavalcade resembled a veritable pageant of fairy chariots."[71]

Alva's eldest son, William K. Vanderbilt Jr., shared his mother's passion for motorcars and frequently added the newest models to his extensive garage. In 1904 he staged the Vanderbilt Cup Race on Long Island, an event so successful that he repeated it the following year. The novelty of the occasion drew a throng of curious members of society, who eagerly

turned out at the unfashionable hour of 6:00 A.M. to witness the proceedings. The grandstand at Jericho Turnpike was crowded with feminine spectators attired in a curious collection of garments that underscored the
novelty of the event: women in white Parisian dresses and large picture
hats stood side by side with ladies clad in sensible British tweeds or plaid
suits. Nor were the men who drove the twenty motorcars more uniform in
their choice of attire: most dressed in riding clothes more suitable to a
hunt, though William Vanderbilt had selected a black satin jacket, black
leather pants, and a pair of goggles that—if sybaritic in nature—at least
concealed the effect of the dust and smoke. At a signal, the motorcars
huffed and sped off, racing through the neighboring villages of Brookville,
Greenvale, and Lakeville at speeds approaching sixty-five miles an hour.
Inevitably, there were accidents: one American driver smashed into a telegraph pole, while another—suffering from a cracked axle—ended up
entrenched in a plowed field. The prize was ultimately taken by Frenchman
Auguste Hemery, who commented, "Someday a dozen people will be killed
if means are not found for keeping American courses free of spectators!"[72]

Accidents became more frequent as "bubbles," as these new motorcars were derisively called, began to clog the roadways, and their owners
treated them as glorified playthings. Alfred Vanderbilt made a game of
racing down Fifth Avenue, attempting to outrun the city's bicycle-
equipped police, who vainly tried to enforce a speed limit of ten miles
per hour. J. P. Morgan once ran down a woman pedestrian on Park Row
and did not even bother to stop; the city police eventually caught up with
him, but the lady in question refused to lodge a complaint when, according to one newspaper, "she learned of the wealth of the occupant in the
coupe."[73]

By far the worst offender, however, was Mamie Fish, who insisted on
driving herself, much to the peril of anyone—and anything—she encountered. Once, staying at Crossways, her house in Newport, she decided to
take a spin around her lawn, but as a contemporary magazine diligently
reported, "the automobile saw a stone wall and made for it, head on. The
automobile won, and a large section of the stone wall fell with a thud.
The motor shook itself free from the debris, and all went well for a while;

but soon the automobile proceeded to lay low a clump of choice shrubbery on the lawn. For the next half hour, Mrs. Fish had a more or less exciting time, and then came the climax. The carriage finally dashed against the steps of the villa, whereupon there was an awful, sudden stop, a crash, and a snap, and the side of the automobile gave way and the day's lesson necessarily came to an end."[74] Even with such a disastrous start, Mamie continued on, her efforts reaching a sort of farcical tragedy in New York City. While driving along the crowded streets, she was met with a pedestrian crossing the street. Mamie—whose abilities never extended to skillful motoring—simply plunged her vehicle headlong into the poor man, knocking him down and proceeding to run over him. Then she put the motorcar in reverse—presumably in an attempt to render assistance—and ran the vehicle over him a second time. Trying to remedy the situation, she put her car in gear and drove over the prostrate man for a third time. Unable to stop the vehicle, she simply sat back and let it crash into a nearby gate where, having finally stalled, she abandoned it and hailed a cab to return home, all without bothering to ask after the victim of her misadventure. Luckily, and amazingly, the man was bruised but otherwise unhurt. There was no question of any lawsuit or attempt at compensation, and he simply limped away from the scene, grateful to be alive.[75]

16

MASTERS OF THE HUDSON

To escape the confines of new york city, the wealthy turned to the European ideal and established large country houses, visited for several months each year. Although the determinedly cynical Frank Crowninshield described a country estate as "an establishment maintained by people of wealth and position who have banished from their home circle the old ideas of family life," most of the retreats carried more symbolic meanings.[1] Not only did members of Gilded Age society consciously attempt to replicate the traditions of the Old World through such estates, but they also compellingly fit into the nineteenth-century view of a romanticized and idealized nature, isolated spots where one could indulge in scenic splendors, bracing air, and recreational opportunities such as walking, riding, fishing, hunting, and sailing. Freed from the usual social concerns and the hustle of city life, they offered bucolic escapes without loss of the trappings of grandeur and the luxuries deemed so necessary to life in the Gilded Age.

Throughout the nineteenth century, the Hudson River Valley saw the emergence of dozens of impressive mansions scattered along its length. From the day Henry Hudson sailed his ship up its waters, the valley became a magnet for the wealthy, with rich Dutch settlers—patroons—establishing their estates next to land grants by the British Crown along the fertile river. Everywhere were reminders of both days past and more recent declarations: the colonial Philippsburg and Van Cortlandt manors, the early-nineteenth-century estates of the Livingston family's Clermont and the Montgomery family's Montgomery Place, Washington Irving's Gothic villa Sunnyside, and the Roosevelt family enclave at Hyde Park.[2] The lushly romantic land-scapes of Frederick Church further painted the Hudson River Valley as a place of tranquil lyricism, where wild cliffs and undisturbed bends evoked the Rhine.

If anyone could be called the master of the Hudson, it was Jay Gould, a man of legendary abilities and suspect business practices, who, more than any other, exemplified the idea of the robber baron. No other man in the Gilded Age was so feared and hated; even the New York papers referred to him as Mephistopheles. Born in 1836 to a family of impoverished farmers in the Catskills, he showed an early aptitude for business; by age fifteen, young Gould worked as a store clerk six days a week, studying books on surveying and engineering by night.[3] After a brief spell as a surveyor, he joined forces with financier Charles Leupp in a new venture, a tannery in the Pocono Mountains. A financial panic in 1857 decimated the company, and Leupp ultimately shot and killed himself, an act for which Gould was unfairly blamed by an angry, howling mob.[4]

Financier Jay Gould, about 1875.

Gould managed to salvage the business, and he used its profits to invest in a number of small railway and steamship lines; eventually he joined forces with legendary speculators Daniel Drew and Jim Fisk, and the trio embarked on a careful campaign to enhance their own riches at the expense of the Erie Railroad. Stock prices were manipulated, and hundreds of thousands of dollars of worthless shares were printed in a gamble that cost many investors, including Commodore Cornelius Vanderbilt, considerable fortunes. The war of the tycoons that followed, with Gould and Vanderbilt each bribing corrupt legislators and judges to gain the upper hand, eventually ended with a bitter truce that left Gould one of the wealthiest men in New York.[5] Gould, it was said, was the only man the equally ruthless Commodore Vanderbilt feared.[6]

In August 1869, Gould and Fisk attempted to corner the American gold market. Gould bribed President Grant's brother-in-law to obtain confidential information on his monetary policies and to try to influence the government's reaction. The result was a panic—Black Friday—on September 24, 1869, when the value of gold sharply plummeted and many investors suffered enormous financial losses.[7] Gould survived the disaster: indeed, he had secretly unloaded his gold shares, suspecting an impending crisis, and in the process made another $11 million ($220 million in 2008), but at the expense of what remained of his good name. Gould went on to help establish the dominance of the Union Pacific Railway, and of Western Union, whose operation he both disrupted and enhanced, leaving him with a fortune of some $80 million ($1.6 billion in 2008), but his business deals, manipulations, and uncanny knack for always getting the better of his opponents forever ruined his reputation, and thereafter Gould was widely regarded as one of the most hated men in America.[8]

This was not entirely fair. Gould, noted one of his biographers, "enjoyed the worst press of any American of his era. Reporters disliked him because he spoke little and said less. When he did speak it was either to advance some purpose of his own or to trick reporters into thinking he had answered their questions when in fact he had evaded them."[9] He was popularly believed, commented one contemporary newspaper, to be "a hard, crafty, bloodless being, with as little graciousness as a wire mousetrap."[10] In 1884 one newspaper decreed: "Mr. Gould's god is his pocket, to fill which he has prostituted every attribute with which he is endowed. Like the Ishmaelite of old, his hand is against every man, and every man's hand is against him. Those who have ventured to look upon him in the light of a friend have invariably found, sooner or later, that they had taken unto their bosom a serpent whose string is death."[11]

Gould's enemies were numerous, and he is said to have distrusted personal friendships. Polite society—and, indeed, any other society—had no use for him, and despite his vast wealth, Gould remained an outcast in New York City. Some shunned him in the mistaken belief that he was a Jew; in fact, the anti-Semitism of the times had not precluded others, notably banker August Belmont, from social acceptance, but Gould lacked the latter's polished manner and willingness to play the game of social niceties.[12] Gould was ostracized precisely because he was ruthless in his business and made no secret of the fact. Even Alva Vanderbilt, from her relatively new and uncertain position of social challenger, once remarked airily, "We never knew the Goulds."[13]

In contrast to Gould's stern public reputation, in his private life he was a quiet, almost shy man. Short and thin, he sported a neatly trimmed beard. He was a dedicated bibliophile, spending his evenings devouring the latest works on a wide variety of subjects, including history, travel, geography, politics, and economics.[14] Gould was conservative in manners and morals; he did not drink or smoke, and owing to constant trouble with his digestion, he ate only the simplest of foods.[15] His passions lay in his family, his books, and his gardening. "Mr. Gould," commented one newspaper, "loves flowers. He cultivates them for the sake of their fragrance and beauty. It is said that he knows not only the common and botanical name of every plant in his extensive greenhouse, but also its exact significance in the vocabulary of sentiment."[16]

Gould's true delight was his family. "To admiring outsiders, including even Jay's harshest critics," wrote Maury Klein, "the Goulds embodied ideals of domestic bliss to a degree that put Victorian convention to shame."[17] He was devoted to his wife, Helen Day Miller, the daughter of a wealthy New York City greengrocer. He married her in 1863, and the couple had six children: George, born in 1864; Edwin, born in 1866;

Helen, born in 1868; Howard, born in 1871; Anna, born in 1875; and Frank, born in 1877. These children were brought up in the suitably baronial splendor of America's most lavish Gothic Revival castle, Lyndhurst, rising over the Hudson at Tarrytown, some twenty miles north of New York City.

Gould came to this exceptionally romantic house, with its crenellations, towers, latticed and stained-glass windows, and deep bays, by accident. By the 1870s, his reputation had not only made him a social pariah in New York City, but also had led to frequent threats that Gould felt endangered his family. Private detectives shadowed his children and paced the sidewalk outside of the Gould house at 579 Fifth Avenue day and night to prevent any incidents, but Jay and Helen decided that the family would be safer in more secluded surroundings, where they could be more easily protected.[18] In 1878 they found Lyndhurst, and obtained a two-year lease before finally purchasing the 550-acre estate in 1880 for some $250,000 ($5 million in 2008).[19] It was quiet and secluded, yet close enough to the city that Gould could sail on his steam yacht from its private dock down the Hudson to his office each morning to attend to business.[20]

The main facade of Lyndhurst, Jay Gould's Hudson River estate.

Lyndhurst began life as Knoll, a villa designed in 1838 by architect Alexander Jackson Davis for General William Paulding, a former mayor of New York, atop a cliff overlooking the Hudson River. Davis, born in New York City in 1803, was one of the foremost proponents of the Gothic Revival style, which had taken hold in Great Britain, popularized by Horace Walpole in his estate Strawberry Hill, and had later spread its influence across Europe. Author Washington Irving's own little Gothic villa lay just down the road from Lyndhurst, and the style, with its asymmetrical character and references to medieval architecture, was thought particularly well suited to the rugged wilds of the Hudson.[21] With its turrets, solid masonry, and evocations of a baronial past, the Gothic Revival offered an expressive presence whose aura of permanence seemed charged with the respectability of centuries of power.

Paulding's original house, as conceived by Davis, was a relatively small, ornately decorated villa with Gothic arches and crenellated gables.[22] In 1864, wealthy merchant George Merritt purchased the estate and commissioned Davis to greatly enlarge the structure, which he renamed Lyndhurst.[23] Davis doubled the size of the existing house, adding a tall, dominant tower and a large wing to the north and raising the central portion of the older structure to accommodate additional rooms.[24] The integration of the old with the new, using the same materials and duplicating the same external elements, was so seamless that the finished, thirty-room structure remained cohesive, "almost," noted one historian, "as if Davis had had the full design in mind from the very start, and had only been waiting for the advent of an even wealthier and more ambitious patron to complete it."[25]

A set of wrought-iron gates, flanked by a gatehouse in the Second Empire style that was manned around the clock to guard against unwelcome intrusions, gave entrance to the estate.[26] Under Merritt, landscape architect Ferdinand Mangold had expanded and improved the grounds, planting clumps of trees and creating artificial mounds dotting the wide lawns to carefully restrict views of the mansion from the sweeping drive to create a heightened sense of drama. Screens of trees also shielded a large, two-storey stable and carriage house; several small cottages for servants; a dock and a boathouse at the bottom of the hillside along the

Hudson; a playhouse known as Rose Cottage for the children; and a kennel where Gould kept seventy-five St. Bernard dogs. Most remarkable of Mangold's additions, however, was the greenhouse, a nearly four-hundred-foot-long, E-shaped structure adjoining a rose garden just north of the house. The largest private greenhouse in the world, it was crowned with a hundred-foot-high iron and glass cupola and onion dome that served as an aviary; when it burned in 1880, Gould had it rebuilt in the Gothic style.[27] Here the feared Gould pottered among his flowers, taking pride in what was said to be the world's largest collection of 8,000 rare orchids, 2,000 azaleas, and more than 250 varieties of exotic palms gathered from around the world.[28]

Eventually the tree-shaded drive revealed the house itself: an asymmetrical structure of light gray Sing-Sing marble bristling with parapets, gables, arches, oriel windows, and towers.[29] Arcaded piazzas stretched to either side of a monumental porte cochere topped with crenellations, while above, arched windows set with elaborately carved stone tracery framed leaded panes and panels of stained glass to lend a suitably medieval atmosphere. Yet even here the rare visitor could find evidence of Gould's familial dedication, as here stood an overtly sentimental statue depicting his two young daughters. A three-storey, crenellated tower on the eastern side encased the grand staircase, overshadowed by a hundred-foot-high, five-storey tower topped with stepped parapets overlooking the Hudson to the west. Every aspect of the house was seductively evocative, with trefoil windows, projecting gables, massed chimneystacks, carved pinnacles,

The ruins of Jay Gould's immense greenhouse at Lyndhurst.

and stepped medieval buttresses, making Lyndhurst quite unlike any other mansion of the Gilded Age.[30]

If the exterior was all monochromatic sobriety, Lyndhurst's interior offered vibrant bursts of unexpected color and life. Wrought-iron and glass doors opened from a vestibule, created when Davis glassed in the former porte cochere, to a heroic world of medieval artifice and quiet, insistent power.[31] In his interiors, Davis deployed an extensive array of colored scagliola, lavish marble, rich fabrics, carved paneling, and ornamental ceiling beams to create a theatrical fantasy. Increasing the coherence of the rooms, the architect also had designed a number of ornately carved chairs and tables, their forms awash with intricate spires to echo the baronial atmosphere that permeated the mansion.[32] The tone was set in the entrance hall, where an arched, ribbed ceiling resting on sculpted corbels topped walls faced in rich, ocher-colored scagliola. A floor of white marble inset with black tiles reinforced a solemn, almost austere quality found throughout the house.[33]

It was a measure of Davis's genius that he worked great contrasts throughout the house, offering surprises and a diversity of experiences at every turn. The somewhat cold impression of the entrance hall was almost immediately dispelled on entering the drawing room to the south. This was a curious amalgam of the medieval with the Victorian, with rich gold silk wall hangings between slender, trefoil-shaped pilasters; from their carved corbels sprouted a tendril of delicate ribs that stretched across the arched, vaulted ceiling. Leaded, diamond-paned French doors, topped with arched lunettes of stained glass to wash the room with color, opened to an arcade that fringed the room on three sides; on the fourth wall, twin chimneypieces of stark white marble added a balancing note of restraint. A large cupid of shimmering marble dominated an alcove formed by the bay window, flanked by sofas and chairs designed in the aesthetic style, cabinets displaying pieces of porcelain, and a forest of potted palms atop Turkish and bearskin rugs strewn across the inlaid parquet floor.[34] It was luxurious and warm, yet remained true to the architect's original vision, invoking a spirit of heroic days long past.

The adjoining reception room offered yet another contrast to the chill formality of the predominant medieval while successfully maintaining its influence. Elaborate leaded- and stained-glass windows dominated the western wall, below a ceiling whose ribbed beams carried brilliantly painted depictions of Raphael's *Hours*. Heavy, overstuffed, and fringed chairs introduced Victorian comfort, but the centerpiece of the room was a carved organ, whose deep chords echoed sonorously throughout the cavernous halls.[35] Gould worked in his office at a magnificent Wooten Patent desk, a marvel of innumerable compartments and swinging doors, beneath a trompe l'oeil ceiling adorned with gilded quatrefoils; in his library he relaxed with the latest books selected from Gothic-style cases fringing the walls and reclined in an elaborately carved chair by Davis, from which he could look through the leaded-glass windows to the Hudson below.[36]

In the corridor, Davis returned to the intimidating medieval, with unadorned walls of ashlar stone rising to a vaulted ceiling that evoked the atmosphere of a forgotten cloister. This rather stark hall led to yet another surprising burst of opulence: the new dining room, added for Merritt at the northern end of the house. The most elaborate of all Lyndhurst's rooms, this was another curious mixture of Gothic detail with high Victorian taste. Bays of arched, stained-glass windows on its eastern and western ends washed the room with light, sending fiery prisms across walls hung in vibrant raspberry-colored paper stenciled in gold. Carved corbels and scagliola columns, painted to resemble heavily veined black marble, upheld an intricately ribbed wooden ceiling; a chimneypiece of red marble, niches filled with white marble sculptures, and elaborately carved chairs covered in aqua-colored leather added visual contrast, combining to form a room of rich, dark textiles enlivened with dramatic bursts of color.[37]

On the second floor, directly over the reception room and extending out above its columned arcade, Davis had transformed the old library into an art gallery. Walls painted to resemble blocks of ashlar offered a neutral backdrop to Gould's extraordinary collection of nineteenth-century European and American paintings, including works by Courbet, Bouguereau, Rousseau, and Corot. Despite the subdued tones of the walls and the persistence of the canvases, it was a room of extraordinary light, rising two storeys to a forest of carved wooden beams and buttresses supporting an arched ceiling pierced by two cupolas. An enormous arched, mullioned window set with stained-glass panels by Tiffany and topped by a matching lunette in the western gable offered dramatic views over the Hudson by day; at night, two immense iron chandeliers set with incandescent electric bulbs bathed the gallery in a soft, welcoming glow.[38] At night, the feared Gould slept in an immense carved Gothic Revival bed beneath a vaulted ceiling of amazing spatial complexity, in the splendor of his baronial mansion as the Catskill storms swept down the valley and thundered against the leaded-glass windows.[39]

"Lyndhurst," wrote Maury Klein, "was not merely a fairytale castle for Gould but also a fortress against a hostile world. Millionaires were always choice prey for cranks and extortionists and Gould's unpopularity made him a prime target." Continuous threats made Gould uneasy and suspicious. The assassinations in 1881 of Tsar Alexander II and President James A. Garfield underscored the unwelcome fact that great wealth and position were no guarantees of safety.[40] Thus Gould never worked late and always made a point of returning to Lyndhurst from New York City to spend the evenings with his wife and children.[41] One relative recalled him as "exceedingly quiet. His words were both few and carefully chosen. He was perfectly poised, always.... I never once saw him give way to anger."[42] When his beloved wife, Helen, died in 1889, Jay was desolate with grief, and his health steadily declined. He suffered from insomnia, indigestion, heart palpitations, and incipient tuberculosis; at night he could often be found outside, wandering up and down beneath the light of the moon, spitting blood into a handkerchief.[43] His oldest daughter, Helen, nursed him through the long, painful, final months of his illness. In one quiet moment he confessed that he was not afraid to die but "hated to leave the younger children" behind as orphans.[44] Finally, fate caught up with the Mephistopheles of Wall Street, and he died on December 2, 1892, at age fifty-six, surrounded by his children. His death made headlines, but few outside of his own family mourned his passing. "Ten Thousand ruined men will curse the dead man's memory," declared *the New York World*, summing up what many in the city must have felt.[45]

As different as imagination could conceive and proudly owned by the social antithesis of the enigmatic Jay Gould, the Mills mansion commanded

The Mills mansion along the Hudson, entrance facade.

a 334-acre estate farther up the Hudson River. In 1888 the coldly elegant and ambitious Ruth Mills inherited the Staatsburg property, purchased nearly a hundred years earlier by her great-grandfather Morgan Lewis. Lewis, who married a Livingston of Clermont, had erected a twenty-five-room, Greek Revival–style mansion, but it was obviously unsuited to the needs of a nineteenth-century family.[46] In 1895 Ruth therefore commissioned McKim, Mead, & White to renovate and enlarge the house into a setting more appropriate to her social position. Her only request was that Stanford White, who took charge of the project, retain the old house as the core of any new construction. This presented numerous challenges. White duly enlarged several existing rooms, but he was forced to add new wings to the north and south to achieve the desired results, in the process doubling the size of the house.[47]

White's new building dominated a tranquil stretch of park, its sloping lawns dotted with classical statuary and banks of trees that screened the house from a meandering drive. The visual impact was therefore all the more dramatic when a final turn revealed a neoclassical mansion of the lightest gray stone, a perfect interpretation of an English country house glistening in an artfully conceived Elysian landscape that consciously evoked an unalterable sense of refined privilege. The facade was all that Ruth had wanted, an overpowering building adorned with Corinthian pilasters, sculpted swags and reliefs, and an ornamental balustrade. Though refined, there was nothing subtle about the structure: at the center of the eastern facade, the architect built an immense and intimidating temple portico said to have been modeled on the north portico of the White House, its entablature supported by six massive Corinthian columns. By the time White had finished, the original Greek Revival house had been completely subsumed into a new, sixty-five-room mansion designed to convey entrenched power and sublime taste.[48]

Within, White designed new, elaborate public rooms, arranged *en enfilade* to provide sweeping vistas from one end of the house to the other, to accommodate the grand entertainments at which Ruth excelled. Two rooms in the old central block were gutted to create a suitably impressive entrance hall, designed in the English style with walls paneled in quartered oak adorned with a gallery of portraits of Livingston ancestors alternating with eighteenth-century Gobelin tapestries; a massive, L-shaped staircase with finely turned wooden balusters swept up to the second floor, beneath a ceiling brimming with dancing cherubs against a cloud-strewn sky.[49] To the south was the drawing room, spanning the full width of the house. Created when White combined two existing rooms, it suffered from the relatively low, twelve-foot ceilings prevalent in the old house. Because raising the ceiling height would intrude into the corridors above, White was forced to work within these proportions, made more claustrophobic by the room's immense length. Attempting to break up the monotony, White added a bowed window overlooking the west terrace and faced the pale blue walls with delicate molding to add visual interest, but the result, crowded by Ruth with elaborately carved and gilded Louis XVI–style sofas and chairs covered in floral tapestry, remained starkly at odds with the regal aspirations of the rest of the house.[50]

White placed the two most important rooms in his new wings, where he could take advantage of appropriately high ceilings and numerous windows to create the desired effect. At the southwestern end of the house was the library. Designed by Jules Allard of Paris, this was a lofty, fifty-foot-long room with paneled walls of carved, quarter-sawn oak adorned with ormolu reliefs. Six-foot-high glass-fronted bookcases filled with elegantly bound but rarely read volumes edged the walls, flanked by Corinthian pilasters with gilded capitals supporting a carved and gilded cornice decorated with reliefs of telescopes, nautical charts, and compasses.[51] It was all coldly splendid and suitably impressive. At the opposite end of the house, a small, elaborately decorated oval reception room opened to the new dining room, created by Allard as the mansion's most opulent space. Echoing the proportions of the library and modeled on the state apartments of Louis XIV at Versailles, this was an overt triumph of irrational display over practical function. Walls sheathed in blue-gray Italian marble reinforced the atmosphere of formal austerity, their monochromatic sobriety contrasting with Flemish tapestries encased in gilded fillets and pilasters topped by rich Corinthian capitals. Even the chimneypiece, composed of contrasting marbles set with gilded mounts, offered a monumental statement, its elaborate scrolls rising to a cornice where golden rocailles, garlands, and cherubs fought for primacy.[52]

Ruth's private apartments in the southeastern corner of the first floor continued the decorative allusions to Versailles. A rococo-style boudoir, its cream-colored walls graced with gilded boiseries and a cornice, evoked the specter of Marie Antoinette, a theme made even more apparent when one passed through mirrored doors into Ruth's Louis XVI–style bedroom.[53] Here, personal presence was sacrificed for a triumphant celebration of seductive power. Dramatic raspberry silk damask panels hung in ivory-colored fillets framed by boiseries carved with sumptuous rocailles and garlands, creating an overwhelming impression of opulence. The same silk damask draped an enormously tall canopy that floated over the bed like an exquisite baldachin, its corners adorned with finials of gathered ostrich plumes.[54] It was an immense secular altar to the idea of the ancien régime, given substance in this Palladian-inspired mansion set in the middle of a classical English park on the wild banks of the Hudson.

Ogden and Ruth Mills generally came to Staatsburg in the fall and remained until the beginning of the New Year, looked after by a butler, footmen, valet, cooks, and maids, who ensured that the house operated flawlessly.[55] In these months there was hunting, shooting, and fishing; riding and coaching on the estate; an occasional boating excursion on the river; and—when winter fell—ice skating on the frozen ponds. In the middle of December a massive tree was erected in the hall, its top rising into the stairwell above. The enlarged mansion was enshrined in all of its gilded glory as Bellomont, the distinguished country seat of the Trenor family, by Edith Wharton in her novel *The House of Mirth*.

If Jay Gould was the shadowy master of the Hudson, and Ruth Mills its frosty queen, Frederick Vanderbilt was its sunny squire. Born in 1856, he graduated from the Sheffield School of Engineering at Yale—the only one of William Henry's four sons to graduate from college—and after the death of his brother Cornelius took control of the family's interests.[56] As director of the New York Central Railroad, he managed through shrewd acumen to transform his $10 million ($200 million in 2008) inheritance into a legacy of $72.5 million ($1.5 billion in 2008).[57] One contemporary described him as "of medium height, a somewhat spare figure, with slightly reddish hair and small mustache, and rather sallow complexion. He is passionately devoted to yachting, and finds his chief pleasure in outdoor sports, caring little or nothing for society." Frederick was, he added, "considered by his associates a thoroughly good fellow, entirely devoid of any snobbishness or nonsense."[58] He was also a great favorite within the Vanderbilt family, "a pleasant, gentle, overly shy person,"

Frederick Vanderbilt.

recalled one younger relative, noted for being "quiet spoken, in no way aggressive, in fact, notably timid."[59]

But all was not quite so proper in the life of "Uncle Fred," as his nieces and nephews called their redheaded relative. In 1878, twenty-two-year-old Fred embarked on an affair with the beautiful Louise Torrance. Not only was she twelve years older than her lover, but also at the time she was in the process of divorcing his cousin Daniel for desertion after six months of marriage. The resulting liaison scandalized the Vanderbilts, but Fred and Louise were desperately in love; as soon as she was free, they quietly married on December 17, 1878, in the Windsor Hotel in New York. His family only learned of the deed three months later.[60]

Hoping to bring his family around to acceptance, Fred launched on an elaborate bit of deception. Within a few months Louise had grown notice-ably larger, and Fred announced she was expecting, thinking that this might win his family's approval. The couple sailed off to Europe; then came a cable from Paris announcing that Louise had given birth to a still-born son. The loss won the couple much sympathy, but it had all been a charade. Fred and Louise had concocted the story, stuffing her gowns with increasingly larger pillows as the "pregnancy" progressed, then invented the child's birth and tragic death to explain his absence on their return to America. Neither Fred nor his "Lulu" was conniving enough to quite carry off the charade, but when the Vanderbilts discovered the truth, they uncharacteristically took pity on the couple and welcomed Louise into the family.[61]

On his father's death Frederick inherited his old house in New York (his mother, Louisa, continued to occupy the magnificent palace at 640 Fifth Avenue), but, disliking society, Fred bought some six hundred acres in the village of Hyde Park on the recommendation of his friend Ogden Mills and in 1895 commissioned McKim, Mead, & White to create an estate fit for a Vanderbilt.[62] Sprawled along the eastern bank of the Hudson, the property had formerly belonged to Colonel Walter Langdon and his wife, Dorothy, daughter of John Jacob Astor. In 1845, after the original house burned, the Langdons replaced it with a Greek Revival–style mansion.[63] Although of modest size, the house suited Fred, and at first he envisioned only minor renovations. Charles McKim, who was responsible for the design, found that the structure was in a bad state—"so bad," McKim wrote, "that it seemed foolish to attempt to build anything on it." Fred was disappointed, but he insisted that any new construction closely follow the arrangement of the Langdon house, much to his wife's displeasure. "There has been a good deal of a fight to do this," McKim reported, "because when it was found the old house had to come down, Mrs. Vanderbilt kicked over the traces and was disposed to build an English house as she called it."[64] Construction of the new house began in September 1896; the steel-framed shell was completed in 1898, but it took another two years—and a reputed $1.9 million ($43.7 million in 2008)—for interior fittings and decoration, and landscaping of the grounds.[65]

From the Albany Post Road, wrought-iron gates opened to a heavily wooded park, originally designed by Belgian André Parmentier in a carefully contrived series of highly romanticized, arcadian scenes, with large, open lawns framed by a fringe of trees.[66] Fred added formal gardens in the Italian style south of the residence, their colorful, sunken parterres centered on fountains and reflecting pools and ornamented with classical statuary and urns.[67] A sweeping drive curved through dense groves of elms, Norwegian spruce, beech, and Japanese maples, past stretches of meadow, and over neoclassical bridges spanning small creeks before reaching the house at the end of a vast lawn.[68]

McKim had created a palace of gray Indiana limestone that mingled elements of the Italianate, Greek Revival, and neoclassical with Beaux Arts sensibilities. Of two principal storeys atop a raised basement, with a third floor nestled above a stringcourse, the mansion was a dignified structure whose clean lines and restraint echoed the character of its owner. McKim adorned the facade with fluted pilasters, carved swags, and a classical balustrade, elongating the structure with double-height porticoes of Corinthian columns at its northern and southern ends. The main, eastern facade was almost severe in its decoration, but McKim graced the building's western side with a dramatic, almost sensual two-storey, semicircular columned portico offering fine views over the Hudson to the distant Catskills.[69]

The house itself was small by Vanderbilt standards; with fifty-four rooms, it was yet intimate, the interiors carried out in Italian Renaissance designs and filled with antiques gathered during Fred and Louise's

The main entrance facade of the Frederick Vanderbilt mansion at Hyde Park.

European travels.[70] At its center lay an elliptical hall designed by Stanford White, with cream-colored walls ornamented by Doric pilasters of gray-green Italian marble above a terrazzo floor. French doors opening to the semicircular portico flanked a massive Italian marble chimneypiece supported by carved caryatids and hung with a seventeenth-century tapestry depicting the Medici family coat of arms; above, an octagonal well ringed by a stone balustrade pierced the ceiling and rose to a skylight that bathed the room in soft light. Furnished as an informal gathering spot, the hall was filled with comfortable overstuffed sofas and high-backed chairs, potted palms, and bearskin rugs to soften the rather formal architectural detail.[71]

Smaller rooms, opening off of the oval hall, occupied each of the four corners of the central block. The most formal was a rococo reception room, its cream-colored walls hung in Aubusson tapestry panels framed by elaborately carved and gilded boiseries. The room's most distinctive feature, however, was above: a painted ceiling depicting a bare-breasted woman riding in a gold chariot, surrounded by other nude women dancing among the white horses, believed to be the work of American artist Edward Simmons.[72] The brazen nudity apparently proved too much for the rather prim Fred, and he later had the ceiling whitewashed.[73]

More dramatic was Fred's library. Used as an informal sitting room, this was a fairly small space of remarkably lavish decoration. Designed by Georges Glaenzer, a French émigré who often worked with McKim, Mead, & White, it was executed in a vaguely Renaissance style, dark and vibrant with contrasting colors and textures. Panels of Santo Domingo mahogany, elaborately carved by Swiss artisans, fringed the lower walls; above them, Glaenzer deployed murals replicating Flemish tapestries alternating with stretches of deep aqua-colored Venetian plaster. Mahogany columns and buttresses framed the walls, supporting an elaborate ceiling of traceried ribs and beams of plaster richly painted in golden tones to simulate wood. Sofas and chairs covered in embroidered green damask flanked an ocher-colored marble chimneypiece, its mantel adorned with a Staffordshire clock and matching candelabra, wedding presents to Fred and Louise from William Henry Vanderbilt.[74]

McKim used the elliptical hall to create a great axial vista within the house that linked its principal rooms. At the southern end was the drawing room, fifty feet long and thirty feet wide, balanced at the northern end by a dining room of identical size. Paneled in Circassian walnut adorned with gilded reliefs, the drawing room was dominated by two large, white marble chimneypieces from Italy flanking French doors to the southern portico. The ceiling, encased by heavily carved and gilded cornices and beams, originally featured murals that the couple later deemed too ornate and removed. Four large seventeenth-century Florentine tapestries, depicting the Trojan War and purchased in France by Stanford White for the room, added notes of color and visual interest to the walls, their tones echoed in the upholstery of the elaborately carved Louis XV–style sofas and armchairs. In one corner stood a gilded Steinway piano adorned with medallion portraits of famous composers, originally commissioned for William Henry Vanderbilt.[75]

Rich, dark walnut also paneled the walls of the dining room, accented with gilded reliefs, fluted pilasters with golden Ionic capitals, and carved lunettes set above the windows. Two Ionic columns of Cippolini marble flanked the main entrance, matching a pair found in the drawing room, while two antique carved Italian Renaissance chimneypieces dominated the northern wall. A large walnut table, ringed by gilded bronze Florentine chairs covered in floral crimson velvet to match the elaborate curtains at the windows, occupied the center of the room, with a smaller table set off to the side for informal dinners; above, an elaborate, seventeenth-century ceiling of carved and gilded coffers was inset with Italian murals. It was all quite splendid, but apparently too much so for Fred, who, on seeing the finished room, asked that some of the gilding details be removed.[76]

Just off the elliptical hall, a marble staircase rose between a balustrade of finely worked metal adorned with bronze medallions to the second floor.[77] Here, in addition to a number of rooms for guests, Fred and Louise each had exquisitely decorated suites over the drawing room. For Fred's bedroom in the southwestern corner, Glaenzer had turned to the splendors of Venice for his inspiration. Columns and panels of carved Circassian walnut ornamented with gilt foliage framed seventeenth-century Flemish tapestries depicting the Garden of Eden; above stretched a ceiling crossed with an intricate network of walnut ribs and beams. A pair of massive, twisted columns wrapped in spirals of gilded leaves framed a bed carved with Gothic arches and spires, set beneath a canopy and hanging of crimson damask elaborately embroidered in gold thread.[78]

If Fred's bedroom was all dark magnificence and subdued colors, Louise's bedroom, in the southeastern corner, offered a stunning, dramatic contrast. Designed by Ogden Codman, this was an attempt, as Lionel and Ottalie Williams noted, "to reproduce the essentials of a queen's bedroom in the Louis XV–period style in all its lavish adornment."[79] Walls of light gray sprouted extravagant gilded boiseries interrupted by pilasters with gilded Corinthian capitals supporting a carved cornice highlighted in gold. A bowed screen of Corinthian columns and an ornamental *ruelle*, or balustrade, separated the bed from the rest of the room in the French manner; family members offered the risqué joke that whenever Fred wanted to visit Louise, he had to deposit a quarter in the railing to gain admission.[80] To contrast with the quiet gray of the rest of the room, Codman hung the bed alcove in hand-embroidered peach damask, providing an appropriately rich backdrop for the canopied bed, which was draped in matching gold-embroidered silk.[81]

Fred and Louise lived quietly at Hyde Park, retreating there at the end of New York City's social season and returning in the fall.[82] Louise would have enjoyed the parties and balls given by her sisters-in-law, but Fred made a point of being in bed by ten each night. Instead she indulged growing passions for astrology, the Christian Science movement, and a love of powerful, historical women. She had an intense interest in Marie Antoinette and Empress Josephine, and often could be found enraptured by biographies of one of her idols.[83] Royalty fascinated her. "When I go driving I do my mental exercises," she once explained. "First I do the kings and queens of England, forward and backward, with their dates, then I do the presidents of this country, forward and backward, with their dates, and sometimes if I take a long drive I get as far as the kings and queens of France."[84] She also became a renowned philanthropist, especially to the children of her servants and to families who lived near the estate, sending groceries and coal, and providing doctors and nurses free of charge to attend to the medical needs of those who could not afford proper care. Each Christmas, wrapped in her thick sable coat, she rode through Hyde Park in a sleigh that had once belonged to Catherine the Great, distributing money and gifts to the less fortunate. She always had a smile, and even delighted in the children's efforts to pelt her with snowballs and snatch the wig from her head.[85]

Fred enjoyed his role as squire of his Hyde Park estate; every morning he rode around the grounds and visited the barns, where he kept Belgian draft horses and a herd of prize-winning Jersey cows that garnered most of his attention and won him numerous prizes at the local Dutchess County Fair.[86] But he was so shy that he would run and hide in his own garden if he saw anyone approaching.[87] He despised his time in New York, when he was forced to deal with family business, though he often could be found strolling along Fifth Avenue, gazing into shop windows. He always carried a checkbook with a $3 million ($63 million in 2008) balance, "just in case I see something I want to buy," he once explained.[88]

Ironically, of all of these Hudson River enclaves, that of the Astors was the most sedate. In the 1850s, William Backhouse Astor II had purchased some twelve hundred acres along the river at Rhinebeck as a country estate, where he could escape the ritualized formality of New York society. Over the years that followed, he developed the property, which he called Ferncliff, adding an enormous agricultural complex. This included an immense dairy with a seventy-foot-high steeple, barns, stables, a smithy, a poultry barn, and a covered racetrack, all executed in a picturesque Tudor style, with half-timbered and stone walls and thatched roofs. Here William could follow the breeding of his cattle and his racehorses, away from the constraints of his wife's social calendar.[89]

A small Gothic-style gatehouse and a menacing set of wrought-iron gates protected a drive that meandered through groves of trees and past gardens adorned with ornamental statuary to the mansion perched above the Hudson. Designed in the Italianate style and ringed by a wide piazza, it was a sprawling building of two principal storeys, with an attic floor tucked beneath the bracketed cornice and a low, hipped roof punctuated by a tall tower. A stone porte cochere opened to a sixty-foot-long hall that gave access to the succession of drawing rooms, reception rooms, the library, and the dining room. Because Caroline Astor so rarely came to Ferncliff, the house reflected her husband's tastes: dark woodwork, heavily carved furniture, bearskin rugs, mounted hunting trophies, and paintings of his favorite racehorses.[90]

When William died in 1892, his only son, Jack, inherited the estate. Caroline had never liked Ferncliff and had spent as little time as possible there, but the exceedingly shy Jack thrived in this isolated environment, and even built a small laboratory, where he could conduct his experiments.[91] Colonel William Mann recorded Jack's time at Ferncliff in his fawning volume *Fads and Fancies:* "What with the breeding stables established by his father, his droves of rare cattle, flocks of sheep, acres of fertile meadow and woodland, his gardens and his orchard, he approaches the English squire as nearly as such a thing is possible in the Republic that he loves."[92]

Jack's most important addition to Ferncliff was an immense pleasure casino. Plans were first discussed in 1898, but it was not until 1902 that he finally commissioned Stanford White to design the pavilion. Originally conceived as a kind of glorified playhouse for adults, the building expanded to encompass an enclosed swimming pool, an indoor tennis court, two squash courts, a library, a steam room, a billiard room, a living hall, dressing rooms for ladies and for gentlemen, five bedrooms, bathrooms, a kitchen, and rooms for servants, making it a mansion in its own right. Jack had not wished for anything quite so large, and difficulties over the scale led to a temporary feud between patron and architect, White admitting that he was "not on architectural speaking terms" with Astor "owing to the rumpus over their athletic courts at Rhinebeck."[93] In a moment of candor, White declared that he understand why people referred to his patron as "Jack Ass."[94] Eventually, however, difficulties were smoothed over, and the casino was completed in 1904.

White's casino was every bit as grand as any palace erected on Fifth Avenue. He modeled the structure on the Grand Trianon at Versailles, repeating the rows of arched windows and Ionic pilasters, and including an allusion to the central, recessed loggia in the white limestone facade.[95] The library, living hall, and billiard rooms followed neoclassical designs inspired by Robert Adam, with leaded-glass domes, marble chimneypieces, and ranks of ornamental Corinthian pilasters framing walls decorated with elaborate moldings. The neoclassical swimming pool, lined in white tile and marble, was lighted by tall plate-glass windows, but the casino's central feature was a two-hundred-foot-long tennis court set beneath an arched ceiling whose canvas panels could be opened to the sky in warm weather.[96] Some $238,000 (approximately $5 million in 2008) was expended on this exquisite plaything, offering mute testament to the extremes—and expenses—to which society would go to seek temporary relief from the gilded monotony of their lives.[97]

17

"THE INLAND NEWPORT"

WHEN THE EASE OF RAIL TRAVEL left previously exclusive destinations such as Saratoga Springs subject to the inroads of unwelcome parvenus and people of moderate means, society began to look elsewhere for its summer pleasures. Some sought refuge along the Hudson River Valley or enjoyed the bracing air of Maine's Mount Desert Island. In the last years of the nineteenth century, members of Gilded Age society also invaded the gently rolling Berkshires in Massachusetts. The Berkshires attracted a wealthy set, though not a particularly fashionable one: most of those who swept into the old colonial villages of Lenox and Stockbridge were merchants and members of the nouveau riche, whose recent fortunes and lack of ancestral pedigrees barred them from complete acceptance elsewhere. Though they termed the area "the inland Newport," the Berkshires were never as sophisticated as that famed Atlantic resort. Boston patrician Frank Crowninshield, whose family often spent holidays there, called the area "dull and dowdy, but full of genteel old families in reduced circumstances who are willing to unbend—if properly propitiated."[1]

What the Berkshires did offer was an ostensible escape from the demands of Gilded Age society. Authors such as Nathaniel Hawthorne,

Henry Wadsworth Longfellow, and Herman Melville had gone there in the first half of the nineteenth century, but it was not until the 1880s that members of Gilded Age society discovered the area's charms. It was the unspoiled, rural nature of the setting, nestled in the protective mountains of western Massachusetts and abundant with pastoral forests and farms, that drew attention. If Newport was all glittering palazzos and endless parties, the Berkshires harkened back to a simpler time; here the emphasis was on the beauty of the surroundings, the rolling hills that burned with color in the summer, the thick forests that erupted into fiery bursts of fall foliage, and the unperturbed spirit of the people who had lived here for decades.

"When we first went to Lenox," recalled Mrs. Burton Harrison, "the lovely hill village had not parted with its old time characteristics of unpretending hospitality. The people who met there, summer after summer, were of the cultured and refined class of American society, knowing each other intimately, and satisfied to exchange simple entertainments in their pretty picturesque homes. . . . I lived there long enough to see a mighty change. The rural hillsides and pastures, bought up at fabulous prices, were made the sites of modern villas, most of them handsome and in good taste. The villas were succeeded by little palaces, some repeating the facades and gardens of royal dwellings abroad. Instead of the trim maidservants appearing in caps and aprons to open doors, one was confronted by lackeys in livery lounging in the halls. Caviar and *mousse aux truffes* supplanted muffins and waffles. Worth and Callot gowns, cut low and worn with abundant jewels, took the place of dainty muslins made by a little day dressmaker. Stables were filled with costly horses, farmyards with stock bearing pedigrees sometimes longer than that of the owner; the dinner hour moved on to eight o'clock, and lastly came house parties, weekends, and the eternal honk and reek of the motorcar."[2]

To accommodate these new arrivals, Lenox developed a coterie of exclusive establishments, including a gentlemen's club, a coaching club, and an archery club. Gradually the influx of society overtook the town, and the decades of church socials, informal picnics, charity bazaars, and ladies' teas were supplanted by more fashionable diversions. "Horse shows and gymkhanas replaced the customary livestock fairs," wrote one visitor, "and

intricate garden parties became a part of regular life. Tents shielded beautifully laid tea tables as elegantly attired ladies and gentlemen crossed
Oriental carpets laid across the grass to partake of refreshments. Tables
draped in crisp white damask held salads, an array of cold chicken, grouse,
and turkey, pâtés de foie gras, tongue sandwiches, salmon mousse, pastries and cakes, punches, champagnes, and iced lemonades, all dispensed
by servants in immaculate liveries."[3]

The principal events of the Lenox season included the horse show and
the Berkshire Hunt. "Lawn tennis parties and archery parties were also
fashionable pastimes," recalled one visitor, "as were boating excursions
on the nearby lakes, and leisurely strolls through the encompassing dense
forests. In the fall there were shoots for grouse and quail, and stalking
for deer, and highly organized hunts that epitomized the Gilded Age idea
of aristocratic leisure, with the men in hunting pink and the ladies in
their long, tight skirts and habits, chasing across the fields on misty
mornings."[4] The season always ended in September with an event
dubbed the Tub Parade, a lengthy procession of carriages, landaus, and
coaches bedecked with flowers that were judged according to the elaboration of their decoration.[5]

If the Berkshires had an undisputed mistress of the Gilded Age, it was
novelist Edith Wharton. Born in 1862, Edith Jones was the product of a
wealthy, distinguished New York family that proudly carried on the
stuffy Knickerbocker traditions. Following the Civil War, her family had
lived in Europe for several years, a period crucial to Edith's artistic development. Already marked as unusual within her family by her intellectual
curiosity, she learned French, German, and Italian and eagerly wandered
through the great villas and gardens of Florence and Rome, absorbing
their beauty and nourishing a love of classical architecture.[6]

The Jones family regularly summered in Newport and spent winters in
New York City. As she grew older, Edith abhorred what she perceived as
the shallow society around her, yet she observed its intricacies with a critical eye. In 1882 she became engaged to Harry Stevens, the handsome
and adventurous son of Marietta, Mrs. Paran Stevens, but reports of the
impending wedding were soon followed by postponements that left
New York society abuzz with gossip. The problem, it was said, was the

Edith Wharton.

ambitious and powerful Mrs. Stevens's acrimonious relationship with proper New York society in general, and with Edith's mother, Lucretia, and her circle in particular. As members of the old guard, the Jones family made no secret of the fact that they looked down on Mrs. Paran Stevens, with her late husband's self-made hotel fortune and rumors that she had once been employed in one of his establishments as a chambermaid; when it became apparent that the Jones family and their milieu would not accept the Stevenses as social equals, Marietta Stevens launched her own whispering campaign, letting it be known that Edith's family were insufferable snobs.[7]

In fact, Harry suffered from incipient—and ultimately fatal—tuberculosis, something he kept carefully concealed from his fiancée. His mother may have informed the Jones family of this fact to save Edith the pain of entering into a union that would almost certainly soon leave her a widow.[8] But there also is some evidence that Marietta Stevens may have sabotaged the relationship for her own financial reasons. When her husband, Paran Stevens, had died, he had left the bulk of his estate in trust for Harry, to be inherited when his son reached age twenty-five, or when he married. With her expensive gowns, glittering parties, frequent travels to Europe, and continual redecoration of her New York City house, Marietta Stevens consistently lived beyond her means, and her desire to maintain control of the $1,250,000 ($25 million in 2008) left by her husband may have led her to do all within her power to keep Harry single as long as possible.[9] If such was her goal, it worked, for the engagement between Harry Stevens and Edith Jones came to an abrupt end; Edith was fortunate, for Harry did indeed die of tuberculosis a mere three years later, but she had the last word, lampooning her former potential mother-in-law as Mrs. Lemuel Struthers in her novel *The Age of Innocence*.

Three years later, Edith married Edward "Teddy" Wharton in a union destined to prove spectacularly unhappy and unrewarding for both partners. Teddy was a popular sportsman from a cultured Boston family, genial and handsome, but he shrank in the shadow of his wife's intellectual pursuits. Edith was never quite able to conceal her feelings of disillusion, and at times she was brutal in her dismissal of her husband; Elsie de Wolfe later remarked that "there was something sharp about her, and she had a forbidding coldness of manner," qualities her unsatisfying marriage brought to the forefront.[10] Teddy's feelings of worthlessness, reinforced subtly and in overt ways by his wife, combined with an already highly strung, unstable personality and led him to seek solace in alcohol. Feeling herself trapped in an unequal and passionless marriage, Edith increasingly turned to a circle of intellectual friends and to her writing for comfort. She was an early proponent of the neoclassical movement in interior design; in 1893 the Whartons purchased a large, shingle-style cottage called Land's End in Newport, and Edith called in Boston architect Ogden Codman Jr. to design the interior, thus beginning an association that eventually resulted in the publication of their influential book *The Decoration of Houses* in 1897.

In the fall of 1899, Teddy took Edith to stay at his mother's summer cottage in Lenox, and she was entranced by the area's natural beauty. Two years later, the couple purchased 113 acres outside of the village and began plans to build their own country estate.[11] "The truth is that I am in love with the place," she wrote to Codman, "climate, scenery, life & all."[12]

The house, which Edith deemed the Mount, was to rise on a wooded hill above tranquil Laurel Lake. At first she hired Codman to help design the estate, but inevitably the friends quarreled. Edith was only moderately wealthy and constantly worried about money; she expected Codman to discount his usual fees in recognition of the work she had obtained for him with members of society. Codman, however, apparently believed that both had benefited equally from the contacts and refused to reduce his prices.[13] In the end, Edith replaced Codman with New York architect Francis Hoppin, who refined Codman's original concepts in consultation with his client. The house was built hastily; to save money, it was constructed of wood concealed with thick coats of white stucco to give the impression of more expensive stone.[14]

The Mount became for Wharton a refuge, an "attempt to carve out her own niche in a social group unsympathetic to, if not suspicious of and puzzled by, her literary concerns," as one author noted.[15] It also was a living experiment, a place where she could investigate her ideas on decoration in practical terms, providing her with an important creative outlet at a time when she felt stifled by her marriage and by the conventions of the day. Although, as she later wrote, her friends often chided her for

The Mount, the Berkshires estate of author Edith Wharton.

"not applying to the arrangement of my own rooms the rigorous rules laid down in *The Decoration of Houses*," she regarded the Mount as something of a fluid entity.[16] Unlike most houses of the Gilded Age, the Mount was an intensely personal expression, designed not to impress society but to provide a refuge amid surroundings deemed suitable to the owner's position and taste, where Edith could immerse herself in an artificially perfected world conducive to her intellectual pursuits.

A long driveway cut through meadows and stretches of woodland artfully disposed to create an Elysian paradise before the main house came into view. Standing in its luminous blanket of white stucco against the surrounding fringe of green trees, the Mount was a curious amalgam of formality and warmth. Ostensibly modeled on the seventeenth-century Belton House in Lincolnshire, England, it repeated its H-shaped plan and distinctive cupola to enforce the allusions, though because the Mount was taller and smaller in width, the proportions were not as pleasing and refined. In adopting what was essentially a Palladian mansion to the wilds of Massachusetts, client and architect infused the structure with a diverse mixture of French and Italian elements that gave it a distinctive quality all its own.[17] The tall brick wall enclosing the forecourt was an entirely French device, while the western, entrance facade, rising three storeys to a hipped roof, mingled the Gallic with the Italianate: the house was built into the side of a hill, and only the two-storeyed eastern facade, opening to a balustraded terrace, conveyed a successful evocation of Belton. The structure was extremely stylized: symmetry was diligently copied, with blank windows concealed by dark shutters to match their working counterparts set in facades that carried stringcourses, dentilated cornices, and corner quoins to further enforce the classical elements of good taste on which *The Decoration of Houses* had been so forcefully insistent.[18]

By the time the external structure was nearing completion, Wharton's break with Codman had ended, and he had designed many of the house's interiors. On the ground floor visitors entered a long, vaulted corridor, a subdued space where a carved fountain dominated a niche and the walls were adorned in an unusual pattern of rippling plaster to suggest water cascading over the surface of a grotto.[19] To the right, the staircase, wrapped with a classically stylized wrought-iron balustrade, ascended to the main floor between walls embellished with painted panels depicting eighteenth-century aristocrats frolicking in a garden.[20] Formal and French in taste, it was nonetheless a quiet, dignified approach, deliberate in its use of minimal decorative detail. The transition was therefore all the more dazzling when one stepped from its upper landing into a long gallery that ran the length of the central block. Here the French gave way to a modified Italianate style, designed to dazzle with the subtlety of its rich yet restrained decorative scheme. Lighted by three tall windows overlooking the forecourt, the gallery offered a strictly formal axial vista from one end of the house to the other in a surrounding of careful spatial complexity. Arches graced a barrel-vaulted ceiling above inset niches and bands of classical molding, but it was the floor that carried the room's primary visual focus: inlaid with muted terrazzo, it was inset with decorative seams of red and white marbles to mirror the arches of the vaults and create a pleasing repetition of pattern.[21] At the northern end, a small den for Teddy occupied one corner, but the real focus of the enfilade was the library. Set at the northeastern end of the house, this was a contemplative space overlooking the gardens, its oak walls pierced by tall, recessed bookcases topped with carved cartouches; additional carved garlands, in the style of the eighteenth-century English master Grinling Gibbons, graced lintels and flanked the marble chimneypiece. Of all interiors in the Mount, it was the room that most evoked the spirit of Belton House.[22]

A thirty-six-foot-long drawing room occupied the center of the house, with French doors opening to the eastern terrace. Here the Palladian and French influences were abandoned in favor of eighteenth-century Georgian. Narrow vertical panels adorned with cascading plaster relief garlands framed the walls, while an elaborate, tiered chimneypiece of French marble, broken pediments atop doorways, and an exuberant ceiling bedecked with sculpted foliage, fruit, rosettes, and swags all deliberately evoked the spirit of renowned English decorator William Kent. A similar decorative scheme was deployed in the adjoining dining room, where stucco reliefs framed ornamental paintings to create the formalized atmosphere deemed appropriate to its function.[23]

In 1904 Edith published *Italian Villas and Their Gardens*, and the Mount presented her with an opportunity to create her own expressive landscape according to classical and Renaissance principles. In this she was assisted by her niece Beatrix Farrand, who was to become the first prominent American female landscape designer. From the eastern terrace, handsome stone staircases flanked by classical balustrades descended to a series of highly formalized gardens laid out along a half-mile axis running parallel to the house. The Red Garden, at the northern end, was the most vibrant exposition, awash in spring and summer with roses in every shade of crimson and pink and surrounding a rectangular pond where a dolphin spouted a thin arc of glistening water into the Berkshire sky. A graveled walk shaded by rows of stately linden trees led to a walled garden at the western end of the lawn. Fringed by the dark green of the surrounding woods, this was a quiet, contemplative space enclosed by solid, ten-foot-high rough stone walls. Open arches allowed pleasant glimpses to the distant Laurel Lake and the shadowed hills beyond, while a circular fountain splashed tranquilly in the soft, dappled light that filtered through the tall, protective firs.[24]

Edith called the Mount "my first real home," a place of "blessed influence."[25] Her friend and fellow novelist Henry James described it as "an exquisite and marvelous place, a delicate French château mirrored in a Massachusetts pond."[26] The Whartons spent several months each summer at the Mount, where, each morning, Edith worked on her latest literary efforts from the comfort of her bed. "I lived and gardened and wrote contentedly." The Mount, she declared, gave her "country cares and joys, long happy rides and drives through the wooded lanes of that loveliest region, the companionship of a few dear friends, and the freedom from trivial obligations which was necessary if I was to go on with my writing."[27]

By the time the Mount was completed, however, the Wharton marriage had all but unraveled. Neither Edith nor her husband made heroic efforts at salvaging the union; while she retreated into her artistic pursuits, Teddy was left to founder under his increasing unhappiness and hypochondria. Eventually he began to secretly embezzle his wife's royalties to fund a series of mistresses, while Edith, too, boldly struck out, launching into her own passionate affair. This unhappy sequence of events played itself out for several years until Edith sold the estate in 1911, moved to France, and two years later divorced her husband. But it was at the Mount that she had finally thrown herself fully into her literary career, and it was here that she largely wrote *The House of Mirth*. Published to great acclaim and financial success in 1905, *The House of Mirth* was a novel redolent of the bitterness of her own life and situation, a scathing indictment of Gilded Age society that shone a harsh and unwelcome light on what she perceived to be its shallow existence and hypocritical manners.

Nearby Elm Court was a sprawling, shingle-style mansion built by William Henry Vanderbilt's second daughter, Emily, and her husband, William Sloane. Sloane, son of the owner of the famous W. J. Sloane & Company in New York, possessed a fraction of his wife's fortune and was widely looked down on as a mere merchant. Indeed, Caroline Astor once rejected the idea of welcoming the Sloanes in her house, saying, "I buy my carpets from them, but then is that any reason why I should invite them to walk on them?"[28] But the fiery, redheaded Emily, full of unexpected passions and strength of character, was determined to have her own way and married Sloane despite the social doubts surrounding the union. She was, recalled her niece Consuelo, "of a joyous nature, and had the look of happy expectancy one sees on the faces of those who love life."[29]

After their marriage in 1872, the couple lived in New York City, first in a fashionable brownstone and then later at 642 Fifth Avenue, the eastern half of William Henry Vanderbilt's famed triple palace.[30] In 1885

Elm Court, the Berkshire cottage of Emily Vanderbilt Sloane, in ruins in 1997.

Emily and her husband decided to build a summer cottage outside of Lenox. Initial plans, conceived by Robert S. Peabody of the Boston architectural firm of Peabody & Stearns and by Frederick Law Olmsted, called for a spacious, shingle-style cottage atop a low hillock. Midway through the design process, however, Emily's father, William Henry Vanderbilt, died, and she inherited $10 million ($200 million in 2008). Unconcerned about cost, the Sloanes asked that the house be expanded into something more suited to their wealth, and a new wing was added, transforming the house into an elongated L-shape.[31] Apparently Sloane was satisfied enough with the result, but Emily seemed possessed of a mania for building, and within a few years she commissioned additional renovations; altogether, the house—christened Elm Court after what was popularly believed to be the oldest and largest elm tree then in existence in America—went through three major additions over the next thirteen years before Emily was satisfied.[32]

Elm Court lay hidden off Old Stockbridge Road behind low, rustic walls that, along with a wild fringe of trees, shielded the estate from inquisitive eyes. A sweeping drive led past expansive open meadows and carefully planted gardens to a walled forecourt, adorned with a splashing fountain copied from one in Rome. The immense, brooding mansion, despite the informality of its materials and almost haphazard appearance, was an intimidating structure, almost threatening in its unrestrained and glowering mass; Elm Court, as completed, was the largest shingle-style house ever built in America, encompassing nearly a hundred rooms, and the second largest of all the Berkshire houses.[33] Like an invasive organism, it had spread across its site over the years as new wings were added. From its marble foundations rose porches and piazzas, towers and wings, gables and dormers, until it resembled some vast, oppressive hotel overgrown with ivy, wisteria, and honeysuckle. A porte cochere angled out into a corner of the forecourt, giving access to wide porches that should have relieved some of the gloom, but hastily tacked-on towers, additions, and half-timbered wings bristling with massed chimneystacks seemed to envelop the structure in a perpetual cloud of darkness. Even worse, in a bizarre move Emily insisted that the house's exterior be decorated in the colors of the Vanderbilt railways, the shingles stained maroon and the trim executed in yellow. "If the colors were good enough for the New York Central," she declared, "they are good enough for me."[34]

Within, a hall lined in white-painted pine gave access to a succession of overly decorated rooms, transformed shortly after the turn of the century when Emily commissioned the firm of Delano & Aldrich to wrap the interiors in colonial revival details. The painted woodwork, dentilated cornices, classical pediments over doorways, and finely molded wainscots below walls hung in floral damask did little to improve the impression; unfortunately, low ceilings, pompously embellished with an abundance of heavy plaster reliefs, only emphasized the claustrophobic proportions, while windows continually strangled by the creeping exterior vines kept the rooms unnaturally dark.[35] In the library, clad in unfortunate flocked velvet wallpaper, shelves "were loaded with splendidly bound volumes arranged in so orderly a fashion that they appeared to be unread," recalled one relative. He suspected that most of the exquisite volumes had been purchased from Charles Lauriat in Boston not for content but because their bindings complemented the pale green on the walls.[36] With its tacked-on wings and spreading tendrils, the interior of Elm Court was a curious maze. "As a child," recalled one of Emily's grandchildren, "I would go up and down the halls and staircases of Elm Court and sometimes arrive at a wall. The halls or staircases led nowhere because of the way the additions were put on."[37]

In complete contrast to the interior, the gardens at Elm Court were all sunshine and expansive vistas, with sweeping lawns, open meadows, and sunken gardens carefully laid out by Frederick Law Olmsted to take advantage of the views over Lake Makheenac. A large greenhouse supplied the 700 roses and 250 carnations needed each week to decorate the sprawling house in an effort to relieve some of the gloom within.[38] The Sloanes came to their Berkshires retreat each June, remaining through the summer season and hosting up to thirty guests at a time.[39] Each morning, the stable order was provided to the guests: this listed the twenty-eight types of carriages and carts available for their use, along with a similar number of horses for riding or driving. "The choice of horses and carriages was larger than the average commercial stable in New York City," recalled one visitor; "on the other hand, if Mrs. Sloane's schedule said you rode at one, you rode at one."[40] In the day, guests could walk, play golf, tennis, or croquet, or ride; Emily insisted that everyone present dine at eight, and, when she retired promptly at ten each night, the lights on the first floor were extinguished as a clear sign that the evening had ended.[41]

Although Emily was generally good-natured, in 1900 she launched on a campaign to ostracize the recently arrived Edith Wharton from Berkshire society. That autumn, Wharton published a short story, "The Line of Least Resistance." The main character, a wealthy merchant prince named Mr. Mindon, was trapped in a marriage of faded passions with Millicent, an impetuous, beautiful heiress who despised her husband's retiring nature and constant gastric complaints. Edith painted the union as little more than a tale of sordid affairs, stupidity, and greed masquerading as social proprieties. One day, Mindon discovered compromising letters between his wife and her constant, amusing companion, Frank Antrim, suggesting that one of his two daughters was not his own.[42]

For Emily and her husband, the detailed portrait and its parallels to reality hit too close to home. At the time Wharton wrote the story, William Sloane's brother Henry had recently divorced his wife, Jessie, after her persistent adultery with August Belmont's son Perry. The beautiful Jessie had scandalized society not only through her flaunted actions but also by willingly abandoning her two children and by marrying Belmont on the same day that her divorce from Sloane was finalized. Various details in "The Line of Least Resistance" were unmistakably drawn from the recent affair, and Emily let it be known that she disapproved of the novelist and would have nothing to do with anyone who associated with her. Wharton's friend Ogden Codman wrote: "Her story about the Sloanes finished her with all the Sloane-Vanderbilt hangers on, who are now barking at her like a lot of yellow dogs. You can see why Mrs. Willy Sloane did not like the story in *Lippincott's* and the Whartons wrote and apologized for it. Mrs. Sloane is the local queen of Lenox so everybody in the place sided with her." With a nod to Edith's own unhappy marriage, he added, "People in glass houses should not throw stones."[43]

In the Berkshires, where the former Vanderbilt heiress held sway over Lenox society, this amounted to social death. As Codman noted, Edith quickly rushed off an apology, disclaiming any connection between her characters and members of the Sloane family. No one was fooled, but Emily graciously accepted the gesture, and with her visit to the Mount for luncheon in 1902, peace was restored.[44]

As a Vanderbilt, Emily took pride of place in the Berkshires' social scene, but in 1891 banker Anson Phelps Stokes made his bid to challenge her supremacy. Born in 1838 in New York City, Stokes was a deeply pious man, in keeping with his descent from the founder and supporter of the London Missionary Society, the American Bible Society, the American Tract Society, and the American Peace Society. In 1861 Stokes became a partner in his family's mercantile company and later organized the banking firm of Phelps, Stokes, & Company, endeavors that made him immensely wealthy. In 1865 he married his cousin Helen Phelps, a woman who shared his conservative moral values, and the couple had nine children: four sons and five daughters.

Stokes, recalled one of his sons, "impressed me always as the English country gentleman." Like his wife, he was "rather aristocratic in his social point of view, but very liberal in his politics." The English association was deliberate and carefully cultivated. "He liked English ways of life and English thought. He generally took his winter vacation by having a couple of weeks hunting in Leicestershire with the Quorn and Pytchley hounds."[45]

In 1891 Stokes purchased just over seven hundred acres on a crest above Lake Makheenac near Lenox, and commissioned local architect H. Neill Wilson to design and build a magnificent summer estate. More than four hundred carpenters, masons, craftsmen, and artists spent two years building the new house.[46] Farms were laid out, and the estate was christened Shadow Brook, the name author Nathaniel Hawthorne had given to the hillside in *The Wonder Book*.[47] Construction was frequently delayed as the house underwent numerous changes; initial designs for a tall, conical roof on its great stone tower were abandoned as unsightly, and Helen Phelps added to the dilemma by once writing to her architect, in the middle of construction, "Please make each room one foot larger in every direction."[48]

By the time it was finished in 1894, Shadow Brook had cost more than $1 million and ($23 million in 2008) and was, with more than a hundred

Shadow Brook, the Berkshire cottage of Anson Phelps Stokes.

rooms, the largest existing private house in America.[49] Its ground floor covered an entire acre.[50] Shadow Brook was a massive, asymmetrical, Tudor-inspired house, overwhelming in size but undoubtedly splendid in its effect. Set on a foundation of locally quarried marble, it stretched and meandered some four hundred feet along the crest of the hillside, dotted with projecting bays, half-timbered gables, loggias, dormers, a four-storey circular tower built entirely of marble, and a dozen chimneystacks, all in imitation of medieval English architecture. The effect, of a rambling house added on to over the passing years, evoked a heroic past of chivalrous gentlemen and noble ladies, a monument redolent of heritage and aristocratic taste that perfectly fit what Stokes had wished for.[51] At night, its windows glowing with light, Shadow Brook, as one man recalled, "looked like a great ship afloat."[52]

Seventeen principal rooms spread over Shadow Brook's first floor, with an equal number confined to an angled service wing. A stone porte cochere opened to a baronial foyer graced with paneled walls and a ceiling adorned with Jacobean strapwork. A massive hall dominated the center of the house, an expansive space more Arts and Crafts than medieval in spirit, where panels of floral damask were set within carved woodwork enameled in soft ivory tones and ornamented with classical pilasters; a carved frieze depicting Pompeian dancing figures fringed a beamed, segmented ceiling. A similar scheme was employed in the drawing room, while the dining room, with its rich wainscot of English oak beneath a ceiling of dark beams, was all quiet Elizabethan probity. In addition to a music room, a morning room, a library, and a breakfast room, Shadow Brook featured an immense ballroom, where privileged couples could swirl beneath a ceiling of elliptical and oval coffers highlighted in gilt. Never quite able to reconcile the period detailing of the exterior with the nineteenth-century comforts employed within, Helen Phelps decorated the rooms with a wildly divergent mixture of furnishings and objets: overstuffed Victorian sofas, Moorish tables, chairs of carved teak from India, and tiger and bearskin rugs.[53]

Shadow Brook, it was popularly believed, was so large that it could comfortably accommodate seventy house guests; on rainy afternoons, Helen Phelps would famously tell her restless brood of nine young children, "Please go up to the attic and ride your bicycles."[54] Yet at times even Shadow Brook's resources were taxed. Once, according to rumor, Anson Phelps Stokes Jr., a member of the class of 1896 at Yale, cabled his mother, "Expect me tonight with crowd of 96 men." Believing that he referred to the number of expected guests and not to his fellow classmates, she replied, "Don't make it more than fifty; have friends already here."[55]

Shadow Brook was a magnificent evocation of the quest for splendor coupled with a ready-made heritage, yet it held its proud designation as the largest existing private house in America only twenty months. In 1895, another Vanderbilt, Emily's brother George, celebrated the completion of his great, 250-room château, Biltmore, in North Carolina.

18

MONARCH OF THE
SMOKY MOUNTAINS

WHILE OTHER MEMBERS of the Vanderbilt family opted for marble mansions in New York or in elite resorts, it was George, William Henry's youngest son, who built the most fantastic of all Gilded Age houses in far-away, distinctly unfashionable North Carolina. Like the house he eventually built, George was an anomaly, both within his family and within his age. Born in 1862, he was an introspective, shy, and quiet young man; unlike his three older brothers, he had little interest in the family business. Instead, George, who suffered from tuberculosis and was educated by private tutors, was enamored of history, art, and architecture. One contemporary called him "the student and litterateur of the family" who "spends much of his time with his books, and delights in delving among musty tomes in old second hand bookstores. . . . He takes great pride and delight in the art gallery, and is thoroughly acquainted with the history of the paintings and the distinguishing characteristics of the artists. Devoted to music, he is an almost nightly attendant at the opera."[1] George grew up to become a handsome young man with the air of a dissipated aesthete, thin and pale, with dark hair, deep-set, piercing blue eyes, and a small, waxed mustache dominating his sallow face.[2] Landscape architect Frederick Law Olmsted described him as "a delicate, refined and bookish man; with considerable humor, but shrewd, sharp, exacting and resolute in matters of business."[3]

George traveled to Europe extensively as his health improved, collecting works of art with the $10 million ($200 million in 2008) legacy he had inherited after his father's death in 1885. He was fluent in French, German, Italian, Spanish, and modern and ancient Greek, could read Sanskrit, and had some proficiency in Hebrew. He seemed oblivious to Gilded Age society, parties, and female companionship, preferring to devote himself to his collections; indeed, at one point he seriously considered becoming a priest.[4] After his father's death, he continued to live with his mother, Louisa, at 640 Fifth Avenue until her death.[5] His father had protected him, and his mother and sisters indulged him terribly, spoiling him and leaving him with a slightly brooding, melancholy, and disdainful air. A gifted linguist and a fine connoisseur, he remained intensely childlike in outlook and in his love of juvenile practical jokes.[6]

In 1888, suffering from recurrent bouts of pneumonia and incipient tuberculosis, George first visited North Carolina's Blue Ridge Mountains and the burgeoning resort town of Asheville. With his mother, he stayed at the Battery Park Hotel, where he fell in love with the picturesque scenery and improved in the beneficial climate.[7] George later said that he "found the air mild and invigorating and I thought well of the climate. I took long rambles and found pleasure in doing so."[8] He was so enamored of the area that he decided to build an estate there, hiring Richard Morris Hunt to design what was initially conceived as a humble spring and winter retreat.[9]

"For a year," reported the New York Times in 1888, "George Vanderbilt has been buying real estate in Western North Carolina."[10] Eventually the estate grew to encompass an astonishing 125,000 acres of forest.[11] The first plans for the estate dated from 1888 and called for a colonial revival–style cottage of fewer than a dozen rooms, flanked by wide piazzas overlooking the mountains; over time, this evolved into a larger house, then a Tudor-inspired mansion, and finally a Beaux Arts palace resembling a French château.[12] Not only did George's vision change, but Hunt also recognized that here he had the unique opportunity to build a house for a cultured patron, unrestrained by such considerations as the width of the plot or a limited budget. It was Hunt's single largest commission, and the result—named Biltmore—was and remains today America's largest private house.

In 1889, Vanderbilt and Hunt traveled extensively through Europe, visiting palaces and examining potential models for the new house, including the Rothschild château of Waddeston Manor in England.[13] Their attention was especially drawn to French châteaux in the Loire Valley, and Hunt carefully noted the details that George most admired, sketching ideas as they went. The pair also scoured markets and auction houses across the Continent, purchasing carpets, tapestries, paintings, sculptures, bronzes, furniture, carvings, and objets d'art to incorporate into the new house.[14]

Hunt's final plans called for a massive, French Renaissance–inspired château set at the edge of a high bluff above the French Broad and Swannanoa rivers, overlooking the pristine forest, Mount Pisgah, and the surrounding Smoky Mountains. Construction began in 1889 and lasted six years. The top of a mountain was cleared and leveled to provide a thirty-five-acre site for the house and its immediate gardens.[15] A massive retaining wall, seventeen feet thick, followed the western edge of the hillside to support the structure, and soon a framework of steel girders and beams arose, sheathed with immense blocks of limestone as the house sprang to life.[16] There was an on-site forge, a smelter, and a brickworks that produced some thirty-two thousand bricks a day at the height of construction; a temporary, three-mile railway spur from Asheville, built at a cost of more than $70,000 ($1.4 million in 2008), allowed direct delivery of the massive blocks of Indiana limestone used in construction to the site, and often as many as a thousand masons, builders, carvers, painters, joiners, and craftsmen worked ten hours a day, six days a week (many local laborers receiving 50 cents a day [$10 in 2008] for their efforts) to create this fantastic baronial vision.[17] The project was so immense that during its construction, Biltmore was the largest single employer in all of North Carolina.[18] No one knew just how much this exquisite folly, with its constant revisions, had cost, but the figure was certainly more than $6 million ($120 million in

2008), and was running to some $45,000 ($900,000 in 2008) a day during the peak of construction.[19]

"The Blue Ridge Palace," recorded the *New York Times,* "will be, when completed, one of the most beautiful homes in the world."[20] Hunt drew on various models, incorporating architectural elements from several Loire Valley châteaux to craft a building that seemed at once familiar and innovative. The Château of Blois, particularly its François I wing, provided much of the inspiration; at Biltmore, Hunt reproduced its arcaded colonnade, its carved and hooded dormers, and its ornamentation and cresting. Biltmore also boasted its own stair tower copied from the famed model at Blois, although Hunt's ascended in the opposite direction. To provide an impressive focal point for the principal facade, the architect looked to another historical model, the house of Jacques Coeur in Bourges, France, duplicating its tower in his impressive central entrance.[21] The result was a combination of varied elements, refracted and refined to create a building that transcended the pastiche of its architectural borrowings to become a deeply expressive, seductive creation in its own right.

The entrance facade of Biltmore, George Vanderbilt's great château in Asheville, North Carolina.

Unfortunately, Hunt never lived to see his masterpiece completed. Increasingly plagued by ill health, he suffered from persistent colds that forced him away from his consuming work, and his son Richard often took over supervision.[22] Richard Morris Hunt was in Newport when, on July 31, 1895, he died unexpectedly. His funeral, at Newport's Trinity Church, was attended by a glittering contingent of his Gilded Age society friends, who had recognized his genius and promoted him as the ultimate architect of the era. He was buried in Newport's Island Cemetery, with George acting as one of his pallbearers.

As Biltmore was rising, work also was under way on the estate's gardens and park. From the beginning, Vanderbilt envisioned the estate as an evocation of a true feudal stronghold, a self-supporting enclave with varied interests. A new model village, designed to resemble a quaint cluster of English-style half-timbered cottages, was laid out at the base of the mountain as housing for servants and employees, complete with a mock-Gothic church. George called in Frederick Law Olmsted, the renowned designer of New York's Central Park, to help him achieve his dream of a thriving, cultivated, and independent community. Olmsted, however, found the terrain difficult and thought that George's plans were a bit too grandiose to be practical. "My advice," Olmsted wrote to Vanderbilt, "would be to make a small park into which to look from your house; make a small pleasure ground and garden, farm your river bottom chiefly to keep and fatten livestock with a view to manure; and make the rest a forest, improving the existing woods and planting the old fields."[23] The intention to develop the entire estate was thus abandoned. Thirty-five acres were to be given over to the formal gardens surrounding the house, with the remaining land devoted to forests and agriculture.[24] Selected spots were cultivated to evoke a typical English landscape, with open meadows, carefully placed clumps of trees, and broad stretches of water to reflect the château and the expansive North Carolina sky.[25]

To help craft this finely tuned naturalistic appearance, Olmsted recommended Gifford Pinchot. The scion of a wealthy Pennsylvania family, Pinchot was one of the earliest forestry experts in America and later headed the Division of Forestry in the Department of Agriculture. Pinchot arrived at Biltmore in 1892, armed with little practical experience but with revolutionary ideas gleaned from his study in France. "Here was my chance," he later wrote. "Biltmore could be made to prove what America did not yet understand, that trees could be cut and the forest preserved at one and the same time. I was eager, confident, and happy as a clam at high tide."[26] Pinchot not only organized the extensive forestry and timber endeavors on the estate, which were intended to help support Biltmore as a sustainable entity, but also assisted in laying out the model farms and the estate's agricultural experiments.[27]

This forest embraced and shielded the house, concealing its splendors and heightening its drama. Beyond the arched entrance lodge, a three-mile-long drive cleaved through this woodland, ascending amid a carefully contrived paradise crafted by Olmsted, meandering through thick forests, over rustic stone bridges spanning tumbling streams, and along banks of flowering azaleas and rhododendrons shadowed by tall, protective pines and hemlocks that underscored the isolation of the estate from the world beyond.[28] Gradually, after a series of twists and turns, the roadway reached a set of pale stone piers set with wrought-iron gates marking the final entry to the center of the estate. A turn brought the esplanade into view, a great nine-acre lawn lined by double rows of tulip trees copied from the classical French *tapis vert*: at the eastern end rose a *rampe douce*, a series of formal, balustraded limestone terraces and staircases ascending to a statue of Diana at the end of a grassed ride.[29] Stone staircases along the southern end of the esplanade descended to a terraced Italian garden, with statuary, parterres, and reflecting pools awash with water lilies and lotuses; beyond this, graveled walks meandered through a colorful shrub garden to a four-acre walled rose garden and conservatory.[30]

At the other end of the esplanade, glistening against the silvery mist of a splashing fountain, the château appeared as if by magic. After acres of pristine forest and the wild beauties of the Smoky Mountains, the pale cream walls of Indiana limestone shone in majestic splendor, a panoply of projecting wings, mullioned windows, and lofty towers rising to a hipped roof of gray slate dappled with carved dormers, massed chimneystacks, and elaborate copper cresting. The sheer scale of the building—with a facade stretching nearly 800 feet along the crest of the hillside, 255 rooms, and more than 175,000 square feet—could have been overwhelming.[31] Hunt, however, viewed the new house as an integral part of the landscape, writing to his wife that "the mountains are just the right size and scale for the château."[32]

In evoking the spirit of a heroic past, with brave warriors and culti- vated ladies, Biltmore managed a feat unequaled in any of the era's other opulent works of domestic historicism: Hunt's interiors, while often luminous and offering unexpected comforts, remained largely true to the French Renaissance exterior. Here there were no gilded salons adorned with rococo boiseries and glittering columns; instead Hunt relied on walls of stone, floors of marble, ceilings of wood, and an assortment of tapestries and carpets to provide contrasting richness, color, and soft- ness. Immense arched doors set in the eastern facade's four-storey central tower opened to a world of quiet grandeur and regal ambitions, where the light of reason washed the shadows of baronial austerity. A cavernous hall faced in limestone and floored in cool marble hinted at antiquity, but Hunt's arrangement was thoroughly modern in approach. He dispelled the cloistered claustrophobia suggestive of his French models by dispos- ing the principal rooms along a complex axis of high, arcaded interior galleries, with cased openings rather than solid doors to further heighten the interrelationships among the spaces.[33]

Arches on the right side of the hall opened to an octagonal, marble- floored, sunken winter garden. A domed and wooden-ribbed skylight hung with eighteenth-century Italian brass lanterns bathed the room in natural light, while groupings of potted palms, ferns, comfortable bam- boo furniture from Paris, and sculpture clustered around a splashing central fountain adorned with a bronze statue, *Boy Stealing the Geese*, sculpted by Karl Bitter.[34] The Bachelors' Wing framed the northern side of the house, providing a smoking room and a gun room, places of quiet refuge for George and his male guests. The largest of these spaces was the billiard room. Conceived as an evocation of Renaissance England, the billiard room offered a warm, intimate atmosphere, its walls sheathed in panels of carved, honey-toned Norwegian oak beneath an elaborately plastered strapwork ceiling. Here guests could play at two carved oak billiard tables, using cue sticks inlaid with ivory and mother-of-pearl to shoot the ivory balls.[35]

South of the entrance hall, an arch opened to a seventy-five-foot-long tapestry gallery. Taking his inspiration from the recently restored Château de Pierrefonds near Compiègne, Hunt adorned the room with twin carved limestone chimneypieces whose hoods bore painted designs, and a ceiling of decorative stenciled beams. It was a comfortable room despite its walls of gray stone wrapped in linen-fold paneling and somber Renaissance details, the muted colors enhanced by three sixteenth-century Brussels tapestries depicting Faith, Prudence, and Charity, part of an original set titled *The Triumph of the Seven Virtues*.[36] The tapestry gallery offered a sweeping approach to one of Biltmore's most dramatic rooms, the library. Here one left the somewhat barren splendors of the Renaissance for a room of baroque triumph. Nearly a hundred feet long, the library was a sumptuous apartment lined with richly carved Circassian walnut paneling and bookcases that held some of George's well-read and much-loved twenty-five thousand volumes; in one corner, a small staircase, enclosed in an elaborate, arched frame and adorned with gilded bronze rails, spiraled up to a mezzanine gallery. Figures carved by Karl Bitter, representing Demeter and Hestia, flanked a monumental chimneypiece of black marble, but it was the ceiling that provided the room's coup de théâtre, an enormous seventeenth-century baroque canvas, *The Chariot of Aurora*, by Giovanni Antonio Pellegrini, which had originally graced the ballroom of the Pisani Palace in Venice.[37]

On the western side of the house, overlooking an ornamental lake and adjoining the entrance hall, Hunt placed an octagonal music room and a salon, both with glorious views over the mountains beyond. For informal meals Hunt created the breakfast room, situated in an octagonal tower whose bay of mullioned windows offered a contrast to the dark richness of walls hung in gilded and handtooled Spanish leather above an ornamental wainscot of red Italian marble. A chimneypiece adorned with blue Jasperware plaques and nestled between fluted columns framing a breast of white marble embellished with a bas-relief heraldic emblem towered to a strapwork ceiling of elaborately composed geometric designs and hanging pendants carved with acorn finials in a nod to the Vanderbilt coat of arms.[38]

Coming after this elegant yet rather subdued room, Hunt's banquet hall offered a magnificent baronial contrast of sparse limestone walls rising seventy-five feet to a vaulted, ribbed wooden ceiling pierced with arched, mullioned dormers. At one end of the hall, above a series of paneled niches, stretched a small organ gallery adorned with ornate reliefs depicting scenes from Wagnerian operas. A monumental triple fireplace dominated the opposite wall, its flaring breast sweeping upward from a triumphant stone relief, *Return of the Chase*, carved by Bitter, to a massive bas-relief of the Vanderbilt family coat of arms. Five immense sixteenth-century Flemish tapestries depicting the romantic triangle among Venus, Mars, and Vulcan hung at intervals along the walls, softening the room's somewhat somber character; above, clustered along a carved cornice, fluttered colorful ornamental banners and flags from the American Revolution and the original thirteen colonies, bathed at night in the glow from two immense iron ring chandeliers. Two tall, canopied Gothic-style thrones of carved oak, designed by Hunt, offered a regal contrast to sixty-four nineteenth-century Italian chairs, clad in crimson damask, that fringed an enormous oak table stretching across a parquet floor arrayed with bear-skin rugs.[39]

Left of the entrance hall, a staircase of white marble spiraled four storeys, around an elaborate seventy-foot-high, three-tiered, seventeen-hundred-pound medieval-style chandelier of wrought iron suspended from a shallow dome on a single pin.[40] Spread across the second and third floors were thirty-four main bedrooms, forty-three bathrooms, quarters for servants, and an immense collection of works of art, including paintings by John Singer Sargent, James McNeill Whistler, Renoir, and Boldini.[41] Panels of carved walnut set against walls covered in a soft, ocher-colored glaze bedecked George's bedroom, a Renaissance-inspired chamber set directly above Hunt's music room. The furnishings, from the canopied seventeenth-century Portuguese bed to the heavily carved, Spanish-style walnut chairs, were hung and upholstered in lush crimson velvet elaborately bordered in gold thread to provide a dramatic burst of color.[42] Contrasting with this rather sparsely decorated chamber, the adjoining oak sitting room echoed the Jacobean style of the billiard room, with walls clad in warm, richly carved oak rising to an ornamental frieze of armorial plaster reliefs and a delicate strapwork ceiling.[43] At the time of Biltmore's planning and construction, George was still a bachelor, and the oak sitting room linked his suite to the other principal apartment, a bedroom lavishly decorated for use by his mother, Louisa. Here one left the subdued Iberian splendors of George's bedroom and the oak sitting room's dignified evocation of Renaissance England and entered the world of Versailles. The most formal of Biltmore's interiors, Louisa's bedroom was an elegant, elongated oval in the Louis XV style, with elaborately carved white rococo woodwork and boiseries against walls hung in vibrant yellow Scalamandré silk. Hangings of rich purple and gold cut velvet cascaded from the bed's canopy and shielded the windows, adding a further lavish touch.[44] The enormous basement included not only the main kitchen and auxiliary kitchens dedicated to pastry and rotisserie cooking, storage, and service rooms, but also a two-lane bowling alley and a seventy-thousand-gallon swimming pool.[45]

George Vanderbilt celebrated the completion of his new château with an inaugural party at Christmas 1895. A string of private railway carriages delivered a host of Vanderbilts—more than thirty family members in all—to Asheville that Christmas Eve: George's mother, Louisa; his brothers Willie, Fred—accompanied by his wife, Louise—and Cornelius, along with his wife, Alice, and their children; and his sisters Emily Vanderbilt Sloane and Eliza Webb, along with their husbands and families. With them, reported the *New York Times*, came "an army of servants." Carriages conveyed them through the town and through the arched lodge, climbing the three miles of winding, snow-banked driveway to George's magnificent new palace. Within, the rooms had been bedecked with garlands of mistletoe, holly, and evergreen boughs mixed with out-of-season flowers from the estate's conservatory; hickory logs crackled and burned against the gray winter twilight, Christmas trees sparkled with candles and tinsel, and the entire house smelled of delicious, welcoming aromas.[46]

Olmsted called the finished result "the most distinguished private place, not only of America, but of the world."[47] Three years later, in 1898, George was finally married, to Edith Stuyvesant Dresser, and the couple had one child, Cornelia, born in 1900. This privileged trio lived amid this isolated, baronial splendor, their needs attended to by a staff of seventy servants. The atmosphere of Biltmore was slightly surreal; in a letter to Edith Wharton, Henry James—who spent several days there—called it "a gorgeous practical joke."[48]

But the triumph was short-lived. Construction costs, unexpected changes, and the sheer scale of the project all spiraled into a seemingly incessant financial black hole; although George was wealthy, his North Carolina château rapidly depleted his available funds. He could not afford to finish Hunt's octagonal music room on the main floor, and screens concealed its brick walls; to disguise the similarly barren adjoining salon, Edith draped the bare ceiling with fabric and hid its unfinished floor beneath thick carpets and piles of pillows.[49] The *New York Times* reported that George, exasperated at the developments, had unexpectedly gone off to India on a tiger hunt after learning one morning that the plumbing had broken: "The sunken foundation, the cracked marbles, the idle sawmill, the unproductive dairy farm, the expensive forestry school, the unprofitable truck farm, and all the failures that had been pointed out came rushing in on him. He could have stood all these, but he could not stand this climax. He had spent $10,000,000 on Biltmore and he could not get a drink of water."[50] George had embarked on the project possessing a legacy of some $13 million ($260 million in 2008); at the time of his premature death in 1914, he was worth less than $1 million dollars ($23 million in 2008), having expended his life and his fortune on the great baronial château in the wilds of North Carolina.[51]

THE KINGDOM BY THE SEA

ABOVE ALL OTHER RESORTS, Newport dominated the summers of Gilded Age society. Elizabeth Drexel Lehr termed it "the very Holy of Holies, the playground of the great ones of the earth from which all intruders were ruthlessly excluded by a set of cast iron rules."[1] With its broad, tree-shaded avenues lined by a succession of fantastic palaces, Newport, declared one visitor, was "perhaps the most artificial place in the world," a picturesque colonial town transformed for ten weeks each summer when the era's elite arrived to parade their finery and preside over lavish parties in opulent mansions that fringed the Atlantic.[2]

Situated at the southern end of Aquidneck Island, Newport was an unlikely destination for Gilded Age society. Founded in the seventeenth century by a group of Puritan dissenters, the town had quickly become not only a haven for various religious communities but also one of America's most important seaports; in 1880, when the sea trade had faded, the U.S. Naval Training Station was established on Harbor Island, followed four years later by the Naval War College. Yet at the beginning of the Gilded Age, Newport was very much a sleepy remnant of times past. From its docks spread a tendril of streets lined with proud colonial houses; they faced onto a square overlooked by the elegantly spired

Trinity Episcopal Church, and rose and fell over an area known as the Point. Dignified Newport society included such luminaries as Julia Ward Howe, Henry Wadsworth Longfellow, Henry James, John La Farge, and a young Edith Wharton. They lived quietly, the gentlemen meeting at the Newport Reading Room to discuss literature, and the ladies spending summer afternoons driving in open carriages to take advantage of ocean breezes.

In the years before the Civil War, Newport hotels catered to middle-class visitors who flocked to its beaches and splashed in the Atlantic, and soon a number of moneyed families from New York, Philadelphia, Boston, and the South began to summer there.[3] They housed themselves in impressive cottages, rambling villas erected in a variety of styles and fringed with verandas overlooking the sea. There were a few large houses, such as George Noble Jones's Kingscote or William Wetmore's Château-sur-Mer, but for the most part, old Newport frowned on ostentatious display. The arrival of the Gilded Age forever shattered this intellectual milieu of quiet probity. The first leader of elite society to regularly summer here was Mrs. August Belmont, who attempted to import something of the grand style of life in New York to annual sojourns at her cottage, By-the-Sea.[4] It was the arrival of Caroline Astor, however, that cemented the town's social reputation. Urged on by Ward McAllister, who owned a farm there, and disillusioned with her husband's Hudson River estate, Caroline followed her adviser to the Atlantic shore.

In 1881 the Astors purchased a villa on Newport's Bellevue Avenue. Originally built for merchant Daniel Parrish by Calvert Vaux in 1852–53, this was a squat, square building of brick cloaked in stucco; an arcaded loggia edged the southern side, balanced by a smaller service wing to the north. Within, a series of enfiladed rooms wrapped around a central corridor, though none was particularly spacious nor refined in decoration.[5] The estate's situation, a five-acre carpet of turf bordering the crashing Atlantic surf, was excellent, however, and its prominent position and lovely views offered enticing possibilities. Caroline commissioned Richard Morris Hunt to rectify the house's shortcomings, with some $2 million ($40 million in 2008) spent on new rooms, imported boiseries, gilded cornices, and refined French furniture to create a suitably regal setting;

even in Newport, Caroline wanted no ambiguity as to the primacy of her position.[6]

Caroline christened her enlarged house Beechwood, after the lofty trees shading a graveled drive that swept from Bellevue Avenue to its rusticated porte cochere. In his renovations, Hunt had followed the house's original Italianate style. Distinctive corner quoins, rounded windows, decorative lintels, and a wide, bracketed cornice ringing a low, hipped

The garden facade of Beechwood, the Astor cottage in Newport, in 1900.

The same view of Beechwood in 1997.

roof added picturesque touches; at the center of the western facade, a gabled projection offered a vertical contrast and broke up the solid massing of the main block. Extending the house to the east, Hunt removed the original loggia and wrapped a wide piazza along the garden facade, a place of quiet refuge shaded by white canvas curtains and dotted with potted palms, tubs of flowers, and clusters of wicker furniture from which to enjoy the views of the ocean.[7]

Hunt's renovations left Beechwood an impressive, quietly elegant house. From the porte cochere, arched glass doors opened to a vestibule and central hall dividing the main block. At the time Caroline commissioned the alterations, she had not yet succumbed to the lavish excesses later arrayed in her new Fifth Avenue château; indeed, despite enlarging the house, she insisted on superb understatement, and the interiors were largely exercises in cautious restraint, offering an unspoken manifestation and reinforcement of her position at the head of society. Thus, in the hall, there were no gilded boiseries, no sculpted cherubs, and no antique tapestries; instead, Hunt deployed classical moldings and a shallow, vaulted ceiling to convey an aura of solid respectability. Vibrant cherry wainscoting and moldings graced an almost somber reception room hung in pale crimson floral silk brocade, while the morning room offered luminous woodwork and lightly toned walls as backdrops to a collection of delicate gilded chairs.

A hint of extravagance followed. In space carved from the former drawing room, Hunt created a rococo music room, a display of formality that signaled the more social aspects of the house. Elaborate boiseries had come from France, disassembled and shipped across the Atlantic. They were carefully pieced together to create a refined, Louis XV–style atmosphere. Sculpted bas-reliefs of musical instruments graced molded panels, their soft tones echoed in a mantle of variegated French marble to create a deft and deliberate contrast to the rooms that had come before.[8]

On the eastern side of the main block, Hunt added two further additions: a new dining room and a ballroom. Decorated in the simple colonial revival style, the dining room featured a barrel-vaulted ceiling, elegant wainscoting and wall moldings originally from England that framed leather panels painted with floral designs, and a monumental black marble chimneypiece surmounted by a portrait of the first John

Jacob Astor.[9] It was the ballroom, however, that was the heart of the house, a baroque fantasy later refined in 1901 by Stanford White at a cost of $47,010 (approximately $1.9 million in 2008).[10] This was a glittering, luminous room designed as a gilded evocation of the ocean just beyond its French doors. White walls adorned with gilded boiseries and rocailles were set with hundreds of mirrors to create a shifting, rushing wave of light and shadow across the floor of oak parquet; ormolu tendrils of seaweed formed glittering sconces, their crystals matched by those of the magnificent chandeliers suspended from a ceiling fringed by a sweeping, wavelike frieze whose *mascarons* and putti gleamed like burnished suns. Here Caroline held her annual summer ball on the first day of July. Invitations were regarded as high prizes, and the privileged crowded into the fine room and flowed out across her velvety lawns to the edge of the ocean sparkling in the distance.

It was only natural that Alva Vanderbilt would follow the path to Newport, though she did so in her own style. According to Harry Lehr, she "loved nothing better than to be knee deep in mortar," and a new summer cottage in Newport offered her the perfect opportunity to indulge in her favorite pursuit.[11] In 1888 Willie presented her with a unique and costly gift to mark her thirty-eighth birthday: carte blanche to design and build an estate here—"the very best living accommodations that money could provide," ran the instructions.[12] This was not quite as generous a gesture as it appeared: Alva was rumored to have extorted the house—and its unlimited budget—from her husband on learning of his infidelity.[13]

What Alva wanted was not merely the elegant mise-en-scène deemed necessary to Newport's increasing lavish summer entertainments but also a statement of power, an unrivaled sign of her preeminent place at the apex of Gilded Age society. To accomplish this, she purchased—not by accident—a plot of land at 600 Bellevue Avenue, adjoining Mrs. Astor's Beechwood, and commissioned Richard Morris Hunt to create a palace that would dazzle in its opulence. To add a hint of intrigue, Alva had a massive fence built around the site to conceal any views of the new structure during its erection, and installed a constant patrol of watchmen supplemented with ferocious St. Bernard dogs.[14]

A palace in Newport offered Alva the opportunity to refine the French taste of her Fifth Avenue château while at the same time exploring other monumental themes to create a building of impressive regality. Like the Fifth Avenue house, this structure was adopted from Gallic models, though in Newport, the period shifted from the Renaissance to the more expressively opulent court of Louis XIV. Hunt drew on the Petit Trianon at Versailles, though his principal, west facade carried a monumental temple portico derived from both the Temple of the Sun in Lebanon and, in a nod to American design, that which graced the northern front of the White House.[15] Marble House, as the building came to be called, contained fewer rooms than did Beechwood, but they were larger and far more sumptuous than anything Newport had yet seen. Some five hundred thousand feet of Italian marble arrived from Europe; rooms were designed and decorated by the firm of Jules Allard in Paris and shipped across the Atlantic; and carpenters, masons, woodcarvers, and painters arrived from New York to complete the mansion.[16] A reported $11 million ($220 million in 2008) went into Marble House's construction and furnishings before the building was finished.[17] The result, as Alva frankly admitted, "was like a fourth child to me."[18]

When Marble House was ready, Alva summoned Newport society to celebrate her new mansion with a magnificent ball. On the night of August 19, 1892, the guests arrived to find the tall privacy walls ringing the estate gone; against the encroaching night and swirling fog that swept in from the Atlantic, they could barely discern the house, which lay in darkened shadow. Then, with a theatrical flourish, thousands of electric lights burst into life, revealing the massive facade. "The sight," reported the *New York Times*, "was one never before seen in Newport. The grand portico was ablaze of lights and liveried attendants were on hand from carriage to cloakroom."[19]

Passing through intricate wrought-iron gates on Bellevue Avenue, guests could look up a sweeping, semicircular drive to this magisterial monument. Here there was no ambiguity: Hunt conceived Marble House as nothing short of a secular temple to Gilded Age society in general and Alva Vanderbilt in particular. A U-shaped building of two principal storeys atop a raised basement, Marble House was an almost austere neoclassical structure, its facade

The main entrance facade of Alva Vanderbilt's Marble House in Newport, showing Richard Morris Hunt's immense portico.

of pale gray Tuckahoe marble enlivened by fluted marble Corinthian pilasters and elaborate stone reliefs ringed by a carved cornice and balustrade. Tall wrought-iron lamp standards cast an eerie glow across the balustraded stone ramp that arced in a gentle curve to Hunt's regal portico, its entablature supported by four fluted Corinthian columns that alluded to classical Greece and provided an intimidating approach to Alva's new palace.[20]

Entrance to Marble House was suitably dramatic. Alighting from their carriages, guests faced an enormous ten-ton finely worked steel-and-glass grille, twenty-five feet long and sixteen feet high, lavishly embellished with

William K. Vanderbilt's monogram, ormolu rocailles, and masks of Apollo set in radiant sunbursts to evoke the spirit of Louis XIV.[21] It was, declared the *New York Times*, "the finest piece of work of this character ever turned out in the United States."[22] Liveried footmen flanked the center of the grille, where double doors, each weighing one and a half tons, were so finely suspended on pivots that they swung open without a sound.[23] They also were unique in all of Newport for another reason: there were no exterior knobs.[24] It was a choice bit of symbolism: only those invited to Marble House could cross its threshold, and those so privileged need not weary themselves by any action so mundane as the opening of a door.

Unlike 660 Fifth Avenue, with its diversity of styles ranging from the baronial and the Renaissance to French rococo and even Moorish, the interior of Marble House offered a more unified vision, a carefully controlled environment designed to transcend mere function and evoke the splendors of Versailles. Marble House contained fewer rooms than did Alva's New York City residence, but they were larger and more excessive in their gilded insistence. The first floor contained only four main rooms opening off the hall, two of which functioned as informal living spaces for the family; the remaining pair, however, were conceived as imaginatively luxurious public spaces, a decision that allowed them to be treated in an almost unbelievably extravagant manner that might have failed had it been pursued throughout the house.

Guests entered a cavernous, twenty-foot-high hall sheathed in rich, almost translucent yellow sienna marble topped by a ceiling awash with plaster garlands of fruit and foliage in gilded relief. Two immense eighteenth-century Gobelin tapestries encased in elaborately carved and gilded fillets offered visual contrast, their vibrant reds echoed in the cut velvet that covered Louis XIV–style gilded bronze armchairs. Consoles embellished with ormolu mounts and tall bronze lamps ornamented with gilded dragons added a lustrous shimmer to the hall; on the southern wall, between a pair of doors, a niche framed a looking glass reflecting a trickling, cast bronze fountain by Jules Allard.[25] It was a surprisingly cool space, subdued in ornament and deliberately restrained in its approach, yet all the more impressive for its undisguised luxury, a splendid backdrop for the formal receptions around which Marble House had been conceived.

Mirrored doors opened to the Gold Room, a stunningly opulent ball-room designed by Jules Allard. Here all was brilliance, the walls sheathed in richly carved panels burnished in twenty-three-carat gold leaf, the ceiling framed by heavily stuccoed and gilded reliefs encircling a painted panel depicting Minerva carrying off Youth. By day, five floor-length windows, draped in brown and gold cut velvet, bathed the room in light; at night, mirrors reflected the two bronze chandeliers, gleaming with clusters of gilded leaves and putti blowing trumpets. A tall chimneypiece of *fleur de pêche* marble, flanked by life-size sculpted bronze figures by Allard representing youth and maturity, offered layer upon layer of extravagance: a gilded bronze garland swept dramatically across the mantel, distinguished by a central mask of Bacchus; above, reflected in the looking glass, stood an ornamental globe of glass and crystal whose revolving sphere marked the passage of time. Everything in the room was designed to dazzle and sparkle; even the green and gold cut velvet uphol-stery on the sofas and chairs was fringed with silk tassels studded with glittering rhinestones.[26]

On the other side of the hall, Jules Allard created a dining room mod-eled on the Salon of Hercules at Versailles. Paired pilasters, with ormolu

The Gold Room in Marble House, Newport.

bases and Corinthian capitals, ringed walls of dark pink Numidian marble from Algeria embellished with gilt bronze spears, pennants, and military helmets; above, the rich colors of an allegorical painting of Mercury leading a goddess to Mount Olympus glowed against a ceiling of gilded stucco relief garlands and hunting trophies. A portrait of Louis XIV after Henri Testelin hung above a marble chimneypiece whose mantel was ornamented with an ormolu mask of Hercules, further emphasizing the allusion to Versailles. Louis XIV–style chairs of cast bronze by Allard flanked the long mahogany dining table; covered in crimson cut-velvet brocade woven with metallic thread and weighing seventy pounds, they were so heavy that footmen had to pull each one out for the guests.[27]

Two semiprivate rooms occupied the projecting northern and southern wings at the rear of the house, framing a terrace overlooking the Atlantic. Leaving the Gold Room, guests entered the one true anomaly in Marble House. Designed in France and shipped across the Atlantic, the Gothic Room offered a fantastic showcase for a collection of medieval and Renaissance art and weaponry that Alva had purchased from Émile Gavet; it also served as an informal drawing room. Walls hung in red damask above a wooden wainscot bristling with carved spires rose to a magnificent ribbed and traceried ceiling adorned with decorative bosses picked out in vibrant blues, reds, greens, and gold. Stained-glass windows cast shifting prisms of light over the pierced bronze chandeliers and a hooded chimneypiece of theatrical pinnacles, crenellations, and arched niches from whose depths peeked sculpted knights.[28] On the other side of the house, tucked behind the service pantry, was the library, a small, intimate room in the rococo style lined with carved English walnut bookcases and crowned with a coved ceiling painted with depictions of the sciences, history, and time.[29]

From the hall, a monumental staircase of Sienna marble, its wrought-iron railing embellished with ormolu foliage, garlands, and sunbursts designed by Jules Allard and Sons, ascended to the floor above.[30] An immense bronze lantern hung from a coved ceiling adorned with gilded heroic figures guarding a mythological painting, its light washing a landing where a copy of Bernini's bust of Louis XIV was flanked by relief portraits in white marble by Karl Bitter of the king's court architect

Jules Hardouin-Mansart and Richard Morris Hunt.[31] Off the landing, at
the mezzanine level, were two small rooms: a study hung in crimson damask and lined with paintings of racehorses for Willie to the left, and to the
right, an elaborate little rococo boudoir for Alva, with carved boiseries
and stucco relief garlands and cherubs.[32] In comparison with the regal
public rooms, the family's private apartments, at least those intended for
the men, seemed models of restraint. In the rooms occupied by Willie and
his two sons, the decoration was subdued, neoclassical in style, with reliance on a few decorative moldings and ornamental mantels to achieve a
measure of privileged comfort.[33] For her only daughter, Consuelo, Alva
created an austere, gloomy Italian Renaissance-style bedroom at the rear
of the house. Dark, carved oak wainscoting; sober, deep crimson silk satin
on the walls; a coffered wooden ceiling; and a grim stone mantelpiece set
the tone for the heavy, inappropriately masculine canopy bed and furnishings.[34] Although its tall windows overlooked the Atlantic Ocean, the room,
as Consuelo recalled, was an oppressive place; certain of the supremacy of
her own taste, Alva had personally selected and placed every article in the
room, and forbade her daughter to add personal items or to disturb in any
way this carefully crafted museum.[35]

Not surprisingly, Alva's French rococo bedroom, above the Gold Room,
was the most elaborate of these private chambers. Arabesque-patterned
lilac damask from Lyon hung on the walls between cream-colored pilasters and panels elaborately carved to match the wainscot and cornice;
festoons of the same lilac silk cascaded from window pelmets carved with
garlands and frolicking cherubs. The motif was repeated in the over-
doors, where carved cherubs bore shields emblazoned with sinuously
scrolled A's, and in the rocailles and garlands that swept around a ceiling
painting of Athena. The suite of rococo-style furniture was luxuriously
impractical, enameled in white and exuberantly awash with putti, scrolls,
and swags.[36]

The effect of Marble House was dazzling, a fantasy of power and
ambition. "No description can possibly give one an idea of how marvel-
ously beautiful it is," wrote one visiting relative. "It is far ahead of any
palace I have ever seen abroad, far ahead of any I have ever dreamed
of."[37] It represented yet another triumph for the unwavering Alva, who

Alva Vanderbilt's bedroom in Marble House, Newport.

kept a staff of thirty-six servants in the Vanderbilt maroon livery to maintain a constant state of perfection for the ten weeks of her summer residence.[38]

Yet even as servants collected the lavish floral displays and restored the rooms in Marble House to their solemn brilliance on the morning after its magnificent debut, Alva was in the midst of a domestic scandal. Over the years, Willie had grown weary of her forceful personality; he was, above all else, a man who treasured domestic tranquillity, and the tempestuous Alva provided little of that. He was disillusioned with her endless round of parties, he was disillusioned with her overarching aspirations, and he was disillusioned at the contemptuous way in which she treated him. Perhaps it was inevitable: it was Alva's ambition, not love, that had led to her marriage, and once she could lay claim to what Willie possessed, she had little use for her husband. "I never understood why my parents ever married," Consuelo would later say. "They had absolutely nothing in common. I don't even think they liked each other very much."[39] While she clung ferociously to social expectations in public, Alva had never been a model of nineteenth-century demure femininity, and, at least behind the safety of her own doors, her rebellious, unorthodox ideas had come to dictate her private behavior. "I don't believe in marriage," she once declared. "I never shall until we have true equality of the sexes. The marriage ceremony itself shows the unfairness of women's positions. When a woman can get up in the pulpit, mumble a lot of words over a couple and say 'go away and sleep together,' then I'll uphold marriage, not before."[40]

By the time she moved into Marble House, Alva had already begun an affair with her husband's best friend, the diminutive Oliver Hazard Perry Belmont (he stood only five feet tall), a man five years her junior. Belmont, recalled Elizabeth Drexel Lehr, was "one of the handsomest men, with his dark eyes, clear cut profile, and slender, faun-like grace."[41] Scion of the wealthy August Belmont and his wife, Caroline, Oliver was a man of few ambitions. He had entered the U.S. Naval Academy at Annapolis but had done so poorly that he was dropped from his class; through the machinations of his father—and the intervention of the secretary of the navy—Oliver was reinstated, although he was never happy at sea and eventually resigned his commission.[42] It was while on holiday in Newport that he met his first wife, Sarah Swan Whiting, whom he married in 1882. The union quickly collapsed when Sarah insisted on

Oliver H. P. Belmont.

taking her mother and two of her sisters with them on their Parisian honeymoon; disheartened, Belmont spent most of their time in Paris drinking and visiting disreputable night spots, eventually abandoning his new wife for an extended tour of Europe. Within a year the couple was divorced.[43]

Happily free of all concerns, Belmont devoted himself to pleasure. Then, in 1888, he joined Willie Vanderbilt aboard the latter's yacht *Alva* on a Mediterranean cruise, and a romance with his best friend's wife quickly developed. By the end of the cruise, society gossips were already whispering about an affair, a situation exacerbated when Belmont joined the couple on a cruise the following year.[44] According to a popular story that made the rounds in society, one afternoon Vanderbilt returned to his house unexpectedly early and discovered Oliver hiding in his bedroom closet. "Willie," one society gentleman declared, "should have shot him!"[45] Instead, his reaction seems to have been relief; already embroiled in his own sexual liaisons, the knowledge of his wife's infidelities freed Willie from any lingering feelings of guilt. That he seemed to welcome the situation was evidenced in November 1893 when, with full knowledge of his wife's feelings, he once again invited Belmont to join the couple on a cruise aboard his new yacht *Valiant* to Europe, the Mediterranean, and India.

But if Willie hoped to maintain his marriage for the sake of convenience, he had neglected to consider the forceful personality of his wife. The cruise went disastrously wrong, and Alva abruptly left *Valiant* in the Mediterranean, leaving her husband and his guests with indisputable evidence that she was no longer content to act in a charade of respectability.[46] As their daughter, Consuelo, recalled, there were many bitter arguments that created an atmosphere of "dread and uncertainty."[47] After several months of heated shouting matches, during which Alva loosed "expletives of a character to turn all the milk in the refrigerators," she simply stopped speaking to her husband; she communicated with Willie only through brutally unkind messages that a reluctant Consuelo was forced to deliver.[48] Eventually the strain became too much, and Willie abandoned his wife for the less hostile surroundings of an apartment at the Metropolitan Club in New York City.[49]

In 1895 Alva shocked society by leaving her husband and initiating divorce proceedings. "I was the first society woman to ask for a divorce," Alva proudly declared, "and within a year ever so many others had followed my example. They had been wanting divorce all the time, but they had not dared to do it until I showed them the way."[50] Although Alva was not, as she claimed, the first woman in society to end her marriage, she was certainly the most prominent, and, with typical hyperbole, the *New York World* declared it to be "the biggest divorce case that America has ever known."[51]

The contemporary press exploded with every salacious detail. Ever gallant, Willie offered up the fact that he already had an American mistress in Paris, the improbably named Nellie Neustretter, which allowed his adulterous wife to claim the role of injured party. A native of Nevada, Neustretter had abandoned her husband and gone to Paris hoping to attract a wealthy lover.[52] She was, declared the *New York World*, "a woman notorious in Europe," upon whom Willie was rumored to have lavished an annual allowance of some $200,000 ($4 million in 2008) along with houses in Paris and Deauville.[53] Although there had been hints about Alva's relationship with Belmont, and no one in society was fooled, publicly, at least, her reputation had been saved.

But the undercurrent of hostility that drove Alva suggested a situation far worse than even the papers of the day dared hint, and a scandal of truly international proportions. Nellie Neustretter almost certainly shared Willie's bed, but Alva was unlikely to have cared about such a minor and even expected indiscretion. What she did not expect and, indeed, could not tolerate, was the rumor that her husband had taken her childhood friend and confidante Consuelo Yznaga as his mistress. Not only had the former Lady Mandeville and, by 1892, the widowed Duchess of Manchester been her closest friend but also, to make matters worse, Alva's sister Virginia had married Consuelo's brother, Fernando Yznaga. Certainly the story was prevalent in society, and the *New York World* dared hint that this was the ultimate cause for the collapse of the union.[54] If such a liaison existed, Alva's discovery of the fact—more than Willie's affair with Nellie—would explain her lingering bitterness over her marriage and perhaps her own reckless, retaliatory move in embarking on an affair with her husband's closest friend.[55]

Whatever the truth, the Vanderbilts were careful to present to the public and to the court only the story of Willie's affair with Nellie upon which he and Alva had agreed. The divorce proceedings began on January 3, 1895, and concluded on March 5, when Judge Barrett of the New York State Supreme Court granted a decree of dissolution. Alva, as the officially wronged party, was awarded a substantial settlement of approximately $2.3 million ($52.9 million in 2008), along with alimony amounting to roughly $200,000 ($4.6 million in 2008) per year and full custody of the couple's three children, Consuelo, William Jr., and Harold. By the terms of the decree, she was free to marry again, while as long as Alva lived, Willie was expressly forbidden to do so, at least in the State of New York, although any union contracted elsewhere would be recognized as valid. She kept Marble House, which had been a birthday present; Willie offered her the French château at 660 Fifth Avenue as well, but she declined, owing to the cost of its maintenance.[56]

"Until Mrs. W. K. Vanderbilt's advent," the *New York World* rather incorrectly told its readers, "the family was unheard of in New York society, except occasionally when it was abused for watering stocks or damning the public. Mrs. W. K. Vanderbilt thought that better things could be done with their opportunities. She took Willie K. by the hand and led the way for all the Vanderbilts into the gay world of society, Fifth Avenue, terrapin, Newport, dry champagnes, servants in livery, men who don't work, women with no serious thoughts, and all the other charms of fashionable existence."[57]

Despite this blistering comment on what the *New York World* deemed the rather shallow existence of everyone involved, Alva emerged triumphant in the eyes of most of the public. Divorce could have ruined a woman of her standing, but she ignored the slurs and married Oliver Belmont on January 11, 1896, in a quiet ceremony conducted by William Strong, the mayor of New York City, at her new house at 24 East 72nd Street.[58] Alva promptly moved out of Marble House (though she continued to have her laundry done there) and down Bellevue Avenue to Belmont's own Newport mansion, the sixty-room Belcourt.[59] Designed by Richard Morris Hunt in 1891, this was one of the town's most peculiar houses, created to evoke a French hunting lodge in the reign of Louis XIII,

Oliver Belmont's Belcourt in Newport, showing the original entrance ramps to the house that allowed carriages to enter the mansion.

and had cost Belmont some $3 million ($60 million in 2008).[60] With its light-colored stone walls ornamented with dull red brick stringcourses and surrounds, its rounded copper dormer windows and high mansard roofs, Belcourt offered the strong medieval atmosphere Alva so loved, but its unique combination of residence and stable was a far cry from the stately opulence of Marble House.[61]

While there was little Alva could do about her new husband's infatuation with horses, she absolutely refused to have them in the main house. The carriage entrances were closed off, and she transformed the former vestibule into an Italian Renaissance–style banquet hall, while several new reception rooms were created from the old carriageway.[62] Alva had a new grand staircase, said to be a copy of one from the reign of François I in the Musée de Cluny in Paris, carved and installed, though she was never entirely happy with the arrangement and had it moved a number of times before her workers threatened to rebel.[63]

At the top of the staircase stretched the grand hall, a somber space hung in deep red silk damask patterned with Belmont's initials above a carved oak wainscot, and dimly lighted by stained-glass windows adorned with

Oliver Belmont's Belcourt in Newport, the facade facing Bellevue Avenue.

his family crest. A similar crimson damask lined the François I music room, where heavy carved stone reliefs above the doorways and chimneypiece depicted medieval hunts of French kings. After such darkly rich interiors, the dining room came as a surprise. An oval room decorated in Louis XV–style rococo, this was all luminous ivory woodwork, fluted Corinthian columns framing floor-length windows, and tall mirrors to reflect the light. Concealed behind a raised cornice circling a shallow dome embellished with sculpted neoclassical reliefs were sixty carbon-filament bulbs, installed in 1894 by Belmont's friend Thomas Edison, in the first use of indirect lighting in the United States.[64] The heart of Belcourt, however, was its Gothic ballroom. Seventy feet long and rising thirty feet to a ribbed, vaulted ceiling pierced with five thirteenth-century stained-glass trefoil dormers to echo the five arched windows below them, this was an extraordinary piece of theater, its gleaming white walls offering the perfect background to Belmont's collection of medieval arms and armor. In a final dramatic flourish, Hunt crafted a twenty-foot-high chimneypiece of Caen stone designed to resemble a castle, bristling with towers, battlements, and carved figures that watched in silence over this expensive bit of fantasy.[65]

Alva found Belcourt utterly wanting in comfort. Although Belmont kept a staff of thirty servants and the house boasted sixty rooms, there was only one bedroom, a severely decorated, medieval-style chamber with stenciled walls, a beamed ceiling, and a hooded, carved fireplace. She quickly rectified this situation, commissioning Hunt to add a suite for her twelve-year-old son, Harold, and, more lavishly, one for herself. In contrast to the rather stark decoration of the majority of the house, Alva's new rooms were frothy rococo concoctions, lined with antique boiseries culled from several châteaux and a collection of fine French furniture. With the interior deemed suitable to her continued social ambitions, and ignoring the collective wrath of the Vanderbilt and Belmont families, Alva boldly resumed entertaining at the side of her new husband.

Notoriety, though, was a difficult thing to escape, particularly for a woman of Alva's social standing in the Gilded Age. Belcourt became a regular fixture for the trolleys and omnibuses of tourists who clogged Bellevue Avenue in the summer, as guides armed with megaphones shouted stories about the mansions and their occupants. Once, Alva was in the midst of a luncheon at Belcourt when she saw the approach of one such cortege. "Oh, here's that dreadful man with the megaphone," she told her guests. "He's going to tell all the tourists about our staircase. Do listen to what he says; it really is too funny for words." They rushed to the windows, craning necks as the man loudly shouted, "Here you see before you the new home of a lady who is much in the public eye, a society lady who has just been through the divorce courts. She used to dwell in the marble halls with Mr. Vanderbilt. Now she lives over the stables with Mr. Belmont."[66]

20

SWELLS IN NEWPORT

JUST THREE MONTHS AFTER MARBLE HOUSE made its stunning debut, another Newport cottage owned by the Vanderbilts captured the attention of the press. In 1885, Cornelius Vanderbilt II had purchased the Breakers, a rambling Queen Anne–style mansion at the tip of Ochre Point, from tobacco merchant Pierre Lorillard. Designed by Peabody & Stearns, this was a rather gloomy house, adorned with spidery towers and monumental chimneystacks and wrapped in wide piazzas overlooking the ocean. In November 1892, disaster struck when a fire broke out; by the time the flames had been doused, all that remained of the Breakers were its tall brick chimneys, standing as lonely sentinels over the mournful, smoking ruins.

With eleven acres dominating the tip of Ochre Point, the estate was too scenic to abandon, and the fire gave Cornelius and his wife, Alice, the opportunity to begin anew, this time with the talents of Richard Morris Hunt. It has often been suggested that Hunt received the commission as the result of a rather expensive rivalry between Alva Vanderbilt and her more retiring sister-in-law Alice, reflecting the latter's wish to erect a structure that would dwarf Marble House in both size and ostentation. At the time, however, Hunt was already employed by the senior Vanderbilts, working with fellow architect George Browne Post in enlarging their New York City residence, and, initially at least, neither Corneil nor his wife envisioned their Newport house in grandiose terms. They wanted a comfortable, luxurious, but relatively modest summer escape; it was Hunt who apparently forced the issue, presenting increasingly elaborate and larger plans and ultimately convincing the couple that the site—as well as their wealth and social position—required something truly monumental.[1] Hunt did not find every aspect of the commission quite so easy. Accustomed to working with the architecturally sympathetic Alva, he soon discovered that her sister-in-law Alice had neither knowledge of his profession nor respect for his work. To Alice, Hunt was merely a glorified hired hand, and her "rudeness," as he put it, "made the work trying occasionally."[2]

Initial designs in the French Renaissance style were rejected, perhaps in an effort to break away from the profusion of châteaux for which Hunt had become so famous.[3] Hunt turned instead to sixteenth-century palazzos of Turin and Genoa, a decision that also evoked the idea of the Vanderbilts as modern-day incarnations of the powerful and artistic Medici family.[4] Work began in the spring of 1893 and took a mere two years; by the time of its completion in 1895, more than $7 million ($140 million in 2008) had been spent to create this piece of extravagance.[5] "In the matter of cost and general appointment," proclaimed the *New York Times* of the new Breakers, "it is said to outrank any private summer residence in the world."[6]

At Ochre Point Avenue, an arched, thirty-foot-high wrought-iron gate barred the unwelcome. Commissioned at a cost of some $75,000 ($1.5 million in 2008), this was a masterpiece of elaborate, gilded rocailles alternating with fleurs-de-lis, oak, and acorn leaves ascending in tendrils to a scrolled oval set with the initials CV.[7] On the other side of this gate, past tranquil lawns shaded by protective elms, lindens, and maples, Hunt's new palace rose in splendor at the head of an angled drive.[8]

A massive building of three principal storeys, the new Breakers dominated Ochre Point, its walls of buff-colored Indiana limestone shimmering luminously in the summer sun. To enrich its triumphal facade, Hunt deployed rows of composite Doric and Ionic columns, stringcourses, carved stone swags and reliefs, and rusticated corner quoins that anchored

The Breakers, the Newport cottage of Cornelius Vanderbilt II, showing the main entrance facade and porte cochere.

the house to its surrounding terrace; above, resting atop a carved, bracketed cornice concealing an attic floor with rooms for thirty-three servants, he crowned the building with a low, hipped roof, a panoply of mottled red terra-cotta tiles that provided a dramatic burst of color.[9] The entrance was severe, but to the southeast, where the house faced the crashing surf from which it derived its name, the architecture was warmer: a central, double arcade linked two projecting wings flanked by shadowed loggias, created a sinuous rhythm of arches that danced across the facade to create a shifting series of shadows and light, while a semicircular bow to the southwest, fringed with a peristyle of Doric columns, added a graceful touch that alleviated any lingering ponderous impressions.[10]

With more than seventy rooms, the Breakers was the largest of the Newport cottages. Beyond the tall gates, guests passed beneath the porte cochere, beyond a massive set of carved oak doors, and through two-ton wrought-iron and glass grilles, ascending a short flight of stairs, where an arch revealed the immense panorama of the great hall.[11] Hunt conceived the room as an echo of an Italian *cortile* (courtyard); an open space

The Breakers, the Newport cottage of Cornelius Vanderbilt II, showing the facade facing the Atlantic Ocean.

would have been impractical given the vagaries of the Atlantic weather, but a double row of tall windows and a trompe l'oeil ceiling, ringed by an ornate carved and gilded cornice and painted to resemble a blue sky strewn with clouds, lent the appropriate sense of airiness. A fifty-foot square rising some forty-five feet high, the great hall was a luminous space of cream-colored Caen stone walls adorned with ornamental panels of colored marbles, decorative masks, sculpted garlands embellished with oak leaves and acorns, and fluted pilasters topped by capitals of carved oak leaves and acorns. Arcades to the north and south not only added axial approaches to suites of rooms but also broke up the hall's rectilinear lines; columns of gray marble with alabaster capitals framed the openings of an encircling upper arcade set with wrought-iron and ormolu railings. From here one could look down on four immense bronze chandeliers with milky opaque globes, designed to match eight tall bronze candelabra standing at intervals across a floor of colored, polished marble.[12] It was a dignified space, cool and quiet, offering a subtle, almost cautious introduction to the delightful and luxuriously unambiguous interiors that followed.

Hunt consigned the decoration of several of the rooms to the firm of Jules Allard & Sons, which in turn commissioned Parisian Richard Bouwens van der Boijen to create elaborate interiors suited to the demands of such a monumental building. The morning room was perhaps the least formal of these spaces, yet even it failed to escape the rich overlay of expensive materials and imposing decor. In a sun-washed space set at the southeastern corner of the building, the morning room's French doors opened to flanking loggias, while tall windows overlooked the carpet of turf stretching to the Atlantic. Conceived as an evocation of the Florentine Renaissance style, with walls of pale gray ringed by elaborately carved and gilded Ionic pilasters, the morning room featured eight corner panels painted on silver leaf and depicting the Muses; stylized representations of the four elements graced sliding mahogany doors; and an allegorical scene of the four seasons danced across a ceiling awash with rocailles and garlands. Against this monochromatic background, a monumental chimneypiece of blue-gray Campian marble, ornamented with ormolu caryatids, cornucopias, and garlands, provided a surprising burst of color. Despite its undisguised richness, the room was far from oppressive, its solemnity relieved by an abundance of natural light and the cheerful cream and rose floral brocade that covered the gilded, Renaissance-style sofas and chairs.[13]

Boijen also designed the adjoining music room, with its semicircular bay, flanked by Ionic columns, opening to a sunken parterre garden. Like the morning room, it featured wall panels of pale gray, this time highlighted with gilt moldings and cartouches. Immense mirrors and plaques of smoky blue Campian marble added to the room's lustrous sparkle during balls and receptions, while gilded sofas and chairs covered in Venetian cut-velvet brocade of deep crimson to match the curtains interjected regal drama. Bands of gilded foliage twisted around Ionic columns, rising to a coffered ceiling picked out in gold and silver leaf, where two immense ormolu and crystal chandeliers framed a painting depicting harmony, music, song, and melody.[14]

Imported Circassian walnut and handtooled green Spanish leather embossed with gold cloaked the walls of the more masculine library, with its Renaissance-style ceiling of carved coffers highlighted with gold and inset with polychrome reliefs. Built-in bookcases inset beneath arched panels embellished with gilded reliefs held an array of leather-bound volumes, but the room was dominated by a massive, sixteenth-century carved limestone chimneypiece. Purchased from the Château d'Arnay-le-Duc, its archaic French inscription was more than a little ironic amid all of this splendor: "Little do I care for riches, and do not miss them, since only cleverness prevails in the end."[15]

More than six tons of pale gray-green Cippolino marble, framed with yellow alabaster arches and inset with colored marble mosaics, faced the walls of the billiard room. Conceived as a thematic representation of ancient Rome, it bore a vaulted ceiling adorned with floral mosaics depicting a mother and her children bathing, arching above a mosaic floor inlaid with a motif of oak leaves and acorns.[16]

The state dining room was the mansion's most opulent interior. Designed for Hunt in the Italian Renaissance style by Richard Bouwens van der Boijin, this was a cavernous, two-storey space of some forty-two by fifty-eight feet faced in Cippolino marble. Circling the room were twelve monumental columns of red and cream alabaster backed by matching pilasters, their gilt bronze Corinthian capitals supporting a cornice clustered with carved and

The state dining room in the Breakers, Newport.

gilded garlands, masks, and life-size sculpted figures. A coved plafond, painted with classical scenes and pierced with oeil-de-boeuf windows, swept up to a central painted panel depicting Aurora, flanked by two twelve-foot ormolu and Baccarat crystal chandeliers that shimmered above a sixteenth-century table of carved oak inlaid with lemonwood marquetry. Renaissance-style reliefs, delicately picked out in silver leaf, decorated an arched panel set with a hooded chimneypiece of blue-gray Cippolino marble ornamented with ormolu appliqués, while rich crimson damask, cascading from gilded pelmets over the windows and covering the thirty-four gilt bronze chairs, reinforced the room's stately, almost overpowering luxury.[17]

From the central arch at the northern end of the great hall, a handsome staircase of Caen stone, fringed by intricate wrought-iron balustrades ornamented in gilded bronze reliefs, rose in twin flights from a landing hung with a twenty-four-foot-long seventeenth-century Flemish tapestry depicting King Darius of Persia offering tribute to Alexander the Great. By day, panels of opalescent and stained glass designed by Newport artist John La Farge and originally installed in Cornelius's New York City residence washed the ascent in natural light; at night, hanging bronze lanterns illuminated the crimson-carpeted steps.[18] Author and Newport resident Edith Wharton had introduced the Vanderbilts to her friend and future collaborator Ogden Codman Jr., and Corneil and Alice commissioned the designer to decorate the family suites on the second floor. In contrast to the lavish scale and monumental appearance of the public rooms, these chambers were more human though unmistakably elegant. Here Codman created a cool refuge of neoclassical taste, with enameled white woodwork, wall panels of floral silk or cretonne, and deep, plush crimson carpets.[19] Amid this restraint, however, the bathrooms were models of extravagance. During construction, they were piped for hot and cold freshwater and seawater, allowing bathers to select their preference, although the tubs, many carved from enormous, single blocks of marble, usually were so cold that servants had to first heat them with lashings of hot water before members of the family could comfortably bathe.[20]

On August 14, 1895, Cornelius and Alice—now christened "Alice of the Breakers" by Harry Lehr—formally inaugurated the new mansion with a debutante ball for their twenty-year-old daughter, Gertrude.[21]

Passing through its immense rooms, with their colored marbles, sparkling chandeliers, and gilded embellishments, guests marveled at the splendid excess of it all. Whatever her own social shortcomings, Hunt had provided the mousy Alice with an incredibly lavish and enchanting fantasy, a carefully crafted theatrical stage that dwarfed Alva's Marble House in both magnitude and unrivaled extravagance.

By the turn of the century, Ward McAllister's distasteful—if tolerated— "swells" had descended on the town, purchasing lots and erecting ever more grandiose summer cottages. Former resident Henry James found the town's transformation a most unwelcome development, particularly the introduction of mansions he termed "white elephants." He complained, "They look queer and conscious and lumpish—some of them, as with an air of the brandished proboscis, really grotesque—while their averted owners, roused from a witless dream, wonder what in the world is to be done with them. The answer to which I think can only be that there is absolutely nothing to be done; nothing but to let them stand there always, vast and blank, for reminder to those concerned of the prohibited degree of witlessness, and of the peculiarly awkward vengeances of affronted proportion and discretion."[22] Visiting French author Paul Bourget was equally discouraged, calling these immense houses models of "excess, abuse, absence of moderation. On the floors of halls, which are too high, there are too many precious Persian and Oriental rugs. There are too many tapestries, too many paintings on the walls of the drawing rooms. The guest chambers have too many bibelots, too much rare furniture, and on the lunch or dinner table there are too many flowers, too many plants, too much crystal, too much silver."[23]

Not all of the town's Gilded Age cottages easily fit such criticisms. Perhaps the most sublime of these was Rosecliff, the shimmering white palace built by Stanford White for Tessie Oelrichs. In 1891, Tessie—along with her sister Virginia—had purchased Rose Cliff, an eleven-acre estate at 548 Bellevue Avenue overlooking the Atlantic. Formerly owned by diplomat and historian George Bancroft, it drew its name from the lush gardens ringing an 1851 Italianate house.[24] "The roses imported or home bred were remarkable for number and variety, which throve close to the edge of the ocean," recalled one Newport resident, "as Mr. Bancroft coaxed them to acknowledge that the sea air was as good for their health and complexions as it was for that of delicate women."[25] While the situation was splendid, the old house was deemed too small, and in 1898 Tessie commissioned White to design a lavish residence to complement the surroundings, with Jules Allard assuming responsibility for several of the main rooms. Work was slowed by a particularly harsh winter, and Tessie insisted on taking up residence in July 1900, before construction could be completed. For the house's first party, screens of potted palms and immense bowers of flowers concealed the still-unfinished interior.[26]

The new Rosecliff, as the building was called, was completed in 1902, but it was two years later, in the summer of 1904, when the house reached its social zenith.[27] To celebrate the Astor Cup yacht race in Newport's Narragansett Sound, Tessie summoned her society friends to an event that quickly became one of Newport's most storied parties, the Bal Blanc. Harry Lehr, who helped plan the event, decreed that the guests should all appear in white: white gowns adorned with translucent diamonds and pearls for the ladies, and eighteenth-century-style white satin coats and knee breeches for the gentlemen. In addition, Tessie and

The entrance facade of Rosecliff, the magnificent Newport cottage built by Stanford White for Tessie Oelrichs.

Harry asked the ladies to powder their hair to imitate eighteenth-century wigs, while the gentlemen were requested to shave off their mustaches and beards, in an effort to replicate the court of Versailles.[28] When they learned of this, many of the male guests rebelled, saying that they would "not make fools of themselves to please Harry Lehr."[29] Instead, most of the gentlemen resorted to hunting costume, or came attired in formal black evening wear, which offered a successful contrast to their partners.[30]

Just after ten on the evening of August 19, 1904, lines of elegant carriages began snaking across Newport and along Bellevue Avenue, conveying privileged guests to Tessie's great fete. For those not previously invited, there could have been no better introduction to its splendors than the theatrical spectacle that Friday night. Turning off Bellevue, carriages followed a spectral ribbon of hundreds of white lights, flickering like pale fiery teardrops against the consuming blackness of night, past sweeping lawns lined with dark trees and dotted with ghostly statuary before Rosecliff burst upon them in all its magnificence.[31] Concealed lights bathed the house in a soft glow, spilling over carefully clipped hedges and banks of flowers set against a glistening facade of white, glazed terracotta ornamented with garlands and putti in shadowed relief. Built in an H-shape, Rosecliff was modeled on the Grand Trianon at Versailles, White creating a spirited evocation of Mansart's original rather than a diligent copy, replacing the central, open colonnade with a ballroom and flanking it with wings that embraced marble terraces overlooking the lawn to the west and the Atlantic to the east. Paired Ionic pilasters played across the main storey, supporting an ornamental stringcourse and a low second floor topped with a classical balustrade circling a concealed attic.[32]

Carriages deposited guests at the end of the southern wing, where glowing lanterns suspended from a gently curved wrought-iron-and-glass canopy marked the main entrance. Footmen in new white and tan liveries specially commissioned for the occasion flanked the elaborate wrought-iron-and-glass doors embellished with ormolu rocailles, heads inclined as the parade of ladies and gentlemen stepped into a luminous, white-walled vestibule adorned with Ionic pilasters and sculpted reliefs.[33] Here stood Tessie, in a gown of white lace sewn with silver thread, her white-powdered hair crowned by three tall ostrich plumes and artfully draped

The elaborate wrought-iron-and-glass canopy over the main entrance to Rosecliff, the Newport cottage of Tessie Oelrichs.

with strands of diamonds and pearls that gleamed as she greeted her guests; at her side was her sister Virginia Vanderbilt, costumed as Marie Antoinette in a gown of white crepe de chine, a collar of diamonds and pearls flashing fire from around her neck.[34]

Masses of palms, white hydrangeas, and hollyhocks framed the guests, who followed a gold-edged red carpet up a short, shallow flight of steps and beneath an open, tripartite Palladian screen of columns to the stair hall, where twin flights of pale Caen stone from above curved down to a landing set with a tall arched window before cascading in a sweep to the marble floor; when viewed from below, this sinuous rococo fantasy formed the shape of a heart, a delightful and feminine touch in this decidedly feminine house.[35] Directly ahead, in the southeastern wing facing the Atlantic, lay the salon, an oddly incongruous yet cohesive mixture of conflicting styles. White had intended to fill the walls with a set of Beauvais tapestries after designs by François Boucher; Tessie, however, balked at their expense and covered the panels between Corinthian pilasters with less costly hangings purchased from Jules Allard. Twenty feet above the guests, two immense ormolu and crystal chandeliers hung

The grand staircase at Rosecliff, Newport.

from an elaborately coffered ceiling, casting prisms of light over the glittering assemblage, which could look with wonder at a tall, Gothic-style chimneypiece of Caen stone bristling with carved ornaments to surprise and amuse against this neoclassical backdrop.[36]

Berger's Hungarian Band and Mullaly's Orchestra provided music as Harry Lehr, dressed as a courtier from Versailles in a white satin surcoat, a white ruffled lace shirt, knee breeches, and silk stockings, led the two hundred guests, who danced in Tessie's sparkling white ballroom at the center of the house.[37] The largest private ballroom in Newport, its eighty-foot length was bedecked with banks of white roses, orchids, and lilies of the valley, the rows of five French doors topped with arched lunettes lining its eastern and western sides thrown open to the warm night air. As they swirled over the parquet floor beneath two immense ormolu and crystal chandeliers, the guests were engulfed in this rococo concoction by Jules Allard, where rows of paired, fluted Corinthian pilasters rose to an elaborately molded plaster frieze, picked out in tones of gray and ivory, topped by a trompe l'oeil ceiling depicting a blue sky strewn with gauzy clouds.[38]

When they tired of dancing, guests could refresh themselves with ices and champagne in the Louis XVI–style dining room at the northwestern corner of the house, where ivory-colored boiseries framed immense eighteenth-century French landscape paintings that glowed in the light from two bronze *doré* and crystal French chandeliers. A few of the gentlemen vanished to the billiard room, its walls of bleached English oak and chimneypiece carved with depictions of Irish kings and an array of nautical motifs offering a solidly masculine retreat in which to smoke. At midnight the guests repaired to the eastern terrace for a formal supper. Here, twelve round tables had been set beneath a temporary arbor of white Corinthian columns, entwined with garlands of smilax and ivy, supporting a canopy of white silk woven with silver birch, garlands of white hydrangea, and hanging baskets of white orchids, all laced with tiny, sparkling white electric lights. From each table, draped in white damask and bedecked with a towering arrangement of white lilies of the valley set with twinkling lights, guests could look across the sloping lawn to the silvery, splashing arc of a fountain where white swans floated in the basin. As they dined, guests were treated to yet another unexpected touch. To celebrate the Astor Cup yacht race, Tessie had wanted a vista of ships to provide a suitably nautical touch. According to legend, she asked the U.S. Navy to anchor its White Fleet in the ocean just off her estate and was genuinely surprised when they refused. In fact, Tessie simply had a string of a dozen full-size silhouettes hastily created, painted white and strung with sparkling white lights, and set upon the dark blue waters of the Atlantic, where their shimmering profiles served as a magnificent trompe l'oeil backdrop. A cotillion, with favors of silver desk sets, table ornaments, toilette sets, clocks, and engraved cigarette cases, ended with a magnificent display of colorful fireworks over the spectral mock white fleet anchored off the estate. Society was enchanted by the extravagant spectacle, which was said to have cost some $30,000 ($690,000 in 2008), and by Tessie's fantastic white palace at the edge of the sea.[39]

Nothing could have offered a greater contrast to Rosecliff's gleaming formality than the Newport house built by local architect Dudley Newton in 1897 for Mamie Fish. With suitable plots of land along Bellevue Avenue not only scarce but also prohibitively expensive, Mamie purchased a site at Ocean Avenue and Jeffrey Road, high on a bluff overlooking Bailey's Beach and the crashing waves of the Atlantic Ocean. At the time it was one of the more remote of Newport's social houses, but this was not its only claim to distinction. Not for Mamie the Italian palazzos, French châteaux, and Gothic castles of her Gilded Age rivals: rather, she asked for a house in the increasingly fashionable colonial revival style. Crossways, as it was called, was a large, white structure, its two-storey facade ornamented with an immense temple portico and gable supported by four monumental Corinthian columns. Within, a great staircase offered a stage upon which Mamie could receive, and there was room for two hundred guests in her large dining room and ballroom.[40] Here she

Crossways, the Newport cottage built by Mamie Fish.

regularly ended the Newport season with her annual Harvest Ball each September, decorating the rooms with an array of fruits and vegetables, sheaves of cornstalks, pumpkins, and garlands of yellow and orange leaves shipped from Maine and Vermont.[41] One society wag, chafing at never having received an invitation to her Newport mansion, once confronted Mamie, snobbishly remarking, "I can never remember the name of your house, Mrs. Fish. Isn't it the Cross Patch?"

"Well, anyhow," she shot back, "it's a patch you'll never cross!"[42]

Within a few years, however, as Mamie's star ascended in the social firmament and her entertainments grew ever larger, she found Crossways too intimate. "I have determined that in order to entertain properly and to have just the degree of exclusiveness one desires," she declared, "it is the proper thing to have a big estate. I have plenty of ground here, but that is not what I want. And besides, I think that Newport is becoming too contracted for the society of the future. It is becoming too much a place for people to come who want to break into society."[43] Nevertheless, she failed to abandon the comforts of her house for a more lavish Newport palace.

"America," recalled Elizabeth Drexel Lehr of the Newport summer season, "will never again, I think, see entertaining on such a lavish, such a luxurious scale. Into those six or seven weeks were crowded balls, dinners, parties of every description, each striving to eclipse the other in magnificence. Colossal sums were spent in the prevailing spirit of rivalry."[44] The cost of summering in Newport could be astronomical. It was not unusual for a family to spend $2,000 to $4,000 ($46,000 to $92,000 in 2008) per week during their stays, with the most magnificent balls occasionally running near $100,000 ($2.3 million in 2008).[45] North Carolina millionaire Pembroke Jones admitted that he regularly set aside $300,000 ($6.9 million in 2008) each year for these ten weeks of Newport entertaining.[46] In the quest to escape what one contemporary termed the "magnificent monotony" of society's Newport entertainments, increasingly bizarre and peculiar displays took place, reaching a kind of zenith with William Fahnestock, who, for the opening of his Newport estate, Bois Doré (Golden Wood), decorated the trees in his garden with artificial fruit made of fourteen-carat gold.[47] When Grand Duke Boris Vladimirovich, cousin of Nicholas II, the last tsar of Russia, visited Newport shortly after the turn of the century, he—no stranger to unparalleled opulence—breathlessly encapsulated this almost overwhelming magnificence, declaring, "I have never dreamt of such luxury as I have seen in Newport! Is this really your America, or have I landed on an enchanted island? Such an outpouring of riches! It is like walking on gold. We have nothing to equal this in Russia."[48]

Society spent its days at leisure. There were drives down Bellevue Avenue and along the rocky Atlantic shoreline fringed by Ocean Avenue, a careful, fashionable promenade enacted each afternoon that offered a "magnificent display of horses and carriages and automobiles, and a still more magnificent display of beautiful women faultlessly dressed, who put themselves on parade and who know they are watched and criticized by the members of their set."[49] Ladies called on each other; gentlemen participated in coaching races and rode; there were yachting parties, afternoons spent watching polo matches at Izzard Field, and archery competitions.[50]

"For those who are hopelessly out of the race," commented one turn-of-the-century writer, "there is little enjoyment in this social Mecca. The only real satisfaction they have is in driving about and being mistaken for 'swells' by persons who know no better. And this explains why so many smart traps are seen on the public beach. In them handsomely gowned women pose and return the stare of the admiring excursionists and boarding house people with that insolently good natured air which they have copied from those who are of the elect, finding solace for their disappointed souls in the remarks of the crowd."[51]

The Newport Casino Club was one of the prime magnets. Built by James Gordon Bennett Jr. at the northern end of Bellevue Avenue between 1879 and 1880, this was a sprawling, shingle-style structure by McKim, Mead, & White, with shops opening to the street, and card rooms, smoking rooms, dining rooms, and a ballroom ranged around a horseshoe-shaped piazza shaded by intricate, ivy-covered lattice screens overlooking the lawn-tennis courts. Although the casino was an exclusive gathering spot, those outside the bounds of proper society still could purchase tickets for a dollar to gaze on America's aristocracy or to watch the matches of the newly formed U.S. National Lawn Tennis Tournament each August from galleries.[52] "A little awestruck crowd of humbler citizens (chiefly female) congregates opposite the club entrance . . . for at any moment may not one of the great dames of the republic . . . appear in the flesh and brighten for a few brilliant moments the monotony of the democratic horizon?" wrote one English visitor.[53]

This voyeuristic tone dominated Newport and led to much resentment. Society, recalled Elizabeth Drexel Lehr, "was only concerned in excluding the townspeople from any of the pastures they considered their own. They themselves might wander at will in the lovely old town with its quaint old-fashioned streets nestling down by the waterfront. But the inhabitants must not dream of returning the compliment. Not for them the sacred purlieus of Bellevue Avenue and Ocean Drive, where they might catch a glimpse of the forbidden splendors of villas which were only occupied for six or seven weeks in the year."[54]

One particular point of contention was Newport's fabled Cliff Walk, a scenic and sometimes precarious trail that meandered some three and a half miles along the ocean. First laid out in the 1860s, this skirted the cliffs from a point known as the Forty Steps near Ochre Point to Rough Point, a spit of land jutting into the ocean at the end of Bellevue Avenue. Residents of the town had always enjoyed strolling along its path, but when the Gilded Age mansions began to rise across Newport, many owners saw the walk—which bordered their lawns—as an unwelcome intrusion. Some attempted to close the Cliff Walk amid an immense out-cry, building stone walls studded with jagged and broken glass bottles, but the townspeople merely pulled them down and flung them into the Atlantic.[55] A few residents, complaining of vandalism, responded by sinking sections of the Cliff Walk below their lawns, or covering seg-ments with tunnels to prevent the public from gazing at their houses.[56] Mrs. John King Van Rensselaer explained, "This may perhaps seem churlish on the part of the rich proprietors to try as they do to exclude the public from access to their grounds, but they could tell many tales of the annoyances they have received from trespassers." She noted that "it is no unusual thing for people to walk up to the houses, sit on the piazza, or even enter the rooms" of those properties bordering the path.[57]

The Cliff Walk was not the only source of controversy. Dissatisfied with the growing numbers of visitors of other classes coming to the public Easton's Beach, Newport's upper-class families adopted Bailey's Beach as their exclusive playground. Owned and operated by the Spouting Rock Beach Association, Bailey's Beach became the ultimate test of one's acceptance into Newport society.[58] "Only the elite could bathe at Bailey's Beach," remembered Elizabeth Drexel Lehr. "It was Newport's most exclusive club. The watchman in his gold-laced uniform protected its sanctity from all interlopers. He knew every carriage on sight, fixed newcomers with an eagle eye, swooped down upon them and demanded their names. Unless they were accompanied by one of the members, or bore an introduction from an unimpeachable hostess, no power on earth could gain them admission. If they wanted to bathe, they could only go to Easton's Beach—'The Common Beach' as the habitués were wont to call it. There they would have the indignity of sharing the sea with the Newport townspeople."[59] Bailey's Beach, recalled one man, "was far from ideal for swimming—not in a class with the superb mile-long stretches of the public beach. At Bailey's, one often had to wallow about in a thick ooze of seaweed, through which tiny marine monsters scooted," and Blanche Oelrichs remembered that it reeked of the "veritable stench of the ocean."[60] Nevertheless, it remained an exclusive enclave, a place of such rigid etiquette that a woman could be thrown off the beach if she neglected to wear the customary black stockings during a dip in the Atlantic.[61]

After ten weeks of parties, promenades, bathing in the sea, and exquisite balls, members of society abandoned their glittering Newport cottages to retreat to quiet country estates in preparation for the coming winter season in New York. Servants rolled carpets in tarpaper and stored them; furniture disappeared beneath fitted dust covers; chandeliers were wrapped in foil and swathed in pale gossamer shrouds; cheesecloth enveloped paintings, clocks, and sculpture; awnings were lowered and shutters carefully closed against the coming winter.[62] A gloomy silence descended over the marble palaces and French châteaux as they awaited their owners' return the following summer.

21

THE SOCIAL SEASON

EACH OCTOBER, as the trees in Central Park shed their foliage and increasingly bitter winds swept off the Hudson and through the city, the great mansions along Fifth Avenue came to life as society returned to New York. Shutters were opened, windows washed, carpets unrolled across newly polished floors, furniture stripped of its protective covers, and chandeliers, paintings, and objets d'art exposed to the light of day. By the time occasional bursts of snow flurries rained down over the crowded streets and sidewalks, society had assembled behind the walls of its Italian palazzos and French châteaux, looking forward with expectation to a fresh round of lavish entertainments.

The winter social season stretched from the middle of November until the onset of Lent.[1] Over these twelve weeks, society flung itself headlong into a persistent rhythm of parties and receptions, dinners and balls, each designed to both dazzle in their opulence and to renew control of the elite over their own milieu. The pace could be exhausting: in one typical season, New York society enjoyed 301 receptions and teas, 205 dinner parties, 35 luncheons, 23 musicales, and 17 balls, not counting evenings at the theater and the opera.[2] For a debutante, this social whirl offered not only the excitement of spectacular diversions but, more importantly, the chance to meet eligible young suitors: during one season, Gertrude Vanderbilt, daughter of Cornelius and Alice, attended 92 dinner parties and dances.[3]

The New York Horse Show, held in the middle of each November, formally inaugurated each new season; it was, recalled one man, "the greatest society and fashionable function of the year."[4] Begun in 1883 and usually held at Stanford White's Madison Square Garden, the horse show always attracted the cream of New York society, who looked over the equine parade from the comfort of private boxes decorated in the black and yellow colors of the Horse Show Association. Thousands of dollars might be exchanged on any given day, as studs and mares were purchased and sold by discerning equestrians. Even the city's shops and restaurants entered into the spirit, bedecking windows with bunting in the association's colors, violets, and chrysanthemums.[5]

The horse show, noted the *New York Times*, marked "the first appearance in town of the crowds of men and women who live a life of feverish pleasure in the whirl of that indefinite thing known as society since their return from the resorts where their butterfly existence has been whiled away during the summer." While horses would be paraded about the ring covered in tan bark, the newspaper declared, "the real show" was "the crowd that will fill the boxes and wander about the promenade in the garden. All of the gay world will be out to see and to be seen, and there will be the very latest things in the way of Parisian hats and tailor made gowns, as well as the latest young things out in society."[6] It was, recalled Elizabeth Drexel Lehr, "a matter of strict form to wear a different costume at each performance—and not to miss any of the events. In New York, the boxes were numbered on the program so that those who came could know who was who."[7] One visiting French aristocrat, surveying the crowd, recalled that every lady present "tried to out-dress and out-pearl some other friend or enemy, while the pitiless radiance of the electric light shines on faces, the majority of which would have given points to Jezebel. Never had I seen such a collection of jewels and furs. Many of the women were perambulating jewelers' shops and their expensive furs baffled any guess as to their value."[8]

The days and weeks following the horse show witnessed society in an ever-changing round of tribal homage paid to a shifting altar of divertissements. In the Gilded Age, nearly every aspect of life during the season fell victim to the rituals of society. "Going to church was a social function," recalled Elizabeth Drexel Lehr. "Everything was religious. The more successful in business you were during the week, the more devoutly you attended church on Sunday. Pierpont Morgan took up the collection at St. Bartholomew's, the Vanderbilt men roared out the hymns untunefully at St. Thomas's."[9] Socially speaking, there were only five churches in New York City, all crowded around Fifth Avenue and its neighboring streets. The few Catholic members of society worshiped in the Gothic magnificence of St. Patrick's Cathedral, but their numbers were scarce; for most of the city's elite, the only denomination that mattered was the prim and proper Episcopal Church. With a passion for all things English, society eagerly seized on the Episcopalian faith, finding comfort and reassurance in its rich panoply of ritual and tradition. Indeed, noted one social historian, "the presence of an Episcopal church could raise the fashion level of a neighborhood."[10]

Certain churches enjoyed patronage by competing social powers. The Astors regularly worshiped at Trinity Church, designed and built in 1845–46 by architect Richard Upjohn on lower Broadway in the Gothic Revival style and adorned with a set of elaborate bronze relief doors added at the turn of the century by sculptor Karl Bitter.[11] The Vanderbilts divided their prayers between two churches. At the northeast corner of Madison Avenue and Forty-fourth Street stood St. Bartholomew's Episcopal Church, built in the 1830s and graced with a magnificent colonnade of Romanesque arches and a relief frieze of biblical scenes framing three sets of immense bronze doors with sculpted panels, given in memory of Cornelius Vanderbilt II, who had taught Sunday school here, by his widow, Alice, after his death in 1899.[12] Then there was St. Thomas's Episcopal Church, at the corner of Fifth Avenue and Fifty-third Street. Built in 1870 by Richard Upjohn in the high Gothic style, its dark brown stone exterior bristled with elaborate carvings and buttresses reaching to a tall spire that glowered over the avenue.

Stained-glass windows by John La Farge suffused the interior with a dim light that washed over a gilded altar and sculptures by Augustus Saint-Gaudens. Renowned for its fine organ and talented choir, St. Thomas's was called "the Vanderbilt church," as most members of that family worshiped here.[13]

The city's most fashionable church, however, was Grace Church, at 800 Broadway. Built in 1846 by architect James Renwick, who also designed St. Patrick's Cathedral, this was a massive, Gothic-style structure of arched doorways, lancet windows, carved finials, and a tall, shimmering spire. It always attracted an exclusive congregation, and it was the place in which those who aspired to join society could often be seen; it was popularly described as "the wealthiest Episcopal church in town."[14] The social nature of the institution was underscored during the tenure of Isaac Brown, a rector who presided over the church during the rise of the Gilded Age. A genial man, Brown was careful not to upset the social balance by filling his sermons with tales of the deserving poor and admonitions against the accumulation of great wealth; he also was a thorough snob who, wrote one historian, catered to the "pomps and vanities" of his wealthy congregation.[15] Brown was reputed to keep a list of eligible, thoroughly vetted young men known as "Brown's Brigade," who could be dispatched to balls if a hostess found herself hard pressed to fill out the ranks of potential dancing partners. Brown advised those aspiring to join New York society on what entertainments to give, whom to include on their invitation lists, and what questionable associations were best avoided. As a result he made Grace Church, in the words of one social historian, "the most fashionable and exclusive of our metropolitan courts of heaven."[16]

Another peculiarity of the city's most fashionable churches was the selling of their pews at exorbitant prices. These prices were determined by their size and prominence, with those on the aisle near the front often going for enormous sums. Although this helped finance the parish, there was something unseemly in the fact that people bid on places within a church, and the money brought in far exceeded mere necessity. Some $321,900 (approximately $6.4 million in 2008) was raised, for example, by auctioning off seats in St. Bartholomew's Church in 1872; Cornelius Vanderbilt paid $1,509 ($30,180 in 2008) for his family's large pew at the front of the church. Considered private assets, these pews bore brass plaques listing the owners' names and were passed down within families through wills.[17]

As ritualized as church attendance was the festive round of social occupations. Although many of the younger ladies had, by the turn of the century, abandoned the almost religious observance of New Year's Day calls, a few of the more dignified and traditionally minded hostesses persisted in this relic of Knickerbocker society. By custom, those who observed this tradition kept an open house from eleven in the morning until five in the afternoon, allowing those visitors paying their respects to appear and disappear throughout the proceedings.[18] Being one of the holdovers from the past, a New Year's Day reception tended to attract a fair number of the "old fossils" derided by Ward McAllister, who took advantage of this familiar custom from the days of their youth to undertake their social obligations.[19]

Eventually most New Year's Day receptions fell victim to the "at home" reception. Ladies always established several set at home days during the season, which were announced in the society columns of the city's papers. These days were largely governed by location: a lady who lived on Fifth Avenue habitually received, by custom established under Caroline Astor, on Tuesdays; if she lived on Madison Avenue, she received on Thursdays. Such geographical considerations were intended to ease the travel necessitated by multiple visits.[20] Aside from the reception of one's circle, an at home also offered ladies opportunities to ease eligible daughters into society functions amid surroundings less demanding and more congenial than formal dinners and balls. Daughters assisted their mothers, pouring tea and politely greeting guests, which allowed for their introduction to the most prominent hostesses of the day.[21]

An at home day called for an extended reception. Widows and elderly ladies were advised to wear dresses of black satin or velvet for such occasions, while cream or white dresses in brocaded silk, subtly embroidered and adorned with lace, were recommended for their younger counterparts; elbow-length gloves were de rigueur.[22] It was customary to offer a variety of refreshments: Lloyd Morris recalled tables draped with "snowy damask cloth that touched the floor," gleaming "with silver and cut glass.

There were salads of chicken and lobster; dainty sandwiches; trays of pastry; dishes of mints and chocolates," and "a fancy ice from the caterer's, a rococo structure of spun sugar, lace paper frills and satin ribbon bows."[23]

Among the rules that governed an at home day was a rigid code that often caused untold worry and unwarranted offense. A hostess, of course, could only approximately anticipate her prospective callers, but she always had to be on guard lest two ladies unknown to each other appear in her drawing room at the same time, for it was considered a strict rule that introductions should not be made during an at home. "It is an awkward and an embarrassing restriction," noted one authority. Such introductions could only properly be made after the hostess asked permission to do so, which often placed both her and her guests in an uncomfortable situation, particularly if some socially superior visitor desired no such acquaintance and pointedly cut the lady presented to her. Thus one might find in the same room two ladies, each befriended by their hostess but ignoring the other's existence, even to refusing to acknowledge polite inquiries on the grounds that they did not know the questioner.[24]

"Unsolicited introductions are bad for both parties," declared one adviser, who noted that above all, ladies must consider not only their positions but also the effect that an undesired introduction would have on her own circle. "Some large-hearted women of society are too generous by half in this way. A lady should by adroit questions find out how a new acquaintance would be received, whether or not it is the desire of both parties to know each other; for, if there is the slightest doubt existing on this point, she will be blamed by both. It is often the good-natured desire of a sympathetic person that the people whom she knows well should know each other. She therefore strives to bring them together at lunch or dinner, but perhaps finds out afterwards that one of the ladies has particular objections to knowing the other, and she is not thanked. The disaffected lady shows her displeasure by being impolite to the pushing lady, as she may consider her. Had no introduction taken place, she argues, she might have *still* enjoyed a reputation for politeness."[25]

Other days in the season might be given over to formal matinees or teas. An adaptation of the French original, a matinee—as enacted by New York society—was a morning reception, usually beginning at eleven and ending at one to allow for any luncheons at two. A matinee offered its hostess not only the opportunity to receive in a less formal manner than necessitated by evening but also the chance to follow Caroline Astor's dictum that the leaders of society should not only entertain but also enlighten and uplift. Thus most matinees were devoted to the presentation of a newly arrived pianist from Germany, a talented painter from Paris, or a brilliant soprano from Italy. Although a matinee was principally conceived for female attendance, ladies often held them on national holidays to ensure the presence of a few gentlemen.[26]

By the turn of the century, the ritual of a formal afternoon tea had largely become, as one lady complained, "a splendid ball by daylight, with every luxury of the season." Although the former custom of inviting a small circles of ladies to exchange gossip and enjoy some small refreshment lingered in a few of New York City's more traditional houses, most often afternoon teas were given not for enjoyment but as an excuse to pay off a multitude of social obligations at the least expense. Increasingly, the afternoon tea became the opportunity for a hostess to gently introduce a debutante daughter into society, from attending her during the greeting of guests to presiding over the tea table itself.[27]

In these long, dark winter nights, society took refuge in elaborate diversions. A few of the older, socially secure, and traditionally minded hostesses still clung to the soirees common in the first years of the Gilded Age. Soirees were considered exceptionally difficult affairs to manage: they existed in a separate category and could not stray into the territory reserved for a dinner or a ball, yet had to offer both entertainment and substantial refreshment. Held in the early evening, a soiree was generally artistic in nature, focusing on a literary reading, a chorale, or a small concert, often accompanied by a small buffet supper. Such an entertainment called for both foresight and diplomacy. In an era of increasingly opulent parties, a quiet circle listening to arias or somber chamber music offered little excitement, and there were few potential guests unlikely to be bored by such proceedings. Eventually, given the problems presented, most ladies abandoned the soiree entirely.[28]

In 1895, Mamie Fish shocked New York society by dining out with a few friends one Sunday evening at Sherry's Restaurant, at a time when ladies had to be escorted and moralists assumed that only actresses and other "loose" women dared to risk the censure of being so observed in public.[29] When the attendants took their wraps, Mamie and her party were found to be in fashionable décolleté; as they crossed the floor to their table, waiters averted their eyes while the rest of the patrons stared, mouths open in astonishment, or moving in loud whispers of "Disgusting!" and "Shameless!" "If they had come in naked they could hardly have caused more of a sensation," recalled Elizabeth Drexel Lehr. "Incredulity, horrified condemnation, outraged virtue registered themselves in varying degrees on every face."[30]

Mamie's brash experiment inaugurated a trend; even the indomitable Caroline Astor finally decided that she must see for herself what all of the fuss was about, and one evening in September 1895 she asked Harry Lehr to escort her to dinner at Sherry's.[31] The next day, the city's newspapers were full of the story. "To see that august lady," declared one reporter, "in a coquettish raiment of white satin, with the tiniest hair dress, at Sherry's on Sunday last, dos-a-dos almost with Lillian Russell, I could hardly believe my eyes. And she seemed to enjoy it, and nodded her head to the ragtime tunes, and took the most gracious interest in everything." Another man summed up the feelings of many when he wrote: "I never dreamed that it would be given to me to gaze on the face of an Astor in a public dining room."[32] The barrier had been breached, and with Mrs. Astor's imprimatur ladies regularly began to dine out, offering yet another evening diversion during the season; nevertheless, there was still a certain aura of prudish decorum, and a woman could find herself hastily asked to leave the premises if she was bold enough to light a cigarette in public.[33]

It was the opera, however, that formed the supreme height of Gilded Age cultural expression. Society was diligent in its devotion to the season at the Metropolitan Opera House in New York, but this had less to do with appreciation of the arts than with the opportunities these evenings offered for ladies to dazzle in their latest Parisian evening gowns and shimmer in their exquisite parures of jewelry. It was, to be sure, a "superlatively artificial" endeavor: for many, music was beside the point as, noted critic Ralph Pulitzer, society "can only endure it. For as a whole its musical sense is quite atrophied."[34] Yet for many, attendance at the opera, presenting themselves as objects of interest and envy, itself constituted the most significant demonstration of their culture. To this end, the opera dominated the winter social season; parties, dinners, and balls were planned around its schedule. Monday and Friday performances were considered the high points of the week; on these evenings, all of the ladies came *en grande toilette*, bedecked with tiaras, diamond necklaces, brooches, stomachers, and bracelets.[35]

For society, evenings at the opera followed an inevitable, precise pattern whose regularity lent an aura of majesty. Lines of sleek carriages and colorfully painted sleighs sped across the city, snow flying from wheels and runners and the bells on harnesses jingling gaily; within, ladies and gentlemen were safely wrapped in furs and woolen greatcoats against the chill night air. They passed beneath the eerie halos of streetlamps that burned against the black night, finally arriving at the immense Metropolitan Opera House, whose facade glowed with windows filled with light. The highest echelons of society—those who held parterre boxes at the opera—swept past the main entrance to private doorways at Thirty-ninth and Fortieth streets, where their carriages deposited them and they left the dark winter night for the blazing warmth of the marble foyer.

A sweep of crimson-carpeted stairs led to the first parterre, the renowned "Diamond Horseshoe." Although the Metropolitan held four tiers of private boxes, socially only the thirty-eight on the first parterre, their doors marked with small silver plaques bearing the names of their owners, mattered.[36] These boxes, held by subscribers and passed down from father to son, encompassed the cream of New York's Gilded Age society: Alva Vanderbilt Belmont had box 6, Mamie Fish box 9, Tessie Oelrichs box 5, the Goelet family box 24, and Clarence Mackay box 28.[37] The box at the center of all attention, however, was box 7, occupied by Mrs. Astor.[38]

A liveried usher escorted the owners to their boxes, where a maid waited to assist the ladies with their wraps. Each box contained a small sitting room, providing a refuge to which gentlemen could retreat to ease their boredom over a cigar and a glass of whiskey.[39] Owners often decorated these rooms with lavish floral displays: heiress Lillian Hammersley regularly had the walls and ceiling of her sitting room festooned with thick garlands of hothouse orchids.[40] Beyond, concealed by thick red velvet curtains, were the loges, each set with two gilded chairs at the front for the ladies, with three or four directly behind them for the gentlemen.[41]

The old Metropolitan Opera House in New York City.

From here they could gaze across the immense white and gold auditorium, lorgnettes or exquisite, bejeweled opera glasses by Lemaire sweeping over gilded columns to the putti clustered at the ceiling, taking in the iridescent flash of diamonds that spread like miniature infernos throughout the parterre.

Although the general audience was seated by eight-thirty, when the orchestra began the overture, no member of society ever appeared in his or her box until the middle of the first act.[43] Then the curtains at the back of the boxes parted, revealing "a radiance of satin, a scintillation of diamonds, a luster of pearls, a glow of rubies."[43] "The audience, if anything," noted one French visitor, "is even more gorgeously gowned and bejeweled than in Paris or London, and far more so than at a similar affair in poor bankrupt Rome, or even in St. Petersburg. If the precious stones and laces are what they look to be, these Americans must spend fortunes upon their women."[44]

Society's decision to largely treat the opera as an opportunity for display even dominated the selection of the Metropolitan season. Wagner was a particular bane: not only did many find his operas inordinately long and too cold but also, more to the point, many were dimly staged and left the auditorium in long stretches of darkness considered "prejudicial to display or scrutiny of a fashionable wardrobe and its gems."[45] The constant commotion in many of the boxes underlined a general lack of enthusiasm for the musical spectacle. Once, on hearing a great din emanating from the sitting room at the back of a box, a guest turned to her hostess to ask if something was amiss. "Oh, don't mind!" the hostess explained. It was only her debutante daughters, "playing bean bags with their callers. They're young, poor things, and must have something to pass away the time."[46] Sir Philip Burne-Jones noted "a pretty continuous flow of conversation in the parterre boxes during the entire performance; and this goes on steadily, irrespective of the music or the artists on the stage. Indeed, the opera in New York has become, for this particular set, little else than a social occasion, for the meeting of friends and talking; and one of them admitted to me that she was always anxious for the opera to come to an end, that she might get away to supper."[47]

It was not only immature debutantes who disrupted the program, for the gathered crowd always eagerly awaited the arrival of Caroline Astor. No matter what time the opera began, or what was being given, Mrs. Astor always appeared in box 7 promptly at nine, in the middle of the first act.[48] "Every feminine eye," recalled one man, followed "her progress to her box," scarcely "able to catalogue and evaluate the flashing, tinkling armor of diamond rings, emerald pendants, brooches, and necklaces with which she was bedecked. These might be supplemented with jeweled sunbursts, butterflies, a tiara, as well as with that most uncompromisingly named adornment—the diamond stomacher." Throughout the evening, he remembered, "hundreds of people who ordinarily wouldn't have had an opportunity to see her in full rig crowded around the box and paid her the tribute of rapt, open-mouthed scrutiny—a tribute which she seemed to enjoy."[49]

Caroline Astor rarely remained at the opera until its end; she received members of her own set and their special guests during the interval, but never left her box to pay homage to another.[50] During the second act she would quietly slip out of her box, on her way to some dinner party or ball.[51]"When her place was vacant," recorded one historian, "others would begin to drift away. Leaving before her was scarcely thinkable, not merely as a violation of protocol, but even more because some bit of byplay might occur that would be the next day's justification for having spent the previous evening at the opera."[52]

All of this spectacle and display not only turned the opera into a social event but also exposed less admirable traits. "Exclusive society, to have any reason for existence, must exclude," wrote one critic. "It must prove that it is select by showing itself in the midst of those whom it is rejecting. If it lived perpetually in a complete and splendid isolation the lower classes would have no ocular proof that they were being excluded, while society itself would have no collective sense of excluding them. The opera gives society a point of contact, and thus of contrast with that horde against whose incursions it is its mission to defend itself. Society's reunion in the visible midst of its foes gives it an esprit de corps, a solidarity, which it could never secure or maintain by uninterrupted aloofness."[53]

———— ❖ ————

22

THE SOCIETY DINNER PARTY

"THOUGH THE DEVICES by which Society is amused are countless," recorded one turn-of-the-century commentator, "no fiction seems to find such lasting favor as the dinner party."[1] In Knickerbocker New York, families dined and entertained at five and six in the afternoon; as nouveau riche society took hold, these entertainments gradually shifted later and later, until no fashionable person would sit down to dinner before eight or nine—an indulgence, recalled one man, "that Old New Yorkers outspokenly termed sinful."[2] "Not only has the hour changed," noted one observer, "but the meal itself has undergone a radical transformation, in keeping with the general increase of luxurious living, becoming a serious although hurried function."[3]

Elaborate dinner parties in the Gilded Age formed part of the highly ritualized milieu of the social elite, offering—as did the opera—opportunities for display and taste; moreover, a dinner party, as a private entertainment, provided reinforcement of exclusivity, enveloping the participants in a mantle of prestige and an iconic brilliance, a reassuring cocoon of privilege. With less than half a dozen recognized leaders of New York society, such invitations were necessarily limited: a dinner for a hundred hosted by Alva Vanderbilt Belmont lacked the exclusivity of one for twelve given by Caroline Astor.[4]

Dinners offered not only reciprocal entertainment of one's friends but also the opportunity to present and parade some particularly important politician or clergyman, a visiting prince or count, or, better yet, the occasional return to New York of one's aristocratic relatives—daughters, sons-in-law, sisters—from Europe. Such dinner parties were intricate affairs, often weeks in the planning. A hundred guests were not uncommon for a very formal dinner, but most consisted of twenty-four to forty-eight people, with smaller parties composed of twelve guests. The first consideration was the guest list. Despite the social rivals who challenged her declining pride of place after 1896, the ultimate prize remained an invitation to dine with Caroline Astor; indeed, noted the *New York Times*, "cards to Mrs. Astor's dinners were regarded here much in the same light as are commands to court functions abroad."[5] The principal object, advised Ward McAllister, was to "make your dinners so charming and agreeable that invitations to them are eagerly sought for and to let all feel that it is a great privilege to dine at your house, where they are sure they will meet only those whom they wish to meet."[6] This could be a delicate balancing act, as feuds and rivalries had to be known and respected to avoid any undue tensions or social repercussions.

Once a guest list was determined, invitations were sent out, always at least three weeks in advance.[7] Formal custom dictated the use of a large card of thick vellum, engraved with the simple formula *Mr. and Mrs. [X] request the pleasure of the company of _____ at dinner*, along with the date, time, and address.[8] These invitations, recalled Elizabeth Drexel Lehr, were always made out by Maria de Baril, a woman "who acted as a sort of social secretary to all the great hostesses of New York" and who made a career of doing their calligraphic work. "The moment an envelope addressed in her delicate handwriting, embellished with the Gothic scrolls which no one dreamt of imitating, appeared on the breakfast tray, one knew that here was an invitation of importance."[9] The daughter of a wealthy Peruvian family whose fortune had disappeared in a financial crisis, Maria kept a suite of rooms at the Hotel Stratford and insisted that most of her prospective clients call on her.[10] "Her handwriting was by no means at the disposal of anyone who could pay for it," said Elizabeth Drexel Lehr. "She had to make certain that invitations emanating from her pen would only be received by people of eminence before she would condescend to dispatch them."[11]

Etiquette demanded an immediate acceptance or regret to these invitations, conveyed on a small vellum card with the message personally written by the recipient. Acceptance of an invitation carried a grave responsibility and could not be easily cast aside. "A dinner obligation, once accepted," declared McAllister, "is a sacred obligation. If you die before the dinner takes place, your executor must attend the dinner."[12] Discretion in accepting was always advised. "If a bachelor receives a dinner invitation from people who are not really 'in the swim,'" advised one turn-of-the-century guide, "he should simply toss it into the fire. This plan will prevent any more invitations from so undesirable a quarter. Were he to answer these people politely, they would certainly annoy him again at a later date."[13]

Once invitations had been dispatched, the hostess consulted with her chef de cuisine. Ordinarily, most ladies left the planning of their dinner menus to their chefs, reviewing their suggestions and perhaps adding or subtracting a dish. This, too, was a matter of some delicacy: McAllister had warned against the "fatal mistake" of "letting two white or brown sauces follow each other in succession, or truffles appearing twice in the dinner" lest the hostess open herself to derision.[14] The chef ordered provisions, shopped for any necessary items, and prepared his kitchen staff. Working with the housekeeper, the hostess determined which rooms in her house would be used in the evening and for what purposes, the types of flowers to order and how they were to be arranged, and what entertainment, if any—whether a quartet, a choral group, or a small orchestra—was desired and needed to be engaged. Flower arrangements usually were ordered several weeks in advance from Klunder, Hodgson, Wadley, & Smythe, or Fleischman, the city's leading florists, and on the day of the dinner a cart loaded with blooms, plants, and greenery would arrive at the house, accompanied by several specialists to arrange them according to instructions.[15]

A meeting with the butler settled a multitude of questions. First there was the issue of seating, alternating ladies and gentlemen, separating husbands from wives, keeping any potential rivals distant, and giving prominence to those deemed most important. An invitation sent to Caroline Astor always complicated a dinner, remembered Lloyd Morris, as "it was understood that she took precedence over all other guests. Thus, when she dined out, she was invariably placed at the right of her host."[16] Once this had been decided, the hostess worked with her butler to determine the style and tone of the dinner. Large, leather-bound folios called plate books, containing depictions and listings of the various china, silver, crystal, and gold services available, were consulted and a service selected, the decoration of the table was discussed, the suggested list of wines and liqueurs to be served was approved, and the number of footmen needed, and what liveries they would wear, would be settled.[17]

The issue of servants was a complicated one, for during a dinner party they were visible symbols of their employer's wealth and status. Generally, a dinner party of twenty-four called for the butler and eight footmen to serve, with several grooms detailed to the front door and additional footmen employed to assist in the cloakroom and in the drawing room and the library. In New York City's most elite houses, elaborate evening liveries in the family's colors and adorned with buttons crested with their monogram were considered de rigueur for footmen attending to a formal dinner. Additionally, a number of maids would be called upon for a dinner party, from assisting in the ladies' dressing room to serving coffee and tea after the meal had ended.[18]

Dinner guests usually arrived thirty minutes before a meal. Liveried grooms waited at the curb, opening carriage or motorcar doors and assisting guests out of their vehicles and up the steps, where another groom bowed as they entered.[19] Here, footmen attired in their frilled shirts, colored waistcoats, brocaded coats, knee breeches, silk stockings, and patent leather shoes directed them to cloakrooms. Ladies deposited their furs, wraps, and muffs, while gentlemen handed over their coats, hats, scarves, and white gloves. These guests were always uniformly attired: ladies in formal evening gowns, long gloves, and an abundance of jewelry, and gentlemen in white tie and tails. In the cloakroom, gentlemen were motioned to a damask-draped table, where a silver tray held a selection of boutonnieres provided by the hostess. A second tray held small white envelopes, each inscribed with a gentleman's name; within he would find a gilt-edged card with the name of the lady he was to escort in to dinner. The gentlemen had no say in such alliances, which were all arranged in advance by the hostess in accordance with her seating plan.[20] "This part of the ceremony," recalled one man, "is usually accompanied by groans and maledictions as the gentlemen tremblingly open their envelopes."[21]

The hostess, often, declared Ralph Pulitzer, wearing an "indelible smile" reminiscent of "Christian martyrs," waited to greet each guest personally before they passed into the drawing room, the butler loudly announcing each name at their approach.[22] Here, a welcoming fire might burn, adding to the luster of the shimmering crystal chandeliers and sconces that caught the sparkling diamonds of the ladies' toilettes and sent prisms of light dancing across gilded chairs. Enormous arrangements of roses, orchids, and lilacs sprouted from priceless Chinese vases, adding their scent to the crackling hickory logs on the hearth and, occasionally, a whiff of incense that lingered from a censer swung through the rooms a few moments before the guests arrived. In some houses a footman might offer guests an aperitif from a silver tray, often a small sherry, although in the age before the arrival of the cocktail this act smacked of bad taste. After fifteen or twenty minutes, the butler appeared and announced, "Madame, dinner is served." The hostess rose and offered her arm to the most important male guest, the gentlemen seeking out the ladies named on their cards and leading them in procession to the dining room.[23] According to etiquette, the hostess always entered the dining room last.[24]

No other Gilded Age entertainment constituted such a labyrinth of ritualized detail as did a formal dinner party, offering layer after layer of intricacies that would quickly reveal any unwelcome arriviste. The dining table was the field of battle. The proliferation of china, silver, and crystal was staggering; with an American Gilded Age sensibility that demanded outlandish luxury, not even royal banquets in European palaces presented such complexities. On the day of a formal dinner, the butler opened the gold and silver safes: often these were small rooms, where a dazzling array of plates, salvers, vases, ewers, and epergnes were displayed in glittering profusion on rows of felt-lined shelves. The pieces selected for use had to be carefully polished, using a rouge paste that served to highlight their appearance before being burnished with chamois cloths to a blinding sheen.[25] Elaborate Meissen, Sèvres, Royal Worcester, or Dresden china services were retrieved from glass-fronted cupboards, each piece protected from its neighbor by felt covers, and loaded onto carts for transport to the dining room; the same ritual was repeated for the multitude of crystal to be used.

One large, long table was preferred for dinners with fewer than fifty guests; only above this number were a number of smaller, round tables used. The table was draped with felt, most often red but occasionally green, followed by a fine white damask cloth from Ireland or France. This was often exquisitely embroidered with floral garlands, cartouches sewn with the owner's monogram, and open scrolls through which the crimson could peek; the top of the white cloth might be further embellished with a runner of crimson velvet, sewn with foliate designs in gold thread and adorned with colorful peacock feathers.[26] Napkins generally matched the white damask of the tablecloth, but at the turn of the century, napkins embroidered with monograms and fringed with gold lace became fashionable.[27]

In the highest echelons of society, service à la Russe—where footmen discreetly appeared at the side of each guest offering the various courses in sequential order—had become fashionable. Service à la Russe had first been adopted by New York's fashionable society in the 1870s under Mrs. Astor and quickly became the standard for elegance, replacing the more cumbersome and elaborate service à la Française, which called for presentation of the entire meal at one time.[28] This also left the table free of platters, dishes, and tureens; in their place, a mirrored plateau might stretch the length of its surface, serving as a miniature stage for various adornments and a massive central floral arrangement. "In the selection of the floral decoration for the table the lady of the house has the final voice," declared one turn-of-the-century guide. "Flowers which have a very heavy fragrance should not be used." For a dinner party, roses, violets, carnations, orchids, and lilacs were advised, though rarely mingled together; the Gilded Age preference was a single, vibrant, and unified splash of color to make a powerful statement. Thus one might find a central silver basket of a hundred Jacqueminot roses rising three or four feet, the base worked with carefully arranged tendrils of ivy that spread across the table, or a vase of tall lilies and palm fronds.[29] At intervals down the plateau were smaller mixed arrangements, epergnes of lavishly cascading roses, orchids, lilies, and ivy.[30] Occasionally a hostess might offer an additional, unexpected arrangement, such as a canopy of roses and lilies woven with ivy, palm fronds, ferns, and boughs of evergreen suspended from the ceiling and set with tiny electric lights shimmering above the diners to "reproduce the sense of dreamland."[31]

Centerpieces could take a variety of forms. Once, Mamie Fish gave a dinner at a table whose center had been cut away and replaced with a long tank filled with goldfish and bobbing models of yachts that circled the perimeter as the guests ate.[32] Another Gilded Age hostess replaced the usual damask-covered mahogany tabletop with a long sheet of plate glass, illuminated from below by hidden electric lights so that the entire surface offered a flattering, reflective glow.[33]

Every object on a table was carefully placed for maximum effect. Tall, gilded candelabra stood at intervals, the flames of their wax candles shielded by white or light pink silk shades; they alternated with silver bowls of pineapple, or epergnes mounded with sugared fruits bedecked with leaves and trailing vines.[34] Such decorative items were used to great effect: Mamie Fish commissioned a gold dinner service for three hundred from Tiffany that included not only place settings but also immense candelabra, a plateau, and intricately decorated epergnes that could be screwed together to form a magnificent, towering centerpiece.[35] It was so elaborate that only her butler knew how to correctly assemble the various pieces—a bit of misfortune, as it once turned out, when Mamie gave the man his notice the day before one of her dinner parties. In retaliation, before leaving her house, he carefully unscrewed the entire service and left it all in a jumbled heap on her dining room floor. No one knew how to reassemble it, and only the hasty arrival of two men from Tiffany managed to save the evening.[36]

Laying the table normally took several hours. The butler worked with white-gloved footmen, carefully measuring each piece placed with a small rod to ensure uniformity. A usual place setting—or cover, as it was known—included ten pieces of silver: on the right side was an oyster fork placed atop the soup spoon, a bread knife, a fish knife, a meat knife, and a salad knife; to the left was a fish fork with curved tines to flake the fish, a meat fork, a salad fork with widely spaced tines to avoid bruising the lettuce, and a fruit fork. When each course was completed, the foot-men would remove the used silver with the plate; for service à la Russe, this arrangement of silver was sometimes minimized, with only the first required utensils set. Additional pieces of silver not already laid would accompany their respective courses, placed on either side of the new plate: a spoon for the Roman punch, a silver or gold spoon and a small fork for dessert, and a small spoon for coffee.[37] Often these services, commissioned from Tiffany or Gorham in New York or Garrard in London, were works of art themselves, composed of silver or ormolu, their ornately scrolled handles decorated with family crests and the initials of the owners.[38]

In place of the usual profusion of china that had accompanied a din-ner party before the introduction of service à la Russe, guests would find only a service plate, or charger. Larger than an ordinary plate, it often was gold, to add contrast to the dinner plates and bowls of Sèvres, Royal Worcester, Meissen, or Dresden china placed upon it.[39] Flanking the service plate was the crystal: an etched tumbler for sparkling water; two flutes for champagne; three glasses for wine; a glass for Burgundy and one for sauterne; an etched, red glass for the claret; and a glass of deep green, Bohemian cut crystal for the hock.[40] Tall, thin glasses for sherry and for Madeira appeared on the table during the latter part of the dinner.[41]

At the center of each service plate stood a damask napkin, folded three times to form a small pyramid holding a dinner roll; a second dam-ask napkin would be brought with the dessert course. Directly above the plate was a hand-lettered place card with the guest's name, flanked by individual silver cellars of salt and of pepper, and a small silver dish of salted nuts. Guests also found a handwritten menu; often these were written in French on gilt-edged vellum cards illuminated with some festive or pastoral scene and held upright in engraved silver or gold holders, making a working knowledge of the language yet another factor that defined the highest echelons of society. If crystal finger bowls were used, they were placed atop lace doilies, with a violet or rose petals floated on the surface.[42] It was customary to provide some small favor for each attendee, set out at his or her place at the table; these were generally painted ribbons, fans, reticules, card cases, tiepins, or little jeweled eggs, although by the turn of the century it was common for hostesses to lavish engraved silver cigarette cases, gold cuff links, and jewelry upon their guests.[43]

Menus were lavish, rarely encompassing fewer than eight courses and sometimes extending to twelve or fourteen, although it was understood that guests were in no way expected to partake of everything offered. A formal dinner often began with oysters on the half shell, although occasionally caviar might be served in their place.[44] Raw oysters were rarely served, and hostesses were cautioned against presenting them fried, which left "a disagreeable odor through the house."[45] These, and all the courses that followed—with the exception of the relevé and the rôte—were prepared and plated in the kitchen or pantry; footmen, using a white damask cloth to hold the rim of the plate and serving from the left of each guest, placed it atop the charger and removed it at the end of the course.

There were generally two soups, a consommé and a bisque; as soon as the oyster or caviar plate was removed, a footman replaced it with a heated soup plate and bowl. Because there generally were two soups, this first bowl—and the one that followed—contained only half a ladleful of soup; at a smaller dinner party, guests usually selected which type of soup they desired.[46] When the soup course was removed, a second, oven-warmed plate was placed atop the service plate. Onto this footmen placed the fish course. Generally this was striped bass in a rich cream sauce, or broiled red snapper, although soft-shell crabs or lobster also were popular choices.[47] McAllister warned that salmon should be served only in a cold mousse during the social season: "The man who gives hot salmon during the winter, I care not what sauces he serves with it, does an injury to himself and his guests."[48]

The relevé followed. This was the principal meat course, and might consist of a fillet of beef, often in a champagne or mushroom sauce; turkey stuffed with truffles; boned chicken stuffed with oysters; or a saddle of roast lamb served with currant jelly.[49] This was one of two courses that guests served themselves, selecting the desired portion from a platter presented at their left side by a footman. The entremets, or entrées, typically followed, although occasionally they would accompany the relevé. These generally consisted of pâté de foie gras, sweetbreads, stuffed mushrooms in cream sauce, artichoke hearts, roasted potatoes, puffed pastries with centers of asparagus or spinach, or terrapin.[50] In the Gilded Age, terrapin became the supreme culinary symbol of a refined table, its popularity so immense that the turtles were eventually harvested to extinction.

After the relevé and the entremets had been cleared, most fashionable dinners followed with a Roman punch. This was not a beverage but rather a rich iced concoction made of beaten egg whites, sugar, lemon juice, and rum, served in faience cups of vessels carved from ice and consumed with small gold spoons as a palate freshener.[51] The rôte followed. This was always roasted, seasonal game served, like the relevé, from platters presented by footmen, and might include capon with truffles, canvasback duck, grouse stuffed with oysters, roast partridge, braised pigeon, woodcock, or venison in wine sauce. A salad always accompanied the rôte, generally a mixture of lettuces with tomatoes and perhaps punctuated with crab or shrimp.[52]

The entremets sucrés, or desserts, formed the final course. Often there was a custard or a pudding, followed by cakes, pastries, petits fours, tortes, *glacé aux marrons,* Bavarian creams, and ices, followed by a cheese and fruit course. Gorgonzola, Brie, and Neufchâtel were highly recommended, as were small, savory pastries stuffed with warm cheese. Generally two types of fruit were offered: pears, apples, grapes, peaches, or strawberries, often sliced and doused in sweet wine or champagne.[53]

These dinners called for a wide variety of wines, champagnes, and liqueurs of exceptional vintage. The butler was charged with their preparation before the dinner began; often he was the only servant entrusted with the keys to the wine cellar, and under his careful supervision—lest any bottles go missing at the hands of an alcoholic footman—the necessary provisions were retrieved and brought up to a pantry adjacent to the dining room. Here the wines would be decanted, the sherry cooled, and the champagne, hock, and sparkling wines set in iced buckets to chill. Generally the butler poured, although in larger dinners this task could be delegated to trusted footmen. "An inexperienced servant," warned one guide, "should never serve the wine; it must be done briskly and neatly, not explosively or carelessly. The overfilling of the glass should be avoided, and servants should be watched, to see that they give champagne only to those who wish it, and that they do not overfill glasses for ladies, who rarely drink anything." Wine, champagne, and liqueurs were always poured on the right side of the guest, in contrast to the service of the food.[54] Sherry or a fine Madeira accompanied the oysters or caviar, followed by hock or Chablis with the fish; sherry or Madeira with the soup; claret, white wine, or dry or sweet champagne with the relevé; Chambertin or Burgundy with the rôte; and a selection of dry and sweet champagnes and liqueurs with the desserts.[55] Madeira, sherry, and Burgundy were placed in cut crystal decanters on the table and passed round to the guests by their host.[56]

Conversation was lively but, following the standards of the day, focused on superficial matters: houses, travel, horses, music, and especially gossip. "At a very large dinner," warned one social guide, somewhat tongue-in-cheek, "the lady beside you is almost certain to be one who entertains generously and, as such, should be treated with a certain degree of politeness. Try to suppress, however, all sentiments purely human in their nature, such as pity, kindness of heart, sympathy, enthusiasm, love of books, music, and art. These ridiculous sentiments are in exceedingly bad taste and should be used but sparingly if at all."[57]

Coffee, sparkling Apollinaris water, and liqueurs signaled the end of the meal. At the conclusion, the hostess generally rose and retired to the drawing room with her female guests to engage in a half hour of conversation over coffee or tea; the gentlemen either remained at the table to smoke, drink port or brandy, and discuss business, or retired to the library to do so. By the turn of the century, however, this polite convention of

segregating the sexes after dinner was often abandoned. "Many indulgent hostesses," commented one chronicler, "now allow young gentlemen to smoke a cigarette at the table, after the eating and drinking is at an
end, rather than break up the delicious flow of conversation which at
the close of a supper seems to be at its best. This, however, should not be
done unless every lady at the table acquiesces, as the smell of tobacco
smoke sometimes gives women an unpleasant sensation."[58]

Occasionally, some entertainment might follow—a piano recital, a choral
group to entertain, or for the more adventurous, perhaps a group of Gypsy
dancers or fortune-tellers. The goal was to provide suitable diversion from
the need of continued conversation. Within an hour after the meal had
ended, sated and stuffed and often growing weary of the endeavor, dinner
guests generally began to look for signals that would allow their leave without any insult to their hostess; by this time, the lady of the house, too, was
usually anticipating retreat to her suite of rooms. Once a general lull had
settled over the gathering, a keen hostess would rise from her chair and,
with a fixed smile that no one could mistake as an invitation to linger,
thank her guests for the pleasure of their company.[59] Thus, with little of the
ceremony that had attended the proceedings, the evening would come to an
end—at least for the guests—while, unseen, the multitude of servants began
hours of washing, scrubbing, polishing, and carefully returning each piece
of silver, china, and crystal to its proper place.

By the turn of the century, formal dinners had largely become demon-
strative spectacles for the display of wealth and taste; that they were often
long and deadly dull escaped no one. Indeed, as Mrs. Winthrop Chanler,
one of Mrs. Astor's relatives, complained, they tended to be "extremely
unrewarding. Nothing was done for the guests' entertainment beyond
providing them with a vast amount of elaborate food."[60] As a result,
despite the elegant atmosphere created, dinners were less culinary experiences than they were opportunities for self-satisfaction, expressions of
the stylized tribal rituals that bound members of Gilded Age society
together in their privileged milieu.

23

SOCIETY BALLS

No ENTERTAINMENT IN GILDED AGE society rivaled a ball. Balls during the season generally took place on week nights following the opera, beginning at eleven and including not only general dancing but also a midnight supper and a cotillion; frequently they ended in the early hours of the morning, with an informal breakfast. On no other occasion were the ladies' gowns so expensive and their toilettes so lavish, the gentlemen so smart and elegant in appearance and manner, and ballrooms so exquisitely festooned with elaborate floral displays and filled with rhapsodic strains.

Until the turn of the century, Gilded Age New York had witnessed two kinds of balls: those given in private houses and those held in fashionable hotels and restaurants. The latter had become a feature of the city's social life only in 1870, when Archibald Gracie King gave the first private ball at Delmonico's.[1] McAllister's Patriarch balls—along with his junior cotillions—followed this pattern of public revelry, but many visiting Europeans found the idea abhorrent. "You have no safeguard for society in America," complained one aristocratic French lady, "but your homes. No aristocracy, no king, no courts, no traditions, but the sacred one of home. Now, do you not run great risks when you abandon your homes, and bring out your girls at a hotel?"[2] This division finally changed after 1897, when the Patriarch balls ceased and it became the fashion for young ladies to formally enter society at private entertainments held in the ballrooms of the city's mansions.

Most Gilded Age hostesses might give one or two balls each winter social season, allowing her to fulfill social obligations and to entertain her friends. Occasionally a ball marked a special event, such as an anniversary or the debut of a daughter, or was held in honor of an important dignitary or visitor from Europe. Invitations to a ball, like those to a dinner party, were usually dispatched up to a month before the event was to occur. By the turn of the century, however, many of the most powerful hostesses took to sending them in the week that the ball was to take place. "At first thought," noted one chronicler of society, "this might seem to be a mistake, giving a suggestion of the impromptu with its attendant geniality and informality, to what should be an august and deliberate ceremonial. But deeper consideration will show that this very briefness of notice is a circumstance full of pomp and prestige. It demonstrates that the hostess is a lady of such caliber that she need fear the rival entertainments of no lesser ladies on the evening of her choice; that her invitations are paramount, to be eagerly accepted, no matter what else her guests had planned for that night. The only danger in this method—that one of the few other hostesses of equal position with herself should chance to choose the same night for a ball of her own—is avoided by each of these hostesses having secured the social rights to a certain week in winter for her annual ball, and on this week none of her equals would think of infringing."[3]

The engraved vellum cards never mentioned the word "ball." Rather, an invitation might read *Mr. and Mrs. [X] request the pleasure of the company of _____ on Monday Evening, January 10, at ten o'clock. Dancing* (or *Cotillion*) but otherwise would contain no further mention of the purpose of the evening. All balls were assumed to be formal affairs; if such were not the case, the invitation would include the word "Informal" inscribed in one corner. If the ball was given for a debutante, and if she had her own calling card, it often would be enclosed with each invitation.[4]

On the day of a ball, servants prepared a designated suite of rooms for the evening. The ballroom floor was scrubbed with scalding water, and milk was then poured over the wood and allowed to dry before being washed off, leaving a glossy sheen across its surface.[5] In addition to the ballroom, servants usually prepared a reception room and a drawing room for general congregation, and a smaller room in which small pastries, canapés, and iced lemonade would be offered throughout the evening. A thoughtful hostess also provided a library or a smoking room as a refuge for the gentlemen; this was deemed particularly important, as the etiquette of a ball declared that no gentleman could smoke in the presence of a lady.[6] The principal rooms were adorned with lavish floral displays: tables and consoles held baskets and vases of carefully arranged, out-of-season roses, orchids, lilacs, and lilies; mirrors were framed with garlands of smilax, evergreen boughs, palm fronds, and ivy wired with tiny electric lights; tall bowers of flowers flanked doorways; and lofty potted palms and orange trees decorated the length of the ballroom, offering the illusion of an exotic tropical garden in the midst of winter.[7]

Except for those entitled to wear a military uniform, gentlemen at a ball were almost uniformly attired in white tie and waistcoat and a black tailcoat. The wearing of white gloves was de rigueur. Not only was a gentlemen never seen without his gloves in the ballroom, but also they served a more delicate purpose: "The perspiration on the hand from dancing will ruin a lady's dress when gloves are not worn," warned one authority.[8] Ladies were always *en grande toilette*, clad in décolleté gowns of heavy brocade, satin, or velvet and bedecked in stunning parures of jewels. For debutantes, light, diaphanous gowns of white satin, chiffon, or tulle were advised; small corsages of flowers, sent by potential partners, perfumed their bodices or hung on velvet or satin ribbons from the waist and sleeves.[9] Each lady also carried a tiny vellum card with a tiny gold pencil, attached by a colored ribbon to her wrist. One side listed the evening's dance program, while the other was used to record the names of partners selected for a particular dance. Young ladies were advised to consider offers carefully and not hastily fill in their dance cards, lest an acquaintance or more desirable partner arrive after their schedule had been set.

Debutantes gathered in distant corners of the ballroom, casting nervous eyes across the seemingly interminable stretch of gleaming parquet to the clusters of prospective partners. This uncertainty, remembered Consuelo Vanderbilt, was a source of pervasive worry to these young ladies. "The terror of not being asked to dance, the humiliation of being a wallflower, ruined the pleasures of a ball for those who were ill favored," she later recalled.[10] Worse yet, they were keenly aware not only of the distant gentlemen assessing their possibilities but also of the censorious dowagers in the security of their gilt chairs, who watched through lorgnettes, evaluating gestures and behavior, "the beauty of their faces or the bounty of their families" as matrimonial material.[11] These chaperones were also poised for the slightest furtive glance or suggestion of some secret assignation; a debutante who behaved in an improper fashion at a ball could expect to find her name crossed off future guest lists, not only bringing shame to herself and her family but also ruining her future prospects.[12]

If ladies controlled most of society, the ballroom, at least, was the province of the gentleman. No lady could ask a gentleman to dance, and while gentlemen might wander freely through the room, it was considered improper for any lady to do so without an escort. A gentleman of good breeding who came to a ball alone was expected, by courtesy, to introduce himself to the hostess and ask that she present him to any ladies who may be without partners but might like to dance.[13] In this way he not only gained the favor of his hostess but also earned a reputation as a reliable gentleman, thus ensuring a continued flow of invitations to similar events.

Gentlemen could ask a lady to dance only if they were formally introduced or if they were known to each other before the ball; if a lady refused one request for a dance in which she was without a partner, etiquette demanded that she remain seated during that round: refusing one gentleman and then accepting the offer of another was considered highly vulgar. "After dancing with a lady, and walking about the room with her for a few times," advised an expert, "a gentleman is at perfect liberty to take the young lady back to her chaperone and plead another engagement."[14] Invitations made in the ballroom to facilitate dancing were to be considered just that; they did not constitute any acquaintanceship beyond that evening, and any gentleman who pressed for such recognition after a ball was likely to be a cad.[15]

Worldly gentlemen and would-be suitors were well versed in the various forms of unspoken communication ladies employed in a ballroom. An entire system of flirting and covert messages had been codified around the use of fans, gloves, and handkerchiefs, and these were deployed with great regularity to evade any attentive chaperones. If a lady bit the tip of a gloved finger, she wished the gentleman to leave; if she dropped her gloves, it indicated that she loved him, whereas a handkerchief twisted in the right hand signaled that her heart belonged to another. A fan held in front of the face with the right hand bade the gentleman to follow her; if quickly swept across her forehead, it meant that they were being watched. If a quick opening and folding of the fan met the gentleman, he at once understood he had been dismissed with an unstated "You are too cruel."[16]

Balls usually opened with a quadrille, a slow, elegant procession down the ballroom floor that emphasized the stateliness of the occasion; this was followed by waltzes, polkas, a gallop, a lancer, and perhaps a mazurka.[17] Dancing was often a difficult operation, given the push of the guests and the lack of space in less commodious ballrooms, as couples swirled across the parquet floor amid a kaleidoscopic sweep of skirts and trains. The heat from such exertions, in heavy gowns and formal dress, enacted in a crowded room, could be stifling. "To put five hundred people into a hot room, with no chairs to rest in, and little air to breathe, is to apply a very cruel test to friendship," warned one guidebook.[18] Some canny gentlemen often brought several sets of extra starched collars to a ball, retiring throughout the evening to a washroom and exchanging them for ones dampened with sweat.[19]

At about one in the morning, a buffet supper was usually served in an adjoining room. Here, guests passing down a line of damask-covered tables might find chafing dishes and platters offering creamed oysters, boned turkey, lobster salad, salmon mousse, sweetbreads, terrapin, salad, bouillon, *bombe glacée*, mousse, cakes, bonbons, ices, coffee, tea, sparkling water, wine, and champagne.[20] "The quantity of silver plate and gold spoons displayed by some rich families on these occasions is very great," one chronicle recorded, "and detectives in evening dress are sometimes employed to watch the supper table. Other entertainers do not use all their best plate and china at a crowded ball, but hire their supplies . . . thus giving themselves greater ease of mind than they could possibly have were so much of their worldly wealth exposed to loss or destruction."[21] Rather than partake of this feast, many gentlemen took advantage of the break and retreated to the library for a quick smoke before the festivities recommenced in the ballroom.

A cotillion followed the supper. In Gilded Age New York, this meant a variety of intricate circle dances collectively called the German. Individual introductions were not deemed necessary for those who joined the circle, but caution was advised, as no one in the circle could refuse to dance if they encountered an unsympathetic partner. Gilded Age cotillions were entrusted to men such as Worthington Whitehouse, Elisha Dyer, and Harry Lehr, recognized leaders in the intricacies of the dance floor and the multitude of possible variations. For the German, the leader and his partner motioned to certain other couples to join them in the *tour de valse* around the ballroom. At its conclusion, the leading pair separated, the gentleman summoning forward two new ladies and his partner two new gentlemen, a cycle repeated until all had participated. Next might come *la chaise*, in which the leader placed his partner in a chair at the center of the room and brought forward two gentlemen, one of whom she selected for the dance; the same ritual was repeated for the gentleman not chosen, and the lady he did not partner was always accompanied by the cotillion leader when the figure was danced. This gave way to *les drapeaux*, in which the leader selected half a dozen ladies and an equal number of gentlemen, presenting all with small flags from different nations; in making the tour de valse, the goal was for each lady to end the figure with the gentleman whose flag matched her own.[22]

The German offered dozens of such figures, including *la corde*, in which gentlemen jumped over ropes stretched across the floor in order to reach their partners, and *les masques*, where ladies selected elaborately masked gentlemen, but a cotillion always ended with *les bouquets*, when several carts of flowers and favors were wheeled to the center of the ballroom.[23] After the leading couple performed a tour de valse, they each selected some small item from the carts and offered it to a new partner, the procedure being repeated until all had toured the room and received a favor. These favors ranged from small bouquets, boutonnieres, colored sashes, antique coins, and fans to rather more expensive items such as ivory shirt studs, jeweled cuff links, watches, brooches, and picture frames. "The cheap, light, fantastic things are the best, and contribute more to the amusement of the company," advised one guide. Yet in a city and a society dedicated to the extravagant gesture, it was not uncommon for these favors to include tickets for antique furniture, or engraved cigarette and card cases from Tiffany & Company.[24] At one ball in 1897, the cotillion favors given by Ava Astor included such luxurious items as leather tobacco pouches with solid silver tops and golf balls inlaid with gold.[25]

The munificence of such gifts, the decades of public acclaim, and the aura of magisterial power all combined to keep the Astors at the apex of New York society. Even after the turn of the century, when her power and influence had begun to wane, nothing better represented the height of fashionable society than attendance at one of Caroline Astor's balls. None was more spectacular in tone and pregnant with meaning than her annual opera ball, usually held on the first or second Monday in January. This was still considered the ne plus ultra of the season, "the one great social event of the year in New York society," declared the *New York Times*.[26] Attendance was the dream of every aspirant, every arriviste, and rumors persisted that for those desperate enough, a bribe of $15,000 ($345,000 in 2008), quietly paid to the proper source, could secure an invitation and thus win admittance to the very heights of recognized society.[27]

For weeks before Mrs. Astor's opera ball, recalled Elizabeth Drexel Lehr, Caroline and Harry Lehr would "sit in solemn conclave scanning the columns of the social register, deciding who should and who should not be invited."[28] By the turn of the century, these guests included a number of those who were more or less permanent fixtures: in addition to Mrs. Astor's daughter Carrie, and her son and daughter-in-law Jack and Ava, this included Alva and Oliver Belmont; Harry and Elizabeth Lehr; Elisha Dyer Jr. and his wife; Richard and Marietta Wilson; Mamie and Stuyvesant Fish; Hermann and Tessie Oelrichs; Ruth and Ogden Mills; Senator Chauncey Depew; the Elbridge Gerrys; Neily and Grace

Vanderbilt; William K. Vanderbilt Jr. and his wife, Virginia; the Goelets; the Townsend Burdens; the Pembroke-Joneses; and various members of the Vanderbilt, Iselin, Canfield, Roosevelt, Van Cortlandt, Livingston, and Cutting families.[29] As such, Caroline's guest lists offered visible evidence of the changes she had wrought in society, creating in her thirty-year reign and through the force of her will what came to be an acceptable mixture of old and new money, of distinguished ancestry and self-made gentlemen.

For those not so honored with a coveted invitation, recalled Elizabeth Drexel Lehr, "life could hold no more bitter mortification." To disguise the crushing shame of exclusion, "doctors were kept busy during the week of the ball, recommending hurried trips to the Adirondacks for the health of perfectly healthy patients; maiden aunts and grandmothers living in remote towns were ruthlessly killed off to provide alibis for their relations"; in short, "any and every excuse" was employed to conceal the fact that the prized vellum card had not been delivered to the devastated hopeful. It was better to feign illness or invent bereavements than admit social defeat.[30]

The night of the ball was, ironically, the one Monday performance in the entire Metropolitan Opera season on which Caroline willingly abandoned the temporary pleasures of public admiration that always accompanied her appearance. She spent the evening in her great château at 840 Fifth Avenue tending to last-minute details as servants banked fires of crackling hickory logs in hearths, lighted chandeliers and sconces, and supervised as workers from Klunder, Hodgson, or Fleischman—the city's finest and most exclusive florists—put the finishing touches on their elaborate decorations and displays. Having rather quickly faded from the Metropolitan Opera as soon as the second act commenced, guests left the cold winter night and stepped into the warmth of a vestibule, where garlands of smilax framed bowers of roses and contrasted with the banks of lilies and poinsettia fringing the walls.[31] They passed between columns entwined with strings of ivy and palm fronds clustered with bunches of white and pink roses, slowly and steadily moving in an elegant line up the wide, white marble stairs, past ranks of impassive footmen in their eighteenth-century-style blue liveries, toward rooms already crowded with the elite of Gilded Age society.[32]

Caroline always received in her drawing room, standing beneath her 1890 portrait by Carolus-Duran, providing a kind of odd, almost Dorian Gray moment in reverse as the passing years took their toll on its living subject.[33] Invariably she was flanked by either her daughter Carrie or by her daughter-in-law Ava, assisting her in greeting the guests. Her gowns on these evenings rarely deviated from one of two accepted palettes: either white or cream satin brocade, or dark blue, purple, or black velvet. These gowns, ordered from Worth in Paris, dazzled with exquisite embroidery in silver or gold thread, sunbursts set with flashing sequins, foliate designs adorned with pearls or other gemstones, or sleeves and flounces of antique lace encrusted with shimmering seed pearls. To add to the lustrous effect, Caroline always wore a tiara and an extravagant collection of necklaces, brooches, jeweled ornaments, and her famous Marie Antoinette stomacher.[34]

The struggle for primacy followed the guests when they entered what many considered to be the very sanctum sanctorum of Gilded Age New York, Caroline's ballroom. At one end, atop a raised dais, stood a crimson velvet banquette, from which she surveyed the proceedings. Known in society as "the throne," the banquette could seat only half a dozen ladies, who were inevitably delighted to discover small cards inscribed with their names set out along its length. Those not so favored often took exclusion as a deliberate public snub. Once a lady who was certain that her long acquaintanceship with Mrs. Astor would be so rewarded was dismayed to find that, on this particular evening, she had not been granted the honor. Erupting into uncontrollable tears, she rushed from the ballroom, sobbing, "She does not love me! I won't stay one minute longer in a house where I am not loved!"[35]

In its form, Caroline's opera ball closely followed the rituals of other such evenings, opening with a quadrille to the music of John Lander's Orchestra that floated down from a second-floor gallery, and continuing with a variety of dances for which a Hungarian band provided a stream of lively tunes. After a few hours, supper was served but, as might be expected, the details not only were exquisite in their execution but also surpassed in magnificence similar efforts at the city's other balls. Caroline preferred a formal, sit-down dinner to the usual buffet supper, placing her guests at forty or fifty round tables erected in her vast dining room. Although the menu was often indistinguishable from any supper given elsewhere, the white-damask-draped console—gleaming with hundreds of carefully burnished pieces of the Astor silver and gold services—and the elaborately wrought candelabra, aglow with pink wax candles imported from Europe softened by little yellow silk shades, created an atmosphere of enshrined privilege and luxury.[36] By the time the cotillion commenced, Caroline had usually slipped away, quietly and often unnoticed, leaving the festivities to others. Her position challenged but never usurped by her rivals, by the turn of the century Mrs. Astor was a shadow queen, presiding over a court of her own creation where an eager society still paid its respectful homage. As the years passed, she gradually ceded her power, but the prestige of her entertainments remained unaltered.

Of all Gilded Age balls, however, none was as blatantly promoted, as extravagantly expensive, or as infamous as that given by Bradley and Cornelia Martin in February 1897. Following the marriage of their daughter Cornelia, they spent much of their time in Scotland and England; three years later they returned to America, determined to dazzle New York City's winter social season. Although the city—indeed, the entire country—was in the midst of a severe economic depression, the couple decided to give the most splendid entertainment imagination could conceive, an evening so monumental in tone and lavish in its expenditure that it would quickly supersede Alva Vanderbilt's great 1883 ball as the greatest event New York had ever witnessed. Yet, according to Frederick Townsend Martin, brother of Bradley Martin, it began innocently enough, and with altruistic motives. One day, he recalled, his brother said, "I think it would be a good thing if we got up something; there seems to be a great deal of depression in trade; suppose we send out invitations for a concert?"

"And pray, what good will that do?" Cornelia supposedly asked. "The money will only benefit foreigners. No, I've a far better idea; let us give a costume ball at so short notice that our guests won't have time to get their dresses from Paris. That will give an impetus to trade that nothing else will."[37]

Such, at least, was the official story, and throughout the controversy that followed, it was to this excuse—that of providing "an impetus to trade"—that the couple steadfastly clung. The Bradley-Martins sent out some twelve hundred invitations, summoning society to an elaborate ball to be held on Wednesday, February 10, 1897, at the Waldorf Hotel.[38] Guests were asked to come in period costume from the sixteenth, seventeenth, and eighteenth centuries.[39] On the instructions of the Bradley-Martins, details of the coming extravaganza were carefully and deliberately leaked to the press, whipping up a storm of publicity surrounding the event. There were rumors—passed without comment or correction—that it was to be the costliest entertainment ever given in America; that thousands were being spent on flowers alone; that a team of professional decorators had been hired to transform the ballroom of the Waldorf into an exact replica of the Hall of Mirrors at Versailles. Each new day brought even more stunning reports from Mrs. Bradley-Martin's social secretary: there would be "five mirrors on the north side of the ballroom," wrote the *New York Times* in a delirium typical of the coverage, "richly but not heavily garlanded in a curtain effect by mauve orchids and the feathery plemusa vine; garlands will be hung irregularly across the mirrors to loop onto the capitals of the columns separating the mirrors; the chandeliers on each column will be decorated with orchids and suspended from each chandelier will be a Rosalind-like pocket filled with Louis XVI roses and ferns. Roses will fall in showers over the balcony and will festoon the columns, not a space on the balcony, wall, or column, that will not be festooned, banked, showered with bride, American Beauty, and pink roses, or lilies of the valley or orchids. The profusion of mauve orchids will stream carelessly to the floor, like the untied bonnet strings of a thoughtless child."[40]

All of this extravagance at a time when thousands were without work and shivering through one of the coldest winters in the city's history created a storm of controversy. Some of the most prominent clergy publicly railed against the reported expenditure. "You rich people put next to nothing in the collection plate," one cleric thundered, "and yet you'll spend thousands of dollars on Mrs. Bradley Martin's ball."[41] Then there was the Reverend Dr. William Rainsford of the city's St. George's Episcopal

Church, who deemed the ball an example of the sybaritic indulgence of the Gilded Age elite. No one was more vocal in his denunciations. From his pulpit Rainsford warned his parishioners against accepting invitations, warning that such useless expenditure and frivolity at a time of suffering was unconscionable. "This affair," he declared, "will draw attention to the growing gulf which separates the rich and the poor, and serve to increase the discontent of the latter needlessly. It is hardly to the point to talk of setting money into circulation. I believe it to be a deplorable thing to do anything that will emphasize the poverty of the poor or augment their discontent. The meat of the matter is that in a time of general depression, with poverty all too prevalent, it is unwise to give to social reformers and would-be revolutionaries any handle for their fanatical efforts."[42]

"Threatening letters arrived by every post," recalled Frederick Townsend Martin, "debating societies discussed our extravagance, and last, but not least, we were burlesqued unmercifully on the stage. I was highly indignant about my sister-in-law being so cruelly attacked."[43] Even the would-be guests began to fear "that some disturbing crank would carry out the threats made to the different people at the ball."[44] Within a few weeks, the coming Bradley-Martin ball had consumed the city; moralists argued and condemned, the press played both sides in reporting every expected extravagance and the growing opposition, and as the event drew nearer, there was talk of riots and very real concerns that some ambitious reformer or anarchist would put a match to the powder keg. So worried were officials that Theodore Roosevelt, the city's assistant police commissioner, ordered ten squadrons of the Metropolitan Police—385 men in all—deployed around the Waldorf in an effort to protect the guests and prevent any possible violence.[45]

By seven on the night of February 10, 1897, crowds of curious onlookers already lined the sidewalks around the Waldorf, held back by a cordon of Metropolitan Police. At ten, footmen with white-powdered hair and bedecked in eighteenth-century blue and gold liveries spread a ribbon of crimson carpet from the main entrance along the pavement, awaiting the arrival of the guests. By ten-thirty, Fifth Avenue was jammed with a seemingly endless stream of closed carriages and brightly painted sleighs conveying their elaborately costumed owners to the hotel; necks craned with each new arrival, but, far from hurling the expected insults, the gathered crowd cheered and even applauded this fantastic parade.[46] Even so, inside the hotel and clad in evening dress, more than a dozen private detectives patrolled throughout the ball, ensuring that no one without an invitation was admitted and that there were no outbursts of violence.[47]

Within, the ballroom of the Waldorf had been completely transformed. Mirrors and antique tapestries lined the walls, framed by garlands of ivy, mauve orchids, and roses woven with tiny, twinkling electric lights between potted palms and tall, gilded candelabra. Everywhere there were cascades of some sixty thousand orchids and roses; even the enormous crystal and ormolu chandeliers had been draped with clusters of pink roses and festooned with asparagus vines. Just before the guests arrived, florists had wandered through the room and along the corridors scattering a trail of rose petals to create an enchanted path to this tropical paradise.[48]

Cornelia Bradley-Martin greeted her guests from atop a crimson dais. Costumed as Mary, Queen of Scots, she wore a gown of black velvet, its skirt split at the front by a deep, inverted V to reveal an underskirt of white satin intricately embroidered with arabesques and flowers in gold and silver thread. Garlands and foliage sewn in silver thread adorned with pearls and precious stones ornamented the bodice, while tiny crystals shimmered on the winged, Elizabethan-style collar of white lace framing the neckline. A twenty-foot-long train of black velvet, lined with cerise-colored satin and embellished with foliate designs in silver thread, cascaded from her waist, creating a cumbersome yet regal wave that followed her as she moved about the room. At her side stood her husband, in a more subdued costume as Louis XV, his pink and white brocaded satin surcoat, knee breeches, and white silk stockings offering a dramatic contrast to Cornelia's inky ensemble.[49]

More magnificent than her costume were Cornelia's jewels, widely reported in the press to be worth more than $100,000 ($2.3 million in 2008). A diamond tiara with pearl spikes crowned her dark hair; three long strands of diamonds draped artistically from her shoulder to a diamond belt, formed from a rivière, circled her waist; her diamond *berthe*, with its trellis of diamonds, rippled over her bodice; and a large quatrefoil pendant of diamonds and rubies graced her décolletage. Adding to the effect, she also wore six pieces that had once formed the French crown jewels: Marie Antoinette's sweeping necklace of diamond and ruby clusters; the Sévigné Brooch, a starburst of diamonds, pinned to her bodice next to a cluster of diamond grapes that had belonged to Louis XIV; two diamond-and-ruby-studded bracelets once owned by Empress Marie Louise, Napoleon's second wife, linked together to form a dog collar around her neck; and Marie Louise's large diamond and pearl pendant, prominently sparkling at the center of her neckline. The effect, noted the *New York Times*, was "a picture of extravagance," and when Cornelia moved, her tiara was "a small sheet of fire, emitting iridescent rays."[50]

Thus costumed and bejeweled, Cornelia Bradley-Martin, the *New York World* faithfully and somewhat snidely reported to its readers, was "a short, stout woman with cold blue eyes, a square, determined face and a nose that looked as though it intended to tilt but stopped short."[51] There was nothing subtle about the impression created, and this extravagance seemed to weigh down the far from svelte hostess. One critic ruthlessly complained that despite her costume, Cornelia did not exactly "look every inch a queen, her horizontal having developed at the expense of her perpendicular," likening her "rather robust physique" to the shape of a beer barrel, and her complexion to that of "an un-licked postage stamp."[52]

In the matter of jewelry, Cornelia's display was outdone by Caroline Astor's, who wore the dark blue velvet gown trimmed with lace in which Carolus-Duran had painted her and some $200,000 ($4.6 million in 2008) worth of jewels.[53] "It was perfectly astonishing," the *New York World* declared, "how Mrs. Astor managed to find a place for so many jewels; they covered her like a cuirass."[54] Frederick Townsend Martin thought that there had never "been a greater display of jewels before or since. In many cases the diamond buttons worn by the men represented thousands of dollars, and the value of the historic gems worn by the ladies baffles description."[55] Nor did the costumes fail to capture attention. The unpredictable Harry Lehr appeared as a rival Louis XV to his host, glittering with thousands of dollars of jewels borrowed from Tiffany; three ladies came as Catherine the Great, eight as Madame de Maintenon, and ten as Madame de Pompadour, and there were a host of courtiers, cavaliers, and courtesans. Striking out in his own unique vein, Richard Welling came as an Indian chief, in a flimsy costume accented with a tall, feathered headdress and a necklace of bear claws and deer teeth jangling around his neck; Oliver Belmont took the opposite approach, completely concealing himself in a suit of gold-inlaid armor, worth some $10,000 ($230,000 in 2008), that was so heavy he could scarcely move.[56] Most daring of all was young Otto Cushing as a Renaissance prince. When he threw back his cloak on entering the ball-room, his flesh-colored tights were so revealing that nothing was left to the imagination, and an audible gasp erupted among the guests; this was too much even for a would-be sophisticate such as Cornelia Bradley-Martin, who promptly asked him to leave.[57]

The Hungarian Orchestra from the Eden Musée and the Twenty-second Regiment Band led by composer Victor Herbert serenaded guests from a balcony draped in clematis and pink roses.[58] The ball opened with the *quadrille d'honneur*, in which Jack Astor led Cornelia Bradley-Martin down the shimmering length of parquet floor, followed by Mamie Fish on the arm of Robert Van Cortlandt, Carrie Astor Wilson with Harry Lehr, and a virtual galaxy of McAllister's fabled four hundred mixed with the city's newer elite.[59] After several hours, dancing gave way to an almost unbelievably lavish twenty-eight-course formal supper that included caviar-stuffed oysters, lobster, roast English suckling pig, terra-pin, canvasback duck stuffed with truffles, and plovers' eggs. According to the *New York World*, the guests "behaved like children afraid of muss-ing their clothes" and simply picked at the waves of food.[60] This feast was washed down with an astonishing four thousand bottles of 1884 Moet et Chandon specially shipped from Europe, a thoughtful gesture, the *New York World* declared, and quite unlike the usual "stint in cham-pagne" at other balls, where guests might have to make do with a mere quart each.[61] The management of the hotel, upset at the financial loss of not serving their own champagne, retaliated by charging a corkage fee of $6,000 ($138,000 in 2008).[62] After supper, the dancing resumed with waltzes and the two-step. By the time the evening had ended, the entire affair, it was estimated, had cost the Bradley-Martins $369,000 (approxi-mately $8.5 million in 2008).[63]

The Bradley-Martin ball, the *New York Times* enthused the following day, had been "in every way the greatest night in the history of New York Society."[64] The city's newspapers stumbled over themselves to convey its extravagant details. "Once in a generation," the *New York Sun* declared, "the rivalry of social ambitions crystallize in an entertainment so stupendous in scope and sumptuous in detail that it makes an epoch in the history of society . . . the fame of the function goes forth to the uttermost parts of civilization."[65] Then, as interest ebbed, the same press, desperate to keep the story alive, rushed to condemn it. Very quickly the critical voices rose to the forefront. Popular commentator William Brann was lavish in his denunciation and summed up what, in the aftermath of the ball, rapidly became the prevailing sentiment: "Mrs. Bradley-Martin's sartorial kings and pseudo-queens, her dukes and Du Barrys, princes and Pompadours, have strutted their brief hour upon the mimic stage, disappearing at daybreak like foul night-birds or an unclean dream, have come and gone like the rank eructation of some crapulous Sodom, a malodor from the cloacae of ancient capitals, a breath blown from the festering lips of half-forgotten harlots, a stench from the sepulcher of centuries devoid of shame." He termed the ball "one more festering sore on the syphilitic body social—another unclean maggot industriously wriggling in the malodorous carcass of a canine."[66]

In the wake of ceaseless, often unfair, but persistently mounting criticism, the Bradley-Martins permanently decamped to Great Britain, a move possibly influenced when the city's assessors dramatically raised their tax rates. Before leaving, however, they gave a farewell dinner for eighty-six of their friends at the Waldorf-Astoria that was, at a cost of $116 ($2,668 in 2008) a plate, nothing short of a proverbial slap in the face of their numerous detractors.[67] To the public at large, and to the censorious generations that followed, the Bradley-Martin ball of 1897 served as a powerful indictment of the abuses of privilege, representing the very worst excesses of Gilded Age society.

24

THE DOLLAR PRINCESSES

WITH MANSIONS, MANNERS, AND MODES of life so diligently copied from European models, it was only natural that New York's Gilded Age elite should turn to the cultural pleasures of Paris and the aristocratic pursuits of St. Petersburg, Berlin, and London to fill the interminable gap in societal entertainment that stretched from Lent to the onset of summers at Lenox and Newport. By the turn of the century, the great capitals of Europe had themselves become an integral part of the American season, the departures of New York City's great hostesses each spring regularly noted in society columns.[1] Caroline Astor followed an almost unvarying routine diligently copied by others, sailing for London in March and spending most of the spring at her apartment on the Champs-Élysées in Paris, with occasional journeys to German resorts to take the waters. She was in London by the second week of May, when the summer exhibition at the Royal Academy inaugurated the English social season. After a month of parties, dinners, balls, and receptions at court, she always returned to America by late June, in time to take up residence in Newport for the summer season.[2]

New, luxurious ocean liners transformed the transatlantic voyage into its own exercise in indulgent luxury, with private suites running several thousand dollars for the weeklong ocean crossing. Vessels of the Cunard, White Star, Inman, Compagnie Générale Transatlantique, Nord Deutscher Lloyd, and Hamburg Amerika Lines provided all the comforts of a mansion on Fifth Avenue, with mahogany-paneled drawing rooms, smoking rooms where warming fires burned in the hearth, and arcaded dining saloons rising through the decks to leaded-glass domes. Frequent travelers tended to have their favorite lines and ships: Cunard offered speed, White Star impeccable service, the American lines familiarity, the French vessels style and fine dining, and the Germans exquisite interiors. In the Gilded Age, such journeys often resembled imperial progresses: a voyage might call for twenty pieces of luggage, including immense steamer trunks carefully packed with every possible necessity and luxury; a string of valets and maids to look after their employers while on board the ship; favorite pets, from whom their owners could not be bear to be parted; and even cases with their own bed linens and pillows, lest they suffer the discomfort of sleeping on unfamiliar and disagreeable sheets and pillows.[3] Surrounded by such splendor and indulged at every turn, these grandes dames and their families arrived on the Continent fully rested, armed with thousands of dollars set aside for shopping, and determined to win entrée to the royal courts of Europe.

Americans often found that unencumbered wealth opened a multitude of doors across Europe. There always was an impoverished aristocrat willing to rent his ancestral manse for a substantial sum, a nobleman fallen on hard times whose title still held important cachet in court circles and who, for some "consideration," was more than happy to promote his new American friends within these rarefied circles. The wife of one diplomat from the United States noted that in turn-of-the-century Europe, it was easy to find aristocratic ladies who "will sell their entrée to any American who wants to buy. They acknowledge that they cannot do without their accustomed rounds of pleasure, of dinners, balls, and hunting. So they get it all and make a good living besides by bringing out their dear kinsmen from the United States."[4]

It was easy to deploy money in Europe to the best social advantage, and the more determined of the visitors armed themselves with ample resources to facilitate the quest. Over the course of a twelve-week

European journey in 1894, George Gould and his family managed to spend an estimated $600,000 ($12 million in 2008), or a staggering $4,615 ($92,300 in 2008) every day on accommodations, travel, purchases, and entertainment.[5] Wealthy Americans on the Continent rarely carried such substantial sums in cash. Instead, they relied on letters of credit, written by their own banks and presented on arrival to officials at a corresponding European financial institution. A letter of credit described in some detail the amount for which the American bank was willing to vouch. On receiving such a letter of credit, the European bank official noted the date on the reverse of the document, recording the amount of money and the type of currency being advanced by his institution. This process was repeated in each country visited, so that relevant funds were provided throughout the journey. At the end of the trip, the final institution returned the document to the issuing bank, which then dispatched checks to cover the sums advanced.[6]

Europe was a place to be seen and to seek acceptance, but rarely for these families was it a place to indulge in historical inquiry and cultural enrichment. There were, of course, exceptions, and many young sons and daughters happily assumed the roles of tourists as an accepted component to completing their educations; but for their parents, these journeys were acquisitive and social. "Such people go to Fontainebleau because they are buying furniture," commented one critic, "and they wish to see the best models. They go to Versailles on the coach and 'do' the Palace during the half-hour before luncheon. Beyond that, enthusiasm rarely carries them. As soon as they have settled themselves at the Bristol or the Rhine begins the endless treadmill of leaving cards on all the people just seen at home, and whom they will meet again in a couple of months at Newport."[7]

Americans scoured Italy, purchasing works of art to adorn their houses in New York and Newport, and luxuriated at Baden-Baden or Marienbad. The French Riviera, especially Cannes and Nice, had long been a destination for members of Europe's aristocratic and royal families seeking cures and relaxation in the warm, restorative climate. Here, amid the rocky shorelines, sandy coves, and cypress, palm, and olive trees arching above the shimmering blue Mediterranean, immense Belle Époque hotels and ornate little white villas witnessed a seasonal migration of courtesans, counts, grand dukes, and princesses, all intent on enjoying themselves and luxuriating in the sunny climate, or retreating to the gilded casino in Monte Carlo to gamble away fortunes. Queen Victoria had been a regular visitor, as was her son Edward VII, and Empress Eugénie, widow of former emperor Napoleon III of France, had a villa there, as did Princess Catherine Yourievskaya, the second, morganatic wife of the assassinated tsar Alexander II, creating an atmosphere of demicourts that lent the region a kind of faded grandeur.

Belle Époque Paris was a magnet for these visiting Americans— splendid, romantic, and slightly dangerous, charming and enticing Gilded Age society to its bosom. Paris was the center of the cosmopolitan world, "the supreme reference point for chic and good taste, the favored space for fashion rivalries, and the magical place for launching new fashions," as one historian wrote.[8] Here, Russian grand dukes gathered with their mistresses, Edward VII had indulged his private passions both as Prince of Wales and as king, and European aristocrats loved, played, and dueled. These Americans sallied forth from the Hôtel Meurice, the Hôtel Bristol, or the Ritz, along broad, tree-lined boulevards, determined to enjoy Parisian society. Ladies gravitated to the Rue de Rivoli and the Rue de la Paix, arming themselves with diamond tiaras and stomachers from Cartier, Boucheron, and other purveyors of exquisite jewels. And then there were the clothes. For many members of America's Gilded Age society, the annual journey to Europe was at least as important for the sartorial opportunities it offered as it was for the social connections to be made, with dutiful pilgrimages to Doucet, Pacquin, and, above all, to the Rue de la Paix and the holy of fashion holies, Maison Worth.

Although a few visiting Americans such as Caroline Astor found themselves embraced by the highest echelons of French society, by the turn of the century the steady, persistent, and often insistent pressing of new money had led most members of the aristocratic old guard, known as the Faubourg St. Germain set, to pointedly snub them. "We know the French do not like us," declared one lady, "but we don't care. We love Paris and we have our own society. We can go to their parties if we want to, but our own are much nicer. Anyhow, we are not dependent on the French for having a good time."[9] Such measures forced many a determined American hopeful to turn to less prominent and less exclusive circles. These visitors, reported one authority, "would be willing to decorate their mansions with orchids, to give a cup of tea to a duchess, however déclassé she might be in her own circle. They are the expatriates who try so hard to forget that they are Americans."[10]

As enticing as was Paris, it was London and its social season that drew Americans like bees to honey. Anglomania was rampant in the Gilded Age, and in the spring, when the great aristocratic houses in London burst into life as their owners celebrated the brief English season, anxious American women crowded the elaborate ballrooms, dropping exaggerated curtsies, and attempting to prove that they were both respectful of and equal to their European models. In time they became, noted one author, "an exclusive social caste as valid at certain European courts as an hereditary titled aristocracy—a powerful class of ultra-fashionable multi-millionaires, who at their present ratio of ascendancy bid fair to patronize royalty itself."[11]

From their suites at the Grand Hotel, the Carlton, the Savoy, Claridge's, the Bristol, and the Langham, these Americans boldly embarked on a deliberate conquest of society.[12] In the years before Queen Victoria's death in 1901, it was the Prince of Wales who set the tone in London society. The queen still presided over formal court functions, but she spent much of her time isolated and away from London, leaving her son Prince Albert Edward, known as Bertie, to lead fashionable society through its entertainments. Attendance at his parties at Marlborough House and Sandringham marked social acceptance, and his circle of friends, known as the Marlborough House Set, broke with convention. Here money, amusing personalities, and—for ladies—beauty opened previously closed social doors. He welcomed not only dignified members of the aristocracy but also wealthy visiting Americans. "As a rule," recalled American heiress Jennie Jerome, who married Lord Randolph Churchill in 1874, people viewed an American girl "as a disagreeable and even dangerous person, to be viewed with suspicion, if not avoided altogether. Her dollars were her only recommendation, and each was credited with the possession of them, otherwise what was her raison d'être?"[13]

In this quest to gain access to royal circles, ladies such as the Duchess of Manchester (Alva Vanderbilt Belmont's friend the former Consuelo Yznaga) and Minnie Stevens, who in 1878 married Lord Alfred Paget, were relied on to make introductions. Minnie Paget, who enjoyed considerable favor with the Prince of Wales, was so successful that it was widely rumored that she accepted bribes from wealthy Americans in exchange for the necessary entrée.[14] "American women have succeeded wonderfully of late years in all foreign society from their beauty, their wit, and their originality," declared one guidebook. "From the somewhat perilous admiration of the Prince of Wales and other Royal Highnesses for American beauties, there has grown up, however, a rather presumptuous boldness in some women, which has rather speedily brought them into trouble, and therefore it may be advisable that even a witty and very pretty woman should hold herself in check in England."[15]

The ultimate goal of much of this travel was conquest by New York's hostesses of the marital circuit for their eligible daughters. By the turn of the century, it had become fashionable to seek aristocratic husbands during these journeys to Europe, men who might be impoverished but who possessed the kind of respectable lineage and proud titles that no amount of American money could buy; in marrying American heiresses, they gained not only wives but also substantial fortunes. As Geoffrey Beard noted, "With declining rents and a fall in the value of property, many English peers needed their capital regenerated."[16] Edith Wharton called these young women "buccaneers," but newspapers of the day termed them "the dollar princesses." By 1900 more than five hundred Gilded Age heiresses had entered into such marriages, usually for titles and convenience, rarely for love.[17] The custom had become so prevalent that in 1896, when Gertrude Vanderbilt married Harry Payne Whitney, one newspaper commented proudly, "It will be an American wedding," adding, "There will be no foreign noblemen in this. . . . The millions all belong in America and they will all remain here. . . . An American boy, an American girl, an American courtship."[18]

The quest to obtain a titled husband was not a Gilded Age phenomenon, but it was certainly more pronounced, the avaricious nature of the attempt more blatant, and the steely determination more apparent, than at any other time in American history. The behavior was well understood; long before Edith Wharton's *The Buccaneers*, Mrs. Burton Harrison published a novel, *Anglomaniacs*, deriding the pursuit of aristocratic husbands, and the trend was lampooned and criticized in newspapers, periodicals, and cartoons.[19] The proudly American Mamie Fish decried the fashion, saying, "The marriages of American girls to impecunious foreign noblemen are very foolish."[20]

The number of alliances between American heiresses and European aristocrats caused considerable consternation in the press. Journalist William Brann, openly hostile to any form of Gilded Age society, recorded, "A nobleman marries such a woman not because he cares for her companionship, but because he needs money which he is too indolent to earn and too cowardly to steal. Having given her his name in exchange for a grubstake, he feels that he has performed his part of the contract, has discharged his entire duty. He understands full well that the woman wedded him solely for his title—that it was social ambition instead of love's passion that brought her to his bed—and he heartily despises her, as all hypocrites do their fellow humbugs. There is no contempt so profound, no hatred so implacable as that with which the impoverished patrician regards the aspiring parvenu; and scarce has the epithalamium ceased ere this feeling begins to make itself manifest. The man who weds a woman solely for her wealth cannot possibly possess the instincts of a gentleman. Though he wear a crown, he is at heart a human hyena, capable of any crime that requires no courage—just the kind of a creature to find a fiendish joy in torturing the helpless, in making a woman's life a hell. All the manhood which the older nobility of Europe ever possessed was bred out by selfish marriages and shameless bawdry years ago. Most royal families were originally established by the plunder and oppression of the weak by the strong. The nobility was composed of the obsequious servants of marauding sovereigns, the hired assassins of crowned hoodlums, its ranks regularly recruited from professional panderers and the spawn of prostitutes. For centuries the European nobility was but a foul cesspool into which emptied the social sewer. The throne was surrounded by ennobled bastards and shameless bawds swayed the sovereign's scepter. . . . Idle lives, vicious habits and inherited disease have degraded the present nobility below even the brutish level of its progenitors—has transformed it into a disreputable omnium-gatherum of wife-beaters and sure-thing gamblers, scorbutic cowards and brazen cuckolds. Here and there may be found a family, lately ennobled, that has not yet become irremediably rotten; but the tendency is almost invariably downward—each succeeding generation drifting further from the distinctive virtues of manhood."[21]

Although there were rare examples of happy transatlantic unions, such as those of Mary Leiter and the future Viceroy of India, George Curzon, and heiress May Goelet and the Duke of Roxburghe, without doubt the most famous of these marriages was that of the ultimate "dollar princess," Alva Vanderbilt's daughter, Consuelo, to the ninth Duke of Marlborough. Born on March 2, 1877, Consuelo was Alva and Willie's only daughter. Hers was a childhood typical of the age: educated at home by tutors, by the time she was eight Consuelo was fluent in French, German, and English.[22] Yet, where many Gilded Age parents took little interest in their children, Consuelo suffered from her mother's almost overwhelming obsession with grooming her with an eye to the future; Consuelo thought that it was Alva's "wish to produce me as a finished specimen framed in a perfect setting, and that my person was dedicated to whatever final disposal she had in mind."[23] To this end, Alva dominated every aspect of her daughter's life: when she thought Consuelo's posture was poor, she forced her to wear a steel rod strapped to her spine; and when the girl once expressed an opinion on clothing, her mother coldly declared that she had no taste. "I don't ask you to think," she told Consuelo. "I do the thinking. You do as you are told."[24] It all amounted, Consuelo would later recall, to "a kind of incessant devotion" tempered by her mother's "autocratic will."[25] "My mother," Consuelo would later say, "treated me like a captive, like something dangerous to be locked away until I could be safety tamed."[26]

The size of her family's fortune helped make Consuelo the finest of marital prizes, but she was also stunningly beautiful, with deep eyes, a swanlike neck, and a lissome figure. "Her frailty and height made her look as if she might break in two in an adverse breeze," recalled Blanche Oelrichs.[27] To help secure a suitable husband for her daughter, Alva turned to her friends Minnie Paget and Consuelo Yznaga. During an

1894 visit to London, Minnie seated Consuelo next to Charles Richard John Spencer-Churchill, the twenty-four-year-old, sleepy-eyed ninth Duke of Marlborough.[28] Known as Sunny to his family, he was one of England's premier aristocrats, and he possessed an immense three-hundred-room country house, Blenheim Palace, near Oxford. With its fourteen acres of leaky roofs and gardens choked with weeds, Blenheim needed money badly, and the Vanderbilts had it.

"I thought him good-looking and intelligent," Consuelo later recalled, but this was the extent of her interest.[29] A year later, Alva and Consuelo returned to Great Britain, this time visiting the duke at his estate. Consuelo was aware that machinations were taking place behind her back, but brushed them off; Alva, however, was not so easily thwarted. Nearly half a century later, Consuelo published her memoirs, relating her own version of what transpired once she had returned to America. Alva raised the idea of marriage to the duke, but Consuelo refused to consider the possibility. Stunned, Alva demanded to know her reasons, and Consuelo confessed that she was in love with, and secretly engaged to, a thirty-year-old businessman named Winthrop Rutherfurd. The scion of a distinguished and wealthy family whose ancestors included Peter Stuyvesant, Rutherfurd was renowned, remembered one man, for his "breath-taking good looks."[30] When Alva learned of this, she exploded into hysterics. Although Winthrop's father, Lewis, was one of the original Patriarchs and had been included in Ward McAllister's fabled list of the four hundred, Alva considered Winthrop too poor and too socially unimportant to marry her daughter.[31] No such marriage, she firmly told Consuelo, would be allowed; her daughter must marry the duke. Alva, her daughter later recorded, threatened to ruin Winthrop unless Consuelo complied with her wishes; when this failed, she locked her daughter into her bedroom and posted a guard.[32]"She intercepted all letters my sweetheart wrote and all of mine to him," Consuelo declared. "She caused continuous scenes. She said I must obey. She said I knew very well I had no right to choose a husband, that I must take the man she had chosen."[33]

Consuelo remembered that Alva's determination knew no bounds. When Consuelo persisted, Alva threatened to actually shoot Rutherfurd, saying that she would certainly be hanged for her crime and that her daughter would bear the responsibility.[34] This campaign of terror, in which Consuelo was virtually imprisoned, went on for three long weeks in the spring of 1895, during which not only did a footman guard her bedroom door but also an intimidating watchman paced beneath her windows.[35] Finally Alva sent word through a servant that her daughter's obstinacy had given her a heart attack and that she was close to death; Consuelo was allowed to leave her room to visit, and finally agreed to do as her mother wished. Within an hour, Alva had amazingly recovered from her "fatal" illness, and Consuelo realized she had been tricked.[36] "I have always had absolute power over my daughter," Alva would later admit. "When I issued an order, nobody discussed it. I therefore did not beg but ordered her to marry the duke."[37]

The duke arrived in Newport in late summer 1895. Alva had planned a magnificent ball at Marble House on Wednesday, August 28, to introduce him to Gilded Age society: footmen in maroon liveries and powdered wigs ushered the five hundred guests into the hall, where the tapestries and bronze fountain had been garlanded with lilac hyacinths and pale pink hollyhocks. Alva, attired in a gown of green and white satin adorned with Spanish lace and wearing Catherine the Great's pearls around her neck, received in her Versailles-inspired dining room; at her side, clad in white, stood a numb Consuelo, the duke flanking his hostess. Three orchestras provided the music that floated through the lofty rooms, serenading the guests when they retreated to the terrace, where thirty-five round tables festooned with pink hollyhocks overlooked a sweep of lawn illuminated by swaying, multicolored Chinese lanterns and tiny electric lights woven into the foliage of the trees, and sat for a midnight supper prepared by three French chefs.[38]

A few days later, the duke met a nervous Consuelo alone in her mother's Gothic Room, "whose atmosphere," she recalled, "was so propitious to sacrifice," and formally asked for her hand in marriage. If the party had seemed to Consuelo like a wake, the proposal—and her acceptance—was the closing of the tomb door. "It was simply horrible," Consuelo would later recall. "He just sat there sweating, starting at me, stuttering, and when I finally nodded my head and agreed he jumped up, wiped his forehead, and ran out of the room to tell my mother."[39] Consuelo later painted these days as filled with desperate unhappiness; her eleven-year-old brother, Harold, continually taunted her, crying, "He is only marrying you for your money!"[40] Money, in fact, seemed to be the foremost thought in the duke's mind. Soon enough, his legal representative arrived from London to discuss a financial settlement and Consuelo's dowry. Willie agreed to bestow fifty thousand shares of the Beech Creek Railroad Company, with a cash value of $2.5 million ($57.5 million in 2008), on the duke to do with as he saw fit; this would pay an annual dividend of some $100,000 ($2.3 million in 2008), and Consuelo also was to receive $100,000 each year for her own expenses.[41] Such negotiations led one critic to comment that while "the Vanderbilts could not afford to pay their workers a few cents more in wages a day, they could afford to pay millions of dollars for matrimonial alliances with foreign titles."[42]

Consuelo Vanderbilt as Duchess of Marlborough in her formal robes for the coronation of King Edward VII in 1902.

Consuelo's marriage took place at St. Thomas's Episcopal Church in New York on Wednesday, November 6, 1895. "It is no exaggeration to say that the preparations for this wedding are the most elaborate ever made in this country," declared the *New York Times*.[43] By 10:00 A.M., a crowd of some two thousand curious onlookers had jammed the sidewalks outside of Alva's new residence on Seventy-second Street and Madison Avenue, held back by a contingent of fifty Metropolitan Police; another seven thousand spectators lined the length of Fifth Avenue to the church, hoping for a glimpse of the bride.[44]

Eighty florists had labored for two days to transform the interior of St. Thomas's into a lush and exotic garden. Enormous garlands of ivy, laurel, palm fronds, holly, and ferns, woven with lilies, and roses hung in cascades from the dome above the altar, while the columns were wreathed with spirals of pink and white chrysanthemums. Trellises of laurel adorned with lilies of the valley and pink chrysanthemums lined the walls of the nave; festoons of white roses and orchids topped the vine-wrapped columns of the organ loft; and the ends of every fifth pew bore four-foot-high sprays of pink and white roses, tied against palm fronds with pink and white satin ribbons that draped artistically to the floor.[45]

The first guests arrived at ten-thirty. Alva, still stinging from the social backlash following her divorce from Willie eight months earlier, had pointedly excluded every member of the Vanderbilt family; the only exception was her mother-in-law, Louisa, who, out of loyalty to her family, refused to attend her granddaughter's nuptials.[46] The rest of the city's Gilded Age society, however, had turned out in full force, led by Caroline Astor, who arrived, as the *New York Times* reported, escorted by her son Jack and attired in an "exquisite costume of gray" and a black toque bedecked with white satin rosettes. She was given a place of honor, just behind the pew occupied by the governor of New York and the British ambassador. Many of the guests, reported the *New York Times*, "insisted on taking seats in the center of the church; others absolutely refused to be seated in the pews assigned to them, either on the side aisles or in the galleries, and still others actually stood on the seats whenever some well-known woman arrived so that they might catch a better glimpse of her gown." The last to arrive was a triumphant Alva. Dressed in a gown of pale blue satin edged with Russian sable and a hat of silver lace with a tall blue aigrette, she was escorted down the aisle by her two sons, William K. Vanderbilt Jr. and Harold. The *New York Times* noted that she looked "very bright and fresh, and wore a decided expression of satisfaction on her face."[47]

The only person missing was the bride. "I spent the morning of my wedding day in tears and alone," Consuelo later wrote. "No one came near me. A footman had been posted at the door of my apartment, and not even my governess was admitted."[48] The footman was Alva's insurance policy to prevent any last-minute escape attempt. Willie K. Vanderbilt collected his daughter and escorted her to the church to walk her down the aisle—the only part Alva allowed him to play in the ceremonies. The push of the crowds was so great that the bride was delayed by twenty minutes, leaving her increasingly anxious mother sitting in St. Thomas's pondering the worst, but finally the fifty-six-piece orchestra, led by Walter Damrosch, burst into the bridal chorus from Wagner's *Lohengrin*, and the procession began. Eight bridesmaids, in long white dresses of white satin with blue sashes at their waists and blue velvet picture hats, preceded the bride.[49] Consuelo's gown, the press dutifully reported, had cost $6,720 ($154,560 in 2008).[50] Of cream satin adorned in flounces of Brussels lace, it had a high neck, a bodice sewn with silver thread foliate designs embellished with seed pearls, and long sleeves puffed at the shoulders; garlands of orange blossoms adorned the full skirt, while the fifteen-foot-long train, which fell from her shoulders, was intricately embroidered with garlands and foliate designs in silver thread shimmering with seed pearls.[51] A long veil enveloped her in a cloud of tulle, but keen observers noted that through the filmy gauze her face "looked sad" and that she "appeared to have been crying."[52] "Numb" was the word Consuelo would later use to describe her feelings at her wedding.[53]

At the conclusion of the ceremony, when the newly married couple walked down the aisle to a march from Wagner's *Tannhäuser*, many in the congregation, the *New York Times* reported, "were surprised to discover that she was fully half a head taller than the bridegroom."[54] In the space of an hour, Consuelo had become Duchess of Marlborough, her mother had won an aristocratic son-in-law, and the duke had received a gift of $2.5 million, which soon disappeared into repairs on Blenheim Palace. The marriage produced two sons, John, the Marquess of Blandford and future tenth Duke of Marlborough, in 1897, and Ivor, in 1898, but the union was—as Consuelo had feared—a disaster; her new husband confessed to her that he had abandoned his true love to wed her, and had done so only "out of duty."[55]

As infamous as Consuelo Vanderbilt's marriage became, it paled in comparison with the era's most notorious transatlantic mésalliance, the marriage of financier Jay Gould's daughter Anna. Born in 1878, Anna was accustomed to luxury and privilege; self-centered and often tactless, she had, from an early age, always been determined to get her own way in all things.[56] Sadly for the ambitious Anna, nature had not endowed her with a beauty to match the munificence of her father's fortune. Society thought her too short and her complexion too sallow; her nose was too prominent, her eyebrows resembled thick caterpillars, and her stubby arms were covered with an unfortunate growth of dark hair.[57]

In 1893 Anna managed to attract the amorous attentions of broker Oliver Harriman. With an ardor that mystified all of New York, Harriman was willing to ignore not only her appearance but also the uncertain social status of her family in favor of the more promising rewards of the Gould fortune and asked for her hand in marriage.[58] Anna accepted with alarming alacrity, no doubt pleased at her good luck, and set off for Paris to select her trousseau. Here, however, she met the twenty-seven-year-old blond, blue-eyed, and elegant Paul Ernest Boniface, Comte de Castellane.[59] Known as Boni, the comte was a renowned bon vivant, a man who, said one contemporary, "had the radiance of the dawn. . . . His complexion was like a sixteen-year-old Swedish girl, and his profile like Louis XV's."[60]

It would be hard to imagine a pair as unlikely as the dour and unattractive Anna and her new dandified acquaintance. With his deliberate, Old World manner, studied charm, and luxurious tastes, Boni, commented one acquaintance, "smelled of Versailles."[61] Elizabeth Drexel Lehr called Boni "elegant and charming, a poser to the day of his death."[62] Lucius Beebe, however, noted that Boni was "the living caricature of what the American newspaper reading public envisioned when they thought of a degenerate, titled, hand-kissing little foreign cad. His stature was diminutive; he reeked of perfume, engaged in duels of a strictly theatrical order, and snowed his naive American victims with the manners and affectation of a *Vielle noblesse* that was already an anachronism in his native France."[63] Boni was a renowned sybarite. Each morning, a string of servants lavishly tended to his needs: one ceremoniously presented his master with a silk robe; a second valet draped it around his shoulders; a footman delivered a delicate faience cup filled with coffee on a silver tray; a barber arrived to shave him, trim his hair, and wax his mustache; a masseuse massaged and rubbed his skin with scented lotions; and a Chinese pedicurist painted his toenails pink.[64] The count's roll of mistresses, courtesans, and whores was so notorious that one wag suggested his coat of arms should include "the penis erectus."[65]

Shrewd and suspicious as she was, Anna saw none of this; instead, dazzled by his epicene beauty and aristocratic title, she quickly and ruthlessly broke off her engagement to Harriman and allowed Boni to pursue her, feigning reluctance all the way. Boni met Anna just as his family was approaching financial ruin.[66] Although he described her as "excessively shy," "childish," and "a trifle malicious," Anna, he declared, "possessed charm and, what is always delightful to a man, possibilities."[67] For Boni, these possibilities focused primarily on her bank account. In the words of Lucius Beebe, he was entranced by the fact that Anna's "family bore a reasonable resemblance to the United States Treasury."[68] Aware of the prevalent gossip painting him as a greedy adventurer, Boni later protested: "I can honestly affirm that Miss Gould's fortune played a secondary part in her attraction for me. She was, in many respects, unusual, and the unusual has always fascinated me."[69] Unusual Anna certainly was, and a far cry from the beautiful ladies who regularly shared his bed. When one of his friends pointed out her aesthetic shortcomings, Boni replied airily, "In light of her dowry, she doesn't look bad at all."[70]

Despite his protests, Boni clearly saw in Anna a means to his family's financial salvation, and for the impoverished count, potential access to her fortune was enough to temporarily and willingly blind him to both her physical shortcomings and her abrasive manner. Anna was clearly captivated by this elegant, handsome young aristocrat, and Boni seized the opportunity, pursuing her back to America, flattering her with constant attentions and acting the part of a devoted suitor. In the winter of 1895 Anna accepted his proposal, much to the surprise of one acquaintance, who candidly commented, "This girl will never be silly enough to accept a man who is foolish enough to want to marry her."[71]

"It is probable that the public, if not society, breathed a sigh of relief last week when it was finally, definitely, and conclusively announced that Miss Anna Gould, daughter of the late Jay Gould, was actually engaged to be married," the *New York Times* declared somewhat incredulously.[72] This was no grand romance: Anna wanted social recognition and a titled husband, and Boni wanted her money. In a charade of happiness, they declared their love, yet neither party was foolish enough to believe that this was to be anything but a marriage based on avarice and mutual benefit. More than any other couple, Anna and Boni exemplified the public perception of Gilded Age society at its worst: vacuous, self-indulgent, and blissfully profligate in their expenditures. Few couples can have been so mismatched in taste and temperament, or so deserved each other. There was an ominous hint of the troubles that lay ahead when, on hearing Boni's suggestion that she convert to Catholicism before their wedding, Anna declared forthrightly: "I shall never become a Catholic, because if I were to do so I should not be able to divorce you, and if I were not happy I would not remain your wife a moment longer than was necessary."[73]

When the couple married in New York on March 4, 1895, Anna won her title and a position in Europe's aristocracy, while Boni received not only an enormous settlement but also, as he had hoped, access to his wife's fortune. Much to Boni's delight, Anna possessed a dowry of some $2 million ($46 million in 2008), with income on a trust of $15 million ($345 million in 2008) that amounted to roughly $700,000 ($16.1 million in 2008) a year—money that would save the de Castellanes from ruin.[74] Awash with such riches, Boni confessed, "I only lived for the moment when I should embark for Europe and there regain my lost paradise of tradition and beauty."[75]

True to his word, Boni launched upon a dedicated crusade to spend his new wife's inheritance. He spent thousands on "marvelous Gobelin tapestries," sculptures, carpets, an "exquisite green and white Sèvres dinner service," furniture, and paintings by Rembrandt, Reynolds, and Van Dyke.[76] An enormous yacht called *Valhalla*, purchased at a cost of $500,000 ($11.5 million in 2008), provided leisure at sea, while thousands of francs disappeared into bad investments and at the elegant casinos of Monte Carlo and Biarritz.[77]

Then there were the houses. "I preferred to exist in a dream world of past splendor, pretty women and interesting people," Boni admitted.[78] He purchased and restored two châteaus, Grignan and his favorite, Marais, an eighteenth-century gem on which he lavished hundreds of thousands of francs. The usual scarlet liveries of his servants, Boni declared, would "have desecrated Marais, so I evolved white coats and pale blue breeches" to create a more unified appearance. Thousands more were spent on the fantastic gardens, with "glowing flower beds gilded by the setting sun, amongst which wandered gigantic Nubians wearing plumed red turbans, holding jaguars or sinuous black panthers in leash," as Boni rhapsodized.[79]

With an increasing architectural megalomania, Boni deemed no house in Paris grand enough for their habitation. Thus, in 1896, he built his extravagant Palais Rose at 40 Avenue du Bois, a massive mansion of pink marble modeled on the Grand Trianon by Jules Hardouin-Mansart at Versailles. Designed by Ernest Sanson, this was an unapologetic exercise in wildly impractical, sybaritic luxury. From the Cour d'Honneur, with its pink marble pilasters, guests passed through a vestibule walled in polychrome marble to the heart of the palace, a copy of the destroyed Escalier des Ambassadeurs at Versailles. This was a grandiose ascent of marble stairs, between panels of contrasting marble ornamented by bas-reliefs and pilasters glowing with gilded capitals, adorned and embellished with antique tapestries, paintings, sculpture, and glittering sconces.[80] "My nephew and his wife," Boni's aunt once commented, "must march up

their grand staircase with peacock feathers stuck up their asses."[81]
Opening from the staircase was an enfilade of exquisite marble salons
copied from the state apartments at Versailles, culminating in a private
theater for six hundred guests.[82]

These extravagant rooms were lighted only with candles; electricity,
Boni declared, was fit only for the use of servants.[83] As a piece of theatrical
fantasy it was without parallel in fin de siècle Paris, costing an estimated
$6 million (approximately $122 million in 2008), with some $160,000
(approximately $3.7 million in 2008) alone expended on the ceiling of
Anna's marble-walled bedroom, where she slept in a gray-satin-draped
bed that had once belonged to Marie Antoinette.[84] To Boni, his Palais
Rose was "a monument of beauty," a visible display of his refined taste,
and a suitably elegant background against which he would stage his enviable entertainments.[85] On nights when the de Castellanes entertained,
Boni lined the marble halls of the Palais Rose with some five hundred
footmen, all bedecked in eighteenth-century scarlet liveries and powdered wigs.[86] So unbelievably lavish was the impression that once Boni
came upon one of his guests rubbing a handkerchief against a column as if
to satisfy himself that all of this extraordinary palace was genuine. "I assure
you," Boni coldly told him, "it is no falser than your face."[87]

In July 1897, to celebrate his wife's birthday, Boni gave one of the most
spectacular of all Gilded Age parties. That evening, some three thousand
guests made their way to the Bois de Boulogne, over lawns covered with
more than nine miles of specially woven red carpet, lined by sixty footmen in scarlet liveries and powdered wigs, and by mounted members of
the Republican Guard with their sabers drawn in salute, to a stage
framed by tall oaks, the whole illuminated with eight thousand specially
commissioned Venetian-glass lamps from Murano. An orchestra of two
hundred musicians played while the corps de ballet of the Paris Opera
danced, their performance interrupted when twenty-five white swans
were released and, scared by the loud strains of Offenbach, attacked the
dancers and the guests. A lavish dinner in a marquee adorned with
twenty-five thousand fresh roses was followed by a magnificent display of
fireworks.[88] Boni was delighted with the whole affair, which was said to

have cost $250,000 (approximately $5.7 million in 2008), although Anna was less than enchanted. "The guests," Boni wrote, "represented the bluest blood of France, the mise-en-scène was unreal, super-artistic and super-sensuous, yet it might have been anywhere and anything so far as Anna was concerned."[89]

Anna's money flowed through the hands of these two supremely self-ish, careless wastrels like water. As profligate as Boni was, Anna, too, was guilty of excess, often spending $20,000 ($460,000 in 2008) a month on the latest gowns from Worth.[90] Worse still, she lacked the capacity to behave diplomatically, and alternated between ennui and shrill outbursts. Anna, Boni declared, "entered our world of traditions from out of a world absolutely destitute of them, and she made no attempt to under-stand the French temperament in those early days."[91] As the years passed, her snobbery grew unchecked: Anna had no concept of her duties and refused to entertain unless it was a ball or a dinner given for guests whose rank was superior to her own. She made no secret of the fact that she disliked the French in general and her husband's family in particular; once, when Boni took her to visit his mother at the family's Château Rochecotte in the Loire Valley, Anna did nothing to disguise her boredom and declared, "with an ever smoldering hatred," that she found the house—and the idea of sharing a roof with her in-laws—appalling.[92] Not even the arrival of three sons, Boniface, George, and Jay—upon whom the couple bestowed the unlikely nick-names of Pittipat, Tippytoe, and Tittymouse, respectively—could save the situation.[93]

The de Castellanes were without doubt the most celebrated, most talked about, and most vilified of all Gilded Age couples at the turn of the century. Scarcely a week went by without their appearance in the gos-sip columns of Paris, London, and New York, a circumstance the vain couple seemed to enjoy but that did little to enhance Boni's standing as a deputy in the French legislature. Worse yet was Boni's predilection for threatening lawsuits and challenging those whom he disliked to duels. When the de Castellanes' wet nurse gave birth to stillborn sons con-ceived out of wedlock, Henri Turot, editor of the *Petite République*, openly accused Boni of being the father. Outraged, Boni publicly challenged Turot to a duel; press coverage of the impending event was so widespread that some four hundred people came out one early July morning in 1898 to watch the notorious count in action. True to form, Boni credited his superior breeding with a victory when he brought Turot down with two wounds to the arm, leaving the editor to flee back to Paris to nurse his wounds.[94] After the editor of *Figaro* attacked the count for his profligate spending, Boni instigated another duel, declaring, "I will probably blow his head off!"[95]

"During the twelve years of our married life," Boni declared, "I never attempted to feather my nest at the expense of my wife."[96] Nevertheless, after six years of such notorious behavior, the de Castellanes were not only deeply unhappy but also deeply in debt, owing more than $4.4 million (approximately $101 million in 2008) to various creditors.[97] The money, Boni openly admitted, had been spent on "my general existence, my châteaux, my palaces, my bibelots, my racehorses, my yachts, my traveling expenses, my political career, my charities, my fetes, my wife's jewels, and loans to my friends," though he insisted that as far as his wife was concerned, "I have actually represented a more than profitable investment for her."[98] Boni simply assumed that Anna could withdraw the money from her accounts, but this was not the case. Jay Gould had left millions for his daughters, but this was in the form of trusts controlled by his eldest son, George, and the principal was not to be touched, nor could any of the incomes be transferred to their husbands.[99] "The dominant idea of the Gould family," Boni wrote, "was to keep the Gould fortune in America; it was nothing short of an obsession with them."[100]

Eventually George Gould arranged for funds to be dispatched when he learned that several French creditors were contemplating lodging suit in America against the family trust; this money, however, took the form of a loan, and called for severe economies by the profligate Boni and Anna.[101] But neither Boni nor Anna was capable of curtailing their sybaritic styles of life and continued on. Soon the Palais Rose was again crowded with thousands of guests attending magnificent dinners served by footmen in lavish new liveries. At the height of this financial crisis

Anna was said to have somehow spent \$120,000 (\$2.7 million in 2008) on clothing in a single month; when the bills came due, there was no money to pay the couturiers.[102]

This situation might have continued indefinitely had not Boni flaunted his affairs across the capital. He once carelessly left love letters to his numerous mistresses scattered on his desk, where his always suspicious wife found and read them; on another occasion Anna crept into her husband's bedroom and found that he had actually left a stuffed dummy in his bed, a clumsy attempt to escape notice while he prowled through the city's seedier nightspots.[103] Anna was content to tolerate her husband's spending but not his increasingly public adultery, and there were constant—and often violent—fights. Once, in the midst of a particularly virulent shouting match, Boni slapped her face as the servants looked on in horror; on another occasion Anna literally tackled her husband to the floor, beating him with her fists and biting him until she drew blood.[104]

A determinedly unsympathetic chronicler recorded that Anna, "too proud to marry an American," a woman who "bartered her beauty for a title, her soul for social distinction," was "one of the most miserable of mortals." Her "syphilitic" husband spent her money on alcohol and women "while neglecting and humiliating his wife in every possible way. So brutal in his treatment, so ostentatious his neglect of the woman who has paid for the very clothes he wears and the bread in his belly, that even the heartless cosmopolites of the wickedest city in the world profess to pity her."[105]

The years of scandal and wretched excess finally ended in January 1906. One day, while Boni was out for a business appointment, Anna made her move. She hired a string of carts and movers and, in four hours, had the Palais Rose stripped of every piece of antique furniture, every painting, every priceless bibelot, every sculpture, every carpet, and even the curtains that hung at the windows. Boni returned to find a curt note from Anna announcing that she had left him and taken their three sons, along with everything that her money had paid for; she had even ordered the heat and electricity cut off, leaving her husband standing alone in his dark and icy marble palace.[106]

In March, Anna sued Boni for divorce; although he desperately tried to win her back, her mind was made up. Eight months later, the French courts granted a civil divorce on the grounds of his persistent infidelity. All of the Gould money disappeared, and a penniless Boni was forced to assume a job, selling the precious antiques he himself so prized. Anna kept her remaining millions, but she was not one to forgive and forget. She extracted her own peculiar form of extreme revenge when, in 1908, she married Boni's cousin Hélie de Talleyrand-Périgord, Prince de Sagan.

25

A BREATH OF SCANDAL

SLOWLY, GRADUALLY, THE OLD ORDER WAS PASSING. In the years after the turn of the century, with Caroline Astor fading in influence and power, and with Alva, Tessie, and Mamie controlling its destinies, New York society plunged headlong into its last gasp of glory. Parties became more lavish and entertainments more eccentric, recalled Frederick Townsend Martin, as "the glitter of tinsel and the tawdry finery of mere wealth" consumed society in its "constant hunt for amusement and novelty."[1] At a dinner given by Mrs. George Westinghouse, guests found a $100 bill wrapped in their napkins; at another dinner, the host handed around cigarettes rolled in $100 bills, each stamped with his initials in gold.[2] One hostess concealed a black pearl in each oyster served to her guests, at a total cost of some $20,000 ($420,000 in 2008); at another party, guests found the center of the table covered in a mound of sand. Miniature silver shovels and pails were set at each place, and before dinner was served the guests had the novelty of digging through the dune for a wealth of diamonds, sapphires, and rubies that formed the party favors.[3]

Such ostentation left Caroline Astor adrift. The frantic search for amusement and the increasing dominance of money as social power buried her concept of the Gilded Age, with its noble instincts and distinguished elite.

In her own way, she attempted to rival the methods employed by others, though inevitably her efforts fell short. Attempting to rise to the occasion, she once announced, "I am having a Bohemian party." Guests were duly intrigued, but disappointed to find that Mrs. Astor's idea of Bohemian was to invite Edith Wharton and J. P. Morgan.[4] Her most daring move was in 1898, when she asked Isadora Duncan to dance before her guests on the lawns at Beechwood in Newport.[5]

"Mrs. Astor," Duncan later recalled, "represented to America what a queen did to England. The people who came into her presence were more awed and frightened than if they had approached royalty. But to me she was very affable. She arranged the performances on her lawn, and the most exclusive society of Newport watched me dance on that lawn." The experience, however, proved unsatisfactory to the mercurial dancer: the money she was offered barely paid for her transportation and the cost of her hotel, and she found the gathered audience utterly wanting in true appreciation: "They looked upon my dancing and thought it charming, they hadn't any of them the slightest understanding of what I was doing. . . . These people seemed so enwrapped in snobbishness and the glory of being rich that they had no art sense whatever."[6]

The need for novelty took ever more bizarre forms. One millionaire gave a hobo dinner, to which all of his wealthy friends came dressed in rags. They sat on broken boxes, buckets, and wooden crates; used dust rags and newspapers as napkins; ate scraps of food served on wooden plates; and drank beer from jars and rusty tin cans.[7] Similarly peculiar was the Servants Ball given by stockbroker Henry Clews and his wife. No one was admitted unless they appeared as a servant. Henry Clews, dressed as a valet and holding a feather duster in one hand and a kitchen pail in the other, manned the front door to greet his guests. Harry Lehr came attired as a butler, and his wife as a lady's maid; Tessie Oelrichs, in a plain maid's dress, was found in typical pose scrubbing the floor, while Oliver Belmont played cloakroom attendant. All of the guests crowded into the kitchen to cook their own supper: Mamie scrambled eggs, Elisha Dyer Jr. boiled lobster, and James Van Alen made spaghetti.[8]

Not surprisingly, Mamie Fish excelled at such endeavors. She gave the Baby Talk Dinner, at which guests spoke only in gibberish; the Barnyard

Ball; the Heavenly Party, at which she hired messenger boys from Western Union to dress in skimpy shorts and parade among the guests as Cupids; and even the Circus Ball, at which a live elephant wandered through the rooms of her house in New York so the guests could feed it peanuts.[9] More infamous was the Dog's Dinner, to which Mamie and Harry Lehr invited a hundred dogs, along with their masters, to a lavish feast. Some owners, seizing on the sheer absurdity of the occasion, outfitted their pets in elaborate little costumes; the canine guest of honor, it was later reported, sported a new collar studded with $15,000 ($315,000 in 2008) worth of diamonds, ranging from one sixth to one carat each.[10] While the owners dined at one table, liveried footmen served their pets a three-course feast of stewed liver and rice, fricassee of bones, and specially baked biscuits. "It must have been appreciated," recalled Elizabeth Drexel Lehr of the canine participants, "for the guests ate until they could eat no more. Elisha Dyer's dachshund so overtaxed its capacities that it fell unconscious by its plate and had to be carried home."[11]

Such extravagance inevitably evoked criticism in the press, but the condemnation was nothing compared to the furor that erupted over the ball Mamie gave in honor of Prince del Drago of Corsica. Mamie and Harry sent four hundred engraved invitations to meet the visiting Italian aristocrat, and for weeks society was aflutter with excitement. On the appointed evening, the elegantly attired guests waited in anticipation. Then Mamie appeared at the top of the staircase and announced the prince: a monkey dressed in a perfectly made, miniature tuxedo, who behaved tolerably well until the festivities bored him. He then proceeded to attack the glittering guests, jumping from table to table before finally perching on a crystal chandelier and throwing champagne glasses at the startled onlookers. Mamie and Harry dissolved in laughter; the guests were somewhat less amused, but none dared reproach Mamie lest they be ostracized, and she continued on unrestrained, causing havoc and confusion at every turn.[12]

One newspaper declared, "It is simply appalling to think of Mrs. Stuyvesant Fish becoming the leader of our society. In that case social life would be a long succession of monkey parties and equally undignified entertainments. I suppose our balls would all be more or less like Indian war dances. It is dreadful to think of distinguished foreigners coming over here and judging us by Mrs. Stuyvesant Fish's entertainments, arranged with the assistance of Harry Lehr. New York society represents America in the eyes of the foreign world, and we should behave with a becoming sense of dignity."[13]

This rising condemnatory tone threatened the underpinnings of a society Caroline Astor had so assiduously and ardently created and attempted to protect, and she took the highly unusual step of offering a public comment on the increasingly bizarre entertainments. In her first— and only—interview, she railed against "the undignified methods employed by certain New York women to attract a following. They have given entertainments that belonged under a circus tent rather than in a gentlewoman's home. Their sole object is notoriety, a thing that no lady ever seeks but, rather, shrinks from. Women of this stamp are few in New York but, alas, they are so appallingly attractive."[14] It was no secret that Caroline was referring to Mamie Fish; when she learned of this, however, Mamie simply dismissed it with a coldly delivered "Mrs. Astor is an elderly woman."[15]

Open criticism of Caroline Astor offered mute evidence of the shift in society. Increasingly withdrawn and isolated, she was no longer able to control the destinies of an entity grown too large and too independent to fall under the authority of a single figure. While she lived, Mrs. Astor retained her once respected position as the recognized doyenne of fashionable New York, but in many ways she was simply a shadow queen, the remnants of her power a mere illusion in the wake of an insistent challenge from more determined elements. All around her, Gilded Age society marched on, caution thrown to the wind, following a path that increasingly and inexorably would lead to their ruin.

Such was the case of one of New York City's most fabled parties. In January 1905, wealthy and handsome insurance heir James Hazen Hyde announced a magnificent costume ball modeled after the court of Versailles, to be held at Sherry's. It would, he proudly declared, "eclipse in splendor any entertainment that had ever been given in New York."[16] This remark underlined just how far standards had fallen: Caroline Astor would never have openly promoted one of her parties in such vulgar language, nor did Hyde aspire to any position at the head of society through the magnificence of his entertainment. It was simply to be a costly, excessive diversion in a life grown bored, and the event soon turned from spectacle to scandal.

Ostensibly, Hyde staged the ball to introduce society to his niece Miss Annah Ripley. He selected the evening of Tuesday, January 31, for the festivities, and commissioned architect Whitney Warren to transform Stanford White's lavish fourth-floor ballroom at Sherry's into a replica of Versailles. Thousands of dollars were spent on marble statuary and tapestries, arbors hung with festoons of roses and ivy, potted palms and immense looking glasses framed by enormous bowers of roses, all woven with tiny electric lights to create a magical effect.[17] Some measure of this extravagance can be gauged from the fact that New York City florist Wadley & Smythe billed Hyde $28,500 ($588,000 in 2008) for the flowers alone.[18]

Some six hundred elaborately costumed guests began to converge on Sherry's just after ten that frigid January night.[19] A length of crimson carpet had been spread across the pavement before the entrance, and a contingent of police held back the hundreds of onlookers who, despite the blistering cold, had turned out to catch even a glimpse of the city's most fashionable society as they entered what the newspapers had trumpeted as one of the most extravagant parties ever given in the metropolis. Within, footmen clad in red-and-blue-striped coats trimmed with gold braid and silver lace, knee breeches, white silk stockings, and powdered wigs—all supplied by the costume workshops of the Metropolitan Opera—directed the guests in hastily learned French to the fourth-floor ballroom.[20]

Here, their host waited atop a dais. Hyde wore a costume created from the formal dress of the New York Coaching Club mingled with a variety of French touches: a vibrant green tailcoat, black satin knee breeches, white silk stockings, and silver shoes with lace bows, with a brilliant red waistcoat providing a splash of dramatic color over his frilled white shirt. On his breast he wore the two crosses of the Légion d'Honneur he had received from the French government in recognition of the favorable business deals he had brokered on their behalf.[21] At his side was his sister Mrs. Sidney Dillon Ripley, attired in a gown of brocaded cerise with lace sleeves, modeled on a portrait of Madame Victoire de France, who had married Louis XIV's son the grand dauphin.[22]

The parade of costumes, recalled guest James W. Gerard, was "magnificent, and the whole thing was beautifully done."[23] Mamie, hair powdered and lavishly dressed in a long white eighteenth-century gown awash with lace, accented her ensemble with a turquoise parure.[24] Edith Gould, wife of Jay Gould's eldest son, George, came costumed as Queen Marie, consort of Louis XV, in a gown of white satin embroidered with pearls and adorned with pearl-encrusted lace sleeves. From two emerald buckles at her shoulders cascaded a long train of green velvet and satin sewn with foliate designs in gold thread ornamented with real emeralds and lined with ermine. On her head, at her throat, on her bodice, and on her arms were rows of glittering diamonds supplemented with strings of pearls and emerald pendant drops—some $250,000 ($5.2 million in 2008) worth of jewels in all; her husband was so worried about possible theft that he had his wife trailed all evening by a private detective clad in period costume.[25] But pride of place went to Mrs. Clarence Mackay, who had come costumed as eighteenth-century French actress Adrienne Lecouvreur in her role as Phèdre. Her gown of silver brocade, sewn with foliate designs and ornamented with turquoises, split at the waist to reveal an underskirt of silver lace; from her shoulders fell a twenty-foot-long train of silver brocade, stunningly enriched by more embroidery and hundreds of gems. The weight of this outfit, literally encrusted with jewels, was staggering, so heavy that Mrs. Mackay could not move without the assistance of her "two little Negro pages," whom she had dressed in pink silk brocade.[26]

Once the guests had been received, Hyde led his sister and his niece to a platform at the end of the ballroom, where they sat in gilded chairs beneath a canopy of blue velvet embroidered with gold fleurs-de-lis and topped with plumes of ostrich feathers.[27] The forty-piece orchestra from the Metropolitan Opera played as guests seated themselves in rows of gilded chairs before the stroke of eleven signaled the beginning of the festivities. Eight gentlemen in black-and-white Pierrot costumes and pointed hats topped with pom-poms led eight debutantes in white gowns wreathed in garlands of roses to the center of the ballroom, grabbing streams of multicolored ribbons hanging from the ceiling and dancing an intricate gavotte.[28] This amateur effort gave way to a more polished gavotte and a minuet, enacted by the ballet corps of the Metropolitan Opera.[29]

At midnight, the doors at the far end of the ballroom were opened and four stout footman, costumed as members of the Swiss Papal Guard, carried in an elaborately decorated sedan chair out of which stepped Mme. Gabrielle Réjane, a French actress then currently appearing in a production of *Ma Cousine* at New York's Liberty Theater.[30] Clad in an appropriate eighteenth-century-style gown, she bowed to the audience and to her host, then ascended the stage, the curtains parting to reveal a backdrop depicting two Renaissance-style salons.[31] The actress enacted a little bedroom farce, carefully written for the occasion by Dario Nicodemi in easily understood French words of one syllable for the sake of the audience.[32] "There was nothing in the slightest degree immoral or suggestive," recalled Albert Crockett, "at least to ears accustomed to English, and certainly eyes could not have detected anything that need offend the tenderest susceptibilities of even mid-Victorian morality. As a matter of fact, the whole entertainment was highly artistic."[33]

At a fanfare of trumpets from the orchestra gallery, Hyde rose from his seat and bade his guests dine. Warren Whitney had designed two adjoining supper rooms to resemble a formal parterre garden: real turf, strewn with rose petals, concealed the parquet floors; pedestals with statuary shimmered next to splashing fountains; and trellises covered with a profusion of ivy and roses laced with tiny electric lights formed the sides of makeshift striped tents.[34] In one room, sixty round tables, each centered on an exquisitely manicured miniature tree adorned with roses and wired with flickering electric lights, filled the floor, while in another, a large, damask-draped horseshoe-shaped table framed a patterned garden.[35] Liveried waiters moved through the rooms, serving an elaborate meal that included *consommé Voltaire, médaillons de foie gras en timbale à la gelée de porto, escalopes de homard à la Réjane, faisan piqué Louis XV, salade Madame de Pompadour, jambon à la gelée princess, glace à la reine,* petits fours, bonbons, and fruits, all washed down with magnums of Pol Roger 1889, Mumm's Extra, and Veuve Clicquot.[36]

After supper, the guests returned to dance in the ballroom above for ninety minutes, before another fanfare signaled a light refreshment of bouillon, sausages, ham, and chicken. Stomachs were already full from the substantial supper, and those who took to the dance floor after partaking of the second repast moved more slowly and heavily under the weight of so much food and the influence of so much alcohol. At six in the morning, a final fanfare signaled a breakfast of New England fish cakes before Hyde bade his sated, overwhelmed guests farewell.[37]

Newspapers offered up all of the extravagant details, including the rumor that the whole affair was said to have cost some $200,000 ($4.2 million in 2008), money—it was strongly suggested—that had come from the coffers of Hyde's Equitable Life Assurance Society; in actual fact, Hyde footed the bill himself, and the amount paid was likely a quarter of the more sensational estimates.[38] Whatever the cost, Hyde's ball scarcely set the record for extravagant entertaining in New York City, but by this time the public mood had shifted. "There was now a great deal of wealth in New York," recalled Albert Crockett. "But there was a tremendous amount of poverty as well, and public opinion was keen and quick to censure lavish expenditures for pleasure, and to scan, with minute attention, the source of the wealth that made such performances possible."[39] Now Americans no longer looked on in awe at such frivolities but instead regarded them with condemnation, as the squandering of resources. On February 19, the New York World published a number of illicitly obtained photographs of the guests. "The impression was devastating," wrote historian Walter Lord. "There was no suggestion of an evening of old-world culture; only shot after shot of bewigged lackeys, foppish young men, and spoiled-looking girls, their powdered hair lumped clumsily above their bland, patched faces. Looking at them, it was easy to believe the rumors of scandalous goings-on."[40] Very quickly, rumor had it that Hyde's ball had been nothing short of an orgy.[41] Hyde's rivals within the Equitable Life Assurance Society seized on the rumors of financial malfeasance and immoral conduct, launching a series of legal investigations so distasteful that, together with the critical headlines, they eventually drove a disgusted Hyde into French exile.[42]

Then, in 1906, came two dramatic events that foreshadowed the collapse of New York's Gilded Age revelries. Hyde's misfortunes had played out in a press consumed with society. In the first years of the Gilded Age, the coverage had been respectful, largely confined to reprinting the guest lists and details of parties forwarded by social secretaries. This changed, however, after the 1880s, when the rise of people such as Alva Vanderbilt and their attempts at obvious self-promotion not only warranted increased coverage but also brought new scrutiny by the increasingly competitive and ferocious yellow press of the day. By the turn of the century, newspapers in New York City, led by highly critical editors such as Joseph Pulitzer and William Randolph Hearst, had begun to offer not just commentary of the wealthy but also criticism of their scandals, both personal and professional.[43]

Without doubt, the principal chronicle of Gilded Age society was *Town Topics*. On the cusp of ruin, it had been purchased by Eugene Mann, who soon sold it to his brother, the enigmatic Colonel William D'Alton Mann. Definitely not a gentleman—though he affected the manners and mode of life fitting to such an appellation—Mann moved easily through the highest echelons of Gilded Age society, where he was always welcomed at exclusive parties. Mann's success rested not on his background or wealth, his wit or his connections, but rather on undisguised fear. The good colonel was, in fact, one of the era's most prolific and successful extortionists and a man who knew all of society's secrets.

Mann, recalled one acquaintance, was "a kindly looking gentleman who wore a flowing white beard, a red bow tie, and a clerical frock coat."[44] Corpulent, his red face fringed with white hair and whiskers, Mann could have passed for a benevolent Santa Claus, but appearances were deceptive.[45] Born in Ohio in 1839, Mann was a genuine colonel and military hero: he had formed the Fifth Michigan Cavalry at the beginning of the Civil War, and led the Seventh Michigan Cavalry alongside General George Custer in the Union Army at the Battle of Gettysburg.[46] At the end of the war he moved to Alabama, where he purchased and published the *Mobile Register*, his first foray into the nineteenth century's burgeoning media.[47] Mann also made a small fortune patenting a luxurious railway carriage whose rights he later sold to the Pullman Company.[48]

On purchasing *Town Topics*, Mann set about transforming it from an accumulation of guest lists at parties and balls passed on by social secretaries to something more disturbing. Using a network of paid spies drawn from a wide swath—butlers who overheard conversations at dinner tables, maids who found compromising letters, coachmen who delivered husbands

Colonel William D'Alton Mann, publisher of *Town Topics*.

to quiet pieds-à-terre where they kept their mistresses, and telegraph operators who regularly sent and received the most intimate of messages—he
quickly uncovered a wealth of high society's secrets. Even Harry Lehr was
suspected of being on the colonel's payroll at times.[49]

No member of Gilded Age society was ever quite certain of the loyalty
of their staff where *Town Topics* was concerned. "Nobody," remembered
one man, "could be sure that the butler or the personal maid wasn't a

spy, that the charming but penniless young cousin wasn't selling his rich relatives down the river."[50] Cagey employers, suspecting a leak, often deliberately spoke of invented scandals in front of their employees. If the false information appeared in print in *Town Topics*, they knew they had been betrayed. There was even suspicion, actively promoted by the magazine, that certain society ladies, chafing from a snub or exclusion from some party, happily confided the darkest secrets of their circles to Mann in an attempt to avenge themselves.[51]

Tessie Oelrich's niece Blanche recalled that *Town Topics* "played an enormous part in everyone's life. Climbing matrons were driven to despair by its jibes; indiscreet young married couples went in terror of its insinuations; hardy financiers whose pile concealed a more than ordinary toll of ruined persons hastened to try and buy off the editor."[52] Within a few years, Mann had turned *Town Topics* into both the most feared—and the most widely read—chronicle of high society. Few would admit that they read it (one proud exception was Mamie Fish), but it became an indispensable guide to the latest scandals.

At a time when any hint of scandal—an affair, problems with drinking, gambling, or drugs, shady financial dealings—could prove ruinous to the thin veneer of respectability in which society so boldly wrapped itself, Mann knew precisely how to attract attention and how to use his information to his own advantage. He composed a column entitled "The Saunterer" that appeared in each issue, in which the good colonel, using tactics that one man recalled bore "a curious resemblance to those that Hitler immortalized in *Mein Kampf*," regularly both chronicled society and at the same time took it to task.[53]

Mann was nothing if not honest about his motives. "New York Society," he once wrote, "cannot become more worthless, meaningless and theatrical than it is today. It is inhabited by jackasses, libertines, and parvenus."[54] "My ambition," he once declared, "is to reform the Four Hundred by making them too deeply disgusted with themselves to continue their silly, empty way of life. I am also teaching the great American public not to pay any attention to these silly fools. If I didn't publish *Town Topics*, someone else without moral responsibility would do so." With a note of self-justification he added, "I am really doing it for the sake of the country."[55]

While mingling the sycophantic with the condemnatory, Mann had little use for members of society. His column, noted Andy Logan, "was populated by individuals who gave receptions, tea dances, and tennis parties, and got married and engaged as much as they did on the town's other society pages. It was also populated by charlatans, transvestites, adulterers (often incestuous), nymphomaniacs, lesbians, and cuckolds."[56] Aided by sitting New York City justice Joseph H. Deuel to help him avoid any libel actions, Mann offered a tantalizing chronicle of society's misdeeds. He invented one of the gossip columnist's staples, the blind item. Mann would report the latest case of adultery, drunkenness, or domestic warfare in elaborate detail, never once mentioning the names of those involved, but dropping enough hints scattered through the article that the guilty could easily be identified by those in the know; he would often follow such a report with an ostensibly harmless piece of society news in which the names of those involved in the actual scandal would be innocently listed. Those who read Town Topics, as Andy Logan wrote, therefore had "no difficulty identifying the bride of the season who had once borne twins out of wedlock, the cotillion leader down with syphilis, or the prominent Philadelphia matron against whom divorce proceedings were brought because of her passionate friendship with a female librarian."[57]

Even when he named names, Mann evinced little caution or discretion. "Miss Van Alen," Town Topics once reported, "suffers from some kind of throat trouble—she cannot go for more than half an hour without a drink." He was scathing in his criticism: "Seldom does a brunette make a pretty bride," read one entry, "and Miss Marie Arnot Haver was no exception." Alva Vanderbilt Belmont, he diligently reported, "dyes her hair. Through covered with diamond rings, her hands are wrinkled like a washerwoman's."[58]

Mann soon realized that often there was more power in not printing an incriminating story; he let it be known that his locked safe held society's secrets, and managed to turn fear of exposure into a profitable industry.[59] Indeed, he declared, "Many a head of hair in the so-called social set would have turned white over night" had he disclosed the information he so carefully amassed. Those guilty of indiscretions, recalled Mann's niece Mildred, "constantly tried to shower the Colonel with gratuities of large sums of money to keep their many frivolous escapades out of print." They "relished it, and by the same token, feared it. They themselves made it what it was."[60]

This willingness to provide financial remuneration helped show Mann the way to further riches. If a story was particularly damaging, he would have it typeset and print a copy—which in fact he never intended to publish—then discreetly let the person involved know that he was set to print damning information and wanted him or her to read it first to correct any errors. On the days before *Town Topics* went to press, Mann was most often seen at his regular table at Delmonico's, enjoying his usual lunch of six double mutton chops, ham, kidneys, and slices of liver, all washed down with expensive champagne and occasionally accompanied by his sudden barks of "Wolf, wolf!" to express his approval.[61]

Throughout the afternoon, worried members of society would arrive for hastily arranged meetings, during which Mann presented his proofs; inevitably the stories were true, and when the subject was suitably horrified, Mann would compassionately offer not to publish in exchange for some consideration. Those impending crises not settled at Delmonico's were usually dealt with at Mann's office, where the corridor and waiting room would be crowded with "unscheduled visitors, who had got word from one source or another than a certain factually accurate but hideously inconvenient report was about to be dispatched to the printers. These invaders (after dark no one seems to have come alone) would take a sweeping look around the outer editorial room and . . . would advance through the open door of Mann's private office." Mann met them all, a stout walking stick at his side and a pistol concealed in his desk drawer in case any violent outbursts ensued. The outcome was always the same: "The high drama was swiftly transformed into a business negotiation. At its conclusion a check changed hands, marked down as a loan or stock purchase or perhaps an advertising contract, the offending item was removed from the next week's edition, and the visitors retired, sighing the long sigh of the reprieved."[62]

The amounts Mann charged for this blackmail varied depending on the person involved and the immensity of the scandal, but inevitably there was talk of the cost of having to reset the entire typeset edition of the magazine and of having to pay off any of his employees who had already seen the information to ensure that it never became public. As for Mann himself, there usually was some consideration of his "thoughtfulness." In reality he pocketed all of the extorted money, the victim never realizing that their particular article had been specially printed as a single copy and never intended for publication.[63]

For those with particularly deep pockets, Mann conceived yet another endeavor to enrich himself. This was an expensive, privately printed folio with gilt-edged pages titled *Fads and Fancies of Representative Americans*, a "volume of achievement and adulation which," wrote Lucius Beebe, "even in an age that gladly paid top prices for flattery, must stand as a landmark of combined naïveté and opulence."[64] Fewer than ninety copies were printed in 1905 for Mann's "subscribers," most of whom paid some $1,500 ($31,500 in 2008) for the privilege of the inclusion of a short biographical entry. Inevitably, many of those who did so had been the subject of Mann's blackmail, and no one quite knows what further amounts of money he extorted for the privilege of inclusion.[65] No one dared ostracize Mann; indeed, he was a regular fixture at several of New York's most fashionable clubs.

One man included in *Fads and Fancies* was President Theodore Roosevelt; distressed at finding a biographical entry in a book widely believed to consist of victims of Mann's blackmail, Roosevelt fired off an angry note to Mann and let it be known that he had not been consulted prior to publication. Mann was angered by this presidential rebuke and thereafter set his sights on Roosevelt's family, hoping to exact revenge.[66]

In 1904 he got his chance. *Town Topics* ran a piece in its regular column written by Mann, "The Saunterer," that attacked President Roosevelt's daughter Alice. The twenty-year-old woman, nicknamed "Princess Alice" for her often imperious nature, had long been a favorite subject for society columnists, who reported her every move, but Mann loaded his account with scandalous innuendo: "From wearing costly lingerie to indulging in fancy dances for the edification of men was only a step. And then came, second step, indulging freely in stimulants. Flying all around Newport without a chaperone was another thing that greatly concerned Mother Grundy. There may have been no reason for the old lady making such a fuss about it, but if the young woman knew some of the tales that are told at the clubs at Newport she would be more careful in the future about what she does and how she does it. They are given to saying almost anything at the Reading Room, but I was really surprised to hear her name mentioned openly there in connection with that of a certain multimillionaire of the colony and with certain doings that gentle people are not supposed to discuss. They also said that she should not have listened to the risqué jokes told her by the son of one of her Newport hostesses."[67]

Although Mann did not mention Alice Roosevelt, her identity was obvious to all who read the account. Alice, who reveled in publicity, seemed not to care: "When I danced the hootchy-kootchy on Grace Vanderbilt's roof at Newport," she said, "you would have thought the world was coming to an end!"[68] But many considered this not only an insult to Alice Roosevelt but also to her father and to the dignity of the presidency itself.[69] Into this storm stepped Norman Hapgood, the young editor in chief of the popular *Collier's Weekly*. Mann had been one of founder Peter Collier's most vociferous critics, and his son Robert, who now helmed the magazine, wanted revenge. Hapgood used the episode with Alice Roosevelt to openly attack *Town Topics* and its publisher: "The most degraded paper of any prominence in the United States is a weekly of which the function is to distribute news and scandal about society. The mind which guides such a publication tests credulity and forces one to take Swift's Yahoo as an unexaggerated truth. The editor in question leads a somewhat secluded life, and well he may. . . . A recent issue of his sewer-like sheet contains as its leading feature an attack on a young girl who happens to be the daughter of the President of the United States. . . . It charges her with all the errors that hurt a woman most, and it makes these charges in a most coarse and leering way." Mann, he declared, had a reputation "somewhat worse than that of an ordinary forger, horse-thief, or second story man."[70]

Mann fired back with his own attacks against Collier, and the increasingly bitter feud eventually led to yet another attack by Hapgood, this time directed specifically against Justice Deuel. "He is part owner and one of the editors of a paper," Hapgood declared, "of which the occupation is printing scandal about people who are not cowardly enough to pay for silence. What kind of public opinion would allow him to remain upon the bench?"[71]

The charge of blackmail was now out in the open. Hapgood and Collier had acted on the advice of New York district attorney William Travers Jerome, carefully raising the rhetoric to create a situation in which Mann would sue and thus an opportunity for a trial at which Jerome hoped to expose the entire operation.[72] The previous July, Edwin Post, husband of the famed etiquette expert Emily Post, had gone to Jerome and lodged a curious complaint. He related that Charles Ahle, one of Mann's agents, had informed him that the editors knew he was keeping a chorus girl as a mistress in a Connecticut apartment, and demanded $500 ($10,500 in 2008) to suppress the story. Post did the unthinkable and confessed his indiscretion to his wife, who advised him to tell the authorities of the attempted extortion. Acting on Jerome's advice, Post arranged to meet Ahle and pay the requested fee; as soon as the envelope was handed over, police arrested Ahle, who quickly spilled the good colonel's secrets. Mann denied all knowledge, but Jerome was determined to expose *Town Topics* and the colonel's methods and put an end to his blackmail.[73]

The plan initiated by Jerome, Collier, and Hapgood worked, and on August 21, 1905, both Mann and Deuel announced that they were each suing both *Collier's* and Hapgood for libel, asking for $100,000 ($2.1 million in 2008) in damages.[74] The trial, which opened on January 15, 1906, caused a sensation. When cross-examined, Deuel denied any blackmail, but his case unraveled when *Fads and Fancies* was admitted into evidence. On the stand, Mann admitted that he had received some $187,500 (approximately $3.9 million in 2008) in what he described as "loans" from many of those included in the book and in society, including $25,000 ($525,000 in 2008) from William K. Vanderbilt, $2,500 from J. P. Morgan, and similar "contributions" from Arabella Huntington, Clarence Mackay, Oliver Harriman, William C. Whitney, and Jack Astor.[75]

None of these people ever asked for security or repayment. What they gained in return, as Mann reluctantly admitted, was inclusion on his list of "immunes," people about whom *Town Topics* never printed a negative word. Mann insisted that there was absolutely no blackmail involved, but under cross-examination he admitted that he barely knew some of those named, leaving the question of why mere acquaintances would lend the publisher substantial sums of money.[76] On the stand, Mann repeated his denials of blackmail, but his clumsy explanations did little to bolster his credibility. When the district attorney presented the publisher with documents signed "OK, WDM," which outlined the schemes, Mann incredulously claimed that this was not his mark of approval. After a handwriting expert testified that Mann had indeed written the notations, the good colonel was recalled to the stand, where he once again denied any knowledge.[77]

In the end, it took the jury just seven minutes to find Hapgood innocent of the charges.[78] The district attorney, certain that Mann had perjured himself, now brought criminal charges against the publisher, and the chaos erupted once again.[79] Mann repeated all his denials of both blackmail and of responsibility for the damning initialed memoranda, but few were persuaded. Perhaps sensing the futility of arguing his client's innocence, defense attorney Martin Wiley Littleton resorted to a new tactic, recounting Mann's service during the Civil War and his time with Custer at Gettysburg. "Send this gallant old hero from this courtroom a free man!" he implored the jury.[80] The plea for sympathy worked: Mann walked away cleared of perjury, but with his reputation irreparably sullied. *Town Topics* was never to enjoy the same fearful hold again, but the trials—along with the embarrassing revelations and suggestions of errant husbands keeping secrets from their wives—helped shatter society's complaisant belief in its own security.

The exposure of *Town Topics* was rapidly followed by an even more startling event, the shocking murder of architect Stanford White. The fifty-two-year-old red-haired and mustachioed White had become one of society's most important tastemakers through his partnership with Charles McKim and William Mead. Their monumental public buildings drew admiration, and none more so than White's new Madison Square Garden. Formally inaugurated in 1890, it included an immense auditorium and arena, a white-and-gold, Louis XVI–style ballroom, a fashionable rooftop café, and a bank of fashionable apartments. Its most distinguishing feature, however, was its 341-foot-tall tower modeled after the campanile of the Cathedral of Giralda in Seville, topped with a gilded, scandalously

Madison Square Garden,
New York

Stanford White's exotic Madison Square
Garden in New York City.

nude statue of Diana by Augustus Saint-Gaudens that provoked a great
deal of comment across the city.[81]

Commissions from the wealthy for increasingly elaborate houses,
including Mamie Fish's second New York residence and Tessie Oelrichs's
romantic Newport cottage, Rosecliff, followed. White became a regular
fixture at parties given by his Gilded Age clients, and he moved in a circle
that included Alva Vanderbilt Belmont, Tessie Oelrichs, and Mamie
Fish.[82] White was a dominating personality. "He seemed to tingle with
potential energy," recalled Margaret Chanler; "there was something meteoric about his exits and his entrances. Restless as a whirlwind, he would
flash into a roomful of people on his way from one show to another, shake
hands here and there, tell us how lovely something was, or how much
he hated something else, and rush out again into the white night of
Broadway, leaving us all exhilarated and a little breathless, as if a foam
created wave had swept through the room."[83] Although White could be
quite fastidious, he was often badly dressed owing to indifference, his
shock of red hair a tangled mess. He once arrived late for dinner with

Tessie Oelrichs, apologizing but adding, "It never takes me more than five minutes to dress."

"So I should imagine," she shot back, "but then, just look at your idea of dressing!"[84]

Though married, White had a notoriously roving eye, and he kept a set of rooms in the tower of the Madison Square Garden complex he designed, as well as a nearby studio at 22 West 24 Street. Here he threw decadent parties for his male friends and regularly entertained young girls in an immense canopied bed surrounded by mirrors.[85] "The process of seduction," wrote White's great-granddaughter, "was a major feature of Stanford's obsession with sex, and it was an inexorable kind of seduction which moved into the lives of very young women, sometimes barely pubescent girls, in fragile social and financial situations—girls who would be unlikely to resist his power and his money and his considerable charm, who would feel that they had little choice but to let him take over their lives. There are indications that Stanford would sometimes adopt the role of a paternal benefactor, and then would take advantage of the trust and gratitude that had been built."[86]

Such was the case with Evelyn Nesbit, whom White first met in 1901, when she was just sixteen. Born in 1884, Evelyn had moved to New York the previous year, attempting to escape the grinding poverty and despair of her youth, and had begun work as an artist's model. Her beauty was exquisite: Charles Dana Gibson was so enraptured that he drew her portrait for *Collier's Weekly*. She eventually got a part as a chorus girl in the production of the popular musical *Floradora*, where she attracted considerable attention. White, who regularly haunted the popular productions seeking out the loveliest showgirls, was immediately taken with her, and soon began to ply her with expensive dinners and imported champagne.[87]

One evening, White brought Nesbit to his Twenty-fourth Street studio; he plied her with glass after glass of champagne. Dizzy with excitement, she let him lead her to his darkened bedroom; the last thing she remembered before passing out was an overwhelming pounding in her ears.[88] When she awoke in his mirrored bed, she was naked but for a small white chemise, and found her legs and the sheets stained with dried blood; standing over her, White said with a leer, "Now you belong to me!"[89]

Realizing what had happened, she screamed; White assured her that all men did these things, imploring her not to tell her mother and cause a scandal, and promising to look after her.[90] "Then," she later recalled, "he told me that only very pretty girls were nice and that the thinner they were the prettier they were, that nothing was so loathsome as a stout or fat woman."[91]

Having dressed and calmed Evelyn, White returned her to her apartment. Evelyn was naive, but she knew that she had been drugged and raped; worse still, she was, according to law, still a minor.[92] Yet she was too dependent on White's financial largesse to aid both herself and her family to sever her ties; Evelyn also was too enamored of the charismatic White and of his extravagant style of life to break off the relationship, and the affair, commenced in violence, continued for several years, during which Evelyn would strip for the architect as he pushed her in a red velvet swing he had installed in his apartment.[93] Although White soon tired of Evelyn, he continued to see her and look after her financially.

Evelyn Nesbit in about 1903, at the height of her affair with architect Stanford White.

Then, in 1903, she met the wealthy, sadistic, and mentally unstable Pittsburgh railroad heir Harry Thaw.[94]

Born in 1871, the tall, fair-haired Thaw was eccentric in his tastes and dangerous in his behavior: having been expelled from any number of private schools, he finally gained admission to Harvard, only to be sent packing after chasing a cabdriver through the streets with a shotgun. Addicted to alcohol, morphine, and cocaine, Thaw seemed to cause problems wherever he went. He once beat a young hotel bellboy, then ordered him to strip while Thaw rubbed salt into his bleeding wounds, and Thaw was rumored to frequently whip the numerous chorus girls he seduced.[95]

Thaw hated Stanford White, and the two often clashed over who could win the temporary affections of the newest beautiful chorus girl. But Thaw was charming to Evelyn and showered her with gifts, and she gradually fell under his spell, at the same time continuing her liaison with White. In May 1903, when Thaw suggested that Evelyn her and mother accompany him to Europe—at his expense—Evelyn eagerly accepted.[96]

Harry K. Thaw, about 1905.

The relationship deepened in Paris, but Thaw became jealous with rage if he spied another man looking at Evelyn, causing public scenes and even overturning tables in a restaurant.[97] He quickly proposed marriage, but uncertain of her feelings and his behavior, as well as her continued relationship with White and remorse over her past, she turned him down.

"Are you a good girl?" Harry asked suspiciously. "Pure? Are you a virgin?" Then Evelyn broke down in tears and admitted that White had raped her and thus made her unsuitable as a wife. This confession sent Thaw into a delirium of rage, and he began to treat Evelyn with a confusing mixture of overwhelming, obsessive love alternating with wild accusations and physical violence. Once, he beat her so badly that she was confined to bed for a week, but he always followed such outbursts with a litany of apologies and expensive presents.[98]

Despite such behavior, Evelyn continued to see Harry; perhaps she was simply loath to abandon the idea of marrying the multimillionaire heir, despite his pathological nature and brutality. In the end, Thaw got his wish and wed Evelyn in April 1905, but marriage seemed only to inflame his passions. He was obsessed with White, whom he blamed for dishonoring his wife; and for her part, Evelyn compounded the situation, alternately reminding her husband of the architect's evil deeds and then risking Harry's ire by comparing him unfavorably to Stanford, always keeping the specter of her former lover alive as a phantom partner in her tumultuous marriage. Such behavior only served to further unhinge an already dangerously fragile Thaw, who constantly complained to city officials about White's immoral conduct, hired a contingent of private detectives to trail him across New York City to record his movements and dig for further scandal, and let it be known that he was armed in case he ever found himself face-to-face with his enemy.[99] Thaw was determined to exact revenge. On the warm summer evening of June 25, 1906, he got his opportunity.

That night, a happy, privileged crowd sat beneath a canopy of vines strung with red, yellow, and blue Chinese lanterns in White's Madison Square Garden rooftop restaurant, enjoying the premiere of the musical *Mamzelle Champagne*.[100] Thaw and Evelyn were dining there when White arrived at eleven that night and made his way through the crowded restaurant, pausing to greet friends before settling at a table near the stage. Thaw was seized with a sudden, uncontrollable rage. As Evelyn looked on, he stood and made his way across the crowded room. On the stage, Harry Short was singing "I Could Love a Million Girls," backed by a chorus of scantily clad showgirls, as Thaw, his frame shrouded in a long, dark coat, strode toward White's table. From his pocket he pulled a small pistol and shouted, "You deserve this! You have ruined my wife!" As a startled White faced him, Thaw fired three shots in quick succession.[101] One bullet struck White's right arm and shoulder as he was turning, the second struck the left side of his nose and penetrated the brain, while the third took out White's left eye in a shower of gore. The famed architect crumpled over the table, pulling its contents down with him as he crashed to the floor.[102]

The restaurant erupted with screams and shouts; chorus girls fainted, and Evelyn rushed to her husband's side, shouting, "My God, Harry, what have you done?" White was dead before he hit the floor, and Thaw, who made no attempt to escape, was promptly arrested and charged with murder, all the while shouting, "He ruined my wife!"[103]

The murder of Stanford White caused a sensation, but it was nothing compared to the maelstrom that erupted within days of his death as word of his sexual proclivities and the story of Evelyn Nesbit Thaw began to leak to the press. The New York Times described to its readers how the architect had "drugged, ruined, and insulted Mrs. Thaw," and the city reveled in the sexual scandal and the lurid details.[104] "It is not pleasant to speak harshly of a man scarcely cold in his grave," William Randolph Hearst declared piously on the pages of his New York Evening Journal. "But beyond the sentimental respect felt for the dead and beyond the horror of dealing with the shameful details of lives unmentionable, there is a duty to the public in the face of a great danger that cannot be ignored. The man in jail for murder is a young man of weak character in a certain way, but of good instincts and impulses. The worst that can be said of him is that he is a victim of heredity, of a false system, of vast inherited wealth, destroying the necessity for self-control, taking away all the incentive upon which a good life is usually based. . . . The flash of that pistol lighted up depths of degradation, an abyss of moral turpitude that the people must think of, because it reveals some of the hidden features of powerful, reckless, openly flaunted wealth."[105] The scandal was so bad, and the oppro-brium surrounding the murdered architect so pervasive, that none of his friends, colleagues, or former patrons dared come to his defense. "Will no one say a word for Stanford White?" William Travers Jerome, the attorney prosecuting Thaw, was forced to plead openly in the press as he prepared his case.[106]

Thaw's trial for murder, which opened on January 23, 1907, kept the sensation alive, as the general public eagerly read tales of White, fashion-able society's great architect who had lived a wicked and unsuspected life, seducing countless women on his now infamous red velvet swing, and rap-ing Evelyn. Thaw's first trial resulted in a hung jury. In 1908 a second jury found Thaw not guilty by reason of insanity; although this was a condition for which ample evidence seemed to exist, Harry's mother wanted nothing left to chance and bribed dozens of witnesses, including alienists and even Evelyn's own mother, to paint her son as temporarily insane.[107]

Thaw was locked away in an asylum, but the increasing dissatisfaction with the city's elite could not so easily be ignored. The entire episode, along with the outrageous parties and revelations of blackmail by *Town Topics*, exposed the dark underbelly of Caroline Astor's prized Gilded Age New York. Previously, wealth and privilege led to entitlement, allow-ing society to behave as it pleased. By 1906 the public no longer found the lavish parties and magnificent palaces riveting. It was the beginning of the end of benevolent indulgence.

26

SAILING TO OBLIVION

At the dawn of the twentieth century, recalled one man, society "drifted onward through the years, secure in the conviction that in the end everything was going to be all right."[1] Gilded Age America, Frederick Townsend Martin noted, "worshiped great wealth," and society held the country in "an enchanted thrall; even the poorest outcasts looked on in wonder and admiration at their glittering palaces along Fifth Avenue."[2] But the scandals and excesses of society ultimately doomed the Gilded Age, as public opinion turned against unrestrained extravagance. Martin, whose brother and sister-in-law's infamous 1897 ball seemed the epitome of the very worst of society's extremes, sensed the passing of the age even before its death knell sounded. He noted that shortly after the turn of the century, an uncomfortable undercurrent had begun to settle over society, a presentiment that something undefined, intangible, ominous hovered unseen at the edges of their privileged lives. As the years passed, former interest and admiration began to turn to condemnation and to hatred, piercing society's "armor of self-complacency and self-satisfaction" and leaving a vague sense of unease at what the future held.[3]

"To us, who, through the heyday of our popularity, simply sat in the sunshine and throve and grew fat in happiness," Martin wrote, "it came as a terrible shock, this change of the popular attitude. At first we laughed at it; then we preached little sermons about it, half jesting, half serious; then we began to talk about it among ourselves; and we held indignation meetings every time we met our friends, and called down the wrath of heaven on these sharp eyed and glib tongued investigators. Finally, and here lies the heart of the matter, we began to read these outpourings of the popular sentiment very seriously indeed. They came, at last, from sources that we dared not disregard. Instead of mere muck-raking expeditions they assumed the proportions of crusades. Instead of the frantic mouthings of mere sensation mongers there confronted us in the columns of the press and in the more sedate and orderly pages of the magazines, the speeches of a President, or sane, sober editorials written by men who knew both sides and who commanded our respect as well as the respect and admiration of the crowd. We recognized—those of us who thought, and saw, and felt—that instead of being a passing phase, as we had dreamed or hoped, this change of popular sentiment was the beginning of a revolution."[4]

Against this ever-shifting background, Caroline Astor remained a figure of tradition, firmly rooted in a past of her own creation, but, as the years passed, she, too, gradually faded into the background. In her reign, noted one commentator, "she enjoyed great power and influence. But it was usefully employed. She preserved the world over which she ruled from many mistakes, directed it with an unerring hand into channels calculated to prove of advantage and of benefit to the body politic, never for one moment relaxed her efforts in behalf of the maintenance of the best standards of culture, refinement, and delicacy, and will remain on lasting record as the personification of that greatest of all virtues in a social leader, namely, charity—not so much of the purse, but of heart and judgment."[5]

January 1905 saw one final burst of glory, when Caroline presided over the last of her opera balls at her Fifth Avenue mansion. The stiff vellum invitation read simply *Mrs. Astor. At Home. January Ninth, Ten o'clock.* Some six hundred guests, including the Harry Lehrs, Mamie and Stuyvesant Fish, William K. Vanderbilt Jr. and his wife, Birdie, Ruth and Ogden Mills, Neily and Grace Vanderbilt, Mr. and Mrs. Isaac Townsend Burden, the Elisha Dyers, and an assortment of other society fixtures swept past the banks of poinsettias, palms, and lilies in the foyer to the drawing room, where Caroline stood between immense cascades of American Beauty roses. Visibly old now and at times appearing to struggle through the proceedings, she wore a Worth gown of deep purple velvet trimmed with panels of blue satin and lace and embroidered in gold thread. All of the old symbols of power were in evidence: atop her black pompadour wig, her famous diamond tiara flashed fire; around her neck stretched a dog collar of diamonds with pearl pendants, while her bodice sparkled with a large diamond corsage brooch and the weight of Marie Antoinette's diamond stomacher. After watching a few dances in the ballroom, and before her guests retreated to a supper at 1:00 A.M., Caroline quietly slipped away to her rooms upstairs, wearied by the ordeal of her continued social obligations.[6]

From the splendid isolation of her château on Fifth Avenue, Caroline denounced the increasingly vulgar displays; people such as Mamie Fish and Alva Vanderbilt Belmont, she said, with their elaborate dinners in honor of monkeys and dogs, were ruining all of the noble instincts and honorable exclusivity she had bestowed on society. Perhaps aware that her time was limited, the ordinarily reclusive Mrs. Astor gave an extraordinary interview in which she reflected on her role in society: "Many people seem to think I could have done a great deal in making New York society as democratic as it is in London and open to anyone of intellectual attainments, as it is over there. But one can only do one's best under the conditions. . . . We have to be more exclusive in New York because in America there is no authority in society." She ended with a candid remark: "I am not vain enough to believe that New York will not be able to get along without me. Many women will rise up to fill my place."[7]

A few months later, seventy-five years old and noticeably frail, Caroline stumbled and fell down her magnificent marble staircase. Servants found her moaning on the floor, her halo of white hair cloaked in blood. A hastily called examining physician discovered that she had suffered numerous deep gashes and contusions; having refused to go to the hospital, she bravely sat in a chair, tightly clutching the arms while the doctor stitched her wounds. Although she recovered physically, Caroline was never the same again. Her famous sharpness faded, replaced with confusion and a growing senility.[8]

The great château on Fifth Avenue fell into a gloomy silence, as rooms once filled with music and laughter were shuttered, their furniture hidden under dustcovers and chandeliers swathed in netting. A skeleton staff of three maids and Thomas Hade, the butler who had been in her employ since 1876, cared for the house, while two nurses and Caroline's physician, Dr. Austin Flint, tended to her needs.[9] Occasionally she was quite lucid, but she spent the majority of her days lost in a haze of dementia. Now "quite small and shrunken," as a granddaughter recalled, Caroline filled her days entertaining the phantoms of the past.[10]

One of Caroline's granddaughters remembered, "She used to think I was my Aunt Helen, long since dead, and spoke of her mother and sisters as though they were living." Once, she became obsessed with the idea that she was pregnant, and ordered a nursery prepared; to indulge her fantasy, an obstetrician was even called in to consult until the delusion passed.[11] In the mornings, Caroline received her butler, discussing details for dinners that would never take place, and discussed guest lists for imaginary balls. But on instructions from her family, the invitations were never sent, and 840 Fifth Avenue remained silent.[12] In the evenings, after her customary carriage ride through Central Park, Caroline received in her silent, empty house. "Unaware that her long reign had ended," recalled Lloyd Morris, "she did not lay aside her scepter; she bore it into the world of illusion that gradually enveloped her. Still erect, still bravely gowned and jeweled, she stood beneath her portrait—quite alone, greeting imaginary guests long dead, conversing cordially with phantoms of the most illustrious social eminence."[13]

In October 1908, time finally caught up with Mrs. Astor. For several years, she had suffered from heart palpitations, and a recurrence at the beginning of the month confined her to her bed.[14] On the evening of Thursday, October 29, Dr. Flint issued a statement to the press acknowledging that she was ill but declaring confidently that Caroline was "resting quietly."[15] The following day, she steadily declined; Flint administered stimulants and oxygen, but at two that afternoon, Caroline lapsed into a coma. At seven-thirty that night, with her daughter Carrie at her side, the fabled Mrs. Astor died at the age of seventy-eight.[16]

"For more than half a century," declared the *New York Times*, the name of Mrs. Astor "has been familiar to people not only in all parts of America but likewise in Europe as the most notable representative and leader of New York society." The paper attempted to sum up her legacy: "She had ideals and strove to live up to them. She did what she could throughout her life to discountenance the frivolities and inanities popularly accredited to an element in society. . . . She preserved the traditions, and if she had no salon in the good old sense, she did not discountenance intelligent conversation or permit the transformation of the social life around her into a vaudeville. She was in short an admirable woman who deserved the honors of her unofficial position and bore its many burdens with unfailing graciousness."[17]

Caroline's funeral took place on Monday, November 2. On that cold, windy day, nearly ten thousand curious, respectfully silent onlookers gathered outside her Fifth Avenue house. After a short service that afternoon in the drawing room, the glass and wrought-iron doors to the vestibule opened and Caroline's coffin, covered in a pall woven of flowers, was carried down the steps and loaded into a hearse. As the rain poured down, crowds along Fifth Avenue watched the hearse make its way to Trinity Church. After a short service, Caroline was interred in Trinity Church Cemetery on Riverside Drive, next to her husband.[18] It was the end of an era.

A year after Mrs. Astor's death, her daughter-in-law Ava finally did something that pleased her husband, suing Jack for divorce. A contingent of private detectives had shadowed him, providing Ava with irrefutable evidence of his infidelity; to rid himself of his hated wife, Jack was willing to ignore the multitude of similar rumors that swirled around Ava. On November 8, 1909, in a "remarkably well-hushed-up" proceeding kept secret from the press until Astor himself released a terse statement, the marriage was finally dissolved; Jack was granted custody of their son, Vincent, while Ava kept custody of their daughter, Alice.[19]

In the summer of 1911, during a visit to Bar Harbor, Jack met seventeen-year-old Madeleine Force; Madeleine was blond, beautiful and, in contrast to Ava, docile and doting, qualities that soon captivated Jack. Two months later, when he declared his intention of marrying Madeleine, the scandal was enormous. At the time, Madeleine was thirty years her future husband's junior, and just a year younger than his son, Vincent; not only had the couple known each other for just a few months but also, it was popularly believed, Madeleine was simply after the Astor millions. Jack quickly got an unwelcome measure of this disapproval when he tried to arrange the nuptials. Authorities for the Episcopal Church in New York City, of which he was not only a member but also a warden, publicly forbade any of their clergy to perform such a union. Thinking he could simply bribe his way around the problem, Jack publicly offered $1,000 ($21,000 in 2008) to a variety of Protestant ministers to conduct the ceremony; all of them refused.[20]

Finally, one minister, the Reverend J. Lambert of Elmwood Temple in Newport, was brave enough to risk public opinion and accepted Jack's offer. On September 9, 1911, with Lambert presiding, Jack finally married Madeleine, the ceremony ironically held in his mother's blue and gold ballroom at Beechwood. To escape the intense public disapproval that continued to swirl around them, the newly married couple sailed to Europe on an extended, six-month honeymoon, visiting Egypt and France.[21] Lambert was not so fortunate: within two months of the wedding, a steady stream of hate mail and public condemnation forced him to resign.[22]

In 1912, Gilded Age society looked forward to yet another season of splendor. In April, John Jacob Astor and his wife booked passage on a new ocean liner for their return to America. A few months earlier, Madeleine had learned that she was pregnant and, despite the battering his reputation had undergone, Jack wanted the child born in the United States. They were joined by Benjamin Guggenheim, scion of America's wealthiest Jewish family and owner of a fortune valued at $95 million ($1.9 billion in 2008); the elderly Isidor Straus, who with his brother Nathan owned Macy's Department Store and who was traveling with his wife of forty-one-years, Ida; and the Wideners: George, his wife, Eleanor, and son, Harry, returning to Newport to inspect progress on Miramar, a magnificent new limestone château designed by Horace Trumbauer that they were building at the edge of the Atlantic using some of their estimated $50 million (just over $1 billion in 2008) fortune.[23]

Madeleine Astor.

At 9:40 A.M. on Wednesday, April 10, the Astors boarded the boat train and left the Gare St. Lazare in Paris, bound for the port of Cherbourg, where they were to embark on their voyage.[24] With them traveled Victor Robbins, Jack's valet; Rosalie Bidois, Madeleine's lady's maid; Caroline Endres, Madeleine's private nurse; and Kitty, the couple's Airedale terrier.[25] Although an array of steamer trunks and valises accompanied them, it could not rival that of American Charlotte Drake Martinez Cardeza, who, after ten months in Europe, was returning to the United States with fourteen steamer trunks, four suitcases, three crates, and a medicine chest, all to be loaded aboard the waiting liner. Together they held seventy dresses; gowns from Worth in Paris; ten fur coats, ermine muffs from Dresden, and a coat of baby lamb's wool from St. Petersburg; thirty-eight feather boas; eighty-four pairs of gloves; thirty-two pairs of shoes (carefully packed in their own Louis Vuitton shoe trunk); a $14,000 ($294,000 in 2008) diamond and Burmese ruby ring and a $20,000 ($420,000 in 2008), seven-carat pink diamond, both from Tiffany; and an enameled music box, shaped like a bird, from Switzerland.[26]

Just after 6:30 P.M., in the fading orange light of sunset, the liner dropped anchor in the harbor at Cherbourg. Along with Jack and Madeleine, 140 other first-class passengers boarded the tender *Nomadic* and left the quayside.[27] Jack and Madeleine seemed in good spirits, playing with Kitty as they sped over the dark waters to the waiting vessel that, as one passenger recalled, was aglow with "tier upon tier of glittering electric lights."[28] A few hours later, the immense liner slowly steamed out of the harbor.[29] The following day, she dropped anchor at Queenstown in Ireland, her last port of embarkation. Crowded tenders ferried the multitude of passengers over the emerald waters; most were working-class—merchants, teachers, factory workers, and farmers—who, along with their families, were on their way to America, to pursue the Gilded Age mythical dream of prosperity, to escape the despair and poverty of their homeland. Late that afternoon, chased by screeching gulls and churning a ribbon of white foam in her wake, the liner steamed west, filled with the disparate ennui and scandals of its wealthy passengers and carrying the hopes and dreams of the less fortunate toward the promised land. *Titanic* would never again see land.

For three days, the liner was a hive of activity. The Astors, Guggenheim, the Wideners, the Thayers of Philadelphia, and other members of the elite wandered the ship's 882-foot length; although only minimal changes marked her out from her sister ship *Olympic*, this new vessel, plowing through the chilly April waters of the North Atlantic on her maiden voyage, was the largest liner in the world. The brainchild of the White Star Line—the *Titanic*-like *Olympic*—could not compete with the Cunard Line's faster *Mauretania* and *Lusitania* in speed, so the owners and builders—among them J. P. Morgan—elected unparalleled luxury and comfort. *Olympic* had impressed through the refinement of her appointments, but *Titanic* was even more sumptuous. Belowdecks, the third-class passengers passed their days in sparse, white-enameled common rooms outfitted with wooden benches; but for those in first class, there was no hint of economy. In the day, ladies could pass the hours in a crisply white writing room adorned with Corinthian columns and Georgian-inspired decor, or sip tea in the Louis XV–style lounge, paneled in carved oak boiseries and crowded with ornate, tapestry-covered sofas and chairs, while gentlemen could retreat to the smoking room, with its stained-glass windows, mahogany-paneled walls ornamented with mother-of-pearl, and comfortable, leather-upholstered furniture.[30]

A magnificent staircase of polished oak, set beneath an intricate wrought-iron and glass dome and flanked by scrolled wrought-iron balustrades ornamented with bronze foliage, swept past a handsome carved panel at the top landing embellished with a clock supported by figures representing Honor and Glory crowning Time, and descended to the decks below.[31] A white-paneled reception room opened to the Jacobean dining saloon, where leather-covered oak armchairs arranged around dozens of tables sat beneath an elaborate ceiling decorated in molded strapwork.[32] The à la carte restaurant, paneled in French walnut and adorned with gilded columns, offered a more intimate, exclusive dining experience, while the Café Parisien, with its lattice-covered walls, wicker chairs and tables, and French waiters, evoked the ambience of an informal sidewalk bistro.[33] In addition to a tiled, exotic Turkish bath and an indoor swimming pool, *Titanic* boasted "a large barber's shop, a dark room for photographers, a clothes-pressing room, a special dining room for maids and valets, a lending library, a telephone system, and a wireless telegraphy installation."[34]

Corridors laid with thick floral carpets stretched to cabins and staterooms. Accommodations, one contemporary journal declared, "of size and style sufficiently diverse to suit the likes and dislikes of any passenger are provided."[35] Jack and Madeleine occupied one of *Titanic*'s special suites, cabins C62–64, amidships on the vessel's port side.[36] These special suites, proclaimed *The Shipbuilder*, were "fitted out with unparalleled luxury." The suite encompassed three staterooms, C62–66, each eighteen by eleven feet and paneled in carved boiseries above a woven floral carpet, with Louis XV–style beds, dressing tables, chests, upholstered sofas, tables, and chairs; a small corridor, two wardrobe rooms, and a private bathroom and lavatory completed the accommodations.[37] For all this luxury, Jack paid just over

$3,000 ($63,000 in 2008) in 1912; by comparison, a third-class ticket cost a mere $30 ($630 in 2008).[38]

On Sunday, April 14, as the ship drew closer to Newfoundland, the air grew noticeably cooler; passengers taking promenades on the decks could watch their misty breath as they spoke. One passenger later recalled an "odor of ice in the air."[39] In the sunlight, some brave souls enjoyed the folding wooden chaises that lined the first-class decks, protected by woolen lap rugs and blankets against the invasive chill; below them—literally—the respectably dressed second-class guests walked, read, and socialized. Chains and warning notices strung across stairways barred them from the privileged realm of first class and protected them from the mass of third-class passengers who crowded the small spaces set aside for their daily turns on deck. *Titanic* was nothing if not a stratification of the rigid social and monetary castes that dominated in 1912. A first-class passenger would no more have slipped past the chains and descended (in every sense of the word) to the ranks of the tartan-garbed masses on the lower decks than a third-class passenger would have dreamed of intruding into the world of high society enacted above.

Throughout the day, five ice warnings poured into *Titanic*'s Marconi room, manned by two operators, Jack Phillips and Harold Bride.[40] Intermittently passed on to the officers and captain or ignored, they indicated that the ship was rapidly approaching small floes, bergs, and even sheets of ice that presented hazards to the vessel's safe navigation. Captain Edward Smith, an amiable company man with years of experience, saw no reason to change his speed or his course. Smith was nothing if not a man of habit, and he maintained the same approach he had used for many years, even as the ships under his command grew more complex, more powerful, and more difficult to maneuver quickly. In 1911 this had resulted in a collision between *Titanic*'s sister ship *Olympic*, helmed by Smith, and a small cruiser, HMS *Hawke*.[41] These new behemoths were simply too enormous for a man of Smith's ability, and he was set to retire at the end of *Titanic*'s voyage. Smith also was under some pressure from a particularly important passenger on this voyage, J. Bruce Ismay, chairman of the White Star Line, who, though he liked to proclaim that he enjoyed no special status or influence aboard the ship, had let it be known that an early arrival in New York would help cement the vessel's reputation as the preeminent liner of the day.

The North Atlantic sunset that Sunday was a glorious wash of fiery crimson, vibrant orange, ethereal pearl, and the encroaching blue-black of the night. As the black velvet sky arced over the vessel, passengers chatted, danced to the music of the ship's small band, and dined. "The tables were gay with pink roses and white daisies," recalled one first-class passenger, "the women in their beautiful shimmering gowns of satin and silk, the men immaculate and well groomed, the stringed orchestra playing music from Puccini and Tchaikovsky. The food was superb: caviar, lobster, quail from Egypt, plover's eggs, and hothouse grapes and fresh peaches."[42]

By eleven, the festivities of the elite were slowly ebbing; meals were finished, port was consumed, and gentlemen escorted their ladies down the grand staircase to comfortably heated cabins. A few men lingered in the smoking room, sipping brandy and enveloped in a haze of cigar smoke. Waiters had cleared the tables in the dining saloon and replaced the linen, china, silver, and crystal for breakfast the following morning. Outside, the ocean was calm, a seemingly endless sheet of black water interrupted by the bow of the vessel as it sliced onward, leaving a trail of white foam in its wake that glistened against the dark ocean.

There was no moon that night; had there been, perhaps lookout Frederick Fleet, perched high in the tiny crow's nest straddling the ship's foremast, might have spotted the white waves breaking around the bases of the monstrous iceberg that suddenly appeared directly in *Titanic*'s path just after 11:35 P.M. *Titanic* was too large, its turning circumference too wide, its immense reciprocating engines too slow to respond within the few minutes available to take her from catastrophe to safety. At 11:40 P.M. *Titanic* struck the berg on her starboard side; invisible spurs submerged beneath the water scraped along the hull, buckling plates and popping rivets in a sweep of damage some three hundred feet long. Ice in the crystal tumblers of drinks being consumed in the smoking room gently rattled; a few decks down, strings of crystals on the light fixtures in cabins jangled as a low rumble filled the hull; farther down still, in the cabins occupied by third-class passengers and in the service area of the ship, the effect was more profound, a momentary, violent shaking that ceased after a minute. As the berg floated away, ghostly pale in the fading light from the ship, it seemed as if this chance encounter was little more than an inconvenience, a novelty to be recalled, a brief moment of excitement on an otherwise tranquil night. But deep in the ship, freezing water was pouring in through holes and gaps in the steel hull plates. *Titanic* had sixteen watertight compartments, which could be sealed—as they were now—by electrically operated sliding doors; but the bulkheads did not extend the height of the ship, meaning that they were of limited use. *Titanic* was designed to stay afloat if any four of her sixteen watertight compartments were breached; the designers had not envisioned any scenario that could possibly result in more damage. But the iceberg exposed six of the sixteen compartments to the sea—a fatal injury. As water filled these first six compartments and the ship settled down by the bow, it would inevitably spill over the transverse bulkheads into the next one, a chain reaction as it flooded, sinking lower and lower until the bow disappeared beneath the ocean and the Atlantic invidiously infiltrated the hull.

Titanic was doomed. Awakened, Captain Smith reluctantly accepted every master's nightmare and ordered the lifeboats prepared for lowering and the passengers mustered on deck. Here, along the boat deck, sixteen lifeboats—eight to each side—stood ranged in two groups, one fore and one aft, with an additional four collapsible canvas-sided boats stowed for emergency use. Among them, they could hold perhaps 1,200; but 2,227 passengers and crew were on *Titanic*. The number of boats required had been laid down by British Board of Trade regulations, based on a vessel's gross tonnage; even though a liner such as *Titanic* far exceeded the tonnage figures upon which these calculations had been made many years earlier, the builders rejected the idea of providing additional lifeboats to compensate for the difference, not wanting to mar the deck with what they firmly believed to be excessive safety measures.[43]

After the iceberg hit the ship, Astor left his suite to investigate. At some point he spoke to Captain Smith, who whispered, "I think it is dangerous."[44] Jack returned and awoke his sleeping wife, telling her that the ship had struck ice; although he assured her that the damage did not appear serious, Jack told her that women and children were asked to follow the captain's orders and temporarily abandon the immense liner. There was no panic; Madeleine quickly donned an outfit, taking the time to adorn herself with several pieces of jewelry. Seeing her, Jack was not satisfied, and asked her lady's maid to retrieve a heavier dress; as a final touch, he insisted that she wear a long fur coat to stave off the cold. Atop her exquisite Parisian haute couture gown that concealed the swell of her pregnancy and over her ankle-length fur coat he placed one of the life belts retrieved from the armoire, composed of hard cork blocks covered in white canvas, before leading Madeleine down the crowded corridor, up the elegant oak staircase, and out onto the sloping deck.[45]

Here, people rushed about, crowding their way in to the lifeboats, gentlemen pushing reluctant wives down into their seats amid screams and cries. Although no one could fail to notice the ever-increasing slant of the deck, for many it seemed impossible that *Titanic* could sink; faced with the perilous uncertainty of an eighty-foot descent in a swaying lifeboat to a freezing sea or remaining aboard the blazing, warm liner, many passengers elected the latter as the lesser of risks. Women refused to be parted from their husbands, sons from their fathers, and small groups of families huddled together in the soft yellow glow of the electric lights, convinced that help was on the way. The atmosphere was even lighthearted as the ship's band, gathered on deck, entertained the passengers with a jaunty selection of rousing ragtime tunes.

Beneath the black sky, to the light of fiery distress rockets fired from the bridge in the hope of attracting the attention of any nearby vessels, the stark white lifeboats were gradually lowered from their davits to the sea; some, designed to take seventy people, carried fewer than a dozen when they hit the ocean. For a time, Jack and Madeleine retreated to the warmth of the gymnasium, near the first-class entrance on the boat deck, where the optimistic instructor was eagerly demonstrating the rowing machines, stationary bicycles, and mechanical horse.[46] Madeleine was uncertain, torn between following her husband's wishes and leaving the ship, and remaining at his side. When she expressed skepticism about the ability of the life belts to keep anyone afloat, Jack picked up one that had been temporarily discarded nearby, pulled a penknife from his pocket, and cut into the canvas, showing her the cork and explaining how it would help with buoyancy in the water.

Over the next hour, Jack wandered out onto the portside boat deck, checking progress on *Titanic* and on lifeboat 4, to which Madeleine was assigned. Second Officer Charles Lightoller had ordered the boat swung out at 12:45 A.M. and had it lowered from the davits to the promenade deck immediately below, thinking it would be easier to load the passengers from this vantage. But he found the large windows on the fore promenade deck sealed shut; by the time several members of the crew had been located to crank open the windows, some forty-five minutes had passed.[47]

Finally, Chief Second Steward George Dodd informed the Astors that the lifeboat was ready, and led them and the other waiting passengers down the Grand Staircase and out onto the promenade deck, where Lightoller stood waiting by the open window, having placed a wooden deck chair against the rail to serve as steps. Jack helped his wife to the makeshift stairs and, aided by Colonel Archibald Gracie, assisted her into the boat.[48] Turning to Lightoller, Jack explained that his wife was "in a delicate condition" and asked if he could accompany her to ensure that she was safe.[49] Although men were being admitted to other lifeboats, Jack was denied. "No, sir," Lightoller told him. "No man is allowed on this boat or any of the boats until the ladies are off."[50]

"The sea is calm," Jack assured Madeleine. "You'll be all right. You're in good hands. I'll meet you in the morning." He leaned forward, kissed her, and, with a smile, stood watching as her boat was slowly lowered toward the black water.[51] It was nearly 2:00 A.M.; lifeboat 4 was the last of *Titanic*'s regular lifeboats to leave the vessel. By this time, water was already washing over the bow; *Titanic* was so low that by the time lifeboat 4 was lowered, the eighty-foot drop from the promenade deck to the sea had shrunk to a mere fifteen feet.[52] As the passengers and seamen began to row the boat away from side of the hull, Madeleine chanced to look up and thought that she spotted Kitty, her favorite terrier, running back and forth along the deck amid the rows of passengers.[53]

As Madeleine's lifeboat slowly pulled away from the ship, she could clearly see for the first time that *Titanic* was in serious trouble. Water was churning over the bow and forecastle, seeping along the decks, and flooding the remaining forward compartments. Against the black of the Atlantic, *Titanic* was awash with light, decks blazing, silhouetting the hundreds gathered on deck, portholes glowing, arc lights shining upon the four buff-colored funnels, now rising at an increasing angle as the bow disappeared beneath the waves and the three gigantic bronze propellers at the stern began to clear the water in the stern's ascent toward the heavens. And although her husband had been denied a place, Madeleine discovered as they rowed away from the ship that a young Irish man had jumped into the boat; spotting him, she quickly threw a shawl over his head and warned him to remain hidden lest he be flung overboard.[54]

For a time Jack stood on deck, watching as the lifeboat carrying his pregnant wife faded slowly into the murk of the night. He wore no life belt; when one man approached him offering one, he refused, saying, "I am not going to jump."[55] From the cold of her distant lifeboat, Madeleine watched as *Titanic* entered its death throes. The water surrounding the vessel was awash with deck chairs, planking, and life preservers amid a sea of thrashing arms and legs as hundreds of passengers struggled to remain afloat; screams and cries for help filled the air. The ever-increasing angle tore away at the ship's structural integrity; with a great grinding noise of steel being torn asunder, the forward funnel snapped its guy wires and crashed into the sea atop a crowd of swimmers, and the dynamos failed, plunging the remaining length of the vessel into darkness. The wet hull glistened, the white superstructure outlined in a ghostly pallor. As Madeleine watched in horror, the ship emitted an internal cacophony of ruin—china and crystal breaking, furniture sliding across floors and smashing to pieces, machinery tearing loose from fittings—as it buckled and ripped apart with an explosion of fire and steam, the bow section breaking free and plunging toward the oceanbed, and the stern rising against the night until it stood at a ninety-degree angle. For a few moments it lingered there, people screaming as they plunged hundreds of feet into the freezing, hard, debris-strewn water to their deaths, before it finally gathered speed and slipped beneath the surface at 2:20 A.M.

In a daze, Madeleine clung to the side of her lifeboat; the cold was pervasive, the shock of what had just taken place overwhelming.[56] Lifeboat 4 had been some nine hundred feet from the hull when *Titanic* finally disappeared; Quartermaster Perkis, in charge of the small, white craft bobbing tranquilly on the icy sea, immediately ordered that the passengers and crew turn the boat around and search for survivors. Madeleine helped man the oars, pulling the boat through the chill waters toward the screaming throng.[57] It took some ten minutes to reach the site where *Titanic* had gone down; less than a dozen swimmers, some unconscious, were plucked from the water, and two men died in the boat within a few minutes from hypothermia.[58] Madeleine Astor's was the only lifeboat to return to search for and rescue survivors; the other fifteen regular lifeboats and the collapsible boats remained at bay while the screams and pleas for help of some fifteen hundred people gradually died away as the icy water took hold.

After a few hours, the icy water began to seep into the crowded lifeboat, swirling around feet encased in elegant Parisian shoes and delicate satin slippers. Finally, against the orange glow of a sunrise that illuminated a sea clotted with ice-blue floes and bergs, the Cunard liner *Carpathia* appeared. Captain Arthur Rostron, having been awakened and told of *Titanic*'s distress signal, had raced his own smaller liner and its 740 passengers at 17.5 knots—the fastest the vessel could go—in an attempt to reach the stricken vessel, but he was too late.[59]

Throughout that early, bitterly cold morning, bright flares went up, and *Titanic*'s lifeboats gradually rowed through the floes of ice toward the waiting liner where, exhausted, their occupants slowly ascended rope ladders to the deck or were lifted in canvas carriers to safety.[60] Once aboard, Madeleine was rushed to the privacy of the ship's infirmary.[61] Gazing out over the sparkling water dotted with an occasional jagged white iceberg or bluish floe, Rostron saw only a few scattered deck chairs, some canvas life belts, and a single corpse bobbing mournfully in the sea; nothing else remained of *Titanic*.[62] Of *Titanic*'s 2,227 passengers and crew, only 705 survived.

Jack Astor's son Vincent was waiting at Pier 54 in New York at 8:00 P.M. on Thursday, April 18, when *Carpathia* finally arrived with his pregnant stepmother, along with her lady's maid and private nurse, who also had been saved, but there was only speculation as to the fate of his father.[63] On April 22, the cable ship *Mackay Bennett* from Halifax, commissioned to search for victims, came across a corpse, no. 124 of the 306 bodies—most kept afloat by their lifebelts—they retrieved from the Atlantic.[64] The details were carefully recorded in a ledger: male, estimated age of fifty, with light-colored hair and mustache, attired in a blue serge suit, a belt with a gold buckle, and a brown shirt with the monogram *JJA* on the collar.[65] It was Jack Astor. An examination revealed that he had not drowned, but had been killed in the sinking: his bloated face and arms were badly crushed and still covered with soot, indicating that he had been struck by falling debris when *Titanic* began its final plunge, perhaps by the forward funnel when it crashed into the water. A diamond ring circled one of his fingers; gold cuff links set with diamonds still clasped the wrists of his shirt; and a gold watch remained in his pocket. In his wallet were £225 (approximately $62,000 in 2008) and $2,440 ($51,240 in 2008).[66] At the time of his death, Jack had been worth some $87 million ($1.8 billion in 2008), but all of his money and privilege could not save him.[67]

Titanic forever crushed the aura of complacency that had hovered uneasily over America's Gilded Age society. It was, recalled Blanche Oelrichs, "as if some great stage manager planned that there should be a minor warning, a flash of horror," to sound the alarm before the impending disaster.[68] The introduction of income taxes the following year, and the outbreak of World War I in 1914, brought a final end to the Gilded Age's years of increasingly unchecked excess and sybaritic pleasures. One by one, the great mansions of New York, the Hudson, the Berkshires, and Newport were shuttered and abandoned, never again to recover from the intrusion of the twentieth century.

EPILOGUE

ON AUGUST 14, 1912, four months after the sinking of *Titanic*, the widowed Madeleine Astor gave birth to a son, John Jacob Astor V. The majority of Jack's considerable estate went to his eldest son, Vincent, with $5 million ($105 million in 2008) to his daughter Alice. Before his death, Jack had established a trust of $3 million to $5 million ($63 to $105 million in 2008) for Madeleine's unborn child, while his widow received income on a $5 million account, with the proviso that such funds would cease if she remarried. She also was granted lifetime residence in Caroline Astor's Fifth Avenue château for as long as she remained unmarried.[1]

In 1916, confounding all perceptions that she had only wed Jack to gain access to his fortune, Madeleine willingly relinquished income from her trust and residence in Hunt's New York palace to marry William Dick, a childhood friend and banker. Two sons were born, but the marriage ended in divorce in 1933; a few months later, Madeleine wed again, this time to an Italian boxer named Enzo Fiermonte. When this union, too, ended in divorce, Madeleine moved to Palm Beach, where she lived quietly. In 1940, at age forty-six, she died from a persistent heart ailment. Her first son, John Jacob Astor V, outlived her by half a century, dying in 1992.

Like their stepmother, the children from Jack's union with Ava also became known for their strings of marriages. After two previous failed unions, Vincent finally found happiness with Mary Brooke Russell before his death in 1959; his widow, the famous philanthropist Brooke Astor, died in 2007. Alice married four times, including exiled Russian prince Serge Obolensky, before she died of a stroke in 1956 at age fifty-four. After her divorce from Jack, their mother had gone to live in England, where in 1919 she married Lord Ribblesdale. Largely estranged from her son Vincent, she left most of her fortune to Alice's children on her death in 1958.[2]

Under the growing pressures that rebelled against the indulgence of the Gilded Age, a number of society women had begun to search for more meaningful ways of life. Not surprisingly, Alva Vanderbilt Belmont was at the forefront of this new movement. Even before *Titanic* and the introduction of income taxes signaled the end of privilege, she had turned her attentions from parties to social issues, spending her fortune on soup kitchens, model houses for the poor, literacy campaigns, and the promotion of birth control. Oliver Belmont helped instill some of this social conscience, publishing a liberal weekly journal, *The Verdict*, in which he denounced corruption and the banking and railroad trusts that exploited the poor, and serving in the U.S. House of Representatives before his death from appendicitis in 1908.

In the wake of Belmont's death, Alva threw herself wholeheartedly into a new passion, women's suffrage. In 1909 she founded the Women's Political Equality League and opened Marble House for suffragette meetings, draping its walls with purple and gold banners emblazoned with Susan B. Anthony's last words, "Failure is Impossible!" Her guests wandered through the house, sipping tea from Alva's latest commission, a thousand-piece tea service whose cups bore the inscription "Votes for Women!"[3] In 1912 Alva led the Women's Vote Parade down New York's Fifth Avenue, dodging eggs and tomatoes thrown from the crowd. When one young woman erupted into tears, Alva comforted her, saying, "Brace up, dear. Pray to God. She will help you."[4] Using her millions, Alva took her campaign across the country, using her name and her money to meet and influence legislators and governors; she picketed the White House in

Washington, D.C., went on hunger strikes, chained herself to buildings, and was arrested, but her determination was eventually rewarded when Congress gave women the vote. Alva spent her last years in France, restoring an old château. She died in January 1933 at age eighty from injuries sustained in an accident. Even in death, Alva caused controversy: her burial in New York bore more resemblance to a suffragette parade than to a funeral, with female pallbearers and strident eulogies delivered in a church adorned with political banners.[5]

Alva's dramatic turn toward women's rights also had led to a remarkable reconciliation with her daughter. Even so, as Consuelo's granddaughter Lady Sarah Spencer-Churchill remembered, the mere mention of Alva's name was enough to provoke violent emotions. "Granny sometimes went white with rage when discussing her mother," Sarah recalled. "Her face tightened, and her body became stiff when Alva came up. Beneath their truce there was still a lot of animosity over a relationship gone sour."[6]

After Consuelo's marriage to the Duke of Marlborough, the couple had been at the forefront of Great Britain's most fashionable aristocratic circles; Consuelo's beauty, charm, and natural sympathy won her many admirers, and in 1902 she was asked by Queen Alexandra to attend her during the coronation of Edward VII. In private, however, the Marlborough relationship soured quickly. "I cannot say what a beast my first husband was," Consuelo later admitted.[7] There were rumors of his infidelity, and Sunny, desperate to rid himself of his hated wife, hired private detectives to trail her, hoping to turn up evidence of any affairs that could then be used against her in divorce proceedings. When no such evidence was forthcoming, Sunny resorted to character assassination, openly claiming that his wife was wildly unfaithful.[8] His own mother was so shocked at his behavior that she openly sided with her daughter-in-law. In 1906 William K. Vanderbilt, who in a bizarre twist had a few years earlier married the twice-widowed Anne Harriman Sands Rutherfurd, former sister-in-law of Consuelo's first love, Winthrop, interceded with Marlborough and urged Sunny not to seek a divorce and thus subject his daughter to malicious gossip. Sunny finally agreed to a legal separation in 1907 and joint custody of their two sons without divorce when Vanderbilt offered him a considerable amount of money.[9] The fracture of the Marlborough marriage was, for a time, one of the principal topics of conversation in American society circles, and even President Theodore Roosevelt weighed in, writing angrily, "The lowest note of infamy is reached by such a creature as this Marlborough, who proposing to divorce the women when *he* at least cannot afford to throw any stone at her, nevertheless proposes to keep and live on the money she brought him."[10]

In November 1920, four months after the death of Consuelo's father, William K. Vanderbilt, the couple finally petitioned for divorce. When the decree came on May 31, 1921, neither party wasted any time moving on: Sunny wed American beauty Gladys Deacon, and Consuelo, who had fallen in love with Frenchman Jacques Balsan, married him that summer. The Balsans, however, were an old Catholic family, and the Duke of Marlborough himself wanted to convert to Catholicism. In 1926, hoping to resolve the situation, the case was appealed to the Papal Rota with a request for an annulment. Consuelo had clearly been coerced into the union, a fact that provided sufficient grounds for such a decree, and Alva even volunteered testimony to this effect.[11]

But there also was substantial evidence suggesting that despite the undoubted pressure exerted by Alva, Consuelo had not been quite the sacrificial lamb depicted in her later memoirs and usually described by history. Consuelo and Sunny were essentially two incompatible individuals who came together in an arranged union typical of the era. The fact that the duke was suspected of numerous infidelities that quickly poisoned the marriage did nothing to bolster the case for coercive fraud, so such circumstances were simply ignored in the case before the Rota.[12] Incompatibility and infidelity offered nothing on which the petitioners could advance the claim of coercion; to obtain the desired annulment, both Consuelo and Sunny seem to have contrived—with the assistance of Alva—a rather more dramatic version of events surrounding the circumstances of their marriage in an attempt to guarantee the desired result. In the end, presented only with tales of Alva's abominable behavior and heavy hand, the Rota accepted that coercion had indeed taken place and annulled the marriage, absolving both Consuelo and her former husband of any personal responsibility in its failure.[13]

Consuelo and Jacques lived happily in France, the former Vanderbilt heiress often returning to America, where she maintained several residences and where, with Alva installed in her own château, the reconciliation between mother and daughter was complete. Jacques died in 1956, and Consuelo died at her house on Long Island in December 1964. According to her will, her body was returned to England, to be buried in the churchyard of St. Martin's at Bladon, next to the grave of her youngest son, Ivor, who had predeceased her. Ironically, in death Consuelo rested within sight of the magnificent Blenheim Palace, where she had spent so many miserable years as chatelaine.

With the passage of time, most of the Vanderbilts faded from view. George died in 1914 after an emergency appendectomy, his massive North Carolina château, Biltmore, eventually passing to the sons of his only daughter, Cornelia. Fred and Lulu, the quiet Vanderbilts of Hyde Park, lived happily at their estate until she died in 1926. Fred moved into a small attic room but continued to oversee what remained of the family business until his death in 1938. The formidable Alice Vanderbilt died in 1940; not until the 1920s did she fully forgive her son Neily for his marriage to Grace, though history eventually proved her initial suspicious instincts correct. By the time of Alice's death, Grace and Neily were largely estranged, he often living aboard his yacht to avoid his wife.[14] Neily died in 1942 while on holiday in Florida.[15] Grace outlived him by just over a decade, but she enjoyed the ultimate revenge: in the wake of Caroline Astor's death, the lady who had once been ostracized by the Vanderbilts proudly assumed the late queen's mantle of doyenne over the remnants of New York society, holding court in her Fifth Avenue mansion and clinging to a way of life that, with each successive year, was rapidly passing into oblivion.[16]

In an eerie echo of Caroline Astor's last years, her social rival Tessie Oelrichs also slipped into dementia, her last days spent in her magical Newport house, Rosecliff. Before her death in 1926, recalled her niece, "she would wander, a fragile and still incredibly beautiful person, her raven hair with its deep wave gone snow-white, through the rooms of her immense marble copy of the Villa Trianon, reseating her guests over and over again, pressing them to take just another ice, one more glass of champagne."[17] The irrepressible Mamie Fish continued to mystify and bewilder, personifying more than any other lady the contradictions of the age, eagerly embracing privilege while loudly declaiming democratic ideals. In 1913 she did the unthinkable for a Gilded Age hostess and ventured into the slums of New York City, personally investigating tenements and the conditions of a sweatshop at which the young female workers had gone on strike. Wandering through this grim world in an immaculate white dress, gloves, hat, and veil, Mamie was startled by the poverty and despair. "I am not a suffragette," she told the women, "and I am not a socialist, but I do think you ought to get seven dollars a week, and I am here to urge you to keep up the fight, though I don't really believe in strikes. And I think it is a pity that there's so much bitterness among the poor against the rich. But you ought to get seven dollars a week." Someone pulled her aside and advised that the workers were actually asking for $9 ($189 in 2008) a week. "Good gracious!" she exclaimed. "We spend that much for a bunch of flowers or a box of candy!" Before leaving, she repeated her support to the strikers, but warned them not to engage in women's suffrage nor to be drawn in by the lure of socialism.[18] She died in May 1915.

With the waning of the Gilded Age, Harry Lehr and his hated wife had taken up permanent residence in Paris. As the years passed, he became increasingly eccentric in his already outlandish behavior, and Elizabeth suspected that her husband's sanity was crumbling. "They say you are mad, poor lamb," Mamie Fish once wrote to Harry. "But in the circles in which we move nobody would ever notice."[19] In January 1929 Harry died of a brain tumor in his native Baltimore. "There was a time," the New York Times reported on his passing, "when his social eccentricities, including bizarre pranks, under the patronage of various wealthy social leaders, made him the most talked about and widely paragraphed man in America."[20] In 1936 Elizabeth Lehr married a third time, to the 5th Baron Decies, who had once been wed to Jay Gould's daughter Helen. Elizabeth died in 1944.[21]

Helen Gould's sister, the distinctly unsympathetic Anna Gould, had three more children with Boni de Castellane's cousin the Prince de Sagan. Family reunions, not surprisingly, were often fraught not only with tension but occasionally violence. Boni, understandably humiliated at not only losing his wife's fortune but also at losing his wife to his cousin, became obsessed with the couple. Once, at a family funeral, he attacked the Prince de Sagan, beating him over his head with a walking stick as he left the church and hurling a string of foul insults that left the startled mourners in shock.

This was not, however, the end of the wretched de Castellane affair. Although Anna had cared little about her former husband's Catholicism, she was vehemently opposed—perhaps out of sheer spite—to his efforts to obtain an annulment from the Vatican, and her continued, festering hatred of Boni drove her to fight him for the next two decades.[22] "Probably not since Henry VIII tried in vain to get an annulment of his marriage with Catherine of Aragon has a matrimonial case been so long in the courts of the Roman Catholic Church," *Time* magazine noted. The first trial before the Papal Rota in 1911 ended with a verdict that upheld the marriage as valid. Boni appealed the decision, and the second trial, in which Anna refused to participate, found that the union did indeed meet the requirements for an annulment. Before the formal verdict could be issued, however, Anna put her millions to good use, lodging a formal complaint and asking for a new hearing. A third trial before the Rota reversed the previous decision, and Boni personally appealed to Pope Benedict XV, who ordered that the Church's supreme tribunal, the Commission of the Apostolic Signatura, review the ever-increasing mountain of evidence. When its six cardinals upheld the previous finding that the marriage had been valid, Boni again appealed, this time to the new Pope Pius XI, who ordered a new trial. The fifth hearing determined that an annulment was warranted, and this time it was Anna who took her case to the pope. Exasperated, Pius XI ordered yet another trial, appointing nine cardinals to review the evidence and make a final ruling. Much to Boni's displeasure, the Apostolic Signatura agreed with the three previous findings that the marriage had been valid and that there were no grounds for an annulment. After six trials, thousands of dollars, and fourteen years of litigation and appeals, Anna emerged victorious, providing a fittingly contentious end to the Gilded Age's most famous and sordid aristocratic marriage.[23]

All three of Anna's sons with Boni predeceased their mother, and one of her sons with Hélie also died young, shooting himself when his parents refused him permission to marry.[24] After Hélie died in 1937, Anna frequently returned to America, living at Lyndhurst, her father's Gothic manse above the Hudson. On her death in 1961, she willed the house and its contents to a trust, allowing it to be opened to an inquisitive public.[25] She had outlived not only Hélie and four of her children but also Boni, who died in Paris in 1932. During World War II Nazis occupied his grand Palais Rose, but it survived the ordeal largely intact. Finally sold in 1962, there was some talk of using its marble halls as a museum but, in a stunning and tragic move, the Paris Historical Monuments Administration declared it to be a building without architectural value. In 1969 it, too, fell victim to the progress of the twentieth century, razed to make way for yet another nondescript block of glass and concrete.

The ever-controversial James Gordon Bennett also spent his last years in France, founding the *Paris Herald* and the *International Herald Tribune*. In maturity, Bennett lost nothing of his penchant for creating havoc. Diners at Maxim's in Paris were often startled to hear a great commotion as he swept into the room, walking casually, arms extended, and deliberately brushed china, silver, and crystal from tables to the floor, never once turning around as the sound of wreckage followed his progress to his regular table. Stunned, guests would rise in protest, only to be calmly reassured that this was one of Bennett's chief amusements; all of the dishes would be promptly replaced with new expensive entrées, wines, and bottles of champagne, at Bennett's expense. He also happily paid for any damage to their clothing. Few objected, and in time it even became a point of pride among certain diners to have had the eccentric Bennett so disrupt their meal.[26] At age seventy-three Bennett, ever the calculating businessman, married the daughter of Baron Reuter, thus uniting the news agency with his newspaper empire. He died in 1918.[27] The infamous Colonel William d'Alton Mann, the era's other celebrated chronicler of society, never recovered from the libel trials that ended the influence of his *Town Topics*. He died in 1920, a figure who once wielded such enormous power all but forgotten by his former millionaire friends.[28]

Evelyn Nesbit and Harry Thaw, the ill-fated couple who had been at the center of so much press attention, divorced after his second trial and incarceration at Matteawan Hospital for the Criminally Insane. A hearing in 1915 adjudged him sane, and Thaw was released, free to enjoy his family fortune until his death in 1947. Thaw's mother had promised Evelyn $1 million in exchange for courtroom testimony that helped paint Harry as a temporarily insane man out to avenge his wife's honor, but once Stanford White's assassin received his verdict, the dowager saw no reason to keep her pledge, and her former daughter-in-law was cut off financially and left to fend for herself. For a time Evelyn attempted to use her notoriety to advantage, launching a vaudeville act and taking roles as an actress in silent films, but her public appeal soon faded. In 1916 she married again, this time to her dancing partner, but within a decade he had left her and the pair was divorced. A long, sad spiral of alcoholism, addiction to morphine, and suicide attempts followed, although Evelyn, always a fighter, managed to overcome them all. In 1967 the once-famous beauty at the center of so many turn-of-the-century headlines died in a nursing home in Santa Monica, California, at age eighty-two.[29]

Time also took its toll elsewhere as, one by one, most of the great houses of New York City fell in the persistent onslaught of twentieth-century progress. The first to go, ironically in view of its tremendous impact and almost universal acclaim, was Alva's château at 660 Fifth Avenue. After Alva declined to accept the house in her divorce settlement, Willie had lived there periodically and rented the property until his death in 1920. Despite being perhaps the single most influential piece of domestic architecture in the city, as well as one of Hunt's undoubted masterpieces, by this time it was considered an anachronism, a bit of theatrical fluff undeserving of serious architectural consideration. In 1925 it was sold to developers for $3.7 million, and it was pulled down the following year. Today the site is occupied by an office block, 666 Fifth Avenue.[30]

That same year, Corneil's widow, Alice, finally abandoned their massive palace at 1 West 57th Street and the building was sold for $7 million. Its lavish interiors were gutted of their fixtures; many of the fittings were purchased by cinema mogul Marcus Loew and distributed to his various theaters, including the Moorish Smoking Room, which now adorns the

Midland Theater in Kansas City. In 1927 this house, too, fell victim to the wrecker's ball; today Bergdorf-Goodman stands on the site.[31]

In 1926 the Astor heirs sold Caroline's Fifth Avenue château, and yet another Hunt masterpiece fell in the name of progress. Today the site is occupied by the elegant and immense Temple Emanu-El, the largest synagogue in the world. It is perhaps a fitting irony for the society doyenne who had once declared, in open contravention to the prejudices of her era, that she would welcome Jews into her intimate circle.

Of these great houses of social power, William Henry Vanderbilt's famous Twin Palace managed to survive the longest. Although the northern pavilion, built for his two married daughters, was pulled down in 1925 and replaced with a skyscraper, the larger, southern mansion was continually occupied from the time of its completion. After William Henry's death, his widow, Louisa, had continued to live at 640 Fifth Avenue until her own death in 1896. George, the couple's youngest son, inherited the mansion and used it as his New York residence. When he died in 1914, it was left to his nephew Neily and his wife, Grace. Grace despised the house, once referring to it derisively as "the Black Hole of Calcutta," and made extensive renovations during which much of the original, heavily ornate decor was stripped and removed.[32] In 1940 Neily sold the house, ironically to William Waldorf Astor's heirs, for $1.5 million, on the proviso that the transfer would not take place until three years after his death and that his widow, Grace, would be allowed to remain in residence for that duration.[33] Following Neily's death in 1942, Grace remained at 640 Fifth Avenue for just two years, finally moving to a smaller mansion, and in 1946 the Twin Palace was razed, replaced—as were so many other Gilded Age residences—with a modern, characterless office block.[34]

It was not only in New York City that the houses of the Gilded Age struggled to survive in the aftermath of taxation and the declining fortunes of their owners. Today, along the Hudson River, all three of the Gilded Age's great estates—Lyndhurst, the Ogden Mills mansion, and the Vanderbilt mansion at Hyde Park—are open to the public, carefully preserved museums offering visitors an intimate look at their former owners' ways of life. The Astor estate at Rhinebeck was not as lucky.

The Italianate house at Ferncliff, already out of fashion by the turn of the century, no longer stands, but Vincent Astor's widow, Brooke, left much of the former estate, including Stanford White's extravagant casino, to New York State.

George Vanderbilt's Biltmore remains not only America's largest privately owned house but also, after dedicated efforts by his grandson William Cecil, it is also one of the country's most popular tourist destinations. Many of the era's other great houses have not been as fortunate. In the Berkshires, Edith Wharton's the Mount is still undergoing extensive restoration after years of use as a girls' school, but its preservation is assured. Nearby Elm Court, the sprawling shingle-style cottage built by Emily Vanderbilt Sloane, offers a more troubling story. After serving as an inn for many years, it was abandoned, falling into disrepair, vandals stripping its rooms of fittings, and weather playing havoc with its fragile structure. One Sunday afternoon in September 1997, with my friend Susanne Meslans, I stumbled over the estate's encircling walls and across its overgrown, weed-choked lawns to take it all in: a massive building, windows boarded over, bits of cornices fallen and crumbling on the surrounding terraces, wind whistling eerily through its empty porches. Yet a new roof, a vibrant splash of red against the dingy brown of the house, hinted that all was not lost. Emily's great-great-grandson, Robert Berle, had begun an extensive and costly restoration, clearing away decades of neglect and returning the rooms to their former glory before again opening the rambling building as an inn. In 2005, however, Berle put Elm Court on the market for some $21 million. There has been talk of expensive condominiums or use of the house as a business center or corporate retreat, but its ultimate fate is uncertain.[35] Misfortune also befell Anson Phelps Stokes's massive Shadow Brook. After a riding accident left him unable to fully enjoy his estate, Stokes sold it, and for several years it was rented as a summer house and also served as an inn. Industrialist Andrew Carnegie purchased the house in 1917, dying there in 1922. His widow sold the immense structure to the New England Society of Jesus, and for many years it was used as a Jesuit retreat before a tragic fire in 1956 destroyed what had once—albeit briefly—been America's largest private house.

But by far, the largest single remaining concentration of Gilded Age estates is in Newport. In a town imbued with an appreciation of its historic past and a proud tradition of preservation, many of these houses survive as recognized landmarks and, through the throngs of curious tourists who crowd their rooms, important assets to the local economy. Marble House, the Breakers, and Rosecliff are pristine jewels, carefully restored and tended by the Preservation Society of Newport County, while Oliver Belmont's eccentric Belcourt Castle, restored by the Tinney family, is Newport's only regularly inhabited Gilded Age cottage open to the public. Caroline Astor's famous Beechwood, after years of private occupancy, also was opened to the public. Here, a theatrical group in turn-of-the-century costumes portrayed characters from the era, unraveling the history of the house and of the Gilded Age for the enjoyment of visitors. In the summer of 2007, however, its owner put Beechwood on the market, asking $16 million in recognition of the house's importance and prime location at the edge of the Atlantic. Like Elm Court, its fate remains uncertain.

The Gilded Age had come to an end. For just forty years, from the establishment of the Patriarch balls until the sinking of *Titanic*, Caroline Astor's artificial, opulent, and ultimately fragile society had dazzled and intrigued, enticed and infuriated. The successful melding of respected lineage with recent money to create an American aristocracy had demanded stringent adherence to rules of behavior both traditional and new. While Caroline remained at the helm, this society could be controlled, its members shepherded through its intricacies, and its aspirants made to properly expiate the sins of their background and the crispness of their money.

Caroline's gradual retreat in the 1890s from society left a social vacuum into which poured not only people such as Alva Vanderbilt Belmont, who attempted to maintain a modicum of dignity, but also hostesses such as Mamie Fish, determined both to enjoy and to ridicule the snobbery surrounding their positions. "My mother," recalled Grace Vanderbilt's son, "could not abide Mamie and her breezy, brash, cruel wit, her breaking with the traditions of the past. It was Mrs. Fish, she always claimed, who created the nucleus of what later became café society."[36]

Grace, like many others, laid the blame for the Gilded Age society's disintegration squarely at the feet of Mamie Fish; if this was not an entirely fair assessment, it underlined the conflict inherent in the era, the struggle between distinction and flamboyance, and the incoherent jumble that eventually emerged in the wake of Caroline's death. In writing of the British monarchy in the nineteenth century, Walter Bagehot warned that the crown's continued hold over society lay in achieving a precarious balance, one that ostensibly allowed even the most humble of subjects to identify with Queen Victoria and her family while at the same time presenting them as inhabitants of a unique realm that existed somewhere between the terrestrial and the celestial. Maintenance of the mystique was pivotal; as Bagehot famously warned, "We must not let daylight in upon the magic."[37] The same was true for Gilded Age society. Its continued successful existence required both public interest and public indulgence. This could be achieved only through careful management and a strong, controlling hand.

Caroline understood the conflicting strains and outside pressures that assailed society. Her views offered a profound reflection of careful diplomacy and constant reassessment of the ever-shifting aspirants to join its ranks. For Caroline Astor, society was not a pleasure but rather a duty imposed by ancestry, tradition, and wealth. It had to preserve all that was worthy and promote all that was noble. Many years later, Neily's son encapsulated this view, recording that his father "had been reared by his parents in the firm belief that they were America's aristocracy, embodying in their lives and actions all that was fine, honorable, and Christian. Theirs was a sacred God-given trust to maintain these standards."[38]

Inevitably, the waning influence wielded by the once-feared and respected *the* Mrs. Astor left this tenuous world adrift, her retreat as doyenne marking, more than any other single event, the ominous moment when the delicate shroud protecting society was inexorably rent and forever cast aside, exposing not the laudatory nor the munificent, but rather the hedonistic and determinedly sybaritic. Scorn soon followed, anger and indignation giving rise to exaggerated tales of excess and moral turpitude. In the years and decades that followed, this became the prevalent view. Gilded Age society as a whole was derided as a manifestation, not of the noble elite envisioned and promoted by Caroline Astor, but rather of a period of bad taste and base instincts, of an avaricious people who cared only about their own continued amusement.

And yet, a century removed from this dramatic turn, it is still possible to look back on the elite of the Gilded Age and, while not ignoring their more blatant failings, to at the very least acknowledge the rich cultural legacy of which we continue to benefit. The great estates along the Hudson, the remaining mansions of the Berkshires, the imposing splendor of Biltmore, and the almost surreal collection of summer cottages still standing in Newport tantalize, inspire, and awe. Endowments, gifts, memorials, and legacies from these fortunes often go unnoticed, from Central Park's Cleopatra's Needle (whose shipping from Egypt and subsequent erection were costs borne by William Henry Vanderbilt) and original grants by the Vanderbilts and Astors that helped establish Vanderbilt University and the New York Public Library to the more refined treasures of the remaining great houses and the objets d'art with which they were once filled.

The history of New York City's Metropolitan Museum of Art offers mute testimony of this social munificence. While the artistic philanthropy of collectors such as Henry Clay Frick and J. P. Morgan is well known, that of the Vanderbilts was in many ways just as significant. In 1887, Cornelius Vanderbilt II purchased Rosa Bonheur's famous painting *The Horse Fair* from the estate of A. T. Stewart for $53,000 ($1.6 million in 2008) and promptly donated it to the Metropolitan Museum, where it quickly became (and remains today) one of the institution's most popular exhibits.[39] On his death in 1899, more canvases and works of art followed, including J. M. W. Turner's *The Grand Canal*.[40] His brother William K. Vanderbilt also made similar significant bequests, donating several pieces of exquisite French furniture, Rembrandt's *The Noble Slav*, and François Boucher's *The Toilette of Venus*, which had hung in Alva's boudoir at 660 Fifth Avenue.[41]

Here we find the embodiment of the best of the Gilded Age. This motivation to endow America with artistic and architectural treasures, to provide it with worthy examples of fine manners and beautiful clothing, and to leave it with a carefully ordered ruling class to help craft the country as a rival to any European kingdom has too often fallen victim to more entertaining tales of scandal and dinners for tuxedoed monkeys, leaving only an impression of hollow glory. But reconciling the sublime with the ridiculous is key to understanding the dichotomy of the age and to assessing the continued appeal of the era and its players in the imagination of the public.

The season of splendor that marked the Gilded Age was brief. Someone such as Alva Vanderbilt Belmont could witness both its beginning and its end, successfully deploying her resources and adjusting her interests to stay au courant with not only the desires of society but also with the increasingly important factor of public opinion. Even those who continued to exist in this rarefied world after 1914, in the wake of World War I, federal income taxes, and a cynical press, were often all too aware of the gathering clouds that, however distant on the horizon, heralded the inevitable coming storm. The final word goes to Grace Vanderbilt, bravely holding on to her position and the phantoms of a lost world in the Twin Palace on Fifth Avenue as skyscrapers rose all around her and new ideas, new reforms, and new society took hold. "Dear, poor Marie Antoinette," she once said sadly. "I feel so sorry for her. If the revolution ever came to this country, I would be the first to go."[42]

NOTES

A NOTE ON CURRENCY

1. King, *Handbook*, 49, 212, 220–223; Friedman, 93.

INTRODUCTION

1. Vanderbilt, *Fortune's Children*, 264.
2. Beer, 72.
3. Van Rensselaer, *Social Ladder*, 36.
4. Myers, 1:97–100; Jaher, *Urban*, 160–162; Wecter, 55–56.
5. Van Rensselaer, *Social Ladder*, 22.
6. Ibid., 30.
7. Almond, 48.
8. Browne, *The Great Metropolis*, 33.
9. Van Rensselaer, *Social Ladder*, 53.
10. Still, 172.
11. Wharton, *Backward Glance*, 6.
12. For further examination see Jaher, *The Rich, the Well Born, and the Powerful*, 263.
13. Gerard, 36.
14. Morris, *Postscript to Yesterday*, 15.
15. Bourget, 51.
16. Pulitzer, 1–2.
17. Persons, 104, 273.
18. McAllister, 160–161.
19. Bourget, 50.
20. Schuyler, 371.
21. Lehr, 57.
22. Beebe, 109.
23. Martin, *The Passing of the Idle Rich*, 13.
24. Veblen, 37–38.
25. Ibid., 53.
26. Burne-Jones, 118.
27. Amory, *The Last Resorts*, 212.

PROLOGUE: NEW YORK CITY, 1903

1. Clews, 449.
2. Baedeker, 22–23.
3. King, *Handbook*, 56, 48; Erenberg, 36.
4. Morris, *Incredible New York*, 3.

5. Clews, 448–449.
6. Bourget, 15–17.
7. Ibid., 17.
8. Burrows and Wallace, 944; Silver, 28.
9. Van Dyke, 178–180.
10. Crockett, 153.
11. Morris, *Incredible New York*, 111.
12. Burrows and Wallace, 668; Morris, *Incredible New York*, 7, 111; Crockett, 24; Churchill, 160; Baker, *Richard Morris Hunt*, 76; Patterson, *Fifth Avenue*, 75; King, *Handbook*, 802.
13. Van Dyke, 195.
14. Morris, *Incredible New York*, 111.
15. Van Dyke, 197.
16. Patterson, *Fifth Avenue*, 36; Tolman, 96; Fifth Avenue Bank, *Fifth Avenue*, 11, 14; Baker, *Stanny*, 167; Lowe, 189; Simon, 22–23.
17. Bennett, 27.
18. Baker, *Stanny*, 223.
19. Platt, 138; Baldwin, 239–241.
20. *New York Times*, December 22, 1996.
21. *New York Times*, March 30, 1903; *New York Times*, December 22, 1996; Stern, Gilmartin, and Massengale, 57.
22. *New York Times*, March 30, 1903; Josephson, 338; Lord, 105; Crockett, 192; Martin, *The Passing of the Idle Rich*, 31.
23. *New York Times*, March 30, 1903.
24. Josephson, 338; Lord, 105; Crockett, 192.

CHAPTER 1: MRS. ASTOR HOLDS COURT

1. For background on the Astor family and John Jacob Astor see Madsen; Wilson; and Myers, 1:109.
2. Patterson, *The Best Families*, 22.

3. Gates, 33; Patterson, *The Best Families*, 22.
4. For more information see Madsen; Myers, especially 1:109–147; Patterson, *The Best Families*, 22; and Kavaler, 27.
5. Kavaler, 1.
6. Gates, 35.
7. Madsen, 268.
8. Gates, 49.
9. Kavaler, 61.
10. Gates, 61; Kavaler, 63.
11. Kavaler, 64.
12. Sinclair, 178–179.
13. Gates, 62; Myers, 3:202.
14. Gates, 58–59.
15. Ibid., 55.
16. Gates, 52; Wecter, 115.
17. Gates, 59, 63; Myers, 1:223.
18. Gates, 63, 69.
19. Wilson, 103.
20. Gates, 69–71.
21. Cowles, 90.
22. Wilson, 103.
23. Wilson, 103; Homberger, 252.
24. Wilson, 103.
25. Gates, 78; Wector, 111.
26. Myers, 1:224.
27. Homberger, 239–240.
28. Gates, 184.
29. Gates, 82; Homberger, 253; Kavaler, 105.
30. Wilson, 95.
31. Cowles, 90.
32. Kavaler, 76.
33. Gates, 74.
34. Kavaler, 107.
35. Wilson, 104.
36. Gates, 72.
37. Gates, 73; Wilson, 103; Madsen, 279; Homberger, 260.
38. Wilson, 194.
39. Lehr, 73.
40. Ibid., 73–74.
41. Gates, 184.
42. Lehr, 72–73.
43. Ibid., 68.
44. Ibid., 10.
45. Ibid., 153.
46. Van Rensselaer, *Social Ladder*, 169.
47. Sherwood, 4.
48. Gale, 227; Amory, *Who Killed Society?* 118; McAllister, 13–15, 25.
49. McAllister, 33–36, 65–68.
50. Lehr, 11–12.
51. Morris, *Not So Long Ago*, 173; Amory, *Who Killed Society?* 118; Lehr, 11.

52. Elliott, 149.
53. McAllister, 222.
54. *New York Times*, October 30, 1908.
55. Kavaler, 115.
56. Morris, *Postscript to Yesterday*, 11.
57. McAllister, 245–246.
58. Van Rensselaer, *Social Ladder*, 171.
59. *New York Tribune*, March 25, 1888.
60. Chanler, 238.
61. Sherwood, 5.
62. Ibid., 241.
63. McAllister, 214.
64. Ibid., 214–215.
65. *New York Tribune*, March 25, 1888.
66. Jaher, *The Rich, the Well Born, and the Powerful*, 268–269.
67. Jaher, *Urban*, 279.
68. Morris, *Incredible New York*, 145.
69. *New York Times*, November 1, 1908.
70. McAllister, 127–128.

CHAPTER 2: THE VAINGLORIOUS VANDERBILTS

1. Beebe, 1.
2. For a more detailed examination of the Vanderbilt antecedents see, generally, Patterson, *The Vanderbilts*, chapter 1, and specifically Croffut, chapter 1.
3. Vanderbilt, *Fortune's Children*, 6–7.
4. Croffut, 17, 28–32.
5. Flynn, 178–179; Vanderbilt, *Fortune's Children*, 8–10; Hoyt, *Vanderbilts*, 82–84; Andrews, 12–15.
6. Vanderbilt, *Fortune's Children*, 10–11.
7. Ibid., 22–23.
8. *New York Times*, January 5, 1877.
9. Rugoff, 55–58; Josephson, 132–134; Andrews, 123–135; Hoyt, *Goulds*, 65–72; Klein, 84–87; Renehan, 115 passim.
10. Patterson, *Vanderbilts*, 42.
11. Patterson, *Vanderbilts*, 22–23; Vanderbilt, *Fortune's Children*, 17–18.
12. Churchill, 10; Vanderbilt, *Fortune's Children*, 21.
13. Patterson, *Vanderbilts*, 22.
14. *New York World*, November 13, 1877.
15. Wecter, 131.
16. Croffut, 108.
17. Vanderbilt, *Queen*, 129.
18. Vanderbilt, *Fortune's Children*, 42–43; Patterson, *Vanderbilts*, 43–45.
19. Vanderbilt, *Fortune's Children*, 44–45.
20. Patterson, *Vanderbilts*, 54.
21. *New York Times*, July 15, 2007; Croffut, 143; Foreman and Stimson, 9; see also

Croffut, appendix D, for the Commodore's will, 286 passim.

22. *New York World*, December 10, 1885.
23. Allen, 17; Croffut, 60.
24. *New York Herald*, December 9, 1885.
25. Depew, 240.
26. Holbrook, 93.
27. *Chicago Tribune*, October 17, 1882.
28. Croffut, 223; Josephson, 187; Clews, 370; Andrews, 194.
29. Fiske, 330; Elliott, 160.
30. Croffut, 248.
31. Balsan, 3.
32. Wector, 134; Flynn, 212; Josephson, 191.
33. *New York Times*, December 9, 1885.
34. Beebe, 16; Black, 666–667; Wecter, 463.
35. Beebe, 15; Morris, *Incredible New York*, 191.
36. Beebe, 14.
37. Quoted in Andrews, 263.
38. Homberger, 231.
39. Kolodin, 4–7; Peltz, 7–9; Beckert, 247.
40. Patterson, *Vanderbilts*, 110.
41. Andrews, 238.
42. Churchill, 69.
43. Vanderbilt, *Fortune's Children*, 179; Croffut, 182.
44. Croffut, 182.
45. Vanderbilt, *Fortune's Children*, 181.
46. *New York Sun*, September 13, 1899.
47. Elliott, 161.
48. Vanderbilt, *Queen*, 20.
49. Balsan, 3.
50. Foreman and Stimson, 51.
51. Croffut, 183.
52. Sloane, 57.
53. Vanderbilt, *Queen*, 18.
54. Vanderbilt, *Without Prejudice*, 162.

CHAPTER 3: ENTER THE CHALLENGER

1. *New York Times*, July 23, 1920.
2. Croffut, 183–184.
3. Balsan, 9, 5.
4. Stuart, 21.
5. Cited in Vanderbilt, *Fortune's Children*, 85.
6. Stuart, 29.
7. Wecter, 336; Balsan, 4.
8. Stuart, 33–38.
9. Gerard, 47.
10. Croffut, 184.
11. Balsan, 5.
12. Lehr, 109.
13. Vanderbilt, *Fortune's Children*, 101; Andrews, 253.

14. Cowles, 90.
15. Churchill, 63.
16. *New York Times*, March 27, 1883; *New York Sun*, March 27, 1883.
17. *New York Times*, March 27, 1883.
18. *New York Sun*, March 27, 1883; Kathrens, *Great Houses*, 27.
19. *New York Times*, March 27, 1883.
20. Croffut, 193.
21. *New York Times*, October 31, 1908.
22. Croffut, 194; Balsan, 6; Andrews, 253–260; Gates, 90.
23. *New York Tribune*, March 27, 1883.
24. *New York Times*, March 27, 1883; *New York Herald*, March 27, 1883.
25. *New York Tribune*, March 27, 1883.
26. *New York Times*, March 27, 1883.
27. *New York Times*, March 27, 1883; Allen, 28, 38.
28. *New York Times*, March 27, 1883; McAllister, 354.
29. Vanderbilt, *Fortune's Children*, 115; *New York Times*, March 27, 1883.
30. Croffut, 197; *New York Herald*, March 27, 1883; *New York Times*, March 27, 1883.
31. Churchill, 61.
32. *New York Tribune*, March 24, 1883; Josephson, 331; Croffut, 196; *New York Herald*, March 27, 1883; the *New York Times*, March 27, 1883.
33. *New York Times*, March 27, 1883.
34. *New York Times*, March 27, 1883; McAllister, 353; Clews, 367.
35. *New York Times*, March 27, 1883.
36. *New York Herald*, March 27, 1883.
37. *New York Times*, March 27, 1883; Croffut, 195–196; *New York Herald*, March 27, 1883; *New York Sun*, March 27, 1883; Wecter, 338.
38. *New York Sun*, March 27, 1883; *New York World*, March 27, 1883.
39. Clews, 366.
40. Churchill, 69.
41. Sinclair, 191; O'Connor, *Astors*, 197.
42. Morris, *Incredible New York*, 154.
43. Van Rensselaer, *Social Ladder*, 65.

CHAPTER 4: THE SOCIETY LADY

1. Cited in Perrot, 85.
2. Morris, *Incredible New York*, 254.
3. *New York Times*, October 30, 1908.
4. Carter, 15.
5. Gates, 82, 79; Wecter, 214; Morris, *Postscript to Yesterday*, 11.

6. Cited in Perrot, 85.
7. Harrison, *The Well-Bred Girl*, 32.
8. Carter, 17.
9. Gates, 88–89.
10. Carter, 18.
11. Sherwood, 162–165.
12. Ibid., 20.
13. Gates, 89.
14. Longstreet, *Social Etiquette of New York*, 8–9.
15. Wharton, *Backward Glance*, 82–83.
16. Sherwood, 27.
17. McAllister, 385.
18. Sherwood, 19.
19. McAllister, 390.
20. Sherwood, 14.
21. McAllister, 300.
22. Sherwood, 14–16.
23. Ibid., 21.
24. Ibid., 18.
25. Ibid., 64–65.
26. Ibid., 21–22.
27. Friedman, 5.
28. Carter, 22.
29. Beckert, 262; Burrows and Wallace, 1,087.
30. Busbey, 92.
31. Montgomery, 51–52.
32. Barrett, 32.
33. Townsend, 36.
34. Harrison, *The Well-Bred Girl*, 6; Busbey, 93.
35. Friedman, 97.
36. Lehr, 112.
37. Kavaler, 121.
38. Gates, 83–84.
39. Homberger, 256.
40. Gates, 87.
41. Wilson, 196; Gates, 84–85; Kavaler, 131.
42. *New York Sun*, March 18, 1892.
43. Wilson, 197; Gates, 75.
44. Wilson, 197; Kavaler, 132.
45. Wilson, 196.
46. Wilson, 198; *New York Journal*, January 9, 1896; Kavaler, 132.
47. Lehr, 74.
48. *New York Journal*, January 9, 1896.
49. *New York Herald*, December 18, 1896.
50. Morris, *Not So Long Ago*, 2.
51. Gates, 98; Mills, 54–55.
52. *New York Times*, September 15, 1908.
53. Lehr, 136.
54. O'Connor, *Golden Summers*, 178–179.
55. Benway, 71.
56. Wector, 126.
57. Amory, *Who Killed Society*, 437.

58. Preservation Society of Newport, *Theresa Fair Oelrichs: A Western Mining Heiress Builds Rosecliff* (hereafter Preservation Society of Newport, *TFO*), 3.
59. Strange, 48–49.
60. Decies, 97; Strange, 91.
61. Barrett, 96–97; Amory, *Last Resorts*, 206.
62. Decies, 94.
63. Ibid., 165.
64. Ibid., 96.
65. Ibid., 96–97.
66. Strange, 49.
67. Wecter, 341.
68. Quoted in Patterson, *Best Families*, 20; O'Connor, *Golden Summers*, 202; Amory, *Last Resorts*, 213.
69. Kathrens, *Great Houses*, 99.
70. *New York Times*, May 27, 1915.
71. Cited in Dunwell, 115.
72. Barrett, 105.
73. Lehr, 154–155.
74. *New York Times*, May 27, 1915.
75. Amory, *Last Resorts*, 174.
76. Decies, 107.
77. Van Rensselaer, *Social Ladder*, 212.
78. Amory, *Last Resorts*, 214.
79. Low, 53.
80. Dressler, 132–134.
81. Low, 53.
82. Belmont, 83.
83. *New York Times*, September 27, 1903.
84. Decies, 108.
85. Ibid., 131.
86. Amory, *Last Resorts*, 216.
87. Decies, 107.
88. Ibid., 105.
89. Ibid., 107.
90. Strange, 57–58.
91. Lehr, 122.
92. Barrett, 104.
93. Lehr, 156; Wecter, 136.

CHAPTER 5: THE SOCIETY GENTLEMAN

1. Morris, *Postscript to Yesterday*, 15.
2. For a discussion of the major painters in the salon and their styles, see Lucie-Smith and Dars, 233–240.
3. Churchill, 38.
4. Lucie-Smith and Dars, 8 passim.
5. Churchill, 41.
6. *New York Times*, December 9, 1885.
7. Croffut, 163, 165–173.
8. Churchill, 40–41.
9. Ibid., 122.

10. Croffut, 167–169.
11. See Hammack, pages 74–75, tables 3–3, 3–4 for breakdowns of economic status and wealth in club members.
12. Amory, *Who Killed Society?*, 201.
13. Morris, *Incredible New York*, 244.
14. Amory, *Who Killed Society?*, 205.
15. Longstreet, *Social Etiquette of New York*, 123.
16. Birmingham, *Right People*, 120.
17. Cited in Homberger, 10.
18. Maurice, 130; Wecter, 260–261; Boyer, 83.
19. Maurice, 132; Hammack, 73.
20. Maurice, 133.
21. Amory, *Who Killed Society?*, 190.
22. Amory, *Who Killed Society?*, 203; Wecter, 264; Hammack, 73.
23. Brown, 51, 70.
24. Lowe, 160.
25. Amory, *Who Killed Society?*, 203; Wecter, 263; Hammack, 73.
26. Baker, *Stanny*, 142-44; Morris, *Incredible New York*, 205; Lowe, 162–165; Stern, Gilmartin, and Massengale, 232.
27. Crockett, 129; Morris, *Incredible New York*, 226–227.
28. Silver, 61; Goldsmith, 85.
29. Crockett, 129.
30. See Black, 4–6, 44; Birmingham, *Grandes Dames*, 225; Wecter, 153.
31. Black, 20 passim.
32. Ibid., 66.
33. Fiske, 28; Homberger, 174; Patterson, *Best Families*, 27.
34. Black, 169–171; Birmingham, *Grandes Dames*, 226; Jenkins, 28.
35. Homberger, 177; Patterson, *Best Families*, 27.
36. Birmingham, *Grandes Dames*, 226; Fiske, 30.
37. Fiske, 31.
38. Elliott, 47; Black, 660.
39. Beebe, 133.
40. Fiske, 32; Beebe, 133–134.
41. Fiske, 36.
42. Barrett, 40.
43. Patterson, *Fifth Avenue*, 52.
44. Beebe, 134.
45. Ibid., 136.
46. Elliott, 153–154; Beebe, 134–135; Barrett, 40; McAllister, 355–158.
47. Beebe, 137.
48. Ibid., 138.
49. Lord, 106.
50. See, for example, Lord, 106–107; Seitz, 267–268.
51. Lord, 108–109; Crockett, 272.
52. Beard, *After the Ball*, 4.
53. Beard, *After the Ball*, 7; Lord, 108.
54. Beebe, 122; Lord, 108.
55. Beard, *After the Ball*, 4; Crockett, 273.
56. Quoted in Homberger, 2.
57. Lord, 108; see Beard, *After the Ball*, chap. 11.
58. Wilson, 200.
59. Gates, 112.
60. Wilson, 202–204.
61. Gates, 112.
62. Gerard, 40.
63. Sinclair, 135.
64. Thomas, *Pride of Lions*, 124.
65. Barrett, 113.
66. Kavaler, 142.
67. Wilson, 201; Gates, 114; Kavaler, 145–146.
68. Wilson, 202; Lehr, 149–150.
69. Lehr, 149–150.
70. Wilson, 206.
71. Kavaler, 148.

CHAPTER 6: THE COURT JESTER

1. *New York Times*, January 20, 1900.
2. Barrett, 26.
3. *New York Times*, April 30, 1889; Wecter, 334.
4. Homberger, 217.
5. Quoted in Patterson, *Best Families*, 115.
6. Dedmon, 222–225.
7. Wecter, 223.
8. Amory, *Who Killed Society?*, 122–123; *New York Times*, February 2, 1895; Homberger, 152.
9. *New York Times*, February 3, 1895.
10. Lehr, 36–37.
11. Ibid., 38.
12. Ibid., 39.
13. Ibid., 54–55.
14. Ibid., 36.
15. Gerard, 41.
16. Barrett, 85.
17. Lehr, 21.
18. Ibid., 42.
19. Gerard, 41.
20. Lehr, 40.
21. Ibid., 50.
22. Jaher, *The Rich, the Well Born, and the Powerful*, 273.
23. Lehr, 26.
24. Crockett, 78.
25. Lehr, 26–28.

26. Ibid., 141.
27. Ibid., 45.
28. Crockett, 78.
29. Gerard, 41.
30. Lehr, 21.
31. Ibid., 24–25.
32. Ibid., 26, 29.
33. Ibid., 31.
34. Ibid., 31–32.
35. Ibid., 32.
36. Ibid., 34.
37. Ibid., 269.
38. Ibid., 38, 42.
39. Ibid., 53.
40. Ibid., 35.
41. Ibid., 65.
42. Ibid., 54.
43. Ibid., 105.
44. Ibid., 2.
45. Ibid., 205.
46. Morris, *Postscript to Yesterday*, 18.
47. Lehr, 216.
48. Ibid., 113.
49. Logan, 138.
50. Vanderbilt, *Queen*, 34.
51. Lehr, 120.
52. Ibid., 122.
53. Ibid.
54. Ibid., 123.
55. Ibid., 122–123.
56. Ibid., 124.

CHAPTER 7: THE ARRIVISTES

1. McAllister, 245.
2. Jaher, *Urban Establishment*, 10.
3. McAllister, 118–119.
4. Burne-Jones, 112—113.
5. Wecter, 246–247.
6. Persons, 282.
7. Longstreet, *Social Etiquette of New York*, 77–79.
8. Gates, 179.
9. Wharton, *Backward Glance*, 11.
10. Lehr, 86.
11. Morris, *Incredible New York*, 143; Brandon, 64–67; Eliot, 85–87.
12. Wecter, 332.
13. Montgomery, 22–23; Eliot, 94; Brandon, 63–64.
14. Foreman and Stimson, 265.
15. Lehr, 108.
16. Ibid., 109.
17. Ibid., 110.
18. Churchill, 168.
19. Lehr, 119.

20. Wilson, 196; see Vanderbilt, *Queen*, 28–30; Vanderbilt, *Fortune's Children*, 206; Fowler, 261.
21. Wilson, 196; Lewis, Turner, and McQuillin, 169.
22. *New York World*, June 8, 1902.
23. Lehr, 55.
24. Kavaler, 127.
25. Gates, 82.
26. Lehr, 72.
27. Wilson, 196.
28. Kavaler, 128.
29. Vanderbilt, *Queen*, 16–17.
30. Vanderbilt, *Queen*, 43–44; Friedman, 103.
31. Vanderbilt, *Queen*, 24.
32. *New York Times*, March 1, 1942.
33. Vanderbilt, *Queen*, 49–50.
34. Friedman, 102.
35. Vanderbilt, *Queen*, 51.
36. Ibid., 13.
37. Vanderbilt, *Queen*, 89–90; Churchill, 177.
38. Vanderbilt, *Queen*, 53.
39. *New York Times*, June 11, 1896.
40. Vanderbilt, *Queen*, 59.
41. Ibid., 60.
42. Vanderbilt, *Queen*, 66; Hoyt, *Vanderbilts*, 306.
43. Friedman, 141
44. *New York Times*, August 4, 1896.
45. *New York Times*, March 1, 1942; Vanderbilt, *Queen*, 132–133.
46. Vanderbilt, *Queen*, 12.
47. Lehr, 139.
48. Downing and Scully, 138–139; see Pardee, 31 passim for Beaulieu today.
49. Lehr, 126; Lord, 105.
50. Low, 165.
51. Vanderbilt, *Queen*, 164–165; *New York Times*, August 26, 1902; Lehr, 125–126.
52. *New York Times*, January 8, 1953; *New York Times*, March 1, 1942.
53. Lehr, 140.
54. Vanderbilt, *Queen*, 239.
55. Tebbel, 128.

CHAPTER 8: THE EDIFICE COMPLEX

1. Wharton, *Backward Glance*, 54–55.
2. Van Dyke, 229.
3. Bourget, 25.
4. Desmond and Croly, 12.
5. Ibid.
6. Van Dyke, 227.
7. Churchill, 173.

8. Seale, 11.
9. Lehr, 7–8.
10. Van Dyke, 228–229.
11. Gregory, *Worldly Ways and Byways*, 53.
12. Van Dyke, 230–231.
13. Pulitzer, 31–32.
14. Quoted in Patterson, *Best Families*, 122.
15. Maurice, 314.
16. Kathrens, *Great Houses*, 13–14; Black, 275.
17. Gerard, 36.
18. Hamlin, 132; Homberger, 174.
19. Birmingham, *Grandes Dames*, 226
20. Cited in Homberger, 176–177.
21. Maurice, 269; Fifth Avenue Bank, 29; Patterson, *Fifth Avenue*, 72.
22. Churchill, 19; Patterson, *Fifth Avenue*, 72.
23. Fifth Avenue Bank, 29.
24. Churchill, 19–20.
25. Maurice, 269; Fifth Avenue Bank, 29; Patterson, *Fifth Avenue*, 72.
26. Lewis, Turner, and McQuillin, 33; Lowe, 12.
27. Churchill, 28; Maurice, 269; Fifth Avenue Bank, 29; Patterson, *Fifth Avenue*, 72; Lewis, Turner, and McQuillin, 33; Boyer, 141.
28. Cited in Boyer, 141.
29. Lehr, 6.
30. Churchill, 30.
31. Lewis, Turner, and McQuillin, 33.
32. Kathrens, *Great Houses*, 14; Patterson, *Fifth Avenue*, 70–72; Lewis, Turner, and McQuillin, 33; Churchill, 28.
33. Churchill, 27–28.
34. Churchill, 32; Kathrens, *Great Houses*, 14; Patterson, *Fifth Avenue*, 70–72; Lewis, Turner, and McQuillin, 35–39.
35. Churchill, 29.
36. Kathrens, *Great Houses*, 14; Patterson, *Fifth Avenue*, 70–72; Lewis, Turner, and McQuillin, 39; Churchill, 29–30.
37. Patterson, *Vanderbilts*, 97.
38. Churchill, 34.
39. Patterson, *Vanderbilts*, 97; Churchill, 29–30.
40. Churchill, 32; Kathrens, *Great Houses*, 14; Patterson, *Fifth Avenue*, 70–72; Lewis, Turner, and McQuillin, 39.
41. Maurice, 269.
42. Lewis, Turner, and McQuillin, 33.
43. Maurice, 301; Stern, Gilmartin, and Massengale, 308; Boyer, 24.
44. Morris, *Incredible New York*, 142.
45. Wharton, *Age of Innocence*, 24–25.

Chapter 9: Palaces on Fifth Avenue

1. *New York Times*, January 5, 1877.
2. King, *Vanderbilt Homes*, 8.
3. Churchill, 11–12; King, *Vanderbilt Homes*, 10. In 1882 the house was destroyed by fire.
4. King, *Vanderbilt Homes*, 11–12.
5. Croffut, 38; Andrews, 4.
6. Seale, 64.
7. Patterson, *Vanderbilts*, 76; Howe, Frelinghuysen, Voorsanger, Jervis, Ottomeyer, Bascou, Wood, and Riefstahl, 80.
8. *New York Tribune*, December 9, 1885.
9. Patterson, *Vanderbilts*, 77.
10. Brown, 93.
11. Lewis, Turner, and McQuillin, 114; Churchill, 43–45; Kathrens, *Great Houses*, 330; Foreman and Stimson, 313; Strahan, 1:7; Howe, Frelinghuysen, Voorsanger, Jervis, Ottomeyer, Bascou, Wood, and Riefstahl, 200; Stern, Gilmartin, and Massengale, 309.
12. Howe, Frelinghuysen, Voorsanger, Jervis, Ottomeyer, Bascou, Wood, and Riefstahl, 200.
13. Quoted in Maher, xvi–xvii.
14. Churchill, 46.
15. Strahan, 1:7; Croffut, 156.
16. Strahan, 1:7.
17. Croffut, 155–156; *New York Daily Tribune*, January 17, 1882; Churchill, 46.
18. Howe, Frelinghuysen, Voorsanger, Jervis, Ottomeyer, Bascou, Wood, and Riefstahl, 258, n. 2.
19. Strahan, 1:4, 7; Croffut, 155; Foreman and Stimson, 313; Lewis, Turner, and McQuillin, 114; King, *Vanderbilt Homes*, 20.
20. Kathrens, *Great Houses*, 330–331.
21. Quoted in Lewis, Turner, and McQuillin, 114.
22. Strahan, 1:v.
23. Ibid., 1:9.
24. Churchill, 47; Patterson, *Vanderbilts*, 90; Strahan, 1:13–14.
25. Croffut, 157; Patterson, *Vanderbilts*, 93.
26. Croffut, 158; Churchill, 47; Foreman and Stimson, 313; Lewis, Turner, and McQuillin, 114; King, *Vanderbilt Homes*, 22; Strahan, 1:21–24.
27. Strahan, 2:51–53.
28. Quoted in Moss, 187.

29. Strahan, 2:47–48; Croffut, 158; Lewis, Turner, and McQuillin, 116; Howe, Frelinghuysen, Voorsanger, Jervis, Ottomeyer, Bascou, Wood, and Riefstahl, 92.
30. Howe, Frelinghuysen, Voorsanger, Jervis, Ottomeyer, Bascou, Wood, and Riefstahl, 203.
31. Strahan, 2:51; Croffut, 158–159; Lewis, Turner, and McQuillin, 116.
32. Croffut, 159–161; Lewis, Turner, and McQuillin, 119; Strahan, 2:34–36, 44; Howe, Frelinghuysen, Voorsanger, Jervis, Ottomeyer, Bascou, Wood, and Riefstahl, 206.
33. Croffut, 159; Lewis, Turner, and McQuillin, 116; King, Vanderbilt Homes, 22; Strahan, 3:59–62; Howe, Frelinghuysen, Voorsanger, Jervis, Ottomeyer, Bascou, Wood, and Riefstahl, 53.
34. Croffut, 160; Churchill, 49; Lewis, Turner, and McQuillin, 116; Strahan, 4:77–80; Howe, Frelinghuysen, Voorsanger, Jervis, Ottomeyer, Bascou, Wood, and Riefstahl, 204–205.
35. Croffut, 160; Lewis, Turner, and McQuillin, 119.
36. Josephson, 342.
37. Croffut, 165–173; Churchill, 43–52; Tomkins, 34–35.
38. Lewis, Turner, and McQuillin, 23.
39. Strahan, 4:96; Hoyt, Vanderbilts, 241; Lewis, Turner, and McQuillin, 120.
40. Croffut, 158; Strahan, 4:99.
41. Croffut, 161; Lewis, Turner, and McQuillin, 120; Strahan, 5:111–112.
42. Strahan, 5:105–106; Croffut, 161; Lewis, Turner, and McQuillin, 120.
43. Croffut, 161; Strahan, 5:108.
44. Strahan, 5:108.
45. New York Times, March 8, 1882.
46. Foreman and Stimson, 51.
47. Ibid., 52.
48. King, Vanderbilt Homes, 30.
49. Churchill, 72–73; Foreman and Stimson, 56–57.
50. Kathrens, Great Houses, 38.
51. Boyer, 149; Still, 210; King, Vanderbilt Homes, 33.
52. Boyer, 149; Churchill, 70; Kathrens, Great Houses, 36–38; Foreman and Stimson, 52, 57–59; Stern, Gilmartin, and Massengale, 309.
53. Quoted in King, Vanderbilt Homes, 32.
54. Goldsmith, 111.
55. Foreman and Stimson, 58.
56. Kathrens, Great Houses, 39; Foreman and Stimson, 54; King, Vanderbilt Homes, 34–35.
57. Foreman and Stimson, 60.
58. Vanderbilt, Without Prejudice, 94.
59. King, Vanderbilt Homes, 36.
60. Kathrens, Great Houses, 38; Foreman and Stimson, 60.
61. Auchincloss, 39.
62. Platt, 22.
63. See Baker, Richard Morris Hunt, chap. 1, for background.
64. See ibid., chap. 3.
65. See ibid., 172 passim, 314 passim.
66. Ibid., 334.
67. Baker, Richard Morris Hunt, 274; Van Pelt, 13–15.
68. Baker, Richard Morris Hunt, 274–281; Van Pelt, 13–18.
69. Lehr, 163.
70. Baker, Richard Morris Hunt, 274–276.
71. Cited in Vanderbilt, Fortune's Children, 144.
72. Baker, Richard Morris Hunt, 373.
73. Churchill, 61.
74. Balsan, 6; Baker, Richard Morris Hunt, 283–287.
75. Baker, Richard Morris Hunt, 176.
76. Ibid., 276–281.
77. New York Tribune, March 27, 1883.
78. Croffut, 194–196; Josephson, 331; Kathrens, Great Houses, 28–29; Balsan, 10–12; Baker, Richard Morris Hunt, 281; King, Vanderbilt Homes, 50–51; New York Times, March 27, 1883.
79. Kathrens, Great Houses, 28–29; King, Vanderbilt Homes, 51; New York Times, March 27, 1883.
80. New York Tribune, March 27, 1883; Josephson, 331; Kathrens, Great Houses, 28–29; Croffut, 195–196, Balsan, 9; Baker, Richard Morris Hunt, 281; New York Times, March 27, 1883.
81. King, Vanderbilt Homes, 52.
82. New York Tribune, March 27, 1883; Josephson, 331; Kathrens, Great Houses, 28–29; Balsan, 9; Baker, Richard Morris Hunt, 281; King, Vanderbilt Homes, 51–52.
83. New York Tribune, March 27, 1883; Josephson, 331; Kathrens, Great Houses, 28–29; Balsan, 8; Baker, Richard Morris Hunt, 281; Foreman and Stimson, 38–39; Vanderbilt, Fortune's Children, 117; King, Vanderbilt Homes, 52; New York Times, March 27, 1883.

84. Foreman and Stimson, 38; King, *Vanderbilt Homes*, 51.
85. Balsan, 8.
86. Stuart, 59; Patterson, *Vanderbilts*, 126; *New York Times*, March 27, 1883; *New York Tribune*, March 27, 1883; Josephson, 331; Kathrens, *Great Houses*, 30; Croffut, 195; Churchill, 58, 62; Balsan, 9; Foreman and Stimson, 40; King, *Vanderbilt Homes*, 53.
87. Friedman, 16.
88. Thorndike, *Magnificent Builders*, 317.
89. Cited in Baker, *Richard Morris Hunt*, 286.
90. Boyer, 146.
91. Stern, Gilmartin, and Massengale, 310.

CHAPTER 10: MRS. ASTOR JOINS THE RACE

1. Kavaler, 106.
2. Gerard, 39; Still, 241; Boyer, 48; Patterson, *Fifth Avenue*, 69; Morris, *Incredible New York*, 10.
3. Still, 241; Roth, 23.
4. *New York Times*, January 22, 1884.
5. Morris, *Incredible New York*, 146; Wecter, 333; Gerard, 39; Still, 241.
6. *New York Times*, January 22, 1884; Morris, *Incredible New York*, 146; Wecter, 333; Gerard, 39; Still, 241; Kavaler, 119.
7. Eliot, 50–51.
8. Gates, 184–189; Amory, *Who Killed Society?*, 474; Madsen, 277; Wilson, 121; Patterson, *Fifth Avenue*, 80–81; Kavaler, 124.
9. Kavaler, 124; Gates, 187.
10. Wecter, 334; Elliott, 147; Morris, *Incredible New York*, 155.
11. Gates, 184–189; Amory, *Who Killed Society?*, 474; Madsen, 277; Wilson, 121; Tebbel, 61.
12. Crockett, 48.
13. Wilson, 197.
14. Gates, 111; Stern, Gilmartin, and Massengale, 254.
15. O'Connor, *Astors*, 236; Kavaler, 133.
16. Myers, 3:239; Kathrens, *Great Houses*, 73–75; Baker, *Richard Morris Hunt*, 346; Stern, Gilmartin, and Massengale, 321.
17. Myers, 3:239.
18. Homberger, 16.
19. Myers, 3:239; Homberger, 236; Kathrens, *Great Houses*, 79; Baker, *Richard Morris Hunt*, 346; Churchill, 114–115.
20. Obolensky, 279.

21. Myers, 3:239; Wilson, 105; Kathrens, *Great Houses*, 75; Homberger, 224; Baker, *Richard Morris Hunt*, 346.
22. Coleman, 62–63. The painting is now in the Metropolitan Museum of Art in New York City.
23. Myers, 3:239; *New York Times*, January 10, 1905.
24. Churchill, 114.
25. Decies, 76–77.
26. Obolensky, 278–279.
27. Myers, 3:239; Wilson, 105; Kathrens, *Great Houses*, 76; O'Connor, *Astors*, 236; *New York Times*, January 10, 1905.
28. Morris, *Incredible New York*, 155.

CHAPTER 11: BUILDING FOR ETERNITY

1. Desmond and Croly, 279.
2. Maher, 237–260; Birmingham, *Grandes Dames*, 188, 191–192; see also http://dgmweb.net/genealogy/FGS/D/DeWorsionJohn-ArabellaDuvalYarrington.shtml.
3. Birmingham, *Grandes Dames*, 187.
4. Maher, 237–260; Birmingham, *Grandes Dames*, 191–192; see also http://dgmweb.net/genealogy/FGS/D/DeWorsionJohn-ArabellaDuvalYarrington.shtml.
5. Maher, 264–276; Birmingham, *Grandes Dames*, 191–192, 194–195.
6. Kathrens, *Great Houses*, 59.
7. Maher, 278–280; Kathrens, *Great Houses*, 60.
8. Birmingham, *Grandes Dames*, 198.
9. Wecter, 129.
10. Howe, Frelinghuysen, Voorsanger, Jervis, Ottomeyer, Bascou, Wood, and Riefstahl, 148.
11. Baker, *Richard Morris Hunt*, 295, 298.
12. Kathrens, *Great Houses*, 55.
13. Ibid., 55.
14. Lehr, 135.
15. Van Rensselaer, *Social Ladder*, 210.
16. Quoted in Patterson, *Best Families*, 122.
17. Kathrens, *Great Houses*, 83; Stern, Gilmartin, and Massengale, 326–329.
18. Tebbel, 151; Sloane, 60.
19. Logan, 138.
20. Tebbel, 151; Kathrens, *Great Houses*, 82–84; Sloane, 60.
21. Churchill, 136–137.
22. Ibid., 138–140.

23. Ibid., 140–143; Wector, 126.
24. Churchill, 135.
25. Ibid., 137.
26. Ibid., 144–145.
27. Kathrens, *Great Houses*, 104–105.
28. Churchill, 137, 141.
29. Churchill, 146; Lowe, 211.
30. Lowe, 211.
31. Kathrens, *Great Houses*, 107, 110; Churchill, 147, 150; Morris, *Incredible New York*, 207.
32. Morris, *Incredible New York*, 207; Churchill, 149.
33. Churchill, 148–149; Lowe, 214.
34. Churchill, 149–150.
35. Lowe, 237; Kathrens, *Great Houses*, 110.
36. Churchill, 150; Morris, *Incredible New York*, 207.
37. *New York Times*, January 5, 1901.
38. Churchill, 151–153.
39. Lowe, 251.
40. Roth, 59.
41. Lowe, 253; Kathrens, *Great Houses*, 100.
42. Baker, *Stanny*, 307–308; Kathrens, *Great Houses*, 100–102; Lowe, 253.
43. Kathrens, *Great Houses*, 102; Decies, 165.
44. Sloane, 88.
45. Kathrens, *Great Houses*, 127; King, *Vanderbilt Homes*, 160.
46. King, *Vanderbilt Homes*, 116; Stern, Gilmartin, and Massengale, 334.
47. Kathrens, *Great Houses*, 128; King, *Vanderbilt Homes*, 162.
48. Sloane, 208; Kathrens, *Great Houses*, 128–129; King, *Vanderbilt Homes*, 162–163.
49. The Burden house is now home to the Convent of the Sacred Heart.

CHAPTER 12: THE UNSEEN ARMIES
1. Fowler, 268.
2. Sutherland, 14.
3. Veblen, 65.
4. Carter, 12–13.
5. Sutherland, 15.
6. Carter, 184.
7. Ibid., 186.
8. Sherwood, 372; Carter, 187–188; Horn, 77.
9. Wecter, 250.
10. Horn, 78–79.
11. Carter, 192.
12. Ibid., 132.

13. Veblen, 57.
14. Lehr, 131.
15. Sutherland, 89.
16. Carter, 38.
17. Ibid., 12.
18. Ibid., 38.
19. Ibid., 217–218.
20. Ibid., 220–222.
21. Carter, 232–235; Horn, 86.
22. Carter, 236.
23. Sherwood, 397–398.
24. Carter, 68–69.
25. Decies, 98.
26. Horn, 49, 57.
27. Carter, 70.
28. Sutherland, 90–91.
29. Horn, 80–81.
30. Sherwood, 372.
31. Amory, *Last Resorts*, 244.
32. Carter, 188.
33. Carter, 132; Kavaler, 133.
34. Horn, 84.
35. Dudden, 194.
36. Carter, 96.
37. Decies, 177.
38. Carter, 89.
39. Ibid., 86.
40. Ibid., 89.
41. Sherwood, 400.
42. Carter, 155.
43. Turbeville, 28.
44. Carter, 168–175; Dudden, 142–143; Flanders, 159.
45. Horn, 69.
46. Carter, 246.
47. Decies, 178.
48. Carter, 203–204; Horn, 74–75.
49. Horn, 87–88.
50. Carter, 64–65.
51. Cable, 88.
52. Carter, 214.
53. Sherwood, 373; Horn, 110.
54. O'Leary, 17.
55. Sutherland, 86.
56. Ibid., 77.
57. Sherwood, 373.
58. Spofford, 37.
59. Dudden, 221.
60. Spofford, 39.
61. Townsend, 33.
62. Carter, 143.
63. O'Leary, 112.
64. Flanders, 138.
65. Carter, 6.
66. Decies, 166–170.

CHAPTER 13: CLOTHING

1. Perrot, 90.
2. Burne-Jones, 54.
3. Carter, 235, 239.
4. King, *Handbook*, 798; Barrett, 28.
5. Beebe, 237; Lehr, 26–27.
6. Cited in Aldrich, 33.
7. Perrot, 120–121.
8. Busbey, 337.
9. Cited in Aldrich, 72.
10. Sherwood, 290; Perrot, 115.
11. Beebe, 237; Lehr, 27.
12. Perrot, 113.
13. Carter, 240.
14. Lehr, 27.
15. Veblen, 179.
16. Collier, 46.
17. Perrot, 27.
18. *New York Times*, September 27, 1903.
19. Churchill, 160.
20. Cited in Coleman, 89.
21. Lehr, 61–62.
22. Carter, 71.
23. Ibid., 27.
24. Ibid., 34.
25. Perrot, 135.
26. Sherwood, 173; Aldrich, 75–76.
27. Perrot, 136; Gernsheim, 83.
28. Carter, 28; Perrot, 41.
29. Perrot, 92–93.
30. Carter, 29.
31. Gernsheim, 74.
32. Sherwood, 289; Harrison, *The Well-Bred Girl*, 25.
33. Sherwood, 170.
34. Ibid., 347.
35. Ibid., 174.
36. Quoted in Patterson, *Best Families*, 87.
37. Lehr, 127; Decies, 59; Sherwood, 179.
38. Decies, 59.
39. Lehr, 128.
40. Perrot, 92.
41. Harrison, *The Well-Bred Girl*, 22; Perrot, 93.
42. Perrot, 93; Gernsheim, 74.
43. Gernsheim, 78.
44. Sherwood, 231–232.
45. Perrot, 93.
46. Sherwood, 231; Perrot, 95.
47. Sherwood, 253.
48. Perrot, 96; Gernsheim, 63, 83; Coleman, 69.
49. See Coleman for lengthy discussion of these gowns and their design.
50. Cited in Perrot, 97.
51. Burne-Jones, 54.
52. Veblen, 167.
53. Lehr, 170.

CHAPTER 14: JEWELRY

1. Morris, *Postscript to Yesterday*, 16.
2. Bourget, 51.
3. Lehr, 59.
4. Phillips, Becker, Dietz, Frelinghuysen, Loring, and Purcell, 55.
5. Nicholls, 55.
6. Collier, 42.
7. Perrot, 99.
8. Cited in Perrot, 99.
9. Dunlop, 2.
10. Sloane, 198.
11. Simon, 180.
12. Loring, 11.
13. Sherwood, 290.
14. Lehr, 59.
15. *New York Times*, January 12, 1924.
16. Hoyt, *Goulds*, 145; Beebe, 263.
17. Munn, 338–339; Lehr, 93.
18. Wecter, 368.
19. Dunlop, 3–6.
20. Wecter, 368.
21. Brann, 1:118.
22. Dunlop, 36; Munn, 212; Loring, 94.
23. Munn, 212; http://jck.polygon.net/archives/1995/07/0795rub.html.
24. Morris, *Incredible New York*, 240; Decies, 126; Beebe, 120; Loring, 42; Phillips, Becker, Dietz, Frelinghuysen, Loring, and Purcell, 104.
25. Cited in Homberger, 208.
26. Lehr, 59.
27. Nicholls, 55.
28. Munn, 334; Vanderbilt, *Fortune's Children*, 170; Stuart, 185.
29. Nicholls, 55.
30. Vanderbilt, *Queen*, 70.
31. Cologni and Nussbaum, 12; Vanderbilt, *Queen*, 12.
32. Cologni and Nussbaum, 12; Vanderbilt, *Queen*, 11; http://www.royal-magazin.de/collection/vanderbilt-jewels.htm.
33. Nicholls, 469, 55; Munn, 334.
34. Sherwood, 185.
35. *New York Times*, October 31, 1908.
36. *New York Times*, January 10, 1897.
37. Gates, 82; Wecter, 214; Morris, *Postscript to Yesterday*, 11; *New York Times*, October 31, 1908.

38. Gates, 82, 79; Wecter, 214; Morris, *Postscript to Yesterday*, 11; *New York Times*, October 31, 1908.
39. *New York Times*, January 10, 1905; Kavaler, 117; Morris, *Incredible New York*, 146.
40. Gates, 82, 79; Wecter, 214; Morris, *Postscript to Yesterday*, 11.
41. *New York Times*, October 31, 1908; Barrett, 18; quoted in Patterson, *Best Families*, 24; Loring, 44–45.
42. *New York Times*, January 10, 1905; Kavaler, 117; Cowles, 142; Barrett, 18.
43. Wecter, 334.
44. Wilson, 105.
45. Carter, 34.
46. Barrett, 18.
47. Hoyt, *Goulds*, 145.
48. Beebe, 264.
49. Crockett, 117–119.

CHAPTER 15: TRANSPORTATION

1. Amory, *Last Resorts*, 4.
2. Brinnin, 200.
3. Allen, 12.
4. Rousmaniere, 90–91.
5. Croffut, 46–47: Brinnin, 200–201; Churchill, 15; Allen, 12.
6. *New York Post*, January 5, 1877.
7. *London Daily News*, June 4, 1853.
8. Robinson, 48–49.
9. Roth, 30.
10. http://www.metmuseum.org/toah/hd/cawh/hod_28.70.3.htm; *New York Daily Graphic*, April 27, 1882; Barrault, 55; Rousmaniere, 98.
11. Longstreet, *We All Went to Paris*, 180.
12. Ibid., 178; Rousmaniere, 99.
13. Beebe, 21.
14. Gates, 75.
15. Robinson, 7.
16. Wilson, 194, 202; Gates, 75.
17. *New York Times*, October 1, 1886.
18. Churchill, 93; Jenkins, 34–35; Black, 707; Robinson, 55; Rousmaniere, 112; Hoyt, *Vanderbilts*, 281–282.
19. Jenkins, 35; Balsan, 12.
20. Barrault, 54; Foreman and Stimson, 178, 227; Balsan, 18; Andrews, 269.
21. Rousmaniere, 100.
22. Ibid., 100–107.
23. Robinson, 89.
24. *New York World*, November 8, 1885.
25. Ibid.

26. *New York World*, November 8, 1885; Robinson, 56; Rousmaniere, 98.
27. Williamson, 83.
28. Beebe, 178.
29. Ibid., 175–176.
30. Churchill, 43; Patterson, *Best Families*, 170; Beebe, 177.
31. Foreman and Stimson, 78, 90.
32. Beebe, 179–180.
33. Ibid., 20.
34. Ibid.
35. Ibid., 180.
36. Ibid., 177.
37. Lehr, 62.
38. Decies, 49.
39. Mead, 101–102.
40. Huggett, 67–71.
41. Morris, *Incredible New York*, 96.
42. Ibid.; Wecter, 438; Croffut, 200; Andrews, 229–230.
43. Morris, *Incredible New York*, 95–96; Patterson, *Vanderbilts*, 32.
44. Patterson, *Vanderbilts*, 68.
45. Aslet, 180–183.
46. Croffut, 205.
47. Sadler and Sadler, 99–100; Smales, 36–37; Baker, *Richard Morris Hunt*, 366; Folsom, 256.
48. Sadler and Sadler, 94; Elliott, 203; Baker, *Richard Morris Hunt*, 363–364; Lehr, 132–133; Platt, 99.
49. Elliott, 203.
50. Lehr, 62.
51. Josephson, 334; Lehr, 62; Huggett, 31.
52. Lehr, 62.
53. Elliott, 133.
54. Morris, *Incredible New York*, 95.
55. Crockett, 155.
56. Morris, *Incredible New York*, 11.
57. Lehr, 15–16.
58. Huggett, 34.
59. Ibid., 39.
60. Aslet, 183.
61. Huggett, 39.
62. Aslet, 183.
63. Wecter, 440; Morris, *Incredible New York*, 149.
64. Beebe, 184.
65. Van Dyke, 182.
66. Beebe, 188.
67. Cited in Homberger, 236.
68. *New York Times*, September 10, 1899.
69. Gerard, 46.
70. Morris, *Not So Long Ago*, 268–269.
71. Gerard, 46.

72. Morris, *Not So Long Ago*, 268–269.
73. Lord, 116–117.
74. Ibid., 115–116.
75. Karolevitz, 157; Morris, *Not So Long Ago*, 270; Beebe, 184; Lord, 116.

CHAPTER 16: MASTERS OF THE HUDSON

1. Crowninshield, 9.
2. For more detailed analyses of Clermont and Montgomery Place in particular see Wecter, 55–56; Moss, 128–131.
3. Hoyt, *Goulds*, 5–11; Renehan, 45–50; Klein, 21 passim.
4. Rugoff, 52–53; Hoyt, *Goulds*, chap. 5; Klein, 43–47, 56–59; Renehan, 65–67.
5. Rugoff, 55–58; Josephson, 132–134; Andrews, 123–135; Hoyt, *Goulds*, 65–72; Klein, 84–87; Renehan, 115 passim.
6. Patterson, *Vanderbilts*, 42.
7. Klein, 102–113; Renehan, 163 passim; Hoyt, *Goulds*, 51–54.
8. Josephson, 205–206; Rugoff, 59–60; Patterson, *Best Families*, 81; Hoyt, *Goulds*, 76–78; Klein, 195 passim.
9. Klein, 4.
10. *New York Sun*, August 30, 1883.
11. Quoted in Klein, 323.
12. Hoyt, *Goulds*, 72.
13. Amory, *Who Killed Society?*, 448–449.
14. Hoyt, *Goulds*, 66.
15. Rugoff, 53.
16. *New York Sun*, August 30, 1883.
17. Klein, 213.
18. Hoyt, *Goulds*, 73.
19. Dwyer, 175; Hoyt, *Goulds*, 73–74.
20. Moss, 155.
21. Williams and Williams, *Great Houses*, 131; Cavalier, 104.
22. Nicolson, 301–303.
23. National Trust, *Lyndhurst*, 4; Dwyer, 171–172.
24. Page, 185.
25. Nicolson, 304.
26. National Trust, *Lyndhurst*, 8.
27. Dwyer, 174; Hoyt, *Goulds*, 74; Griswold and Weller, 75; Cavalier, 105.
28. Beebe, 13; Randall, 90; Hoyt, *Goulds*, 74–75; O'Connor, *Gould*, 203.
29. National Trust, *Lyndhurst*, 3; Nicolson, 301.
30. Moss, 148–149; Dwyer, 172; Hoyt, *Goulds*, 73; McAlester and McAlester, 100–103.
31. Page, 188.
32. Cavalier, 104.
33. Dwyer, 171; Williams and Williams, *Great Houses*, 136; McAlester and McAlester, 104.
34. Williams and Williams, *Great Houses*, 135; Nicolson, 306.
35. Williams and Williams, *Great Houses*, 136; Page, 188.
36. McAlester and McAlester, 107.
37. Williams and Williams, *Great Houses*, 136; McAlester and McAlester, 109; Nicolson, 309; Page, 190.
38. Hoyt, *Goulds*, 75; Williams and Williams, *Great Houses*, 136; McAlester and McAlester, 104, 109; Nicolson, 309.
39. McAlester and McAlester, 104, 109.
40. Klein, 217.
41. O'Connor, *Gould*, 206.
42. Ibid., 208–209.
43. Hoyt, *Goulds*, 79, 88; O'Connor, *Gould*, 265; Klein, 404.
44. O'Connor, *Gould*, 278.
45. The *New York World*, December 3, 1892.
46. Baker, *Stanny*, 296; Dwyer, 89–91; White, 174.
47. Randall, 122; Baker, *Stanny*, 296; Dwyer, 94–95; White, 177; Lowe, 208.
48. Ibid.
49. White, 174.
50. Dwyer, 95; White, 177.
51. Dwyer, 92; Randall, 118–122; White, 179.
52. Randall, 122; White, 179.
53. Dwyer, 94.
54. *The New York State Preservationist*, 6, no. 1 (Fall/Winter 2002): 7; White, 181.
55. Dwyer, 95.
56. Croffut, 265.
57. Andrews, 329.
58. Croffut, 184–185.
59. Field, 30.
60. Amory, *Who Killed Society?*, 490; Croffut, 185; *New York Tribune*, February 18, 1879; Foreman and Stimson, 198; Field, 33.
61. Field, 33; Foreman and Stimson, 199–200.
62. Foreman and Stimson, 200; White, 191.
63. Dwyer, 98, 101; Foreman and Stimson, 196–197; Snell, 29.
64. Cited in Hewitt, 130.
65. Patrick, 8; Roth, 156; Hewitt, 128; Dwyer, 103; Foreman and Stimson, 207.
66. Dwyer, 98; Foreman and Stimson, 196.
67. Snell, 46; McAlester and McAlester, 255.
68. Randall, 113; Griswold and Weller, 73.

69. Hewitt, 130; Foreman and Stimson, 203–204; Williams and Williams, *Treasury*, 201; White, 193; Folsom, 198.
70. McAlester and McAlester, 249.
71. Dwyer, 99; Foreman and Stimson, 209; Williams and Williams, *Treasury*, 205; White, 193; McAlester and McAlester, 250; Snell, 14, 33.
72. Hewitt, 133; Randall, 110; Williams and Williams, *Treasury*, 208; Snell, 36.
73. Folsom, 197.
74. Hewitt, 133; Dwyer, 98; Foreman and Stimson, 208; McAlester and McAlester, 251; Snell, 33–34.
75. Dwyer, 100; Williams and Williams, *Treasury*, 206; Snell, 36–37.
76. Dwyer, 101; Williams and Williams, *Treasury*, 208; McAlester and McAlester, 251; Snell, 37.
77. Snell, 39.
78. Dwyer, 105; Foreman and Stimson, 208; Williams and Williams, *Treasury*, 210; Snell, 40, 42.
79. Williams and Williams, *Treasury*, 208–209.
80. Field, 32.
81. Foreman and Stimson, 208; Dwyer, 103; Williams and Williams, *Treasury*, 209; Snell, 42.
82. Hewitt, 130; Dwyer, 97; Snell, 15–16.
83. Hewitt, 128.
84. Amory, *Last Resorts*, 41.
85. Foreman and Stimson, 198, 211–212; Snell, 23, 26.
86. Snell, 21; McAlester and McAlester, 255; Hewitt, 128; Randall, 113.
87. Hewitt, 128.
88. Amory, *Who Killed Society?*, 490.
89. Wilson, 103; Randall, 136–141.
90. Randall, 136, 141; Wilson, 103; Cowles, 68.
91. Wilson, 200.
92. Quoted in Aslet, 70.
93. Baker, *Stanny*, 299.
94. Lowe, 214.
95. Ibid., 212–214.
96. Randall, 136–138; Baker, *Stanny*, 299; Aslet, 170; Obolensky, 279.
97. Roth, 23.

Chapter 17: "The Inland Newport"

1. Crowninshield, 106–107.
2. Harrison, *Recollections Grave and Gay*, 310–311.
3. Sherwood, 331.
4. Ibid., 344.
5. Owens, 62.
6. Dwight, 15.
7. Brandon, 67–68.
8. Lewis, *Ladies*, 76–77.
9. Brandon, 68; Dwight, 31.
10. de Wolfe, 107.
11. Metcalf, 160.
12. Letter of Edith Wharton to Ogden Codman, August 1, 1900, quoted in Marshall, 15.
17. Jackson and Gilder, 194; Metcalf, 162; Dwight, 90.
14. Metcalf, 164, 169.
15. Craig, 23.
16. Wharton, *Backward Glance*, 110.
17. Metcalf, 164–165.
18. Ibid., 164–167.
19. Metcalf, 168; Craig, 102.
20. Craig, 106.
21. Metcalf, 168–169; Craig, 106–107.
22. Metcalf, 169; Craig, 107–110.
23. Jackson and Gilder, 197; Metcalf, 169; Owens, 174; Craig, 110–111.
24. Griswold and Weller, 13; Craig, 119–122.
25. Wharton, *Backward Glance*, 124.
26. Letter of Henry James, October 17, 1904, in Edel, 4:325.
27. Wharton, *Backward Glance*, 125.
28. Lehr, 74.
29. Balsan, 3.
30. Sloane, 7.
31. Jackson and Gilder, 99–102.
32. Oakes, 31; Owens, 163.
33. Oakes, 31.
34. Jackson and Gilder, 102–103; Foreman and Stimson, 138–140; Lewis, *American Country Houses*, 94; King, *Vanderbilt Homes*, 131.
35. Patterson, *Vanderbilts*, 208.
36. Field, 26.
37. Owens, 163.
38. Foreman and Stimson, 140.
39. Foreman and Stimson, 130; Sloane, *Maverick,* 92–93.
40. Owens, 73–74.
41. Ibid., 120.
42. See "The Line of Least Resistance" (details may be found on page 489) for the complete tale.
43. Dwight, 100–101.
44. Metcalf, 162; Dwight, 101.
45. Cited in Jackson and Gilder, 157.
46. Owens, 110.
47. Ibid., 180.

48. Ibid., 27.
49. Jackson and Gilder, 152.
50. Ibid., 152–153; Owens, 180.
51. Owens, 18; Jackson and Gilder, 153–156.
52. Owens, 30.
53. Jackson and Gilder, 153–156.
54. Owens, 30.
55. The story seems to have made its first appearance in print in the June 30, 1897, edition of *Town and Country*. This original version is quoted by both Patterson, *Best Families,* 160, and by Jackson and Gilder, 15. The *Town and Country* tale gave the figure of ninety-seven men. In a set of private memoirs, Anson Phelps Stokes Jr. admitted, "There is a basis of truth to the whole story, but it has been much exaggerated." See Jackson and Gilder, 22, for further discussion of the tale.

CHAPTER 18: MONARCH OF THE SMOKY MOUNTAINS

1. Croffut, 186.
2. Ibid., 185.
3. Roper, 389.
4. Foreman and Stimson, 275.
5. Andrews, 333.
6. Aslet, 4–5.
7. Bryan, 29.
8. Cited in Rybczynski, 379.
9. Baker, *Richard Morris Hunt,* 412.
10. *New York Times,* November 2, 1888.
11. Baker, *Richard Morris Hunt,* 412.
12. Bryan, 38–41.
13. Ibid., 42.
14. Baker, *Richard Morris Hunt,* 332.
15. Vanderbilt, *Fortune's Children,* 275.
16. Baker, *Richard Morris Hunt,* 424.
17. Ibid., 415–416; Bryan, 99–101; Carley and Rennicke, 14.
18. Covington, 21.
19. Hewitt, 2.
20. *New York Times,* December 7, 1889.
21. Bryan, 42–45; Foreman and Stimson, 281; Carley and Rennicke, 14.
22. Baker, *Richard Morris Hunt,* 416.
23. Roper, 416.
24. Griswold and Weller, 164.
25. Hall, 200–201; Rybczynski, 384; Bryan, 33–36.
26. Pinchot, 49.
27. Rybczynski, 384.
28. Hewitt, 6; Baker, *Richard Morris Hunt,* 420; Hall, 205; Carley and Rennicke, 85.

29. Calkins, 64; Carley and Rennicke, 86.
30. Desmond and Croly, 431; Baker, *Richard Morris Hunt,* 412; Rybczynski, 383; Calkins, 64-65; Carley and Rennicke, 88–91.
31. Carley and Rennicke, 14; Desmond and Croly, 431; Baker, *Richard Morris Hunt,* 421, 424.
32. Cited in Baker, *Richard Morris Hunt,* 414.
33. Baker, *Richard Morris Hunt,* 424; Carley and Rennicke, 24; Aslet, 9–10.
34. McAlester and McAlester, 236; Platt, 58; Carley and Rennicke, 24.
35. Baker, *Richard Morris Hunt,* 424; Williams and Williams, *Great Houses,* 181; Carley and Rennicke, 27.
36. Williams and Williams, *Great Houses,* 180; McAlester and McAlester, 237; Carley and Rennicke, 37.
37. Williams and Williams, *Great Houses,* 180–181; Moss, 202; Baker, *Richard Morris Hunt,* 428; McAlester and McAlester, 237; Carley and Rennicke, 39.
38. Williams and Williams, *Great Houses,* 182; Carley and Rennicke, 30.
39. Baker, *Richard Morris Hunt,* 424, 428; Williams and Williams, *Great Houses,* 178; Bryan, 133; Patterson, *Vanderbilts,* 173; McAlester and McAlester, 238–239; Carley and Rennicke, 28, 108.
40. Williams and Williams, *Great Houses,* 177; Folsom, 62; Carley and Rennicke, 40.
41. Carley and Rennicke, 9.
42. Williams and Williams, *Great Houses,* 182; McAlester and McAlester, 239; Carley and Rennicke, 44.
43. Carley and Rennicke, 46.
44. Williams and Williams, *Great Houses,* 182; Carley and Rennicke, 49.
45. Carley and Rennicke, 61–63.
46. *New York Times,* December 26, 1895; *New York Tribune,* December 26, 1895; Covington, 23.
47. Cited in Baker, *Richard Morris Hunt,* 416.
48. Letter of Henry James to Edith Wharton, February 8, 1905, in Edel, 4:244.
49. Covington, 25, 170–171. The music room was completed in the 1970s, while the salon has kept the fabric-draped ceiling but incorporated more permanent decorations.
50. *New York Times,* December 27, 1897.
51. Andrews, 335; Tebbel, 121.

CHAPTER 19: THE KINGDOM BY THE SEA

1. Lehr, 100.
2. Low, 160.
3. Elliott, 41; O'Connor, *Golden Summers*, 23–24.
4. Van Rensselaer, *Newport*, 32.
5. Kowsky, 39–42; Yarnall, 56; Vaux, 306.
6. Yarnall, 56.
7. Yarnall, 56; Kowsky, 39–42; Barrett, 83.
8. Gates, 177.
9. Wilson, 106; Gates, 177.
10. Roth, 23.
11. Lehr, 161.
12. Baker, *Richard Morris Hunt*, 352.
13. Ibid., 352–362; Yarnall, 137.
14. Baker, *Richard Morris Hunt*, 352–353; Foreman and Stimson, 226.
15. Baker, *Richard Morris Hunt*, 353; Mulvagh and Weber, 148; Wecter, 339.
16. Panaggio, 32; Warburton, 26; Foreman and Stimson, 223.
17. Baker, *Richard Morris Hunt*, 352.
18. Cited in Vanderbilt, *Fortune's Children*, 146.
19. *New York Times*, August 20, 1892.
20. Baker, *Richard Morris Hunt*, 353; Yarnall, 138; Desmond and Croly, 426; Foreman and Stimson, 221–222; Williams and Williams, *Treasury*, 113–114.
21. Williams and Williams, *Treasury*, 114; Mulvagh and Weber, 148; Platt, 95; Preservation Society of Newport, 6.
22. *New York Times*, April 26, 1892.
23. Yarnall, 139; Baker, *Richard Morris Hunt*, 353, 358; Preservation Society of Newport, 6.
24. King, *Vanderbilt Homes*, 59.
25. Mulvagh and Weber, 148; Benway, 38; Baker, *Richard Morris Hunt*, 358, 362; Foreman and Stimson, 223; Williams and Williams, *Treasury*, 114–115; King, *Vanderbilt Homes*, 61; Preservation Society of Newport, 5.
26. Benway, 38; Baker, *Richard Morris Hunt*, 358, 362; Foreman and Stimson, 223; Williams and Williams, *Treasury*, 116; Mulvagh and Weber, 148; King, *Vanderbilt Homes*, 62; Preservation Society of Newport, 6–7.
27. Benway, 38–40; Baker, *Richard Morris Hunt*, 358; Foreman and Stimson, 223; Balsan, 21; Williams and Williams, *Treasury*, 119–120; Mulvagh and Weber, 148; Patterson, *Vanderbilts*, 140; King,

Vanderbilt Homes, 61; Preservation Society of Newport, 10.
28. Benway, 41; Balsan, 20; Baker, *Richard Morris Hunt*, 358; Foreman and Stimson, 223; Williams and Williams, *Treasury*, 116–117; King, *Vanderbilt Homes*, 62.
29. Benway, 41; Baker, *Richard Morris Hunt*, 358; Platt, 95; King, *Vanderbilt Homes*, 59; Preservation Society of Newport, 9.
30. Platt, 95; Preservation Society of Newport, 11; Benway, 38.
31. Benway, 43; Baker, *Richard Morris Hunt*, 358, 362; Foreman and Stimson, 223; Williams and Williams, *Treasury*, 114–115; Preservation Society of Newport, 14.
32. Preservation Society of Newport, 13; Benway, 41–43; Platt, 98.
33. Preservation Society of Newport, 16; Platt, 98; Benway, 43.
34. Preservation Society of Newport, 15.
35. Balsan, 20.
36. Brough, 55; Benway, 43; Baker, *Richard Morris Hunt*, 362; Williams and Williams, *Treasury*, 121; Platt, 98; Preservation Society of Newport, 14–15.
37. Sloane, 26.
38. Benway, 36.
39. Lady Sarah Spencer-Churchill to the author, May 2000.
40. Lehr, 141.
41. Ibid., 14.
42. Black, 517–518, 597.
43. Ibid., 659–660, 663–664.
44. Ibid., 707.
45. Slocum, 48.
46. *New York Times*, January 12, 1896.
47. Balsan, 23.
48. Logan, 243; Balsan, 4.
49. *New York Tribune*, March 6, 1895.
50. Lehr, 109.
51. *New York World*, March 6, 1895.
52. Brough, 64.
53. *New York World*, March 6, 1895.
54. Ibid.
55. Stuart, 109–110; Vanderbilt, *Fortune's Children*, 248. In a conversation with the author, Alva's great-granddaughter, Lady Sarah Spencer-Churchill confirmed that this possible explanation was certainly discussed within the family and believed by many to have been true.
56. *New York World*, March 6, 1895; *New York Times*, March 6 1895; *New York Times*, January 12, 1896.
57. *New York World*, March 6, 1895.

58. *New York Times*, January 12, 1896.
59. Baker, *Richard Morris Hunt*, 362.
60. Yarnall, 139.
61. Baker, *Richard Morris Hunt*, 364.
62. Platt, 99; Baker, *Richard Morris Hunt*, 363–364.
63. Lehr, 132; Yarnall, 140.
64. Folsom, 260; Platt, 101.
65. Downing and Scully, 173; Yarnall, 140; Baker, *Richard Morris Hunt*, 364.
66. Lehr, 133.

CHAPTER 20: SWELLS IN NEWPORT

1. Foreman and Stimson, 249.
2. Cited in Vanderbilt, *Fortune's Children*, 186.
3. Yarnall, 141.
4. Baker, *Richard Morris Hunt*, 366.
5. Smales, 12; Foreman and Stimson, 249.
6. *New York Times*, April 21, 1895.
7. Smales, 33; Foreman and Stimson, 251; Benway, 49; Sirkis, 94; Folsom, 256.
8. Vanderbilt, *Fortune's Children*, 185; Smales, 32, 35.
9. Vanderbilt, *Queen*, 14; Yarnall, 141; Williams and Williams, *Great Houses*, 191–192; Smales, 15.
10. Baker, *Richard Morris Hunt*, 366–367; Desmond and Croly, 425–426; Foreman and Stimson, 249–251; Williams and Williams, *Great Houses*, 192; Smales, 29–31.
11. Smales, 15.
12. Benway, 51; Baker, *Richard Morris Hunt*, 370; Foreman and Stimson, 252; Williams and Williams, *Great Houses*, 195; King, *Vanderbilt Homes*, 42; Smales, 17–19.
13. Williams and Williams, *Great Houses*, 198–199; Smales, 22; Benway, 51.
14. Foreman and Stimson, 252; Williams and Williams, *Great Houses*, 198; Smales, 21–22; Benway, 51.
15. Benway, 51–52; *New York Times*, April 21, 1895; Baker, *Richard Morris Hunt*, 370; Foreman and Stimson, 253; Williams and Williams, *Great Houses*, 199; Folsom, 254; Smales, 19–21.
16. Benway, 53; *New York Times*, April 21, 1895; Baker, *Richard Morris Hunt*, 370; Foreman and Stimson, 253; Smales, 25.
17. Baker, *Richard Morris Hunt*, 370; Williams and Williams, *Great Houses*, 196, 198; King, *Vanderbilt Homes*, 43; Smales, 25–26; Benway, 53–44.

18. Benway, 51; Yarnall, 142; Williams and Williams, *Great Houses*, 195; Smales, 17–19.
19. Benway, 55–57; Metcalf, 12; Smales, 27.
20. Smales, 27; Baker, *Richard Morris Hunt*, 366; Foreman and Stimson, 249, 254; Vanderbilt, *Without Prejudice*, 104.
21. Lehr, 217.
22. James, 224–225.
23. Bourget, 49.
24. Ferguson, 2–3; Preservation Society of Newport, *TFO*, 3; Benway, 73.
25. Van Rensselaer, *Newport*, 61.
26. Baker, *Stanny*, 297; Benway, 70; Ferguson, 9–11; Yarnall, 156–157; White, 203.
27. Baker, *Stanny*, 297; Benway, 70; Ferguson, 11; Yarnall, 156–157; White, 203.
28. *New York Times*, August 18, 1904.
29. *New York Times*, August 20, 1904.
30. Baker, *Stanny*, 297; Morris, *Postscript to Yesterday*, 6; Lehr, 213; O'Connor, *Golden Summers*, 244–245; *New York Times*, August 20, 1904; Preservation Society of Newport, *TFO*, 6.
31. *New York Times*, August 18, 1904.
32. *New York Times*, August 20, 1904; White, 199, 208; Mulvagh and Weber, 202; Baker, *Stanny*, 297–298; Benway, 70; Ferguson, 9–11; Yarnall, 156–157.
33. Baker, *Stanny*, 297; Morris, *Postscript to Yesterday*, 6; Lehr, 213; O'Connor, *Golden Summers*, 244–245; *New York Times*, August 20, 1904; Preservation Society of Newport, *TFO*, 6.
34. *New York Times*, August 20, 1904.
35. Ferguson, 15–17; Baker, *Stanny*, 298; Benway, 76; Yarnall, 156–157; White, 208; Preservation Society of Newport, *TFO*, 4; *New York Times*, August 20, 1904.
36. Preservation Society of Newport, *TFO*, 4–5; Baker, *Stanny*, 298; Mulvagh and Weber, 208; Benway, 76.
37. Baker, *Stanny*, 297; Morris, *Postscript to Yesterday*, 6; Lehr, 213; O'Connor, *Golden Summers*, 244–245; *New York Times*, August 20, 1904; Preservation Society of Newport, *TFO*, 6.
38. Baker, *Stanny*, 298; Benway, 76; Ferguson, 20; Yarnall, 156–157; Mulvagh and Weber, 202; Preservation Society of Newport, *TFO*, 5.
39. Baker, *Stanny*, 297–298; Morris, *Postscript to Yesterday*, 6; Mulvagh and Weber, 208; Benway, 77; Lehr, 213; O'Connor, *Golden Summers*, 244–245; *New York*

Times, August 20, 1904; Preservation Society of Newport, *TFO*, 5–6; Ferguson, 22. Paul Miller, architectural historian for the Preservation Society of Newport County, helpfully pointed out to me that while the story of Tessie's request to the navy appears in nearly every publication, extensive research has shown that this oft-repeated spectacular example of Gilded Age entitlement is, in fact, only a legend.

40. Yarnall, 177.
41. Lehr, 81; Decies, 91, 105.
42. Lehr, 131.
43. Quoted in Patterson, *Best Families*, 70.
44. Lehr, 126.
45. Warburton, 6.
46. Lehr, 126.
47. Busbey, 335; Lord, 108; Elliott, 164.
48. Lehr, 125.
49. Low, 161–162.
50. Elliott, 199.
51. Davis, 482.
52. Lewis, *American Country Houses*, 16–17; Warburton, 20; Baker, *Stanny*, 67; Yarnall, 99–101; Mulvagh and Weber, 92; O'Connor, *Golden Summers*, 145–146; Lowe, 77–80; Platt, 144; Downing and Scully, 162.
53. Burne-Jones, 133–134.
54. Lehr, 129.
55. Folsom, 246.
56. *New York Times*, July 11, 1897.
57. Van Rensselaer, *Newport*, 56–57; see also Lowenthal, particularly 131–133.
58. O'Connor, *Golden Summers*, 15.
59. Lehr, 128.
60. Barrett, 127; Strange, 111.
61. Belmont, 85.
62. Morris, *Postscript to Yesterday*, xxii; Townsend, 6.

CHAPTER 21: THE SOCIAL SEASON

1. Gregory, *Worldly Ways*, 179.
2. Almond, 156–158.
3. Friedman, 52.
4. Crockett, 95.
5. Baker, *Stanny*, 164; Wecter, 189.
6. *New York Times*, November 12, 1893.
7. Decies, 194.
8. de Castellane, 38.
9. Lehr, 65.
10. Cable, 36.
11. Baker, *Richard Morris Hunt*, 373–374; Burrows and Wallace, 717; King, *Handbook*, 310.

12. Tolman, 176–177.
13. Tolman, 184; Maurice, 284; Burrows and Wallace, 1,087.
14. King, *Handbook*, 320; Fifth Avenue Bank, 16; Burrows and Wallace, 717; Baker, *Richard Morris Hunt*, 73.
15. Jaher, *The Rich, the Well Born, and the Powerful*, 262.
16. Wecter, 209–210.
17. Homberger, 113–115.
18. Sherwood, 230.
19. Ibid., 236.
20. Carter, 23.
21. Sherwood, 248.
22. Ibid., 231–232.
23. Morris, *Postscript to Yesterday*, xvi–xvii.
24. Sherwood, 44.
25. Ibid., 45–46.
26. Ibid., 240.
27. Ibid., 247–248.
28. Ibid., 244.
29. Thomas, *Delmonico's*, 199.
30. Lehr, 185.
31. Cowles, 132.
32. Lehr, 70–71.
33. Ibid., 186.
34. Pulitzer, 49–50.
35. Chanler, 250.
36. Homberger, 232–233; Pulitzer, 60.
37. Homberger, 232–233; Cowles, 106.
38. Homberger, 225.
39. Burne-Jones, 102.
40. Lehr, 9.
41. Pulitzer, 52.
42. Ibid., 51.
43. Ibid., 52.
44. Collier, 42.
45. Kolodin, 73.
46. Harrison, *Reminiscences Gay and Grave*, 297.
47. Burne-Jones, 119.
48. Kolodin, 66; *New York Times*, October 31, 1908.
49. Gerard, 40.
50. Kolodin, 66.
51. Gates, 95.
52. Kolodin, 67.
53. Pulitzer, 54–55.

CHAPTER 22: THE SOCIETY DINNER PARTY

1. Carter, 257.
2. Gerard, 20.
3. Gregory, *Worldly Ways*, 175.
4. Almond, 112–114.

5. *New York Times*, November 1, 1908.
6. McAllister, 255.
7. Carter, 257.
8. Sherwood, 66–67.
9. Lehr, 77.
10. Wecter, 237.
11. Lehr, 77.
12. McAllister, 299.
13. Crowninshield, 37.
14. McAllister, 258.
15. Carter, 257.
16. Morris, *Postscript to Yesterday*, 11.
17. Carter, 257.
18. Ibid., 201.
19. Pulitzer, 13.
20. Carter, 262; McAllister, 291.
21. Crowninshield, 36.
22. Pulitzer, 17.
23. Carter, 263–264.
24. McAllister, 291.
25. Harrison, *My Life in Service*, 110.
26. Carter, 125, 259, 267.
27. Sherwood, 367.
28. Flanders, 275.
29. Sherwood, 275.
30. Ibid., 356.
31. Ibid., 286.
32. Quoted in Patterson, *Best Families*, 70.
33. Ibid., 85.
34. Sherwood, 270.
35. Beebe, 386.
36. Lehr, 132.
37. Sherwood, 273, 360–362.
38. Ibid., 267.
39. Ibid.
40. Carter, 268.
41. Sherwood, 271.
42. Carter, 260, 360.
43. Sherwood, 276–277.
44. Carter, 261.
45. Sherwood, 311, 313.
46. Ibid., 273.
47. Sherwood, 312–313, 316; Carter, 229.
48. McAllister, 260.
49. Sherwood, 312–313, 316; Carter, 230; McAllister, 262.
50. Carter, 229–230; Sherwood, 311–313; McAllister, 263.
51. Black, 171; Sherwood, 268, 274, 360.
52. Sherwood, 308, 310, 312, 316, 320.
53. Sherwood, 308, 360–361; Carter, 261.
54. Sherwood, 274.
55. Sherwood, 274, 312; Carter, 229–230, 261; McAllister, 281–283.
56. Sherwood, 272, 302.
57. Crowninshield, 38.
58. Sherwood, 312.
59. Crowninshield, 39.
60. Chanler, 236.

CHAPTER 23: SOCIETY BALLS

1. Homberger, 187.
2. Sherwood, 147.
3. Pulitzer, *Society*, 94–95.
4. Sherwood, 71, 142–143.
5. Aldrich, 117.
6. Sherwood, 148.
7. Ibid., 356.
8. Cited in Aldrich, 35.
9. Sherwood, 143.
10. Balsan, 27.
11. Pulitzer, 115.
12. Harrison, *The Well-Bred Girl*, 14–15.
13. Sherwood, 144.
14. Ibid.
15. Ibid., 48, 145.
16. Aldrich, 103–105.
17. See Aldrich, 15, 132–133.
18. Sherwood, 147.
19. Turbeville, 130.
20. Sherwood, 145; Aldrich, 61–62.
21. Cited in Aldrich, 62.
22. Sherwood, 155–157.
23. Aldrich, 182–185.
24. Sherwood, 156–157.
25. *New York Times*, January 19, 1897.
26. *New York Times*, October 31, 1908.
27. O'Connor, *Golden Summers*, 59.
28. Lehr, 74.
29. See *New York Times*, January 19, 1897, and January 10, 1905.
30. Lehr, 75–76.
31. Kolodin, 66–67; see *New York Times*, January 22, 1884; January 19, 1897; and January 10, 1905.
32. For example, see *New York Times*, January 22, 1884; January 19, 1897; and January 10, 1905.
33. *New York Times*, January 30, 1900.
34. See *New York Times*, January 22, 1884; January 19, 1897; and January 10, 1905.
35. Lehr, 77.
36. *New York Times*, January 22, 1884; January 19, 1897; and January 10, 1905.
37. Martin, *Things I Remember*, 238–239.
38. Dunlop, 27.
39. Beckert, 1–2.
40. *New York Times*, February 3, 1897.
41. Martin, *Things I Remember*, 239.
42. *New York Times*, January 23, 1897.

43. Martin, *Things I Remember*, 240.
44. *New York Tribune*, February 11, 1897.
45. Almond, 184; Beard, *After the Ball*, 166; Beebe, 117; Crockett, 73; *New York Times*, February 11, 1897.
46. Beebe, 117; Beard, *After the Ball*, 166; Crockett, 73; *New York Times*, February 11, 1897.
47. Crockett, 73.
48. *New York Times*, February 3, 1897; Josephson, 339; Crockett, 73–74.
49. Martin, *Things I Remember*, 240; Beebe, 120; *New York Times*, February 21, 1897; *New York World*, February 12, 1897; Wecter, 369; Crockett, 74.
50. *New York Times*, February 21, 1897; *New York World*, February 12, 1897; Beard, *After the Ball*, 167; Wecter, 369; Munn, 212.
51. *New York World*, February 12, 1897.
52. Brann, 1:120.
53. Lehr, 70.
54. *New York World*, February 12, 1897.
55. Martin, *Things I Remember*, 241.
56. Ibid.; Gerard, 71; *New York Times*, February 12, 1897; *New York World*, February 12, 1897; Lehr, 49.
57. de Wolfe, 116.
58. Crockett, 74–75.
59. *New York Sun*, February 12, 1897; *New York World*, February 12, 1897.
60. *New York World*, February 12, 1897.
61. Crockett, 81; *New York World*, February 12, 1897.
62. Beebe, 119.
63. Crocket, 75–76; Beebe, 120.
64. *New York Times*, February 12, 1897.
65. *New York Sun*, February 12, 1897.
66. Brann, 1:123.
67. Gates, 99.

CHAPTER 24: THE DOLLAR PRINCESSES

1. Almond, 116.
2. Gates, 97.
3. Beebe, 155.
4. Widow of American Diplomat, 202.
5. Quoted in Patterson, *Best Families*, 80.
6. Beebe, 157.
7. Gregory, *Worldly Ways*, 22.
8. Perrot, 4.
9. Williams, *It Was Such Fun*, 162.
10. Widow of American Diplomat, 50.
11. Nicholls, 83.
12. Sherwood, 467.

13. Cornwallis-West, 60.
14. Eliot, 94.
15. Sherwood, 477.
16. Beard, *Gentleman*, 63.
17. Amory, *Who Killed Society?*, 229.
18. Quoted in Eliot, 31.
19. Amory, *Who Killed Society?*, 229.
20. *New York Times*, September 27, 1903.
21. Brann, 1:355.
22. Balsan, 16.
23. Ibid., 25.
24. Ibid., 5, 11.
25. Lady Sarah Spencer-Churchill to the author, May 2000.
26. Ibid.
27. Strange, 26.
28. Balsan, 40.
29. Ibid., 30.
30. Vanderbilt, *Queen*, 45.
31. Brugh, 57–58.
32. Balsan, 36.
33. *New York Times*, November 25, 1926.
32. Balsan, 37.
33. Lady Sarah Spencer-Churchill to the author, May 2000.
36. Balsan, 37–38.
37. *New York Times*, November 25, 1926.
38. Balsan, 38; *New York Herald*, August 29, 1895; *New York Times*, August 29, 1895; Barrett, 115.
39. Lady Sarah Spencer-Churchill to the author, May 2000.
40. Balsan, 40.
41. Wecter, 408.
42. Myers, 2:273.
43. *New York Times*, November 3, 1895.
44. Vanderbilt, *Fortune's Children*, 164–165.
45. *New York Times*, November 7, 1895; *New York World*, November 7, 1895.
46. Balsan, 41.
47. *New York Times*, November 7, 1895.
48. Balsan, 41.
49. *New York Times*, November 7, 1895.
50. *New York World*, November 2, 1895.
51. Balsan, 42; *New York Times*, November 7, 1895.
52. *New York Herald*, November 7, 1895.
53. Lady Sarah Spencer-Churchill to the author, May 2000.
54. *New York Times*, November 7, 1895.
55. Balsan, 45.
56. O'Connor, *Goulds*, 301.
57. Ibid.; Brandon, 80; Longstreet, *We All Went to Paris*, 149; Lehr, 227.

58. Renehan, 306.
59. Hoyt, *Goulds*, 147–148.
60. Cited in Brandon, 81.
61. Skinner, 84.
62. Lehr, 227.
63. Beebe, 18.
64. Skinner, 82.
65. Longstreet, *We All Went to Paris*, 150, 153.
66. Hoyt, *Gould*, 148.
67. de Castellane, 15.
68. Beebe, 19.
69. de Castellane, 16.
70. Cologni and Nussbaum, 9.
71. de Castellane, 21.
72. *New York Times*, February 10, 1895.
73. de Castellane, 45.
74. Hoyt, *Goulds*, 208–209.
75. de Castellane, 51.
76. Ibid., 136–140.
77. Hoyt, *Goulds*, 206–209; de Castellane, 152.
78. de Castellane, 166.
79. Ibid., 176.
80. Rousset-Charny, 83–84.
81. Longstreet, *We All Went to Paris*, 151.
82. Rousset-Charny, 87–88; Beebe, 29; Jenkins, 47.
83. Skinner, 85.
84. Brandon, 91–93, 100; Rousset-Charny, 88.
85. de Castellane, 166.
86. Ibid., 170.
87. Decies, 115.
88. de Castellane, 143–145; Jenkins, 47; Longstreet, *We All Went to Paris*, 149.
89. de Castellane, 144.
90. Hoyt, *Goulds*, 212.
91. de Castellane, 131.
92. Ibid., 135–136.
93. O'Connor, *Gould*, 307.
94. de Castellane, 146–148; *New York Times*, July 2, 1898.
95. *New York Times*, January 26, 1900.
96. de Castellane, 207–208.
97. Ibid., 16.
98. Hoyt, *Goulds*, 210; Brandon, 100.
99. de Castellane, 227, 16.
100. Klein, 485.
101. de Castellane, 41.
102. Hoyt, *Goulds*, 210; Brandon, 100.
103. Brandon, 92.
104. Hoyt, *Goulds*, 243; Brandon, 92.
105. Brann, 1:354.
106. Hoyt, *Goulds*, 245; Pearson, 142; de Castellane, 277.

CHAPTER 25: A BREATH OF SCANDAL

1. Martin, *Passing*, 13–14, 30.
2. Ibid., 36; Amory, *Who Killed Society?*, 521; Wecter, 181.
3. Martin, *Passing*, 39; Josephson, 338.
4. de Wolfe, 108.
5. Morris, *Postscript to Yesterday*, 13–14.
6. Duncan, 43.
7. Martin, *Passing*, 33.
8. Lehr, 212.
9. Kavaler, 137; Patterson, *Best Families*, 72; Morris, *Incredible New York*, 253.
10. Lehr, 211; Martin, *Passing*, 32.
11. Lehr, 211.
12. *New York Times*, September 20, 1908; *New York Times*, January 4, 1929; Lehr, 138.
13. Lehr, 138–139.
14. *New York Times*, September 20, 1908.
15. Kavaler, 137.
16. Lehr, 58.
17. Baker, *Stanny*, 345; Beebe, 121–123; Lord, 109.
18. Beebe, 124.
19. Lord, 109; *New York Herald*, February 1, 1905; *New York Times*, February 5, 1905.
20. Beard, *After the Ball*, 173; Lehr, 58; *New York Herald*, February 1, 1905; *New York Times*, February 5, 1905.
21. Beard, *After the Ball*, 171; Lord, 110.
22. Beard, *After the Ball*, 173; *New York Herald*, February 1, 1905; *New York Times*, February 5, 1905.
23. Gerard, 73.
24. Beebe, 124–125; Simon, 117.
25. Beebe, 124–125; Beard, *After the Ball*, 174; Lord, 109; *New York Herald*, February 1, 1905; *New York Times*, February 5, 1905.
26. Beard, *After the Ball*, 174; Lord, 112; Gerard, 73; *New York Herald*, February 1, 1905; *New York Times*, February 5, 1905.
27. Beard, *After the Ball*, 174.
28. Ibid.; Lord, 110.
29. Beard, *After the Ball*, 175; *New York Herald*, February 1, 1905; *New York Times*, February 5, 1905.
30. Beebe, 123; Crockett, 273.
31. Beard, *After the Ball*, 175.
32. Lord, 110; Beebe, 125; *New York Times*, February 5, 1905; *New York Herald*, February 1, 1905.
33. Crockett, 273–274.

34. Baker, *Stanny*, 345; *New York Times*, February 1, 1905; Beebe, 121–123; Lord, 109.
35. Beard, *After the Ball*, 172; *New York Herald*, February 1, 1905; *New York Times*, February 5, 1905.
36. Beebe, 126; Beard, *After the Ball*, 175; Lord, 111; *New York Herald*, February 1, 1905; *New York Sun*, February 5, 1905; *New York Times*, February 5, 1905.
37. Beebe, 125–126; Beard, *After the Ball*, 175; Lord, 111; *New York Times*, February 5, 1905.
38. Beebe, 121; Lehr, 58; Beard, *After the Ball*, 4–5.
39. Crockett, 285.
40. Lord, 113.
41. Gerard, 73.
42. Amory, *Who Killed Society?*, 520; Lord, 114.
43. Ponce De Leon, 142.
44. Morris, *Incredible New York*, 256.
45. Logan, 11.
46. Ibid., 112.
47. *New York Times* Times, May 18, 1920.
48. Wecter, 371; *New York Times*, May 18, 1920; Logan, 67 passim.
49. Beebe, 96–97; Barrett, 121.
50. Barrett, 121.
51. Ibid.
52. Strange, 67.
53. Barrett, 121.
54. Logan, 20.
55. *New York Times*, July 7, 1905.
56. Logan, 138.
57. Ibid., 138–139.
58. Ibid., 139.
59. Morris, *Postscript to Yesterday*, 20.
60. Brann, 1966.
61. Logan, 12.
62. Ibid., 141–142.
63. Beebe, 98–99.
64. Ibid., 99.
65. Crockett, 263; Beebe, 100–101; Caldwell, 13; Logan, 59–62.
66. O'Connor, *Golden Summers*, 119.
67. Logan, 48.
68. Amory, *Who Killed Society?*, 541.
69. Lewis, *Ladies*, 228.
70. *Collier's*, November 5, 1904, 63.
71. *Collier's*, August 5, 1905, 43.
72. Logan, 52.
73. Ibid., 24–29.
74. Logan, 53; O'Connor, *Courtroom Warrior*, 161.

75. Logan, 165.
76. Ibid., 173–174.
77. Logan, 163; O'Connor, *Courtroom Warrior*, 162–163.
78. O'Connor, *Courtroom Warrior*, 163.
79. Logan, 187.
80. Ibid., 208.
81. Baker, *Stanny*, 149 passim; Lowe, 136–142; Burrows and Wallace, 147–148; Baldwin, 199–201; Silver, 52.
82. Baker, *Stanny*, 319.
83. Chanler, 256.
84. Lehr, 187.
85. Baker, *Stanny*, 132, 273–277; Lessard, 202.
86. Lessard, 203.
87. Baker, *Stanny*, 321–322; Thaw, *Prodigal Days*, 8–28.
88. Baker, Stanny, 321–324; Thaw, *Prodigal Days*, 40–41; *New York Times*, February 8, 1907.
89. Baker, *Stanny*, 325; Thaw, *Prodigal Days*, 41–42.
90. Baker, *Stanny*, 325.
91. Thaw, *The Traitor*, 232.
92. Lessard, 253.
93. Thaw, *The Traitor*, 230; Baker, *Stanny*, 325.
94. Thaw, *Prodigal Days*, 52.
95. Baker, *Stanny*, 331; *New York Times*, July 14, 1906; *New York Tribune*, July 14, 1906.
96. Baker, *Stanny*, 331.
97. Thaw, *Prodigal Days*, 100–104.
98. Baker, *Stanny*, 332–333.
99. Lessard, 218.
100. Lowe, 320.
101. Thaw, *The Traitor*, 145; Lord, 115.
102. Baker, *Stanny*, 373–376.
103. Thaw, *The Traitor*, 145–146.
104. *New York Times*, June 29, 1906.
105. *New York Evening Journal*, June 29, 1906.
106. Lessard, 16.
107. Amory, *Who Killed Society?*, 367; Lowe, 325. See Baker, *Stanny*, chap. 25, for more information on Thaw's trials.

CHAPTER 26: SAILING TO OBLIVION

1. Martin, *Passing*, 104.
2. Ibid., 111.
3. Ibid., 123.
4. Ibid., 114–116.
5. *New York Times*, November 1, 1908.

6. Ibid., January 10, 1905.
7. Ibid., September 15, 1908.
8. Gates, 100.
9. Ibid., 101; *New York Times*, September 20, 1908; Kavaler, 140; Patterson, *First Four Hundred*, 40–41; *New York World*, January 8, 1905.
10. Gates, 101.
11. Ibid.
12. *New York Times*, October 30, 1908.
13. Morris, *Incredible New York*, 258.
14. *New York Times*, October 30, 1908.
15. Ibid., and October 31, 1908.
16. Ibid., October 31, 1908.
17. Ibid., November 1, 1908.
18. Ibid., and November 2, 1908.
19. Gates, 118; Cowles, 142; Amory, *Who Killed Society?*, 480; Wilson, 207.
20. Davie, 79.
21. Wilson, 206–207.
22. Davie, 79–80.
23. Brinnin, 375; Kathrens, *American Splendor*, 191, 197.
24. Eaton and Haas, *Journey*, 49.
25. Eaton and Haas, *Titanic*, 75.
26. Lord, 270; Geller, 70.
27. Eaton and Haas, *Journey*, 49–50.
28. Russell, 10.
29. Eaton and Haas, *Journey*, 49–50.
30. *Ocean Liners Past*, 77.
31. Ibid., 69.
32. Ibid., 69–71.
33. *Ocean Liners Past*, 133; Lynch and Marschall, 59.
34. *Ocean Liners Past*, 69.
35. Ibid.
36. These are the couple's presumed stateroom assignments. Jack's valet is known to have occupied C62, while Madeleine's private nurse had cabin C45. The issue of precise occupation of staterooms on *Titanic* remains an ongoing work of scholarship, but it seems likely, based on available evidence, that these were indeed the Astors' accommodations during the fatal voyage. See Eaton and Haas, *Titanic*, 75; http://www.encyclopedia-titanica.org/cabins.html.
37. *Ocean Liners Past*, 90–91.
38. Eaton and Haas, *Titanic*, 75; see also *Titanic Commutator* 10, no. 3 (November 1995–January 1996): 35.
39. *Report on the Loss of the Titanic*, v.
40. Ibid., 26–27.
41. *Ocean Liners Past*, 160 passim.

42. Williamson, 112.
43. Heyer, 23.
44. Committe on Commerce, 74.
45. Gates, 121.
46. Lynch and Marschall, 63; *Ocean Liners Past*, 90.
47. Eaton and Haas, *Titanic*, 149.
48. Lynch and Marschall, 130.
49. Amory, *Who Killed Society?*, 480.
50. Kuntz, 409.
51. Gates, 121–122.
52. Eaton and Haas, *Journey*, 75; Lynch and Marschall, 130.
53. Gates, 121–122.
54. Kuntz, 433.
55. Amory, *Who Killed Society?*, 480.
56. Gates, 122.
57. Kuntz, 493.
58. Lynch and Marschall, 114; Eaton and Haas, *Journey*, 75.
59. *Report on the Loss of Titanic*, 41.
60. Gates, 122.
61. Eaton and Haas, *Titanic*, 179.
62. *Report on the Loss of Titanic*, 41.
63. Lynch and Marschall, 166.
64. Ibid., 174.
65. Eaton and Haas, *Journey*, 108.
66. Ibid., Kavaler, 168; Amory, *Who Killed Society?*, 480; Brinnin, 375.
67. Patterson, *Best Families*, 22.
68. Strange, 110.

EPILOGUE

1. Davie, 309; *New York Times*, March 28, 1940.
2. *New York Times*, June 11, 1958.
3. Vanderbilt, *Fortune's Children*, 260–261.
4. Wecter, 340.
5. *New York Times*, January 26, 1933; *New York Times*, February 2, 1933.
6. Lady Sarah Spencer-Churchill to the author, May 2000.
7. Sloane, 191.
8. See Vickers, 106–107.
9. Lewis, *Ladies*, 229.
10. Cited in Vickers, 108.
11. Balsan, 192.
12. See Stuart, 466.
13. Montgomery, 176–179.
14. Patterson, *Vanderbilts*, 280.
15. *New York Times*, March 1, 1942.
16. Ibid., January 8, 1953.
17. Strange, 53–54.
18. *New York Tribune*, February 8, 1913.
19. Beebe, 238.

20. *New York Times*, January 4, 1929.
21. Ibid., June 14, 1944.
22. Ibid., November 30, 1961.
23. *Time*, April 13, 1925.
24. *New York Times*, May 29, 1933.
25. Ibid., December 1, 1961.
26. Beebe, 140.
27. *New York Times*, May 16, 1918.
28. Ibid., May 18, 1920.
29. *Los Angeles Times*, January 19, 1967.
30. Foreman and Stimson, 41, 45.
31. Ibid., 67; King, *Vanderbilt Homes*, 36.

32. Vanderbilt, *Queen*, 240.
33. Patterson, *Vanderbilts*, 280.
34. Foreman and Stimson, 323.
35. *Boston Globe*, October 30, 2005.
36. Vanderbilt, *Queen*, 171.
37. Bagehot, 86.
38. Vanderbilt, *Queen*, 200.
39. Tomkins, 71.
40. Patterson, *Vanderbilts*, 124.
41. Tomkins, 190; Patterson, *Vanderbilts*, 125–126.
42. Vanderbilt, *Queen*, 200.

BIBLIOGRAPHY

BOOKS

Aldrich, Elizabeth. *From the Ballroom to Hell: Grace and Folly in Nineteenth Century Dance.* Evanston, Ill: Northwestern University Press, 1991.

Allen, Armin Brand. *The Cornelius Vanderbilts of the Breakers: A Family Retrospective.* Newport, R.I.: The Preservation Society of Newport County, 1995.

Almond, Gregory A. *Plutocracy and Politics in New York City.* Boulder, Colo.: Westview Press, 1997.

Amory, Cleveland. *The Last Resorts.* New York: Harper & Brothers, 1952.

———. *Who Killed Society?* New York: Harper & Brothers, 1960.

Andrews, Wayne. *The Vanderbilt Legend.* New York: Harcourt, Brace, 1941.

Aslet, Clive. *The American Country House.* New Haven, Conn: Yale University Press, 1990.

Auchincloss, Louis. *The Vanderbilt Era.* New York: Charles Scribner's Sons, 1989.

Baedeker, Karl. *The United States.* New York: Baedeker, 1893.

Bagehot, Walter. *The English Constitution.* Cambridge, U.K.: Cambridge University Press, 2001.

Baker, Paul R. *Richard Morris Hunt.* Cambridge, Mass: MIT Press, 1980.

———. *Stanny: The Gilded Life of Stanford White.* New York: Free Press, 1989.

Baldwin, Charles G. *Stanford White.* New York: Dodd, Mead, 1931.

Balsan, Consuelo Vanderbilt. *The Glitter and the Gold.* London: William Heinemann, 1953.

Barrault, Jean-Michel. *Yachting: The Golden Age.* London: Hachette, 2004.

Barrett, *Richmond. Good Old Summer Days.* New York: Appleton-Century, 1941.

Beard, Geoffrey. *The Compleat Gentleman.* New York: Rizzoli, 1993.

Beard, Patricia. *After the Ball: Gilded Age Secrets, Boardroom Betrayals, and the Party That Ignited the Great Wall Street Scandal of 1905.* New York: HarperCollins, 2003.

Beckert, Sven. *The Monied Metropolis: New York and the Consolidation of the American Bourgeoisie, 1850–1896.* Cambridge, U.K.: Cambridge University Press, 2001.

Beebe, Lucius. *The Big Spenders.* Garden City, N.Y.: Doubleday, 1966.

Beer, Thomas. *The Mauve Decade: American Life at the End of the Nineteenth Century.* New York: Alfred A. Knopf, 1926.

Belmont, Eleanor Robson. *The Fabric of Memory.* New York: Farrar, Strauss, & Cudahy, 1957.

Bennett, Arnold. *Your United States: Impressions of a First Visit.* New York: 1912.

Benway, Ann. *A Guidebook to Newport Mansions.* Newport, R.I.: Preservation Society of Newport County, 1984.

Birmingham, Stephen. *The Grandes Dames.* New York: Simon & Schuster, 1982.

———. *The Right People: The Social Establishment in America.* Boston: Little, Brown, 1959.

Black, David. *The King of Fifth Avenue: The Fortunes of August Belmont.* New York: Dial Press, 1981.

Bourget, Paul. *Outre-Mer: Impressions of America.* New York: Charles Scribner's Sons, 1895.

Boyer, M. Christine. *Manhattan Manners: Architecture and Style, 1850–1900.* New York: Rizzoli, 1985.

Brandon, Ruth. *The Dollar Princesses: Sagas of Upward Nobility, 1870–1914.* New York: Alfred A. Knopf, 1980.

Brann, William Cowper. *Brann the Iconoclast: A Collection of the Writings of W. C. Brann.* Waco, Tex.: Herz Brothers, 1911.

Brinnin, John Malcolm. *The Sway of the Grand Saloon: A Social History of the North Atlantic.* New York: Barnes & Noble, 1986.

Brough, James. *Consuelo: Portrait of an American Heiress.* New York: Coward, McCann, & Geoghegan, 1979.

Brown, Henry Collins. *Fifth Avenue Old and New, 1824–1924.* New York: Fifth Avenue Association, 1924.

Browne, Junius Henry. *The Great Metropolis: A Mirror of New York.* Hartford, Conn.: American Publishing, 1869.

Bryan, John M. *Biltmore Estate: The Most Distinguished Private Place.* New York: Rizzoli, 1994.

Burne-Jones, Sir Philip. *Dollars and Diplomacy.* New York: D. Appleton, 1904.

Burrows, Edwin G., and Mike Wallace. *Gotham: A History of New York City to 1898.* Oxford, U.K.: Oxford University Press, 1999.

Busbey, Katherine G. *Home Life in America.* London: Metheun, 1910.

Cable, Mary. *Top Drawer: American High Society from the Gilded Age to the Roaring Twenties.* New York: Athenaeum, 1984.

Caldwell, Mark. *A Short History of Rudeness.* New York: St. Martin's Press, 2000.

Calkins, Carroll C., edi. *Great Gardens of America.* New York: Coward-McCann, 1969.

Carley, Rachel, and Rosemary Rennicke. *A Guide to Biltmore Estate.* Asheville, N.C.: The Biltmore Company, 1997.

Carter, Mary Elizabeth. *Millionaire Households and Their Domestic Economy.* New York: D. Appleton, 1903.

de Castellane, Boni. *How I Discovered America: Confessions of the Marquis Boni de Castellane.* New York: Alfred A. Knopf, 1924.

Cavalier, Julian. *American Castles.* New York: A. S. Barnes, 1973.

Chanler, Margaret. *Roman Spring.* Boston: Little, Brown, 1934.

Churchill, Allen. *The Splendor Seekers.* New York: Grosset & Dunlap, 1974.

Clews, Henry. *Fifty Years in Wall Street.* New York: Irving, 1908.

Coleman, Elizabeth Ann. *The Opulent Era: Fashions of Worth, Doucet and Pingat.* New York: Thames & Hudson, 1989.

Collier, Price. *America and the Americans, From a French Point of View.* New York: Charles Scribner's Sons, 1897.

Cologni, Franco, and Eric Nussbaum. *Platinum by Cartier: Triumphs of the Jewelers' Art.* New York: Harry N. Abrams, 1995.

Committee on Commerce, United States Senate. *Titanic Disaster: Report of the Committee on Commerce, United States Senate.* Washington, D.C.: U.S. Government Printing Office, 1912.

Cornwallis-West, Mrs. George. *The Reminiscences of Lady Randolph Churchill.* New York: Century, 1908.

Covington, Howard E. *Lady on The Hill: How Biltmore Estate Became an American Icon.* New York: John Wiley & Sons, 2006.

Cowles, Virginia. *The Astors: Story of a Transatlantic Family.* London: Weidenfeld & Nicolson, 1979.

Craig, Theresa. *Edith Wharton: A House Full of Rooms: Architecture, Interiors, and Gardens.* New York: Monacelli Press, 1996.

Crockett, Albert Stevens. *Peacocks on Parade.* New York: Sears, 1931.

Croffut, William A. *The Vanderbilts and the Story of Their Fortune.* New York: Belford, Clarke, 1886.

Crowninshield, Francis W. *Manners for the Metropolis.* New York: D. Appleton, 1909.

Davie, Michael. *The* Titanic: *The Full Story of a Tragedy.* London: Bodley Head, 1986.

Dayton, Abram C. *Last Days of Knickerbocker Life in New York.* New York: G. W. Harlan, 1882.

Decies, Elizabeth, Lady (Elizabeth Wharton Drexel Dahlgren Lehr). *The Turn of the World.* Philadelphia: J. B. Lippincott, 1937.

Dedmon, Emmett. *Fabulous Chicago.* New York: Random House, 1953.

Depew, Chauncey M. *My Memories of Eighty Years.* New York: Charles Scribner's Sons, 1924.

Desmond, Harry W., and Herbert Croly. *Stately Homes in America from Colonial Times to the Present Day.* New York: Appleton, 1903.

de Wolfe, Elsie. *After All.* New York: Harper & Brothers, 1935.

Downing, Antoinette F., and Vincent J. Scully. *The Architectural Heritage of Newport, Rhode Island.* New York: Clarkson Potter, 1967.

Dressler, Marie. *My Own Story.* Boston: Little, Brown, 1934.

Dudden, Faye. *Serving Women: Household Service in Nineteenth Century America.* Middletown, Conn.: Wesleyan University Press, 1983.

Duncan, Isadora. *My Life.* Garden City, N.Y.: Garden City, 1927.

Dunlop, M. H. *Gilded City: Scandal and Sensation in Turn of the Century New York.* New York: William Morrow, 2000.

Dunwell, Frances F. *The Hudson River Highlands.* New York: Columbia University Press, 1991.

Dwight, Eleanor. *Edith Wharton: An Extraordinary Life.* New York: Harry N. Abrams, 1994.

Dwyer, Michael Middleton. *Houses of the Hudson River.* New York: Bulfinch Press, 2003.

Eaton, John P., and Charles A. Haas. Titanic: *A Journey Through Time.* New York: W. W. Norton, 1999.

———. Titanic: *Triumph and Tragedy.* New York: W. W. Norton, 1995.

Edel, Leon, ed. *Henry James's Letters.* Cambridge, Mass: Harvard University Press, 1984.

Eliot, Elizabeth. *Heiresses and Coronets.* New York: McDowell, Obolensky, 1959.

Elliott, Maud Howe. *This Was My Newport.* Cambridge, Mass.: Mythology, 1944.

Erenberg, Lewis. *Steppin' Out: New York Nightlife and the Transformation of American Culture, 1890–1930.* Westport, Conn.: Greenwood Press, 1981.

Ferguson, J. Walton. *Rosecliff.* Newport, R.I.: Preservation Society of Newport County, 1977.

Field, Frederick Vanderbilt. *From Right to Left.* Westport, Conn.: Lawrence Hill, 1983.

Fifth Avenue Bank. *Fifth Avenue: Glances at the Vicissitudes and Romance of a World-Renowned Thoroughfare.* New York: Fifth Avenue Bank, 1915.

Fiske, Stephen. *Off-Hand Portraits of Prominent New Yorkers.* New York: G. R. Lockwood & Son, 1884.

Flanders, Judith. *Inside the Victorian Home.* New York: W. W. Norton, 2003.

Flynn, John T. *Men of Wealth: The Story of Twelve Significant Fortunes from the Renaissance to the Present Day.* New York: Simon & Schuster, 1941.

Folsom, Merrill. *Great American Mansions and Their Stories.* Mamaroneck, NY: Hastings House, 1963.

Foreman, John, and Robbe Pierce Stimson. *The Vanderbilts and the Gilded Age.* New York: St. Martin's Press, 1991.

Fowler, Marian. *In a Gilded Cage.* Toronto: Random House, 1993.

Friedman, B. H. *Gertrude Vanderbilt Whitney.* Garden City, N.Y.: Doubleday, 1978.

Gale, Robert L. *The Gay Nineties in America: A Cultural Dictionary of the 1890.* Westport, Conn.: Greenwood Press, 1992.

Gates, John D. *The Astor Family.* Garden City, N.Y.: Doubleday, 1981.

Geller, Judith B. Titanic: *Women and Children First.* New York: W. W. Norton, 1998

Gerard, James W. *My First Eighty-three Years in America: The Memoirs of James W. Gerard.* Garden City, N.Y.: Doubleday, 1951.

Gernsheim, Alison. *Victorian and Edwardian Fashion.* New York: Dover, 1981.

Goldsmith, Barbara. *Little Gloria, Happy At Last.* New York: Alfred A. Knopf, 1980.

Gregory, Alexis. *Families of Fortune: Life in the Gilded Age.* New York: Rizzoli, 1993.

Gregory, Eliot. *Worldly Ways and Byways.* New York: Charles Scribner's Sons, 1899.

Griswold, Mac, and Eleanor Weller. *The Golden Age of American Gardens.* New York: Harry N. Abrams, 1991.

Hall, Lee. *Olmsted's America.* Boston: Bulfinch Press, 1995.

Hamlin, Talbot. *Greek Revival Architecture in America.* New York: Oxford University Press, 1944.

Hammack, David C. *Power and Society: Greater New York at the Turn of the Century.* New York: Russell Sage Foundation, 1982.

Harrison, Constance Cary. *Recollections Grave and Gay.* New York: Charles Scribner's Sons, 1911.

———. *The Well-Bred Girl in Society.* Garden City, N.Y.: Doubleday, 1904.

Harrison, Rosina. *My Life in Service.* New York: Viking, 1975.

Hewitt, Mark Alan. *The Architect and the American Country House, 1890–1940.* New Haven, Conn.: Yale University Press, 1990.

Heyer, Paul. Titanic *Legacy: Disaster as Media Event and Myth.* Westport, Conn: Praeger, 1995.

Holbrook, Stewart H. *The Age of the Moguls.* Garden City, N.Y.: Doubleday, 1954.

Homberger, Eric. *Mrs. Astor's New York: Money and Social Power in a Gilded Age.* New Haven, Conn.: Yale University Press, 2002.

Horn, Pamela. *The Rise and Fall of the Victorian Servant.* Gloucester, U.K.: Alan Sutton, 1986.

Howe, Katherine S., Alice Cooney Frelinghuysen, Catherine Hoover Voorsanger, Simon Jervis, Hans Ottomeyer, Marc Bascou, Ann Claggett Wood, and Sophia Riefstahl. *Herter Brothers: Furniture and Interiors for a Gilded Age.* New York: Harry N. Abrams, 1994.

Hoyt, Edwin P. *The Goulds: A Social History.* New York: Weybright & Talley, 1969.

———. *The Vanderbilts and Their Fortune.* Garden City, N.Y.: Doubleday, 1962.

Huggett, Frank E. *Carriages at Eight: Horse-Drawn Society in Victorian and Edwardian Times.* New York: Charles Scribner's Sons, 1979.

Jackson, Richard S., and Cornelia Brooke Gilder. *Houses of the Berkshires, 1870–1930.* New York: Acanthus Press, 2006.

Jaher, Frederic Cople, ed. *The Rich, the Well Born, and the Powerful.* Champaign: University of Illinois Press, 1973.

———. *The Urban Establishment.* Champaign: University of Illinois Press, 1982.

James, Henry. *The American Scene.* New York: Charles Scriber's Sons, 1946.

Jenkins, Alan. *The Rich Rich: The Story of the Big Spenders.* New York: G. P. Putnam's Sons, 1978.

Josephson, Matthew. *The Robber Barons: The Great American Capitalists, 1861–1901.* New York: Harcourt, Brace, 1934.

Karolevitz, Robert F. *This Was Pioneer Motoring*. Seattle: Superior Publishing, 1968.

Kathrens, Michael C. *American Splendor: The Residential Architecture of Horace Trumbauer*. New York: Acanthus Press, 2002.

———. *Great Houses of New York, 1880–1930*. New York: Acanthus Press, 2005.

Kaveler, Lucy. *The Astors: A Family Chronicle of Pomp and Power*. New York: Dodd, Mead, 1966.

King, Moses. *King's Handbook of New York City*. New York: Moses King, 1892.

King, Robert. *The Vanderbilt Homes*. New York: Rizzoli, 1989.

Klein, Maury. *The Life and Legend of Jay Gould*. Baltimore: Johns Hopkins University Press, 1986.

Kolodin, Irving. *The Story of the Metropolitan Opera, 1883–1950: A Candid History*. New York: Alfred A. Knopf, 1953.

Kowsky, Francis R. *Country, Park, & City: The Architecture and Life of Calvert Vaux*. New York: Oxford University Press, 1998.

Kuntz, Tom, ed. *The* Titanic *Disaster Hearings: The Official Transcripts of the 1912 Senate Investigation*. New York: Pocket Books, 1998.

Lehr, Elizabeth Drexel. *King Lehr and the Gilded Age*. London: Constable, 1935.

Lessard, Suzannah. *The Architect of Desire: Beauty and Danger in the Stanford White Family*. New York: Dial Press, 1996.

Lewis, Alfred Allan. *Ladies and Not-So-Gentle Women*. New York: Viking Penguin, 2000.

Lewis, Arnold. *American Country Houses of the Gilded Age: Sheldon's "Artistic Country Seats."* New York: Dover, 1982.

Lewis, Arnold, James Turner, and Steven McQuillin. *The Opulent Interiors of the Gilded Age*. New York: Dover, 1987.

Logan, Andy. *The Man Who Robbed the Robber Barons*. New York: W. W. Norton, 1965.

Longstreet, Abby Buchanan. *Social Etiquette of New York*. New York: D. Appleton, 1879.

Longstreet, Stephen. *We All Went to Paris: Americans in the City of Light, 1776–1971*. New York: Macmillan, 1972.

Lord, Walter. *The Good Years*. New York: Harper & Row, 1960.

Loring, John. *Tiffany Diamonds*. New York: Harry N. Abrams, 2005.

Low, A. Maurice. *America at Home*. London: George Newnes, 1910.

Lowe, David Garrard. *Stanford White's New York*. New York: Watson-Guptill, 1996.

Lucie-Smith, Edward, and Celestine Dars. *How the Rich Lived: The Painter as Witness, 1870–1914*. New York: Padding Press, 1976.

Lynch, Don, and Ken Marschall. Titanic: *An Illustrated History*. New York: Hyperion/Madison Press, 1992.

Madsen, Axel. *John Jacob Astor: America's First Multimillionaire*. New York: John Wiley & Sons, 2001.

Maher, James T. *The Twilight of Splendor*. Boston: Little, Brown, 1975.

Marshall, Scott. *The Mount: Home of Edith Wharton*. Lenox, Mass.: Edith Wharton Restoration, 1997.

Martin, Frederick Townsend. *The Passing of the Idle Rich*. Garden City, N.Y.: Doubleday, Page, 1911.

———. *Things I Remember*. London: Eveleigh Nash, 1913.

Maurice, Arthur B. *Fifth Avenue*. New York: Dodd, Mead, 1918.

McAlester, Virginia and Lee. *Great American Houses and Their Architectural Styles*. New York: Abbeville Press, 1994.

McAllister, Ward. *Society as I Have Found It.* New York: Cassell, 1890.

Mead, Theodore H. *Horsemanship for Women.* New York: Harper & Brothers, 1887.

Metcalf, Pauline C., ed. *Ogden Codman and the Decoration of Houses.* Boston: Boston Athenaeum/David R. Godine, 1988.

Mills, C. Wright. *The Power Elite.* Oxford, U.K.: Oxford University Press, 2000.

Montgomery, Maureen E. *Gilded Prostitution: Status, Money, and Transatlantic Marriages, 1870–1914.* London: Routledge, 1989.

Morris, Lloyd. *Incredible New York.* New York: Random House, 1951.

———. *Not So Long Ago.* New York: Random House, 1949.

———. *Postscript to Yesterday.* New York: Random House, 1947.

Moss, Roger W. *The American Country House.* New York: Henry Holt, 1990.

Mowbray, Jay Henry. *The Sinking of the* Titanic. Washington, D.C.: George Bertron, 1912.

Mulvagh, Jane, and Mark A. Weber. *Newport Houses.* New York: Rizzoli, 1989.

Munn, Geoffrey C. *Tiaras: A History of Splendour.* Woodbridge, Suffolk, U.K.: Antique Collectors' Club, 2001.

Myers, Gustavus. *History of the Great American Fortunes.* Chicago: Charles H. Kerr, 1911.

National Trust for Historic Preservation. *Lyndhurst: A Guide to the Estate and Grounds.* Washington, D.C.: National Trust for Historic Preservation, 1995.

Nichols, Charles Wilbur de Lyon. *The 469 Ultra-Fashionables of America.* New York: Broadway, 1912.

Nicolson, Nigel. *Great Houses of the Western World.* New York: G. P. Putnam's Sons, 1968.

Oakes, Donald T., ed. *A Pride of Palaces: Lenox Summer Cottages 1883–1933.* Lenox, Mass.: Lenox Library Association, 1981.

Obolensky, Prince Serge. *One Man in His Time.* New York: McDowell, Obolensky, 1958.

Ocean Liners of the Past: Olympic *and* Titanic *1911.* Reprint, Wellingsborough, Northamptonshire, U.K.: Patrick Stephens, 1988.

O'Connor, Harvey. *The Astors.* New York: Alfred A. Knopf, 1941.

O'Connor, Richard. *Courtroom Warrior.* Boston: Little, Brown, 1963.

———. *The Golden Summers.* New York: G. P. Putnam's Sons, 1974.

———. *Gould's Millions.* Garden City, N.Y.: Doubleday, 1962.

O'Leary, Elizabeth. *From Morning to Night: Domestic Service in Maymont House and the Gilded Age South.* Charlottesville, Va.: University of Virginia Press, 2003.

Owens, Carole. *The Berkshire Cottages.* Stockbridge, Mass.: Cottage Press, 1984.

Page, Marian. *Historic Houses Restored and Preserved.* New York: Watson-Guptill, 1976.

Panaggio, Leonard J. *Portrait of Newport II.* Newport, R.I.: Bank of Newport, 1994.

Pardee, Bettie Bearden. *Private Newport.* New York: Bulfinch Press, 2004.

Patrick, James B., ed. *Vanderbilt Mansion.* Little Compton, R.I.: Fort Church, 1988.

Patterson, Jerry E. *The Best Families: The Town & Country Social Directory, 1846–1996.* New York: Harry N. Abrams, 1996.

———. *Fifth Avenue: The Best Address.* New York: Rizzoli, 1998.

———. *The First Four Hundred: Mrs. Astor's New York in the Gilded Age.* New York: Rizzoli, 2000.

———. *The Vanderbilts.* New York: Harry N. Abrams, 1989.

Pearson, Hesketh. *The Marrying Americans.* New York: Coward McCann, 1961.

Peltz, Mary Ellis. *Behind the Gold Curtain: The Story of the Metropolitan Opera, 1883–1950.* New York: Farrar, Straus, 1950.

Perrot, Philippe. *Fashioning the Bourgeoisie: A History of Clothing in the Nineteenth Century.* Princeton, N.J.: Princeton University Press, 1994.

Persons, Stow. *The Decline in American Gentility.* New York: Columbia University Press, 1973.

Phillips, Clare, Vivienne Becker, Ulysses Grant Dietz, Alice Cooney Frelinghuysen, John Loring, and Katherine Purcell. *Bejewelled by Tiffany.* New Haven, Conn.: Yale University Press, 2006.

Pinchot, Gifford. *Breaking New Ground.* Seattle: University of Washington Press, 1974.

Platt, Frederick. *America's Gilded Age: Its Architecture and Decoration.* New York: A. S. Barnes, 1976.

Ponce De Leon, Charles L. *Self-Exposure: Human-Interest Journalism and the Emergence of Celebrity in America, 1890–1940.* Chapel Hill, N.C.: University of North Carolina Press, 2002.

Preservation Society of Newport County. *Marble House.* Newport, R.I.: Preservation Society of Newport County, 1965.

Pulitzer, Ralph. *New York Society on Parade.* New York: Harper & Brothers, 1910.

Randall, Monica. *Phantoms of the Hudson Valley: The Glorious Estates of a Lost Era.* New York: Overlook Press, 1995.

Renehan, Edward J. Jr. *Dark Genius of Wall Street: The Misunderstood Life of Jay Gould.* New York: Basic Books, 2005.

Report on the Loss of the SS Titanic. Parliamentary Report. New York: St. Martin's Press, 1990.

Robinson, Bill. *Legendary Yachts.* New York: Macmillan, 1971.

Roper, Laura Wood. *F.L.O.: A Biography of Frederick Law Olmsted.* Baltimore: Johns Hopkins University Press, 1973.

Roth, Leland M. *The Architecture of McKim, Mead & White, 1870–1920: A Building List.* New York: Garland, 1978.

Rousmaniere, John. *The Luxury Yachts.* Alexandria, Va.: Time-Life Books, 1981.

Rousset-Charny, Gerard. *Les Palais Parisiens de la Belle Époque.* Paris: Délégation à l'action artistique de la Ville de Paris, 1990.

Rugoff, Milton. *America's Gilded Age.* New York: Henry Holt, 1989.

Rybczynski, Witold. *A Clearing in the Distance: Frederick Law Olmsted and America in the Nineteenth Century.* New York: Scribner, 1999.

Sadler, Julius Trousdale, and Jacqueline D. J. Sadler. *American Stables: An Architectural Tour.* Boston: New York Graphic Society, 1981.

Seale, William. *The Tasteful Interlude: American Interiors through the Camera's Eye, 1860–1917.* New York: Praeger, 1975.

Seitz, Don C. *Joseph Pulitzer: His Life & Letters.* New York: Simon & Schuster, 1924.

Sherwood, Mary Elizabeth Wilson. *Manners and Social Usages.* New York: Harper & Brothers, 1897.

Silver, Nathan. *Lost New York.* New York: Schocken Books, 1971.

Simon, Kate. *Fifth Avenue: A Very Social History.* New York: Harcourt Brace Jovanovich, 1978.

Sinclair, David. *Dynasty: The Astors and Their Times.* London: J. M. Dent, 1983.

Sirkis, Nancy. *Newport: Pleasures and Palaces.* New York: Viking, 1963.

Skinner, Cornelia Otis. *Elegant Wits and Grand Horizontals.* Boston: Houghton Mifflin, 1962.

Sloane, Florence Adele. *Maverick in Mauve.* Edited by Louis Auchincloss. Garden City, N.Y.: Doubleday, 1983.

Smales, Holbert T. *The Breakers.* Newport, R.I.: Preservation Society of Newport County, 1979.

Snell, Charles W. *Vanderbilt Mansion.* Washington, D.C.: National Park Service, 1960.

Spofford, Harriet Elizabeth Prescott. *The Servant Girl Question.* Boston: Houghton Mifflin, 1881.

Stern, Robert A. M., Gregory Gilmartin, and John Montague Massengale. *New York, 1900: Metropolitan Architecture and Urbanism 1890–1915.* New York: Rizzoli, 1983.

Still, Bayard. *Mirror for Gotham: New York as Seen by Contemporaries from Dutch Days to the Present.* New York: New York University Press, 1956.

Strahan, Edward. *Mr. Vanderbilt's House and Collection.* New York: George Barrie, 1883–1884.

Strange, Michael [Blanche Oelrichs]. *Who Tells Me True.* New York: Charles Scribner's Sons, 1940.

Stuart, Amanda Mackenzie. *Consuelo and Alva Vanderbilt.* New York: HarperCollins, 2005.

Sutherland, Daniel E. *Americans and Their Servants: Domestic Service in the United States from 1800 to 1920.* Baton Rouge: Louisiana State University Press, 1981.

Tebbel, John. *The Inheritors: A Study of America's Great Fortunes and What Happened to Them.* New York: G. P. Putnam's Sons, 1962.

Thaw, Evelyn Nesbit. *Prodigal Days: The Untold Story of Evelyn Nesbit.* New York: Julian Messner, 1934.

Thaw, Harry K. *The Traitor.* Philadelphia: Dorrance, 1926.

Thomas, Lately. *Delmonico's: A Century of Splendor.* Boston: Houghton Mifflin, 1967.

———. *A Pride of Lions: The Astor Orphans.* New York: William Morrow, 1971.

Thorndike, Joseph. *The Magnificent Builders and Their Dream Houses.* New York: American Heritage Publishing Company, 1978.

Tolman, William Howe. *The Better New York.* New York: Baker & Taylor, 1904.

Tomkins, Calvin. *Merchants and Masterpieces: The Story of the Metropolitan Museum of Art.* New York: E. P. Dutton, 1970.

Townsend, Reginald T. *God Packed My Picnic Basket.* New York: Hastings House, 1970.

Turbeville, Deborah. *Newport Remembered.* Text by Louis Auchincloss. New York: Harry N. Abrams, 1994.

Vanderbilt, Arthur T. *Fortune's Children: The Fall of the House of Vanderbilt.* New York: William Morrow, 1989.

Vanderbilt, Cornelius Jr. *Queen of the Golden Age: The Fabulous Story of Grace Wilson Vanderbilt.* New York: McGraw-Hill, Inc., 1956.

Vanderbilt, Gloria Morgan. *Without Prejudice.* New York: E. P. Dutton, 1936.

Van Dyke, John C. *The New New York: A Commentary on the Place and the People.* New York: Macmillan, 1909.

Van Pelt, John V. *A Monograph of the William K. Vanderbilt House.* New York: J. V. Van Pelt, 1925.

Van Rensselaer, Mrs. John King. *Newport: Our Social Capital.* Philadelphia: J. B. Lippincott, 1905.

———. *The Social Ladder.* New York: Henry Holt, 1924.

Vaux, Calvert. *Villas and Cottages.* New York: Harper & Brothers, 1857.

Veblen, Thorstein. *The Theory of the Leisure Class: An Economic Study of Institutions.* New York: Macmillan, 1899.

Vickers, Hugo. *Gladys, Duchess of Marlborough.* New York: Holt, Rinehart, & Winston, 1979.

Warburton, Eileen. *In Living Memory: A Chronicle of Newport, Rhode Island, 1888–1988.* Newport, R.I.: Newport Savings and Loan Association/Island Trust Company, 1988.

Wecter, Dixon. *The Saga of American Society.* New York: Charles Scribner's Sons, 1937.

Wharton, Edith. *The Age of Innocence.* New York: Scribner's, 1993.

————. *A Backward Glance*. New York: D. Appleton-Century, 1934.

White, Samuel G. *The Houses of McKim, Mead & White*. New York: Rizzoli, 1998.

Widow of an American Diplomat. *Intimacies of Court and Society*. New York: Dodd, Mead, 1912.

Williams, Henry Lionel, and Ottalie K. Williams. *Great Houses of America*. New York: G. P. Putnam's Sons, 1969.

————. *A Treasury of Great American Houses*. New York: G. P. Putnam's Sons, 1970.

Williams, Mrs. Hwfa. *It Was Such Fun*. London: Hutchinson, 1935.

Williamson, Ellen. *When We Went First Class*. Garden City, N.Y.: Doubleday, 1977.

Wilson, Derek. *The Astors, 1763–1992: Landscape with Millionaires*. New York: St. Martin's Press, 1993.

Yarnall, James L. *Newport Through Its Architecture: A History of Styles from Postmedieval to Postmodern*. Hanover, N.H.: University Press of New England/Salve Regina University Press, 2005.

Articles

Davis, Hartley. "Magnificent Newport." *Munsey's Magazine*, no. 23, July 1900.

Lowenthal, Larry. "The Cliff Walk at Newport." *Newport History* 61, no. 212, part 4, Fall 1988.

Russell, Edith. "I Was Aboard the *Titanic*." Titanic *Commutator* II, issue 21, Spring 1979.

Schuyler, Montgomery. "A Newport Palace." *Cosmopolitan,* no. 29, August 1900.

Slocum, Eileen G. "Memories of Bellevue Avenue: The Story of A Newport Family." *Newport History 67*, no. 230, Summer 1995.

Wharton, Edith. "The Line of Least Resistance." *Lippincott's Magazine* no. 66, October 1900.

Newspapers and Periodicals

Specific dates are referenced in the citations in the notes section.

Boston Globe

Chicago Tribune

Collier's

London Daily News

Los Angeles Times

New York Daily Graphic

New York Herald

New York Journal

New York Post

New York State Preservationist

New York Sun

New York Times

New York Tribune

New York World

Time

Titanic *Commutator* (published by the *Titanic* Historical Society)

Other Media

Preservation Society of Newport County. "Theresa Fair Oelrichs: A Western Mining Heiress Builds Rosecliff." Unpublished docent guide. Newport, RI: Preservation Society of Newport County, no date.

Brann, Mildred Mann. "*Colonel Mann and Town Topics.*" Manuscript in the possession of Tracey M. DeMartini, 1966.

http://dgmweb.net/genealogy/FGS/D/DeWorsionJohn-ArabellaDuvalYarrington.shtml.

http://jck.polygon.net/archives/1995/07/0795rub.html.

http://www.royal-magazin.de/collection/vanderbilt-jewels.htm.

http://www.encyclopedia-titanica.org/cabins.html.

http://www.metmuseum.org/toah/hd/cawh/hod_28.70.3.htm

INDEX